Human Development

ACROSS THE LIFESPAN

FIFTH EDITION

Human Development

ACROSS THE LIFESPAN

John S. Dacey
Boston College

John F. Travers
Boston College

Boston   Burr Ridge, IL   Dubuque, IA   Madison, WI   New York   San Francisco   St. Louis
Bangkok   Bogotá   Caracas   Kuala Lumpur   Lisbon   London   Madrid   Mexico City
Milan   Montreal   New Delhi   Santiago   Seoul   Singapore   Sydney   Taipei   Toronto

McGraw-Hill Higher Education ⚛

A Division of The **McGraw-Hill** Companies

HUMAN DEVELOPMENT ACROSS THE LIFESPAN, FIFTH EDITION

Published by McGraw-Hill, a business unit of The McGraw-Hill Companies, Inc., 1221 Avenue of the Americas, New York, NY 10020. Copyright © 2002, 1999, 1996 by The McGraw-Hill Companies, Inc. All rights reserved. No part of this publication may be reproduced or distributed in any form or by any means, or stored in a database or retrieval system, without the prior written consent of The McGraw-Hill Companies, Inc., including, but not limited to, in any network or other electronic storage or transmission, or broadcast for distance learning.

Some ancillaries, including electronic and print components, may not be available to customers outside the United States.

♲ This book is printed on recycled, acid-free paper containing 10% postconsumer waste.

1 2 3 4 5 6 7 8 9 0 QPD/QPD 0 9 8 7 6 5 4 3 2 1

ISBN 0–07–241364–6

Editorial director: *Jane E. Karpacz*
Senior sponsoring editor: *Rebecca H. Hope*
Senior developmental editor: *Sharon Geary*
Senior marketing manager: *Chris Hall*
Project manager: *Richard H. Hecker*
Production supervisor: *Enboge Chong*
Coordinator of freelance design: *Rick D. Noel*
Cover designer: *Nicole Dean*
Cover image: © *Stone Images (image no. AR3712-001)*
Senior photo research coordinator: *Carrie K. Burger*
Photo research: *LouAnn K. Wilson*
Supplement producer: *Tammy Juran*
Media technology lead producer: *David Edwards*
Compositor: *ElectraGraphics, Inc.*
Typeface: *10/12 Garamond*
Printer: *Quebecor World Dubuque, IA*

The credits section for this book begins on page C-1 and is considered an extension of the copyright page.

Library of Congress Cataloging-in-Publication Data

Dacey, John S.
   Human development across the lifespan / John S. Dacey, John F. Travers.—5th ed.
      p. cm.
   Includes bibliographical references and index.
   ISBN 0–07–241364–6   (alk. paper)
   1. Developmental psychology.   I. Travers, John F.   II. Title.

BF713 .D33   2002
155—dc21
                                                            2001030616
                                                            CIP

www.mhhe.com

This book is dedicated with deep affection
to the two people who have helped us the most—
Linda Dacey and Barbara Travers,
our wives.

Brief Contents

Contents

PART III

Infancy

CHAPTER 5

Physical and Cognitive Development in Infancy 101

CHAPTER 6

Psychosocial Development in Infancy 131

PART IV

Early Childhood

CHAPTER 7

Physical and Cognitive Development in Early Childhood 155

PART VIII
Middle Adulthood

CHAPTER 15

Physical and Cognitive Development in Middle Adulthood   *381*

CHAPTER 16

Psychosocial Development in Middle Adulthood   *405*

PART IX
Late Adulthood

CHAPTER 17

Physical and Cognitive Development in Late Adulthood   *431*

In this first decade of the twenty-first century, American society has clearly adopted the goal that greater opportunities should be available for all its members to develop their potential more fully. To achieve this goal, it will be essential that we know as much as possible about human development—how we change from the helplessness of infancy to the competence of adulthood to the wisdom of old age.

Perhaps the human saga is not written as clearly as we would like. As Thomas Jefferson once noted, although the human condition is not open to complete scrutiny, it is, nevertheless, susceptible to considerable improvement. Clues providing insights into the riddle of human development are beginning to multiply. Genetic discoveries are occurring at a rate that can only be described as breathtaking.

As the population of our nation continues to change, we have become more sensitive to the influence that culture exerts on development. We recognize that children learn in many different ways; we see how different cultures view developmental stages such as adolescence and old age from different perspectives; we understand more about how society changes us, but also how we can influence society.

Basic Themes of Human Development Across the Lifespan

Reflecting the exciting changes that are taking place in our knowledge of human development, we have woven our narrative around several integrating themes: the biopsychosocial model, the cultural context of development, the roles of age and gender, and applications to daily living. We return to these themes in each chapter as a means of making more meaningful the basic knowledge of human development.

The Biopsychosocial Approach

The *biopsychosocial approach* will help you to integrate the wealth of information that you will find in the pages to come. By thinking of lifespan development as the product of the interaction of biological, psychological, and social forces, you will better appreciate the complexity of development. For example, biological influences on development range from the role of genes in development to adult health concerns; psychological influences include all aspects of cognitive and personality development; social influences refer to such powerful forces as family, school, peers, and the media. The biopsychosocial approach helps to explain how the interaction of these forces is the key to understanding human development.

Contextual Influences on Development

Our goal in urging you to adopt a sociocultural perspective is to help you develop a greater understanding of those who seem "different." If you adopt this perspective, you will come to realize that different people have different worldviews that decisively influence their thinking. People from different cultures do not always think like each other and, as we will stress, these differences are assets. Recognizing how diverse people are in their thinking and behavior will help you to identify and comprehend variations in how individuals are raised, how they think, and how they become functioning members of their culture.

In various places throughout the book, we will be discussing the four major tenets of the contextual model: the relative plasticity of life; the historical embeddedness of all development; the diversity of development; and the bidirectionality of the causes of all human behavior. Since we feel so strongly about the importance of these factors, you will find a discussion of sociocultural issues in each chapter. We also open several sections of the book with a sociocultural perspective on the issues to be discussed.

The Roles of Age and Gender

Inasmuch as this book is organized chronologically, we will be explaining the influence of age in every chapter. In some ways, the effects of age are quite apparent and in other ways its effects are subtle and complex. As concerns about gender equity have received more publicity, the stereotypes about males and females are slowly eroding. If people are treated according to stereotypical characteristics, then their potential is immediately limited. Although gender stereotyping is only one part of the gender story, it illustrates the importance of the relationship between gender and development. For example, children at an early age construct social categories from the world around them, attach certain characteristics to these categories, and label the categories. This process may be positive because it helps to organize the world; it may also be negative if the characteristics associated with the category are limiting—"girls just can't do math." We'll examine how this theme plays out, both positively and negatively, throughout the lifespan.

Applications to Daily Living

The study of lifespan development is an exciting, rapidly changing, and highly relevant subject that can shed light on the developmental changes that you witness in yourself and see in your friends and family members of all ages. To help you put the theories and research of this book into a meaningful framework, we have written several **An Applied View** boxes for each chapter. These range from the appeal of street gangs for some children, to the role of television in a child's life, to an adolescent's search for identity, and to problems that the adult children of alcoholics encounter.

We have also included boxes that ask you to interact with the text's material. Called **An Informed View,** these boxes are intended to help you think about and act on topics we have just discussed in the chapter. In these activities, you are invited to reflect on what your knowledge and your experience tell you about these matters. We do not present answers in these boxes. Rather, we hope you apply your best judgment to the issues we raise.

Major Changes in the Fifth Edition

Thanks to suggestions from students who used the fourth edition of our text and the insightful comments of reviewers, we have made the following substantial changes in the fifth edition:

- An innovation from the previous edition is the changing of **What's Your View** boxes to **An Informed View.** These new boxes, which appear once or more in each chapter, not only ask students to take a side on a "hot" developmental issue, but also suggest further readings that should help to provide a better basis for the formation of that stance. In some cases, these boxes will contain a World Wide Web icon that will prompt you to visit the text's web site for additional information. As a result, students are encouraged to think more critically about the major issues in the field today, and not just jump to a snap judgment.

- In addition to appearing at the end of the text in the glossary, definitions of key terms now appear within the margins of the text. This enhancement makes it easier for students to identify important terms and study them in preparation for exams.

- We have continued to add new examples of the biopsychosocial approach in this edition.

- Because we believe that the quotations that appear in each chapter in our book set the tone for that chapter, we have provided one as an opening, along with a vignette about human development, in each chapter.

- Earlier in this preface we mentioned that development is a lifelong process, which implies that lifespan psychology books must constantly change to accommodate fresh insights into the developmental process. To meet this challenge, we have made the following key changes in our chapters:

Chapter 1. Lifespan Psychology—An Introduction

We have reshaped major sections of Chapter 1: new approaches to the meaning and characteristics of lifespan psychology, completely changed our analysis of the views of lifespan psychology, and refocused the importance of biopsychosocial interactions.

Chapter 2. Theories of Development: Interpreting the Lifespan

We have changed Chapter 2 to reflect the latest direction in the field. For example, we have used developmental contextualism as an illustration of the growing importance of systems analysis to understand development. How the various human systems interact is now recognized as a most promising technique to unlock developmental secrets.

Chapter 3. The Biological Basis of Development

The ART section (Assisted Reproductive Techniques) was completely redone to reflect current research. Also, cloning was discussed. The Human Genome Project was almost totally rewritten to keep up with the startling news about the mapping of the human genome. This section received highly favorable reviews.

Chapter 4. Pregnancy and Birth

The major changes in this chapter are a reorganization of topics, a much-expanded version of maternal influences on prenatal development, and a new approach to prematurity (identification of categories, etc.).

Chapter 5. Physical and Cognitive Development in Infancy

We rewrote major sections of this chapter. For example, we expanded our discussion of brain development in infancy. We also reworked the section on perceptual development—visual and auditory. Although we maintained a strong position in Piagetian thought, we noticeably enlarged our treatment of information processing in infancy.

Chapter 6. Psychosocial Development in Infancy

We continued our emphasis on the importance of interactions and relationships on development and extended the notion of "ghosts in the nursery" with regard to parental expectations. We also increased our analysis of father attachment. We completely rewrote the section on emotions and emotional development, which received excellent reviews.

Chapter 7. Physical and Cognitive Development in Infancy

Once again, we expanded our discussion of brain development in the early childhood period. We reorganized the discussion of the importance of drawing in a child's life. We introduced the latest research concerning children's theory of mind and linked it to information processing theory—a major change. The analysis of language development began with a presentation of Roger Brown's work, which we thought would help readers to grasp this important topic.

Chapter 8. Psychosocial Development in Early Childhood

In our discussion of parenting techniques, we introduced the pros and cons of punishment. Our presentation of family included the different effects of culture on the interactions among family members. The work on divorce was updated to include the latest statistics and research suggesting the differential effects of divorce on boys and girls. We introduced several new important studies on the developmental outcome of day care. The section on gender development was completely reworked—updating and expanding the theory section, analyzing the role of culture, and introducing the latest research on the emotional life of boys, including violence.

Chapter 9. Physical and Cognitive Development in Middle Childhood

We pointed out the importance of nutrition during these years. We then totally revamped our discussion of intelligence to make it more meaningful for readers. Since reviewers seemed to focus on problem solving and critical thinking, we GREATLY expanded our discussion of critical thinking; we discussed taxonomies, the use of questions, the kinds of strategies children develop, etc. We refined and added to our analysis of reading skills with regard to language development.

Chapter 10. Psychosocial Development in Middle Childhood

We have made sweeping changes for this edition. We introduced a section on the development of violence (which has attracted so much attention today) and tied it to early clues for troublesome behavior. Following this discussion, we then tied the topic to impulse control, one of the most significant issues for today's children. We made many changes in the peer section, detailing their important influence on development. In this edition, we decided—for obvious reasons—to link our discussion to schools and development. We brought in new work on the role of learning and problem solving. From there, we turned to the impact of television on development, using the National Television Violence Study. We concluded with an analysis of resilient children and, in this edition, introduced a section on the characteristics of resilient children.

Chapter 11. Physical and Cognitive Development in Adolescence

We included important new evidence on the secular trend—although menarche (first menstruation) is not starting any earlier, breast development is beginning sooner, and this has important ramifications for the social treatment of preadolescent girls. We also have a new section on body image and eating disorders, as well as new evidence on patterns of mental illness in the teen years.

Chapter 12. Psychosocial Development in Adolescence

New statistics on developments in the typical family, sexual behavior and sexually transmitted diseases, and on pregnancy and the impact of divorce in the United States are provided in this chapter. There is also a new section on the use of the drug Ecstasy, as well as new statistics on other drug use today.

Chapter 13. Physical and Cognitive Development in Young Adulthood

We have included a considerable amount of new information in the area of the effect of lifestyle on health. There is also a new section on the phenomenon of the dual-career family.

Chapter 14. Psychosocial Development in Young Adulthood

New information on the sexual behavior of young adults is presented in this chapter, as well as an increased treatment of gender roles and their importance in the development of the members of this age group. We also include a new set of statistics on changing American marriages and families.

Chapter 15. Physical and Cognitive Development in Middle Adulthood

There's a new section on recent information on the climacteric for both men and women. Exciting new work on the way that memory operates has been included in this edition. We have also added several new studies to our section on the special problems of the working woman.

Chapter 16. Psychosocial Development in Middle Adulthood

We have added information about recent studies concerning the relationships between siblings and between middle-aged friends. A new section on sex and love in middle adulthood has also been included.

Chapter 17. Physical and Cognitive Development in Late Adulthood

We have expanded the sections on sensory abilities (especially hearing and eyesight) of elderly persons. We have made significant revisions on the subjects of health and appearance. In our coverage of Alzheimer's disease, we have added sections on new research on the causes and ways of treating this devastating problem. Our information on the concept of wisdom has also been expanded.

Chapter 18. Psychosocial Development in Late Adulthood

We have incorporated updated material on the sexual behavior of elderly adults, as well as a considerable amount of new information on the elderly and their families. There's new information on grandparenting (especially their role as primary parents). We have taken a new look at personality development among this age group, and have revised the information we present on Erikson's point of view.

Chapter 19. Dying and Spirituality

We have a major new section on causes of suicide. We have considerably expanded our coverage of physician-assisted suicide and of the role of the hospice in helping the elderly prepare themselves for death when they are terminally ill. We have also increased our coverage of the rapidly expanding area of spirituality.

Teaching—Learning Features of the Fifth Edition

You will enjoy and learn from this book to the extent that its topics, organization, and clarity make its contents meaningful to you. Helping you to master the book's contents in as uncomplicated a manner as possible has been the most important pedagogical goal of our work. To accomplish this task, we have built a number of features into each chapter, described here. The *Student Owner's Manual* that follows this preface also walks you through these features by pairing examples of features with explanations of their use.

- *Chapter Outlines.* The major topics of each chapter are presented initially so that you may quickly find the subject you need. An outline helps you to retain material (a memory aid) and is an efficient method for reviewing content.

- *Opening Quotation.* Each chapter opens with a quotation that sets the tone for what follows.

- *Opening Vignette.* Each chapter opens with a vignette that illustrates the chapter's content. These vignettes are intended to demonstrate how the topics described in the chapter actually work in the daily lives of human beings, young and old.

- *Chapter Questions.* Following the introductory section of each chapter, we present a concise list of questions that are answered in the chapter to guide your reading. When you finish reading the chapter return to the list and test yourself to see if you can respond to their intent; that is, can you analyze, can you apply, can you identify, can you define, can you describe?

- *View Boxes.* We have designed our boxes to expand on the material under discussion and to do so in a manner calculated to aid student retention. The view boxes are of three types:

  1. *An Informed View.* Here we present controversial issues and you are asked to give your opinion after you have studied the facts. In some cases these boxes are accompanied by an icon indicating that additional information can be found on the World Wide Web.

  2. *An Applied View.* Here you will see how the topics under discussion apply to an actual situation, in settings such as a classroom or a medical facility.

  3. *A Sociocultural View.* Here we analyze the contributions of different cultures to individual development, as well as research on newly discovered influences of aging, gender, and other social factors.

- *Conclusion & Summary.* At the end of each chapter you will find a brief concluding statement that summarizes the main themes of the chapter. This statement provides you with a quick check of the purpose of the chapter and the content covered. Immediately following the brief concluding section is a more detailed set of summary statements that are grouped according to the major topics of the chapter. This section should help you to review the chapter quickly and thoroughly.

- *Key Terms.* In addition to the list that appears at the end of each chapter, you will also find definitions of key terms within the chapter's margins. These terms are highlighted and explained in the context of the chapter. We urge you to spend time mastering the meaning of each of these terms and relate them to the context in which they appear.

- *What Do You Think?* Following the Key Terms, you will find a series of questions intended to have you demonstrate your knowledge of the chapter's content, not only by applying the material to different situations but also by asking you to be creative in answering the question or solving the problem.

- *Suggested Readings.* Interspersed in appropriate places throughout the text, you will find an annotated list of four or five books or journal articles that we think are particularly well suited to supplement the contents of the chapter. These references are not necessarily textbooks; they may not deal specifically with either education or psychology. We believe, however, that they shed an illuminating light upon the chapter's material.

- *Student Study Guide.* We include a student study guide in the body of the text, in the form of Guided Review sections, as one means of making the material as meaningful as possible and to aid retention.

Supplementary Materials

The supplements listed here may accompany Dacey & Travers' *Human Development Across the Lifespan,* Fifth Edition. Please contact your local McGraw-Hill representative for details concerning policies, prices, and availability as some restrictions may apply.

For the Instructor

Instructor's Manual and Test Bank

Developed by Rebecca Walker-Sands, Central Oregon Community College, the *Instructor's Manual* to accompany the fifth edition of *Human Development Across the Lifespan* has been revised and expanded to include new teaching ideas and features available for instructors. Features in this edition of the *Instructor's Manual* include, for each chapter, a summary outline, learning objectives, key terms, lecture suggestions, classroom or student activities, and questions for review and discussion. In addition, we have included supplementary resources for both video/film and web site use for the human development instructor. The summary outline and learning objectives closely follow the text and highlight the important concepts and topics from each chapter. The learning objectives are also used in the test bank to help instructors select supporting questions. Key terms from the text are listed to show which terms need to be emphasized within lectures. Complete lecture suggestions that give entertaining, yet educational, ideas on how to enliven classroom discussion of the text material are provided as well. In addition, classroom activities serve to provide hands-on suggestions for applying course material to students' everyday lives in and out of the classroom. Questions for review and discussion are available for each chapter to aid instructors in promoting class participation and/or as essay question assignments.

The *Test Bank* portion of the *Instructor's Manual/Test Bank* provides instructors with a resource of over 1,500 test questions specifically related to the main text. This testing tool includes multiple-choice questions for each chapter from which to develop test materials. In addition, each test item is identified by type as either factual, conceptual, or applied for easier test development.

Computerized Test Bank CD-ROM

This computerized test bank contains all of the questions in the print version, and is now available on a hybrid CD-ROM that functions in both Windows and Macintosh platforms. These questions can be rearranged and customized using Microtest III, a powerful yet easy-to-use test generating program by Chariot Software Group. Professors may choose questions, instructions, headings, and even fonts. Tests may be personalized by adding or importing instructors' own questions to those already in the test bank.

Instructor's Resource CD-ROM

This teaching tool offers instructors the opportunity to customize McGraw-Hill materials to create their lecture presentations. Resources include the *Instructor's Manual, Computerized Test Bank,* PowerPoint presentation slides, and the *Image Database for Developmental Psychology.*

PageOut—Build your own course web site in less than an hour

You don't have to be a computer whiz to create a web site. Especially with an exclusive McGraw-Hill product called PageOut™ that requires no prior knowledge of HTML. No long hours of coding. And no design skills on your part. www.pageout.net

The McGraw-Hill Developmental Psychology Image Database & Overhead Transparencies

This set of 200 full-color images was developed using the best selection of our human development art and tables and is available in electronic format on the text's web site and as part of our *Instructor's Resource CD-ROM,* as well as in a print overhead transparency set. These images have been selected to correspond with the instructor's manual. Plus, instructors can add their own lecture notes to the electronic images as well as organize the images to correspond to their particular classroom needs.

Online Learning Center

This extensive web site, designed specifically to accompany Dacey & Travers' *Human Development Across the Lifespan,* Fifth Edition, offers an array of resources for both instructor and student. PowerPoint Presentations, the Developmental Psychology Image Database, Web Links, and more resources can be found by logging on to the text site at www.mhhe.com/dacey5

Annual Editions—Human Development 2001/2002

Published by Dushkin/McGraw-Hill, is a collection of 45 articles on topics related to the latest research and thinking in human development. These editions are updated annually and contain helpful features including a topic guide, an annotated table of contents, and unit overviews, and a topical index. An instructor's guide containing testing materials is available.

Sources: Notable Selections in Human Development

A collection of over 40 articles, book excerpts, and research studies that have shaped the study of human development and our contemporary understanding of it. The selections are organized topically around major areas of study within human development. Each selection is preceded by a headnote that establishes the relevance of the article or study and provides biographical information on the author.

Taking Sides

A debate-style reader designed to introduce students to controversial viewpoints on the field's most crucial issues. Each issue is carefully framed for the student, and the pro and con essays represent the arguments of leading scholars and commentators in their fields. Instructor's guide containing testing materials is available.

Guide to Lifespan Development for Future Educators & Guide to Life-Span Development for Future Nurses

New course supplements that help students apply the concepts of human development to education. Each supplement contains information, exercises, and sample tests designed to help students prepare for certification and understand human development from a professional perspective.

For the Student

Making the Grade CD-ROM

This user-friendly CD-ROM offers 15–25 multiple-choice practice test questions, with feedback, per chapter. By providing these materials, along with a Learning Assessment questionnaire to help students identify their learning styles, the CD gives students an opportunity to test their comprehension of the course material.

Online Learning Center

The official web site for the text contains chapter outlines, practice quizzes that can be e-mailed to the professor, links to relevant web sites, and other interactive activities such as crosswords and flashcards. www.mhhe. com/dacey5

Acknowledgments

We would like to express our deep appreciation to our editors at McGraw-Hill, Rebecca Hope, Sharon Geary, and Rick Hecker, for their diligent attention to items big and small in this edition. We are also most grateful to our graduate assistants, Janet Morganelli and Erica Lolli, who helped in ways too plentiful to describe to shepherd this edition to publication. Finally, we would like to acknowledge the excellent contributions of the following reviewers:

Dan Bellack,
Trident Technical College

Montie A. Campbell,
Oklahoma Baptist University

Suzanne E. Cortez,
Northern Kentucky University

Laurie Dickson,
Northern Arizona University

Estelle Friedman,
Quinnipiac College

Robin Des Jardin,
John Tyler Community College

Richard Kandus,
Mount San Jacinto College

Michael S. Kelly,
Henderson State University

Patricia S. Laser,
Bucks County Community College

Madelyn Mack,
University of West Alabama

Eric A. Mansfield,
Western Illinois University

Cheryl McGill,
Florence Darlington Technical College

Mary Mindess,
Lesley College

Leslie Minor-Evans,
Central Oregon Community College

Carol Pandy,
Los Angeles Pierce College

Shelley Parker,
New Brunswick Community College—Fredericton Campus

Therese Schuepfer,
Northeastern Illinois University

Jill F. Shoen,
Northern State University

Jillene G. Seiver,
Green River Community College

Edward Snodgrass,
Meridian Community College

Vincent J. Sullivan,
Pensacola Jr. College

Mary Ellen Vandenburg,
Potomac State College of West Virginia University

Carol Yoder,
Indiana State University

John S. Dacey, Ph.D., is professor at Boston College in the Department of Counseling, Developmental Psychology, and Research Methods. He began his career as a junior high social studies teacher. Now a college teacher and a researcher in adolescent and adult development, he is the author of 12 books and nearly 30 articles on parenting, creativity, and general human development. His most recently published book is entitled *Your Anxious Child.* He is currently finishing a book on parental techniques for promoting family cohesion.

John Travers has worked with young people all his professional life, beginning with his own four children. Early in his career, he worked with children ages five to eighteen in a recreational setting. He has taught in elementary and high school and now teaches undergraduate and graduate students at Boston College, where, among a faculty of 1000, he was recognized as one of eight outstanding teachers in the university. He has also been honored as Teacher of the Year. His undergraduate and graduate teaching has been in the field of developmental psychology. Teaching, counseling, and writing have been constant themes in his professional life. He has written 15 books and approximately 30 professional articles.

Owner's Manual: A Guide to Content Features

CHAPTER 3

The Biological Basis of Development

Chapter Outlines

The major topics of each chapter are presented initially so that you may quickly find the subject you need.

On October 6, 1998, Frank and Ellen Smith arrived at Dr. James Otis's office a few minutes early for their appointment. Married for seven years, they had been unable to conceive and had found that their problem was caused by male infertility, in this case, a low sperm count. As they attempted to learn more about their problem, they discovered that they were not alone; estimates are that one in six heterosexual couples has a fertility problem.

Other couples whom they had met in their search for a solution had recommended Dr. Otis as a physician who was sympathetic, knowledgeable, and successful in using DI—donor insemination. (Currently, close to 100,000 women in the United States will use DI each year.) Frank and Ellen chose this procedure because the screening process in accepting sperm for freezing lowers the risk of sexually transmitted diseases (STDs) and also provides detailed information about the donor: race, ethnic background, blood type, hair and eye color, physical characteristics, and personal background information.

The Smiths found that Dr. Otis was exactly as he had been described. Unhurried and calm, he told the couple just what would be expected of them. He also stressed that he received sperm from a large, nationally known, respected sperm bank. He explained that freezing techniques had improved in the last few years. Cryobiology, the study of how best to freeze living tissue, had made great strides by adding chemicals such as glycerol to liquid nitrogen at a temperature of –190 degrees C. This technique protects cells and tissues by preventing any damage that could be caused by the formation of ice crystals.

Frank and Ellen felt reassured by their discussion with Dr. Otis. They couldn't afford the time and money required for adoption, but from their reading they had decided their chances of conceiving through donor insemination were good. Healthy couples with no other problems have a 70 to 80 percent success rate within one year. This figure compares with a natural conception rate of 85 to 90 percent for fertile couples.

The Smiths were also pleased that Dr. Otis had so carefully explained the procedure to them. After carefully tracking a woman's menstrual cycle and searching for accurate

Opening Vignette

Each chapter opens with a vignette that illustrates the chapter's content. These vignettes are intended to demonstrate how the topics described in the chapter actually work in the daily lives of human beings, young and old.

With approximately 5 million individuals in the United States who are thought to be infertile, many couples are consulting fertility specialists.

not stand alone; they are related to other aspects of science, that is, they should be tested experimentally and applied to actual situations. Only in this way can the truthfulness and usefulness of any theory be assessed.

In this chapter, we'll first turn to the major theorists who for many years have guided our thinking about development: Sigmund Freud, Erik Erikson, Jean Piaget, Lev Vygotsky, B. F. Skinner, and Albert Bandura. Next we'll discuss the present status of developmental theory and several issues related to the direction of developmental theory. Finally, we'll use Richard Lerner's notion of contextualism to reflect recent thinking regarding new directions in developmental analysis, which we hinted at in chapter 1.

Psychoanalytic theory
Freud's theory of the development of personality.

Chapter Objectives

After you read this chapter, you should be able to answer the following questions.

◆ How does psychoanalytic theory explain development across the lifespan?
◆ What is the relationship between psychosocial crises and lifespan development?
◆ How did Piaget explain cognitive development?
◆ What impact does culture have on lifespan development?
◆ What is the behavioral perspective on development?
◆ What is the status of current developmental theory?

The Psychoanalytic Approach

On a beautiful spring day in 1885, Sigmund Freud sat down and wrote a startling letter to his fiancee. Telling her that he had just about completed a massive task—destroying his notes, letters, and manuscripts of the past fourteen years, a destructive act that he would repeat several times in his lifetime—Freud revealed his mistrust of future biographers. Yet, in spite of his efforts, the autobiographical nature of much of his published works and his vast correspondence left a lasting legacy.

Freud's ideas no longer dominate developmental psychology as they did in the early part of the 20th century. Yet his insistence on the early years as decisive in development has remained a potent and controversial concept (Cairns, 1998). In more than 100 years of psychological research, it is impossible to think of anyone who has played a larger role than Sigmund Freud. Even his most severe critics admit that his theory on the development of personality is a milestone in the social sciences (Ferris, 1997).

Let's begin by examining Freud's ideas about the structure of the mind.

Dr. Sigmund Freud was a medical doctor who proposed the psychoanalytic theory of development.

Sigmund Freud suggested that babies react to needful feelings such as hunger in several steps. First they become aware of the need, then they cry; next they imagine that the need has been met, and then they fall back to sleep. Slowly they learn that imagination is no substitute for real satisfaction of a need.

Chapter Objectives

This is a concise list of questions that are answered in the chapter to guide your reading. Once you've finished the chapter, you should be able to analyze, apply, identify, define, and describe.

A Sociocultural View

These provide analysis of different cultures to individual development, as well as reseach on newly discovered influences of aging, gender, and other social factors.

Suggested Readings

Interspersed throughout the text are titles of book and journal articles that are particularly well suited to supplement the contents of the chapter.

Guided Review Questions

Acting as an integrated study guide, these questions help you to study what you've just learned.

Chapter 1 Lifespan Psychology: An Introduction • 13

A Sociocultural VIEW   *The Impact of the Cultural Climate*

Understanding cultural differences will move our relationships with others to a level of mutual understanding in all settings. As an illustration, think of the changing American classrooms, where children and teachers from many different cultures are now coming together. Many minority children have had to make major adjustments to the dominant culture in the classroom (Chen & others, 1997). Teachers who are aware of the differences between the home culture and that of the school can do much to ensure that these children succeed academically and personally to achieve their potential (Greenfield & Suzuki, 1998).

A good example of this kind of endeavor can be seen in Kim's (1990) description of Hawaiian children's school experiences. Many Hawaiian children achieve at the lowest academic level and are labeled as lazy and disruptive by some teachers. Yet these same children are equally responsible at home—cooking, cleaning, taking care of their brothers and sisters. They demonstrate considerable initiative and a high performance level. When something needs to be done, they get together and make a group effort to do whatever is necessary. When they find themselves in an individualistic, competitive classroom, however, their performance suffers.

In a series of experiments, teachers were encouraged to model desired behaviors and not assign specific tasks to students. By the end of the academic year, the students would begin the day by examining the schedules of their learning centers and then divide themselves into groups that assigned tasks to individual members, obtained materials,

and used worksheets. Although their achievement scores improved significantly, once the students were returned to regular classrooms for the fourth grade, a familiar pattern of problems appeared (Kim, 1990).

The classroom is not the only location in which cultures merge. In the business world, people of various cultures work side by side; those designated as minorities may have leadership positions in which members of the dominant culture report to them. As companies become more global and as the number of international markets increases steadily, the workplace is beginning to resemble the classroom as a meeting place of cultures.

Our goal in urging you to adopt a multicultural perspective is to help you reach a level of significant understanding of those who seem different. If you adopt this perspective, you will come to realize that different people have different worldviews that decisively influence their thinking. People from different cultures do not all think alike. Recognizing how diverse people are in their thinking and behavior will help you to identify and comprehend variations in people's backgrounds and how they become functioning members of their culture. In this way, you will work, play, or study more congenially with others, thus fostering more positive relations in our society.

Finally, cultural awareness should also make us aware that we are all alike in important ways. It's mainly in our behavior, the manner in which we deal with the demands of our environments, that we differ.

An excellent introduction to the changing cultural conditions in our country is *Multicultural Education of Children and Adolescents*. This text, by M. Lee Manning and Leroy Baruth and published in Boston by Allyn and Bacon (1995) is thorough, well-written, and practical.

- To assess current cultural change initiatives, such as intervention programs in the United States, and program development in other countries, such as Peru's Human Development Institute, which encourages development through the schools (Harrison, 2000).

Contributors to Biopsychosocial Interactions

If you examine table 1.4 carefully, you'll note several characteristics listed for the biological, psychological, and social aspects of interactions. These certainly aren't exhaustive but indicate several developmental features that affect growth during the lifespan. More importantly, however, we would like you to think about the interactions that occur among the three categories and how these interactions affect development. To give a simple example, genetic damage (biological) may negatively affect cognitive development (psychological), and lead to poor peer relationships (social).

We believe that by recognizing the significance of biopsychosocial interactions, you'll better understand and remember the material of any chapter. This perspective also helps to emphasize those social-cultural features that so powerfully influence development through the lifespan.

---

16 • Part I Introduction

Guided Review

15. A belief in _____ is to hold the opinion that early experiences in a child's life continue to exert influence throughout the lifespan.
16. Those who believe that developmental change occurs because of a slow and steady progression believe in _____.
17. Today's developmental psychologists interpret the influence of nature and nurture as one of an _____ between the two.

Developmental Research

Having identified several key developmental issues and theoretical viewpoints, we must now ask: How can we obtain reliable data about these topics so that we may better understand them?

Today we use many approaches to understanding human behavior. Each has its strengths and weaknesses; none is completely reliable. Most developmental psychologists employ one of three data collection methods: descriptive studies, manipulative experiments, and naturalistic experiments. In the first type, information is gathered on subjects without manipulating them in any way. In the second two, an experiment is performed before the information is gathered.

An Applied VIEW   *When Are Research References Too Old?*

Probably for the rest of your career, you will be reading research—articles, chapters in books, monographs, and so on. When should you decide that a reference is too old to be credible any longer? As with so many aspects of social science, the answer is "It all depends." Guidelines exist, however, so let's try to understand them by looking at several references. Before reading our decision, you might try to guess what a good judgment would be.

As many as one-third of adolescents receive less than 70 percent of their minimum daily requirement for the most common minerals such as calcium and iron (U.S. Department of Health, Education, and Welfare, 1972).

Since eating habits of adolescents are likely to change with the times (depending, among other things, on the economic condition of the country), this statistic is unreliable because about 30 years have passed since the data were collected.

Although the average number of homosexuals who are contracting AIDS each year is decreasing, they are still the most vulnerable group (U.S. National Center for Health Statistics, 1990).

This study is much more recent, but it too is suspect because we know that the AIDS epidemic is changing very rapidly. In fact, heterosexual females are now experiencing the greatest rate of increase per capita.

Noise-induced hearing loss is recognized as the second most common cause of irreversible hearing loss in older persons (Surjan & others, 1973).

Here is another study that is quite dated, but because there is no known reason to believe that aging factors have changed much over the years, if the study was well designed, we may still accept the results.

The major crisis in the first year and one-half of human life is the establishment of basic trust (Erikson, 1963).

This statement is not a research finding but rather represents Erikson's belief as reflected in his psychosocial theory of human development. As such, it is accurate because that is exactly what Erikson said.

Can you think of other factors that influence the timeliness of research references? Can you think of other criteria for judging them?

Answers

15. stability 16. continuity 17. interaction.

An Applied View

These provide examples to demonstrate how the chapter material relates to real-life situations.

An Informed View

These highlight controversial issues, challenging you to give your opinion after you have studied the facts.

---

56 • Part II Beginnings

In Vitro Fertilization (IVF)

In vitro fertilization (IVF) is the external fertilization technique you are probably most familiar with. The steps in IVF are as follows (Curtis & Barnes, 1994):

1. The woman is usually treated with hormones to stimulate maturation of eggs in the ovary, and she is observed closely to determine the timing of ovulation (i.e., the time at which the egg leaves the surface of the ovary).
2. The physician makes an incision in the abdomen and inserts a laparoscope (a thin tubular lens through which the physician can see the ovary) to remove mature eggs.
3. The egg is placed in a solution containing blood serum and nutrients.
4. **Capacitation** takes place—this is a process in which a layer surrounding the sperm is removed so that it may penetrate the egg.
5. Sperm are added to the solution; fertilization occurs.
6. The fertilized egg is transferred to a fresh supporting solution.
7. Fertilized eggs (usually three) are inserted into the uterus.
8. The fertilized egg is implanted in the uterine lining.

Capacitation Removal of layer surrounding sperm.

An Informed VIEW   *To Clone or not to Clone*

Dolly, the most famous lamb in history, was born at 5:00 p.m. on a warm summer's day, July 5, 1996. It was a remarkably quiet introduction to one of the most controversial events of the twentieth century. Dolly was a clone, that is, she was not the product of the union of a sperm and egg. Ian Wilmut, a quiet, unassuming embryologist, combined the udder cell of a 6-year-old sheep with the egg of another sheep, after first removing the genetic material from the egg. The udder cell's genes now assumed command of the growth and development of the newly fertilized egg. The result: Dolly, an identical twin of the original sheep that supplied the udder cell. *But the identical twin was born six years later!* (Kolata, 1998).

Dolly, a cloned lamb, is destined to become the most famous lamb in history.

Until Dolly's birth, scientists had mainly discounted the possibility of cloning from adults since their only success had come from cloning the cells of embryos. Attempts using adult cells consistently failed until researchers discovered that the secret lay in the growth cycle of cells. As part of their normal cycle, cells enter into resting periods called G0 (gap zero). As long as the cell is in the G0 state, the egg would accept the DNA of the adult cell and use it to direct growth.

You have probably anticipated the next stage in the chronology of cloning. Is it possible to clone a human? As you can imagine, this question has ignited a firestorm of controversy. Do the benefits of cloning (replicating perfect farm animals, adding genes so that a cow might have valuable drugs in its milk, allowing childless couples to have children, developing organs to use in transplants) suggest that cloning humans is a necessary next step? Or do the negative features of cloning (sacrificing embryos to obtain one healthy clone, the possibility of genetic monsters, unresolved issues about the self—are we the product of our genes or not; if not, what makes us *us*?) outweigh any potential benefits?

Considering the inevitable collision between available technology and the forces arrayed against cloning, do you think the cloning of humans will ever occur? If you would like to have a more informed view on this issue, you may want to read one or more of the references in this chapter. (For example, Gina Kolata (1998) has written a fascinating account of the background and techniques of this process.) You may also wish to learn more about it by going to our web site at http://www.mhhe.com/dacey 5.

For an excellent summary of the cloning process, see Gina Kolata, *Clone*, which was published by William Morrow & Co. in 1998.

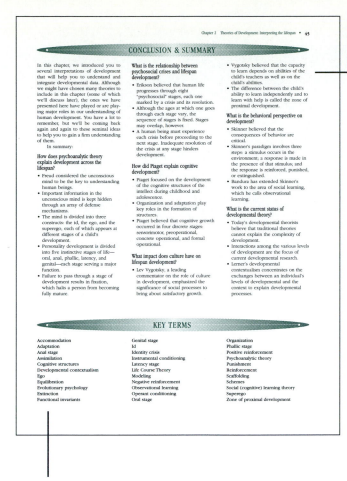

Chapter 2   Theories of Development: Interpreting the Lifespan • 45

CONCLUSION & SUMMARY

In this chapter, we introduced you to several interpretations of development that will help you to understand and integrate developmental data. Although we might have chosen many theories to include in this chapter (some of which we'll discuss later), the ones we have presented here have played or are playing major roles in our understanding of human development. You have a lot to remember, but we'll be coming back again and again to these seminal ideas to help you to gain a firm understanding of them.

In summary:

How does psychoanalytic theory explain development across the lifespan?

• Freud considered the unconscious mind to be the key to understanding human beings.
• Important information in the unconscious mind is kept hidden through an array of defense mechanisms.
• The mind is divided into three constructs: the id, the ego, and the superego, each of which appears at different stages of a child's development.
• Personality development is divided into five instinctive stages of life—oral, anal, phallic, latency, and genital—each stage serving a major function.
• Failure to pass through a stage of development results in fixation, which halts a person from becoming fully mature.

What is the relationship between psychosocial crises and lifespan development?

• Erikson believed that human life progresses through eight "psychosocial" stages, each one marked by a crisis and its resolution.
• Although the ages at which one goes through each stage vary, the sequence of stages is fixed. Stages may overlap, however.
• A human being must experience each crisis before proceeding to the next stage. Inadequate resolution of the crisis at any stage hinders development.

How did Piaget explain cognitive development?

• Piaget focused on the development of the cognitive structures of the intellect during childhood and adolescence.
• Organization and adaptation play key roles in the formation of structures.
• Piaget believed that cognitive growth occurred in four discrete stages: sensorimotor, preoperational, concrete operational, and formal operational.

What impact does culture have on lifespan development?

• Lev Vygotsky, a leading commentator on the role of culture in development, emphasized the significance of social processes to bring about satisfactory growth.

• Vygotsky believed that the capacity to learn depends on abilities of the child's teachers as well as on the child's abilities.
• The difference between the child's ability to learn independently and to learn with help is called the zone of proximal development.

What is the behavioral perspective on development?

• Skinner believed that the consequences of behavior are critical.
• Skinner's paradigm involves three steps: a stimulus occurs in the environment; a response is made in the presence of that stimulus; and the response is reinforced, punished, or extinguished.
• Bandura has extended Skinner's work to the area of social learning, which he calls observational learning.

What is the current status of developmental theory?

• Today's developmental theorists believe that traditional theories cannot explain the complexity of development.
• Interactions among the various levels of development are the focus of current developmental research.
• Lerner's developmental contextualism concentrates on the exchanges between an individual's levels of developmental and the context to explain developmental processes.

KEY TERMS

Accommodation
Adaptation
Anal stage
Assimilation
Cognitive structures
Developmental contextualism
Ego
Equilibration
Evolutionary psychology
Extinction
Functional invariants

Genital stage
Id
Identity crisis
Instrumental conditioning
Latency stage
Life Course Theory
Modeling
Negative reinforcement
Observational learning
Operant conditioning
Oral stage

Organization
Phallic stage
Positive reinforcement
Psychoanalytic theory
Punishment
Reinforcement
Scaffolding
Schemes
Social (cognitive) learning theory
Superego
Zone of proximal development

Conclusion & Summary

Following a brief summary of the chapter's main themes, a detailed set of summary statements help you to review the chapter quickly and thoroughly.

Key Terms

This represents a list of those terms that are essential to understanding the ideas and suggestions of that chapter.

Chapter Review Test

Use this end-of-chapter test to check your understanding of the chapter's key points.

What Do You Think?

This series of questions challenges you to demonstrate your knowledge of the chapter's content, not only by applying the material to different situations but also by asking you to be creative in answering the question or solving the problem.

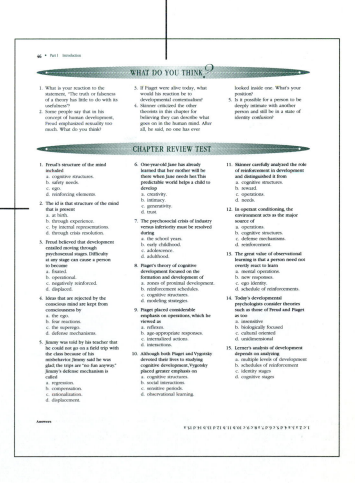

46 • Part 1   Introduction

WHAT DO YOU THINK?

1. What is your reaction to the statement, "The truth or falseness of a theory has little to do with its usefulness"?
2. Some people say that in his concept of human development, Freud emphasized sexuality too much. What do you think?
3. If Piaget were alive today, what would his reaction be to developmental contextualism?
4. Skinner criticized the other theorists in this chapter for believing they can describe what goes on in the human mind. After all, he said, no one has ever looked inside one. What's your position?
5. Is it possible for a person to be deeply intimate with another person and still be in a state of identity confusion?

CHAPTER REVIEW TEST

1. Freud's structure of the mind included
   a. cognitive structures.
   b. safety needs.
   c. ego.
   d. reinforcing elements.

2. The id is that structure of the mind that is present
   a. at birth.
   b. through experience.
   c. by internal representations.
   d. through crisis resolution.

3. Freud believed that development entailed moving through psychosexual stages. Difficulty at any stage can cause a person to become
   a. fixated.
   b. operational.
   c. negatively reinforced.
   d. displaced.

4. Ideas that are rejected by the conscious mind are kept from consciousness by
   a. the ego.
   b. fear reactions.
   c. the superego.
   d. defense mechanisms.

5. Jimmy was told by his teacher that he could not go on a field trip with the class because of his misbehavior. Jimmy said he was glad; the trips are "no fun anyway." Jimmy's defense mechanism is called
   a. regression.
   b. compensation.
   c. rationalization.
   d. displacement.

6. One-year-old Jane has already learned that her mother will be there when Jane needs her. This predictable world helps a child to develop
   a. creativity.
   b. intimacy.
   c. generativity.
   d. trust.

7. The psychosocial crisis of industry versus inferiority must be resolved during
   a. the school years.
   b. early childhood.
   c. adolescence.
   d. adulthood.

8. Piaget's theory of cognitive development focused on the formation and development of
   a. zones of proximal development.
   b. reinforcement schedules.
   c. cognitive structures.
   d. modeling strategies.

9. Piaget placed considerable emphasis on operations, which he viewed as
   a. reflexes.
   b. age-appropriate responses.
   c. internalized actions.
   d. interactions.

10. Although both Piaget and Vygotsky devoted their lives to studying cognitive development, Vygotsky placed greater emphasis on
   a. cognitive structures.
   b. social interactions.
   c. sensitive periods.
   d. observational learning.

11. Skinner carefully analyzed the role of reinforcement in development and distinguished it from
   a. cognitive structures.
   b. reward.
   c. operations.
   d. needs.

12. In operant conditioning, the environment acts as the major source of
   a. operations.
   b. cognitive structures.
   c. defense mechanisms.
   d. reinforcement.

13. The great value of observational learning is that a person need not overtly react to learn
   a. mental operations.
   b. new responses.
   c. ego identity.
   d. schedule of reinforcements.

14. Today's developmental psychologists consider theories such as those of Freud and Piaget as too
   a. insensitive
   b. biologically focused
   c. cultural oriented
   d. unidimensional

15. Lerner's analysis of development depends on analyzing
   a. multiple levels of development
   b. schedules of reinforcement
   c. identity stages
   d. cognitive stages

Answers

PART I

Introduction

The basic premise of lifespan psychology is that ontogenesis (individual development) extends across the entire life course and that lifelong adaptive processes are involved.

Paul Baltes

Lifespan Psychology: An Introduction

T he year was 1955.

During those 365 days, the psychologists Emmy Werner and Ruth Smith (1992) began to collect data on every child born on the island of Kauai, a part of the Hawaiian chain. That year a total of 837 children were born.

Amazingly, Werner and Smith studied 505 of these children from their prenatal days until they were in their early thirties. (The drop in the number of children studied was due to some of the children dying, some moving to other islands, and some moving to the U.S. mainland.)

Of these 505 children, one in three was born with the threat of serious developmental difficulties, such as the effects of a difficult birth or an environment that triggered formidable challenges. Some faced the prospect of a life of grinding poverty. Others experienced divorce, desertion, alcoholism, or mental illness.

Two out of three children in this vulnerable group were exposed to four or more of these risk factors. And yet, one in three of these high-risk children developed into a confident, competent young adult.

How can we explain this phenomenon? What developmental forces were at work that enabled certain children to overcome dramatically difficult obstacles, and yet permitted others to succumb? In a sense, the children of Kauai provide us with a window through which we can view the events that shape the lifespan, the biological, psychological, and environmental interactions that make us what we are. ❂

The encouraging story of the children of Kauai testifies to the remarkable changes that occur in the course of the lifespan. But much more is hidden in the chronicle of these lives. What combination of biological, psychological, and environmental forces interacted at what levels to produce these differences? What were the processes at work that *explain* what happened? These are the questions that will guide our work together as we explore the mysteries of the lifespan.

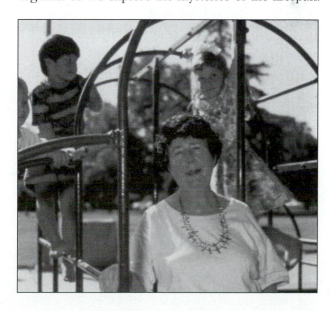

Emmy Werner's studies have provided invaluable insights into the characteristics of resilient children.

Chapter Objectives

After you read this chapter, you should be able to answer the following questions.

◆ How would you define and describe lifespan development?

◆ What are the different views of lifespan development?

◆ What role do biopsychosocial interactions play in lifespan development?

◆ What are the major issues in lifespan development?

◆ What is the role of research in studying lifespan development?

Thinking about Lifespan Development

When you pick up this book and open to chapter 1, you have every right to expect some clues about what lifespan psychology is, this subject that will demand your attention for the next 14 or 15 weeks. So first let's be technically accurate about what you'll be studying. **Lifespan psychology** *studies human development from conception to death.* In our work, we'll adopt a *normative* approach to development—the typical or average developmental path that people follow—but also point out individual variations where necessary.

Lifespan psychology
Lifespan psychology studies human development from conception to death.

Why Study the Lifespan?

As a discipline, lifespan psychology gathered momentum when developmental psychologists began to realize that development didn't cease when human beings passed from adolescence to adulthood. Rather, development is a lifelong process (Smith & Baltes, 1999). But there also can be no argument with the idea that each age (infancy, adolescence, etc.) has its own developmental agenda and contributes to the entire lifespan. Consequently, lifespan psychology has several objectives.

• To offer an organized account of development across the lifespan.

• To identify the interconnections between earlier and later events.

• To account for the mechanisms responsible for lifespan development.

• To specify the biological, psychological, and environmental factors that shape an individual's development (Baltes, Lindenberger, & Staudinger, 1998).

What Is Development?

Development Focus upon the changes that occur in the lifespan.

The second term you want to be clear about is development. **Development** *is about change* and is the focus of this book. Here are several ideas that help to explain the challenge and excitement of studying development across the lifespan.

• First is a warning: *Development is not explained by age alone.* Although age gives a rough estimate of when behavior appears, it tells us nothing about *why* a particular behavior appears at a specific time (Overton, 1998). In other words, what are the mechanisms that were responsible? People change as they grow older, but to explain these changes by age alone is misleading (Rutter & Rutter, 1993). For example, most children will talk and walk at about one year of age. Why? Is it simply because the child is one year of age? But Einstein didn't talk until he was four years of age. Or is a combination of other forces responsible: brain development, hormonal input, parental encouragement, etc.? Age is an acceptable index of when common behaviors typically appear, but it is not an explanation. What causes the differences in timing when young girls first experience menarche (first menstruation)? It can't be age. As Lerner (1998) noted, the appearance of menarche is due to interactions involving biology, culture, physical features of the ecology, and socioeconomic resources (nutrition, medical care, etc.).

- *Development is discontinuous as well as continuous.* For example, skills that we mastered in our youth may well be lost in old age.

- *Timing exerts an important influence on development.* An unwanted teen-age pregnancy is likely to produce a different parenting style than a planned, wanted pregnancy in early adulthood.

- *Development includes behaviors that change in form, but result from the same process.* For example, attention in infancy appears different from problem-solving ability in later years, but there's a significant link between the two.

- *Development demands careful examination of cause-and-effect relationships.* For example, a child who did well in school may go on to graduate studies, an auspicious career, and socioeconomic success. Passing tests, however, didn't alter the child's personality or intelligence. The proper academic credentials and a network of social relationships associated with schools gave her invaluable social advantages.

If you think about your own life—starting school, perhaps going off to college, beginning a job, getting married, having a child—you begin to appreciate the complexity of development. Since it's usually difficult to look at ourselves objectively, let's examine the life of an outstanding individual—Bill Cosby—whose rise to fame and wealth with all its accompanying triumphs and tragedies offers an insightful view into what is meant by lifespan development.

William Henry Cosby Jr. was born to Anna and William Cosby on July 12, 1937 at three A.M. The Cosbys were poor and as his mother said, "The only thing I had to give him was plenty of love, and oh, dear God, I gave him all I had. But success comes from within and Bill was determined to be something." (Smith, 1997, p. 7) The family was desperately poor, held together by a mother's love and hard work. His father left and Bill, as the oldest son, assumed responsibility for his three younger brothers, one of whom died at 6 years of age.

After attending a ghetto elementary school, Cosby dropped out of high school and worked a succession of jobs with little prospects for the future. Eventually he joined the Navy. His interest in humor never left him and as he studied the techniques of the famous comics of his day (Jack Benny, George Burns), he convulsed his friends with his stories. After four years in the navy, he decided to apply to Temple University as a 23-year-old freshman. The admissions officials were impressed and awarded him an athletic scholarship (football and track).

He continued to polish his comedy routines before college groups and audiences in small Philadelphia clubs during the summer. More of a storyteller than a joketeller, Cosby often gave six shows a night and then worked until dawn analyzing why some routines worked and others didn't. Finally, he had to make a decision—to stay in school or turn to full-time comedy. The lure of the stage won and although his reputation slowly grew, the breakthrough came with a guest appearance on the Johnny Carson Show. Cosby had arrived. He then moved on to star with Robert Culp in the *I Spy* series, a radical departure for the networks in which an African-American actor was on an equal basis with his white co-star.

Happily married to Camille Henry and with a growing family, Cosby moved to Amherst, Massachusetts, where he was admitted to graduate school at the University of Massachusetts, eventually receiving a doctorate. Success followed him: *The Bill Cosby Show, Fat Albert,* and *The Electric Company.* But as the years passed, failure also dogged him. Several ventures in television and the movies were criticized, but as Cosby said about himself, he was nothing if not persistent.

In spite of considerable skepticism, Cosby persuaded NBC to air a family show—no dirt, no off-color jokes, no innuendos. Bill Cosby as Dr. Huxtable and the Cosby Show were a smash hit. But for Cosby, success is always a close relative of sorrow. The tragic and untimely death of his son Ennis is the most recent example. Yet he continues on, fighting for racial equality, donating breathtaking amounts of money to charity, bringing pleasure and happiness to untold millions.

A young Bill Cosby.

Bill Cosby and his wife, 1965.

Bill Cosby and his TV family.

A serious Bill Cosby.

You would enjoy reading Ronald Smith's biography of Bill Cosby, *Cosby: The life of a comedy legend,* published in 1997 by Prometheus Books.

(*Personal Note.* One of the authors (JFT), while lunching at a restaurant outside of Boston, looked up to see Bill Cosby and several colleagues being seated at the next table. Cosby, in Boston to film a children's television program, looked around the room and noticed what was obviously a retirement party at another table. Observing the group with its tinge of sadness, Cosby stood up and walked over to the table. Within a matter of moments, the mood at the table became hilarious. He then moved to other tables, creating the same effect. Typical Cosby.)

In our work, we'll trace the significant changes that occur at various times in the lifespan, emphasizing that the potential for development is a constant in our lives, from youth to old age. Although these changes may not be as dramatic, tragic, and heartwarming as those we have just traced in Bill Cosby's life, they are important to us as individuals making progress through our own lifespans.

With these ideas in mind, then, we'll first explore the meaning of lifespan development in this chapter and attempt to indicate its importance to you by illustrating how peaks and valleys come into all of our lives. Although we all chart an individual course, we can still identify many similarities in our lives. We walk, we talk, we attend school, and we search for a satisfying career. Yet within this sameness, we all have and choose different experiences that shine a unique light on our journey through the lifespan.

Following this discussion, we would like you to think about various aspects of development, particularly how different viewpoints affect the way you interpret developmental change. Next we turn to several issues that are crucial in any analysis of a person's passage through the lifespan. Then we'll examine those research techniques that will help you to assess and interpret the issues, theories, and studies you'll meet in the coming pages. As Hetherington (1998) noted, current research emphasizes the scientific and multidisciplinary nature of developmental studies. Finally, we urge you to recognize the importance of biopsychosocial interactions as a means of guiding your reading and integrating the many and varied paths of development.

Guided Review

1. Lifespan psychology studies human development from _____ to _____.
2. Development is about _____.
3. Development cannot be explained by _____ alone.
4. Behavior may change in form, but results from the _____ process.

The Meaning of Lifespan Development

As you can tell from our brief discussion at the chapter's opening, development is a lifelong process—complex, intriguing, and filled with unanswered questions. One of our goals is to identify those developmental features that are common to us all: We grow physically; we become more comfortable with abstract ideas as the years pass; we attempt to control our emotions as we mature. But you should also begin to wonder about and look for answers to the question: If we're alike in so many ways, why are people so different from one another (called **inter-individual differences**)? Finally, how can we explain the differences in the potential for change within individuals (called **intra-individual differences**)?

Inter-individual differences
Differences between individuals.

Intra-individual differences
Differences in the potential for change within an individual.

Characteristics of Lifespan Development

Puzzling over these and similar questions, the well-known lifespan psychologist Paul Baltes and his colleagues (Baltes, Lindenberger, & Staudinger, 1998) identified several characteristics that attest to the uniqueness of lifespan studies.

- *A lifelong process.* No one developmental period (infancy, middle childhood, early adulthood, etc.) is dominant in the course of development. The later adult years are as important as infancy in understanding the lifespan.

- *Multidirectional.* Constant changes take place in the dynamic between biology and culture during a person's lifespan. *Thus development includes both gain and loss* (Smith & Baltes, 1999). For example, childhood is a period marked by obvious *growth;* adulthood seems to be a time of *maintenance* (and perhaps resiliency); old age forces us to adjust to *loss* (memory, for example, declines in the later years).

- *Selection.* As a result of the interaction of our genes with the environment, we make choices throughout the lifespan to further healthy development (or at least what we think is healthy development). We choose to eat certain foods to acquire energy; we may also choose not to eat if weight seems to be a problem.

- *Plasticity.* The potential for change exists throughout the lifespan. For example, it's possible to improve memory in older adults by training exercises (see chapter 17).

Answers

1. conception, death 2. change 3. age 4. same

- *Embedded in history*. Development is influenced by sociocultural conditions at any given time. For example, modern women have decidedly different developmental paths today than their grandmothers.

Studying lifespan development should provide you with insights into your own behavior and the behavior of others. Because of this, you should achieve better personal and professional relationships with those around you (Strough & others, 1996). To help you fulfill this objective, we have included *An Informed View?, A Sociocultural View,* and *Applied View* boxes. Also, for purposes of research and analysis we've divided the lifespan into the segments seen in table 1.1, while urging you to remember that each segment is part of a whole.

Guided Review

5. The infancy period extends from _____ to _____ years.
6. Later adulthood includes the years over _____.
7. The differences in potential for change within individuals is called _____ differences.
8. Development is a _____ process.

TABLE 1.1   DEVELOPMENTAL PERIODS OF THE LIFESPAN

Period	Characteristics
Prenatal (conception to birth)	Nine months of rapid growth in which organs and systems appear; extreme sensitivity to negative influences.
Infancy (birth to 2 years)	Continued rapid growth; brain development provides the basis for the emergence of motor, cognitive, and psychosocial accomplishments.
Early childhood (2 to 6 years)	Physical growth slows somewhat; substantial gains in cognitive and language development; the interplay between socialization and individuation shapes personality and influences adjustment.
Middle childhood (7 to 11 years)	School becomes a major force in development; physical, cognitive, and psychosocial abilities become apparent.
Adolescence (12 to 18 years)	The changes of puberty affect all aspects of development; thought becomes more abstract, academic achievement begins to shape the future; the search for identity continues unabated.
Early adulthood (19 to 34 years)	Higher education or the beginning of work beckons; relationships are a major focus of these years; marriage and children become central concerns of the lifespan.
Middle adulthood (35 to 64 years)	Heightened responsibility; may include care of children and aging parents; growing community involvement; peak period for leadership and influence; a time of physical change (e.g., menopause).
Later adulthood (65+)	Retirement; declining health and strength; adjusting to death of loved ones; facing one's own mortality; changing lifestyle to enhance "successful aging," enjoying greater wisdom.

Answers

Chart Your Own Lifespan

Endeavoring to illustrate how important knowledge of the lifespan is to each of us, Sugarman (1986) has devised a simple exercise that you can do quickly. Using a blank sheet of paper, assume that the left edge of the page represents the beginning of your life and the right edge where you are today. Now draw a line across the page that indicates the peaks and valleys that you have experienced so far.

For example, the chart for one of the authors of this book (JFT) is shown below.

In this chart, the first valley was a financial reversal for the author's parents. The first peak represents happy and productive high school years, followed by entry into teaching, and then marriage a few years later. The deep valley was a serious accident followed by years of recuperation and then the birth of children and the publication of a first book. You can see that it looks like a temperature chart. Try it for yourself.

Sugarman (1986) suggested that when you finish, sit back and ask yourself these questions:

- Are there more peaks than valleys?
- Is there a definite shape to my chart?
- Would I identify my peaks and valleys as major or minor?
- What caused the peaks and valleys?

- Could I have done anything to make the peaks higher and the valleys more shallow?
- What happened during the plateaus?
- What's my view of these highs and lows in my life?

You have drawn a picture of your lifespan and the questions that you have just answered are actually the subject matter of lifespan development.

Different Views of Lifespan Development

John Smith, age 17, won a four-year full scholarship at a prestigious Eastern university, capping a brilliant elementary and secondary school career. At graduation, those in attendance were buzzing about his spectacular performance.

"What do you expect; his father is brilliant, you know. The apple doesn't fall far from the tree."

"I know his father's bright, but his family must have helped him. His brother went through the same program two years ago."

As you begin to consider the possible paths that lifespan development takes and the forces that shape its direction, you may examine all the information you're about to acquire from a particular perspective. That is, you may think that once parents pass along their genes to their children, development is fixed on an unchanging path, as in the explanation of John Smith's success—biology provides most of the answers. Or you may believe that John's genes flourished in the environment he was born into. The interaction between the environment and biology tells us what we need to know about development, the second explanation. Consequently, even those who lean to one explanation or the other (biology or the environment) believe that some type of interaction holds the clues that help us to understand human growth.

Since some developmental psychologists still believe that either biology or the environment is mainly responsible for development, let's briefly examine each of these viewpoints.

A Biological Perspective

The chief claim of those adhering to a biological explanation of development points to the critical role of the genes, which establishes the rate and nature of development. In other words, maturation occurs according to a predetermined biological timetable. For example, our mental functioning is closely tied to the structure and organization of the brain. (See chapter 5 for a more detailed account of this concept.)

Although psychological development is linked to biological maturation, to what extent does biological maturation play a significant role in individual psychological differences? (For an excellent discussion of this topic see Gottlieb, Wahlsten, & Lickliter, 1998.) It's tempting to entertain the possibility of a cause-and-effect relationship between the two when you consider physical development and certain behaviors. Think of two 14-year-old boys, one of whom looks like a mature man while the other looks like a young boy. The larger, older-looking boy may have started drinking and engaging in sexual behavior and it's possible to speculate that his precocious development caused these behaviors. *But* that boy may have begun these behaviors not only because of his size: He was also accepted by and associated with bigger, older boys who engaged in similar actions. Consequently, we can't ignore the influence of experience on biological maturation.

Biological explanations of development gradually lost their appeal in the 1960s and 1970s, only to reemerge in the 1980s and 1990s with the enormous explosion of genetic knowledge, as seen in the *Human Genome Project* with its goal of mapping all the human genes. Once the study of genetics moved away from an unwavering fatalistic position—your genes are your destiny—it was easier to accept a genetic role in a wide range of behavior, both normal and abnormal. Today we realize that our genes help to expose us to certain environments. For example, parents who pass on a particular set of genes also provide a particular type of environment. Genes likewise contribute to our personalities. Happy, cheerful children receive pleasant, friendly reactions from those around them. Finally, we realize that our genes help us to select our environments. Intelligent children usually like to read, do well in school, go to college, and enjoy scholastic success (Rutter & Rutter, 1993, pp. 16–21). Consequently, today we recognize biology's contributions to all aspects of development. (See chapter 3 for a more detailed discussion of genetic action.)

A Bioecological Perspective

Reciprocal interactions
Similar to transactional model; recognizes the child's active role in its development; I do something to the child, the child changes; as a result of the changes in the child, I change.

Bioecological model
The belief that the interactions between person and environment are best explained by a system analysis.

Proximal processes
Bronfenbrenner's term for the reciprocal interactions between a person and the environment.

The environment acts in ways that we are only beginning to comprehend. For example, psychologists have for some time recognized the importance of **reciprocal interactions** in development. Reciprocal interactions mean that we respond to those around us in a way that causes them to change; their responses to us then change, which in turn produces new changes in us. These *bidirectional interactions* are an unending process that doesn't rely exclusively on either heredity or environment. Rather it uses the interactions between the two to describe and explain developmental changes that occur from birth, if not sooner.

Thanks to the systems analysis of Uri Bronfenbrenner (Bronfenbrenner, 1978, 1989; Bronfenbrenner & Morris, 1998), we now realize that there are many environments acting on us. Bronfenbrenner's perspective, called the **bioecological model,** contains four major components. The first component, **proximal processes,** refers to the reciprocal interactions between a person and the environment (often called the *context* of development). Feeding and playing with a child, peer play, and school learning with teachers are all examples of proximal processes. Bronfenbrenner & Morris (1998) refer to proximal processes as the primary engines of development.

The second component is the *person* involved, especially an individual's temperament or disposition that activates the proximal processes. Third is the person's *context,* those environmental features that either foster or interfere with development. Finally, developmental changes occur over *time,* the fourth component of the bioecological model.

Bronfenbrenner visualized the environment as a set of nested structures, each inside the next. He identified the deepest level of the environment that affects development as the **microsystem** (for example, the home or school). Next is the **mesosystem,** which refers to the relationship among microsystems. A good example is seen in a child's school achievement. Those children who are fortunate enough to be in a family that maintains close and warm relationships with the school can be expected to do well in their classroom work.

The **exosystem,** Bronfenbrenner's next level, is an environment in which the developing person is not actually present, but which nevertheless affects development. For example, an adolescent has a friend whose parents, unlike her own parents, are relaxed about late hours, no pressure to complete assignments, etc. These different parenting practices may eventually cause conflict with her own parents. The **macrosystem,** Bronfenbrenner's final level, is the blueprint of any society, which is a kind of master plan for human development within that society. Think for a moment about the differences that people in the mainland Chinese society have encountered when compared to the experiences of American citizens.

But these systems also interact over time (sometimes called the **chronosystem**); they don't remain isolated from each other. Consider the youngster whose father has just lost his job (changes in the exosystem), which then causes the family to move to another location with different friends and schools for the child (changes in the micro- and mesosystems). These examples illustrate how a bioecological analysis emphasizes the significance of context in development.

Microsystem The home or school.

Mesosystem The relationship among microsystems.

Exosystem An environment in which a person is not active but affects development.

Macrosystem The blueprint of any society.

Chronosystem The effect of time on development.

Guided Review

9. Those adhering to a biological perspective on development believe that _____ proceeds by a predetermined biological timetable.
10. The outstanding proponent of a systems analysis of development is _____ _____ .
11. Changes in you that cause changes in me are called _____ _____ .

The Importance of Biopsychosocial Interactions

Biopsychosocial interactions The idea that development proceeds by the interaction of biological, psychological, and

Today, however, most developmental psychologists emphasize the role of **biopsychosocial interactions** in development. Thinking of lifespan development as the product of the interaction of biological, environmental, as well as psychological forces, helps you to better understand and appreciate the complexity of development. Consequently, the goal of lifespan psychology is to probe the multiple and integrated layers (genetic, physical, behavioral, environmental) that drive development. Keeping these interactions in mind also provides you with a guide to explore cross-cultural and sociocultural issues that greatly enrich our understanding of human development (Garcia Coll & others, 1996).

Answers

9. maturation 10. Urit Bronfenbrenner 11. reciprocal interactions

Understanding Children's Cultures

We think it's important to recognize the contributions a particular culture makes to the development of its children. Think of **culture** as the customs, values, and traditions inherent in one's environment. Different cultures have different developmental expectations for their children. Asian children, for example, are encouraged to avoid emotional displays, a characteristic that does not necessarily apply to Asian-American children. We also urge you to remember that the *biology plus environment equals development* equation plays out within the confines of a particular culture. Consequently, understanding people's behavior demands an understanding of their cultures (Greenfield & Suzuki, 1998).

To help you grasp the significance of culture in development you should remember that there are three answers to the question: How well do you understand the cultures of your friends, workmates, or your neighbors?

1. You may understand at a *superficial* level, that is, you know only the facts that make up a person's cultural history.

2. You may understand at an *intermediate* level, that is, you understand the central behaviors that are at the core of a person's social life. Language usage is a good example here. Does a child's culture tolerate, even encourage, calling out, which could be a major problem for teachers not familiar with the acceptable behaviors of this child's culture.

3. You may understand at a *significant* level, that is, you grasp the values, beliefs, and norms that structure a person's view of the world and how to behave in that world. In other words, you change psychologically as a result of your interactions with a different culture (Casas & Pytluk, 1995).

Consequently, as we begin our work of studying lifespan development we want to impress on you the need to be aware that "different does not mean deficient." We have integrated examples of the cultural influence on development in a dual manner: through *A Sociocultural View* boxes and by age-specific examples. In this way we hope to accomplish several objectives:

- To understand the relationship between culture and development.

- To identify the values and attitudes that promote healthy development.

- To trace the impact of cultural transmission, such as parenting practices and the influence of peers, schools, and media.

Culture   Those values, beliefs, and behaviors characteristic of a large group of people, for example, those of Hispanic origin.

We pride ourselves on being a nation of immigrants, a country that welcomes newcomers with the promise of unrestricted opportunity. To achieve this objective during a time of increasing immigration demands consideration and tolerance for those of different color, nationality, and beliefs.

An excellent introduction to the changing cultural conditions in our country is *Multicultural education of children and adolescents.* This text, by M. Lee Manning and Leroy Baruth and published in Boston by Allyn and Bacon (1995) is thorough, well written, and practical.

• To assess current cultural change initiatives, such as intervention programs in the United States, and program development in other countries, such as Peru's Human Development Institute, which encourages development through the schools (Harrison, 2000).

Contributors to Biopsychosocial Interactions

If you examine table 1.2 carefully, you'll note several characteristics listed for the biological, psychological, and social aspects of interactions. These certainly aren't exhaustive but indicate several developmental features that affect growth during the lifespan. More importantly, however, we would like you to think about the interactions that occur among the three categories and how these interactions affect development. To give a simple example, genetic damage (biological) may negatively affect cognitive development (psychological), and lead to poor peer relationships (social).

We believe that by recognizing the significance of biopsychosocial interactions, you'll better understand and remember the material of any chapter. This perspective also helps to emphasize those social-cultural features that so powerfully influence development through the lifespan.

A Sociocultural View — The Impact of the Cultural Climate

Understanding cultural differences will move our relationships with others to a level of mutual understanding in all settings. As an illustration, think of the changing American classrooms, where children and teachers from many different cultures are now coming together. Many minority children have had to make major adjustments to the dominant culture in the classroom (Chen & others, 1997). Teachers who are aware of the differences between the home culture and that of the school can do much to ensure that these children succeed academically and personally to achieve their potential (Greenfield & Suzuki, 1998).

A good example of this kind of endeavor can be seen in Kim's (1990) description of Hawaiian children's school experiences. Many Hawaiian children achieve at the lowest academic level and are labeled as lazy and disruptive by some teachers. Yet these same children are remarkably responsible at home—cooking, cleaning, taking care of their brothers and sisters. They demonstrate considerable initiative and a high performance level. When something needs to be done, they get together and make a group effort to do whatever is necessary. When they find themselves in an individualistic, competitive classroom, however, their performance suffers.

In a series of experiments, teachers were encouraged to model desired behaviors and not assign specific tasks to students. By the end of the academic year, the students would begin the day by examining the schedules of their learning centers and then divide themselves into groups that assigned tasks to individual members, obtained materials, and used worksheets. Although their achievement scores improved significantly, once the students were returned to regular classrooms for the fourth grade, a familiar pattern of problems appeared (Kim, 1990).

The classroom is not the only location in which cultures merge. In the business world, people of various cultures work side by side; those designated as minorities may have leadership positions in which members of the dominant culture report to them. As companies become more global and as the number of international markets increases steadily, the workplace is beginning to resemble the classroom as a meeting place of cultures.

Our goal in urging you to adopt a multicultural perspective is to help you reach a level of significant understanding of those who seem different. If you adopt this perspective, you will come to realize that different people have different worldviews that decisively influence their thinking. People from different cultures do not all think alike. Recognizing how diverse people are in their thinking and behavior will help you to identify and comprehend variations in people's backgrounds and how they become functioning members of their culture. In this way, you will work, play, or study more congenially with others, thus fostering more positive relations in our society.

Finally, cultural awareness should also make us aware that we are all alike in important ways. It's mainly in our behavior, the manner in which we deal with the demands of our environments, that we differ.

TABLE 1.2 ELEMENTS OF BIOPSYCHOSOCIAL INTERACTIONS

Bio	Psycho	Social
Genetics	Cognitive Development	Attachment
Fertilization	Information Processing	Relationships
Pregnancy	Problem Solving	Reciprocal Interactions
Birth	Perceptual Development	School
Physical Development	Language Development	Peers
Motor Development	Moral Development	Television
Puberty	Self-efficacy	Stress
Menstruation	Personality	Marriage
Disease	Body Image	Family

Guided Review

12. The biopsychosocial model illustrates the interaction of _____ and _____ in development.
13. The values, beliefs, and behaviors that characterize a large group of people refer to that group's _____ .
14. You react to a culture at the _____ , _____ , or _____ levels of understanding.

Issues in Lifespan Development

In lifespan psychology, as in any discipline, several issues or themes appear with sufficient frequency to warrant special mention. Here we'll discuss several issues that affect your understanding of development and that appear repeatedly throughout the book.

Continuity versus Discontinuity

Do you think you are basically the same person you were when you were 3 years old? 12 years old? 20 years old? Or do you feel quite different? How would you explain your answer? These questions introduce the issue of continuity versus discontinuity, that is, do developmental changes appear as the result of a slow but steady progression **(continuity)** or as the result of abrupt changes and stages **(discontinuity)**?

As a rather dramatic illustration, consider the phenomenon known as attachment in infancy. Sometime after 6 months of age, babies begin to show a decided preference for a particular adult, usually the mother. We then say that the infant has attached to the mother. During any time of stress—anxiety, illness, appearance of strangers—the baby will move to the preferred adult. With regard to continuity or discontinuity, does attachment appear suddenly as completely new and different behavior, or do subtle clues signal its arrival? (For an excellent overview of this topic, see Rutter & Rutter, 1993.)

Continuities and discontinuities appear in all our lives because the term development implies change. Puberty, leaving home, marriage, and career all serve to

Continuity   The lasting quality of experiences; development proceeds steadily and sequentially.

Discontinuity   Behaviors that are apparently unrelated to earlier aspects of development.

shape psychological functioning. Continuities will occur, however, because our initial experiences, our early learning, and our temperaments remain with us. The form of the behavior may change over the years but the underlying processes remain the same. For example, the conduct disorders of childhood (stealing, fighting, truancy) may become the violence of adulthood (theft, wife abuse, child abuse, murder, personality disorders). Surface dissimilarities may be evident in the types of behavior, but the processes that cause both kinds of behavior may be identical, thus arguing for continuity in development (Rutter & Rutter, 1993).

Other behaviors in our lives, however, seem to be quite different from those that preceded them; for example, walking and talking. We also negotiate transitions at appropriate times in our lives, such as leaving home, beginning a career, getting married, adjusting to the birth of children. Events such as these have caused some developmental psychologists such as Michael Lewis (1997) to note that accidents, wars, famines, disease, and chance encounters have always been our bedfellows. Consequently, Lewis (1997) believes that the study of developmental change is actually the study of complex, often random, and certainly unpredictable conditions.

Most developmental psychologists now believe that both continuity and discontinuity characterize development. For example, Rutter and Rutter (1993), after examining the connections between childhood and adulthood, conclude that continuities and discontinuities both exercise their influence in a complicated mixture of direct and indirect effects.

Stability versus Change

Whether children's early experiences (either positive or negative) affect them throughout their lifespan is a question that today intrigues developmental psychologists. If a child suffers emotional or physical neglect, abuse, or malnutrition, does it mean the child is scarred for life? Or if a child has been encouraged to adopt a caring attitude toward others, will such positive behavior persevere? If you answer yes, you believe in **stability;** if your answer is no, then you accept the likelihood of change.

Stability A belief that children's early experiences affect them for life.

We know, for example, that human beings show amazing resiliency, which testifies to our ability to change (Kagan, 1998). The Werner & Smith study (1992) mentioned at the beginning of the chapter is remarkable evidence of resiliency. Yet resiliency has its limits, which testifies to the lingering effects of stability (Rutter & Rutter, 1993). Most developmental psychologists would argue for the presence of both stability and change throughout our lives.

Nature versus Nurture

An enduring issue in developmental psychology has been the question of which exercises a greater influence on development, our inborn tendencies (nature) or our surrounding world (nurture)? The issue today is often framed in a slightly different way—which is more decisive for our development, our genes or our environments? Again, most developmental psychologists lean toward an interplay between these two forces in shaping development. We (the authors) would argue strongly that the *interaction* between genes and environment explains the individual developmental paths each of us follows through our lifespans. Our belief is that human beings, using their genetic heritages, interact with their environments, not as passive recipients but as active shapers of their destinies. We'll discuss this idea in greater length throughout our work, especially in chapter 6.

These issues help to identify lifespan psychology as a dynamic discipline, one with great theoretical and practical implications. But, as fascinating as these issues are, we can't forget the integrated nature of development. With these ideas in mind to help you interpret developmental data, we turn now to those research techniques that developmental psychologists use in resolving questions about the lifespan.

Guided Review

15. A belief in _____ is to hold the opinion that early experiences in a child's life continue to exert influence throughout the lifespan.
16. Those who believe that developmental change occurs because of a slow and steady progression believe in _____ .
17. Today's developmental psychologists interpret the influence of nature and nurture as one of an _____ between the two.

Developmental Research

Having identified several key developmental issues and theoretical viewpoints, we must now ask: How can we obtain reliable data about these topics so that we may better understand them?

Today we use many approaches to understanding human behavior. Each has its strengths and weaknesses; none is completely reliable. Most developmental psychologists employ one of three data collection methods: descriptive studies, manipulative experiments, and naturalistic experiments. In the first type, information is gathered on subjects without manipulating them in any way. In the second two, an experiment is performed before the information is gathered.

An Applied View

When Are Research References Too Old?

Probably for the rest of your career, you will be reading research—articles, chapters in books, monographs, and so on. When should you decide that a reference is too old to be credible any longer? As with so many aspects of social science, the answer is "It all depends." Guidelines exist, however, so let's try to understand them by looking at several references. Before reading our decision, you might try to guess what a good judgment would be.

As many as one-third of adolescents receive less than 70 percent of their minimum daily requirement for the most common minerals such as calcium and iron (U.S. Department of Health, Education, and Welfare, 1972).

Since eating habits of adolescents are likely to change with the times (depending, among other things, on the economic condition of the country), this statistic is unreliable because about 30 years have passed since the data were collected.

Although the average number of homosexuals who are contracting AIDS each year is decreasing, they are still the most vulnerable group (U.S. National Center for Health Statistics, 1990).

This study is much more recent, but it too is suspect because we know that the AIDS epidemic is changing very rapidly. In fact, heterosexual females are now experiencing the greatest rate of increase per capita.

Noise-induced hearing loss is recognized as the second most common cause of irreversible hearing loss in older persons (Surjan & others, 1973).

Here is another study that is quite dated, but because there is no known reason to believe that aging factors have changed much over the years, if the study was well designed, we may still accept the results.

The major crisis in the first year and one-half of human life is the establishment of basic trust (Erikson, 1963).

This statement is not a research finding but rather represents Erikson's belief as reflected in his psychosocial theory of human development. As such, it is accurate because that is exactly what Erikson said.

Can you think of other factors that influence the timeliness of research references? Can you think of other criteria for judging them?

One-time, one-group studies
Studies carried out only once on one group of studies.

Longitudinal studies The experimenter makes several observations of the same individuals at two or more times in their lives. Examples are: determining the long-term effects of learning on behavior; the stability of habits and intelligence; and the factors involved in memory.

Cross-sectional studies This method compares groups of individuals of various ages at the same time in order to investigate the effects of aging.

Sequential (longitudinal/ cross-sectional) studies
A cross-sectional study done at several times with the same groups of individuals.

Descriptive studies
Information is gathered on subjects without manipulating them in any way.

Manipulative experiments
The experimenter attempts to keep all variables (all the factors that can affect a particular outcome) constant except one, which is carefully manipulated.

Treatment The variable that the experimenter manipulates.

Developmental psychologists also use one of four time variable designs: **one-time, one-group studies; longitudinal studies; cross-sectional studies;** and a combination of the last two, called **sequential studies.** Each type of study varies according to the effect of time on the results.

Data Collection Techniques

The three data collection techniques are described in the following sections.

Descriptive Studies

Descriptive studies are quite common. Most are numerically descriptive; for example, how many 12-year-olds versus 17-year-olds think the government is doing a good job? How much money does the average 40-year-old woman have to spend per week? How many pregnant teenage girls were or were not using birth control? How happily or unhappily does the average 66-year-old man view his sex life? Some studies ask people their opinions about themselves (called self-report studies) or other people. These studies may use interviews or questionnaires. Other studies describe people simply by counting the number and types of their behaviors (called observational studies). A third type of study, case studies, presents data on an individual or individuals in great detail, in order to make generalizations about a particular age group.

An example of the case study approach is Mack and Hickler's *Vivienne: The Life and Suicide of an Adolescent Girl* (1982). After Vivienne's death, the researchers obtained the family's permission to read her diary, poems, and letters. They also interviewed her relatives, friends, and teachers to shed light on her thinking as she came closer and closer to committing this tragic act. Although their findings may explain the suicide of only this one person, the researchers' hope was to discover the variables that caused such a decision. A more recent case study approach is of the biographical type. For example, Gardner (1997) closely examined the biographies of four eminent persons: Wolfgang Mozart, Sigmund Freud, Virginia Woolf, and Mahatma Gandhi. From these four cases, he built a new theory about creative innovation.

Descriptive studies have the advantage of generating a great deal of data. Because the sequence of events is not under the observer's control, however, causes and effects cannot be determined. That is, just because two variables are associated does not mean that one causes the other.

Typically, the association between variables is established through a statistical technique known as correlation. This technique provides a numerical evaluation of how great the degree of association is between any two variables. For instance, height and weight are associated with each other, but not perfectly. The taller people are, the more they weigh, but this is not always true; the correlation between height and weight for a typical sample of people is moderately high. Although there is a definite association, we would not say the height causes weight, or vice versa—they are simply correlated. We examine the correlation between variables to see how high they are. If high, we may want to set up experiments to further examine the relationship.

Manipulative Experiments

In the quest for the causes of behavior, psychologists have designed many **manipulative experiments.** In these, the investigators attempt to keep all variables (all the factors that can affect a particular outcome) constant except one, which they carefully manipulate; this is called a **treatment.** If differences occur in the results of the experiment, they can be attributed to the variable that was manipulated in the treatment. The experimental subjects must respond to some test the investigator selects to determine the effect of the treatment. Figure 1.1 illustrates this procedure.

In the figure, E is the experimental group and C is the control group, which receives no special treatment; *x* stands for the treatment; and the lowercase *b* and *a*

Figure 1.1

The classic experiment.

From John F. Travers, *The Growing Child*, Scott, Foresman and Company, Glenview, IL, 1982. Reprinted by permission of the author.

refer to measurements done before and after the experiment. The two groups must have no differences between them, either before or during the experiment (except the treatment). Otherwise, the results remain questionable.

An example would be a study in which sixth and seventh grade inner city students were taught relaxation techniques as part of a conflict prevention program (Dacey, deSalvatore & Robinson, 1997). Most students benefited from the instruction, but boys were much more apt to use the physiological relaxation technique taught in the program, whereas girls were more likely to employ the cognitive method that was taught.

Though manipulative experiments often can lead us to discover what causes what in life, they have some problems. How do you know your results are reliable? Was the treatment similar to normal conditions? Do subjects see themselves as special because you picked them and thus react atypically? For these reasons, researchers may turn to naturalistic experiments.

Naturalistic Experiments

Naturalistic experiments In these experiments, the researcher acts solely as an observer and does as little as possible to disturb the environment. "Nature" performs the experiment, and the researcher acts as a recorder of the results.

In **naturalistic experiments,** the researcher acts solely as an observer and does as little as possible to disturb the environment. "Nature" performs the experiment, and the researcher acts as a recorder of the results. (Note: Do not confuse these experiments with descriptive studies that are done in a natural setting, such as a park; those are not experiments.) An example is the study of the effects of the Northeast blizzard of 1978 by Nuttall and Nuttall (1980). These researchers compared the reactions of those people whose homes were destroyed with the reactions of people whose homes suffered only minor damage.

Only with a naturalistic experiment do we have any chance of discovering causes and effects in real-life settings. The main problems with this technique are that it requires great patience and objectivity, and it is impossible to meet the strict requirements of a true scientific experiment.

Time Variable Designs

Time variable designs The number of times and the number of groups that are studied in a research project.

In the following sections, we'll describe the four **time variable designs.**

One-Time, One-Group Studies

As the name implies, one-time, one-group studies are those that are carried out only once on one group of subjects. Thus investigating causes and effects is impossible because the sequence of events cannot be known.

Longitudinal Studies

The **longitudinal study,** which makes several observations of the same individuals at two or more times in their lives, can answer important questions. Examples are determining the long-term effects of learning on behavior; the stability of habits and intelligence; and the factors involved in memory.

A good example of a longitudinal growth study is that of Werner and Smith (1992) who investigated the long-term effects of birth problems. They found that even when the problems were of a serious nature, some children proved to be remarkably resilient.

The chief advantage of the longitudinal method is that it permits the discovery of lasting habits and of the periods in which they appear. A second advantage is the possibility of tracing those adult behaviors that have changed since early childhood. Longitudinal research, however, has many problems. It is expensive and often hard to maintain because of changes in availability of researchers and subjects. Changes in the environment can also distort the results. For example, if you began in 1960 to study changes in political attitudes of youths from 10 to 20 years of age, you would probably have concluded that adolescents become more and more radical as they grow older. But the war in Vietnam would surely have had much to do with this finding. The results of the same study done between 1970 and 1980 would probably not show this trend toward the radical.

Cross-Sectional Studies

Cross-sectional studies compare groups of individuals of various ages at the same time to investigate the effects of aging. For example, if you want to know how creative thinking changes or grows during adolescence, you could administer creativity tests to groups of 10-, 12-, 14-, 16-, and 18-year-olds and check on the differences of the average scores of the five groups. Jaquish and Ripple (1980) did just this, but their subjects ranged in age from 10 to 84!

As with each of the other research designs, a problem occurs with this method. Although careful selection can minimize the effects of cultural change, it is possible that the differences you may find may be due to differences in age cohort, rather than maturation. Age cohorts are groups of people born at about the same time. Each cohort has had different experiences throughout its history, and this can affect the results as well as the actual differences in age. Figure 1.2 compares the longitudinal and cross-sectional approaches.

Sequential (Longitudinal/Cross-Sectional) Studies

When a cross-sectional study is done at several times with the same groups of individuals (such as administering creativity tests to the same five groups of youth, but at three different points in their lives), the problems mentioned before can be alleviated. Table 1.2 illustrates such a study. Although this type of research is complicated and expensive, it may be the only type that is capable of answering important questions in the complex and fast-changing times in which we live.

Table 1.3 shows how each of the data collection methods may be combined with each of the time variable designs. For each of the cells in this table, a number of actual studies could serve as examples. Can you see where each study mentioned in this section would go?

To conclude this section, figure 1.3 compares the various research techniques. By controlled, we mean the degree to which the investigator can control the relevant variables. By inclusive, we mean the degree to which all relevant information is included in the data.

Figure 1.2

Comparison of the longitudinal and cross-sectional approaches.

TABLE 1.2 ILLUSTRATION OF A LONGITUDINAL/CROSS-SECTIONAL STUDY

Creativity Test

Test 1 March 4, 1999	Test 2 March 4, 2001	Test 3 March 4, 2003	
Group A (12-years-old)	Group A (14-years-old)	Group A (16-years-old)	Mean Score Group A
Group B (14-years-old)	Group B (16-years-old)	Group B (18-years-old)	Mean Score Group B
Group C (16-years-old)	Group C (18-years-old)	Group C (20-years-old)	Mean Score Group C
Mean Score 1999	Mean Score 2001	Mean Score 2003	

From John F. Travers, *The Growing Child,* Scott, Foresman and Company, Glenview, IL, 1982. Reprinted by permission of the author.

TABLE 1.3 RELATIONSHIPS OF DATA COLLECTION TECHNIQUES AND TIME VARIABLE DESIGNS

Data Collection Techniques

Time Variable Designs	Descriptive	Manipulated	Naturalistic
One-time, one-group	_____	_____	_____
Longitudinal	_____	_____	_____
Cross-sectional	_____	_____	_____
Sequential	_____	_____	_____

Guided Review

18. In a manipulative experiment, the experimenter attempts to keep all the variables constant except one, which is called the _____ .
19. A study that observes the same individuals two or more times in their lives is known as a _____ study.
20. Comparing groups of individuals of various ages at the same time is an example of _____ research.

Figure 1.3

A comparison of research techniques.

Answers

An Applied
VIEW   *Understanding the Research Article*

As you continue your reading and work in lifespan development, your instructor will undoubtedly ask you to review pertinent articles that shed light on the topic you're studying. Many of these articles present the results of an experiment that reflects the scientific method.

The typical research article contains four sections: the *Introduction,* the *Method* section, the *Results* section, and *Discussion* (Moore, 1983). We'll review each of these sections using a well-designed study—*The Effects of Early Education on Children's Competence in Elementary School,* published in *Evaluation Review* (Bronson & others, 1984)—to illustrate each of the four sections.

Abstract

1. The Introduction
   The introductory section states the purpose of the article (usually as an attempt to solve a problem) and predicts the outcome of the study (usually in the form of hypotheses). The introduction section also contains a review of the literature. In the introductory section of the article by Bronson and her associates, the researchers state that their intent is to coordinate the effects of early education programs on the performance of pupils in elementary school. They concisely review the pertinent research and suggest a means of evaluating competence.

2. The Method Section
   The method section informs the reader about the subjects in the experiment (Who were they? How many? How were they chosen?), describes any tests that were used, and summarizes the steps taken to carry out the study. In the study by Bronson and her associates, the subjects were 169 second-grade children who had been in an early education program and 169 other children who had not been in the preschool program. The outcome measure was a classroom observation instrument. The authors then explained in considerable detail how they observed the pupils.

3. The Results Section
   In the results section, the results gathered on the subjects is presented, together with the statistics that help us to interpret the data. In the article we are using, the authors present their data in several clear tables and show differences between the two groups using appropriate statistics.

4. Discussion
   Finally, the authors of any research article will discuss the importance of what they found (or did not find) and relate their findings to theory and previous research. In the Bronson article, the authors report that the pupils who had experienced any early education program showed significantly greater competence in the second grade. The authors conclude by noting the value of these programs in reducing classroom behavior problems and improving pupils' competence.

   Conclusion

   Don't be intimidated by research articles. Look for the important features and determine how the results could help you to understand people's behavior at a particular age.

CONCLUSION & SUMMARY

In this chapter we urged you to think about lifespan development as a rich, multilayered complex of interactions. We presented a model of development—the biopsychosocial model—that forms the structure of this book. We urge you to use this model to help you grasp and retain the material and meaning of the various chapters. We have also identified the various age groups that constitute the lifespan and that are the focus of this book. As a result of reading about the strengths and weaknesses of different research methods, you should be more analytical and critical of the studies that are presented.

Lifespan study can aid us in adjusting to a society in which rapid change seems to be an inevitable process. By acquiring insights into your own development and recognizing the developmental characteristics of people of differing ages, you can hope to have more harmonious relationships with others.

How would you define and describe lifespan development?

- As psychologists realized that development did not cease at adolescence but continued into adulthood and old age, lifespan psychology assumed an important place in developmental psychology.
- To understand development is to accept the positive and negative features of change.
- The timing of experiences as well as the transitions during the lifespan help us to gain insights into developmental processes.
- Development cannot be explained by age alone.

What are the characteristics of lifespan development?

- Individual differences lead to differences in the potential for change.
- No one developmental period dominates the course of human development.

- The dynamic between biology and culture changes constantly during a person's life.
- A major feature of the heredity-environment interaction is the necessity for people to make continual choices to further healthy development.

What are the different views of lifespan development?

- A biological perspective on development emphasizes the powerful impact the genes have on development.
- The bioecological model recognizes the importance of proximal processes in development.
- The need for more sophisticated perspectives on development has highlighted the place of reciprocal interactions in development.

What role do biopsychosocial interactions play in lifespan development?

- Biopsychosocial interactions in human development refer to the interactions of biological, psychological, and social forces.

- Biopsychosocial interactions occur at multiple levels of the developing person, from the genetic to the environmental levels.
- Analyzing development from a biopsychosocial perspective helps to identify the complexities of human development.

What are the major issues in lifespan development?

- Any analysis of lifespan development must address key developmental issues, such as the importance of culture and development, if it is to present a complete picture of development.
- Many psychologists believe that development occurs as a steady progression of small accomplishments (for example, most infants begin to move on the floor by pulling themselves on their stomachs; they then move to a position on their hands and knees and move much more quickly, which is an example of continuous development); other psychologists believe that development occurs in spurts or stages, such as the marked

difference between crawling and walking, which is an example of discontinuity.
- The controversy over stability versus change continues to divide developmental psychologists.
- Resiliency is a fact of human development that requires cautious interpretation.

What is the role of research in studying lifespan development?

- To explain the various ages and stages of development, we must use the best data available to enrich our insights and to provide a thoughtful perspective on the lifespan.
- Good data demand careful research methods, otherwise we would be constantly suspicious of our conclusions.
- The most widely used research techniques include descriptive studies, manipulative experiments, and naturalistic experiments.
- Developmental psychologists also use four time variable designs: one-time, one-group; longitudinal studies; cross-sectional studies; and sequential studies.

KEY TERMS

Bioecological model
Biopsychosocial interactions
Chronosystem
Continuity
Cross-sectional studies
Culture
Descriptive studies
Development
Discontinuity

Inter-individual differences
Intra-individual differences
Lifespan psychology
Longitudinal studies
Manipulative experiments
Macrosystem
Mesosystem
Microsystem
Naturalistic experiments

One-time, one-group studies
Proximal processes
Reciprocal interactions
Sequential studies
Stability
Time variable designs
Treatment

WHAT DO YOU THINK?

1. We urged you to refer to the biopsychosocial model as you continue your reading of the text. Can you explain its potential value? Now think of an example in your own life, or in the life of a family member, and describe how biological, psychological, and social factors interacted to produce a particular effect. Do you think the model helped you to explain that person's behavior?

2. We presented several issues that thread their way through lifespan studies; for example, culture and development, the role of sensitive periods, continuity versus discontinuity, stability versus change. Why do you think these are issues? Examine each one separately and defend your reasons for stating that each has strong developmental implications.

3. Throughout the chapter, we have stressed the important role that the environment or context plays in development. What do you think of this emphasis? Although this is only the first chapter of your reading, recall your own life and think about the influence (both positive and negative) that those around you have had. Use these personal experiences in your answer.

CHAPTER REVIEW TEST

1. Development is about
   a. change.
   b. age.
   c. gender.
   d. genes.

2. Development is
   a. a lifelong process.
   b. age focused.
   c. topically restricted.
   d. circular in nature.

3. Lifespan psychology assumes that development is
   a. unidimensional.
   b. chronologically explained.
   c. multidirectional.
   d. age limited.

4. Developmental psychologists not only attempt to explain inter-individual differences, but also
   a. personal processes.
   b. reinforcement schedules.
   c. cognitive barriers.
   d. intra-individual differences.

5. A model that uses the interaction of biological, psychological, and social influences to explain development is the
   a. psychoanalytic.
   b. cognitive.
   c. biopsychosocial.
   d. behavioral.

6. When one person's reactions bring about change in the behavior of another person, this is called
   a. transfer.
   b. reciprocal interactions.
   c. accommodation.
   d. psychosocial crisis.

7. The resurgence of interest in biological explanations of development is due to
   a. government subsidies.
   b. the influence of learning theorists.
   c. recent genetic research.
   d. studies of prenatal development.

8. Who believed that a system analysis of development was most fruitful?
   a. Watson
   b. Piaget
   c. Gesell
   d. Bronfenbrenner

9. When we refer to the values, beliefs, and characteristics of a people, we are referring to
   a. culture.
   b. race.
   c. ethnicity.
   d. customs.

10. The relationship among microsystems is referred to as the
    a. mesosystem.
    b. exosystem.
    c. macrosystem.
    d. ecosystem.

11. More complex explanations of development depend on the idea of
    a. genes.
    b. reciprocal interactions.
    c. naturalistic research.
    d. stimulus-response experiments.

12. Descriptive studies
    a. determine cause and effect.
    b. manipulate variables.
    c. require experimenter control.
    d. generate considerable data.

13. When an experimenter keeps all variables constant but one, that one is called
    a. determined.
    b. predicted.
    c. descriptive.
    d. treatment.

14. An example of a cross-sectional study is
    a. comparing individuals of various ages at the same time.
    b. continued observations of the same individuals.
    c. careful description by the researcher.
    d. one that requires no manipulation.

15. The typical research article contains four sections. Which item is not included in a research article?
    a. introduction
    b. method
    c. results
    d. author biography

Answers

1.a 2.a 3.c 4.d 5.c 6.b 7.c 8.d 9.a 10.a 11.b 12.d 13.d 14.a 15.d

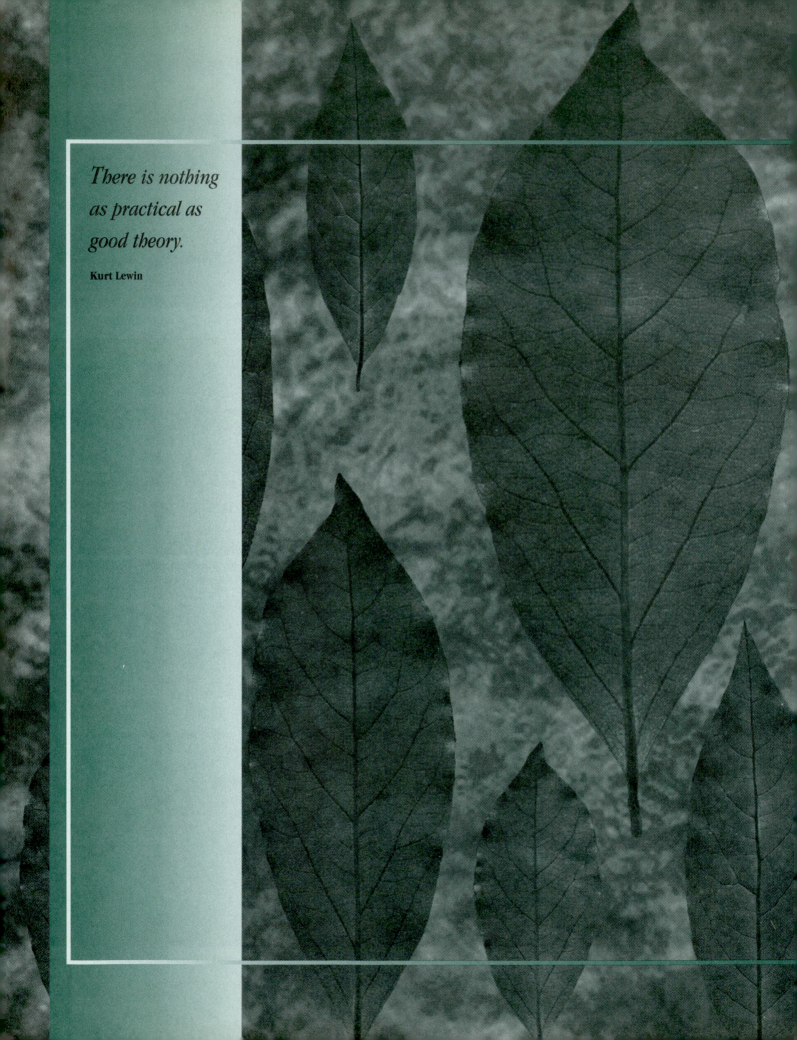

There is nothing as practical as good theory.

Kurt Lewin

Chapter Outline

I n this chapter, you'll read about several of the leading developmental theories. After you have finished your reading, we would like you to analyze the information in the following case study and interpret it according to a theory (or theories) you have just studied. For example, let's assume you use Skinner's ideas on reinforcement. You would want to mention the need for positive reinforcement: Was Thomas receiving needed reinforcements at home and school? Could anything be done about it? Do you think proper reinforcement would improve Thomas' behavior? Another of your classmates may believe that Erikson's work is more applicable. Discuss and compare the various interpretations. Or is the answer to Thomas' problems to be found, as Lerner suggests, in the interactions among various levels of development? There are no right or wrong answers, rather we would like you and your classmates to discuss your various interpretations and actually see how theory guides your analysis of behavior.

I. Background Information

A. Thomas: 8 years old
    White
    Public school
    First grade (not promoted)
    Sixth of six children
B. Home Conditions

The mother is 42 years old, separated from her husband, and almost totally blind. Four of the six children live with her in a low-income section of the city. The oldest son and a married daughter do not reside in the home.

II. The Problem

Thomas, bothered by asthma, exhibits frequent temper tantrums and is failing the first grade for the second time.

III. History

Thomas is the youngest of six children; his birth was accompanied by marital and family problems. The pregnancy was unplanned and unwanted, and the father left home before the child was born. Thomas was born prematurely, had immediate difficulty with breathing, and was put in a respirator for twenty days before coming home.

Feeding, motor development, and verbal development were all normal, but he manifested considerable separation anxiety; that is, he cried excessively when his mother left him alone. He still shows signs of this behavior at 8 years of age, although less frequently. The mother states that he is "fidgety" (cannot remain still) and that he worries about his small size.

IV. Impressions

After several interviews with both the boy and his mother, the case worker commented that both mother and child display clear signs of anxiety. A definite theme of aggression and violence runs through Thomas' conversation. Teachers report that he exhibits little motivation and bothers other children in class. He has a very short attention span and shows increasing aggressiveness.

The interviewer reported that the mother seeks constant reassurance and experiences great difficulty with the disciplining of her children. The interviewer stated that the combination of an insecure mother and an unhappy, aggressive son whom she is finding difficult to control points to serious developmental problems for Thomas.

V. Summary

Thomas continues to do very poorly in school. He wants love from and dependence on his mother, yet simultaneously seeks independence and escape from his mother's control. This conflict produces ambivalent feelings toward his mother. That is, he displays considerable anger toward his mother for trying to control him; he bitterly resents his father's absence.

Instead of expressing his anger, he remains passive, especially in school, which is the primary cause of his poor scholastic performance. Thomas' behavior resolves his conflict, however, since he can remain with his mother but also strike back at her with his school failure. ✪

At first glance James Watson and Francis Crick looked like any other young instructors at England's Cambridge University. But there was soon to be something quite different about them. On a winter's day in 1953, they shocked the biological world and took the first step toward their future Nobel prizes when they burst into a pub near their laboratory and announced to their astonished colleagues that "they had discovered the secret of life." Just hours before, they had finally determined the exact model of DNA. After years of theory building, testing, failure, and theory revision, Watson and Crick persevered and triumphed. The search for the DNA model is an excellent example of the importance of theory.

You may be inclined to say, "The facts, please, just the facts," like many of us often do. But facts alone are insufficient for interpretation, insight, and application. Always needed is some focus, some structure to give meaning to the facts. In life-span development that focus is found in theory, the perspective that leads us, sometimes clearly, sometimes grudgingly, to understanding. We believe that theories do not stand alone; they are related to other aspects of science, that is, they should be

Francis Crick and James Watson with their model of DNA, which won them the Nobel prize in 1962.

tested experimentally and applied to actual situations. Only in this way can the truthfulness and usefulness of any theory be assessed.

In this chapter, we'll first turn to the major theorists who for many years have guided our thinking about development: Sigmund Freud, Erik Erikson, Jean Piaget, Lev Vygotsky, B. F. Skinner, and Albert Bandura. Next we'll discuss the present status of developmental theory and several issues related to the direction of developmental theory. Finally, we'll use Richard Lerner's notion of contextualism to reflect recent thinking regarding new directions in developmental analysis, which we hinted at in chapter 1.

Psychoanalytic theory
Freud's theory of the development of personality.

Chapter Objectives

After you read this chapter, you should be able to answer the following questions.

◆ How does psychoanalytic theory explain development across the lifespan?

◆ What is the relationship between psychosocial crises and lifespan development?

◆ How did Piaget explain cognitive development?

◆ What impact does culture have on lifespan development?

◆ What is the behavioral perspective on development?

◆ What is the status of current developmental theory?

Dr. Sigmund Freud was a medical doctor who proposed the psychoanalytic theory of development.

The Psychoanalytic Approach

On a beautiful spring day in 1885, Sigmund Freud sat down and wrote a startling letter to his fiancee. Telling her that he had just about completed a massive task—destroying his notes, letters, and manuscripts of the past fourteen years, a destructive act that he would repeat several times in his lifetime—Freud revealed his mistrust of future biographers. Yet, in spite of his efforts, the autobiographical nature of much of his published works and his vast correspondence left a lasting legacy.

Freud's ideas no longer dominate developmental psychology as they did in the early part of the twentieth century. Yet his insistence on the early years as decisive in development has remained a potent and controversial concept (Cairns, 1998). In more than 100 years of psychological research, it is impossible to think of anyone who has played a larger role than Sigmund Freud. Even his most severe critics admit that his theory on the development of personality is a milestone in the social sciences (Ferris, 1997).

Let's begin by examining Freud's ideas about the structure of the mind.

Sigmund Freud suggested that babies react to needful feelings such as hunger in several steps. First they become aware of the need, then they cry; next they imagine that the need has been met, and then they fall back to sleep. Slowly they learn that imagination is no substitute for real satisfaction of a need.

> ### TABLE 2.1 SOME COMMON DEFENSE MECHANISMS
>
> **Repression**   Unconsciously forgetting experiences that are painful to remember. Example: failure to remember an incident of sexual abuse.
>
> **Compensation**   Attempting to make up for an unconsciously perceived inadequacy by excelling at something else. Example: learning to play the guitar if unable to make the soccer team.
>
> **Rationalization**   Coming to believe that a condition that was contrary to your desires is actually what you had wanted all along. Example: being glad a trip was canceled, because "it would have been boring anyway."
>
> **Introjection**   Adopting the standards and values of someone you are afraid to disagree with. Example: joining a gang.
>
> **Regression**   Reverting to behaviors that were previously successful when current behavior is unsuccessful. Example: crying about getting a low grade in school with the unconscious hope that the teacher will change the grade.
>
> **Displacement**   When afraid to express your feelings toward one person (e.g., anger at your teacher), expressing them to someone less powerful, such as your sister.

From John F. Travers, *The Growing Child,* Scott, Foresman and Company, Glenview, IL, 1982. Reprinted by permission of the author.

Structures of the Mind

Id   One of the three structures of the psyche according to Freud; the source of our instinctive desires.

Ego   One of the three structures of the psyche according to Freud; mediates between the id and the superego.

Superego   One of the three structures of the psyche according to Freud; acts as a conscience.

Freud divided the mind into three structures: the **id,** the **ego,** and the **superego,** which appear at different stages of a child's development. They are empowered by the libido, Freud's term for psychic energy, which is similar to the physical energy that fuels bodily functions. The characteristics of the three structures of the mind are as follows:

- *The id.* This structure, the only one present at birth, contains all of our basic instincts, such as our need for food, drink, dry clothes, and nurturance. The simplest of the structures, it strives only to secure pleasure.

- *The ego.* The ego is the central part of our personality, the (usually) rational part that does all the planning and keeps us in touch with reality. It begins to develop from the moment of birth. Freud believed that the stronger the ego becomes, the more realistic, and usually the more successful, a person is likely to be.

- *The superego.* Throughout infancy, we gain an increasingly clearer conception of what the world is like. Toward the end of the first year our parents and others begin to teach us what they believe is right and wrong and expect us to begin to behave according to the principles they espouse.

Now starts the never-ending battle between the desires of the id and the demands of the superego, with the ego struggling unceasingly for compromises between these two powerful forces.

Freud also believed that an array of defense mechanisms keeps important information in the unconscious mind from awareness, an attempt to decrease anxiety in the conflict between the id and the ego. These mechanisms are unconscious attempts to prevent awareness of unpleasant or unacceptable ideas. Table 2.1 describes some of the most common defense mechanisms.

The Developing Personality

For Freud, personality development means moving through five stages, each of which he assigns to a specific age range. Each stage is discrete from the others and has a major function, which is based on a pleasure center. Unless this pleasure center is stimulated appropriately (not too much, not too little), the person becomes fixated (stuck at that stage) and is unable to become a fully mature person. Here are the five stages.

Oral stage Freud's belief that the mouth is the main source of pleasure from 0 to 1½ years.

Anal stage Freud's belief that the anus is the main source of pleasure during the years 1½ to 3 years.

Phallic stage Freud's belief that the sex organs become the main source of pleasure from 3 to 5 years.

Latency stage Freud's belief that the sex drive becomes dormant 5 to 12 years.

Genital stage Freud's belief in a resurgence of a strong sex drive from 12 years and beyond.

Maturity is a high price to pay for growing up.

Tom Stoppard

Ferris, Paul. (1998). *Dr. Freud: A life*. Washington, D.C.: Counterpoint. A highly personal account of the life of one of the most controversial figures of the twentieth century, a revealing portrait of the man, his ideas, and his technique.

- The **oral stage** (0 to 1½ years old). The oral cavity (mouth, lips, tongue, gums) is the pleasure center. Its function is to obtain an appropriate amount of sucking, eating, biting, and talking.

- The **anal stage** (1½ to 3 years old). The anus is the pleasure center. The function here is successful toilet training.

- The **phallic stage** (3 to 5 years old). The glans of the penis and the clitoris are the pleasure centers in this stage and in the two remaining stages. The major function of this stage is the healthy development of sexual interest, which is achieved through masturbation and unconscious sexual desire for the parent of the opposite sex. Resolution of the conflicts caused by this desire (called the Oedipal conflict in males and the Electra conflict in females) is the goal.

- The **latency stage** (5 to 12 years old). During this stage, sexual desire becomes dormant, which is especially true for males through the defense mechanism of introjection (see table 2.1). Boys refuse to kiss or hug their mothers and treat female age-mates with disdain. Because our society is more tolerant of the daughter's attraction to her father, the Electra complex is less resolved and girls' sexual feelings may be less repressed during this stage.

- The **genital stage** (12 years old and older). At this stage a surge of sexual hormones occurs in both genders, which brings about an unconscious recurrence of the phallic stage. Normally, however, youths have learned that desire for one's parents is taboo, and so they set about establishing relationships with members of the opposite sex who are their own age. If fixation occurs at any stage, anxiety results, and defense mechanisms will be used to deal with it.

Guided Review

1. For Freud, the best way to understand the human being is through the _____ .

2. An unconscious attempt to avoid awareness of unpleasant ideas is called _____ .

3. The structure of the mind containing our basic instincts is called _____ .

4. When a person attempts to excel at one thing because of feeling inadequate in another, this is called _____ .

5. Reverting to behaviors of an earlier age is called _____ .

6. In the developing personality, when pleasure is derived from such behaviors as sucking, this is the _____ stage.

Psychosocial Crises and Development

Influenced by Freud, but searching for a different perspective, Erik Erikson, the chief proponent of a psychosocial theory of development (as opposed to Freud's psychosexual) wrote *Childhood and Society* (1963), a perceptive and at times poetic description of human life. Erikson's view of human development flowed from his extensive study of people living in an impressive variety of cultures: Germans, East Indians, the Sioux of South Dakota, the Yuroks of California, and wealthy adolescents in the northeastern United States (Erikson, 1959, 1968). His ideas also stem from intensive studies of historical figures such as Martin Luther (Erikson, 1958) and Mahatma Gandhi (Erikson, 1969).

Answers

1. unconscious 2. repression 3. id 4. compensation 5. regression 6. oral

Psychologist Erik Erikson is best known for his theory of psychosocial crises.

According to Erikson, human life progresses through a series of eight stages. Each of these stages is marked by a crisis that needs to be resolved so that the individual can move on. Erikson used the term crisis in a medical sense; that is, it is like an acute period during illness, at the end of which the patient takes a turn for the worse or better. Table 2.2 gives an overview of his psychosocial theory.

Erikson's Eight Psychosocial Stages

Let us look at each stage more closely.

1. *Basic trust versus mistrust* (birth to 1 year old). In the first stage, which is by far the most important, infants should develop a sense of basic trust. For Erikson, trust has an unusually broad meaning. To the trusting infant, it is not so much that the world is a safe and happy place but rather that it is an orderly, predictable place, that is, infants learn about causes and effects. Trust flourishes with warmth, care, and also discipline.

2. *Autonomy versus shame and doubt* (2 to 3 years old). When children are about 1½ years old, they should move into the second stage, characterized by the crisis of autonomy versus shame and doubt. Children begin to gain control over their bodies and toilet training usually begins during these years. Erikson agreed with other psychoanalysts about the importance of toilet training and believed that the sources of generosity and creativity lie in this experience. Toilet training is not the only accomplishment of the period; children of this age usually start acquiring self-control.

3. *Initiative versus guilt* (4 to 5 years old). The third crisis, initiative versus guilt, begins when children are about 3 years old. Building on the ability to control themselves, children now acquire some influence over others in the family and begin to successfully manipulate their surroundings. They don't merely react, they also initiate. If parents and others make children feel incompetent, however, they develop a generalized feeling of guilt about themselves. Erikson believed that play was particularly important during these years, both as an aid to a child's identity and as a safe way to reduce tension by dealing with problems in a symbolic way (Csikszentmihalyi & Rathunde, 1998).

TABLE 2.2 ERIK ERIKSON'S PSYCHOSOCIAL THEORY OF DEVELOPMENT

Age (years)	Stage	Psychosocial Crisis	Psychosocial Strength	Environmental Influence
1	Infancy	Trust vs. mistrust	Hope	Maternal
2–3	Early childhood	Autonomy vs. shame, doubt	Willpower	Both parents or adult substitutes
4–5	Preschool, nursery school	Initiative vs. guilt	Purpose	Parents, family, friends
6–11	Middle childhood	Industry vs. inferiority	Competence	School
12–18	Adolescence	Identity vs. identity confusion	Fidelity	Peers
18–35	Young adulthood	Intimacy vs. isolation	Love	Partners: spouse/lover friends
35–65	Middle age	Generativity vs. stagnation	Care	Family, society
Over 65	Old age	Integrity vs. despair	Wisdom	All humans

From *Childhood and Society* by Erik H. Erikson. Copyright 1950, © 1963 by W.W. Norton & Company, Inc., renewed © 1978, 1991 by Erik H. Erikson. Used by permission of W.W. Norton & Company, Inc.

4. *Industry versus inferiority* (6 to 11 years old). The fourth stage corresponds closely to the child's elementary school years. Now the task is to go beyond imitating ideal models and acquire the needed information and skills of their culture. Children expand their horizons beyond the family and begin to explore the neighborhood. Their play becomes more purposeful, and they seek knowledge to complete the tasks that they set for themselves. A sense of accomplishment in making and building should prevail, otherwise children may develop a lasting sense of inferiority.

5. *Identity and repudiation versus identity confusion* (12 to 18 years old). The main task of the adolescent is to achieve a state of identity. Erikson, who originated the term **identity crisis,** used the word in a special way. In addition to thinking of identity as the general picture one has of oneself, Erikson referred to it as a state toward which one strives. If you are in a state of identity, the various aspects of your self-image would be in agreement with each other; they would be identical.

6. *Intimacy and solidarity versus isolation* (18 to 35 years old). In the sixth stage, intimacy with others should develop. Erikson is speaking here of far more than sexual intimacy. He is talking about the essential ability to relate one's deepest hopes and fears to another person, and to accept in turn another person's need for intimacy.

7. *Generativity versus stagnation* (35 to 65 years old). Generativity means the ability to be useful to ourselves and to society. As in the industry stage, the goal here is to be productive and creative thus leading to a sense of personal fulfillment. Furthermore, a sense of trying to make the world a better place for the young in general, and for one's own children in particular, emerges. In this stage many people become mentors to younger individuals, sharing their knowledge and philosophy of life. When people fail in generativity, they begin to stagnate, to become bored and self-indulgent, unable to contribute to society's welfare. Such adults often act as if they are their own child.

8. *Integrity versus despair* (65 years old and older). To the extent that individuals have been successful in resolving the first seven crises, they achieve a sense of personal integrity. Adults who have a sense of integrity accept their lives as having been well spent. They feel a kinship with

Identity crisis   Erikson's term for those situations, usually in adolescence, that cause us to make major decisions about our identity.

According to Erikson, a sense of intimacy with another person of the opposite gender should develop between the ages of 18 and 25. If it does not, a sense of isolation results.

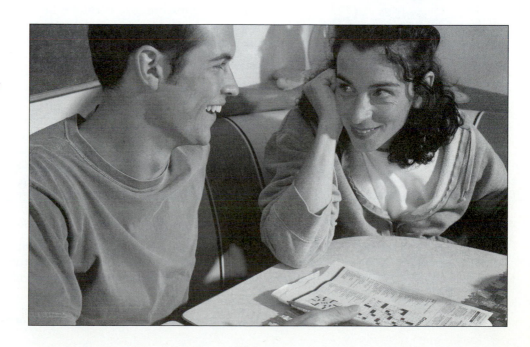

people of other cultures and of previous and future generations. They have a sense of having helped to create a more dignified life for humankind. They have gained wisdom.

If, however, people look back over their lives and feel they have made the wrong decisions, or more commonly, that they have too frequently failed to make any decision at all, they see life as lacking integration. They feel despair at the impossibility of "having just one more chance to make things right." They often hide their terror of death by appearing contemptuous of humanity in general, and of those of their own religion or race in particular. They feel disgust for themselves.

> Live so that when your children think of fairness and integrity, they think of you.
>
> H. J. Brown

> Erikson, Erik. (1958). *Young man Luther.* New York: Norton. Martin Luther was the main force behind the Protestant Reformation. In Erikson's penetrating analysis of the causes behind Luther's actions, we have a wonderfully clear example of Erikson's ideas about adolescence in general and negative identity in particular.

Guided Review

7. Each of Erikson's stages is highlighted by a _____ that must be resolved before passage to the next stage.
8. At each stage the individual is pressured by _____ needs and the demands of _____ .
9. In Erikson's first stage, it is critical for infants to learn that their world is a _____ place.
10. During Erikson's fifth stage, which occurs during or after adolescence, it is frequently necessary to resolve an _____ _____ .

The Cognitive Developmental Approach

Imagine for a moment that your name is Jean Piaget. You were born in Neuchatel, Switzerland in 1896 and are now 15 years old. You began your scholarly career at the age of 10(!) and published numerous papers on birds, shellfish, and other topics of natural history. Based on these publications, you have just been offered the curator's position at the prestigious Geneva Natural History Museum. What would you do? Realizing that the museum officials didn't know his age, Piaget rejected the offer and went on to finish secondary school, complete his Ph.D. in biology, and write more than 50 influential books during his lifetime.

Piaget's training as a biologist had a major impact on his thinking about cognitive development. His fascination with the processes that led children to make incorrect answers in reasoning tests caused him to turn his attention to the analysis of children's developing intelligence. As Rutter & Rutter (1993) noted, one of Piaget's great legacies is the attention he focused on the role that cognitive mechanisms play in development.

Jean Piaget was among the first to study normal intellectual development.

Jean Piaget's Theory

Have you ever been in a restaurant and wondered why some babies try to find the toy they knocked off their tray, while others make no attempt to retrieve it or even look for it? This apparently simple behavior and other things that babies say and do fascinated the Swiss psychologist, Jean Piaget (1896–1980), who sought to understand the *cognitive structures* of the intellect (1953, 1966; Flavell, 1963). How did Piaget explain cognitive development?

Key Concepts in Piaget's Theory

Stages Piaget believed that intelligence matures as we develop increasingly effective **cognitive structures.** (Think of these structures as the blueprints that enable us to organize and adapt to our world.) Piaget believed that cognitive development

Cognitive structures Piaget's term to describe the basic tools of cognitive development.

Answers

means that we form more sophisticated cognitive structures as we pass through four stages: the *sensorimotor stage* (birth to 2 years old); the *preoperational stage* (2 to 7 years old); the *concrete operational stage* (7 to 11 years old); and the *formal operational stage* (11 years old and up). Thus, Piaget believed that cognitive functioning begins as responses to concrete phenomena—babies know only what they can touch, taste, or see. Our ability to use symbols and to think abstractly increases with each subsequent stage until we are able to manipulate abstract concepts and consider hypothetical alternatives. Piaget's stages of cognitive development are illustrated in table 2.3.

Functional Invariants   Piaget stated that we can form cognitive structures because we have inherited a method of intellectual functioning that enables us to respond to our environment. At the heart of this method are two psychological mechanisms, **adaptation** and **organization.** Because we use these same two mechanisms constantly throughout our lives from birth through adulthood, Piaget named them **functional invariants.**

Piaget believed that adaptation consists of **assimilation** and **accommodation.** When we assimilate something we incorporate it; we take it in. Think of eating. We take food into the structure of our mouths and change it to fit the shape of our mouths, throats, and digestive tract. We take objects, concepts, and events into our minds similarly: We incorporate them into our mental structures, changing them to fit the structures as we change the food to fit our physical structures. For example, you are now studying Piaget's views on cognitive development. These ideas are unique and will require effort to understand them. You are attempting to comprehend them by using the cognitive structures you now possess. You are assimilating Piaget's ideas; that is, you are mentally taking them in and shaping them to fit your cognitive structures.

But we also change as a result of assimilation; that is, we accommodate to what we have taken in. The food we eat produces biochemical changes; the stimuli we incorporate into our minds produce mental changes. *We change because of what we take in; we are also changed by it.* For example, not only are you taking in Piaget's ideas, but they are also changing your views on intelligence and cognitive development. The change in your cognitive structures will produce corresponding behavioral changes; this is the process of accommodation.

Thus, the adaptive process is the heart of Piaget's explanation of learning. As we try to "fit" new material into existing cognitive structures, we try to strike a balance between assimilation and accommodation, a process that is called **equilibration.** For example, we all make mistakes but by continued interaction with the environment, we correct these mistakes and change our cognitive structures (we have accommodated).

But our mental life doesn't consist of random activities; it is organized. The cognitive structures that we form enable us to engage in ever more complex thinking. Physical structures can again provide an analogy for Piaget's ideas on organization. To read this text you are balancing it, turning the pages, and moving your eyes. All

Adaptation   One of the two functional invariants in Piaget's theory.

Organization   One of the two functional invariants in Piaget's theory.

Functional invariants
In Piaget's theory, functional invariants refer to the psychological mechanisms of adaptation and organization.

Assimilation   Piaget's term to describe the manner in which we incorporate data into our cognitive structures.

Accommodation   Piaget's term to describe the manner by which cognitive structures change.

Equilibration   Piaget's term to describe the balance between assimilation and accommodation.

TABLE 2.3 PIAGET'S STAGES OF COGNITIVE DEVELOPMENT		
Stage	**Age**	**Major Features**
Sensorimotor	Birth to 2 years	Infants use their bodies to form cognitive structures
Preoperational	2 to 7 years	Use of symbols; rapid language growth
Concrete operational	7 to 11 years	Can reason about physical objects
Formal operational	11+ years	Abstract thinking leads to reasoning with symbols

of these physical structures are organized so that you can read. Likewise, for you to understand this material, your appropriate cognitive structures are organized so that they can assimilate and accommodate.

Schemes   Organization and adaptation are inseparable; they are two sides of the same coin. Every intellectual act is related to other similar acts, which introduces Piaget's notion of schemes. **Schemes** *are organized patterns of thought and action,* that is, they are the cognitive structures and behavior that make up an organized unit. Schemes help us to adapt to our environment and may be best thought of as the inner representation of our activities and experiences. A scheme is named by its activity: the grasping scheme, the sucking scheme, the kicking or throwing scheme.

To give you an idea of how schemes develop, consider a baby reaching out and touching something, say a blanket. The child immediately begins to learn about the material (e.g., its heaviness, its size); the child is forming a cognitive structure about the blanket. When the child combines knowledge about the blanket with the act of reaching for it, Piaget called this behavior a scheme—in this case, the grasping scheme.

How does Piaget's theory actually "work"? If you think of his theory in this way it may help: Stimuli come from the environment and are filtered through the functional invariants. The functional invariants, adaptation and organization, use the stimuli to form new structures or change existing structures. For example, you may have had your own idea of what intelligence is, but now you change your structures relating to intelligence because of your new knowledge about Piaget. Your content or behavior now changes because of the changes in your cognitive structures. The process is as follows:

Environment
(filtered through)
the Functional Invariants
(produce)
Cognitive Structures
(which combine with behavior to form)
Schemes

Although Piaget has been criticized for not stressing the role and impact of culture in cognitive development, his theory was rooted in interactionism, that is, in the experiences of the individual (Turiel, 1999). Another theorist, however, who put culture at the center of his work, was Lev Vygotsky.

The Cultural Framework Approach

A telling example of culture's importance occurred when several American psychologists went to Ruwanda to help with the massive psychological problems caused by the savagery and violence the people had experienced (Seppa, 1996). They found that traditional Western therapeutic methods, such as individualized therapy, were useless. Cultural values change, but slowly (Harrison, 2000). Successful programs in Africa demand programs that help restore social supports and relationships. They also discovered that urging patients to "talk it out" simply did not work. Using song, dance, and storytelling, which their patients found natural and comforting, proved to be more successful.

Incidents such as this testify to the value of the work of the Russian psychologist Lev Vygotsky (1896–1934) who has attracted considerable attention because of his emphasis on social processes. Born in Russia in 1896, Vygotsky was educated at Moscow University and quickly turned his attention to educational psychology, developmental psychology, and psychopathology. For Vygotsky, the clues to understanding mental development are in children's social processes; that is, cognitive growth depends on children's interactions with those around them. The adults around children interact with them in a way that emphasizes those things that a culture values.

Schemes   Piaget's term to describe the patterns of behavior that infants use to interact with their environment.

Lev Vygotsky placed great emphasis on the role of social processes in intellectual development.

Tragically, tuberculosis claimed Vygotsky in 1934. His work today, because of its cultural emphasis, is more popular than it was when he died. In contrast to Piaget who, as we have seen, believed that children function as "little scientists," Vygotsky turned to social interactions to explain children's cognitive development.

Lev Vygotsky's Theory

If you understand Vygotsky's basic ideas, you'll be able to grasp how his theory works. For example, Vygotsky identified dual paths of cognitive development— *elementary processes* that are basically biological, and *psychological processes* that are essentially sociocultural (Vygotsky, 1978). Children's behaviors emerge from the intertwining of these two paths. For example, brain development provides the physiological basis for the appearance of external or egocentric speech, which gradually becomes the inner speech children use to guide their behavior. (See chapter 5 for Vygotsky's interpretation of inner speech in language development.)

Three fundamental themes run through Vygotsky's work: the unique manner in which he identified and used the concept of development, the social origin of mind, and the role of speech in cognitive development.

1. Vygotsky's *concept of development* is at the heart of his theory. He thought that elementary biological processes are qualitatively transformed into higher psychological functioning by developmental processes. In other words, such behaviors as speech, thought, and learning are all explained by development. Let's concentrate on speech for a moment.

   Think of the "noises" that babies make in their speech development— crying, cooing, babbling—all of which are accompanied by physical movement. Children gradually begin to point at objects and adults tell them the name—ball, cup, milk. First words come, children start to string words together, talk aloud, and, finally, use speech much the way adults do. Instead of seeing a series of independent accomplishments, Vygotsky viewed these changes as *a series of transformations brought about by developmental processes*. As Cairns (1998) noted, Vygotsky believed that a developmental analysis of speech helps to provide clues as to how speech and thought are interrelated.

2. To understand cognitive development, we must examine *the social and cultural processes* shaping children (Wertsch & Tulviste, 1992). But how do these processes affect cognitive development? Vygotsky argued (1978) that any function in a child's cultural development appears twice, on two planes: first, in an interpsychological category (social exchanges with others), and, second, within the child as an intrapsychological category (using inner speech to guide behavior).

   The question now is: What happens to transform external activity to internal activity? For Vygotsky, the answer is to be found in the process of *internalization*. As he stated, the transformation of an interpersonal process (egocentric speech) into an intrapersonal process (inner speech) is the result of a long series of developmental events (Vygotsky, 1978, p. 57). He termed this internalization process "the distinguishing feature of human psychology," the barest outline of which is known.

3. Although Vygotsky lacked hard data to explain this belief, he believed that *speech* is one of the most powerful tools humans use to progress developmentally.

   > . . . . the most significant moment in the course of intellectual development, which gives birth to the purely human forms of practical and abstract intelligence, occurs when speech and practical activity, two previously completely independent lines of development, converge (Vygotsky, 1978, p. 24).

Let's now turn to one of Vygotsky's most famous ideas, the notion of the *Zone of Proximal Development*.

The Zone of Proximal Development

Vygotsky (1978) argued forcefully that learning must be matched with a pupil's developmental level, which is too frequently identified by an intelligence test score. He stated that we cannot be content with the results of intelligence testing, which only identifies a student's developmental level at the time of testing.

For example, after administering a Stanford-Binet Intelligence Test, we find that a pupil's IQ on this test is 110, which would be that student's current level of mental development. We then assume that the pupil can only work at this level. Vygotsky argued, however, that with a little help, pupils might be able to do work that they could not do on their own.

We know that pupils who have the same IQ are quite different in other respects. Motivation, interest, health, and a host of other conditions produce different achievement levels. For example, our student with an IQ of 110, when working alone may be able to do only addition problems, but solve subtraction problems with a teacher's help.

Zone of proximal development The distance between a child's actual developmental level and a higher level of potential development with adult guidance (what children can do independently and what they can do with help).

To explain this phenomenon, Vygotsky introduced his notion of the **zone of proximal development.** He defined the zone of proximal development as the distance between a child's actual developmental level, as determined by independent problem solving, and the higher level of potential development as determined by problem solving under adult guidance or in collaboration with more capable peers. In other words, it's the difference between what children can achieve with guidance, and what they can achieve through individual effort (Valsiner, 1998).

Remember: *The zone of proximal development is not something within the child.* It's a characteristic of a child's activity within a specific social environment (Steward, 1995). Vygotsky's ideas on what constitutes the kind of assistance to be given children were general—demonstration, leading questions, introducing the beginning elements of the solution (Vygotsky, 1978).

Scaffolding Helping children move from initial difficulties with a topic to a point where, with help, they gradually learn to perform the task independently.

These ideas of Vygotsky led to the notion of **scaffolding.** Think of scaffolding as a way of helping children move from initial difficulties with a topic to a point where, with help, they perform the task independently. Picture a child learning to play tennis. She volleys fairly well, but has difficulty serving. Watching her, you notice that when she tosses the ball into the air and starts to swing, her grip slips slightly. You mention this to her and suggest that she change her grip. She tries, but still has difficulty. You remind her of the proper finger placement; she continues to practice; gradually it all comes together, and you fade gracefully into the background.

Scaffolding applies to children's school work as well. Let's assume that a mother approaches her son's math teacher. Worried about her son's math, trying to help, but feeling uncomfortable with anything mathematical, she accurately concludes

An Applied View

Literary Lunches

Another example of the value of Vygotsky's zone of proximal development can be seen in a phenomenon called *Literary Lunches*. This idea, which is becoming quite popular across the country, has teachers inviting several senior citizens to read the same book as middle school students. Then both students and adults meet for lunch to discuss the book. The seniors help the students to grasp the more subtle themes in the story, while the students help the seniors to realize that most of the students in our schools are good people with ideas of their own. The understanding of both groups is extended and enriched by their interactions.

In one class recently, both groups read the enormously popular *Nothing but the Truth* by Avi, the author of many outstanding books for young people. In this story, the conflict between a student and teacher has community-wide ramifications that hurts everyone involved. This story led to an animated discussion of character development in which the students gained a greater perspective of the forces working on adults, and the seniors acquired a more sympathetic idea of the pressures on students—Vygotsky's zone of proximal development in action.

she couldn't fake math skills she doesn't have. So the teacher suggests that she show her son how important math is in the consulting work she does part-time, in keeping score in the tennis games she loves, in shopping, and in anything the mother can think of that makes math relevant. The teacher could also suggest that she shop for books and computer software for math games that require problem-solving and logical thinking skills and play them with her son.

While all of this is going on, the teacher urges the mother to constantly tell her son, "You're not bad in math; you just need to catch up on a few things." In this case, the teacher and the mother, while not forcing anything on the child, provide support (a scaffold) that will gradually be withdrawn.

As Vygotsky noted (1978), instruction is effective only when it proceeds ahead of development. That is, teaching awakens those functions that are already maturing and that are in the zone of proximal development. Although teaching and learning are not identical to development, they can act to stimulate developmental processes.

Finally, table 2.4 will help you to identify the most significant differences between Vygotsky and Piaget.

Guided Review

11. Piaget's major concern was with the development of _____ _____.

12. Piaget believed that cognitive development occurred by passage through cognitive _____.

13. _____ are mental, internalized actions.

14. Vygotsky differed from Piaget in that he was more interested in the role that _____ _____ played in cognitive development.

15. Vygotsky believed that for learning to be effective, it must be matched with a pupil's _____ level.

16. The difference between a child's actual developmental level and the level of potential development is what Vygotsky called the _____ of _____ _____.

TABLE 2.4 KEY DIFFERENCES BETWEEN PIAGET AND VYGOTSKY

	Piaget	Vygotsky
Perspective	Individual child constructs view of world by forming cognitive structures—"the little scientist"	Child's cognitive development progresses by social interactions with others ("social origins of mind")
Basic psychological mechanism	Equilibration—child acts to regain equilibrium between current level of cognitive structures and external stimuli	Social interaction, which encourages development through the guidance of skillful adults
Language	Emerges as cognitive structures develop	Language begins as preintellectual speech and gradually develops into a sophisticated form of inner speech; one of the main forces responsible for cognitive development
Learning	Assimilation and accommodation lead to equilibration	Learning results from the interaction of two processes: biological elementary processes (such as brain development), plus sociocultural interactions
Problem solving	Child independently searches for data needed to change cognitive structures, thus enabling child to reach solution	Two aspects of problem solving: 1. key role of speech to guide "planful" behavior; 2. joint efforts with others

Piaget or Vygotsky? Vygotsky or Piaget? From your reading, you have learned that Piaget and Vygotsky disagreed on the emphasis they placed on the basic processes of cognitive development. Piaget believed that children act as scientific investigators, acquiring knowledge as they build more and richer cognitive structures. Although it's unfair to state that Piaget ignored social and cultural influences on development, he did, however, focus on the independent, self-reliant path that children take in constructing their world.

Vygotsky turned to a child's culture and stressed social interactions as the driving force in cognitive development. If social exchanges with adults are lacking or inadequate, children's opportunities to reach, or even approach, their cognitive potential, are sharply limited.

Analyzing Vygotsky's interpretation of the zone of proximal development and the notion of scaffolding, Greenfield (1999) raised an interesting possibility. She argued that those societies encouraging scaffolding are stable and in a tradition-maintaining state. Dynamic and more innovative societies, however, encourage independent, trial-and-error experimental behavior in their citizens.

It's an intriguing idea. Think about a country you're familiar with (other countries as well as the United States). Do you agree with Greenfield's conclusion? Can a society shift from one mode to another? If you would like to have a more informed view on this issue, you may want to read one or more of the articles referenced in this chapter (such as Greenfield, 1999).

You may also wish to learn more about it by going to our web site at http:/www.mhhe.com/dacey5.

The Behavioral Approach

Reinforcement Usually refers to an increase in the frequency of a response when certain pleasant consequences immediately follow it.

Our final explanation of human development takes us into the world of learning and learning theory. Two of its best-known proponents are B. F. Skinner, famous for his insights into the role of **reinforcement,** and Albert Bandura, who called our attention to the power of modeling in development.

Skinner and Operant Conditioning

About three years before Skinner died, the wife of one of the authors (JFT) called Skinner's office at Harvard to request any available photos of his early work. To her surprise, Skinner himself answered the phone. Slightly nonplussed, she identified herself and told him what she wanted. Sensing her nervousness, Skinner told her a funny story about the rats in one of his early experiments, and said he would be delighted to send along some copies. In a very real sense, Skinner demonstrated the proper use of positive reinforcement.

B. F. Skinner (1904–1990) received his doctorate from Harvard and after teaching for several years at the Universities of Minnesota and Indiana, he returned to Harvard. Convinced of the importance of reinforcement, Skinner developed an explanation of learning that stressed the consequences of behavior. What happens after we do something is all-important. Reinforcement has proven to be a powerful tool in the developing, shaping, and control of behavior, both in and out of the classroom. Prominent in American psychology for over 60 years, Skinner inspired and stimulated research and theory. As Lattal (1992) noted, when Skinner spoke, psychologists listened.

Skinner's Views

Skinner has been in the forefront of psychological and educational endeavors for the past several decades. Innovative, practical, tellingly prophetic, and witty, Skinner's work has had a lasting impact. In several major publications—*The Behavior of Organisms* (1938), *Science and Human Behavior,* (1953), *Verbal Behavior* (1957), *The Technology of Teaching* (1968), *Beyond Freedom and Dignity* (1971), *About Behaviorism* (1974)—and in a steady flow of articles, Skinner reported his experiments and developed and clarified his theory. He never avoided the challenge of applying his findings to practical affairs. Psychology, education, religion, psychotherapy, and other subjects have all felt the force of Skinner's thought.

Harvard psychologist B. F. Skinner is identified with operant conditioning.

Operant conditioning
Skinner's form of conditioning in which a reinforcement follows the desired response; also known as instrumental conditioning.

In his theory, called **operant conditioning** (also called *instrumental conditioning*), Skinner demonstrated that the environment has a much greater influence on learning and behavior than previously realized. Skinner argued that the environment (parents, teachers, peers) reacts to our behavior and either reinforces or eliminates that behavior. Consequently, the environment holds the key to understanding behavior.

Skinner argued that if the environment reinforces a certain behavior, it's more likely to result the next time that stimulus occurs. Thus, if the teacher asks a particular question again, the student is more likely to give the right answer, because that response was reinforced. If the response is punished, the response is less likely in the future. If the response is simply ignored, it also becomes less likely in the future. Each of these three concepts—*reinforcement, punishment,* and no response (which Skinner calls *extinction*)—needs further explanation.

Skinner preferred the term reinforcement to reward. Defining reinforcement as anything that makes a response more likely to happen in the future, Skinner identified two kinds of reinforcement. **Positive reinforcement** refers to any event that, when it occurs after a response, makes that response more likely to happen in the future. **Negative reinforcement** is any event that, when it ceases to occur after a response, makes that response more likely to happen in the future. Notice that both types of reinforcement make a response more likely to happen. Giving your daughter candy for doing the right thing would be positive reinforcement. Ceasing to twist your brother's arm when he gives you back your pen would be negative reinforcement.

Positive reinforcement
Refers to those stimuli whose presentation as a consequence of a response strengthens or increases the rate of the response.

Negative reinforcement
Refers to those stimuli whose withdrawal strengthens behavior.

Research into operant conditioning continues unabated. For example, Dragoi & Staddon (1999) noted that dynamic theories of operant conditioning turn to historical (past reinforcing events) as well as recent reinforcements. By using reinforcements that occurred at different times, operant conditioning becomes a more powerful, flexible tool in predicting behavior.

What does operant conditioning have to do with development? In Skinner's opinion, human development is the result of the continuous flow of learning that comes about from the operant conditioning we receive from the environment every day. For Skinner, development is a continuous, incremental sequence of conditioned acts that fulfill children's needs as quickly and completely as possible. Ideally, then, the demands of normal living are introduced at a controlled rate that helps a child to master them without acquiring negative feelings (Thomas, 1992).

 An Applied View   **Who Can Find the Raisin?**

Probably the best way to understand Skinner's view of behaviorism is to apply its principles to teaching someone. For this suggested activity, you need two cups, a raisin, and two squares of paper of different colors, big enough to cover the cups.

For 1- to 2-year-olds, you must start very simply. Follow these steps:

1. Place a raisin in one of the cups and cover that cup with a large square of either color.

2. Cover the empty cup with the large square of the other color. Do this so that the child cannot see what you are doing.

3. Ask the child to guess which cup the raisin is in by pointing to one of the squares. If the child gets the right one, he or she wins the prize. If not, say, "Too bad. Maybe you'll get it next time. Let's try again."

4. Now, out of the child's sight, switch the positions of the cups, but cover the cup with the raisin with the same square. Do this until the child regularly guesses correctly. This is called continuous reinforcement. Generally speaking, the older the child, the quicker the learning.

5. Now cut out two large circles, each a different color, and repeat steps 1 through 4 using circles instead of squares. Does the child learn more quickly this time?

For older children, the game can be made more and more complex. Use a greater variety of shape combinations, and use three or even four cups. Finally, try to get the child to verbalize what he or she thinks is the principle behind this activity. Perhaps the child could even invent another way of doing it! As you perform this experiment, you will gain insights into the behaviorist ideas of reinforcement and extinction.

Skinner, B. F. (1948). *Walden two*. New York: Macmillan. Many students find it hard to see how Skinner's behaviorism would function in everyday life. In this novel, we see how a community based on his principles would operate. In fact, for a while at least, several such communities really existed. Reading *Walden two* will provide you practical insights into Skinner's work.

Modeling   Bandura's term for observational learning.

Social (cognitive) learning theory   Bandura's theory that refers to the process whereby the information we glean from observing others influences our behavior.

These ideas about change in human behavior have been enhanced by the ideas of Albert Bandura and his associates. They extend the behaviorist view to cover social behavior.

Bandura and Social Cognitive Learning

Albert Bandura, one of the chief architects of social learning theory, has stressed the potent influence of **modeling** on personality development (Bandura, 1997). He called this *observational learning*. In a famous statement on **social (cognitive) learning theory,** Bandura and Walters (1963) cited evidence to show that learning occurs through observing others, even when the observers do not imitate the model's responses at that time and get no reinforcement. For Bandura, observational learning means that the information we get from observing other people, things, and events influences the way we act.

Social learning theory has particular relevance for development. As Bandura and Walters noted, children often do not do what adults tell them to do but rather what they see adults do. If Bandura's assumptions are correct, adults can be a potent force in shaping the behavior of children because of what they do.

The importance of models is seen in Bandura's interpretation of what happens as a result of observing others:

- By observing others, children may acquire new responses, including socially appropriate behaviors.

- Observation of models may strengthen or weaken existing responses.

- Observation of a model may cause the reappearance of responses that were apparently forgotten.

- If children witness undesirable behavior that is either rewarded or goes unpunished, undesirable behavior may result. The reverse is also true.

Bandura, Ross, and Ross (1963) studied the relative effects of live models, filmed human aggression, and filmed cartoon aggression on preschool children's aggressive behavior. The filmed human adult models displayed aggression toward an inflated doll; in the filmed cartoon aggression, a cartoon character displayed the same aggression.

Later, all the children who observed the aggression were more aggressive than youngsters in a control group. Filmed models were as effective as live models in transmitting aggression. The research suggests that competent models are more readily imitated than models who lack these qualities (Bandura & Walters, 1963). You can see, then, how modeling can be a powerful force in development. (For a more detailed account of how recent research supports these conclusions, see chapter 10.)

Guided Review

17. Skinner's view of learning is referred to as _____ or _____ conditioning.
18. This explanation of learning depends heavily on the role of the _____.
19. When a response is _____, it is more likely to reoccur.
20. Bandura's social learning theory, also called observational learning, stresses the role of _____ in learning.
21. Observation of models may _____ or _____ existing responses.

Let's conclude our discussion of developmental theory by turning to new ideas and new controversies.

Answers

17. operant, instrumental 18. environment 19. reinforced 20. modeling 21. strengthen, weaken

Developmental Theory: Current Status, Future Direction

E. O. Wilson, biologist, advocate of evolutionary psychology, and author of two Pulitzer Prize winning books, recently focused on psychology's role in unifying science in the twenty-first century. Arguing that the social sciences and the natural sciences are converging, Wilson noted that psychologists can help bridge remaining gaps between the two worlds because they bring perspectives from both a biological and social perspective. He stated (in Azar, 1999):

> **Most of the issues that vex humanity daily cannot be solved without integrating knowledge from the natural sciences with that of the social sciences and humanities.**

In a sense, Wilson's words define the task for today's developmental theorists who argue that traditional theories cannot cope with exploding and pertinent knowledge from varied sources (biological, social, cultural, psychological).

The world of developmental theory is changing as you read these words and we want you to be aware of the latest thinking of today's theorists. A persistent criticism of such traditional theorists as Piaget and Freud is that they were simply too unidimensional to explain the complexity of development. That is, they focused on only one aspect of development. For example, Piaget was consumed by the lure of cognitive development, and Freud spent his lifetime delving into the secrets of personality development. But as Lerner noted (1998), in current developmental theories, the person is not simply "biologized, psychologized, or sociologized."

And yet, we should continue to turn to these theorists for guidance along particular developmental paths. For example, Piaget remains a trusted guide for unlocking many of the enigmas of cognitive development. Erikson's sensitive understanding of psychosocial crises provides cogent clues to the identity problems many adolescents face. We can integrate the knowledge these great theorists have generated to further our vision of the lifespan. With gratitude, then, we'll use their insights throughout our work in this book.

Such restricted viewpoints, however much they have helped us to understand the processes involved in development, present an inadequate portrayal of the richness and dynamism of the lifespan. The nuances of human development can't be captured by theories limited to one facet of development—motor, cognitive, or language. Rather, a developmental systems perspective is needed, one that encompasses previously hard-won knowledge and now searches for explanations in the relationships among the multiple levels that contribute to development (Lewis, 2000).

Interactions Among Levels of Development

As Gottlieb (1997, p. 138) noted, today's developmental psychologists are analyzing activity at four levels: genetic, neural, behavioral, and environmental. *But more importantly, researchers and theorists are scrutinizing the interactions among these levels,* which is the meaning of the multidirectional nature of development mentioned in chapter 1. Figure 2.1 illustrates interactions of the multiple levels of development.

The genes act to produce a particular physical constitution, which contributes to an individual's behavior, helping that individual to select a particular environment (peers, activities, etc.). But the environment also acts to influence behavior, physical status, and even genetic activity; in other words, each level interacts with all other levels. An attempt to capture this type of analysis is seen in the work of Richard Lerner and developmental contextualism (1991, 1998).

Developmental Contextualism

We know today that heredity and environment produce their results in a complex, interactive manner that reflects the role of reciprocal interactions. By stressing the

Figure 2.1

Interactions of multiple levels of development.

Source: Dacey & Travers, 1994; Gottlieb, 1997; Lerner, 1998.

E = Environment B = Behavior C = Constitution G = Genes

Developmental contextualism
An interpretation of development that emphasizes the reciprocal interactions between all our characteristics and the environment.

complexity of developmental analysis, those adhering to a reciprocal interaction perspective have made it clear that there are no simple cause-and-effect explanations of development. All of us, children, adolescents, and adults, experience a constant state of reorganization as we move through the life cycle (Lerner, Fisher, & Weinberg, 2000).

Developmental contextualism, popularized by Richard Lerner (1991, 1998), is the current version of a perspective that begins with the idea that all of our characteristics, psychological as well as biological, function by reciprocal interactions with the environment (often referred to as the *context*). In this way, developmental contextualism leads to the belief that we *construct* our view of the surrounding world.

Context is an inclusive term that attempts to portray environmental complexity by identifying four major forces of our development:

1. *The physical setting,* such as the home, classroom, and workplace.

2. *Social influences,* such as our family, peers, and significant others.

3. *Our personal characteristics,* such as physical appearance, temperament, and language fluency.

4. *The influence of time,* that is, change brought about by the sheer chronology of our lives; to put it simply, the longer we're able to survive, the more changes we experience with their inescapable and inevitable consequences for our development.

These forces are illustrated in figure 2. 2.

Exchanges between individuals and the multiple levels of their contexts are the basic change processes in development (Horowitz, 2000; Lerner, 1998). Consequently, the crucial element in our development is the changing relationship between our complexity and a multilayered context. If you think about this deceptively simple statement, you can appreciate the need to study development, not from any single perspective, like biology or environment but from a more sophisticated analytical appraisal. *No single level of organization is seen as the primary or the ultimate causal influence on behavior and development* (Dixon & Lerner, 1999).

For example, consider what happens when you interact with your environment. Your genes provide a blueprint that is passed on to the cells, tissues, and organs of your body, influencing the growth of such widely divergent features as your brain development and temperament (to name only two). On the other hand, the intricate and involved layers of the context, ranging from your family to your peers to your wider social sphere, simultaneously weave their networks of influence. Simple explanations? Hardly. What is needed is a developmental perspective equally as intricate as the behavior it attempts to clarify.

An easy-to-obtain and brief, but careful analysis of developmental contextualism by Richard Lerner can be found in *Developmental psychology,* January, 1991, Volume 27 (1), 27–32.

Figure 2.2

A developmental contextual model of person–context interaction.

From R. Lerner, *Developmental Psychology*, vol. 27, 1991, pp. 27–32, Figure 1, p. 30. Copyright 1991 by the American Psychology Association. Reprinted with permission.

Life Course Theory A theory referring to a sequence of socially defined, age-graded events and roles that individuals enact over time.

Evolutionary developmental psychology An explanation of development that rests upon the assumption that our physiological and psychological systems resulted from evolution by selection.

Final Theoretical Notes

Although we have used developmental contextualism as an example of the changes taking place in the search for developmental explanations, other ideas continue to emerge. **Life Course Theory,** proposed by Glen Elder, refers to a sequence of socially defined, age-graded events and roles that individuals enact over time (Elder, 1998, p. 941). Such *biological* facts as birth, puberty, and death derive their meaning in the life course as *social* facts. Consequently, the developmental implications of an individual's life are related to changing social and historical conditions.

Evolutionary developmental psychology is an explanation of development that assumes our physiological and psychological systems resulted from evolution by selection. In 1859 Charles Darwin published his *On the Origin of Species* in which he concluded that natural selection was the basic principle of change. Ongoing selection processes depend on gene action and provide the basis for evolutionary events to occur (Plotkin, 1997). It's the study of how our genes are expressed during development and how the context of development influences the expression of genetic action (Geary & Bjorklund, 2000).

Evolutionary ideas had little impact on psychological thought until approximately 1959, which was the centennial year of the publication of *On the Origin of Species.* Conferences and publications devoted to Darwin's work sparked renewed interest in his ideas and encouraged theorists and researchers to search for obscure biological causes of behavior.

At about the same time, this impetus received support from an unrelated and unexpected source: the cognitive revolution. Widely and wildly popular with psychologists, studies of cognition provided respectability to explanations of behavior that were not immediately visible (Plotkin, 1997; Geary & Bjorklund, 2000).

In tracing the roots of evolutionary psychology, Pinker (1997) stated that evolutionary psychology brings together two scientific revolutions. One is the cognitive revolution that began in the 1950s and 1960s, which helped us to understand why we have the kind of mind we do. The other is the change in evolutionary biology that explained the ability of living things to adapt by selection. Thus the physiological and psychological mechanisms needed for healthy development are those that survive the process of natural selection. Conversely, developmental psychologists have expressed reservations lest the notion that "biology is destiny" becomes too easily accepted, thus diminishing the environmental input·into development (Geary & Bjorklund, 2000).

Table 2.5 summarizes several features of the theories discussed in this chapter.

Guided Review

22. A major criticism of Freud and Piaget is that their theories are too _____.
23. Modern developmental theorists have turned their attention to the _____ among multiple levels of development.
24. Lerner's work is referred to as _____ _____.
25. A term used to describe the influence of environmental complexity on development is _____.

TABLE 2.5 COMPARING THEORIES OF DEVELOPMENT

	Psychoanalytic	Psychosocial	Cognitive	Cultural	Behavioral	Contextual
Major Figures	Freud	Erikson	Piaget	Vygotsky	Skinner Bandura	Lerner
Major Ideas	Passage through the psychosexual stages	Passage through the psychosocial stages	Development of cognitive structures through stages of cognitive development	Social processes embedded within a culture influence development	Power of operant conditioning; role of modeling in development	Development occurs as an individual's characteristics interact with that person's context.
Essential Features	Id, ego, superego; psychosexual stages	Psychosocial crises; psychosocial stages	Formation of cognitive structures; stages of cognitive development	Social processes; zone of proximal development	Reinforcement of responses; observational learning; modeling	Interaction among multiple levels of development
Source of Developmental Problems	Conflict during development leads to fixation, regression, and personality problems	Inadequate resolution of psychosocial crises	Weak formation of cognitive structures	Environmental support lacking or insufficient	Lack of reinforcement, incorrect pairing of stimuli and responses	Faulty exchanges between the individual and the multiple levels of the context.
Goal	Sexually mature individual	A sense of personal integrity	Satisfactory formation and use of cognitive structures	Recognition and use of social processes to guide development	The acquisition of conditioned acts to fulfill needs	Satisfactory relationships between the individual and a multilayered context.

Answers

22. unidimensional 23. interactions 24. developmental contextualism 25. context

CONCLUSION & SUMMARY

In this chapter, we introduced you to several interpretations of development that will help you to understand and integrate developmental data. Although we might have chosen many theories to include in this chapter (some of which we'll discuss later), those we have presented here have played or are playing major roles in our understanding of human development. You have a lot to remember, but we'll be coming back again and again to these seminal ideas to help you to gain a firm understanding of them.

How does psychoanalytic theory explain development across the lifespan?

- Freud considered the unconscious mind to be the key to understanding human beings.
- Important information in the unconscious mind is kept hidden through an array of defense mechanisms.
- The mind is divided into three constructs: the id, the ego, and the superego, each of which appears at different stages of a child's development.
- Personality development is divided into five instinctive stages of life—oral, anal, phallic, latency, and genital—each stage serving a major function.
- Failure to pass through a stage of development results in fixation, which halts a person from becoming fully mature.

What is the relationship between psychosocial crises and lifespan development?

- Erikson believed that human life progresses through eight "psychosocial" stages, each one marked by a crisis and its resolution.
- Although the ages at which one goes through each stage vary, the sequence of stages is fixed. Stages may overlap, however.
- A human being must experience each crisis before proceeding to the next stage. Inadequate resolution of the crisis at any stage hinders development.

How did Piaget explain cognitive development?

- Piaget focused on the development of the cognitive structures of the intellect during childhood and adolescence.
- Organization and adaptation play key roles in the formation of structures.
- Piaget believed that cognitive growth occurred in four discrete stages: sensorimotor, preoperational, concrete operational, and formal operational.

What impact does culture have on lifespan development?

- Lev Vygotsky, a leading commentator on the role of culture in development, emphasized the significance of social processes to bring about satisfactory growth.

- Vygotsky believed that the capacity to learn depends on abilities of the child's teachers as well as on the child's abilities.
- The difference between the child's ability to learn independently and to learn with help is called the zone of proximal development.

What is the behavioral perspective on development?

- Skinner believed that the consequences of behavior are critical.
- Skinner's paradigm involves three steps: a stimulus occurs in the environment; a response is made in the presence of that stimulus; and the response is reinforced, punished, or extinguished.
- Bandura has extended Skinner's work to the area of social learning, which he calls observational learning.

What is the current status of developmental theory?

- Today's developmental theorists believe that traditional theories cannot explain the complexity of development.
- Interactions among the various levels of development are the focus of current developmental research.
- Lerner's developmental contextualism concentrates on the exchanges between an individual's levels of development and the context to explain developmental processes.

KEY TERMS

Accommodation	Functional invariants	Organization
Adaptation	Genital stage	Phallic stage
Anal stage	Id	Positive reinforcement
Assimilation	Identity crisis	Psychoanalytic theory
Cognitive structures	Latency stage	Reinforcement
Developmental contextualism	Life Course Theory	Scaffolding
Ego	Modeling	Schemes
Equilibration	Negative reinforcement	Social (cognitive) learning theory
Evolutionary developmental psychology	Operant conditioning	Superego
	Oral stage	Zone of proximal development

WHAT DO YOU THINK?

1. What is your reaction to the statement, "The truth or falseness of a theory has little to do with its usefulness"?

2. Some people say that in his concept of human development, Freud emphasized sexuality too much. What do you think?

3. If Piaget were alive today, what would his reaction be to developmental contextualism?

4. Skinner criticized the other theorists in this chapter for believing they can describe what goes on in the human mind. After all, he said, no one has ever looked inside one. What's your position?

5. Is it possible for a person to be deeply intimate with another person and still be in a state of identity confusion?

CHAPTER REVIEW TEST

1. Freud's structure of the mind included
   a. cognitive structures.
   b. safety needs.
   c. ego.
   d. reinforcing elements.

2. The id is that structure of the mind that is present
   a. at birth.
   b. through experience.
   c. by internal representations.
   d. through crisis resolution.

3. Freud believed that development entailed moving through psychosexual stages. Difficulty at any stage can cause a person to become
   a. fixated.
   b. operational.
   c. negatively reinforced.
   d. displaced.

4. Ideas that are rejected by the conscious mind are kept from consciousness by
   a. the ego.
   b. fear reactions.
   c. the superego.
   d. defense mechanisms.

5. Jimmy was told by his teacher that he could not go on a field trip with the class because of his misbehavior. Jimmy said he was glad; the trips are "no fun anyway." Jimmy's defense mechanism is called
   a. regression.
   b. compensation.
   c. rationalization.
   d. displacement.

6. One-year-old Jane has already learned that her mother will be there when Jane needs her. This predictable world helps a child to develop
   a. creativity.
   b. intimacy.
   c. generativity.
   d. trust.

7. The psychosocial crisis of industry versus inferiority must be resolved during
   a. the school years.
   b. early childhood.
   c. adolescence.
   d. adulthood.

8. Piaget's theory of cognitive development focused on the formation and development of
   a. zones of proximal development.
   b. reinforcement schedules.
   c. cognitive structures.
   d. modeling strategies.

9. Piaget placed considerable emphasis on operations, which he viewed as
   a. reflexes.
   b. age-appropriate responses.
   c. internalized actions.
   d. interactions.

10. Although both Piaget and Vygotsky devoted their lives to studying cognitive development, Vygotsky placed greater emphasis on
    a. cognitive structures.
    b. social interactions.
    c. sensitive periods.
    d. observational learning.

11. Skinner carefully analyzed the role of reinforcement in development and distinguished it from
    a. cognitive structures.
    b. reward.
    c. operations.
    d. needs.

12. In operant conditioning, the environment acts as the major source of
    a. operations.
    b. cognitive structures.
    c. defense mechanisms.
    d. reinforcement.

13. The great value of observational learning is that a person need not overtly react to learn
    a. mental operations.
    b. new responses.
    c. ego identity.
    d. schedule of reinforcements.

14. Today's developmental psychologists consider theories such as those of Freud and Piaget as too
    a. insensitive.
    b. biologically focused.
    c. cultural oriented.
    d. unidimensional.

15. Lerner's analysis of development depends on analyzing
    a. multiple levels of development.
    b. schedules of reinforcement.
    c. identity stages.
    d. cognitive stages.

Answers

1. c 2. a 3. a 4. d 5. c 6. d 7. a 8. c 9. c 10. b 11. b 12. d 13. b 14. d 15. a

PART II

Beginnings

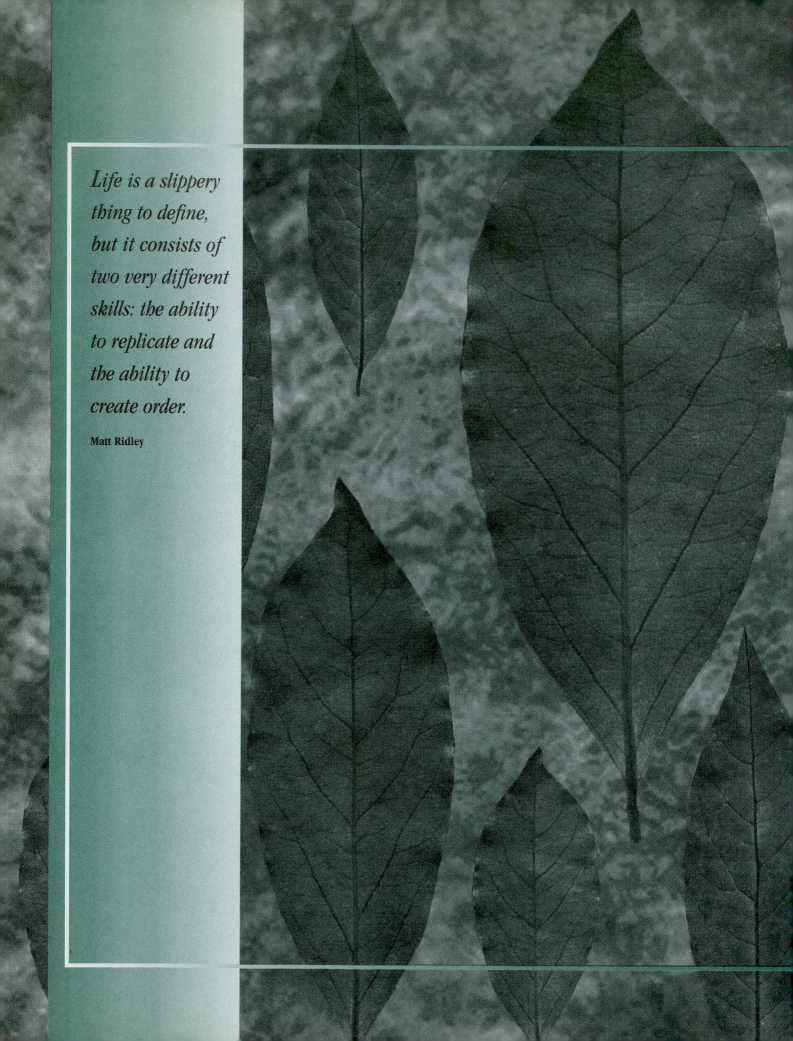

Life is a slippery thing to define, but it consists of two very different skills: the ability to replicate and the ability to create order.

Matt Ridley

The Biological Basis of Development

F rank and Ellen Smith arrived at Dr. James Otis' office a few minutes early for their appointment. Married for seven years, they had been unable to conceive and had found that their problem was caused by male infertility, in this case, a low sperm count. As they attempted to learn more about their problem, they discovered that they were not alone; estimates are that one in six heterosexual couples has a fertility problem.

Other couples whom they had met in their search for a solution had recommended Dr. Otis as a physician who was sympathetic, knowledgeable, and successful in using DI—donor insemination. (Currently, close to 100,000 women in the United States will use DI each year.) Frank and Ellen chose this procedure because the screening process in accepting sperm for freezing lowers the risk of sexually transmitted diseases (STDs) and also provides detailed information about the donor: race, ethnic background, blood type, hair and eye color, physical characteristics, and personal background information.

The Smiths found that Dr. Otis was exactly as he had been described. Unhurried and calm, he told the couple just what would be expected of them. He also stressed that he received sperm from a large, nationally known, respected sperm bank. He explained that freezing techniques had improved in the last few years. Cryobiology, the study of how best to freeze living tissue, had made great strides by adding chemicals such as glycerol to liquid nitrogen at a temperature of –190 degrees C. This technique protects cells and tissues by preventing any damage that could be caused by the formation of ice crystals.

Frank and Ellen felt reassured by their discussion with Dr. Otis. They couldn't afford the time and money required for adoption, but from their reading they had decided their chances of conceiving through donor insemination were good. Healthy couples with no other problems have a 70 to 80 percent success rate within one year. This figure compares with a natural conception rate of 85 to 90 percent for fertile couples.

The Smiths were also pleased that Dr. Otis had so carefully explained the procedure to them. After carefully tracking a woman's menstrual cycle and searching for accurate

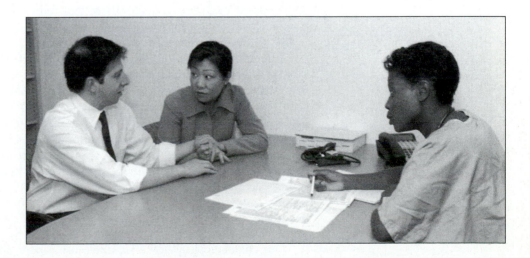

With approximately 5 million individuals in the United States who are thought to be infertile, many couples are consulting fertility specialists.

clues to the time of ovulation by examining her vaginal mucus and urine, the physician injects the semen through the cervix with a needleless syringe. Their hopes and expectations were justified: Ellen conceived and gave birth to a healthy baby boy. ✪

We guarantee that by the time you finish reading this chapter, you'll be a different person. Don't laugh. It's true. In the next 30 to 40 minutes, many of your genes will be changed by mutations, that is, errors will have occurred in your personal genetic messages.

Pondering this idea, the English geneticist Steve Jones (1993) described how our copying process—the process that makes hundreds of millions cells each second, each with its own copy of the original genetic message—can go wrong. With about 100 trillion cells in the human body and with millions of them constantly dividing, the possibility of error is mind-boggling. Thankfully, most of these mutations (or changes) are harmless, but others can be disastrous, such as those producing cancer cells. So you see, by the time you answer the questions at the end of the chapter, you are literally a different person.

We would like you to think of this chapter in the same way you would draw a map. In this case, however, you'll be studying the inherited map of yourself, now being traced in exquisite detail in the *Human Genome Project* (HGP). But you may well ask, What value is a map of our genes? Aside from the contribution it is making to human knowledge, the potential it offers for identifying and curing disease is inestimable. Other more mundane but practical contributions can be seen in the following example.

In 1902 a murder was committed that shocked even the sophisticated residents of Paris. The brutality of the crime and the cleverness of the murderer suggested that its solution would be difficult, if not impossible. Yet using the latest technology of those times, the famous French detective, Alfonse Bertillon, quickly identified the killer. You have probably guessed by now that the murderer left his fingerprints at the scene of the crime, which was the evidence that convicted him. Eighty-three years later, near Leicester, England, the killer of two young girls was arrested and convicted because of genetic material found at the site of the crime. The "DNA" fingerprint discovered, because of its uniqueness, was considered to be a statement of personal identity. These two incidents are telling testimony both to the rapid advancement of biological research and to the importance of biological data in our lives (Jones, 1993).

In this chapter you'll read about the fertilization process, during which the sperm and egg unite. Today, however, we can no longer refer to "the union of sperm and egg." We must ask additional questions: Whose sperm? Whose egg? Where did the union occur? Was it in the woman's body? Which woman will carry the fertilized egg? You can see, then, that fertilization is a process filled with the potential for conflict and controversy because of new techniques that enable fertilization to occur outside of a woman's body.

Sometime in your life you probably have said, "Oh, I've inherited that trait." That's the easy answer. How did you inherit that characteristic? Do you remember that DNA you heard about in your science classes? Here you'll learn that the discovery of DNA involved some of the world's greatest biologists in a race to be the first to find the "secret of life." Today scientists are engaged in a struggle to "map the human genome" in the Human Genome Project, which is an endeavor to identify our genetic endowment—the approximately 100,000 genes that lie in the nucleus of every cell. Once these genes are identified and located efforts can be made to combat thousands of genetic diseases! Perhaps equally as exciting is the attempt to identify "susceptibility" genes, which do not of themselves cause disease but make certain individuals susceptible to such diseases as breast cancer, colon cancer, and Alzheimer's.

Our characteristics, however, don't just appear; they're passed on from generation to generation. Following our discussion of genes, we'll trace the manner in which hereditary traits are transmitted. Unfortunately, we are all too well aware that occasionally the transmission of traits produces abnormalities, which we also discuss. Finally, no discussion of human heredity is complete without acknowledging the ethical issues that have arisen because of these new developments. Answers still elude us, but at least we can ask several critical questions: Should scientists be allowed to implant specific genes to satisfy a couple's preferences? Should society determine that certain types of genes be implanted to ensure "desirable" products? No easy questions, these, but you can be sure that they will arise in the future.

Chapter Objectives

After you read this chapter, you should be able to answer the following questions.

◆ How does fertilization, both natural and external, occur?

◆ What are the mechanisms of heredity and what could go wrong?

◆ What are the major features and anticipated uses of the Human Genome Project?

The Fertilization Process

The fusion of two specialized cells, the sperm and the egg (or ovum), mark the beginning of development and the zygote (the fertilized ovum) immediately begins to divide. This fertilized ovum contains all of the genetic material that the organism will ever possess.

The Beginnings

Any discussion of fertilization today must account for the advances that both research and technology have made available. Consequently, our discussion will include external fertilization techniques, such as **in vitro fertilization** (the famous "test-tube" babies). Table 3.1 contains a glossary of many terms you will find in this discussion. Be sure to refer to it when you meet an unfamiliar term. Otherwise, the amazing richness of the genetic world can escape you.

In our analysis of genetic material and its impact on our lives, we'll attempt to follow the manner in which we receive genes from our parents, so our story begins with the male's sperm and the female's egg.

The Sperm

Certain cells are destined to become the sperm and eggs. The chief characteristics of the sperm are its tightly packed tip (the acrosome), containing 23 chromosomes, a short neck region, and a tail to propel it in its search for the egg (Wolpert, 1991). Sperm are so tiny that estimates are that the number of sperm equal to the world's population could fit in a thimble. Sperm remain capable of fertilizing an egg for about 24 to 48 hours after ejaculation (Moore & Persaud, 1998). Of the 200 million sperm that enter the vagina, only about 200 survive the journey to the woman's fallopian tubes, where fertilization occurs.

The major purpose of a male's reproductive organs is to manufacture, store, and deliver sperm. The sperm has as its sole objective the delivery of its DNA to the egg. Males, at birth, have in their testes those cells that will eventually produce sperm. At puberty, the number of chromosomes is halved and actual sperm are formed. Simultaneously, the pituitary gland stimulates the hormonal production that results in the male secondary sex characteristics: pubic hair, a beard, and a deep voice.

The Ovum (Egg)

The egg is larger than the sperm, about the size of the period at the end of this sentence. The egg is round and its surface is about the consistency of stiff jelly. You may find it hard to believe, but a whale and a mouse come from eggs of about the same size. In fact, the eggs of all mammals are about the same size and appearance. When females are born, they already have primal eggs. From 1 to 2 million eggs have been formed in the ovaries. Since only one mature egg is required each month for about

In vitro fertilization
Fertilization that occurs "in the dish"; an external fertilization technique.

(a)

(b)

The sperm (a), in its search for the egg (b), carries the 23 chromosomes from the male.

TABLE 3.1 A GENETIC GLOSSARY

Acrosome Area at the tip of the sperm that contains the chemicals enabling the sperm to penetrate the egg's surface.

Allele Alternate forms of a specific gene; there are genes for blue eyes and brown eyes.

Autosome Chromosomes other than the sex chromosomes.

Chromosome Stringlike bodies that carry the genes; they are present in all of the body's cells.

DNA Deoxyribonucleic acid, the chemical structure of the gene.

Dominance The tendency of a gene to be expressed in a trait, even when joined with a gene whose expression differs; brown eyes will appear when genes for blue and brown eyes are paired.

Fertilization The union of sperm and egg to form the fertilized ovum or zygote.

Gametes The mature sex cells, either sperms or eggs.

Genes The ultimate hereditary determiners; they are composed of the chemical molecule deoxyribonucleic acid (DNA).

Gene locus The specific location of a gene on the chromosome.

Genotype The genetic composition of an individual.

Heterozygous The gene pairs for a trait differ; a person who is heterozygous for eye color has a gene for brown eyes and one for blue eyes.

Homozygous The gene pairs for a trait are similar; the eye color genes are the same.

Meiosis Cell division in which each daughter cell receives one-half of the chromosomes of the parent cell. For humans this maintains the number of chromosomes (46) at fertilization.

Mitosis Cell division in which each daughter cell receives the same number of chromosomes as the parent cell.

Mutation A change in the structure of a gene.

Phenotype The observable expression of a gene.

Recessive A gene whose trait is not expressed unless paired with another recessive gene; both parents contribute genes for blue eyes.

Sex chromosome Those chromosomes that determine sex; in humans they are the 23rd pair, with an XX combination producing a female, and an XY combination producing a male.

Sex-linkage Genes on the sex chromosome that produce traits other than sex.

Trisomy Three chromosomes are present rather than the customary pair; Down syndrome is caused by three chromosomes at the 21st pairing.

Zygote The fertilized egg.

From John F. Travers, *The Growing Child,* Scott, Foresman and Company, Glenview, IL, 1982. Reprinted by permission of the author.

35 years, the number present far exceeds the need. Eggs are usually fertilized about 12 hours after they are discharged from the surface of the ovary or they die within 12 to 24 hours (Moore & Persaud, 1998). From this brief discussion, you can identify the major differences between eggs and sperm. Eggs are massive compared to sperm; eggs are well-equipped with cytoplasm, while sperm have very little.

The Menstrual Cycle

The pituitary gland secretes a hormone that stimulates the ripening of eggs, and after two weeks one egg, which has ripened more than the others, is discharged from the ovary's surface (Curtis & Barnes, 1994). (Figure 3.1 illustrates the relationship of the ovum to the ovary, the fallopian tubes, and the uterus.) This process, called ovulation, triggers a chemical reaction that inhibits the ripening of further eggs. It also prepares the uterine lining for a potential fertilized ovum.

If fertilization does not occur, the prepared uterine lining is shed in menstruation and the entire process begins again. As a woman approaches the end of her egg-producing years, these last ova have been present for as many as 40 years. This may explain why the children of older women are more susceptible to genetic defects. The eggs have been exposed to environmental hazards (such as radiation) too long to escape damage (Jones, 1993; Moore & Persaud, 1998).

Figure 3.1

The relationship of ovary, egg, fallopian tube, and uterus.

From John F. Travers, *The Growing Child*, Scott, Foresman and Company, Glenview, IL, 1982. Reprinted by permission of the author.

Figure 3.2

Fertilization of the egg. The sperm, carrying its 23 chromosomes, penetrates the egg, with its 23 chromosomes. The nuclei of sperm and egg fuse, resulting in 46 chromosomes.

From John F. Travers, *The Growing Child*, Scott, Foresman and Company, Glenview, IL, 1982. Reprinted by permission of the author.

Ovulation   Egg bursts from the surface of the ovary.

Fallopian tubes   Passageway for the egg once it is discharged from the ovary's surface.

Zygote   The fertilized egg.

Implantation   Fertilized egg attaches and secures itself to uterine wall.

Blastocyst   Name of the fertilized egg after initial divisions.

Implantation

When the egg is discharged from the ovary's surface (a process called **ovulation**), it is enveloped by one of the **fallopian tubes.** The diameter of each fallopian tube is about that of a human hair, but it almost unfailingly ensnares the egg and provides a passageway to the uterus. If fertilization occurs, it takes place soon after the egg enters the fallopian tube. Figure 3.2 illustrates the fertilization process.

Fusion of the two cells is quickly followed by the first cell division. As the fertilized egg, now called the **zygote,** travels toward **implantation** within the uterus, cell division continues. The cells multiply rapidly and after about seven days reach the uterine wall. The fertilized egg is now called a **blastocyst.** The journey is pictured in figure 3.3.

Although individuals may change in the course of their lives, their hereditary properties do not change. The zygote (the fertilized egg), containing all 46 chromosomes, represents the "blueprint" for our physical and mental makeup. Under ordinary circumstances, environmental conditions leave the 46 chromosomes unaltered. (We know today that environmental agents such as drugs, viruses, or radiation may cause genetic damage.)

Once fertilization occurs, the zygote is not yet free from risk. Let's use a figure easy to work with and assume that 100 eggs are exposed to sperm. Here is the estimated mortality rate from fertilization to birth:

84 are fertilized
69 are implanted
42 survive one week
37 survive seven weeks
31 survive to birth

Thus, nature's toll results in about a 70 percent mortality rate.

Twins

Occasionally, and for reasons that still elude us, twins are born. Most twins occur when a woman's ovaries release two ripened eggs (rather than one) and both are

Figure 3.3

From ovuation to implantation.

From John F. Travers, *The Growing Child,* Scott, Foresman and Company, Glenview, IL, 1982. Reprinted by permission of the author.

Dizygotic Nonidentical twins.

fertilized by separate sperm. These twins are called nonidentical, or **dizygotic.** Their genes are no more alike than those of siblings born of the same parents but at different times.

Less frequently, twins develop from a single fertilized egg that divided after conception. Interestingly, identical twins usually do not result when the fertilized egg initially divides into two cells; separation occurs later when the dividing egg consists of several hundred cells (Wolpert, 1991). This process leads to identical, or

Monozygotic Identical twins.

monozygotic, twins whose genes are identical; that is, they share the same genotype (Bouchard, 1994).

Monozygotic twins are born with remarkable consistency, about 3 or 4 per thousand births, regardless of race. The rate of nonidentical (dizygotic) twin births, however, varies considerably from country to country. For example, in the United States about 8 to 10 pairs of dizygotic twins are born per 1,000 live births. The rate is about the same in Great Britain and other European countries. In Asia about 2 or 3 pairs of dizygotic twins are born per 1,000 live births. In Africa, about 20 pairs of dizygotic twins are born per 1,000 live births (Jones, 1993; Lytton, Singh, & Gallagher, 1995).

Infertility

Although the fertilization process just described is the normal process for most women, there are exceptions. For some couples, like Frank and Ellen Smith in the chapter's opening, *infertility,* for whatever reason, is a serious problem. Today hundreds of thousands of childless couples desperately desire children. These couples share a growing problem in our society: infertility.

Causes of Infertility

Estimates are that about one in six American couples meet the criteria for infertility: an inability to achieve pregnancy after two years. Several reasons have been offered for this increased rate. In males, the number and quality of sperm are often suspected; rarely are structural or hormonal abnormalities the culprit. For example, the number of *sexually transmitted diseases (STDs),* especially *chlamydia* (usually a silent infection that may lurk in a woman's pelvic organs), show a marked acceleration. These, in turn, can lead to *pelvic inflammatory disease (PID),* which then can cause infertility. Also, a growing number of women are delaying childbearing until their thirties or later. Older women are more likely to become infertile if they have had abdominal surgery, or if they experienced **endometriosis,** a condition that increases with age. (Endometriosis, typically found in the lining of the uterus, is the growth of endometrial tissue outside of the uterus.) *Intrauterine devices (IUDs)* were popular through the 1970s. Although discredited because of the hazards they introduce, especially the risk of infection, they still are responsible for some problems seen today. Here is a summary of the most common infertility problems (Marrs & others, 1997).

Endometriosis   A condition in which tissue normally found in the uterus grows in other areas, such as the fallopian tubes.

- Ovulation and/or sperm problems   40%
- Sperm/mucus interaction   15%
- Fallopian tubes and/or uterus   15%
- Pelvic environment   15%
- Unexplained   15%

Simply because a woman does not become pregnant within a specific time doesn't necessarily indicate infertility. Couples should wait for two years before suspecting infertility if a woman is in her twenties, one year if she is between 30 and 35, and six months if she is over 35. Even if a couple finds that they are indeed infertile, they needn't abandon their hopes of parenthood. Many reproductive techniques are available today.

The new technologies we are about to discuss offer couples new hope. Hundreds of in vitro fertilization centers and sperm banks now exist around the country.

Assisted Reproduction

Although you are probably most familiar with in vitro fertilization, another process, *artificial insemination by donor (AID),* is by far the most widely used procedure. Many new forms of *assisted reproductions technologies (ART)* are now available (Marrs & others, 1997):

- *In vitro fertilization,* in which fertilization of egg with sperm occurs in a dish.

- *Gamete intrafallopian transfer (GIFT),* in which sperm and egg are placed in the fallopian tube with the intent of achieving fertilization in a more natural environment (also known as *embryo transfer).*

- *Zygote intrafallopian transfer (ZIFT),* in which the fertilized egg is transferred to the fallopian tube.

- *Sperm and egg donation,* in which males and females either donate or sell their sperms and eggs. Today hundreds of sperm banks operate in the United States. Sixteen cryobanks store and sell frozen sperm, which are frozen in liquid nitrogen at −190 degrees C and remain potent for years. Women who will offer their eggs are in great demand. For example, a childless couple placed the following ad in the monthly magazine of a prestigious Eastern university:

  $50,000 to an intelligent, athletic egg donor who must be at least 5'10" have a 1400+ SAT score and possess no major family medical issues. (Sege, 1999)

- *Cryopreservation,* which refers to freezing embryos for future use.

- *Surrogate motherhood,* in which one woman carries another woman's enbryo for nine months.

Consequently, today a child may have as many as five parents:

- A sperm donor (father or other male).

- An egg donor (mother or other female).

- A surrogate mother.

- The couple who raises the child.

In Vitro Fertilization (IVF)

In vitro fertilization (IVF) is the external fertilization technique you are probably most familiar with. The steps in IVF are as follows (Curtis & Barnes, 1994):

1. The woman is usually treated with hormones to stimulate maturation of eggs in the ovary, and she is observed closely to determine the timing of ovulation (i.e., the time at which the egg leaves the surface of the ovary).

2. The physician makes an incision in the abdomen and inserts a laparoscope (a thin tubular lens through which the physician can see the ovary) to remove mature eggs.

3. The egg is placed in a solution containing blood serum and nutrients.

4. *Capacitation* takes place—this is a process in which a layer surrounding the sperm is removed so that it may penetrate the egg.

5. Sperm are added to the solution; fertilization occurs.

6. The fertilized egg is transferred to a fresh supporting solution.

7. Fertilized eggs (usually three) are inserted into the uterus.

8. The fertilized egg is implanted in the uterine lining.

An Informed VIEW   *To Clone or Not to Clone*

Dolly, the most famous lamb in history, was born at 5:00 P.M. on a warm summer's day, July 5, 1996. It was a remarkably quiet introduction to one of the most controversial events of the twentieth century. Dolly was a clone, that is, she was not the product of the union of a sperm and egg. Ian Wilmut, a quiet, unassuming embryologist, combined the udder cell of a 6-year-old sheep with the egg of another sheep, after first removing the genetic material from the egg. The udder cell's genes now assumed command of the growth and development of the newly fertilized egg. The result: Dolly, an identical twin of the original sheep that supplied the udder cell. *But the identical twin was born six years later!* (Kolata, 1998).

Until Dolly's birth, scientists had mainly discounted the possibility of cloning from adults since their only success had come from cloning the cells of embryos. Attempts using adult cells consistently failed until researchers discovered that the secret lay in the growth cycle of cells. As part of their normal cycle, cells enter into resting periods called G0 (gap zero). As long as the cell is in the G0 state, the egg would accept the DNA of the adult cell and use it to direct growth.

You have probably anticipated the next stage in the chronology of cloning: Is it possible to clone a human? As you can imagine, this question has ignited a firestorm of controversy. Do the benefits of cloning (replicating perfect farm animals, adding genes so that a cow might have valuable drugs in its milk, allowing childless couples to have children, developing organs to use in transplants) suggest that cloning humans is a necessary next step? Or do the negative features of cloning (sacrificing embryos to obtain one healthy clone, the possibility of genetic monsters, unresolved issues about the self—are we the product of our genes or not; if not, what makes us *us*?) outweigh any potential benefits?

Considering the inevitable collision between available technology and the forces arrayed against cloning, do you think the cloning of humans will ever occur? If you would like to have a more informed view on this issue, you may want to read one or more of the references in this chapter. (For example, Gina Kolata (1998) has written a fascinating account of the background and techniques of this process.)

You may also wish to learn more about it by going to our web site at http://www.mhhe.com/dacey5.

Dolly, a cloned lamb, is destined to become the most famous lamb in history.

For an excellent summary of the cloning process, see Gina Kolata, *Clone*, which was published by William Morrow & Co. in 1998.

During this period, the woman is being treated to prepare her body to receive the fertilized egg. For example, the lining of the uterus must be spongy or porous enough to hold the zygote. The fertilized egg must be inserted at the time it would normally reach the uterine cavity. About 27,000 IVF procedures are done every year in the United States with an estimated success rate at about 20 percent (CDC, 1995; Curtis & Barnes; 1994; Marrs & others, 1997).

Adoption

For many couples who remain childless in spite of several attempts at external fertilization, adoption (to take a child of other parents voluntarily as one's own) offers a viable option. Today's traditional middle to upper-middle class white couples who decide to adopt face competition from single adults, older adults, and homosexual adults. Because single parenthood is widely accepted today, more single women are keeping their children. The increasing use of contraception and the legality of abortion have also caused a sharp reduction in the number of available children, leading to heightened interest in adopting children from other nations. Nevertheless, more children are available for adoption than is commonly thought: older children, minority children, and handicapped children (Henry, 1999). Although these children are available for immediate adoption, the waiting period for healthy white infants may run into years (Brodzinsky, Lang, & Smith, 1995).

Closed adoption   Natural parents knew nothing about the adopting parents.

Adoption procedures were formerly closed **(closed adoption)** and the biological parents were completely removed from the life of their child once the child was surrendered for adoption. The bonds between birth parent(s) and child were legally and permanently severed; the child's history was sealed by the court. These procedures were done with the best intentions, but it was as if the child had no genetic past. Supposedly the natural parents and the adoptive couple were saved from emotional upset. Many biological mothers, however, reported in later interviews that they never recovered from the grieving process.

Today, however, when a pregnant woman approaches an adoption agency, she gets what she wants. She can insist that her child be raised by a couple with specific characteristics: nationality, religion, income, number in family. She can ask to see her child several times a year, perhaps take the youngster on a vacation, and telephone the child frequently. The adoption agency will try to meet these demands. This process is called **open adoption,** and although many adoptive couples dislike the arrangement, they really have no choice. Thus we see a new definition of adoption: the process of accepting the responsibility of raising an individual who has two sets of parents.

Open adoption   Natural parent has considerable input into the adoption process.

When couples choose to adopt, they should carefully consider the age of the child. They may find one age group more appealing than others. Each developmental period—infancy, early childhood, middle childhood, adolescence—has its own strengths and weaknesses that they should consider as potential adoptive parents. They should also realize that once children know they are adopted and understand what that means, the relationship with their adoptive parents inevitably changes. This "moment of truth" affects both parents and children. For example, children must cope with the idea of being relinquished, which is not an easy task. Parents must accept the idea that their children will want to know more about their biological parents, which is a natural concern.

Finally, a troubling new development has entered the adoption scene. If you recall, in the in vitro process only about 2 or 3 embryos out of about a dozen are implanted in the woman. What happens to the rest? Estimates are that the roughly 300–400 in vitro clinics in the United States now have about 200,000 embryos stored. Of these, thousands have been donated to infertile couples thus creating a new form of adoption. What is troubling about this new procedure is the lack of any regulations to deal with critical issues: screening for disease, donor rights and responsibilities, donor identification (similar to the process for open adoption). This new technique promises to raise controversial legal and ethical issues.

A Sociocultural View

Foreign Adoption—An Odyssey

Recently, friends of ours, Steve and Nancy, decided to adopt a Romanian infant girl of 15 months. Their story is both touching and moving, as well as a detailed chronicle of what's involved in the process.

The young couple examined the pros and cons of both domestic and foreign adoptions and ultimately decided on a foreign adoption. They felt there were too many complications with most domestic adoptions, less certain outcomes, and often very lengthy waits. The downside of an international adoption is that generally the children are older and often spend a year or more in an orphanage.

The adoption agency they worked with was certified by the Romanian government. The agency had a Romanian husband and wife team working to identify adoptable children and assist with negotiating the process in Romania and also helping the adoptive parents once in Romania. The son of this couple works for the agency in the U.S.A. and communicates regularly with his parents.

Steve and Nancy were told they must use one of the certified agencies in order to adopt. They also needed to follow Massachusetts laws for a detailed home study, including criminal background checks. In addition they had to apply to the Immigration and Naturalization Services (INS) for approval. They were also checked by the FBI. The only input they had to the adoption process was to specify a child as young as possible; the agency matches children and parents. On a second adoption, however, prospective parents are allowed to specify the sex.

They found going through the Romanian system a difficult process. They were told about Katie in June and anticipated going to Romania the following September to get her. Katie is from Iasi, near the Ukrainian border. The home study done on Steve and Nancy plus their INS paperwork were submitted to the Romanian Adoption Review Committee, which approved them as adoptive parents. The birth parent(s) must also give their permission for the child to be adopted.

Once the adoption committee approves both parents and children, the paperwork goes back to the local courts for finalization. Next, a hearing is held followed by an appeal period. Ultimately the adoption paperwork was completed in early January. They had to wait three weeks for Katie's passport and then went back to Romania to bring her home.

At the orphanage, Steve and Nancy were able to see only the main entry way and a small room off to the side. They were told that this orphanage was the best in the country. Supposedly, the director was well educated, with degrees in early childhood education. The orphanage seemed bright and clean, and the children are taken outside to play, which is very unusual in Romania. There were Disney characters on the wall and Polaroid pictures of the

The number of international adoptions is increasing although the process remains complicated.

children visiting with their version of Santa Claus. They couldn't learn much about the children's diet or stimulation other than Katie had oranges and in all likelihood bananas. They also learned little about staffing conditions (ratio of staff to children, education of staff, etc.).

When they brought Katie home in late January, she was almost 15 months old. She was slightly anemic when she arrived, but an iron based formula quickly corrected the problem. Today Katie is an excellent eater and enjoys almost everything except fruit juices. She adjusted quickly to her new parents and their home. She had no difficulty with eating or sleeping, nor was she irritable. The only problem was a viral infection that lasted for about 5 weeks. The social worker visited about 3 weeks after they arrived home and again at the 2+ month mark. In that time she noticed how much more interactive Katie had become. They recently had their final home study visit, and the social worker was very pleased with Katie's development.

Katie will be 22 months old on September 4 and is a normal toddler. She's very active, has good motor skills, is beginning to exhibit a temper when she does not get her own way, and tests Steve and Nancy to see how much she can get away with—very normal reactions for an almost 2-year-old. The only problem seems to be a language delay, but comprehension seems to be normal. A speech pathologist has recommended a re-evaluation in 4 months, with the belief that her language skills will explode before then. She is now mimicking much of what Steve and Nancy say to her, thus it would appear that she will swiftly overcome this language delay.

In summary, Katie came into a warm, loving environment, has adjusted well, and seems on the way to a normal and happy childhood.

Nevertheless, we can agree that:

As a means of ensuring the physical and emotional well-being of children, adoption has proven to be an unqualified success. Adopted children fare significantly better than children reared in institutional environments or in foster care (Brodzinsky, Lang, & Smith, 1995).

Guided Review

1. _____ is the process uniting sperm and egg.
2. A fertilized egg is known as a _____ .
3. The _____ gland secretes hormones that stimulate the ovaries to ripen and release an egg each month.
4. The most well-known example of an external fertilization technique is _____ fertilization.
5. The most popular external fertilization technique is _____ .
6. Estimates are that _____ in _____ American couples are infertile.
7. A form of adoption that today is becoming more popular is _____ adoption.

Mitosis Cell division in which the number of chromosomes remains the same.

Meiosis Cell division in which the number of chromosomes is halved.

Figure 3.4

A mitotic division is a cell division in which each daughter cell receives the same number of chromosomes as the parent cell—46.

Heredity at Work

The original cell, the possessor of 46 chromosomes, begins to divide rapidly after fertilization, until the infant has billions of cells at birth. The cells soon begin to specialize: some become muscle, some bone, some skin, some blood, and some nerve cells. These are the somatic, or body, cells. The process of division by which these cells multiply is called **mitosis** (see figure 3.4). In a mitotic division, the number of chromosomes in each cell remains the same.

A second type of cell is also differentiated: the germ, or sex, cell that ultimately becomes either sperm or egg. These reproductive cells likewise divide by the process of mitosis until the age of puberty. But then a remarkable phenomenon occurs—another type of division called **meiosis,** or reduction division (see figure 3.5). Each sex cell, instead of receiving 46 chromosomes upon division, now receives 23.

Mitosis is basically a division of cells in which each chromosome is duplicated so that each cell receives a copy of each chromosome of the parent cell. What is doubled in mitotic division is the amount of deoxyribonucleic acid (DNA), the chief component of the genes. Meiosis, which occurs only in germ cell reproduction, is responsible both for the shuffling of hereditary characteristics received from each parent and for their random appearance in offspring. During the reduction division, the chromosomes separate longitudinally so that 23 go to one cell and 23 to another.

For the male, reduction division begins to occur just before puberty. For the female, the process differs slightly. Since she is required to produce only one mature egg a month, there is no provision for an indefinitely large number of eggs, as there is for sperm. A woman normally sheds only 300 to 400 mature ova in her lifetime, whereas the normal male in a single ejaculation emits hundreds of millions of sperm.

At birth the female's ovaries contain tiny clusters of all the eggs that will mature in later years. Just before puberty, the final phases of the reduction division occur, and mature eggs are formed. It is as if there is a lengthy waiting period, from birth until about the age of 12 or 13, before the process is finally completed. The 23 chromosomes with their hereditary content are present at birth but must await the passage of time before biological maturity occurs in the female.

Answers

1. Fertilization 2. zygote 3. pituitary 4. in vitro 5. AID 6. one, six 7. open

Figure 3.5

A meiotic division is a cell division in which each daughter cell receives one half of the chromosomes of the parent cell—23.

Genotype An individual's genetic composition.

Phenotype The observable expression of gene action.

DNA (Deoxyribonucleic acid) The chemical structure of the gene that accounts for our inherited characteristics.

Now that we have traced the process by which fertilization occurs and discovered what is passed from parents to child, we still need to know "why I am who I am." This leads us to a discussion of chrosomomes and genes.

Chromosomes and Genes

After the sperm and egg unite, the new cell (the potential individual) possesses 23 pairs of chromosomes, or 46 chromosomes, which represents our total biological heritage. Until 1956, the number of human chromosomes was thought to be 48 (Korf, 1996). The sperm actually determines sex, since it alone can carry a Y chromosome. Thus there are two kinds of sperm: the X chromosome carrier and the Y chromosome carrier. The Y carrier is smaller than the X, which contains more genetic material. The Y carrier is also lighter and speedier and can reach the egg more quickly. But it is also more vulnerable.

One member of each pair of chromosomes has been contributed by the father and one by the mother. Each pair, except the 23rd, is remarkably alike. The 23rd pair defines the individual's sex: an XX combination indicates a female; XY indicates a male. The male, from conception, is the more fragile of the two sexes. Estimates are that 160 males are conceived for every 100 females. However, so many males are spontaneously aborted that only 105 males are born for every 100 females. A similar pattern appears in neonatal life and continues throughout development, until women finally outnumber men, reversing the original ratio. Consequently, certain conclusions follow:

- Structurally and functionally, females resist disease better than males.

- The male is more subject to hereditary disease and defect.

- Environmental elements expose the male to greater hazards.

- Females are born with and retain a biological superiority over males.

The significance of the chromosomes lies in the material they contain—the genes. Each gene is located at a particular spot on the chromosome, called the gene locus. The genes, whose chemical structure is DNA, account for all inherited characteristics, from hair and eye color to skin shade, even the tendency toward baldness.

Genetic Information

How much information is contained in this biological heritage? Each chromosome contains the equivalent of about 3 billion letters. Since the average word contains six letters, each chromosome incorporates information equal to about 500 million words. At about 300 words per typical printed page, this translates into the equivalent of about 2 million pages. The average book consists of about 500 pages. Thus the information in one human chromosome corresponds to that in 4,000 books.

To avoid any misunderstanding, however, we want to reemphasize that development results from the interaction of heredity and environment. It's the process by which our **genotype** (our genetic heritage) is expressed as a **phenotype** (our observable characteristics). Genes always function in an environment, and environmental circumstances affect the way the genes express themselves.

Our discussion now brings us to the discovery of DNA, one of the great achievements of the twentiethth century.

DNA: Structure and Function

We know that each chromosome contains thousands of genes, which are small sections of **DNA** (deoxyribonucleic acid). Each of these thousands of genes has a role in the growth and development of each human being (Cohen, 1997). The amazing chemical compound DNA is the chemical key to the life force in humans, animals,

Figure 3.6

The DNA double helix. (a) The overall structure that gave DNA its famous name. (b) A closer examination reveals that the sides of the spiral are connected by chemicals similar to the rungs of a ladder.

From John F. Travers, *The Growing Child,* Scott, Foresman and Company, Glenview, IL, 1982. Reprinted by permission of the author.

(a)   (b)

and plants and is the molecular basis of the genes. Each cell in your body contains about 6 feet of DNA, and, if all the DNA in your cells were stretched out, it would reach to the moon and back 8 thousand times (Jones, 1993). Genes not only perform certain duties within the cell but also join with other genes to reproduce both themselves and the whole chromosome (see figure 3.6).

Each gene follows the instructions encoded in its DNA and sends these instructions, as chemical messages called RNA (ribonuceic acid), into the surrounding cell. The RNA acts swiftly, forming a particular protein at the staggering rate of 100 molecules per second! These new products then interact with the genes to form new substances (Rensberger, 1996). The process continues to build the millions of cells needed for various bodily structures (Curtis & Barnes, 1994).

Examine figure 3.6 and note how the strands intertwine. The strands, similar to the sides of a ladder, are connected by chemical rings: adenine (A), guanine (G), cytosine (C), and thymine (T) (Jackson, 1996). The letters are not randomly connected: A joins with T, G with C. If a code were written as AGCTTGA, it must appear as:

A G C T T G A

T C G A A C T

Thus, one sequence determines the other.

A remarkable feature of DNA is its ability to reproduce itself and ensure that each daughter cell receives identical information. During mitosis the DNA splits as readily as a person unzips a jacket (Curtis & Barnes, 1997). Each single strand grows a new mate, A to T and G to C, until the double-helix model is reproduced in each daughter cell.

Figure 3.7

(a) At the top is the chromosome structure of a male, and (b) at the bottom is the chromosome structure of a female. The 23rd pair is shown in the bottom right box of each figure; notice that the Y chromosome of the male is smaller. To obtain this chromosomal picture, a cell is removed from the individual's body, usually from the inside of the mouth. The chromosomes are magnified extensively and then photographed.

(a)

(b)

Watson, J. (1968). *The double helix.* Boston: Atheneum. This book has become a scientific classic. It is James Watson's personal, colorful look at the discovery of DNA and is guaranteed to hold your attention. If you are the least bit intimidated by the thought of reading about your genetic heritage, this book should eliminate your concerns. (Available in paperback.)

The four letter possibilities, AT, TA, GC, and CG, seem to limit genetic variation. But when we consider that each DNA molecule is quite lengthy, involving thousands, perhaps millions of chemical steps (TA, GC, AT, CG, AT, CG, TA), the possible combinations seem limitless. Recent estimates indicate that there may be as many as three thousand million DNA letters involved (Jones, 1993). The differences in the DNA patterns account for the individual genetic differences among humans and for differences between species (Figure 3.7 illustrates the chromosomal arrangement of a typical male and female).

Guided Review

8. Cell division in which each daughter cell receives the same number of chromosomes as the parent cell is called _____.
9. A reduction division in which the number of chromosomes is halved is called _____.
10. The chemical key to life is _____.
11. The amount of _____ _____ is doubled in each mitotic division.
12. A remarkable feature of DNA is its ability to _____ itself.
13. In genetic coding, A is linked with _____ and G is linked with _____.
14. The genetic composition of an individual is referred to as the _____, whereas the observed expression of a gene is called the _____.

Answers

8. mitosis 9. meiosis 10. DNA 11. deoxyribonucleic acid 12. reproduce 13. T, C 14. genotype, phenotype

The strong resemblance of these family members to each other is testimony to the role of heredity in our makeup.

Alleles   Different forms of a gene.

Homozygous   Identical alleles for a trait.

Heterozygous   Different alleles for a trait.

Dominant   The tendency of a gene to be expressed in a trait.

Recessive   A gene whose trait is not expressed unless paired with another recessive gene, for example, both parents contribute genes for blue eyes.

Mutations   Abrupt hereditary changes.

Polygenic inheritance   Many genes contribute to the formation of a particular trait.

Cytogenetics   The study of chromosomes.

How Traits Are Transmitted

Genes that control a particular trait, say for a cleft chin, can have alternate forms called **alleles** (Rensberger, 1996). As we have seen, if two alleles are identical (either for cleft or non cleft), the person is **homozygous** for the trait (cleft). If the alleles are different, then the organism is **heterozygous** (Cole & Cole, 1996). As genetic research continued, however, studies showed that the patterns of inheritance were not quite as simple and direct as originally thought. The effects of any gene are influenced not only by the alleles of that trait, but also by other genes and also by the environment. The story behind the transmission of traits is fascinating.

Working in a quiet monastery garden, the Austrian monk Gregor Mendel provided the impetus for modern genetics. His great achievement was to demonstrate that inherited characteristics are passed on by discrete elements called *genes*. As a result of cross-breeding pea plants (e.g., purple with white, yellow with green), Mendel discovered genetic principles that still guide us. By the last year of his experiments, it's estimated that Mendel had counted more than 300,000 peas! (Henig, 2000)

For example, cross-breeding purple with white produced all purple in the first generation. Consequently, Mendel called purple the **dominant** characteristic in this combination. When white appeared in later generations, he referred to white as the **recessive** characteristic. Studying his results, Mendel realized that the appearance and disappearance of various characteristics could be traced to separate factors. Some came from the maternal parent, others from the paternal parent, which led to his hypothesis that every individual carries pairs of factors for each trait. Members of each pair then separate from generation to generation. His discovery is called the *principle of segregation,* and helps to explain why blue-eyed babies occasionally appear in typically brown-eyed families.

Mendel's work, first reported in 1865, was ignored until 1900 when other biologists discovered his work. Using his ideas, new strides were made. For example, abrupt changes in genes are possible, a phenomenon called **mutations.** Think of mutations as inherited accidents, which may have adverse effects on any individual, but rarely affect evolutionary change (Jones, 1993). Other advances included the notion of *incomplete dominance,* that is, some characteristics seem to blend (red + white = pink). Occasionally *codominance* results in both pure characteristics appearing. Blood types are a good example: Type AB has red blood cells with the distinctive characteristics of both Type A and Type B. We now know, however, that most traits result from the interaction of many genes, and also that most genes influence more than a single trait (Curtis & Barnes, 1994). When many genes interact to produce a particular trait, the process is called **polygenic inheritance.** Such traits as height and weight are examples of polygenic inheritance.

Unfortunately, the line of transmission is occasionally broken and hereditary abnormalities occur.

Hereditary Disorders

Since hereditary abnormalities can reside either in the chromosomes or the genes, we'll analyze each of these separately.

Examples of Chromosomal Disorders

The study of chromosomes is called **cytogenetics** and thanks to new research techniques that enlarge prints of the chromosomes 2,000 to 3,000 times, our knowledge has increased tremendously. Although the chance of a chromosomal error in pregnancy is small, the risk increases with the age of the woman. Increasing age of the father may also be a factor, though less significant (Feinbloom, 1993). A discussion of chromosomal disorders follows.

Down syndrome is caused by a deviation on the 21st pair of chromosomes. These children have distinctive facial features and are usually motorically and mentally retarded.

Down syndrome Genetic abnormality caused by a deviation on the 21st pair of chromosomes.

Klinefelter syndrome Males with the XXY chromosomal pattern.

Turner syndrome Females with the XO chromosomal pattern.

Sickle-cell anemia A chromosomal disorder resulting in abnormal hemoglobin.

Down syndrome is caused by a deviation on the 21st pair of chromosomes; the individual may have 47 chromosomes. This defect was discovered in 1866 by a British doctor, Langdon Down, and produces distinctive facial features, small hands, a large tongue, and possible functional difficulties such as mental retardation, heart defects, and an added risk of leukemia.

The appearance of Down syndrome is closely related to the mother's age: Chances of giving birth to a child with Down syndrome are about 1 in 750 between the ages of 30 and 35; 1 in 300 between 35 and 39; and 1 in 80 between 40 and 45. After 45 years the incidence jumps to 1 in 40 births. Under age 30 the ratio is only 1 in 1,500 births. Recent evidence suggests that in one-third of the cases, the extra chromosome may come from the father (Blackman, 1997).

Although the exact cause of Down syndrome remains a mystery, the answer may lie in the female egg production mechanism, which results in some eggs remaining in the ovary for 40 or 50 years. The longer they are in the ovary, the greater the possibility of damage. Research during the last 40 years has led to improvements in life expectancy, overall health, and quality of life of Down syndrome children (Saal, 1998). Management of the mental retardation associated with Down syndrome has also advanced: better educational programs, early intervention techniques, and specific therapies (e.g., speech programs), which in turn have produced better functioning and socialization.

Other disorders relate to the sex chromosomes. If you recall, the 23rd pair of chromosomes are the sex chromosomes, XX for females, XY for males. Estimates are that 1 in every 1,200 females and 1 in every 400 males has some disorder in the sex chromosomes. Occasionally a male will possess an XXY pattern rather than the normal XY. This is called **Klinefelter syndrome** (named after Dr. Harry Klinefelter in 1942), a disorder that may cause small testicles, reduced body hair, possible infertility, and language impairment. Klinefelter's occurs in about 1 in 1,000 male births; the condition may be helped by injections of testosterone. Another pattern that appears in males is XYY, which may cause larger size and increased aggression— about 1 in 1,000 male births (Bock, 1993).

Females occasionally possess an XO pattern (lack of a chromosome) rather than XX. This is called **Turner syndrome** and is characterized by short stature, poorly developed secondary sex features (such as breast size), and usually sterility (about 1 in 2,500 female births).

Examples of Genetic Disorders

This section discusses the incidence and characteristics of several specific genetic disorders. Even as this is being written, thanks to the Human Genome Project, new genetic discoveries are being announced daily. (For an excellent analysis of genetic disorders, see McKusick, 1992.)

Jews of Eastern European origin are struck hardest by Tay-Sachs disease, which causes death by the age of 4 or 5. At birth the afflicted children appear normal, but development slows by the age of 6 months, and mental and motor deterioration begin. About 1 in every 25 to 30 Jews of Eastern European origin carries the defective gene, which is recessive; thus danger arises when two carriers marry. The disease results from a gene failing to produce an enzyme that breaks down fatty materials in the brain and nervous system. The result is that fat accumulates and destroys nerve cells, causing loss of coordination, blindness, and finally death. Today there are reliable genetic tests to identify carriers, and amniocentesis (see chapter 4) can detect the genetic status of a fetus of carrier parents (Cherry, 1992).

Sickle-cell anemia, which mainly afflicts those of African descent, appeared thousands of years ago in equatorial Africa and increased resistance to malaria. Estimates are that 10 percent of the African-American population in the United States carry the sickle-cell trait. Thus, two carriers of the defective gene who marry have a one in four chance of producing a child with sickle-cell anemia.

The problem is that the red blood cells of the afflicted person are distorted and pointed. Because of the cells' shape, they encounter difficulty in passing through

Cystic fibrosis Chromosomal disorder producing a malfunction of the exocrine glands.

Human Genome Project The attempt to identify and map the 50,000 to 100,000 genes that constitute the human genetic endowment.

Phenylketonuria (PKU) Chromosomal disorder resulting in a failure of the body to break down the amino acid phenylalanine.

Spina bifida A genetic disorder resulting in the failure of the neural tube to close.

Sex-linked inheritance Characteristics associated with genes on the sex chromosomes.

Hemophilia A genetic condition causing incorrect blood clotting; called the "bleeder's disease."

Fragile X syndrome A sex-linked inheritance disorder in which the bottom half of the X chromosome looks as if it is ready to fall off; causes mental retardation in 80% of the cases.

Hemophilia is an example of sex-linked inheritance, which affected several of the royal families of Europe (such as the Romanovs, pictured here).

the blood vessels. They tend to pile up and clump, producing oxygen starvation accompanied by considerable pain. The body then acts to eliminate these cells, and anemia results.

In the population of the United States, **cystic fibrosis** (CF) is the most severe genetic disease of childhood, affecting about 1 in 1,200 children. About 1 in 30 individuals is a carrier. The disease causes a malfunction of the exocrine glands, the glands that secrete tears, sweat, mucus, and saliva. Breathing is difficult because of the thickness of the mucus. The secreted sweat is extremely salty, often producing heat exhaustion. Cystic fibrosis kills more children than any other genetic disease.

Cystic fibrosis has been deadly for several reasons: Its causes remained unknown, and carriers could not be detected. Thus until a child manifested the breathing and digestive problems characteristic of the disease, identification was impossible. The CF gene now has been identified, however, and new research offers hope. Discovery of the CF gene has made possible the detection of carriers, a tremendous legacy of the **Human Genome Project.**

Phenylketonuria (PKU) results from the body's failure to break down the amino acid phenylalanine, which then accumulates, affects the nervous system, and causes mental retardation. Most states now require infants to be tested at birth. If PKU is present, the infants are placed on a special diet that has been remarkably successful.

But this success has produced future problems. Women treated successfully as infants may give birth to retarded children because of a toxic uterine environment. Thus at the first signs of pregnancy, these women must return to a special diet. The "cured" phenylketonuric still carries the faulty genes.

Spina bifida (failure of the spinal column to close completely) is an example of a genetic defect caused by the interaction of several genes with possible environmental involvement. During the formation of the nervous system (see chapter 4), if the developing neural tube does not close, spina bifida results, which can cause mental retardation. Studies have shown that if women take extra folic acid when they're pregnant, the number of cases of spina bifida decreases (Blackman, 1997).

Disorders also occur because of what is known as **sex-linked inheritance.** If you recall, the X chromosome is substantially larger than the Y (about three times as large). Therefore the female carries more genes on the 23rd chromosome than the male. This difference helps to explain sex linkage. Think back now to the difference between dominant and recessive traits. If a dominant and recessive gene appear together, the dominant trait is expressed. An individual must have two recessive genes for the recessive trait (say, blue eyes) to appear. But on the 23rd set of chromosomes, nothing on the Y chromosome offsets the effects of a gene on the X chromosome.

Perhaps the most widely known of these sex-linked characteristics is **hemophilia,** a condition in which the blood of hemophiliacs does not clot properly. Several of the royal families of Europe were particularly prone to this condition. Another sex-linked trait attributed to the X chromosome is color blindness. The X chromosome contains the gene for color vision and if it is faulty, nothing on the Y chromosome counterbalances the defect.

In 1970 a condition called **fragile X syndrome** was discovered. In this disorder, the end of the X chromosome looks ready to break off. In 1991 the gene for fragile X (FMR1) was discovered. Difficult to diagnose in the first year of life, fragile X seems to cause no physical problems. But as time passes, many of these children are learning disabled or mentally retarded. As Hart (1998) noted, Fragile X also is a common cause of inheritable developmental delay. Fragile X appears in about 1 in 2,000 live births.

These are the more frequent chromosomal and genetic diseases, which are summarized in table 3.2. (Other diseases also have, or are suspected of having, a strong genetic origin: diabetes, epilepsy, heart disorders, cancer, arthritis, and some mental illnesses.)

To end this part of our work on a more optimistic note, let's turn our attention to the promising and exciting discoveries of the Human Genome Project.

TABLE 3.2 CHROMOSOMAL AND GENETIC DISORDERS

Chromosomal Disorders

Name	Effects	Incidence
Down syndrome	47 chromosomes; distinctive facial features, mental retardation, possible physical problems	Varies with age; older women more susceptible (under 30—1 in 1500 births; 35–39—1 in 300 births)
Klinefelter syndrome	XXY chromosomal patterns in males; possible infertility, possible psychological problems	About 1 in 1000 male births
Turner syndrome	One X chromosome missing in female, lack of secondary sex characteristics, infertile	About 1 in 2500 female births
XYY syndrome	XYY chromosomal pattern in males; tend to be large, normal intelligence and behavior	About 1 in 1000 male births

Genetic Disorders

Name	Effects	Incidence
Tay-Sachs disease	Failure to break down fatty material in central nervous system; results in blindness, mental retardation, and death (usually by 4 or 5 years of age)	One in 25 Jews of Eastern European origin is a carrier
Sickle-cell anemia	Blood disorder produces anemia and considerable pain; caused by sickle shape of red blood cells	About 1 in 10 African-Americans is a carrier
Cystic fibrosis	Body produces excessive mucus, causing problems in the lungs and digestive tract; may be fatal; suspect gene recently identified	About 1 in 2000 births
Phenylketonuria (PKU)	Body fails to break down amino acid (phenylalanine); results in mental retardation; treated by special diet	About 1 in 15,000 births
Spina bifida	Neural tube problem in which the developing spinal column does not close properly; may cause partial paralysis and mental retardation	About 1 in 1000 births (depending on geographical area)

From John F. Travers, *The Growing Child,* Scott, Foresman and Company, Glenview, IL, 1982. Reprinted by permission of the author.

The Human Genome Project

On June 26, 2000, Dr. Francis Collins (Director of the National Human Genome Research Institute) and Dr. J. Craig Venter (President of Celera Genomics) announced at a White House ceremony that they had completed a "rough draft of the human genome." As we have seen, it requires over 3 billion chemical letters (A,T,C,G) to identify the DNA instructions by which an individual develops from an embryo to an adult. The Human Genome Project has been nothing less than an attempt to identify and map the 50,000 to 100,000 genes that constitute our genetic makeup (Cohen, 1997; Hart, 2000).

Much remains to be done: sequencing the genome (determining the exact order of the 3 billion chemical letters), finding the specific location of the genes and determining their functions, correcting disease-causing genes, etc. (Wade, 2000). In the process, HGP is revolutionizing biology, medicine, and pharmacology, to say nothing of its ethical, legal, and social ramifications. For example, forms of hypertension, schizophrenia, and Alzheimer's have been targeted by an emerging drug therapy (Cohen, 1997). The genes responsible for cystic fibrosis and Huntington's disease have been identified, as well as the breast cancer susceptibility gene (BRCA1). Some genetic defects have been identified only days after fertilization (Rensberger, 1996). Despite controversy and some disappointing results, gene therapy continues to offer promise for treating hemophilia, certain forms of cancer, and babies with defective immune systems (Stolberg, 2000).

The first complete draft of the human genome promises great potential, although much work remains to be done.

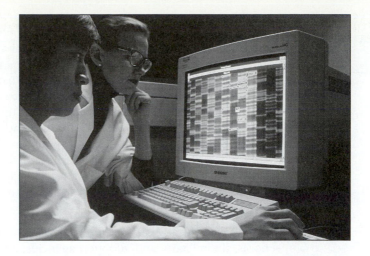

Although there are hundreds of diseases caused by a single gene, for thousands of others the contribution is much more obscure. For example, some diseases need an environmental trigger (which may be the case for schizophrenia), whereas in other diseases such as bipolar depression, several genes must interact (Bodmer & McKie, 1995; Goode, 2000).

How the Human Genome Project Began

Two gatherings of America's top biologists in the 1980s are credited as the forerunners of the project. In 1985, a group of scientists met at the University of California at Santa Cruz to discuss the possibility of mapping the human genome. Although many participants at this meeting were sure it *could* be done, they remained skeptical that it *should* be done because of the enormous expense. Because of the widespread benefits that would come from the project, however, almost all of the scientists present agreed that it deserved continued consideration. In March 1986, a meeting of international scientists took place in Santa Fe, New Mexico. This meeting is considered to be the actual beginning of the Human Genome Project. The National Institutes of Health (NIH), with the assistance of the Department of Energy (DOE), assumed leadership of the project (Cole, 1998). As a result of these meetings, the following goals were identified.

- Continued mapping of the human genome, that is, mapping the 100,000 genes present in each chromosome.

- Identification of all the genes in the genome.

- Advance DNA sequencing. (Sequencing is the process of determining the order of the nucleotides—A, T, C, and Gs—along a DNA strand.)

- Development of new and improved technologies.

- Continued investigation of the ethical, social, and legal aspects of the project.

In spite of these successes, the difficulty of the task that remains can't be discounted. Although there are hundreds of diseases caused by a single gene, for thousands of others the contribution is much more obscure. Studies of genetic susceptibility will undoubtedly follow the same pattern. The genes that make people susceptible to certain diseases do not, by themselves, cause disease. Rather, the combination of a particular environmental factor with a particular gene is needed (Ridley, 2000). Once the mechanisms that cause a susceptibility gene to spring into action are more fully understood, such preventative measures as screening techniques and drug therapy will save many lives. Could it be possible that at birth people will be given a DNA test and then issued a small card or computer chip that indicates what type of health problems they are likely to encounter?

Ethical, Legal, and Social Implications

Unfortunately, this explosion of knowledge is also leading to uncertain, even dangerous, consequences. (As you read this, companies are being formed to recruit people to donate their DNA to help find genes that cause disease.) For example, if a family member is susceptible to a particular disease, do insurance companies have the legal right to deny this person, and perhaps the entire family, health insurance? Where are the lines drawn between public and private interests? How private/public is a person's medical history? Grappling with this and similar issues has led the *National Institutes of Health* and the *Department of Energy* to join forces and create a program for studying the ethical, legal, and social implications of the Human Genome Project—the ELSI program. Several of the issues that have been identified include the following.

- *Fairness in the use of genetic information* by insurers, employers, courts, schools, the military, and adoption agencies, among others. Who has access to this information, and how will it be used?

- *Privacy and confidentiality of genetic information.* Who owns and controls the information?

- *Psychological impact.* Is there any stigma attached because of a person's genetic makeup?

- *Genetic testing.* If there's a specific family history of a disorder, what is the role of genetic testing?

- *Reproductive issues.* What role does genetic information play in decision making and reproductive rights?

- *Clinical issues.* What type of and how much education are necessary for health care providers? What are desirable standards and quality control measures?

- *Commercialization.* Who controls property rights and accessibility of data?

Finally, a good way to summarize our work in this chapter is to remember that the outcome of genetic action can only result from its interaction with environmental experiences. An example of this conclusion can be found in the work of Robert Plomin and his associates (1995), who investigated genetic effects on the family environment. Noting that children don't passively accept environmental influences, these researchers pointed out that children select, modify, and even create their environments. Thus research steadily supports the conclusion that the path of development is determined not only by heredity but also by the environment into which children are born—heredity interacting with environment.

Cook-Deegan, R. (1995). *The gene wars: Science, politics, and the Human Genome.* New York: Norton. You will find this an excellent, readable account of the Human Genome Project. The personal histories are especially appealing.

Guided Review

15. _____ first made us aware of dominant and recessive characteristics.
16. When several genes contribute to a trait, this is called _____ inheritance.
17. Down syndrome is perhaps the best-known _____ disorder.
18. _____ anemia and _____ disease are examples of genetic disorders.
19. Mapping the human genes is the goal of the _____ _____ _____ .
20. The results of the latest genetic research reinforce the belief that development is explained by the _____ of genes and the environment.

Answers

15. Mendel 16. polygenic 17. chromosomal 18. Sickle-cell, Tay-Sachs 19. Human Genome Project 20. interaction

CONCLUSION & SUMMARY

In this chapter we explored the biological basis of our uniqueness. We considered not only the power and beauty of nature in establishing our genetic endowment but also the growing influence of technology. The genes the mother and father provide unite to produce a new and different human being. Yet this new life still shows many of the characteristics of both parents. We saw how this newness and sameness has challenged researchers for decades.

Beginning with the discoveries of Mendel and still continuing, the secrets of hereditary transmission remain at the forefront of scientific endeavor, especially given the impetus of the Human Genome Project. Today's work, building on our knowledge of DNA, provides hope for the future while simultaneously raising legal and ethical questions that have yet to be resolved.

How does fertilization, both natural and external, occur?

- Knowledge of hormonal control of the menstrual cycle is crucial for understanding fertilization.
- The study of twins, especially monozygotic twins, has long fascinated psychologists.
- The increasing number of infertile couples has led to a growing demand for external fertilization.
- The most widely used external fertilization technique is AID (artificial insemination by donor).
- The success rate of external fertilization procedures has improved with increasing knowledge.
- Today's adoption procedures include both closed and open adoption.

What are the mechanisms of heredity and what could go wrong?

- Mitosis and meiosis are the means of cell division.

- DNA is the chemical key to life.
- Understanding how traits are transmitted requires a knowledge of the workings of dominant and recessive genes.
- Chromosomal defects include: Down syndrome, Klinefelter syndrome, and Turner syndrome.
- Genetic defects include: Tay-Sachs, sickle-cell anemia, cystic fibrosis, phenylketonuria, and spina bifida.

What are the major features and anticipated uses of the Human Genome Project?

- The Human Genome Project is an endeavor to map all of the genes.
- HGP will have major implications for the identification, prevention, and medication of disease.
- Ethical, legal, and social issues require resolution in the light of new discoveries.

KEY TERMS

Alleles	Genotype	Open adoption
Blastocyst	Hemophilia	Ovulation
Closed adoption	Heterozygous	Phenotype
Cystic fibrosis (CF)	Homozygous	Phenylketonuria (PKU)
Cytogenetics	Human Genome Project	Polygenic inheritance
Dizygotic	Implantation	Recessive
DNA	In vitro fertilization (IVF)	RNA (ribonucleic acid)
Dominant	Klinefelter syndrome	Sex-linked inheritance
Down syndrome	Meiosis	Sickle-cell anemia
Endometriosis	Mitosis	Spina bifida
Fallopian tubes	Monozygotic	Turner syndrome
Fragile X syndrome	Mutation	Zygote

WHAT DO YOU THINK?

1. Several controversies have occurred lately about surrogate mothers and the children they bear. Do you have any strong feelings about surrogacy? Can you defend it? Regardless of your personal feelings, can you present what you see as the pros and cons of surrogacy?

2. In your reading, perhaps you noticed that the process of in vitro fertilization depended on research findings from studies of the menstrual cycle. Can you explain this, paying particular attention to the administering of hormones and the timing of their administration?

3. James Watson and Francis Crick received a Nobel prize for their discovery of the double-helix structure of DNA. Why is the discovery of DNA so important in our lives? Can you think of anything you have read about in the newspapers or seen on television that derives from this discovery?

CHAPTER REVIEW TEST

1. From ovulation to implantation takes about
   a. seven days.
   b. two weeks.
   c. one month.
   d. nine months.

2. The union of sperm and egg is a process known as
   a. mitosis.
   b. fertilization.
   c. meiosis.
   d. mutation.

3. In vitro fertilization takes place
   a. in the fallopian tube.
   b. in the uterus.
   c. outside the woman's body.
   d. in the ovary.

4. Which of the following is not a female secondary sex characteristic?
   a. higher voice
   b. wider hips
   c. breasts
   d. thick hair

5. The process by which eggs are ripened and released is called
   a. ovulation.
   b. mitosis.
   c. fertilization.
   d. implantation.

6. Each sex cell carries a total of _____ chromosomes.
   a. 23
   b. 24
   c. 47
   d. 46

7. _____ twins are likely to occur when a woman's ovaries release two ripened eggs that are fertilized by separate sperm.
   a. Nonidentical
   b. Identical
   c. Siamese
   d. Monozygotic

8. Which factor is not thought to be a cause of infertility in men?
   a. influenza
   b. low sperm count
   c. defective sperm
   d. genetic disease

9. Which of the following statements is true?
   a. XX indicates male.
   b. XY indicates male.
   c. XO indicates male.
   d. X- indicates male.

10. Which of the following is an example of a genetic disorder?
    a. sickle-cell anemia
    b. Turner syndrome
    c. Klinefelter syndrome
    d. Down syndrome

11. When a natural mother relinquishes her child, but retains input into the process of adoption, it's called _____ adoption.
    a. closed
    b. foreign
    c. selected
    d. open

12. Which of the following is an example of a chromosomal disorder?
    a. spina bifida
    b. chronic disease syndrome
    c. phenylketonuria
    d. Turner syndrome

13. _____ is the most widely used external fertilization technique.
    a. IVF
    b. AID
    c. SART
    d. PID

14. Which combination is not possible?
    a. AT
    b. TA
    c. GT
    d. GC

15. DNA possesses the remarkable ability to _____ itself.
    a. accommodate
    b. reproduce
    c. assimilate
    d. disengage

16. Which of the following populations is more likely than others to be afflicted with sickle-cell anemia?
    a. Eastern Europeans
    b. African-Americans
    c. Asians
    d. Hispanics

17. Down syndrome is caused by
    a. the body's failure to break down amino acids.
    b. the fragile X syndrome.
    c. a deviation on the 21st pair of chromosomes.
    d. an XO pattern.

18. An example of sex-linked inheritance includes
    a. PKU.
    b. neural tube defects.
    c. Tay-Sachs disease.
    d. hemophilia.

19. The Human Genome Project is an endeavor to identify and map
    a. certain substances within cells.
    b. all human genes.
    c. cell divisions.
    d. nucleotides within DNA.

20. Which of the following is not suspected of having a strong genetic origin?
    a. polio
    b. epilepsy
    c. diabetes
    d. cancer

Answers

1. a 2. b 3. c 4. d 5. a 6. a 7. a 8. a 9. b 10. a 11. d 12. d 13. b 14. c 15. b 16. b 17. c 18. d 19. b 20. a

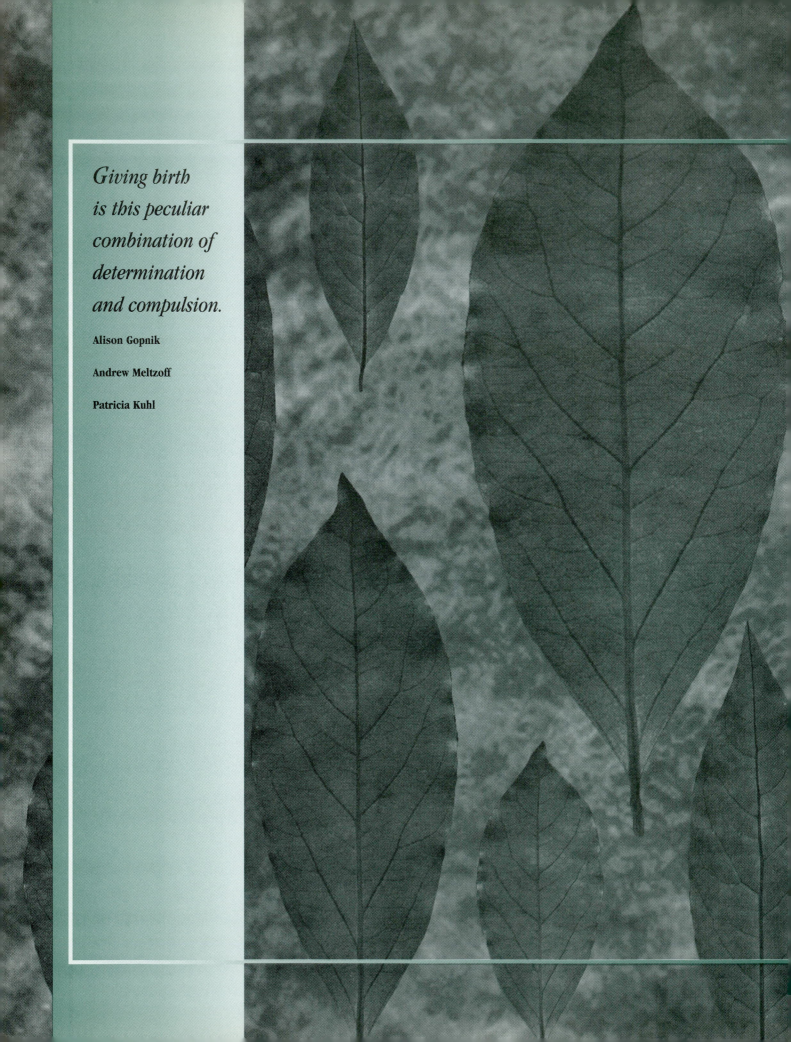

Giving birth is this peculiar combination of determination and compulsion.

Alison Gopnik

Andrew Meltzoff

Patricia Kuhl

Ellen and Kevin were delighted. The parents of a 3-year-old boy, they were now looking forward to their second child. Kevin, having shared in the birth of their first child, was calmer but even more excited as he looked forward to the events of this pregnancy and birth. Ellen, a healthy 31-year-old, was experiencing all the signs of a normal pregnancy. The morning sickness abated at 12 weeks. She felt movement at 17 weeks, and an ultrasound at 20 weeks showed normal development. Weight gain, blood glucose levels, blood pressure, and AFP (alpha-fetoprotein) test results were all within acceptable ranges.

Since this was Ellen's second pregnancy, she felt more comfortable with her changing body. Visits to the obstetrician were pleasant and uneventful. At 28 weeks, loosening ligaments caused her pelvis to irritate the sciatic nerve at the base of the spine. Her obstetrician recommended Tylenol, a heating pad, and rest. He also recommended a visit to an orthopedist to confirm the treatment. Ellen refused to take any medication and decided not to bother with a second opinion. Since she felt she could tolerate the pain for the 12 weeks until delivery, she would not be X-rayed or take even a mild painkiller. She rationalized that the back pain was acceptable because it accompanied a normal pregnancy.

At 31 weeks, Ellen noticed episodes of unusual movement and became concerned. A week later, fearing that the baby might be in distress, she called the obstetrician to describe the jabs, pokes, and excessive movements she was experiencing. The doctor immediately scheduled a biophysical profile: an eight-point check of the internal organs and another ultrasound.

Ellen nervously gulped the required 32 ounces of water an hour before the examination. Arriving at a glistening new medical center, she was quickly escorted to an examining room. The technician was both professional and serious as he looked for a problem (increasing Ellen's anxiety). The examination included a thorough check of the baby's heart chambers, a type of EKG (electrocardiogram) measurement, and an assessment of blood flow—all displayed in vibrant colors. The cord, internal organs, position of the baby, and body weight were all evaluated. Ellen was able to listen to the baby's heartbeat while watching the heart chambers function.

Later that day, Ellen's obstetrician called to tell her the results: no apparent medical problems, just an unusually active baby. Ellen and Kevin sagged with relief. They also received a bonus: a reassuring ultrasound image of their unborn child's face—in living color! ✪

Ultrasound is frequently used when questions arise about a pregnancy. Soundwaves directed onto the uterus bounce off the bones and tissues of the fetus and are formed into an image.

One of the authors (JFT) frequently (perhaps too often) tells an amusing story about the birth of his second child. Badly hurt in an automobile accident and temporarily using a wheelchair, he was determined to drive his wife to the hospital when the magic moment arrived. Sure enough, the time arrived (2 o'clock in the morning, of course) and he successfully maneuvered to the hospital. While he parked the car, his wife went in search of a wheelchair. As the two of them struggled down the corridor to the nurses' station, the puzzled nurse on duty looked from one to the other and tactfully asked, "Could you tell me which one of you I'm supposed to admit?"

The baby born after this less than auspicious beginning was Ellen, the subject of the chapter's opening. Her journey through the nine months of pregnancy is quite typical: normal prenatal development accompanied by occasional worrisome moments. Given current concern about the quality of life for a woman and her developing child, we can understand the importance placed on prenatal development. In fact, today's acceptance of the impact that these nine months have on an individual's future has led to greater emphasis on *prepregnancy* care. If you think about this for a moment, it makes considerable sense because some women don't realize they're pregnant for two or three months. By then, rapid growth has occurred (as we'll see, such growth is particularly true of the central nervous system) with the potential for serious damage if elements such as alcohol and drugs have been abused.

In this chapter, we'll first explore the prenatal world, that nine-month period that provides nourishment and protection and serves as a springboard for birth. Next we'll turn to those agents that can influence prenatal development. These are both physical and psychological and can be either positive or negative. We'll then look at birth itself, the completion of a journey that has involved remarkable development. For various reasons, some fetuses can't endure this nine-month journey, so our final focus in this chapter will be the special case of these early, or premature, births. In the past few years, great advances—technological, medical, and psychological—have resulted in an increasing number of premature babies surviving.

Chapter Objectives

After reading this chapter, you should be able to answer the following questions.

- ◆ What kinds of development occur during the prenatal period?
- ◆ What influences prenatal development and what cautions should be taken?
- ◆ What are the circumstances and possible difficulties of the birth process?

The Prenatal World

Although it may be difficult to imagine, you are the product of one cell, the zygote, or fertilized egg. Once the union of sperm and egg takes place, in only a matter of hours (about 24–30) that one cell begins to divide rapidly. The initial phase of the event occurred in a very protected world—the prenatal environment.

Fertilization through the embryonic period: The moment of fertilization.

Implantation Fertilized egg attaches and secures itself to uterine wall.

Once the egg is released from the ovary, it passes into the fallopian tube. Fertilization occurs in the first part of the fallopian tube, about three days after the egg has entered the tube. The fertilized egg must now pass through the remainder of the fallopian tube to reach the uterus, a journey of about three to four days to travel five or six inches. During its passage through the fallopian tube, the zygote receives all of its nourishment from the tube (Moore & Persaud, 1998). Figure 4.1 illustrates passage into the uterus and **implantation.**

During the prenatal months, we can identify three fairly distinct stages of development: germinal, embryonic, and fetal.

The Germinal Period

Germinal period The first two weeks following fertilization.

The **germinal period** extends through the first two weeks. The passage through the fallopian tube takes three to four days and then the fertilized egg floats in the uterine cavity for about three more days before beginning implantation. During these days, it receives nourishment from the glands of the uterine wall (Kellogg,

Blastocyst When the fertilized egg reaches the uterus (about 7 days), it's known as a blastocyst.

Placenta The placenta supplies the embryo with all its needs, carries off all its wastes, and protects it from danger.

Umbilical cord Contains blood vessels that go to and from the mother through the arteries and veins supplying the placenta.

2000; Moore & Persaud, 1998). The zygote is now 1 week old and called a **blastocyst.** During the second week, the blastocyst becomes firmly implanted in the wall of the uterus. From its outer layer of cells, the **placenta, umbilical cord,** and **amniotic sac** begin to develop. The inner cell layer develops into the embryo itself. Figure 4.2 illustrates the developmental significance of the blastocyst.

The placenta and the umbilical cord serve critical functions during development. The placenta supplies the embryo with all its needs, carries off all its wastes, and protects it from danger. The placenta has two separate sets of blood vessels, one going to and from the baby through the umbilical cord, the other going to and from the mother through the arteries and veins supplying the placenta.

Figure 4.1

Passage of the zygote into the uterus.

Figure 4.2

During the second week, the blastocyst becomes firmly implanted in the wall of the uterus and the placenta, umbilical cord, and embryo itself begin to form from its outer layer of cells.

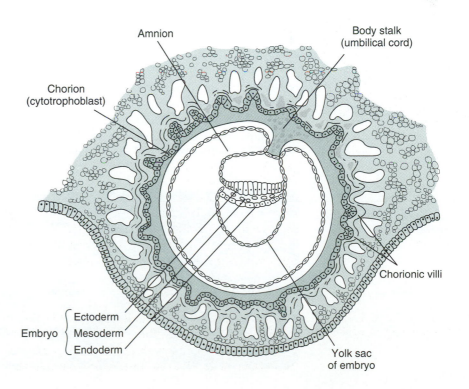

We can summarize the first two weeks following conception as follows:

Week 1: The zygote moves through the fallopian tube to the uterus and rapid cell division begins within the first 30 hours (Kellogg, 2000).

Week 2: The blastocyst adheres to the uterine wall and begins to form the placenta, umbilical cord, and amniotic sac. (The amniotic sac will contain amniotic fluid, which is essentially fetal urine.)

The Embryonic Period

In the **embryonic period,** from the third through the eighth week, a recognizable human being emerges. The nervous system develops rapidly, which suggests that the embryo at this time is in a sensitive period, that is, a time when certain experiences have a significant impact. For example, with the rapid formation of many different organ systems, any negative agent (drugs, disease) can have long-lasting effects.

In an astonishing display of nature's power, the brain evidences a rate of growth and development that almost defies belief. And yet, if you stop and think about it, this tremendous growth surge is vital for survival, given the control the brain exercises over such critical functions as breathing. Estimates are that in a relatively brief time during brain maturation, at least 100 billion (some estimates run as high as 200 billion) brain cells are formed (Shatz, 1999).

The beginning of this amazing phenomenon (about the third prenatal week) lies in a process called *neural induction* when a chemical signal is sent from the mesoderm to the ectoderm thus signalling the onset of nervous system development. Nerve cells proliferate rapidly in the *neural tube* but quickly leave this area and commence a sometimes tortuous journey to the region of the brain where they will become functional. This phase, called *cell migration,* begins during the seventh prenatal week. Each of these 100 billion nerve cells, now called *neurons,* will make connections (called synapses) with other neurons. Estimates are that human beings can form more than 10 trillion synapses (Damasio, 1999).

While this building process is going on, recent discoveries (Shatz, 1996, 1999) suggest that the developing brain's electrical activity helps to shape the structure of the brain. In other words, the brain's early electrical activity isn't just a by-product of the building process but is an integral part of shaping the brain's physical makeup.

Perhaps the most remarkable change in the embryo is **cellular differentiation.** Three distinct layers are being formed: the **ectoderm,** which will give rise to skin, hair, nails, teeth, and the nervous system; the **mesoderm,** which will give rise to muscles, skeleton, and the circulatory and excretory systems; and the **endoderm,** which will give rise to lungs, liver, and pancreas. (See figure 4.3 for details.)

Usually by the completion of the fourth week, the heart begins to beat—the embryo's first movement. The accompanying photographs show that during the fifth week eyes and ears begin to emerge, body buds give clear evidence of becoming arms and legs, and the head area is the largest part of the rapidly growing embryo.

During the sixth and seventh weeks, fingers begin to appear on the hands, the outline of toes is seen, and the beginnings of the spinal cord are visible. In the

---

Embryonic period   Third through the eighth week following fertilization.

This 4-week-old embryo now has a beating heart, body buds are beginning to emerge, and the eye region is becoming discernible.

Cellular differentiation
Embryonic cells are destined for specific functions.

Ectoderm   The outer layer of the embryo that will give rise to the nervous system, among other developmental features.

Mesoderm   The middle layer of the embryo that gives rise to muscles, skeleton, excretory system.

Endoderm   The inner layer of the embryo that will give rise to the lungs, liver, and pancreas, among other developmental features.

Figure 4.3

Development from the three layers of the blastocyst.

Ectoderm	Mesoderm	Endoderm
Central nervous system	Circulatory system	Respiratory system
Peripheral nervous system	Skeleton	Digestive system
Outer skin layers	Muscles	
Mammary and pituitary glands	Excretory system	
	Reproductive system	

Blastocyst

Organogenesis   The formation of organs during the embryonic period.

Coming to the end of the embryonic period, this 7-week-old embryo has begun to assume a more human appearance. It is now about 1 inch in length with discernible eyes, ears, nose, mouth, arms, and legs.

Fetal period   The period extending from the beginning of the third month to birth.

germinal period, the number and differentiation of cells rapidly increase; in the embryonic period, the organs are formed, a process called **organogenesis** (Sadler, 1995). After eight weeks, 95 percent of the body parts are formed and general body movements are detected.

We can summarize the embryonic period as follows (Kellogg, 2000):

Weeks 3+: Rapid development of nervous system

Week 4: Heart beats

Week 5: Eyes and ears begin to emerge, body buds for arms and legs, embryo is about 3/8 inch long

Week 6 and 7: Embryo is about 1/2 to 3/4 inches long, fingers and toes visible, beginning of spinal cord, liver begins to form red blood cells

Week 8: Embryo is now about 1 inch long, about 95 percent of body parts differentiated—arms, legs, beating heart, nervous system

The embryonic period can be hazardous for the newly formed organism. During these weeks embryonic tissue is particularly sensitive to any foreign agents during differentiation, especially beginning at the third or fourth week of the pregnancy. Estimates are that about 30 percent of all embryos are aborted at this time without the mother's knowledge; about 90 percent of all embryos with chromosomal abnormalities are spontaneously aborted.

At the end of this period, a discernible human being with arms, legs, a beating heart, and a nervous system exists. It is receiving nourishment and discharging waste through the umbilical cord, which leads to the placenta. The placenta itself never actually joins with the uterus but exchanges nourishment and waste products through the walls of the blood vessels (Moore & Persaud, 1998). The future mother begins to experience some of the noticeable effects of pregnancy: the need to urinate more frequently, morning sickness, and increasing fullness of breasts.

The Fetal Period

The **fetal period** extends from the beginning of the third month to birth. During this time, the fetus grows rapidly both in height and weight. The sex organs appear during the third month, and it is possible to determine the baby's sex. Visible sexual differentiation begins, and the nervous system continues to increase in size and complexity.

By the fourth month, the fetus is about 8 to 10 inches in length and weighs about 6 to 8 ounces. The fourth to the fifth month is usually the peak growth period. During this time, the mother begins to feel movement. The fetus now swallows, digests, and discharges urine. Growth is rapid during the fourth month to accommodate an increasing oxygen demand (Nilsson & others, 1993). The fetus produces specialized cells: red blood cells to transport oxygen and white blood cells to combat disease.

The fetus is now active—sucking, turning its head, and pushing with hands and feet—and the mother is acutely aware of the life within her. Figure 4.4 represents the fetus in the fourth month.

By the end of the fifth month, the baby is 10 to 12 inches long and weighs about a pound. The fetus sleeps and wakes like the newborn does, even manifesting a favorite sleep position. Rapid growth continues in the sixth month, with the fetus gaining another 2 inches and one pound, but slows during the seventh month. Viability, the ability to survive if born, is attained. After six months very few new nerve and muscle cells appear, since at birth the nervous system must be fully functioning to ensure automatic breathing.

Development of the Senses

During the two final fetal months, organ development prepares the fetus for the shock of leaving the sheltered uterine world. The senses are ready to function; some, in fact, are already functioning. For example, the fetus is able to hear

Figure 4.4

The fetus at 4¹/₂ months—a time of rapid growth and considerable activity.

sound—the silent world of the fetus is a myth—and responds to auditory stimuli. The fetus hears many environmental sounds—voices, stomach rumblings, and the pulsing of the mother's heart. Hearing ability commences during the last trimester and is well developed at birth (Howard-Glenn, 2000).

• **Touch**   Touch refers to the reaction to pressure, temperature, and pain, and seems to produce a generalized response. The sense of touch becomes functional by the beginnng of the third month (Blass & Ciaramitaro, 1994).

• **Taste**   Taste buds appear as early as the third fetal month and seem to be more widely distributed in fetal life than in adult life. Initially taste buds appear on the tonsils, palate, and part of the esophagus. In the adult, taste cells are restricted to the tongue. Although the mechanism for taste is present before birth, the presence of the amniotic fluid limits the taste response until after birth (Smith & Blass, 1996).

• **Smell**   Like taste, the neurological basis for smell appears before birth, thus there exists the possiblity of response (Cole & Cole, 1996). But since the nasal cavity is filled with amniotic fluid, it is not likely that the sense of smell functions before birth. Premature infants, in the last month, can smell substances when air enters the nasal cavity.

• **Hearing**   As previously noted, most fetuses can hear sound by the fourth month. The auditory mechanism is well developed structurally in later fetal life, but since the middle ear is filled with fluid, the fetus cannot respond to sounds of normal intensity. Strong auditory stimuli, however, produce a response (Berk, 1997).

An Applied View   *Fetal Surgery*

"By the time I saw her, it was just too late." These words have been uttered by frustrated surgeons for many years, but now thanks to sophisticated surgical procedures, it may not be too late. Today, the promise of surgery before birth offers hope to many anguished parents. Three types of fetal surgery have received considerable attention.

First, to cure a condition in which the brain ventricles fill with fluid and expand (called *fetal hydrocephalus*), surgeons now operate within the womb. In 1986, after repeated failures to insert shunts into the fetus' brain, the Fetal Medicine Society asked surgeons to cease their attempts. Recently, with improved techniques, successful attempts have been reported (Foreman, 1999).

The surgeon must pierce the woman's abdomen and uterine wall, penetrate the fetal skull, and then insert a tube (catheter) into the brain to drain this region until birth. This procedure is called "open fetal surgery"; newer techniques employing ultrasound and thin instruments are being developed (Foreman, 1999). Unless this condition is treated, fluid presses against the walls (membranes) of the fetal brain ventricles and can cause mental retardation or even death.

In a second type of fetal surgery to correct a blocked urinary tract in the fetus (called *fetal hydronephosis*), the surgeon removes the fetus from the womb, operates, and then returns the fetus to the uterus. The surgeon then adds

either saline solution (salt water) or amniotic fluid that has been saved and warmed and, finally, sews the uterus. This surgery could not be accomplished unless drugs preventing labor were available. If the condition is not corrected, the lungs of the fetus cannot develop. The blocked urinary tract causes urine to stay in the bladder, which can actually burst. Or urine can back up into the kidneys, causing serious damage. The major problem is that the fetus stops producing amniotic fluid, which is mainly fetal urine. The fetus swallows amniotic fluid, which causes the lungs to grow. Without the amniotic fluid, the lungs don't grow; and at birth, the fetus simply can't breathe.

Finally, to correct a condition in which the fetus has a hole in its diaphragm (the muscle separating the abdomen from the chest cavity), surgeons make an incision across the uterus and cut into the fetal chest and abdomen. (This condition is called *diaphragmatic hernia*.) Surgeons push back into the abdomen any abdominal organs that might have moved through the hole in the diaphragm into the chest cavity. They then close the hole. Without this surgery, the abdominal organs that have pushed into the chest cavity restrict the growth of the lungs and eventually the fetus cannot breathe.

***Kolata, G. (1990). *The baby doctors*. New York: Dell. You should find this book fascinating, a riveting account of the types of surgery now being performed on fetuses and newborns.

• *Vision*   There is general agreement that the absence of adequate retinal stimulation eliminates the possibility of true sight during prenatal life. By the end of pregnancy, the uterus and the mother's abdominal wall may be stretched so thin that light filters through, exposing the fetus to some light and dark contrast. Visual development begins in the second week following fertilization and continues until after birth (Brazelton & Nugent, 1995). At birth, the eye is sufficiently developed to differentiate light and dark. (For an excellent discussion of the senses, see Craig & Rollman, 1999.)

Thus the foundation of the nervous system forms in the first few weeks following conception; by six weeks the reflexes are active and electrical brain activity appears. Touching the fetal forehead as early as nine weeks causes the fetus to turn away, and if the soles of its feet are stroked, the toes curl up. The entire body is sensitive to touch. By mid-pregnancy, the inner ear is fully developed, and the fetus reacts with movement to external sound.

During amniocentesis, the fetal heart rate changes and movement increases, suggesting that the fetus has sensed tactile stimulation. Muscular development of the eyes enables the fetus to move its eyes during sleep or to change its position. From about the 16th week the fetus is sensitive to any light that penetrates the uterine wall and the amniotic fluid. Toward the end of pregnancy, a bright light pointed at the mother's abdomen causes the fetus to move. The fetus begins to swallow amniotic fluid early in the pregnancy and demonstrates taste by turning toward and swallowing more of a sweet substance injected into the amniotic fluid.

This description of fetal life leads to an inevitable conclusion: Given adequate conditions, the fetus at birth is equipped to deal effectively with the transition from its sheltered environment to the extrauterine world.

We can summarize these developments as follows:

Third month: Sex organs appear
Fourth month: Rapid growth, red blood cells, white blood cells; active sucking
Fifth month: Hears sound, sleeps, 10 to12 inches long, 1 pound
Sixth month: Rapid growth, 12 to 14 inches, 2 pounds
Seventh month: Growth slows, viability attained
Eighth and ninth months: Preparation for birth; senses ready to function, brain is 25 percent of adult weight

Prenatal learning   The possibility of learning during the fetal period.

At the end of the ninth month, the fetus (just before birth) is about 20 inches long, weighs about 7 pounds, 6 ounces, and its brain at birth is 20 to 25 percent of its adult weight. Table 4.1 summarizes the course of prenatal development.

An Applied VIEW

Prenatal Learning: Fact or Fiction?

As an example of the importance of these prenatal days, consider this question: Is it fact or fantasy to think that **prenatal learning** is a possibility? Although we cannot as yet answer this question with certainty, several clues will help us.

One of the leading centers of research into fetal life is at the University of North Carolina. Here, Anthony DeCasper and his colleagues are attempting to piece together the puzzle of fetal learning in a series of experiments. For example, they had infants suck on a nipple attached to a tape recorder. Fast sucking activated a recording of their mothers' voices, and slower sucking produced another woman's

voice. The babies showed a preference for their mothers' voices, as indicated by fast sucking.

Taking these results one step further, DeCasper asked a group of pregnant women to read a children's story aloud twice a day for six weeks before their expected delivery day. At birth the infants' patterns showed that they preferred the familiar story to one they had never heard (DeCasper & others, 1994). Obviously, some fetal "learning" had occurred. Results are sufficiently promising to stimulate continued research. (For a discussion of this phenomenon across species, see Smotherman & Robinson, 1996.)

TABLE 4.1 MILESTONES IN PRENATAL DEVELOPMENT

Age	Accomplishment
3 weeks	Nervous system begins to form
4 weeks	Heart begins to beat
5 weeks	Head continues rapid growth
8 weeks	Almost all body parts are differentiated
12 weeks	Possible to visually determine baby's sex Growth of head slows Formation of red blood cells by liver slows
14 weeks	Begins to coordinate limb movements Slow eye movements occur
16 weeks	Ultrasound shows clearly defined bone structure
20 weeks	Possible to hear heartbeat with fetoscope Baby covered by fine downy hair called lanugo Eyebrows and head hair visible Fetal movements called quickening are felt by mother
21 weeks	Rapid eye movements commence Substantial weight gain
24 weeks	Fingernails can be seen
28 weeks	Eyes open and close Lungs capable of breathing
32 weeks	Skin pink and smooth Chubby appearance
38 weeks	Nervous system can carry out some integrative functions Reacts to light Usually assumes upside-down position as birth approaches

Source: Kellogg, 2000; Moore & Persaud, 1998; Olds, London, & Ladewig, 1996.

Guided Review

1. The fertilized egg passes through the _____ _____ on its way to the uterus.
2. The fertilized egg secures itself to the uterine wall, which is called _____.
3. The embryonic period extends from the _____ to the _____ week of development.
4. The three distinct layers during the embryonic period are the _____, the _____, and the _____.
5. The period beginning with the third month of pregnancy and extending to birth is known as the _____ period.
6. The peak growth period in prenatal development is during the _____ and _____ months.
7. For fetal surgery to be successful, _____ must be prevented.

Influences on Prenatal Development

When we speak of "environmental influences" on children, we usually think of the time beginning at birth. But remember: At birth an infant has already had 9 months of prenatal living, with all of this period's positive and negative features. For

Answers

1. fallopian tube 2. implantation 3. third, eighth 4. ectoderm, mesoderm, endoderm 5. fetal 6. fourth, fifth 7. labor

example, researchers have recently discovered that morning sickness, with all its unpleasant connotations, has a powerful survival value (Brody, 2000). Nausea and vomiting protects both mother and fetus from infection and dangerous chemicals. Women who experience morning sickness are significantly less likely to miscarry.

Many women today experience the benefits of the latest research about prenatal care. Diet, exercise, and rest are all carefully programmed to meet the needs of the individual woman. Where women, especially pregnant teenagers, lack such treatment, the rates of prenatal loss, stillbirths, and neonatal (just after birth) mortality are substantially higher.

In spite of this care, some children still experience problems, which introduces the concept of **developmental risk.** Developmental risk is a term used to identify those children whose well-being is in jeopardy. Such risks incorporate a continuum of biological and environmental conditions. These range from the very serious (genetic defects) to the less serious (mild oxygen deprivation at birth). What now seems clear is that *the earlier the damage (a toxic drug or maternal infection), the greater the chance of negative long-term effects.*

As we begin our discussion, remember that almost all drugs (including aspirin), unnecessary medication, and risky chemicals at work or at home—should be avoided. Most pregnant women today are also cautious about the amount of caffeine and sweeteners they use. For example, the FDA has cautioned pregnant women to moderate their consumption of caffeine-containing foods and beverages. These simple precautions will eliminate danger for most women and their babies. Specifically, what causes a child to be developmentally at risk?

Developmental risk Children who may be susceptible to problems because of some physical or psychological difficulty ("at-risk" children).

The effects of teratogens.

Teratogens Any agents that can cause abnormalities, e.g., drugs, chemicals, infections, pollutants.

Teratogens

With regard to developmental risk, our major concern here is with those substances that exercise their influence in the prenatal environment, a time of increased sensitivity. Teratogenic agents, which are any agents that cause abnormalities, especially demand our attention (Moore & Persaud, 1998). **Teratogens** that can cause birth defects are drugs, chemicals, infections, pollutants, or a mother's physical state, such as diabetes. Table 4.2 summarizes several of the more common teratogenic agents and the times of greatest potential risk.

By examining Table 4.2, you can see that these teratogenic agents fall into two classes: infectious diseases and different types of chemicals.

Infectious Diseases

Some diseases that are potentially harmful to the developing fetus and that are acquired either before or during birth are grouped together as the STORCH diseases (Blackman, 1997): Syphilis, Toxoplasmosis, Other infections, Rubella, Cytomegalovirus, and Herpes.

Syphilis A sexually transmitted disease that, if untreated, may affect the fetus.

Syphilis **Syphilis** is sexually transmitted and, if untreated, may affect the fetus. It makes no difference whether the mother contracted the disease during pregnancy or many years before. If the condition remains untreated, about 25 percent of the infected fetuses will die any time during or after the second trimester. (Another 25 percent die soon after birth.) Of those who survive, serious problems such as blindness, mental retardation, and deafness may affect them (Blackman, 1997). Given the advances in antibiotic treatments, the incidence of congenital syphilis has steadily decreased, although there has been a recent upsurge.

Toxoplasmosis Caused by a protozoan, it may cause damage to the nervous system; transmitted by animals, especially cats.

Toxoplasmosis **Toxoplasmosis** is caused by a protozoan (a single-celled microorganism called *toxoplasma gondii*) that is transmitted by many animals, especially cats, or occasionally from raw meat. The infection is usually harmless in adults, but can cause serious problems for the fetus (Olds, London, & Ladewig, 1996). The results include both spontaneous abortions, premature deliveries and neurological problems such as mental retardation, blindness, and cerebral palsy. Low birth weight, a large liver and spleen, and anemia also characterize the disease. Although

TABLE 4.2 TERATOGENS, THEIR EFFECTS, AND TIME OF RISK

Agent	Possible Effects	Time of Risk
Alcohol	Fetal Alcohol Syndrome (FAS), growth retardation, cognitive deficits	Throughout pregnancy
Aspirin	Bleeding problems	Last month, at birth
Cigarettes	Prematurity, lung problems	After 20 weeks
DES	Cancer of female reproductive system	From 3 to 20 weeks
LSD	Isolated abnormalities	Before conception
Lead	Death, anemia, mental retardation	Throughout pregnancy
Marijuana	Unknown long-term effects, early neurological problems	Throughout pregnancy
Thalidomide	Fetal death, physical and mental abnormalities	The first month
Cocaine	Spontaneous abortion, neurological problems	Throughout pregnancy
AIDS	Growth failure, low birth weight, developmental delay, death from infection	Before conception, throughout pregnancy, during delivery, during breast feeding
Rubella	Mental retardation, physical problems, possible death	First three months, may have effects during later months
Syphilis	Death. congenital syphilis, prematurity	From five months on
CMV	Retardation, deafness, blindness	Uncertain, perhaps 4 to 24 weeks
Herpes simplex	CNS damage, prematurity	Potential risk throughout pregnany and at birth

estimates are that as many as 20 to 30 percent of women have been exposed to the infection, the incidence of toxoplasmosis is about 1 per 1,000 live births (Moran, 2000).

Other Infections This category includes such diseases as influenza, chicken pox, and several rare viruses.

German measles (rubella) A typically mild childhood disease caused by a virus.

Rubella (German measles) When pregnant women hear the name German measles (the technical term is **rubella**), warning signals are raised, and with good reason. Women who contract this disease may give birth to a baby with a serious defect: congenital heart disorder, cataracts, deafness, or mental retardation. The risk is especially high if the disease appears early in the pregnancy, when a spontaneous abortion may result. The infection appears in less than 1 per 1,000 live births.

Any woman who has had German measles as a child cannot assume she is immune, so a pregnant woman should take the precaution of a blood test. The American Medical Association recommends that any woman of childbearing age who has not been vaccinated for German measles be immunized. These women should then avoid becoming pregnant for at least three months. The incidence of congenital rubella has dropped in the United States to about 20 cases per year (Blackman, 1997).

Cytomegalovirus (CMV) A virus that can cause damage ranging from mental retardation, blindness, deafness, and even death.

Cytomegalovirus (CMV) **Cytomegalovirus (CMV)** is the most common STORCH infection, with an incidence of about ten per thousand live births. CMV is a disease that can cause damage ranging from mental retardation to blindness, deafness, and even death. One of the major difficulties in combating this disease is that there is no specific treatment for it. The greatest risk to the fetus is during the mother's first pregnancy; in later pregnancies, the risk is lower (Blackman, 1997).

Herpes simplex An infection that usually occurs during birth.

Herpes Simplex In the adult, type I **herpes simplex** virus usually appears in the mouth, whereas type II herpes appears in the genital area. If the disease is passed on to the fetus (usually during the passage through the birth canal), a child develops symptoms during the first week following birth. The central nervous system seems to be particularly susceptible to this disease, with serious long-term consequences. The incidence is less than 1 per 1,000 live births.

The Special Case of AIDS

AIDS (Acquired Immune Deficiency Syndrome) A condition caused by a virus that invades the baby's immune system, thus making it vulnerable to infections and life-threatening illnesses.

The final infection we wish to discuss is **AIDS (Acquired Immune Deficiency Syndrome).** Since medical concern became public in the early 1980s, worldwide estimates are that about 12 million adults and children have died. As many as 33 million adults and children are living with HIV/AIDS (U.S. Census Bureau, 1999). Further estimates are that 1,000 children become infected each day and that 350,000 children will die this year of HIV/AIDS related illnesses. About 20 percent of all newly reported AIDS cases are women (Moran, 2000). In the United States, 7,000 to 8,000 women infected with HIV virus will give birth this year.

Statistics showing that only one in four babies born of mothers infected with HIV develops AIDS have long puzzled investigators. Studies have shown that these figures are directly related to the amount of the virus that the mother is carrying (Altman, 1994). That is, the more extensive the infection, the greater the chance that the baby will be born with the virus. Consequently, treatment with zidovudine ZDU—formerly called azidothymidine (AZT)—or other treatments early in the pregnancy may help to prevent the transmission of the virus (Fox, 1997).

An infected mother can pass the HIV virus to the fetus during pregnancy, during delivery, and after birth, occasionally through breast milk. Through 1991, 1 million children worldwide had been born infected with the HIV infection. These figures help to explain the growing and intensifying movement to provide schoolchildren with AIDS education as soon as they can grasp the concepts involved.

We know today that AIDS is a disorder that cripples the body's disease-fighting mechanisms, and that the virus causing it can lie dormant for years (Curtis & Barnes, 1994). What triggers full-blown AIDS remains unknown, but remember that AIDS is the end stage of the infection and is not in itself a disease.

With regard to the fetus, estimates are that an infected mother transmits HIV from 30 percent to 50 percent of the time. Thus, 50 to 70 percent of these fetuses remain unaffected. When the virus is transmitted, a condition called *AIDS embryopathy* may develop. This causes growth retardation, small head size (microcephaly), flat nose, and widespread, upward-slanted eyes, among other characteristics. AIDS is also associated with higher rates of preterm disease, low birth weight, and miscarriage.

This cocaine-addicted baby was born prematurely and suffers from such behavior disturbances as tremulousness, irritability, and muscular rigidity.

For those fetuses who become infected, AIDS has a shorter incubation period than for adults. Symptoms may appear as early as six months after birth and include weight loss, fever, diarrhea, and chronic infections. Once symptoms appear, babies rarely survive more than five to eight months (Hochhauser & Rothenberger, 1992).

Chemicals

Thalidomide A popular drug prescribed during the early 1960s that was later found to cause a variety of birth defects when taken by women early in their pregnancy.

Many women of childbearing age in the United States use one or more of the following drugs: alcohol, cocaine, marijuana, or nicotine. Fifteen percent of these women use drugs with sufficient frequency to cause damage to a fetus during pregnancy. Estimates are that 30 to 40 percent of pregnant women smoke; 60 to 90 percent use analgesics during pregnancy; 20 to 30 percent use sedatives; and an undetermined number continue to use illicit drugs (Stimmel, 1991). Also, a number of women continue to use drugs before they realize they are pregnant.

Prescription drugs such as **thalidomide** have also produced tragic consequences. During the early 1960s, this drug was popular in West Germany as a sleeping pill and an antinausea measure that produced no adverse reactions in women. In 1962 physicians noticed a sizable increase in children born with either partial or no limbs. In some cases, feet and hands were directly attached to the body. Other outcomes were deafness, blindness, and occasionally, mental retardation. In tracing the cause of the outbreak, investigators discovered that the mothers of these children had taken thalidomide early in their pregnancies.

DES (Diethylstilbestrol)
In the late 1940s and 1950s, DES (a synthetic hormone) was administered to pregnant women supposedly to prevent miscarriage. It was later found that the daughters of the women who had received this treatment were more susceptible to vaginal and cervical cancer.

DES (diethylstilbestrol) is another example of a teratogenic drug. In the late 1940s and 1950s, DES (a synthetic hormone) was administered to pregnant women, supposedly to prevent miscarriage. Researchers found that the daughters of the women who had received this treatment were more susceptible to vaginal and cervical cancer. These daughters also experienced more miscarriages when pregnant than would be expected. Recent suspicions have arisen about the sons of DES women; they seem to have more abnormalities of their reproductive systems.

As knowledge of the damaging effect of these agents spreads, women have grown more cautious once they realize they are pregnant. We know now that these agents pass through the placenta and affect the growing embryo and fetus. We also know that certain prenatal periods are more susceptible to damage than others; for example, the embryonic period. Figure 4.5 illustrates times of greater and lesser vulnerability.

To keep a pregnancy as safe as possible, a woman should begin by avoiding the obvious hazards.

Smoking Smoking negatively affects everything about the reproduction process: fertility, conception, possible spontaneous abortion, fetal development, labor and delivery, and a child's maturation. Smoking is probably the most common environmental hazard in pregnancy, and it results in a smaller than normal fetus. Babies of smoking mothers may have breathing difficulties and low resistance to infection, and they seem to suffer long-lasting effects after birth.

Figure 4.5

Teratogens and the timing of their effects on prenatal development. The danger of structural defects caused by teratogens is greatest early in embryonic development. This is the period of organogenesis, which lasts for several months. Damage caused by teratogens during this period is represented by the dark-colored bars. Later assaults by teratogens typically occur during the fetal period and, instead of structural damage, are more likely to stunt growth or cause problems of organ function.

Modified from K.L. Moore and T.V.N. Persaud, *The Developing Human: Clinically Oriented Embryology*, 5th ed. Copyright © 1993 W.B. Saunders Company, Philadelphia, PA. Reprinted by permission.

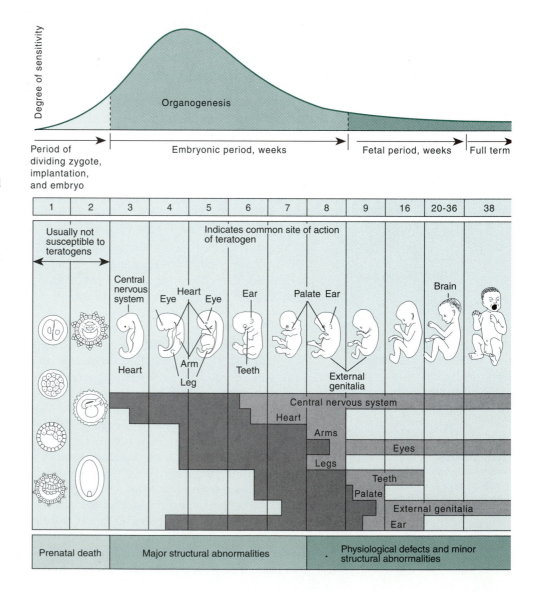

Maternal smoking produces a condition called intrauterine growth retardation *(IUGR)*. The birth weight of neonates whose mothers smoked during pregnancy is about 200 grams less than normal. Those infants whose mothers stopped smoking before the 16th week showed the greatest improvement in their birth weights (Moore & Persaud, 1998).

Fetal alcohol syndrome (FAS) Refers to babies when their mothers drink alcohol during pregnancy.

Alcohol Women who consume alcohol daily during their pregnancy can produce damage in their babies, especially a condition called **fetal alcohol syndrome (FAS).** Identifying FAS depends on several characteristics (Moore & Persaud, 1998; Ronge, 1998):

- A history of the mother's alcohol consumption.

- Physical abnormalities (small head, widely spaced eyes, thin upper lip, and possible defects in limbs, joints, face, and heart).

- Growth deficiency (thin, short, gross reduction in brain weight).

- Central nervous system dysfunction (includes mild to moderate retardation, irritability, hyperactivity, and possible learning disabilities).

Recently, prenatal exposure to alcohol has been linked to so many different neurodevelopmental problems that the terms *alcohol-related neurodevelopmental disorder* and *alcohol-related birth defects* have been propsed to identify these children (American Academy of Pediatrics, 2000).

The brains of these children do not function normally with the result that the children have difficulty structuring their time and remembering what they have to do. Impulsivity and reduced attention span work against them when they're faced with problems, and they often show poor social judgment (Ronge, 1998).

Babies born to women who drank heavily during their pregnancies may manifest distinctive characteristics such as those shown in this photo.

Maternal Influences

Among the significant influences on prenatal development are maternal nutrition and maternal emotions.

Maternal Nutrition

Examining pregnancy from a wellness perspective, it's possible to identify several components that affect a woman's condition.

- An environment that provides an adequate food supply and protection against stress.

- Family history and genetic traits.

- Lifestyle (diet, exercise, substance use, personal values).

- Prenatal care (Balcazar & Mattson, 2000).

Because a fetus depends on its mother for nourishment, most women today are keenly aware of the need to have a proper diet that will help them to give birth to a healthy, happy baby.

Women of childbearing age who wish to have children need to evaluate their weight and nutritional habits well before pregnancy. In this way they can establish good eating habits and attempt to maintain normal weight for their size. How much weight to gain is always an important question for pregnant women. In a typical pregnancy, a woman will gain 25 to 30 pounds.

If a woman is overweight beginning her pregnancy, a weight gain of 15 to 25 pounds is recommended (depending on health, nutritional status, etc.). Underweight women are urged to reach their ideal weight plus 25 to 35 pounds during pregancy (Balcazar & Mattson, 2000).

A pregnant teenager may need more calories than an adult woman. A weight gain of up to 35 pounds may be necessary for her to produce a baby of normal weight. Here we see one of the problems of teenage pregnancy: A young girl is still growing and needs additional calories for herself. If she resists this need because of a concern for appearance or a desire to conceal her pregnancy, the fetus may not receive enough nourishment (Alexander & Korenbrot, 1995).

The woman's physician will usually recommend supplements to her regular diet, such as additional protein, iron, calcium, sodium, fiber, folic acid, and vitamins. We have previously mentioned the dangers of alcohol, cigarette smoking, and caffeine.

The effects of drugs, disease, and diet, although dramatic, are not the only influences on prenatal development. How a woman feels about her pregnancy is also highly significant.

Maternal Emotions

Most pregnant women experience a wide range of emotions that are typically not sufficiently intense to affect the fetus. Seriously stressed mothers often have babies who are restless, irritable, and have feeding problems or bowel difficulties. (For an excellent discussion of the antecedents of infant temperament, see DiPietro & others, 1996). Although the fetus is not perfectly insulated from the mother's stress, unless the stress that the mother experiences is unusually severe and prolonged, the effects on the fetus are usually of short duration (Marrs & others, 1997).

No direct evidence is available that indicates a mother's emotions affect prenatal growth. Nevertheless, data continue to accumulate suggesting that a woman under stress releases hormones that may influence prenatal development. A mother's emotions trigger the release of chemicals that cross the placenta within seconds of her emotional reaction. Short periods of intense emotions don't seem to cause any lasting negative effect on the fetus. Prolonged periods of intense emotions, however, may cause negative reactions in the baby (Stoppard, 1993).

Most women report mood swings that seem to peak in the third trimester. Hormonal changes, body image changes, and identity crises may occur as pregnancy progresses, which may produce temporary feelings about pregnancy and parenthood. For example, at one moment a woman may be thrilled at the prospect of a new baby, and the next feel worried about her new responsibilities (Stoppard, 1993). Most women believe that their major task during pregnancy is to keep themselves and their babies healthy and safe (Rubin, 1995).

Nevertheless, prenatal problems arise, and today's diagnostic techniques often enable early detection of these difficulties.

Diagnosing Fetal Problems

Some women have a greater chance of developing difficulties during pregnancy or delivering a child with problems. To cope with these conditions, the rapidly expanding field of fetal diagnosis not only identifies problems but also offers means of treatment. About one percent of infants suffer from some genetic defect, whereas another 0.5 percent suffer from defective chromosomes. As a result, prenatal testing is steadily becoming more common, especially for older women.

For example, children born with cystic fibrosis or sickle-cell anemia acquire these diseases from parents who are both carriers. Tests are now available to determine whether a person is a carrier of a particular genetic disease. If both potential partners are carriers, the chances of children acquiring the disease can be calculated. Among the diagnostic tools now available are the following.

Amniocentesis

Probably the technique you have heard most about is **amniocentesis,** which entails inserting a needle through the mother's abdomen, piercing the amniotic sac, and withdrawing a sample of the amniotic fluid. (Amniocentesis may be done from the 15th week of pregnancy on.) The fluid sample provides information about the child's sex and almost 70 chromosomal abnormalities (Moore & Persaud, 1998).

Here a pregnant woman is undergoing amniocentesis. Amniotic fluid is withdrawn and analyzed to determine sex and any chromosomal abnormalities. Amniocentesis may be done from the 15th week onward.

Amniocentesis A process that entails inserting a needle through the mother's abdomen, piercing the amniotic sac and withdrawing a sample of the amniotic fluid.

A Sociocultural VIEW

Different Attitudes Toward Pregnancy

Pregnancy is seen quite differently by different cultures. You have just read a typical American view of the issues surrounding a woman during the prenatal months. Physical matters, such as the need for proper diet and exercise, are stressed (Cole, 1999). For example, women are warned about any deficiencies in vitamins and minerals (especially iodine and iron). Psychological matters, such as emotional health, were also mentioned as important influences on prenatal development. These concerns are typical of most Western societies and are real concerns.

Other cultures, however, view pregnancy and birth quite differently. Consequently, identifying cultural values is a key factor in understanding a group's attitudes toward prenatal care and birth practices. Appreciating the roles of males and females, family lifestyles, and the place of children in a culture helps to explain reactions to pregnancy. It's also important to remember that individual differences exist *within* a culture (Olds, London, & Ladewig, 1996). For example, does a traditional Japanese family hold the same values as a Japanese family that has absorbed American culture?

One way of grappling with these issues is to answer the following questions (Mattson, 2000).

Defining Pregnancy and Birth

Antepartum (Before Birth)	Intrapartum (Birth and Delivery)	Postpartum (After Birth)
Who controls the preparations for birth?	Who controls the labor and delivery process?	Who controls postnatal care?
What are the guidelines for a safe delivery?	Who attends the birth?	What are the norms for mother-child contact following birth?
Who provides knowledge about the birth process?	Where is the birth location? What are labor and delivery positions? What kind of intervention is acceptable in the birth process?	Are there any dietary rules? What are permissible maternal activities? Are there any birth rituals?

Adapted from: S. Mattson, 2000.

Alpha-Fetoprotein (AFP) Test

Occasionally, AFP (a protein produced by a baby's liver) escapes from the spinal fluid in those fetuses with neural tube problems (Jasper, 2000). It then passes into the mother's bloodstream. Spina bifida babies (see chapter 3) show a raised level of AFP, which may be detected in the mother's blood by a test called MSAFP (Maternal Serum Alpha Fetoprotein).

Fetoscopy

Fetoscopy A procedure in which a tiny instrument called a fetoscope is inserted into the amniotic cavity making it possible to see the fetus.

In a **fetoscopy,** a tiny instrument called a fetoscope is inserted into the amniotic cavity, making it possible to see the fetus. If the view is clear, defects of hands and legs are visible. (Fetoscopy is usually performed after the 16th week.) Today, doctors avoid fetoscopy if possible because of potential injury to the fetus and use a relatively new method for obtaining fetal blood: *percutaneous umbilical blood sampling,* which draws pure fetal blood from the umbilical cord (Olds, London, & Ladewig, 1996). A needle is inserted through the abdomen and uterus into the blood vessels of the umbilical cord. Not only can this aid genetic diagnosis, it also permits blood transfusions to the fetus (Nightingale & Goodman, 1990).

Chorionic Villi Sampling (CVS)

Chorionic villi sampling (CVS) A procedure in which a catheter (small tube) is inserted through the vagina to the villi and a small section is suctioned into the tube.

The outer layer of the embryo is almost covered with chorionic villi, fingerlike projections that reach into the uterine lining. A catheter (small tube) is inserted through the vagina to the villi, and a small section is suctioned into the tube. **Chorionic villi sampling (CVS)** is an excellent test to determine the fetus' genetic structure and may be performed beginning at 8 weeks, usually between 8 and 12 weeks. Results are available in 3 hours to 7 days as compared with 2 to 4 weeks for amniocentesis (Jasper, 2000).

Ultrasound The use of sound waves to produce an image that enables a physician to detect structural abnormalities.

Ultrasound

Ultrasound is a procedure that uses sound waves to produce an image that enables a physician to detect structural abnormalities. Useful pictures can be obtained as early as 7 weeks. Ultrasound is frequently used in conjunction with other techniques such as amniocentesis and fetoscopy (Sadler, 1995).

Guided Review

8. _____ _____ is the term used to describe children whose well-being is in jeopardy.
9. The acronym _____ indicates some of the potentially harmful diseases that can affect the developing fetus.
10. A harmful agent that can cause abnormalities in the developing fetus is called a _____ .
11. _____ is the most common environmental hazard in pregnancy and can result in a smaller than normal fetus.
12. Amniocentesis can be used after the _____ week of pregnancy.
13. A comprehensive test to determine the fetus' genetic structure is _____ _____ _____ .

The Birth Process

The odyssey that began approximately nine months earlier for approximately 4 million American women each year reaches its climax at birth (Guyer, Hoyert, Martin, Ventura, MacDorman, & Strobino, 1999) In spite of what you may have heard, no one knows exactly what causes labor to begin or why it begins about 280 days after the first day of the last menstrual period. Before this moment arrives, the mother has to make certain decisions. Does she, for example, ask the physician to use an anesthetic, or does she want natural childbirth? Both methods have their advantages and disadvantages. Does she want the father with her during labor and birth (Sears & Sears, 1994)?

Natural childbirth provides an unforgettable experience for the mother (and often the father, a common practice today), but it is hard, painful work. The use of analgesics prevents much of the birth pain, but women today are sensitive to the possibility that any drug may affect the baby adversely, decreasing alertness and activity for days after birth (Brazelton & Nugent, 1995).

At birth, we see one of the great shifts among the interactions of the biopsychosocial framework (Cole, 1999). From the warm, cozy prenatal environment, the newborn enters a dry, cold world. The newborn must struggle for oxygen and nutrition. For the first time the newborn encounters other human beings and parents have their initial glimpse of their child. The interactions that lead to a particular parent-child relationship now commence.

Stages in the Birth Process

A woman usually becomes aware of the beginning of labor by one or more of these signs:

- The passage of blood from the vagina. Occasionally, with a softening of the cervix, the mucous plug is expelled with a small amount of blood. Called a *bloody show,* this usually signifies that labor will begin in about 24 to 48 hours (Olds, London, & Ladewig, 1996).

Answers

8. Developmental risk 9. STORCH 10. teratogen 11. Smoking 12. 15th 13. chorionic villi sampling

- The passage of amniotic fluid from the ruptured amniotic sac through the vagina.

- Uterine contractions and accompanying discomfort.

The first two clues are certain signs that labor has begun; other pains (false labor) are occasionally mistaken for signs of true labor. Three further stages of labor can also be distinguished:

1. *Stage One: Dilation.* The neck of the uterus (the cervix) dilates to about four inches in diameter. **Dilation** is the process responsible for labor pains and may last for 12 or 13 hours, or even longer. When labor begins, the duration of the contractions is about 30 seconds, which increases to about 60 seconds (range: 45–90 seconds) as labor continues (Olds, London, & Ladewig, 1996).

    Think of the baby at this stage as enclosed in a plastic cylinder. It is upside down in the mother's abdomen, with the bottom of the cylinder under the mother's rib and the tip buried deep in her pelvis. The cervix is about one-half inch long and almost closed. Before the next stage, expulsion, occurs, the diameter of the cervix must be stretched to a diameter of four inches. (The comedienne Carol Burnett has said that the only way you can imagine this feeling is if you pulled your upper lip over your head!)

2. *Stage Two: Expulsion.* With the cervix fully dilated, the fetus no longer meets resistance and the uterine contractions drive it through the birth canal. Uterine pressure at this stage is estimated to be 60 pounds. This **expulsion** phase should be completed about two hours after the cervix becomes fully dilated for those giving birth for the first time, about half that time for women who have previously given birth (Olds, London, & Ladewig, 1996). This is the phase when most fathers, if they are present, become exultant. They describe the appearance of the head of the baby (called the *crowning*) as an unforgettable experience.

    Note that the times for expulsion (90 minutes and 30–45 minutes) are averages. If this second stage of labor is prolonged—with no evidence of a problem—surgical intervention remains unnecessary. Occasionally, women spend five or six hours (or more) in a normal first birth.

3. *Stage Three: The Afterbirth.* In the **afterbirth** stage, the placenta and other membranes are discharged. This stage is measured from the birth of the baby to the delivery of the placenta and may last only a few minutes. If the spontaneous delivery of the placenta is delayed, it may be removed manually. Figure 4.6 illustrates the birth process.

When a pregnancy ends spontaneously before the 20th week, a spontaneous abortion, commonly called a **miscarriage** has occurred. After the 20th week, the spontaneous end of a pregnancy is called a **stillbirth** if the baby is born dead, or a premature birth if the baby survives. Occasionally a pregnancy occurs outside the uterus. In an **ectopic pregnancy,** the fertilized egg attempts to develop outside the uterus, usually in one of the fallopian tubes, sometimes referred to as a *tubal pregnancy.* About 1 in every 200 pregnancies is ectopic.

Immediately after birth and continuing for about 6 weeks, women enter the *postpartum period,* a time of physical and psychological adjustment to pregnancy and birth. Hormonal changes after birth, a sense of anticlimax after completing something anticipated for so many months, sheer fatigue, and tension about care of the baby (especially after a first birth) may cause temporary feelings of depression in the new mother. These feelings usually leave quickly, but if they persist longer than two or three weeks help should be sought.

Cultural Variations of the Birth Process While the biological processes involved in labor and birth are similar everywhere, the experience of giving birth varies in

---

Dilation Stage one of the birth process during which the cervix dilates to about 4 inches in diameter.

Expulsion Stage two of the birth process during which the baby passes through the birth canal.

Afterbirth Stage three of the birth process during which the placenta and other membranes are discharged.

Miscarriage The term that describes when a pregnancy ends spontaneously before the 20th week.

Stillbirth The term used to describe, after the 20th week, the spontaneous end of a pregnancy.

Ectopic pregnancy A pregnancy in which the fertilized egg attempts to develop in one of the fallopian tubes.

Figure 4.6

Stages in the birth process.

Stage one:
Baby positions
itself

Stage two:
Baby begins
to emerge

Stage three:
Placenta is
expelled

accordance with cultural traditions (Cole & Cole, 1996). These expectations determine procedures and identify behaviors, emotions, and reactions to be expected.

For example, the Hmong women of Laos give birth in a squatting position, some Native American women remain upright, and Pueblo women may kneel during the birth process. Vietnamese women attempt to maintain self-control and even keep smiling during labor, but the Ibo of Nigeria consider childbirth as an illness. These cultural variations require consideration by those supporting the woman during child birth (Olds, London, & Ladewig, 1996).

Birth Complications

For most women, the birth process, as painful as it may be, proceeds normally. Occasionally, however, problems arise. The following are a few of the more common complications.

Forceps Delivery

When certain conditions prevail—extreme fatigue, inadequate contraction strength, cardiac problems, etc.—the physician will withdraw the baby with forceps during the first phase of birth (Smith, 2000). A **forceps delivery** presents some danger of rupturing blood vessels or causing brain damage but, with new guidelines, forceps delivery is considered quite safe.

A decision about a forceps delivery depends on two conditions: those involving the fetus and those related to the mother. Is the fetus in distress? Is the baby in the correct position? Has the mother sufficient strength for the final push? Specifically, a forceps delivery may be called for when the woman has been in the second stage of labor for several hours or when an emergency arises for either the mother (shock, exhaustion) or the fetus (clear signs of fetal distress such as a slowing heart rate).

Breech Birth

During the last month of pregnancy, most babies move into a head down (vertex) position. Most babies who don't turn during this time will be in **breech birth** presentation position. It's almost as if the baby were sitting in the uterus, head up and feet and buttocks down. Several conditions can contribute to a breech presentation: more than one fetus in the uterus, an abnormally shaped uterus, a placenta partially (or even fully) covering the uterine opening, and prematurity.

About four out of every hundred babies are born feet first, or buttocks first, while one out of a hundred is in a crosswise position (transverse presentation). Breech births can be worrisome because the baby must be carefully guided through the birth canal, but most breech babies are born well and healthy. The major concern is with premature babies who, given the size of their heads in proportion to the rest of their bodies, often require a cesarean birth. Today efforts are being made to reduce the increased number of breech births by cesarean section (Olds, London, & Ladewig, 1996).

Cesarean Section

If for some reason the child cannot come through the birth canal, surgery is performed to deliver the baby through the abdomen, in a procedure called **cesarean section.** For example, a cesarean may produce a healthier baby than does prolonged labor and difficult birth. Among the conditions suggesting a cesarean include: mother's health, fetal distress, a pelvis too small for a safe vaginal delivery, an abnormal presentation position, and previous cesareans that increase the possibility of uterine rupture (Smith, 2000).

A cesarean section is considered major surgery and is not recommended unless necessary. About one-fourth of all live births in the United States are cesarean, a figure many consider to be excessive. (In England, the cesarean birth rate is 12 percent, in Scotland 14 percent, and in Sweden 11 percent.) Leading obstetricians suggest that a 12 percent cesarean bith rate is a desirable goal. Today many women attempt a vaginal delivery following a cesarean if the conditions that caused the original cesarean are no longer a concern and if only one fetus is present. The success rate for a natural delivery after having had a cesarean is from 60 percent to 80 percent.

Anoxia (Lack of Oxygen)

If anything should happen during the birth process that interrupts the flow of oxygen to the fetus, brain damage or death can result. A substantial need for oxygen exists

Forceps delivery A procedure in which the physician, for safety, will withdraw the baby with forceps during the first phase of birth.

Breech birth A birth in which the baby is born feet first, buttocks first, or in a crosswise position (transverse presentation).

Cesarean section A surgery performed to deliver the baby through the abdomen if for some reason the child cannot come through the birth canal.

Anoxia (lack of oxygen)
A condition that possibly can cause brain damage or death if it occurs during the birth process.

Rh factor An incompatibility between the blood types of mother and child; if the mother is Rh-negative and the child Rh-positive, miscarriage or even infant death can result.

Prepared childbirth
Combination of relaxation techniques and information about the birth process.

during birth because pressure on the fetal head can cause some rupturing of the blood vessels in the brain. After the umbilical cord is cut, delay in lung breathing can also produce **anoxia.** Failure here can cause death or brain damage. Controversy surrounds infants who have experienced anoxia, survived, but show evidence of mental dullness. Whether the damage is permanent is difficult to predict (Niijhuis, 1992).

The Rh Factor

Rh factor refers to a possible incompatibility between the blood types of mother and child. If the mother is Rh-negative and the child Rh-positive, miscarriage or even infant death can result. During birth some of the baby's blood inevitably enters the mother's bloodstream. The mother then develops antibodies to destroy fetal red blood cells. This usually happens after the baby is born, so the first baby may escape unharmed. During later pregnancies, however, these antibodies may pass into the fetus' blood and start to destroy the red blood cells of an Rh-positive baby.

Estimates are that about 10 percent of marriages are between Rh-negative women and Rh-positive men. Today, a protective vaccine called RhoGam (an RH immune globulin) has almost eliminated the possibility of Rh incompatibility when Rh-negative women are identified (Olds, London, & Ladewig, 1996). In a case where the first baby's blood causes the mother to produce antibodies, exchange blood transfusions may be given to the baby while still in the uterus.

An Informed VIEW Do Childbirth Strategies Matter?

A range of birth options is now available to couples. About one percent of women, for example, are choosing home births with the guidance of trained delivery specialists such as midwives. Midwives assist with about 50 percent of all nonhospital deliveries. One reason for the popularity of home delivery is that most babies experience few complications and little if any birth difficulty.

Hospital procedures are also changing. For example, birthing rooms may be available, which have a more relaxed and homelike atmosphere than the typical delivery room. Some hospitals may provide birthing beds or birthing chairs for greater comfort. Still, between 95 and 99 percent of all births occur in hospitals.

Childbirth preparation typically involves the ideas of several theorists. For example, **prepared childbirth,** or the Lamaze method after French obstetrician *Fernand Lamaze,* is the most popular method used in the United

States today. For several sessions women are informed about the physiology of childbirth and instructed in breathing exercises and methods of muscle relaxation. These techniques are intended to relieve fear and pain.

Other strategies include the *Bradley* method, which focuses on breathing and the cooperation of a partner, and the *Kitzinger* method, which focuses on the use of sensory memory and relaxation techniques. Regardless of the technique used (or a combination of techniques), the basic principles of childbirth education include the following (Mullaly, 2000).

- Partner participation and support.
- Learning about relaxation techniques to combat anxiety and pain.
- Acquiring breathing patterns to help cope with pain and facilitate labor.
- Knowledge about the birth process and any available options.

Hospital, home, or birthing center? Each has its advantages and disadvantages. What is your reaction to these strategies and settings?

If you would like to have a more informed view on this issue, you may want to read one or more of the references in this chapter, such as Smith, 2000.

The presence of the father during birth can be a source of physical and psychological support for the mother. Fathers present during birth describe it as an "unforgettable experience."

You may also wish to learn more about it by going to our web site at http://www.mhhe.com/dacey5.

The Special Case of Prematurity

The average duration of pregnancy is 280 days. Occasionally, however, some babies are born early; they are **premature** or preterm, often called "preemies." Formerly these babies had high mortality rates, but with today's sophisticated technology their chances of survival are much greater. Before we discuss the condition of these babies and the reasons for their early appearance, let's establish some pertinent facts.

Prematurity A condition that occurs less than 37 weeks after conception and is defined by low birth weight and immaturity.

Facts about Prematures

A preterm infant is one born before the completion of a 37-week gestation period, and who "fits" one of three categories.

- *Borderline*. These infants are typically born between 37 and 38 weeks gestation, and weigh about 5.8 to 7.3 pounds. In other words, they're similar to full-term babies, but just a little earlier and lighter.

- *Moderate*. These infants are born between 31 and 36 weeks gestation, and weigh from 3.5 to 5.8 pounds. Thus these babies can be classified as low birth weight babies (LBW).

- *Extreme*. These infants are born between 24 and 30 weeks gestation, and weigh from 1 to 3.5 pounds at birth. They are classified as very low birth weight babies (VLBW) and account for 84 percent of neonatal deaths (babies of all gestational ages) (Putman, 2000).

This third classification—very low birth weight (VLBW)—is defined as below 1,500 grams (about 3 pounds). These babies are particularly prone to infection of the amniotic fluid and death by pneumonia (Barton, Hodgman, & Pavlova, 1999). Their chance of survival improves during the first days after birth, but they are at significant risk for later death even after 84 days (Cooper, Berseth, Adams, & Weisman, 1998).

Causes of Prematurity

About 300,000 to 400,000 of all infants born in the United States each year are classified as premature. Although it is still impossible to predict which women will begin labor prematurely, prematurity has been linked to certain conditions. For example, *maternal risk* for preterm labor is closely associated with infection. *Also, once a woman has given birth prematurely,* the risk of prematurity in the next pregnancy is about 25 percent. *Multiple births* (a growing phenomenon due to the increasing use of fertility drugs) also produce babies whose birth weights are lower than that of a single baby. *Stress* has likewise been identified as a cause of prematurity (Azar, 1999). *Age* has shown a high correlation with prematurity. If the mother is under 17 or over 35, the risk is substantially increased.

Other causes include the following.

- *Low socioeconomic status (SES)*. In underdeveloped countries as many as one infant in four is born prematurely. In the United States more premature babies are born to poor than affluent women.

- *Smoking* remains a significant factor in any discussion of prematurity. Growth delays and lung maturity are among the conditions attributed to smoking.

- *Alcohol* also increases the likelihood of prematurity. About 60 percent of American women drink. For those taking 10 drinks per week while pregnant, the chance of having a low birth weight baby doubles.

- Cervical problems, high blood pressure, unusual stress, diabetes, and heart disease may all be related causes. Even when all of these causes are enumerated, explaining exactly what happened in any given pregnancy still is difficult, if not impossible.

Although these infants may differ from full-term babies in the early days of their development, these differences eventually may disappear. Most prematures reach developmental levels similar to those of full-term babies. The only difference is that it takes premature babies a little longer to get there (Fox, 1997).

However, too often a negative stereotype hinders their progress (Azar, 1999). The premature infants are seen as vulnerable, fragile, and less competent, *even when they had caught up with babies who had experienced a normal birth*. For example, observers were told that a healthy looking 9-month-old infant had been premature. They then described the baby as "weaker, less physically mature, less sociable, and less cognitively competent," a tendency that Stern and Karraker (1992) call "prematurity stereotyping."

One conclusion seems inevitable: The younger and smaller the infant, the greater the risk for later difficulties. For example, babies born before 37 weeks gestation are at risk for SIDS at a rate five times higher than that for full-term babies (Hodgman, 1998). Although we can't predict the developmental outcome of these babies with a high degree of certainty, we can conclude that although the vast majority of low birth weight children function within the normal range, they have higher rates of subnormal growth, health conditions, and inferior neurodevelopmental outcomes than do normal birth weight children (Hack, Klein, & Taylor, 1995, p. 191).

 Avery, M.C. & G. Litwack. (1983). *Born early*. New York: Little, Brown. Vital data, good writing, and a positive outlook make this an excellent introduction to the topic of prematurity. It has become a classic in the premature literature.

An Applied View — Guidelines for Parents of Prematures

Although the new technology designed for prematures is marvelous, these babies need to sense parental love. In what has become a classic discussion of the treatment of prematures, Helen Harrison (1983) has proposed several guidelines that parents of prematures can use, even with the technological nature of the premature nursery.

 With advances in the treatment of prematures (temperature control, nutrition), the outlook for these babies has greatly improved. Psychological insights into the development of prematures have led to the conclusion that parental support and stimulation are needed during the baby's hospitalization to ensure that attachment proceeds as normally as possible.

- *Try to understand the baby.* Begin by observing carefully, learning what upsets and soothes. How does the baby respond to different types of stimulation? How long does it take to calm the baby after some upset? What kinds of clues are being given to signal discomfort (changes in skin color, muscular reaction, breathing rate)?
- *Use as much body contact as possible.* Since these babies came into the world early, they often seem physically insecure (when compared to the normal infant after birth). Touching the baby with the whole hand on back or chest and stomach often relaxes the premature. Massaging both relaxes and shows affection.
- *Talk to the baby.* Studies have repeatedly shown that prematures, while seemingly unresponsive, show better rates of development when exposed to the mother's voice as often as possible.

When the premature infant can be taken from the incubator and given to the parent, a delicate moment has arrived. Some parents find it difficult to react positively to a premature; they feel guilty, occasionally harbor feelings of rejection, and must fight to accept the situation. They are simply overwhelmed. Usually this reaction passes quickly. On the occasion of this initial contact, parents should have been well prepared for holding a baby that is still entangled in wires and tubes.

Guided Review

14. Labor usually begins _____ days after the first day of the last menstrual period.
15. The spontaneous end of pregnancy is called a _____ if it occurs before the 20th week.
16. A fertilized egg that develops in a fallopian tube is called an _____ pregnancy.
17. _____ _____ can cause a woman to feel a little "down" for a few days following delivery.
18. Births occurring less than 37 weeks after conception are said to be _____ .
19. After the 20th week of pregnancy, the spontaneous end of pregnancy resulting in death is known as a _____ .
20. Age and _____ help to categorize prematurity.

CONCLUSION & SUMMARY

In this chapter, you have seen how a human being begins its journey through the lifespan. Nature's detailed choreography of prenatal development provides a remarkably complex yet elegantly simple means of ensuring the survival of generations. Once conception occurs, uniting the genetic contribution of both mother and father, the developmental process is under way, sheltered for the first nine months in the protective cocoon of the womb.

For some, the process is interrupted and the uterine stay is shortened. Today these prematures, thanks to technological advances, have a heightened chance of survival and of normal physical and psychological development.

What kinds of development occur during the prenatal period?

- The germinal period is the time when the fertilized egg passes through the fallopian tube.

- The embryonic period is a time of rapid development and great sensitivity.
- The fetal period is a time of preparation for life outside the womb.
- The senses develop during the prenatal months and are ready to function at birth.

What influences prenatal development and what precautions should be taken?

- Developmental risk is a term that applies to those children whose welfare is in jeopardy.
- Teratogens are those agents that cause abnormalities.
- Infectious diseases and chemical agents are the two basic classes of teratogens.
- Today AIDS is recognized as a potential danger for newborns.
- Maternal nutrition and emotions are important influences during pregnancy.

- Advancing technology has provided diagnostic tools for the detection of many fetal problems.

What are the circumstances and possible difficulties of the birth process?

- Birth occurs as a series of three stages.
- Complications such as breech presentations, anoxia, and the Rh factor are among the difficulties that can develop during the birth process.
- Childbirth strategies are evolving that are designed to ease the transition from womb to world.
- Today the outlook for prematures is much more optimistic than in previous times.

KEY TERMS

Afterbirth
AIDS (Acquired Immune Deficiency Syndrome)
Amniocentesis
Anoxia (lack of oxygen)
Blastocyst
Breech birth

Cellular differentiation
Cesarean section
Chorionic Villi Sampling (CVS)
Cytomegalovirus (CMV)
DES (Diethylstilbestrol)
Developmental risk
Dilation

Ectoderm
Ectopic pregnancy
Embryonic period
Endoderm
Expulsion
Fetal alcohol syndrome (FAS)
Fetal period

Answers

14. 280 15. miscarriage 16. ectopic 17. Postnatal depression 18. premature 19. stillbirth 20. weight

Fetoscopy
Forceps delivery
German measles (rubella)
Germinal period
Herpes Simplex
Implantation
Mesoderm
Miscarriage

Organogenesis
Placenta
Prematurity
Prenatal learning
Prepared childbirth
Rh Factor
Stillbirth
Syphilis

Teratogens
Thalidomide
Toxoplasmosis
Trophoblast
Ultrasound
Umbilical cord

WHAT DO YOU THINK?

1. Considerable discussion has occurred recently about the possibility of prenatal learning. Where do you stand on this issue? Be sure to support your opinion with facts from this chapter.

2. You probably have heard how careful women must be when they are pregnant. They are worried about such things as smoking and drinking. Do you think we have become too nervous and timid about these dangers? Why?

3. Turn back to table 4.2. From your own knowledge (relatives and friends, for example), indicate which of these teratogens you think are most common. Select one and explain why you think it is a common threat and what could be done to help prevent it. (Lead paint is a good example.)

4. Significant medical and ethical questions surround such techniques as fetal surgery. Assume that a physician does not inform a woman that her fetus is a good candidate for fetal surgery. The baby is stillborn. Is the doctor guilty of malpractice or any crime? Can you think of other examples?

CHAPTER REVIEW TEST

1. It takes a fertilized egg about _____ to travel through the fallopian tube to the uterus.
   a. 3 days
   b. 14 days
   c. 30 days
   d. nine months

2. It then takes another _____ days for the fertilized egg to implant.
   a. 3 days
   b. 7 days
   c. 14 days
   d. 30 days

3. The first two weeks following fertilization are called the _____ period.
   a. embryonic
   b. fetal
   c. germinal
   d. pregnancy

4. A _____ is a one-week-old zygote.
   a. fetus
   b. embryo
   c. blastocyst
   d. trophoblast

5. During the _____ period the nervous system develops rapidly.
   a. embryonic
   b. fetal
   c. gestational
   d. germinal

6. Which system does not develop from the mesoderm?
   a. Muscular
   b. Skeletal
   c. Circulatory
   d. Respiratory

7. Development is most vulnerable to outside agents during the _____ period.
   a. embryonic
   b. germinal
   c. fetal
   d. sensitive

8. The peak growth period for the fetus is during the _____ and _____ months.
   a. first, second
   b. fourth, fifth
   c. sixth, seventh
   d. eighth, ninth

9. Red blood cells transport _____ and white blood cells to combat disease.
   a. oxygen
   b. amniotic fluid
   c. teratogens
   d. villi

10. Which of the following statements is true?
    a. The earlier the damage, the greater the chance of negative long-term effects.
    b. The fetus is safe from all harm while in the womb.
    c. Babies are usually born on the day predicted.
    d. A fetus hears no sound until birth.

11. Toxoplasmosis is
    a. a sexually transmitted disease.
    b. a virus capable of causing deafness or cataracts.
    c. a disease capable of causing mental retardation or death.
    d. a problem caused by the genetic makeup of the father.

12. Which of the following will not result from exposure to rubella?
    a. Congenital heart disorder
    b. Skeletal deformity
    c. Deafness
    d. Mental retardation

13. _____ is not a STORCH infection.
    a. RDS
    b. CMV
    c. Herpes simplex
    d. Toxoplasmosis

14. It is almost impossible for a mother to pass the AIDS virus to her baby through
    a. delivery.
    b. handling.
    c. pregnancy.
    d. breast milk.

15. In a typical pregnancy, a woman will gain about ___ to ___ pounds.
    a. 25 to 30
    b. 30 to 35
    c. 35 to 40
    d. 40 to 45

16. A woman's emotions can affect her pregnancy indirectly by a release of her
    a. villi.
    b. teratogens.
    c. hormones.
    d. Rh factor.

17. _____ is a technique in which a needle is inserted through a pregnant woman's abdomen and into the amniotic sac in order to obtain a fluid sample.
    a. Ultrasound
    b. Chorionic villi sampling
    c. Amniocentesis
    d. Non-stress test

18. Prematurity is *not* associated with
    a. vitamin therapy.
    b. low SES.
    c. multiple births.
    d. cigarette use.

19. _____ was a pioneer in the technique of prepared childbirth.
    a. Leboyer
    b. Lamaze
    c. DeCasper
    d. Salk

20. Mental retardation, hyperactivity, and primary growth retardation can be symptoms of
    a. Fetal Alcohol Syndrome (FAS).
    b. Rh factor.
    c. prematurity.
    d. anoxia.

21. Premature babies of very low birth weight are
    a. not normally at severe risk.
    b. not permitted visits by their parents.
    c. more likely to develop cerebral palsy.
    d. more likely to have problems later in life.

Answers

1.a 2.a 3.c 4.c 5.a 6.d 7.a 8.b 9.a 10.a 11.c 12.d 13.a 14.b 15.a 16.c 17.c 18.a 19.b 20.a 21.d

PART III

Infancy

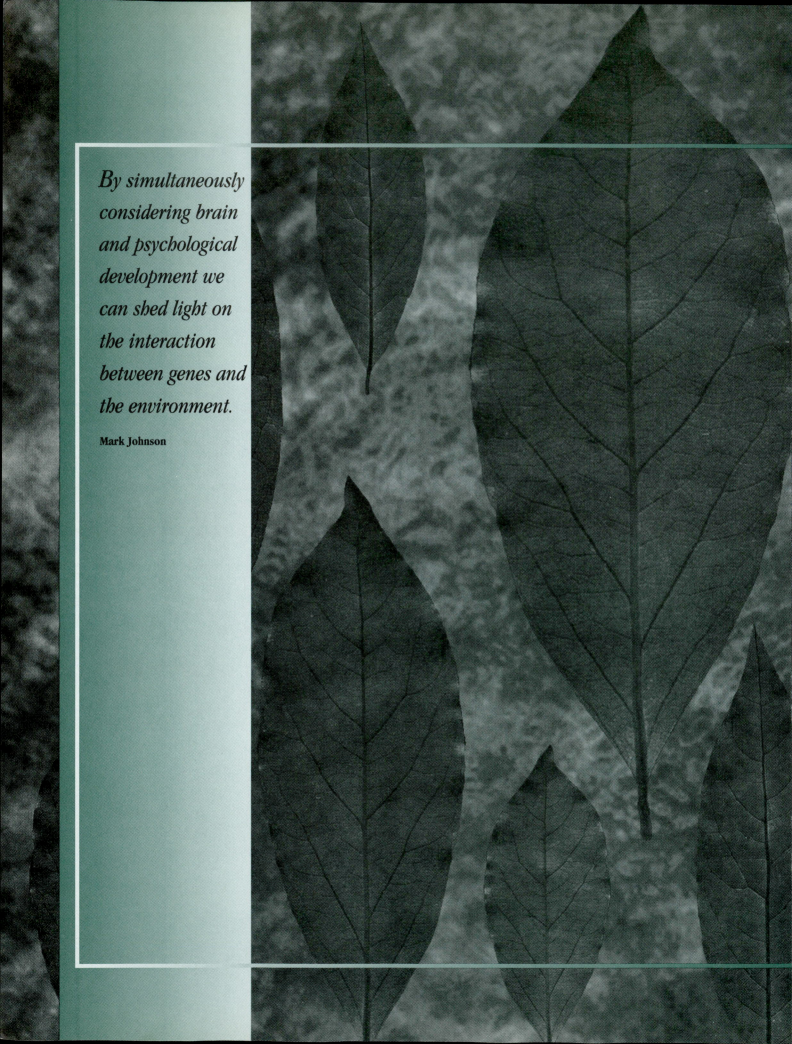

By simultaneously considering brain and psychological development we can shed light on the interaction between genes and the environment.

Mark Johnson

Chapter Outline

Liz gazed at the infant girl in her arms. Although she had carried this tiny creature within her for nine months, it was still a stranger. Would it be easy to take care of? Who would she really look like? Would she do well in school? Of course she would be smart!

As these thoughts flashed through her mind, she remembered a course in child psychology she had taken and the theorists she had studied. What was it that Freud had said? Oh, Yes: "From the very first children have a copious sexual life." Liz smiled. That must have been a popular idea in Victorian days.

Or the behaviorist, John Watson, who believed that infants are a source of potential stimulus-response connections. He believed that if you turn your attention to an infant early enough, you can make that infant into anything you want—it's all a matter of conditioning!

As she struggled to recall what these theorists said about infancy, Piaget's name flashed across her memory. Rather than seeing children as small sponges waiting for something to be poured into them, Piaget believed that children actively construct their own views of the world during these early years. One of the first psychologists to question the apparently passive state of infants, he argued that infants are much more competent than originally thought and during infancy they build the cognitive structures that are the foundation of their intelligence.

How had the instructor referred to a newborn? Neonate; yes, that was it. She had read the books on infancy, especially those by T. Berry Brazelton and knew what to expect: feedings, sleep patterns, possible illnesses. But what really was a neonate? What was an infant? Maybe I should check Brazelton's work again; he's speaking at the university tomorrow night. Catching herself in these musings, she began to laugh. ☻

The tall, athletic-looking man walked quickly across the stage and put his notes on the podium. He then looked up and smiled at the crowd filling the university theatre. They had come to hear T. Berry Brazelton, professor of pediatrics at Harvard Medical School, founder of the Child Development Unit at Boston's Childrens Hospital and probably America's most popular pediatrician, talk about the importance of the infancy years.

With his belief that infants are both competent and complex, Brazelton, in his own practice, his writings, and in television appearances, has been one of the leaders in changing our views of infancy. Thanks to his work and that of his colleagues (see Brazelton & Nugent, 1995), we now recognize how much infants contribute to their own development in these early years.

To help you understand an infant's world, in this chapter you'll first trace the infant's physical development and then examine the methods used to assess the well-being of infants following birth. Next you'll follow various paths of infant development: motor, perceptual, cognitive, and language. You'll also begin to discern the issues and themes discussed in chapter 1. For example, stability is particularly important in any discussion of infancy. That is, do the events that occur in infancy leave an indelible mark that lasts a lifetime?

Chapter Objectives

After reading this chapter, you should be able to answer the following questions.

◆ What are the major physical accomplishments of the infancy period?
◆ How do infants acquire information about their world?
◆ What are the differences between Piaget's view of cognitive development in infancy and that of information processing?
◆ How do infants acquire their language?

Physical Development in Infancy

Infancy is a time of rapid physical and nervous system development, accomplishments that ensure an infant's survival and ability to cope with its world. The typical newborn weighs about 7½ pounds and is about 20 inches in length. In one year after its birth, an infant's length increases by one-half and its weight almost triples. Infancy sees exciting changes in psychomotor development.

Developmental Milestones of Infancy

In his careful analysis of physical growth and development, Tanner (1990) described growth as like the weaving of a cloth whose design never repeats itself. The underlying threads, each coming from the reel at its own rhythm, interact with one another continuously, in a manner always highly regulated and controlled.

To help you visualize the rapid growth that occurs during infancy, consider table 5.1.

As their baby's growing physical competence becomes observable, parents begin to treat their child differently, recognizing greater individuality and maturity. Different parenting practices now spring into action and these varied practices reflect the culture into which a child is born. The manner in which Balinese mothers carry their children affects children's motor development; infants in Ghana show superior motor abilities due to their considerable physical freedom; the expectations of Jamaican mothers help their infants to sit and walk relatively early (Bornstein, 1995). In other words, different families in different cultures go about parenting in different ways.

TABLE 5.1 DEVELOPMENTAL MILESTONES OF INFANCY

Age (mos.)	Height (in.)	Weight (lbs.)
3	24	13–14
6	26	17–18
9	28	20–22
12	30	22–24
18	32	25–26
24	34	27–29

Growing children experience changes in shape and body composition, in the distribution of tissues, and in their developing motor skills, and these changes then influence cognitive, psychosocial, and emotional development. For example, the infant's head at birth is about a quarter of the body's total length, but in the adult it is about one-seventh of body length. Different tissues (muscles, nerves) also grow at different rates, and total growth represents a complex series of changes. Underlying this rapidly unfolding and complex process is, of course, proper nutrition.

Nutrition

Developed countries have nearly eliminated malnutrition, although the familiar suspects of poverty, illness, and neglect can still cause considerable nutritional damage. In developed countries, the issue focuses on concerns about the relative benefits of breast versus formula feeding.

Although breast versus formula has almost always caused controversy, it's interesting to note that breast-feeding in the United States declined noticeably from 1984 to 1989 (Lutz & Przytulski, 1997). Given the recent attention to the benefits of breast-feeding and the national goal of having 75 percent of mothers breast-feed, the trend has been reversed.

The composition of breast milk varies during the first weeks following birth. For the first 3 or 4 days, it's known as *colostrum,* a thin, yellowish fluid that is high in proteins. *Transitional milk* then appears until about the end of the second week. Finally, *mature milk* is available (Moore, 1997).

Breast-feeding leads to two advantages that can't be duplicated by formula feeding. First is the protection against disease offered by a mother's milk. Breast-fed babies seem to have a lesser degree of illness than formula-fed babies, an important consideration in developing countries. Second, breast-fed babies are less at risk for allergic reactions than are formula-fed babies.

On the other hand, one of the advantages of formula feeding is that others, including the father, can feed the baby. Commercial formulas are good, containing more proteins than breast milk. Assuming that the formula is appropriate, nutritional problems should not arise. In the United States, infants are usually well-nourished either through breast or formula feeding. Other considerations, such as returning to work, may influence a woman's decision to either breast or formula feed (Lutz & Przytulski, 1997).

Newborn infants have a special need for protein, given the rapid tissue building occurring during these days. Their high metabolic rates also consume large amounts of their energy, thus they require substantial amounts of proteins, fats, carbohydrates, minerals and vitamins—especially iron, zinc, and calcium (Moore, 1997). Infants are usually ready for solid food at about 4 to 5 months. Table 5.2 presents a recommended schedule for the introduction of solid food (Tamborlane, 1997).

TABLE 5.2 INTRODUCING SOLID FOODS

Age	Foods
0–4 months	Breast milk or formula
4–6 months	Iron fortified cereals made with rice or barley
6–7 months	Strained fruits and vegetables
	Fruit juices, teething foods
8–9 months	Pureed meats, potatoes, rice, or pasta
10–12 months	Finger foods, toast strips, yogurt, and an increased variety of foods

In the course of one year, then, infants progress from either breast- or bottle-feeding to a variety of table foods.

Let's turn now to the remarkable role of the brain in development.

Brain Development

The adult human brain weighs about 3 to 4 pounds and contains about 100–200 billion neurons (Gopnik, Meltzoff, & Kuhl, 2000). As we have seen, nervous system development begins during the embryonic period when neurons reproduce at the rate of about 250,000 per minute. During infancy, connections among the neurons begin to increase notably (as much as 100 to 1,000 connections for each of the billions of neurons). This amazing complexity provides the biological basis for cognitive development (Fischbach, 1992). Estimates are that the baby's brain at birth is

Shown here are the brain's lobes and functional areas.

about a quarter of its adult size. At 6 months it's about 50 percent of its adult weight, 60 percent at 1 year, 75 percent at 2½ years, 90 percent at 6 years, and 95 percent at 10 years. The developmental pattern is seen in figure 5.1.

The human brain (unlike that of other primates) continues to grow rapidly after birth, especially during the first two years (Howard, 2000). The myelin sheath, which helps the passage of nerve impulses, isn't complete until about 6 years of age, and the brain isn't considered to be physically mature until puberty. Thus about 75 percent of the human brain develops outside of the womb in direct relationship with its environment (Shore, 1996).

Our knowledge of the brain has increased dramatically with new discoveries in the neurosciences. Thanks to technological advances such as the *MRI* (Magnetic Resonance Imaging) and the *PET* scan (Positive Emission Tomography), brain researchers now have a much more detailed view of the brain and its activity levels. As new data emerge, new speculations about the relationship of brain to behavior inevitably arise.

Another example of startling new breakthroughs in brain research is the ability to grow new brain cells to replace damaged brain cells (in mice). It was long thought that brain cells, once damaged, could never be replaced. However, recent research (Saltus, 2000) has discovered that neural brain cells migrate through the brain, attach to damaged nerves, and transform themselves into the appropriate nerves cells. As a result, the future looks brighter for sufferers of such diseases as Parkinson's and Lou Gehrig's disease.

Current thinking concerning brain behavior interactions (referred to as *probabilistic epigenesis*) reflects the system analysis of development discussed in chapter 2.

Figure 5.1

Brain development.

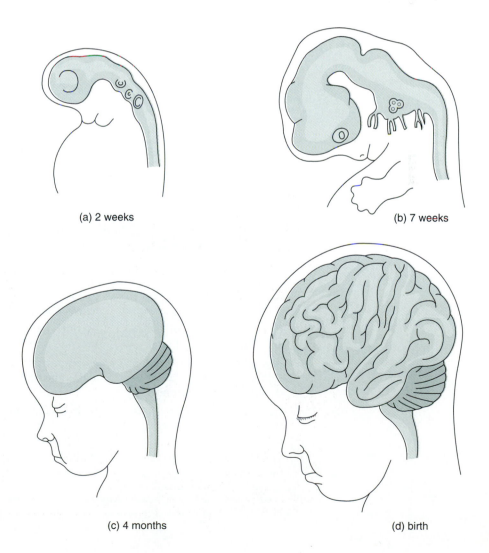

(a) 2 weeks

(b) 7 weeks

(c) 4 months

(d) birth

(For an excellent discussion of this topic see Johnson, 2000.) Consequently, these new findings have forced us to change our thinking about the brain and its functions, as seen in table 5.3.

For example, at birth, the baby's experiences add a new dimension to the brain's wiring process. The range of a baby's pleasant and unpleasant experiences begin to shape an infant's emotional life; the degree to which parents talk to their babies the more complex will be their wiring for language; when babies have the opportunity to interact with appropriate toys and objects, the more refined their circuitry for motor control becomes. In other words, the brain keeps rewiring itself even after it's turned on (Gopnik, Meltzoff, & Kuhl, 2000).

Each of the brain's four lobes (frontal, parietal, temporal, and occipital) exercises specialized functions. For example, the frontal lobe contains the motor area for control of all the skeletal muscles (which shows rapid growth for survival purposes); the parietal lobe seems to be the controlling center for the body's sense areas; the temporal lobe manages auditory functions; the occipital lobe analyzes visual information. Brain structures for thinking are diffused throughout the cortical area, which makes considerable sense when you think (!!!) about answering a question. You listen to the question (auditory area); you respond by speaking (motor area); you search your memory.

At birth, of course, the infant must assume those life-sustaining functions that the mother provided for nine months, which leads us to an analysis of the important role that native reflexes play.

Neonatal Reflexes

Reflex When a stimulus repeatedly elicits the same response.

Think of a **reflex** as an automatic response to certain stimuli. Popular examples include the eye blink and the knee jerk. All of the activities needed to sustain life's functions are present at birth (breathing, sucking, swallowing, elimination). These reflexes serve a definite purpose: The gag reflex enables infants to spit up mucus; the eye blink protects the eyes from excessive light; an antismothering reflex facilitates breathing.

In an attempt to rank an infant's reflexes in order of importance, Harris and Liebert (1992) note that the most crucial reflexes are those associated with breathing. Breathing patterns are not fully established at birth, and sometimes infants briefly stop breathing. These periods are called **apnea,** and although there is some concern that apnea may be associated with sudden infant death, these periods are quite common in all infants. Usually they last for about 2 to 5 seconds; episodes

Apnea Brief periods when breathing is suspended.

TABLE 5.3 RETHINKING THE BRAIN

Old Thinking	New Thinking
A brain's development depends solely on genes.	Brain development depends on the interactions between genes and experience.
Experiences before three years are relatively insignificant.	Experiences during infancy are critical for the structure of the brain and its future potential.
A good relationship between a child and parents facilitates development and learning.	A secure relationship not only aids development, it also affects the way the brain is wired.
Brain development proceeds steadily, that is, in a linear fashion.	Brain development is essentially non-linear, that is, there are ideal times for different kinds of experiences.
The brain is less active during the early years.	During these years, an infant's brain may be twice as active as an adolescent's or adult's.

Adapted from R. Shore. (1997). *Rethinking the brain: New insights into early development.* New York: Families and Work Institute.

that extend from about 10 to 20 seconds may suggest the possibility of a problem. Sneezing and coughing are both reflexes that help to clear air passages.

Next in importance are those reflexes associated with feeding. Infants suck and swallow during the prenatal period and continue at birth. They also demonstrate the rooting reflex, in which they'll turn toward a nipple or a finger placed on the cheek and attempt to get it into the mouth. Table 5.4 describes some of the more important neonatal reflexes.

Newborn Abilities

Neonate Term for an infant in the first days and weeks after birth.

In the days immediately following birth until about two weeks to one month, the infant is called a **neonate.** During this period, babies immediately begin to use their abilities to adapt to their environment. Among the most significant of these are the following:

- *Infants display clear signs of imitative behavior at 7 to 10 days.* (Try this: Stick out your tongue at a baby who is about 10 days old. What happens? The baby will stick its tongue out at you!) Here neonates are telling us that they have the ability to imitate almost immediately after birth, an ability that should alert parents to immediately demonstrate desirable behavior for their children to learn and imitate. Infants' imitation of such tongue movements as just described is well-established in babies as young as a few hours to more than six weeks of age (Jones, 1996).

- *Infants can see at birth* and, if you capture their attention with an appropriate object (such as a small, red rubber ball held at about 10 inches from the face), they will track it as you move the ball from side to side. Infants react to color at between 2 and 4 months; depth perception appears at about 4 to 5 months (Brazelton & Nugent, 1995).

- *Infants not only can hear at birth (and prenatally),* but they also can perceive the direction of the sound. In a famous yet simple experiment, Michael Wertheimer (1962) sounded a clicker (similar to those children play with) from different sides of a delivery room only 10 minutes after an infant's birth. The infant not only reacted to the noise, but attempted to turn in the direction of the sound, indicating that children immediately tune into their environment (Olds, London, & Ladewig, 1996).

TABLE 5.4 NEONATAL REFLEXES

Name of Reflex	How Elicited	Description of Response
Plantar grasp	Press thumbs against the balls of the infant's foot	Toes tend to curl
Babinski	Gently stroke lateral side of sole of foot	Toes spread in an outward and upward manner
Babkin	Press palm of hand while infant lies on back	Mouth opens; eyes close
Rooting	Gently touch cheek of infant with light finger pressure	Head turns toward finger in effort to suck
Sucking	Mouth contacts nipple of breast or bottle	Mouth and tongue used to manipulate (suck) nipple
Moro	Loud noise or sudden dropping of infant	Stretches arms and legs and then hugs self; cries
Grasping	Object or finger is placed in infant's palm	Fingers curl around object
Tonic neck reflex	Place infant flat on back	Infant assumes fencer position: turns head and extends arm and leg in same direction as head
Stepping	Support infant in upright position; soles of feet brush surface	Infant attempts regular progression of steps

From John F. Travers, *The Growing Child,* Scott, Foresman and Company, Glenview, IL, 1982. Reprinted by permission of the author.

Sample photographs of a model's happy, surprised, and sad expressions, and an infant's corresponding expressions

Courtesy of Dr. Tiffany Field and *Science*. From Field, et al., Model and Infant Expressions from "Discrimination and Imitation of Facial Express by Neonates" in *Science*, fig. 2, Vol. 218, pp. 179–181, October 8, 1982. Reprinted by permission of the American Association for the Advancement of Science.

- *Infants are active seekers of stimulation.* Infants want—actually need—people, sounds, and physical contact to stimulate their cognitive development and to give them a feeling of security in their world. Remember that infants are engaged in a subtle, though powerful battle to establish control over their bodies. For example, they are struggling to regulate their bodily functions such as eating, breathing, and heart rate. But for brief moments, perhaps for only 15 or 20 seconds, they stop these efforts and pay close attention to the environment in a search for stimulation. This happens even when they are hungry.

  One of the authors takes students to Boston's Children Hospital for observation visits, and attempts to find a nurse bottle-feeding an infant. Watching what happens when someone moves into the baby's field of vision, they are surprised at the baby's reaction. *The baby stops sucking and stares intently at that person's face!* Not for long, but long enough to interrupt feeding. Now you may not be too impressed with this but think about it. An infant's hunger drive is extremely powerful, yet, momentarily, the need for stimulation is even stronger indicating that infants show a willingness, even a need, to interact with other human beings.

- *Infants, using these abilities, begin their efforts to master the developmental tasks of the first two years:* learning to take solid foods, learning to talk, learning to walk.

Neonatal Assessment Techniques

Although all infants are born with these reflexes and abilities, not all possess them to the same degree. For example, some neonates demonstrate much weaker reflex action than others, a condition that affects their chances of surviving. Consequently, efforts to develop reliable measures of early behavior, called *neonatal assessment,* have increased sharply.

An Informed VIEW

Neonates: Competent or Helpless?

Before continuing your reading, try to decide how competent you think a newborn baby is. In one view, infants are empty, unresponsive beings merely waiting for things to be done to and for them. They become active, healthy babies only because of maturation and the actions of those around them.

In another view, newborns are seen as amazingly competent and capable of much more than is now expected of them. Adherents of this belief view infants as "Super Babies," capable of prodigious accomplishments from birth, if not before. Consequently, from the first months of an infant's life, infants need some form of education.

In a third view, infants are seen as neither passive objects nor as superbabies, designed for instant greatness. Newborn babies are seen as bringing abilities with them into the world, a cluster of competencies that enables them to survive but also permits them to engage in a wider range of activities than was previously suspected (Brazelton & Nugent, 1995).

The expectations that parents have for their babies determine how they treat them and these expectations have important physical, cognitive, and psychosocial consequences. Babies "tune into" their environments—they react to the tone of an adult's voice, they sense how they're being handled (gently or roughly)—and are quite skillful in detecting the moods of those around them.

Ask your parents to think back on their childbearing days and try to recall how competent they thought babies were. Ask them if it made any difference in how they treated you. If you have brothers or sisters or friends with children, ask them what they expected a new-born baby would be like? Combining their practical outlook on infancy with what you have read, decide which of the above three views of infancy you think is most realistic. Which will most help infants to fulfill their potential?

If you would like to have a more informed view on this issue, you may want to read one or more of the references in this chapter, such as Brazelton & Nugent's account of newborn behavior.

You may also wish to learn more about it by going to our web site at http://www.mhhe.com/dacey5.

Three basic classifications of neonatal tests are used to assess infant reflexes and behavior: the *Apgar scale, neurological assessment,* and *behavioral assessment.*

Apgar A scale to evaluate a newborn's basic life signs.

1. *The Apgar.* In 1953 Virginia Apgar proposed a scale to evaluate a newborn's basic life signs. The **Apgar** is administered one minute after birth, and repeated at three-, five-, and ten-minute intervals. Using five life signs—heart rate, respiratory effort, muscle tone, reflex irritability, and skin color—an observer evaluates the infant by a three-point scale. Each of the five dimensions receives a score of 0, 1, or 2. (0 indicates severe problems, whereas 2 suggests an absence of major difficulties.)

Neurological assessment

Identifies any neurological problem, suggests means of monitoring the problem, and offers a prognosis about the problem.

2. *Neurological Assessment.* The **neurological assessment** is used for three purposes:

   • Identification of any neurological problem

   • Constant monitoring of a neurological problem

   • Prognosis about some neurological problem

   Each of these purposes requires testing the infant's reflexes, which is critical for neurological evaluation and basic for all infant tests.

Brazelton Neonatal Behavioral Assessment Scale A neonatal assessment technique that includes a baby's state of consciousness.

3. *Behavioral Assessment.* The **Brazelton Neonatal Behavioral Assessment Scale** (named after T. Berry Brazelton) has become a significant worldwide tool for infant assessment. Brazelton and Nugent (1995) believe that the baby's state of consciousness (sleepy, drowsy, alert, fussy) is the single most important element in the examination. The Brazelton test also permits us to examine the infant's behavior, which, as we have mentioned, is sensitive to cultural differences.

For example, during the administration of the Brazelton, one of the tests involves gently placing a piece of cheese cloth over the eyes and nose of the baby. This is intended to measure the baby's defensive reactions, so important for survival. Most African- and Anglo-American babies quickly turned their heads away or tried to push the cloth away. Chinese American babies, however, remained still and breathed through their mouths (Brazelton & Nugent, 1995; Kagan, 1994). (For an excellent discussion of the role of culture in the origins of individual differences in neonatal behavior, see Nugent & others, 1995.)

All three of these assessment techniques provide clues about the infant's ability to function on its own and have proved to be invaluable tools in diagnosing problems in the early days of infancy. Tests such as these, plus careful observation, have given us much greater insight into infant development. These tests have also helped us to realize that infants are much more competent than we previously suspected.

Given the rapid development of the brain and the survival value of the reflexes, we should expect motor development to proceed rapidly, which is just what happens.

Motor Development

Parents are fascinated by their child's motor development: Is she sitting up on time? Shouldn't she be crawling by now? I wonder if she'll ever walk. Why can't she hold her head steady? Motor development occurs in both head-to-feet direction (called *cephalocaudal*), as well as a *proximodistal* direction (from the center of the body to the extremities).

For many years, research into infant locomotion has been at a standstill mainly because of the belief that neuromuscular maturation was the primary agent of motor development. Recently, however, modern investigators using high-speed film, computerized video recordings, and infrared emitting diodes, have provided new insights into changes in coordination, balance, and strength in infants' locomotion.

Studies have shown that continuity of walking movements in the first year may be masked by underlying changes in the infant's muscle distribution, body fat, and the differential effect of gravity. For example, newborns with chubby legs stepped less than slender-legged infants. But when the slender-legged infants were weighted with an amount usually gained over the first months of life, they stopped stepping (Adolph, 1997).

Here are several important characteristics of motor control.

Note the steady development of body control in this picture, especially the head and upper body. Control of the lower body and legs follows by several months.

Head Control

The most obvious initial head movements are from side to side, although the 1-month-old infant occasionally lifts its head when in a prone position. Four-month-old infants can hold their heads steady while sitting and will lift their head and shoulders to a 90 degree angle when on their abdomens. By the age of 6 months, most youngsters can balance their heads quite well.

Locomotion: Crawling and Creeping

Crawling Locomotion in which the infant's abdomen touches the floor and the weight of the head and shoulders rests on the elbows.

Creeping Movement is on hands and knees and the trunk does not touch the ground; creeping appears from nine months in most youngsters.

Crawling and creeping are two distinct developmental phases. In **crawling,** the infant's abdomen touches the floor and the weight of the head and shoulders rests on the elbows. Locomotion is mainly by arm action. The legs usually drag, although some youngsters push with their legs. Most youngsters can crawl after age 7 months.

Creeping is more advanced than crawling, since movement is on hands and knees and the trunk does not touch the ground. After age 9 months, most youngsters can creep.

Most descriptions of crawling and creeping are quite uniform. The progression is from propulsion on the abdomen to quick, accurate movements on hands and knees, but the sequence is endlessly varied. Youngsters adopt a bewildering diversity of positions and movements that can only loosely be grouped together.

Most youngsters somewhere in the 7 to 9 month period begin to pull themselves up to a standing position. Their legs are now strong enough to support them while standing.

Locomotion: Standing and Walking

After about age 7 months, infants when held will support most of their weight on their legs. Coordination of arm and leg movements enables babies to pull themselves up and grope toward control of leg movements. The first steps are a propulsive, lunging forward. Gradually a smooth, speedy, and versatile gait emerges. The world now belongs to the infant.

Once babies begin to walk, their attention darts from one thing to another, thus quickening their perceptual development (our next topic). Tremendous energy and mobility, coupled with a growing curiosity, push infants to search for the boundaries of their world. It is an exciting time for youngsters but a watchful time for parents, since they must draw the line between encouraging curiosity and initiative and protecting the child from personal injury. The task is not easy. It is, however, a problem for all aspects of development: What separates unreasonable restraint from reasonable freedom?

Finally, we want to call your attention to changes in theorizing about and research into motor development. Reflecting current thinking about development (see chapters 1 and 2), recent studies have incorporated a multicausal explanation of motor development (Lockman & Thelen, 1993; Thelen, 1995). For example, in analyzing the stepping reflex previously discussed (see p. 110), Thelen (1995) commented on the disappearance of this behavior by two or three months. Yet kicking, which has the same movement pattern as stepping, is *not* lost. How can these differences be explained? Thelen (1995) pointed to a change of posture, plus weight gain (the legs get heavier) plus the pull of gravity as the multicausal answer.

Table 5.5 summarizes milestones in motor development.

Neonatal Problems

Not all infants enter the world unscathed. Occasionally the developmental sequence that we have just discussed does not run smoothly. Among the most prominent of possible problems are the following.

TABLE 5.5 MILESTONES IN MOTOR DEVELOPMENT

Age	Head Control	Grasping	Sitting	Creeping, Crawling	Standing, Walking
1–3 months	Can lift head and chest while prone	Grasps objects, briefly holds objects, carries objects to mouth	Sits awkwardly with support		
4–8 months	Holds head steady while sitting, balances head	Develops skillful use of thumb	Transition from sitting with slight support to brief periods without support	Crawling movements appear at about 7 months (trunk touches floor)	
8–12 months	Has established head control	Coordinates hand activities, handedness begins to appear	Good trunk control, sits alone steadily	Creeping (trunk raised from floor) begins at 9–10 months and continues until steady walking	Can stand and take steps holding on to something; by 12 months will pull self up
12–14 months		Handedness pronounced, holds crayon, marks lines	Can sit from standing position		Stands alone; begins to walk alone
18 months					Begins to run

From John F. Travers, *The Growing Child*, Scott, Foresman and Company, Glenview, IL, 1982. Reprinted by permission of the author.

Toilet Training—Easy or Difficult?

By the end of their child's infancy period, most parents begin to think about toilet training. One important fact to remember is that voluntary control of the sphincter muscles, which are the muscles that control elimination, does not occur until about the 18th month. For some children, however, control is not possible until about 30 months.

Evidence suggests that children are ready to participate in toilet training at about 18 months of age and may be completely trained between 2 and 3 years of age. Attempting to train children before they are ready can only cause anxiety and stress for the child and frustration for the parents (Brazelton & others, 1999).

Toilet training should commence when bladder control and rectal muscles are sufficiently mature.

Children really can't be trained; they learn when to use the toilet. Certain signs of readiness can alert parents when they can initiate the process. For example, necessary muscle control does not occur until well into the second year and a child must be able to communicate, either by words or gesture, the need to use the bathroom.

At about 2 years, almost all children want to use the toilet, to become more "grown-up," and to rid themselves of the discomfort of wet or soiled diapers. Parents should try to obtain equipment that the child feels most comfortable with—either a chair that sits on the floor or one that fits over the toilet seat.

Most parents expect their children to be toilet trained by the end of infancy, usually sometime between 2 and 3 years of age. Physiologically, most children are ready to learn control; socially it is desirable; psychologically it may be traumatic unless parents are careful. Here are several suggestions that can help parents (Gorski, 1999).

- Recognize the time of day and children's moods when they are most approachable.
- Work with children's attention span; plan distractions that will keep them comfortable on a potty chair.
- Accept a child's frustration level and work within those limits.
- Provide as much support and encouragement as a particular child needs.

Failure to Thrive

Failure-to-thrive (FTT)
A condition in which the weight and height of infants consistently remain far below normal (the bottom 3% of height and weight measures).

The weight and height of **failure-to-thrive (FTT)** infants consistently remain far below normal. They are estimated to be in the bottom 3 percent of height and weight measures. They account for about 3 percent of pediatric hospital admissions.

There are two types of FTT, organic and nonorganic. *Organic FTT* accounts for 30 percent of FTT cases, and the problem is usually some gastrointestinal disease, occasionally a problem with the nervous system. *Nonorganic FTT,* much more difficult to diagnose and treat, lacks a physical cause. Consequently, researchers have looked to the environment and identified problems such as poverty, neglect, and often ignorance of good parenting practices. The seriousness of this problem is evident from the outlook for FTT infants: Almost 50 percent of them will continue to experience physical, cognitive, and behavioral problems (Blackman, 1997).

Sudden Infant Death Syndrome

Sudden infant death syndrome (SIDS) Death of an apparently healthy infant, usually between 2 and 4 months of age; thought to be a brain-related respiratory problem.

Discussion of the survival value of reflexes introduces one of the most perplexing problems facing both parents and researchers, **sudden infant death syndrome (SIDS).** An estimated 4,000 infants 2 to 4 months old die each year from SIDS. There is little warning, although almost all cases are preceded by mild cold symptoms and usually occur in late winter or early spring (American Academy of Pediatrics, 2000).

SIDS rarely occurs before age 1 month or after age 1 year; most victims are between 2 and 4 months old. Deaths peak between November and March. Boys are more vulnerable than girls, in this case by a 3 to 2 margin (Donner, 1997).

SIDS is particularly devastating for parents because of the lack of warning. These infants are apparently normal. Parents put them in a crib for a nap or for the night and return later to find them dead (hence the common name, "crib death"). You can imagine the effect this has on parents, particularly the feelings of guilt: What did I do wrong? Why didn't I look in earlier? Why didn't I see that something was wrong? Today, special centers have been established to counsel grieving parents. (One disturbing recent statistic has raised concern: There is a larger proprtion of SIDS deaths in day-care centers than in parent care. For an analysis of this research, see Moon & colleagues, 2000.)

Although no definite answers to the SIDS dilemma have yet been found, current research points to a respiratory problem. Control of breathing resides in the brain stem, and autopsies have indicated that the SIDS infant may not have received sufficient oxygen while in the womb, a condition known as *fetal hypoxia.* Consequently, parents are being urged to be extremely cautious when their babies are sleeping: Keep them on their back as much as possible, be alert to overheating, and avoid soft, loose bedding (American Academy of Pediatrics, 2000; Klonof-Cohen, 1997). These cautionary practices have resulted in a decrease in post-neonatal SIDS mortality (Malloy & Freeman, 2000).

A startling twist in the analysis of SIDS deaths has recently led researchers to attribute *some* of these deaths to child abuse. One possible cause is called *Munchausen by proxy,* in which a parent deliberately injures or kills a child to attract attention. Munchausen by proxy is a variant of adult Munchausen in which victims inflict harm on themselves, again to seek attention and sympathy.

In a bizarre episode, researchers, baffled by unexplained illnesses in children who were being treated at an Atlanta hospital, hid video cameras in 41 rooms. In more than *half* the cases mothers were inflicting injury on the child. One mother injected her child with her own urine; another gagged herself to vomit and then said the vomit was the child's; another injected chemicals into her child's feeding tube causing chronic fatigue (Hall & others, 2000). Remember, however, in the vast majority of SIDS cases (estimates range from 95–98 percent), the parents are blameless. This bizarre finding will undoubtedly lead to more detailed studies.

Sleeping Disorders

Most sleeping disorders are less serious than FTT or SIDS. Nevertheless, infant sleeping problems negatively affect growth and trouble parents. As Ferber (1985, p. 15) stated:

> The most frequent calls I receive at the Center for Pediatric Sleep Disorders at Children's Hospital in Boston are from a parent or parents whose children are sleeping poorly. When the parent on the phone begins by telling me "I am at the end of my rope" or "We are at our wits' end" I can almost predict what will be said next.

Ferber went on to explain that typically the parent has a child between the ages of 5 months and 4 years who does not sleep readily at night and wakes repeatedly. Parents become tired, frustrated, and often angry. Frequently the relationship between the parents becomes tense.

Usually a sleeping disorder has nothing to do with parenting. Also, usually nothing is wrong with the child, either physically or mentally. Occasionally problems do exist; for example, a bladder infection or, with an older child, emotional factors causing night terrors. A sleep problem is not normal and should not be waited out.

Neonates sleep more than they do anything else (usually from 14 to 15 hours per day) and have three sleep patterns: light or restless, periodic, and deep. Little if any activity occurs during deep sleep (about 25 percent of sleep). Neonates are mostly light sleepers and have the brain wave patterns associated with dreaming (although infants probably do not dream).

Some internal clock seems to regulate sleep patterns, with most deep sleep spells lasting approximately 20 minutes. At the end of the second week, a consistent and predictable pattern emerges. Neonates sleep in short stretches, about seven or eight hours. The pattern soon reverses itself, and infants assume an adult's sleep schedule. Sleep patterns in infants range from about 16 to 17 hours in the first week to 13 hours at age 2.

Adults also need to exercise caution when they take children into their own beds. From January 1990 to December 1997, 515 children under 2 died while sleeping with adults (Wright, 1999); 394 of these resulted from the baby becoming wedged between the mattress and the wall or headboard. The remaining 121 deaths occurred when an adult rolled over and smothered the child. The *American Academy of Pediatrics* recommends the following procedures.

- Place infants on their backs on a firm mattress that meets current safety standards.

- Remove all pillows, quilts, and comforters, and any soft toys from the crib.

- If using a blanket, tuck it around the mattress and be sure it reaches only to the baby's chest (Wright, 1999).

Respiratory Distress Syndrome

Respiratory distress syndrome (RDS) A problem common with premature babies that is caused by the lack of a substance called surfactant, which keeps the air sacs in the lungs open.

The last of the disorders to be discussed is **respiratory distress syndrome (RDS)** (also called hyaline membrane disease). Although this problem is most common with prematures, it may strike full-term infants whose lungs are particularly immature.

RDS is caused by the lack of a substance called *surfactant,* which keeps open the air sacs in the lungs. When surfactant is inadequate, the lung can collapse. Since most babies do not produce sufficient surfactant until the 35th prenatal week, you can see why it is a serious problem for premature infants. (Only 10 percent of a baby's lung tissue is developed at full-term birth.)

Full-term newborns whose mothers are diabetic seem especially vulnerable to RDS. Babies whose delivery has been particularly difficult also are more susceptible. The good news is that today 90 percent of these youngsters will survive and, given early detection and treatment, the outlook for them is excellent.

Field, T. (1990). *Infancy.* Cambridge, MA: Harvard University Press. A clear, simple, and carefully written account of infancy by a well-known commentator on these years.

Guided Review

1. About _____% of the brain develops outside of the womb.
2. A _____ is a behavior in which a repeated stimulus elicits the same response.
3. The _____ is a neonatal assessment technique that measures how an infant interacts with the environment.
4. Motor development occurs in a _____ and _____ direction.
5. The weight and height of _____ infants consistently remain below normal.

Perceptual Development

From what we've said so far, the current picture of an infant is that of an active, vibrant individual vigorously searching for stimuli. How do infants process these stimuli? Answering this question moves us into the perceptual world. We know now that babies not only receive stimuli, they interpret them. Perception begins our experience and interpretation of the world. It is also our basis for the growth of thought, the regulation of emotions, interactions in social relationships, and for

Answers

1. 75 2. reflex 3. Brazelton 4. cephalocaudal, proximodistal 5. FTT

progress in almost all aspects of development (Bornstein & Arterberry, 1999). Before attempting to chart perceptual development, let's explore the meaning of perception in more detail.

The Meaning of Perception

Infants acquire information about the world and constantly check the validity of that information. This process defines *perception:* getting and interpreting information from stimuli. Infants are particularly ingenious at obtaining information from the stimuli around them. They attend to objects according to the perceptual information the objects contain. As Bornstein (1995) noted, during infancy the capacity to take in information through the major sensory channels, to make sense of the environment, and to attribute meaning to information improves dramatically.

Seeking information leads to meaning. Objects roll, bounce, or squeak—in this way infants learn what objects are and what they do. In the first year of life, infants discern patterns, depth, orientation, location, movement, and color (Bornstein & Arterberry, 1999). During infancy, babies also discover what they can do with objects, which furthers their perceptual development. For example, Lewkowicz (1996) reported that when an investigator used both her voice and face as stimuli, 4-, 6-, and 8-month-old infants responded better to the combination of stimuli than to face or voice alone.

Remember: Infants are born ready to attend to changes in physical stimulation. Stimuli presented frequently cause a decrease in an infant's attention **(habituation).** If the stimuli are altered, the infant again attends, indicating awareness of the difference. For example, if you show an infant a picture (flower, birds, anything attractive), the child is first fascinated, then becomes bored; the child has habituated. If you now change the picture, you again capture the child's attention.

Infants, however, encounter a wide variety of objects, people, and events, all of which differ in many dimensions: color, size, shape. They must learn how to react to each, and how they react depends on many factors. For example, Clifton, Perris, and Bullinger (1991) found that when 6- and 7-month-old infants were in a dark setting and were presented with objects that made a sound, they reached accurately for the objects as long as they were within their reach. When the objects were out of reach, the infants were far less accurate. They thus perceive distance and direction and seem able to define their auditory space as long as an object is within reach of the body.

In a classic study, Brooks and Lewis (1976) studied how infants responded to four different types of strangers, a male and female child, a female adult, and a female

midget. In this way, facial configurations and height were varied. The infants reacted to the children by continuous looking and some smiling. They reacted to the midget with considerable puzzlement but no positive response such as smiling or movement toward her. They reacted to the adult by sporadic looking, averting their eyes, frowning, and even crying. Thus the infants used size and facial configuration cues.

We may conclude, then, that perception depends on both learning and maturation. An infant's perceptual system undergoes considerable development following birth, resulting from greater familiarity with objects and events in the world as well as from growth.

Habituation   A process in which stimuli that are presented frequently cause a decrease in an infant's attention.

Infants quickly begin to attend to the objects in their environments, thus constructing their views about how the world "works."

Visual Perception

Infants are born able to see and quickly exhibit a preference for patterns. Do infants prefer looking at some objects more than others? In a pioneering series of experiments, Robert Fantz provided dramatic documentation of an infant's perceptual ability. Fantz (1961) stated that the best indicator of an infant's visual ability is eye activity. Infants who consistently gaze at some forms more than others show perceptual discrimination; that is, something in one form holds their attention.

Using a "looking chamber" in which an infant lies in a crib at the bottom of the chamber and looks at objects placed on the ceiling, Fantz could determine the amount of time that infants fixated on different objects. In one of his experiments, Fantz tested pattern perception by using six objects, all flat discs 6 inches in diameter: face, bull's-eye, newsprint, red disc, yellow disc, and white disc. The face attracted the greatest attention (human faces are remarkably complex), followed by the newsprint, the bull's-eye, and then the three plain-colored discs (none of which received much attention). Infants, then, show definite preferences based on as much complexity as they can handle (Lewkowicz, 1996).

Visual Adaptation

Studying visual development spurs speculation about how growing visual skill helps infants to adjust to their environment. Gibson and Walk (1960), in their famous *visual cliff* experiment, reasoned that infants would use visual stimuli to discriminate both depth and distance.

The visual cliff is a board dividing a large sheet of heavy glass. A checkerboard pattern is attached flush to one half of the bottom of the glass, giving the impression of solidity. The investigators then placed a similar sheet on the floor under the other half, creating a sense of depth—the visual cliff.

Thirty-six infants from ages 6 to 14 months were tested. After the infant was placed on the center board, the mother called the child from the shallow side and then the cliff side. Twenty-seven of the youngsters moved onto the shallow side toward the mother. When called from the cliff side, only three infants ventured over the depth. The experiment suggests that infants discriminate depth when they begin crawling.

To conclude, we can state that by 2 to 4 months of age, infant perception is fairly sophisticated. Infants perceive figures as organized wholes; they react to the relationship among elements rather than single elements; they perceive color; and complex rather than simple patterns fascinate them. They scan the environment, pick up information, encode and process information. Why? Because they are well-equipped to hear, to orient to, to perceive, and to distinguish sounds (Bornstein & Arterberry, 1999).

A child's depth perception is tested on the visual cliff. The apparatus consists of a board laid across a sheet of heavy glass, with a patterned material directly beneath the glass on one side and several feet below it on the other.

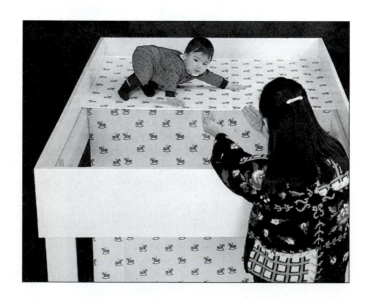

Auditory Perception

In chapter 4, we described how Anthony DeCasper's experiment illustrated how both a fetus and infant will recognize its mother's voice. Hearing and auditory discrimination is well-developed at birth since sounds are carried to the fetus through the amniotic fluid as a series of vibrations. Infants display a remarkable sensitivity to differences in the quality of sounds. For example, some babies may prefer music to other sounds and one type of music to another; they can discriminate their mothers' voices from those of other women. They also can locate where a sound comes from, and newborns will even turn their heads to the sound of a rattle or bell (Hetherington & Parke, 1999).

Although important in itself, this perceptual sensitivity underscores the importance of auditory perception in language development. For example, infants begin to differentiate the sounds of their language and tune into the speech they hear around them. By four months of age, infants can detect the match between heard and seen vowels, looking preferentially at a "talking head" producing the sounds (Werker & Tees, 1999). It's as if nature has determined that infants must immediately attend efficiently to the important information in the speech surrounding them.

Guided Review

6. The decrease in an infant's attention to stimuli presented frequently is called _____ .

7. Newborn infants show a preference for _____ .
8. A child's depth perception is tested on an apparatus called a _____ _____ .

9. Neonates require about _____ hours of sleep per day.
10. Perception depends on _____ and _____ .

Cognitive Development

How do infants develop an understanding of the world around them? Can infants really think? If they can, what is their thinking like? How do we explain the cognitive changes in the first two years of life? As you read this section, keep in mind the possible relationship between physical growth (especially the brain) and cognitive development. (For a further discussion of this topic, see Diamond, 2000.)

In their first year of life, infants seem to proceed through several stages. In the first month, they have no idea that objects are permanent—out of sight, out of mind. From 1 to 4 months, infants will continue to stare at the spot where an object disappeared and then turn their attention to something else. From 4 to 8 months, infants begin to show signs that an object still exists even if they can't see it; they'll look for a toy after they drop it; they love playing peek-a-boo. From 8 to 12 months, infants develop the notion of **object permanence** and will continue to hunt for a hidden object.

Recent studies indicate that object permanence is related to later cognitive development suggesting that roots of cognition lie in infancy. For example, Rose and his associates (1991) compared object permanence (among other cognitive indicators) in premature infants at 1 year with IQ measures at 5 years. They found a significant relationship between the two, suggesting developmental continuities in cognition.

Object permanence   Refers to children gradually realizing that there are permanent objects around them, even when these objects are out of sight.

Answers

To discover how infants develop such concepts as object permanence, we now turn to the work of the great Swiss scholar, Jean Piaget. You previously read about several of his important ideas in chapter 2; here we'll examine his interpretation of infancy in some detail.

Piaget's Sensorimotor Period

Egocentrism Child focuses on self in early phases of cognitive development; term associated with Piaget.

Piaget (1967) states that the period from birth to language acquisition is marked by extraordinary mental growth and influences the entire course of development. **Egocentrism** describes the initial world of children. Everything centers on them; they see the world only from their point of view. Very young children lack social orientation. They speak at and not to each other, and two children in conversation may be discussing utterly unrelated topics. (Likewise, egocentric adults know that other viewpoints exist, but they disregard them.) The egocentric child simply is unaware of any other viewpoint.

Sensorimotor period Piaget's term for the first of his cognitive stages of development (0 to 2 years).

The remarkable changes of the **sensorimotor period** (about the first two years of life) occur within a sequence of six stages. Most of Piaget's conclusions about these stages were derived from observation of his own three children. (Jacqueline, Lucianne, and Laurent have become as famous in psychological literature as some of Freud's cases or John Watson's Albert.)

Stage 1 During the first stage, children do little more than exercise the reflexes with which they were born. For example, Piaget (1952) stated that the sucking reflex is hereditary and functions from birth. At first infants suck anything that touches their lips; they suck when nothing touches their lips; then they actively search for the nipple. What we see here is the steady development of the coordination of arm, eye, hand, and mouth. Through these activities, the baby is building a foundation for forming cognitive structures. (For a more extended discussion of the antecedents of these behaviors, see Smotherman & Robinson, 1996.)

Primary circular reactions Infants repeat some act involving their bodies; term associated with Piaget's theory.

Stage 2 Piaget referred to stage 2 (from about 1 to 4 months) as the stage of first habits. During stage 2, **primary circular reactions** appear, in which infants repeat some act involving their bodies. For example, they continue to suck when nothing is present. They continue to open and close their hands. Infants seem to have no external goal, no intent in these actions other than the pleasure of self-exploration. But they are learning something about that primary object in their world: their own bodies.

Secondary circular reactions Infants direct their activities toward objects and events outside themselves.

Stage 3 **Secondary circular reactions** emerge during the third stage, which extends from about 4 to 8 months. During this stage, infants direct their activities toward objects and events outside themselves. Secondary circular reactions thus produce results in the environment, and not, as with the primary circular reactions, on the child's own body.

For example, Piaget's son, Laurent, continued to shake and kick his crib to produce movement and sound. He also discovered that pulling a chain attached to some balls produced an interesting noise, and he kept doing it. In this way, babies learn about the world "out there," and feed this information into their developing cognitive structures.

Coordination of secondary schemes Infants combine secondary schemes to obtain a goal.

Stage 4 From about 8 to 12 months of age, infants **coordinate secondary schemes** to form new kinds of behavior. Now more complete acts of intelligence are evident (Piaget & Inhelder, 1969).

The baby first decides on a goal (finding an object that is hidden behind a cushion). The infant attempts to move objects to reach the goal. In stage 4, part of the goal object must be visible behind the obstacle. Here we see the first signs of intentional behavior.

Tertiary circular reaction
Repetition with variation; the infant is exploring the world's possibilities.

When infants begin to move things to get what they want, they are "coordinating secondary schemata." This is a clear signal of advancing cognitive development.

Stage 5 **Tertiary circular reactions** appear from 12 to 18 months of age. In the tertiary circular reaction, repetition occurs again, but it is repetition with variation. The infant is exploring the world's possibilities. Piaget thought that the infant deliberately attempts to provoke new results instead of merely reproducing activities. Tertiary circular reactions indicate an interest in novelty for its own sake.

How many times have you seen a baby standing in a crib and dropping everything on the floor? But listen to Piaget: Watch how the baby drops things, from different locations and different heights. Does it sound the same when it hits the floor as the rug? Is it as loud dropped from here or higher? Each repetition is actually a chance to learn. Thanks to Piaget, you will be a lot more patient when you see this behavior.

Stage 6 During stage 6, the sensorimotor period ends and children develop a basic kind of *internal representation*. A good example is the behavior of Piaget's daughter, Jacqueline. At age 20 months, she approached a door that she wished to close, but she was carrying some grass in each hand. She put down the grass by the threshold, preparing to close the door. But then she stopped and looked at the grass and the door, realizing that if she closed the door the grass would blow away. She then moved the grass away from the door's movement and then closed it. She had obviously planned and thought carefully about the event before acting. Table 5.6 summarizes the accomplishments of the sensorimotor period.

Progress through the sensorimotor period leads to four major accomplishments:

- *Object permanence:* Children realize that permanent objects exist around them; something out of sight is not gone forever.

- *A sense of space:* Children realize environmental objects have a spatial relationship.

- *Causality:* Children realize a relationship exists between actions and their consequences.

- *Time sequences:* Children realize that one thing comes after another.

By the end of the sensorimotor period, children move from purely sensory and motor functioning (hence the name sensorimotor) to a more symbolic kind of activity.

TABLE 5.6 OUTSTANDING CHARACTERISTICS OF THE SENSORIMOTOR PERIOD

The Six Subdivisions of This Period

Stage 1: During the first month the child exercises the native reflexes, for example, the sucking reflex. Here is the origin of mental development, for states of awareness accompany the reflex mechanisms.

Stage 2: Piaget referred to stage 2 (from 1 to 4 months) as the stage of primary circular reactions. Infants repeat some act involving the body, for example, finger sucking. (Primary means first, circular reaction means repeating the act.)

Stage 3: From 4 to 8 months, secondary circular reactions appear; that is, the children repeat acts involving objects outside themselves. For example, infants continue to shake or kick the crib.

Stage 4: From 8 to 12 months, the child "coordinates secondary schemes." Recall the meaning of schema—behavior plus mental structure. During stage 4, infants combine several related schemata to achieve some objective. For example, they will remove an obstacle that blocks some desired object.

Stage 5: From 12 to 18 months, tertiary circular reactions appear. Now children repeat acts, but not only for repetition's sake; now they search for novelty. For example, children of this age continually drop things. Piaget interpreted such behavior as expressing their uncertainty about what will happen to the object when they release it.

Stage 6: At about 18 months or 2 years, a primitive type of representation appears. For example, one of Piaget's daughters wished to open a door but had grass in her hands. She put the grass on the floor and then moved it back from the door's movement so that it would not blow away.

From John F. Travers, *The Growing Child,* Scott, Foresman and Company, Glenview, IL, 1982. Reprinted by permission of the author.

As infants acquire the ability to form representations of objects, they begin to move through their environments more skillfully.

Criticisms of Piaget

Although Piaget has left a monumental legacy, his ideas have not been unchallenged. Piaget was a believer in the stage theory of development; that is, development is seen as a sequence of distinct stages, each of which entails important changes in the way a child thinks, feels, and behaves. However, the acquisition of cognitive structures may be gradual rather than abrupt and is not a matter of all or nothing; for example, a child is not completely in the sensorimotor or preoperational stage. A child's level of cognitive development seems to depend more on the nature of the task than on a rigid classification system.

In one of the first important challenges to Piaget, Gelman and Baillargeon (1983), changed the nature of the task as follows:

• by reducing the number of objects children must manipulate

• by allowing children to practice (e.g., teaching children conservation tasks)

• by using materials familiar to children

These researchers found that children can accomplish specific tasks at earlier ages than Piaget believed. Such criticisms have led to a more searching examination of the times during which children acquire certain cognitive abilities. For example, Piaget believed that infants will retrieve an object that is hidden from them in stage 4, from 8 to 12 months. Before this age, if a blanket is thrown over a toy that the infant is looking at, the child stops reaching for it as if it doesn't exist.

To trace the ages at which object permanence appears, Baillargeon (1987) devised an experiment in which infants between 3½ and 4½ months old were seated at a table where a cardboard screen could be moved back and forth, either forward (toward the baby) until it was flat on the table or backward (away from the baby) until the back of the cardboard touched the table.

Baillargeon then placed a painted wooden block behind the cardboard screen so that the infant could see the block when the screen was in a forward, flat position. But when the screen was moved backward, it came to rest on the block, removing it from the infant's sight. Occasionally Baillargeon secretly removed the block so that the screen continued backward until it rested flat on the table. The 4½-month-old infants looked surprised at the change (they looked at the screen longer); even some of the 3½-month-olds seemed to notice the "impossible" event. These findings suggest that infants may develop the object permanence concept earlier than Piaget originally thought.

Information Processing in Infancy

Piaget, as we have seen, argued forcefully that cognitive development proceeds by progression through discrete stages. Information processing theorists, however, argue just as strongly that cognitive development occurs by the gradual improvement of such cognitive processes as attention and memory.

An underlying assumption of information processing theory is that individuals are not passive recipients of stimuli. Rather, they are actively involved in their own development, which fits nicely with current interpretations of infancy. Consequently, any mental activity that involves noticing, taking in, mentally manipulating, storing, combining, retrieving, and acting on information describes information processing. Changes in these processes are the focus of developmental information processing theorists (Lutz & Sternberg, 1999).

To help you visualize how these processes work in information processing theory, consider Figure 5.2.

Now let's examine how infants "use" these processes.

Figure 5.2

An information processing model.

Infants and Attention

Infants attend to different stimuli for a variety of reasons: intensity, complexity of the stimuli, visual ability, and novelty. Consequently, they find human faces, voices, and movements particularly fascinating. Attending to and reacting to those around them occupies much of their time. They quickly become skilled at discriminating facial expressions and responding accordingly (Flavell, 1999). Yet we must introduce a note of caution here.

For example, how would you interpret this behavior? On a recent visit to a shopping mall with my wife, one of us (JFT) was sitting on a bench waiting for her to return. A young mother with three children—I would guess their ages to be about 8 years, 5 years, and 3 or 4 months—stopped at a nearby bench. The mother explained to the older children that she was going into the store for a few minutes to pick out a birthday card. She would be able to see them from the store and asked them to watch their baby sister whom they obviously loved.

When she left, the children began to do all sorts of things—smiling, patting, funny faces—to keep their sister's attention until finally the infant turned away for relief from such intense (for her) stimulation. Of course, this only spurred the boys to redouble their efforts and she then began to spit up. The baby simply could not handle the "stimulus overload."

What happened here? Think about what attention means for the developing infant.

- *Their attention becomes selective,* that is, people (especially infants) can't attend to everything.

- *Their attention involves cognitive processing,* that is, infants don't just passively accept stimuli—they actively process incoming information.

- *Their attention is limited,* that is, infants especially can attend only to a limited number of things at the same time (Flavell, 1999).

When we consider these limitations during the infancy years, we realize that babies simply lack the cognitive maturity—call it an adequate gate-keeping mechanism—that permits them to control all of the stimuli that assault them. A good rule of thumb to remember is that infants are drawn to stimuli of moderate intensity.

The adults around them must assume responsibility for monitoring the sights and sounds that their infants experience to shield them from too intense stimulation. Most mothers intuitively read their babies' signals and react appropriately, which reflects sensitive responsiveness to a child's needs. (See Brazelton & Nugent, 1995, for an analysis of an infant's ability to attend to and control stimuli.)

Infants and Memory

As infants progress through these first two years, behavior appears that can only be attributed to memory. (For an excellent discussion of current research into memory, see Kuhn, 2000; Samuelson & Smith, 2000.) The last half of the first year appears to be a time of rapid growth in memory ability (Schacter, 1996). To explain what's occurring, Siegler (1998) identified four sources of memory development.

- *Basic capacities* are present and functioning, such as association and recognition.

- *Strategies,* such as following with eyes, pointing, naming, and selective attention begin to emerge (Herbert & Hayne, 2000).

- *Content knowledge* grows steadily and aids memory.

Although infants have limited cognitive skills, they use these basic processes to form immediate memories.

Testing infant memory is difficult because infants can't tell us whether or what they remembered. Consequently, investigators have relied on experiments that measure the time that infants look at familiar and novel objects, which is referred to as *habituation/dishabituation procedures.* For example, Kail (1990) presented two groups of infants with a bull's-eye pattern and a set of stripes. One group saw the bull's-eye first and then the stripes; the other group had the procedure reversed: first the stripes and then the bull's-eye.

If both groups looked longer at the second presentation (the stripes for the first group and the bull's-eye for the second), it shows that they preferred the novel stimuli, thus giving evidence of infant memory. That is, they remembered the first and habituated and were then more interested in the novel stimulus. Research has shown that infants' rates of habituation and preferences for novelty are related to later measures of childhood IQ (Schneider & Bjorklund, 1998).

Newborns seem to recognize events they have heard or seen before (recall DeCasper's work that we mentioned in chapter 4). By 2 to 3 months, infants will remember an event for several days, perhaps as long as a week. Memory continues to improve as infants "economize," that is, rather than remembering specific events, they begin to integrate their experiences (Shields & Rovee-Collier, 1992). This helps to explain how they find hidden objects (such as in the object permanence experiments); they can now recall things and events (Kail, 1990). We may conclude that memory during infancy is highly specific to the conditions surrounding the original encoding and that the last items forgotten are the first to be retrieved (Hayne & Rovee-Collier, 1995).

Siegler, R. (1998). *Children's thinking.* (3d ed.). Upper Saddle River: Prentice Hall. An exellent, well-documented account of how children develop their thinking skills during infancy.

An Applied View   *Infantile Amnesia*

If memory seems to develop early in our lives, why do we have difficulty in remembering most of our experiences in infancy? You undoubtedly look with considerable skepticism at those individuals who claim to remember events from the first days of their lives. More common is a phenomenon called infantile amnesia, which refers to an inability to recall events from early in life. Infantile amnesia refers to our inability to remember much before the age of four. Memories much before the age of of six or seven years are rare (Schneider & Bjorklund, 1998; Schneider & Pressley, 1997).

How do we explain this phenomenon? The passage of time is an inadequate explanation, as is a psychoanalytic interpretation that we tend to repress infant sexual experiences. Recent explanations point to the gradual maturation of the brain's frontal lobes, which seems to be involved in memory. A second explanation relates to language development. For example, you and I try to remember the names of people and events, but infants do not encode such information verbally. As infants listen to and begin to

comprehend the stories they hear around them, they impose a logical construction upon them that they tend to remember.

Finally, there may be crucial differences in the way that infants encode information compared to older children and adults. That is, do infants encode information in a way that they can later retrieve? As Siegler (1998) notes, the world looks quite different from the perspective of a 12-month-old infant and a 19-year-old adult. The general knowledge we acquire as we mature helps us to encode information more precisely and clearly, thus making retrieval that much easier.

You can see that these three recent explanations are not mutually exclusive, but may interact with each other as our memory sharpens with time. For example, brain maturation is a must for healthy cognitive development; hearing others explain what's happening around them helps infants to encode information more meaningfully; improved encoding helps children to retrieve information more rapidly and accurately.

Guided Review

11. Piaget's first stage of cognitive development is known as the _____ period.
12. _____ describes a phase of child development in which children perceive the world only from their point of view.
13. _____ _____ is when a child realizes that an object out of sight is not gone forever.
14. A major assumption of information-processing theory is that children are not _____ recipients of stimuli.
15. Two important information processes of infancy are _____ and _____.

Language Development

A friend of one of us recently expressed amazement at the way his grandson was talking. "You know," he said, "it seems like only the other day that he was just making noises. But when I asked him today if we were still pals, he said, 'No, we're firefighters.' And he's not quite two." Here we see an excellent example of the tremendous growth of language during infancy.

The forerunners of language appear immediately after birth in infant gazes and vocal exchanges with those around them. With no formal learning and often exposed to dramatically faulty language models, children learn words, meanings, and how to combine them in a purposeful manner. To guide you through the complexity of language development, here are several transitions that help to explain children's amazing accomplishments (Bloom, 1998).

- The first transition occurs at the end of the first year and continues in the second year with the appearance of words and the acquisition of a basic vocabulary (McLaughlin, 1998).

- The second transition occurs when children change from saying only one word at a time to combining words into phrases and simple sentences about the end of the second year.

- The final transition occurs when children move beyond using simple sentences to express one idea to complex sentences expressing multiple ideas and the relations between them.

Acquiring Their Language

How does this uniquely human achievement occur? Students of language, attempting to explain the richness and complexity of children's language, are convinced that this feat is possible because of two accomplishments. First, *children learn the rules of their language,* which they then apply in a wide variety of situations. Second, by the end of the second year, *children begin to fast map;* that is, they learn to apply a label to an object without anyone telling them. Even when children don't understand a word, they acquire information about it from the surrounding context (Hulit & Howard, 1997).

The process of acquiring language goes on at a furious pace until, at about the age of 5 for most children, they have acquired the fundamentals of their language. By the time children enter elementary school, they are sophisticated language users. After that, it's a matter of expanding and refining language skills, a task that often defines success or failure. The speed of acquisition and the fact that it generally

Answers

11. sensorimotor 12. Egocentrism 13. Object permanence 14. passive 15. attention, memory

occurs, without overt instruction, for all children, regardless of great differences in a range of social and cultural factors, have led to the belief that there is some "innate" predisposition in the human infant to acquire language (Yule, 1996).

As an example of the world into which language development takes children, consider some of the intricacies of the English language that we, as adults, understand completely. Do you realize that you drive on a parkway and park on a driveway? Do you realize that you eat *ghoti* quite frequently? (*gh* as in tough, *o* as in women, *ti* as in nation—put them all together and you're eating fish.)

Since understanding how children acquire their language is a difficult task, we have decided to use the five stages of Roger Brown's seminal work (1973), coupled with recent research on grammar, meaning, and usage as a means of providing you with a usable framework for tracing language development usage (Bloom, 1998; Hulit & Howard, 1997; Tager-Flusberg, 1997). Brown was particularly interested in the development of grammar, which he measured by a technique called the *mean length of utterance (MLU)*. This simply refers to counting the morphemes (meaningful units of language) in each utterance and dividing by the number of utterances. A child who uses 215 morphemes in 100 utterances has a MLU of 2.15.

In Brown's Stage One (12 to 26 months, MLU of 1.0 to 2.0), children develop first words, begin to combine them, and use them as a form of conversation. Stage One opens when children produce thir first meaningful words and closes when they start to put words together. During the infancy years children progress from one word at the beginning of the stage to 200–300 words at the end of the stage, ask questions, use negatives, make demands, and use language to get things done (Hulit & Howard, 1997).

A Sociocultural View   *Context and Language*

The Russian psychologist, Lev Vygotsky, whose ideas we discussed in chapter 2, proposed a contextual view of language development that attracted considerable attention. Vygotsky (1978) believed that *speech* is one of the most powerful tools humans use to progress developmentally. Speech, especially *inner speech,* plays a critical role in Vygotsky's interpretation of cognitive development. In *Thought and Language* (1962), he clearly presented his views about the four stages of language development.

1. The first stage, which he called *preintellectual speech,* refers to such elementary processes as crying, cooing, babbling, and bodily movements that gradually develop into more sophisticated forms of speech and behavior. Although human beings have an inborn ability to develop language, we must then interact with the environment if language development is to fulfill its potential. Michael Cole (1996) employs a garden metaphor to help explain these issues: Think of a seed planted in damp earth in a jar and then placed in a shed for two weeks. The seed sprouts, a stem emerges, and then leaves appear. But for further development the plant must now interact with sunlight.

2. Vygotsky referred to the second stage of language development as "naive psychology," in which children explore the concrete objects in their world. At this stage, children begin to label the objects around them and acquire the grammar of their speech.

3. At about 3 years of age *egocentric speech* emerges, that form of speech in which children carry on lively conversations, whether anyone is present or listening to them.

4. Finally, speech turns inward (inner speech) and serves an important function in guiding and planning behavior.

For example, think of a 5-year-old girl asked to get a book from a library shelf. The book is just out of her reach, and as she tries to reach it, she mutters to herself, "Need a chair." After dragging a chair over, she climbs up and reaches for the book. "Is that the one?" "Just a little more." "OK." Note how speech accompanies her physical movements, guiding her behavior. In two or three years, the same girl, asked to do the same thing, will probably act the same way, with one major exception: she won't be talking aloud. Vygotsky believed she would be talking to herself, using inner speech to guide her behavior, and for difficult tasks she undoubtedly would use inner speech *to plan her behavior.*

In many cases, children who aren't permitted these vocalizations *can't accomplish the task!* In fact, the more complex the task, the greater the need for egocentric speech. Note how Vygotsky and Piaget disagreed about the function of egocentric speech: Piaget believed it simply vanishes; Vygosky believed it's an important transitional stage in the formation of inner speech.

With this brief background, let's turn our attention to what we know about language development. All children learn their native language at about the same time and in a similar manner. During the infancy period, children at about 3 months use sounds in a similar manner to adults and at about 1 year they begin to use recognizable words. The specific sequence of language development during infancy appears in table 5.7.

Key Signs of Language Development

In the first year, babies continue to learn the sounds of their language (Sansavini, Bertoncini, & Giovanelli, 1997). Here's a question for you to think about: Since the fetus responds to sound (as we've seen), do you think it's possible that language acquisition begins *before* birth?

Let us help you out here. Remember: When a newborn baby is presented with something new, its heart rate slows. Researchers asked several pregnant women to repeat the sentences *Hello, baby. How are you today?* while they rested. Each time the mother asked the question, the fetal heart rate slowed (Golinkoff & Hirsh-Pasek, 2000). It seems indeed that fetuses listen to their mothers' voices.

During the first two months, babies seem to develop sounds that are associated with breathing, feeding, and crying. **Cooing** (sounds like vowels) appears during the second month (McLaughlin, 1998). Between five and seven months, babies play with the sounds they can make, and this output begins to take on the sounds of consonants and syllables, the beginning of **babbling.** Babbling probably appears initially because of biological maturation. At seven and eight months, sounds like syllables appear—da-da-da, ba-ba-ba (a phenomenon occurring in all languages), a pattern that continues for the remainder of the first year (Pinker, 1994).

Cooing Early language sounds that resemble vowels.

Babbling Infant produces sounds approximating speech between 5 and 6 months.

Babbling, producing vowel and consonant sounds, encourages parents to interact verbally with their children.

TABLE 5.7 LANGUAGE DEVELOPMENT DURING INFANCY	
Language	**Age**
Crying	From birth
Cooing	2–5 months
Babbling	5–7 months
Single words	12 months
Two words	18 months
Phrases	2 years

Vocables Consistent sound patterns to refer to objects and events.

Phonology The sounds of a language.

Semantics The meaning of words.

Syntax Rules for constructing sentences.

Pragmatics Rules for taking part in a conversation.

Language explosion Rapid acquisition of words beginning at 18 months.

Holophrastic speech The use of one word to communicate many meanings and ideas.

Holophrase Children's first words that usually carry multiple meanings.

Telegraphic speech Initial multiple-word utterances, usually two or three words.

Late in the babbling period, children use consistent sound patterns to refer to objects and events. These are called **vocables** and suggest children's discovery that meaning is associated with sound. For example, a lingering "L" sound may mean that someone is at the door. The use of vocables is a possible link between babbling and the first intelligible words.

First Words

Around their first birthday, babies produce single words, about half of which are for objects (food, clothing, toys). Throughout the world children's first words express similar menings. These words refer to people, animals, toys, vehicles, and other objects that fascinate children (Siegler, 1998). Children quickly learn the sounds of their language **(phonology),** the meanings of words **(semantics),** how to construct sentences **(syntax),** and how to communicate **(pragmatics)** (Gleason, 1997).

At eighteen months, children acquire words at the rate of 40 new words per week (Woodward & Markman, 1998). This rapid increase in vocabulary lasts until about 3 years of age and is frequently referred to as the **language explosion.** Vocabulary constantly expands, but estimating the extent of a child's vocabulary is difficult because youngsters know more words than they articulate.

Estimates are that a 1-year-old child may use from two to six words, and a 2-year-old has a vocabulary ranging from 50 to 250 words. Children at this stage also begin to combine two words (Pinker, 1994). By first grade, children may understand 10,000 words, and by fifth grade they understand about 40,000 words (Woodward & Markman, 1998).

Holophrases If you have the opportunity, listen to a child's speech when single words begin to appear. You will notice a subtle change before the two-word stage. *Children begin to use one word to convey multiple meanings.* For example, youngsters say "ball" meaning "give me the ball," "throw the ball," or "watch the ball roll." They have now gone far beyond merely labeling this round object as a ball. Often called **holophrastic speech** (one word to communicate many meanings and ideas), it is difficult to analyze. These first words, or **holophrases,** are usually nouns, adjectives, or self-inventive words and often contain multiple meanings. As mentioned previously, "ball" may mean not only the ball itself but "throw the ball to me."

When the two-word stage appears (anytime from 18 to 24 months), children initially struggle to convey tense (past and present) and number (singular and plural). They also experience difficulty with grammatical correctness. Children usually employ word order ("me go") for meaning, only gradually mastering inflections (plurals, tenses, possessives) as they begin to form three-word sentences. They use nouns and verbs initially and their sentences demonstrate grammatical structure. (Although the nouns, verbs, and adjectives of children's sentences differ from those of adults, the same organizational principles are present.)

Children begin to use multiple words to refer to the things that they previously named with single words. Rather than learning rules of word combination to express new ideas, children learn to use new word forms. Later, combining words in phrases and sentences suggests that children are learning the structure of their language.

Telegraphic Speech At about 18 to 24 months of age children's vocabularies begin to expand rapidly, and simple two-word sentences appear. Children primarily use nouns and verbs (not adverbs, conjunctions, or prepositions), and their sentences demonstrate grammatical structure. These initial multiple-word utterances (usually two or three words: "mommy milk"—give me the milk) are called **telegraphic speech.** Telegraphic speech contains considerably more meaning than superficially appears in the two or three words.

Word order and inflection (changing word form: e.g., "word"/"words") now become increasingly important. During the first stages of language acquisition, word order is paramount. At first, children combine words without concern for inflections, and it is word order that provides clues as to their level of syntactic (grammatical) development. Once two-word sentences are used, inflection soon appears, usually with three-word sentences. The appearance of inflections seems to follow a pattern: first the plural of nouns, then tense and person of verbs, and then possessives.

A youngster's effort to inject grammatical order into language is a good sign of normal language development. Several things, however, signal delay or difficulty in language acquisition. When children begin to babble beyond one year, problems may be present. For example, deaf children continue to babble past the age when other children begin to use words (Cole & Cole, 1996).

As we complete this initial phase of examining infant development, remember that all phases of development come together in an integrated manner. Motor development is involved when a child moves excitedly toward its mother on her return. Language development is involved when infants intensify their relationships with their mothers by words that are now directed toward her. Cognitive development is probably less obvious but just as significant: Children are excited by their mothers' return because they remember their mothers. Consequently, a sound principle of development remains—all development is integrated. Table 5.8 summarizes several of the developmental highlights we have discussed in this chapter.

Pinker, S. (1994). *The language instinct.* New York: Morrow. You would enjoy this fascinating, well-written account of the nature of language and how humans acquire their language.

Guided Review

16. _____ is sounds that approximate speech.
17. One word used to communicate many meanings is called _____ speech.
18. Vygotsky's work reflects a _____ view of language development.
19. A good sign of normal language development is a child's attempt to build _____ order into language.
20. For Vygotsky, _____ _____ plays a key role in cognitive development.

TABLE 5.8   DEVELOPMENTAL CHARACTERISTICS OF INFANCY

Age (Months)	Height (in.)	Weight (lbs.)	Language Development	Motor Development	Cognitive (Piaget)
3	24	13–14	Cooing	Supports head in prone position	Primary circular reactions
6	26	17–18	Babbling—single syllable sounds	Sits erect when supported	Secondary circular reactions
9	26	20–22	Repetition of sounds signals emotions	Stands with support	Coordinates secondary schemata
12	29.5	22–24	Single words—mama, dada	Walks when held by hand	Same
18	32	25–26	3–50 words	Grasps objects accurately, walks steadily	Tertiary circular reaction
24	34	27–29	50–250 words, 2–3 word sentences	Walks and runs up and down stairs	Representation

Answers

CONCLUSION & SUMMARY

Our view of an infant today is of an individual of enormous potential, one whose activity and competence are much greater than originally suspected. It is as if a newborn enters the world with all its systems ready to function and eager for growth. What happens during these first two years has important implications for future development. Setbacks—both physical and psychological—will occur, but they need not cause permanent damage. From your reading in chapter 1, you realize that human infants show remarkable resiliency.

What are the major physical accomplishments of the infancy period?

- Newborns display clear signs of their competence: movement, seeing, hearing, interacting.
- Infants' physical and motor abilities influence all aspects of development.
- Techniques to assess infant competence and well-being are widely used today.
- Motor development follows a well-documented schedule.
- Infants can develop problems such as SIDS and FTT for a variety of reasons.

How do infants acquire information about their world?

- Infants are born with the ability to detect changes in their environment.
- Infants are capable of acquiring and interpreting information from their immediate surroundings.
- Infants from birth show preferences for certain types of stimuli.

What are the differences between Piaget's view of cognitive development in infancy and that of information processing?

- Infants, even at this early age, are attempting to answer questions about their world, questions that will continue to occupy them in more complex and sophisticated forms throughout their lives.
- One of the first tasks that infants must master is an understanding of the objects around them.
- Piaget's theory of cognitive development has shed considerable light on the ways that children grow mentally.
- A key element in understanding an infant's cognitive development is the role of memory.

How do infants acquire their language?

- Infants show rapid growth in their language development.
- Language acquisition follows a definite sequence.
- Language behaviors in infancy range from crying to the use of words and phrases.

KEY TERMS

Apgar
Apnea
Babbling
Brazelton Neonatal Behavioral Assessment Scale
Cooing
Coordination of secondary schemes
Crawling
Creeping
Egocentrism
Failure to thrive (FTT)

Habituation
Holophrases
Holophrastic speech
Language explosion
Neonate
Neurological assessment
Object permanence
Phonology
Pragmatics
Primary circular reactions
Reflex

Respiratory distress syndrome (RDS)
Secondary circular reactions
Semantics
Sensorimotor period
Sudden infant death syndrome (SIDS)
Syntax
Telegraphic speech
Tertiary circular reactions
Variable accommodation
Vocables

WHAT DO YOU THINK?

1. The shift from considering an infant as nothing more than a passive sponge to seeing infants as amazingly competent carries with it certain responsibilities. We can't be overly optimistic about a baby's abilities. Why? What are some of the more common dangers of this viewpoint?

2. Testing infants has grown in popularity these past years. You should consider some cautions, however. Remembering what you have read about infants in this chapter, mention several facts you would be careful about.

3. You have been asked to babysit your sister's 14-month-old baby. When you arrive, the mother is upset because she has been repeatedly picking up things that the baby has thrown out of the crib. With your new knowledge, you calm her down by explaining the baby's behavior. What do you tell her?

4. After reviewing the infancy work, what do you think about this period as "preparation for the future"? Select one phase of development (e.g., cognitive development) and show how a stimulating environment can help to lay the foundation for future cognitive growth.

CHAPTER REVIEW TEST

1. Which of the following is not a reflex?
   a. Breathing
   b. Sucking
   c. Swallowing
   d. Laughing

2. A _____ reflex is elicited by gently touching the infant's cheek.
   a. Moro
   b. rooting
   c. Babkin
   d. Babinski

3. _____ are brief periods when an infant stops breathing.
   a. Apnea
   b. Rooting
   c. Babbling
   d. Primary circular reactions

4. Depth perception in infants appears at
   a. birth.
   b. 7 to 10 days.
   c. 2 to 4 months.
   d. 4 to 5 months.

5. The Brazelton test assesses an infant's
   a. interaction with the environment.
   b. respiratory effort.
   c. reflex irritability.
   d. hearing.

6. Neurological assessment is not used for which of the following purposes?
   a. Identification of a neurological problem
   b. Treatment of a neurological problem
   c. Monitoring a neurological problem
   d. Prognosis about a neurological problem

7. The final area of the brain to develop is the
   a. sensory region.
   b. motor area.
   c. visual area.
   d. auditory area.

8. _____ is a disorder caused by the lack of a substance called surfactant.
   a. SIDS
   b. RDS
   c. AIDS
   d. FTT

9. When infants demonstrate a decrease in attention, this is called
   a. repression.
   b. habituation.
   c. egocentrism.
   d. permanence.

10. The Brazelton test is a type of
    a. survival assessment.
    b. motor assessment.
    c. play assessment.
    d. behavioral assessment.

11. Infants from _____ show preferences for certain types of stimuli.
    a. birth
    b. 10 days
    c. two months
    d. six months

12. An infant's search for novelty during the sensorimotor period is seen in
    a. object permanence.
    b. secondary circular reactions.
    c. coordination of secondary schemes.
    d. tertiary circular reactions.

13. Infants initially show memory ability during
    a. the first and second weeks.
    b. the first three months.
    c. third to sixth month.
    d. sixth to 12th month.

14. In the development of language, children about 1 year of age begin to use recognizable
    a. vocables.
    b. holophrases.
    c. phrases.
    d. sentences.

15. According to Piaget, the acquisition of language in children depends on
    a. cognitive structures.
    b. biology.
    c. reinforcement.
    d. language acquisition devices.

16. By _____ months a child begins to run.
    a. 9
    b 12
    c. 24
    d. 18

17. Which of the following is not a major accomplishment of the sensorimotor period?
    a. Reversibility
    b. Sense of space
    c. Causality
    d. Time sequence

18. _____ argue that cognitive development occurs by the gradual improvement of such cognitive processes as attention and memory.
    a. Psychoanalysts
    b. Behaviorists
    c. Humanists
    d. Information processing theorists

19. A 2-year-old child may have a vocabulary of as many as _____ words.
    a. 250
    b. 500
    c. 1,000
    d. 2,000

20. _____ believed the roots of language and thought were separate and only become linked through development.
    a. Chomsky
    b. Lenneberg
    c. Vygotsky
    d. Piaget

Answers

1. d, 2. b, 3. a, 4. d, 5. a, 6. b, 7. c, 8. b, 9. b, 10. d, 11. a, 12. d, 13. d, 14. a, 15. c, 16. d, 17. a, 18. d, 19. a, 20. c

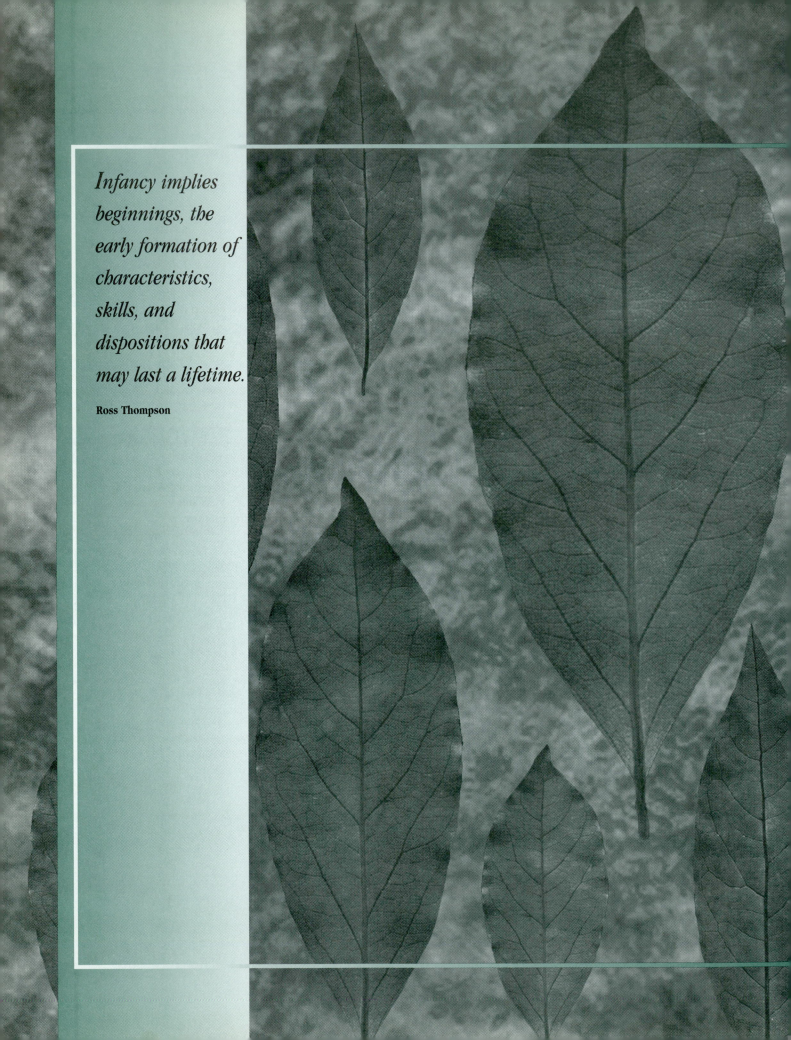

Infancy implies beginnings, the early formation of characteristics, skills, and dispositions that may last a lifetime.

Ross Thompson

CHAPTER 6

Chapter Outline

The reciprocal interactions between parents and their children are at the heart of the attachment process.

anice watched with exasperation as her 1-year-old son, Joseph, sat crying. Her friend Laura had dropped in for a cup of coffee and had started to play with Joseph when he began to cry and pull away from her. Janice had noticed this happening often lately and was concerned that something was bothering him. She could tell that her friend, who had no children, was hurt; Janice wondered whether the problem was serious enough to call her doctor for advice. Joseph looked fine and seemed to show no symptoms of any illness, which made her hesitate.

Later that day, after her friend had left and Joseph was taking his nap, Janice thought about his behavior. If he wasn't sick, what was the problem? She was concerned that he might be so shy that he could have difficulty with relationships and in making friends. She was also bothered that she could be doing something wrong. Joseph was a first child; could she be keeping him too close to her and perhaps subconsciously resisting any contacts he might have with others?

Janice decided to take Joseph shopping the following day and visit the local bookstore. The next morning Joseph was bright and cheerful and kept himself busy with a toy while Janice browsed through the books in the child-care section of the bookstore. At first she turned to those books that dealt with specific problems, but she didn't know what to look for, so she turned to more general discussions of child rearing. Still not satisfied, she was about ready to give up when she came across a book that described the milestones that occur during infancy.

Sure enough, there it was. "Beginning in the second half of the first year, infants start to show anxiety in the presence of strangers. This behavior is probably the first clue you will notice that tells you attachment is developing." Janice read the words again, relieved and delighted; Joseph was perfectly normal. Now, however, she was determined to learn more about attachment. ✪

In showing his fear of strangers, Joseph was demonstrating perfectly normal behavior. His intense relationship with his mother is an example of what's called attachment. Typically attachment is between children and mothers although it may be between children and someone else who is important to them, such as their father, grandmother, or aunt. Using these interactions with their mothers as a blueprint for future relationships, children like Joseph predict what to expect from others, which then shapes the path of their social development.

In one of the schools I visit, a first-grader's grandmother affectionately meets her grandson every afternoon after school. Tony's mother is in drug counseling and his grandmother is caring for him.

Beginning at about six months of age, infants show signs of distress when approached by a stranger.

Watching them walk down the street one afternoon, with Tony excitedly telling his grandmother all that happened that day, I was struck by the obvious attachment of this little boy to his grandmother.

Children learn what to expect from others because, as we have seen, their rapid brain and cognitive development enables them to take in and interpret information, and some of this information is about how others, especially parents, treat them. Although they may not grasp everything that's going on around them, children understand the quality of their treatment: caring/cold, loving/hostile. *These initial relationships, then, are the foundation for a child's social development.*

These are the years that Erikson believed resulted in a sense of trust or mistrust. On the one hand, infants develop the feeling that the world is a safe and secure haven or a place where a sense of confidence is never acquired, producing uncertainty about self and others.

To help us untangle this important network, we'll first discuss the meaning and importance of relationships (such as the active role that infants play in their own development). Next, we'll explore a special relationship—attachment—that has attracted so much attention these past few years. We'll then examine how the temperaments of children and their parents structure the kind of relationships they form. Finally, we'll see how these forces interact to affect emotional development. Let's begin by looking at several basic ideas about relationships.

Chapter Objectives

After reading this chapter, you should be able to answer the following questions.

◆ What is the role of relationships in psychosocial development?

◆ How would you assess the importance of attachment in psychosocial development?

◆ How does temperament affect the relationship between parents and their children?

◆ How do children develop and control their emotions?

The Meaning of Relationships

Think of a relationship as *a pattern of intermittent interactions between two people involving interchanges over an extended period of time* (Hinde, 1993). A child's relationships incorporate many aspects of development: physical aspects such as walking, running, and playing with a peer; *language aspects,* which enable youngsters to share their lives; *cognitive aspects,* which allow them to understand one another; *emotional aspects,* which permit them to make a commitment to another; and *social aspects,* which reflect both socialization and individuation. In other words, a relationship is a superb example of the influence of biopsychosocial interactions.

Infants are ready to respond to social stimulation, but it's not just a matter of responding passively. Infants in their own way initiate social contacts. Many of their actions (such as turning toward their mothers or gesturing in their direction) are forms of communication. Hinde (1993), too, noted that the interchange between infants and their environments is an active one. Those around infants try to attract their attention, but the babies actively select from these adult actions. In other words, infants begin to structure their own relationships according to their individual temperaments.

They do this within the family context. The interactions occurring among the other family members—parent-parent, parent-other children, sibling-sibling—produce a ripple effect that colors the parent-child relationship. Marital conflict, for example, inevitably spills over into the relationship between parents and their children and may produce unexpected results such as physical illness or tension in the child (Caspi, 1998). Consequently, the nature of the relationship between parents and their children emerges from the temperament of each, and the interactions that occur (Rubin, Bukowski, & Parker, 1998).

We can usually label relationships, using adjectives such as warm, cold, rejecting, and hostile. But we must be cautious. Any relationship may be marked by apparently contradictory interactions. A mother may have a warm relationship with her child as evidenced by hugging and kissing, but she may also scold when scolding is needed for the child's protection. *To understand the relationship, we must understand the interactions.*

For most people, relationships with other people are the most important part of their lives.
Robert Hinde

How Do Children Develop Relationships?

Infants quickly focus on their mothers as they recognize them as sources of relief and satisfaction. Mothers, in turn, rapidly discriminate their infants' cries: for hunger, attention, or fright. Thus infants learn to direct their attention to their mothers and a pattern of interactions is established. How do we explain this development? Three motives seem to be at work:

- *Bodily needs*—food, for example—lead to a series of interactions that soon become a need for social interaction.

- *Psychological needs* can cause infants to interrupt one of their most important functions, such as feeding. Children, from birth, seem to seek novelty; they require increasingly challenging stimulation. For infants, adults become the source of information as much as the source of bodily need satisfaction.

- *Adult response needs*. Adults satisfy needs, provide stimulation, and initiate communication, thus establishing the basis for future social interactions.

How do these three influences—at work during the infant's early days—affect the development of relationships?

The Developmental Sequence
Bodily need satisfaction, a search for novelty, and adult responses to the infant's overtures form a basis for the appearance of social interactions similar to the following sequence.

- *During the first three weeks* of life, infants are not affected much by an adult's appearance. The only exception, as noted, is during feeding periods.

- *From about the beginning of the fourth week,* infants begin to direct actions toward adults. Emotional reactions also appear at this time, with obvious signs of pleasure at the sight and sound of adults, especially females.

- *During the second month,* more complex and sensitive reactions emerge, such as smiling and vocalizations directed at the mother, plus animated behavior during interactions.

- *By 3 months of age,* the infant has formed a need for social interactions. That need continues to grow and be nourished by adults until the end of the second or beginning of the third year, when a need for peer interactions develops (Hinde, 1992).

Synchrony The ability of parents to adjust their behavior to that of an infant.

Symmetry An infant's capacity for attention; style of responding influences interactions.

Entrainment Term used to describe the rhythm that is established between a parent's and an infant's behavior.

Autonomy Infants realize that they have a share in controlling their interactions with others.

Infants immediately begin to take in information from their environment, and mothers are an important source of this information. From mothers, infants begin to develop a sense of how the world will treat them.

Brazelton, T.B. & B. Cramer. (1990). You should enjoy reading *The earliest relationship.* (Reading, MA: Addison-Wesley), an excellent, readable account of how relationships develop, presented from both a pediatric and psychoanalytic perspective.

Reciprocal interaction Interactions that result in mutual changes.

1. Characteristics of the Developing Relationship

As these early interactions commence, several characteristics begin to identify the emergence of a successful relationship (Brazelton & Cramer, 1990). The first of these is **synchrony,** which refers to the ability of parents to adjust their behavior to that of an infant. Immediately after birth, infants are mostly occupied by their efforts to regulate such systems as breathing and heart rate, which demands most of their energy and attention. Once parents recognize these efforts—the baby's "language" (Brazelton & Cramer, 1990)—they can use their own behavior—talking softly, stroking—to help their infants adapt to environmental stimuli. This mutual regulation of behavior defines synchrony.

Another characteristic is **symmetry,** which means that an infant's capacity for attention and style of responding influence any interactions. In other words, how children interact with their parents reflects their temperaments. As Brazelton and Cramer (1990, p. 122) note, in a symmetric dialogue parents recognize an infant's thresholds, that is, what and how much stimuli an infant can tolerate.

Other characteristics include **entrainment,** a characteristic that identifies the rhythm that is established between a parent's and infant's behavior. For example, when the infant reaches toward the mother, the mother says something like, "Oh, yes, Timmy." The sequence involved in entrainment leads to playing games such as the mother making a face at the baby and the infant trying to respond similarly. Once infants realize that they have a share in controlling the interactions (about 6 months of age), they begin to develop a sense of **autonomy.** With these interactions, infants are beginning to form relationships and learn about themselves.

Guided Review

1. A relationship is a pattern of intermittent _____.
2. Infants quickly begin to _____ their relatonships.
3. _____ _____ is an important influence on developing relationships.
4. The nature of a relationship emerges from the _____ of the partners.
5. A relationship is an excellent example of _____ interactions.

2. The Role of Reciprocal Interactions

We realize today that children are not born as passive sponges; they immediately seek stimulation from their environment and *instantly interpret, and react to, how they are being treated,* a process called **reciprocal interactions.** Think of it this way: You react to me in a particular manner and I change. As a result of the changes that occur in me, you change. Back-and-forth, on-and-on it goes, constantly changing the relationship. Consequently, we can now examine an infant's psychosocial development from a totally new and exciting perspective. Not only do infants attempt to make sense of their world as they develop cognitively, they also "tune into" the social and emotional atmosphere surrounding them and immediately begin to shape their relationships with others.

Thinking about the type of interactions parents have with their children helps you to appreciate how the relationship has developed. For example, consider the kinds of things parents do with their children and the way they do them—all involving interactions. They play. They discipline. They explain. They provide correction and feedback. They answer questions. In other words, they're exercising their parental role in all of these interactions with their children. Analyzing these interactions helps you to realize that parents change as a result of their child's behavior

Answers

1. interactions 2. structure 3. Family context 4. characteristics 5. biopsychosocial

Parents' own experiences and their expectations of their children's behavior help to shape the relationships they develop with their children.

and their children change in turn because of their parents' reactions. These *reciprocal interactions* demonstrate continuity over time and are a powerful force in the development of relationships (Freitag & others, 1996).

But infants also exercise some control over the interactions. We, as adults, respond to infants partly because of the way that they respond to us. An infant's staring, cooing, smiling, and kicking can all be employed to maintain the interactions. Thus these early interactions establish the nature of the relationship between parent and child, giving it a particular tone or style.

To understand the developing relationship between parents and infants remember that infants "tune into" their environment from birth. Thus they react to far more than their parents' behavior: They react to the way their parents handle them, the tone of voice a parent uses, and the playful nature of interactions. Consequently, the quality of the interactions instantly begins to establish the nature of the relationship (Hart & others, 1997).

Parental Roles: Expectations for a Relationship

Finally, parents bring basic preconceived ideas about the role they should play in their relationships with their children. Technically, *role* usually refers to behavior, or certain expectancies about behavior, associated with a particular position in society. Mothers and fathers have certain expectations about how parents should act. *How they exercise that power and how their children react to their suggestions and encouragements, their demands and commands ultimately determine the success of the relationship.* In an ideal world, their ideas, their expectations, and their sense of their role as a parent should mesh perfectly with their child's personality and abilities.

Ghosts in the Nursery

Let's pause for a moment and consider one source of their expectations about their parental role. Selma Fraiberg, a well-known child psychiatrist, has referred to the presence of *ghosts in the nursery,* which can have many consequences (1987). Do parents feel their own parents looking over their shoulder, telling them how to

Different Cultures, Different Interactions

From birth children are exposed to and shaped by the culture surrounding them. Their cultural context includes everything from sleeping arrangements and feeding practices to the child's value systems, school experiences, and interpersonal interactions. In a multicultural society, children are influenced by both their *home* culture and *societal* culture (Greenfield & Suzuki, 1998).

Parents from a particular culture share a common system of beliefs, values, practices, and behaviors that differ from those of parents in other cultures. But those from different cultural backgrounds differ in their views of infant competence, how to respond to crying, and what developmental skills are most significant (Coll, 1990). Consequently, infants are subject to different parental behaviors that are shaped by a particular culture.

These different parental practices commence immediately following birth. For example, sleep patterns in the United States are directed at a typical day-night cycle, that is, there is pressure to sleep through the night as soon as possible. For rural Kenyan infants, on the other hand, the

idea of getting on a schedule is quite different. They sleep with their mothers and nurse on demand. At one month their longest sleep period is about three hours, which increases very little for the first eight months. This simple example illustrates how children are shaped by cultural practices (Coll, 1999).

But merely identifying specific differences in raising children in different cultures limits our perspective on development. As Garcia Coll and others (1996) have noted, to understand the development of children demands knowledge of how such variables as racism, prejudice, discrimination, and other sources of oppression influence developmental outcomes.

In addition, studies of children of color need to move from conceptualizing developmental outcome as either negative or positive to a more balanced conceptualization that reflects both the strengths and weaknesses in developmental processes and competencies of these children (Coll & others, 1996, p. 1895).

bring up their child, ideas that they may well have rejected or even rebelled against? Does their child remind them of someone from their past, and they begin to react as they did to that other person? Do they tend to imitate a friend whom they admire? Or have they been impressed by the ideas of some "expert" they have read about or have seen on television?

When parents are aware that ghosts from their past may influence them, they are able to overcome these relics and move on to positive relations with their children. Examining mother-grandmother relationships, Wakschlag, Chase-Lansdale, and Brooks-Gunn (1996) found that the quality of the existing mother-grandmother relationship is indeed related to parenting of the next generation. When the mother-grandmother relationship is open, flexible, and autonomous, the mothers demonstrated these qualities in their own parenting. Their findings also suggest that when the relationship between a mother and child is negative, *any intervention should include the grandmother.*

Figure 6.1 illustrates the sequence by which the first interactions, combined with developmental changes, gradually lead to specific relationships.

As the interactions between mother and child increase and become more complex, let's now examine the attachment that develops between the two.

Figure 6.1

The origin and development of relationships.

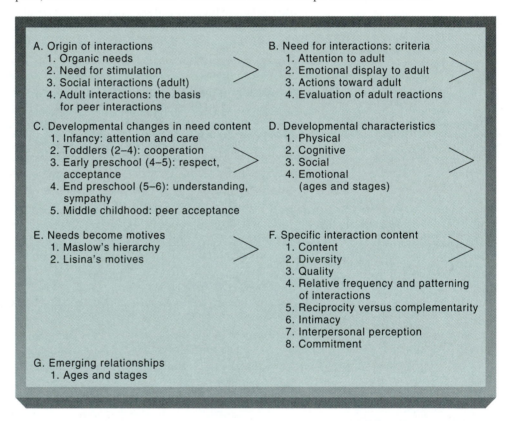

A. Origin of interactions
1. Organic needs
2. Need for stimulation
3. Social interactions (adult)
4. Adult interactions: the basis for peer interactions

B. Need for interactions: criteria
1. Attention to adult
2. Emotional display to adult
3. Actions toward adult
4. Evaluation of adult reactions

C. Developmental changes in need content
1. Infancy: attention and care
2. Toddlers (2–4): cooperation
3. Early preschool (4–5): respect, acceptance
4. End preschool (5–6): understanding, sympathy
5. Middle childhood: peer acceptance

D. Developmental characteristics
1. Physical
2. Cognitive
3. Social
4. Emotional
(ages and stages)

E. Needs become motives
1. Maslow's hierarchy
2. Lisina's motives

F. Specific interaction content
1. Content
2. Diversity
3. Quality
4. Relative frequency and patterning of interactions
5. Reciprocity versus complementarity
6. Intimacy
7. Interpersonal perception
8. Commitment

G. Emerging relationships
1. Ages and stages

Guided Review

6. Infants' interactions with their mothers are motivated by three categories of needs: _____, _____, _____.
7. _____ is the ability of parents to adjust their behavior to that of an infant.
8. The need for social interactions appears at about _____ months of age.
9. Infants' capacity for attention and style of responding that influences their interactions is called _____.
10. The rhythm that develops between a parent's and infant's behavior is called _____.

Answers

6. bodily, psychological, adult response 7. Synchrony 8. three 9. symmetry 10. entrainment

Attachment

Because the roots of future relationships are formed during the first days of life, we may well ask: How significant is the mother-infant relationship in those first days and weeks after birth? Infants who develop a secure attachment to their mothers have the willingness and confidence to seek out future relationships (Waters, Hamilton, & Weinfield, 2000). We know that infants learn what to expect from others because of these early relationships (Thompson, 1998).

Among the first researchers to recognize the significance of relationships in an infant's life were John Bowlby and Mary Salter Ainsworth.

3. Bowlby's Work

John Bowlby was not a man easily forgotten. With his shock of unruly white hair, confident manner, and brilliant mind, he was a commanding presence in the initial days of the attachment battles. Early in his professional career, Bowlby had been affected by the plight of children suffering from negative family experiences early in life (such as prolonged separation from their mothers). This led to his basic premise: A warm, intimate relationship between mother and infant is essential to mental health.

Ethology The study of behavior in natural settings.

Using concepts from psychology and **ethology** (ethology is the study of behavior in natural settings, Hinde, 1993), Bowlby formulated his basic premise: A warm, intimate relationship between mother and infant is essential to mental health because a child's need for its mother's presence is as great as its need for food. A mother's continued absence can generate a sense of loss and feelings of anger. (In his 1969 classic, *Attachment,* Bowlby states quite clearly that an infant's principal attachment figure can be someone other than the natural mother.)

Background of Attachment Theory

Bowlby and his colleagues, especially James Robertson, initiated a series of studies in which children aged 15 to 30 months were separated from them. (They had been placed either in hospitals or residential nurseries.) A predictable sequence of behaviors followed. *Protest,* the first phase, may begin immediately and persist for about one week. Loud crying, extreme restlessness, and rejection of all adult figures mark an infant's distress. *Despair,* the second phase, follows immediately. The infant's behavior suggests a growing hopelessness: monotonous crying, inactivity, and steady withdrawal. *Detachment,* the final phase, appears when an infant displays renewed interest in its surroundings, but a remote, distant kind of interest. Bowlby describes the behavior of this final phase as apathetic, even if the mother reappears.

From observation of many similar cases, Bowlby defined **attachment** as follows:

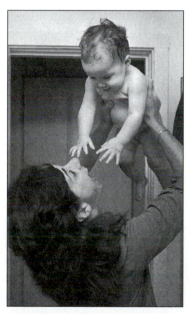

Both mother and child bring their own characteristics to the relationship (facial expressions, movements, vocalizations), and as they do, the interactions between the two become more complex and an attachment slowly develops between the two.

> Attachment behavior is any form of behavior that results in a person attaining or maintaining proximity to some other clearly identified individual who is conceived as better able to cope with the world. It is most obvious when the person is frightened, fatigued, or sick, and is assuaged by comforting and care-giving. At other times the behavior is less in evidence (1982, p. 668).

Bowlby also believed that while attachment is most obvious in infancy and early childhood, it can be observed throughout the life cycle (Waters & colleagues, 2000; Hamilton, 2000; Kerns & colleagues, 2000). Table 6.1 presents a chronology of attachment behavior.

Attachment Intended to keep a child (or adult) in close proximity to a significant other.

Attachment Research

A child's behaviors indicate attachment only when they are specifically directed at one or a few persons rather than to others. When infants first direct their attention to their mothers, they are attempting to initiate and maintain interactions with their mothers. Children also attempt to avoid separation from an attachment figure,

TABLE 6.1 CHRONOLOGY OF ATTACHMENT DEVELOPMENT

Age	Characteristics	Behavior
4 months	Perceptual discrimination; visual tracking of mother	Smiles and vocalizes more with mother than anyone else; shows distress at separation
9 months	Separation anxiety; stranger anxiety	Cries when mother leaves; clings at appearance of strangers (mother is primary object)
2–3 years	Intensity and frequency of attachment behavior remains constant	Notices impending departure, indicating a better understanding of surrounding world
3–4 years	Growing confidence; tendency to feel secure in a strange place with subordinate attachment figures (relatives)	Begins to accept mother's temporary absence; plays *with* other children
4–10 years	Less intense attachment behavior, but still strong	May hold parent's hand while walking; anything unexpected causes child to turn to parent
Adolescence	Weakening attachment to parents; peers and other adults become important	Becomes attached to groups and group members
Adult	Attachment bond still discernible	In troubled times, adults turn to trusted friends; elderly direct attention toward younger generation

Source: From John Bowlby, "Attachment and Loss: Retrospect and Prospect" in *American Journal of Orthopsychiatry,* 52:664–678. Reprinted with permission from the *American Journal of Orthopsychiatry.* Copyright © 1982 by the American Orthopsychiatric Association, Inc.

Bowlby, J. (1969). *Attachment.* New York: Basic Books. Here is Bowlby's classic statement about attachment. This book is very readable and is a reference with which you should be familiar.

particularly if faced with a frightening situation (Waters & Cummings, 2000). Attachment theorists believe that a mother's (or some other adult's) sensitivity helps to determine the degree and quality of an infant's security. But as we have seen in our discussion of reciprocal interactions, the child also contributes to the relationship (Thompson, 1998, 2000).

To assess the quality of attachment, a student of Bowlby's, Mary Salter Ainsworth, devised the *strange situation.* Ainsworth (1973, 1979; Ainsworth & Bowlby, 1991), who accepted Bowlby's theoretical interpretation of attachment, devised the strange situation technique to study attachment experimentally.

4. *The Strange Situation Technique*

Ainsworth had a mother and infant taken to an observation room. The child was placed on the floor and allowed to play with toys. A stranger (female) then entered the room and began to talk to the mother. Observers watched to see how the infant reacted to the stranger and to what extent the child used the mother as a secure base. The mother then left the child alone in the room with the stranger; observers then noted how distressed the child became. The mother returned and the quality of the child's reaction to the mother's return was assessed. Next the infant was left completely alone, followed by the stranger's entrance, and then that of the mother. These behaviors have been used to classify children as follows:

- *Securely attached children,* who used their mothers as a base from which to explore. Separation intensified their attachment behavior; they exhibited considerable distress, ceased their explorations, and at reunion sought contact with their mothers.

- *Avoidantly attached children,* who rarely cried during separation and avoided their mothers at reunion. The mothers of these babies seemed to dislike or were indifferent to physical contact.

- *Ambivalently attached children,* who manifested anxiety before separation and who were intensely distressed by the separation. Yet on reunion they displayed ambivalent behavior toward their mothers; they sought contact but simultaneously seemed to resist it.

ä • *Disorganized/disoriented children,* who show a kind of confused behavior
at reunion. For example, they may look at the mother and then look away,
showing little emotion (Main, 1996).

Ainsworth also believed that attachment knows no geographic boundaries.
Reporting on her studies of infant-mother attachment in Uganda, Ainsworth (1973)
noted that of 28 infants she observed, 23 showed signs of attachment. She was
impressed by the babies' initiative in attempting to establish attachment with their
mothers and noted that the babies demonstrated this initiative even when no threat
of separation or any condition that could cause anxiety existed. In tracing the
developing pattern of attachment behavior, Ainsworth (1973) stated:

> The baby did not first become attached and then show it by proximity-
> promoting behavior, but rather that these are the patterns of behavior
> through which attachment grows (p. 35).

Ainsworth reported other studies conducted in Baltimore, Washington, and Scotland
indicating that cultural influences may affect the ways in which different attachment
behaviors develop. Nevertheless, although these studies used quite different subjects
for their studies, all reported attachment behavior developing in a similar manner.

Infants' reactions to the Strange Situation technique demonstrate the powerful
impact of culture. For example, studies of traditional Japanese families indicated a
large proportion of anxious/resistant infants, but no anxious/avoidant infants. Since
Japanese mothers rarely leave their children in anyone else's care, the children
become upset when left alone with a stranger. Studies of German children indicate
a low percentage of securely attached infants, which does not suggest a large number of insensitive parents. Rather German parents reflect a cultural belief that parents should remain somewhat distant from their children and discourage bodily
contact when the children become mobile (Cole & Cole, 1996).

5. New Directions in Attachment Research

An added tool in attachment research has been the development of the *Adult
Attachment Interview,* which examines the responses of parents to determine if they
maintain a coherent, relevant discussion of their early attachments (Main, 1996).
Their answers are then linked to the quality of their children's attachment. Based
on their responses, adults are classified as follows.

• *Autonomous.* These individuals value relationships, believe that their
attachments help their development, and their answers were consistent and
coherent.

• *Dismissing.* These individuals denied the influence of attachments on their
lives, showed memory lapses, and their positive expressions about their parents
were inconsistent and contradictory.

• *Preoccupied.* These individuals speak of their parents in an angry, incoherent
manner.

• *Unresolved/disorganized.* These individuals reflected a sense of unresolved loss
in their answers.

Differences in responses to the questions of the AAI (that is, how truthful, clear, and
orderly are the responses) predict the attachment categories of their infants (secure,
insecure, etc.), *both before and after birth* (Main, 1996).

Continued research into the application of the AAI has focused on asking
respondents to look back on their own childhood attachment. During a one-hour
interview, people are asked to support their memories by supplying evidence. For
example, they are asked to furnish five adjectives describing their relationship to
each parent. Later during the interview, they're questioned about specific incidents

supporting their earlier answers. Parental responses have been coded into categories that relate to the quality of their infants' attachment (see table 6.2).

Attachment researchers are also examining representational processes; that is, they're focusing on the relationship between early attachment and a child's drawings and stories in middle childhood. For example, when presented with instances of children who were separated from their mothers, secure 6-year-olds made up positive, constructive responses about the child in the story. But disorganized children gave frightened responses: "The mother is going to die," "The girl will kill herself." Continued studies (Weinfield, Sroufe, & Egeland, 2000; Lewis, Feiring, & Rosenthal, 2000) indicate that in high-risk samples (divorce, desertion, abuse, maternal depression) stability of attachment from the early years to adulthood was lacking.

TABLE 6.2 THE ADULT ATTACHMENT INTERVIEW

Adult Attachment Interview	Strange Situation Response
Secure—Autonomous—Coherent, values attachment, accepts any unpleasant, earlier experiences	*Secure*
Dismissing—Positive statements are unsupported or contradicted; they claim earlier unpleasant experiences have no effect	*Avoidant*
Preoccupied—Seems angry, confused, passive, or fearful; some responses irrelevant	*Resistant—Ambivalent*
Unfocused—Disorganized—Loses train of thought during discussion of loss or abuse; lapses in reasoning (speaks of dead people as alive)	*Disorganized/Disoriented*

An Informed View   *Parents, Attachment, and Future Relationships*

We cannot exaggerate the importance of the initial encounters that infants have with the adults around them. The sensitive responsiveness of parents is closely linked to the development of secure attachment in children. This relationship, in turn, helps children to feel socially competent.

Analyzing parents' role in the development of social competence in their children, Rubin, Bukowski, & Parker (1998) reached several conclusions.

- The interactions between parents and their children provide a context within which socal competencies can develop.
- The relationship between a parent and a child allows the child freedom to explore, practice, and refine social skills.
- Within the parent-child relationship, children form assumptions and expectations about other people.

For most children, the mother-infant relationship is initially the most significant. Their interactions are frequent, intense, and instructive and become the building blocks for all future relationships. As attachment emerges from these interactions, children develop an internal model of the mother as a source of support and of the self as socially competent and worthy of a positive response from others. Thus secure attachment promotes positive social expectations with others and a sense of self-worth that will carry forward into future relationships (Rubin, Bukowski, & Parker, 1998).

Here's a project for your class. Either you or some of your classmates probably have relatives with infants. For those of you who do, observe the mother and child interacting. What's their reaction to this "mutual reciprocity"? What was the infant doing? How did the mother react to the baby's signals? Use these reports for class discussion and combine them with your reading of this chapter.

Do you still agree with the conclusion that the early mother-infant relationship shapes future relationships? Can you "fit" your interpretation of the importance of these early interactions with the reports of your classmates?

If you would like to have a more informed view on this issue, you may want to read one or more of the articles referenced in this chapter, such as Ainsworth & Bowlby's 1991 article.

You may also wish to learn more about it by going to our web site at http:/www.mhhe.com/dacey5.

Finally, researchers are placing greater emphasis on the cultural impact on attachment. Theorists have long held that culture influences specific behaviors and that there is a substantial core of attachment that is immune from cultural influence. For example, infants displaying insecure-ambivalent is seen in the United States as a manifestation of incompetence, but not necessarily so in Japan (Rothbaum & colleagues, 2000). Consequently, the more universal aspects of the theory are receiving closer scrutiny.

Note how we've focused on the attachment between mothers and their children because most of the research has examined this relationship. What can we say about the attachment between fathers and their infants?

Fathers and Attachment

Socialized into being the family breadwinner, "traditional" fathers provided strong moral and material support for their families, meted out discipline to their children, but did little else. They paced the waiting room during childbirth, rarely if ever changed a diaper or warmed a bottle, and generally steered clear of the nursery, leaving the responsibility of child rearing almost entirely to their wives (Parke & Brott, 1999).

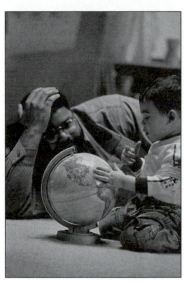

The interactions between a father and his child tend to be more physical than those between a mother and her child. The qualitatively different types of stimulation a child receives from each parent would seem to suggest implications for the staffing of day-care centers and preschool facilities.

Historically, it has often been said that fathers are a biological necessity, but a social accident. Disagreeing with this view, Parke & Brott (1999) noted that today's fathers are pretty much the same as they were before: some are involved; some are even raising their children by themselves; some remain uninvolved. Although we have concentrated on the mother in our discussion of attachment, the father's role in the process has attracted growing interest.

As fathers became more involved in child care, questions have arisen about an infant's attachment to both mother and father. Do infants react differently to each parent? Studies have consistently shown that fathers, particularly in modern societies, are actively involved in nurturing their children and that primary-caretaker fathers do an excellent job (Parke & Brott, 1999).

Commenting on the attachment between father and child, Bowlby (1988) noted that the patterns closely resembled those between mothers and their children. A finding that intrigued Bowlby was that there was no correlation between the attachment patterns for each parent; that is, an infant may have a secure attachment with the mother but not necessarily with the father, or with the father but not necessarily the mother.

We can summarize these findings by stating that at 7 or 8 months of age, when attachment behavior (as defined by Bowlby and Ainsworth) normally appears, infants are attached to both mothers and fathers and prefer either parent to a stranger. The evidence indicates, then, that fathers can establish a close and meaningful relationship with their infants immediately from birth (Cox & others, 1992; Phares, 1992).

Differences in Mother/Father Behavior

Research has also focused on demonstrating the differences between mothers' and fathers' behavior (nurturant versus playful), the similarity between parental behaviors (both exhibit considerable sensitivity), and the amount of involvement in the infant's care. Mothers are more verbal, tend to offer toys, and play more conventional games. In a relaxed setting, both parents seem to have equal attractions as attachment figures. When infants are hungry or sick, however, they turn more to their mothers.

Fathers, however, provide more unpredictable, less rhythmic, and more exciting stimulation than mothers. Children learn to expect these behaviors from their fathers and enjoy playing with them (Lamb, Hwang, Ketterlinus, & Francasso, 1999). Examining the antecedents of father-son attachment, Belsky (1996) studied 126 fathers and their sons in the strange situation. He found that fathers of secure infants were more extraverted and agreeable than fathers of insecure infants. They tended to have better marriages, and had a harmonious relationship between work and family. Infant temperament did not seem to distinguish between security and insecurity.

As you can tell from this brief summary, more research is needed to help us understand the dynamics of the interaction between fathers and their infants. Although estimates are that probably thousands of studies have been done about the mother-child relationship, to date only seventeen known studies have compared the child's attachment to his father (Lewis, 1997). To conclude this section, we can turn to Lewis' statement (1997) that the presence of an adult male, usually the father, is quite important for children's development. (For an excellent discussion of the father's role in development in our modern society, see Cabrera & colleagues, 2000.)

Since we know that both adults and children contribute to the quality of attachment, let's turn now to the role that temperament plays in this process.

Guided Review

11. An early researcher into the significant relationships in an infant's life was _____.

12. Following separation from their mothers, Bowlby found a predictable sequence of behaviors: _____, _____, _____.

13. Attachment characterized by separation or stranger anxiety usually begins at the age of _____ months.

14. Studies showed that by _____ months of age, infants interact differently with their parents than with strangers.

15. _____ is known for the strange situation technique.

Temperament

One of the most important dynamics in parents' relationship with their children is **temperament.** Temperament technically means constitutionally based individual differences in emotional, motor, and attentional reactivity and self-regulation (Rothbart & Bates, 1998). Simply put, a child's temperament refers to a unique and stable style of behaving (Thompson, 1999). *Each child is different at birth and must be treated differently.*

For example, Kagan (1997) has noted that 4-month-old infants who show a tendency to become upset at unfamiliar stimuli are more likely to become fearful and subdued during early childhood. Thus temperament is a critical personality trait, especially in the first days and weeks after birth, a trait that is both stable and persistent. Talking recently with a mother of ten-year-old identical twins about what she could expect, she turned and said, "Even from birth, I could tell them apart by the differences in their reactions to things around them like faces, voices, and colors." In other words, their temperament provided the clues to their identity.

The Origins of Temperament

Temperament appears to have a constitutional component that is observable, at least partially, during the first few days of life (Rothbart & Bates, 1998). Studies that used the same measure of temperament—Bayley's *Infant Behavior Record* (IBR)— all found significant genetic influences on temperament (Caspi, 1998).

Temperament A child's basic personality.

Answers

11. Bowlby 12. protest, despair, detachment 13. 9 months 14. 8 15. Ainsworth

For example, results of the *Colorado Adoption Project,* which compared matched adopted and non-adopted children, showed a clear genetic influence on temperament (Plomin & others, 1997). The ongoing *MacArthur Longitudinal Twin Study,* designed to study more than 330 same-sex twin pairs, has initially reported genetic influences on individual differences at 14 months of age; for example, behavioral inhibition and observed shyness showed a significant genetic influence (Emde & others, 1992). (For an excellent discussion of this topic, see Caspi, 1998.)

As Kagan noted (1992, 1997), given the individual differences in the biochemistry of the brain, it is little wonder that a child could be vulnerable to either sadness or anxiety. Thus, evidence continues to suggest a genetic role in temperament, with all that implies for the mother-infant relationship.

And yet, since our work is based on a reciprocal interaction basis, we can't overlook the interactions between genes and the environment. Examining this developmentally interactive process, Thompson (1999) reached the following conclusions.

- A child's temperament may mesh well or poorly with the demands of the social setting. As we'll see, this goodness of fit between temperament and environment has a major impact on personality and adjustment. But keep in mind also that a child's environment changes dramatically through the years, changes that have powerful effects on development and adjustment.

- Temperament influences how a child selects and responds to different aspects of the environment (individuals, settings, etc.). This in turn will affect how people respond to the child. (Reciprocal interactions at work!)

- Temperament colors how a child perceives and thinks about the environment.

- Temperament may interact with environmental influences in a way we simply don't understand.

Thus temperament is a biologically based but developmentally evolving feature of behavior (Thompson, 1999).

What are some implications of these temperamental differences, and how do they influence parent-child relationships?

6. *Implications of Temperamental Differences*

Two child psychiatrists, Stella Chess and Alexander Thomas (1987), were struck by the individuality of their own children in the days immediately following birth, differences that could not be attributed solely to the environment. Intrigued, they devised the **New York Longitudinal Study** of 141 children. Chess and Thomas discovered that even with children as young as 2 or 3 months of age, they could identify and categorize three types of temperament:

- **Easy children,** characterized by regularity of bodily functions, low or moderate intensity of reactions, and acceptance of, rather than withdrawal from, new situations (40 percent of the children).

- **Difficult children,** characterized by irregularity in bodily functions, intense reactions, and withdrawal from new stimuli (10 percent of the children).

- **Slow-to-warm-up children,** characterized by a low intensity of reactions and a somewhat negative mood (15 percent of the children).

They were able to classify 65 percent of the infants, leaving the others with a mixture of traits that defied neat categorization. Table 6.3 summarizes their classification scheme.

If parents recognize similar characteristics in their children—the need for sleep at a certain time; a unique manner of reacting to strangers or the unknown; the intensity or concentration on a task—they can use their knowledge of such characteristics to build a *goodness-of-fit* relationship.

New York Longitudinal Study
Long-term study by Chess and Thomas of the personality characteristics of children.

Easy children   Term used to describe calm, relaxed children; associated with Chess and Thomas.

Difficult children   Term to describe restless, irritable children; associated with Chess and Thomas.

Slow-to-warm-up children
Term used to describe children with low intensity of reactions; may be rather negative when encountering anything new.

TABLE 6.3 CATEGORIES OF TEMPERAMENT

Behaviors	Easy Children	Difficult Children	Slow-to-warm-up Children
Activity level	Varies	Low to moderate	Varies
Rhythmicity (Regularity)	Very regular	Irregular	Varies
Approach or withdrawal	Positive approach	Withdrawal	Initial withdrawal
Adaptability	Very adaptable	Slowly adaptable	Adaptable
Sensory threshold (level of stimulation necessary to produce a response)	High or low	Tends to be low	High or low
Quality of mood	Positive	Negative	Slightly negative
Intensity of reactions	Low or mild	Intense	Moderate
Distractibility	Varies	Varies	Varies
Persistence and attention span	High or low	High or low	High or low

Goodness of Fit

If the interactions between parents and their children are compatible, *a goodness of fit* exists, that is, parents' demands and expectations are compatible with their children's temperament, abilities, and other characteristics (Chess & Thomas, 1987). Goodness of fit signifies the match between the properties of the environment with its expectations and demands, and the child's capacities, characteristics, and style of behaving.

Poorness of fit exists when parental demands and expectations are excessive and not compatible with a child's temperament, abilities, and other characteristics. Poorness of fit produces stress and is often marked by developmental problems (Chess & Thomas, 1987). A simple way of phrasing this concept is to ask parents and their children how they get along together.

Maintaining Goodness of Fit

Although goodness of fit established in infancy produces a good beginning for a child, no guarantee exists that this fit between parental demands and expectations and a child's temperament and capacities will last (Chess & Thomas, 1987). Children change and so do their parents' expectations, and as relationships become more complex (e.g., during adolescence) the goodness of fit may also change.

For example, the parents of an infant with a low threshold for stimulation—a door closing or a light coming on may disturb her—may have adapted to her temperament. Later in school, however, the child may need extra time for homework or lose attention during a long lesson. Unless such environmental demands are made in light of the child's temperament, the goodness of fit could rapidly deteriorate.

Knowing their children's temperament can help parents adjust their style (their way of doing things) to their needs. For example, soon after the birth of her second daughter, a young woman (a friend of one of my daughters, let's call her Diane) came to see me (JFT). Her story was a classic example of how temperament affects relationships. Her first child, a normal, healthy baby girl needed a great deal of physical contact; she thrived on being held and stroked.

Three years later, a second daughter was born, one with a quite different temperament. Not only was it quickly apparent that this child didn't enjoy being held, she actively resisted physical contact. Diane, understandably, was quite upset because she realized that even at this early age, she wasn't getting along with the second daughter as well as the first. From the stiffening of her second daughter's body when she was held, Diane sensed a tension between the two of them.

Most of us have definite preferences and Diane's second daughter was no different. The solution was to help Diane find another way of reaching her child. My advice was to use verbal stimulation in as gentle and personal a manner as possible, that is, make sure the infant knew that her mother was talking to her. Rather than embracing her baby with hugs and kisses, Diane initiated physical contact when necessary (feeding, changing), but concentrated on softly talking to her child.

It seemed to work. Today Diane and her daughter enjoy a warm, comfortable relationship, which resulted from her efforts to make those early interactions as positive as possible. What Diane accomplished was not simple or easy. She could have felt rebuffed by her child's seeming resistance, especially when she compared this child with her first child. These feelings, in turn, could have caused her to respond mechanically to her baby. But she instinctively realized something was wrong—a poorness of fit—and took measures to correct it.

Sensitive Responsiveness

Sensitive responsiveness
Refers to the ability to recognize the meaning of a child's behavior.

The importance of parents' and children's temperaments in establishing a goodness-of-fit relationship (parents react differently to different children) has introduced the concept of **sensitive responsiveness.** For example, as we have seen, babies are temperamentally different at birth. An example of sensitive responsiveness would be that although most infants like to be held, some dislike physical contact. How will a mother react to an infant who stiffens and pulls away, especially if previous children liked being held? There's no escaping the importance of infant temperament in the development of attachment (Seifer, Schiller, & Sameroff, 1996).

Infants instantly tune in to their environment. They give clues to their personalities so that a mother's and father's responses to their child's signals must be appropriate for *that* child, that is, greater parental sensitivity produces more responsive infants. A good example of this is seen in research indicating that responsive parenting in the first few years of life provides a foundation for the development of behavioral regulation and social competence in young children (Wakschlag & Hans, 1999). Twenty-six percent of the children whose mothers were unresponsive during infancy developed disruptive behavior by 10 years of age, while none of those with highly responsive mothers showed similar behavior. (For a thoughtful discussion of this topic, see Thompson, 1998.)

Now let's turn to the role that relationships, reciprocal interactions, attachment, and temperament play in a child's emotional development.

Guided Review

16. Temperament is another example of the interaction of _____ and _____ .

17. _____ and _____ are identified with the New York Longitudinal Study.

18. _____ is an individual's behavioral style in interacting with the environment.

19. Compatibility between parental and child behavior is known as _____ _____ _____ .

20. When the behavior of parents and children are incompatible, this is called _____ _____ _____ .

Answers

16. genes, environment 17. Chess, Thomas 18. Temperament 19. goodness of fit 20. poorness of fit

Early Emotional Development

While we were working on this section of the book, one of us (JFT) tried to relax by watching a hockey game on television. Bad choice. With a few seconds left in the game one of the players savagely swung his stick at the head of a member of the other team who immediately dropped to the ice, severely injured. Needless to say, there was a history of bad blood between the two players and the repercussions of this violent encounter are still being played out.

Still, it dramatically illustrated the powerful role that emotions play in our lives. What was there in the emotional development of this player that would cause him to act so brutally? Does the answer lie in brain functioning? We know, for example, that the brain's limbic system (especially the amygdala) has a critical function in triggering our alarm system (Goldman-Rakic, 1999).

But we also know that as humans we are able to exercise considerable *emotional regulation* in our lives. In the first year of life, infants gradually develop the ability to inhibit or minimize the duration and intensity of emotional reactions. (For an excellent discussion of emotional regulation see Thompson, 1999; Saarni, Mumme, & Campos, 1998.) So our task is clear: Exactly what do we mean by emotional development?

Emotions and Emotional Development

As you read about the impact of attachment and early relationships on psychosocial development, you can understand how a child's emotional life is also affected (Pollak & colleagues, 2000). (See Warhol, 1998, for an overview of the importance of emotions in development.) The study of emotions has had a checkered career in psychology. From the peaks of popularity, interest in emotions and their development plunged to the depths of neglect. Today we see once again a resurgence of enthusiasm for the study of emotional development (Lemerise & Arsenio, 2000).

Theorists recently have moved in one of two directions. The *structuralists* believe that our emotional experiences fall into different emotional states, each with its unique source of arousal, cognitive appraisal, and subjective feeling: We become angry; we know fear and anxiety; we have feelings of sadness. These emotional states are deeply immersed in our human nature, develop early in life, and are critical for our survival.

Functionalists, on the other hand, believe that emotions act to maintain satisfactory relations between a person and the environment. Thus the goal of emotions is to help make cognitive appraisals of a situation, identify and seek appropriate goals, establish satisfactory social relationships, and regulate our emotional behavior, among other behaviors (Thompson, 1999). In other words, emotions help us function more effectively.

Defining Emotion

But what do we mean by *emotion?* Although philosophers and psychologists have trembled at the thought of defining emotion for almost as long as attempts have been made, the following definition hints at what underlies this emotional (!) term.

> *Emotion is a feeling(s) and its distinctive thoughts, psychological and biological states, and range of propensities to act* (Goleman, 1995, p. 289).

Goleman then goes on to ask the controversial question: Is it possible to classify the basic emotions? Answering his own question, he proposes several fundamental families of emotion, together with representative members of each family.

- *Anger:* fury, resentment, animosity
- *Sadness:* grief, sorrow, gloom, melancholy

- *Fear:* nervousness, apprehension, dread, fright

- *Enjoyment:* happiness, joy, bliss, delight

- *Love:* acceptance, trust, devotion, adoration

- *Surprise:* shock, astonishment, amazement, wonder

- *Shame:* guilt, embarassment, mortification, humiliation

You would enjoy reading Daniel Goleman's remarkably clear analysis of emotions, *Emotional intelligence* (1995). New York: Bantam.

You probably would disagree with Goleman—what about blends such as jealousy? You could accurately point out that too much is missing from these categories.

Yet efforts such as these undoubtedly will continue since Paul Ekman's discovery that specific facial expressions for fear, anger, sadness, and enjoyment are recognized by people of all cultures around the world, thus suggesting their universality (Ekman & Davidson, 1994). Once Ekman stated that emotions evolved for their adaptive value in dealing with fundamental life tasks and identified four of these emotions, the stage was set and the task was identified: link these fundamental tasks with basic emotions. Let's now attempt to discover how emotions develop.

Emotional Communication   One of the great adaptive values of emotions, of course, is their ability to communicate feelings and shared experiences. The mother who plays peek-a-boo with her baby, the father who tickles his infant, the parent who runs toward the child with alarm on her face and shouts, "Don't go out in the street"—all are conveying meaning with their emotional behavior. But do infants understand the emotional message being sent? For them to comprehend emotional meanings, infants must be able to

- react to the feeling component of the message.

- discriminate one emotional signal from another.

- recognize the specific meaning of different emotions.

- realize that the emotional signal refers to *something* (another person, an event, an object).

Research has shown that from the first days after birth infants are sensitive to the quality and discernible features of an emotional signal, they recognize the emotional content of the message, and that the message may refer to external events as well as internal states (Saarni, Mumme, & Campos, 1998).

Signs of Emotional Development

One method of tracing emotional development has been suggested by Izard (1982, 1994). Using infants' facial expressions, Izard identified the initial appearance of various emotions as follows.

- At birth, infants display interest, disgust, distress, and startle states. Interest aids cognitive development; disgust furthers chances of survival (avoiding noxious, dangerous substances); distress helps infants to receive needed attention.

- During the first four months anger, sadness, surprise, and joy emerge.

- The true social smile appears sometime in the 2 to 3 month period.

- Fear and shyness are apparent in the 5 to 8 month period.

Izard and his colleagues (1995) noted that emotional expressions exhibit both continuity and change. For example, we all become angry at times (continuity), but how we express the anger changes, for example, compressing our lips.

Another attempt to trace emotional development in infancy has been made by Kopp (1993). Combining research results with personal observation over many years, she has proposed the following sequence.

Age	Behavior
1 month	distress
2 months	pleasure
3 months	smiles
7 months	fear, anger
12 months	jealousy
18 months	irritable, stubborn
24 months	intense, responsive to others' moods

The appearance of these various emotions may vary slightly from theorist to theorist, but the basic explanation of *how* they develop is identical. Emotional development occurs as the result of an infant's dispositional tendencies combined with a complex interaction between growing cognitive skills and social interactions.

As we conclude this section, a word of warning: In examining the appearance of the various emotions, remember that *different* responses may be made to any *one* emotion. A smile, for example, may signal joy, scorn, a social greeting or some other emotion (Saarni, Mumme, & Campos, 1998). Recognizing that several issues surround emotional development will help you to understand this important part of children's lives (Dunn, 1994).

Analyzing Emotional Expressions

As children grow, the circumstances that elicit an emotion change radically, that is, the emotional experiences at different ages vary drastically. The amusement a 6-month-old child shows when tickled by her mother is far different from a 16-year-old's amusement at a funny story told by a friend. We may label both "amusement," but is the emotion the same?

Remember also that complex new emotions appear as children grow. For example, as early as 2 or 3 years of age children begin to display shame, guilt, and jealousy. These new emotions emerge from a child's increasing cognitive maturity and, as they do, they have a strong influence on self-esteem (Dunn, 1994). For example, embarassment or shame at giving a wrong answer in school may weaken a child's sense of competence.

As emotions appear, children must grapple with the issue of regulating them. Impulse control (see chapter 10) becomes an important learning experience early in life, strongly influenced by a child's temperament and how the environment (family, school, peers) reacts to emotional outbursts. We see here once again the importance of recognizing how biopsychosocial interactions affect behavior.

Emotional development seems to move from the general (positive versus negative emotions) to the specific—general positive states differentiate into such emotions as joy and interest; general negative states differentiate into fear, disgust, or anger. These primary emotions emerge during the first six months. Sometime after 18 months of age (recall Piaget's explanation of cognitive development), secondary emotions appear that are associated with a child's growing cognitive capacity for self-awareness. For emotions such as embarassment to appear, children must have developed a sense of self (Rothbart, 1994).

The Smile

One of the first signs of emotion is a baby's smile, which most parents immediately interpret as a sign of happiness. Two-month-old infants are often described as "smilers." Frequent and socially significant smiles emerge in the 2 to 3 month period (Kagan, 1998). Babies smile instinctively at faces—real or drawn—and this probably reflects the human tendency to attend to patterns. Infants gradually learn that familiar faces usually mean pleasure, and smiling at known faces commences as early as the fifth month (Lewkowicz, 1996). Infants quickly learn that smiling is a key element in securing positive reinforcement from those around the infant.

This 3-month-old infant is responding to its mother's face by smiling. In these interactions we see the roots of a child's psychosocial development.

Summarizing, then: Infants smile at any high-contrast stimuli, the human beings around them, and discovering a relationship between their behavior and events in the external world. When infants smile, they elicit attention from those around and begin to associate the human face with pleasure.

Smiling has a developmental history and, "for no reason" (that is, before infants discriminate among faces), appears soon after birth (Izard, 1994; Goleman, 1995). These smiles are usually designated as "false" smiles because they lack the emotional warmth of the true smile. By the baby's third week, the human female voice elicits a brief, real smile. By the sixth week the beginnings of the true social smile appear, especially in response to the human face.

Finally, as we conclude this chapter, we would like to emphasize that current research on emotional development reinforces the reciprocal interaction base of this book: Emotional expression appears immediately after birth, acquires definite meaning, and expands rapidly because of the socially interactive nature of emotional communication.

Guided Review

21. _____ expressions for emotions are recognized by people of all cultures around the world.
22. _____ believe that emotional experiences reflect individual emotional states.
23. _____ believe that emotions act to maintain satisfactory relationships between a person and the environment.
24. Emotional communication refers to the _____ associated with an emotional signal.
25. Inhibiting and minimizing emotional reactions is called _____ _____.

CONCLUSION & SUMMARY

The role of relationships in development has achieved a prominent place in our attempts to understand a child's growth. From the initial contacts with the mother to the ever-expanding network of siblings and peers at all ages, relationships exert a powerful and continuing influence on the direction of development.

We are slowly acquiring data about the function of relationships. For example, we have seen how important and persistent are the first interactions with parents and the importance of temperament and attachment. The interaction of these forces affects future relationships and the nature of emotional development. Recent research has led to significant findings about the quality of relationships.

What is the role of relationships in psychosocial development?

- Relationships involve almost all aspects of development.
- Infants, as active partners in their development, help to shape their relationships.
- To understand relationships, we must analyze and understand the reciprocal interactions involved.
- The development of social interactions seems to follow a definite schedule.
- Parents' role expectations affect their relationships with their children.

How would you assess the importance of attachment in psychosocial development?

- Bowlby and his colleagues, studying the separation of children from their parents, identified attachment as

an important part of psychosocial development.
- Ainsworth's strange situation technique is designed to assess the security of an infant's attachment.
- Attachment is a cross-cultural phenomenon that knows no geographic boundary.
- Attachment develops early in life and offers clues to psychosocial development.
- The *Adult Attachment Interview* helps to assess the quality of a child's attachment.
- The issue of attachment to fathers has attracted considerable interest.

How does temperament affect the relationship between parents and their children?

- Temperament refers to a child's unique way of interacting with the environment.

Answers

21. Facial 22. Structuralists 23. Functionalists 24. meaning 25. emotional regulation

- An infant's temperament immediately affects interactions with adults.
- The work of Chess and Thomas helps us to understand the concept of goodness of fit.
- To maintain a goodness of fit, parents must constantly adapt their parenting style to match the developmental changes in their children.

How do children develop and control their emotions?

- The brain plays a major role in the development and appearance of emotions.
- As emotional development occurs, children acquire a necessary degree of emotional regulation.

- Theories of emotional development reflect either a structuralist or functionalist perspective.
- Current research produced a schedule tracing the appearance of the various emotions.
- One of the first signs of emotional behavior is an infant's smile.

KEY TERMS

Attachment
Autonomy
Difficult children
Easy children
Entrainment

Ethology
New York Longitudinal Study
Reciprocal interactions
Sensitive responsiveness
Slow-to-warm-up children

Symmetry
Synchrony
Temperament

WHAT DO YOU THINK?

1. Probably the basic issue for you to grasp is the extent of an infant's abilities: physical, social, and psychological. Do you think that infants are as we have described them in chapters 5 and 6, or do you think that we have over- or underestimated their competencies?

2. Depending on your answer to question 1, explain how you interpret an infant's participation in developing relationships. That is, given an infant's ability to smile, coo, and make physical responses,

how much control do you believe infants exercise in their interactions with adults?

3. As you read about the resurgence of interest in emotional development, how did you react to the developmental schedules that were presented? Do you think that theorists and researchers possess the skill and knowledge to be able to accurately identify the appearance of specific emotions at specific times?

4. Although Mary Ainsworth's research is the basis for our belief in the importance of attachment in social development, criticism has been directed at her studies because of the small number of subjects and the lack of consideration of the subjects' temperaments. Do you think these are valid criticisms? Do they raise questions in your mind about the universality of her conclusions?

CHAPTER REVIEW TEST

1. An extended series of interactions doesn't necessarily imply a
   a. relationship.
   b. goodness of fit.
   c. friendship.
   d. communication.

2. Which of the following statements is not in agreement with an understanding of sensitive responsiveness?
   a. All children are temperamentally similar at birth.
   b. Children instantly tune into their environment.

   c. Children give clues to their personalities.
   d. Children, from birth, engage in reciprocal interactions.

3. A true relationship has
   a. language aspects.
   b. cognitive aspects.
   c. physical aspects.
   d. all of the above.

4. More sensitive mothers have infants who are more
   a. restless.
   b. nervous.
   c. detached.
   d. responsive.

5. Parents and infants both exercise control over the
   a. siblings.
   b. interactions.
   c. labeling.
   d. temperament.

6. What parents see as their _____ affects parent-child relationships.
   a. interactions
   b. function
   c. background
   d. role

7. Children's _____
   contribute significantly to their
   interactions with their
   environments.
   a. ages
   b. gender
   c. temperaments
   d. culture

8. Chess and Thomas described a
   child with a low intensity of
   reactions and a somewhat negative
   attitude as
   a. slow to warm up.
   b. difficult.
   c. easy.
   d. depressed.

9. Constitutionally based individual
   differences are known as
   a. interactions.
   b. attachments.
   c. temperament.
   d. parental signposts.

10. The author of the Strange Situation
    test is
    a. Ainsworth.
    b. Bowlby.
    c. Brazelton.
    d. Kagan.

11. _____ is a characteristic
    that identifies the rhythm that is
    established between a parent's and
    infant's behavior.
    a. Synchrony
    b. Autonomy
    c. Entrainment
    d. Symmetry

12. According to Bowlby,
    _____ behavior is any
    form of behavior that results in a
    person attaining or maintaining
    proximity to some other clearly
    identified individual who is
    conceived as better able to cope
    with the world.
    a. detachment
    b. attachment
    c. protest
    d. emotional

13. Which statement is true?
    a. Only mothers have the potential
       to induce attachment.
    b. Fathers and mothers act quite
       differently with their infants.
    c. There is a sensitive period for
       parent-infant bonding.
    d. No sensitive period exists for
       parent-infant bonding.

14. The study of behavior in natural
    settings is known as
    a. ethology.
    b. physiology.
    c. anthropology.
    d. molecular biology.

15. Bowlby's work on attachment
    began to notice the behavior
    of infants who experienced
    _____ from their
    mothers.
    a. attention
    b. separation
    c. neglect
    d. habituation

16. The true social smile appears at
    about _____ months.
    a. eight
    b. six
    c. four
    d. two

17. Which is *not* a possible explanation
    of an infant's smile?
    a. Infants smile at human beings
       around them.
    b. Infants smile at high-contrast
       stimuli.
    c. Infants smile at discovering a
       relationship between their
       behavior and external events.
    d. Infants smile at environmental
       noise.

18. Inhibiting or minimizing the
    intensity of emotional reactions
    is known as emotional
    a. guidance.
    b. latitude.
    c. regulation.
    d. short-circuiting.

19. _____ believe that
    emotions act to maintain
    satisfactory relations between
    the person and the environment.
    a. Structuralists
    b. Functionalists
    c. Behaviorists
    d. Cognitivists

20. One of the great adaptive
    values of emotions is that they
    _____ feelings and
    shared experiences.
    a. communicate
    b. sublimate
    c. actualize
    d. repress

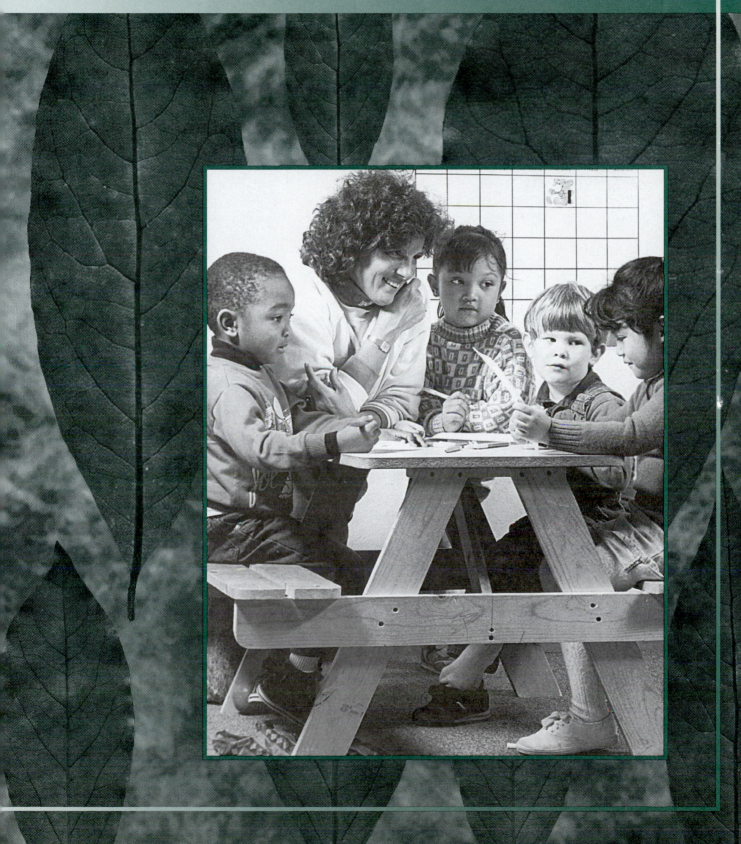

*One of the most
important areas
children must
learn to regulate
is their cognitive
functioning. They
must develop the
ability to exercise
conscious control
over their
attention and
memory processes.*

Martha Bronson

CHAPTER 7

Physical and Cognitive Development in Early Childhood

iz, whom we met in chapter 5, felt she now had a good idea of what perpetual motion meant. Her two children, 3-year-old Maddi and 5-year-old Jackie, engaged in nonstop activities from the time they woke up in the morning until they went to bed—with great reluctance. (Be thankful for small favors, she thought; Maddi still took a long afternoon nap.) At least you could talk to Jackie, who was excited about entering kindergarten in September.

But Maddi—oh, that Maddi! She had discovered the thrill of saying "no" loudly and emphatically, was into everything, and sometimes pretended not to hear Liz's warnings. Liz was worried about what seemed to be a steady stream of threats she directed at Maddi. She was concerned that so many negative incidents could affect her relationship with Maddi.

These thoughts came to Liz as she opened a letter from the preschool where Maddi was registered for the fall. Also included was a form for her to fill out, and as she read the items, she became even more concerned.

The first item asked for a description of Maddi. Liz answered honestly that she was healthy, vigorous, active, and seemed to be progressing well. She was toilet trained, helped in dressing herself, and seemed quite independent. Liz thought Maddi was unusually curious, always poking into things, opening drawers, and looking into closets. Liz was often embarrassed by this behavior when she and Maddi visited other homes. On the other hand, Maddi was putting her words together nicely and played fairly well with other children.

In the next part of the form, Liz was asked several specific questions: How independent was Maddi? Was she left-handed or right-handed? Were there particular activities that Maddi really enjoyed, such as drawing? Did she like pretend play?

Liz answered the questions carefully: Maddi seemed quite independent; she didn't cling and could play by herself. She used her right hand for drawing and throwing. She loved to draw and Liz was able to understand what Maddi was trying to tell in her pictures. In her games and play, she often used objects for different purposes, such as a stick for a broom.

As Liz responded to the questions, she realized that Maddi seemed to be a fairly normal 3-year-old (whatever that might mean, Liz thought a little gloomily). Still, she was bothered by Maddi's incessant questioning and outbursts of negativism. Since she and Maddi were scheduled for an interview at the preschool the next week, Liz decided to mention her worries to the instructor who would be interviewing them. After all, preschool teachers worked constantly with children of this age.

The following week, while Liz talked with one of the instructors, Maddi played happily with a variety of toys. When the instructor commented that Maddi seemed quite well-adjusted, Liz had the opportunity to mention how worried she was. The instructor listened and then began to laugh, saying that Maddi seemed to be perfectly normal for her age. She mentioned that Maddi was at that age when she wanted as much information as possible to feed her inquiring mind, which was steadily becoming involved in more symbolic activities, such as telling a story with her drawings and using one thing to represent another.

As Liz listened, she was delighted because these were just the things that Maddi was doing. She was acting as most youngsters of her age do. The instructor then went on to describe what Liz could expect for the next year or so. ✪

Have you ever seen a 2-year-old strutting around in one of those prophetic T-shirts that says:

Watch out—I just turned two!

Cries of frustration, frequently uttered by tired parents, don't mark parents like Liz as uncaring or heartless. Rather, they are a too human reaction to the reality of dealing with a dynamo. Boundless energy, constant curiosity, and growing mental maturity all characterize children from 2 to 6 years of age. By age 2, typical children walk, talk, and eagerly explore their environment, gradually acquiring greater mastery over their bodies.

The rounded bodies of infancy give way to the slimmer torsos of early childhood, muscles begin to firm, bones begin to harden, and continued brain development provides a foundation for a world of symbolic promise. When these changes combine with feelings of confidence—"No, no, I can do it"—parents and other adults working with children of this age face challenges that can try their patience.

Cognitively, it's the time of Piaget's *preoperational period,* which traces a child's mental odyssey during these years. During these years children also begin to form a theory of mind. Many of today's early childhood youngsters will also experience some form of preschool education. Finally, these are the years when children acquire their language so rapidly that we refer to the "language explosion."

In this chapter we'll first trace the important physical changes of the period. We'll then analyze cognitive development and trace the growing symbolic ability of the early childhood youngster. We'll conclude our discussion by analyzing how children of these years begin to control their environment by their use of rapidly developing language skills.

Chapter Objectives

After reading this chapter, you should be able to answer the following questions.

◆ What are the major physical and motor accomplishments of the early childhood years?

◆ How do Piaget's views on cognitive development differ from information processing theorists?

◆ What types of early childhood education seem most promising?

◆ How does children's language acquisition proceed during these years?

Early childhood youngsters find the world a fascinating place. Giving these children the freedom to explore and learn, coupled with sensible restrictions, encourages the development of mastery.

Physical and Motor Development

Growth in childhood proceeds at a less frantic pace than in infancy. Children during this period grow about another 12 inches and continue to gain weight at the rate of about 5 pounds a year. Body proportions are also changing, with the legs growing faster than the rest of the body. By about age 6, the legs make up almost 45 percent of body length. At the beginning of this period, children usually have all their baby teeth; and at the end of the period, children begin to lose them. Boys and girls show about the same rate of growth during these years.

Figure 7.1

The human growth curve.

From John F. Travers, *The Growing Child,* Scott, Foresman and Company, Glenview, IL, 1982. Reprinted by permission of the author.

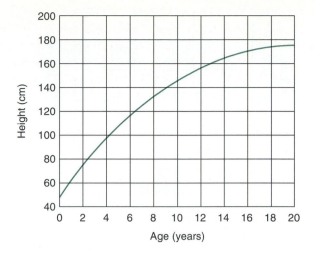

Features of Physical Development

Look at figure 7.1, the human growth curve. (Note that 10 centimeters equal 4 inches.) This curve strikingly illustrates the regularity of physical growth. Most parts of the body (except the brain and the reproductive organs) follow this pattern (Tanner, 1989). With the exception of the two spurts at infancy and adolescence, growth is highly predictable for almost all boys and girls, given satisfactory conditions.

The Sequence of Early Childhood Growth

We know that different cells, tissues, and organs grow at different rates. (Some tissues never lose the ability to grow, such as hair, skin, and nails.) In humans, for example, body length at birth is about four times the length of the face at birth, so the head is relatively large. But the head grows more slowly than the trunk or limbs, so that they gradually become proportional.

Parents and children alike are quite conscious of the appearance and loss of "baby" teeth and the arrival of the first permanent teeth. At about 2½ years all of the primary teeth have come through, which most children begin to lose between 5 and 6 years. At about this time, the first permanent teeth appear. Children continue to lose their primary teeth and gain new permanent teeth at about the same time. The timing can be different for some children, however, so that gaps between teeth may appear or new teeth arrive before the baby teeth have fallen out, causing a space problem that may require professional attention.

Children's rapidly developing motor skills are clearly seen in their drawings from uncontrolled scribbling to controlled "within the lines" attempts to their own creative expressions.

Continuing Brain Development

We traced the brain's rapid development during the prenatal period and the infancy years, and now we see a slowing process take hold. The brain's growth spurt effectively begins to decelerate during the early childhood years. Brain growth occurs as follows.

- At birth, the brain is about 25 percent of its adult weight.

- At 6 months about 50 percent.

- 75 percent of adult brain weight is present at 2 to 2½ years

- 90 percent of adult brain weight is present at 5 to 6 years

- By 10 years about 95 percent of adult brain weight has developed.

These figures clearly indicate a slower growth pattern. In other words, while it took 2½ years to grow 75 percent, another 3½ years sees brain growth increasing only by 15 percent. Figure 7.2 illustrates this process.

Figure 7.2

Slowing growth of the brain.

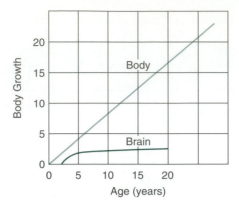

The nature of the changes occurring during the early childhood years is interesting to trace. Microscopic examinations have repeatedly shown an increase in dendrites, accompanied by growth in the number of synapses. These changes, while not changes in structure, nevertheless help to explain the growing cognitive ability of 2 to 6 year olds. The neural foundation is being laid for children to form more connections, providing a network that furthers cognition and learning (Johnson, 1998, 1999; Howard, 2000).

Thus the brain continues its development, but the process resembles more a filling in of the structure that has grown to this point. For example, a child's experiences feed back into the developing nervous system and facilitates the multiplication and growth of cells. The new and exciting stimuli of the early childhood years also encourage the formation of new connections among the neurons that developed during infancy. (See chapter 5 for a review of early brain development.)

By the age of 2, the cortex has grown to a point where it more closely resembles the cortex of an adult brain. The cerebellum, which is that part of the brain controlling balance and fine motor skills, continues to grow fairly rapidly. The sensory area receives visual, auditory, and tactile stimuli that children must analyze and interpret, thus furthering their potential for cognitive development. Consequently, we can say that continued brain growth during the early childhood years parallels cognitive and language accomplishments, another example of the continued impact of biopsychosocial forces (Johnson, 1998).

Lateralization

During the early childhood years, as the brain continues to exercise its powerful control of behavior, children show a decided preference for using one hand or foot over the other. This preference, called **handedness,** starts to appear toward the end of infancy and becomes well established by the age of 5 or 6.

Which hand do you use for writing? If you were to kick a football, would you use the leg on the same side of your body as the hand you use for writing? Pick up a pencil or ruler and assume it is a telescope. Which eye do you use? Are you using the same side of the body that you used for writing and kicking? Your answers to these questions should give you some idea of the meaning of cerebral **lateralization.**

Although these observable behaviors and their tongue-twisting names—handedness, footedness, eyedness—have long intrigued parents, psychologists, neuropsychologists, and educators, details of *how* they appear still elude us. Today three possible explanations have been proposed (Johnson, 1999).

1. *The biased gene model* turns to heredity for the solution. A gene predisposes most of us to right-handedness and left hemisphere control of speech, for example.

2. *The biased brain model* pinpoints neuroanatomical differences around the time of birth. That is, there are anatomical differences between the cerebral hemispheres. The planum temporale, involved in the production of language, is larger in the left hemisphere for most adults.

Handedness Children's preference for using one hand over the other.

Lateralization Refers to a preferred side of the brain for a particular activity.

Figure 7.3

Lateralization of handedness.

3. *The biased head model* argues that laterality results from the tendency of infants to turn their heads to one side. Since most infants turn their heads to the right, the right hand, then, becomes the preferred hand for reaching. An extension of the biased head model links preferential head turning to position in the uterus.

Whichever one of these models turns out to be correct, it's clear that hemispheric specialization functions as early as 4 to 5 months for such cognitive functions as language and face processing.

Consequently, although the hemispheres seem to be almost identical, our discussion reveals important differences between the two. These differences are clues to your brain's organization. If you are right-handed, for example, your left cerebral hemisphere is lateralized for handedness and also for control of your speech—you are "left lateralized." Figure 7.3 illustrates lateralization.

Influences on Physical Development in Early Childhood

In an excellent overview of physical development, Tanner (1989) indicated how the interaction of heredity and environment produces the rate and kinds of physical growth. Among the chief contributing forces are the following:

- *Genetic elements.* Hereditary elements, as we have seen, are of immense importance to the regulation of growth. The genetic growth plan is given at conception and functions throughout the entire growth period.

- *Nutrition.* Active preschoolers need a well-balanced diet—bread, cereal, fruit, vegetables, meat, milk—and they also require several wholesome snacks. Parents, for as long as possible, should restrict sweets and soda drinks. Almost as important, they should begin to develop good eating habits (Lutz & Przytulski, 1997; Tamborlane, 1997).

- *Disease.* Short-term illnesses cause no permanent retardation of the growth rate, although they may cause some disturbance if the child's diet is consistently inadequate (an abundance of empty calories). Major disease usually causes a slowing of growth, followed by a catch-up period if circumstances become more favorable.

- *Psychological disturbance.* Stress can produce decided effects on physical development, beginning with the prenatal period. For example, stress and anxiety are associated with low birth weight and early delivery (Azar, 1999). During the early childhood years, children experience the trauma of leaving home for preschool and kindergarten, adjusting to new adults and peers. If these events are coupled with any trouble at home (conflict, divorce), the impact on the children can be decidedly negative. There is always the danger that adverse experiences can—not always—cause a negative self-concept (Rutter & Rutter, 1993). (We'll explore this topic at greater length in chapter 10.)

The energy of the early childhood years is seen in the physical activities of the period: constant motion followed by periods of rest and nutrition.

Motor skills Skills (both gross and fine) resulting from physical development enabling children to perform smooth and coordinated physical acts.

- *Socioeconomic status.* Children from different social classes differ in average body size at all ages. Tanner gives the example of differences in height between British children of the professional class and those of laborers. Children of the professional class are from 1 inch taller at age 3 and 2 inches taller at adolescence. A consistent pattern appears in all such studies, indicating that children in more favorable circumstances are larger than those growing up under less favorable economic conditions. The difference seems to stem from nutrition, sleep, exercise, and recreation.

- *Secular trends.* During the past hundred years the tendency has been for children to become progressively larger at all ages. This is especially true in Europe and America.

This brief overview of physical development again illustrates the importance of the biopsychosocial model. For example, you may be tempted to think that physical growth is essentially biological, mainly determined by heredity. Note, however, the role played by nutrition and socioeconomic status. The interaction among biological, psychological, and social influences testifies to the power of the biopsychosocial model in explaining development.

Growing Motor Skills

When early childhood children reach the age of 6, no one—neither parents nor teachers—is surprised by what they can do physically. Think back to the infancy period and recall how often we referred to what children couldn't do. Stand, walk, run. We tend to take the accomplishments of the 6-year-old for granted, but a great deal of neuromuscular development had to occur before these motor skills became so effortless.

We are concerned here with two types of **motor skills:** *gross* (using the large muscles) and *fine* (using the small muscles of the hands and fingers). Thanks to perceptual and motor development, 3- and 4-year-old children can hold crayons, copy triangles, button their clothes, and unlace their shoes. Table 7.1 summarizes the development of motor skills.

The physical picture of the early childhood youngster is one of energy and growing motor skill. Adequate rest is critical and parents should establish a routine to avoid problems. For example, to reconcile a rambunctious child with the necessity of sleep, parents should minimize stimulation through a consistent, easily recognized program: washing, toothbrushing, storytelling, and gentle but firm pressure to sleep. Careful and thoughtful adult care should prevent undue difficulties.

The Special Case of Drawing

Children love to draw and their art work has long attracted the attention of scholars as far back as John Ruskin in 1857 with his book, *The Elements of Drawing.* In

TABLE 7.1 THE EMERGENCE OF MOTOR SKILLS

Age	Gross Skills	Fine Skills
2	Runs, climbs stairs, jumps from object (both feet)	Throws ball, kicks ball, turns page, begins to scribble
3	Hops, climbs stairs with alternating feet, jumps from bottom step	Copies circle, opposes thumb to finger, scribbling continues to improve
4	Runs well, skillful jumping, begins to skip, pedals tricycle	Holds pencil, copies square, walks balance beam
5	Hops about 50 feet, balances on one foot, can catch large ball, good skipping	Colors within lines, forms letters, dresses and undresses self with help, eats more neatly
6	Carries bundles, begins to ride bicycle, jumps rope, chins self, can catch a tennis ball	Ties shoes, uses scissors, uses knife and fork, washes self with help

a finely tuned sequence, which no one has to teach them, children move from the pincer movements of infancy to random scribbles to skillful creations. As they do, certain questions arise: Why do children scribble? What are they trying to say in their art? Why do they draw stick figures when they know people don't look that way (Schirrmacher, 1998)?

In analyzing children's art, it's important to remember that their drawings are the expression of *what they are capable of doing.* That is, the early childhood youngster is limited in eye-hand coordination, motor ability, and manual dexterity. But their drawings, as crude as an adult may think they are, tell us much about a child's personality and emotional state.

According to Kellogg (1979), who collected over one million children's drawings and paintings, the first stage of children's art development consists of 20 basic scribbles. Kellogg believed that children's art work passes through four stages: placement (where on the paper the child places the drawing), shape, design, and pictorial. By age 2 years, children have achieved 17 placement patterns. At 3 years, they're using circles, crosses, squares, and rectangles.

Random scribbling Drawing in which children use dots and lines with simple arm movements.

For example, 2-year-olds grab markers and scribble enthusiastically (using dots and lines) and seem fascinated by their ability to produce lines as a result of their movements. Parents and preschool teachers should encourage this **random scribbling** as a necessary first step in children's creative growth. During this phase of random scribbling, which continues until about age 3, children are free from any evaluation of their drawings; they're simply having fun.

Controlled scribbling Drawing in which children carefully watch what they are doing, when before they looked away.

Three-year-olds hold a crayon with their whole hand and then begin to use their wrists, which permits them to draw curves and loops. Called **controlled scribbling,** they become engrossed with geometric figures and are beginning to realize their lines can represent objects. Now their art matches their cognitive development and reflects their growing symbolic power. For example, they'll point to their creation and say, "That's a man." This phase lasts until about age 4.

Four- and 5-year-olds show greater control and attention to what they are doing, deliberately attempting to create representations of objects. For example, they'll use a circle to represent a head or the sun. Young children produce exciting creations, using a combination of symbols that vary widely from child to child

---

An Informed View   *Children's Love of Drawing—What Happens?*

Many questions have arisen about children's love of drawing. Noting how drawings develop, from the scribbles of the 2-year-old to the 3-year-old's interest in design to the 4- and 5-year-old's drawing representations, Gardner (1982) commented on the liveliness and enthusiasm of their work. And then suddenly it stops, usually by the end of the early childhood period for most children. Why?

Children limit their artistic efforts to copying forms or cease drawing altogether after the peak of creativity has been reached. This "reach for realism" may be a critical stage of development during which children reflect their cognitive level by following rules and obeying the dictates of convention. With growing cognitive ability, and a decrease in egocentrism, children may well compare their efforts with those of others and become discouraged—their work just isn't as good—and they lose interest. It isn't until adolescence that a small number of children again manifest that

creative spark. At this time inborn talent and a supportive environment help a child develop those skills needed to withstand immersion in rules and correct thinking.

Children like to draw and paint, to express themselves through their artistry. They lose their interest, however, when they see no goal, when making another pattern no longer fascinates them. With no new objectives and challenges, children's enthusiasm vanishes, interest evaporates, and they turn their attention to other fields. How would you explain this phenomenon?

If you would like to have a more informed view on this issue, you may want to read one or more of the references in this chapter, such as Kellogg's (1979) classic work.

You may also wish to learn more about it by going to our web site at http://www.mhhe.com/dacey5.

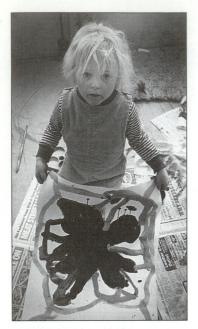

The early childhood years are a time when children show a great love for drawing. Not only are their drawings a sign of motor development, but they also indicate levels of cognitive development and can be emotionally revealing.

(Wachowiak & Clements, 1997). Artistic expression seems to peak by the end of the early childhood period. During these years, children begin to paint and hold the brush with thumb and fingers. They hold the paper in place with the free hand. They give names to their drawings and begin to show representation (using one thing for another—see the cognitive section of the chapter).

Children's drawings not only are good clues to their motor coordination but, as we'll see, provide insights into their cognitive and emotional lives, another example of how a biopsychosocial perspective helps us to understand development.

Guided Review

1. The period of early childhood extends from the age of _____ to the age of _____.
2. During this period a child can grow as much as _____ inches and gain about _____ pounds per year.
3. By the end of this period, children begin to lose their _____ _____.
4. Hemispheric specialization is often referred to as _____.
5. By 2 to 2½ years of age, the brain has achieved about _____% of its adult weight.
6. The belief that a gene predisposes us to handedness is called the _____ theory.
7. Much of our knowledge about the development of children's art is based on the millions of children's drawings collected by _____.
8. A child using his/her left hand to draw, signals that the _____ cerebral hemisphere is lateralized for handedness.
9. Motor skills fall into two types _____ and _____.
10. Gardner has attributed the loss of a child's artistic creativity to the _____ _____ _____.

Cognitive Development

Physical developments, while observable and exciting, are not the only significant changes occurring during early childhood. Early childhood youngsters expand their mental horizons by their increasing use of ideas and by their rapid growth in language. This growing cognitive ability is a fact; explaining it is much more difficult. To help us understand what is happening and how it happens, we turn once more to Piaget.

Piaget's Preoperational Period

Preoperational   Piaget's second stage of cognitive development, extending from about 2 to 7 years.

For Piaget, **preoperational** refers to children who cannot take two things into consideration at the same time—take something apart and put it together again, who cannot return to the beginning of a thought sequence, that is, who cannot comprehend how to reverse the action of 2 + 2, who cannot believe that water poured from a short, fat glass into a taller, thinner one retains the same volume—these children are at a level of thinking that precedes operational thought.

An example of the limitations of preoperational thought is seen in the preschooler's notion of death. Studying 157 children ages 3 to 17 who had experi-

Answers

1. 2, 6 2. 12, 5 3. baby teeth 4. Lateralization 5. 75 6. biased-gene 7. Kellogg 8. right 9. gross, fine 10. "reach for realism"

enced a parent's illness and death, Christ (2000) discovered that children 3 to 5 years could not accept the finality of the parent's death. For months, they would ask when the parent was coming back. They needed repeated concrete explanations of what death meant.

Several examples of preoperational thinking are as follows:

Realism Refers to when children learn to distinguish and accept the real world.

Animism Children consider objects as alive and conscious that adults consider inert.

Artificialism Children attribute human life to inanimate objects.

- **Realism,** which means that children slowly distinguish and accept a real world. They now have identified both an external and internal world.

- **Animism,** which means that children consider a large number of objects as alive and conscious that adults consider inert. For example, a child who sees a necklace wound up and then released explains that it is moving because it "wants to unwind." Piaget believed that comparison with the thoughts of others slowly conquers animism as it does egocentrism.

- **Artificialism,** which consists of attributing human creation to everything. For example, when asked how the moon began, some of Piaget's subjects replied, "because we began to be alive." As egocentrism decreases, youngsters become more objective and they steadily assimilate objective reality to their cognitive structures. They proceed from a purely human or divine explanation to an explanation that is half natural, half artificial: The moon comes from the clouds but the clouds come from people's houses. (The decline of artificialism parallels the growth of realism.)

Features of Preoperational Thought

Representation Child's growing ability to engage in abstract thinking.

For Piaget, the great accomplishment of the preoperational period is a growing ability to represent, which is how we record or express information. For example, the word "car" is a **representation** since it represents a certain idea. Pointing an index finger at a playmate and saying "Stick 'em up" is also an example of representation.

Other activities typical of preoperational children reflect their use of internal representation and include the following (Piaget & Inhelder, 1969).

Deferred imitation Imitative behavior that continues after the disappearance of the model to be imitated.

Deferred Imitation Preoperational children can imitate some object or activity that they have previously witnessed; for example, they walk like an animal that they saw at the zoo earlier in the day. Piaget gave the example of a child who visited his home one day and while there had a temper tantrum. His daughter Jacqueline, about 18 months old, watched, absolutely fascinated. Later, after the child had gone, Jacqueline had her own tantrum. Piaget interpreted this to mean that Jacqueline had a mental image of the event.

Symbolic play The game of pretending; one of five preoperational behavior patterns.

Symbolic Play Children enjoy pretending that they are asleep, or that they are someone or something else. Piaget argued eloquently for recognizing the importance of play in a youngster's life. Obliged to adapt themselves to social and physical worlds that they only slightly understand and appreciate, children must make intellectual adaptations that leave personality needs unmet. For their mental health, they must have some outlet, some technique that permits them to assimilate reality to self, and not vice versa. Children find this mechanism in play, using the tools characteristic of symbolic play. (We'll discuss the role of play in greater detail in chapter 8.)

Drawing Piaget's use of the term to indicate a growing symbolic ability.

Drawing We have previously discussed drawing in a broad context but here Piaget concentrated on its cognitive elements. Children of this age project their mental representations into their drawings. Highly symbolic, their artwork reflects the level of their thinking and what they are thinking. Encourage children to talk about their art.

These children, playing doctor and patients, are furthering all aspects of their development. They are discovering what objects in their environment are supposed to do, they are learning about the give and take of human relationships, and they are channeling their emotional energies into acceptable outlets.

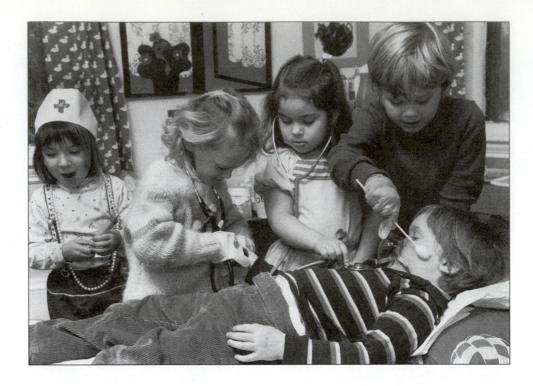

Reproductive images   Mental images that are faithful to the original object or event being represented.

Anticipatory images   Piaget's term for images that enable the child to anticipate change.

Mental Images   Mental images appear late in this period because of their dependence on internalized imitation. Piaget's studies of the development of mental images between the ages of 4 and 5 showed that mental images fall into two categories. **Reproductive images** are images restricted to those sights previously perceived. **Anticipatory images** are images that include movements and transformations. At the preoperational level, children are limited to reproductive images.

A good illustration of the difference between the two types of images is Piaget's famous example of matching tokens. Piaget showed 5- and 6-year-old children a row of red tokens and asked them to put down the same number of blue tokens. At this age, children put one blue token opposite each red one. When Piaget changed the arrangement, however, and spread out the row of red tokens, the children were baffled because they thought there were more red tokens than blue. Thus, children of this age can reproduce but not anticipate, which reflects the nature of their cognitive structures and level of cognitive functioning.

Language   For preoperational children, language becomes a vehicle for thought. Children of this age need ample opportunities to talk with adults and with each other. (See the language section of this chapter.)

Limitations of Preoperational Thought

Although we see the steady development of thought during this period, preoperational thought still has limitations. To know an object is to act on it, to modify it, to transform it, and to join objects in a class. The action is also reversible. If two is added to two, the result is four; but if two is taken away from four, the original two returns. Preoperational children can't perform such operations on concepts and objects.

Several reasons account for the restricted nature of preoperational thought. In the period of preoperational thought, children cannot assume the role of another person or recognize that other viewpoints exist, a state called **egocentrism.** This differs from sensorimotor egocentrism, which is primarily the inability to distinguish

Egocentrism   Child focuses on self in early phases of cognitive development; term associated with Piaget.

oneself from the world. For example, children may believe that the moon follows *them* around; everything focuses on them.

In Piaget's classic experiment, a child is shown a display of three mountains varying in height and color. The child stands on one side of the table, looking at the mountains; a doll is then placed at various spots around the mountains. The child is next shown several pictures of the mountains and asked to pick the one that shows what part of the mountains the doll saw. Egocentric children pick the photo that shows the mountains as they saw them.

Another striking feature of preoperational thought is the centering of attention on one aspect of an object and the neglecting of any other features—called **centration.** Consequently, reasoning is often distorted. Preoperational youngsters are unable to decenter, to notice features that would give balance to their reasoning. A good example of this is the process of **classification.** When youngsters from age 3 to age 12 are asked, "What things are alike?", their answers proceed through three stages. First, the youngest children group *figurally,* that is, by similarities, differences, and by forming a figure in space with the parts. Second, children of about age 5 or 6 group objects *nonfigurally.* They form the elements into groups with no particular spatial form. (For an interesting discussion of the development of children's analysis of spatial patterns, see Tada & Stiles, 1996.)

At this stage, the classification seems rational, but Piaget and Inhelder (1969) provide a fascinating example of the limitations of classification at this age. If in a group of 12 flowers, there are 6 roses, preoperational youngsters can differentiate between the other flowers and the roses. But when asked if there are more flowers or more roses, they are unable to reply because they cannot distinguish the whole from the part (see figure 7.4). This understanding does not appear until the third phase of classification, at about the age of 8.

Another limitation of the period is the lack of **conservation.** Conservation means understanding that an object retains certain properties, no matter how its form changes. The most popular illustration is to show a 5-year-old two glasses, each half filled with water. The child agrees that each glass contains an equal amount. But if you then pour the water from one of the glasses into a taller, thinner glass, the youngster now says that the new glass contains more liquid (see figure 7.5).

Youngsters consider only the appearance of the liquid and ignore what happened. They also do not perceive the reversibility of the transformation. In their minds they do not pour the water back into the first glass.

Finally, preoperational thought lacks **reversibility.** A truly cognitive act is reversible if it can use stages of reasoning to solve a problem and then proceed in reverse, tracing its steps back to the original question or premise. The preoperational child's thought is irreversible and entangles the child in a series of contradictions in logic.

Centration A feature of preoperational thought—the centering of attention on one aspect of an object and the neglecting of any other features.

Classification The ability to group objects with some similarities within a larger category.

Conservation Children conserve the essence of something even though surface features change.

Reversibility The ability to reverse thinking.

Figure 7.4

Lack of genuine classification.

From John F. Travers, *The Growing Child,* Scott, Foresman and Company, Glenview, IL, 1982. Reprinted by permission of the author.

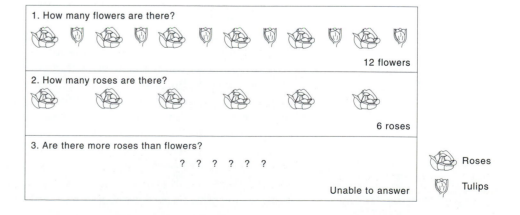

Figure 7.5

Piaget used the beaker task to determine whether children had conservation of liquid. In 1, two identical beakers (A and B) are presented to the child; then the experimenter pours the liquid from B into beaker C, which is taller and thinner than A and B. The child is asked if beakers B and C have the same amount of liquid. The preoperational child says no, responding that the taller, thinner beaker (C) has more.

From John W. Santrock and Steve R. Yussen, *Child Development: An Introduction,* 4th ed. Copyright © 1989 Wm. C. Brown Communications, Inc., Dubuque, Iowa. All rights reserved. Reprinted by permission.

In the water-level problem, for example, the child believes that the taller, thinner glass contains more water. Youngsters cannot mentally reverse the task (imagine pouring the contents back into the original glass). At the conclusion of the preoperational period, children slowly decenter and learn reversibility as a way of mental life.

Challenges to Piaget

As you can well imagine, Piaget's theory, which has been with us for more than 70 years, has been tested, retested, challenged, and refuted in many respects. Training studies have repeatedly shown that early childhood youngsters possess more cognitive competence than Piaget believed. For example, 4-year-old nonconservers can be taught to conserve (Bjorklund, 2000).

Evidence continues to mount supporting the conclusion that Piaget underestimated the cognitive abilities of young children: They conserve, classify, and overcome egocentrism earlier than Piaget realized. For example, preschoolers show clear evidence that they understand basic concepts that Piaget believed were too advanced for them. As Siegler (1998) noted, although some preschoolers may not understand the number concept, they know a lot about numbers.

Children's Theory of Mind

Theory of mind Children's realization that others' thoughts affect their behavior.

Many developmental psychologists believe that today's cognitive psychology is actually the psychology of children's **theory of mind.** Emerging from the tradition of Piaget's seminal ideas and the theory and research relating to metacognition, theory of mind studies now dominate the field. These studies investigate the beliefs, desires, knowledge, and thoughts of children's mental states (Flavell, 1998).

For example, in one study (called a *false-belief* task) an experimenter showed a 5-year-old a candy box with pictures of candy on the cover. When asked what's in it, she replied, "Candy." She then looked inside and was surprised to find crayons, not candy. The experimenter then asked her what another child would find in the box. "Candy," was the firm reply.

Next, the experiment was done with a 3-year-old, who said she expected to find candy inside. But when asked the second question, the 3-year-old said, "Crayons!" She insisted that she thought the box always contained crayons. That is, children of this age don't realize that people think and act in accordance with the way they represent the world rather than the way the world actually is (Flavell, 1999). But it is during the early childhood years that children discover mind. The question facing us is: How?

The Role of Information Processing in Discovering Mind

If you recall in chapter 5, we noted that information processing theorists argued that cognitive development occurred by improvement of such cognitive processes as attention and memory. During the early childhood years the amount of information a child can attend to steadily increases.

Span of apprehension   The amount of information a person can attend to at one time.

For example, studying what is called **span of apprehension** (how much information people can attend to at one time), Cowan and his colleagues (1999) compared first graders with fourth graders and discovered that the first graders could attend to 2.5 items while fourth graders attended to 3 items. This is a significant difference that testifies to true developmental growth. Bjorklund (2000) has summarized the development of attention as a lengthy process in which children translate what they know into appropriate actions and then rely on these strategies to gather new information. As Siegler (1998) noted, the selectivity with which children focus their attention on relevant items increases greatly between three and eight years.

Rehearsal   Repeating information to aid memory.

Much the same holds true for memory. During the early childhood years, children begin to develop memory strategies, such as rehearsal, organization, and retrieval. For example, **rehearsal** (repeating target information) shows a clear developmental pattern. In a classic study, Flavell, Beach, and Chinsky (1966) studied list learning in 5-, 7-, and 10-year-olds. The results showed that as rehearsal increased with the older children, recall also improved. Eighty-five percent of the 10-year-olds displayed spontaneous rehearsal, while only 10 percent of the 5-year-olds did so.

Organization   Imposing structure on information to aid recall.

Organization (discovering or imposing structure on a set of items to guide behavior) follows much the same developmental path as attention. When children are given a randomized list of items that can be sorted into categories (fruit, cars, tools, etc.), older children cluster the items and improve their recall. Preschool children, however, cluster items only by chance, but studies have shown that training exercises can improve their ability to organize (Bjorklund, 2000).

Retrieval   Obtaining information from memory.

Retrieval (obtaining information from memory) takes two forms: recognition and recall. Most children find recognition tasks fairly simple, but recall tests offer a more serious challenge. Helping younger children to recall demands that the circumstances under which they first acquired the material need to be repeated. Older children spontaneously use retrieval cues more often than preschoolers.

You can see, then, how rapidly improving cognitive processes such as attention and memory help children to acquire a theory of mind. As children's cognitive processes show steady growth, their theory of mind also shows developmental changes similar to the following (Bartsch & Wellman, 1995; Flavell, 1999).

- Around two years of age children acquire a *desire psychology,* which is an expression of simple emotions and desires about what they're attending to. Cross-cultural studies consistently show a similar pattern of mental state language in children: desire, thinking, and knowing. Studying theory of mind development in Mandarin- and Cantonese-speaking children, Tardif and Wellman (2000) found that although the pattern of development was similar, the Chinese-speaking children used desire terms much earlier than English-speaking children.

- About three years of age, children begin to talk about beliefs and thoughts as well as desires. Nevertheless, they still explain people's behavior by desires rather than beliefs. This level of understanding is called *desire-belief* psychology.

- At approximately four years of age, children begin to understand that what people think and believe, as well as what they desire, affect how they behave. This level is referred to as *belief-desire* psychology.

For a thoughtful, readable introduction to the theory of mind work, see Janet Astington. (1993). *The child's discovery of the mind.* Cambridge, MA: Harvard University Press.

Experience seems to be the explanatory mechanism here. That is, children see people behaving in a way that can't be explained by desire alone. The notion of belief is also required.

An Applied View
Children and Their Humor

"Why did daddy tiptoe past the medicine cabinet?"
"Because he didn't want to wake the sleeping pills."

Jokes such as these have spurred Paul McGhee (1979, 1988; McGhee & Panoutsopoulous, 1995) to analyze children's humor and trace its developmental path. Noting that little is known about how children develop humor, McGhee turned to cognitive development as a possible explanation. Although humor also has psychodynamic and social features (Clay, 1997), McGhee believes that its cognitive properties offer the best basis for unraveling its secrets.

McGhee begins by noting that the basis of most children's humor is incongruity, which is the realization that the relationship between different things just isn't "right." Using this as a basis, he traces four stages of incongruous humor. He treats stages as does Piaget: The sequence of stages remains the same, but the ages at which children pass through them varies.

- *Stage 1: Incongruous Actions toward Objects.* Stage 1 usually occurs sometime during the second year, when children play with objects. They are able to form internal images of the object and thus start to "make believe." For example, one of Piaget's children picked up a leaf, put it to her ear, and talked to it as if it were a telephone, laughing all the time. One of the main characteristics of stage 1 humor is the child's physical activity directed at the object.
- *Stage 2: Incongruous Labeling of Objects and Events.* Stage 2 humor is more verbal, which seems to be its most important difference from

stage 1. McGhee (1979) notes that the absence of action toward objects is quite noticeable. Piaget's 22-month-old daughter put a shell on the table and said, "sitting." She then put another shell on top of the first, looked at them and said, "sitting on pot." She then began to laugh. Children in this stage delight in calling a dog a cat, a foot a hand, and then start laughing.

- *Stage 3: Conceptual Incongruity.* Around age 3, most children begin to play with ideas, which reflects their growing cognitive ability. For example, stage 3 children laugh when they see a drawing of a cat with two heads.
- *Stage 4: Multiple Meanings.* Once children begin to play with the ambiguity of words, their humor approaches the adult level.

"Hey, did you take a bath?"
"No. Why, is one missing?"

Children at stage 4 (usually around age 7) understand the different meaning of take in both instances. Stage 3 children could not understand the following joke:

"Order! Order! Order in the court."
"Ham and cheese on rye, your honor."

Stage 4 youngsters appreciate its ambiguity.

You can see how cognitive development is linked to humor: The effective use of humor with children can help stimulate new learning and creative thinking, instill an interest in literature, facilitate social development, and enhance emotional development and adjustment.

Guided Review

11. According to Piaget, _____ is the means that permits children to assimilate reality to self.
12. Attributing human activity or creation to things is known as _____ .
13. To understand that an object retains properties no matter how its form changes is called _____ .
14. Researchers have used _____-_____ tasks to study a child's theory of mind.
15. When children understand that what people believe affects what they do, they are at the _____-_____ level.

Answers

11. play 12. artificialism 13. conservation 14. false-belief 15. belief-desire

Early Childhood Education

Early education programs, often referred to as preschool and kindergarten programs, usually take one of two directions. They are either physically, socially, and emotionally oriented or more cognitively centered, which is not to say that programs are exclusively social or cognitive; typically elements of both occur in all programs (Bredekamp & Copple, 1997).

Given today's concern with educational achievement, many preschool programs rely on the ideas of individuals such as Piaget or Montessori.

Piaget and Montessori

Hauser-Cram, P., D. Pierson, D. Klein Walker, & T. Tivnan, (1991). *Early education in the public schools.* San Francisco: Jossey-Bass. An excellent review of early childhood programs designed according to developmentally appropriate principles.

In these programs, which are based on a developmental theory of behavior, children are encouraged to learn through interacting with their environments and to be active participants in constructing knowledge. Early childhood programs stress integrated subject matter; for example, mathematics is taught by having the children weigh different objects and measure amounts to cook. Peer relationships are stressed and the line between work and play fades. Teachers encourage, mediate, and try to extend children's thinking (Hauser-Cram & others, 1991).

Although Piaget himself never advocated using his developmental theory in this manner, you can see how his ideas could form the basis for early childhood programs. His emphasis on a child's progression through intellectual stages of development has clearly defined program implications (use of concrete materials, etc.). Since Piaget's is an *interactive* theory, children's energy and activities can be directed at interesting cognitive outcomes rather than having children passively accept facts.

In contrast, Montessori (1967) was a strong proponent of early childhood programs. She believed that developing children pass through different physical and mental growth phases that alternate with periods of transition, suggesting that children possess different types of minds at different periods. These periods differ so sharply that Montessori referred to them as a series of new births.

Absorbent mind Montessori's term for a child's ability to absorb experiences from the environment (0 to 6 years).

She described three major periods of development. The first stage, which is called the **absorbent mind** phase to indicate a child's tremendous ability to absorb experiences from its environment, extends from birth to age 6. The second stage, which is referred to as the **uniform growth** phase to identify these years as a time of considerable stability, extends from age 6 to age 12. Finally, the third stage extends from 12 to 18 years.

Uniform growth Montessori's term to describe the developmental period in which children show considerable stability.

A youngster reaches this level by what Montessori calls the **prepared environment.** For children under age 6, the prepared environment includes sensorial materials, such as rods to teach lengths, cubes to teach size, and bells to teach musical pitch, materials for the acquisition of cultural geography, history, art, and arithmetic, and materials and techniques necessary for the development of a child's religious life. Montessori also devised concrete materials to encourage learning in 6- to 12-year-old children.

Prepared environment Use of age-appropriate materials to further cognitive development.

The stages we have just described lead to what is perhaps the best known of Montessori's ideas, that of **sensitive periods.** Montessori believed that there are times when a child was especially *sensitive* or ready for certain types of learning. One of the earliest and most vital of these periods is concerned with the attainment of their language, which, as we have seen, children acquire effortlessly, a good example of Montessori's sensitive periods.

Sensitive periods Montessori's term for ideal times of readiness for learning.

Project Head Start

Head Start Early intervention program intended to provide educational and developmental services to disadvantaged children.

Other preschool programs, such as **Head Start,** have also helped disadvantaged children. Originally conceived as part of President Lyndon Johnson's War on Poverty in the 1960s, *Project Head Start* was headed by Sargent Shriver who had been astounded on examining the distribution of poverty in the United States. Data indicated that about one-half of the nation's 30 million poor were children and most of these were under age 12. His main objective thus became the preparation of poor children for entrance into kindergarten and the first grade. As Hauser-Cram and others (1991) noted, Head Start was intended to provide educational and developmental services to preschool children from low-income families.

Improving children's health became a primary goal; children received pediatric and neurological assessments plus two nutritious meals a day (Zigler & Muenchow, 1992). Head Start programs had six components: preschool education, health screening and referral, mental health services, nutrition education and hot meals, social services for the child and family, and parental involvement (Zigler & Styfco, 1994). Since its beginning, Head Start has served more than 13 million children.

The IQ Controversy

Unfortunately, several of the early claims about the gains to be realized from Head Start programs revolved around changes in IQ; some proponents stated that as a result of participation in Head Start, a child's IQ would increase one IQ point a month. In the mid-1960s, critical evaluations of intelligence tests had not reached today's level of sophistication, but even then certain individuals such as Edward Zigler, a member of the Head Start Planning Committee, deplored reliance on increases in IQ scores as the means of evaluating Head Start.

His fears were quickly justified as follow-up studies of Head Start children showed a "fadeout effect." That is, although graduates of these preschool programs showed immediate gains in intelligence and achievement test scores, after several months in the public schools, the Head Start children seemed to lose these cognitive benefits (Zigler & Styfco, 1994, p. 128). Nevertheless, even if Head Start graduates do not maintain *academic* gains, they have improved their readiness for school and the advantages of Head Start extend to other parts of their lives.

Today, with the rapid increase in the number of working women and the stunning rise of children living in poverty, the need for early intervention programs to aid these children seems more compelling than ever. As Stipek & Ryan (1997) noted, disadvantaged children are every bit as eager to learn as their advantaged peers, but they have much further to go with regard to their intellectual skills and too often never catch up. In her summary of the need for greater support of preschool programs, Kassebaum (1994) pointed out that 21 percent of all American children live in poverty; 25 percent of all children live with a single parent; 25 percent of all babies

Zigler, E. & S. Muenchow. (1992). *Head start.* New York: Basic Books. A fascinating, well-written history of the early intervention movement and its role in attempting to prepare disadvantaged children for a successful school experience.

Head Start was designed to offer developmental and educational services to preschool children from low-income families. With the increasing number of children living in poverty, such programs can provide much needed services.

are born to unmarried mothers; every night at least 100,000 children are homeless; the United States ranks 20th in the world with regard to infant mortality.

These statistics cry out for attention because the children they represent not only suffer educational disadvantages but they also face other developmental difficulties. For example, as we have seen, they are more frequently the premature babies; their families suffer devastating and widespread deprivation; the children themselves are more subject to physical illness and lowered cognitive performance. As more of these children enter the public schools, is it any wonder they are unable to meet the ordinary demands of the classroom (Hauser-Cram & others, 1991)? It is in meeting their needs that we see the value of programs such as Head Start and the hope of bringing these children successfully into the mainstream of school life and the wider community. If we are to succeed, we must identify the skills, both academic and social, that our students need.

Good Preschools

Several features distinguish good preschools: low teacher-child ratio, specially trained teachers, availability of resources, and recognition of children's individual differences. These programs are all child centered; that is, they are designed to emphasize individual children and to provide children with enriching, enjoyable experiences suitable for their years, which is especially desirable given the social needs of early childhood youngsters. Most studies of peer relationships during the early childhood period (2–6 years) have been conducted in day-care centers and nursery schools. Note the age progression in developing relationships: Social contacts occur more frequently among 5-year-olds than 3-year-olds. Aggressive interactions are quite common in the period, although aggression decreases in proportion to friendly interactions (especially true among middle-class boys).

Particularly interesting are the changes in quarreling during these years. As in their other social exchanges, older youngsters (4, 5, and 6 years) engage in fewer but longer quarrels with members of their own sex (Berk, 1997). Boys quarrel more frequently among themselves than girls, usually over objects, gradually changing from physical to verbal aggression toward the end of the period. Although solitary activity persists, older children of this period are more obviously bidding for the attention of their peers.

As you can tell from our discussion thus far, children of these years have marched firmly into a symbolic world, a major part of which is language.

Guided Review

16. Preschool programs are usually oriented to either _____ or _____ / _____ / _____ development.
17. Two individuals who have had great influence on the nature of preschool programs are _____ and _____ .
18. A major goal of Project Head Start was improving children's _____ .

Language Development

Did you ever try to learn a second language, perhaps in high school or college? Do you remember the difficulties you experienced with everything from pronunciation to vocabulary? Yet youngsters naturally and easily acquire their native language, a task of such scope and intricacy that its secrets have eluded investigators for centuries. During the early childhood period, language figuratively "explodes." At

Answers

16. cognitive, physical, social, emotional 17. Piaget, Montessori 18. health

The attention that adults (especially parents) give children encourages positive interactions and leads to satisfactory and fulfilling relationships. Adult attention will also further language development and enhance a child's self-concept.

Simply by making noises with our mouths, we can reliably cause precise new combinations of ideas to arise in each other's minds.

Steven Pinker

Fast mapping Techniques to help children detect word meanings.

Phonology Describes how to put sounds together to form words.

Syntax Describes how we learn to put words together to form sentences.

Semantics Describes how to interpret the meaning of words.

Pragmatics Describes how we learn to take part in a conversation.

Receptive language Language that children use to show an understanding of words without necessarily producing them.

about the same age children manifest similar patterns of speech development, whether they live in a ghetto or in a wealthy suburb.

Within a short span of time and with almost no direct instruction, children completely analyze their language. Although refinements are made between ages 5 and 10, most children have completed the greater part of the process of language acquisition by the age of 4 or 5. Recent findings have also shown that when children acquire the various parts of their language, they do so in the same order. For example, in English, children learn *in* and *on* before other prepositions, and they learn to use *ing* as a verb ending before other endings such as *ed* (Hulit & Howard, 1997).

These are the years of Brown's Stages Two, Three, Four, and Five. (See chapter 5 for a discussion of Stage One.) The accomplishments of each of these stages are as follows (Brown, 1973; Owens, 1996; Hulit & Howard, 1997; Bloom, 1998).

- *Stage Two* (27 to 30 months). Children begin to use pronouns and phrases and clauses to form sentences similar to adults. As you probably know all too well, they love to use negatives, and begin to ask endless questions.

- *Stage Three* (31 to 34 months). At this stage children refine their use of pronouns and auxiliary verbs. They also show considerable improvement in their ability to carry on a conversation.

- *Stage Four* (35 to 40 months). Children now demonstrate a major new achievement called *embedding,* which refers to combining clauses and phrases. *I know what you did.*

- *Stage Five* (41 to 46 months). Embedding becomes more complex, grammar continues to improve, and children become better conversationalists during these years.

Language acquisition is a tremendous accomplishment; if you remember how you may have tried to learn a foreign language as an adult, you'll recall how difficult it was to acquire vocabulary and to master rules of grammar and the subtleties of usage. Yet preschool children do just this with no formal training. By the time they are ready to enter first grade, most children have a vocabulary of about 8,000 words; use questions, negative statements, and dependent clauses; and have learned to use language in a variety of social situations. They are relatively sophisticated language users.

Language as Rule Learning

As children acquire the basics of their language, they are also learning the guidelines that make language such a powerful tool. For example, by the age of 4 or 5, children will also have discovered that rules exist for combining sounds into words, that individual words have specific meanings, and that there are rules for combining words into meaningful sentences, and for participating in a dialogue. These rules help children to detect the meaning of a word with which they are unfamiliar. Called **fast mapping,** this technique enables children to use context for a word's meaning, thus helping them to continue rapid vocabulary development. (See also chapter 5.)

We can summarize these accomplishments as follows.

- The rules of **phonology** describe how to put sounds together to form words.

- The rules of **syntax** describe how to put words together to form sentences.

- The rules of **semantics** describe how to interpret the meaning of words.

- The rules of **pragmatics** describe how to take part in a conversation.

As we trace the path of language development in the early childhood years, you should remember a basic distinction that children quite clearly demonstrate. At about 1 year (the infancy period), children show an ability for **receptive language**

Whole Language: Lasting Improvement or Passing Fad?

Building on a growing knowledge of language development, many educators, long dissatisfied with the teaching of reading and writing, have adopted a new strategy. Called *whole language,* this strategy refers to a technique by which the four language modes (speaking, listening, reading, and writing—including spelling and handwriting) are studied in a more natural context, as a whole and not as a series of isolated facts.

For those communities whose schools have turned to the whole language approach, the teaching of discrete language subskills (phonics, spelling, punctuation, etc.) no longer is the main focus. Rather teachers attempt to integrate all four language modes with other subjects (history, literature, science). Whole language advocates argue that meaning should be the goal of language instruction (Ovando & Collier, 1998).

How the Whole Language Concept "Works"

Shifting from dependence on a basal language series to whole language requires teachers to rethink their assumptions about literature and language learning. For example, in the whole language strategy, many teachers will work with themes: friendship, loyalty, and honesty. First children will read a story that illustrates the theme. This is known as *experiencing the literature.* Next the teacher may read a related story or poem; pupils are listening to the literature.

Now the teacher may attempt to *expand* the concepts that the children experienced in their literature and simultaneously work on vocabulary using various techniques. Next children may read the selection cooperatively (taking turns with their partners or reading aloud about a particular character in the story). They can then discuss the characters in the story.

At this point, the children may *respond* to the literature by completing a story form (sentences with missing words, explaining the beginning and ending, telling how the story's problem was solved). The teacher may ask them to evaluate the characters' actions in the story or give their own opinions about the story. Some children may explore language; that is, if they need help with vocabulary or phonics, or with general reading strategies, they are guided to appropriate activities.

The children now shift from reading to writing. For example, they may write a paragraph explaining a particular part of the story. They use the words they have learned in their reading and apply them to their writing. They can be taught how to proofread and to revise in this phase.

With their reading and writing experiences completed, and if time permits, children may *extend their reading experiences.* That is, if the theme of their work is friendship, they may do independent research that could include examples of friendship in stories, friendship between leaders of nations, or friendship between people of different cultures.

The ideal time for the introduction of whole language is during the early childhood period. Children of this age are experiencing a rapid natural growth of language and enjoying the newfound power that language confers, which is the rationale for harnessing this exuberance and using it to further their learning.

Yet many critics of the whole language approach believe that children can miss many necessary fundamentals, such as systematic phonics instruction. The controversy swirling around whole language shows no sign of abating in the immediate future.

Expressive language
Language that children use to express their own ideas and needs.

("show me your nose"—they receive and understand these words). Now, in early childhood, they produce language themselves, **expressive language** (McLaughlin, 1998). How do children acquire these language milestones?

The Pattern of Language Development

As mentioned earlier, all children learn their native tongue, and at similar ages they manifest similar patterns of language development. The basic sequence of language development during early childhood is that at about 2½ years, most children produce complete sentences, begin to ask questions, and use negative statements. At about 4 years they have acquired the complicated structure of their native tongue, and in about two or three more years they speak and understand sentences that they have never previously used or heard.

As children grow, specifying the extent of their vocabularies is difficult. Do we mean spoken words only? Or do we include words that children may not use but clearly understand? Building a vocabulary is an amazing accomplishment. For example, the vocabulary of every language is categorized; that is, some words are nouns, some are verbs, still others are adjectives, prepositions, or conjunctions. If English had only 1,000 nouns and 1,000 verbs, we could form 1 million sentences (1,000 × 1,000).

But nouns can be used as objects as well as subjects. Therefore the number of possible three-word sentences increases to one billion (1,000 × 1,000 × 1,000).

One billion sentences is the result of a starkly impoverished vocabulary. The number of sentences that could be generated from English, with its thousands of nouns and verbs, plus adjectives, adverbs, prepositions, and conjunctions, staggers the imagination. Estimates are that it would take trillions of years to say all possible English sentences of twenty words. In this context, the ability of children to acquire their language is an astounding achievement. Although most youngsters experience problems with some tasks during this period—difficulty with reading or mathematics—they acquire their language easily and in just a few years.

Language Irregularities

Overextensions Children's tendency to apply a word too widely.

When speech emerges, certain irregularities appear in children's speech that are quite normal and to be expected. For example, **overextensions** mark children's beginning words. Assume that a child has learned the name of the house pet, *doggy*. Think what that label means: an animal with a head, tail, body, and four legs. Now consider what other animals "fit" this label: cats, horses, donkeys, and cows. Consequently, children may briefly apply *doggy* to all four-legged creatures; they quickly eliminate overextensions, however, as they learn about their world.

Overregulation Children's inappropriate use of language rules they have learned.

Overregularities are a similar fleeting phenomenon. As youngsters begin to use two- and three-word sentences, they struggle to convey more precise meanings by mastering the grammatical rules of their language. For example, many English verbs add *ed* to indicate past tense.

> I want to play ball.
> I wanted to play ball.

Other verbs change their form much more radically.

> Did Daddy come home?
> Daddy came home.

Most children, even after they have mastered the correct form of such verbs as come, see, and run, still add *ed* to the original form. That is, youngsters who know that the past tense of *come* is *came* will still say:

> Daddy comed home.

Again, this phenomenon persists only briefly and is another example of the close link between language and thought. We know that from birth, children respond to patterns. They look longer at the human face than they will at diagrams because the human face is more complex. (Remember the Fantz study?) Once they have learned a pattern such as adding *ed* to signify past tense, they have considerable difficulty in changing the pattern.

An interesting development occurs as children's sentences grow longer: Their use of word order becomes closely linked to grammar rather than merely reflecting meaning. That is, their language has become more syntactic. Inflections such as "s" and "ed" are correctly added to words and, thanks to Roger Brown's groundbreaking work (1973), we now know quite a bit more about these grammatical morphemes (s, ed). He studied fourteen morphemes, including the three "s" inflections—plural (girls), possessive (girl's), and verb endings (runs).

Using them correctly requires considerable language sophistication. Children who correctly add *ed* to a word tell us in no uncertain terms that something happened in the past. Brown also discovered that *all* children acquire these fourteen morphemes in the same sequence. For example, although the three "s" look exactly alike, children learn the plural usage first, followed by the possessive, and finally the verb inflection.

During the early childhood years, children begin to display a growing mastery of meaning. As we mentioned, their vocabulary continues to increase quite dramatically, and they begin to combine words to refine their meaning. Yet they also display a sense of constraint in the way they use words, that is, they quickly learn to suggest the correct meaning for the correct word.

"That's right," suggesting correctness.
"That's right," suggesting direction.

Summarizing, then, as children come to the end of the early childhood period, several language milestones have been achieved:

- Children become skillful in building words; adding suffixes such as *er, man*, and *ist* to form nouns (the person who performs experiments is an *experimenter*).

- They begin to be comfortable with passive sentences (the glass *was broken* by the wind).

- By the end of the early childhood period, children can pronounce almost all English speech sounds accurately.

- As we have noted, this is the time of the "language explosion" and vocabulary has grown rapidly.

- Children of this age are aware of grammatical correctness.

Moskowitz, B. (1979). The acquisition of language. *Scientific American,* 239, 92–108. If you are like most readers encountering the basics of language development for the first time, you probably would like to do more reading about it. This article (still one of the best) is clear, thorough, and well written. You should find it easily in your library. You will find it helpful.

Bilingualism

Why doesn't Odette feel competent? She's in an English as a second language class. We're going to get her to learn English. There's no reason for her to worry about her accent. She's sitting there with a lot of Spanish kids. They have a funny accent, too.

This conversation, unfortunately true, reflects the problem that many children in the United States, who do not speak or write English as their native language, face on a daily basis. Happily, as we have become more sensitive to the needs of all our students, incidents such as this occur with less frequency.

All evidence points to the conclusion that our country today is more diverse ethnically and linguistically than ever before. Consequently, a major question faced language experts and educators: What is the most effective way to teach English to non-English-speaking students while at the same time helping them to maintain the richness and cultural values of their own languages?

To help make these figures more meaningful, consider this: The New York City school system, in the last several years, has enrolled more than 150,000 immigrant children. But suburban school systems are also experiencing the same increase. In one system of 5,300 students, the children speak 25 languages; in a larger Northeast system, the children speak 46 languages. How have the schools responded to these challenges?

Bilingual Education Programs

In a landmark decision in 1974 *(Lau v. Nichols)*, the U.S. Supreme Court ruled that LEP students *(Limited English Proficiency)* in San Francisco were being discriminated against because they were not receiving the same education as their English-speaking classmates. The school district was ordered to provide means for LEP students to participate in all instructional programs. The manner of implementing the decision was left to the school district under the guidance of the lower courts. This decision provided the impetus for the implementation of bilingual education programs in the United States.

Two different techniques for aiding LEP pupils emerged from this decision. In the *English as a second language program* **(ESL),** students are removed from class

ESL   English as a second language.

An Applied View — Meet Genie—A Child You''ll Never Forget

The tranquility of Temple City, California, was shattered in November, 1970 by disquieting, almost unbelievable, news. Screeching headlines described the discovery of a young girl who had been "held prisoner" by her family for thirteen years. Her mother, almost completely blind and feeling the ravages of an abusive marriage, sought assistance for the blind in the local welfare office. With Genie, she mistakenly stumbled into a social services office where an alert eligibility worker became fascinated, not by the mother, but by the girl.

No wonder. The 13-year-old girl weighed only 59 pounds and was 54 inches tall. She was even in worse condition than she looked. She wasn't toilet trained, she couldn't chew solid food, and she could barely swallow. She drooled continuously and had no compunction about spitting—no matter where she was. And these were only Genie's less obnoxious characteristics. Perhaps most important of all, she couldn't talk.

After her discovery, investigators began to trace the road that led Genie to her present state. At about 20 months of age, she received a rare physical examination by a pediatrician who stated that she seemed a little "slow," which the father interpreted as meaning that she was profoundly retarded. With the physician's label ringing in his ears, Genie's father, Clark, developed a weird and abusive style of child-rearing for his youngest child.

He kept her in a small bedroom tied to an infant's potty seat. Trapped in this harness, Genie couldn't move anything but her hands and feet. She sat there, day after day, month after month, year after year. At night, she was placed in a sleeping bag designed by her father that kept her arms motionless much like a straitjacket. She was then placed in a crib with an overhead cover and wire mesh sides. She heard nothing—no human voices (only when her father swore at her), no radio, no language. When she made noise, her father beat her. She quickly learned to keep quiet rather than be beaten by a board her father kept in the room.

The room contained no other furniture, no pictures, one ceiling bulb. She was allowed to play with two dirty plastic raincoats, empty cottage cheese containers, and empty spools of thread. Her diet was baby foods, cereal, and an occasional soft-boiled egg. If she choked and spit out any food, he rubbed her face in it. Almost totally blind, Genie's mother was helpless; she was at the mercy of her husband. Finally, things became so bad that Clark relented, and called Genie's maternal grandparents, who took Genie and her mother with them, which eventually led to Genie's discovery. Her parents were arrested. Despondent about the emotional valleys in his life, Clark killed himself. Genie was hospitalized and became the object of intensive and prolonged study.

The startling case of Genie illustrates the durability of language but also demonstrates its vulnerability. After treatment in the Children's Hospital of Los Angeles, Genie was placed in a foster home where she acquired language, more from exposure than any formal training. Estimates are that she has acquired as much language in eight years as the normal child acquires in three. She continues to have articulation problems and difficulty with word order.

Although Genie made remarkable language progress, difficulties persist. For example, she does not appear to have mastered the rules of language (her grammar is unpredictable), she continues to use the stereotypic speech of the language-disabled child, and she seems to understand more language than she can produce. Thus the case of Genie suggests that while language is difficult to retard, sufficiently severe conditions can affect progress in language. Here we see the meaning of a sensitive period when applied to language development.

If you'd like to learn more about this tragic case, Rymer, R. (1993). *Genie: A scientific tragedy.* New York: Harper. This is one of the best summaries of Genie's years of hell.

and given special English instruction (called *ESL pullout*). The intent is to have these pupils acquire enough English to allow them to learn in their regular classes that are taught in English. Today, however, ESL programs have moved away from this model and turned to what is known as *ESL content*. Specially trained teachers have second language expertise with both language and content objectives for each lesson (Ovando & Collier, 1998).

With the *bilingual* technique, three major goals are identified (Brisk, 1998; Ovando & Collier, 1998).

- The continued development of the student's primary language.

- Acquisition of a second language, usually English.

- Instruction in content subjects using both languages.

Students are taught partly in English and partly in their native language. The objective here is to help pupils to learn English by subject matter instruction in their own language and in English. Thus they acquire subject matter knowledge simultaneously with English. Bilingual programs also allow students to retain their cultural identities while simultaneously progressing in their school subjects. In today's schools, bilingual education has become the program of choice.

Bilingual education programs can also be divided into two categories. First are those programs (sometimes called *transitional* programs) in which the rapid development of English is to occur so that students may switch as soon as possible to an all-English program. Second are those programs (sometimes referred to as *maintenance* programs) that permit LEP students to remain in them even after they have become proficient in English. The rationale for such programs is that students can use both languages to develop mature skills and to become fully bilingual. Transitional programs are the most widely used in the schools.

A third type of bilingual program, called **bilingual immersion,** has become increasingly popular in the United States. Originally introduced in Canada in the 1960s, the program has children spend 90 percent of their day using the minority language in kindergarten and first grade. The majority language is introduced in grades two or three, and usage gradually increases until subjects are taught equally in both languages by grades four and five (Ovando & Collier, 1998).

The controversy surrounding bilingual education programs recently came to a head in the state of California when voters decided to replace bilingual programs with structured English immersion (SEI). SEI programs have several variations, but each is characterized by extensive use of English and the use of English-as-a-second language methodology (Baker, 1999).

Whatever program is chosen, a consensus seems to have gathered around techniques that in no way show disrespect to a student's language. For example, schools effective with culturally different populations are sufficiently flexible to accommodate a range of dialects that learners bring to school. Teachers are urged to allow dialects in social and recreational settings and encourage these students to use Standard English in school settings (Manning & Baruth, 1996).

Table 7.2 summarizes several of the outstanding characteristics of early childhood youngsters.

Bilingualism immersion
Students are taught partly in English and partly in their own language.

TABLE 7.2 SOME DEVELOPMENTAL CHARACTERISTICS OF EARLY CHILDHOOD

Age (yrs.)	Height (in.)	Weight (lbs.)	Cognitive Development	Language Development	Motor Development
2½	36	30	Continued symbolic development; thought still egocentric	Can identify object by use	Can walk on tiptoes; can jump with both feet off the floor
3	38	32	Discriminates 4 objects from 5; mental images are representations of objects	Answers questions; uses brief sentences	Can stand on one foot; jumps from bottom of stairs; rides tricycle
3½	39	34	Understands that thoughts differ from objects; some signs of conservation of number	Begins to build sentences	Continues to improve 3-year-old skills; begins to play with others
4	41	36	Continued growth of symbolic ability; proficient at counting	Names and counts several objects; uses conjunctions; understands prepositions	Walks downstairs, one foot to step; skips on one foot; throws ball overhand
4½	42	38	Begins to understand concept of time	Mean length of utterance 4.5 words	Hops on one foot; dramatic play
5	43	41	Some understanding of conservation of weight; begins to use rehearsal to help memory	Begins to show language mastery; uses words apart from specific situation	Skips alternating feet; walks straight line; stands for longer period on one foot
5½	45	45	Continuing signs of conservation; still tends to focus on perceptual aspects	Asks meaning of words; more complex sentences of 5 or 6 words	Draws recognizable person; continues to develop throwing skill

From John F. Travers, *The Growing Child,* Scott, Foresman and Company, Glenview, IL, 1982. Reprinted by permission of the author.

A Sociocultural VIEW

Teaching Non-English-Speaking Students: Bilingual Education or ESL?

About 40% of our public school students are from ethnically diverse backgrounds, and these students may be at risk because of an English language deficit. Bilingual education, which offers these students course instruction in their native language while they study English separately is a major commitment because academic fluency takes about seven years. Many issues concerning bilingual education generate conflicting, often heated, opinions such as the following:

Issue

Bilingual education is the way American public schools should educate non-English-speaking students.

Answer—Pro Students in bilingual education are not penalized because of a language deficit. They are able to stay currrent with their studies because they are taught in their native language, which helps to maintain students' self-esteem while they gain proficiency in English.

Answer—Con Bilingual education is not that helpful to these students. Students who eventually succeed in the marketplace are proficient in English. Bilingual education wastes valuable time reinforcing students' native languages instead of teaching them English.

Issue

English as a Second Language (ESL) is a good alternative program to bilingual education.

Answer—Pro ESL is a desirable program because most of a student's course work is in English, with separate time allotted for specific English language instruction. Students are grouped according to grade level and the ESL teacher uses the student's classroom curriculum.

Answer—Con ESL does not give students support in their native language. In spite of English language training these students fall behind. Older students in particular may have difficulty with this technique.

With children bringing many different languages into the classroom, concerns have arisen that an English language deficit may affect achievement.

Issue

Since English is the official language of government and commerce in the United States, classroom instruction in public school classrooms should be in English.

Answer—Pro One of the goals of public school education is fluency in spoken and written English. If students are in an environment where only English is spoken, they will learn the language more quickly. These students may have initial difficulty but once they have acquired English proficiency, they typically catch up.

Answer—Con Non-English-speaking students are often put in with students younger than themselves while gaining English proficiency. Or if they are put in with their peers, they suffer because they cannot keep up with the course work. Both of these conditions result in a loss of self-esteem for the students, which can then affect total academic performance and may cause the student(s) to drop out of school altogether.

Guided Review

19. Most children have completed the greater part of language acquisition by the age of
    _____ .
20. _____ describes how to put sounds together to form words.
21. Calling all four-legged, furry animals doggy would be an example of
    _____ .
22. _____ traced children's language development by using mean length of
    utterance.
23. The two chief methods for instructing non-English-speaking students are
    _____ and _____ .
24. LEP refers to _____ _____ _____ .
25. A program that has children initially spend 90% of their time using the minority
    language is called _____ _____ .

CONCLUSION & SUMMARY

Thus far in our discussion of the early childhood years, we have seen that although the rate of physical growth slows somewhat, it still continues at a steady pace. Physical and motor skills become more refined. Cognitive development during these years leads to a world of representation in which children are expected to acquire and manipulate symbols. Language gradually becomes a powerful tool in adapting to the environment.

What are the major physical and motor accomplishments of the early childhood years?

- Growth continues at a steady, less rapid rate during these years.
- Brain lateralization seems to be well-established by the age of 5 or 6.
- Height is a good indicator of normal development when heredity and environment are considered in evaluating health.

- Increasing competence and mastery are seen in a child's acquisition of motor skills.

How do Piaget's views on cognitive development differ from information processing theorists?

- These years are the time of Piaget's preoperational period and the continued appearance of symbolic abilities.
- During these years children develop a theory of mind.
- Children's growing cognitive proficiency is seen in their use of humor.
- Many current early childhood programs have a cognitive orientation.

What types of early childhood education seem most promising?

- Many preschool programs are based on the ideas of Piaget and Montessori.

- Project Head Start was originally designed to offer educational and developmental services to disadvantaged children.
- Several positive social and emotional outcomes seem to be associated with Head Start programs.

How does children's language acquisition proceed during these years?

- Children acquire the basics of their language during these years with little, if any, instruction.
- All children seem to follow the same pattern in acquiring their language.
- Children whose native language is not English need a carefully designed program to support their native language and to help them acquire English as efficiently as possible.

KEY TERMS

Absorbent mind	Bilingualism immersion	Controlled scribbling
Animism	Centration	Deferred imitation
Anticipatory images	Classification	Drawing
Artificialism	Conservation	Egocentrism

Answers

19. 5 20. Phonology 21. overextension 22. Brown 23. bilingual education, ESL 24. Limited English Proficiency 25. bilingual immersion

ESL
Expressive language
Fast mapping
Handedness
Head Start
Lateralization
Motor skills
Organization
Overextensions
Overregulation

Phonology
Pragmatics
Preoperational
Prepared environment
Random scribbling
Realism
Receptive language
Rehearsal
Representation
Reproductive images

Retrieval
Reversibility
Semantics
Sensitive periods
Span of apprehension
Symbolic play
Syntax
Theory of mind
Uniform growth

WHAT DO YOU THINK?

1. As you can tell from the data presented in this chapter, early childhood youngsters continue their rapid growth, although at a less frantic rate than during infancy. Consider yourself a parent of a child of this age (boy or girl) for a moment. How much would you encourage them to participate in organized, directed physical activities (swimming, dancing, soccer, etc.)? Be sure to give specific reasons for your answer.

2. As you read Paul McGhee's account of the development of children's humor, could you explain his stages by comparing them with Piaget's work? Do you think this is a logical way to proceed? Why?

3. When you consider the tragic case of Genie compared to the enormous language growth of most children, what comes to your mind? Does it change your opinion about how language develops? In what way? What do you think this case implies for the existence of a sensitive period for language development?

CHAPTER REVIEW TEST

1. By the age of 3 a child should be able to
   a. jump from stairs.
   b. draw a recognizable person.
   c. stand on each foot alternately.
   d. throw a ball overhand.

2. By the age of five to six years, _____% of adult brain weight is present.
   a. 70
   b. 80
   c. 90
   d. 100

3. When children show a preference for one hand or the other, this illustrates brain
   a. lateralization.
   b. synapses.
   c. dendrites.
   d. initiative.

4. A frequent cause of psychological disturbance for children can be
   a. brain adaptation.
   b. muscle growth.
   c. equilibration.
   d. stress.

5. Using the large muscles is referred to as _____ motor skills.

   a. fine
   b. peripheral
   c. gross
   d. anatomical

6. Which of the following factors is not known to influence physical development?
   a. Genetic elements
   b. SES
   c. Disease
   d. Ethnicity

7. Which of the following would not be considered a motor skill?
   a. Running
   b. Skipping
   c. Tying shoes
   d. Singing

8. Controlled scribbling appears at about age
   a. 5.
   b. 3.
   c. 4.
   d. 2.

9. Which of the following behaviors is not associated with the preoperational period?
   a. Symbolic play
   b. Drawing

   c. Language
   d. Walks steadily

10. A child's belief that inanimate objects are real and conscious is known as
    a. artificialism.
    b. delusion.
    c. animism.
    d. centration.

11. By the time children are ready to enter first grade they have a vocabulary of about _____ words.
    a. 8,000
    b. 6,500
    c. 3,000
    d. 1,200

12. McGhee notes that the basis of most children's humor is
    a. irony.
    b. play on words.
    c. incongruity.
    d. sarcasm.

13. Effective use of humor is not credited with stimulating
    a. motor development.
    b. creative thinking.
    c. social development.
    d. emotional development.

14. Montessori's ideas concerning
_____ periods are
important in planning preschool
programs.
 a. lengthy
 b. class
 c. sensitive
 d. time

15. Project Head Start was initiated in
the
 a. 1960s.
 b. 1970s.
 c. 1980s.
 d. 1990s.

16. Studying language processes in a
natural way refers to
 a. whole language.
 b. language acquisition.

 c. language rules.
 d. metalinguistic awareness.

17. The rules of _____
describe how to put words
together to form sentences.
 a. phonology
 b. semantics
 c. syntax
 d. pragmatics

18. When students are removed from
class to receive special instruction
in English, this is called
 a. removal.
 b. ESL pullout.
 c. class insertion.
 d. focused instruction.

19. A 3-year-old stating, "Daddy comed
home" is an example of
 a. overextension.
 b. mispronunciation.
 c. overregulation.
 d. delayed development.

20. Children who receive 90% of their
instruction in a minority language
are in _____
_____ programs.
 a. bilingual immersion
 b. sheltered language
 c. autonomous
 d. gramatically correct

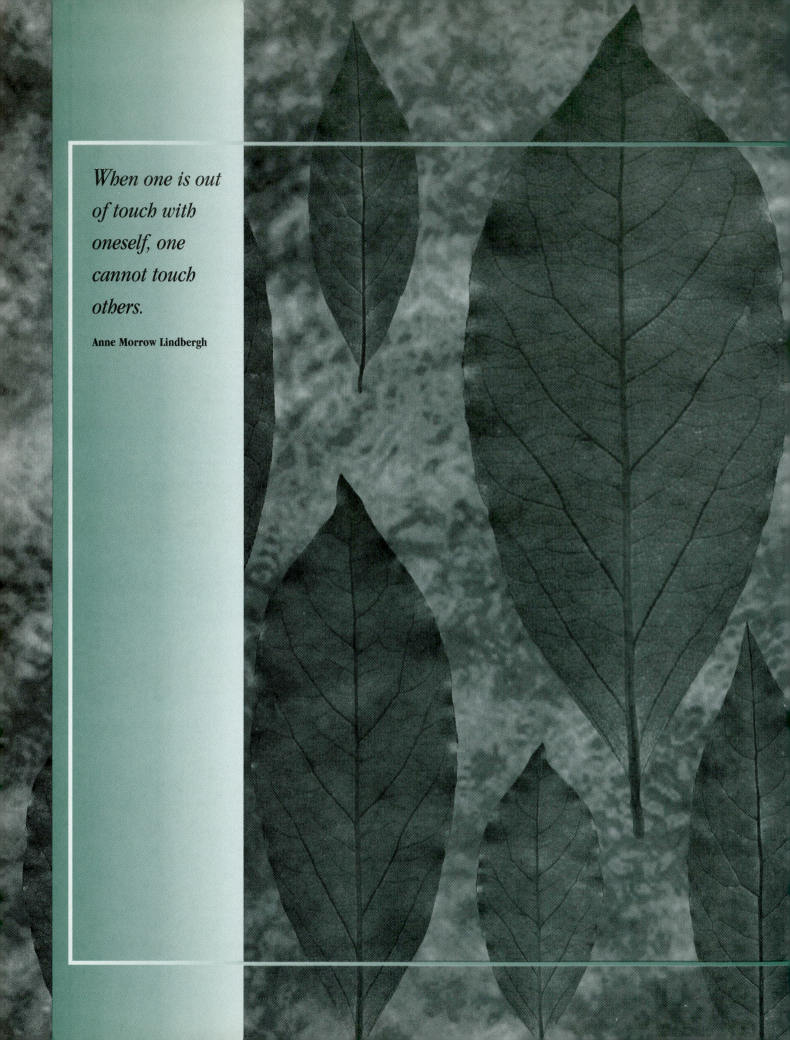

*When one is out
of touch with
oneself, one
cannot touch
others.*

Anne Morrow Lindbergh

Chapter Outline

Barbara is a former nurse who now takes care of four neighborhood children, ranging in age from 9 months to 4 years. A neat, careful person who loves children (she has two of her own away at school), she is sensitive to their needs and aware of the developmental changes constantly occurring in her four children. Barbara is in great demand by neighborhood families because of these traits, but she refuses to take more than four children at a time.

It's eight o'clock in the morning and Gina, a 4-year-old dynamo, is at the door with her mother, Janice. Janice takes courses at the local college and leaves Gina with Barbara three days each week. Barbara smiles at the thought of Gina. Pretty, bright, and active, with springs in her legs, Gina usually leads the other children (and Barbara) on a merry chase. When you talk to her, Gina constantly bounces up and down.

Janice and Gina walk into the front room, which is spotless and filled with toys arranged attractively along the walls. It's apparent that this home is designed for children: bright, cheerful, and safe. Janice and Barbara talk about Gina for a few minutes; she had a cold the previous day and had a restless night, but Janice says she seems fine now. Upon seeing her 3-year-old friend, Amy, Gina darts over and begins to hug her.

Barbara and Janice watch as Gina asks Amy if she wants to see her new dance. (Gina takes a dance class and will be in a recital soon.) Without waiting for an answer, she goes through her dance and takes a deep bow. Amy laughs happily as Janice and Barbara applaud. Gina then takes Amy's hand and pulls her toward the backyard with its swings and sandbox.

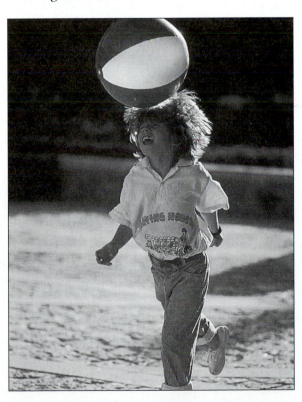

It's so easy to tell how Gina feels by observing her play, Barbara thinks. Today she seems to be feeling better, has her energy back, and wants to play physically. At other times, Barbara has seen Gina working out a conflict with Janice by playing with dolls and assigning them mother-daughter roles. In her pretend play world, there were "mommy" dolls, "good" dolls, "bad" dolls, and "napping" dolls. As Barbara watches, she thinks to herself, as she does so often, what a wonderful time these years are. ✿

In one of the great classics describing the early childhood years, Selma Fraiberg immortalized them as *The Magic Years*. Children believe that their thoughts and actions bring about the events they witness around them. Wonderful at times, such as when they see themselves as the heroic firefighter saving others, magical thought can also be upsetting, such as when they blame themselves for their parents' divorce. Our goal in this and the preceding chapter is to understand this magical world of the child.

During the early childhood years, children blossom into quite distinctive personalities. Although personality differences are apparent at birth, they now flourish until even the most casual observer notices a child's "personality." Children of this age are entering a period in which they must learn to reconcile their individuality with the demands of the world around them. New abilities, new friends, new ideas come up against parental restrictions and parents often find themselves searching for an ideal mix of firmness and love.

How they accomplish this leads us to Erikson's stages of autonomy vs. shame and doubt, and initiative vs. guilt. If children are encouraged to *develop* as well as *control* their newfound abilities, they acquire feelings of competence and independence that can only further development. As Erikson noted, parental control during these years must be firmly reassuring so as to protect children from shame and doubt. They can then move on to using their growing sense of intiative in a manner that frees them from any sense of guilt.

Children's personalities take on definite shadings. Their interactions with those around them begin to take shape, setting the stage for the kind of relationships they will form in the future. They now begin the process of widening their circle of relationships. Children from 2 to 6 will make new friends: in the family, in the neighborhood, in preschool. Some youngsters of this age are also faced with adjusting to a new sibling (or siblings), which can be a time of great frustration if not handled carefully.

To help understand these issues, in this chapter we'll examine the modern family, tracing the stages through which it proceeds (including the growing importance of day care and divorce), how children continue to develop their sense of self and gender identity, and the role of play in their development. Our initial task, though, is to examine that great socializing agent—the family.

Chapter Objectives

After reading this chapter, you should be able to answer the following questions.

◆ What role does family play in development during these years?

◆ How do children of this age acquire a sense of self?

◆ How do children come to understand the meaning of their gender?

◆ What is the value of play to children of these years?

The Family in Development

You've probably heard the old saying that "a family that grows together, stays together." True, as most cliches are, but it's a deceptively simple statement. Can today's families truly grow together, given the constant changes in family life? A modern family may have both parents working; it may be a single parent family; it may be unrelated people living together; it may be a blended family (divorce and remarriage).

Homeless Those who live in shelters, or on the street, or in parks.

It could also be a **homeless** family. The homeless today represent a different population from the days when they were seen as alcoholic men clustered together on skid rows. The so-called new homeless population is younger and much more mixed: more single women, more families, and more minorities. Families with young children may be the fastest-growing segment of today's homeless. On any given night, 100,000 children in this country will be homeless (Walsh, 1992). They are also characterized by few social contacts, poor health, low school achievement, a high level of contact with the criminal justice system, and poverty. (For an analysis of the impact of poverty and homelessness on development, see Duncan & Brooks-Gunn, 2000.)

It may also be a family with *foster children.* Today there are about 750,000 children in foster care (Simms, Dubowitz, & Szilagyi, 2000). Although most of these children enter foster care with many problems, many don't receive adequate care while in placement. When children are placed in foster care, the responsible officials must provide for continuity of care.

And yet, most developmental psychologists agree that, in spite of these radical changes, the family remains the most important institution influencing child development (Zigler & Finn-Stevenson, 1999).

A Changing View of the Family

If you think about the family as a unit, it's clear that today's family is experiencing rapidly changing dynamics. Changes occur in the individual members, caregivers, the circumstances surrounding the family, and unexpected transitions that demand changing responses from the family unit. For example, the United States Supreme Court recently ruled that parents have the fundamental right to make decisions concerning the care, custody, and control of their children. This legal decision involved parental rights to determine how frequently grandparents may visit their grandchildren and signalled the court's recognition of the difficulty in identifying the "average American family" (Greenhouse, 2000).

As social conditions change—working mothers, single-parent families—fathers have become more involved in child care. Children thus see their parents in roles different form the more stereotypical views of the past.

Consequently, families develop a unique style or climate for adapting to change while simultaneously attempting to maintain its integrity. The style or climate that emerges has developmental consequences for the family's children and here again we note major cultural differences across North America, Asia, and Africa (Grusec, Goodnow, & Kucynski, 2000; Parke & Buriel, 1998). As Etounga-Manguelle (2000) noted, although there are wide differences across these vast continents, there are also shared values, attitudes, and institutions. For example, African parents typically avoid individual praise and emphasize integration into a wider family group, providing numerous examples of such integration (Weisner, 2000).

Parents and Their Children

Parents do many things—select clothes, limit television time, impose rules—but they alone can't determine the nature of the relationship with their children. Parents and children are in it together, for better or worse. Studying 88 2-child, 2-parent families, Perozynski and Kramer (1999) discovered that parents used strategies based not only on their perception of how effective the strategy was, but also how well they could carry out the strategy.

We'll wrestle with parent-child issues throughout the chapter, but if there's one thing we've learned about the relationships between parents and their children it's this: What's right means what works for parents and their children in their culture.

Children of different ages, with different problems, and from different cultures require different types of parenting. We're quite sure now that parents and children actually *construct* their relationships; no one model fits all children and parents.

Children's **socialization** emerges from the thousands of reciprocal interactions occurring among them and their family members over a period of many years. For example, studying 116 children aged 4 years 9 months to 6 years 5 months, Isley and her colleagues (1999) found that teachers rated the children who expressed more positive feelings about their parents as more socially competent. Also, parents who expressed positive feeling toward their youngsters had children with better social outcomes in kindergarten and first grade.

Let's turn now to Diane Baumrind's pioneering work on parenting style.

Socialization Refers to the need to establish and maintain relations with others and to regulate behavior according to society's demands.

Parenting Behavior

Analyzing the relationship between parental behavior and children's competence, Baumrind (1967, 1971, 1986, 1991) discovered three kinds of parental behavior: authoritarian, authoritative, and permissive. Here is what she means by each of the types.

Authoritarian parents
Baumrind's term for parents who are demanding and want instant obedience as the most desirable child trait.

Authoritarian Parents **Authoritarian parents** are demanding, and for them instant obedience is the most desirable child trait. When there is any conflict between these parents and their children (Why can't I go to the party?), no consideration is given to the child's view, no attempt is made to explain why the youngster can't go to the party, and often the child is punished for even asking. It's a simple case of "Do it my way or else!"

An Informed VIEW   *The Puzzling Topic of Punishment*

No child is perfect, which introduces the controversial subject of punishment. Most parents are puzzled about what to do when their children misbehave and their reactions can range from using harsh physical punishment to a permissive, "hands-off" approach. Neither of these techniques is desirable, but what are some acceptable alternatives?

First, what is meant by punishment? Punishment may take one of two paths: Something unpleasant is done to a child (scolding, hitting), or something pleasant is withdrawn (removal from an exciting game). Either type of punishment has certain effects:

- *It is confined to the immediate situation and may have absolutely no effect in the future.* For example, most of you have been scolded for chewing gum in school, yet if you look around your present classroom, you'll probably see some of your classmates chewing away.
- *Punishment may produce a future effect if it is sufficiently severe and causes intense, unpleasant emotional responses.* The danger here, of course, is that conditioned stimuli can cause negative, accompanying reactions: a child may fear a teacher, which then leads to a fear and dislike of all teachers and schools.

If parents punish their child, they should quickly have that child do something that they can praise. They should also be precise in what they punish so that their child knows exactly what behavior to avoid. For example, it makes little sense to say, "You're not going out with that crowd again." Who? Where? What was done? Above all, no one parent should be singled out as "the punisher."

Most child experts, including pediatricians, oppose the use of corporal punishment for many reasons, chief of which is that it too often leads to child abuse. Non-physical methods, such as positive reinforcement whenever possible, time-out, or removal of privileges are the desired methods (American Academy of Pediatrics, 1998). Still, spanking is used regularly by many parents who believe it is the most effective form of punishment. Would you spank your child? Were you spanked as a child?

If you would like to have a more informed view on this issue, you may want to read one or more of the articles referenced in this chapter, such as the analysis presented by the American Academy of Pediatrics (1998).

You may also wish to learn more about it by going to our web site at http://www.mhhe.com/dacey5.

A particularly useful analysis of the role of punishment in child care can be found in American Academy of Pediatrics. (1998). Guidance for effective discipline. *Pediatrics,* 101(4), 723–728.

Authoritative parents
Baumrind's term for parents who respond to their children's needs and wishes, believing in parental control, they attempt to explain the reasons for it to their children.

Permissive parents Those parents who take a tolerant, accepting view of their children's behavior.

If you want to examine the research and implications of parenting in more detail, you would find M. Bornstein (Ed.), 1995, *Handbook of parenting* very helpful.

TABLE 8.1 PARENTAL BEHAVIORS AND CHILDREN'S CHARACTERISTICS

	Parental Behaviors		
	Authoritarian	Authoritative	Permissive
Children's characteristics	Withdrawn	Self-assertive	Impulsive
	Lack of enthusiasm	Independent	Low self-reliance
	Shy (girls)	Friendly	Low self-control
	Hostile (boys)	Cooperative	Low maturity
	Low need achievement	High need achievement	Aggressive
	Low competence	High competence	Lack of responsibility

Authoritative Parents **Authoritative parents** respond to their children's needs and wishes. Believing in parental control, they attempt to explain the reasons for it to their children. Authoritative parents expect mature behavior and will enforce rules, but they encourage their children's independence and search for potential. They try to have their youngsters understand that both parents and children have rights. In the resolution of socialization versus individuation, authoritative parents try to maintain a happy balance between the two.

Permissive Parents **Permissive parents** take a tolerant, accepting view of their children's behavior, including both aggressive and sexual urges. They rarely use punishment or make demands of their children. Children make almost all of their own decisions. Distinguishing indulgence from indifference in these parents can be difficult.

Authoritative parents are high on control (they have definite standards for their children), high on clarity of communication (the children clearly understand what is expected of them), high in maturity demands (they want their children to behave in a way appropriate for their age), and high in nurturance (a warm, loving relationship exists between parents and children). Thus, according to Baumrind's work, authoritative parents are most desirable. Table 8.1 presents the relationship between Baumrind's classes of parenting behavior and children's characteristics.

Baumrind's findings have held firm over the years. As Holmbeck and others (1995) stated, authoritative parents have adolescents who achieve better and demonstrate more positive social adjustment than children whose parents adopted either authoritarian or permissive parenting styles.

Yet it's important to remember that Baumrind's findings don't necessarily indicate a cause-and-effect relationship between her categories and a child's characteristics. These findings apply to white, middle-class families with both parents present. Children reared in single-parent families may experience quite different parenting behaviors. We must also recognize that children's temperaments affect *how* they're treated. Baumrind has acknowledged the influence of temperament, but has also argued that parenting behavior must have a decided impact on a child's behavior.

No discussion of the family's influence on development would be complete without examining the role of siblings.

Siblings and Development

The two girls couldn't be more different. Twelve-year-old Christine was tall, blonde, smart, and athletically gifted. Nine-year-old Beth was tall, dark, smart, and couldn't walk across the room without falling over something. Christine, outgoing and nonchalant; Beth, quiet and intense. Christine, older and the center of attention, also liked to tease Beth to the point of tears, a

A Sociocultural VIEW   Families in Their Cultures

From birth, children are influenced by their culture in almost every way we can imagine: feeding practices, sleeping arrangements, accepted values, educational expectations, school experiences, and interpersonal relations. Yet, if we examine "culture" carefully, we see that two cultures affect children, the culture of the home and the culture of the society. Consequently, children are raised in a dual climate of culture within the home and the culture of the surrounding world (Greenfield & Suzuki, 1998).

Differences in the culture of the society are often seen in maternal behaviors. Japanese mothers, for example, encourage their children to be dependent on them, whereas American mothers ecourage independence in their children. When American observers witnessed a disruptive Japanese preschooler in class, they criticized the Japanese teacher and the classroom atmosphere, thus absolving the child. Japanese preschool teachers, however, believed that the child was at fault, thus blaming the child (Cole, 1999).

An example of the impact of the culture of the family is seen in the manner in which interpersonal relationships within the family play a large role in the socialization of African-American children (Banks, 1993). Parents attempt to prepare their children for interactions with both peers and teachers and teach them how to act in social situations. Thus, parents are trying to provide a set of guidelines for behaving in novel situations that reflect the network of connections and kinship functions with which they are most comfortable (Manning and Baruth, 1996).

Any analysis of the family's influence on development must consider parental goals. An example of this is seen in a culture's adoption of authoritarian parenting methods, which isn't necessarily associated with negative child development. Chinese-American families use what appears to be authoritarian methods to foster harmonious relationships and these are a sign of parental concern. Latino families may

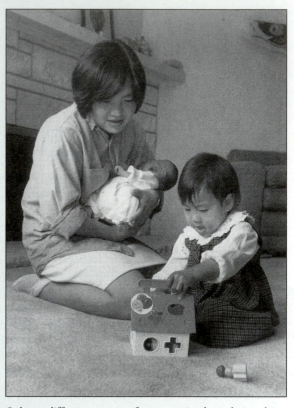

Culture differences are often seen in the relationships between parents and their children.

use authoritarian techniques to achieve the developmental goal of respect for others (Greenfield & Suzuki, 1998).

Consequently, it's important to remember that references to *culture* invariably refer to *cultural differences* and not *cultural deficits*.

---

habit their parents tried to stop. As Christine grew older and her interests broadened (read boys), her relationship with Beth became much smoother and both girls seemed to have worked out a comfortable way of living with each other.

Siblings   Brothers and sisters.

Growing up with **siblings** (brothers and sisters) is quite different from growing up without them. Brothers and sisters, because of their behavior toward one another, create a different family environment. When you examine sibling relationships from this perspective, you can see how they affect development. In the early years, young brothers and sisters can provide security for babies who may feel frightened by strangers or anything different (Eisenberg & Fabes, 1998).

About 80% of children have siblings, which means that they grow up in a special network of relationships that affects their development in unique ways.

Judy Dunn

Older siblings become models for younger children to imitate. They can become sounding boards for their younger brothers and sisters; that is, the younger siblings can try out something before approaching a parent. Older siblings often ease the way for the younger by trying to explain to parents that what happened wasn't all that bad. In this way, bonds are formed that usually last a lifetime, longer in most cases than those between husband and wife or parent and child.

Sibling Relationships through the Years

Several cultural factors contribute to the formation of a lifelong bond between siblings. For example, *longer lifespans* mean that brothers and sisters spend a longer period of their lives together than ever before, as long as 70 or 80 years! When parents have died, the siblings' own children have left, and spouses have died, siblings tend to tighten the bond and offer each other needed support. *Geographic mobility* means unavoidable separation. Friendships are lost; schools and teachers change; adjustments to new situations must be made, but the sibling relationship usually remains intact. *Divorce and remarriage* typically bring unhappiness and hurt, and the need for support. During these troubled days, siblings may well be a trusted source of support and stability. For many children, the one anchor to be found is a brother or sister.

Studying stability in sibling relationships, Dunn and her associates (1994) found considerable continuity from early childhood to the beginning of adolescence in the positive and negative feelings of siblings toward each other. Many reasons contributed to the stability of these behaviors, especially the ongoing family dynamics. The siblings seemed to grow closer with adversity; that is, when one sibling had troubles with someone at school or became ill, other siblings offered support and sympathy. Gender differences also appeared: Adolescent girls were closer to their younger sisters than were adolescent boys with their younger sisters. Dunn and her associates (1994) attributed this finding to the tendency of adolescent boys to become more intensely involved with their male peer group.

How Siblings Help Each Other

Siblings act as nonthreatening sounding boards for each other. New behaviors, new roles, and new ideas can be tested on siblings, and their reactions, whether positive or negative, lack the doomsday quality of many parental judgments. The emotional atmosphere is less charged. They exchange clothes as teenagers, borrow money before a paycheck, provide support in life's crises, in other words, they offer valuable services for each other.

Siblings also form subsystems that are the basis for the formation of powerful coalitions, often called the **sibling underworld.** Older siblings can warn their younger brothers and sisters about parental moods and prohibitions, thus averting problems. Older siblings frequently provide an educational service to parents by informing them of events outside the home that parents should be aware of.

We also know, however, that sibling relationships can be negative. We're not talking here of the temporary squabbles that cloud any relationship. If aggressive and aversive conflict between siblings is prolonged, conduct problems may occur. When sibling conflict is coupled with parental rejection, high levels of aggressive behavior result (Garcia, Shaw, Winslow, & Yaggi, 2000).

Also, *rivalry,* whatever the cause, may characterize any bond. An older sibling can contribute to that sense of inferiority that Erikson identified as the crisis of this period. Imagine the difficulty of a firstborn sibling forced to share parental attention, especially if the spacing between the children is close (less than two years). If the firstborns must also care for younger children, they can become increasingly frustrated.

The boyhood of President John F. Kennedy is a good example of the turbulence and support that siblings share. An older, stronger, and charming brother, Joe, at times made life miserable for the future president, resulting in quarreling and even fighting. John responded by frequently becoming the nasty little brother, irritating his older sibling when he could. Occasionally the two of them would join forces to torment the two younger brothers, Robert and Edward. Yet all four brothers shared a powerful bond that helped them survive the crises and tragedies that were to strike the Kennedy family.

Siblings play a major role in development. For those children with brothers and sisters, older siblings can act as models, help younger brothers and sisters in times of difficulty, and help smooth relations with adults.

Sibling underworld
Interactions among siblings, usually unknown to parents.

What Siblings Really Think   In a classic study of sibling relationships, Helen Koch (1960), a long-time student of developing relationships, found that school-age children have unique and often conflicting attitudes about their siblings. For example:

- Some children said they played frequently with their brothers and sisters; others rarely did.

- About one-third of the children said they fought constantly; another one-third said they seldom quarreled.

- Some said they liked playing with a sibling; others much preferred a friend.

When Koch asked the youngsters if they would be happier without their siblings, she received definite answers. One-third replied they would be happier without the sibling. (Could you make her disappear? She's too bossy.) The majority, however, said they preferred keeping the sibling (although they phrased their answers in less than glowing terms: "I'll keep him. He's bad but not that bad"). The children's replies reflected many of the functions that siblings provide for each other: help, money, support, even advice.

Guided Review

1. When a divorce is followed by remarriage, the resulting family is called a _____ family.
2. Many parents use parenting strategies that they don't believe are effective, such as _____ _____.
3. The sibling subsystem in a family is often called the _____ _____.
4. Parents who rely on verbal persuasion, positive reinforcement, and indirect methods of control are demonstrating _____ parenting behavior.
5. About _____ percent of children have siblings.

Children of Divorce

The changes and stress associated with divorce typically cause multiple problems for all concerned—children, mothers, and fathers. Today's divorce rate is still about 50 percent of all first marriages and about 62 percent of remarriages. Sixty percent of the divorces in the United States involve children. Consequently, children can experience the upset of divorce, usually several years in a single-parent home, and then the changed circumstances of a remarriage (Hetherington & Stanley-Hagan, 1995). What do we know about the family's reaction to divorce?

Families and Divorce

We think of divorce today as a sequence of experiences. The conflict and disagreements that lead to divorce undoubtedly begin long before the divorce itself and influence any children who witness parental unhappiness (Kitzmann, 2000). This is especially true for boys who tend to be more exposed to parental conflict than girls (Parke & Buriel, 1998). Following the divorce, parents often are less sensitive to their children as they struggle with their own needs. Their discipline becomes erratic and with the decline in the quality of parental care comes an increase in the problem behavior of their children (Lamb, Hwang, Ketterlinus, & Fracasso, 1999).

Children develop within a complex network of family relationships. What they are exposed to during these years can have long-lasting consequences.

Answers

1. blended 2. passive nonintervention 3. sibling underworld 4. authoritative 5. eighty

After about two years, family arrangements usually stabilize, a remarriage may have occurred, and children and parents are on the road to adjustment (although boys may still be more aggressive and disobedient). As we turn our attention to the children's reaction to the divorce remember that the divorce itself, that is, the actual separation, may *not* be the major cause of any problem behavior. Too many other factors have intervened (exposure to conflict, economic decline, erratic parenting, etc.). But how do early childhood youngsters react to divorce?

Children's Adjustment to Divorce

Any analysis of divorce *must* begin with consideration of a child's level of cognitive development. Early childhood youngsters are at Piaget's preoperational level, which means they are still quite egocentric. Their ability to engage in abstract thinking is still limited, and they lack that vital aspect of cognition—the ability to reverse their thinking. This colors their reaction to their parents' divorce; for example, they may think that *they* are responsible.

As we mentioned, in the two or three years following the divorce, most children adjust to living in a single-parent home. This adjustment, however, can once again be shaken by what a parent's remarriage means: losing one parent in the divorce, adapting to life with the remaining parent, the addition of at least one family member in a remarriage. Figure 8.1 illustrates these transitions in a child's life.

During the early childhood years, children demonstrate intense separation anxiety and fear of abandonment by both parents, which leads to the tendency to blame themselves for the divorce (Lamb, Hwang, Ketterlinus, & Fracasso, 1999; Hetherington & Stanley-Hagan, 1995). Immediately following the divorce, mothers seem to show less affection toward their children and treat their sons more harshly (threatening them, for example). Fathers, conversely, seem to become more permissive and indulgent. As time passes, relationships stabilize and life becomes more predictable.

Although these short-term effects appear in early childhood, long-term effects are also apparent. For example, there seems to be a sleeper effect that appears in some girls: at adolescence they may have difficulty with heterosexual relations. Boys may continue to be behavior problems and have a high dropout rate in high school (Parke & Buriel, 1998).

Divorced Fathers

For more information and reasoned discussion of the impact of divorce on children, we strongly recommend any of the writings of E. Mavis Hetherington.

As mentioned earlier, about 12 percent of all single parents are fathers, most of whom are divorced. The children in their families are usually older than those who remain with mothers and are more likely to be male. Fathers typically maintain their standard of living. They become the custodial parent when mothers were judged to be incompetent or simply didn't want custody and the fathers accepted the idea of single parenthood. Single fathers have less control problems than mothers and do a better job of assigning household responsibilities. Like their maternal counterparts, they report feelings of uncertainty and incompetence about their parenting skills in these new circumstances (Weinraub & Gringlas, 1995).

Even when the mother has custody of the children, the father can—and should—remain an important figure in a child's life (Cabrera & others, 2000). Estimates are that only about a third of divorced fathers see their children once a week, a figure that decreases with time. This *retreat from parenthood* may be due to: distance, finances, remarriage, and how the mother sees her role as *maternal*

Figure 8.1

Transitions in marriage.

gatekeeper. Almost one-half of mothers with custody refuse to permit the father to see the child at all. They may be protecting the child from an incompetent father, or punishing the divorced father, or attempting to obtain better support (Parke & Brott, 1999).

Day Care

There's nothing new about parents' search for quality nonparental day care. It's one of the oldest problems faced by human society. Historically, it's possible to identify four goals of quality child care (Lamb, 1998).

1. Child-care policies in many countries are intended to encourage female employment, thus increasing equal employment opportunities.

2, Child care, especially preschools, provide a foundation for children of different cultures, an entry into the new culture.

3. Child-care facilities enable women to seek employment, thus encouraging family self-sufficiency and reducing the need for welfare.

4. Child care, if properly designed, can enrich children's lives.

As economic conditions and the changing role of women in modern societies cause more women to move into the workplace, one question remains to be answered: What happens to children while their mothers are at work? Obviously someone must be caring for these youngsters, which raises questions about *au pairs, nannies,* and *day care.* How competent are the individuals who offer these services?

Au Pairs and Nannies

Au pairs, for example, are young women, often English, who want to spend time in America, typically 12 months because of the length of their work permits (U.S. Information Agency, 1996). They agree to provide child-care services for up to 45 hours working no more than 5½ days a week (Peters, 1997). The United States Information Agency, which oversees the process, recently stated that about 10,000 au pairs are working in the United States in any given year.

Au pairs must be at least 18 and not more than 25, and possess a secondary school certificate. They are screened, determined to be of good character, and have a driver's license since America is such a car-oriented society. They receive anywhere from $100 to $130 per week plus room and board. The au pair-family relationship demands compatibility given the live-in arrangements and the daily contact. If problems arise, however, conditions can deteriorate quickly. (You may be interested in reading about the famous Louise Woodward case in Massachusetts in which the au pair was accused of murder in the death of a child in her care.)

Nannies present a different picture. Older, usually better educated, and higher paid (about $300 per week), they seem to provide a more stable environment for

(a) Day care has become an important phenomenon in our society as more and more mothers join the workforce. Research indicates that developmental outcomes are closely linked to the quality of day care. (b) Among the variety of day-care settings, home day-care centers are quite numerous. Often run by a family member or neighbor, they are smaller and more informal than large centers.

(a)

(b)

children. English nannies, for example, are often former nursery nurses with considerable experience. They typically receive careful developmental training such as a course that discusses age characteristics, nutrition, work with exceptional children, how to handle problems, etc. Many parents worry about the close relationship that develops between a child and nanny, often feeling threatened by a growing attachment between the two. What's needed before care is actually begun is a frank discussion between the parents and nanny about duties, responsibilities, and limitations, particularly regarding the need for privacy for both parties.

Today, however, when we hear the term "caregiver," we tend to think of day care. What are the long-term developmental consequences of day-care placement? Is the day-care center healthy and stimulating? Is it safe?

Facts about Day Care

Reliable facts about day care are hard to come by, chiefly because of the lack of any national policy that would provide hard data. About 35,000 to 40,000 "places" provide day-care services (i.e., principal income is from offering child care). "Places" is perhaps the best way to describe these facilities because of the wide variety of circumstances that exist.

For example, one mother may charge another mother several dollars to take care of her child. A relative may care for several family children. Churches, businesses, and charities may run large operations. Some may be sponsored by local or state government as an aid to the less affluent. Others are run on a pay-as-you-go basis. Almost everyone agrees that the best centers are staffed by teachers who specialize in day-care services (about 25 percent of day-care personnel).

Types of Day Care

Today the term *day care* has come to mean a variety of nonparental care arrangements: family day care, care by nonparental relatives, in-home babysitters, nursery schools, and day-care centers. Children may spend from 5 to 55 hours per week in these settings (Lamb, 1998). But regardless of the type of day-care setting, the one key element that affects a child's development is the *quality* of care provided. Sorting out what is known about types of day-care centers, we can group them as follows (Clarke-Stewart & others, 1995).

Care in the Child's Home   In this type of care, a relative is usually the caregiver, which is fairly common, but as Clarke-Stewart and others noted (1995), we probably know less about this care than any other. Although such an arrangement has several advantages (e.g., the child is familiar with the setting and the caregiver, the schedule can be flexible), several disadvantages also occur (e.g., the caregiver is usually untrained, the child misses peer activities).

Family Day Care   Here caregivers provide service in their homes, which may or may not be licensed and the number of children may range from 1 (family day-care home) to 12 (group day-care home). Family day-care homes are the most numerous and the least expensive. They are typically located near the child's home so transportation is no problem. A family atmosphere exists while simultaneously enabling a child to interact with a limited number of children of various ages. A major disadvantage is that in this type of day care the provider is the least accountable of providers. These settings typically are informal, unprofessional, and short-lived with little or no supervision (Clarke-Stewart & others, 1995).

Day-Care Centers   These centers are what people mean when they refer to "day care." They may be for profit (the number of these is increasing) or they may be nonprofit and they may provide for fewer than 15 or more than 300 children, whom they group by age. The average day-care center offers care for 60 children (Clarke-Stewart et al., 1995). Here is a summary of many of the day-care centers.

- *Private day-care centers* run for profit have no eligibility requirements and will accept almost anyone who can pay the fee. Typically staffed by two or three people (usually not professionally trained), these centers may operate in a converted store or shop. They probably are minimally equipped with toys and educational activities and usually offer no social or health services.

- *Commercial centers* are also private and run for profit. They may be part of a national or regional chain with uniform offerings and facilities. They usually are well-equipped with good food and activities. The centers are a business; KinderCare, for example, runs about 900 centers. Costs may run as high as $200 per week for infants in the best centers, $180 for children under three, and $160 for those over three. With subsidized day care, costs usually run from $60 to $120 (Peters, 1997).

- *Community church centers* are often, but not always, run for children of the poor. The quality of personal care (attention, affection) is usually good, but church centers often have minimal facilities and activities.

- *Company centers* are often offered as fringe benefits for employees. They are usually run in good facilities with a well-trained staff and a wide range of services.

- *Public service centers* are government sponsored, well run, and have high quality throughout. Unfortunately, few of these are available and they are designed to serve children of low-income families.

- *Research centers* are usually affiliated with a university and represent what the latest research says a day-care center should be. Most studies of day care have been conducted in these centers. But since the centers are of the highest quality, the results of such studies do not give a true picture of day care throughout the country.

Day Care: A National Concern

As you can see, the country has moved into a different era with regard to day care. Working mothers are now in the majority, and their numbers promise to increase. Given these events, regulation of day care has taken on new urgency. Legislative battles over standards for day-care centers have been constant, but the best the federal government has been able to do is to propose general standards.

Despite the minimal salaries of day-care workers, costs are high because day care is labor intensive. Staff-child ratios usually average from 1:8 to 1:10, much too high considering children's needs and safety. But a new attitude is developing, one with political consequences. National surveys have consistently shown that more than one-half of the voters think a national policy regarding day care should be formulated.

Developmental Outcomes of Day Care

Two recent investigations have helped to shed light on how early child-care experiences influence development.

The National Institute of Child Health and Human Development (NICHD) studied over 1,000 families and their children beginning at one month of age and continuing through 36 months of age (NICHD, 1998, 1999, 2000). Data collected consisted of demographic information, child-care usage, children's behavioral functioning, mother-child interactions, and quality of the home environment.

Children were assigned to contrasting child-care groups. Those in the full-time child-care group experienced 30 or more hours of non-parental care per week beginning at 4 months of age. Children in the maternal-care group never averaged more than 10 hours per week by someone else (NICHD, 1998).

The researchers were intent on answering one question: Do different child-care experiences affect the cognitive and socioemotional development of children when they were three years old? Results indicated that nonparental-care did *not* weaken the influence of family factors—developmental outcomes were similar for children with and without early-care experiences (NICHD, 1998). Although no significant differences were found between the two groups in attachment security (NICHD, 1999) some minor differences were found. For example, more hours in child care predicted less maternal sensitivity and less positive child engagement. Higher quality child care predicted greater maternal sensitivity.

A second major study addressed the question: Does quality intervention at an early age aid the cognitive development of children born into poverty and hardship? *The Carolina Abecedarian Project* (Campbell & Ramey, 1994) studied 111 families and their infants. Based on such characteristics as parental education and income, the poor school achievement of older siblings, and other family problems, these 111 children were identified as at risk for school failure. They were assigned to either a treatment or control group. Both groups received identical nutritional supplements and health services.

Children in the treatment group were placed in a year-round day-care program until they entered school. During the first three years, instructors focused on improving the children's cognitive, language, and social skills. After three years, the program was expanded to include prereading and math concepts. A continuing thread through these years was the effort by parents and instructors to provide nurturing and supportive interactions with the children.

Follow-up studies have revealed continuing and significant differences between the two groups.

- At the end of the third year, the IQs of the children in the treatment group were significantly higher than those in the control group.

- By 15 years of age, those who were in the treatment group showed better academic progress, higher IQ scores, higher levels of grade retention, and less need for remedial services (Zigler & Hall, 2000).

- At age 15, twice as many of the control group were in special education classes.

- At 21 years of age, 35 percent of the children who were originally in the treatment group compared to 14 percent of the control group attended college. Another 30 percent of the treatment group held good jobs (Wilgoren, 1999).

We can also conclude from this remarkable study that the earlier quality intervention is offered to children, the more satisfactory and longlasting will be the results. To test this belief the researchers of the Carolina Project conducted a second study within the framework of the original. When the children of both groups entered kindergarten, half of the treatments and half of the controls were provided with a special teacher who offered additional educational activities to both groups. Little difference was found between these children and those who did not receive the supplemenray treatment. In other words, waiting until 4 or 5 years of age may be too late.

The Effects of Day Care: Conclusions

What can we infer, then from the existing day-care research?

- In the United States, the majority of children under 5 years of age receive some kind of nonparental day care (Harvey, 1999; Zigler & Finn-Stevenson, 1999).

- Early enrollment in day care is associated with less harmonious mother-child relationships (Lamb, 1998).

- Enrollment in day care during the early childhood years does not aid or impede positive relationships with peers (Lamb, 1998).

- The quality of care offered affects the maturity of the children (Clarke-Stewart & others, 1995).

- Nonparental child care seems to be associated with increased behavior problems (Lamb, 1998).

TABLE 8.2 CHARACTERISTICS OF QUALITY DAY CARE

Site Features	Functional Features
Good staff-child ratio	Concern with personal care
Superior staff education	Supervised motor activities
Good staff training	Attention to language
Higher staff wages	Opportunity for creativity
Attractive, safe environment	Social relationships encouraged

Guided Review

6. Nearly _____ of today's marriages will probably end in divorce.
7. A major factor in understanding children's reactions to divorce is level of _____ _____.
8. High quality day care has a positive effect on children's _____ achievement.
9. The developmental outcomes of day care are difficult to assess because most children are in _____ settings.
10. _____ day-care settings are the most numerous probably because they are the least _____.

- High quality child care has a positive effect on children's intellectual development (Clarke-Stewart & others, 1995; Harvey, 1999; Lamb, 1998; Zigler & Finn-Stevenson, 1999; Burchinal & others, 2000).

Table 8.2 illustrates those features associated with quality day care.

Finally, we repeat our earlier warning: Be cautious interpreting what you read and hear about the consequences of day care.

The Self Emerges

Imagine for a moment you're looking in a mirror. What do you see? Don't laugh; *you see you*. But what exactly do you see? When you look in the mirror, you see yourself, of course. But there are two sides to this vision of yourself. The first is referred to as the "I" self, that part of you that is doing the actual looking. The second part of what you see is the "Me" self, that is, the "Me" is the person observed, a dichotomy that remains alive and well today (Harter, 1993, 1998).

We have the great American psychologist, William James, to thank for this division of the self into two distinct parts. James believed that the "I" part of the self was the knower, that is, the "I" that thinks, makes judgments, recognizes it's separate from everything it sees, and controls the surrounding world. The "Me," on the other hand, is the object of all of the "I's" thinking, judging etc. Think of the "Me" as your self-image, which helps you to understand how the "I" develops feelings of self-esteem: As a result of the "I" evaluating the "Me's" activities, the self is judged good or bad, competent or incompetent, masterful or fumbling.

The infant shown here touching his nose and mouth against the mirror reveals the development of a sense of self, which most infants accomplish by about 18 months of age.

Answers

6. one-half 7. cognitive development 8. intellectual 9. private 10. Family, expensive

An Applied View

When I and Me Are We

Born in Taiwan, adopted by American Caucasian parents, product of an American upbringing, Julia Ming Gale often looks in the mirror and asks herself, "Who am I?" In her mind she sees a young woman with curly red hair, green eyes, and freckles, an image that causes her considerable sadness. Adopted by parents with two children of their own, the Gales had lived in Taiwan for three years, studied the Chinese language, had many Chinese friends, and kept a number of Chinese items in their American home—books, scrolls, and furniture.

But Ming's world was Caucasian and she couldn't recall a time when she didn't feel Caucasian, even though every time she looked in the mirror she faced an inescapable reality: the face looking back at her was Chinese. Periodic reminders of her Chinese heritage plagued her. Once doing the dishes, her younger brother came in with a friend. Telling his friend she was the maid and didn't speak any English, her brother was joking, but Ming still remembers the hurt. Bewildered, she began to fantasize that her birth mother was some famous Asian woman.

Nevertheless, her inner self didn't want to be any more Chinese than she had to be and she resisted any efforts her parents made to encourage the flourishing of her Chinese roots. She just wanted to be treated as another Caucasian.

By the time she was 12, she learned she had been born in Taiwan, not in China, which only increased her sense of cultural rootlessness. She was bothered that she couldn't claim the culture she grew up in. She even tried to force herself to "go Chinese," but it didn't work. Wanting to be Caucasian, she couldn't bridge the gap between the two cultures.

When her parents realized what she was going through, they tried to help her reconcile her conflicts. Ming, at age 24, has slowly started to explore her Chinese background through language lessons, taking courses in Chinese history, and readings that show her interest in both China and adoption. The career she has chosen reflects her own background: helping Chinese adoptees discover their identities, to help them live with the duality that caused her so much pain.

In Ming's case two selves existed in conflict and she spent 24 years trying to reconcile the differences between them. A novelist couldn't dramatize a better example to illustrate how knowing who they are shapes children's development, giving them the poise and assurance to undertake challenges they may otherwise shun. Too often children feel a conflict between the self they want to be and what they actually see themselves as, two different versions of the same self, When "I" and "Me" are "We."

The Development of Self

How do children construct a sense of self, this sense of who they are and what makes them different from everyone else? In a famous and ingenious study of self-development, the psychologists Michael Lewis and Jean Brooks-Gunn (1979) devised different strategies for uncovering how children discover they are distinct from their surroundings.

- Working with infants between 5 and 8 months old, the investigators placed them before a mirror. The children looked at themselves intently, smiled at their images, and even waved at the mirror, but gave no indication that they knew they were looking at themselves.

- Next, infants between 9 and 12 months reached out to the mirror to touch their bodies and turned toward other people or objects reflected in the mirror.

- The researchers then dabbed red rouge on the noses of infants between 15 and 18 months. When they saw themselves in the mirror, they pointed to their noses (on their own faces, not in the mirror) and tried to rub off the rouge.

- Finally, between 21 and 24 months, infants used their names and correctly applied personal pronouns. When placed with other same-sex infants in front of the mirror, they accurately identified themselves.

We're safe in saying, then, that children will usually have acquired a sense of self by 18 months of age and that after 2 years of age children clearly distinguished themselves from others (Pipp-Siegel & Foltz, 1997).

After infants take this initial step on the path to self-development and understanding, the next phase centers on the early childhood years. Children's growing—even astonishing—ability to understand things provides them with ever-deepening insights into themselves. When asked to tell who she was, a 4-year-old replied as follows.

> I go to preschool. I like it. I play with my brother a lot. I have dark brown hair. I like to talk. (Oh yes!)

These remarks are characteristic of preschoolers, particularly in the initial years of the period. That is, children's self-evaluations are both positive (perhaps unrealistically so) and concrete (Harter, 1998).

Here are the comments of a 6-year-old girl when asked to describe herself.

> I'm the youngest in my family. I'm happy most of the time. I like riding my bike. I eat a lot and I like different kinds of food. I have brown eyes. I have lots of freckles. I like almost everybody and I have lots of friends. Sometimes I get a little scared. When I'm a little older, I want to be a babysitter and I'll protect people. When I grow up I'm going to be a librarian.

Changes in the Developing Self

The quotations we have just seen are fairly sophisticated. Note the more abstract ideas of happiness, friendship, and protecting others, concepts that usually appear at later ages. Most children of her age focus on the physical—hair color, color of eyes, etc.—or on tangible objects such as food, toys, even freckles. As children grow, their sense of self isn't limited to their reflections in a mirror; they have acquired language and are able to tell us what they think of themselves.

Note how children change from identifying themselves by physical characteristics (hair or eye color) to more social and emotional characteristics (feeling good or bad about themselves). In these later years, they usually begin to compare themselves to others. These changes occur because of the changes taking place in the developing self. Thompson (1999), attempting to explain these changes, used a model of the self consisting of five features.

- At the core of self-development is a sense of *subjective self-awareness* that reflects James' "I-self." I'm the one doing the acting, thinking, etc.

- But the self also includes *self-representations,* that is, who you think you are. As cognitive development continues, self-recognition deepens and becomes the basis for distinguishing yourself from others.

- An important element in self-development is *an autobiographical personal narrative* that integrates events in your life to the self.

- *Self-evaluations* steadily become more significant as children recognize the opinions of others.

- Finally, the *social self* is influenced by social interactions with others and early childhood youngsters gradually become interested in what others think of them.

During the early childhood years these various aspects of the self help children not only to better understand themselves but to comprehend the thoughts and emotions of others (Thompson, 1999).

Another powerful input into a child's sense of self is that of gender.

I can't marry her. She's too much like myself. I hate myself.

Jerry Seinfeld

The Role of Gender in Development

Now little girls sway
Like buds in May
    And tremble upon the stalk.
But little boys wear
An arrogant air
    And they swagger when they walk.

As you read these words by Phyllis McGinley, do they bring to mind the stereotypes we have about boys and girls? In our modern society, a major concern is how children acquire their sense of gender in a way that they themselves and their society find acceptable. "Acceptable" means many things to many people, and although gender roles for boys and girls, men and women are slowly, even grudgingly, changing, sharp differences of opinion are still evident. For example, many parents want their children to follow traditional gender roles (sports for boys, dolls for girls), while other parents want to break down what they consider rigid gender-role stereotypes. In discussing these issues, let's first clarify the meaning of several terms used in any analysis of gender and development.

Definition of Terms

Developmental psychologists, responding to Unger's plea (Unger & Crawford, 1996), have urged that we use the terms sex and gender more carefully. In this new context, sex refers to biological maleness or femaleness (for example, the sex chromosomes), whereas gender suggests psychosocial aspects of maleness and femaleness (for example, changing gender roles).

Within this framework, we can now distinguish among gender identity, gender stereotypes, and gender roles.

- *Gender identity* is a conviction that one belongs to the sex of birth.

- *Gender stereotypes* reflect those beliefs about the characteristics associated with male or female.

- *Gender role* refers to culturally acceptable sexual behavior.

Theories of Gender Development

Let's now examine how the various theorists have explained gender development. Among the most popular of today's explanations and among those which have generated most of the research are the following.

Biological Explanations Advocates of biological explanations of gender development have turned to the rapidly growing body of research relating to chromosomal and hormonal input. About the sixth prenatal week the fetal gonads develop and begin to secrete hormones that influence gender development. An important question then arises: Do hormones also cause gender differences in brain development? Perhaps the best way we can answer this question is to conclude that, although the evidence is limited, some structural differences are apparent (females seem to have a larger corpus callosum than males) and some processing differences (females may process information with both hemispheres more than males) (Eisenberg, Martin, & Fabes, 1996; Ruble & Martin, 1998). It's important, however, to remember that the brains of males and females are much more similar than they are different.

Social Learning Theory Explanations Social learning theorists believe that parents, as the distributors of reinforcement, reinforce appropriate gender-role behaviors. By their choice of toys, by urging "boy" or "girl" behavior, and by reinforcing this behavior, parents encourage their children to engage in gender-appropriate behavior.

Children quickly learn what objects, activities, and friends are gender appropriate.

Today's social learning theorists have incorporated cognition in their explanations (Bandura, 1997; Eisenberg, Martin, & Fabes, 1996; Ruble & Martin, 1998; Unger & Crawford, 2000). For example, if parents have a good relationship with their children, they become models for their children to imitate, encouraging them to acquire additional gender-related behavior. They also learn appropriate gender behavior from other male and female models (such as those in television shows) who display different kinds of behavior.

Cognitive Development Explanations A second explanation, quite popular today, is cognitive-developmental, which derives from Kohlberg's speculations about gender development (1966). Using Piaget's work, Kohlberg believed that children acquire their gender identity and then begin the process of acquiring sex-appropriate behavior. In other words, as a result of cognitive development—in a sense, constructing their own world—children begin to build the concepts of maleness and femaleness (Unger & Crawford, 2000).

Gender Schema Explanations A newer, and different, cognitive-developmental explanation is called gender schema theory. A schema is a mental blueprint for organizing information, and children develop a schema for gender. Children form a network of mental associations about gender, which they use as a guide to interpret and store information about male and female (Ruble & Martin, 1998). In other words, children use their cognitive abilities to form schema about gender and then shape any gender information coming from the environment to change and expand the existing schema. The gender schema then becomes a powerful tool in connecting many ideas that otherwise seem unrelated (Lips, 2001).

Psychoanalytic-Identification Explanations In traditional Freudian theory (see chapter 2), children become sex typed usually from 4 to 6 years of age because they identify with the same-sex parent. Fear of castration by the father because of the child's desire for the mother explains a boy's sex typing; explanations of identification for girls remains vague in this theory. More recent explanations rely on a boy's and girl's different ways of knowing, which then translates into different ways of knowing boys as differentiated from girls, such as seen in Carol Gilligan's work. (See chapter 9.)

Males and females grow up in quite different learning environments with important psychological implications for development.

Jeanne Block

Acquiring Gender Identity

One of the first categories children form is sex-related; there is a neat division in their minds between male and female. For example, children first indicate their ability to label their own sex and the sex of others between 2 and 3 years of age. By 4 years of age, children are aware that sex identity is stable over time. They then come to the realization that sex identity remains the same despite any changes in clothing, hair style, or activities (Ruble & Martin, 1998; Szkrybalo & Ruble, 1999; Lips, 2001).

Becoming Boys and Girls

Children move from the observable physical differences between the sexes and begin to acquire gender knowledge about the behavior expected of male and female. Depending on the source of this knowledge, gender-role stereotyping has commenced and attitudes toward gender are being shaped. What do we know about the forces influencing this process?

Family Evidence clearly suggests that parents treat boy and girl babies differently from birth by the toys they supply, by their room furnishings, and the type of gender behavior they encourage (Ruble & Martin, 1998). Adults tend to engage in rougher play with boys; give them stereotypical toys (cars and trucks), and speak differently to them. By the end of the second year, parents respond favorably to what they consider appropriate sexual behavior (i.e., stereotypical) and negatively to cross-sex play (boys engaging in typical girl's play and vice versa). Parents also treat girls' misbehavior as more serious than boys'. They criticize girls more severely for failure and hold them to higher levels of self-regulation (Ferguson & others, 1999).

Observations of toddlers and their parents at home disclosed that both mothers and fathers differentially reinforced their children's behavior. That is, parents reinforced girls for playing with dolls and boys for playing with blocks, girls for helping their mothers around the house and boys for running and jumping (Fagot, 1995; Leaper, Anderson, & Sanders, 1998).

Parents usually are unaware of the extent to which they engage in this type of reinforcement (Lips, 2001). In a famous study (Will, Self, & Data, 1976) 11 mothers were observed interacting with a 6-month-old infant. Five of the mothers played with the infant when it was dressed in blue pants and called "Adam." Six mothers later played with the same infant when it wore a pink dress and was called "Beth." The mothers offered a doll to "Beth" and a toy train to "Adam." They also smiled more at Beth and held her more closely. The baby was actually a boy. Interviewed later, all the mothers said that boys and girls were alike at this age and *should be treated identically*.

Since about 80 percent of children have siblings and spend considerable time with each other, sibling relationships also exercise a considerable influence. An older brother shows a younger brother how to hold a bat; a younger sister watches her older sister play with dolls; siblings quarrel among themselves. Same-sex siblings seem to exercise a greater influence on gender-typed activities by modeling or reinforcing gender-appropriate behavior. The influence of other-sex siblings on gender-typing is inconsistent, however (Maccoby, 1998; Ruble & Martin, 1998).

Peers

Boys and girls have different expectations about their friends; girls quickly learn that relationships are a crucial part of their lives, while boys are urged to be independent and self-reliant (Lips, 2001). When children start to make friends and play, these activities foster and maintain sex-typed play. When they engage in "sex-inappropriate" play (boys with dolls, girls with a football), their peers immediately criticize them and tend to isolate them ("sissy"; "tomboy"). Although we see increasing inroads into these stereotypes (girls in Little League and youth hockey, for example), the tendency to sexually compartmentalize behavior increases with age until most adolescents react to intense demands for conformity to stereotypical gender roles.

Here, again, we see the influence of imitation and reinforcement. Children learn about gender-appropriate behavior by observing their friends (Ruble & Martin, 1998). During development, youngsters of the same sex tend to play together, a custom called **sex cleavage** and one that is encouraged by parents and teachers: boys guided to more large-group activities, girls forming more intense small groups (Fagot, 1995). If you think back on your own experiences, you can remember your friends at this age—either all male or female. In adolescence, despite dating and opposite sex attraction, both males and females want to live up to the most rigid interpretations of what their group thinks is ideally male or female. You can understand, then, how imitation, reinforcement, and cognitive development come together to intensify what a boy thinks is masculine and a girl thinks is feminine.

Sex cleavage Youngsters of the same sex tend to play and do things together.

Media

Another influence on gender development, one that carries important messages about what is desirable for males and females and one that reaches into the home, is the media, especially television. Television has assumed such a powerful place in the socialization of children that it is safe to say that television is almost as significant as family and peers. What is particularly bothersome is the stereotypical behavior that it presents as both positive and desirable. The more television children watch, the more stereotypical is their behavior (Lips, 2001).

In spite of such shows as *Murphy Brown* and *Dr. Quinn,* the central characters of shows are much more likely to be male than female, the theme will be action-oriented for males, and the characters typically engage in stereotypical behavior (men are the executives and leaders, women are the housewives and secretaries). Much the same holds true for television commercials. There is little doubt that children notice the different ways television portrays males and females. When asked to rate the behavior of males and females, children aged 8 to 13 responded in a rigidly stereotypical manner: Males were brave, adventurous, intelligent, and make good decisions. Females, on the other hand, cried easily and needed to be protected (Lips, 2001).

With this brief examination of the biological and environmental forces that contribute to gender and the theories that attempt to explain the process, let's next look at what happens when gender stereotypes are formed.

Gender Stereotyping

It's clear from our discussion that children learn more about gender than how to recognize boys and girls; they quickly enter the world of gender stereotyping (Eisenberg, Martin, & Fabes, 1996). Gender stereotyping is the belief that we have about the characteristics and behavior associated with male and female. In other words, from an early age we form an idea of what a male and female should be, begin to accumulate characteristics about male and female, and assign a label to that category. This process certainly simplifies our ability to deal with our world: That rough, noisy person is a boy; that gentle, soft-spoken, obedient person is a girl. (As a result of such stereotyping, the "feminine" boy or "masculine" girl often has difficulties with their peers.)

Even the world of computer games mirrors society's stereotyping. In 1998, the top six selling computer games for girls were all Barbie games. One game, *Barbie's Fashion Designer* sold an astonishing 500,000 copies in its first two months on the market. Boys' games, however, take them into a virtual world where enemies are vanquished, space is explored, and aliens are battled. So the stereotype is further entrenched: girls' games teach about social relationships and boys' games teach about power and mastery.

When the characteristics associated with a label create a negative image, problems arise. "Oh, girls can't do math; girls can't do science; girls are always crying; girls can't be leaders." At this point we start to treat the individual according to the stereotypes we associate with male or female. If you think about this for a moment, you can see some potential pitfalls, especially in the classroom. (For an excellent summary of the place of women in education, see Sadker & Sadker, 1994, pp. 15–41.)

Although sexual equality is widely accepted today—legally, professionally, and personally—gender stereotyping is still alive and well. But are males and females actually that different?

Children often find opposite-sex toys extremely attractive. Many parents encourage the use of such toys to help their children avoid the development of stereotypical gender-role attitudes.

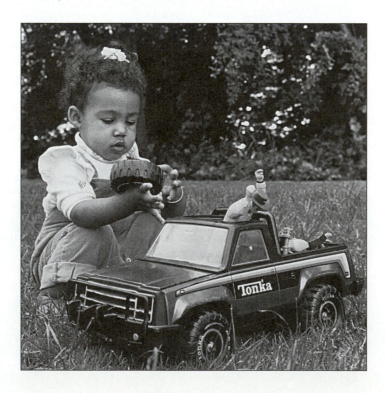

An important part of the early childhood years is the role of play in physical, cognitive, social, and self-development.

An Informed VIEW   *The Emotional Life of Boys*

"Nobody's going to make me do anything I don't want to do. If they try, they better be ready for trouble. I don't care what happens. I can take care of myself."

These macho words, spoken by a 13-year-old boy, illustrate the bravado that unfortunately too often leads to aggression. Boys exhibiting this kind of behavior have become a source of concern for those attempting to understand the causes for a dramatic increase in male violence. The tragic murders at Columbine High School in Littleton, Colorado, brought to public attention a question that researchers and developmental psychologists have been wrestling with for several years: What is happening in the development of some boys that leads to wild acts of violence, even murder?

The public's concern with causes of these brutal assaults is reflected in the popularity of such books as James Garbarino's *Lost Boys* (1999), Dan Kindlon and Michael Thompson's *Raising Cain* (1999), and William Pollack's *Real Boys* (1998). There is a growing recognition that the emotional lives of some boys is so distorted that brutality and murder are inevitable results. Why? Among the reasons offered are:

- Schools are "antiboy," that is, they tend to ignore the greater physical restlessness and activity of boys.
- Many members of our society, especially fathers, encourage a tough guy, macho image for their sons.
- Boys' environments are frequently a daily mix of aggression, fighting, bullying, and taunting.

- At the same time, others such as teachers, women, and psychologists are urging boys to display greater sensitivity.
- The hero image—long neglected in our society—too often is seen in violent entertainment and sports' figures.

Pollack (1998) stresses that parents, communities, and schools develop plans to help boys avoid feelings of alienation, prevent academic decline, and present image-enhancing role models. He identified two sources of a boy's reluctance to display his feelings.

1. The overuse of shame in the "toughening up" process of boys.
2. The emphasis society places on a boy separating emotionally from his mother at an unnecessarily early age (usually by six years).

The problem is not that we introduce our boys to the world—that's what parents should be doing—it's how we do it. We expect them to step outside the family too abruptly, with too little preparation for what lies in store, too little emotional support, not enough opportunity to express their feelings, and often with no option of going back or changing course. That's because we believe disconnection is important, even essential, for a boy to "make the break" and become a man (Pollack, 1998, p. xxiv).

If you would like to have a more informed view on this issue, you may want to read one or more of the articles referenced in this chapter.

www   You may also wish to learn more about it by going to our web site at http:www.mhhe.com/dacey5.

Guided Review

11. The "I" is the _____; the "Me" is the _____.
12. Children usually acquire a sense of self by _____ months of age.
13. When children develop a mental blueprint concerning gender, this is called
    _____ _____ _____.
14. Psychologists today are more alert to the proper use of the terms _____
    and _____ to indicate the interacton of _____ and
    _____ to explain gender.
15. Gender stereotyping is reflected in the world of _____ games.

Answers

11. knower, known 12. 18 13. gender schema theory 14. sex, gender, biology, environment 15. computer

The Importance of Play

Think about play for a moment, what you remember from your childhood or what you see as an older brother, sister, or even parent. Why do children play? You'd probably answer that children play to have fun, to do things they had learned, or to relieve the anxieties of going to the dentist or doctor. In their play, children demonstrate each of these explanations: fun, learning, and emotions. When children play, they learn about themselves, others, and their world and play becomes the medium through which these processes occur.

Among the characteristics of play are the following (Garvey, 1990):

- Play must be enjoyable and valued by the player.

- Play has no extrinsic goals; that is, play is intrinsically motivated.

- Play is spontaneous and voluntary; no one is forcing a child to play; it is freely chosen by the child.

- Play demands that a child be actively engaged.

- Play has systematic relations to other behavior that is not play.

We'll see later that play is linked to other developmental considerations such as cognition, emotion, and the like. But for now, let's define **play** as *an activity that children engage in because they enjoy it for its own sake.*

Why do we play? Attempting to answer this question takes us into the realm of what interests us as human beings throughout our lifespan. We're curious about the social and physical world and reach out to explore it and master and control processes and produce desired effects by our own. Children play in a wide variety of situations: alone or with others, with objects, and with ideas, simply, but also with great skill (Bronson, 1995). During the early childhood years, play assumes a more social nature and children, using their growing symbolic ability, enter the world of pretend play (Rubin, Coplan, Nelson, & Lagace-Sequin, 1999).

The Meaning of Play

Play allows children to explore their environment on their own terms and to take in any meaningful experiences at their own rate and on their own level (e.g., running through a field and stopping to look at rocks or insects). Although students of play no longer believe that children engage in play as practice for tasks that will be useful to them as adults, you can see remnants of that belief in the notion that gaining experience in culturally valued roles remains a function of play (Uzgiris & Raeff, 1995).

For example, Vygotsky (1978) argued that children's imaginary situations provide zones of proximal development that function as mental support systems. Typically, adults provide these zones of proximal development by their suggestions, hints, and guidelines. But as Vygotsky noted, children tend to play at a level above their average age and above their daily behavior. (See chapter 2 for an analysis of Vygotsky's work.)

Yet we must enter a disclaimer, perhaps more from a lack of evidence than anything else. Research specifically designed to show that play encourages development is lacking. Studies of Central American Mayan children indicate that they spend less time playing during their early years than North American children, but equal them in their performance on standardized tests of development (Cole & Cole, 1996).

Children also play for the sheer exuberance of it, which enables them to exercise their bodies and improve motor skills. Such uninhibited behavior permits children to relieve tension and helps them to master anxiety (Watson, 1995). You probably remember the story of the child playing dentist after a visit to a dentist's office. Keep in mind, however, in our discussion, the interactive nature of play: Children can't play certain kinds of games until they reach a specific cognitive level, but they

Play Play is an activity that children engage in because they enjoy it for its own sake.

Play may be one of the most profound expressions of human nature and one of the greatest innate resources for learning and invention.

Martha Bronson

TABLE 8.3 TYPES OF PLAY

Play Type	Age	Definition	Examples
Functional play	1–2 years	Simple, repetitive motor movements with or without objects	Running around, rolling a toy car back and forth
Constructive play	3–6 years	Creating or constructing something	Making a house out of toy blocks, drawing a picture, putting a puzzle together, using Legos
Make-believe play	3–7 years	Acting out roles	Playing house, school, or doctor; acting as a television character
Games with rules	6–11 years	Understanding and following rules in games	Playing board games, cards, baseball, etc.

Source: After Berk, 1997.

can't reach that level without environmental encouragement, some of which comes through their play.

Play in childhood may also influence the learning skills and conscious learning interests of the future. What children learn as "fun" becomes the foundation for intrinsic motivation now and later. Think back yourself: What kind of play did you really enjoy? Do you think it contributed to your success today? (Discuss this in class; it should provide some funny moments.) (Table 8.3 presents several types of play and the ages at which they occur.)

Developmental Aspects of Play

With this interactive model in mind, we can see that children play for various reasons, such as the following.

Cognitive Development

Play aids cognitive development; cognitive development aids play. Through play, children learn about the objects in their world, what these objects do (balls roll and bounce), what they are made of (toy cars have wheels), and how they work. To use Piaget's terms, children "operate" on these objects through play and also learn behavioral skills that will help them in the future.

Once children leave infancy and enter the early childhood years, Piaget classified the games that children play as follows.

*   *Practice games,* which are mainly characteristic of the sensorimotor period, carry into the initial early childhood years.

*   *Symbolic games,* which typically begin at about 18 to 24 months, are seen when children pretend to be asleep, or washing their hands. Piaget believed that during these years children use their growing symbolic ability to extend their real world.

*   *Games with rules* begin during the early childhood (symbolic) years but are more typical of the 7- to 11-year period. (Table 8.4 presents a schedule of appropriate games for various ages.)

Social Development

Play helps social development during this period because the involvement of others demands a give-and-take that teaches early childhood youngsters the basics of forming relationships. Social skills demand the same building processes as cognitive skills. That is, children begin to share symbolic meanings through their use of pretend play (Rubin, Coplan, Nelson, & Lagace-Sequin, 1999).

For a more detailed presentation of Piaget's work on play see Piaget, J. (1951). *Play, dreams, and imitation in childhood.* New York: Norton.

TABLE 8.4 APPROPRIATE GAMES

Age	Appropriate Materials	Developmental Concerns
Older toddlers (2 years)	Simple games with few pieces; game pieces that are not too small (2–4 inches); simple matching games with few pairs (lotto-type); giant dominoes; magnetic fishing games	Enjoy games that they can do alone or with one other child and/or adult
Preschool and kindergarten children (3 through 5 years)	More complex matching games (more pieces), including lotto; dominoes (picture, color number); simple card games (Concentration); first board games (4–5 years); picture bingo (matching letter/number bingo at about age 5); games involving construction or balancing	Development of turn taking, concentration, attention to detail, and understanding of rule-based interaction supported by early games; can play games in which outcome is determined by chance, not strategy; may play with one or two peers but may have difficulty losing
Primary school children (6 through 8 years)	Simple guessing or deductive games, strategy games, trading games, card games, bingo, dominoes, marbles, checkers, Chinese checkers; word games, arithmetic games (simple adding games)	Increasing interest in games but hate to lose; can play competitive games by age 8; increasing capacity for cooperative interaction and use of strategy nurtured by games, but games should have relatively few rules and not require complicated strategies

Source: Bronson, M.B., 1995. *The Right Stuff for Children Birth to 8: Selecting Play Materials to Support Development,* Washington, D.C.: NAEYC. Reprinted with permission from the National Association for the Education of Young Children.

An Applied VIEW   *Children and Their Toys*

When parents shop for their children's toys, they should ask themselves a basic question: What kind of activities can this toy lead to? Too often, the answer is "nothing good." Today's toys frequently promote violence, involve candy, or depend on electronic technology, turning the child into a passive observer—push the button and watch.

From what we have said, you can see how important it is to provide appropriate play materials to match the needs and goals of children. As Bronson (1995) noted, the play materials we supply our children are loaded with multiple messages. They not only cause children to do certain things (because of the nature of the toy), they also convey clearly what parents think is acceptable. For example, some parents would never give a child a toy gun; others think guns are a normal part of growing up.

Play materials are typically grouped into four categories: social and fantasy; exploration and mastery; music, art, and movement; gross motor play. *Social and fantasy play materials* include items that encourage the use of imagination and the mental representation of objects and events, as well as a deeper understanding of people and the rules we live by. Play materials in this category are often used in dramatic play, solitary fantasy play, and role play.

Exploration and mastery play materials increase children's knowledge about the physical world, encouraging them to devise ways to enrich their comprehension of "how things work." Puzzles, pattern-making games, sand, water, and string encourage children's search for knowledge. *Music, art, and movement play materials* aid in the development of artistic expression, and include arts, crafts, and instruments. Finally, *gross motor play materials* foster large muscle development and skills, and would include playground and gym equipment, push-and-pull toys, and sports equipment.

Bronson (1995) suggests the following developmental guidelines for purchasing toys.

- *Birth to 12 months.* Simple toys such as rattles and mobiles are appropriate.
- *12 to 24 months.* In their search for cause-and-effect relations and their own need to learn self-control, blocks, stacking toys, and stuffed animals give them the opportunity to explore and experiment.
- *2 to 3 years.* Toys that make use of size, shape, color, and texture, balls that help motor skills to develop, and objects for pretend play are suited for these years.
- *3 to 5 years.* Simple board games, art materials, and building sets such as Lego are good for these years.

At three years of age, children prefer playmates of their own sex. Girls show a stronger preference than boys at this age, but from four to five years it is boys who show a stronger sex preference, although mixed sex groups still occur. But gender differentiation from three to five years becomes ever more apparent. During free play sessions in preschool and day-care centers, children of the same sex are the close partners, a trend that holds across cultures. (For an excellent discussion of this topic see Maccoby, 1998.)

Why are some 5- and 6-year-olds more popular with their classmates than others? Watching closely, you can discover the reasons: decreasing egocentrism, recognition of the rights of others, and a willingness to share. These social skills do not simply appear; they are learned, and much of the learning comes through play.

Emotional Development

The work of Freud and Erikson that we discussed in chapter 2 suggests that play can provide an emotional release for children. That is, play helps children to master those intense, sometimes overpowering, experiences all children encounter. In their play, they avoid the right or wrong, life-and-death feelings that accompany interactions with adults. Children can be creative without worrying about failure and work out their emotional tensions through play.

Guided Review

16. Any analysis of play must take into consideration that children play because they _____ it for its own sake.
17. Play is associated with four aspects of development: _____, _____, _____, and _____ .
18. When parents buy toys, they should be concerned with the type of _____ the toy can lead to.
19. _____ work reflects play's role in cognitive development.
20. The play material we furnish children are laden with _____ _____ .

CONCLUSION & SUMMARY

At the beginning of the early childhood years, most children meet other youngsters. By the end of the period, almost all children enter formal schooling. Their symbolic ability enriches all of their activities, although limitations still exist. Given their boundless energy and enthusiasm, early childhood youngsters require consistent and reasonable discipline. Yet they should be permitted to do as many things for themselves as possible to help them gain mastery over themselves and their surroundings.

By the end of the early childhood period, children have learned much about their world and are prepared to enter the more complex, competitive, yet exciting world of middle childhood.

What role does family play in development during these years?

- The meaning of "family" in our society has changed radically.
- How parents treat their children has a decisive influence on developmental outcomes.
- Baumrind's types of parenting behavior help to clarify the role of parents in children's development.
- Research has demonstrated how divorce can affect children of different ages.
- Divorce plus remarriage produces a series of transitions to which children must adjust.
- Many children attend some form of day care, and the developmental outcomes of these experiences are still in question.

How do children of this age acquire a sense of self?

- The emergence of the self follows a clearly defined path.

Answers

16. enjoy 17. physical, cognitive, social, emotional 18. activities 19. Piaget's 20. multiple messages

- At the core of self-development is a sense of subjective self-awareness.

How do children come to understand the meaning of their gender?

- Various theories have been proposed to explain how children achieve their sense of gender.

- Youngsters acquire their gender identity during the early childhood years.
- Modeling is an important influence on children's gender development.
- Children initially seem to acquire an understanding of gender before they manifest sex-typed behavior.

What is the value of play to children of these years?

- Play affects all aspects of development: physical, cognitive, social, and emotional.
- The nature of a child's play changes over the years, gradually becoming more symbolic.

KEY TERMS

Authoritarian parents
Authoritative parents
Homeless

Permissive parents
Play
Sex cleavage

Siblings
Sibling underworld
Socialization

WHAT DO YOU THINK?

1. With today's accepted changes in the gender roles of males and females, do you think that a boy or girl growing up in these times could become confused about gender identity? Does your answer also apply to gender roles? Why?
2. Think back on your days as a child. Can you put your parents'

behavior in any of Baumrind's categories? Do you think it affected your behavior? Explain your answer by linking your parents' behavior to some of your personal characteristics.
3. In this chapter you read about the "sleeper" effect of divorce (effects show up quite a bit later). Do you

agree with these findings? Can you explain them by the child's age at the time of the divorce? (Consider all aspects of a child's development at that age.)
4. You probably have read about child abuse in some day-care centers. Do you think there should be stricter supervision? Why? By whom?

CHAPTER REVIEW TEST

1. Selma Fraiberg identified the early childhood period as
   a. Children and Their Parents.
   b. The Magic Years.
   c. Stress and Storm.
   d. Society and Its Children.

2. A child who is aggressive and demonstrates a lack of responsibility is associated with _____ parenting behavior.
   a. authoritative
   b. permissive
   c. authoritarian
   d. doting

3. Today's homeless population is
   a. mostly alcoholic men.
   b. skid row inhabitants.
   c. younger and more mixed than previously.
   d. socially more limited.

4. About _____ percent of first marriages end in divorce.
   a. 75
   b. 80

   c. 50
   d. 25

5. Almost _____ percent of second marriages will end in divorce.
   a. 48
   b. 62
   c. 74
   d. 83

6. Divorce is thought of today as a _____ of experiences.
   a. sequence
   b. repression
   c. assimilation
   d. amalgamation

7. After divorce, familiy conditions usually stabilize in about _____ years.
   a. two
   b. three
   c. four
   d. five

8. About _____ _____ places provide day-care services.
   a. 15,000 to 25,000

   b. 25,000 to 35,000
   c. 35,000 to 45,000
   d. 45,000 to 55,000

9. _____ are older, better educated, and higher paid care givers.
   a. Au pairs
   b. Nurses
   c. Nannies
   d. Grandparents

10. In the United States, the majority of children under _____ years receive nonparental care.
    a. 2
    b. 3
    c. 4
    d. 5

11. The most important feature of day care is the _____ of care provided.
    a. time
    b. degree
    c. extent
    d. quality

12. Probably the best type of day care is found in the _____ center, which may not provide an accurate picture of all centers.
    a. research
    b. company
    c. commercial
    d. family run

13. The American psychologist who discussed the "I" and "Me" elements of the self was
    a. Edward L. Thorndike.
    b. William James.
    c. B. F. Skinner.
    d. John Watson.

14. The beliefs that we have about the characteristics and behavior we associate with male and female is called
    a. accommodation.
    b. gender practices.
    c. gender stereotypes.
    d. gender equality.

15. In cognitive development theory, children first acquire their
    a. gender identity.
    b. appropriate gender behavior.
    c. psychic stability.
    d. conditioned behavior.

16. Social learning theory depends on the concept of _____ to explain the acquisition of appropriate gender behavior.
    a. schema
    b. assimilation
    c. reinforcement
    d. adaptation

17. When children of the same sex tend to play together, it is referred to as
    a. sex differentiation.
    b. sex cleavage.
    c. sex bias.
    d. sex dichotomy.

18. True play has no _____ goals.
    a. divergent
    b. coercive
    c. intrinsic
    d. extrinsic

19. Play materials are grouped into _____ categories.
    a. 4
    b. 6
    c. 8
    d. 10

20. Piaget classified games as practice, with rules, and
    a. complex.
    b. routine.
    c. simple.
    d. symbolic.

Answers

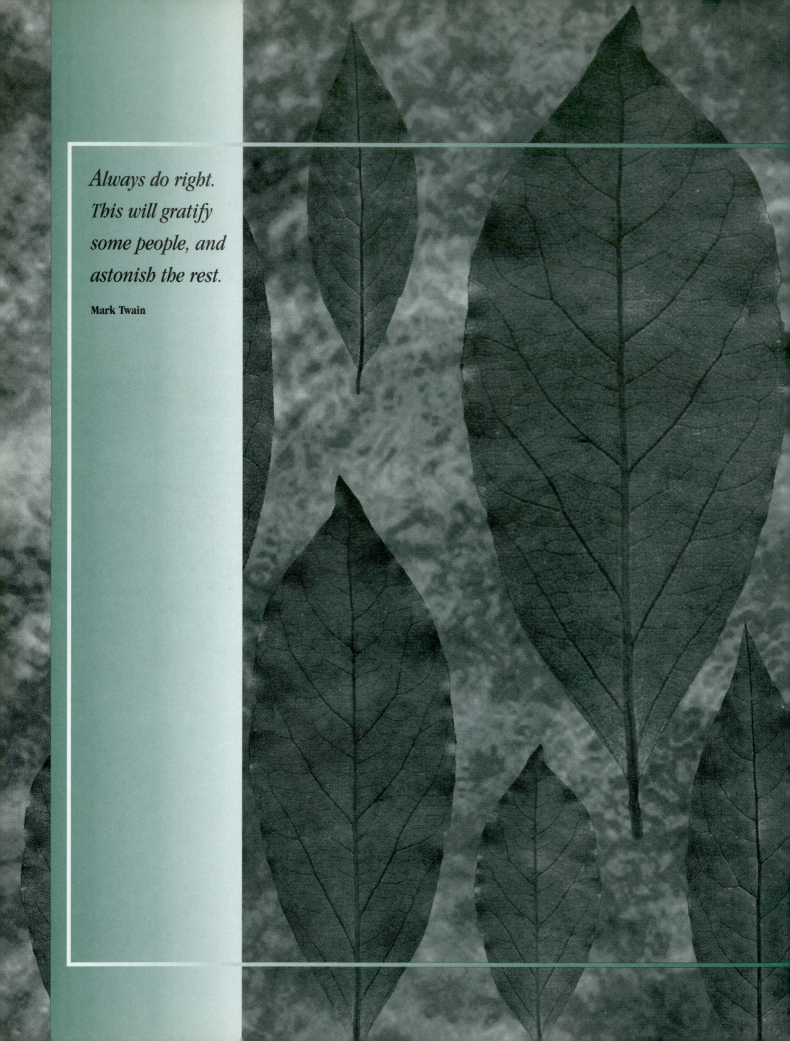

*Always do right.
This will gratify
some people, and
astonish the rest.*

Mark Twain

CHAPTER 9

Physical and Cognitive Development in Middle Childhood

Chapter Outline

Cognitive theory has made us aware that children's language reveals much about their level of mental functioning.

It was the week after school opened and 5-year-old Kenny Wilson and his 11-year-old sister Alice had just transferred to the Brackett School District. Mrs. Allan, the principal, took both pupils to their new classrooms and introduced them to their teachers.

"Good morning, Kenny. I'm delighted that you're going to be in this classroom," said Mrs. Groves, the first-grade teacher. "Some of the boys and girls in this room live near you. By the way, do you like your new house?"

Kenny, at first nervous, began to respond to Mrs. Groves' warm manner. "Oh, yes. I have my own bedroom. It has big windows."

Mrs. Groves laughed. "Can you see the moon from your window?" she asked.

"You bet. It follows me around the room," said Kenny.

At the same time, Alice was talking with Mr. Gallo, the sixth-grade teacher. "Welcome to the Brackett sixth grade, Alice. I think you'll enjoy being here," said Mr. Gallo. "Can you give me an idea of the kind of work you were doing?"

"Well, the social studies teacher was helping us with research skills," said Alice. "We were doing a project on Egypt and we had to pick one specific topic like housing. Then we outlined it and made a report to the class."

"That sounds as if you were doing good work, Alice. You'll like it here; we're doing a lot of the same things."

Both teachers were listening to and observing their pupils as they spoke, searching for clues that would help them work with these new pupils in their classrooms. And the clues were there, as you can tell from both conversations. Although each pupil spoke well, there are significant differences in both the thinking and speech of the two students. For example, Kenny's statement that the moon follows him around furnishes clues to his level of cognitive development, which we described in chapter 7 when we discussed cognitive development during the early childhood years.

Alice's skillful explanation of her use of research methods also revealed a level of cognitive development that one would expect of a typical sixth grader. Understanding the developmental achievements of children Alice's age—in middle childhood—will be our task in the next two chapters. ✹

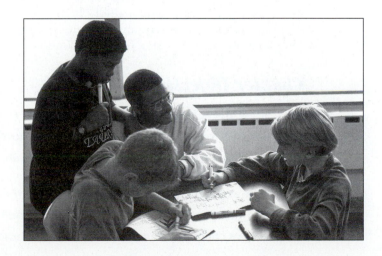

Marty was 20 years old, a fit, athletic-looking student who rarely missed class and seemed to be doing quite well although his work had fallen off somewhat recently. When he asked for an appointment to talk with me, I sensed that he was a troubled young man. Entering my office the next day, the first thing he said was, "Professor, I might not be as regular in coming to class as I've been all semester. I took a job and have to work until midnight." This surprised me because I knew he was an outstanding hockey player on a full scholarship.

I mentioned that I thought it would be difficult to work, keep up classes, and play hockey. "That's just it," he said, "I quit hockey." He noticed my reaction and told me a story that's becoming all too familiar. An outstanding skater almost from the time he could walk, he had played well at all levels (midgets, mites, juniors, high school, and now college). But now, he said, he was burned out. Unrelenting pressure from coaches, peers, and professional scouts had brought him to the point where he just couldn't take any more.

What does this have to do with middle childhood youngsters (about 7 to 11 years of age)? Everything. These years see the emergence of talents that children have been previously nurturing and now, especially during the 9- to 11-year period, suspected skills become full-blown. Whether these be athletic, artistic, mathematical, musical, or whatever, parents, teachers, coaches, adults in general must be sensitive not only to children's abilities but also to their developmental needs and limitations—*they are still children*.

Consequently, this chapter, which analyzes the physical, cognitive, and moral milestones of middle childhood, will often take on the appearance of a mystery. Much is happening to 6- to 12-year-old youngsters that eludes initial detection. Cognitive complexities and subtle moral reasoning characterize these years between childhood and adolescence.

To help you discover clues to important developmental achievements, in this chapter we begin by tracing physical and motor development during the middle childhood years. We'll then turn again to Piaget and analyze his concrete operational period, that time of cognitive development when youngsters begin to engage in truly abstract thinking. Here we'll pause and examine the world of intelligence, which has caused so much controversy. Today's children are expected to do much more with their intelligence than just sit and listen and memorize: They're expected to develop thinking skills and to solve problems. We'll explore both of these worlds (thinking and problem solving) and then trace the moral and language development of middle childhood youngsters.

As observers of this phase of lifespan development, we can't allow ourselves to be deceived by an apparent lull in development. Too much is going on. Deep-seated developmental currents are changing the very process by which children reason and make their moral decisions. Think about what you read in this chapter; probe into what lies behind a child's behavior. It will help you to understand the developmental achievements that prepare a youngster to move from these last years of childhood to the different demands of adolescence.

Chapter Objectives

After reading this chapter, you should be able to answer the following questions.

◆ How would you describe physical and motor development during these years?

◆ What are some of the competing views of cognitive development during the middle childhood years?

◆ How do children develop thinking and problem-solving strategies?

◆ How would you trace children's progress in moral development?

◆ How does children's language change during these years?

Physical Development

In contrast to the rapid increase in height and weight during the first years of life, physical development proceeds at a slowed pace during middle childhood. Most children gain about 2 inches in height per year. The same pattern applies to weight gains. By 6 years of age, most children are about seven times their birth weight.

Nutrition

The physical picture of the middle childhood youngster is one of energy and growing motor skills. Parents often worry that their child isn't eating enough, but given the slower growth rate of these years, less food is needed. Rather it's the quality of the food that's important; junk foods and excessive fats and sugars are to be avoided. Some parents in developed countries have children who are on vegetarian diets. In other cases, the children themselves dislike meat or avoid it because of their love of animals.

Vegetarian diets are in many ways desirable, but care must be taken that nutrients such as iron and zinc are obtained. Also, some fat is necessary. If the fat content of a diet falls below 20 percent, growth can be stunted. At the other extreme, obesity has many adverse consequences. These include an increasing susceptibility to physical problems, and a diminished sense of self that can cause psychological difficulties (Lutz & Pryzltulski, 1997).

Obesity

With a slower growth rate children need fewer calories (Moore, 1997). Although their need for protein, vitamins, and minerals remains high, some children begin to accumulate empty calories from high-sugar and high-fat foods. Thus obesity, with its social, psychological, and medical consequences, looms on the horizon. (The best way to think of obesity is an excessive amount of fat on the body.) Recent research indicated that children who are overweight between the ages of 10 and 17 years will probably have a lifetime problem regardless of whether their parents were thin or fat (Whitaker & others, 1997). Even with slim parents, children who are overweight during the preteen and teen years have a 64 percent chance of becoming obese adults.

To help their children avoid obesity, parents should follow several safeguards (Lutz & Przyltulski, 1997).

- Carefully monitor their children's time spent watching television; the sarcastic label "couch potato" is, unfortunately, all too true given the tendency to munch while watching.

- Encourage appropriate physical activity *on a year-round basis.*

- Serve as much fruit and vegetables as possible.

- Watch fat intake because it is the most concentrated source of calories.

- Start early to make children aware of what they're eating.

- If a child is overweight, don't become obsessed with it; remember that obesity may well be a genetic problem.

Middle childhood youngsters show steady growth, usually good health, and an increasing sense of competence. Physical growth is relatively slow until the end of the period, when girls' development may spurt. Actually, American girls are reaching puberty earlier than previously realized according to recent research (Herman-Giddens & others, 1997). Nearly one-half of African-American girls and 15 percent of white girls begin to develop sexually by 8 years of age. In other words, girls in the second and third grades are facing issues of puberty (breast development, growth of pubic hair).

Variables such as genetic influence, health, and nutrition may also cause wide fluctuations in the growth of these children. Two youngsters may show considerable physical variation and yet both be perfectly normal. Consequently, although most children achieve the major developmental milestones, development may well differ between cultures, subcultures, and ethnic groups.

Physical Changes in Middle Childhood

Changes in height and weight are not the only noticeable physical differences. The relatively new field of developmental cognitive neuroscience has unearthed significant brain changes during these years. The developmental changes in EEG (electroencephalogram) patterns from four to nine years correspond to changes in attention and working memory during these years (Case, 1998; Bjorklund, 2000). Note in Figure 9.1 the increase in working memory capacity between 4.5 to 6.5 years, and the decrease from 6.5 to 9 years.

This recent research supports the belief that important biological changes accompany the many developmental changes seen in the 5- to 7-year period—often called the "five to seven year shift" (Sameroff & Haith, 1996).

Body proportion changes also. Head size comes more in line with body size. An adult's head size is estimated to be about one-seventh of total body size; the preschooler's is about one-fourth. This difference gradually decreases during the middle childhood years. Also, the loss of baby teeth and the emergence of permanent teeth change the shape of the lower jaw. By the end of the period, the middle childhood youngster's body is more in proportion and more like an adult's.

Changes in arms, legs, and trunk size also occur. The trunk becomes thinner and longer, and the chest becomes broader and flatter. Arms and legs begin to stretch but as yet show little sign of muscle development. Hands and feet grow more slowly than arms and legs, which helps to explain some of the awkwardness that we see during these years. Children are tremendously active physically and gradually display a steady improvement in motor coordination (Tanner, 1989).

Healthy, active children of this age—both boys and girls—also demonstrate considerable motor skill. Lansdown and Walker (1991) summarized motor development during these years:

- Skill increases with maturity until, by the end of the period, some youngsters are highly skilled and much in demand for various sports.

- Boys are stronger than girls.

- Girls may be more graceful and accurate.

Figure 9.1

Increases in working memory.

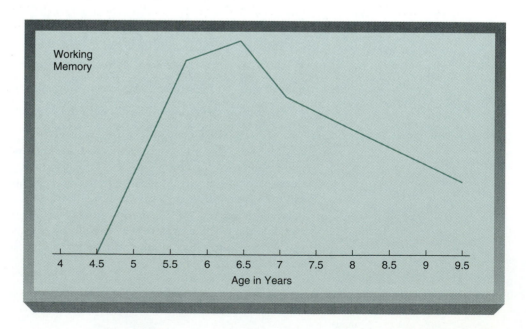

The middle childhood years are a time when children demonstrate considerable competence. Their continuing mastery of their bodies and their environment lead to emerging skills that are readily observable.

- Sex differences—especially strength—become more obvious toward the end of the period.

- Balance matures by the end of the period.

- Fine motor skills (writing and drawing) improve noticeably.

Table 9.1 summarizes the major physical/motor changes in middle childhood.

Guided Review

1. Girls as young as 8 years of age today are faced with the issues of _____ .
2. Motor development during these years shows an increasing degree of _____ .
3. Changes in height, weight, and _____ _____ are major physical changes in middle childhood.
4. Changes in brain wave patterns parallel changes in _____ _____ during these years.

TABLE 9.1 PHYSICAL AND MOTOR DEVELOPMENT IN MIDDLE CHILDHOOD

Age (years)	Height (in.)		Weight (lb.)		Motor Development
	Girl	Boy	Girl	Boy	
7	48	49	52	53	Child has good balance; can hop and jump accurately.
8	51	51	60	62	Boys and girls show equal grip strength; great interest in physical games.
9	52	53	70	70	Psychomotor skills such as throwing, jumping, running show marked improvement.
10	54	55	74	79	Boys become accurate in throwing and catching a small ball; running continues to improve.
11	57	57	85	85	Boys can throw a ball about 95 feet; girls can run about 17.5 feet per second.
12	60	59	95	95	Boys can run about 18.5 feet per second; basketball popular with girls.

From John F. Travers, *The Growing Child,* Scott, Foresman and Company, Glenview, IL, 1982. Reprinted by permission of the author.

Answers

1. puberty 2. coordination 3. body proportion 4. working memory

Cognitive Development

Middle childhood youngsters now begin formal schooling, and their cognitive abilities help them to meet the more demanding tasks set by the school. One way of understanding how children's thinking enables them to master new challenges is to analyze Piaget's explanation of these years—the **concrete operational period.**

Piaget and Concrete Operations

Concrete operational period
Piaget's third stage of cognitive development during which children begin to employ logical thought processes with concrete material.

Picture a 5-year-old child (in Piaget's preoperational stage), an 8-year-old child (in Piaget's concrete operational stage), six black tokens, and six orange tokens. Make a row of the black tokens. If you give the 5-year-old child the orange tokens with instructions to match them with the black tokens, the child can easily do it. When the tokens are in a one-to-one position, a 5-year-old can tell us that both rows have the same number.

• • • • • •

o o o o o o

But if we spread the six black tokens to make a longer row, the 5-year-old will tell us that the longer row has more tokens!

• • • • • •

o o o o o o

Present the 8-year-old with the same problem. The child will think it is a trick—both rows obviously still have the same number. Why? This child is in Piaget's **concrete operational period** and thinking is much more flexible. Concrete operational children *operate mentally* on their environment. For example, they can reverse their thinking. During the period of concrete operations, children gradually employ logical thought processes with *concrete* materials, that is, with objects, people, or events that they can see and touch. They also concentrate on more than one aspect of a situation, which is called **decentering.**

Decentering The process by which concrete operational children can concentrate on more than one aspect of a situation.

Accomplishments of the Concrete Operational Period

Among children's cognitive achievements of these years are the following.

Conservation The understanding that an object retains certain properties, no matter how its form changes.

- **Conservation** appears. If you think back to Piaget's famous water jar problem (see chapter 7), children in the concrete operational stage now mentally pour the water back. By reversing their thinking in this manner, they *conserve* the basic idea: the amount of water remains the same.

Seriation The process by which concrete operational children can arrange objects by increasing or decreasing size.

- **Seriation** means that concrete operational children can arrange objects by increasing or decreasing size.

Classification The process by which concrete operational children can group objects with some similarities within a larger category.

- **Classification** enables children to group objects with some similarities within a larger category. Brown wooden beads and white wooden beads are all beads.

Reversibility Retracing one's thoughts.

- **Reversibility** enables children to retrace their thoughts.

Numeration The process by which concrete operational children grasp the meaning of number, the oneness of one.

- **Numeration** means that children understand the concept of numbers; for example, children understand oneness—that one boy, one girl, one apple, and one orange are all one of something.

Features of Concrete Operational Thinking

Children at the level of concrete operations can solve the water-level problem, but the problem or the situation must involve concrete objects, hence the name of the period. In the water-level problem, for example, children no longer concentrate

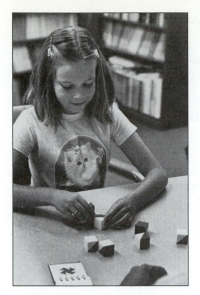

Middle childhood youngsters are at Piaget's stage of concrete operations. Now they demonstrate increasing mental competence, such as classifying.

solely on the height of the water in the glass; they also consider the width of the glass. But as Piaget noted, concrete operational children nevertheless demonstrate a true logic, since they now can reverse operations. Concrete operational children gradually master conservation—that is, they understand that something may remain the same even if surface features change.

Figure 9.2 illustrates the different types of conservation that appear at different ages. For example, if preoperational children are given sticks of different lengths, they cannot arrange them from smallest to largest. Or if presented with three sticks, A, B, and C, they can tell you that A is longer than B and C, and that B is longer than C. But if we now remove A, they can tell you that B is longer than C, but not that A is longer than C. They must see A and C together. The child at the level of concrete operations has no difficulty with this problem.

Piaget's Legacy

As we end our analysis of Piaget's theory of cognitive development, what conclusions are possible.

• Piaget forced us to reconsider prevailing views on how children think.

• Thanks to Piaget we have a deeper understanding of children's cognitive development.

• He made us realize that children are active cognitively (not just passive recipients) as they construct their mental worlds.

• Piaget attempted to explain and not just describe children's thinking.

Figure 9.2

Different kinds of conservation appear at different ages.

From John F. Travers, *The Growing Child,* Scott, Foresman and Company, Glenview, IL, 1982. Reprinted by permission of the author.

Conservation of	Example	Approximate age
1. Number	Which has more?	6–7 years
2. Liquids	Which has more?	7–8 years
3. Length	Are they the same length?	7–8 years
4. Substance	Are they the same?	7–8 years
5. Area	Which has more room?	7–8 years
6. Weight	Will they weigh the same?	9–10 years
7. Volume	Will they displace the same amount of water?	11–12 years

But, as we have seen, serious questions have emerged about Piaget's beliefs.

- By changing the nature of the task (e.g., reducing the number of objects children must manipulate), researchers have found that children accomplish specific tasks at earlier ages than Piaget thought (Haith & Benson, 1998).

- By allowing children to practice (e.g., teaching children conservation tasks), and by using familiar materials, young children can be trained to master concrete operational tasks.

- Research has rejected Piaget's belief that cognitive development proceeds through four discrete stages. For an excellent discussion of recent research on Piagetian concepts by French and Swiss psychologists, see Larivee, Normandeau,

An Applied View
Footprints in the History of Intelligence

The story of Alfred Binet and his search for the meaning and measurement of intelligence is one of the most famous in the history of psychology. In 1904 Binet was asked by the Parisian Minister of Public Instruction to formulate some means of identifying children most likely to fail in school. The problem was very difficult, because it meant finding some means of separating the normal from the truly retarded, of determining the lazy but bright who were simply poor achievers, and of eliminating the **halo effect** (assigning an unwarranted high rating to youngsters because they are neat and attractive).

Accepting this task meant that Binet had to begin with his own idea of intelligence, since it's impossible to fashion the means to measure something unless you know what that something is. Binet's view of intelligence contained three elements.

1. There is *direction* in our mental processes; they're directed toward the achievement of a particular goal and the discovery of adequate means of attaining the goal. In the preparation of a term paper, for example, you select a suitable topic and also the books and journals necessary to complete it.

2. We possess the ability to *adapt* by the use of tentative solutions, that is, we select and utilize some stimuli and test their relevance as we proceed toward our goal. Before writing the term paper, for example, you may make a field trip to the area you're researching, or to save time, you may decide to use relevant sources on the Internet or library resources.

3. We also possess the ability *to make judgments* and to criticize solutions. Frequently called *autocriticism,* this implies an objective evaluation of solutions. You may, for example, complete a paper, reread it, decide that one topic included is irrelevant, and eliminate it. This is autocriticism at work.

The items in Binet's early test reflected these beliefs. When an item seemed to differentiate between normal and subnormal, he retained it; if no discrimination appeared, he rejected it. Binet defined normality as the ability to do the things that others of the same age usually do. The fruits of his and his coworkers' endeavors was the publication in 1905 of the *Metrical Scale of Intelligence.*

Since their publication, Binet's mental age scales have pointed the way for intelligence testing. The success of the Binet scale led a leading American psychologist, Lewis Terman, to adapt it for American usage. Terman's revision, called the Stanford-Binet, first appeared in 1916 and was revised in 1937 and 1960. The fourth edition appeared in 1985 (Thorndike, Hagan, & Satler).

Another effort to measure intelligence appeared in the work of David Wechsler who devised a series of tests intended to measure intelligence through the lifespan. Like Binet, Wechsler believed in a global theory of intelligence, that is, intelligent people, as measured on these tests, will be superior at anything they attempt. There are three forms of his test:

- *The Wechsler Adult Intelligence Scale—Revised (WAIS-111)* contains both verbal and performance items.

- *The Wechsler Intelligence Scale for Children—111 (WISC-111)* is designed for children 5 to 15 years old.

- *The Wechsler Preschool and Primary Scale of Intelligence—Revised (WPPSI-R)* is designed for children 4 to 6½ years old.

Considerable controversy has developed around these tests, mainly because those who have used them deviated from Binet's goal: to provide a means of identifying those students who needed help and *not* to classify people into rigid categories. Today we know that intelligence test scores change over the course of the lifespan for a variety of reasons. We also realize that these tests, which are highly verbal, are unfair to children from backgrounds different from middle-class white Americans. (For an extended discussion of these issues, see Travers and others, 1993.)

& Parent (2000). Their emphasis on individual differences reflects Robert Siegler's adaptive strategy choice model discussed on p. 229 of this chapter.

Although Piaget has left an enduring legacy, his ideas aren't the only explanation of cognitive development. Other psychologists, not entirely happy with Piaget's views, have devised new ways of explaining children's cognitive abilities.

New Ways of Looking at Intelligence

In our discussion of cognitive development from infancy through the middle child-hood years, we have identified limitations in Piaget's theory. Addressing these short-comings, several recent theories have been proposed to explain intelligence and cognitive development. Two of these explanations by Howard Gardner and Robert Sternberg are particularly significant.

Gardner and Multiple Intelligences

Multiple Intelligences
Gardner's theory that attributes seven types of intelligence to humans.

Howard Gardner (1983, 1991, 1993, 1997) has forged a tight link between thinking and intelligence with his theory of **Multiple Intelligences.** An especially intriguing aspect of Gardner's work is the insight it provides into those individuals who are capable of penetrating mathematical vision but who are baffled by the most obvi-ous musical symbols. Gardner attempted to explain this apparent inconsistency by identifying eight equal intelligences.

1. *Linguistic intelligence.* The first of Gardner's intelligences is language—linguistic intelligence. For example, tracing the effects of damage to the language area of the brain, researchers have identified the core operations of any language: phonology, syntax, semantics, and pragmatics. Gardner considered language a preeminent example of human intelligence.

    As we shall soon see, during these years children change their use of language to a more flexible, figurative form. Gardner commented on this by noting that middle childhood youngsters love to expand on their accomplishments. They use appealing figures of speech: "I think I'll get lost," meaning that they're about ready to leave.

2. *Musical intelligence.* One has only to consider the talent and career of Yehudi Menuhin to realize that musical ability is special. At 3 years of age, Menuhin became fascinated by music, and by 10 he was performing on the international stage. The early appearance of musical ability suggests some kind of biological preparedness—a musical intelligence. The right

A child's intelligence may be expressed in many ways: physical, cognitive, psychosocial.

hemisphere of the brain seems particularly important for music, and musical notation clearly indicates a basic symbol system. Although not considered intelligence in most theories, musical skill satisfies Gardner's criteria and so demands inclusion.

In regard to the middle childhood years, Gardner noted that most children (except for those who are musically talented) cease musical development after school begins. For the talented, up to the age of 8 or 9, talent alone suffices for continued progress. Around 9 years of age, serious skill building commences, with sustained practice until adolescence, when these children must decide how much of their lives they want to commit to music. In general, society accepts musical illiteracy.

3. *Logical-mathematical intelligence.* Unlike linguistic and musical intelligences, logical-mathematical intelligence, Gardner believed, evolves from our contact with the world of objects. In using objects, taking them apart, and putting them together again, children gain their fundamental knowledge about "how the world works." By this process, logical-mathematical intelligence quickly divorces itself from the world of concrete objects. Children begin to think abstractly.

Gardner then used Piaget's ideas to trace the evolution of thinking. The development of logical-mathematical thinking, as explored by Piaget, is used as an example of scientific thinking. You may want to review Piaget's ideas concerning the unfolding of intelligence to better understand Gardner's views.

4. *Spatial intelligence.* Brain research has clearly linked spatial ability to the right side of the brain. Here Gardner relied heavily on Piaget, noting that an important change in children's thinking occurs during these years, especially with the appearance of conservation and reversibility. Middle childhood youngsters can now visualize how objects seem to someone else. During these years, children can manipulate objects using their spatial intelligence, but this ability is still restricted to concrete situations and events. (For further discussion of spatial development in children, see Tada & Stiles, 1997.)

Gardner, H. (1983). *Frames of mind.* New York: Basic Books. Gardner's book, which is available in paperback, is an excellent example of the new perspective on studying intelligence. Recognizing that we all seem to demonstrate different abilities, Gardner makes an appealing case for the existence of several intelligences.

5. *Bodily-kinesthetic intelligence.* Gardner stated that our control of bodily motions and the ability to handle objects skillfully are defining features of an "intelligence"—bodily-kinesthetic intelligence. You may be puzzled by this statement, given that we normally divide the mind and reasoning from our physical nature. This divorce between mind and body is often accompanied by the belief that our bodily activities are somehow less special. But Gardner urged us to think of mental ability as a means of carrying out bodily actions. Thus thinking becomes a way of refining motor behavior, which raises the age-old question: Does increasing mental ability affect the performance of a bodily skill?

6 & 7. *Interpersonal and intrapersonal intelligence.* Gardner referred to interpersonal and intrapersonal intelligences as the personal intelligences. Interpersonal intelligence builds on an ability to recognize what is distinctive in others, while intrapersonal intelligence enables us to understand our own feelings. Autism is a good example of a deficit in this intelligence. Often competent in a certain skill, autistic children may be utterly incapable of ever referring to themselves.

8. Gardner recently identified the eighth of his intelligences as *naturalist intelligence,* by which he meant the human ability to discriminate among living things as well as a sensitivity to our natural world. (Table 9.2 summarizes Gardner's theory.)

Triarchic model of intelligence A three-tier explanation of intelligence proposed by Robert Sternberg.

Metacomponents Sternberg's term for those components that help us to plan, monitor, and evaluate our problem-solving strategies.

Performance components Sternberg's term for those components that help us to execute the instructions of the metacomponents.

Knowledge-acquisition components Sternberg's term for those components that help us to learn how to solve problems in the first place.

Sternberg's Triarchic Model of Intelligence

Robert Sternberg (1988, 1990, 1995, 1996) has designed a **triarchic model of intelligence,** which focuses on the following three aspects of intelligence.

1. *The components of intelligence.* These are the information processing skills or components that contribute to intelligent behavior: **metacomponents,** which help us to plan, monitor, and evaluate our problem-solving strategies; **performance components,** which help us to execute the instructions of the metacomponents; and **knowledge-acquisition components,** which help us to learn how to solve problems in the first place (Sternberg, 1988). For example, consider writing a term paper. The metacomponents help you to decide on the topic, plan the paper, monitor the actual writing, and evaluate the final product. The performance

TABLE 9.2 GARDNER'S MULTIPLE INTELLIGENCES

Type of Intelligence	Meaning
Linguistic	Communication, a preeminent example of human intelligence.
Musical	Linked to brain location and a basic symbol system.
Logical-mathematical	What we usually mean by "intelligence."
Spatial	Linked to brain location and symbol systems.
Bodily-kinesthetic	Smooth development of bodily movements and adaptation.
Interpersonal and intrapersonal	Linked to frontal lobe of brain; recognize what is distinctive in others.
Naturalist	Ability to discriminate among categories.

components help you in the actual writing of the paper. You use the knowledge-acquisition components to do your research.

2. *Experience and intelligence.* The second contribution to intelligent behavior is experience, which improves our ability to deal with novel tasks and to use pertinent information to solve problems. Think of the first time you used a word processing program—nervous, hesitant, afraid of making mistakes—and compare those days to the rapid and expert techniques you now use.

3. *The context of intelligence.* The third contribution to intelligent behavior in Sternberg's model refers to the ability to adapt to our culture. We learn how to do those practical things that help us to survive in our society, such as changing the washer in the kitchen sink, driving a car, getting along with others. In other words, skills that are not academic. (Figure 9.3 summarizes Sternberg's theory.)

Since 1987, Sternberg and Gardner have worked together to develop a theory-based curriculum called *Practical Intelligence for School* (PIFS), which combines the major features of both theories. For example, joining Gardner's logical-mathematical intelligence with Sternberg's metacomponents, students are taught to complete a math worksheet accurately and then transfer their new knowledge to figuring out the steps for balancing a budget. Or using Gardner's linguistic intelligence and Sternberg's metacomponents, students focus on the steps in problem solving and organizing their thoughts to give directions to another student.

Guided Review

5. Concrete operations is characterized by the following cognitive accomplishments: conservation, classification, seriation, numeration, and _____.
6. Sternberg's triarchic model of intelligence includes _____, _____, and _____-_____ components.
7. _____ is associated with the theory of multiple intelligences.
8. Gardner would describe an ability to recognize what is distinctive in others as an example of an _____ intelligence.

Figure 9.3

The Triarchic model of intelligence.

The Components of Intelligence   Experience and Intelligence   Context and Intelligence

working together

produce

Intelligent Behavior

Thinking and Problem Solving

As our society moves from an industrial base to one committed to information technology, the skills that children need to adapt to these new directions likewise change. Unless parents and teachers equip themselves with the ability to teach innovative skills, children will be woefully unprepared to meet new demands (Ceci, 1996). Since a swift proliferation of knowledge characterizes an information technology, mastery of available content will not suffice once children leave home and school and attempt to become productive citizens. Rather, they need thinking skills and problem-solving strategies that enable them to adapt to constant change. That is, critical thinkers are self-correcting; they discover their own weaknesses and act to remove obstacles and faults.

Children and Thinking Skills

Once children have accumulated knowledge, they must plan what to do with the material, like a carpenter who has secured a desirable piece of wood and now has to decide how to shape it. Children need to shape their facts so that they squeeze

A Sociocultural View   *Immigrant Children and Tests*

Children's ability to take tests often powerfully influences the results of the test, especially intelligence tests. Tests can scare students or cause them anxiety. Test anxiety may come from parental pressure, their own concerns, or the testing atmosphere. At any rate, merely taking a test may affect a child's performance, which often is especially true for pupils with different cultural experiences. Language, reading, expectations, and behavior all may be different and influence test performance.

These children want to succeed, as reflected in interviews with many of them: Almost 50 percent were doing one to two hours of homework every night. (Twenty-five percent of the Southeastern Asian students reported more than three hours each night.) We have spoken throughout our work of the need for sensitive responsiveness. Here is an instance in which being sensitive to the needs of multicultural children will only aid their adjustment and achievement in school.

The goals are clear; the task itself is difficult. Since social and cultural groups differ in the extent to which they share the values that underlie testing and the values that testing promotes, any national testing system raises questions of equity (Madaus, 1994). The values of the test makers and the test takers aren't necessarily identical. For example, different cultural groups may have different intellectual traditions that tests, of whatever design, may not measure. As Madaus (1994) pointed out, who gains and who loses once again raises the issue of equity.

When children feel comfortable, they do better; this is particularly true for test taking. Multicultural children need information about why the test is being given, when it is being given, what material will be tested, and what kinds of items will be used. These are just a few topics to consider. In addition, language should not be a barrier to performance. For example, children need to understand the terms in the directions of the test—what analyze means; what compare means; what discuss means.

Helping multicultural students in this way means extra time and effort for teachers. But it is teaching, just as teaching English or history is teaching. As more and more multicultural students become users of classroom tests, they shouldn't do poorly because they don't understand the mechanics of the test.

as much value from them as possible. It's not enough just to obtain knowledge; children need to apply what they have learned, to integrate it with other facts, and then to stand back and ask themselves if they could do any better. Parents and teachers attempting to help children improve their thinking skills shouldn't focus merely on questions or on facts. They should try to stretch children's thinking abilities by asking questions that require application, analysis, synthesis, and evaluation such as those based on thinking skills programs.

A Thinking Skills Taxonomy

In 1956, Benjamin Bloom and his colleagues published a classic work entitled *Taxonomy of Educational Objectives, Handbook 1: Cognitive Domain.* (Think of a taxonomy as a classification scheme. Bloom's taxonomy is currently being updated by Anderson and Krathwohl and their colleagues and is expected to be published in 2002.) Bloom's taxonomy has enjoyed widespread acceptance and today forms the core of many thinking skills programs. The main purpose of the taxonomy is to provide a classification of the goals of our educational system (Bloom, 1956, p. 1). The taxonomy consists of three major sections: the cognitive, the affective, and the psychomotor domains. Our concern here is with the cognitive taxonomy, which is divided into the six major classes listed below:

> 1.00 *Knowledge*—recall of specific facts
> 2.00 *Comprehension*—understanding what is communicated
> 3.00 *Application*—generalization and use of abstract information in concrete situations
> 4.00 *Analysis*—breakdown of a problem into subparts and detection of relationships among the parts
> 5.00 *Synthesis*—putting together parts to form a whole
> 6.00 *Evaluation*—using criteria to make judgments

The use of a taxonomy of thinking skills provides a useful organization of knowledge about thinking and facilitates answering questions such as:

- What do we know about children—their developmental paths, needs, and interests?

An Applied View

How Would You Answer These Questions?

1. Imagine that you were lucky enough to obtain two tickets to the great Broadway musical *Phantom of the Opera* for $100. As you walk down the street to the theater, you discover that you have lost the tickets. You can't remember the seat numbers. Would you go to the ticket window and buy another pair of tickets for $100?

2. Imagine that you are on the way to the theater to buy tickets for the Broadway play *Phantom of the Opera.* They will cost you $100. As you approach the ticket window, you discover that you have lost $100. Would you still pay $100 for the tickets?

These questions, originally posed by Tversky and Kahneman (1981) elicit some interesting answers. How did you answer them? Among their subjects, 46 percent answered yes to question 1, while 88 percent answered yes to question 2. Note that many more people said they would buy

new tickets if they had lost the money rather than the tickets. Yet the two situations are almost identical—in each instance you would have lost $100.

How can we explain the difference in the responses? Tversky and Kahneman believed that the way a problem is framed helps to explain our response. As they stated:

> The frame that a decisionmaker adopts is controlled partly by the formulation of the problem and partly by the norms, habits, and personal characteristics of the decisionmaker (1981, p. 453).

The point here is that our personal characteristics (such as motivation, persistence, and the like) and how questions and problems are structured influence our decisions. We can help children reach better decisions by teaching them the skills and strategies discussed in this chapter.

As children's decision-making abilities improve with age, they can be futher aided by helping them to improve their thinking and problem-solving skills.

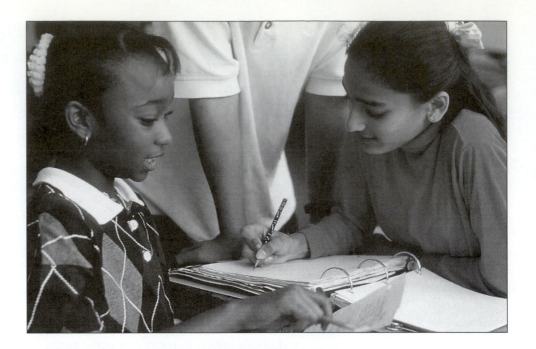

- What is in the nature of the subject matter that can help to shape objectives?

- What does the psychology of learning tell us about the appropriate placement of objectives in the learning sequence? Do the ways that students learn suggest a series of steps that must be mastered?

With today's interest in thinking skills, many concerned parents and teachers have turned to Bloom's categories of analysis, synthesis, and evaluation as the best means available for children to master higher order thinking skills. Table 9.3 provides an example of Bloom's ideas, plus a sample of the kinds of questions you can ask your students to sharpen their thinking skills. (We used the American Civil War as an example.)

Helping children improve their thinking skills introduces the important role played by questions. *Parents and teachers should not focus merely on questions about facts; rather they should stretch children's thinking abilities by asking questions that require application, analysis, synthesis, and evaluation.*

Using Questions to Improve Thinking Skills

Even before Socrates, questioning was one of teaching's most common and effective techniques. Teachers and parents ask hundreds of questions, especially about science, geography, history, or literature. Using questions is a specific example of how to help children improve their thinking skills. Good questions cause children to *pay attention,* to *process information,* to *organize their ideas,* and to *compose an answer,* a neat summary of thinking and problem solving (Cruickshank, Bainer, & Metcalf, 1995).

Three issues are critical in framing thoughtful questions (Cruickshank, Bainer, & Metcalf, 1995).

1. *How to ask questions.* Questions should be clearly and concisely phrased. You could well follow Michael Gelb's advice (1996) to use a reporter's classic questions: *What? Where? When? Who? How? Why?* The language of the question must be appropriate for the children's cognitive level and focus their attention on clear objectives. In other words, don't muddy the waters by introducing unnecessary words or expressions. Also, avoid questions that merely require a "yes" or "no" answer. Effective questions cause children to *think about* what's asked and to compose an answer. Finally, ask only one question at a time. Too often adults think about another aspect of the material they're using and piggyback one or more questions on to the original.

TABLE 9.3 USING BLOOM'S TAXONOMY

Level of Thinking	Sample Questions
Knowledge— recalling specific facts	When did the Civil War begin? When was the Civil War completed? Who was President of the Confederacy during the Civil War?
Comprehension— understanding what is communicated	Why would Americans want to fight against each other? Can you give me a brief summary of the Civil War in your own words?
Application— generalizing and using abstract information	Why did the North want to keep a large army around Washington? Where would you put the Southern cities on this map?
Analysis— dividing a problem into subparts	Can you think of several causes of the Civil War? What were the main features of the Battle of Gettysburg?
Synthesis—putting together parts to form a whole	Why do you think Lee surrendered at Appomatox? Could you write a few sentences describing Lee's personality?
Evaluation—using criteria to make judgments	Many people criticize Grant for losing so many men. Do you think Lincoln made the right decision in putting him in charge of the Union armies? Do you think Lincoln made a mistake in leaving McClellan as head of the Army of the Potomac for so long?

From Elliott, Kratochwill, Littlefield, and Travers. *Educational Psychology: Effective Teaching, Effective Learning.* Copyright 2000, McGraw-Hill. Used by permission of The McGraw-Hill Companies.

Give careful attention to the level of thought your question is demanding. Table 9.4 illustrates the use of Bloom's taxonomy in organizing questions.

2. *Obtaining good answers.* One of the best ways to encourage children to give their best responses is *to give them enough time to answer.* Research has shown that a wait time of about 3 to 5 seconds results in the best answers (Cruickshank, Bainer, & Metcalf, 1995).

3. *Following-up the responses.* Once children have responded, you (parents, teachers, adults) must react. Try to avoid saying. "OK," and then moving on. You should clarify, expand, and synthesize when you can. Never let an incorrect answer stand.

Parents and teachers are the primary motivators of a middle childhood youngster's cognitive potential to think critically. By appealing to a child's enthusiasms and abilities, adults encourage these youngsters to begin using "a thinking disposition" and to use their thinking abilities to attack the problems they face, both in and out of school.

Problem-Solving Strategies

One of the authors of this text (JFT) recently was asked to give a talk to a group of parents on thinking skills and problem-solving strategies for children. To begin, he presented the following problem.

Two motorcyclists are 100 miles apart. At exactly the same moment they begin to drive toward each other for a meeting. Just as they leave, a bird flies from the front of the first cyclist to the front of the second cyclist. When it reaches the second cyclist, it turns around and flies back to the first. The bird continues flying in this manner until the cyclists meet.

TABLE 9.4 USING BLOOM'S TAXONOMY TO FRAME QUESTIONS

Level of Thinking	Examples of Questions
Knowledge	Who did _____? When was _____ completed? Identify the _____ in the list. What does 2 + 6 equal?
Comprehension	Provide a good title for the story you read. In your own words, what was the main theme of the story?
Application	Use the word corrrectly in a sentence. Design a model that illustrates your understanding of the concept.
Analysis	Categorize all of the elements of the problem. What is the function of _____? How is A related to B?
Synthesis	Identify the common pattern resulting from all of the pictures. Summarize the various points that were made by stating a rule. Integrate the various pieces of information to create a profile of the person.
Evaluation	Judge the best method for testing the hypothesis. Rank order the projects, using stated criteria, from best to worst. Decide which problems were solved correctly.

From Elliott, Kratochwill, Littlefield, and Travers. *Educational Psychology: Effective Teaching, Effective Learning.* Copyright 2000, McGraw-Hill. Used by permission of The McGraw-Hill Companies.

The cyclists both travel at the rate of 50 miles per hour, while the bird maintains a constant speed of 75 miles per hour. How many miles will the bird have flown when the cyclists meet?

Examining this problem, you may immediately begin to calculate distance, miles per hour, and constancy of speed. Actually, this is not a mathematical problem; it's a word problem. Carefully look at it again. Both riders will travel for one hour before they meet; the bird flies at 75 miles per hour; therefore, the bird will have flown 75 miles. No formula or calculations are needed, just a close examination of what is given.

The talk to the parents was in the evening. They were tired, and not too attentive. Then they became downright mad at themselves for not getting the correct answer. Now he had their attention, and the parents were determined not to be tricked again. He next asked them to think of something that had frustrated them recently—in other words, a problem—and how they had felt if they couldn't reach a solution. Finally, he reminded the parents that their children have similar feelings when they are baffled by an arithmetic word problem, or bewildered about how to start a term paper.

Characteristics of Good Problem Solvers

Solving a problem occurs when a person has a particular goal in mind that can't be attained immediately because obstacles are present. Thus there are four criteria needed for problem solving to occur: goals, obstacles, strategies for overcoming the obstacles, and an evaluation of the results (Bjorklund, 2000). We know a great deal about problem-solving strategies today and this knowledge can be of great value to children. To give you one example, simply reassuring them that there's nothing to be afraid of when they face a problem and urging them to look for the facts that are given in a problem greatly improves their problem-solving abilities.

Can children be good problem solvers? Can we help them to improve? We think so, given what we know about the characteristics of good problem solvers. For example, *good problem solvers have a positive attitude toward problems,* believing

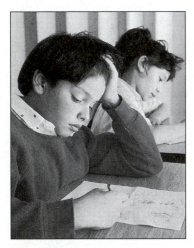

Teaching children the basics of problem solving will improve their abilities to recognize and solve problems, both in and out of the classroom.

they can solve them by careful, persistent analysis. *They're concerned with accuracy,* which is a wonderful attitude to foster in children, one that carries over to all aspects of their lives. *They learn to take a problem apart,* to break it down into its smallest, manageable parts, and then integrate the parts into a manageable whole that leads to a solution. Finally, *they learn not to guess and jump at answers,* a valuable tool to remember whenever they are challenged by a problem, in or out of school (Thornton, 1995).

Improving Children's Problem-Solving Strategies

Obviously some people are better at problem solving than others due to intelligence, experience, or education. But it's possible to improve anyone's ability to solve problems, even children's. Some children and adults don't do well with problems because they're afraid of them. "I'm just not smart enough"; "I never could do these." Here is a good example. Group the following numbers in such a way that when you add them, the total is 1,000.

8 8 8 8 8 8 8 8

Unintimidated elementary school children get the answer almost immediately. Some of you won't even bother trying; others will make a halfhearted effort; still others will attack it enthusiastically. What is important is how you think about a problem. In the eights problem, think of the only number of groups that would give you 0 in the units column when you add them—five. Try working with five groups and you will eventually discover that:

888 + 88 + 8 + 8 + 8 gives you 1,000.

Many of the daily problems children face are vague and ill-defined and if they lack problem-solving strategies, their task is next to impossible. Recent research (Siegler, 1996, 1998; Chen & Siegler, 2000) indicates that most children devise a wide variety of strategies to solve their problems and, depending on the nature of the task, they'll select what they think is the most appropriate strategy. This is the **adaptive strategy choice model** of Robert Siegler (1996). Those strategies that produce successful solutions increase in frequency, while those that do not decrease in frequency. Children have multiple strategies available at all ages, but a child's age dictates which strategies are most frequently used.

Adaptive strategy choice model   Successful strategies increase in frequency.

What Kinds of Mistakes Do Children Make?

Most errors are made not because children (and adults) lack information about the problems, but mainly because they don't attend to the problem or fully employ their reasoning processes. For example, try this problem.

> In a different language liro cas means red tomato, dum cas dan means big red barn, and xer dan means big horse. What is the word for barn in this language? (a) dum (b) liro (c) cas (d) dan (e) xer

Here we have a fairly simple problem, but one demanding a systematic comparison of phrases and a careful matching of words. Poor problem solvers often jump at the first clue, with the result that they choose b, c, d, or e.

Among the most common sources of error are the following:

- *Failure to observe and use all the relevant facts of a problem.* Did you account for each word in the language problem?

- *Failure to adopt systematic, step-by-step procedures.* The problem solver may skip steps, ignore vital information, and leap to a faulty conclusion. Did you make a check, or some other mark, against each word?

- *Failure to perceive vital relationships in the problem*. Did you discover the pattern that led to *dum* as the correct answer?

- *Frequent use of sloppy techniques in acquiring and applying vital information*. Did you guess at the meanings of any of the words? Did you try to eliminate the irrelevant words?

Following is a strategy to help children overcome these mistakes, by developing effective problem-solving techniques.

The DUPE Model

DUPE Problem-solving model (Determine a problem exists, Understand its nature, Plan for its solution, and Evaluate the solution).

Many models have been proposed to help people solve a wide variety of problems. Often these models employ acronyms to assist people in problem solving (e.g., SAC—Strategic Air Command; NATO—North Atlantic Treaty Organization; HOMES—The names of the Great Lakes: Huron, Ontario, Michigan, Erie, Superior). For our purposes we'll use an acronym that you'll remember easily and transfer to any problems (or teach to a child). The acronym is **DUPE** and its intent is to convey the message: *Don't let yourself be deceived*. The meaning of each letter is as follows:

D—*Determine* just exactly what is the nature of the problem. Too often meaningless elements in the problem deceive us; it is here that attention to detail is so important. How would you go about solving this problem?

> There is a super psychic who can predict the score of any game before it is played. Explain how this is possible.

This problem, taken from Bransford and Stein (1993), poses a challenge to most of us because, as the authors noted, a reasonable explanation is difficult to generate. If you are having difficulty, it is probably because you have made a faulty assumption about the nature of the problem. You were not asked about the final score; the score of any game before it is played is 0 to 0. We deliberately presented a tricky problem to stress that you must attend to details.

U—*Understand* the nature of the problem. Realizing that a particular problem exists is not enough; you must also comprehend the essence of the problem if your plan for solution is to be accurate. For example, we frequently hear that a pupil's classroom difficulties are due to hyperactivity. Thus the problem is determined; but understanding the cause of the hyperactivity—physical, social, psychological—requires additional information. Here is an example of the need to understand the nature of a problem.

> Tom either walks to work and rides his bicycle home or rides his bicycle to work and walks home. The round trip takes one hour. If he were to ride both ways, it would take 30 minutes. If Tom walked both ways, how long would a round trip take?

This problem illustrates a basic problem-solving strategy of dividing a problem's information into subgoals to help understand what's required. Think for a moment: What are the givens? How long would it take to ride one way? (15 minutes) How long is a round trip? (1 hour) How long does it take to walk one way? (45 minutes) How long is the round trip if Tom walked both ways? (45 + 45 = 90 minutes)

P—*Plan your solution*. Now that you know that a problem exists and you understand its nature, you must select strategies that are appropriate for the problem. It is here that memory plays such an important role (Siegler, 1998). The accompanying box illustrates various memory strategies that aid memory.

E—*Evaluate your plan*, which usually entails two phases. First you should examine the plan itself in an attempt to determine its suitability. Then you must decide how successful your solution was.

Bransford, B. & B. Stein, (1993). *The IDEAL problem solver*. New York: Freeman. An excellent little book that explores the mysteries of problem solving in an engaging and practical way.

An Applied VIEW

The Role of Memory

Most children have good memories that can be improved with adult help, which, in turn, helps them in solving problems. All memory strategies, however, are not equally effective. The appropriateness of the strategy depends on what you are asked to do. Try this memory problem.

The following list contains 25 words. Take 90 seconds to study these words. When time runs out, write as many of the words as you can without looking at the list.

paper	fruit	street	wheel
white	step	juice	time
spoke	shoe	car	note
ball	word	judge	run
banana	touch	hammer	table
dark	page	bush	official
walk			

How did you do? Or more importantly from our perspective, how did you do it? Were these among the strategies you used?

1. Rehearse each word until you have memorized it: car, car, car.

2. Rehearse several words: paper, white, spoke; paper, white, spoke.

3. Organize the words by category. Note that several words are related to cars; others could be grouped as fruit; still others could be categorized as relating to books.

4. Construct a story to relate as many of the words as possible.

5. Form images of words or groups of words.

You may have tried one or a combination of these strategies, but note that you were not told to memorize them in any particular manner. If you had received specific instructions, each of these strategies would not have been equally effective. For example, when we are asked to remember a particular telephone number, the tendency is to rehearse it for as long as we need to recall it. If you had been directed to memorize the words in the list in a certain order (e.g., the way that they were presented), grouping them by categories would not have been efficient. Thinking of a story to link them in the correct order would have been much more efficient.

Guided Review

9. A program designed to aid the development of thinking skills was devised by _____.

10. A memory strategy in which you go over material repeatedly is called _____.

11. The adaptive strategy choice model was proposed by _____.

12. Good problem solvers share distinct characteristics such as a positive _____ and a concern for _____.

13. The letters in DUPE mean _____, _____, _____, and _____.

Moral Development

We want children to be good, truthful, kind, wise, just, courageous, and virtuous. We also want them to behave, *in all circumstances,* according to an internalized code of conduct that reflects these desirable characteristics. Internalization of moral standards, which entails a shift from reliance on external controls to internal mechanisms, is a significant milestone in the socialization process (Koenig, Cicchetti, & Rogosch, 2000). How do children reach this ideal state? As we attempt to answer this question, we would like you to keep three issues in mind as we study children's moral development.

Answers

9. Bloom 10. rehearsal 11. Siegler 12. attitude, accuracy 13. determine, understand, plan, evaluate

1. *How do children think about moral development?* Here we'll present the theories and relevant research that shed light on this question. We'll then trace the powerful influence of gender and social class on children's thinking about moral issues.

2. *How do children feel about moral matters?* The role of emotions in morality deserve our attention because of the manner in which emotions interact with how children think and behave in moral situations. To make this more meaningful, think of yourself for a moment. For example, how do you "feel" when you know you hurt someone else by something you said, even if you didn't mean to. The answer is that you feel awful. So do children when they do the same thing.

3. *How do children behave in moral situations?* Do children's thoughts and emotions dictate how they act morally? An intriguing question, one that both fascinates and frustrates us, and one that will challenge our ingenuity to answer.

As we begin our analysis of children's moral progress, remember that moral behavior is a complex mixture of *cognition* (thinking about what to do), *emotion* (feelings about what to do or what was done), and *behavior* (what is actually done). To untie this tightly formed knot, psychologists today have appealed to a variety of theoretical explanations, ranging from psychoanalytic to cognitive to behavioristic views. Within these theoretical perspectives consideration is given to issues such as emotion, culture, gender, individual judgment, social influences, and personal reflection (Turiel, 1998).

A summary of children's moral development should help to put the theories and research in a more meaningful perspective.

The Path of Moral Development

Initially, young children (birth to about 2 or 3 years) begin to learn about right and wrong from their parents; these teachings immediately begin to interact with children's natural inclination to do good. So from an early age—as soon as possible—most parents try to combine direction with understanding. Continually forcing children to obey, as we know, loses its effectiveness as they grow older. During these early years, modeling is especially effective. Lacking cognitive sophistication, young children who have a good relationship with their parents usually are enormously impressed by what they see their parents doing.

The next phase (about 2 to 6 years) reflects children's growing cognitive maturity and their developing ability to decide what's right or wrong. They now begin to interact with a variety of authority figures—teachers, counselors, religious, coaches, directors—who make reasonable demands on them. These individuals assume great importance in children's lives and usually reinforce parental concerns about moral behavior. By their directions, explanations, expectations, and by pointing out the consequences of children's behavior for others (a process called *induction*), they provide welcome support to parents' efforts.

Yet telling the truth remains a difficult developmental task for children. Studying 72 children from 3 years 1 month to 6 years 3 months, Polak and Harris (1999) found a decided increase in children's use and understanding of deceptive strategies. Growing deception occurred in a three-step process. First, the younger children showed a clear tendency to deliberately deny obvious misdemeanors. Next, as understanding of deceptive strategies grows, denial of misdeeds becomes more widespread. In these first two phases, however, the children find it difficult to sustain their deception by pretending ignorance. It isn't until the third phase that children become more clever at feigning ignorance.

As children move into the next phase (about 7 to 11+ years), they interact more frequently and intensely with their siblings in their family lives, with their schoolmates in classroom experiences, and with their friends in games and other social activities. Here they again encounter the reality of rules not established by parental edict. (For an excellent discussion of the differential impact of peers and parents in moral development, see Walker, Hennig, & Krettenauer, 2000.) As a result they learn about making and following regulations as well as deriving insights into those children who break the rules. In this way, children are both participants (in games and activities where they must obey the rules) and authority figures (occasionally they will be among those who make the rules). In a sense, they are reflecting the relationship between truth and rightness (Chandler, Sokol, & Wainryb, 2000).

Parents and Moral Development

Are parents influential in their children's moral development? A team of psychologists at Pennsylvania State University probed the question of why children show marked differences in their sensitivity to moral issues, differences that have been widely documented (Dunn & others, 1995). The researchers concentrated on uncovering the possible reasons for these differences. Studying 6-year-old children, they made two important findings.

1. Children whose mothers treated them reasonably but firmly after transgressions seemed more sensitive to matters of right and wrong. These mothers also insisted that their children consider the harm or discomfort done to the *other* child.

2. Those children with older siblings who were friendly and supportive seemed more morally mature.

These findings testify to the significant input parents have into their children's moral development, which begins with the type of family relations they encourage. If parents urge (perhaps insist is a better word) their children to help and encourage each other, and if they deal with misbehavior with a judicious blend of firmness and understanding, they will have illuminated the moral pathway quite brightly for their children. Parents who also encourage their children to express their opinions about moral issues and who themselves model a higher level of moral behavior help to advance their children's insights into matters of right and wrong.

Let's now turn our attention to how children think about matters of right and wrong.

> A cadet does not lie, cheat, or steal, or tolerate those who do.
>
> *The West Point Honor Code*

Piaget's Explanation

Youngsters realize that the opinions and feelings of others matter: What they do might hurt someone else. By the end of the middle childhood period, children clearly include intention in their thinking. For 6-year-olds, stealing is wrong because they might get punished; for the 11- or 12-year-old, stealing may be wrong because it takes away from someone else. During these years, children move from judging acts solely by the amount of punishment to judging acts based on intention and motivation.

Marbles and Morality

As might be expected, Piaget examined the moral development of children and attempted to explain it from his cognitive perspective (Piaget, 1932). Piaget formulated his ideas on moral development by observing children playing a game of marbles. Watching the children, talking to them, and applying his cognitive theory to their actions, he identified how children actually conform to rules.

While observing the children playing marbles Piaget also asked them their ideas about fairness and justice, what is a serious breach of rules, and how punishment should be administered. From this information, he devised a theory of moral development:

• Up to about 4 years, children are not concerned with morality. Rules are meaningless, so they are unaware of any rule violations.

- At about 4 years, they begin to believe that rules are fixed and unchangeable. Rules come from authority (e.g., parents, God) and are to be obeyed without question. This phase of moral development is often called *heteronomous morality* (or *moral realism*). Children of this age make judgments about right or wrong based on the consequences of behavior; for example, it is more serious to break five dishes than one.

  They also believe in *immanent justice;* that is, anyone who breaks a rule will be punished immediately—by someone, somewhere, somehow! In an interesting cross-cultural comparison, Shweder (1991) noted that South Asian scholars found Piaget's idea of immanent justice both uncanny and naïve. Uncanny because Hindu thought believes that nature is just and will dictate that the consequences of sin are suffering. Naïve because faith in a just world does not decline with age and cognitive development.

- From 7 to about 11 years of age, children begin to realize that individuals formulate social rules, which can be changed. This phase is referred to as *autonomous morality* (or the *morality of reciprocity*). At this age, children think punishment for any violation of rules should be linked to the intent of the violator. The person who broke five cups didn't mean to, so should not be punished any more than the person who broke one.

Piaget's ideas about moral development led to the advancement of a more complex theory devised by Lawrence Kohlberg.

Kohlberg's Theory

Among the more notable efforts to explain a child's moral development has been that of Lawrence Kohlberg (1975, 1981). Using Piaget's ideas about cognitive development as a basis, Kohlberg's moral stages emerge from a child's active thinking about moral issues and decisions. Kohlberg formulated a sophisticated scheme of moral development extending from about 4 years of age through adulthood.

Moral dilemma A modified clinical technique used by Kohlberg in which a conflict is posed for which subjects justify the morality of their choices.

To discover the structures of moral reasoning and the stages of moral development, Kohlberg (1975) employed a modified clinical technique called the **moral dilemma,** in which a conflict leads subjects to justify the morality of their choices. In one of the best known, a husband needs a miracle drug to save his dying wife. The druggist is selling the remedy at an outrageous price, which the woman's husband cannot afford. He collects about half the money and asks the druggist to sell the drug to him more cheaply or allow him to pay the rest later. The druggist refuses. What should the man do: steal the drug or permit his wife to die rather than break the law? By posing these conflicts, Kohlberg forces us to project our own views.

Kohlberg's theory traces moral development through six stages by successive transformations of cognitive structures (see table 9.5). Middle childhood youngsters are typically at Kohlberg's *preconventional level of morality.* Only as they approach ages 10 to 12 do they begin to edge into the *conventional level of morality,* where acts are right because that's the way it's supposed to be (determined by adult authority). The *postconventional level of morality* comes at age 13 and over.

According to Kohlberg, moral judgment requires us to weigh the claims of others against self-interest. Thus youngsters must overcome their egocentrism before they can legitimately make moral judgments. Consequently, we again see how the blend of cognitive development and cultural beliefs shape the nature of moral thinking (Narvaez & others, 1999).

Finally, anyone's level of moral development may not be the same as their moral behavior. To put it simply, people may know what is right but do things they know are wrong. Recent research suggests that when children are in a stage of developmental transition, Kohlberg's moral concepts are less influential in moral decisionmaking, that is, children are unsure how to interpret actual events (Thoma & Rest, 1999). Table 9.5 summarizes Kohlberg's theory.

TABLE 9.5 KOHLBERG'S STAGES OF MORAL DEVELOPMENT

Level I. Preconventional (about 4 to 10 years)

During these years children respond mainly to cultural control to avoid punishment and attain satisfaction. There are two stages:

Stage 1. Punishment and obedience. Children obey rules and orders to avoid punishment; there is no concern about moral rectitude.

Stage 2. Naïve instrumental behaviorism. Children obey rules but only for pure self-interest; they are vaguely aware of fairness to others but obey rules only for their own satisfaction. Kohlberg introduces the notion of reciprocity here: "You scratch my back, I'll scratch yours."

Level II. Conventional (about 10 to 13 years)

During these years children desire approval, both from individuals and society. They not only conform, but actively support society's standards. There are two stages:

Stage 3. Children seek the approval of others, the "good boy–good girl" mentality. They begin to judge behavior by intention: "She meant to do well."

Stage 4. Law-and-order mentality. Children are concerned with authority and maintaining the social order. Correct behavior is "doing one's duty."

Level III. Postconventional (13 years and over)

If true morality (an internal moral code) is to develop, it appears during these years. The individual does not appeal to other people for moral decisions; these decisions are made by an "enlightened conscience." There are two stages:

Stage 5. An individual makes moral decisions legalistically or contractually; that is, the best values are those supported by law because they have been accepted by the whole society. If there is conflict between human need and the law, individuals should work to change the law.

Stage 6. An informed conscience defines what is right. People act, not from fear, approval, or law, but from their own internalized standards of right or wrong.

Source: Based on L. Kohlberg, "A Cognitive-Developmental Analysis of Children's Sex-Role Concepts and Attitudes" in *The Development of Sex Differences,* edited by E. Maccoby, Stanford University Press, Stanford, CA, 1966.

Not all students of moral development agree with Kohlberg. Strenuous objections have been made to Kohlberg's male interpretation of moral development, especially by Carol Gilligan.

Gilligan's *In a Different Voice*

The importance Kohlberg placed on justice triggered serious doubts by those who believe that he ignored gender differences. Carol Gilligan, in particular, questioned the validity of Kohlberg's theory for women (1982). She argued that the qualities Kohlberg associated with the mature adult (autonomous thinking, clear decision-making, and responsible action) are qualities that have been traditionally associated with "masculinity" rather than "femininity."

Characteristics that supposedly define the "good woman" (gentleness, tact, concern for the feelings of others, display of feelings, caring) all contribute to a different concept of morality. As a result, the different images of self that boys and girls/men and women acquire lead to different interpretations of moral behavior: women, concerned with caring and a strong interpersonal focus; men, raised with the belief that rights and justice are paramount.

Women's moral decisions are based on an *ethics of caring* rather than a *morality of justice,* which led Gilligan to argue forcefully for a different sequence for the moral development of girls and women. For example, initially, any moral decisions a girl has to make centers on the self and her concerns are pragmatic: Will it work for me? Gradually, as her attachment to her parents continues, self-interest is redefined in light of "what one should do." A sense of responsibility for others appears (the traditional view of women as caretakers), and goodness is equated with self-sacrifice and concern for others.

Gilligan believes that women, with growing maturity, begin to include concern for self with their concern for others. In other words, is it possible to be responsible to one's self as well as to others? Women now realize that recognizing one's

An Applied VIEW   *Moral Development at Home and in the Classroom*

Many schools are now using moral dilemmas as a teaching tool in their classrooms. These are thought-provoking dialogues that probe the moral bases for people's thinking. They're real or imaginary conflicts involving competing claims, for which there is no clear, morally correct solution. As you can imagine, both teachers and parents are interested in using them to further children's moral development. Here are several suggestions.

- *With younger children,* they might try something like this: Set the scenario with a newly arrived foreign student. Yasmin has just arrived from Lebanon, and she is being mocked by some classmates because of differences in language and customs. Ask children what they would do if their friends would no longer play with them if they were friendly with Yasmin. Would they risk their friendships by being nice to the new girl?

Because most younger children have had little experience in resolving moral dilemmas, at first adults should act as a guide during the discussion and only later introduce more complex issues that require resolution at the stage above their present moral level.

- *Asking why* helps children to identify the dilemma and discover their level of moral reasoning. For example, after discussing Hong Kong's reunion with China with your older students, why not ask them what people should do if, while working on a Hong Kong newspaper, they were forbidden to write a story critical of the Chinese government. Their family's lifestyle and security could be at stake. Yet the writer feels strongly about freedom of the press. (Ask your students why theirs is a good solution.)

- *Complicating the situation* adds a new dimension to the problem. Pose this problem to older children: Imagine an official in the Cuban government with family in the United States. He is torn between trying to retain power in Cuba and moving to the United States and rejoining his family. Begin by discussing loyalty, then gradually introduce complications, such as civil conflict, family ties, regional or national commitment, and then ask, "What would you have done?"

Effective discussions of moral dilemmas also require an atmosphere, both at school and in the home, conducive to moral instruction, which can be encouraged by attention to the following four points:

1. *You must create an atmosphere of trust and fairness in which children are willing to reveal their feelings and ideas about the moral dilemma with which the group is wrestling.* Adults must work to bring children to the point where they will share their beliefs with others.

2. *Such an atmosphere results from respecting children and valuing their opinions.* Adults who are decent and fair in their relations with children and treat them with respect can do much to create a positive atmosphere for moral instruction.

3. *Adults must be sensitive to what children are experiencing.* They must be alert especially to those who find a discussion painful, for whatever reason. Make every effort to provide a forum—within the group or in private conversation—for them to express their feelings on their terms.

needs is not being selfish but rather being honest and fair, that is, the idea of doing good includes others but also one's self. Finally, women resolve the conflict between concern for self and concern for others because of their maturing ability to view their relationships from a broader perspective, which results in a guiding principle of nonviolence. Harmony and compassion govern all moral action involving self and others, which ultimately defines both femininity and adulthood.

To both their credit, neither Gilligan nor Kohlberg argued for the superiority of either a male or female sequence of moral development. Nevertheless, does the difference in emphasis on what constitutes the basis of moral development—caring or justice—carry the seeds of inevitable clashes of opinion when boys and girls/men and women look at moral issues? It shouldn't, because the replies of boys and girls to moral dilemmas show both justice and caring themes.

Continuing to refine her ideas about the sequence of moral development for women, Gilligan, Lyons, and Hanmer (1990) noted that adolescent girls face problems

An Informed VIEW

Teaching Moral Values: In the School or in the Home?

Increasing crime and violence in this country is an issue of national attention. In particular, incidents of violence in American schools, such as the murders in Littleton, Colorado, stunned the nation. Many feel the time has come to formally teach moral values in our classrooms, but others disagree.

Issue: A formal in-school program of moral education should be mandatory in all schools.

Answer—Pro A growing consensus has emerged that violence, particularly among the young, is a national problem. As such, the schools, which contact all of our children, would be a logical place to introduce formal programs devoted to moral education. Such programs would guarantee all students access to these ideas and behaviors and would maintain uniformity of the content.

Answer—Con The school day is already too short. Something we are now teaching would have to be eliminated to include another subject. An informal treatment of these issues, designed to suit the problems of individual communities and integrated across the curriculum of the community's schools makes better sense.

Issue: Educators are best suited to develop and implement a program that instills values for children.

Answer—Pro Educators understand best how to develop and teach ideas. Since children spend the greatest part of the day in school, they should receive moral education within the educational system.

Answer—Con More and more schools are being asked to take up the responsibilities that have traditionally rested with the family, which is one reason that

achievement scores have fallen. The schools can only do so much. Families and religious settings are the best contexts within which to impart moral values, not the public school.

Issue: Educators are well suited to develop the content of a moral education curriculum.

Answer—Pro Since teachers are assuming more and more responsibility for all aspects of their students' lives, they are the ideal choice to determine what their students need in a program of moral education. Schools can present a developmentally sensitive curriculum using aspects of ideas like respect, service, and integrity appropriately.

Answer—Con Whose values or morality will the school teach? We are an ever-increasing multicultural nation. Our many backgrounds mean we have many ways of looking at these issues. How do we decide whose view to choose?

Important and sensitive issues are involved here. Should issues that reach into the heart of families, but also impact on society-at-large be confined to home discussion? Yet, is it possible that classroom discussion could conflict with the values taught at home? What do you think about this sensitive issue?

If you would like to have a more informed view on this issue, you may want to read one or more of the articles referenced in this chapter, such as Narvaez & others (1999).

 You may also wish to learn more about it by going to our web site at http:/www.mhhe.com/dacey5.

---

of connections: What is the relationship among self, relationships, and morality? Must women exclude themselves and be thought of as a "good woman," or exclude others and be considered selfish? The answer seems to reside in the nature of the connections that women make with others.

Finally, we must return to the notions of habit and reflection in the expression of moral beliefs. Although habit, in the sense of doing the right thing that a child did in the past, usually suffices, circumstances change. As they do, children (especially as they grow older) must decide if the habits of the past still are sufficient in a time of new temptation. Children must reflect and decide on what now seems to them to be morally correct behavior. These choices can lead children to new heights of moral awareness and commitment (Damon, 1995).

Whether boy or girl, middle childhood youngsters, through their rapid cognitive development, are aware of right and wrong. How do we know this? They write answers to questions; they talk to us. Thus, language development is another clue to their growing maturity.

Guided Review

14. According to Piaget, when children believe that anyone who breaks a rule will somehow be punished, this is called _____ _____.
15. The phase of moral development when children realize that individuals formulate social rules is known as _____ _____.
16. A _____ _____ was Kohlberg's clinical technique whereby a conflict leads subjects to justify the morality of their choices.
17. Middle childhood youngsters are, for the most part, at Kohlberg's _____ level of morality.
18. _____ has challenged Kohlberg's theory with regard to women.

Language Development

As we have noted, by the time children enter kindergarten they have a vocabulary of about 8,000 words and have acquired most of the basic grammar of their language. They use questions, negative statements, clauses, and compound sentences (Gleason, 1997). During the middle childhood years, they communicate constantly with their peers and their language is rich with jokes, riddles, aggressive statements, and forms they learn from television and movies. They appear to be quite sophisticated in their knowledge, but considerable development is still to come. By the end of the period, middle childhood youngsters understand about 50,000 words and are similar to adults in their language usage (McLaughlin, 1998).

Changes in Usage

To help you understand the changes that occur during these years, table 9.6 summarizes several of the major accomplishments.

The most obvious example of developmental change in language during these years is an increase in pragmatic sophistication, which illustrates the interaction between language and socialization. Children are not only continuing to add new words to their vocabulary, but they are devising new ways to use these words (Hulit & Howard, 1997). These changes reflect their growing ability to engage in more abstract thinking.

During middle childhood the relationship of language development (in the sense of mastering a native tongue) to reading becomes crucial. Between the ages of 6 and 10, children must interpret written words wherever they turn: from signs on buses and streets as they go to school, to schooling that is massively verbal. When you consider a middle childhood youngster's competence, especially cognitive and linguistic, you conclude that they should be able to read effectively. The topics that engage reading researchers reflect the cognitive abilities of these children.

The Importance of Reading

You must be familiar with the picture: The 2- or 3-year-old sitting there solemnly examining an open book—probably upside-down! But this picture conveys the importance of reading in our society—in school for knowledge, on computers for practical usage, at home for pleasure. You can tell from our discussion of language development from infancy through the middle childhood years that language and reading are not simultaneous accomplishments. Rather, reading is built on solid language skills and facilitated by advancing cognitive abilities (Bjorklund, 2000; Siegler, 1998; Ely, 1997).

Answers

14. immanent justice 15. autonomous morality 16. moral dilemma 17. preconventional 18. Gilligan

TABLE 9.6 LANGUAGE CHANGES 7–11 YEARS

Age in Years	Phonology	Syntax	Semantics	Pragmatic
7	Manipulates sound units	Comprehends *because*	Uses *left, right*	Narration shows beginning and end
8	Produces all sounds and blends	Uses passives; can judge grammatical correctness	Comfortable with multiword definitions	Begins to recognize nonliteral meanings
9		Comprehends and uses *tell* and *promise*	Word definitions become more conventional	Sustains concrete story topic
10		Uses pronouns; understands difference between *definitely, probably,* and *possibly*	Uses *in* and *on* correctly	Stories show problem resolution, less extraneous detail, more complex episodes
11		Comprehends *if* and *though*	Moves to abstract definitions; understands psychological states	Sustains abstract topics

Source: Based on data from Owens, 1996.

For example, children (and adults) are rather limited information processors. Consequently, we're faced with the dilemma of understanding how good readers distribute their attention across the many processes needed for efficient reading. It's a formidable task. Children must learn to identify letters, connect them to sounds, decipher spelling patterns, and, finally, comprehend what all of this means. The key to this complex process seems to be that good readers process printed words automatically and use their cognitive processes for comprehension. *Automaticity* refers to the ability to automatically process lower level perceptual information needed to decode words so that the reader can concentrate on using more complex cognitive processes for comprehension (Bjorklund, 2000; Siegler, 1998; Hiebert & Raphael, 1996).

Stage and Nonstage Models of Reading Acquisition

In attempting to explain the acquisition of reading skills, theorists are divided between those who adhere to a stage model of reading acquisition and those who believe in a nonstage explanation. *Stage theorists* state that children's abilities and tasks change qualitatively over time. *Nonstage theorists,* on the other hand, argue that reading should unfold naturally, much as a child's language develops.

Every effort should be made to instill a love of reading in children, both for academic success and the lifelong pleasure reading affords.

An example of stage theory is seen in the work of one of today's leading reading specialists, Jeanne Chall, who has proposed a five-stage model leading to reading proficiency (Chall, 1983; Chall, Jacobs, & Baldwin, 1990). The features of the middle childhood stages are seen as follows.

Decoding The technique by which we recognize words.

- *Stage One—ages 6 to 7 years.* Children learn the relationship between letters and sounds and begin to read simple text. They usually experience direct instruction in letter-sound relations (phonics) and use high-frequency words in their reading.

- *Stage Two—ages 7 to 8 years.* Children demonstrate greater fluency in reading simple stories. They combine improved **decoding** skills with fast mapping to meaning in their reading selections.

- *Stage 3—ages 9 to 13 years.* Reading is now used as a tool to obtain knowledge (science and social science textbooks, novels, magazines).

The two major goals of reading acquisition are seen in Chall's stages: efficient word identification and the comprehension of increasingly difficult material.

Nonstage theorists describe reading acquisition as a seamless process in which there is considerable overlapping of skill development, that is, continuous development within various reading categories. For example, it's possible to classify young readers as **emergent, developing,** or **independent.** Don't think of these categories as neat, separate compartments but merely as descriptive tools. Let's look briefly at each of these categories.

Emergent readers Children who can identify letters and recognize some common words; they know what books "do" and they attempt to read by using semantic and syntactic cues.

- *Emergent Readers* are at the beginning of the reading adventure. From stories read to them, they learn that books tell interesting stories and that words and pictures lead to understanding. There seems to be a developmental continuum from preschoolers to proficient readers, which is referred to as *emergent literacy.* These are the years when the skills, knowledge, and attitudes that are the developmental precursors to formal reading are formed (Whitehurst & Lonigan, 1998).

Developing readers Children who are beginning to understand the relationship between sound and symbol and pay close attention to the print in their efforts at decoding.

- *Developing Readers* are becoming true readers. They have established the habit of reading for meaning, and are encouraged to use their own experiences to enrich the meaning of stories. They have learned to use words, illustrations, and their own knowledge, supplemented by analyzing letter-sound associations within the story's context, to predict word meanings.

Independent readers Children who can read ably and without assistance using all of the cueing systems.

- *Independent Readers* are those children who read on their own and when they are alone. These children are competent, confident readers who use all of their skills to derive as much meaning from their reading as possible.

Strategies of Maturing Readers

In discussing the strategies that children of all ages use to obtain meaning from words, Booth (1994) stated that readers sample the text, confirming or rejecting possible meanings. They read along, pause to reflect on what they've read, perhaps skip words that they'll come back to, and reread to clarify meaning. As they do, they search for several types of cues in the text. The first type of cue that Booth (1994) identified are **pragmatic cues,** that is, those practical signals that help discover meaning. For example, a novel differs from a textbook, a shopping list differs from a statistical table.

Pragmatic cues Practical signals used to discover meaning.

Semantic cues Readers relate words to what they signify.

Syntactic cues Using language rules to combine words into sentences.

Phonological cues Using sounds to form words.

Readers then relate the words themselves to what they signify, that is, to known facts and ideas. Using these **semantic** (meaning) **cues,** readers integrate this new information with what they already understand, which is remarkably similar to Piaget's discussion of assimilation and accommodation. **Syntactic cues** (knowledge of rules) enable readers to apply the rules of oral language that they have acquired to predict the meaning of words. Finally, readers use **phonological cues** (sound knowledge) to assess the relationship between the sounds of words and their written symbols.

TABLE 9.7 TYPICAL LANGUAGE ACCOMPLISHMENTS OF MIDDLE CHILDHOOD

Age (years)	Language Accomplishment
6	Has vocabulary of several thousand words; understands use and meaning of complex sentences; uses language as a tool; possesses some reading ability.
7	Improving motor control helps writing skills; can usually print several sentences; begins to tell time; losing tendency to reverse letters (b,d).
8	Motor control continues to improve, aiding both printing and writing; understands that words may have more than one meaning (ball); uses total sentence to determine meaning.
9	Describes objects in detail; little difficulty in telling time; writes well; uses sentence content to determine word meaning.
10	Describes situations by cause and effect; can write fairly lengthy essays; likes mystery and science stories; acquires dictionary skills; possesses good sense of grammar.

Booth (1994) now uses these cues to identify the emergent, developing, and independent readers we previously mentioned. First are the *emergent readers,* who can identify letters and recognize some common words. They know what books "do" and they attempt to read by using semantic and syntactic cues. Next are *developing readers,* who are beginning to understand the relationship between sound and symbol. They pay close attention to the print in their efforts at decoding. Readers at this level use all four of the cueing systems previously mentioned. Finally, there are *independent readers,* who can read ably and without assistance using all of the cueing systems.

As children come to the end of the middle childhood years, most are in the independent reader category. They use their language more symbolically and understand abstract concepts such as time. (Again, note the agreement with Piaget's description of the concrete operational years.) Through these years, which are the elementary school years, children continue to expand the length of their oral sentences and continue to refine their understanding of the structure and function of language (Barchers, 1994).

You can understand why reading is so important to children of this age. As they move through the school curriculum, their work becomes increasingly verbal: They read about the history of their country, the story of science, the symbols of mathematics, or any subject you can mention. A youngster who has a reading problem is a youngster in trouble. Table 9.7 summarizes some of the language accomplishments of the middle childhood years.

Guided Review

19. Middle childhood youngsters begin to use language for their own _____.
20. The most obvious language accomplishment of these years is in the development of _____.
21. A noted stage theorist of reading acquisition is _____.
22. When children learn that books tell interesting stories, they are called _____ readers.
23. When children read on their own or when they're alone, they're called _____ readers.

Answers

19. purposes 20. pragmatics 21. Chall 22. emergent 23. independent

CONCLUSION & SUMMARY

From our discussion so far, we know several things about middle childhood youngsters. But are they capable of meeting the problems they face? Yes and no. They can assimilate and accommodate the material they encounter but only at their level. For example, elementary school youngsters up to the age of 10 or 11 are still limited by the quality of their thinking. They are capable of representational thought but only with the concrete, the tangible. They find it difficult to comprehend fully any abstract subtleties in reading, social studies, or any subject.

With all of the developmental accomplishments of the previous six or seven years, youngsters want to use their abilities, which means that they sometimes experience failure as well as success, especially in their school work. Physically active, cognitively capable, and socially receptive, much is expected of these children, especially in school as we shall see.

How would you describe physical and motor development during these years?

- These are good years physically as middle childhood youngsters consolidate their height and weight gains.
- Middle childhood youngsters develop considerable coordination in their motor skills.

What are some of the competing views of cognitive development during the middle childhood years?

- Among the major cognitive achievements of this period are conservation, seriation, classification, numeration, and reversibility.
- Children of this age show clear signs of increasing symbolic ability.
- Sternberg and Gardner have proposed new ways of explaining intelligence.

How do children develop thinking and problem-solving strategies?

- Children today need critical thinking skills to adapt to sophisticated, technological societies.

- Good problem solvers have several observable characteristics.
- The DUPE model offers suggestions for improving problem-solving skills.

How would you trace children's progress in moral development?

- Piaget formulated a four-stage theory of moral development that is tightly linked to his explanation of cognitive development.
- Kohlberg proposed six levels of moral development that follow a child's progress from about 4 years of age to adulthood.
- Gilligan has challenged the male-oriented basis of Kohlberg's work.

How does children's language change during these years?

- Children's language growth during these years shows increasing representation and facility in conversing with others.
- During these years children develop several strategies to help them with their reading.

KEY TERMS

Adaptive strategy choice model
Classification
Concrete operational period
Conservation
Decentering
Decoding
Developing readers
DUPE

Emergent readers
Independent readers
Knowledge-acquisition components
Metacomponents
Moral dilemma
Multiple intelligences
Numeration
Performance component

Phonological cues
Pragmatic cues
Reversibility
Semantic cues
Seriation
Syntactic cues
Triarchic model of intelligence

WHAT DO YOU THINK?

1. Imagine an 11-year-old boy—let's call him Tim—who lives in the suburbs of a large northeastern city. He shows signs of becoming a great baseball player (a pitcher). His father realizes that his son could eventually win a college scholarship and go on to become a professional if he continues to develop. He decides that Tim should not play pickup games with his friends, because he might hurt himself. He also decides that the family should move to the South so Tom can play ball all year. Neither his wife nor Tim's sister wants to move. As a family friend, you have been asked for advice. What would you suggest?

2. You are a fourth-grade teacher and you turn to Janice and say, "Janice, Barbara is taller than Janie, who is taller than Liz. Who's the tallest of all?" Janice just looks at you. You sigh and think, "Where's Piaget when I need him?" How would you explain Janice's behavior?

3. Billy (9 years old) cuts through the parking lot of a supermarket on the way home from school. In the bike rack by the wall he sees a beautiful racing bike that he really wants. It seems to be unlocked and no one is around. With Kohlberg's work as a guide, what do you think is going through Billy's mind?

CHAPTER REVIEW TEST

1. Psychological characteristics of middle childhood include all but
   a. seriation.
   b. numeration.
   c. moral reasoning.
   d. random scribbling.

2. An average 11-year-old who stands 57 inches weighs about _____ pounds.
   a. 50
   b. 85
   c. 100
   d. 115

3. Which statement is not true?
   a. Girls and boys in the middle childhood years show equal grip strength.
   b. Girls are stronger than boys during middle childhood.
   c. Middle childhood boys and girls show equal interest in physical games.
   d. Balance matures by the end of middle childhood.

4. Which of the following is out of order? Conservation of
   a. number.
   b. volume.
   c. liquids.
   d. length.

5. The acquisition of the number concept is known as
   a. classification.
   b. seriation.
   c. numeration.
   d. conservation.

6. Sternberg's theory is based on components, experience, and
   a. context.
   b. gender.
   c. age.
   d. chromosomes.

7. A popular Taxonomy of Educational Objectives was devised by
   a. Sternberg.
   b. Gardner.
   c. Piaget.
   d. Bloom.

8. Howard Gardner's theory of multiple intelligences includes _____ equal intelligences.
   a. 4
   b. 5
   c. 8
   d. 10

9. In Sternberg's theory, learning how to solve problems is a function of
   a. metacomponents.
   b. genetic endowment.
   c. environment.
   d. knowledge-acquisition components.

10. When we plan, monitor, and evaluate our problem-solving strategies, we are using
    a. knowledge-acquisition components.
    b. performance components.
    c. metacomponents.
    d. general intelligence.

11. Mental age scales were used by _____ in creating his intelligence test.
    a. Binet
    b. Bloom
    c. Gardner
    d. Piaget

12. Recognizing what is distinctive in others is an example of which of Gardner's intelligences?
    a. Linguistic
    b. Interpersonal, intrapersonal
    c. Logical-mathematical
    d. Bodily-kinesthetic

13. Which of Gardner's intelligences results from contact with the objects of the world?
    a. Musical
    b. Interpersonal, intrapersonal
    c. Linguistic
    d. Logical-mathematical

14. One problem with tests is that test takers and test makers may differ in their
    a. relationships.
    b. circumstances.
    c. conditions.
    d. values.

15. The adaptive strategy choice model was devised by
    a. Bjorklund.
    b. Bransford.
    c. Skinner.
    d. Siegler.

16. Gilligan's developmental sequence is based on
    a. social justice.
    b. female superiority.
    c. an ethic of care.
    d. moral reasoning.

17. Piaget's ideas on moral development came from
    a. structured interviews with children.
    b. moral dilemmas.
    c. an ethic of care.
    d. observations of children playing marbles.

18. The major change in language development during the middle childhood years is in _____ sophistication.
    a. pragmatic
    b. phonetic
    c. syntactic
    d. semantic

19. A belief that reading should develop naturally much as language does is characteristic of _____ theorists.
    a. nonstage
    b. stage
    c. quantitative
    d. trait

20. Processing lower level information quickly and with a minimum of cognitive input is called
    a. emergent.
    b. independent.
    c. automaticity.
    d. inputting.

Answers

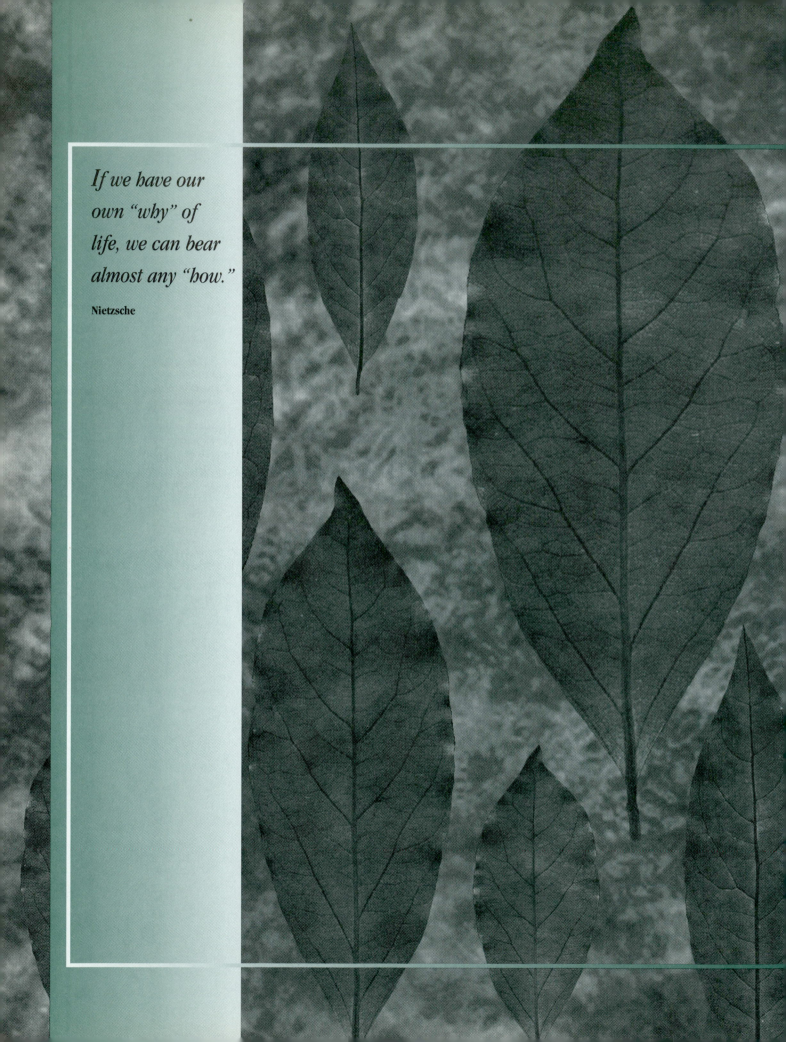

If we have our own "why" of life, we can bear almost any "how."

Nietzsche

CHAPTER 10

Psychosocial Development in Middle Childhood

Support and encouragement
are needed during the middle
childhood years if a realistic
sense of self-esteem is to develop.

The two pre-teenage boys were sitting on the top row of the spectator seats, talking quietly until the game began. (Let's call them Jack and Bill.) It was a beautiful spring afternoon and baseball was in the air as the two high school teams prepared to get the game underway. The two boys stopped talking for a moment and waved at one of the players, obviously a friend of theirs. As the umpire motioned the first batter of the visiting team into the batter's box to start the game, a tall, striking-looking man paused at the foot of the stands and scanned the seats. Seeing the two boys in the top row, he quickly climbed the steps to join them.

"Hi guys. What are you doing here? No classes today for you private school softies?"

Both boys laughed; they obviously were at ease with the older man and his brand of humor. Jack then replied, "No, we started exams today and got out at noon. We're about a week ahead of Phil (the older man's son). But don't forget, we started earlier in September."

"Sure, Sure, Sure. All I get from you two are excuses, excuses, excuses."

Bill turned to him and said, "Well, at least Phil has a longer season; I'd love to still be playing." (Both boys played varsity baseball on their school team.)

The man shrugged and said, "I dunno. If the season ended sooner, I wouldn't feel I had to come here and watch that kid of mine make a fool of himself. Game after game; sometimes I wonder what's wrong with him. But, you know, fathers are supposed to be here."

Both boys stared at the field and didn't say anything. They liked Phil's father. He was nice to them and always was glad to see them, but they couldn't understand his reaction to Phil. Nothing that he did seemed to please his father. And to make matters worse, his father had no hesitation in criticizing—sometime belittling—Phil in front of others, including Phil's friends.

Just as his father finished speaking, Phil entered the batter's box. Both Jack and Bill noticed how Phil glanced up at his father as he moved to the plate. "Here we go again," said his father, "I suppose it'll be another strikeout."

Jack and Bill were too respectful to say what they thought, but both of them, when they were talking later, mentioned how glad they were that their fathers either voiced their support or kept quiet when things went bad. Jack summed up their feelings nicely. "I don't know how Phil takes that, day after day. If that were my father, I wouldn't even go out for team. No one needs that kind of stuff." ✷

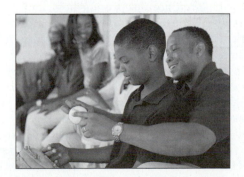

(The preceding story, unfortunately true, involved a friend of one of the authors.) Too often we tend to overlook the long-term consequences of the way parents, teachers, and adults in general sometimes treat children. Phil, the son in the story, today is a timid, anxious man with little drive and no confidence in himself. Will he ever achieve to the extent he might have if his self-concept hadn't been so severely shaken during those early years?

As Erikson stated, these are the years when children are ready for "entrance into life." As he noted, their sense of *industry* leads them to form productive relationships with others, thus helping them avoid any feelings of inferiority.

We have encountered too many similar cases over the years not to recognize the importance of a child's self-esteem. Consequently, in this chapter, we want to study its role in healthy development, while simultaneously avoiding many of the pitfalls and exaggerated claims surrounding any discussion of this important topic. For example, if parents do this or don't do that, will their children be geniuses, presidents, Mars-walking astronauts, or Hollywood movie stars? Well, maybe, but unfortunately it just doesn't work that way, as we'll see.

Among the prime influences on a child's developing sense of self is peer opinion, which at this age is becoming a powerful motivator of behavior. School, with its important network of social contacts and the emphasis placed on achievement, provides constant feedback that powerfully affects a child's feeling about self. The media, especially television with its stereotypical models, furnishes children with artificial, often self-destructive, goals of what the self should be. Finally, all children face occasional stress. Although some children find themselves under unrelenting pressure, how these children cope with stress leaves an indelible mark on their feelings about themselves.

Chapter Objectives

After reading this chapter, you should be able to answer the following questions.

◆ What are the key elements in children acquiring a personally satisfying and competent sense of self?

◆ How influential are peers during these years?

◆ What are some effects that different schools and teachers have in the middle childhood years?

◆ Does television affect, either positively or negatively, children's development?

◆ What are some of the major stressors of the middle childhood years?

The Changing Sense of Self

In chapter 8, we described the emerging sense of self and self-concept and traced their developmental path. Here we'll continue our narrative by demonstrating the tight link between realistic self-esteem and the attainment of competence. What do we mean by *self-esteem?* A good way to think of it is as a feeling of confidence and self-satisfaction with one's self (Thompson, 1999). How do children develop a sense of self-esteem?

During the middle childhood years, children's developing sense of self helps to shape their personal goals. For example, any discrepancy between the perceived ideal self and the real self can be a strong motivating force. Thanks to their growing cognitive ability, children become more objective during these years, and as they do, begin to compare their achievements with those of others (Harter, 1998). In a sense, children are discovering how they "measure up" against others. They come to realize, for example, while they may excel at math, someone else is a much better writer, and that someone else is an outstanding athlete.

Children during these years begin to employ a complex and sophisticated self-evaluation that results in a more balanced assessment of personal strengths and weaknesses. They recognize that they have both desirable and undesirable qualities. The middle childhood years see a declining self-esteem because of these more realistic assesssments and social comparisons.

These changes occur in the context of a growing social self as children more and more perceive themselves as a part of their social context (Thompson, 1999). Consequently, their sense of self and self-esteem are tightly interwoven with their satisfaction with their appearance, their need for support from those they love and trust, and a belief in their own competence.

Self-Esteem and Competence

Self-concept   Children's evaluation of themselves and their competencies.

Self-esteem   How children rank themselves compared to others (self-worth).

Competence   Children's sense of self-esteem; related to athletic competence, peer popularity, physical appearance, and behavior.

Susan Harter, a developmental psychologist at the University of Denver, has been a long-time student of the self, self-development, **self-concept,** and **self-esteem** and her research has been a beacon of light in an otherwise murky field (Harter, 1993). Studying 8- to 13-year-old children, Harter and her colleagues identified five types of **competence** that seem to be central to a child's level of self-esteem: scholastic competence, athletic competence, likability by peers, physical appearance, and behavioral conduct. Trying to determine what produces a child's sense of self-esteem, Harter posed a basic question.

> **How does children's evaluation of their competency affect the level of their self-esteem?**

Devising a questionnaire that tapped children's perception of their competence, the researchers used items such as the following.

> **Some kids have trouble figuring out the answers in school.**

but

> **Other kids can almost always figure out the answers.**

Children would then indicate which of the answers best described them, thus creating a profile of their feelings of competence. The results were fascinating.

Children don't feel they do equally as well in all five types of competence Harter identified. Most children show a "sawtooth" profile, indicating that they feel good about themselves in some activities but not so good in others. Not only that but some children who have noticeably different profiles have quite similar levels of self-esteem. Other children, with similar profiles, have vastly different levels of self-esteem. Here's an example of the children's profiles.

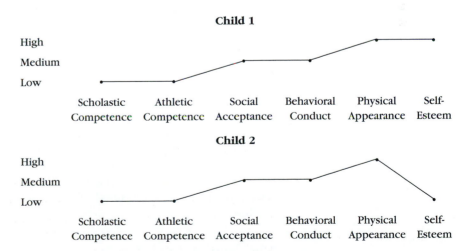

You can see in this example that each child has a similar profile but a much different level of self-esteem. Their self-esteem was affected only by the things they viewed as important (social acceptance, looks, etc.). The first child does not see school or athletics as important, therefore not doing well academically or athletically doesn't matter. The other child, however, probably does value sports and studies, and feels inadequate with an accompanying loss of self-esteem.

In the second phase of her study, Harter probed to discover how what others think about children affects their self-esteem. She used questions similar to the following:

Some kids have classmates that like the kind of person they are.

but

Other kids have classmates who do not like the kind of person they are.

The results were as you probably anticipated. Children who receive considerable support from the important people in their environment had a high regard for themselves. Those who obtain little, if any, support from their significant others showed the lowest self-esteem. Taken together, these findings provide penetrating insights into how children acquire their sense of self-esteem.

Ever the honest researcher, Harter proposed several troublesome questions about the information she and her colleagues uncovered. For example, in all of her studies there was a strong link between what children thought of their physical appearance and their level of self-esteem. In fact, what children think of their looks is the leading predictor of their self-esteem. As Harter asks, is self-esteem only skin deep?

Harter asked her subjects whether they felt that their appearance determined their self-esteem or did their sense of worth lead them to favorably evaluate their looks. She discovered that those who believed their looks determined their self-esteem felt worse about their appearance, had lower self-esteem, and were more subject to bouts of depression.

Summarizing, then, children and young adolescents for whom personal appearance and the opinion of others determined their sense of self had lower levels of self-esteem. Those who believed that their sense of self caused others to think highly of them and who felt that their sense of self-esteem led to feelings of competency had higher levels of self-esteem. The lesson is clear for those working with children: To help children enhance their self-esteem encourage them to examine their sense of worth carefully, but not to look through the glass darkly.

Parents and educators must walk a thin line between providing the necessary support and encouragement for children to face "the great battle of life" on the one hand and the equal necessity of keeping children's feet securely planted in reality on the other. We again want to emphasize the need to praise and recognize children's honest achievements.

But if an adult's reactions are an island of praise in a sea of neutral, even negative evaluations, eventually children will ignore them. Children shouldn't be subjected to a salvo of criticisms, but reactions to their efforts can't be transparently false. You can't fool children; they cut right through any sham, especially if something is meaningful to them. It's better to be honest. "You didn't do that well this time, but I know if you study (practice, rehearse, whatever the activity) hard, you'll do better next time." Honest evaluation, coupled with support and encouragement, go a long way toward deserved self-esteem.

There is, however, a flip side to this positive look we've taken at the self. For their own good, and the good of those around them, children must develop self-control.

Children and Self-Control

On June 3, 1986, the state of Florida charged 9-year-old Jeffrey Bailey with murder. Making sure no one else was around, he had pushed a 3-year-old boy who couldn't swim into the pool. He pulled up a chair to watch the boy drown. Later, when the police had pieced together the circumstances of the murder, they arrested Jeffrey, who was described as calm, nonchalant, and enjoying the attention (Magid & McKelvey, 1987).

This story, as startling as it is true, is only one of many that appears with increasing frequency in our nation's newspapers and television news reports. Murder is the most dramatic example of a life gone wrong, but the increasing rate of assaults, robberies, and arson raises a basic question: What happens to children to turn them into killers, thieves, and arsonists? Why didn't they ever develop those critical inner controls?

What Is Self-Control?

Self-control   Restraint exercised over impulses, emotions, and desires.

Just exactly what is meant by **self-control?** As you know, self-control refers to many different types of behaviors: mastering fear, controlling eating, restricting drinking, keeping your temper in check, and refusing drugs. We'll focus on that element of self-control that saves children from unnecessary conflicts, unreasonable aggression, and senseless violence. A dictionary definition of self-control is a good starting point: restraint exercised over one's own impulses, emotions, or desires. In other words, children should possess the ability to control their actions in appropriate ways; they must develop a sense of inner control (Dacey & Fiore, 2000).

Let's examine several key reasons that help us to understand why some children become aggressive, even violent, adolescents and adults.

The Roots of Violent Behavior

Each year more than 150,000 adolescents are arrested for violent crimes, more than 300,000 are assaulted seriously enough to require medical care, and 3,500 are murdered. Teenagers in the United States are four times more likely to be murdered than teenagers in 21 other industrialized countries (Coie & Dodge, 1998). What happened in the development of these individuals to produce such reactions?

One answer seems to be that most of these young people have had past experiences with violence (Garbarino, 1999; Kindlon & Thompson, 1999; Purugganan & colleagues, 2000). Consequently, an unmistakable association between past and future antisocial behavior leads to the maxim that the best predictor of violence is past antisocial behavior. (Think of violence as behavior intended to harm another person.)

Another possible explanation is the exposure a child has to violence (Osofsky, 1995; Rich, 1999; Walker, 2000). Exposure to violence may lead to two different kinds of behavior: the development of aggressive behavior, or emotional behavior that ranges from temporary upset to clear signs of post-traumatic stress disorder (Osofsky, 1995; Weissberg & Greenberg, 1998).

The causes of violent and criminal behavior are multiple and complex. Nevertheless, most modern scientists believe that a tendency to commit crime is established early in life, *perhaps as soon as the preschool years,* and the behavior of these children provides ample clues to their possible future antisocial behavior. Aggression has been well-established in preschoolers and recent research (Coie & Dodge, 1998; Crick, Casas, & Mosher, 1997; Galen & Underwood, 1996) has indicated that these early signs of aggression are closely associated with social-psychological maladjustment.

A critical age for early signs of emerging delinquency is 7 to 12 years when children search for friends and want to become accepted members of a group. Some children, for whatever reason, tend to join groups that encourage antisocial acts (Tomada & Schneider, 1997). They may be drawn to a particular group because a friend is a member; it may be a sign of rebellion (my mother doesn't like those kids, but I think they're neat); it may just seem a daring thing to do.

During the middle childhood years, most children engage in less frequent aggressive behavior, except for a select few that become increasingly troublesome. When aggression appears during these years, it's more hostile and directed at individuals rather than objects or situations. Unfortunately, aggressive children display a continuity of antisocial behavior throughout their lives. For example, disobedience, defiance, aggression toward peers, and similar behaviors at the age of three years continues into later childhood.

Three developmental pathways of chronic offenders have been identified.

- During the preschool years chronic offenders display hyperactive and oppositional behavior (stubbornness, defiance, bullying, running away).

- Frequent aggressive behavior is observable during the school years (lying, shoplifting, numerous fights, fire setting).

- Varied forms of delinquency appear in adolescence (stealing cars, attacking individuals, breaking and entering, selling drugs) (Coie & Dodge, 1998).

Consequently, early antisocial behavior predicts serious, adult antisocial behavior. But it's important to note that less than one-half of the early offenders go on to become serious problems as adolescents and adults. The best clue to early antisocial behavior continuing into adulthood is that the earlier the age of onset of behavior problems, the greater the chance of adult antisocial behavior.

Clues to Troublesome Behavior

If two boys are from the same family, with the same opportunities, why does one turn to a life of crime while the other leads a law-abiding life? Was there some subtle genetic transmission? Were the family relations similar for both boys? Were their friends radically different? Examining each case helps us to identify the causes of crime for that child. Family conditions may be the cause for one child but not another; that is, one child may experience the environment quite differently than another (Henrich, Brown, & Aber, 2000).

Does anything distinguish delinquents from nondelinquents. What are some characteristics of children who become delinquent?

- There may be something *genetic* at work; for example, both members of identical twin pairs are more likely to be involved in delinquency than nonidentical twins. (For an excellent and thorough analysis of the interaction of genes and the environment in the development of antisocial behavior, see Rutter, 1997.)

- *Males* are more prone to criminal behavior than females, and younger males are more likely to commit crimes at a higher rate than older males; age is a major factor in understanding criminal behavior (Coie & Dodge, 1998).

- *Attitudinally,* most children prone to behavior problems are hostile, defiant, resentful, suspicious, and resistant to authority (Weissberg & Greenberg, 1998).

- *Psychologically,* delinquents are more interested in the concrete than the abstract and are generally poor problem solvers (Elliott & others, 2000).

- *Socioculturally,* delinquents are frequently reared in homes that offer little understanding, affection, stability, or moral clarity. For example, some parents frequently, although, unconsciously, reinforce aggressive behavior in an effort to defuse an explosive situation. A mother may tell a child to do something; the child refuses and becomes aggressive toward the mother. The mother may then "back off" and the child's aggressive behavior has been positively reinforced (Noam, 1998).

These findings testify almost unerringly to the conclusion that the causes of antisocial behavior are multiple, complex, and interactive and that these interactions begin at an early age (Walker, 2000). The roots of violence may stretch as far back as infancy. For example, children who do not form bonds with anyone (see chapter 4) constitute one of the largest deviant populations in the country (Wilson, 1993). These children cannot form relationships; they describe their reactions to others as making "no connections."

The words of convicted serial killer Ted Bundy hang like icicles in the chilling world of those deprived of friends and relationships (Magid & McKelvey, 1987).

An Applied VIEW   *The Bully*

Is there any reader who did not have nightmares sometime during school about that "monster" who loved to tease, humiliate, threaten, and fight? Tough boys see themselves as very popular, very aggressive, and very competent (Rodkin & Farmer, 2000). Many of their peers see them in that same way, which raises the disturbing topic of bullies. Even today most middle-school principals will list bullying among their major worries.

Who is the *bully?* Olweus (1993, 1995) identified bullies as those who are overly aggressive and possess considerable physical strength. *Peer victimization,* on the other hand, describes those children who are anxious, insecure, cautious, and sensitive with low self-esteem. Many have been treated violently themselves, attended schools that treated violence ineffectively, or are members of a peer group that encourages aggression. As a result, these children avoid school, if possible, and even at an early age begin to lead lonely lives (Coie & Dodge, 1998).

Four causes are apparent in the development of a bully:

- *Indifference* (usually by the mother), in itself a form of silent violence
- Parents who are *permissive* with an aggressive child
- Parents who typically resort to *physical punishment;*
- A *temperamentally aggressive* child

Be alert for this type of behavior; often teachers and parents are the last to know since the victim is reluctant to talk about it. Among Olweus' suggestions for dealing with bullies are the following:

- Supervise recreation periods more closely
- Intervene immediately to stop bullying
- Talk to both bully and victim privately and insist if such behavior does not stop both school and parents will become involved.

> I didn't know what makes things tick. I didn't know what made people want to be friends. I didn't know what made people attractive to one another. I didn't know what underlay social interactions.

📖 Magid, K. & C. McKelvey. (1987). *High risk: Children without a conscience.* New York: Bantam. An excellent, readable account of the development of violent children.

As the screeching headlines of our newspapers tell us, children are becoming more and more involved in serious crime and violence. Consequently, identifying the causes of such behavior and formulating the means to prevent it become more urgent. The task is difficult, expensive, and lengthy but well worthwhile to prevent violence from becoming an accepted part of children's lives.

Children and Impulse Control

For children to be successful in any of their endeavors and enjoy pleasant relationships with others, they must exercise restraint in deciding what to do, how to do it, what to say, and how to say it. In other words, controlling their impulses becomes an increasingly important feature in their lives.

Psychologists have found the study of impulsivity alluring, similar to standing at a window and peering into the depths of a child's personality. And what they see is not only revealing but has serious long-term developmental implications. (You may also have seen **impulsivity** referred to as a child's lack of ability to delay gratification or, of course, self-control.) Children who are reflective as opposed to impulsive seem destined to achieve at higher levels, attain greater emotional maturity, and gain appreciable personal popularity (Mischel & Mischel, 1983).

Impulsivity A child's lack of ability to delay gratification.

Impulsivity and Development

What do we know about impulsivity and the developmental path it follows? Like the tributaries of a river joining to form the major body, the streams of research into impulsivity converge on delay of gratification studies. Picture this setting: Children are placed in a position in which they are presented with something they enjoy—candies, toys—and told if they don't eat the candy or play with the toy until the researcher returns, they can have two pieces of candy or an even bigger toy. The researcher then leaves the room and observers watch the children through one-way mirrors. The results were as you would expect: Some children ate the candy immediately or played with the toy; others resisted by trying to distract themselves.

The truly amazing part of this work, however, was the follow-up research. The same children who displayed impulsivity at 4 years of age were the more troubled adolescents; they had fewer friends; they experienced more psychological difficulties such as lower self-esteem; they were more irritable and aggressive, and less able to cope with frustration. Whereas the 4-year-olds who delayed their gratification could better handle frustration, were more focused and calm when challenged by any obstacle, and were more self-reliant and popular as adolescents. The behavior of the 4-year-olds on delay of gratification tests predicted success in both elementary and secondary schools, and even turned out to be a powerful predictor of how they would do on their SATs (Mischel & Mischel, 1983).

Transformations

Transformation Children learn to think about what they shouldn't do in different terms.

Parents can help children to develop self-control when they're young by urging them to think of other things. As they grow a little older, perhaps by first grade, a phenomenon called **transformation** appears; that is, they learn to think about what they shouldn't do in different terms. If they're instructed not to eat marshmallows, for example, they may think of the marshmallows as white clouds. From this time on, children do well at devising their own strategies as they become more competent with their growing cognitive abilities. In fact, research indicates that children exercise greater self-control when using strategies they've devised rather than using those suggested by adults.

But what to do with Johnny, sitting, standing, jumping, calling out, giving the impression of being driven by demons? A victim of attention-deficit hyperactivity disorder (often called hyperactivity), self-control seems to represent another world for Johnny. It's during the elementary school years that ADHD becomes an obvious problem for the 3 percent to 5 percent of children who experience this disorder. For a variety of possible reasons—neurological, emotional, environmental—they simply can't pay attention, sit still, and focus on schoolwork. Medications (such as Ritalin) and psychotherapy have helped to introduce inner peace and stability into their lives (American Academy of Pediatrics, 2000; Elliott & others, 2000).

Middle childhood youngsters will bring to their interactions with those outside of the family the characteristics that they formed within the family circle. With this in mind, let's turn now to the impact of peers on development.

Guided Review

1. A feeling of confidence and satisfaction with one's self is defined as
   _____.

2. Harter's work attempted to link level of self-esteem with various types of
   _____.

3. Level of self-esteem is affected powerfully by what children think of their
   _____ _____.

4. The best predictor of future antisocial behavior is _____
   _____.

5. The resistance to temptation studies are an example of a child's ability to control
   _____.

Answers

1. self-esteem 2. competence 3. physical appearance 4. past behavior 5. impulses

During middle childhood, peer relationships become increasingly important for social development. Children are attracted to those who share their interests, who play well with them, and who help them to learn about themselves.

Peers exercise a powerful influence on a child's development.

The Influence of Peers

Do you sometimes wonder if we exaggerate the influence of peers? If you have any doubts, here is an example of the far-reaching power of peer relations, one that should answer this question. In the 1940s, Anna Freud (Sigmund Freud's daughter) and Sophie Dann worked with six German-Jewish orphans whose parents had died in the Nazi gas chambers. The six children were together in a concentration camp for several years, enduring horrible conditions, with few adult contacts.

When the war ended, the children were taken to England to recover. It soon became clear to observers that although the children showed some effects of their ordeal—thumbsucking, fearfulness, restlessness—they were strongly attached to each other, to the point where they would comfort each other if disturbed and become upset if separated. With the loving care that the children received over the next years, coupled with their continued relationships with their peers, they gradually showed normal patterns of development, a moving example of the strength and significance of peer relationships (Freud & Dann, 1951).

Interactions, Relationships, and Groups: The Middle Childhood Years

Peer   Refers to youngsters who are similar in age to other children, usually within 12 months of one another.

We typically use the word **peer** to refer to youngsters who are similar in age, usually within 12 months of each other. But equal in age does not mean equal in everything, for example, intelligence, physical ability, or social skills. Nevertheless, interactions with peers constitute an important developmental context for children, providing a range of experiences that affect their adaptation across the lifespan (Rubin, Bukowski, & Parker, 1998).

Understanding children's relationships with their peers requires an analysis of several levels of social complexity (Cillessen & Bukowski, 2000).

- *Individual.* Each child brings a unique blend of skills and temperament to any relationship, which structures the type and quality of interactions between partners. (Here you may want to review the relationship discussion in chapter 6.)

- *Interactions.* These vary with the particular social situation and the characteristics of the partners.

- *Relationships.* Any relationship is influenced by, once again, the characteristics of the children involved, and past and anticipated interactions (Stepp, 2000).

- *Groups.* Groups, through shared beliefs help define the type and range of relationships and interactions (Rubin & others, 1999).

During these years, the interactions involving peers increase dramatically to about 30 percemt of all social interactions. The size of the peer group increases with a lessening of adult supervision in a variety of settings: malls, schools, telephones, e-mail. As we mentioned in the preceding section, aggression becomes more verbal and personally hostile. Children of these years become much more concerned with acceptance by their peer group and gossip is more prevalent (who's in, who's out). Friendship assumes a greater role in determining acceptance or rejection (Rubin & others, 1999).

Children's Friendships

Friend A nonfamilial relationship that offers feelings of warmth and support.

Middle childhood youngsters, with the abilities that we have traced, can reach logical conclusions about their friends. Children of this age search for **friends** who are psychologically compatible with them. For example, does Jimmy share my interests? Does he want to do the same things I do? Children begin to realize, especially toward the end of the middle childhood period, that friends must adapt to each other's needs. One explanation of these developmental changes in peer relations is seen in Selman's theory of **social perspective-taking.**

Social perspective-taking The idea that children's views on how to relate to others emerge from their personal theories about the traits of others.

Social Perspective-Taking In his efforts to clarify children's interpersonal relationships, Selman proposed a theory of social perspective-taking levels that springs from a social cognitive developmental framework. Selman (1980) stated that you can't separate children's views on how to relate to others from their personal theories about the traits of others. Thus, children construct their own version of what it means to be a self or other.

As a result of careful investigations of children's interactions with others, and guided by such theorists as Piaget, Flavell, Mead, and Kohlberg, Selman has identified several levels of social perspective-taking and noted that in the middle childhood years a youngster gradually realizes that other people are different and have ideas of their own, thanks to a diminishing egocentrism. By the end of middle childhood, a youngster's view of a relationship includes self, someone else, and the kind of relationship between them, and also the desire to conform becomes important, especially at the end of the period. Table 10.1 summarizes a child's thinking at each level.

Peers in Middle Childhood

Think of the world these children are now encountering. Their physical and cognitive abilities enable them to move steadily, although slowly, toward others such as neighborhood friends. Upon entering school, they increase their contacts and begin to realize that other children have ideas that may differ from their own. How children react to these different opinions may reflect their own home conditions (Kerns, Klepac, & Cole, 1996).

With school entrance children's lives change dramatically. Their interactions with others contain revealing clues about the path of their future social development.

TABLE 10.1 SOCIAL PERSPECTIVE-TAKING	
Level 0: 3–6 years. Undifferentiated and egocentric, Children have no accurate idea of relations.	**Friendship** depends on physical closeness.
Level 1: 5–9 years. Differentiated and subjective. Focus remains on self.	**Friendship** depends on someone doing what a child wants or a child does what another wants.
Level 2: 7–12 years. Relationships become more reciprocal.	**Friendship** depends on desirable interactions. A "meeting of the minds."
Level 3: 10–15 years. Recognizes that interpersonal interactions include self, others, and the relationship.	**Friendship** includes mutual interest and sharing.
Level 4: 12+ years. Accepts complexity of individuals, interactions, and relationships.	**Friendship** depends on open and flexible relationships to satisfy complex needs.

During these years some children still find it difficult to tear themselves away from their mothers and have considerable difficulty in relating to their peers. Where is the problem here, with the mother or the child?

In one of the schools we visited, we noticed the mother of a fifth grade boy walking him to school every day while holding his hand. We discovered that the boy, while not a problem in school, was having difficulty with the other boys in his class and tended to drift off by himself or play with younger children. How to reach the mother, of course, was the issue because the boy was doing fairly well in school and was causing no difficulties. The matter was resolved by having the teacher gently point out the growing independence of boys of this age and by having the mother become a "room mother," where she could see the typical behavior of fifth grade boys.

During these years, children discover they must get along with peers, which forces them to think about their relationships, a major step in social development (Cassidy & others, 1996). For example, their growing abilities enable them to make definite judgments about the behavior of their peers. They become more astute at detecting meaning in facial expressions and in the way something is said. Since teachers have now become a force to be reckoned with, children no longer may ignore the wishes and ideas of those around them.

Given the increase in friends during the school years, we should examine the role of schooling itself. How does it influence the development of middle childhood youngsters?

One's friends are that part of the human race with which one can be human.

George Santayana

Guided Review

6. Children who are within 12 months of age of each other are called _____.
7. Equal in age does not mean equal in _____.
8. Understanding children's relationships requires an analysis of different levels of _____ _____.
9. Selman's theory is referred to as _____ _____ _____.
10. Children in middle childhood gradually come to see that other points of view exist due to diminishing _____.

Answers

6. peers 7. everything 8. social complexity 9. social perspective-taking 10. egocentrism

Schools and Middle Childhood

In our discussion of the effects of schooling on development, one question is critical: Do schools affect development during these years? Common sense dictates that any environment in which children sharpen their intellectual skills, learn how to get along with others, work with a diverse cultural group of peers, and assess their self-concepts in competition with others must have a powerful effect on development.

For example, during these years in school, the tendency for same-sex playmates intensifies, which is true of agricultural as well as industrial societies. In Western societies, although teachers encourage mixed-sex activities (seating arrangements, spelling bees, organized playground games) same-sex preferences appear in lunch rooms, corridors, and unsupervised playground activities. Go to a Little League and watch what happens between innings on boy-girl teams. The girls sit together; the boys sit together. Estimates are that same-sex preferences peak from eight to eleven years (Maccoby, 1998).

Many of today's schools, recognizing the varied backgrounds of their students, have developed curricula to meet their specialized needs. For example, some schools have programs to help adopted children: appropriate assignments, adoption-friendly terms, specialized readings (Seidman, 2000).

Are Schools Really That Important?

Unfortunately, however, as we enter the twenty-first century, there are few definitive answers to our question (Eccles & Roeser, 1999; Paris & Cunningham, 1996). It's only recently that researchers have looked beyond the academic and intellectual to examine how school influences a child's identity, self-esteem, beliefs, and behavior (Eccles & Roeser, 1999). Given the physical, cognitive, and social changes that occur in children of these years, it's only reasonable to expect schools to play an influential role.

This influential role, however, may be either positive or negative. Summarizing the need for changes in educational practices, Manning and Baruth (1996) noted that:

- African-American students suffer academically because their learning styles focus on cooperative behavior and content about people.

- Navajo children often interpret tests as games, resulting in lower achievement scores.

- Although curricular materials are beginning to reflect our nation's diversity, Native-American, Asian, and Hispanic-American children are underrepresentd in the curriculum.

- Many teachers still call on and praise Anglo students more than others.

Same-sex preferences persist in unsupervised activities during the middle childhood years, although schools strive for mixed activities.

Compelling data such as these suggest that teachers and administrators recognize, accept, and accommodate the needs of an increasingly diverse school population.

One of the few attempts to examine a school's effect on intellectual development has been the work of Michael Rutter. Rutter, an internationally respected researcher of children's issues, in a massive and meticulously conducted study of school effectiveness, found startling differences between schools in their impact on children (1983). His data led to several conclusions.

- Children are more likely to show good behavior and good scholastic achievement if they attend some schools rather than others.

- Differences between the schools are not due to the size or age of the buildings or the space available.

- Differences between the schools are due to a school's emphasis on academic success, teacher expectations of student success, time-on-task, skillful use of rewards and punishment, teachers who provide a comfortable and warm classroom environment, and teachers who insist on student responsibility for their behavior.

These criteria graphically demonstrate that *good instructional leadership* is critical, which means that principals, teachers, students, and parents agree on goals, methods, and content. Home-school cooperation supports good leadership, which in turn produces *an orderly environment* that fosters desirable discipline, academic success, and personal fulfillment. When teachers *sense the support of parents and administrators,* they intuitively respond in a manner that promotes student achievement and adjustment, encourages collegiality among teachers, and produces a warm, yet exciting atmosphere (Elliott & others, 2000; Travers & others, 1993).

Let's now examine several issues that affect children's development in our schools.

> Our schools should develop the reasoning faculties of our youth, enlarge their minds, cultivate their morals, and instill in them precepts of virtue and order.
>
> Thomas Jefferson

Schools and Development

As children pass through the elementary grades, they no longer satisfy society's needs by playing happily and behaving nicely. Now they face challenges to achieve and, like it or not, they face daily competition. They not only experience steady developmental changes, they also encounter constant subject matter change. It's almost as if knowledge that had been forced below a level of consciousness has burst through restraining barriers, and, as if to make up for lost time, has exploded before their eyes.

Children, in the midst of all these discoveries, have a unique opportunity to acquire learning that will shape their future as never before. Interestingly, studies of children in Los Angeles, Tokyo, East and West Berlin, Moscow, and Prague have shown that children, across cultures, have similar developmental patterns in their beliefs about the importance of effort, ability, luck, teachers, and unknown causes as explanations of school success (Little & Lopez, 1997).

Schools, Development, and Learning

Learning   A process that results in the modification of behavior.

With all the demands made on schools today, we occasionally forget that children go to school to learn, which raises the interesting question: What does **learning** have to do with development? The answer almost jumps out at us if we think carefully about what "learning" means. (See Siegler (2000) for a pertinent discussion of the rebirth of interest in children's learning.)

Children learn. They learn in school, often with difficulty, and out of school, usually with ease. One of my students, Liz (a college first year student) does fairly well on her classwork, but rebels against reading assignments. Yet this same student has a part-time sales position in the jewelry department of a well-known, large store which requires her to spend hours reading about emeralds, jade, and diamonds. She does this cheerfully and successfully.

A Sociocultural VIEW — Poverty, Culture, and Education

Research has demonstrated a powerful relationship between poverty and a child's health, behavior, and achievement. For example, poor children repeat grades and drop out of high school more than two times their nonpoor peers (Duncan & Brooks-Gunn, 2000).

In his biting commentary on current conditions in America's schools, Kozol (1991) drew some vivid comparisons. In schools populated with children of the poor, students are crowded into small, squalid spaces, and in some cities overcrowding is so bad that some schools function in abandoned factories. Students eat their lunches in what was previously the building's boiler room. Reading classes are taught in what used to be a bathroom; science classes have no microscopes; one counselor serves 3,600 students in the elementary grades. In the high school of this district, a single physics section exists for 2,200 students; two classes are being taught simultaneously in one classroom.

As an example of these kinds of schools, listen to Kozol's words.

> The city was so poor there had been no garbage pickup for four years. . . . On the edge of the city is a large chemical plant. There is also a very large toxic waste incinerator, as well as a huge sewage treatment plant. . . . The city has one of the highest rates of infant mortality in Illinois, the highest rate of fetal death, and also a very high rate of childhood asthma.
>
> The schools, not surprisingly, are impoverished. . . . The entire school system had been shut down after being flooded with sewage from the city's antique sewage system. "I did meet several

wonderful teachers in the school, and I thought the principal of the school was excellent. The superintendent *is also a very impressive person*" (Kozol, 1991, p. 5).

A more affluent district in the same state presents a different picture. A greenhouse is available for students interested in horticulture; the physical sciences department offers 14 courses; there are 18 biology electives. The school's orchestra has traveled to the former Soviet Union. Beautifully carpeted hallways enourage students to sit and study; computers are everywhere. The ratio of counselors to students is 1 to 150. Parents of these students recently raised money to send the school choral group to Vienna. Given these different conditions, is it any wonder that different educational outcomes are inevitable?

These conditions can either be improved or made worse by the family's belief in education. As Garbarino and Benn noted (1992), parents may not be present in the classroom but they have a profound influence on the way their children view school and learning. The extent to which the family supports the school's objectives directly affects their child's academic performance. Too often low parental expectations for their children reflect the parents' own educational experiences. If parents had encountered difficulties in school, they may exercise a negative impact on their children's attitudes, expectations, and performance. The reverse also holds true.

Our discussion points to an inescapable conclusion: Schools must be as good as possible because they frequently are the only escape routes from poverty, crime, and violence.

Or consider Ellen, an 11-year-old sixth-grader who complains constantly that "I can't do math; I just don't like it." This same student—for reasons hard to understand—was selected to head the school bank (a cooperative banking project in conjunction with a local bank in an effort to introduce students to the idea of money management). She performed flawlessly.

What Is Learning? Most psychologists would agree that *learning is a process that results in the modification of behavior*. But what exactly does that mean? If we examine learning carefully, several characteristics emerge.

- *A motivated student.* One of the safest statements we can make is that learning will not occur without motivation (at least the positive learning schools desire). For example, children's beliefs about their self-efficacy and competence affect their success (or failure) with academic work.

- *An obstacle.* Some challenge blocks a child's path to a goal: The search for meaning in a reading passage, the solution to a problem, the answer to a math example. How a child and teacher handle this block is crucial to development. You can immediately see obvious implications: The effect on the child's relationship with the teacher, a liking or distaste for school, the impact on self-concept, self-esteem, and self-efficacy (Travers & others, 1993).

- *The presence of environmental stimuli.* The teacher—through discussion, materials, and peer interactions—provides clues for the children. How children react to these clues, how they attend to important stimuli, and how they interact with their peers all contribute to cognitive, social, and cultural aspects of development.

- *Perception of the situation.* Children bring their memory and experiences to bear on the challenge they face. At this phase of learning, a key feature emerges—the need to combine as many clues as possible to solve the problem. Here is where teachers offer crucial support by helping their students to search for and integrate the information children find in their reading, in their discusssions, in their interactions with fellow students. Both social and academic skills merge in this endeavor.

- *Select a response.* Children decide what to do. Their cognitive abilities, their psychosocial input (interactions with teachers and peers), and their self involvement all contribute to their continued, *integrated* development (Stepp, 2000).

- *An Appropriate Goal.* Children need the advice of teachers, parents, and their peers in deciding what goals to pursue and how to go about obtaining them. The selection of realistic, attainable goals is an important element in any child's healthy development. (For a detailed discussion of learning see Elliott & others, 2000; Travers & others, 1993.)

   Summarizing forty years of research on schooling, Eccles and Roeser (1999) reach several conclusions.

- Although school resources are important, the organizational, social, and instructional processes have the greatest impact on children's development.

- Schools produce their effects at different levels: the school as a whole, the classroom, and interpersonal interactions.

- Children's perceptions of the school are powerful predictors of their adjustment, adaptation, and achievement.

- A school's effects on behavior are determined by individual, psychological processes.

Guided Review

11. The impact of schools on _____ has been a neglected research topic.
12. A massive study showing that schools do indeed make a difference in children's development was conducted by _____ _____.
13. _____ is a process that results in the modification of behavior.
14. For achievement to occur, children need to face _____.
15. Children's _____ of school affects their adjustment and achievement.

   Are there other influences that affect achievement, learning, and development in school? Study after study suggests, clearly and precisely, the negative effect that television viewing exercises on school achievement. (For an excellent summary of these studies, see Comstock and Scharrer, 1999.) Let's look at the world of television now in more detail.

Answers

11. development 12. Michael Rutter 13. Learning 14. obstacles 15. perception

An Applied VIEW
Translating Knowledge into Practice

One of the best illustrations of how scientists think and how the great scientists shift their thinking from the highly technical to the practical, applies to the Nobel prize winner, Richard Feynman (Gleick, 1992). Admittedly a genius, Feynman showed his abilities early in life. Fascinated by mathematics and an inveterate tinkerer, as a boy of 10 or 11 years he designed his own radios, invented a burglar alarm for his house, and invented a gadget for rocking his sister's cradle. He taught himself the tricks of mental arithmetic and speculated about the possibility of using atomic power for rockets. Even while deeply immersed in the atomic bomb project, Feynman, always intrigued by puzzles, taught himself how to pick locks, open safes, and infuriate his colleagues.

But it was the Challenger disaster and Feynman's ability to convert the highly technical to the readily understandable that demonstrated the utility of scientific thinking. If you recall, considerable speculation had centered on the O-rings that were designed to keep gases from escaping from the rocket. Feynman believed that at low temperatures (32 degrees) the O-rings would become brittle and permit gases to escape with disastrous consequences.

Appointed a member of the committee to uncover what had caused the tragedy, Feynman became disgusted by the bureaucratic thinking that was gripping the committee. To dramatize his ideas, on the morning of one of the hearings, he rose early, found a taxi, and cruised Washington, searching for a hardware store that would be open. He bought a C-clamp and a pair of pliers. When the hearing began, he asked for a glass of ice water and dropped a piece of O-ring into the glass. Onlookers immediately detected changes in the O-ring, changes that made failure of the critical seals inevitable. Feynman's simple experiment demonstrated scientific thinking at its best, the translation of theory into action.

You're probably saying to yourself that's fine thinking for a Nobel prize winner, but students in grade school? The answer is—yes. Good science instructors will teach children to think in a similar manner: Don't be satisfied with the obvious. Do other, better, solutions exist? What steps do I take for answers? Remember, it's not the subject matter that's important; it's the way of thinking. Disturbed by estimates that fewer than 10% of high school graduates have the skills necessary to perform satisfactorily in college-level science courses, science teachers today are using a more "hands-on" approach to their teaching. Instead of having students memorize lengthy formulas, they have them doing experiments starting in the early grades.

Television and Development

Do you have a television set in your home? Did you laugh at what appears to be a ridiculous question? You probably have at least one, more likely two or three. Ninety-nine percent of American homes today have at least one set, while 87 percent of homes have a VCR. Children spend at least twice as much time watching TV than they do in school (Rich, 1999).

Although today's children are immersed in a media world (movies, television, video games, CD-ROM, audiotapes, videotapes), television is the most widely used and undoubtedly has a greater effect on development than other media (Huston & Wright, 1998). Is television viewing as extensive as claimed? With 1,600 television stations, with more than 224 million television sets, and with most homes having a choice of at least 10 channels (many of them offering programs 24 hours per day), America is a land of television viewers (Comstock & Scharrer, 1999).

Television has become one of the great means of socialization in a child's life. As such, and recognizing the relationship between program content and a child's age, adults should be particularly careful in what children watch.

One of the more worrisome aspects of children's television viewing is its relatively unsupervised nature. Findings from the Kaiser Family Foundation study (1999) of 3,000 children from the ages of 2 through 18 indicate that children spent more than 38 hours per week using some kind of media outside of school. The daily usage breakdown was as follows.

An Applied View   *The Extent of Television Watching*

For an idea of the role that television plays in our society, try to answer these questions, which have been drawn from several national surveys:

1. What percentage of American homes have a TV set?

2. How long (on the average) is the set on per day?

3. By age 85, how many years of television has the average viewer seen?

4. How many hours of TV does the average viewer watch per week?

5. By age 18, a student has watched how many hours of TV?

6. By age 15, how many killings has a child seen on television?

7. Is there evidence that television influences a child's behavior?

If you had any doubts about the extent of television viewing, these figures should dispel them.

Answers

1. 99 2. 7 hours 3. 9 years 4. 28 hours 5. 15,000 hours 6. 13,000 killings 7. yes

---

• 3 hours of television per day

• 1 hour of computer games

• 48 minutes of recorded music

• 44 minutes of reading

• 39 minutes of radio

More than half the children had television sets in their bedrooms. In other words, children's bedrooms are becoming media centers. Half of the children said they had no parental rules about television, and 58 percent told researchers they lived in homes where television is on during meals.

Are there developmental effects from all of this viewing?

Television and Cognitive Development

The moment we concede that children learn from watching television, certain questions arise:

• How active are children in the process?

• To what do they attend?

• How much do they understand?

• How much do they remember?

Answering these questions gives us insight into how TV watching and cognitive development are associated. For example, when you studied Piaget's work, especially his views on operations, you saw how he insisted that children were active participants in their cognitive development. They actively construct their cognitive world.

Cognitive theorists, reflecting Piaget's views, believe that children understand what they see according to their level of cognitive development. The cognitive structures that children form can be altered by what they see on television. Children attend to what they see; they learn from what they see; and they remember what they see. They can also apply these new ideas in new settings.

Specifically, we know that:

• *Children remember what is said,* even when they are not looking at the screen. Auditory attention is also at work—voices, sound changes, laughing, and applause (Huston & Wright, 1998).

- *The amount of time spent looking at the set is directly related to age.* By age 4, children attend to TV about 55 percent of the time, even when there are many other distractions in the room (Comstock, 1993). During the middle childhood years viewing time increases steadily (Huston & Wright, 1998).

- *Specific features of programs attract children:* women, movement, and camera angles; they look away during stills and animal shots (Wright & others, 1994).

- *Children quickly learn to relate sound to sight:* chase music means a chase scene (Wright & others, 1994). (Note the ideal combination of auditory and visual effects that produces powerful attractions.)

- *Television viewing and school achievement* are positively and negatively related. The amount of time spent viewing seems to be a key factor: anything over 30 hours per week seems to interfere with academic achievement. Positive outcomes from general television viewing include vocabulary enhancement for students with language difficulties and improved spatial skills. (For an excellent discussion of the relationship between viewing time and reading, see Huston & Wright, 1998.)

We can also conclude that much of what children see on television is not just content. They also learn TV's codes: sound effects, camera techniques, and program organization. Some researchers believe that changes in children's behavior following the viewing of televised violence come from their responding to fast action, loud music, and camera tricks (Clifford & others, 1995).

Children understand television programs according to their level of development, and their level of development is affected by their television viewing. For example, in a study of 261 subjects age 5 and 7 years, Wright and his colleagues (1994) found that the older children better understood that the fictional characters in the shows they watched differed from the way they acted in real life, a finding that supports Piaget's conclusions about the concrete operational period.

Television and Violence

In 1977 Ronny Zamora, a 15-year-old, shot and killed the 82-year-old woman who lived next door to him in Florida. Not guilty, pleaded his lawyer, Ellis Rubin, by reason of the boy's having watched too much television. From watching television Ronny had become dangerously inured to violence (Stossel, 1997, p. 87). Ronny's lawyer, however, didn't sway the jury; Ronny was convicted of first-degree murder.

After decades of research, we can safely conclude that televised violence may cause aggressive behavior in the children who observe it (Comstock & Paik, 1994). Is this a serious problem? Are children exposed to excessive television violence? In a recent survey of children and the media, Strasburger and Donnerstein (1999) discovered the following:

- Children view an estimated 10,000 to 15,000 acts of violence each year.

- Sixty-one percent of all shows contain violence, with children's programming being the most violent.

- Twenty-six percent of all violent acts involved the use of guns.

- Researchers concluded that children learn their attitudes about violence at a very young age and, once learned, the attitudes can be lifelong.

- The issue of desensitization is of constant concern and has not been adequately addressed.

- Children can learn that violence is acceptable to resolve conflicts and achieve goals.

As a specific example of televised violence, a survey by the *Center for Media and Public Affairs* of one day's programming (on April 7, 1994) tallied 2,605 violent acts shown on TV that day (Stossel, 1997).

Liebert, R.L., J. Sprafkin, & R.M. Liebert. (1992). *The early window.* 4th ed. New York: Pergamon. This paperback is one of the best single sources on the impact of television on our society today. Once you read this, you'll understand why TV is considered a major socializing force in a child's life.

There is another side to television's role in development, however: Its potential for the development of *prosocial behavior* that furthers all aspects of development. Nancy Eisenberg (1992, 1998, 1999), who has done so much to further our thinking about this important topic, has defined prosocial behavior as voluntary behavior intended to benefit others (such as helping, sharing, and comforting).

Prosocial behavior, although it may have an ulterior motive (such as rewards or approval), may also include elements of altruistic behavior, that is behavior motivated by concern and sympathy for others (Eisenberg & Fabes, 1998; Hastings & colleagues, 2000; Hoffman, 2000). Viewing programs specifically designed to promote prosocial

behavior lead to changes in children's behavior (Huston & Wright, 1998). On the other hand, research shows that it's easier to measure cognitive viewing than social/emotional outcomes of television viewing. Given the uncertainty of the research, do you think that it's possible to increase prosocial behavior by television viewing, or are most shows just too violent and sexual?

If you would like to have a more informed view on this issue, you may want to read one or more of the references (such as Eisenberg & Fabes, 1998) in this chapter.

You may also wish to learn more about it by going to our web site at http:/www.mhhe.com/dacey5.

Consequently, you cannot ignore the possible long-term negative effects of violence on TV, particularly when you realize the power of observational learning (Crick, 1996). Most children watch television with few, if any, parental restrictions. (Our concern here is with middle childhood youngsters who tend to watch adult shows.)

In a 10,000-hour, three-year study of television violence (the *National Television Violence Study*—NTVS) (1996) found that 60 percent of sampled programs contained violence. The context of the violent scenes suggested the probability of future negative effects on children. Especially when:

- Bad characters were never punished.

- More than 70 percent showed no remorse for the violence.

- More than 40 percent of the violent scenes included humor.

- More than 50 percent of the violent scenes gave no clue as to the pain inflicted.

- More than 40 percent of the violence was committed by attractive (hero) models.

Commenting on these findings, Shifrin (1998, p. 23) noted that, depending on the child's developmental level, cartoons and fantasy-type violence, i.e., sanctioned violence, cannot be dismissed simply because it is unrealistic.

The effects of viewing televised violence are more forceful for children than adults, particularly if the children believe that the televised violence is real. Another major concern, of course, is the possibility of children becoming desensitized because of their exposure to a steady diet of televised violence. Over time children can begin to lose their sense of reality and fantasize about their own aggressive behavior.

Finally, parents can guide their children's television viewing by considering the following five questions (Rich, 1999):

1. Who is the author and what is the purpose of this show?

2. What techniques are used to attract the children's attention?

3. What values are being presented?

4. Will children interpret the show's message differently from adults?

5. What is lacking in the presentation?

Guided Review

16. Children spend more than _____ hours per week using multimedia.
17. Television viewing and school achievement are both _____ and _____ related.
18. _____ _____ is closely associated with the idea of prosocial behavior.
19. Children understand television according to their level of _____.

Stress in Childhood

Do you recall the Elian Gonzalez case? He was the 6-year-old child who was rescued at sea crossing from Cuba with his mother. His mother died on the trip, but Elian was brought to Florida to live with relatives. His father came to the United States seeking his son and a tug-of-war began between the father and the relatives. The United States government intervened and forcibly removed the boy from the home of the relatives and returned him to his father. Regardless of how you feel about this case, there can be little doubt that this 6-year-old boy experienced severe stress.

Although most children of this age don't go through Elian's ordeal, they begin to encounter stressful situations that range from the severe (parental conflict, divorce, abuse) to the less severe (doing chores, arguing about television-viewing time). They spend more of their time away from home, and new contacts and new tasks can upset them. There is no escape; we all have faced similar circumstances. Were we scarred for life by these encounters? Probably not. Yet for some children, an inability to cope with stress has serious consequences, and today we are more alert to the signs of childhood stress.

But first, let's link what is known about childhood stress to development. We begin by admitting that no definition of stress exists that satisfies everyone. Let's use this definition: **Stress** *is anything that upsets our equilibrium—both psychological and physiological.*

Stress Anything that upsets our equilibrium—both psychological and physiological.

Types of Stress

Table 10.2, based on Brenner's excellent and practical work (1984), summarizes specific childhood stressors.

When each of us faces stress, we react differently. To begin with, not all of us would agree on what stress is. For example, some people are probably terrified of flying, whereas others see it as a pleasant, relaxing adventure. Although many reasons help to explain these different responses, we can isolate several important individual differences.

Why Children React Differently to Stress

Stress, regardless of the source, produces a variety of reactions. Think of your own childhood when your parents were really angry with you. How did you react? Some children react in the same way to anything stressful, either with high anxiety, fear,

Answers

16. 38 17. positively and negatively 18. Nancy Eisenberg 19. development

TABLE 10.2 SPECIFIC CHILDHOOD STRESSORS	
Type	**Example**
Two-parent families	Changes associated with normal growth: new siblings, sibling disputes, moving, school, working parents
One-parent families	Multiple adults, lack of sex-role model, mother vs. father
Multiparent families	New relationships, living in two households
Death, adoption	Parental death, sibling death, possible institutional placement, relationships with different adults
Temporary separation	Hospitalization, health care, military service
Divorce	Troubled days before the divorce, separation, the divorce itself
Abuse	Parental, sibling, institutional; sexual, physical, emotional
Neglect	Physical (food, clothes), emotional (no response to children's needs for attention and affection)
Alcoholism	Secrecy, responsibility for alcoholic parent, suppress own feelings

Children need emotional support from those in their environment. Even under the most difficult circumstances (divorce, death of a parent, hospitalization), the presence of a "significant other" can help a child to cope, to deal with stress in an appropriate manner for the child's developmental level.

Temperament   How children interact with the environment.

Child abuse   Commonly includes physical abuse, sexual abuse, emotional maltreatment, and neglect.

and say to themselves, "They'll get over it." Although we could list many reasons for these varied responses, several important individual differences are at work.

- *Sex.* Whether it's temporary separation, divorce, or hospitalization, boys are more vulnerable to stressful events in their lives. Boys are more likely to be exposed to the conversations and tensions surrounding separation, divorce, or illness, or any other stressor, while parents frequently try to shelter girls from as much unpleasantness as possible. Also parents may not be as sympathetic to the signs of a boy's distress as they are to a girl's (Rutter, 1996).

- *Age.* Children of different ages respond differently to distress. Below the age of 6 months, they simply don't have the cognitive capacity to recognize the various types of stress. During the early childhood years (2–6), children don't really understand what's happening and tend to blame themselves for any problems. But in middle childhood—particularly toward the end of the period—children are exposed to a wider range of stressors: tobacco, alcohol, other drugs, exposure to violence, and accidents. Their greater cognitive ability makes them more vulnerable to the stress caused by a parent's death. On the other hand, they have much better coping resources than younger children (Collins, Harris, & Susman, 1995).

- *Temperament.* Recall that children are all born with unique **temperaments,** differences that affect the way they interact with the environment. Consequently, their temperament influences the intensity of their reactions after a stressful event, such as parental separation (Kagan, 1994). In other words, there seem to be inborn temperamental differences that influence children through the later years, and probably for life.

Let's focus now on one of the stressors we've mentioned—abuse—which, unfortunately, has become a major problem in modern society.

Abused Children

Most people consider the United States to be a nation of child lovers, thus discussing **child abuse** always comes as a shock. Before we begin to discuss this topic, we should agree on what is meant by the term. Four major types of abuse are commonly identified: physical abuse, sexual abuse, emotional maltreatment, and neglect (Cicchetti & Toth, 1998).

Child abuse has always been with us, but it has only been a matter of public awareness for the past 25 years. Abuse still remains an elusive subject that defies precise definition and identification (Jackson & Nuttall, 1997). With a population becoming ever more diverse, parents may not consider certain practices as abusive. For example, in Cambodia fever may be treated with *cao gao,* in which hot coins are rubbed over a child's back or chest (Wyckoff, 1999).

Physical and sexual abuses that leave evidence are easy to detect and describe (if they are reported), but other forms of abuse that emotionally wound youngsters are perhaps never detected. Professionals believe that abusive behavior involves direct harm (physical, sexual, deliberate malnutrition), intent to harm (which is difficult if not impossible to detect), and intent to harm even if injury does not result (Ladd & LeSieur, 1995).

The Nature of the Problem

Courage is the price life exacts for granting peace.
Amelia Earhart

Although child abuse is an age-old problem, not until recently did it become widely publicized. In the 1920s, Dr. John Caffey, studying bone fractures and other physical injuries, suggested that parents might have caused the injuries. The skepticism that greeted his conclusions prevented him from officially reporting his findings until the late 1940s. In 1961 C. Henry Kempe and his associates startled the annual meeting of the American Academy of Pediatrics by their dramatic description of the **battered child syndrome.**

Battered child syndrome
Classic physical abuse.

Parental Characteristics

You may well ask: What kind of person could ever hurt a child? Although the parental characteristics leading to child abuse are not rigidly defined, several appear with surprising frequency. Here are some of the most frequently found characteristics (Cicchetti & Roth, 1998; Rogosh & others, 1996):

• The parents themselves were abused as children.

• They are often loners.

• They refuse to recognize the seriousness of the child's condition.

• They resist diagnostic studies.

• They believe in harsh punishment.

• They have unreasonable expectations for the child. (Children should never cry or drop things.)

• They lack control and are often immature and dependent.

• They feel personally incompetent.

A cycle of abuse becomes clear. The most consistent feature of the histories of abusive families is the repetition, from one generation to the next, of a pattern of abuse, neglect, and parental loss or deprivation. In each generation we find, in one form or another, a distortion of the relationship between parents and children that deprives children of the consistent love and care that would enable them to develop fully. Parents perceive the child as disappointing or unlovable, especially in times of stress and crisis. Finally, for most children, no lifeline exists; that is, no helpful sources can be accessed in times of crisis.

The Special Case of Sexual Abuse

Sexual abuse refers to any sexual activity between a child and an adult whether by consent or force. It includes fondling, penetration, oral-genital contact, intercourse, and the use of children in pornography. Estimates are that between 50,000 and

500,000 children are sexually abused each year (200,000 is the usual figure given, but these figures remain suspect because of the suspected enormous number of unreported cases). Most of the victims are female, but the number of male victims is on the rise (Burkhardt & Rotatori, 1995).

Obtaining reliable data about the sexual abuse of children is extremely difficult. One example of a lack of good data relates to child abuse in day-care settings. Estimates are that the incidence rate of the sexual abuse of children under the age of 6 years in day care is 5.5 per 10,000 children compared to 8.9 per 10,000 children abused at home. The accuracy of these figures is indeed questionable and the topic cries out for extensive, objective research (Jackson & Nuttall, 1997).

Effects of Sexual Abuse

Abused children feel that they have lost control and are helpless when an adult sexually abuses them. All of their lives children have been taught to obey adults, so they feel forced to comply. This is particularly sensitive because most abusers are known to the family: a relative, friend, or some authority known to the children. For example, in a survey of one county in the state of Massachusetts, one-third of the rape victims under 17 were attacked by fathers, stepfathers, male relatives, or mothers' boyfriends. (About 80 percent of the victims were girls.) Between 50 percent to 60 percent of the other children were assaulted by someone familiar to them (Hart, 2000).

What are the developmental effects of an adult's violation and betrayal of a child? Different ages seem to suffer different types of effects (Kendall-Tackett & others, 1993). For example, the highest rate of problems was found in the 7- to 13-year-old group. Forty percent of the abused children of this age showed serious disturbances; 17 percent of the 4- to 6-year-old group manifested some disturbance. About 50 percent of the 7- to 13-year-old group showed greatly elevated levels of anger and hostility compared with 15 percent of the 4- to 6-year-olds. Increase of anxiety, fear, and distress were common to all age groups.

Do adults who were sexually abused as children suffer long-term consequences? Among the possible effects are the following: depression (probably the most common finding), above-normal levels of tension, aggression, a negative self-concept, and sexual problems, often becoming sexually promiscuous (Kendall-Tackett, 1993).

Sexual abuse is a problem that every reader will find repugnant. Yet we can offer some positive conclusions. We are now better able to identify these children and provide help. Treatment techniques offer hope for the future. As the problem becomes more widely publicized, parents, teachers, and concerned adults are becoming more sensitive to the possibility of the occurrence of sexual abuse (Lynskey & Fergusson, 1997).

As we examine these children who have experienced severe stress, what can we learn from them that would benefit others? There are no guarantees of successful coping, for obvious reasons: the intensity of the stress, the immaturity of the children, and the amount of support they receive (Liem, James, O'Toole, & Boudewyn, 1997). Yet we also know that a small number of children seem oblivious to stress, at least for a time.

Resilient Children

The mother of three children was beset by mental problems. She refused to eat at home because she was sure someone was poisoning her. Her 12-year-old daughter developed the same fear. Her 10-year-old daughter would eat at home only if the father ate with her. Her 7-year-old son thought they were all crazy and always ate at home. The son went on to perform brilliantly in school and later in college and has now taken the first steps in what looks like a successful career. The older daughter is now diagnosed schizophrenic, whereas the younger girl seems to have adjusted after a troubled youth. How do we explain these different reactions?

First, understand what *resilient* means. A technical definition would be that resilience refers to a dynamic process encompassing positive adaptation within the context of significant adversity (Luthar, Cicchetti, & Becker, 2000). These children have endured terrible circumstances and come through, not unscathed, but skilled at fending off feelings of inferiority, helplessness, and isolation (Heller, Larrieu, D'Imperio, & Boris, 1999). What we know about these children points to their ability to recover from either physiological or psychological trauma and return to a normal developmental path (Cicchetti & Toth, 1998).

Identifying Resilient Children

Resilient children Children who sustain some type of physiological or psychological trauma yet remain on a normal developmental path.

Who are these **resilient children** who grow up in the most chaotic and adverse conditions, yet manage to thrive? Clues may be found in a remarkable long-term study conducted by Emmy Werner and Ruth Smith called *Overcoming the Odds* (1992). They studied all of the children (837) born on the island of Kauai in the year 1955. (Kauai is an island in the Hawaiian chain.) What's unusual about this study is that the authors studied 505 of these children from their prenatal days until they were 31–32 years of age. (The drop in numbers from the original 837 was due to some of the subjects dying, some moving to other islands, or to mainland U.S.A.)

Of the 505 individuals followed over the 30-plus years, one in three was born with the odds stacked dramatically against them. They either experienced birth problems, grew up in poverty, or were members of dysfunctional families (desertion, divorce, alcoholism, and mental illness). Two children out of three in this particularly vulnerable group encountered four or more risk factors before they were 2 years old and developed serious learning and/or behavior problems. *Nevertheless, one of three of these high risk children developed into a competent, confident young adult by the age of 18.* What protective factors were at work in these children that let them overcome daunting adversity?

Characteristics of Resilient Children

Remember that the children we're focusing on here were battered by stressful events including desertion, divorce, discord, alcoholism, mental illness, neglect, and abuse. These conditions delivered a series of sledgehammer blows to their development, yet one of three of these children turned out to be a success in their personal and professional lives. They made good marriages, had happy families, and were good workers. What personal characteristics were at work here?

One way to answer this question is to search for the characteristics that mark the lives of resilient children.

• *They possess temperaments that elicit positive responses from those around them.* They are the easy children described in chapter 4. Eating and sleeping habits are quite regular; they show positive responses when people approached them; they adapt to changes in their environment. They exhibit a considerable degree of self-regulation (Bronson, 2000). In spite of their suffering, they are friendly, likable children who possess an inner quality that protects them from their hostile surroundings and enables them to reach out to an adult who could offer critical support.

• *Many of these children have a special interest or talent.* For example, some are excellent swimmers, dancers, and artists. Others have a special knack for working with animals. Still others show talent with numbers quite early. Whatever their interest, it served to absorb them and helped to shelter them from their environment. They use their talent to take advantage of the support systems available to them, whether in school, church programs, or community.

These activities seem to provide the encouragement and stability often lacking in their home lives.

- *They are sufficiently intelligent to acquire good problem-solving skills,* which they then use to make the best of things around them; they attract the attention of helpful adults; they do well in school, where they are usually popular. Interestingly enough, their obvious competence elicits support from others, which produces a good sense of self. In turn, higher levels of self-esteem at age 18 produce individuals less inclined to have later bouts of emotionl disturbance. In other words, they use their abilities to adapt successfully to their circumstances.

- When children from troubled families (now the successful adults) recaptured the times when they were struggling and linked them to their present happy circumstances, *they usually mention some person—grandparent, aunt, neighbor, teacher, religious figure, coach—who appeared on the scene in the nick of time.* The support, warmth, advice, and comfort offered by this friend-in-need and in-deed usually was crucial (Dacey & Fiore, 2000).

- Children who are buffeted by events outside of the family, such as economic hardships, often find that one parent—frequently the mother—forms a tight bond with them. Her behavior in accepting the hard times and doing everything she can to overcome crippling adversity sets a lasting example for her children. Here, as in everything else we've discussed, you can see the benefits and power of modeling.

Such characteristics—a genuinely warm, fairly easygoing personality, an absorbing interest, and the ability to seek out a sympathetic adult—help to distance them emotionally from a drugged, alcoholic, or abusive parent (sometimes a parent with all of these problems). You can understand, then, how our efforts to learn more about resilient children also help us to provide paths of intervention and prevention of undesired outcomes of adverse conditions (von Eye & Schuster, 2000).

> There is no single set of qualities or circumstances that characterizes all such resilient children. But psychologists are finding that they stand apart from their more vulnerable siblings almost from birth. They seem to be endowed with innate characteristics that insulate them from the turmoil and pain of their families and allow them to reach out to some adult—a grandparent, teacher, or family friend—who can lend crucial emotional support (Werner & Smith, 1992).

You will be both informed and encouraged by reading Werner, E. & R. Smith. (1992). *Overcoming the odds: High risk children from birth to adulthood.* Ithaca, NY: Cornell University Press.

Table 10.3 summarizes the characteristics of resilient children.

TABLE 10.3 CHARACTERISTICS OF RESILIENT CHILDREN

Age	Characteristics
At birth	Alert, attentive.
1 year	Securely attached infant.
2 years	Independent, slow to anger, tolerates frustration well.
3–4 years	Cheerful, enthusiastic, works well with others.
Childhood	Seems to be able to remove self from trouble, recovers rapidly from disturbance, confident, seems to have a good relationship with at least one adult.
Adolescence	Assumes responsibilities, does well in school, may have part-time job, socially popular, is not impulsive.

Guided Review

20. Anything that upsets our equilibrium, both psychological and physiological is known as _____ .
21. The highest rate of problems resulting from sexual abuse was found in children aged _____ to _____ .
22. _____ , _____ , and _____ are examples of external sources of stress.
23. Gender must be considered in responding to stress. _____ are more vulnerable to stress than _____ .
24. Children who succeed under adverse conditions are called _____ children.

CONCLUSION & SUMMARY

In this chapter, we followed middle childhood youngsters as they moved away from a sheltered home environment and into a world of new friends, new challenges, and new problems. Whether the task is adjusting to a new sibling, relating to peers and teachers, or coping with difficulties, youngsters of this age enter a different world.

But the timing of their entrance into this novel environment is intended to match their ability to adapt successfully, to master those skills that will prepare them for the next great developmental epoch, adolescence. With their entrance into a widening world, middle childhood youngsters require those skills that will enable them to cope successfully

Inevitably, though, they face times of turmoil, which, as we have seen, can come from internal or external sources. For some youngsters, these periods of stress are brief interludes; for others, there is no relief for years. Children cope uniquely using temperamental qualities and coping skills as best they can.

What are the key elements in children acquiring a personally satisfying and competent sense of self?

- The link between self-esteem and competence grows stronger during the middle childhood years.
- The development of self-control becomes a key element in a child's success, both cognitively and psychosocially.

How influential are peers during these years?

- During the middle childhood years, children begin to form close friendships.
- Children who have difficulty with their peers are often bothered by personal problems.
- Middle childhood youngsters learn to recognize the views of others.
- Children form and test social relations during these years.

What are some effects that different schools and teachers have on children in the middle childhood years?

- Children must learn to adjust to a wide variety of classmates, many of whom may be children of different cultures.
- School-age children are encountering considerable change in both curriculum and instructional methods.

Does television affect, either positively or negatively, children's development?

- Television is the school's great competitor for children's time and attention.
- Some children spend more time watching television than they do in school-related activities.
- Controversy surrounds the issue of the effects of television violence.
- Television is also credited with the potential for encouraging prosocial behavior.

What are some of the major stressors of the middle childhood years?

- Children react differently to stress according to age, gender, and temperament.
- Some children, called resilient children, overcome the adverse effects of early stressors.
- Several theories have been proposed to explain how children become violent.
- Children acquire coping skills that enable them to adjust to stress in their lives.

Answers

20. stress 21. 7, 13 22. Family, school, peers 23. Males, females 24. resilient

KEY TERMS

Battered child syndrome
Child abuse
Competence
Friend
Impulsivity

Learning
Peer
Resilient children
Self-concept
Self-control

Self-esteem
Social perspective-taking
Stress
Temperament
Transformation

WHAT DO YOU THINK?

1. Recall Harter's studies investigating the association between self-esteem and physical appearance. Would you agree that the association is as strong as she found in her subjects? Could you make additional suggestions for helping children find other means of evaluating themselves?

2. It is generally accepted that friendships and groups become more important during the middle childhood years. With your knowledge of the developmental features of these years, do you think children of this age are ready for group membership?

3. For individuals to experience stress, they must understand the forces that are pressing on them. Do you think middle childhood youngsters are capable of such an interpretation of the events surrounding them?

4. Great concern exists today about the increasing rate of violence among children. Do you think the problem is as serious as the media indicate? From your knowledge of this topic, do you think the predictors of early criminal behavior are useful?

CHAPTER REVIEW TEST

1. Children who have similar levels of competence may have quite different levels of
   a. cognitive development.
   b. friendship.
   c. television viewing.
   d. self-esteem.

2. A peer is defined as one who is
   a. equal in intelligence.
   b. in the same grade.
   c. within 12 months of age.
   d. in a nearby house.

3. Which of the following differences between schools has little impact on children's development?
   a. Emphasis on academic success
   b. Teacher expectations
   c. Time-on-task
   d. Size of school

4. Impulse control at 4 years of age predicted
   a. the nature of interactions with siblings.
   b. future academic success.
   c. the health of a child.
   d. physical competence.

5. Friends provide certain resources for children that adults lack. Which of the following is not a resource provided by friends?
   a. Membership in the sibling underworld
   b. Opportunity for learning skills
   c. Chance to compare self with others
   d. Chance to belong to a group

6. Selman's theory of interpersonal relationships is known as
   a. observational learning.
   b. social perspective-taking.
   c. linguistic interpretation.
   d. accommodation.

7. A critical factor in effective schools is
   a. condition of the school.
   b. recreational facilities.
   c. number of tenured teachers.
   d. good instructional leadership.

8. Learning is a process that results in the _____ of behavior.
   a. modification
   b. efficient use of language
   c. assimilation
   d. repression

9. The author of a scathing criticism of schools in low SES environments is
   a. Bruner.
   b. Skinner.
   c. Kozol.
   d. Deming.

10. In a recent survey, 50% of the children had TV sets in their
    a. cars.
    b. kitchens.
    c. bedrooms.
    d. porches.

11. Television can also further _____ behavior.
    a. regressive
    b. accommodating
    c. subliminal
    d. prosocial

12. Which of the following is not considered a severe stressor of childhood?
    a. Parental alcoholism
    b. School life
    c. Abuse
    d. Separation from parent

13. Child abusers often share parental characteristics. Which of the following is not such a characteristic?
    a. Perpetrator abused as a child
    b. Have unreasonable expectations for the child
    c. Often immature and dependent
    d. Low SES

14. There may be as many as _____ sexually abused children per year in the United States.
    a. 75,000
    b. 250,000
    c. 500,000
    d. 1,000,000

15. Which is not a long-term effect of sexual abuse?
    a. Permissive parenting
    b. Depression
    c. Negative self-concept
    d. Sexual problems

16. Although middle childhood youngsters are more exposed to stressful situations, they possess a better ability to
    a. cope.
    b. ignore.
    c. retreat.
    d. achieve.

17. Stress has the tendency to upset our
    a. denial patterns.
    b. equilibrium.
    c. sublimations.
    d. trust.

18. Which of the following does not account for individual differences in the reaction to stress?
    a. Age
    b. Sex
    c. Temperament
    d. Athletic ability

19. Children react differently to stress according to all but
    a. age.
    b. gender.
    c. temperament.
    d. race.

20. Among the protective factors for resilient children is
    a. temperament.
    b. interactive error.
    c. geographic mobility.
    d. assimilation.

Answers

1. d 2. c 3. d 4. b 5. a 6. b 7. d 8. a 9. c 10. c 11. d 12. b 13. d 14. c 15. a 16. a 17. b 18. d 19. d 20. a

PART VI

Adolescence

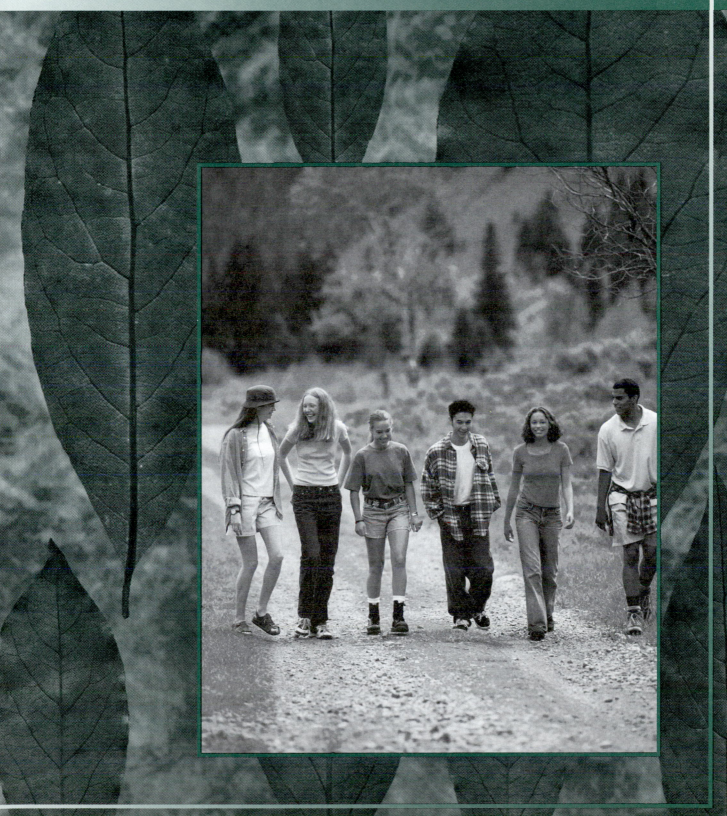

*If men and
women are to
understand each
other, to enter
into each other's
nature with
mutual sympathy,
and to become
capable of genuine
comradeship, the
foundation must
be laid in youth.*

Havelock Ellis

CHAPTER 11

Physical and Cognitive Development in Adolescence

Are adolescents today forced to deal with too many pressures?

Peter and Lynn are wide awake at two in the morning, but they are not having a good time. They are having a teenager. Matty, their son, was due home two hours ago. He is sixteen, his curfew is midnight, and they have heard nothing from him. They are wide awake and angry, and most of all, they are worried.

But this is not going to be one of those nights that changes anyone's life. Nobody is going to die. Nothing of this night will be on the news. This is the ordinary night nobody writes about. Matty is going to come home in another half hour hoping his parents have long since gone to sleep, so he can assure them tomorrow that he was in "only a little past twelve." When his hopes are dashed by the sight of his wide-awake parents, he will have an excuse about somebody's car and somebody else's mother and a third person who borrowed the first person's jacket with his car keys and left the party early, and maybe it's just because it's now nearly three in the morning, but the story will sound to Peter and Lynn so freshly made up that all its pieces barely know how to fit together.

Lynn won't be thinking about it now, but only six years ago—not a long time to her—she had been struck by how independent Matty had become. This clingy kid who seemed to need her so much had become a little 10-year-old fellow full of purpose and plans, in business for himself, with a sign on his bedroom door—"Adults Keep Out." A part of her missed the little boy who didn't want to be left alone, but a bigger part of her was pleased for both of them by this development. But six years later, at 2:30 in the morning, it will not occur to her to say, "Matty, my son, I'm so impressed by the way you are able to take care of yourself, by how much you can do for yourself, by the way you just go wherever you want to and come home whenever you want to, by how little you seem to need your dad and me. You're really growing up, son. Your dad and I just wanted to stay up until 2:30 in the morning to tell you how proud we are!" No, what will occur to Lynn to say is something more like "This isn't a hotel here, buddy!" ... Peter and Lynn want something more of Matty now than they wanted when he was 10 (Kegan, 1994, p. 15–16). ✿

Famed Harvard psychologist Robert Kegan believes we all want a lot from teens like Matty. We want him ". . . to be employable, a good citizen, a critical thinker, emotionally self-reflective, personally trustworthy, and possessed of common sense and meaningful ideals. This is a lot to want. It grows out of our concern for ourselves, our concern for others who live with Matty, and our concern for Matty himself. Will he be up to all these expectations?" (p. 19)

Kegan suggests that in general, our expectations of our teenagers are too high. There is considerable evidence today that the great majority of adolescents pass safely through this stage of life and become reasonably happy adults who make contributions to their families, friends, and communities. Nevertheless some researchers are finding that our youths are under greater stress than in previous decades (e.g., Reisberg, 2000), and that this is being reflected in an increase in a variety of high-risk behaviors (see the Applied View box on page 278). In this and the next chapter, we will look closely at the most revealing studies and try to come to some conclusions about the nature of adolescence today. We begin by looking at some ways to better define our subject.

Chapter Objectives

After reading this chapter you should be able to answer the following questions.

◆ How should we define adolescence?

◆ What are the leading theories that attempt to explain adolescence?

◆ What are the key factors of physical development in adolescence?

◆ How does cognition develop during the adolescent years?

How Should We Define Adolescence?

> "Who are you?" said the caterpillar. Alice replied, rather shyly, "I—I hardly know, Sir, just at present—at least I know who I was when I got up this morning, but I must have changed several times since then."
>
> Lewis Carroll, *Alice in Wonderland,* 1865

In writing his brilliant story, Carroll presaged in many ways current views of adolescence. For example, Graber and Brooks-Gunn (1996) stated that:

> Current approaches to studying adolescence frequently consider the precursors and outcomes of a variety of transitions, a constellation of events that define the transition period, or the timing and sequence of events that occur within a transitional period. For example, puberty and school events are frequently studied as key transitions signaling the entry into adolescence; finishing school or beginning one's full-time job are examined as transitional events that define the exit from adolescence or entry into adulthood. . . . The term **transition-linked turning points** is used to characterize this framework (pp. 768–69).

Transition-linked turning points   A constellation of events that define the transition period or the timing and sequence of events that occur within a transitional period.

Lerner (1996; see chapter 1) characterized the adolescent transition as being distinguished by four traits:

• *Relative plasticity*. There is always the potential for change, although past and contemporary contextual conditions may oppose severe limitations.

• *Relationism*. The basis for change lies in the multiple levels of the individual's relationships with others.

• *Historical embeddedness*. No level of organization functions as a result of its own isolated activity. All change is meaningful only in the context of the historical time in which it occurs.

• *Diversity and individual difference*. In the past, developmental psychology has emphasized the ways that all humans are alike (that is why we have behaviorist and stage theories). More and more, the emphasis is on the variety of ways individuals learn to cope with themselves and their environments.

In this chapter, some of the theories and research that we review conform to these newer views and some do not. Nowhere can the science of developmental psychology be seen to be more in transition than in its study of adolescence. Therefore, although we attempt to report the best of the newer work, we also retain an interest in the older, still classic contributions.

When Does Adolescence Start?

At what point did your adolescence begin? Many answers have been offered:

- When you began to menstruate, or when you had your first ejaculation.

- When the level of adult hormones rose sharply in your bloodstream.

- When you first thought about dating.

- When your pubic hair began to grow.

- When you became 11 years old (if a girl); when you became 12 years old (if a boy).

- When you developed an interest in the opposite sex.

- When you (if a girl) developed breasts.

- When you passed the initiation rites set up by society: for example, confirmation in the Catholic Church; bar mitzvah and bas mitzvah in the Jewish faith.

- When you became unexpectedly moody.

- When you became 13.

- When you formed exclusive social cliques.

- When you thought about being independent of your parents.

- When you worried about the way your body looked.

- When you entered seventh grade.

- When you could determine the rightness of an action, independent of your own selfish needs.

- When your friends' opinions influenced you more than your parents' opinions.

- When you began to wonder who you really are.

Although at least a grain of truth exists in each of these statements, they don't help us much in defining adolescence (Roche & Tucker, 1997). For example, although most would agree that menstruation is an important event in the lives of women, it really isn't a good criterion for determining the start of adolescence. The first menstruation (called menarche) can occur at any time from 8 to 16 years of age. We would not say that the menstruating 8-year-old is an adolescent, but we would certainly say the nonmenstruating 16-year-old is one.

Probably the most reliable indication of the onset of adolescence is a sharp increase in the production of the four hormones that most affect sexuality: progesterone and estrogen in females, testosterone and androgen in males. But determining this change would require taking blood samples on a regular basis, starting when youths are 9 years old. Not a very practical approach, is it?

Clearly, identifying the age or event at which adolescence begins is not a simple matter. We will need to look at it much more closely, from the standpoints of biology, psychology, sociology (biopsychosocial interactions). An American psychologist was the first to offer a specific theory to explain development in the teen years, one based almost entirely on biology.

G. Stanley Hall

G. Stanley Hall (1844–1924) is known as the father of adolescent psychology. Building on Charles Darwin's theory of evolution, Hall constructed a psychological theory of teenage development, published in two volumes and entitled *Adolescence* (1904). A major aspect of his theory was his speculation that this stage of life is characterized by "storm and stress," that most teens are by nature moody and untrustworthy. This stereotype has had many advocates ever since (Kegan, 1994).

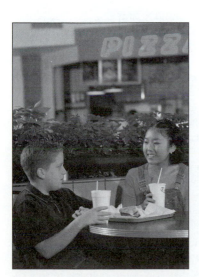

Is interest in the opposite sex the best sign that a young person has reached puberty? What other indicators could you name?

Although Hall is to be admired for his efforts to bring objectivity to adolescent psychology through the use of empiricism, it has been suggested that he had several personal agendas. He was a strong preacher against what he viewed to be teenage immorality and was especially concerned that educators try to stamp out the "plague of masturbation," which he considered to be running rampant among male youth. Here is a little speech that he recommended high school teachers and clergy give to their youthful charges:

> If a boy in an unguarded moment tries to entice you to masturbatic experiments, he insults you. Strike him at once and beat him as long as you can stand, etc. Forgive him in your mind, but never speak to him again. If he is the best fighter and beats you, take it as in a good cause. If a man scoundrel suggests indecent things, slug him with a stick or a stone or anything else at hand. Give him a scar that all may see; and if you are arrested, tell the judge all, and he will approve your act, even if it is not lawful. If a villain shows you a filthy book or picture, snatch it; and give it to the first policeman you meet, and help him to find the wretch. If a vile woman invites you, and perhaps tells a plausible story of her downfall, you cannot strike her; but think of a glittering, poisonous snake. She is a degenerate and probably diseased, and even a touch may poison you and your children (1904, p. 136).

Is adolescence typically a stage during which hormones run rampant, causing irrational and antisocial behavior? It is true that some misbehavior occurs (see the Applied View box), but there is also evidence that it is a time when many good deeds are done.

A book that also deals with the stereotype of lack of civility among adolescents is: William Goldman's *Lord of the flies.* New York: Coward-McGann. This tale of a group of teenage boys whose plane crashes on a Pacific island, killing the adults, is excellent reading. You watch the subgroups develop and proceed to the shocking ending.

An Applied View

An Average Day in the Life of Some North American Teens

Today (and every other day this year), some teens get into trouble:

- 8,441 teens become sexually active.
- 2,756 teens become pregnant.
- 1,340 babies are born to teen mothers.
- 2,754 babies are born out of wedlock.
- 638 babies are born to mothers receiving late or no prenatal care.
- 2,699 babies are born into poverty.
- 95 babies die before their first birthday.
- 2 children younger than 5 are murdered.
- 248 children are arrested for violent crimes.
- 176 children are arrested for drug abuse.
- 12,720 children are arrested for alcohol abuse or drunk driving.
- 135,000 children bring guns to school.
- 2,350 children are in adult jails.
- 167,500 students ages 16 to 24 drop out each school day.

On the other hand, today (and every other day this year), teenagers have engaged in many kinds of activities that enrich their own lives and those of the people around them. The great majority of them never engage in the kinds of misbehaviors noted above.

It is impossible to know exactly how many are involved in altruistic activities. (It is interesting that we know much more about teenagers' negative actions, isn't it?) Here are some examples of what we mean:

- Have joined a service-oriented club (e.g., Scouts, 4-H, Future Farmers of America)
- Became members of Junior Achievement
- Competed in an athletic event
- Became a candy-striper (volunteer nurse's aide)
- Joined Students Against Drunk Driving
- Taught another teen in a peer tutor program
- Served food in a shelter for the homeless
- Volunteered at a day-care center or a nursing home for the elderly
- Answered phones on a drug abuse or suicide hotline
- Delivered newspapers, stocked supermarket shelves, or in some other way earned money at a part-time job

Obviously, we would wish that all adolescents were more interested in the ideals represented by these activities. Can you think of ways that you could help make this happen?

Why, then, has the "storm and stress" view of adolescence been so prevalent in the popular press? Could it be that there has been a bias in the research itself?

Guided Review

1. Graber and Brooks-Gunn hold that the precursors and outcomes of a variety of transitions are one kind of _____ _____ _____ .
2. Lerner characterized the adolescent transition as being distinguished by four traits: relative plasticity, historical embeddedness, diversity and individual difference, and _____ .
3. G. S. Hall, the father of adolescent psychology, saw child development paralleling the development of the human race, with adolescence being a time both of civilization and of storm and _____ .

Theories of Adolescence

In this section, the theories of three famous adolescent theorists are reviewed. These theories were not chosen because they fully explain adolescence, but because they have done such a good job of spurring our thinking about the nature of this period. Thus it is with theories in general: they are respected not because they are true, but because they are generative.

> True, my theory is no longer accepted, but it was good enough to get us to the next one!
>
> Donald Hebb

Anna Freud's Psychological Theory

The daughter of Sigmund, Anna Freud (1895–1983) believed that his definition of adolescence was too sketchy. She suggested (1968) that her father had been too involved with his discovery that sexuality begins not at puberty but in early infancy.

An Informed VIEW   *Is a Bias Built into Adolescent Research?*

Hall is hardly the only adolescent psychologist who can be accused of bias in his thinking. In a fascinating study, Enright and colleagues (1987) looked at 89 articles published during two economic depressions and two world wars to see if these events had an influence on research. The results were striking:

> In times of economic depression theories of adolescence emerge that portray teenagers as immature, psychologically unstable, and in need of prolonged participation in the educational system. During wartime, the psychological competence of youth is emphasized and the duration of education is recommended to be more retracted than in depression (p. 541).

Is it likely that youths were viewed as immature during financial depressions in order to keep them from competing with adults for scarce jobs? Is their maturity seen as greater during wartime because they are needed to perform such adult tasks as soldiering and factory work? If so, is this societal bias conscious or unconscious? What do you think? Perhaps a search of the popular press for articles about teens, some written in war times and some when the economy was stagnant, would enlighten your thinking.

As you read the other theories in this chapter, see if you can spot what you believe to be biases in them. Do they emphasize some aspects of adolescent life at the expense of others? Is one more moralistic than the others?

If you would like to have a more informed opinion on this issue, you might want to learn more about it by going to our web site at http://www.mhhe.com/dacey5.

A Sociocultural View

Is Adolescence a Cultural Phenomenon?

In Western cultures, extended schooling keeps children out of full-time productive work so they do not start observing and participating in the adult economic world as they do in, for example, Guatemala. Schooling has become a substitute for adult roles. For instance, a college student spends years studying nursing (or chemistry or psychology), but he is not a nurse (chemist, psychologist). Extended schooling, then, artificially stretches the period from childhood to adulthood. This delay or waiting period is unique in human history. Combined with the decreasing age of reaching menarche in

middle-class Western girls, adolescence can be prolonged more than 10 years! Compare this to the Efe, hunters and gatherers in Zaire, who marry and assume adult roles soon after puberty. Is adolescence just a theoretical construct (see chapter 2)? Is it peculiar to cultures with extended schooling? Has an extended adolescence altered our definition of maturity? What if our increasing need for high-level education were to extend adolescence into the middle or even late 20s? Would this change the meaning of adolescence? What do you think?

Erikson wrote a fascinating book on Martin Luther: *Young man Luther.* New York: Norton. Erikson picked Luther as a subject because, in Erikson's view, he was a famous case of someone who struggled with his sense of identity. This book also closely examines the Protestant Reformation and so may appeal to you if you are interested in the beginnings of the Protestant religions.

State of identity If individuals were in a state of identity (an ideal circumstance), the various aspects of their self-image would be in agreement with each other; they would be identical.

Identity crisis Erikson's term for those situations, usually in adolescence, that cause us to make major decisions about our identity.

Repudiation Striving toward a state of identity means committing to one lifestyle and repudiating (giving up) all the other possibilities, at least for the present.

As a result, he overemphasized the importance of that earlier stage in the total developmental picture. Anna Freud spent the major part of her professional life trying to extend and modify psychoanalytic theory as applied to adolescence.

Anna Freud saw the major problem of adolescence as being the restoration of the delicate balance between the ego and the id, which is established during latency and disrupted by puberty. Latency, she felt, is the time when children adopt the moral values and principles of the people with whom they identify. Childhood fears are replaced with internalized feelings of guilt that are learned during this period. The id is controlled during latency by the strength of the superego. At puberty, however, the force of the id becomes much greater and the delicate balance is destroyed.

The problems brought about by this internal conflict cause the adolescent to regress to earlier stages of development. A renewed Oedipal conflict (see chapter 2) brings about fears that are entirely unconscious and often produce intense anxiety. Therefore, the unconscious defenses of the ego tend to multiply rapidly, especially the typical ones of repression, denial, and compensation. The problem, of course, is that the use of these defense mechanisms causes new stresses within the individual and tends to further increase the level of anxiety.

Anna Freud described two additional adolescent defense mechanisms:

- Asceticism, in which, as a defense against the sexual, "sinful" drives of youth, the teenager frequently becomes extremely religious and devoted to God.

- Intellectualization, in which the adolescent defends against emotionality of all kinds by becoming extremely intellectual and logical about life.

Anna Freud may be seen as emphasizing the psychological aspect of the bio-psychosocial model.

Erik Erikson's Psychosocial Theory

According to Erik Erikson (1902–1994), the main task of the adolescent is to achieve a **state of identity.** Erikson (1963, 1975), who originated the term **identity crisis,** used it in a special way. In addition to thinking of identity as the general picture one has of oneself, Erikson referred to it as a state toward which one strives. If you were in a state of identity, the various aspects of your self-images would be in agreement with each other; they would be identical.

Repudiation of choices is another essential aspect of a person's identity. Striving for identity means that we have to repudiate (give up) all the other possibilities,

Members of the Hitler Youth Corps were victims of "premature foreclosure," in which their identity was designed for them without their having any choice.

Identity status Marcia's four aspects of identity formation.

at least for the present. All of us know people who seem unable to do this. They cannot keep a job, they have no loyalty to their friends, they are unable to be faithful to a spouse. For them, "the grass is always greener on the other side of the fence." Thus they must keep all their options open and must not repudiate any choices, lest one of them should turn out to have been "the right one."

Erikson suggested that identity confusion is far more likely in a democratic society because so many choices are available. In a totalitarian society, youths are usually given an identity, which they are forced to accept. The Hitler Youth Corps of Nazi Germany in the 1930s is an example of a national effort backed by intense propaganda to get all the adolescents in the country to identify with the same set of values and attitudes. In democratic societies, where more emphasis is placed on individual decisionmaking, choices abound; some children may feel threatened by this overabundance of options. Nevertheless, a variety of choices is essential to the formation of a well-integrated identity.

Erikson saw adolescence as a period of moratorium—a "time out" period during which the adolescent experiments with a variety of identities, without having to assume the responsibility for the consequences of any particular one. The moratorium period does not exist in preindustrial societies. Erikson stated that indecision is an essential part of the moratorium. Tolerance of it leads to a positive identity. Some youths, however, cannot stand the ambiguity of indecision. This leads to "premature foreclosure." The adolescent who makes choices too early usually comes to regret them. He or she is especially vulnerable to identity confusion in later life.

Although some youths tend to be overly idealistic, Erikson believed that idealism is essential for a strong identity. In young people's search for a person or an idea to be true to, they are building a commitment to an ideology that will help them unify their personal values. They need ideals to avoid the disintegration of personality that is the basis of most forms of mental illness.

Identity Status

Erikson's ideas on adolescence have generated considerable research on identity formation. The leader in this field is James Marcia, who has made a major contribution to our understanding through his research on **identity status.** He and his colleagues have published numerous studies on this topic (Marcia, 1980, 1983; Berzonsky & Kuk, 2000; vanHoof, 1999; Waterman, 1999).

Marcia believes that two factors are essential in the attainment of a mature identity. First, the person must undergo several crises in choosing among life's alternatives, such as the crisis of deciding whether to hold or to give up one's religious beliefs. Second, the person must come to a commitment, an investment of self, in his or her choices. Since a person may or may not have gone through the crisis of choice and may or may not have made a commitment to choices, four combinations, or statuses, are possible for that person to be in.

Status 1. *Identity confusion:* No crisis has been experienced and no commitments have been made.

Status 2. *Identity foreclosure:* No crisis has been experienced, but commitments have been made, usually forced on the person by the parent.

Status 3. *Identity moratorium:* A number of crises have been experienced, but no commitments are yet made.

Status 4. *Identity achievement:* Numerous crises have been experienced and resolved, and relatively permanent commitments have been made.

Table 11.1 summarizes these definitions.

Erikson's eight stages (in addition to the six described in this book thus far, there are the stages of generativity and integrity) follow each other in a more or less unchangeable sequence. Research indicates that Marcia's identity statuses have a tendency toward an orderly progression, but not so clearly as Erikson's stages. Carol Gilligan and others have focused on possible gender differences in identity formation.

TABLE 11.1 SUMMARY OF MARCIA'S FOUR IDENTITY STATUSES

	Identity Status			
	Confusion	Foreclosure	Moratorium	Achievement
Crisis	Absent	Absent	Present	Present
Commitment	Absent	Present	Absent	Present
Period of adolescence in which status often occurs	Early	Middle	Middle	Late

They have concluded that women are less concerned than men with achieving an independent identity status. Women are more likely to define themselves by their relationships and responsibilities to others. Society gives women the predominant role in transmitting social values from one generation to the next. This role requires a stable identity, and therefore a stable identity appears to be more important to women than it is to men.

John Hill's Biopsychosocial Theory

Psychologist John Hill was one of the first to produce a biopsychosocial theory of adolescence (Adams & others, 1996; Hill, 1996; Hill & Holmbeck, 1986). Figure 11.1 illustrates his theory. The concentric rings are meant to portray the interrelatedness of the three factors. Biological factors are in the center because they are present at birth, as are some of the psychological factors. However, all the psychological and social factors begin playing a part immediately after birth. The major point is that each is imbedded in the other two. The meaning of each is inextricably connected to the other two. A fourth factor running through the others is time—not only the aging process from early to late adolescence, but also the events going on during this historical period.

Figure 11.1

John Hill's theory of adolescence.

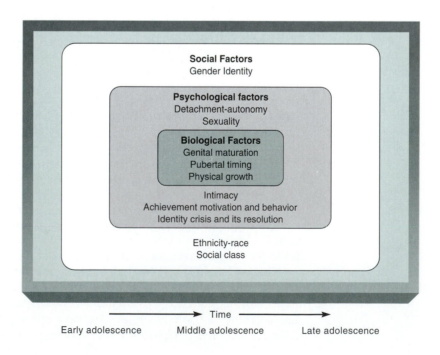

The biological factors Hill considered important are considered later in this chapter, and the social factors are reviewed in chapter 12. However, some additional comment in Hill's conception of the psychological factors is required here.

By detachment, Hill did not mean emotional independence from parents, as did many other theorists of his time. According to their view (which was primarily psychoanalytic), because teens are shifting their sexual attachments from their parents to their peers, there is bound to be a lot of "storm and stress." It was seen as natural for parents and their adolescent children to fight with each other on a regular basis. Hill rejected this view on the basis of actual research of his own and others. He saw the shift as more a matter of moving from dependence to interdependence (see chapter 12).

The nature of the shift, he felt, was more a matter of growing autonomy, which means ". . . independence in decision making and feelings of confidence in personal goals and standards of behavior" (1973, p. 37). There is a lessening of dependence, but the emphasis should be placed on increases in autonomy.

As to sexuality, once again Hill disagreed with the psychoanalytic view, which was that change in one's sense of a sexual self follows a gradual continuous pattern. He argued that puberty is brought on not only by physiological changes of a rather abrupt nature (menarche, nocturnal emissions, the growth spurt). Rather the social changes involved in acquiring the new self-concept of adolescence force teens to view themselves in a whole new light sexually. Thus the change is discontinuous, not gradual.

The new adolescent ability to become intimate with another, Hill believed, is basically tied to sexuality. It begins with feelings of affection for a close friend (which are not overtly sexual but are more intimate than the feelings that characterized earlier relationships). For most people, intimacy and sexual attraction then move to focus on opposite-sex friends. The integration of intimacy and sex, Hill believed, is one of the basic tasks of adolescence.

Achievement motivation and behavior are related to the standard of excellence individuals set for themselves and the relative proficiency they see themselves as having. Achievement behavior is different from achievement motivation, because the former may be affected by other motives too (having a good time, for instance). This difference is a particularly good example of the role that social context may play. For example, a girl may be highly motivated to play the violin, but if her friends treat that activity with contempt, and if she cares more and more about their opinions as she passes into adolescence, then the violin is likely to be relegated to its case.

Finally, Hill paid Erikson the compliment of saying that his concept of identity integrates much of what is known about adolescence. Hill felt that the six psychological factors he highlighted (see figure 11.1) fit well with and added to the concept of psychological identity. He did caution, however, that more research would be needed to determine if the adolescent years are always the time in which identity issues are most likely to be addressed (Adams & others, 1996). His concern has been borne out: it is now clear that many young people, especially college students, do not come to a clear identity crisis until they are in their early twenties, if then.

Although much progress in understanding the building blocks of adolescence has been made since Anna Freud, Erik Erikson, and John Hill theorized about it, it is abundantly clear that our progress would have been far less without their splendid insights.

In summary, it may be said that the adolescent's personality is undergoing many changes, but these changes are probably no more traumatic than at any other stage of life. There is the danger of overreliance on defense mechanisms. Another danger is staying in the moratorium period too long. The major concern is to begin to form an adult identity, which means choosing certain values and repudiating others. It is considered necessary to work one's way from identity confusion through the moratorium to an achieved identity, while avoiding foreclosure. In the next two sections of this chapter, we will be dealing with the two foundations of adolescence: physical and cognitive development.

Physical Development

To better understand physical development in adolescence, we'll answer the following questions in this section: What parts of our body are involved? When does puberty start? What are the effects of timing?

> The girls are clearly beginning to look like young ladies, while the boys with whom they have thus far played on scarcely equal terms now seem hopelessly stranded in childhood. This year or more of manifest physical superiority of the girl, with its attendant development of womanly attitudes and interests, accounts in part for the tendency of many boys in the early teens to be averse to the society of girls (King, 1914, p. 13).

Your Reproductive System

Today more is known about many aspects of **puberty,** such as how the organs of our reproductive system function together. Just as important, we are learning how to present this knowledge to adolescents effectively.

The Female Sexual System

The parts of the female sexual system are defined here and are illustrated in figure 11.2.

- *Bartholin's glands.* A pair of glands located on either side of the vagina. These glands provide some of the fluid that acts as a lubricant during intercourse.

- *Cervix.* The opening to the uterus located at the inner end of the vagina.

- *Clitoris.* Comparable to the male penis. Both organs are similar in the first few months after conception, becoming differentiated only as sexual determination takes place. The clitoris is the source of maximum sexual stimulation and becomes erect through sexual excitement. It is above the vaginal opening, between the labia minora.

- *Fallopian tubes.* Conduct the ova (egg) from the ovary to the uterus. A fertilized egg that becomes lodged in the fallopian tubes, called a fallopian or ectopic pregnancy, cannot develop normally and if not surgically removed will cause the tube to rupture.

- *Fimbriae.* Hairlike structures located at the opening of the oviduct that help move the ovum down the fallopian tube to the uterus.

Gretchen, my friend, got her period. I'm so jealous, God. I hate myself for being so jealous, but I am. I wish you'd help me just a little.

Judy Blume

Puberty A relatively abrupt and qualitatively different set of physical changes that normally occur at the beginning of the teen years.

Prior to the twentieth century, it appears that children moved directly from childhood into adulthood with no period of adolescence in between.

Answers

Figure 11.2

The female reproductive system.

- *Hymen.* A flap of tissue that usually covers most of the vaginal canal in virgins.

- *Labia majora.* The two larger outer lips of the vaginal opening.

- *Labia minora.* The two smaller inner lips of the vaginal opening.

- *Mons pubis or mons veneris.* The outer area just above the vagina, which becomes larger during adolescence and on which the first pubic hair appears.

- *Ova.* The female reproductive cells stored in the ovaries. These eggs are fertilized by the male sperm. Girls are born with more than a million follicles, each of which holds an ovum. At puberty, only 10,000 remain, but they are more than sufficient for a woman's reproductive life. Because usually only one egg ripens each month from the midteens to the late forties, a woman releases fewer than 500 ova during her lifetime.

- *Ovaries.* Glands that release one ovum each month. They also produce the hormones estrogen and progesterone, which play an important part in the menstrual cycle and pregnancy.

- *Pituitary gland.* The "master" gland located in the lower part of the brain. It controls sexual maturation and excitement and monthly menstruation.

- *Ureter.* A canal connecting the kidneys with the bladder.

- *Urethra.* A canal leading from the bladder to the external opening through which urine is excreted.

- *Uterus.* The hollow organ (also called the womb) in which the fertilized egg must implant itself for a viable pregnancy to occur. The egg attaches itself to the lining of the uterus from which the fetus draws nourishment as it matures during the nine months before birth.

- *Vulva.* The external genital organs of the female.

The Male Sexual System

The parts of the male sexual system are defined here and are illustrated in figure 11.3.

- *Cowper's glands.* Located next to the prostate glands. Their job is to secrete a fluid that changes the chemical balance in the urethra from an acidic to an alkaline base. This fluid proceeds up through the urethra in the penis, where it is ejaculated during sexual excitement just before the sperm-laden semen. About a quarter of the time, sperm also may be found in this solution, sometimes called preseminal fluid. Therefore, even if the male withdraws his penis before he ejaculates, it is possible for him to deposit some sperm in the vagina, which may cause pregnancy.

Figure 11.3

The male reproductive system.

- *Epididymis.* A small organ attached to each testis. It is a storage place for newly produced sperm.

- *Foreskin.* A flap of loose skin that surrounds the glans penis at birth, often removed by a surgery called circumcision.

- *Glans penis.* The tip or head of the penis.

- *Pituitary gland.* The "master" gland controlling sexual characteristics. In the male it controls the production of sperm, the release of testosterone (and thus the appearance of secondary sexual characteristics such as the growth of hair and voice change), and sexual excitement and maturation.

- *Prostate gland.* Produces a milky alkaline substance known as semen. In the prostate the sperm are mixed with the semen to give them greater mobility.

- *Scrotum.* The sac of skin located just below the penis, in which the testes and epididymis are located.

- *Testes.* The two oval sex glands, suspended in the scrotum, that produce sperm. Sperm are the gene cells that fertilize the ova. They are equipped with a tail-like structure that enables them to move about by a swimming motion. After being ejaculated from the penis into the vagina, sperm attempt to swim through the cervix into the uterus and into the fallopian tubes, where fertilization takes place. If one penetrates an egg, conception occurs. Although the testes regularly produce millions of sperm, the odds against any particular sperm penetrating an egg are enormous. The testes also produce testosterone, the male hormone that affects other aspects of sexual development.

- *Ureter.* A canal connecting each of the kidneys with the bladder.

- *Urethra.* A canal that connects the bladder with the opening of the penis. It is also the path taken by the preseminal fluid and sperm during ejaculation.

- *Vas deferens.* A pair of tubes that lead from the epididymis up to the prostate. They carry the sperm when the male is sexually aroused and about to ejaculate.

When Does Puberty Start?

Is the beginning of adolescence marked by any one physiological event? The sequence of bodily changes in puberty is surprisingly constant. This holds true whether puberty starts early or late and regardless of the culture in which the child is reared. Table 11.2 lists the sequences of physiological change.

TABLE 11.2 THE SEQUENCE OF PHYSIOLOGICAL CHANGE IN MALES AND FEMALES

Females

- Change in hormonal balance
- The beginning of rapid skeletal growth
- The beginning of breast development
- The appearance of straight, pigmented pubic hair
- The appearance of curly, pigmented pubic hair
- Menarche (first menstruation)
- Maximum growth spurt (when growth is at its fastest rate)
- The appearance of hair on the forearms and underarms

Males

- Change in hormonal balance
- The beginning of skeletal growth
- The enlargement of the genitals
- The appearance of straight pigmented pubic hair
- Early voice changes (voice "cracks")
- First ejaculations (wet dreams, nocturnal emissions)
- The appearance of kinky, pigmented pubic hair
- Maximum growth spurt
- The appearance of downy facial hair
- The appearance of hair on the chest and underarms
- Late voice change (the voice deepens)
- Coarse, pigmented facial hair

Note: For more on these physiological changes, see Muuss (1996).

Hormonal balance One of the triggering mechanisms of puberty that may be used to indicate the onset of adolescence.

Menarche Onset of menstruation.

Which of these physical events in the life of the adolescent might we choose as the actual beginning of puberty? Change in **hormonal balance** is first, but its beginning is difficult to pinpoint. Skeletal growth, genital growth, pubic hair, breast development, voice change, growth spurt—all are inconvenient to measure. **Menarche** has been suggested as the major turning point for girls, but many women do not recall menarche as a particularly significant event. Hormonal changes actually precede menarche by about two years, or as early as eight or nine years of age. Sometimes the first ejaculation is suggested as the beginning of adolescent puberty for males, but this too is often a little-remembered (and possibly repressed) event.

Despite the fact that puberty is primarily thought of as a physical change in an adolescent, the psychological impact can be significant (Dorn & others, 1999; Kosan, 2000). This is especially true with menstruation. Even in these "enlightened" times, too many girls experience menarche without being properly prepared. As a result, an event in a young girl's life that should be remembered as the exciting, positive beginning of the transition to adulthood is instead viewed as a negative, sometimes frightening, experience. Research suggests that better preparation for first menstruation results in more positive attitudes about it (Masters & others, 1995). The same is no doubt also the case for a male's first ejaculation. Accurate and accessible information about the changes our bodies undergo benefits adolescents for whom physical changes often lead to sexual activity (Bingham & Crockett, 1996).

Given our understanding of the physiology of adolescents and differences in individual psychology and culture, we would have to conclude that no single event but, rather, a complex set of events marks the onset of puberty, a process whose effects may be sudden or gradual. Thus biology alone cannot give us a definition of adolescence; we will need to include psychological and social factors to achieve that.

The Effects of Timing on Puberty

In a general sense, the onset of puberty affects all adolescents in the same way. However, the age at which these changes begin has some very specific effects on the adolescent's life. (The photograph in figure 11.4, taken in 1914, illustrates how 14-year-old adolescents can differ greatly in their stage of physiological development—and did so even many years ago!)

In this section, eight adolescents (four females and four males) are compared to illustrate the differences that often occur among children even though they are all in the **normal range of development.** Each adolescent is 14 years old. The first female and male are early maturers, the second are average maturers, and the third are late maturers. They all fall within the typical range of all adolescents.

The Early-Maturing Female: Ann

At 5 feet 5 inches and 130 pounds, Ann is considerably bigger than her age-mates. Her growth accelerated when she was 8 years old, and by the time she was 10½, her **maximum growth spurt** crested. She is still growing taller but at a slower rate. Her motor development (coordination and strength) had its greatest rate of increase two years ago. She is stronger than her age-mates, but her strength and coordination have reached their maximum.

She started menstruating three years ago, at age 11, and her breasts are already in the secondary (adult) stage. Her pubic and underarm hair are also at an adult stage. She has clearly entered a period in which the **maturation** process is accelerated.

The Average-Maturing Female: Beth

Although Beth is also 14, she is different in almost every way from Ann. She represents the typical adolescent today in the sense of being average in her measurements

Normal range of development The stages of pubertal change occur at times that are within the normal range of occurrence.

Maximum growth spurt The period of adolescence when physical growth is at its fastest.

Maturation The process of physical and mental development due to physiology.

A Sociocultural View — Culture and the Imaginary Audience

" 'Chin, chong, chin, chong, ah so! Yellow-face, can you see out of those eyes?!' Every day for nearly one year, I heard those words as I rode the bus to middle school. I was 11 years old in the seventh grade."

This experience was related by a young Korean girl. At that time she believed that she must have done something to deserve such anger. She experienced immense humiliation and pain. She wanted to be like the other children. "With the onset of puberty, my body began to change, and I did not want to change into something even more different from the other girls." Because she could not change her slanted eyes or her skin color, she decided she must learn to speak perfect English.

When she was 11, this young woman worked hard on her English to please an imaginary audience—all those peers whom she imagined were watching her every move. By the time she was 14, their opinion became much less important to her, and she began to feel pride in her ethnic identity.

Phinney (1996) has found that ethnic identity development has stages that parallel those of Marcia's ego statuses in adolescents: a combined foreclosure-diffusion stage in which teenagers had not explored their ethnic identity yet; ethnic identity search/moratorium; and ethnic identity achievement. This study found that the greater a teen's ethnic identity achievement, the higher was her or his self-esteem. In an interesting series of studies, Rotheram-Borus (1993) found that in an integrated school, biculturalism (identification with American culture and with the ethnic background of their parents) was common (44–45 percent). In a school with high cross-ethnic tension, however, most students (over 70 percent) were most strongly committed to the ethnic identity of their parents. Ethnicity, then, seems to become a more powerful conditioner of one's identity if one experiences strong ethnic tension in one's surroundings.

and physical change. It is clear that from the standpoint of personality and behavior, no "average" adolescent exists.

Beth is 5 feet 3 inches tall and weighs 120 pounds. She reached her maximum growth spurt two years ago and is also starting to slow down. She is presently at the peak of her motor development.

Her breasts are at the primary breast stage; she is beginning to need a bra, or thinks she does. She started menstruating two years ago. She has adult pubic hair, and her underarm hair is beginning to appear.

The Late-Maturing Female: Cathy

Cathy is at the lower end of the normal range of physical development for a 14-year-old girl. She is only 4 feet 8 inches tall, weighs 100 pounds, and is just beginning her growth spurt. She is not too happy about this; she feels that the other girls have advantages in relationships with boys.

Cathy's breasts are at the bud stage; her nipples and encircling areolae are beginning to protrude, but she is otherwise flat-chested. She has just begun menstruation. Pubic hair growth has started, but as yet no hair has appeared under her arms.

The Early-Maturing Male: Al

Al finds that at 5 feet 8 inches tall, he towers over his 14-year-old friends. He reached his maximum growth spurt approximately two years ago and weighs 150 pounds. He is now about two years before the peak of his motor development. His coordination and strength are rapidly increasing, but contrary to the popular myth he is not growing clumsier.

As adolescents reach their peak of motor development, they usually handle their bodies better, although adults expect them to have numerous accidents. It is true that when one's arms grow an inch longer in less than a year, one's hand-eye coordination suffers somewhat. However, the idea of the gangling, inept adolescent is more myth than fact.

Al's sexual development is also well ahead of that of his age-mates. He already has adult pubic hair, and hair has started to grow on his chest and underarms. He began having nocturnal emissions almost two years ago, and since then the size of his genitals has increased almost 100 percent.

The Average-Maturing Male: Bob

Interestingly, Bob is exactly the same height as his "average" female counterpart, Beth, at 5 feet 3 inches tall. At 130 pounds, he outweighs her by 10 pounds. He is currently in the midst of his maximum growth spurt and is four years away from reaching the peak of his coordination and strength.

Figure 11.4

Comparison of male and female growth (King, 1914).

Dealing with Early or Late Development

Petersen and others (1988) found an increased risk of sexual abuse for the early-maturing female. Significantly early or late development has been linked to depression and eating disorders in both boys and girls (Rierdan & others, 1988), so it is important for practitioners working with adolescents to be aware of negative reactions to their physical change (or lack of it). If you know a teen who is significantly early or late in body development, be on the lookout for psychological problems. If you find evidence of such problems, make arrangements for the youth to have access to appropriate professional attention.

On the other hand, you should understand that "normal" covers a wide band of developmental time. We should help teens who "hate" their bodies because they are not perfectly average to be more accepting. Finally, if you do feel there is a problem, say nothing to the teen until you have an experienced person's advice on the best course of action.

Three books that provide additional information are: (1) Judy Blume's *Are you there, God? It's me, Margaret.* New York: Bradbury. Although written for teens, this book has a wealth of insights into pubertal change, at least for females. (2) R. H. Curtis' *Mind and mood: Understanding and controlling your emotions.* New York: Scribner's. According to Curtis, knowing more about emotions and how they affect the body can help in understanding and controlling them. (3) McCoy and Wibbelsman's *The teenage body book.* Los Angeles, CA: The Body Press. An excellent reference book for teenagers and those who work with them.

Secular trend The phenomenon (in recent centuries) of adolescents entering puberty sooner and growing taller and heavier.

Being a late maturer can often be a source of derision.

His sexual development began about a year ago with the start of nocturnal emissions, and he is just now starting to grow pubic hair. As yet he has no hair on his chest or under his arms. However, his genitals have reached 80 percent of their adult size.

The Late-Maturing Male: Chuck

Chuck is also similar in stature to his counterpart, Cathy. They are both 4 feet 8 inches tall, although at 90 pounds, Chuck is 10 pounds lighter than Cathy. He is a year and a half away from his maximum growth spurt and must wait six years before his motor development will peak.

Chuck's sexual development is also lagging behind those of the other two boys. His genitals are 50 percent larger than they were two years ago, but as yet he has no pubic, chest, or underarm hair. He has not yet experienced nocturnal emissions, although these are about to begin.

The preceding descriptions illustrate the great variability in adolescent growth and in adolescent responses to growth. Keep in mind, however, that self-image and peer relationships are not entirely determined by physique. "Average-sized" adolescents do not always lead a charmed life, and many late and early maturers are quite comfortable with themselves.

The Secular Trend

The average teenagers 100 years ago were physically similar in most ways to Cathy and Chuck, the late maturers described above. This fact is part of the phenomenon called the **secular trend.** The secular trend refers to the decreasing age of the onset of puberty, including a significant drop in the average age at which females in a particular country reach menarche. Earlier puberty affects other developmental factors such as sexual attraction (Alsaker, 1996; McClintock & Herdt, 1996). In Western countries, the average age of menarche has declined about three months per decade over the past hundred years. In the United States, 17 was the average age in the late eighteenth and early nineteenth centuries. By the beginning of the twentieth century, it was 14.5.

Today the average age of menarche is 12.5 years, about the same as it was in 1955. For white girls the average age is 12.9, for African-Americans, 12.2 (Kaplowitz, 2000). Most researchers feel that improved nutrition, sanitation, and health care are responsible for the trend, and that we are now at a period of leveling off. There is some evidence that breast development is continuing to occur earlier, however, and that this places even more stress on early maturers. For example, premature development of breasts may make young teens sex objects. Suspected causes for earlier occurrence of these aspects of puberty are:

- Lack of exercise—obesity can promote hormone production.

- More fat in diet—same result.

- Presence of hormone—like chemicals in milk and meat (although the evidence for this is scanty (Kaplowitz, 2000).

The findings of the Dorn and associates (1999) study found that girls misreport the onset of menarche by as much as several months. This suggests that girls experience menarche as a series of developmental experiences rather than a single event. Studies of female athletes and dancers have shown that a lack of fat can delay menarche or can stop menstruation after it has begun. Childhood conflict also influences pubertal timing (Kim & others, 1997). In their study of female athletes, Malina and associates (1998) found that size of family affects menarche. They learned that girls with larger families had later menarche than girls with small families. The delay averaged 2.3 months for each additional sibling in the girls' families. The authors did not offer an explanation for why this should be so. Muscari and associates (1998) found no relationship between the age of menarche of the girls they studied and the age of menarche of their mothers.

Christy Henrich, a gymnast who died of anorexia.

Anorexia nervosa
A syndrome of self-starvation that mainly affects adolescent and young adult females.

Figure 11.5 details the age ranges considered normal for development. Adolescents who experience these changes earlier or later may have no medical problem, but consulting a doctor is probably a good idea. If a glandular imbalance exists, the doctor can usually remedy the problem with little difficulty.

In summary, we may say that the vast majority of human bodies proceed toward maturity in the same way, but that in the last few centuries the timing of the process in females has changed radically. Although timing is affected mainly by biology, psychological and social forces clearly influence it, too. An example of the biological consequences of psychological and social factors is the eating disorder.

Body Image and Eating Disorders

Although still rather rare, eating disorders are so serious (about one-third of those who develop an eating disorder die) it is necessary to review what we know about them here. Eating disorders are the third most common chronic condition among adolescents. The two main types, anorexia and bulimia nervosa, have in common the profound concern about shape and weight (Pilote, 1998). While some symptoms are unique to one disorder, there are numerous parallels between anorexia and bulimia.

Gender, puberty, weight, and age all impact body image and eating behaviors in adolescents. Young boys believe that their sexual appeal is based on their ability to develop their bodies. Postpubertal males tend to have high self-esteem and are confident in their ability to control their own lives. On the other hand, postmenarcheal females often experience dissatisfaction with their new size and shape. This dissatisfaction can lead to feelings of inadequacy, loss of control, and decreased self-esteem, which are all risk factors for eating disorders (O'Dea & Abraham, 1999).

Anorexia nervosa is a syndrome of self-starvation that mainly affects adolescent and young adult females, who account for 95 percent of the known cases. Professionals suspect that many males may also be victims (e.g., those who must maintain a low weight for sports), but their illness is covered up (O'Dea & Abraham, 1999). "The essential features of anorexia nervosa are that the individual refuses to maintain a minimally normal body weight, is intensely afraid of gaining weight, and exhibits significant disturbance in the perception of the shape or size of his or her body. In addition, post menarcheal females with this disorder are amenorrhiec. (The term *anorexia* is a misnomer because loss of appetite is rare.)" (American Psychiatric Association, 1994.)

Health professionals have seen an alarming rise in the incidence of this disorder among young women in the last 15 to 20 years. Whether anorexia nervosa has actually increased or whether it is now being more readily recognized has yet to be determined.

Figure 11.5

Normal age ranges of puberty.

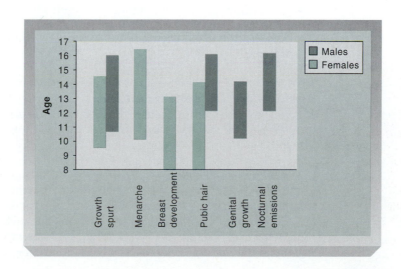

According to the DSM-IV (1996), the specific criteria for anorexia nervosa are the following:

- Refusal to maintain body weight at or above a minimally normal weight for age and height (e.g., weight loss leading to maintenance of body weight less than 85 percent of that expected; or failure to make expected weight gain during period of growth, leading to body weight less than 85 percent of that expected).

- Intense fear of gaining weight or becoming fat, even though underweight.

- Disturbance in the way in which one's body weight or shape is experienced, undue influence of body weight or shape on self-evaluation, or denial of the seriousness of the current low body weight.

- In postmenarcheal females, amenorrhea, i.e., the absence of at least three consecutive menstrual cycles. (A woman is considered to have amenorrhea if her periods occur only following hormone, e.g., estrogen, administration.)

Bulimia nervosa This disorder is characterized by "episodic binge eating accompanied by an awareness that the eating pattern is abnormal, fear of not being able to stop eating voluntarily, and depressed mood and self-deprecating thoughts following the eating binges."

Bulimia nervosa is a disorder related to anorexia nervosa and sometimes combined with it. It is characterized by "binge eating and inappropriate compensatory methods to prevent weight gain. In addition, the self-evaluation of individuals with bulimia nervosa is excessively influenced by body shape and weight" (American Psychiatric Association, 1996).

Bulimia has been observed in women above or below weight, as well as in those who are normal. According to the DSM-IV (1996), the specific criteria of bulimia are the following:

- Recurrent episodes of binge eating. An episode of binge eating is characterized by both of the following:

    eating, in a discrete period of time (e.g., within any 2-hour period), an amount of food that is definitely larger than most people would eat during a similar period of time and under similar circumstances.

- A sense of lack of control over eating during the episode (e.g., a feeling that one cannot stop eating or control what or how much one is eating).

- Recurrent inappropriate compensatory behavior in order to prevent weight gain, such as self-induced vomiting; misuse of laxatives, diuretics, enemas, or other medications; fasting; or excessive exercise.

- The binge eating and inappropriate compensatory behaviors both occur, on average, at least twice a week for 3 months.

- Self-evaluation is unduly influenced by body shape and weight.

- The disturbance does not occur exclusively during episodes of anorexia nervosa.

Anorectics and bulimics share emotional and behavioral traits, despite their clinical differences. The most characteristic symptoms specific to these disorders are the preoccupation with food and the persistent determination to be slim, rather than the behaviors that result from that choice (Cauffman & Steinberg, 1996).

The Athletic Body and Eating Disorders At the age of 15, gymnast Christy Henrich narrowly missed making the United States Olympic team. Following the trials, a judge told Christy that she should lose a few pounds—at the time, Christy was 4 feet 10 inches and weighed 90 pounds! Comments such as these led to Christy having anorexia and bulimia. At one point Christy's weight was down to 47 pounds. In July 1994, as her parents and coach were helping her recover, Christy died of multiple organ failure at the age of 22. Her coach claims that gymnastics and its emphasis on slimness are not responsible for Christy's illness and death. He claims her intense drive to win contributed to her eating disorder. The gymnastic training system encourages young female athletes to keep their weight down, and many gymnasts live on diets of fruits, laxatives, and painkillers. In 1976 the average age of a U.S. gymnast was 18, with an average weight of 106 pounds. In 1992, the average age of a U.S. gymnast was 16, with an average weight of 83 pounds—a drop of 23 pounds! Cathy Rigby, a former gymnast who won a gold medal at the 1968 Olympics, fought a 12-year battle with anorexia and bulimia. Now recovering from her illness, Cathy states that gymnasts are trained to be slim through fear, guilt, and intimidation (Ryan, 1995). This trend appears to continue. In a recent study of college athletes, Picard (1999) found that females involved in sports that stress a lean figure, place restrictions on weight, and compete at higher levels demonstrated more symptoms of disordered eating and were at higher risk for developing an eating disorder.

The Role of Stress

The relationship between stress and emotional illness is well-established. Therefore it is important to know to what extent adolescents feel that their lives are stressful. The most reliable source for this information is the Higher Education Research Institute, which has been studying this question for the last 35 years (Reisberg, 2000). Of the over 260,000 students interviewed at 462 colleges by the Institute, 30 percent say they feel "overwhelmed by all I have to do." This is up from 16 percent in 1985. The concern is almost twice as great among women (39 percent) than among men (20 percent). A significant part of this pressure comes from the need to work. In 1982, 16 percent of entering freshmen felt they would have to get a full-time job while attending college; in 1999, that figure had risen to 25 percent. More women than men (45 percent to 33 percent) believed that they would need to work at least part-time to pay for college.

Many adolescents who find that sports teams at schools are not available to them are looking for alternatives to sitting on the couch and watching television. As a result, fitness programs for teens are becoming popular in places such as the YMCA. The goal of the program is to help teens exercise on a regular basis to improve their overall level of fitness (Anderson, 1998).

Other teens are turning to long hours at work as a means of spending their high level of energy, not always with good results. Teenagers are working more and more, and as a result, they are getting injured more frequently on the job. Over two-fifths of their occupational fatalities occur when they are engaged in work prohibited by child labor laws (Wright, 2000). For children under 18, national laws prohibit:

- driving a motor vehicle

- operating power-driven equipment

- working in hazardous jobs such as wrecking, roofing, mining, excavating, demolition, logging, or saw milling

- working in meat packing or slaughtering.

  In addition, children under 16 may not:

- bake or cook

- work on a ladder or scaffold

- load or unload trucks, railroad cars, or conveyors

- work in a warehouse

- work in construction, building, or manufacturing.

Guided Review

9. Puberty is a relatively abrupt and qualitatively different set of physical changes in boys and girls that usually occurs at the beginning of the _____ years.
10. Although there is a rather wide normal range of development as relates to the onset of puberty, early- or late-maturing children can be affected socially and _____ .
11. _____ -maturing boys are often peer group leaders.
12. One hundred years ago the average-maturing girl was physically much like the late-maturing girl today. This phenomenon is called the _____ _____ .
13. _____ _____ is a syndrome of self-starvation characterized, in part, by an intense fear of becoming obese, disturbance of body image, and significant weight loss.

Cognitive Development

I was about 12 when I discovered that you could create a whole new world just in your head! I don't know why I hadn't thought about it before, but the idea excited me terrifically. I started lying in bed on Saturday mornings till 11 or 12 o'clock, making up "my secret world." I went to fabulous places. I met friends who really liked me and treated me great. And of course I fell in love with this guy like you wouldn't believe! (Susan Klein, an eighth-grade student.)

Adolescence is a complex process of growth and change (see, for example, Rushton & Ankney, 1997). Because biological and social changes are the focus of attention, changes in the young adolescent's ability to think often go unnoticed. Yet growth spurts in the parietal and frontal lobes of the brain, as well as subcortical regions, make possible tremendous changes in the quality of a teenager's thinking. It has recently been discovered (Seltz, 2000) that there are actually two growth spurts, one at around 12 and 13 and a second in the later teen years. It is during early and middle adolescence that thinking ability reaches Piaget's fourth and last level—the level of abstract thought (see chapter 2). To understand how abstract thought develops, we have to know more about cognition itself.

Variables in Cognitive Development: Piaget

Let us pause to review Jean Piaget's theory (described in chapter 2). He argued that the ability to think develops in four stages:

- The sensorimotor stage (birth to 2 years), in which the child learns from its interactions with the world.

- The preoperational stage (2 to 7 years), in which behaviors such as picking up a can are gradually internalized so that they can be manipulated in the mind.

- The concrete operational stage (7 to 11 years), in which actions can be manipulated mentally, but only with things. For example, a child of 8 is able to anticipate what is going to happen if a can is thrown across the room without actually having to do so.

- The formal operational stage (11 years +), in which groups of concrete operations are combined to become formal operations. For example, the adolescent comes to understand democracy by combining concepts such as putting a ballot in a box and hearing that the Senate voted to give money for the homeless. This is the stage of abstract thought development.

Answers

Young teens compete at a chess tournament.

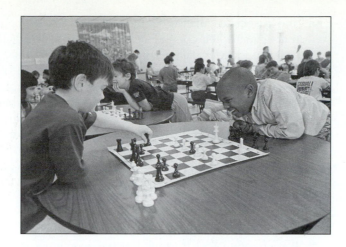

We are like other animals, especially the primates, in many ways. They, too, can make plans, can cooperate in groups, and may well have simple language systems. But the ability to perform formal operations is what truly separates us (although we cannot say that all humans reach this stage, either). Piaget's conception of the formal operation is a remarkable contribution to psychology.

It was also Piaget who first noted the strong tendency of early adolescents toward democratic values because of this new thinking capacity. This is the age at which youths first become committed to the idea that participants in a group may change the rules of a game, but once agreed on, all must follow the new rules. This tendency, he believes, is universal; all teenagers throughout the world develop this value.

Having considered Piaget's ideas about adolescent cognition in some detail earlier in this book, let us turn now to a review of the findings of those researchers who have been diligently following him.

Culture and gender can also influence cognitive development. Piaget's theory seems to assume that the ideal person at the end point of cognitive development resembles a Swiss scientist. Most theorists focus on an ideal end point for development that, not too surprisingly, ascribes their own valued qualities to maturity.

Piaget (1973) acknowledged that his description of the end point might not apply to all cultures, since evidence had showed cultural variation. If one stresses the influence of context (sociocultural and individual) on development as Vygotsky (1978) and Barbara Rogoff (1990) do, then one sees multiple directions for development rather than only one ideal end point. For example, it may well be that for some agricultural societies, sophisticated development of the concrete operational stage would be far more useful than minimal formal operational thinking. That is, an understanding of the complicated workings of a machine may be concrete, but that does not make that type of thinking inferior to another person's ability to do formal operations. Thus believing that the formal operations stage is always superior would be intellectual snobbism.

Gender also plays a role in the definition of formal operations. Gilligan (1982) said that most theories of development define the end point of development as being male only, and that they overlook alternatives that more closely fit the mature female. She believed that if the definition of maturity changes, so does the entire account of development. Using men as the model of development, independence and separation are seen as the goals of development. But if women are used as the models, relationship with others or interdependence are the goals of development. Gilligan contends that this gender difference also leads to distinctions in the development of thinking about morality.

In a rare study that investigated all three aspects of the biopsychosocial approach, Casey and associates (1997) sought to explain the superiority of males on the Mathematics Scholastic Aptitude Test (SAT-M). Some scholars have argued that this perennial result is due to a male genetic advantage in doing math, whereas others have attributed it to female math anxiety, which they learn early in life. Casey and associates measured the relationships among sex and spatial skills (innate traits), math self-confidence and geometry knowledge (psychological variables), and math anxiety (a socially induced trait).

(It should be noted that the sources of each of these variables are themselves biopsychosocial, at least to some degree.) Through a complex statistical technique known as path analysis, the researchers established that attitudinal variables accounted for only 36 percent of the variation in SAT-M scores, and spatial skills accounted for 64 percent. This finding does not mean that the greater math ability of boys is inevitable, however. Numerous approaches to the difference might be taken. For example, we could encourage girls to get more experience playing with toys and games and in sports that require a high degree of spatial skill.

Adolescent Egocentrism

Parents often feel frustrated at the seemingly irrational attitudes and behaviors of their adolescent children. One explanation is the reemergence of a pattern of thought that marked early childhood, egocentrism. **Adolescent egocentrism,** a term coined by Elkind (1978), refers to adolescents' tendency to exaggerate the importance, uniqueness, and severity of social and emotional experiences. Their love is greater than anything their parents have experienced. Their suffering is more painful and unjust than anyone else's. Their friendships are most sacred. Their clothes are the worst or the best. Developmentally speaking, adolescent egocentrism seems to peak around the age of 13 (Elkind & Bowen, 1979), followed by a gradual and sometimes painful decline.

Elkind sees two components to this egocentrism. First, teenagers tend to create an **imaginary audience** (Montgomery & others, 1996; Vartanian, 1997; Rycek & others, 1999). They feel they are on center stage, and the rest of the world is constantly scrutinizing their behavior and physical appearance. This accounts for some of the apparently irrational mood swings in adolescents. The mirror may produce an elated, confident teenager ready to make an appearance. Then one pimple on the nose can be cause for staying inside the house for days. In fact, school phobia can become acute during early adolescence because of concerns over appearance.

The second component of egocentrism is the **personal fable.** This refers to adolescents' tendency to think of themselves in heroic or mythical terms (Siegel & Shaughnessy, 1995; Vartanian, 1997). The result is that they exaggerate their own abilities and their invincibility. This type of mythic creation on the part of an adolescent can sometimes lead to increased risk-taking, such as drug use, dangerous driving, and disregard for the possible consequences of sexual behavior. Many teenagers simply can't imagine an unhappy ending to their own special story.

Another explanation for these seemingly irrational behaviors and attitudes may be found in the adolescent brain. In a recent study conducted by Yurgelun-Todd (1998), adults and adolescents were shown photos depicting fear. The adults accurately identified the emotion; however, most adolescents incorrectly identified the pictured emotion. Their inaccurate responses included emotions such as anger and worry. After studying brain scans of the teens and adults, Yurgelun-Todd found that the amygdala (the part of the brain which is responsible for emotional responses) played a large role in the teens' reactions. In contrast, the prefrontal cortex (the part of the brain that is responsible for reason and thought) played a large role in the adults' responses. These differences between the adolescent and adult brain may explain why teens are often seen to be so emotional.

Critical Thinking

Although we discussed critical thinking at some length in chapter 9, we should make a number of points about its role in adolescence. The distinction between convergent and divergent thinking is helpful here, because critical thinking is made up of these two abilities.

All morality consists in a system of rules, and the essence of all morality is . . . in the respect which the individual acquires for these rules.

Jean Piaget

Adolescent egocentrism The reversion to the self-centered thinking patterns of childhood that sometimes occurs in the teen years.

Imaginary audience Adolescents' perception that the world is constantly scrutinizing their behavior and physical appearance.

Personal fable Adolescents' tendency to think of themselves in heroic or mythical terms.

Young teenagers today are being forced to make decisions that earlier generations didn't have to make until they were older and more mature, and today's teenagers are not getting much support and guidance.

David Elkind

Convergent thinking
Thinking used to find one correct answer.

Convergent thinking is used when we solve a problem by following a series of steps that close in on the correct answer. For example, if we were to ask you to answer the question, "How much is 286 times 469?" you probably could not produce it immediately. However, if you used a pencil and paper or a calculator, you would almost certainly converge on the same answer as most others trying to solve the problem. Only one answer is correct. Critical thinking uses convergent thinking.

Divergent thinking, on the other hand, is just the opposite. This is the type of thinking used when the problem to be solved has many possible answers. For

Divergent thinking Thinking used when a problem to be solved has many possible answers.

Many students enjoy divergent thinking more than convergent thinking.

example, what are all the things that would be different if it were to rain up instead of down?

Other divergent questions are "What would happen if we had no thumbs?" and "What should we do to prevent ice buildup from snapping telephone lines?" Divergent thinking can be right or wrong, too, but considerably greater leeway exists for personal opinion than with convergent thinking. Not all divergent thinking is creative, but it is more likely to produce a creative concept. To be a good critical thinker, analyzing statements accurately is not enough. Often you will need to think divergently to understand the possibilities and the implications of those statements, too.

In the next section, we make a distinction between critical and creative thinking, but it is important that we not make too great a distinction. Paul (1987) describes this concern well:

> Just as it is misleading to talk of developing a student's capacity to think critically without facing the problem of cultivating the student's rational passions—the necessary driving force behind the rational use of all critical

---

An Informed VIEW

What's Your View: Should Critical Thinking about Interpersonal Problems Be Taught in Our Schools?

Critical thinking is of tremendous importance to teens, as they learn to cope with the changes that life brings. One arena in which this skill is of great usefulness is in working out interpersonal problems. Here, too, we may easily see how an understanding of the concept of bidirectionality (see the section on contextualism in chapter 1) also plays a role. The roots of interpersonal problems almost always involve bidirectional causes. Most teens are well aware of how the actions of others affect them, but sometimes fail to see how their own actions may bring about negative reactions. Here is where following the five phases of critical thinking comes in. Practicing this procedure can greatly alleviate some of the hurt feelings and misunderstandings that inevitably occur.

Many educators agree that teaching critical thinking as it applies to school subjects is appropriate, but cannot agree that they should also apply these lessons to real-life teen problems. If you were a secondary teacher (or counselor or administrator), would you include adolescent interpersonal relations in your teaching of critical thinking? What's your view?

If you would like to have a more informed opinion on this issue, you might want to read one of the articles on the subject referenced in chapter 9.

You might also wish to learn more about it by going to our web site at http://www.mhhe.com/dacey5.

An Applied View

Video Games and Cognitive Development

The emergence of video games as a popular pastime among children and adolescents in the late 1970s created a firestorm of controversy. Parents and educators were warned that there may be detrimental consequences to prolonged exposure.

Research from the early 1990s offers a different perception of this form of play. Strong evidence indicates that just as various forms of play in all societies prepare children for the demands of adulthood, video games are an important cultural artifact to teach skills that relate to the mastery of computer technology. Video games may also enhance hand-eye coordination, decisionmaking, numerical concepts, and the ability to follow directions. Additionally, video games have been shown to improve divided attention in both expert and novice video game players.

In 1998 the video game industry topped $6.3 billion. Despite rating systems and parental disapproval, adolescents find violent video games to be highly accessible. Most of the games are used on home computer systems. Research has found that parents prefer not to engage in dialogue with their teens regarding the violent and aggressive nature of these games (Leland, 1998). Recent research by Wiegman and van Schie (1998) found that children, especially boys, who favored aggressive video games showed more aggression and less prosocial behavior. Also, children with lower intelligence were more likely to play aggressive video games. However, it cannot be overlooked that even violent and aggressive video games provide opportunities for visualization and learning through analysis of clues (Leland, 1998).

---

thinking skills—so too it is misleading to talk of developing a student's ability to think critically as something separate from the student's ability to think creatively. . . . The imagination and its creative powers are continually called forth (p. 143).

Creative Thinking

This is the story about a very curious cat named Kat. One day Kat was wandering in the woods where he came upon a big house made of fish. Without thinking, he ate much of that house. The next morning when he woke up he had grown considerably larger. Even as he walked down the street he was getting bigger. Finally he got bigger than any building ever made. He walked up to the Empire State Building in New York City and accidentally crushed it. The people had to think of a way to stop him, so they made this great iron box which made the cat curious. He finally got inside it, but it was too heavy to get him out of again. There he lived for the rest of his life. But he was still curious until his death, which was 6,820,000 years later. They buried him in the state of Rhode Island, and I mean the whole state (Ralph Titus, a seventh-grade student).

The restless imagination, the daring exaggeration, the disdain for triteness that this story demonstrates—all are signs that its young author has great creative potential. With the right kind of encouragement, with the considerable knowledge we now have about how to foster creativity, this boy could develop his talents to his own and society's great benefit (Dacey, 1989a and c, 1998; Dacey & Lennon, 1998; Esquivel, 1995). Creative thinking appears to have many elements—divergent thinking, fluency, flexibility, originality, remote associations. We will look more closely at these elements when we get to adult creativity later in this book, but one element that seems to be of special importance in adolescence is the use of metaphor.

Creativity, Giftedness, and the IQ

As Feldman (1979; 1994) has pointed out, many studies of "giftedness" have been conducted, but only a few of exceptionally creative, highly productive youths have been undertaken. This is a serious omission because, as you will see later in this book, adolescence is a sensitive period in the growth of creative ability. Feldman believes that this unfortunate situation is mainly the fault of "the foremost figure in

Many gifted teens have the need to express their feelings artistically.

the study of the gifted," Lewis M. Terman. Terman (1925) was well known for his research on 1,000 California children whose IQs in the early 1920s were 135 or higher. Terman believed these children to be the "geniuses" of the future, a label he kept for them as he studied their development over the decades. His was a powerful investigation and has been followed by scholars and popular writers alike.

Precisely because of the notoriety of this research, Feldman argues, we have come to accept a numerical definition of genius (an IQ above 135), and a somewhat low one at that. Feldman notes that the *Encyclopedia Britannica* now differentiates two basic definitions of genius: the numerical one fostered by Terman; and the concept first described by Sir Francis Galton (1870, 1879): "creative ability of an exceptionally high order as demonstrated by actual achievement."

Precociousness The ability to do what others are able to do, but at a younger age.

Prodigiousness The ability to do qualitatively better than the rest of us are able to do; such a person is referred to as a prodigy.

Feldman says that genius, as defined by IQ, really only refers to **precociousness** —doing what others are able to do, but at a younger age. **Prodigiousness** (as in child prodigy), on the other hand, refers to someone who is qualitatively higher in ability from the rest of us. This is different from simply being able to do things sooner. Further, prodigiousness calls for a rare matching of high talent and an environment that is ready and open to creativity. If such youthful prodigies as Mozart in music or Bobby Fischer in chess had been born 2,000 years earlier, they may well have grown up to be much more ordinary. In fact, if Einstein had been born 50 years earlier, he might have done nothing special—particularly because he did not even speak well until he was five!

So if prodigies are more than just quicker at learning, what is it that truly distinguishes them? On the basis of his intensive study of three prodigies, Feldman states that

Child prodigies are distinguished by the passion with which they pursue their interests. Here we see the young Wolfgang Amadeus Mozart performing for a group of admiring adults. He was not merely precocious— able to perform at levels typical of older children; he was prodigious—able, at a young age, to write music that professional musicians still perform.

Perhaps the most striking quality in the children in our study as well as other cases is the passion with which excellence is pursued. Commitment and tenacity and joy in achievement are perhaps the best signs that a coincidence has occurred among child, field, and moment in evolutionary time. No event is more likely to predict that a truly remarkable, creative contribution will eventually occur (1979, p. 351).

In summary, critical and creative thinking are similar in that they both employ convergent and divergent production. The main difference between them is that critical thinking aims at the correct assessment of existing ideas, whereas creativity is more aimed at the invention and discovery of new ideas. Although each requires a certain amount of intelligence, creativity also depends on such traits as metaphorical thinking and an independent personality.

Robert Sternberg (2000a and b) said the intelligent person can recall, analyze, and use knowledge, whereas the creative person goes beyond existing knowledge and the wise person probes inside knowledge and understands the meaning of what is known (see chapter 18). It should be noted that these conclusions appear to hold true not only for adolescence, but for all periods of the lifespan.

Mental Health Issues

A number of psychologists and psychoanalysts (most notably Freud) have suggested that having distressing, turbulent, unpredictable thoughts that in an adult would be considered pathological is normal in adolescence. This disruptive state is partly characteristic of the identity stages of confusion and moratorium. Identity confusion is sometimes typified by withdrawal from reality. Occasional distortions in time perspective can occur. Mental disturbance also often makes intimacy with another person impossible. These characteristics are also seen in the moratorium stage, but they tend to be of much shorter duration. Mental health issues are pertinent for numerous reasons including: many adult disorders originate in childhood events, childhood mental illness is common, and many of these illnesses have a poor prognosis (Barnes, 1998; Gerhardt et al., 1999).

How common and how serious are these problems? The picture is not clear. Researchers have concluded that true psychopathology (mental illness) is relatively rare during adolescence. It is impossible to determine the frequency of mental illness, however, because of current disagreements over its definition. The summary of numerous studies gives us considerable reason to believe that "adolescent turmoil," though common, does not really constitute psychopathology.

Studies do indicate that when adolescents become seriously disturbed and do not receive appropriate treatment quickly, the chances of their "growing out" of their problems are dim (James & Nims, 1996; Tolbert, 1996).

There is evidence that living in an adoptive family is less of a factor in the emotional adjustment of adoptees than the mental health of biological parents. A recent study conducted by Ge and associates (1996a) found that the hostile and antisocial behaviors sometimes displayed by adopted children were in fact related to the psychiatric disorders of their biological parents. McGue and associates (1996b) discovered that adolescents raised by adoptive parents are less well adjusted than children born to those same parents. Although adopted and birth children may be raised in the same environment, it appears that adopted children may face a more complicated transition into adolescence. McGue and associates concluded that "These findings provide further evidence of the minimal effect of common rearing on sibling psychological similarity, at least within the broadly constituted U.S. middle class" (p. 604).

Furthermore, the family environment may perpetuate adolescent depression and antisocial behavior. Pike and associates (1996) stated that responses to negativity questionnaires by parents and siblings showed significant relationship to unhealthy adolescent adjustment. Family factors were also examined by Henry and associates (1996), with regard to violent and nonviolent behaviors of adolescents. The authors concluded that whereas childhood temperament is associated with the adolescent's being convicted of primarily violent offenses, family characteristics were associated with both violent and nonviolent criminal behavior of adolescents.

Adolescent suicide represents the second leading cause of death among 15- to 19-year-olds. Fortunately, this issue is receiving increased attention, and school suicide prevention programs are being implemented throughout the United States. Dr. Keith King (in an article in the *American Academy of Pediatrics News,* February, 2000, p. 23) suggests a number of myths that seriously undercut the effectiveness of these programs:

Myth 1. Adolescent suicide is a decreasing problem in the United States. While the suicide rate for the general population has remained relatively stable since the 1950s, the suicide rate for adolescents has more than tripled since then. Presently, the suicide rate for 15- to 24-year-olds stands at 13.8 per 100,000.

Myth 2. Adolescent homicide is more common than suicide. For adolescents 15–19 years of age, suicide is the second leading cause of death, and homicide is the third leading cause of death.

Myth 3. Most adolescent suicides occur unexpectedly, without warning signs. Nine out of 10 adolescents who commit suicide give clues to others before the suicide attempt. Warning signs for adolescent suicide include:

- Depressed mood,
- Substance abuse,
- Loss of interest in once-pleasurable activities,
- Decreased activity level,
- Decreased attention,
- Distractability,
- Isolation,
- Withdrawing from others,
- Sleep changes,
- Appetite changes,
- Morbid ideation (e.g., thinking about death),
- Offering verbal cues ("I wish I were dead"),
- Offering written cues (notes, poems),
- Giving possessions away.

Factors that place a teenager at increased risk for suicide include:

- Having a previous suicide attempt,
- Having low self-esteem,
- Having a recent relationship breakup,
- Being impulsive,
- Being homosexual,
- Coming from an abusive home,
- Having easy access to a firearm,
- Having low grades,
- Being exposed to suicide or suicidal behavior by another person.

Myth 4. Adolescents who talk about suicide do not attempt or commit suicide. One of the most ominous warning signs of adolescent suicide involves talking repeatedly about one's own death.

Myth 5. Most adolescents who attempt suicide fully intend to die. Most suicidal adolescents do not want suicide to happen. Rather, they feel torn between wanting to end their psychological pain through death and wanting to continue living.

Myth 6. Educating teens about suicide leads to increased suicide attempts, since it provides them with ideas and methods about killing themselves. Since three-fourths of teenage students state that if they were contemplating suicide they would first turn to a friend for help, peer assistance programs have been implemented throughout the nation. Further, educational programs help students identify peers at risk and help them receive the asistance they need.

Myth 7. Adolescents cannot relate to a person who has experienced suicidal thoughts. Data from a recent survey of 16,000 high school students found that one in five students had seriously considered attempting suicide in the previous year. More than half of students had experienced thoughts about suicide at least once.

Myth 8. No difference exists between male and female adolescents regarding suicidal behavior. Adolescent females are three times more likely than adolescent males to have thought about suicide and to have attempted suicide. However, adolescent males are five times more likely to die from the suicide attempt.

Myth 9. Because female adolescents are less likely to die from a suicide attempt than males, their attempt need not be taken as seriously. One of the most powerful predictors of a completed suicide is a prior suicide attempt.

Myth 10. The most common method for adolescent suicide completion involves drug overdose. Guns are the most frequently used method for completing suicide among teens, accounting for about two-thirds of all completed suicides. Hanging is the second most common method (18 percent).

Myth 11. All adolescents who engage in suicidal behavior are mentally ill. Most adolescents who attempt suicide have no mental disorder.

Myth 12. If adolescents want to commit suicide, there's nothing anyone can do to prevent its occurrence. School professionals who are aware of the signs of suicide and of the risk factors listed above are frequently able to prevent suicides.

The transition from junior high school to high school can be a stressful time for adolescents. The stress may come from many different sources, such as peers, parents, siblings, and teachers. It is a time when more emphasis is placed on grades and academic achievement. It is also a time of increased pressure to date and experiment with cigarettes, drugs, and alcohol. Isakson and Jarvis (1999) conducted a longitudinal study of adjustment to high school. They found that the more the teen felt a sense of belonging in the school and the higher the teen's GPA, the easier the transition. This was also true for students who saw their parents as supportive.

Types of Mental Disorders

The question of what kinds of mental illness afflict adolescents has not received much attention, but interest is increasing (Reimer, 1996). Several studies (Dori & others, 1999; Haliburn, 2000; Grilo, 2000) have suggested that the prevalence of major depression and the incidence of suicide is increasing in adolescent populations, particularly among males.

Ethnic differences in depressed adolescents were examined by Greenberger and Chen (1996). They found that the ethnic variations among adolescents did not account for significant differences. However, whether the subjects were in the early or late stages of adolescent development produced more striking differences with regard to their perceived relationships with their parents. The perceived relationships accounted for more variance in depressed mood in early adolescents. Parental hostility toward teens when they were in the seventh, eighth, and ninth grades was observed by Ge and associates (1996a) as predictors of adjustment problems and depressive symptoms among these children when they were in the tenth grade. Although depression rates are about equal for boys and girls before they reach

A source on this subject is Gibson's *The butterfly ward.* New Orleans: Louisiana State University Press. This set of short stories tells what it is like to be between sanity and insanity. It is a sensitive look at the world of the mentally ill, both in and out of institutions.

puberty, after it starts, girls are about twice as likely to feel seriously depressed as boys. A detailed description of the research on adolescent suicide rates and causes is presented in chapter 19.

In conclusion, adolescence is not a time of turmoil and distress for most teens. Rates of mental disturbance among teens are very similar to rates of disturbance among adults. As you will recall, however, adolescents (and adults) are experiencing increasingly high levels of daily stress.

Guided Review

14. In exploring cognitive development, we examine Piaget's four stages of cognitive development: sensorimotor, preoperational, _____ operational, and formal operational.
15. Formal operational means that a person can form _____ mental operations.
16. Elkind presents the concept of adolescent egocentrism, which includes an _____ _____ and the personal fable.
17. Thinking skills can be separated into convergent (coming together with a single correct answer) and _____ (exploring the many possible answers to a question).
18. David Feldman claims that some children are precocious (doing what others do, but at a younger age), while other children are _____ (having a qualitatively greater ability than the rest of us).
19. _____ _____ is sometimes typified by withdrawal from reality.

CONCLUSION & SUMMARY

Defining adolescence is a complex task. Deciding when it begins and ends is even more complicated. We know that any definition must be biopsychosocial in order to be comprehensive. We know that, biologically, there is a marked increase in the flow of sex-related hormones, as well as a maximum growth spurt and the appearance of secondary sex characteristics. Psychologically, a new sense of self and the formation of the identity take shape, and cognitive changes such as formal operations, the personal fable, and the imaginary audience occur. The social world of the teen undergoes many changes, including the inauguration of new privileges and new responsibilities. These changes constitute the bare bones of a definition, but even all the information in this and the following chapter only begin to tell the whole story.

We wish that all children could complete puberty with a normal, healthy body and body image. We wish they could negotiate adolescence so successfully that they become energetic, self-confident adults.

Unfortunately, we know that this is not always the case. Some youths suffer from a negative self-concept because, although they differ from the norm only slightly in their body development, they perceive this as "catastrophic." Others deviate significantly from the norm because of some physiological problem. Of particular concern for females is our society's obsession with thinness. Taken together, the various aspects of puberty can cause the adolescent quite a bit of chagrin.

The only solution is to get some perspective on these problems. The good news is that just when they need it, most adolescents develop improved mental abilities that enable them to get a more realistic view of themselves. Cognitive development is a complex matter, one about which we understood very little before this century. Our best

evidence is that the intellect develops in stages. Contrary to earlier beliefs, thinking in childhood, adolescence, and adulthood are qualitatively different from each other. Furthermore, cognitive development has a number of other aspects: social cognition, information processing, egocentric thinking, critical thinking, creative thinking, and mental health.

How Should We Define Adolescence?

- Most experts state that the majority of adolescents are happy and productive members of their families and communities.
- Hall's interpretation of adolescent development was greatly influenced by his observation that it is a period of storm and stress.
- It is likely that youths are viewed as immature during financial depressions in order to keep them from competing with adults for

Answers

14. concrete 15. abstract 16. imaginary audience 17. divergent 18. prodigious 19. Identity confusion

scarce jobs; their maturity is seen as greater during wartime because they are needed to perform such adult tasks as soldiering and factory work.

What are the leading theories that attempt to explain adolescence?

- Anna Freud believed that the delicate balance between the superego and the id, being disrupted by puberty, causes the adolescent to regress to earlier stages of development.
- According to Erik Erikson, human life progresses through eight "psychosocial" stages, each of which is marked by a crisis and its resolution. The fifth stage applies mainly to adolescence.
- Although the ages at which one goes through each Eriksonian stage vary, the sequence of stages is fixed. Stages may overlap, however.
- John Hill's biopsychosocial theory, with its emphasis on the six factors of dependence, autonomy, sexuality, intimacy, achievement, and identity, offers the most inclusive theory of adolescence.

What are the key factors of physical development in adolescence?

- Theories of adolescence in the early twentieth century were largely based on personal bias, because little empirical data existed.
- Those who work with adolescents need complete knowledge of the reproductive systems of both sexes.
- The order of physical changes in puberty is largely predictable, but the timing and duration of these changes are not.

- The normal range in pubertal development is very broad, and includes early, on-time, and late maturers.
- The adolescent's own perception of being normal has more influence on self-esteem than objective normality.
- Maturity of appearance affects whether adolescents are treated appropriately for their age.
- Early maturing is usually a positive experience for boys but may be negative for girls.
- Late maturing is often difficult for both boys and girls.
- Two of the most disruptive problems for adolescents are the eating disorders known as anorexia and bulimia nervosa.
- Adolescent girls develop eating disorders more than any other group.
- Developmental, cultural, individual, and familial factors are associated with the development of eating disorders.
- Teens are working longer and longer hours, and this has resulted in a serious increase in injuries on the job.

How does cognition develop during the adolescent years?

- Piaget focused on the development of the cognitive structures of the intellect during childhood and adolescence.
- The infant and child pass through Piaget's first three stages: sensorimotor, preoperational, and concrete operational.
- Piaget's highest stage of cognitive development, that of formal

operations, begins to develop in early adolescence.
- Adolescents focus much attention on themselves and tend to believe that everybody is looking at them. This phenomenon is called the imaginary audience.
- Many adolescents also hold beliefs about their own uniqueness and invulnerability. This is known as the personal fable.
- Critical thinking combines both convergent thinking, in which there is only one correct answer, and divergent thinking, in which there are many possible answers to a problem.
- Effective decisionmaking, a formal operational process, is a part of critical thinking.
- Creative thinking includes divergent thinking, fluency, flexibility, originality, and remote associations.
- Conventional schooling often has a dampening effect on students' willingness to risk doing creative, metaphorical thinking.
- Criticism of genius, as defined by IQ, holds that IQ indicates only precociousness but cannot account for prodigiousness.
- The idea that those who develop mental illness during adolescence will "grow out of it" is not supported by research. Depression can be an especially dangerous illness at this age.
- Adolescence is not a time of turmoil and distress for most teens. Rates of mental disturbance among teens are very similar to rates of disturbance among adults.

KEY TERMS

Adolescent egocentrism
Anorexia nervosa
Bulimia nervosa
Convergent thinking
Divergent thinking
Hormonal balance
Identity crisis

Identity status
Imaginary audience
Maturation
Maximum growth spurt
Menarche
Normal range of development
Personal fable

Precociousness
Prodigiousness
Puberty
Repudiation
Secular trend
State of identity
Transition-linked turning points

WHAT DO YOU THINK?

1. Should children be taught about their body functions in school? Should this teaching include sexuality? If so, at what grade should it start?
2. How do sociocultural influences

impact adolescent cognitive development? How do these influences differ for girls and boys?
3. Why do you suppose people develop eating disorders?

4. Why should adolescents be more prone than other age groups to having "imaginary audiences" and "personal fables"?

5. Do you believe you can "disinhibit" (free up) your creative abilities? How should you start? Why don't you?

6. What are some of the ways we can help adolescents to have better mental health?

CHAPTER REVIEW TEST

1. Which of the following is part of the male reproductive system?
   a. Fimbriae
   b. Vas deferens
   c. Cervix
   d. Ova

2. What controls sexual characteristics in both males and females?
   a. Pituitary gland
   b. Bartholin's glands
   c. Cowper's glands
   d. Epididymis

3. What marks the onset of puberty?
   a. Menarche for females; the first ejaculation for males
   b. The growth spurt for females and males
   c. The beginning of breast development for females; the enlargement of the genitals for males
   d. No single event marks the onset of puberty.

4. Adolescents who are dependent and childlike, who feel a growing dislike for their bodies, and who become more introverted and self-rejecting because of it are most likely to be
   a. early-maturing males.
   b. early-maturing females.
   c. average-maturing males.
   d. late-maturing females.

5. The identity status in which numerous crises have been experienced and resolved, and relatively permanent commitments have been made is called
   a. identity moratorium.
   b. identity achievement.
   c. foreclosed identity.
   d. confused identity.

6. The decreasing age of the onset of puberty is referred to as
   a. early physical maturation.
   b. early psychological maturity.
   c. the evolutionary trend.
   d. the secular trend.

7. Specific criteria for anorexia nervosa include
   a. weight loss of at least 25 percent of original body weight.
   b. onset before age 25.
   c. distorted attitudes toward eating and weight.
   d. All of the answers are correct.

8. One of the traits by which Lerner characterized the adolescent transition is
   a. independence.
   b. eating disorders.
   c. relative plasticity.
   d. negative body image.

9. From the standpoint of adolescence, the most important of Erikson's eight stages is the _____ stage.
   a. identity
   b. autonomy
   c. intimacy
   d. industry

10. What occurs during Piaget's formal operational stage?
    a. Concrete operations combine to become formal operations.
    b. Preoperations turn into formal operations.
    c. Parts of the sensorimotor stage turn into formal operations.
    d. The preoperational stage and the sensorimotor stage combine to become formal operations.

11. One of the criticisms of Piaget's theory of cognitive development is that it
    a. is too broad.
    b. does not address abstract thought.
    c. is too complex.
    d. does not account for culture and gender influences.

12. To think of oneself in heroic or mythical terms is known as
    a. egocentrism.
    b. imaginary audience.
    c. the personal fable.
    d. invincibility.

13. When teenagers believe they are being scrutinized for their behavior and physical appearance, they are
    a. egocentric.
    b. creating a personal fable.
    c. creating an imaginary audience.
    d. exaggerating their abilities and skills.

14. According to John Hill's biopsychosocial theory, which three factors are most involved?
    a. Biological, achievement, and social
    b. Biological, psychological, and sexual
    c. Intimacy, dependency and autonomy
    d. Biological, psychological, and social

15. To solve problems that have only one correct answer, we are using
    a. divergent thinking.
    b. convergent thinking.
    c. creative thinking.
    d. critical thinking.

16. New ideas are to creative thinking as existing ideas are to
    a. convergent thinking.
    b. critical thinking.
    c. divergent thinking.
    d. preoperational thinking.

Answers

1.b 2.a 3.d 4.d 5.b 6.d 7.d 8.a 9.a 10.a 11.d 12.c 13.c 14.d 15.b 16.b

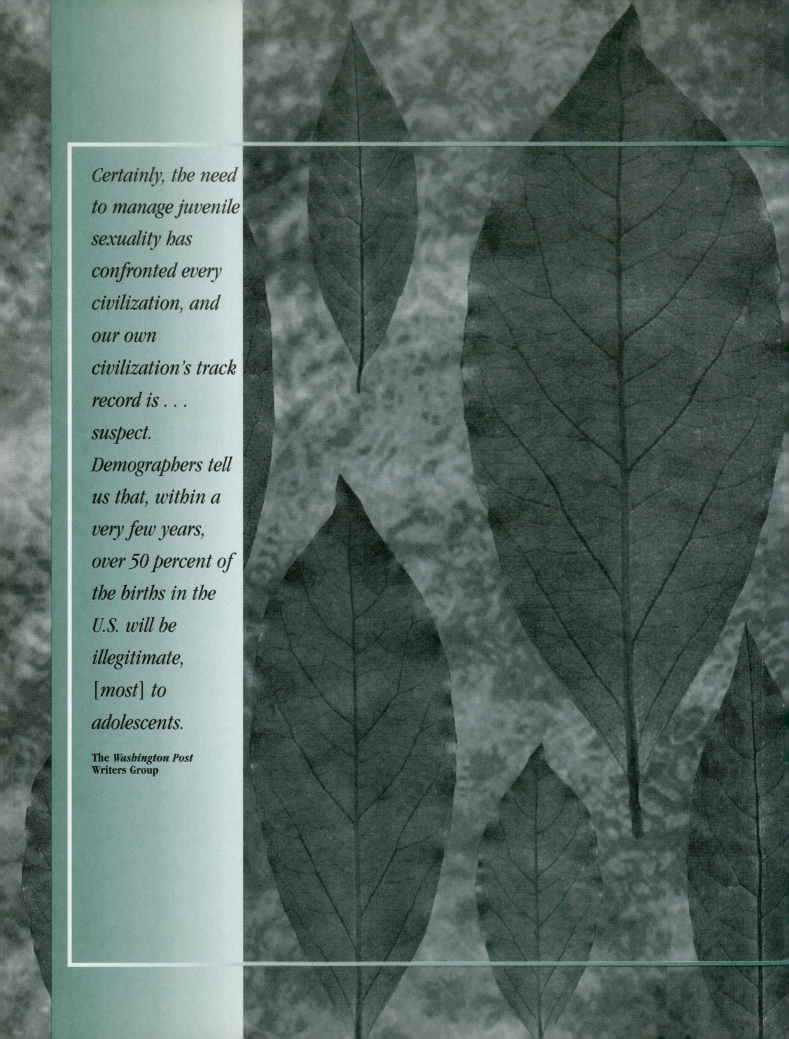

Certainly, the need to manage juvenile sexuality has confronted every civilization, and our own civilization's track record is . . . suspect. Demographers tell us that, within a very few years, over 50 percent of the births in the U.S. will be illegitimate, [most] to adolescents.

The *Washington Post* Writers Group

CHAPTER 12

Psychosocial Development in Adolescence

I n the last chapter and in this one, evidence is presented of a serious increase in several types of high-risk behaviors (such as eating disorders, binge drinking, use of illegal substances, and unprotected sex) among a significant group of today's adolescents. In a comparison of these youths with their parents, who became adults in the 1970s, William Pfaff (1997) offers a possible explanation for this phenomenon:

> The post-1960s generation felt itself liberated to set its own principles of life. . . . People now were to be free, independent, 'self-actualizing' individuals.
>
> What counted was each person's freedom to do whatever he or she wanted to do, within the professed limitation that it did not restrict anyone else's freedom to do whatever they wanted to do. All this, as we now know, did not work out in an entirely positive way. . . .
>
> . . . A great many of the children of [today's] generation feel that they have been deserted by their parents. They have been given no standards. . . . This new generation is saying: You failed to transmit to us positive values in which you believed. We now must look for them elsewhere (p. 15). ✿

Is Pfaff's description of the situation today the explanation for the increase in high-risk activities? He is describing a relatively momentary trend in family life, one that seems likely to change as today's teens become parents. As you read the various sections of this chapter, ask yourself whether you believe Pfaff's explanation is sufficient, or whether you think there could be other forces, perhaps more biological or psychological, that also play a role in why adolescents are behaving as they are.

The topics in this chapter examine the evidence, pro and con, on Pfaff's position. Following a discussion of the changing life of the family, we look closely at peer relations and sexuality. We also cover four topics of psychosocial development that no one is happy about: sexually transmitted infections, teenage pregnancy, substance abuse, and criminal behavior.

"This song is dedicated to our parents, and is in the form of a plea for more adequate supervision."

© The New Yorker Collection 1991. Edward Koren from cartoonbank.com. All Rights Reserved.

Chapter Objectives

After reading this chapter you should be able to answer the following questions.

◆ What changes have occurred to American families and their roles in adolescent life in recent years?

◆ What is the nature of peer relations during the teen years?

◆ How do teens deal with sexual relations?

◆ What new information do we have about sexually transmitted infections?

◆ How is the modern teenage parent dealing with the stresses that parenthood entails?

◆ What recent information do we have on adolescent illegal behavior?

Changing American Families and Their Roles in Adolescent Life

It is, after all the simplest things we remember: A neighborhood softball game, walking in the woods at twilight with Dad, rocking on the porch swing with Grandma.

Now, no one has time to organize a ballgame. Our woods have turned to malls. Grandma lives three states away. How will our children have the same kind of warm memories we do? (Barbara Meltz)

Of all the changes in American society in recent years, those affecting families have probably been the most extensive (also see chapter 8). Let's begin with a look at the changing roles of families in modern society.

The Loss of Functions

In 1840 the American family fulfilled six major functions (Sebald, 1977). Table 12.1 lists those functions and suggests which elements of society now perform them.

Today professionals have taken over the first five functions—economic-productive, educational, religious, recreational, medical. It appears that the family has been left to provide but one single function—affection—for its members. In the nineteenth century, parents and children needed each other more than now, for the following three major reasons:

• *Vocational instruction.* For both males and females, the parent of the same sex taught them their adult jobs. Most men were farmers and most women, housewives. Parents knew all the secrets of work, secrets passed on from generation to generation. Today nearly 100 percent of men work at jobs different from their fathers, and an increasing percentage of women are not primarily housewives, as their mothers were.

TABLE 12.1 THE CHANGING ROLES OF FAMILIES

Former Family Roles	Societal Elements That Perform Them Now
Economic-productive	Factory, office, and other business
Educational	Schools
Religious	Church or synagogue
Recreational	Commercial institutions
Medical	Doctor's office and hospital
Affectional	Still the family's role

- *Economic value.* Adolescents were a vital economic asset on the farm; without children, the farm couple had to hire others to help them. Work was a source of pride to the children. It was immediately and abundantly clear that they were important to the family. Today, instead of being an economic asset, most children are an economic burden on the family's resources.

- *Social stability.* When families almost never moved from their hometowns, parents were a crucial source of information about how to live in the town, knowing all the intricacies of small-town social relationships. One depended on one's parents to know what to do. Today, when the average American moves every five years, the adults are as much strangers in a new place as the children. In fact, with Dad, and now frequently Mom, driving out of the neighborhood to work, the children may well know the neighborhood better than their parents do.

A number of other factors also influence adolescent family life. Mullis and associates (1999) studied social support among adolescents. They found that the more adolescents felt supported in a social context, the closer they reported being to their mothers. A study by Weigel and associates (1998) confirmed this finding. In another study, the social support of family was found to be positively related to self-reliance and good grades and negatively related to problem behavior in African-American adolescents (Taylor, 1996). Bankston and Caldas (1998) found that academic achievement in African-American adolescents is lowest for those whose schoolmates lived with single mothers. Greater parental religious practices can also have positive affects on adolescents' academic and socioemotional adjustment during this stage of their lives (Brody & others, 1996). Molina and Chassin (1996) found that parent alcoholism did not moderate the effects of puberty, but Mexican-American and white children experienced more conflict with their parents than nonalcoholic parents and their children. Parental values also play an important role in predicting problem behaviors in adolescents. For example, Garnier and Stein (1998) found that adolescents' values were similar to their mothers' values. Although delinquency was not likely to occur in families with humanistic/egalitarian values, this style did not protect against substance abuse. Adolescents were less likely to engage in hard drug use.

Fergusson and Lynskey (1996) examined the factors that affect resiliency in 940 New Zealand 16-year-olds who had experienced significant family adversity. The factors most associated with the absence of high-risk behaviors (i.e., resiliency)

A humorous look at adolescence and the family in earlier times may be found in Carson McCullers' *Member of the wedding.* New York: Bantam. Twelve-year-old Frankie yearns desperately to join her brother and his bride on their honeymoon. She learns a great deal about the transition from childhood to maturity from the devoted housekeeper.

An Applied View

How Well Do Parents Know What Their Teens Are Doing?

The *Who's Who* organization recently (1997) surveyed 3,370 teenagers 16- to 18-year-olds, all of whom have an "A" or a "B" average and are planning to attend college. Because these students are among the highest achievers in the United States one might assume that their parents would be reasonably well aware of their activities. As the chart below reveals, there are some serious discrepancies.

There are at least three important questions that are posed by these data: Why is there such a great distance between what the teens say they do and what their parents believe? Might these "good students" be underreporting their actual activities? As you will see in other chapters of this book, in some cases these students' rates of behavior are lower than for more ordinary students, and in some cases higher—why do you suppose this is so?

Do You Think That Your Child . . .	Parental Myth	Teen Reality
Has contemplated suicide?	9%	26%
Has cheated on a test?	37%	76%
Has had sex?	9%	19%
Has friends with drug problems?	12%	36%
Has driven a car while drunk?	3%	10%
Has worries about pregnancy?	22%	46%

Source: *Who's Who Special Report,* 1997.

were higher than average IQ, low novelty seeking, and lower than average affiliation with delinquent peers. The findings emphasized the important role of positive peer models during this age period.

The Effects of Divorce

A smoothly functioning family can provide support and nurturance to an adolescent during times of stress (Young & others, 1997). But when the family is itself in a state of disarray, such as during a divorce, not only is the support weakened, but the family often becomes a source of stress (Fergusson & Lynskey, 1996).

Divorce has become commonplace in American society. Even with slight decreases in the divorce rate in recent years, more than one million divorces still occur every year, which is roughly half the number of marriages performed during the same time (U.S. Bureau of the Census, 1996). Divorce tends to occur most in families with a newborn, and second most in families with an adolescent present. Estimates suggest that divorce affects as much as one-third to one-half of the adolescent population.

What, then, are the effects of divorce on the development of the adolescent? Unfortunately, conclusions are often based as much on speculation as on research findings, due to problems in the research. Divorcing parents often refuse to let themselves or their children participate in such studies, which makes random samples difficult to obtain.

Nevertheless, the divorcing family clearly contributes additional stress to a developing adolescent. One obvious effect is economic. The increased living expenses that result from the need to pay for two domiciles most often leads to a significant decrease in the standard of living for the children. Most adolescents, particularly young adolescents, are extremely status conscious, and status is often obtained with the things money can buy (clothes, stereos, cars, etc.). Young adolescents may well resent being unable to keep up with their peers in this regard. Older adolescents are better equipped to cope with this type of additional stress, both psychologically and financially, because they can enter the workforce themselves.

Simons and associates (1999) found that adolescent adjustment problems can often be attributed to divorce-related issues. For example, both girls and boys from divorced families tend to be more depressed than their same-aged peers from intact families. Divorce increases the mother's chances of being depressed, which often

Divorce has many negative effects on children. One positive is that some fathers spend more time in conversation with their children.

reduces the quality of her parenting. Another obvious effect of a divorce is the absence of one parent. Often custodial rights are given to one parent (usually the mother), and so the children are likely to lose an important source of support (usually that of the father). What support the noncustodial parent provides is sometimes jeopardized by the degree of acrimony between the divorced parents. One or both of the parents may attempt to "turn" the adolescent against the other parent. This sometimes results in disturbing, negative tales about a mother or father, forcing adolescents to cope with adult realities while they are still young.

Such distractions also can disrupt the disciplinary process during adolescence. Under any circumstances, administering consistent and effective discipline during this time often requires the wisdom of King Solomon. A difficult job for two parents becomes the primary responsibility of one. Preoccupied parents, perhaps feeling guilty over subjecting the child to a divorce, find it difficult to provide the consistent discipline that the child was used to previously. It should be noted however, that for adolescents in general, decreased contact with parents also produces these problems. Despite the popular belief that parental remarriage increases a child's ability to tackle academic challenges, Jeynes (1999) found that those from reconstituted families often scored lower academically than their peers from single-parent divorced families.

Not surprisingly, adolescents from divorced families tend to be more vulnerable as a result of the stressors both during and after divorce (Thompson, 1998). For instance, the absence of a father can lead to aggressive behavior and poor adjustment. Imitating feuding parents was found to be another cause of aggressive behavior. In addition to father absence and parental conflict, economic distress is a common result of divorce. Adolescents who experience poverty as a result of increased financial stress on the family are more prone to depression and feelings of abandonment due to the new pressures of one of their single parents, usually their mother, having to get a job.

Some adolescents are able to adapt to the stress of a divorce. Researchers attribute their resilience to personality characteristics such as self-esteem, access to support systems, family unity, and a good relationship with peers and at least one parent (Thompson, 1998).

Because the father typically leaves a family during divorce, there are often more negative effects for males than for females (Hetherington & others, 1989). Wolfinger (1998) found an increased likelihood of problem drinking in men due to parental divorce. The chances of being a smoker were also greatly increased as a result of divorce. During the teenage years, the father often assumes primary responsibility for disciplining the male adolescents in the family. An abrupt change in disciplinary patterns can lead some adolescents to exhibit more antisocial and delinquent behavior. For example, divorce may force adolescents into growing up faster and disengaging from their families. Early disengagement from a family can actually be a good solution for teens, if they can devote themselves to school activities and rewarding relationships with friends or teachers (Hetherington & others, 1989). The single-parent family is likely to influence the timing of when a girl leaves home. A study conducted by Cooney and Mortimer (1999) indicated that girls from a single-parent home are more likely to leave home after high school. The likelihood of this departure is increased if the adolescent has a child of her own or if she is responsible for a great deal of the housework.

For girls, there can be greater problems if the father does not leave the family but has an unhealthy relationship with his wife. A study conducted by Jacobvitz and Bush (1996) examined the perception of family relationships in the minds of adolescent females. They found that the father-daughter alliance, which occurs when fathers turn to their daughters instead of their wives for intimacy and affection (as a consequence of an emotionally unfulfilling marriage), contributed most to daughters' depression, anxiety, and decreased self-esteem.

Despite the negative aspects we've outlined, you should keep in mind that not all aspects of a divorce have a negative impact on adolescents. Divorce is often a better alternative than keeping a stressful, unhappy family intact. In fact, a few studies that have compared adolescents from the two groups have shown that teenagers from divorced families do better in general than adolescents from intact but feuding families (Hetherington & others, 1989). This inference has recently been challenged by Wallerstein and associates (1999), who studied 131 children of divorce in California. They concluded that most of the children were unhappy as a result of the divorce. They state that "Children don't care if parents sleep in separate beds if the household runs well and if the parenting holds up" (p. 2).

Hines (1997) summarizes the research findings:

> For the adolescent undergoing multiple developmental changes, divorce and its related transitions present additional challenges, promoting growth for some and constituting developmental vulnerabilities for others. A review of the literature on adolescent development, family relations and the impact of divorce on adolescents reveals that adolescents experience divorce differently from younger children and that a positive parent-adolescent relationship can ameliorate the negative effects of divorce (p. 375).

Guided Review

1. Five functions that were provided by the family but are now provided elsewhere: educational, religious, recreational, medical, and _____ .
2. Within families that experience divorce, there are some interesting gender differences. Divorce generally has more adverse effects on _____ than on _____ .
3. In a study on parenting styles in which at least one of the adolescents in a family was highly creative, parents were found to employ a style of parenting called _____ .
4. Divorce tends to occur most often in families with a newborn and second most in families with an _____ .
5. The three styles of parenting most often identified by researchers are authoritarian, permissive, and _____ .

The Nurturing Parent

Authoritarian parenting style
Parents strive for complete control over their children's behavior by establishing complex sets of rules.

Permissive parenting style
Parents have little or no control over their children and refrain from disciplinary measures.

Authoritative parenting style
Parents are sometimes authoritarian and sometimes permissive, depending to some extent on the parents' mood.

Nurturing parenting style
Parents use indirect methods and modeling to influence their child's behavior.

As we discussed in chapter 8, most family researchers have agreed that three styles of parenting exist (Darling, 1999): the **authoritarian, permissive,** and **authoritative parenting** styles. In an extensive study of 56 families in which at least one of the adolescents was highly creative (Dacey, 1998; Dacey & Kenny, 1997; Dacey & Lennon, 1998), a picture of a fourth style clearly emerged. The parents in these families were found to be devotedly interested in their children's behavior, but they seldom make rules to govern it. Instead, by modeling and family discussions, they espouse a well-defined set of values and expect their children to make personal decisions based on these values.

After the children make decisions and take actions, the parents let the children know how they feel about what was done. Even when they disapprove, they rarely punish. Most of the teens in the study said that their parents' disappointment in them was motivation enough to change their behavior. All of the parents agreed that if their child were about to do something really wrong, they would stop her or him, but that this virtually never happens. This has been termed the **nurturing parenting style** (Dacey & Packer, 1992). Only some of the parents in the study were found to be highly creative, but all appear committed to this approach.

Answers

1. economic 2. boys, girls 3. nurturing 4. adolescent 5. authoritative

The success of nurturing parents is based on a well-established principle: People get better at what they practice. These parents provide their children with ample opportunities to practice decisionmaking skills, self-control, and, most vital of all, creative thinking. They serve as caring coaches as their children learn how to live. This research demonstrates the profoundly positive effects a healthy family can have on a person.

Peer Relations

Important debates have existed in the field of adolescent psychology concerning the value and influence of peer and parental relationships during adolescence. Recent research has helped to resolve some of these debates. The importance of parent and peer relationships and the ways in which peer relationships change during the adolescent years will be the focus of this section.

Developmental Patterns of Peer Groups

Peer groups are important in adolescent development. Although it is clear that friendships are vital throughout life, there seems to be something special about the role of the peer group during adolescence.

The role of peers as a source of activities, support, and influence increases greatly (Dumont & Provost, 1999). Perhaps it is for these reasons that adults and the media have been interested in and anxious about the role of the peer group. Brown (1990) described four specific ways in which the peer group changes from childhood to adolescence.

- As previously mentioned, adolescents spend much more time with peers than do younger children. As early as sixth grade, the early adolescent begins withdrawing from adults and increases time spent with peers. During high school, middle adolescents spend twice as much time with their peers as they spend with parents and other adults.

- Adolescent peer groups receive less adult supervision and control. Teenagers try to avoid close supervision by parents and teachers and are more independent and find places to meet where they are less closely watched. Even at home, teenagers seek privacy and places where they can talk to friends without being overheard by parents and siblings.

- Adolescents begin interacting more with peers of the opposite sex. Although boys and girls participate in different activities and friendship groups during middle childhood, the sexes mix increasingly during the adolescent years. Interaction with members of the opposite sex seems to increase at the same time as adolescents distance themselves from their parents.

- During adolescence, peer groups become more aware of the values and behaviors of the larger adolescent **subculture.** They also identify with certain **crowds,** which are groups with a reputation for certain values, attitudes, or activities. Common crowd labels among high school students include "jocks," "brains," "druggies," "populars," "nerds," "burnouts," and "delinquents." Interestingly, although the adolescent subculture changes over time, these crowds seem to exist in some form across all periods in which the adolescent subculture has been studied.

Brown and associates (1997) made an important distinction between crowds and cliques, which are subgroups within crowds:

> Some might suppose that crowd labels are little more than vague, stereotypical categories, and because the constraints on selecting a crowd for oneself are substantial, the crowd niche would matter less to adolescents than their clique niche. Remember, however, that the clique

Although rigidly segregated into gender groups during middle childhood, boys and girls become much more willing to interact with each other as adolescence proceeds.

Subculture   A subgroup within a culture, in this case a social culture.

Crowds   Groups known for certain values, attitudes, or activities.

affiliation indicates merely who an adolescent's close friends are; crowd affiliation indicates who an adolescent is—at least in the eyes of peers. It is a very personal evaluation of the adolescent by those whose opinions matter. Thus, it is not surprising that adolescents resist being labeled or pigeonholed as part of one crowd (p. 184).

Brown (1990) also thought about why peer groups change in the preceding ways during adolescence and suggested several explanations. He maintained that the biopsychosocial changes of adolescence affect the development of a teenager's peer relationships. First, puberty seems to increase adolescents' interest in the opposite sex and contributes to withdrawal from adult activities and increased time with peers. Although adolescents are in the process of becoming less dependent on their parents they tend to increase their dependence on peers.

It is well known that teenagers, especially girls, spend a lot of time talking to their peers, much of it over the telephone. A recent study by Boehm and associates (1999) reviewed the issues discussed by adolescent girls around the country while calling a peer hotline. Peer relationships was the most frequently discussed topic (46 percent–60 percent), followed by family problems (10 percent–20 percent). The concerns of the girls were quite similar.

Functions of Peer Groups

In contrast with the popular view that peers are a negative influence during adolescence, peer influence serves important social and psychological functions. When adolescents do not have the chance to be part of a peer group, they miss out on important learning experiences. Kelly and Hansen (1990) described six important positive functions of the peer group. The group can help teens to:

- *Control aggressive impulses.* Through interaction with peers, children and adolescents learn how to resolve differences in ways other than direct aggression. Observing how peers deal with conflict can be helpful in learning assertive, rather than aggressive or "bullying," behavior.

- *Obtain emotional and social support and become more independent.* Friends and peer groups provide support for adolescents as they take on new responsibilities. The support adolescents get from their peers helps them to become less dependent on their family for support.

- *Improve social skills, develop reasoning abilities, and learn to express feelings in more mature ways.* Through conversation and debate with peers, adolescents learn to express ideas and feelings and expand their problem-solving abilities. Social interactions with peers give adolescents practice in expressing feelings of caring and love, as well as anger and negative feelings.

- *Develop attitudes toward sexuality and gender-role behavior.* Sexual attitudes and gender-role behaviors are shaped primarily through peer interactions. Adolescents learn behaviors and attitudes that they associate with being young men and women.

- *Strengthen moral judgment and values.* Adults generally tell their children what is right and what is wrong. Within the peer group, adolescents are left to make decisions on their own. The adolescent has to evaluate the values of peers and decide what is right for him or her. This process of evaluation can help the adolescent to develop moral-reasoning abilities.

- *Improve self-esteem.* Being liked by a large number of peers helps adolescents feel good about themselves. Being called up on the telephone or being asked out on a date tells adolescents that they are liked by their peers, thereby enhancing feelings of positive self-esteem.

It is clear that the formation of intimate friendships is an important adolescent goal. One of the most important aspects of these friendships during adolescence is the growing trend for them to become sexual.

Guided Review

6. Brown describes four ways in which the peer group changes from childhood to adolescence. These are (1) adolescents spend more time with peers; (2) adolescent peer groups receive less adult supervision; (3) adolescents begin interacting more with peers of the _____ _____; and (4) peer groups become aware of values of the larger adolescent subculture.
7. Girls from _____ _____ _____ are more likely to leave home after high school than peers.
8. The influences of the peer group serve important social and _____ functions.
9. Whereas peers teach adolescents about social relationships outside the family, adults provide a source of guidance in forming _____ and setting goals.

Sexual Behavior

Few aspects of human behavior have changed more in this century than sexual behavior. Until the 1980s the popular belief about sex was, "They're talking more about it now, but they're not doing anything more about it!" This may have been true in earlier times, but no longer.

Evidence shows that the forces that traditionally kept the majority of adolescents from engaging in sex are no longer powerful. In her study of female teen magazines, Durham (1998) indicates that not only do the magazines contain many articles pertaining to teen sex, they also support social stereotypes that girls should be sexually subordinate to boys. Available data show that U.S. adolescents are becoming sexually active at increasingly earlier ages. Early sexual activity appears to have declined recently, however, probably due to a growing concern about AIDS and other sexually transmitted diseases. A study conducted by the National Survey of Family Growth (HHS News, 1997) indicates that in the current group of 15- to 19-year-olds, the percentage who have had sex is about 50 percent, down from a peak of 55 percent several years earlier. Results of studies vary, but the most likely percentage of college sophomores who are no longer virgins is about 75 percent for both males and females. In their comparison of the sexual risk-taking behaviors of athletes and their non-athletic counterparts, Savage and Holcomb (1999) found that athletes were less likely to have engaged in risk-taking behaviors. They were also less likely to be sexually active.

Stages of Sexuality

Many psychologists believe that human sexuality develops in three steps (Brooks-Gunn & Paikoff, 1993):

1. Love of one's self **(autosexuality)**
2. Love of members of one's own sex **(homosexuality)**
3. Love of members of the opposite sex **(heterosexuality)**

These stages appear to be natural, although some argue that it is as natural to stay in the second stage as to go on to the third.

Autosexuality The stage at which the child becomes aware of sexual pleasure, and consciously experiments with masturbation.

Homosexuality Love of members of one's own sex.

Heterosexuality Love of members of the opposite sex.

Answers

6. opposite sex 7. single-parent families 8. psychological 9. values

In the autosexual stage, the child becomes aware of himself or herself as a source of sexual pleasure and consciously experiments with masturbation. The autosexual stage begins as early as 3 years of age and continues until the child is about 6 or 7, although in some children it lasts for a considerably longer period of time.

When the child enters kindergarten, the homosexual phase comes to the fore (please note that this does not necessarily refer to sexual touching, but rather to the direction of feelings of love). For most children from the age of 7 to about 13, best friends, the ones with whom he or she dares to be intimate, are people of the same sex. Feelings become especially intense between ages 10 and 12, when young people enter puberty and feel a growing need to confide in others. They naturally are more trusting with members of their own sex, who share their experiences. Occasionally these close feelings result in overt sexual behavior (one study found this to be true more than one-third of the time). In most cases, however, it appears that such behavior results from curiosity rather than latent homosexuality of the adult variety.

The great majority of teenagers move into the third stage, heterosexuality, at about 13 or 14 years, with girls preceding boys by about a year. We discuss these three phases in the following sections.

Autosexual Behavior

Masturbation is probably universal to human sexual experience (Meston & others, 1996; Wiederman & others, 1996). Although most people still consider it an embarrassing topic, it has always been a recognized aspect of sexuality, legitimate or not. Most 4- to 5-year-olds masturbate, are chastised for it, and stop, then start again at an average age of 14. If masturbation is so popular, why has it been considered such a problem?

Although most psychiatrists feel that no intrinsic harm exists in masturbation and believe it to be a normal, healthy way for adolescents to discharge their sexual drive, some teens (mainly boys) feel such a sense of shame, guilt, and fear that they develop the "excessive masturbation" syndrome. In this case, masturbation is practiced even though the child feels very bad about it. These feelings are reinforced by solitude and fantasy, which leads to depression and a debilitating sense of self-condemnation. A recent result of these feelings is a sharp increase in 900 phone line sex calls. Some teens are now being treated for an addiction to making 900 calls.

In summary, most psychiatrists argue that masturbation in childhood is not only normal but helpful in forming a positive sexual attitude. It cannot be obsessive at 4, so it should be ignored at that age. However, it can be obsessive at 14, and if the parents suspect this to be the case, they should consult a psychologist.

Homosexual Behavior

The Psychoanalytic Theory of Homosexuality

Psychoanalytic theory of homosexuality Freud's theory that if the child's first sexual feelings about the parent of the opposite sex are strongly punished, the child may develop a permanent homosexual orientation.

Freud's **psychoanalytic theory of homosexuality** suggested that if the child's first sexual feelings about the parent of the opposite sex are strongly punished, the child may identify with the same-sex parent and develop a permanent homosexual orientation. Because researchers have noted many cases in which the father's suppression of the homosexual's Oedipal feelings was not particularly strong, this theory is not held in much regard today.

The Learning Theory of Homosexuality

Learning theory of homosexuality The belief that homosexuality is the result of learned experiences from significant others.

The **learning theory of homosexuality** offers another explanation: Animals that are low on the mammalian scale follow innate sexual practices. Among the higher animals, humans included, learning is more important than inherited factors. According to this theory, most people learn to be heterosexual, but for a variety of little-understood reasons, some people learn to be homosexual.

Clearly, some of the stereotypes about homosexuals are untrue and unfair. What generalizations, if any, do you believe can fairly be made about all homosexuals?

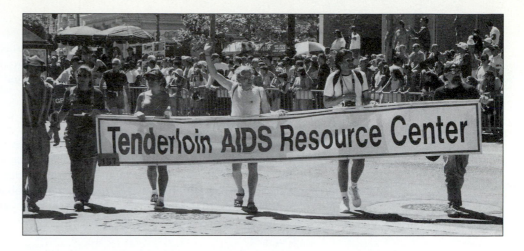

The Biopsychosocial Theory of Homosexuality

No direct proof exists that people become homosexual because of genetic reasons. However, a number of studies (D'Augelli & Patterson, 1995; Diamant & McAnulty, 1995; Hu, 1995; Patterson, 1995) have offered some evidence of genetic predisposition (an inborn tendency). Some theories argue that the fetus' brain reacts to sex hormones during the second through sixth month of gestation in a way that may create such a predisposition. In other words, those who favor a **biopsychosocial theory of homosexuality** suggest that if the biological predisposition is present and certain psychological and social factors (as yet unknown) are in place, then the contention of many homosexuals that their sexual orientation was not a matter of choice would be confirmed. The research of psychologist Daryl Bem (1996) has found support for a biopsychosocial approach. He found that genetic inheritance influences temperament, which then interacts with a long chain of psychological factors that influence whether the person will be homosexual or heterosexual. Because our current culture strongly favors heterosexuality, most people turn out that way. In another cultural setting, things might be different, he believes.

In general, the mental health of gay, lesbian, and bisexual adolescents is frequently dependent on how they perceive their parents' acceptance of their sexual orientation. Floyd and associates (1999) found that perceived parental acceptance was the best predictor of the youth's overall sense of well-being.

Biopsychosocial theory of homosexuality The theory that some factor in a person's DNA affects temperament, which affects sexual orientation.

An Informed *View*   *Is Homosexuality a Matter of Choice?*

On the one hand, we have the behavioral, psychoanalytic, and biopsychosocial theorists giving their explanations of how homosexuality is learned. On the other hand, we have many homosexuals who believe that their sexual orientation became clear so early in life that it could only have been caused genetically. Proponents of each of these positions agree that being homosexual is not a matter of choice for the homosexual. Thus it is argued that they should be accepted the same as heterosexuals, or at the very least be given sympathy, because their role in today's society is not an easy one.

Others believe that homosexuality is a matter of free choice and that those who choose it are behaving in an immoral way. Homosexuals don't have to be that way; they want to. What's your view? Do you think interviewing some gays and lesbians on this question would deepen your understanding?

If you would like to have a more informed opinion on this issue, you might want to read one of the articles on the subject referenced in this chapter (e.g., Bem, D'Augelli & Patterson, Freud).

You might also wish to learn more about it by going to our web site at http://www.mhhe.com/dacey5.

Heterosexual Behavior

At the beginning of this section, we presented some statistics on teen sexuality that may have surprised you. To get a clearer picture of this situation, you will need to look at the data that a number of other studies have provided on heterosexual teen behavior.

First Coitus

Although sexuality develops throughout life, most people view first intercourse as the key moment in sexual development. When this moment occurs is influenced by numerous factors (Lerner & Semi, 1997). For example, the more the adolescent engages in risk behaviors such as drug and alcohol abuse and delinquency, the earlier first coitus is likely to take place (Santelli & others, 1998). Emotional distress encourages earlier sex, especially when caused by divorce and peer conflicts (Feldman, 1995).

Early first coitus is highly associated with a number of adverse outcomes. The National Center for Health statistics found that 22 percent of girls who had sex before they turned 15 described their first encounter as "not voluntary," and over one-third stated that their partner was a male over 18, which constitutes statutory rape in most states (HHS News, 1997). Rosenthal (1996) studied 171 girls, average age 14.5. She

An Applied View

How to Talk to Teens about Sex (or Anything Else, for That Matter)

Adolescents are more likely to talk to adults who know how to listen—about sex, alcohol, and other important issues. But certain kinds of responses, such as giving too much advice or pretending to have all the answers, have been shown to block the lines of communication.

Effective listening is more than just "not talking." It takes concentration and practice. Below are six communication skills that are useful to anyone who wants to reach adolescents. By the way, these skills can also enhance communication with other adults.

Rephrase the person's comments to show you understand. This is sometimes called reflective listening. *Reflective listening* serves four purposes:

- It assures the person you hear what she or he is saying.
- It persuades the person that you correctly understand what is being said (it is sometimes a good idea to ask if your rephrasing is correct).
- It allows you a chance to reword the person's statements in ways that are less self-destructive. For example, if a person says "My mother is a Stinking drunk!" you can say "You feel your mother drinks too much." This is better, because the daughter of someone who drinks too much usually can have a better self-image than the daughter of a "stinking drunk."
- It allows the person to "rehear" and reconsider what was said.

Watch the person's face and body language. Often a person will assure you that he or she does not feel sad, but a quivering chin or too-bright eyes will tell you otherwise. A person may deny feeling frightened, but if you put your fingers on her or his wrist, as a caring gesture, you may find that the person has a pounding heart. When words and body language say two different things, always believe the body language.

Give nonverbal support. This may include a smile, a hug, a wink, a pat on the shoulder, nodding your head, making eye contact, or holding the person's hand (or wrist).

Use the right tone of voice for what you are saying. Remember that your voice tone communicates as clearly as your words. Make sure your tone does not come across as sarcastic or all-knowing.

Use encouraging phrases to show your interest and to keep the conversation going. Helpful little phrases, spoken appropriately during pauses in the conversation, can communicate how much you care:

"Oh, really?"

"Tell me more about that."

"Then what happened?"

"That must have made you feel bad."

Remember, if you are judgmental or critical, the person may decide that you just don't understand. You cannot be a good influence on someone who won't talk to you.

found that 42 percent of them were sexually experienced, having had first intercourse at an average age of 13.1 years. Of these girls, half had had an adverse outcome—a sexually transmitted infection, a pregnancy, or an abnormal Pap smear.

When do most Americans first experience intercourse? The statistics vary, but all research confirms that this experience occurs at a younger age than it did for previous generations (Kinsman & others, 1998; Stevens-Simon & Kaplan, 1998; Rosenthal, 1996). A more recent study of nearly 1,400 sixth graders found that at the beginning of the school year, 30 percent had had sexual intercourse, and an additional 5 percent had done so by the end of the year (Kinsman & others, 1998). From these data, it seems clear that the downward extension of sexual experience is continuing. Table 12.2 and 12.3 offer a national picture for high school students.

Sexual Abuse

When adolescents are abused, typically it is by someone they know and trust. It is often just a continuation of abuse that started during childhood. The most common type of serious sexual abuse is incest between father and daughter. This type of relationship may last for several years. The daughter is often manipulated into believing it is all her fault and that if she says anything to anyone, she will be seen as a bad person, one who may even be arrested and jailed. The outcome is usually another adolescent statistic: a runaway or even a prostitute (Gary & others, 1996; Jezel & others, 1996; Karp & others, 1995).

TABLE 12.2	PERCENTAGE OF TEENAGERS WHO HAVE HAD SEXUAL INTERCOURSE (AGE 15–19)	
Age	**Females**	**Males**
15	24	27
16	39	45
17	52	59
18	65	68
19	77	85

Source: *1995 National Survey of Family Growth* and *1995 National Survey of Adolescent Males*.

A Sociocultural View

Adolescent Sexual Activity: A Look at Risk Factors in Three Ethnic Groups

Perkins and associates (1998) studied the sexual activity of adolescents in three ethnic groups. They were interested in whether there were differences between African-Americans, Latinos, and European-Americans concerning the effects of risk factors on sexual activity. Examples of risk factors include alcohol use, religiosity, grade point average, and sexual and physical abuse. Perkins and his colleagues found a "relationship between the level of risk and the rate of sexual activity for adolescents, regardless of ethnicity." Heavy alcohol use was the strongest risk factor associated with increased sexual activity for males and females from all ethnic groups. Sexual and physical abuse were also strong predictors of increased sexual activity in females from all ethnic groups. These results suggest that ethnic group is much less important than has been thought. Further, it emphasizes the role of other nonsexual causes for teenage sexual behavior. The results emphasize the need to help eliminate or decrease risk factors in adolescents' lives if we are to ensure their safety.

TABLE 12.3 AVOIDING PREGNANCY

Most sexually experienced women and their partners use a contraceptive, primarily the pill or condoms.

By Age

More than seven out of 10 sexually active girls aged 15 to 17 use contraceptives, a figure that rises to nearly nine out of 10 young women 20 to 24.

Age	Pill	Condom	Other*	Total (%)
15–17	38	29	5	72
18–19	52	24	8	84
20–24	60	13	15	88

By Race and Ethnicity

Young Hispanic women aged 15 to 19 trail blacks and whites in use of contraceptives.

Race	Pill	Condom	Other*	Total (%)
Hispanic	37	26	2	65
Black	58	17	2	77
White	45	28	8	81

By Income

Seven out of 10 low-income young women aged 15 to 19 use contraceptives, as do eight of 10 higher-income women.

Income Level	Pill	Condom	Other*	Total (%)
Low**	41	27	3	71
High	47	27	9	83

*Other methods include the diaphragm, sponge, spermicide, and IUD.

**Low income means from 100–199 percent of the poverty level. For example, a family of four that earned $14,000 to $28,000 in 1992 would be considered low income.

Source: Leeming and associates (1996), *Issues in Adolescent Sexuality.* Needham Heights, MA: Allyn & Bacon.

Most sexual offenses are discussed with a friend or with no one. Very few are reported to parents, police, social workers, or other authorities. It has also been found that the effects of abuse may influence a youth's future relationships. Directly following the experience, children may engage in such "acting out" behaviors as truancy, running away, sexual promiscuity, and damage to school performance and family relationships (Gary & others, 1996).

Adolescents are not only the victims of sexual abuse; they also are perpetrators of it (Ryan & Lane, 1997). Juveniles are responsible for about one-third of all reported abuses (Finkfelhor, 1996). This share of responsibility for abusive acts has remained steady for several decades (Snyder & others, 1996).

Several researchers (Al-Mateen & others, 1996; Tingus & others, 1996) have called for improved education to sensitize people to prevent incest, as well as improved reporting systems, legal definitions, and treatment of victims. These may help us better understand and intervene, so that victims can receive professional attention earlier that may reduce the long-term effects of abuse.

Sexuality in the lives of late adolescents and young adults in the last decade of this century is very different from in earlier decades (although perhaps not so different from several centuries ago). What is the relationship between this fact and the problem covered in the next section about sexually transmitted infections? That is a complex question.

> ## Guided Review
>
> 10. Some psychologists describe three stages of human sexuality. These include autosexuality, _____, and heterosexuality.
> 11. Currently the three theories that attempt to explain homosexuality include psychoanalytic theory, _____ theory, and the biopsychosocial theory of homosexuality.
> 12. It is estimated that by the end of adolescence, more than 80 percent of the boys and _____ percent of the girls will have been sexually active.
> 13. Rather than talking to _____ about sexual abuse, teens choose to talk with friends or tell no one at all.
> 14. Considering some of the reasons for adolescent sexual activity, it is not surprising that nearly 70 percent of twelfth graders report having had _____ _____ .

Sexually Transmitted Infections

In this section, we cover research on AIDS and other infections that are sexually contagious.

AIDS

Sexually transmitted infections (STIs) A class of infections that are transmitted through sexual behavior.

AIDS (acquired immune deficiency syndrome) A condition caused by a virus that invades the body's immune system, making it vulnerable to infections and life-threatening illnesses.

Human immunodeficiency virus (HIV) The virus that leads to AIDS.

Not long ago, when people thought about **sexually transmitted infections (STIs),** gonorrhea came to mind. In the 1970s, it was herpes. Today, **AIDS (acquired immune deficiency syndrome)** causes the most concern (Brown & others, 1996; CDC, 2000; Children's Defense Fund, 1999, Johnson & others, 1996).

AIDS was first diagnosed at Bellevue–New York University Medical Center in 1979 and has quickly approached epidemic proportions. What is known about AIDS is that a virus attacks certain cells of the body's immune system, leaving the person vulnerable to any number of fatal afflictions such as cancer and pneumonia. In addition, the disease can directly infect the brain and spinal cord, causing acute meningitis.

The virus that leads to AIDS—**human immunodeficiency virus (HIV)**—is transmitted through the transfer of substantial amounts of intimate bodily fluids such as blood and semen. The virus is most likely to be transferred through sexual contact, the sharing of hypodermic needles, and, much less likely, through blood transfusions (a test for AIDS is now available at blood banks and hospitals). In addition, the virus can be transmitted from an infected mother to an infant during pregnancy, birth, or through breast-feeding. In fact, there will be over 80,000 orphans in the year 2000 in the U.S. due to the effects of AIDS (Children's Defense Fund, 1999). Table 12.4 shows the concentrations of AIDS in each of several age groups, as well as the percentages of cases by race/ethnicity. In the most recent report available (C.D.C.P., 1997), powerful new drugs were credited with bringing about a 6 percent decline in AIDS cases in the United States, the first decline since the epidemic began in the 1980s.

In the initial stages of the spread of the disease in this country, HIV has most often been found in certain segments of the population such as male homosexuals and intravenous drug users and, to a much lesser degree, among hemophiliacs. But that could easily change over time. In some Central African countries, where AIDS is thought to have originated, HIV is found equally among men and women throughout the population. After a slow start, large-scale education efforts by grassroots

Answers

10. homosexuality 11. learning 12. 70 13. parents 14. sexual intercourse

First diagnosed in 1979, AIDS quickly approached epidemic proportions.

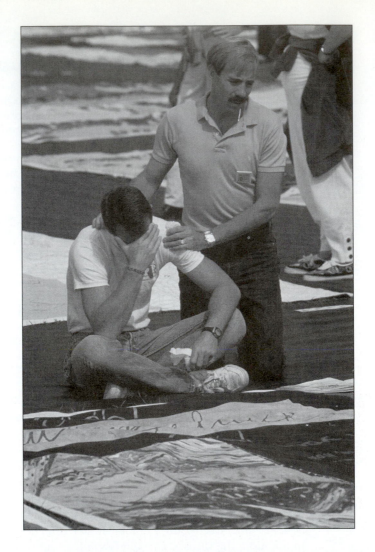

TABLE 12.4 AIDS CASES BY AGE AND RACE/ETHNICITY

Age	White	Black	Hispanic	Asian/Pacific Islander	American Indian/ Alaska Native
Under 5	1,011	4,212	1,524	31	25
5–19	1,632	2,865	1,267	51	32
20–29	51,716	46,951	25,878	910	497
30–39	148,406	122,459	62,760	2,376	1,058
40–49	85,040	76,415	32,809	1,509	471
50–59	26,796	21,791	9,823	481	113
60+	10,219	8,027	3,514	188	37

Source: *Center for Disease Control, Surveillance Report,* Vol. 12, No. 1, 2000.

organizations, as well as by state and federal government agencies, have begun to get these messages out, but the problems remain extremely serious (Cooksey, Rindfuss, & Guilkey, 1996).

First, as mentioned, the virus has been identified with a few select groups. If you're not gay or a drug user, you might think you don't have to consider preventive measures. However, a person exposed to HIV may not show any symptoms for as many as 15 years. Further, this same person can expose other people to the virus during this incubation phase. Some people have reacted to this by becoming more particular about their sexual partners. Monogamous relationships were on the rise again during the 1980s, after the "liberated" days of the sexual revolution of the 1960s and 1970s. And as condom use increases, the educational message seems to be getting through. But many still ignore the dangers, and the consequences may be years away.

This may be particularly true among adolescents. Adolescents currently constitute only about 1 percent of all diagnosed cases of AIDS in the United States (CDC, 2000). But given the long incubation period and the research findings that suggest that adolescents are not very well informed about AIDS, many researchers think this may be an underestimation. Adolescents are also more prone than the general public to misconceptions and prejudices generated by the frightening new disease.

For example, some adolescents have the misconception that AIDS can be transmitted through casual contact such as kissing or hugging someone with AIDS, or sharing their utensils or bathroom facilities. Such misconceptions unnecessarily increase fear and anxiety in everyone. AIDS prevention efforts aimed at adolescents often have as their main goal the dispelling of such myths (Greene & others, 1996; Sigelman & others, 1996).

Other Sexually Transmitted Infections (STIs)

Often lost in the public focus on the burgeoning AIDS problem is a truly epidemic increase in the prevalence of other STIs. Because of its fatal nature, AIDS gets most of the press and the major funding. But STIs such as gonorrhea, syphilis, chlamydia, and herpes are running rampant compared with AIDS, particularly among adolescents. The effects of such venereal diseases range from the mildly annoying to the life-threatening.

Some of the more common STIs (other than AIDS) include the following:

Chlamydia Bacterial infection that may cause infertility; now the most common STI, there often are no symptoms.

- *Chlamydial infection.* **Chlamydia** is now the most common STI, with about 4 million new cases each year (CDC, 1997). Often chlamydia has no symptoms. It is diagnosed only when complications develop. It is particularly harmful for women and is a major cause of female infertility. Untreated, chlamydia can lead to pelvic inflammatory disease (see the information to follow). As with all of these diseases, it can be transmitted to another person whether symptoms are present or not. The news about this infection, however, is excellent. A seven-day course of antibiotic treatment has been found to be very effective.

Gonorrhea Well-known venereal infection accounting for between 1.5 and 2 million cases per year.

- *Gonorrhea.* The well-known venereal disease **gonorrhea** infects 750,000 persons per year in the U.S. (CDC, 1977). Approximately the same amount of cases go unreported each year, and occur among adolescents and young adults (Sexually Transmitted Diseases Sourcebook, 1997). Gonorrhea is caused by bacteria and can be treated with antibiotics. When penicillin was introduced in the 1940s, the incidence of gonorrhea declined dramatically. The most common symptoms are painful urination and a discharge from the penis or the vagina.

Pelvic inflammatory disease (PID) Infection that often results from chlamydia or gonorrhea, and frequently causes prolonged problems, including infertility.

- *Pelvic inflammatory disease.* **Pelvic inflammatory disease (PID)** frequently causes prolonged problems, including infertility. It is usually caused by untreated chlamydia or gonorrhea. These infections spread to the fallopian tubes, resulting in PID. The scarring the infection causes often prevents successful impregnation. More than 1 million new cases per year occur in the United States (Sexually Transmitted Diseases Sourcebook, 1997), with infection rate highest among teens. Women who are most likely to get it are those who use an intrauterine device for birth control, have multiple sex partners, are teenagers, or have had PID before. PID is so widespread that it causes $2.6 billion in medical costs per year!

Genital herpes An incurable sexually transmitted infection, with about 500,000 new cases every year.

- *Genital herpes.* **Genital herpes** is an incurable disease, with about 500,000 new cases every year. Spread by a virus during skin-to-skin contact, the major symptom of genital herpes is an outbreak of genital sores, which can occur as often as once a month. Estimates suggest about 30 million people in this country suffer from this infection. Unlike chlamydia, problems associated with herpes are mainly emotional and social rather than medical. People with herpes often experience embarrassment and low self-esteem about their bodies.

Syphilis   A sexually transmitted infection that presents a great danger in that in its early stage there are no symptoms. If untreated, it can be fatal.

- *Syphilis*. Like gonorrhea, **syphilis** is no longer the killer it was before penicillin. However, this sexually transmitted disease still accounts for 134,000 new cases per year. Caused by bacteria, the first sign of syphilis is a chancre ("shan-ker"), a painless open sore that usually shows up on the tip of the penis and around or in the vagina. This disease must be treated with antibiotics or it can be fatal.

Hepatitis B   A viral infection transmitted through sex or shared needles.

- *Hepatitis B*. About 300,000 new cases of **hepatitis B** occur each year in the United States (Sexually Transmitted Diseases Sourcebook, 1997). This viral disease is transmitted through sexual contact and also through the sharing of infected needles. Although a preventive vaccine is available, those who are most at risk for hepatitis B (intravenous drug users, homosexual men, and inner-city heterosexuals) usually do not have the vaccine readily available to them.

Figure 12.1 depicts the relative percentage of new cases of each type of STI in the United States each year.

Studies have shown that the age group at greatest risk for STIs is individuals between 10 and 19 years old (Steers & others, 1996). This age group is particularly difficult to educate in any area concerning sexuality. The obstacles to education include individuals who refuse to take the information seriously, and parents who won't let the information be taught.

The AIDS crisis and the STI epidemic have several features in common. On the negative side, misconceptions contribute to both problems. Many young people believe that only promiscuous people get STIs, and that only homosexuals get AIDS. Having multiple sexual partners does increase the risk of contracting STIs, but most people do not view their sexual behavior, no matter how active, as being promiscuous. Recent research also suggests machismo gets in the way of proper condom use, an effective prevention technique for all STIs. A "real man" doesn't use condoms. And, finally, when people do contract a disease, strong social stigmas make accurate reporting difficult.

On the positive side, the preventive and educational measures are basically the same for AIDS and other STIs: Dispel the myths, increase general awareness and acknowledgment of the problem, and encourage more discriminating sexual practices. Perhaps some of the educational efforts made on behalf of AIDS prevention and treatment will have a helpful effect on the current STI epidemic. Historically the health focus on STIs has been on treatment, typically with antibiotics, but recently the Public Health Service has shifted its focus to prevention for all STIs. So perhaps comprehensive efforts of this kind that emphasize all STIs will prove fruitful.

Figure 12.1

The relative percentage of new cases of each type of STI in the United States each year.

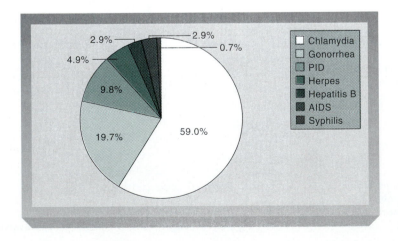

In summary, it seems safe to say that major changes in adolescent sexual practices have occurred in recent decades. Many of them must be viewed with considerable alarm, especially when we consider the tragic increases in STIs and pregnancy.

Guided Review

15. The nature of our concern about sexually transmitted infections has changed since the spread of AIDS, or _____ _____ _____ syndrome.
16. HIV attacks the body's _____ _____, thus leaving the person vulnerable to a number of fatal afflictions.
17. Other sexually transmitted infections include chlamydia, _____, pelvic inflammatory disease, syphilis, genital herpes, and hepatitis B.
18. Studies show that the age group at greatest risk for sexually transmitted infections is _____.

The Teenage Parent

"You're pregnant," the doctor said, "and you have some decisions to make. I suggest you don't wait too long to decide what you'll do. It's already been seven weeks, and time is running out!"

"Look, it just can't be true!" I replied. I was trying to convince myself that the clinic doctor was lying. It wasn't supposed to be like this! I was tired of the bitter quarrel I had been having with the doctor. I resented him with every passion. How could I let myself be seen like this?

I had been fearing this answer. I suppose I knew the truth all along, but I really didn't want to face it. I didn't want an abortion, that much I was sure of. Besides, where would I get the money?

For ages now, I had been thinking my period would come any day. Now the truth was in the open! I walked out of the office and headed aimlessly down the street. I looked around and saw only ugliness. I thought about God and how even He had deserted me. It all hurt so much.

"How could this have happened to me?" I thought. "Good girls don't get pregnant!" All of the things my mother had told me were lies. According to her, only the "fast girls got pregnant." The ones who stayed out late and hung around with boys. I wasn't part of that category!

I looked down at my stuffed belly and thought about my family. Would they be understanding? After all, they had plans for my future. They would be destroyed by the news.

"I'm not a tramp," I said to myself. "Then again, I'm only 16 and who would believe that Arthur and I really are in love?"

The feelings of this unmarried girl are all too typical. Each year, about one million teenage girls in the United States become pregnant. About half of those pregnancies result in live births; one-third result in abortions; and one-sixth result in miscarriages (see Table 12.5). Lillie-Blanton and associates (1996) cites four risk factors that predict teen pregnancy: poverty, early school failure, early behavior problems, and family problems. However, young girls can also be protected from the risk of teen pregnancy if they have a positive relationship with their parents and positive connections to their community or school.

Answers

15. acquired immune deficiency 16. immune system 17. gonorrhea 18. adolescence

Except for the youngest adolescents, birthrates for adolescents have been dropping in recent years. However, the extent to which young adolescents have been becoming pregnant is certainly a cause for great concern because physically, emotionally, and economically, they are at the greatest risk.

TABLE 12.5	TEENAGE PREGNANCY RATES BY YEAR: 1986–1996 WOMEN AGES 15–19	
Year		**Number of Pregnancies (per 1,000 women)**
1996		97.3
1994		106.1
1992		111.9
1990		117.1
1988		111.4
1986		106.7

Source: Alan Guttmacher Institute: *Teenage Pregnancy,* April 1999.

Guided Review

19. The largest increase in the pregnancy rate is occurring among those under the age of _____ .
20. Early coitus has been found to be highly associated with three adverse conditions: _____ , _____ , and _____ _____ _____ .
21. Contrary to the stereotype, most teenagers who become pregnant had been in a relationship for at least _____ _____ .

Illegal Behavior

Although they are not necessarily developmental in nature, we include brief sections on substance abuse and criminal behavior in this chapter because they often play a role in other aspects of development during adolescence. For the most part, that role clearly is negative.

Substance Abuse

It is difficult to say precisely how widespread substance abuse is. Studies differ from year to year, from region to region, and disappointingly, from one another (even when year and region are the same). Nevertheless there have been some sound studies. For

Answers

19. 15 20. STIs, pregnancies, abnormal Pap smears 21. six months

An Applied View

Talking to Teens about Pregnancy

Nurses, teachers, and counselors frequently have opportunities to help teens to clarify their attitudes toward pregnancy, whether they are currently involved with a pregnancy or not. For a number of reasons, these conversations seldom take place, however.

Sometimes those who work with teens feel that discussing pregnancy with them means pushing their own values on them. Others feel that this subject is very delicate and should not be discussed outside the church or home.

Others refrain from discussing it because they feel like they just don't know enough (readers of this book, of course, will not have to be concerned about this problem!). It does seem reasonable to make sure that teens have the objective facts about pregnancy and its repercussions for baby, mother, and father. Does this make sense to you?

It should be noted that some of the suggestions for talking to teens about sex in the box on page 318 are useful here, too.

example, see Table 12.6. Gfroerer and associates (1997) learned that high school dropouts had the highest rate of illicit drug and cigarette use, and college students had the highest rate of alcohol use. In fact, Bogenschneider and associates (1998) studied parental awareness of alcohol use among teens and found that "less than one third of parents were aware of their adolescents' drinking."

Contrary to the stereotype, several studies have found that adolescents of color are often less susceptible to substance abuse than European-American youths, in part because of religious influence (Flannery & others, 1996; Schulenberg & others,

TABLE 12.6 PERCENTAGES REPORTING LIFETIME, PAST YEAR, AND PAST MONTH USE OF ILLICIT DRUGS AMONG PERSONS AGED 12 TO 17

Drug	Time Period		
	Lifetime	Past Year	Past Month
Any Illicit Drug	27.6	20.3	10.9
Marijuana and Hashish	18.7	14.4	7.7
Cocaine	2.4	1.6	0.5
Crack	0.6	0.4	0.1
Heroin	0.4	0.3	0.2
Hallucinogens	5.7	3.8	1.1
LSD	3.8	2.4	0.6
PCP	0.9	0.4	0.1
Inhalants	9.1	4.6	1.9
Non-medical Use of Any Psychotherapeutic	10.9	7.0	2.9
Pain Relievers	8.2	5.3	2.2
Tranquilizers	2.5	1.5	0.5
Stimulants	3.9	2.1	0.7
Methamphetamine	1.4	0.7	0.3
Sedatives	0.8	0.5	0.2
Any Illicit Drug Other Than Marijuana	18.3	12.0	5.3

Source: Substance Abuse & Mental Health Services Administration. (1999) National Household Survey on Drug Abuse, http://www.samhsa.gov/oas/NHSDA/1999/Highlights.htm

Two excellent books on this topic are : (1) Cohen and Cohen's *A six-pack and a fake I.D.: Teens look at the drinking question.* New York: M. Evans. According to the authors of this book, the decision to drink or not to drink is personal rather than moral. (2) Harris' *Drugged athletes: The crisis in American sports.* New York: Four Winds Press. Harris provides an overview and discusses specific problems of drugs in sports at all levels.

1996). This appears not to be true of Native American teens, however (Mitchell, 1996). The adolescents most at risk for substance abuse are those who live with their fathers (fathers alone or married to their step-mother) (Hoffmann & Johnson, 1998). Teens living in families in which birth mothers and fathers are still together were found to have the lowest risk of abuse. Adolescent males studied by Schulenberg and associates (1996) exhibited other risk factors such as drinking "to get drunk," which was related to lack of self-efficacy and was predictive of binge drinking later in life.

A recent study on tobacco use (CDC, 2000) surveyed middle and high school students in order to determine the prevalence of cigarette, smokeless tobacco, cigar, pipe, bidi, and kretek use. The data indicate that 12.8 percent of students in grades 6–8 use some form of tobacco. Cigarettes (9.2 percent) were the most common type in use by both males and females and among racial and ethnic groups. Some adolescents, especially girls, believe that smoking will either help them lose weight or keep them from gaining weight. However, a recent study (Bolch, 1998) found that smokers are just as likely to gain weight as nonsmokers.

Use of new tobacco products such as kreteks (5.8 percent) and bidis (5.0 percent) has become popular among high school students. The overall prevalence of tobacco use was 34.8 percent among highschoolers with males using all forms of tobacco more than females (CDC, 2000).

The study predicts that if this pattern of tobacco use continues, an estimated 5 million Americans who were 18 years old or younger in 1995 could suffer from a smoking-related illness that could cause premature death.

Criminal Behavior

Although much could be said about juvenile delinquency, it is so changeable and varying by region, gender, and social class that we will not be able to go into it all here. Instead, we will limit this discussion to one aspect of adolescent criminal behavior, gang behavior, which has been moving in a most disturbing direction lately.

Gangs often offer youths the fulfillment of basic needs (Popenoe, 1996; Sanyika, 1996; Vigil, 1996). Some of their functions clearly coincide with those of the larger society. Gangs typically provide protection, recognition of the desire to feel wanted, and rites of passage that mark achievement, status, and acceptance, such as the initiation rite of a potential gang member.

The gang provides many adolescents with a structured life they never had at home. What makes the gang particularly cohesive is its function as a family substitute for adolescents whose strong dependency needs are displaced onto the peer group. The gang becomes a family to its members (Dishion & others, 1995).

The formation of juvenile gangs typically follows a sudden increase in this country of new ethnic groups due to immigration. The children of new immigrants have a difficult time breaking through cultural barriers such as a new language and racism. Perceiving their prospects of succeeding in the new society as bleak, some of these children form gangs, which provide the structure and security discussed, but also serve as an outlet to attack the society that seemingly will not accept them. In times past, these gangs were composed of Jewish, Irish, and Italian Americans. Today's gangs are frequently formed by Latinos, Asian Americans, and African-Americans. The gang becomes a vehicle for tearing its members away from the main social structures and authorities, in particular the family and school.

But today's gangs have some disturbing differences from those of years past (Sheley & others, 1995). They are much more heavily armed and seemingly much more willing to use their weapons. Movies like *West Side Story* depict gang members carrying knives, chains, and pipes. Today's urban gangs are often armed with AK-47 assault rifles and UZI submachine guns, grenades, and even cluster bombs. There is a new youth movement that has its members shunning illegal behavior, criminal behavior, and substance abuse (Sege, 1998). These adolescents call themselves "straight edge." Their social lifestyle, which includes activities such as listening to loud music and skateboarding, offers an alternative to the negative peer pressures of smoking, drinking, taking drugs, and engaging in casual sex. Although these "straight edge" teens adhere to abstinence, their group has been described as having "militant fringes" which sometimes spiral into violence.

To what can we attribute the growth of gang membership? Numerous studies have pointed to the absence of an effective father's presence, or at least the presence of an effective male role model (Popenoe, 1996; Vigil, 1996). For many, the violence of gang life is a means of proving masculine capability, which the absence of a father figure has unconsciously put in doubt. Fortunately, professionals are improving in their ability to assess violence risk (Borum, 1996; Grisso & Tomkins, 1996). In addition, a number of new programs, such as those that feature collaborative work situations, are having some success in combating this problem (Wolford & others, 1996).

As early as the early 1960s, Leonard Bernstein's *West Side Story* signaled society's concern that glib sociological excuses would only worsen the handling of behavior disorders. Public opinion and public institutions are turning back to a punishment model.

John Meeks

A Sociocultural View — *Portrait of a Gang Girl*

Tamika was just the gang leader's girlfriend. Then he went to jail, and now the gang depends on her to hold things together (LeBlanc, 1994).

She feels that being in the gang gives her a sense of family; it provides her with companions on the streets that she used to walk alone when she would run away from the father who sexually abused her. Gang life gives her more than a way to hang out with the boys; it also affords her the comfort, protection, and public code of behavior she desires.

Few after-school programs exist for mid-teen girls like Tamika. She prefers handball and softball to cheerleading, and would enjoy exercising her mathematical skills, except that people wouldn't "get down with that." The Brooklyn Navy Yard gang she belongs to is a loosely formed group of Puerto Rican teens who hang out, drink beer, and occasionally get into trouble. Tamika's grandmother's house, where she lives, is an hour's train ride from the Navy Yard, but she makes that journey every day because for her, the confusion there is more predictable and less personal than it is at home.

Although Tamika's gang isn't particularly violent, the members do commit small crimes such as mugging to get money. The gangs depersonalize the victims of their crimes, and prefer mugging to begging overwhelmed parents for money, because mugging only lasts a few minutes. Many of the members come from homes where parents are rarely sober, and these teens feel shame, guilt, and obligation for their family. The goal of the gang is not theft, but rather to promote pride in its cultural heritage.

Tamika's boyfriend, Manny, is currently in prison, which allows her freedom she wouldn't otherwise enjoy with him around. Ordinarily, when Manny goes out with friends, Tamika would be in "lock down," which means that she couldn't leave his mother's apartment. She wouldn't drink beer or smoke without him; she would be more quiet, and go to school regularly. In Manny's absence, Tamika has become close with another male member of the gang, Cee-lo, who provides her with sharp objects, such as paper clips and broken pens, which she uses to cut herself. The feeling of cutting helps her escape, she explains.

Aside from the scars on her body, Tamika also has a tattoo of the name Ruby inside a heart. Ruby, Tamika's grandmother, is the person Tamika loves more than anyone in the world. Tamika is proud of the way her grandmother cares for her: how she gets upset when Tamika is late and doesn't call; how worried she gets if Tamika doesn't come home. One of Tamika's dreams is to get rich and send her grandmother to a beautiful place where she doesn't have to work.

While Tamika waits for Manny's release from prison, she continues to search for the feeling of belonging that is diminishing in her gang. Although she considers joining other gangs, it is important to her that girls are appreciated as much as the boys. She doesn't want to join any organization that doesn't understand the most basic strengths girls have to offer: heart and knowledge.

A member of the Los Angeles Girl bloods gang.

Guided Review

22. In general, the study by Johnston and associates found a slight _____ in abuse of substances in recent years.
23. Some of the functions of a gang include protection, recognition of desire to feel wanted, rites of passage that mark _____, status, and acceptance.
24. Gangs can be cohesive because of their function as a _____ _____ for adolescents with strong dependency needs.
25. Gangs can become a vehicle for tearing their members away from the main _____ _____ of society.

CONCLUSION & SUMMARY

For each of the aspects of social interaction reviewed in this chapter—family interactions, peer relations, sexual behavior, sexually transmitted infections, teenage parenthood, criminal behavior—all adolescents must deal with one consistent trend: fast-paced change. Some of this change derives from ground swells in today's society, and some results from the nature of adolescence itself. Here again we see the biopsychosocial model demonstrated.

There are many changes ongoing in the American family. Many functions formerly fulfilled by the family are now the province of other agencies. The stress of divorce has a variety of outcomes, many of which we are learning to understand and deal with. The nurturing parenting style appears to promote many desirable traits.

Interactions among teenage peers change with each generation. Gang behavior is a growing threat to healthy development. Yet perhaps nothing has had a more resounding impact on adolescent life than the recent changes in our attitudes toward sexuality. The four areas of greatest change have been in homosexuality, sexually transmitted infections (including AIDS), the earlier and more widespread participation in sex by teenage females, and the increase in pregnancy and childbearing among younger teenagers.

Some observers have suggested that the biggest problem facing adolescents today, and one intertwined with those just listed, is the difficulty in knowing when childhood and youth have ended

and adulthood has begun. When the societal lines between these stages of development are blurred, youths cannot be blamed for not knowing how to behave. We will look into this phenomenon more fully in chapter 13.

As to a comprehensive definition of adolescence (the goal of this section of the book), we have seen that only by including biological, psychological (both cognitive and affective), and social factors can we begin to define this complex stage of life. We have reviewed numerous such factors: the sequence of physiological changes that occur in virtually every teen's body as well as the timing of those changes; the remarkable advances made in cognitive abilities; the social and emotional alterations that occur in relations with family, peers, and the larger society. Together these provide markers for the onset of the adolescent period. You should be aware, however, that a really adequate biopsychosocial definition cannot be presented in two chapters of a book, or even in one whole book. We learn more about this complex subject every day, and so our definition must be considered still in process.

What changes have occurred to American families and their roles in adolescent life in recent years?

- American families have lost five of their six main functions; the only remaining one is providing affection for family members.

- A number of effects of divorce pertain only to adolescents.
- There are four recognized parenting styles: authoritarian, permissive, authoritative, and nurturing.

What is the nature of peer relations during the teen years?

- Peer groups provide adolescents with a source of social activities and support, and an easy entry into opposite-sex friendships.
- The biological, psychological, cognitive, and social changes of adolescence affect the development of a teenager's peer relationships.
- Peer groups serve to control aggressive impulses, encourage independence, improve social skills, develop reasoning abilities, and form attitudes toward sexuality and sexual behavior. They may also strengthen moral judgment and values and improve self-esteem.
- Peer groups also aid in the development of self-concept and allow an adolescent to try out a new identity.

How do teens deal with sexual relations?

- Many teenagers are becoming sexually active at increasingly younger ages.
- Sexuality develops in three stages, from love of self to love of members of the same gender to love of members of the opposite gender.
- Masturbation is believed to be a harmless and universal form of human sexual expression.

- Homosexual behavior has been surrounded by many myths throughout history.
- Several theories suggest different origins of homosexual orientation: psychoanalytic, learning, and biopsychosocial.
- Many researchers now believe that homosexual orientation may already be set by adolescence.
- Many teens still obtain a great deal of information and misinformation about sex from their peers.
- Youths from stable family environments are less likely to engage in premarital sexual relations.
- Effective listening skills are essential for parents who wish to maintain good communication with their adolescents.
- Teenagers misuse sex for many nonsexual reasons, including a search for affection, rebellion against parents, venting anger, and alleviating boredom.
- Many adolescent runaways and prostitutes are the products of sexual abuse, often by someone they know, a family member, or parent.

What new information do we have about sexually transmitted infections?

- Today a high prevalence of sexually transmitted infections (STIs) is found in sexually active adolescents.
- AIDS (acquired immune deficiency syndrome) causes the most concern, because it is currently incurable and fatal. As yet, it is not very common in adolescents, but because it usually lies dormant for 10 to 15 years, it is a cause for great concern.
- Other STIs that affect adolescents are increasing in epidemic proportions, including chlamydia, gonorrhea, genital herpes, syphilis, and hepatitis B.
- In spite of increased availability and information about contraceptive methods, many teenagers continue to engage in unprotected sex.

How is the modern teenage parent dealing with the stresses that parenthood entails?

- Teenage pregnancy and parenthood are on the rise among younger teens. With rare exceptions, this situation causes a lot of heartache for the teenage parents, their parents, and their child.

- Teenage mothers who receive emotional support from their families, who continue in school, and who have no additional children while they are still teenagers are likely to have better-adjusted children and avoid the cycle of poverty.
- When teens possess strong self-esteem, feelings of hope concerning the future, and job and academic skills for entry into the job market, they are less likely to become teenage parents.

What recent information do we have on adolescent illegal behavior?

- Drug and alcohol abuse is still prevalent among teens. Tobacco use is on the rise again as is use of marijuana, cocaine, and LSD.
- Gangs typically have a high degree of cohesion and organization, a consistent set of norms, clearly defined leaders, and coherent organization for warfare.
- Gangs have become much more violent in the past decade, probably in part as a response to increased drug trafficking.

KEY TERMS

AIDS (acquired immune deficiency syndrome)
Authoritarian parenting style
Authoritative parenting style
Autosexuality
Biopsychosocial theory of homosexuality
Chlamydia

Crowds
Genital herpes
Gonorrhea
Hepatitis B
Heterosexuality
Homosexuality
Human immunodeficiency virus (HIV)
Learning theory of homosexuality

Nurturing parenting style
Pelvic inflammatory disease (PID)
Permissive parenting style
Psychoanalytic theory of homosexuality
Reflective listening
Sexually transmitted infections (STIs)
Subculture
Syphilis

WHAT DO YOU THINK?

1. Do you think that your adolescent peer group followed the developmental patterns described in this chapter?
2. What are some of the most important effects that your teenage peer group had on your life?
3. Do you agree with the theorists who claim that there are three stages in the development of love and sexuality and that this development is natural?

4. In what ways do you believe family life in the United States will be different in 50 years from the ways it exists today?
5. If you were the mayor of a medium-size city, what actions would you take to try to reduce the incidence of sexually transmitted infections?
6. A number of large, urban high schools are creating day-care facilities for the babies and

children of high school students. Do you think public schools should be providing these services? What services, if any, should junior and senior high schools provide to teenage parents?

In what cases should juvenile offenders be tried as adults? Should they always be treated as adults? Should they be treated differently because of their age? What things need to be considered?

CHAPTER REVIEW TEST

1. Brown (1990) states that the peer group can change in four ways during adolescence: adolescents spend more time with peers; they receive less adult supervision; they interact more with peers of the opposite sex; and they
   a. interact with peers in a work setting.
   b. become sexually active.
   c. begin to identify with certain crowds.
   d. interact more with peers in school and service activities.

2. Most family researchers have agreed that the three styles of parenting are
   a. authoritarian, permissive, and devoted.
   b. permissive, aggressive, and impassive.
   c. authoritarian, authoritative, and permissive.
   d. aggressive, impassive, and devoted.

3. What reason is cited in the text for why there may be a decline in early sexual activity?
   a. Concern about AIDS and other STIs
   b. Prevailing conservative attitudes
   c. More people devoting time to making money
   d. The increasing influence of religion

4. The first stage of sexuality
   a. is heterosexuality.
   b. is homosexuality.
   c. is autosexuality.
   d. depends on the individual.

5. Parents who practice a nurturing parenting style are
   a. interested in their child's behavior but seldom prescribe rules, relying instead on modeling and family discussions to instill a well-defined set of values.
   b. controlling but loving in guiding their children through development.
   c. nurturing but providing little structure in the family.
   d. nurturing yet strictly controlling of the way in which the family functions.

6. The genetic theory on homosexuality claims that
   a. people learn to be homosexual.
   b. as children homosexuals identified with the same-sex parent.
   c. persons born with a predisposition toward homosexuality can be influenced by the environment to either select or avoid homosexuality.
   d. many homosexuals are in denial about their genetically predisposed orientation.

7. Although he has a girlfriend, Steve wants to prove to his friends that he can "score" with a number of different girls in school. Steve's nonsexual motive for sex is to
   a. get affection.
   b. confirm his masculinity.
   c. ensure fidelity of his girlfriend.
   d. obtain greater self-esteem.

8. A female adolescent who "acts out" by running away, engaging in sexual promiscuity, or damaging her school performance may be a victim of
   a. drug abuse.
   b. peer pressure.
   c. extreme loneliness.
   d. sexual abuse.

9. The CDC estimates how many people in the United States are currently infected with the initial virus of AIDS?
   a. 50,000
   b. 100,000
   c. 500,000 to 600,000
   d. 1 to 1.5 million

10. Intravenous drug users, homosexual men, and inner-city heterosexuals are groups most at risk for contracting
    a. syphilis.
    b. genital herpes.
    c. hepatitis B.
    d. gonorrhea.

11. The highest rates of teen pregnancy occur for those
    a. under age 15.
    b. 15 to 16 years of age.
    c. 16 to 18 years of age.
    d. 18 to 19 years of age.

12. Sara is an African-American teenager who grew up in a poor, single-parent home, and has low occupational aspirations. Sara fits the profile of a
    a. drug abuser.
    b. gang member.
    c. pregnant teenager.
    d. domestic abuse victim.

13. Risk factors that predict teenage pregnancy are
    a. early school failure.
    b. early behavior problems.
    c. both a and b.
    d. neither a nor b.

14. Important racial differences can be found in recent research on teenage pregnancy. It seems that studies of low-income nonwhite girls focus on societal factors, whereas studies of white, middle-class girls tend to focus on
    a. social causes.
    b. psychological causes.
    c. cognitive ability causes.
    d. moral reasoning ability causes.

15. John joins a gang because it serves as a pseudo-family for him. Most likely John has strong _____ needs that are being displaced onto the peer group.
    a. dependency
    b. friendship
    c. financial
    d. All of the answers are correct.

16. Recent research indicates that gangs have which of the following characteristics?
    a. They possess a consistent set of norms and expectations that are understood by all gang members.
    b. Members have lower expectations of success than do nonmembers.
    c. Members are as likely to have divorced parents as are nonmembers.
    d. Members are more likely to score high on IQ tests than are nonmembers.

Answers

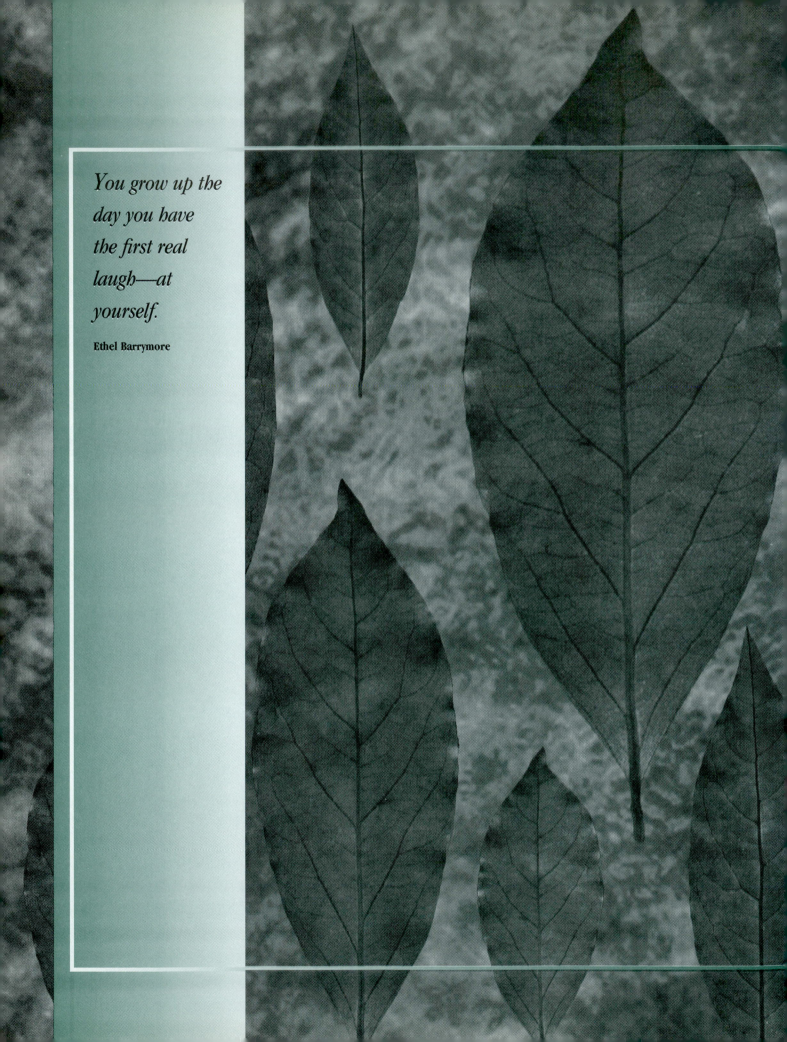

You grow up the day you have the first real laugh—at yourself.

Ethel Barrymore

CHAPTER 13

Physical and Cognitive Development in Early Adulthood

Chapter Outline

Yudia cannot believe how rapidly her feelings keep changing. One moment she is curious and excited, the next, nervous and afraid. Tonight begins her *igubi*, the rite that celebrates her induction into adulthood. Yudia has longed for this day most of her 11 years, but now she wonders if she really wants the responsibilities of a grown-up.

Though it seems much longer, only a week has passed since the excruciating beginning of her initiation. The memory of it is already dimming: the bright fire, her women relatives pinning her down on the table, her grandmother placing a thin sharp stone against her vulva, the searing pain.

The women had held and consoled her, empathizing fully with her feelings. Each had been through the same agony. For them, too, it occurred shortly after their first menstruation. They had explained to her that this was just the beginning of the suffering she must learn to endure as an adult woman. All during the past week, they had been teaching her—about the pain her husband would sometimes cause her, about the difficulties of pregnancy and childbirth, about the many hardships she must bear stoically. For she is Kaguru, and all Kaguru women accept their lot in life without complaint.

It has been a hard week, but tonight the pleasure of the *igubi* will help her forget her wound. There will be singing, dancing, and strong beer to drink. The ceremony, with its movingly symbolic songs, will go on for two days and nights. Only the women of this Tanzanian village will participate, intoning the time-honored phrases that will remind Yudia all her life of her adult duties.

In a large hut less than a mile from the village, Yudia's male cousin Mateya and seven other 13-year-old Kaguru boys huddle close, even though the temperature in the closely thatched enclosure is a stifling 110 degrees. Rivulets of sweat flow from their bodies and flies dot their arms, backs, and legs. They no longer pay attention to the flies, nor the vivid slashes of white, brown, and black clay adorning all their faces. Their thoughts are dominated by a single fear: Will they cry out when the elder's sharpened stone begins to separate the tender foreskin from their penises? Each dreams of impressing his father, who will be watching, by smiling throughout the horrible ordeal.

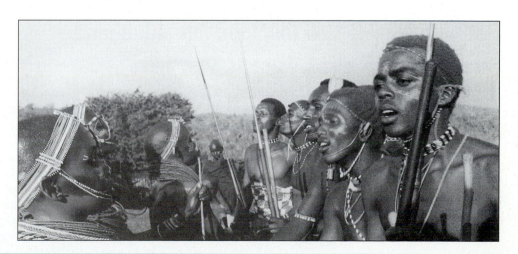

Initiation into adulthood differs greatly in various parts of the world.

Three months of instruction and testing have brought the young men to this point. They have learned many things together: how to spear their own food, how to tend their tiny gardens, how to inseminate their future wives, and most important, how to rely on themselves when in danger.

The last three months have been exhausting. The boys have been through many trials. In some, they had to prove they could work together; in others, their skill in self-preservation was tested. For most of them, being out of contact with their mothers was the hardest part. They have not seen any of the female members of their families since they started their training. Unlike Yudia's initiation, which is designed to draw her closer to the adult women of the tribe, Mateya's initiation is designed to remove him forever from the influence of the females and to align him with the adult men.

Now it is evening. Mateya is the third to be led out to the circle of firelight. Wide-eyed, he witnesses an eerie scene. His male relatives are dancing in a circle around him, chanting the unchanging songs. The grim-faced elder holds the carved ceremonial knife. Asked if he wishes to go on, the boy nods yes. Abruptly the ritual begins: The hands of the men hold him tight; the cold knife tip touches his penis; a shockingly sharp pain sears his loins; he is surprised to hear a piercing scream; then, filled with shame, he realizes it comes from him.

Thus far, Yudia's and Mateya's initiations have been different. Mateya's has been longer and harder than Yudia's. She is being brought even closer to the women who have raised them both, but Mateya must now align himself with the men.

The initiations are similar, though, in that both youths have experienced severe physical pain. In both cases, the operations were meant to sensitize them to the vastly greater role sex will now play in their lives. Furthermore, their mutilations made them recognizable to all as adults of the Kaguru tribe.

At this "coming out" ceremony, males and females also receive new names, usually those of close ancestors. This illustrates the continuity of the society. The beliefs of the tribe are preserved in the continuous flow from infant to child to adult to elder to deceased and to newborn baby again. When all is done, Yudia and Mateya can have no doubt that they have passed from childhood to adulthood. ✪

Chapter Objectives

After reading this chapter you should be able to answer the following questions.

◆ How are American youths being initiated into adulthood today?

◆ What are the significant factors affecting physical development in early adulthood?

◆ How does cognition change during the early adult years?

◆ What patterns of work typify young adults today?

Initiation into Adulthood

Hazing The practice of initiating individuals into group membership through arduous and demeaning tasks.

The horrors of the college fraternity initiation have been softened by legal restrictions and by more humane attitudes. Nevertheless, most of us have heard of cases of maimings and even deaths of young men who have been put through **hazing,** the initiation rite that precedes full acceptance into fraternity membership. Hazing continues to exist not only in fraternities, but in the military as well. A recent report of hazing aboard a Coast Guard cutter (Brelis, 1998) describes humiliating and degrading acts of verbal and physical abuse to new recruits. Although many military groups have anti-hazing policies, hazing activities are reported to be common.

Why do some people, and the groups they wish to be associated with, seem to enjoy holding initiation rites so much? And why are so many adolescents, many of them otherwise highly intelligent and reasonable, willing and eager to endure such pain? Is it simply because they want to join the group, to feel that they belong?

There seems to be more to it than that. Throughout the world, adolescents readily engage in such activities because they seem to want to be tested, to prove to themselves that they have achieved the adult virtues of courage, independence, and self-control. And the adults seem to agree that adolescents should prove they have attained these traits before being admitted to the "club of maturity."

The Transition to Adulthood in the United States

How are youths inducted into adulthood in the United States? Are Western initiation rites adequate? In the rural past of the United States, it used to be fairly clear when one became an adult. In their late teens or early 20s, individuals usually got married and assumed an adult role. Males were accepted as partners in the family farm or business; females became housewives. This has changed in many ways.

This is not to say that Americans have no activities that signal the passage to maturity. We have a number of types of activities, which usually happen at various stages and ages of adolescence. Here is a list of the types and some examples of each:

Religious

Bar mitzvah or bas mitzvah
Confirmation
Participating in a ceremony, such as reading from the Bible

Sexual

Menarche (first menstruation)
Nocturnal emissions (male "wet dreams")
First sexual encounter

Social

"Sweet Sixteen" or debutante parties
Going to the senior prom
Joining a gang, fraternity, or sorority
Beginning to shave
Being chosen as a member of a sports team
Moving away from one's family and relatives
Joining the armed forces
Receiving a bridal shower
Getting married
Becoming a parent
Voting for the first time

Educational

Getting a driver's license
Graduating from high school
Going away to college

Economic

Getting a checking or credit card account
Buying a first car
Getting a first job

This list offers a good example of the biopsychosocial approach. Some of the occurrences are mainly biological (menarche), some psychological (going away to college), and some social (getting married). Which activities help in the passage from adolescence to adulthood? How might we improve this passage? In this and chapter 14, we will look at the developmental trends and needs of young adults, which will help us to better answer these important questions.

Implications of the Lack of an Initiation Ceremony

For most adolescents in our society today, the teen years are a kind of "time out," a moratorium for trying out different ways of being. More and more, we are having doubts that this moratorium is turning out to be effective. In fact, it appears that crime is one of the ways that some youths are initiating themselves into adulthood. Males especially seem to need to do something dangerous and difficult. Males who are raised without fathers or father substitutes are especially vulnerable to the attractions of criminality (Dacey & Kenny, 1997).

In the 1960s and early 1970s, American youths sought to establish their identities by imitating the very rituals of the preindustrial tribes described earlier in this chapter. Known as "hippies" and "flower children," they attempted to return to a simpler life. Many of them returned to the wilderness, living on farms and communes away from the large cities in which they were brought up. Many totally rejected the cultural values of their parents. The most famous symbol of their counterculture was the Woodstock musical marathon in 1969. With its loud, throbbing music, nudity, and widespread use of drugs, the event was similar to many primitive tribal rites. Yet these self-designed initiation rites also seem to be unsuccessful as passages to maturity. Most of the communes and other organizations of the youth movement of the 1960s have since failed.

Organized sport is another attempt to include initiation rites in American life. The emphasis on athletic ability has much in common with the arduous tasks given to preindustrial youths. In particular, we can see a parallel in the efforts by fathers to get their sons to excel in Little League Baseball and Pop Warner Football. Fathers (and often mothers) are seen exhorting the players to try harder, to fight bravely, and when hurt, to "act like a man" and not cry.

Thus, in delinquency, the counterculture, and sports, we see evidence that members of several age groups today yearn for the establishment of some sort of initiation rite. Adolescents and adults alike seem to realize that something more is needed to provide assistance in this difficult transitional period. But what?

Traditional initiation rites are inappropriate for American youths. In preindustrial societies, individual status was ascribed by the tribe to which the person belonged. Social scientists call this an ascribed identity. The successes or failures of

An Applied VIEW

The Components of Maturity

Think of the woman and the man who are the most mature persons you know—people with whom you are personally familiar, or people who are famous. Then ask yourself, "Why do I think these people are so much more mature than others?" In the spaces to the right, for both the male and the female, create a list of the characteristics that seem to distinguish them in their maturity.

How much do the lists differ? Is male maturity significantly different from female maturity? Which of the two people is older? Which of the two do you admire more? Which of the two are you more likely to want to imitate? Were you able to think of many candidates for this title of "most mature adult," or was it difficult to think of anyone? Are either or both of the people you picked professionals? Are either or both of these persons popular with their own peer group? What is the significance of your answers to you?

Female	Male
1.	1.
2.	2.
3.	3.
4.	4.
5.	5.
6.	6.
7.	7.
8.	8.
9.	9.
10.	10.

each tribe determined the prestige of its members. Family background and individual effort usually made little difference. In earlier times in the United States, the family was the prime source of status. Few children of the poor became merchants, doctors, or lawyers. Today, personal effort and early commitment to a career path play a far greater role in the individual's economic and social success. This is called an achieved identity (see chapter 11). For this reason (and others), preindustrial customs are not compatible with Western youths today.

It has been suggested that sports play the same role in life as the arduous tasks performed by youths in centuries past: learning coordination, cooperation, and the other skills necessary in adult work. Can you think of ways that sports might serve as initiation rites?

Guided Review

1. Rites of passage use _____ to capture elements of adult life that have been denied youths and are now accessible to them as they are initiated into adulthood.
2. In the United States today, initiation activities occur in religious, _____, social, educational, and _____ settings.
3. The "time out" period, when adolescents explore possibilities and continue their education, is called the adolescent _____ .
4. Organized sports, countercultural involvement, and _____ _____ are evidence that adolescents yearn for the establishment of some form of initiation rite.

Physical Development

Adult psychologist Malcolm Knowles (1989) has stated:

> As I see it, there are four definitions of "adult." First, the biological definition: we become adult biologically when we reach the age at which we can reproduce.... Second, the legal definition: we become adult legally when we reach the age at which the law says we can vote, get a driver's license, marry without consent.... Third, the social definition: we become adult socially when we start performing adult roles.... Finally, the psychological definition: we become adult psychologically when we arrive at a self-concept of being responsible for our own lives, of being self-directing. From the viewpoint of learning, it is the psychological definition that is most crucial. But it seems to me that the process of gaining a self-concept of self-directedness starts early in life, ... and grows cumulatively as we become biologically mature, start performing adult-like roles, ... and take increasing responsibility for making our own decisions. So we become adult by degree as we move through childhood and adolescence, and the rate of increase by degree is probably accelerated if we live in homes, study in schools, and participate in youth organizations that foster our taking increasing responsibilities. But most of us probably do not have full-fledged self-concepts of self-directedness until we leave school or college, get a full-time job, marry, and start a family (p. 6).

You might enjoy a book by Maya Angelou on this subject: *I know why the caged bird sings.* New York: Random House. Ms. Angelou recounts her childhood in rural Arkansas. Her strength and resilience model the building of a strong personal and cultural identity.

Let us begin our exploration of young adulthood with a consideration of Knowles' first criterion, physical development. We address three main questions about physical development in this section: When is peak development reached? What is organ reserve? What are the effects of lifestyle?

Answers

1. rituals 2. sexual, economic 3. moratorium 4. delinquent activities

The Peak Is Reached

Early adulthood is the life period during which physical changes slow down. Table 13.1 provides some basic examples of physical development in early adulthood.

In sports, young adults are in their prime condition as far as speed and strength are concerned. A healthy individual can continue to partake in less strenuous sports for years. As the aging process continues, however, the individual will realize a loss of the energy and strength felt in adolescence.

Early adulthood is also the time when the efficiency of most body functions begins to decline. For example, cardiac output and vital capacity start to decrease. As Table 13.2 clearly shows, these declines are quite steady right through old age. It is important to remember that this chart gives the average changes; considerable differences will occur from individual to individual.

Organ Reserve

Organ reserve That part of the total capacity of our body's organs that we do not normally need to use.

Organ reserve refers to that part of the total capacity of our body's organs that we do not normally need to use. Our body is designed to do much more than it is usually called upon to do. Much of our capacity is held on reserve. As we get older, these reserves grow smaller. The peak performance that each of our organs (and muscles, bone, etc.) is capable of declines. A 50-year-old man can fish all day with his 25-year-old son and can usually take a long walk with him without becoming exhausted, but he has no chance at all of winning a footrace against him.

TABLE 13.1 SUMMARY OF PHYSICAL DEVELOPMENT IN EARLY ADULTHOOD
Height
Female: maximum height reached at age 18.   Male: maximum height reached at age 20.
Weight (age 20–30)
Female: 14-pound weight gain and increase in body fat.   Male: 15-pound weight gain.
Muscle Structure and Internal Organs

From 19–26: Internal organs attain greatest physical potential. The young adult is in prime condition as far as speed and strength are concerned.
 After 26: Body slowing process begins.
     Spinal disks settle, causing decrease in height.
     Fatty tissue increases, causing increase in weight.
     Muscle strength decreases.
     Reaction times level off and stabilize.
     Cardiac output declines.

Sensory Function Changes
The process of losing eye lens flexibility begins as early as age 10 and continues until age 30. This loss results in difficulty focusing on close objects.   During early adulthood, women can detect higher-pitched sounds than men.
Nervous System
The brain continues to increase in weight and reaches its maximum potential by the adult years.

Source: Bureau of the Census, 1996.

TABLE 13.2 APPROXIMATE DECLINES IN VARIOUS HUMAN FUNCTIONAL CAPACITIES WITH AGE

	Percent of Function Remaining		
	30 Years	**60 Years**	**80 Years**
Nerve conduction speed	100	96	88
Basal metabolic rate	100	96	84
Standard cell water	100	94	81
Cardiac index	100	82	70
Glomerular filtration rate	100	96	61
Vital capacity	100	80	58
Renal plasma flow	100	89	51
Maximal breathing cap	100	80	42

From Alexander P. Spence, *Biology of Human Aging,* © 1989, p. 8. Adapted by permission of Prentice-Hall, Inc., Englewood Cliffs, NJ.

This is why people are aware of little decline during the early adult years and often do not experience a sharp decline in most of their everyday activities even into middle age. Our organ reserves are diminishing, but we are unaware of it because we call on them so seldom.

Of course, some individuals regularly try to use the total capacity of their organ reserves. Professional athletes are an example. Here again we see the biopsychosocial model in action. Biology sets the limits, but psychological factors (e.g., personal pride) and social factors (e.g., the cheering crowd) determine whether the person "gives it her all."

The Effect of Lifestyle on Health

Young adults are healthier than older adults in just about every way. All of the body's systems reach peak functioning at this age. Less illness occurs, too. For example, young adults have fewer hospitalizations and visits to the doctor's office than older adults, and those that do occur are caused mainly by injuries. Even catching a cold happens more rarely at this stage than at any other stage of life (U.S. Bureau of the Census, 1996). According to the Center for Disease Control (CDC) (1999), there are approximately one and a half times less reported AIDS cases during young adulthood than in middle adulthood. Non-Hispanic whites and non-Hispanic blacks make up more than half of these reported cases.

Good health is clearly related to factors such as genetics, age, and the medical treatment locally available. But these factors are generally beyond the control of the individual. Increasingly, people are beginning to realize that their style of life plays an enormous role in their own health.

The impact of lifestyle on health is dramatically illustrated by the observations in the book *The Healing Brain* (Ornstein & Sobel, 1987). These researchers determined that the miraculous technological gains in medicine over the last 100 years have not had as great an impact on health as one might think. It is true that at birth, we can expect many more years of life than people could in the last century. However, a person who has reached the age of 45 today has a life expectancy of only a couple years more than the person who had reached the age of 45 a hundred years ago, in spite of all the money and effort now spent on medicine after that age.

As a counterexample, Ornstein and Sobel offer the people of Nevada and Utah, two states and populations that are similar in geography, education, income, and availability of medical treatment. Yet Nevada's death rate is 40 percent higher than

Utah's. Utah is largely composed of Mormons who live a relatively quiet and stable lifestyle, including very low incidences of smoking and drinking. In Nevada, people drink and smoke much more heavily, and it shows. The rates of cirrhosis of the liver and lung cancer are 100 to 600 percent higher in Nevada than in Utah. A man who reaches the age of 45 in Utah can expect to live 11 years more than the man who reaches age 45 in Nevada. The point is that simple, cost-free choices under the control of the individual are much more effective at improving health than all the expensive, time-consuming medical advances of the last century. Perhaps our priorities are misplaced.

Based on this information, we could conclude that a simple difference in style of life can have more of an effect on health than medical advances. Let's look at the influence on health of some specific lifestyle choices.

Choices of Foods

Cholesterol A substance in the blood that adheres to the walls of the blood vessels, restricting the flow of blood and causing strokes and heart attacks.

Nutrition plays an important role throughout human development, from neonates to the elderly. By the time we reach middle adulthood, however, increasing evidence demonstrates the influence of nutrition on two major health concerns, heart disease and cancer. Medical science has recently established a link between heart disease and a substance in the blood, **cholesterol.** Cholesterol has been found to leave deposits along the walls of blood vessels, blocking the flow of blood to the heart and resulting in a heart attack. The main culprit in high levels of cholesterol has been found to be diets high in fat. Typically Americans consume 40 percent of their total calories as fat. The American Heart Association (1998) recommends changes in diet, such as eating fish and poultry instead of red meat, yogurt and cottage cheese instead of cheese, margarine instead of butter, fewer eggs, and drinking skim milk instead of whole milk, as ways of lowering cholesterol in the body. Exercise is also very helpful.

A similar link has been found between diet and certain types of cancer, such as cancer of the breast, stomach, intestines, and the esophagus. The American Cancer Society has also come out with a set of recommendations for an improved, healthy diet. They too recommend lowering fat intake to no more than 30 percent of the daily caloric total and following a diet that is high in fiber, a substance that helps the digestive process. High-fiber foods include leafy vegetables such as cauliflower, broccoli, and brussels sprouts, as well as whole-grain cereals and breads. The proliferation of new products that feature lower levels of fat and higher levels of fiber indicates that the American public is taking this new knowledge to heart (no pun intended).

Obesity has become an epidemic in this country. According to Jeffrey P. Koplan, director of the CDC (1999), "Overweight and physical inactivity account for more than 300,000 premature deaths each year in the United States, second only to tobacco-related deaths. Obesity is an epidemic and should be taken seriously as any infectious disease epidemic." Anyone who is 10 percent over the normal weight for their height and build is considered overweight. Anyone who is 30 percent over the normal weight is considered obese. Obesity has been a very serious health concern and is rapidly getting worse. The CDC (1999) reports that 17.9 percent of the U.S. population was obese in 1998, compared to only 12 percent in 1991. The rate of obesity increased in every state, for both women and men, across all ages, races, and educational levels. The highest increase was found among young adults, people who had some college education and Latinos. Regionally, the South accounted for the largest increase in obesity. Of the Southern states, Georgia's increase in obesity was 101 percent!

What are the main causes of obesity? According to Koplan (1999), lack of physical activity and the convenient American lifestyle are the culprits. Exercise has taken a backseat to television, labor-saving machinery, and automobiles.

Use of Alcohol

Most people consume alcohol to attain the relaxed, uninhibited feeling that alcohol tends to produce. The fact is, alcohol dulls the senses. Specifically, it decreases reaction times in the brain and nervous system. Continued drinking may affect the sex life of males, by making it difficult for them to attain and keep an erection.

An Applied View

Dealing with Adult Children of Alcoholics

According to Atkinson (1999), clear agreement exists on three aspects of alcoholism: Alcoholism runs in families; children of alcoholics (COA's) run a higher risk of developing alcoholism than other children; children of alcoholics tend to marry alcoholics. She also found that children of alcoholics usually manifest six characteristics. They

- judge themselves without mercy
- have diminished capacity to feel
- constantly seek approval and affirmation
- are impulsive (tendency to react rather than act)
- have feelings of guilt when sticking up for themselves

- involve themselves in relationships where the other person can be rescued or pitied

Atkinson reports that studies have estimated it may be as high as one out of every four Americans is a child of an alcoholic. In addition to the six characteristics noted above, children of alcoholics also exhibit additional emotional struggles. For example, they experience feelings of shame, low self-esteem, fear, guilt, difficulty trusting others, anger, and fear of abandonment. Very often, COA's demonstrate dysfunctional behaviors and emotions. She suggests that they rarely recognize the root of these problems. Perhaps this is one reason why COA's are more likely to attempt and commit suicide.

Even though problems associated with alcoholism (e.g., with family, the law, and one's health) have been highlighted in the popular press, college presidents continue to regularly rank alcohol abuse as the number one problem on campuses (Wechsler & others, 1999). Binge drinking (defined as five or more drinks in a row for men, and four or more drinks in a row for women, one or more times during a two-week period) has become widespread. The practice is not only harmful for those who drink, but also for those in their immediate environment. For example, bingeing is associated with injuries from fights and automobile accidents. Honan (1997) noted increasing numbers of drug arrests on major college campuses according to an annual survey of campus crime. For example, almost all sexual assaults at one major west coast university were alcohol related. Some college officials attribute the rise in arrests to stricter enforcement of the laws, rather than an actual increase in substance abuse. However, the rise in the number of arrests is worth noting, because arrests for other crimes, such as murders, robberies, and burglaries has decreased (F.B.I., 2000).

Ironically, some research has indicated that a daily, moderate intake of alcohol may be beneficial (although not for those over the age of 50—see chapter 15). Such small amounts of alcohol seem to produce a protein in the blood that helps lower cholesterol. Unfortunately, the addictive qualities of alcohol make it impossible for many people to drink in only moderate amounts. This is why treatment programs such as the very successful Alcoholics Anonymous ask their clients to abstain totally from alcohol rather than try to control their drinking (Michels & others, 1999).

Use of Tobacco

Although the use of tobacco has been falling rapidly, at about 1 percent per year since 1987, it continues to be the leading preventable cause of death in the United States. Currently more than 400,000 deaths per year have been attributed to cigarette smoking in this country (CDC, 2000), adding up to over $50 billion in medical costs. Every year, more people die from smoking than from alcohol, AIDS, drug abuse, murders, car accidents, suicides, and fires—combined! (CDC, 2000). Cigarette smoking has been proven to cause lung and esophageal cancer, heart disease, and chronic lung disease. It also contributes to various other types of cancers (kidney, bladder, and pancreatic). Smokers are 14 times more likely to die from cancer of the lungs, and twice as likely to die of a heart attack as nonsmokers. Cigarette smoke is a combination of tar, nicotine, carbon monoxide, and various other chemicals. Smoking increases heart rate and blood pressure, it constricts blood vessels and reduces oxygen supply to tissue, thereby straining the heart.

An Informed VIEW

Can Drinking Alcohol Have Positive Effects?

In most articles you may have read about alcohol consumption, it has been associated with a variety of negative biological and psychological effects. Earlier research seemed to indicate that alcohol had no redeeming qualities. More recently, studies have indicated that moderate use of alcohol may have some beneficial effect. For example, anti-clotting properties of alcohol may account for decreased risk of coronary disease and heart attack (Klatsky, 1999).

Do you think the consumption of alcohol can have positive physiological and social effects? What advice would you get if you called your local Board of Health? The Alcoholics Anonymous Central Service Office? The Ask-A-Nurse Hotline?

If you would like to have a more informed opinion on this issue, you might want to read one of the articles on the subject referenced in this box.

You might also wish to learn more about it by going to our web site at http://www.mhhe.com/dacey5.

Cigar smoking has also recently become fashionable with young adults. This is evidenced by the popularity of trendy cigar bars and cigar clubs in cities across the United States. Even magazines, devoted almost exclusively to cigars, have continued in popularity. Such magazines often feature a celebrity smoking a cigar on the front cover. It is estimated that 5 percent of young adults smoke cigars (Substance Abuse and Mental Health Services Administration, 1999). Cigar smoking, like cigarette smoking, puts individuals at risk for cancer and heart disease. Health officials, including the Surgeon General, are now calling for warning labels, similar to those found on cigarettes, to be placed on cigar packages. The Surgeon General, David Satcher, warns, "the absence of such a warning on cigars could lead consumers to erroneously conclude that cigars do not carry health risks."

Peer pressure from friends is the major reason that young adults smoke. Young people who smoke tend to be extraverted and more disobedient toward authority than nonsmokers. Some young adults see smoking as a way of appearing older and more mature. Others, especially girls, believe that smoking will either help them lose weight or keep them from gaining weight. A recent study (Balch, 1998) indicates that smokers are just as likely to gain weight as nonsmokers. Young adults who go on to college smoke less than those who do not continue their education. Among young women, smoking is associated with being less athletic and more social, studying less, getting lower grades, and generally disliking school more than nonsmoking females.

The use of tobacco among college students has risen an alarming 28 percent since 1993. In an effort to learn more about the trend in cigarette use among young adults, Wechsler and associates (1998) studied the smoking behavior of college students between 1993 and 1997. Students were randomly selected from 116 colleges nationwide. The sample consisted of over 15,000 young men and women in 1993 and over 14,000 students in 1997. Students completed a self-report questionnaire which assessed several types of behavior, including smoking behavior. Results of the study indicated an increase in smoking rates among all ethnic groups of college students, yet none as high as whites. Smoking prevalence was higher among freshman, sophomores, and juniors, higher at public schools, higher at residential schools (as opposed to commuter schools), and higher at less-competitive schools. Wechsler and associates point to the rise in adolescent smoking in the early 1990s as a factor in the rise in smoking behavior among college students.

You may also involuntarily be exposed to the dangers of tobacco use. A growing body of research is documenting the deleterious effects of passive smoking. Passive smoking is the breathing in of the smoke around you that others produce. Over 4,000 chemical compounds have been identified in tobacco smoke. Each year, an estimated 3,000 nonsmoking Americans die of lung cancer due to breathing in second-hand smoke. (CDC, 2000). (The role of smoke in the health of children is covered in chapter 4.) Evidence also indicates that children can be affected when their mothers smoke. The CDC reports that approximately 300,000 young children are plagued with lower respiratory tract infections due to the effects of second-hand smoke. This mounting evidence has led to a flurry of legislation prohibiting smoking in certain public areas such as elevators, airplanes, and restaurants and the designation of smoking areas in workplaces.

The message does seem to be reaching the public. Overall, fewer people smoke now than at any time in the past 25 years (with the exception of teenage females). Numerous stop-smoking programs spring up all the time. These programs run the gamut from classic behavioral techniques to hypnosis. But perhaps the most telling evidence that smoking is on the decline in the United States is the reaction of the giant tobacco companies. In recent years these companies have increasingly targeted foreign markets (a growing ethical controversy, because these markets are typically Third World countries) while diversifying their domestic market with different and healthier products.

Physical Fitness

One of the most popular trends of recent years has been the so-called fitness craze. Health benefits are the obvious reason for this enthusiasm for exercise. Studies have shown that women who walk briskly for three hours a week can reduce their risk of heart attack by one-third (Shin, 1999). This risk is cut in half if walking is increased to five hours per week. Moderately intense exercise, such as brisk walking, also reduces the risk of stroke, osteoporosis, some types of cancer and diabetes.

Many corporations are now providing the time and facilities for employees to build regular exercise into their workday. The reasoning is that work time lost in this way is more than made up for by more productive employees, who end up losing less time due to illness. In one new trend, some health insurance programs are offering free access to exercise facilities, again looking at the long-term gain of having healthier members.

The pressure felt by young people, especially women, to stay physically fit and attractive is enormous. Nelson and associates (1999) report that eating disorders among young adults are becoming more common. They found that young adults with maladaptive eating behaviors and attitudes were more likely to experience psychological disturbance than those men and women who had good eating habits and attitudes. They also found a higher number of males with eating disturbances than expected. They conclude that anorexia among men may be more prevalent than once thought.

Guided Review

5. Early adulthood is the time when the efficiency of most body functions begins to _____.

6. Although physical ability has peaked, bodily responses in adulthood are supplemented by _____ _____; that is, the part of the total capacity of our body's organs that we do not normally need to use.

7. Our lifestyle affects our health, mainly through our choices of foods, use of alcohol, use of tobacco, and _____ _____.

8. Cholesterol, a substance in the blood related to heart attack, can be controlled by _____.

9. Alcohol not only affects the person who drinks it. _____ children of alcoholics often have problems, including difficulty finishing projects, having fun, and constantly seeking the _____ of others.

10. College presidents regularly rank _____ _____ as the number one problem on campuses.

11. Eating disorders among young adults are becoming _____ common.

Answers

5. decline 6. organ reserve 7. physical fitness 8. diet 9. Adult, approval 10. alcohol abuse 11. more

Cognitive Development

There are important characteristics that distinguish young adult learners from older learners (Darkenwald & Novak, 1997; Edwards & Usher, 1997; Saul, 1997). For instance, younger students prefer less formal learning methods, more physical movement in learning, and dislike variety in learning styles. Young adult learners are less achievement-oriented than older students. They are more anxious and impulsive and perceive themselves as less abstract in their thinking than the older students. In addition to learning factors, a major emphasis of research has been on the relationship between intellectual and ethical growth.

Intellectual/Ethical Development

Perry (1968a, 1968b, 1981) studied the intellectual/ethical development of several hundred Harvard college students, a group of males ages 17 to 22. These students responded to several checklists on their educational views and were interviewed extensively on the basis of their responses. The results of these studies led Perry to suggest a sequence of intellectual and ethical development that typically occurs during the transition from late adolescence to early adulthood. This sequence consists of nine positions, which indicate progress from belief in the absolute authority of experts to the recognition that one must make commitments and be responsible for one's own beliefs.

Perry's nine stages are divided among three broader categories, as follows:

Dualism Perry's initial phase of ethical development, in which "things are either absolutely right or absolutely wrong."

I. **Dualism** ("Things are either absolutely right or absolutely wrong.")
- Position 1: The world is viewed in such polar terms as right versus wrong, we versus they, and good versus bad. If an answer is right, it is absolutely right. We get right answers by going to authorities who have absolute knowledge.
- Position 2: The person recognizes that uncertainty exists, but ascribes it to poorly qualified authorities. Sometimes individuals can learn the truth for themselves.
- Position 3: Diversity and uncertainty are now acceptable but considered temporary because the authorities do not know what the answers are yet. The person becomes puzzled as to what the standards should be in these cases.

Relativism The second phase in Perry's theory. An attitude or philosophy that says anything can be right or wrong depending on the situation; all views are equally right.

II. **Relativism** ("Anything can be right or wrong depending on the situation; all views are equally right.")
- Position 4a: The person realizes that uncertainty and diversity of opinion are often extensive and recognizes that this is a legitimate status. Now he or she believes that "anyone has a right to an opinion." It is now possible for two authorities to disagree with each other without either of them being wrong.
- Position 4b: Sometimes the authorities (such as college professors) are not talking about right answers. Rather, they want students to think for themselves, supporting their opinions with data.
- Position 5: The person recognizes that all knowledge and values (including even those of an authority) exist in some specific context. It is therefore relative to the context. The person also recognizes that simple right and wrong are relatively rare, and even they exist in a specific context.
- Position 6: The person apprehends that because we live in a relativistic world, we must make some sort of personal commitment to an idea or concept, as opposed to looking for an authority to follow.

Commitment The third phase in Perry's theory, in which the individual realizes that certainty is impossible but that commitment to a certain position is necessary, even without certainty.

III. **Commitment** ("Because of available evidence and my understanding of my own values, I have come to new beliefs.")

- Position 7: The person begins to choose the commitments that she or he will make in specific areas.
- Position 8: Having begun to make commitments, the person experiences the implications of those commitments and explores the various issues of responsibility involved.
- Position 9: The person's identity is affirmed through the various commitments made. There is a recognition of the necessity for balancing commitments and the understanding that one can have responsibilities that are expressed through a daily lifestyle. Perry (1981) described this position:

> This is how life will be. I will be whole-hearted while tentative, fight for my values yet respect others, believe my deepest values right yet be ready to learn. I see that I shall be retracing this whole journey over and over—but, I hope, more wisely (p. 276).

Some students move through these stages in a smooth and regular fashion; others, however, are delayed or deflected in one of three ways:

- **Temporizing.** Some people remain in one position for a year or more, exploring its implications but hesitating to make any further progress.

- **Escape.** Some people use opportunities for detachment, especially those offered in positions 4 and 5, to refuse responsibility for making any commitments. Because everyone's opinion is "equally right," the person believes that no commitments need be made and, thus, escapes from the dilemma.

- **Retreat.** Sometimes, confused by the confrontation and uncertainties of the middle positions, people retreat to earlier positions.

Perry's theory has been criticized because all of the subjects of his research were male. However, his work spurred considerable research on females, which we now overview.

"Women's Ways of Knowing"

In a continuing collaborative study, Belenky and associates (1986,1997) set out to answer the questions, "Do female ways of knowing develop differently from those of males? If so, how do they come to learn and value what they know?" The study was rooted in Perry's work and the work of Carol Gilligan, whose groundbreaking research on the morality of care and responsibility versus the morality of rights and justice was covered in chapter 9.

Belenky and her associates conducted a series of lengthy and intense interviews with 135 women of diverse socioeconomic backgrounds. The researchers found five general categories of ways in which women know and view the world. Though some of the women interviewed clearly demonstrated a progression from one perspective to the next, the researchers contend that they are unable to discern a progression of clear-cut stages, as did Perry and Gilligan. The five perspectives are silence, received knowledge, subjective knowledge, procedural knowledge, and constructed knowledge.

1. **Silence.** Females in the silence category describe themselves as "deaf and dumb." These women feel passive and dependent. Like players in an authority's game, they feel expected to know rules that don't exist. These women's thinking is characterized by concepts of right and wrong, similar to the men in Perry's first category of dualism. Questions about their growing up revealed family lives filled with violence, abuse, and chaos. The researchers noted that "gaining a voice and developing an awareness of their own minds are the tasks that these women must accomplish if

Temporizing   Some people remain in one position for a year or more, exploring its implications but hesitating to make any further progress.

Escape   Others refuse responsibility for making any commitments because everyone's opinion is "equally right."

Retreat   According to Perry's theory of ethical development, when someone retreats to an earlier ethical position.

Silence   Belenky's first phase of women's thinking, characterized by concepts of right and wrong.

they are to cease being either a perpetrator or victim of family violence" (Belenky & others, 1986, p. 38).

Received knowledge
Belenky's second phase of women's thinking; characterized by being awed by the authorities but far less affiliated with them.

2. **Received knowledge.** Women in the received knowledge category see words as central to the knowing process. They learn by listening and assume truths come from authorities. These women are intolerant of ambiguities and paradoxes, always coming back to the notion that there are absolute truths. Received knowers seem similar to the men that Perry described as being in the first stage of dualism, but with a difference. The men Perry interviewed felt a great affiliation with the knowing authority. The women of this perspective were awed by the authorities but far less affiliated with them. In contrast to the men of Perry's study, women of received knowledge channel their energies and increased sense of self into the care of others.

Subjective knowledge
Belenky's third phase of women's thinking; characterized by some crisis of male authority that sparked a distrust of outside sources of knowledge, and some experience that confirmed a trust in women thinkers themselves.

3. **Subjective knowledge.** The researchers noted that women in the subjective knowledge category often had experienced two phenomena that pushed them toward this perspective: some crisis of male authority that sparked a distrust of outside sources of knowledge, and some experience that confirmed a trust in themselves. Subjectivists value their "gut" or firsthand experience as their best source of knowledge and see themselves as "conduits through which truth emerges" (p. 69). The researchers note that subjectivists are similar to males in Perry's second category of relativism in that they embrace the notion of multiple truths.

Procedural knowledge
Belenky's fourth phase of women's thinking; characterized by a distrust of both knowledge from authority and the female thinker's own inner authority or "gut."

4. **Procedural knowledge.** The women in the procedural knowledge category have a distrust of both knowledge from authority and their own inner authority or "gut." The perspective of procedural knowledge is characterized by an interest in form over content (how you say something rather than what you say). Women in this category also have a heightened sense of control. This category is similar to Perry's position 4b, where students learn analytic methods that authorities sanction. But analytic thinking emerges differently in women because they are less likely to affiliate with authorities.

The researchers describe women as having two kinds of procedural knowledge: separate knowing and connected knowing. These terms are reminiscent of Gilligan's work. Separate knowers are analytical and try to separate the self, to reveal the truth. Connected knowers learn through empathy with others.

Constructed knowledge
Belenky's fifth phase of women's thinking; characterized by an integration of the subjective and procedural ways of knowing (types 3 and 4).

5. **Constructed knowledge.** Those in the constructed knowledge category have integrated the subjective and procedural ways of knowing (types 3 and 4). Women of this perspective note that "all knowledge is constructed and the knower is an intimate part of the known" (p. 137). They feel responsible for examining and questioning systems of constructing knowledge. Their thinking is characterized by a high tolerance of ambiguity and internal contradiction. Indeed, the women whose ways of knowing are of this perspective often balance many commitments and relationships, as well as ideas.

The work of Perry and Belenky and her associates (as well as that of Piaget, Kohlberg, and Gilligan, discussed earlier in this book) has greatly advanced our knowledge of intellectual and ethical development in the late adolescent and early adult years. It has also produced much controversy. Many questions remain to be answered. For example, does socioeconomic level make any difference? What about cultural background? We hope that the research in this area will provide further insights into how we can help youths progress through this period successfully. We could say the same for the next aspect of development we will review, love in young adulthood.

I think the one lesson I have learned is that there is no substitute for paying attention.

Diane Sawyer

Guided Review

12. William Perry examined the intellectual and ethical changes in Harvard males and found them to move through three broad categories of change. These categories include _____ (things are absolutely right or wrong), relativism (all views are equal), and _____ (holding to beliefs based on the best available evidence and values).

13. Perry describes nine stages within these three categories. Some students move through the stages smoothly, others are delayed by _____, escape, and _____.

14. Mary Belenky and her colleagues, building on Perry's work and the work of Carol Gilligan, examined the _____ and _____ development of women.

15. Belenky and others found five general categories of ways in which women view the world. The five perspectives include silence, _____ _____, subjective knowledge, procedural knowledge, and _____ _____.

Patterns of Work

Waste of time is thus the deadliest of sins. Loss of time through sociability, idle talk, luxury, or more sleep than is necessary for health (six hours) is worthy of absolute moral condemnation. Thus inactive contemplation is also valueless, or even reprehensible if it is at the expense of one's daily work.

—Max Weber, *The Protestant Ethic and the Spirit of Capitalism*

Weber, a philosopher and economist, was a leading spokesperson on the role of labor at the turn of the century. How differently we view that role today! Table 13.3

TABLE 13.3 THE PRIMARY ROLES OF WORK

Years	Approximate Primary Role of Work
Early history	Search for food.
8000 B.C.E.	Cultivation of cereal, grains, domestication of animals.
5000 B.C.E.	Greater division of labor, surplus production of goods, trade.
500 B.C.E.	Work seen as degrading and brutalizing by upper classes; done as much as possible by slaves.
500	Serfdom (lord of manor system replaces slavery).
1350	Black Death makes workers scarce. Move to towns; guilds of craftpersons formed. Cottage industry, capitalism start.
1750	Inventions cause "industrial revolution," demise of small business. Factory system takes advantage of cheap labor.
1900	Unions, government regulations, electricity and automation, new management policies greatly improve life of workers.
1950	Computers, technology create world of highly skilled, white-collar workers.
1970	Age of information processing.
2000	Age of global communication

From John Dacey, *Adult Development,* Scott, Foresman and Company, Glenview, IL, 1982. Reprinted by permission of the author.

Answers

12. dualism, commitment 13. temporizing, retreat 14. ethical, intellectual 15. received knowledge, constructed knowledge

Getting a Job

How many jobs have you held so far in your life? Do you remember how you got them? What do the people who hire workers consider when they are hiring? Do blue-collar jobs have significantly different criteria than white-collar jobs?

To find out, you might interview the managers of a bank and a supermarket and ask what they look for in a new employee. Are there differences in behavioral, attitudinal, cognitive, or appearance criteria? Why or why not?

Careers, like rockets, don't always take off on schedule. The key is to keep working on the engines.

displays a brief summary of the history of work in Western society and indicates how much our attitudes toward work have changed. Changes in the world of work have been coming more rapidly in recent years than ever before. Working in the United States today is complicated. The rest of this section is devoted to explicating the major trends, their causes, and likely results.

The Phenomenon of the Dual-Career Family

The traditional family pattern of the husband who goes off to work to provide for his family and the wife who stays home and manages that family is almost extinct. Now, work has come to be a means for attaining power (Blustein, 2000). Economic realities and the women's movement have led to the development of a growing family dynamic—**the dual-career family.** The goals of the American Dream, achievement and self-sufficiency, have not changed. What has changed, however, is the increase in career opportunities for women. This may explain why women move from lower paying jobs with fewer prospects to higher paying industries (Stern & others, 1998). Heckert and associates (1998) learned that marital disruption can be predicted by the relative household earnings of husbands and wives. For example, Ono (1998) found that when the wife does not work, a low salary earned by the husband has a negative effect on the marriage. However, no marital disruption was found relative to the husband's low salary when the wife also earned a salary. Wilkie and associates (1998) found that marital satisfaction is often determined by what each partner perceives to be fair. However, husbands and wives differ on their definition of fairness.

Something else that has not changed is that, despite their increased presence in the workforce, women are still considered responsible for the maintenance of the family. Women often choose jobs that fit in well with the needs of their family. Women tend to work shorter hours and change the nature of their work more often than men do.

Today it is more difficult for some to define themselves according to their jobs (Seppa, 1997). As the number of two-income households continues to

Dual-career family A family in which both the mother and the father are working, usually full time.

On the average, a working mother does about 80 percent of the caretaking chores in a family, as opposed to the 20 percent done by a working husband.

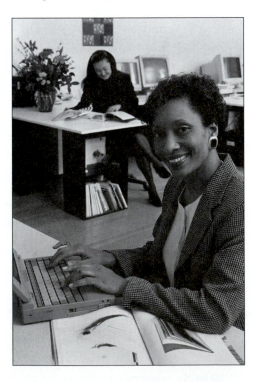

grow, women are taking many of the new high-growth jobs (although this is almost ex-clusively an upper- and middle-class white phenomenon—Fouad & Brown, 2000). It affects men's traditional image as chief provider in the family (Patton & McMahon, 1999), and men are getting more satisfaction from taking on more responsibility for child care. Although many people welcome more equal division of responsibility in marriages, the effects of such positive changes have psycholog-ical ramifications for men, who now may find they have lost their role as dominant breadwinner as they become a more active parent.

This conflict may not be a serious problem for future generations of workers, as children are socialized very differently today. In Seppa's view (1997), boys raised by working mothers are likely to have new views of adult gender roles, and a new def-inition of masculinity will arise. Women's contributions to family income will provide positive benefits to the family, and men will need to define themselves in a way that differs from the old idea that they must compete to be successful. Compared to the rapid changes for women brought on by the feminist movement, this new definition of men is likely to emerge at a slower pace, but will, nevertheless, be the cause of role adjustments for many (Blustein, 1999).

Guided Review

16. The nature of work has changed, moving from a primary focus on food gathering (early human history) to a factory system (1750–1950) to an emphasis on _____ _____ (2000).
17. Research indicates that a new definition of male attitudes toward work in the family is likely to emerge at a (slower, faster, about the same) pace as has been the case for females.
18. It has been found that men have to adjust psychologically to the increased role of their wives as providers: (working class, white-collar) workers have adapted best to this change.
19. In a dual-career family, men can get more satisfaction by taking on an increased responsibility for _____ _____, as well as household duties.

CONCLUSION & SUMMARY

We began this chapter by comparing how youths are inducted into adulthood in preindustrial tribes in other parts of the world and in the modern United States. We concluded that our situation is much more complex than that of the tribes and that the absence of clear ini-tiation rites still causes problems for us.

Young adulthood is a period during which many changes are taking place. The peak of physical development is reached, and the decline of certain abil-ities begins. These declines are almost

never apparent, however, because of organ reserve. Our style of life has a powerful effect on this development, including our diet, use of alcohol, drugs and nicotine, and physical fitness.

The major change occurring in the area of cognitive development involves progress from dualistic thinking through relativism to the ethical/intellectual stage of commitment. Research also suggests that there are five "women's ways of knowing."

The nation's workers experience a

very different environment than their predecessors of 50 years ago, as we leave the industrial age and enter the age of "information processing." Many problems still must be solved—espe-cially the treatment of persons of color and women.

How are American youths being initiated into adulthood today?

• Initiation rites in other cultures offer a formal ceremony marking the transition from child to adult.

Answers

- Some researchers have suggested parallels to the initiation process in the crimes juveniles are often required to commit in order to become a member of a gang, and in the sequence of experiences that so often lead to drug addiction.
- The purpose of initiation rites in preindustrial societies is to cushion the emotional disruption arising from the transition from one life status to another.
- Entry into adulthood is far more complex for adolescents today, largely due to the increase of sophisticated technologies and the need for many more years of formal education.
- Organized sports, the adolescent counterculture, and delinquency all provide some sort of trials that must be passed for acceptance into adulthood.
- Five types of activities signal the passage to maturity in America today: religious, sexual, social, educational, and economic.

What are the significant factors affecting physical development in early adulthood?

- Early adulthood is the period during which physical changes slow down or stop.
- The human body is designed to do much more than it is usually called upon to do. Much of its total capacity is held in "organ reserve."
- Lifestyle, food choices, alcohol and tobacco use, and physical fitness all play an enormous role in the health of a young adult.

How does cognition change during the early adult years?

- Perry suggested three categories of intellectual and ethical development that typify transition from late adolescence to early adulthood: dualism, relativism, and commitment. By avoiding the three obstacles that might impede their progress (temporizing, escape, or retreat), young adults should be able to

achieve commitments that are the hallmark of the mature person.
- Belenky and associates suggest women know and view the world through five perspectives: silence, received knowledge, subjective knowledge, procedural knowledge, and constructed knowledge.

What patterns of work typify young adults today?

- The traditional family pattern of the husband who goes off to work to provide for his family and the wife who stays home and manages that family is almost extinct now.
- Women often choose jobs that fit in well with the needs of their family. Women tend to work shorter hours and change the nature of their work more often than men do.
- Economic realities and the feminist movement have given rise to dual-career families in which both husband and wife work outside of the home.

KEY TERMS

Cholesterol	Escape	Relativism
Commitment	Hazing	Retreat
Constructed knowledge	Organ reserve	Silence
Dualism	Procedural knowledge	Subjective knowledge
Dual-career family	Received knowledge	Temporizing

WHAT DO YOU THINK?

1. Do you remember any experiences from your own youth that were particularly helpful in your transition to adulthood?
2. Societal changes have led to a change in the nature of initiation rites into adulthood. Are young adults better off today as a result, or should we try to return to the societal structures of the past?

3. The media offers countless advertisements to help a person look younger, feel better, be better. Why are these ads so effective? What do they say about Western society?
4. Most college students are making the transition from Perry's category of dualism to relativism and, finally, to commitment. What types of behaviors might you observe

from a college student at each of these levels of intellectual development?
5. Many of the problems in the American family today have been attributed to the phenomenon of the dual-career couple. Is there any truth to this perception? In what ways do two working parents alter (positively and negatively) the family's operation as a unit?

CHAPTER REVIEW TEST

1. A bar mitzvah or bas mitzvah is an example of a(n) _____ rite of passage.
   a. religious
   b. sexual
   c. social
   d. educational

2. Many adolescents are willing to endure pain to be initiated into groups because
   a. they want to be tested.
   b. they want to prove to themselves that they are courageous.
   c. they want to prove to themselves that they have self-control.
   d. all of the above.

3. Because we seldom call on its total capacity, people often are not aware of the decline of their
   _____ _____
   during early adulthood.
   a. aerobic capacity
   b. blood pressure
   c. heart rate
   d. organ reserve

4. Research indicates that heart disease and cancer are linked to
   a. nutrition.
   b. other related diseases.
   c. childhood habits.
   d. None of the above.

5. Lack of exercise, snacking, and use of labor-saving devices are the main causes of
   a. leukemia.
   b. cancer.
   c. obesity.
   d. diabetes.

6. A survey among college students on alcohol use showed that alcohol consumption was directly related to
   a. low grade-point average.
   b. poor relations with peers.
   c. memory loss.
   d. length of time needed to earn a college degree.

7. What is the major reason that young adults smoke?
   a. Stress
   b. Economic reasons
   c. Peer pressure
   d. Get a fix

8. According to the Center for Disease Control (CDC) (1999), there are approximately _____ times less reported AIDS cases during young adulthood than in middle adulthood.
   a. one and a half
   b. two
   c. two and a half
   d. three

9. Among young adult females, maximum height is usually reached at age _____; for males it is age
   _____
   a. 18, 25.
   b. 19, 16.
   c. 18, 20.
   d. 18, 18.

10. Research indicates that children of alcoholics usually manifest a number of specific characteristics. They often
    a. judge themselves without mercy.
    b. have diminished capacity to feel.
    c. constantly seek approval and affirmation.
    d. All of the above.

11. Honan (1997) noted increasing numbers of _____ on major college campuses according to an annual survey of campus crime.
    a. injuries from fights and automobile accidents
    b. drug arrests

   c. sexual assaults
   d. All of the above

12. Perry's stages of dualism, relativism, and commitment refer to a person's
    a. relationship development.
    b. intellectual and ethical development.
    c. ability to make moral decisions.
    d. interpersonal relationships.

13. In a study of women's perspectives on knowledge (Belenky & others), received knowledge refers to
    a. the view that words are central to the knowing process.
    b. an experience that resulted in a distrust of outside sources of knowledge.
    c. a distrust of knowledge from authority.
    d. learned passivity and dependency in relationships.

14. Belenky's category of procedural knowledge is most similar to which of Perry's stages?
    a. Dualism
    b. Commitment
    c. Affirmation
    d. Relativism

15. The ability to recognize that certainty is impossible but _____ to a certain position is necessary, even without certainty, describes Perry's third stage.
    a. aspiring
    b. commitment
    c. ambivalence
    d. disgust

16. Today, women are taking on many of the
    a. minimum wage jobs.
    b. new, high-growth jobs.
    c. old, less-skilled jobs.
    d. none of the above.

Answers

Spend as much solo time with your children as you can, starting from the day they're born. Being alone with children not only strengthens your bond with them, it also helps you develop your own personal and problem-solving skills.

William Doherty

CHAPTER 14

Psychosocial Development in Early Adulthood

The modern American family is quite different from those of the last century. Those families were larger and much more likely to live near each other in the same city or town. What are the advantages and disadvantages of this tendency?

When things go wrong in society, we immediately inquire into the condition of family life. When we see society torn apart by crime, we cry, "If only we could return to the good old days when family was sacred." But were the good old days so good? Was the family ever free of violence? Many people who come to therapy these days were raised in the so-called golden age of the family, and they tell stories of abuse, neglect, and terrifying moralistic demands and pressure. Looked at coldly, the family of any era is both good and bad, offering both support and threat. This is why adults are so ambivalent about visiting their families and spending time with them: they want the emotional rewards of the sense of connection. But they also want the distance from painful memories and difficult relationships.

You may disagree with this assessment of the American family, but most researchers agree that the rapid changes this institution has been experiencing may well be cause for concern, if only because the family is the foundation from which so many other social and emotional elements of our lives spring. No aspects of young adult lives are more vital than those dealt with in this chapter: marriage and the family, work and leisure, and personal development. ✪

Chapter Objectives

After reading this chapter you should be able to answer the following questions.

◆ What factors are affecting American marriages and families?

◆ What problems do young adults face in developing a healthy personality?

◆ What are the relationships between sexual identity and gender roles?

◆ How do young adults deal with the interpersonal relationships of sexuality and love?

Marriage and the Family

When two people are under the influence of the most violent, most divisive and most transient of passions, they are required to swear that they will remain in that excited, abnormal, and exhausting condition continuously until death do them part.

George Bernard Shaw

Changing American Marriages and Families

Finding critics of marriage is not difficult (e.g., Kathrin Perutz's book, *Marriage Is Hell*). Not many Americans are paying attention, though. Almost 95 percent of Americans get married at some point in their lives. To better understand the present situation, let us take a look at the trends in marriage and family relations.

The U.S. Census Bureau defines a family as ". . . a group of two or more people (one of whom is the householder, the person in whose name the housing unit is owned or rented) living together and related by birth, marriage or adoption" (Household and Family Characteristics, 1999). The average U.S. family household consists of 3.18 people, down from 3.58 in 1970. Latino families are larger, with an average of 3.92 members, than either African-American or non-Latino white families, which average 3.42 and 3.02 members, respectively.

About 56 percent of all American adults (under 11 million people) are married and living with their spouses, according to the U.S. Commerce Department (1999). Among those between 25 and 34 years of age, about 35 percent have never been married. Of African-Americans in this age group, 53 percent have never been married. Nearly 30 percent of all children under 18 years of age live with just one parent, and of them, 84 percent live with their mother (down from 94 percent in 1990). One of the major changes in the families of young adults is that the number of single fathers increased by 25 percent in the latter half of the 1990s (Casper & Bryson, 1999).

Today 25 percent of all people who get married for the first time are likely to marry someone who has been married before. In 20 percent of all marriages, both partners were married previously. Trends in the rates of first marriage, divorce, and remarriage since the early twentieth century reflect patterns of change in economic and social conditions in the United States. These changes can be clearly seen in Table 14.1. One of the most interesting trends has been the change in the average age at first marriage. At the turn of the century, the average age for females was almost 22 years, and for males almost 26 years. With the exception of the late Depression and war years, the trend *had* been toward earlier and earlier marriages.

This trend led demographers to make erroneous predictions. For example, they predicted that marriages in 1990 would come even earlier, at about age 20 for both males and females. Several other investigators said the same thing in the late 1960s. But these miscalculations only demonstrate the difficulty of predicting the behavior of human beings.

The average age at first marriage in the United States has gradually increased since the record lows during the mid-1950s (Table 14.1). Small increases in the age

TABLE 14.1   MEDIAN AGE AT FIRST MARRIAGE, BY SEX: 1890 TO 1998

Year	Men	Women
1998	26.7	25.0
1996	27.1	24.8
1994	26.7	24.5
1990	26.1	23.9
1985	25.5	23.3
1980	24.7	22.0
1970	23.2	20.8
1960	22.8	20.3
1950	22.8	20.3
1940	24.3	21.5
1930	24.3	21.3
1920	24.6	21.2
1910	25.1	21.6
1900	25.9	21.9
1890	26.1	22.0

Source: From "Marital Status and Living Arrangements: March 1998 (update)" in *Current Population Reports,* P-20 (No. 514), U.S. Bureau of the Census, Washington, D.C., 1999.

at first marriage occurred from 1955 to 1975. However, sharper increases have occurred in the last two decades. This U-shaped curve (from a high age in the 1890s to a relatively low age in the 1950s back to a high age today) is an excellent example of contextualism (see chapter 1). One example of the effect of the current context for marriage is the rising number of women who have entered the workforce during this period.

An interesting change has been the nearly triple rise in the proportion of young adults who have not married during the past two decades. Eighty percent of men aged 20 to 24 years had never married in 1991, up from 55 percent in 1970. In this same time period, the rate went from 19 percent to 47 percent for men 25 to 29 years old, and from 9 percent to 27 percent for men aged 30 to 34. As expected, because men marry later, men have higher proportions of the never-married in all age groups (U.S. Bureau of the Census, 1999).

Another aspect of young adult relationships is cohabitation, which involves sharing a residence and personal assets, and sometimes having a child, without being married. Brown and Booth (1996) compared the relationships of married couples to those of couples who are cohabitors. Although cohabitors generally reported poorer relationship quality than the married couples, they also reported more frequent interaction with their partners than did married couples. In general, however, the relationships do not differ significantly. Recently, however, cohabitation has been associated with alcohol problems for both men and women. Horwitz and White (1998) found that cohabiting women, when compared to married women, reported more problems with alcohol. Cohabiting men reported significantly more problems with alcohol than married men. In terms of depression, however, Horwitz and White found no differences between cohabiting couples and married couples.

More Americans are marrying outside of their racial groups, according to the major 1990 U.S. Census data (Reyes, 1997). Table 14.2 provides a comparison of interracial marriages in the 1950 and 1990 for African-Americans and whites.

White men who had served in the military were three times as likely to marry outside their racial group as men who had never served. White women in the military were seven times as likely to marry outside their racial group as men who had never served.

The recent trend in increased divorced rates is probably caused, at least in part, by four factors:

• Liberalization of divorce laws.

• Growing societal acceptance of divorce and of remaining single.

• The reduction in the cost of divorces, largely through no-fault divorce laws.

• The broadening educational and work experience of women that has contributed to increased economic and social independence, a possible factor in marital dissolution.

Other factors that affect divorce rates are ethnicity, the wife's workforce participation, husband's employment status, and residence status. A recent study conducted by Brunstein and associates (1996) has shown that when one partner provides social

TABLE 14.2 A COMPARISON OF INTERRACIAL MARRIAGES IN 1950 AND 1990 FOR AFRICAN-AMERICAN AND WHITE WOMEN AND MEN		
Racial Group	**1950**	**1990**
African-American Women	1%	4%
White Women	>1%	3%
African-American Men	>2%	8%
White Men	1%	4%

Three marvelously well-written books that deal with this subject area are: (1) John Fowles' *The magus* (revised edition). Boston: Little, Brown. This is surely one of the best psychological mystery stories ever written. (2) Mary Gordon's *Final payments.* New York: Random House. (3) John Updike's *Rabbit, run.* New York: Knopf. This is the first of four books that chronicles the development of an ordinary man whose nickname is "Rabbit."

support related to the personal goals of the other partner, the result is higher satisfaction with the relationship. Personal goals may include objectives both within and outside of the spouses' relationship, such as career projects or major life transitions.

Although adults are certainly concerned about every aspect of their family lives, the crucial part of family life for most of them is how they manage their relationship with their spouse. Their major concern is: "What kind of marriage will I have, and how can I make it a happy marriage?" Simpson and associates (1996) have found that the level of attachment between spouses contributes to marital satisfaction. Couples who are most securely attached look to each other as a base of comfort and security when faced with stress or when they are upset. Those couples who are less secure or more ambivalent experience more anxiety and try to solve most problems by themselves.

Researchers have also asked the question, "When a marriage produces a sense of well-being, is that due to the state of marriage itself, or because mentally healthy people are more likely to marry than those with problems?" Horvitz and associates (1996) completed a study of 450 males and females age 12, 15 and 18 years old in a longitudinal study that took place from 1982 to 1994. They concluded that:

> . . . with controls for premarital rates of mental health, young adults who get married and stay married experience higher levels of well-being than those who remain single. In addition, although men—but not women—who become married report less depression, women—but not men—who become married report less problems with alcohol. . . . When both male-prevalent and female-prevalent outcome measures are used, both men and women benefit from marriage (p. 895).

Surprisingly, Roberts and Leonard (1998) found that high levels of drinking by either husband or wife did not affect the quality of marriage. Of course, as in the Oscar winning movie, *Days of Wine and Roses,* the marriage of the two leading characters became happier when the abstaining wife began to drink with her husband. After a while, however, their relationship deteriorated as a result of their abuse of alcohol. On the other hand, decreased marital satisfaction has long been linked to the addition of children to the marriage. The transition to parenthood has been implicated as a risk factor for married couples. Some researchers view this transition as a crisis period that slowly improves as the child grows older.

An Informed View

Is the Increase in the Number of Working Mothers Seriously Harming the American Family?

No doubt you have recently heard at least one politician wringing his or her hands over what serious shape the American family is in. In chapter 12, we reported on many of the changes affecting the relationship between parents and children in today's families—for example, the loss of such family functions as job training and economic dependence. Some even worry that the family itself is on the way out. They prophesize that professionals will have ever-increasing roles in raising our children, as more and more American women seek careers.

Are other countries as concerned about this as we are? There are countries in which the family has always been of tremendous importance—Asian countries such as Japan and China, and Western countries such as Italy and Spain,

for example. Is this becoming a big problem for them? What about Russia, where 50 percent of children 1 to 3 years old, and 90 percent of children 4 to 5 years old, are in day care? Do you think they have solved the problem of how to raise children when both parents work full time? What's your view?

If you would like to have a more informed opinion on this issue, you might want to read one of the articles on the subject referenced in this chapter (e.g., Brunstein & associates, Simpson & associates).

 You might also wish to learn more about it by going to our web site at http://www.mhhe.com/dacey5.

Cox and associates (1999) observed couples before and after the birth of their first child to determine the impact of the child on the marriage. Several interesting findings emerged:

- Couples reported higher marital satisfaction if the pregnancy was planned.

- Lower marital satisfaction was reported by couples who had depressive symptoms before the birth of the child.

- Marital satisfaction decreased over time for parents of girls.

- Marital satisfaction was higher if at least one partner demonstrated positive problem-solving communication skills.

Types of Marriage

Attitudes toward marriage, and therefore types of marriage, vary greatly throughout the world. Despite many variations in the ways humans begin their married lives, there are basically four kinds of marriage throughout the world: monogamy, polygamy, polyandry, and group marriage.

Monogamy is the standard marriage form in the United States and most other nations, in which there is one husband and one wife. In **polygamy,** there is one husband but two or more wives. In earlier times in this country, this form of marriage was practiced by the Mormons of Utah. There are still some places in the world where it exists, but the number is dwindling. **Polyandry** is a type of marriage in which there is one wife but two or more husbands. The rarest type of marriage, it is practiced only in situations where there are very few females. **Group marriage** includes two or more of both husbands and wives, who all exercise common privileges and responsibilities. In the late 1960s this form of marriage received considerable attention, but it accounts for a minuscule percentage of the world's population and has lost considerable popularity in recent years.

Homosexual marriages, although not officially sanctioned in many parts of the world, are beginning to be accepted in some religions. Such marriages, according to Wyers (1987), can provide individuals with an intimate, mature relationship. Kurdek (1998) conducted a longitudinal study that compared heterosexual married couples to gay and lesbian cohabiting couples. The study examined whether there were differences between the groups with regard to relationship quality. The quality of the relationship was comprised of five dimensions: constructive problem solving, intimacy, equality, autonomy, and barriers to leaving. These dimensions were measured by subject self-report. Although there were some differences between the groups, the findings suggest that, overall, married heterosexual couples "are more similar to than different from cohabiting gay or lesbian partners." At the same time, though, this type of relationship presents a number of unique challenges to the

Monogamy   The standard marriage form in the United States and most other nations, in which there is one husband and one wife.

Polygamy   A marriage in which there is one husband but two or more wives.

Polyandry   A marriage in which there is one wife but two or more husbands.

Group marriage   A marriage that includes two or more of both husbands and wives, who all exercise common privileges and responsibilities.

Homosexual marriage   Though not accepted legally, the weddings of homosexuals are now accepted by some religions.

Two lesbian women hold their Vermont License and Certificate of Civil Union at the town hall in Williston, VT. They were among the first to take advantage of the new state legislation providing same-sex couples with legal benefits similar to marriage in July of 2000.

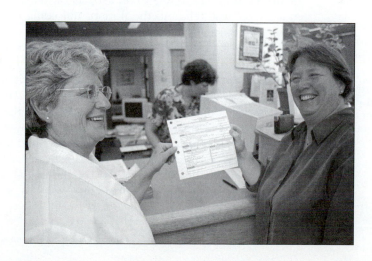

couple. Aside from prejudice and lack of understanding from society at large, in the United States many social service networks and agencies are unprepared to offer services to gay and lesbian men and women (p. 148).

Guided Review

1. The sharpest increases in the average age at first marriage have occurred in the last two decades. One reason for this trend may be that higher numbers of women have entered the _____ during this time.
2. Of Latinos, African-Americans, and whites, _____ have the largest families.
3. Societal acceptance of divorce and of remaining single has been (increasing, decreasing, staying about the same) lately.
4. Four factors are attributed to a recent trend in increased divorce rates. These factors include _____ of divorce laws, growing social acceptance of divorce, reduction in cost of divorces, and the broadening educational and work experience of women.
5. Basically, four types of marriage exist in the world: monogamy, polygamy, _____, and group marriage.

Personal Development

In this section, we discuss the theories of Daniel Levinson and Erik Erikson. Each of these theories is somewhat dated, but each offers insights into the development of the adult personality that are still of great value. We also consider gender differences in individuation.

The Adult Life Cycle: Levinson

Yale psychologist Daniel Levinson, who died in 1994, was one of the most respected researchers in adult developmental psychology. Working with his colleagues at Yale, he derived a theory of adult development based on intensive interviews with 40 men and 40 women. Rather than depend on questionnaire data from a large number of individuals, Levinson decided that intensive interviewing and psychological testing with a small number of representative cases would more likely provide him with the information for a theory of adult development. Because of the number of hours necessary in this study (almost 20 hours were spent on interviews with each subject), Levinson decided to limit the number of cases so that he could get more detailed information.

Key to Levinson's (1978, 1986, 1990a) theory of adult development is the notion of **life course.** Life refers to all aspects of living—everything that has significance in a life. Course refers to the flow or unfolding of an individual's life. Life course, therefore, looks at the complexity of life as it evolves over time.

Equally important to Levinson's theory is the notion of **life cycle.** Building on the findings of his research, Levinson proposed that there is "an underlying order in the human life course; although each individual life is unique, everyone goes through the same basic sequence" (1986, p. 4). The life cycle is a general pattern of adult development, whereas the life course is the unique embodiment of the life cycle by an individual.

Through his studies, Levinson further defined parts of the life cycle. He defined the life cycle as a sequence of eras. Each era is biopsychosocial in character: It is composed of the interaction of the individual, complete with his or her own biological and psychological makeup, with the social environment. Each era is

Life course Levinson's term. Life refers to all aspects of living—everything that has significance in a life; course refers to the flow or unfolding of an individual's life.

Life cycle Levinson's term. The life cycle is a general pattern of adult development, whereas the life course is the unique embodiment of the life cycle by an individual.

Answers

1. workforce (or job market) 2. Latinos 3. increasing 4. liberalization 5. polyandry

An Applied View

Responsibility for Self

One of the clearest indexes of maturity is the ability to be responsible for your own life and behavior. This exercise asks a number of questions involving responsibility for your own behavior.

1. Name two major purchases you have made in the past year by yourself without a strong influence by anyone else.

   _____

   _____

2. Wherever it is that you live, do your parents support you, or do you pay for your own housing?

   _____

3. Are you completely in charge of what time you come home at night, or do you have to answer to someone else?

   _____

4. Are you the sole person who decides what clothing you wear?

   _____

5. To what extent have your parents influenced your career, that is, whether you have chosen to go to college or work, the acceptability of your grades or pay, and so on?

   _____

6. Are you able to make independent decisions about your sex life? Do you let your parents know what you have decided?

   _____

You might compare your answers with those of some of your friends to get a relative idea of how responsible you are for your life.

Transition Levinson's concept that each new era begins as an old era is approaching its end. That "in-between" time is a transition.

Life structure The underlying pattern or design of a person's life at a given time.

important in itself and in its contribution to the whole of the life cycle. A new era begins as the previous era approaches its end. That in-between time is characterized as a **transition.**

The intricacies of Levinson's theory of adult life course and life cycle are further elaborated by his concept of the adult **life structure.** Life structure is the underlying pattern or design of a person's life at a given time. Levinson noted that "a theory of life structure is a way of conceptualizing answers to a different question: 'What is my life like now?'" (1986, p. 6). The primary components of a life structure are the relationships that an individual has with significant others. It is through relationships that we "live out" various aspects of ourselves. Levinson regarded relationships as actively and mutually shaped. Life structure may have many components, but generally only one or two components are central in the structure at a given time. The central component(s) is the one that most strongly influences the life structure of the individual.

Structure building During structure-building periods, individuals face the task of building a stable structure around choices they have made.

Structure changing A process of reappraising the existing life structure and exploring the possibilities for new life structures characterizes the structure-changing period.

The evolutionary sequence of the life structure includes an alternating series of **structure-building** and **structure-changing** transitions. During the structure-building periods, individuals face the task of building a stable structure around choices they have made. They seek to enhance the life within that structure. This period of relative stability usually lasts five to seven years. During that time, the stability of the life structure affords individuals the freedom to question their choices and to consider modifying their life.

This process of reappraising the existing life structure and exploring new life structures characterizes the structure-changing period. This period usually lasts around five years. Its end is marked by the making of critical life choices around which the individual will build a new life structure. Levinson noted that the individual decides at this point, "This I will settle for" (1986, p. 7).

In considering the periods of stability and change in the adult life cycle, Levinson noted, "We remain novices in every era until we have had a chance to try out an entry life structure and then to question and modify it in the mid-era transition" (1986, p. 7). Individuals enter into new stages of adult development as they become focused on certain developmental tasks. You will understand these tasks better when we describe each stage in the following pages.

Levinson gave equal weight to periods of stability and transition. This captures the evolution of the focus of an individual and the flowing quality of adult development. Unlike most theories of child development, in which development takes the form of positive growth, Levinson's study of adult development recognized a coexistence of growth and decline.

Seasons of a Man's Life: Levinson

Levinson made two separate studies, one of men (1978) and one of women (1990b) (both to be further described in chapter 16). In his first study, which was solely of men, 40 male subjects ranging in age from 35 to 45 were selected, representing four categories (10 each): blue-collar workers paid on an hourly basis, middle-level executives, academic biologists, and novelists.

The hourly workers and the executives were employees of an industrial firearms manufacturer or an electronics plant (about half from each). The biologists were employed at two highly rated universities located between Boston and New York. Of the writers, some were highly gifted novelists whose work had already been accepted by critics; others were less well known but were regarded as promising and worthy of serious consideration. Of course, this sample cannot be considered to represent the average male in the United States, but the diversity of the people selected in social class origins, racial, ethnic, and religious backgrounds, education, and marital status does make it typical of a great deal of American society today.

The study concentrates on the choices made by each man during his life and how he has dealt with the consequences of his choices, especially as they affect the main components of living: occupation, marriage, and family. After studying these components, Levinson suggested that there are four main seasons of life: (1) childhood and adolescence—birth to 22 years; (2) early adulthood—17 to 45 years; (3) middle adulthood—40 to 65 years; and (4) older adulthood—60 years and older.

Obviously, considerable overlap occurs between each of his stages. Between these major stages are substages that help to bring about the transitions necessary for development. Figure 14.1 gives a description of various stages and substages. Levinson himself concentrated on the early and middle adult periods, leaving further consideration of the childhood and late adult periods to others.

He believed that "even the most disparate lives are governed by the same underlying order—a sequence of eras and developmental periods" (1978, p. 64). The purpose of these developmental transitions is to cause greater individuation. **Individuation** refers to our becoming more individual; we develop a separate and special personality, derived less and less from our parents and teachers and more from our own behavior.

Although Levinson hypothesized more than 10 substages in the course of life, he chooses to concentrate on three phases in male development. These are the novice phase, the settling-down phase, and the mid-life transition (the latter two are discussed in chapter 16).

The Novice Phase

The **novice phase** of human development extends from age 17 to 33 and includes the early adult transition, entering the adult world, and the age-30 transition (see figure 14.1). In this phase of life, four major tasks are to be accomplished. The individual in the novice phase should form

- *The dream.* "Most men construct a vision, an imagined possibility that generates vitality" (p. 91).

- *Mentor relationships.* Each man should find someone who is older, more experienced, and willing to make suggestions at each of the choice points in his early adult life.

- *An occupational decision.* A man should begin to build on his strengths and to choose a vocation that values those strengths.

Individuation Refers to our becoming more individual; we develop a separate and special personality, derived less and less from our parents and teachers and more from our own behavior.

Novice phase Period of ages 17–33 that includes early adult transition, according to Levinson.

Figure 14.1

Model of Levinson's theory. Levinson's initial phase of human development extends from ages 17 to 33 and includes the early adult transition, entering the adult world, and the age-30 transition.

From *The Seasons of a Man's Life* by Daniel Levinson, copyright © 1978 by Daniel J. Levinson. Used by permission of Alfred A. Knopf, a division of Random House, Inc.

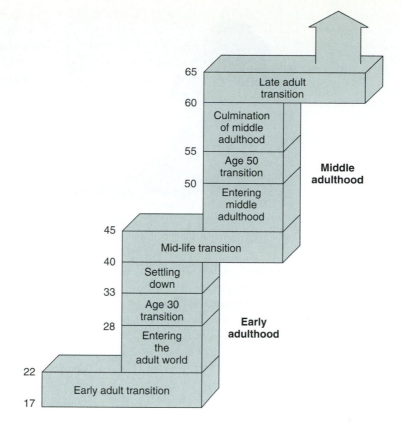

- *Love relationships*. Each man should make decisions on a marriage partner, the number of children, and the type of relationship that he wants to have with wife and children.

The Mentor

Mentoring The act of assisting another, usually younger, person with his or her work or life tasks.

In Greek mythology, Mentor was the guardian of Telemachus, the son of Odysseus. The concept of **mentoring** has received considerable attention in recent years (Bly, 1990; Cannister, 1999; Hamilton & Darling, 1996; Nolinske, 1995). Cannister (1999) found that young men involved in mentor relationships reported improved spiritual well-being over time compared to peers without mentors. Of particular interest are Robert Bly's notions on the subject (which, by the way, he calls "male mothering").

Bly suggested that two events have wreaked havoc with the modern American male's sense of himself. The first, which began in the first half of the nineteenth century, was the Industrial Revolution. As a result of this, fathers were forced to leave home, where they traditionally worked by the side of their sons, and seek employment in factories. The second, which began in the 1960s with "no-fault" divorce, led to the proliferation of single-parent families, about 90 percent of which are headed by females.

An insightful book on this topic is Robert Bly's *Iron John*. Reading, MA: Addison-Wesley. A teacher of both poetry and philosophy, Bly combines the two in this fascinating tale of a journey into the self. Among other insights, he explores the modern young man's grief over his inability to become close to his father.

With each of these events, much of the teaching and appreciation that boys used to get from their ever-present fathers was lost. Mothers have tried to make up for this loss, but because of deep-seated gender differences, only another male can induct a boy into adulthood successfully (see chapter 13). Bly believed that only those young men who achieve a mentor relationship with some other older man are likely to attain a mature personality. This man may be an uncle, one of the father's friends, or some older man at work. Without such a person, the young man will not be brave enough to confront himself, and he will sink into a defensive, self-deluding lifestyle. Bly also suggested that because the typical conflicts that exist between sons and fathers are absent in the mentor relationship, the mentor actually can be more helpful to the young man.

A solid relationship with an older mentor is crucial to the career success of a young adult, according to Levinson. Why is it, do you think, that older males are more likely to take a mentoring attitude toward their younger colleagues than are older females toward their younger colleagues?

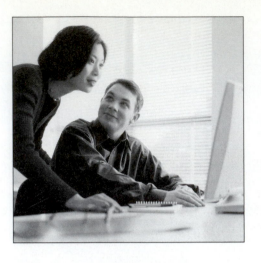

Levinson found that after each man selects a dream, mentor relationship, occupation, and love relationship, at around age 30 (plus or minus two years) he comes to reexamine his feelings about the four major tasks. Important decisions are made at this time, such as an alteration of the dream, a change in mentor, a change in occupation, and sometimes a change in marital status. For some, this transitional period proves to be very smooth. In most cases, however, it challenges the very foundations of life itself. Although he often keeps it to himself, the typical male at this stage undergoes a seriously disturbing period of self-doubt. Fortunately, most emerge from these doubts with a clearer understanding of their strengths and weaknesses, and a clearer view of what they wish to make of themselves.

Thus, for Levinson, the transition from late adolescence to early adulthood (and also for the years to come) tends to proceed in stages as orderly as those we have seen in the earlier stages of life. More variation occurs as we grow older, because we are controlled less and less by our genetic inheritance and more and more by the environment in which we find ourselves, and by our own individual decisions. This growing independence from our genes and our early experiences is reflected clearly in these two theories. Even if we have had a hard childhood, with alcoholic parents and traumatic accidents, we should be developing the ability to be in charge of our lives. As we grow older, we have the opportunity, and indeed the responsibility, to reinvent ourselves. Of course, how we reinvent ourselves depends on our culture. Some have suggested that Levinson's theory is culturally limited to the United States. What do you think? The next personality theorist we will cover, Erikson, would certainly have agreed.

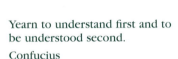

Yearn to understand first and to be understood second.

Confucius

Intimacy versus Isolation: Erikson

We last talked about Erikson's theory in chapter 11, where we discussed his fifth stage (adolescence), identity and repudiation versus identity confusion. Now we will consider his sixth stage, intimacy and solidarity versus isolation. This stage applies to what he defined as young adulthood, ages 18 to 25.

In his definition of intimacy, Erikson stated that it should include

1. Mutuality of orgasm

2. with a loved partner

3. of the other sex

4. with whom one is able and willing to share a mutual trust

5. and with whom one is able and willing to regulate the cycles of

    a. work

    b. procreation

    c. recreation

    so as to secure to the offspring, too, all the stages of a satisfactory development (1963, p. 266).

Erikson pointed out, however, that sexual intercourse should not be assumed to be the most important aspect of intimacy between individuals. He was speaking here of far more than sexual intimacy. He was talking about the ability to relate one's deepest hopes and fears to another person and to accept another's need for intimacy in turn.

Intimacy   Erikson's stage that represents the ability to relate one's deepest hopes and fears to another person and to accept another's need for intimacy in turn.

Those who have achieved the stage of **intimacy** are able to commit themselves to concrete affiliations and partnerships with others and have developed the "ethical strength to abide by such commitments, even though they may call for significant sacrifices and compromises" (1963, p. 262). This leads to **solidarity** between partners.

Solidarity   Erikson's term for the personality style of persons who are able to commit themselves in concrete affiliations and partnerships.

Erikson was fond of quoting Freud's response when asked what he thought a normal person should be able to do well: "Lieben und arbeiten"—"to love and to work." To Freud, then, sharing responsibility for mutual achievements and the loving feelings that result from them are the essence of adulthood. Erikson fully agreed with this. Thus when Freud uses the term genitality to describe this same period, he does not merely mean sexual intercourse; he is referring rather to the ability to share one's deeply held values, needs, and secrets with another through the generosity that is so important in intimacy.

It must be admitted, nevertheless, that Freud was far more concerned with the physical aspects of sex than Erikson, who deserves major credit for moving the school of psychoanalysis away from its fascination with genitalia and toward a greater concern for adult intimacy in general.

Distantiation   The readiness of all of us to distance ourselves from others when we feel threatened by their behavior.

The counterpart of intimacy is **distantiation.** This is the readiness all of us have to distance ourselves from others when we feel threatened by their behavior. Distantiation is the cause of most prejudices and discrimination. Propaganda efforts mounted by countries at war are examples of attempts to increase distantiation. It is what leads to **isolation.**

Isolation   The readiness all of us have to isolate ourselves from others when we feel threatened by their behavior.

Most young adults vacillate between their desires for intimacy and their need for distantiation. They need social distance because they are not sure of their identities. They are always vulnerable to criticism, and because they can't be sure whether the criticisms are true or not, they protect themselves by a "lone wolf" stance.

Although intimacy may be difficult for some males today, Erikson believed that it used to be even more difficult for females. "All this is a little more complicated with women, because women, at least in yesterday's cultures, had to keep their identities incomplete until they knew their man" (1978, p. 49). Now that less emphasis occurs in the female gender role on getting married and pleasing one's husband, and more emphasis is on being true to one's own identity, Erikson believed that both sexes have a better chance of achieving real intimacy.

The 1960s were a time when many grassroots action groups, such as Students for a Democratic Society, came into being. They were anxious to promote "justice, peace, equality, and personal freedom."

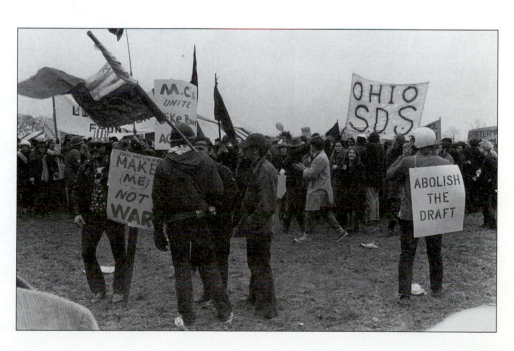

A growing number of theorists, however, many of them feminist psychologists, argue that females still have a harder time "reinventing" themselves, because of the way our society educates them. In the next section, we present their position.

Guided Review

6. Daniel Levinson's theory looks at adult development by examining life _____ (the unique development of the individual) and the life _____ (the general pattern of adult development).
7. Life structure is the underlying pattern or design of a person's life at a given time. It is _____ in character, with a primary component being the _____ that an individual has with significant others.
8. Erik Erikson's sixth stage of psychosocial development, intimacy versus isolation, focuses on building a _____ as opposed to Levinson's more career-oriented approach.

Sexual Identity and Gender Roles

The problem lay buried, unspoken, for many years in the minds of American women. It was a strange stirring, a sense of dissatisfaction, a yearning that women suffered in the middle of the twentieth century in the United States. Each suburban wife struggled with it alone, as she made the beds, shopped for groceries, matched slipcover material, ate peanut butter sandwiches with her children, chauffeured Cub Scouts and Brownies, lay beside her husband at night—she was afraid to ask even of herself the silent question—"Is this all?" (Betty Friedan, 1963, p.1)

This paragraph, which opened Betty Friedan's famous book, *The Feminine Mystique,* marked the beginning of a major reexamination of the female gender role. Today we are still undergoing a searching societal inquiry into the appropriate gender roles of both sexes. But are we any nearer to the answers we seek?

Consider this statement that the famed Greek philosopher Aristotle made more than 2,000 years ago: "Woman may be said to be an inferior man." Most of us would disagree with his viewpoint publicly. On the other hand, its underlying attitude is

The beginning of the "feminist revolution" in the 1960s opened an era of changing views toward gender roles. Do you believe that society's views of gender roles are significantly different today from what they were ten years ago?

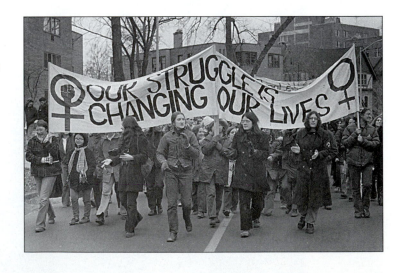

still widespread. People today are far less willing to admit to a belief in female inferiority, but many still act as though it were so. However, the influence of the women's movement, as well as of science and other forms of social change, is profoundly affecting the way we view sexual identity and gender role (Harding, 1998).

First, we should make a distinction between the two. Sexual identity results from those physical characteristics that are part of our biological inheritance. They are the genetic traits that make us males or females. Genitals and facial hair are examples of sex-linked physical characteristics. Gender role, on the other hand, results largely from the specific traits in fashion at any one time and in any one culture. For example, women appear to be able to express their emotions through crying more easily than men, although no known physical cause accounts for this difference. The results of studies have shown that people have different ideas about how their sexual identities formed (Eliason, 1995). Although some subjects claimed not to have thought about the formation of their sexual identities, others stated that society was responsible for their heterosexuality or that gender determined their sexual identities. Other themes were issues of choice versus innate feelings toward sexuality, having no alternative to heterosexuality, and the influence of religion in determining sexual identity.

People may accept or reject their sexual identity, their gender role, or both. For example, Jan Morris, a British author, spent most of her life as the successful author James Morris. Although born a male, she deeply resented the fact that she had a male sexual identity and hated having to perform the male gender role. She always felt that inside she was really a woman. The cause of these feelings may have been psychological—something that happened in her childhood, perhaps. Or the cause may have been genetic—possibly something to do with hormone balance. Such rejection is rare, and no one knows for sure why it happens. Morris decided to have a transsexual operation that changed her from male to female. The change caused many problems in her life, but she says she is infinitely happier to have her body match her feelings about her gender role.

Aspects of Gender Role

Some people are perfectly happy with their sexual identity but don't like their gender role. Gender role itself has three aspects:

- *Gender-role orientation.* Individuals differ in how confident they feel about their sex identity. Males often have a weaker gender-role orientation than females. (This will be discussed later in the chapter.)

Some people are so unhappy with their sexual identity that they have it changed surgically. Renee Richards (a) before the surgery, and (b) the female tennis star, used to be a man by the name of Richard Raskind.

(a)

(b)

- *Gender-role preference.* Some individuals feel unhappy about their gender role, as did Jan Morris, and wish either society or their sex could be changed, so that their gender role would be different. The feminist movement of the last few decades has had a major impact on many of the world's societies in this regard.

- *Gender-role adaptation.* Adaptation is defined by whether other people judge individual behavior as masculine or feminine. If a person is seen as acting "appropriately" according to her or his gender, then adaptation has occurred. People who dislike their gender role or doubt that they fit it well (e.g., the teenage boy who fights a lot because he secretly doubts he is masculine enough) may be said to be poorly adapted.

The traditional view holds that sexual identity is the result of interaction between sex chromosome differences at conception and early treatment by the people in the child's environment. Once culture has had the opportunity to influence the child's sexual identity, it is unlikely to change, even when biological changes occur. Even in such extreme cases of **chromosome failure** as gynecomastia (breast growth in the male) and hirsutism (abnormal female body hair), sexual identity is not affected. In almost all cases, those with one of these problems desperately want medical treatment so they can keep their sexual identities.

Although sexual identity becomes fixed rather early in life, gender roles usually undergo changes as the individual matures. The relationships between the roles of the two sexes also have altered considerably in the past few decades.

Erik Erikson's Studies

Erik Erikson's ideas (see chapters 2 and 11) about the biological determinants of male and female gender roles came from his studies of early adolescents (1963). He tossed wooden blocks of various shapes and sizes on a table and asked each child to make something with them. Girls, he found, tend to make low structures like the rooms of a house. Having finished these structures, the girls then use other blocks as furniture, which they move around in the spaces of the rooms. Boys, on the other hand, tend to build towers, which, after completion, they usually destroy.

Erikson likened the roomlike structures of the girls to their possession of a womb, and the towerlike structures of the boys to their possession of a penis. He felt that these differences account for greater aggressive behavior in males. Penis and tower alike are seen as thrusting symbols of power. He attributed these behaviors to inherited tendencies of the two sexes. Thus in this regard, Erikson may be seen as supporting the biological point of view.

Evolutionary Psychology

A more recent theory that also reflects the biological viewpoint is known as evolutionary psychology. Proponents of this view hold that actual behaviors, including those typically seen in the two genders, are programmed into our genes (Shackleford & Buss, 1997). Gender-bound behaviors are thought to have evolved over the millennia because they serve some useful purpose. Hence males and females are genetically predisposed to react to the environment in specifically different ways. In this regard, we are no different from other mammals. In most species, for example, the male is responsible for guarding the family group (herd, pride) and the female is responsible for watching over the young. Likewise, over the many centuries of human development, males have been rewarded for being competitive and females for being cooperative. As you would expect, many researchers and most feminists disagree with this biological explanation, arguing that gender-related behaviors are more likely the result of learning that occurred in childhood (Harding, 1998).

Chromosome failure
Biological changes such as enlarged breasts in males and abnormal body hair in females.

An excellent reference book on this topic is Judy Blume's *Letters to Judy: What your kids wish they could tell you* (1987). New York: G. P. Putnam's Sons. Blume offers letters from young adults who confide their concerns over the stresses of friendships, families, abuse, illness, suicide, drugs, sexuality, and other problems.

For more on this subject, read *Adulthood* (1978). New York: Norton. Edited by Erikson, this collection of essays explains what it means to become an adult and is written by experts from a wide variety of fields.

Androgyny

One gender-role researcher, Sandra Bem (1975, 1999), argued that typical American roles are actually unhealthy. She said that highly masculine males tend to have better psychological adjustment than other males during adolescence, but as adults they tend to become highly anxious and neurotic and often experience low self-acceptance. Highly feminine females suffer in similar ways.

Bem believed we would all be much better off if we were to become more androgynous. The word is made up of the Greek words for male, andro, and for female, gyne. It refers to those persons who are more likely to behave in a way appropriate to a situation, regardless of their sex. For example, when someone forces his way into a line at the movies, the traditional female role calls for a woman to look disapproving but to say nothing. The androgynous female would tell the offender in no uncertain terms to go to the end of the line. When a baby left unattended starts to cry, the traditional male response is to try to find some woman to take care of its needs. The androgynous male would pick up the infant and attempt to comfort it.

Androgyny is not merely the midpoint between two poles of masculinity and femininity. Rather, it is a more functional level of gender-role identification than either of the more traditional roles. Figure 14.2 illustrates this relationship. Not surprisingly, Bursik (1995) found that people with higher levels of ego development are more likely to be androgynous.

Another criticism has been leveled by Harris (1994), who examined an instrument developed by Bem, the Bem Sex Role Inventory (BSRI), which is used to evaluate one's definitions of masculinity and femininity. He conducted an interesting study to determine if the BSRI is valid for people with different cultural backgrounds. Results showed that the BSRI was valid in terms of general American cultural definitions, but that it was less reliable among Hispanic-American and African-American subjects. Harris suggested that researchers develop culture-specific sex role inventories to take into account the various backgrounds of cultural groups in America.

Before we look at the relationship between gender roles and sexuality, we need to examine one other factor. This is the difference between female and male identity.

Androgyny Functional level of gender-role identifications that incorporate male and female qualities.

Male versus Female Identity

> Identity precedes intimacy for men. . . . For women, intimacy goes with identity, as the female comes to know herself as she is known, through her relationships with others (Gilligan, 1982, p.12).

Sigmund Freud would have concurred with this statement by Gilligan, but for reasons with which many modern women would disagree (Grant, 1999). According to feminist Betty Friedan, Freud believed that women need to accept their own nature, which he thought of as sexually passive and subordinate.

The view of the feminists is that because females are trained to believe in the necessity of their maintaining relationships within the family, and because this role often involves self-sacrifice, women find it harder to individuate—that is, to develop

Figure 14.2

Relationships among the three gender roles.

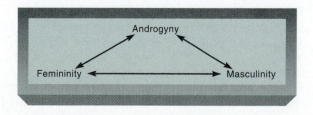

For most young adults, society's gender roles determine the kind of careers they can have.

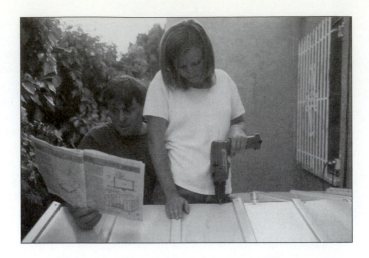

a healthy adult personality of their own. They argue that for the young adult male, identity formation "involves separating himself from dependency on his family and taking his place in the adult world as an autonomous, independent being, competent, with a clear sense of career and confidence in his ability to succeed" (Wolfson, 1989, p. 11).

For the young adult female, career and self-assurance are not so emphasized. Winning the attention and then the commitment of a man are more important aspects of her identity, and intimacy is the major goal. This is seen as unhealthy. As Wolfson (1989) put it, "It is difficult to have a sense of yourself that is internally consistent and congruent if your identity is dependent on the identity of someone else. 'I am who you are' is very different from 'I am who I am'" (p. 12).

This new point of view arose in the 1960s, primarily with Betty Friedan's book. The **feminist movement** fostered a new commitment to women's issues and to studies of women themselves. For example, as a result of her research on the female perspective (see chapter 9), Harvard psychologist Carol Gilligan and others (1982, 1990) has come to believe that

> for girls and women, issues of femininity or feminine identity do not depend on the achievement of separation from the mother or on the progress of individuation. Since masculinity is defined through separation while femininity is defined through attachment, male gender identity is threatened by intimacy while female gender is threatened by separation (1982, p. 9).

Research has also pointed to two other concerns about women's identity formation. One has been the tendency of society to "objectify" women, which means seeing them as a particular type of creature or object rather than as individuals. This may impart results from a difference in the way men in women view sexuality. As Everaerd and associates describe the difference, "The contrast between men and women would then be that in [sexual] experience, women process more situational cues and men more physiological cues" (2000, p. 88). In other words, the better part of a man's sexual drive comes from the inside, whereas for women, it tends to come from stimuli in the outside world. Thus men are more likely to view their partners as the object of their physiological drive. Psychoanalyst Erich Fromm (1955) suggested that "To be considered an object can lead to a deep inner sense that there must be something wrong and bad about oneself" (p. 323). There can be little doubt that women have suffered as a result of this difference: take for example the fact that an extremely high percentage of sexual abuse has been perpetrated by males

Feminist movement The efforts of some women to secure more equitable standards in workplace, society, and home.

(Calhoun & Wilson, 2000). These authors report that on average, over half of the women on the nation's college campuses record having experienced some sort of sexual victimization. Hamby and Sugarman (1999) found that males are more likely to cause psychological, as well as physical, abuse.

The second concern involves the ability to admit vulnerability. Men are taught to avoid showing any signs of vulnerability, while women are taught being vulnerable can be a virtue. In fact, feminist writers (Grant, 1999; Jeffreys, 1998) have argued that the so-called "sexual revolution" has not really occurred. Although men have become somewhat more vulnerable and open to being emotional, they argue, women have been urged to be even more vulnerable to desires of men. Obviously more work is needed to resolve this question of the role of gender in the development of the adult personality. Erikson (1963) himself appears to have endorsed this point of view, by stating that

> there will be many difficulties in a new joint adjustment of the sexes to changing conditions, but they do not justify prejudices which keep half of mankind from participating in planning and decision-making, especially at a time when the other half [men], by its competitive escalation and acceleration of technological progress, has brought us and our children to the gigantic brink on which we live, with all our affluence (p. 293).

For example, recent studies have repudiated the old idea that both sexes respond to stress with a "flight-or-fight" response (see chapter 16). That is, when threatened, ancient structures that have evolved in our brains cause us to want to attack or run away. This appears to be truer of males than of females. Because women have higher concentrations of oxytocin in their brains, they are more likely to respond when threatened with a **"bend-and-bond" response.** In other words, they are more likely to seek a compromise solution to a conflict, which is followed by a sense of improved relationship with the potential enemy (Douglas & others, 2000; Neumann & others, 2000; Ulvas, 1998).

Bend-and-bond response The more typically female response to threats.

This gender difference is reflected in a number of ways. Let's take, for example, a question which has been asked by a number of researchers lately: "Is Generation X (the current generation of young adults) characterized by values and goals that differ from past generations?" This is the question researchers Eskilson and Wiles (1999) asked 462 college students from four different universities. They were asked to picture their lives in ten years and rate how important it would be to succeed in various domains of their life. They were also asked to consider obstacles that might stop them from achieving their goals. Not surprisingly, Generation X students did not differ from preceding generations relative to their fundamental concerns for the future. Men and women both valued economic success, while women found family goals to be more important than men. A surprising finding was that economic success was rated as more important by minority students than by white students. Finally, minority students of both genders and white women listed discrimination as a probable obstacle in their future.

Are such gender differences cast in concrete? Apparently not. Despite our new understanding of the differences in male and female biology, society and its new child-rearing practices are clearly guiding males toward less aggressive gender roles, and away from placing such a high value on competition. As a result, developmental theorists are coming to agreement on a view of identity that holds that men and women are really more like each other, especially in our need to interrelate, than we have realized. It may be that males and females have seemed so different only because we have been taught to think so—the self-fulfilling prophecy.

In each of the theories described in this section on personality, the roles of biological, psychological, and social forces are evident. No one force completely dominates. Once again, we see the power of the biopsychosocial theory, which points to the complex interaction of all three forces in the explanation of human behavior.

Guided Review

9. With regard to gender roles, many people are not willing to admit a belief in female _____ but act as if it were so.
10. Sexual identity refers to our physical characteristics, whereas gender roles refer largely to the specific social _____ in fashion at a given time in a culture.
11. The three parts of gender identity are: gender-role _____, gender-role preference, and gender-role adaptation.
12. Erik Erikson believes that gender differences are _____ determined, based on his experiments with girls and boys as they played with building blocks.
13. According to Bem, _____ is characterized by more functional levels of role identification than by either male or female roles.

Interpersonal Relations

As young adults relate to each other, two of the most important human conditions with which they must deal are sexual behavior and love.

Sexuality

Sexuality plays a significant role in most of our lives. As with gender roles, genetically controlled drives shape our sexual relations. However, such relationships are also molded in powerful ways by psychological forces, and lately, social forces have had a decided impact. A good example of this is "pack dating," which has been occurring at colleges across the country (Gabriel, 1997). Instead of pairing off, undergraduates go out to dinner, movies, and parties in groups. Although these packs may bolster students' confidence and sense of identity, it may keep them from forming deeper, more committed relationships. One possible reason for this behavior is that students from families in which parents have divorced may fear that there is no such thing as a successful romantic relationship. Pack dating resolves this dilemma by allowing one to have sexual relations while avoiding intimacy and deep involvement.

Some experts suggest that pack dating may be an attempt, in part, to deal with the risk of disease. Although HIV infection rates appear to be relatively low on campuses, rates of other STIs, such as venereal warts and chlamydia, are soaring. Because HIV can remain dormant for up to 15 years before becoming AIDS, we really don't know its incidence. Choosing a sex partner from a small circle of friends allows a person to know the histories and habits of the potential partners, which could possibly reduce risk of contracting an STI.

Another explanation for pack dating is that students simply don't have time for relationships. Many students hold at least one job while carrying a full course load, and others are focused on earning grades that will help get them into graduate school.

However, not all college students engage in pack dating. Some choose to become emotionally and physically involved with only one partner and enjoy spending time alone with that person. Knox and associates (1998) were interested in learning why people choose a particular person to date or to marry. They found that both men and women felt it was important to choose a partner similar to themselves in terms of age, values, and education. They also found that men and women valued different characteristics in a partner. Women also stressed the importance of occupation and religious values as well as the desire to have children. Men, on the other hand, were more influenced by the physical attractiveness of a partner.

Answers

9. inferiority 10. characteristics 11. orientation 12. biologically 13. androgyny

Marital Practices

Intercourse between a husband and wife is the only type of sexual activity totally approved of by American society. Sexual closeness also tends to lessen significantly with the birth of each child, except in cases where the couple has taken specific steps to maintain the quality of their sexual relationship.

A number of findings of the Janus Report (Janus & Janus, 1993) are relevant to the marital behavior and attitudes of young adults. Among the most important findings are:

• Women who lived with their spouses before marriage are more likely to be divorced than women who didn't; men, less likely. Couples still married had lived together, on the average, for a shorter period of time before marriage than those who are now divorced.

• Among the divorced, men cite sexual problems as the primary reason for the divorce three times more frequently than women. Women cite extramarital affairs twice as frequently as men. But both cite emotional problems as the most frequent cause of divorce.

• Among the divorced respondents, 39 percent of the men and 27 percent of the women reported using no contraception.

Another important question that we might ask has to do with frequency of sexual relations among young adults. There is an old joke, which suggests the following guidelines: under 25, twice daily; between 25 and 35, try weekly; between 35 and 45, try weekly; between 45 and 55, try weekly; after 55, try, try, try. This joke is a good example of an inaccurate stereotype. In fact, as we will detail later, young adults engage in sex with each other at about the same rate as adults over the age of 55, and less than middle-aged adults. Most adults are more sexually active when they have a regular partner, but because of the much higher average age of marriage mentioned earlier in this chapter, a fairly high percentage do not have sex at all or only rarely.

As Everaerd and associates (2000) have stated, "But frequency follows desire, and not the other way around. Desire will vary with sexual sensitivity and availability of attractive partners, and will generally decrease in the long-lasting relationships and with age" (p. 82). Thus statistics about the frequency of the sexual activity among young adults do not necessarily describe very well what most of them are doing.

In the next section we turn to an examination of the deepest aspect of human relationship, love. The words written about love over the course of human history are uncountable. In this book, we will limit ourselves to describing the developmental aspects of this emotion: the seven forms of love that psychologist Robert Sternberg has suggested, and psychoanalyst Erich Fromm's definition of the essence of love.

Passion   Sternberg's term for a strong desire for another person, and the expectation that sex with them will prove physiologically rewarding.

Intimacy   Sternberg's term for the ability to share one's deepest and most secret feelings and thoughts with another.

Commitment   Sternberg's term for the strongly held conviction that one will stay with another, regardless of the cost.

The Seven Forms of Love: Sternberg

Sternberg (Beall & Sternberg, 1995; Sternberg, 1986, 1990 a and b, Sternberg & Davidson, 1995) argued that love is made up of three different components:

• **Passion.** A strong desire for another person, and the expectation that sex with them will prove physiologically rewarding.

• **Intimacy.** The ability to share one's deepest and most secret feelings and thoughts with another.

• **Commitment.** The strongly held conviction that one will stay with another, regardless of the cost.

For more and more engaged couples, premarital counseling is becoming a part of their plan to marry.

For an expanded view of this subject, read Robert Sternberg's "The triangular theory of love." *Psychological Review, 93:* 129-35, and "Love as a story." *Journal of Social and Personal Relationships, 12* (4): 541-46. These articles, too, offer a penetrating view of this most elusive topic.

Each of these components may or may not be involved in a relationship. The extent to which each is involved defines the type of love that is present in the relationship. Sternberg believed that the various combinations actually found in human relations produce seven forms of love (see table 14.3).

This is not to say that the more of each, the better. A healthy marriage will usually include all three, but the balance among them is likely to change over the life of the marriage. For example, early in the marriage, passion is likely to be high relative to intimacy. The physical aspects of the partnership are new, and therefore exciting, although probably not enough time has passed for intimacy to develop fully. This is a dangerous time in the marriage, because when intimacy is moderate, the couple may misunderstand each other in many situations or may make unpleasant discoveries about each other. Such problems are often much more painful than they are later, when deeper intimacy and commitment have developed.

Passion, Sternberg states, is like an addiction. In the beginning, the smallest gesture can produce intense excitement. As the relationship grows older, however, larger and larger "doses" are needed to evoke the same feelings. Inevitably, passion loses some of its power. Of course, wide differences exist among couples. Some never feel much passion, whereas others maintain at least moderately passionate feelings into old age. Some appear to have strong commitments from the earliest stage of their association (love at first sight?), whereas others waver for many years.

By and large, however, research indicates that love does grow with time. Sprecher (1999) did a longitudinal study of people whose relationships had remained intact for long periods of time. She found that participants' reports of their feelings of love, commitment, and satisfaction in their relationship increased steadily, in most cases, the longer the relationship lasted.

Sternberg's theory has numerous implications for couples, and for marriage therapists as well. For example, more and more couples are engaging in premarital counseling. In this, they analyze with their counselor the three factors of love, and how each person feels about them. This often helps them to avoid later problems and to get their relationship off to a good start. For some, it provides information that makes them realize that although their passion is high, their intimacy and commitment may not be, and they wait until these develop or decide not to get married at all. In their analysis of responses to the "Love Attitudes Scale," Butler and associates (1995) found that factor structure by age to be quite similar. That is, the attitudes of young adults were seen to have much in common with those of middle adulthood. It is hoped that findings such as those made by Sternberg and Butler and associates will improve counseling efforts, which will in turn help to bring about a decrease in our nation's high divorce rate. One caution: at least one review of Sternberg's model (Szuchman & Muscarella, 2000) states that although "conceptually interesting," the model has yet to be emperically validated.

TABLE 14.3 STERNBERG'S SEVEN FORMS OF LOVE

Liking	Intimacy, but no passion or commitment
Infatuation	Passion, but no intimacy or commitment
Empty love	Commitment, but no passion or intimacy
Romantic love	Intimacy and passion, but no commitment
Fatuous love	Commitment and passion, but no intimacy
Companionate love	Commitment and intimacy, but no passion
Consummate love	Commitment, intimacy, and passion

From R. J. Sternberg, "The Triangular Theory of Love" in *Psychological Review 93:* 119–35. Copyright (c) 1986 by the American Psychological Association. Reprinted with permission.

Validation: Fromm

In his highly enlightening book on this subject, *The Art of Loving* (1968), Erich Fromm gave us a highly respected understanding of the meaning of love. First, he argued, we must recognize that we are prisoners in our own bodies. Although we assume that we perceive the world around us in much the same way as others, we cannot really be sure. We are the only one who truly knows what our own perceptions are, and we cannot be certain they are the same as other people's. In fact, most of us are aware of times when we have misperceived something: We heard a phrase differently from everyone else; had a hallucination when under the influence of a fever, alcohol, or a drug; and so on.

Thus we must constantly check on the reality our senses give us. We do this thousands, maybe millions, of times every day. Let us give you an example. We assume you are sitting or lying down while you are reading this book. Did you make a conscious check of the surface you are sitting or lying on when you got on

---

How's Your Individuation Index?

A number of theorists have stressed that maturity involves becoming more and more of an individual as one goes through life's stages; that is, one becomes less dependent on the opinions of one's parents, other relatives, teachers, and friends. The person is better able to determine her or his own personality, using these other influences only as guides. Thus one index of maturity level is the extent to which one is "individuating." Fill in the blanks below to get an idea of your own individuation.

1. Can you think of any occasion within the last month when your friends asked you to do something with them and you refused?

   _____

   _____

   _____

2. Can you think of three important decisions you have made within the past year that were definitely not influenced by your parents?

   _____

   _____

   _____

3. Can you name at least two things about yourself that you used to hate but that you now feel are not all that bad?

   _____

   _____

4. Can you name at least two people who used to have a big influence on your life but who are no longer able to influence you very much?

   _____

   _____

5. Can you name two things that you now like to do by yourself that you previously didn't like to do?

   _____

   _____

6. Can you name two beliefs or values you hold with which your friends would disagree?

   _____

   _____

7. Can you name three things you do of which your parents would disapprove? Three things of which they would approve?

   _____

   _____

   _____

8. Do you think you organize your time differently from most of your friends? Name three ways in which you do things differently from them.

   _____

   _____

   _____

9. Are you an "individual"? Suggest five ways in which you are different from everybody else.

   _____

   _____

   _____

   _____

The answers to these questions do not prove or disprove that you are fully mature. They should help you gain some insight into yourself. Do you like your answers?

it? Probably not. Nevertheless your brain did. You know that if it had been cold, sharp, or wet, you would have noticed. That it is none of these things is something your unconscious mind ascertained without your having to give it a thought.

With some mentally ill people, this is the major problem. Their "reality checker" isn't working right. They cannot tell fact from imagination. They dwell in "castles in the air," out of contact with the real world. We need the feedback from all our senses, doing repeated checks at lightning speeds, to keep in contact with reality.

Fromm's point is this: As important as these "reality checks" on our physical environment are, how much more important are the checks on our innermost state—our deepest and most important feelings and thoughts! To check on the reality of these, we must get the honest reactions of someone we can trust. Such a person tells us, "No, you're not crazy. At least I feel the same way, too!" Even more important, these individuals prove their insight and honesty by sharing with us their own secret thoughts and feelings. In Fromm's words, others give us **validation.**

Validation is essential to our sanity. We are social animals, and we need to know that others approve of us (or, for that matter, when they don't). When someone regularly makes you feel validated, you come to love them. This is the essence of what Erikson has called intimacy. Intimacy fulfills what Maslow calls the need for self-esteem (see chapter 2).

There is, however, great risk in receiving validation. The person who gives it to you is able to do so only because you have let him or her in on your deepest secrets. This gives the person great power, for good or for ill. Because that individual knows you and your insecurities so well, she or he has the capability to hurt you horrendously. This is why many divorces are so acrimonious. No one knows how to get you better than a spouse with whom you have shared so many intimacies. This is why it is said that "There is no such thing as an amicable divorce."

Nevertheless, we truly need love and the validation that leads to it. As studies of mental illness make clear, those who try to live without love risk their mental health.

Validation Fromm's term for the reciprocal sharing of deep secrets and feelings that allows people to feel loved and accepted.

Guided Review

14. Unlike previous generations of young adults, who tended to pair off for social events, today _____ _____ is more common.
15. Research on marital intercourse indicates that sexual closeness between many couples tends to (lessen, increase) significantly with the birth of each child.
16. According to the Janus Report, _____ are more likely to cite sexual problems as the primary reason for divorce than _____.
17. Research indicates that as couples spend more time in a relationship, their feelings of love, commitment, and safety (decrease, stay about the same, increase).
18. Robert Sternberg examined the nature of love, claiming that love is made up of three different components: passion, _____, and commitment.
19. A healthy marriage, according to Sternberg, will involve _____ among all three of his components.
20. Erich Fromm's concept of _____ is closely related to what Erikson calls intimacy.

CONCLUSION & SUMMARY

By now you can see that the study of human development is mainly the study of change. Few chapters in this book, however, have described a more changing scene than this one.

Americans are getting married later for a variety of reasons. They are staying married for shorter periods, having fewer children, and are more reluctant to remarry if they become divorced or widowed. As we discussed previously, the functions of the family itself have changed tremendously in this century, and some have even predicted the family's demise.

Answers

14. pack dating 15. lessen 16. men, women 17. increase 18. intimacy 19. balance 20. validation

Perhaps the liveliest area in developmental study in recent years has been the field of personality research. More and more we are realizing that, just as in childhood and adolescence, adulthood has predictable stages. Distinct life cycles apparently exist, the goals of which are individuation and maturity. As we do more research, differences between male and female development are becoming apparent.

Next we looked at definitions of sexual identities and gender roles, and at specific aspects of each. We examined Erikson's studies and looked into the concept of androgyny.

Pack dating is an important change in the interpersonal relationship patterns among young adults. It is difficult to categorize the current sexual practices of young adults because their partnerships tend to change more than previously. Love, too, may be variously explained, for example with the theories of Sternberg and Fromm.

What factors are affecting American marriages and families?

- Almost 95 percent of Americans get married at some point in their lives.
- Basically four kinds of marriage exist throughout the world: monogamy (one husband, one wife), polygamy

(two or more wives), polyandry (two or more husbands), and group marriage (two or more of both husbands and wives). Homosexual marriages are also beginning to win acceptance.

What problems do young adults face in developing a healthy personality?

- Levinson suggested that adults develop according to a general pattern known as the life cycle. Each individual's personal embodiment of the life cycle is known as his or her life course.
- Levinson also described stages of development unique to men.
- According to Erikson's theory, early adulthood is defined in terms of intimacy and solidarity versus isolation.

What are the relationships between sexual identity and gender roles?

- Sexual identity results from those physical characteristics and behaviors that are part of our biological inheritance.
- Gender role, on the other hand, results partly from genetic makeup and partly from the specific traits in fashion at any one time and in any

one culture.
- Views of acceptable gender-role behaviors have changed considerably during the past 20 years. Androgyny is now considered an acceptable alternative to masculine and feminine gender roles.
- Men are more likely to react to stress with a "fight-or-flight" response, whereas women are more likely to react with a "bend-and-bond" response.

How do young adults deal with the interpersonal relationships of sexuality and love?

- Less dating has replaced the tendency to pair off for social events among other students today.
- The stimuli for male sexual behavior find their sources primarily in internal motives, whereas for females, external stimuli tend to be more powerful.
- Sternberg argues that love is made up of three different components: passion, intimacy, and commitment.
- Fromm states that people need to have their deepest and most important thoughts and feelings "validated" by others who are significant to them.

KEY TERMS

Androgyny
"Bend-and-bond" response
Chromosome failure
Commitment
Distantiation
Feminist movement
Gender-role adaptation
Gender-role orientation
Gender-role preference
Group marriage

Homosexual marriage
Individuation
Intimacy
Isolation
Life course
Life cycle
Life structure
Mentoring
Monogamy
Novice phase

Pack dating
Passion
Polyandry
Polygamy
Solidarity
Structure-building transitions
Structure-changing transitions
Transition
Validation

WHAT DO YOU THINK?

1. Which of the four types of marriage described in this chapter do your parents have? Your grandparents?
2. Which of the types of marriages described in this chapter are likely to exist 100 years from now?

3. Levinson believed that forming a mentor relationship is an essential part of the novice phase. Have you formed such a relationship? What are its characteristics?
4. To be intimate, you must know your own identity. But to achieve

an identity, you need the feedback you get from being intimate with at least one other person. How can this catch-22 be resolved?
5. How would you explain the change from pair to pack dating? How can you tell if you are truly in love?

CHAPTER REVIEW TEST

1. Since 1890, the average age at first marriage in the United States has
   a. increased for males and decreased for females.
   b. increased for females and decreased for males.
   c. increased for both males and females.
   d. decreased for both males and females.

2. A group marriage can be defined as
   a. when there is one husband and two or more wives.
   b. when there is one wife and two or more husbands.
   c. when one husband marries two or more sisters.
   d. when there are two or more of both husbands and wives, who all exercise common privileges and responsibilities.

3. The recent trend in increased divorce rates may be caused by which of the following?
   a. Liberalization of divorce laws
   b. Growing societal acceptance of divorce and remaining single
   c. Increases in the educational and work experience of women
   d. All of the above

4. The role of a _____, according to some theorists, is to provide an individual with guidance during life transitions, assistance with decisionmaking, and a clearer view of what the individual wishes to make of himself or herself.
   a. teacher
   b. mentor
   c. partner
   d. sibling

5. Compared to the baby-boom generation, the current generation of young adults (Generation X) has values which are quite
   a. different.
   b. superior.
   c. inferior.
   d. similar.

6. In Sternberg's conceptualization of love, when a person is able to share his or her deepest feelings and thoughts with another, they are experiencing

   a. passion.
   b. commitment.
   c. intimacy.
   d. true love.

7. Androgyny refers to
   a. persons who are more likely to behave in a way appropriate to a situation, regardless of their sex.
   b. women who have higher than average male elements in their personalities.
   c. men who have higher than average female elements in their personalities.
   d. the midpoint between the two poles of masculinity and femininity.

8. If someone forced his way into a line at a football game, an androgynous female
   a. would accept the fact that he probably had good reason to cut in line.
   b. would be angry, but not let her feelings show.
   c. would look disapproving.
   d. would tell the offender to go to the end of the line.

9. According to Levinson, the purpose of the developmental periods in our lives is to cause greater individuation, which refers to
   a. our developing separate and special personalities, derived less and less from our parents and teachers and more from our own behavior.
   b. the realization that one does not need to be in a relationship to attain happiness.
   c. the recognition of our distinct interests.
   d. the inability for peers to have great influence on major life decisions.

10. Erikson used the term distantiation to describe
    a. the distance we keep between ourselves and others during personal conversation.
    b. our ability to distance ourselves from our families of origin.
    c. the time we need to progress between one developmental stage to the next.

    d. the readiness all of us have to distance ourselves from others when we feel threatened by their behavior.

11. Whose theories find fault with Erikson because of his belief that women are judged through their relationships with others?
    a. Erikson and evolutionary psychologists
    b. Gilligan and Erikson
    c. Friedan
    d. Bem and Erikson

12. Researcher Carol Gilligan states that because femininity is defined through attachment, female gender is most threatened by
    a. divorce.
    b. personal loss.
    c. separation.
    d. dispassionate males.

13. Over the last two decades, one reason for the increase in the age of people at first marriage may be higher numbers of women
    a. entering the workforce.
    b. traveling alone.
    c. afraid of divorce.
    d. having children.

14. The term biopsychosocial refers to the interactions of biology, psychology, and _____ in relation to the individual.
    a. sociology
    b. theology
    c. environment
    d. heredity

15. Men are more likely to react to stress with a _____ response, whereas women are more likely to react with a _____ response.
    a. assertive, subversive
    b. "bend-and-bond," "fight-or-flight"
    c. "fight-or-flight," "bend-and-bond"
    d. positive, negative

16. The person who used the term validation to describe our need, as humans, to feel loved and accepted is
    a. Fromm.
    b. Levinson.
    c. Bem.
    d. Erikson.

Answers

1. c 2. d 3. d 4. b 5. a 6. c 7. a 8. d 9. a 10. d 11. c 12. c 13. a 14. c 15. c 16. a

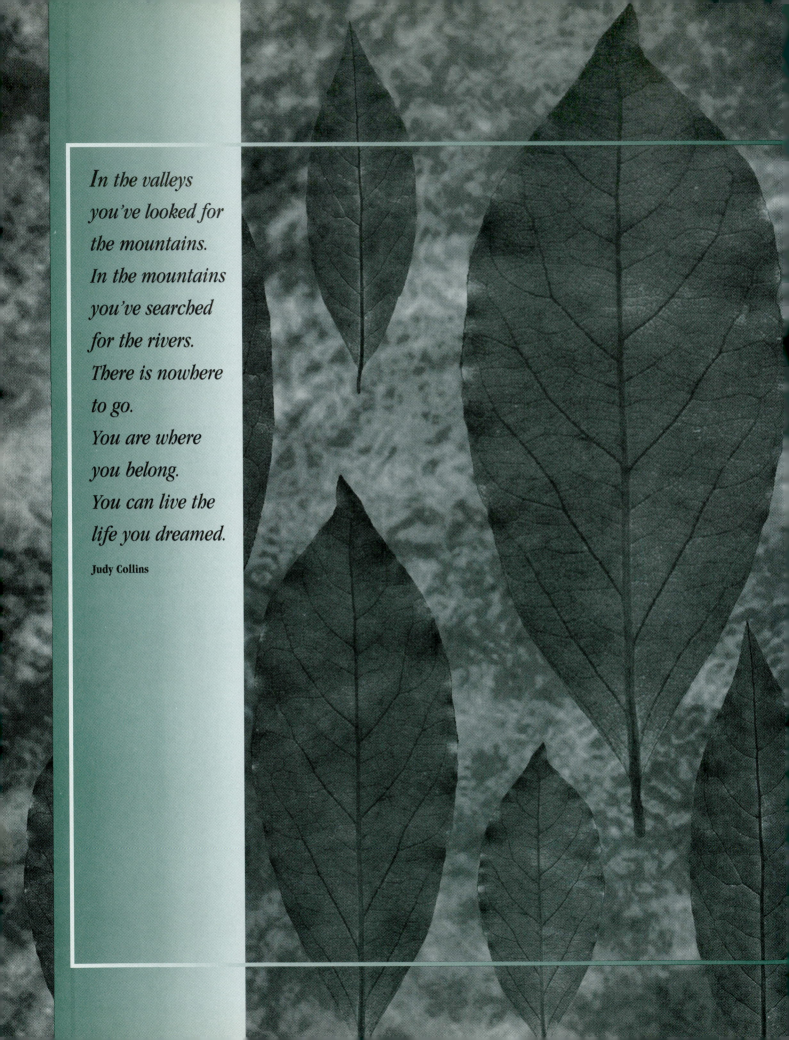

In the valleys
you've looked for
the mountains.
In the mountains
you've searched
for the rivers.
There is nowhere
to go.
You are where
you belong.
You can live the
life you dreamed.

Judy Collins

CHAPTER 15

Physical and Cognitive Development in Middle Adulthood

The idea that there is a "middle" phase in adult life is a rather modern idea. Most non-Western and preindustrial cultures recognize only a mature stage of adulthood, from about 25 to about 60 years old, followed by a stage of old age decline. Many Western scientists (including the authors of this book) now recognize four stages of adult life: young adulthood (approximate age range from 19 to 34); middle adulthood (approximate age range from 35 to 64); young elderly (approximate age range from 65 to 79); and old elderly (80+).

One non-Western country that does recognize middle adulthood is Japan. The Japanese word for middle age, *sonen,* refers to the "prime of life," the period between early adulthood and senility. Another quite positive word often used for the middle adult years in Japan is *hataraki-zakari,* meaning the "full bloom of one's working ability."

Not all Japanese words for middle adulthood are quite so joyful. The word *kan-roku* means "weightiness" or "fullness," both as in bearing a heavy load of authority, and in being overweight.

Why do you suppose industrialized cultures like North America and Japan have several words for middle adulthood, and other cultures have no words at all? ✤

Chapter Objectives

After reading this chapter, you should be able to answer the following questions.

◆ What kinds of physical changes affect people in middle adulthood?
◆ What are the main factors affecting a person's intellectual development in middle adulthood?
◆ What are the patterns of work that we most often see in this life stage?

Physical Development

"You're not getting older, you're getting better!"

You may hear middle-aged people saying this to each other. They hope that the changes they are experiencing are minor and not too negative, but let's face it, physical systems do decline with age. As you will see, biological forces greatly influence physical development, but be on the lookout for ways that psychological and social forces are at work as well. Now let us take a closer look at some of these functions.

Health

In general, concerns about health rise in the middle years. For example, a person's image of what they will be like in the future becomes increasingly health-related in mid-life. This is not to say that middle-aged people are sickly. Their worries probably result more because they experience a greater number of serious illnesses and deaths of their loved ones than do younger people, and from the fact that the changes in their bodies are more abrupt than in the bodies of young adults.

Basal metabolism rate (BMR)
The minimum amount of energy an individual tends to use when in a resting state.

Self-fulfilling prophecy
Making an idea come true simply by believing it will.

An interesting book on this topic is Janet Woititz's *Adult children of alcoholics.* Lexington, MA: Health Communications, Inc. Woititz describes the characteristics of the adult children of alcoholics but insists that these are not character defects. This book provides readers with basic tools that will enable them to achieve greater self-knowledge and understanding.

As one moves into middle adulthood, weight gain becomes a matter of concern. For example, about one-half of the United States adult population weighs over the upper limit of the "normal" weight range. For some, this is the result of genetic inheritance—about 40 percent of the people with one obese parent become obese, as compared with only 10 percent of those whose parents are not obese (CDC, 2000). Others become overweight simply because they do not compensate for their lowering **basal metabolism rate (BMR).**

BMR is the minimum amount of energy an individual tends to use when in a resting state. As you can see from figure 15.1, this rate varies with age and gender. Males have a slightly higher rate than females. The rate drops most quickly during adolescence, and then more slowly during adulthood. This is caused by a drop in the ratio of lean body mass to fat, thus lowering your BMR. Therefore, if you continue to eat at the same rate throughout your life, you will definitely gain weight. If you add to this a decreased rate of exercise, the weight gain (sometimes called "middle-age spread," referring to wider hips, thicker thighs, a "spare tire" around the waist, and a "beer belly") will be even greater. If you expect this to happen, it probably will (another **self-fulfilling prophecy**).

Cardiovascular Health

Cardiovascular reaction to stressful challenges is normal (Manuck, 1994). Jennings and associates (1997) investigated the causes when reactions are abnormal. They presented 902 men of ages from 46 to 64 with four tasks designed to measure their reactivity. They examined the subjects for cardiovascular disease such as hypertension (abnormally high blood pressure) and recorded their use of medications. They concluded that age and disease contributed about equally as causes of reactivity, with medications being a smaller independent influence.

Effects of Alcohol

Anyone over the age of 50 should "go on the wagon" and stay there, according to Teri Manolio of the National Heart, Lung and Blood Institute (cited in AARP, 1990b, p. 7). Even one or two drinks each day can be dangerous, because they can cause enlargement of the left ventricle of the heart. Such enlargement causes the heart to work harder and often can cause irregular heartbeats. If a person's heart is already enlarged, the danger is even greater. These data come from the Framingham (Massachusetts) Heart Study, which has also furnished the following findings:

- The older the person and the larger the number of drinks per day, the greater the risk.

- The risk is smaller for women.

- Men who are obese or have high blood pressure are at the greatest risk.

Figure 15.1

The decline of basal metabolism rate through the life cycle. BMR varies with age and sex. Rates are usually higher for males and decline proportionally with age for both sexes.

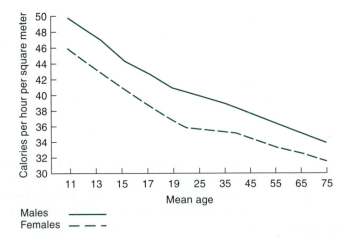

Males ——————
Females — — — —

Muscular Ability

Muscle growth is complete in the average person by age 17, but improvements in speed, strength, and skill can occur throughout the early adult years. In fact, most people reach their peak around age 25—females somewhat earlier than that and males somewhat later. Variations in peak muscular ability depend very much on the type of activity. Consider, for example, the 20-year-old female Olympic gymnast who is thought of as an "old lady" because peak ability in this area tends to come at around age 16.

The current popularity of aerobic activities may be reversing this trend in middle age weight gain and muscle loss. Aerobic activity such as swimming and brisk walking appears to help maintain general health because it demands that the heart pump a great deal of blood to the large muscles of the legs.

In the middle period of adulthood (35 to 64) there is a common but unnecessary decline in muscular ability. Unfortunately, the majority of people in this stage of life do not get much exercise. Both males and females may undergo a marked change in lifestyle. Growing success in one's chosen field often leads to greater leisure and indulgence in the so-called finer things of life.

Sensory Abilities

The five physical senses—vision, hearing, smell, taste, and touch—are responsible for gathering information about the world around us. Although the stereotyped image of an older person losing hearing or vision is sometimes made fun of, the gradual loss of function of one of the senses is a serious concern for all of us. We often take everyday experiences such as reading a good book, watching television, driving a car to the grocery store, tasting or even smelling a good meal, or just holding a child in our arms for granted. Yet all these experiences depend on one or more of the five senses. What changes in sensory ability can we expect as we pass through middle adulthood? The following trends are only general and vary widely from one individual to another.

Because of changes in the eye that occur when we reach our forties, glasses are often necessary.

Vision

Vision is the sense that we most depend on for information about what's going on around us. The eye begins to change physically at about age 40. The lens becomes less elastic and more yellow. The cornea begins to lose its luster. By age 50 the cornea is increasing in curvature and thickness. At 50, the iris begins to respond less well to light (Whitbourne, 1996).

What do these physical changes mean for our vision? In general, our eyes don't adapt to sudden intense light or darkness as effectively as they once did. The ability to focus on nearby objects decreases, leading to a diagnosis of farsightedness and possibly a prescription for bifocals. The ability to detect certain colors can also be hampered by age-related changes in the eye. As the lens yellows, shades of blue and green become more difficult to discern. For most people, these changes in visual ability pose a problem only when lighting is reduced, such as in night driving.

Hearing

Hearing also seems to be susceptible to decline at about age 40. This is when we begin to lose the ability to detect certain tones. As you progress from middle to old age, certain frequencies, the higher ones in particular, may need to be much louder for you to hear them (Whitbourne, 1996). Our ability to understand human speech also appears to decrease as we grow older. The most likely result is an inability to hear certain consonants. Cognitive capacity may play a role in the fact that the ability to listen to speech in a crowded environment (e.g., a party) declines faster than the ability to listen to someone alone with no background noise.

Our visual system is a more reliable sense than our auditory system. In fact, in contrast to the success that medical science has made in fighting blindness, deafness in the United States appears to be increasing. In 1940 you could expect to find deafness in 200 out of every 10,000 people in this country. Forty years later, you could expect to find it in 300 (Hunt & Lindley, 1989). Bear in mind, however, that these effects are partly a result of choice. Cross-cultural studies have shown that our relatively loud, high-tech culture contributes to our society's general loss of hearing.

One curious aspect of the age-related decline in hearing is that, of the five senses, hearing is easily the most stigmatized loss. People who wouldn't think twice about getting prescription eyeglasses will refuse to get a hearing aid or even admit they are suffering a hearing loss.

Smell

Olfactory sense The sense of smell, which uses the olfactory nerves in the nose and tongue.

Although not used as often as vision or hearing, the **olfactory sense** does a little more than just tell us when dinner is about ready. First, the olfactory sense works closely with our taste buds to produce what we think of as the "taste" of a given food. In fact, it is difficult in studies to separate which sense—taste or smell—is actually contributing to the decline in performance on a certain task. Besides bringing us pleasurable smells, this sense warns us against spoiled foods, smoke or fire, and leaking gas (Stevens & Cain, 1987).

Various studies suggest that our sense of smell decreases as we grow older (Stevens & Cain, 1987). The decline seems to begin slowly around age 50 and increases rapidly after age 70.

Taste

As we mentioned, our sense of taste is closely tied to our sense of smell, which makes studying age-related effects on taste very difficult. Recent studies have suggested that older adults may experience a decline in the ability to detect weak tastes but retain their ability to discriminate among those foods that have a strong taste, such as a spicy chicken curry (Spence, 1989). The decline in the ability to taste (and smell) may account in part for the decrease in weight that many elderly persons experience.

In general, we can say that although our senses do decline somewhat throughout middle age, we are finding more and more ways to compensate for the losses, so they cause only slight changes in lifestyle. Another physical concern in our middle years is the climacteric.

The Climacteric

Climacteric Refers to a relatively abrupt change in the body, brought about by changes in hormonal balances.

Menopause The cessation of menstruation.

Male change of life Change in hormonal balance and sexual potency.

Climacterium Refers to the loss of reproductive ability.

The word **climacteric** refers to a relatively abrupt change in the body, brought about by changes in hormonal balances. In women, this change is called **menopause.** It normally occurs over a four-year period at some time during a woman's forties or early fifties (Masters & Johnson, 1966). The climacteric also refers to the **male change of life,** whereas menopause refers only to the cessation of menstruation, most often between the ages of 48 and 52. The term **climacterium** refers to the loss of reproductive ability. This occurs at menopause for women, but men tend to be quite old when they are no longer able to produce fertile sperm. In aging men there is a decline or loss of both libido (the part of sexuality involving conscious experience) and potency (the physical capacity to react to sexual stimuli), although there is a lesser decline in libido (Davidson, 1989). Whereas in females the body ceases to produce certain hormones, the sex hormone that controls normal sex behavior in males, testosterone, has been shown to remain fairly stable over age groups (Rowland & others, 1993). These findings suggest that while men may experience a decrease in physiological function, other factors are important to the overall satisfaction of one's sex life.

The main physical change in menopause is that the ovaries cease to produce the hormones estrogen and progesterone, although the adrenal glands continue to produce some estrogen. Does this decline in hormonal output always cause significant changes in female behavior? The question is difficult to answer. At the onset of menopause, symptoms are often affected by women's attitudes toward sexuality, lifestyle, function within the family, and hormone levels (Huerta & others, 1995). These factors interact as they impact a woman's life in different ways throughout the climacteric. Some researchers feel that negative feelings are related to a lack of social support at this time in a woman's life (Montero & others, 1993).

Undoubtedly a lack of understanding of menopause, coupled with normal fears of growing old, accounts for at least some of the negative feelings about menopause. It should be noted that many women have positive feelings. For example, they no longer have to be concerned about becoming pregnant.

Matthews and associates (1990) found no negative mental health consequences from menopause for the majority of middle-aged women sampled. In a study of Israeli women, those from traditional backgrounds (Moslem Arab villagers) and modern backgrounds (Central European immigrants) were found not to regret the loss of fertility brought on by menopause (Datan, 1995). Also on the positive side, Sheehy (1992) found that menopause is a time of "coalescence," a time of integration, balance, liberation, confidence, and action. A menopausal woman no longer worries about pregnancy; many feel relief when their children leave the nest.

The menopausal woman moves from the old age of youth to the youth of old age or, in other terms, she moves into a second adulthood. Many women in their fifties may find themselves in the prime of their lives (Fodor & Franks, 1990). They have good health, autonomy, security in their major relationship, freedom, higher income, status, and confidence. Brown (1982) found that many postmenopausal women in a variety of cultures experience greater powers, freedoms, and higher-level responsibilities when their children become adults; but as one study cautions, it may be that only women of higher status feel this increase in power (Todd & others, 1990).

For those women who experience serious problems with menopause, **hormone replacement therapy (HRT)** can offer considerable relief. About 12 million women in the United States take estrogen alone and about 8.6 million women are on the combined estrogen-progesterone regimen (NIH, 2000). When estrogen was first instituted, HRT was found to increase the risk of cancer. Today, however, it is given in quite low levels and is combined with progesterone, which greatly reduces the risk (Col & others, 1997; Tavani & La Vecchia, 1999). The choice of whether or not to take hormone replacement therapy is a difficult one for postmenopausal women and must be undertaken on a case-by-case basis. In many women, hormone replacement can increase life expectancy by lowering the risk of developing coronary heart disease or hip fracture. However, hormone replacement therapy is linked with increases in breast cancer (Ross & others, 2000; Schairer & others, 2000). Menopausal women are advised to consult with their gynecologists so they can weigh their risk factors for coronary heart disease, hip fracture, and breast cancer before deciding whether to undergo hormone replacement therapy.

At one time, it was thought that the male hormone balance parallels that of the female. According to a well-designed study conducted by the National Institute on Aging (1998), however, the level of testosterone declines only very gradually with age. Dr. Mitchell Hermann, who conducted the study on men from age 25 to 89, said that his findings contradict earlier results because most of those previous studies were of men in hospitals and in nursing homes who were afflicted with obesity, alcoholism, or chronic illness. All of his subjects were healthy, vigorous men.

Hermann suggested the decrease in sexual potency that men experience in later years is probably not the result of hormone changes, but rather slowing down in the central nervous system, together with a self-fulfilling prophecy (men expect to become impotent, so they do). There have been numerous speculations in the popular press about the nature of "male menopause," as it is referred to in Jed Diamond's book by that name (reviewed in White, 1997), but scientifically speaking the effects of hormonal changes on the appearance and emotional state of men are unclear at the present.

It seems likely that as we better understand precisely how hormone balances change and how the different changes interact with each other, the impairments that have been attributed to these changes will decrease.

Hormone replacement therapy (HRT)

Two works that include sections on middle-aged physical development are: (1) The Boston Women's Book Collaborative. *Our bodies, growing older.* Boston: Author. An excellent update of the popular *Our bodies, our selves,* this book is for middle-aged and elderly women. (2) Nilsson, L. and J. Lindberg. *Behold man: A photographic journey of discovery inside the body.* New York: Delacorte. A book of photographs, many of them pictures enlarged thousands of times. This is a magnificent description of the human body.

Although middle-aged people are generally healthier than the elderly, chronic health problems are especially prevalent for poor African-American middle-aged women. African-Americans also sustain 39 percent more work-related injuries and diseases than whites and thus are more likely to drop out of the labor force before retirement (Jackson & Gibson, 1985). These socioeconomic and racial differences are a good place to see how the biopsychosocial model operates. What role would you say each of these three major forces play in causing these differences?

Health also plays a role in the cognition of middle-aged adults. In the next section, we examine this important developmental capacity.

Guided Review

1. Adulthood has recently been thought of as having four stages: young adulthood (19 to 34 years of age), _____ _____ (35 to 64 years of age), _____ _____ (65 to 79 years of age), and old elderly (80+ years of age).
2. Basal metabolic rate is the _____ amount of energy an individual uses when in a resting state.
3. Our basic metabolism rate decreases with age, meaning that if we eat the same amount all our lives we will _____ weight.
4. According to recent research people over the age of 50 should be concerned about the effects of alcohol as its use can result in enlargement of the _____, causing it to work harder.
5. All five senses decline during middle adulthood, but _____ loss has the greatest social stigma attached to it.
6. "Climacteric" is the term used for the abrupt change that occurs in the body due to changes in _____ bal·nces.
7. The term "menopause" refers to the _____ change of life, which includes the cessation of menstruation.
8. A number of women experience positive consequences from menopause, including a time of coalescence, of integration, and _____.
9. _____ _____ therapy can be used to offer relief to women who are experiencing problems with regard to menopause.

Cognitive Development

I am all I ever was and much more, but an enemy has bound me and twisted me, so now I can plan and think as I never could, but no longer achieve all I plan and think.

—William Butler Yeats

Of course, the "enemy" Yeats refers to is age. Was he right in believing he could think as well as ever or was he just kidding himself? The question of declining intelligence across adulthood has long concerned humans.

Intelligence

Indeed, no aspect of adult functioning has received more research than intelligence. Most of the debate has been over whether intelligence declines with age, and if so, how much and in what ways. As a result of this considerable research, investigators

Answers

have reached considerable agreement as to how cognition develops during adulthood. The leading theory is that of J. L. Horn, who argued that intelligence does decline in some ways, but in other ways it does not. The picture is probably more complicated than either of the first two positions reveals. Evidence indicates that

- One type of intelligence declines, whereas another does not.

- Some individuals decline, whereas others do not.

- Although decline does eventually occur, it happens only late in life.

Fluid intelligence   Involves perceiving relationships, educing correlates, maintaining span of immediate awareness in reasoning, abstracting, concept formation, and problem solving.

Crystallized intelligence Involves perceiving relationships, educing correlates, reasoning, abstracting, concept of attainment, and problem solving.

Horn has described two dimensions of intelligence: fluid and crystallized. The two can be distinguished as follows: **fluid intelligence** depends on the proper functioning of the nervous system. It is measured by tasks that show age-related declines (speeded tasks, tests of reaction time). **Crystallized intelligence** demonstrates the cumulative effect of culture and learning of task performance and is measured by tests of verbal ability and cultural knowledge (Labouvie-Vief & Lawrence, 1985).

Horn (1975, 1978) hypothesized that whereas crystallized intelligence does not decline and may even increase, fluid intelligence probably does deteriorate, at least to some extent (see figure 15.2). Horn and his colleagues (1981) found that this decline in fluid intelligence averages three to seven IQ points per decade for the three decades spanning the period from 30 to 60 years of age.

Some older research has suggested that some kinds of achievement may rely more on one type of intelligence than on the other (Lehman, 1964). For example, in fields such as mathematics, music, chemistry, and poetry, the best work is usually produced at a relatively young age and therefore may rely most on fluid intelligence. Other major achievements, such as in history, astronomy, philosophy, writing, and psychology, usually occur later in life, which may indicate greater reliance on crystallized intelligence.

A number of cross-sectional studies have attempted to validate Horn's theory. A good example is the work of Alan Kaufman and associates (1989). They studied groups of subjects ages 20 to 74 who were given the revised version of the WAIS-R. These researchers wanted to see whether the level of education subjects had completed would have any effect on their performance on the WAIS-R, and the relationship those performance scores would have to the age of each subject group. Results of the study appear to support Horn's theory of fluid and crystallized intelligence. Test scores showed a decline in verbal IQ, performance, and full-scale IQ. However, when education was accounted for statistically, the decline in subjects' scores for verbal IQ disappeared, yet remained for performance and full-scale IQs.

Figure 15.2

Horn's three types of intelligence.

From J. L. Horn, "Remodeling Old Models of Intelligence" in *Handbook of Intelligence: Theories, Measurements, and Applications,* edited by B. B. Wolman, Wiley & Sons, New York, 1985.

A subsequent study showed that ethnic differences occur in tests of crystallized abilities, regardless of educational attainment (Kaufman & associates, 1993). As was pointed out in chapter 2, however, cross-sectional designs like this may be flawed. The problem is that people of different ages, having grown up at different periods, have necessarily had different life experiences. Therefore, the results may be more due to this cohort effect than to aging.

A longitudinal study avoids this weakness because it looks at the same group of people over an interval of time. Schaie and Hertzog (1983) conducted a longitudinal study on cognitive abilities and found evidence that they decline as one ages. The evidence for a decline after the age of 60 was strong. They also found evidence that this process starts after the age of 50, although it is probably not observable in everyday life. Making the situation even more complex, Hertzog's latest research suggested that a decline in speed of performance makes declines in intelligence look worse than they are. "It may be the case that a substantial proportion of the age changes actually observed by Schaie in his longitudinal studies is not loss of thinking capacity per se but, rather, slowing in rate of intelligent thought" (Hertzog, 1989, p. 650). Perhaps you simply need more time to think and respond when you get older.

You should recall from chapter 1, however, that longitudinal studies may suffer from the problem that studies done at different points in time may be distorted by historical effects. Only a sequential design can resolve this difficulty and as of this time, no such study has been carried out.

The lifelong efforts of K. Warner Schaie (summarized in Schaie, 1994) are noteworthy; he has made powerful attempts to understand the adult life course of intellectual abilities. The Seattle Longitudinal Study examined, but was not limited to, the presence or absence of age-related changes and difference in individuals. Consequently, this study has provided data on the importance of age-related changes, variables that may explain such changes, and the basis for future interventions. By adopting the sequential format of studying a cross-sectional sample every seven years since 1956, Schaie has eliminated many limitations that accompany a strictly cross-sectional study or a longitudinal study.

New Views of Intelligence

Part of the debate is a matter of definition. What, exactly, is intelligence? How is it measured? It is certainly composed of several different cognitive abilities, such as memory, language, reasoning, and the ability to manipulate numbers. Each of these mental processes can, in turn, be divided into various subprocesses.

Different definitions of intelligence lead to different measures of it. Each measure emphasizes different mental abilities. For example, if you define intelligence as rank in class or school achievement, then cognitive abilities such as verbal comprehension and general information may be much more important than rote memory and perceptual tasks. In fact, most of the commonly used IQ tests measure only a few of the cognitive abilities that could be measured. Under these circumstances, the question of whether intelligence declines with age becomes unanswerable. Clearly, more specific questions must be asked.

Increasingly, general intelligence is being abandoned as a scientific concept and subject of study. More and more, researchers are proposing several quite distinct cognitive abilities. Horn has now added supporting abilities to the concepts of fluid and crystallized intelligence. These include short-term memory, long-term memory, visual processing, and auditory processing. Howard Gardner (1983) contended that there are seven different cognitive abilities. His list includes linguistic, musical, logical-mathematical, spatial, bodily-kinesthetic, self-understanding, and social understanding abilities.

Robert Sternberg has challenged traditional views of intelligence tests on the grounds that they measure only crystallized intelligence. He believes we should think of intelligence tests as measures of achievement, thus a person's intelligence may change over the course of a lifetime. In his view (1995), successful intelligence

If you want to learn more on this subject, read Gardner's *Frames of mind: The theory of multiple intelligences* (New York: Basic Books). It offers a comprehensive view of the numerous faces of intelligence.

consists of analytic components (solving problems), creative components (deciding what problems to solve), and practical components (devising effective solutions). He suggests that intelligence isn't so much a matter of quantity, but rather a matter of balance, of knowing when and how to use the analytic, creative, and practical intelligence components. This ability peaks in the middle adult years. Because most people in these years have a better understanding of themselves, they can capitalize on their strengths and compensate for their weaknesses.

Dual-process model A model of intelligence that says there may be a decline in the mechanics of intelligence, such as classification skills and logical reasoning, but that the pragmatics are likely to increase.

Baltes (1993) suggested another resolution to the question of how intelligence develops with age. They have proposed a **dual-process model** of intelligence. This model considers the interaction of the potential and the biological limits of the aging mind. Gains and losses are recognized as part of intellectual development. There is likely to be a decline in the mechanics of intelligence, such as classification skills and logical reasoning. These mechanics are largely dependent on genetics, and are comparable to fluid intelligence. Clearly, variables such as memory play an important role in this. Pragmatics of intelligence remain stable or increase with age, and include social wisdom, which is defined as good judgment about important but uncertain matters of life. Culture is the major influence on pragmatic intelligence.

This model seems to offer the most reasonable position. There are just too many famous people whose thinking obviously got better as they got older. To name a few: George Burns, Coco Chanel, Benjamin Franklin, Albert Einstein, Mahatma Gandhi, Helen Hayes, Michelangelo, Grandma Moses, Georgia O'Keefe, Pope John XXIII, Eleanor Roosevelt, Bertrand Russell, George Bernard Shaw, Sophocles, Frank Lloyd Wright, and so on and so on. It is no coincidence that these people also maintained their creative abilities well into old age.

Finally, intelligent mental operations may be broken down into sub-categories, most of which appear to peak at the beginning of middle age. These categories are (Moshman, 1998): case-based reasoning (including analogical, precedent-based, and legal reasoning); law-based reasoning (including logical, rule-based, principal, and scientific reasoning); and dialectical reasoning (including dialectical reflection and argument reasoning).

As we have said, a key factor in the ability to continue to be productive well into the later years is memory. Thus, an important question is what is memory? Certainly intelligence cannot be separated from memory. Your mind can process information like lightning, but if you cannot recall the proper information, processing abilities are useless. Does memory decline with age? The stereotype is of the doddering old person who can't quite seem to remember the names of his grandchildren. But the research does not always confirm the existence of a decline.

Memory

The study of memory has caused considerable excitement in the scientific community in the last few years, as great strides have been made in solving the mystery of how it works (e.g., Bito & others, 1996; Frankland & others, 1997; Kamino & others, 1997; Kaestner & others, 1996; Kiebler & others, 1996; McGaugh & Guzowski, 1997). Although all the microbiological studies thus far have involved animals, experiments with human subjects are planned.

Sea Slugs, Fruit Flies, Mice, and CREBs

On the basis of the research on the animals studied thus far (sea slugs, fruit flies, and mice), it is clear that the memory process is controlled by the flow of a variety of proteins. This flow is governed by a master protein known as CREB. There are four distinct steps in the process (see figure 15.3):

- An electrochemical signal sent from another neuron moves up the dendrite of the receiving neuron, which triggers a reaction in it.

- If the signal is of a certain type, it also triggers a reaction in the neuronal nucleus that activates CREB proteins.

Figure 15.3

Diagram explaining the memory process at the neuronal level.

1. A nervous signal arrives from another nerve cell, triggering production of a chemical inside the nerve cell.

2. The chemical travels to the cell's nucleus, where it in turn triggers the activation of the CREB protein.

3. The active CREB protein targets a site on the cell's DNA, where it flicks on a set of nearby genes.

4. & 5. The proteins made by the genes may induce growth in the dendrite to strengthen the connection, the presumed structural basis of memory.

Neuron in brain

Protein

Neuron in brain

CREB

- A site on the cell's DNA is targeted, which then "turns on" a set of nearby genes.

- Proteins produced by these genes travel back down the dendrite to the synaptic junction and strengthen the connection to the emitting axon by producing more neurotransmitter receiving points. This makes the next transmission from the sending neuron more likely to pass across the junction. In essence, this is the definition of memory.

Thus CREBs are the central factor in what will and what will not be remembered (Hawkins & Kandel, 1996). To be more specific, there are CREB activator proteins and CREB inhibitor proteins (DelVecchio & others, 1995; Tully & Yin, 1996). It has been found that animals given a dose of the inhibitor protein have impaired memory and those given the activator protein have much sharper memory storage ability. For example, fruit flies typically need 10 training sessions to associate an odor with an electric shock. Those that were inhibited could form no lasting memories at all. Those given the activator protein dose learned the association in one trial! Neurobiologist Timothy Tully stated that:

> "This implies these flies have photographic memory. They are just like students who could read a book once, see it in their mind, and tell that the answer is in paragraph 3 on page 274" (cited in Wickelgren, 1996, p. 3).

Both aspects of CREB proteins are essential to all thought. We need to remember the essential items, while not memorizing trivia, such as the habitual use of the word "like." It has also been found that short learning periods with rest or recreation in between facilitates long-term memory, presumably so that CREB activator proteins can be rejuvenated (Tully & Yin, 1996).

How humans operate the CREB process is not yet known, but it appears likely that highly intelligent persons are better at it than others. Where this inquiry will lead is an interesting question. Will we someday ingest synthetic CREB activator when involved in a complex learning task, or a CREB inhibitor when we wish to withdraw from the stimulation of our busy environment?

Memory in Middle Adulthood

Not surprisingly, a number of studies have found deterioration in some types of memory function as people age. For example, prospective memory is the memory "required to carry out planned actions at the appropriate time, such as meeting a friend for lunch or taking a medication. Prospective memory involves retrieval of

The "grande dame" of modern dance, Martha Graham's contributions to choreography make her one of the most creative adults in the twentieth century.

an intention to act that has been stored in long-term memory" (Hertzog & others, 1997, p. 314). This type of memory may decline with age. Hertzog and associates (1997) found that middle adults have more difficulty than younger adults with prospective memory, particularly when it involves monitoring of time.

On the other hand, some researchers have produced differential results. For instance, Whiting and Smith (1997) found that middle adults have more difficulty than younger adults in memory tasks requiring more cognitive effort, such as recall. More automatic processes, such as recognition, do not decline as much with age. Also, middle adults have more difficulty than younger adults in spatial learning, according to Gold and associates (1997). In a study of how adults learn a route from one location to another, middle adults had greater difficulty in remembering the route than younger adults, but were as good at recognition of landmarks along the route.

The Development of Creativity

As the world changes more and more rapidly, it becomes more difficult to define creativity as a separate ability from originality, utility, and productivity (Aiken, 1998). At the same time, the role of creativity has become an even more important aspect of cognitive functioning. In this section, we explore the development of creative ability in the adult years. But first, here is a description of the characteristics of creative adults.

Traits of the Highly Creative Adult

A number of studies (reviewed in Dacey, 1989a and 1989c; Dacey & Fiore, 2000; Dacey & Kenny, 1997; Dacey & Packer, 1992) have compared highly creative and average adults in a number of important traits. In general, highly creative adults

- like to do their own planning, make their own decisions, and need the least training and experience in self-guidance.

A Sociocultural View

Cultural Bias and Cognitive Decline

A chief result of Schaie's studies (1994) has been the identification of variables that reduce the risk of cognitive decline. These are as follows:

- The absence of cardiovascular and other chronic diseases.
- Living in favorable environmental circumstances, such as those who are above average in wealth tend to enjoy.
- Substantial involvement in activities found in stimulating environments such as travel and extensive reading.
- Having a flexible personality style.
- Being married to a spouse who has a high cognitive functioning level.
- Engaging in activities that require quick perception and thinking (such as verbal jousting with friends).
- Being satisfied with one's life accomplishments through mid-life.

No doubt all of these variables are biopsychosocial in origin. We can probably do little about the biological factors involved. Now that these variables have been identified, however, there may be many actions we as a society could take to affect the psychological and environmental elements. Can you think of any?

Furthermore, some of these variables are particularly related to economic level, culture, and lifestyle. Two of the most important are rating one's self as being satisfied with one's life accomplishments and reporting a flexible personality style at mid-life. These in turn tend to be related to having a high socioeconomic level, a complex and intellectually stimulating environment, being married to a spouse with high cognitive status, maintaining high levels of perceptual processing speed, and the absence of chronic diseases, especially cardiovascular disease. In summary, the richer you are and the higher your social class, the less your cognitive abilities decline.

These findings are strong evidence for a class bias in cognitive decline. What reasons can you give to explain the results?

The "artistic" type of person, according to Holland, has a preference for ambiguous, free, unsystematized activities.

- do not like to work with others and prefer their own judgment of their work to the judgment of others. They therefore seldom ask others for opinions.

- take a hopeful outlook when presented with complex, difficult tasks.

- have the most ideas when a chance to express individual opinion is presented. These ideas frequently invoke the ridicule of others.

- are most likely to stand their ground in the face of criticism.

- are the most resourceful when unusual circumstances arise.

- can tolerate uncertainty and ambiguity better than others.

- are not necessarily the "smartest" or "best" in competitions.

   In their compositions, creative adults typically

- show an imaginative use of many different words.

- are more flexible; for example, in a narrative they use more situations, characters, and settings. Rather than taking one clearly defined train of thought and pursuing it to its logical conclusion, creative adults tend to switch the main focus quickly and easily and often go off on tangents.

- tend to elaborate on the topic assigned, taking a much broader connotation of it to begin with, and then proceeding to embellish even that.

- are more original. (This is the most important characteristic. The others need not be evidenced, but this one must be.) Their ideas are qualitatively different from the average person's. Employers frequently react to the creative person's work in this way: "I know what most of my people will do in a particular situation, but I never know what to expect from this one!"

Now let us turn to the research on the development of creativity.

Psychohistorical Studies of Creative Achievement

Lehman (1953) examined biographical accounts of the work of several thousand individuals born since 1774. He studied the ages at which these persons made their creative contributions. He compared the contributions of deceased persons with those still living. On the basis of his study, he concluded that

> on the whole it seems clear that both past and present generation scientists have produced more than their proportionate share of high-quality research not later than at ages 30 to 39, and it is useless to bemoan this fact or to deny it (p. 26).

Figure 15.4 portrays Lehman's general results.

Figure 15.4

Graph of Lehman's findings.

Data from H. C. Lehman, *Age and Achievement,* Princeton University Press, Princeton, NJ, 1953.

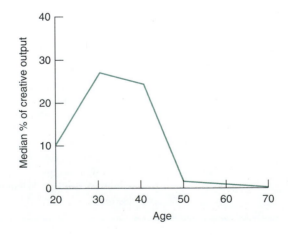

In his report of his own research on this subject, Dennis (1966) criticized Lehman's work, stating that it included many individuals who died before they reached old age. Dennis points out that this biased the study statistically, because we cannot know what proportion of creative contributions these deceased people would have made had they lived longer.

Dennis studied the biographies of 738 creative persons, all of whom lived to age 79 or beyond, and whose contributions were considered valuable enough to have been reported in biographical histories. He did this because he believed "that no valid statements can be made concerning age and productivity except from longitudinal data involving no dropouts due to death" (1966, p. 8).

He looked at the percentage of works done by these persons in each of the decades between the ages of 20 and 80. When creative productivity is evaluated in this way, the results are quite different. Dennis found that scholars and scientists (with the exception of mathematicians and chemists) usually have little creative output in their twenties. For most of them, the peak period is between their forties and sixties, and most produce almost as much in their seventies as they did in their earlier years. The peak period for artists tended to be their forties, but they were almost as productive in their sixties and seventies as they were in their twenties. Figure 15.5 depicts these relationships.

Dennis offered an interesting hypothesis to explain the difference in creative productivity between the three groups. The output curve of the arts rises earlier and declines earlier and more severely because productivity in the arts is primarily a matter of individual creativity. Scholars and scientists require a greater period of training and a greater accumulation of data than do others. The use of accumulated data and the possibility of receiving assistance from others causes the scholars and scientists to make more contributions in later years than people in art, music, and literature. Most of the productive persons in Dennis' study were males. It would be interesting to investigate the patterns of productivity among a comparable all-female group.

Studies by Simonton (1975, 1976, 1977a, 1977b) have attempted to resolve the differences between the Lehman and Dennis research. In general, Simonton found evidence that quantity declines with age, which favors Lehman, but that quality does not, which favors Dennis. Unfortunately, because of differences in design and criteria (e.g., differing data sources, differing criteria for inclusion in the studies), it cannot be said that this issue is fully resolved at this time (Simonton, 1993).

We started this section on cognitive development by looking at the measurement of changes in intelligence over the adult years. Then we reviewed what we know about creative development. Now we will consider a third aspect, one that attempts to pull together a variety of intellectual factors.

A highly respected source on the topic of creativity is *The Journal of Creative Behavior*. Pick up any volume of this fascinating journal at your library and browse through it. A wide variety of interesting topics is covered, and more often than not the articles are written creatively.

Figure 15.5

Graph of Dennis' findings.

Data from W. Dennis, "Creative Productivity Between 20 and 80 Years," in *Journal of Gerontology* 21:1–8, 1966.

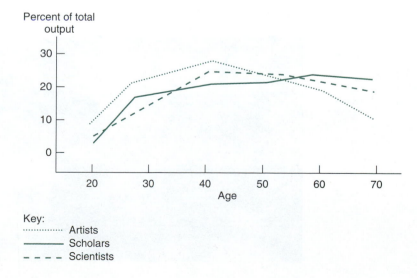

Key:
.... Artists
———— Scholars
– – – – Scientists

An Informed VIEW

Do Most People Become More Creative as They Grow Older?

Think of five people over 35 whom you know and most admire. Write their names here:

_____   _____

_____   _____

_____

Now, ask yourself, how many of these people are among the most creative people you know? If most are, do you think there is something about growing old that contributes to creativity? If your answer is no, what do you think does contribute? Would you say that, on the average, most people get more creative as they grow older?

If you would like to have a more informed opinion on this issue, you might want to read one of the articles on the subject referenced in this chapter (e.g., Jaquish & Ripple, Simonton).

You might also wish to learn more about it by going to our web site at http://www.mhhe.com/dacey5.

Learning Ability

Is there a serious drop from early to late adulthood in the ability to learn? Despite some classic studies (e.g., Eisdorfer & Wilkie, 1973; Hulicka, 1967; Knowles, 1989; Taub, 1975), considerable disagreement over this matter still exists.

For example, many studies have shown a marked decline in paired associate learning (the ability to remember associations between two lists of words) (Kimmel, 1974). Obviously, memorizing pairs of words is itself of no great importance, but much essential learning is based on this skill. In most of these studies, however, the measure of how well the associations have been learned is speed of response. Do older persons perform poorly because they are slower to learn, or only because they take longer to show what they have learned? As Botwinick (1977) reported:

> The research strategy has been to vary both the amount of time the stimulus is available for study and the amount of time that is available for response. A general finding is that elderly people need more time for responding than typically is provided; they are at a disadvantage when this time is not available. When sufficient time for response is available, the performance of elderly people is only slightly inferior, or not inferior at all, to that of young people (p. 278).

Does the apparent drop in learning ability from early to late adulthood occur strictly because of ability, or because of factors such as motivation and dexterity?

An Applied View — *Obstacles and Aids to Creativity*

We may agree that creativity is a valuable trait and should be fostered, but how? A number of theorists offered excellent suggestions (see, for example, Sternberg & Davidson, 1995), but educator Ralph Hallman's suggestions (1967) on the obstacles and aids to creativity are still classic. According to him, creativity has several persistent obstacles:

- *Pressures to conform.* The pressure on the individual to follow standardized routines and inflexible rules is probably the major inhibitor. Authoritarian parents, teachers, and managers who demand order are responsible for destroying a great deal of creative talent.
- *Ridicule of unusual ideas.* This destroys one's feelings of worth and makes one defensive and compulsive.
- *An excessive quest for success and the rewards it brings.* An overconcern with material success is often the result of trying to meet the standards and demands of others to obtain the rewards they have to give. In the long run, this distorts one's view of reality and robs one of the strength of character to be creative (Amabile & others, 1986).
- *Intolerance of a playful attitude.* Innovation calls for playing around with ideas, a willingness to fantasize and make believe, and a healthy disrespect for accepted concepts. Creative persons often are seen as childlike and silly and their activity wasteful, but these are only appearances. As Hallman remarks, "Creativity is profound fun."

In addition to recommending that we avoid these obstacles, Hallman urges that we promote the following aids in ourselves and others:

- *Engage in self-initiated learning.* Most people who are in charge of others (managers, teachers, parents) find it hard to encourage others to initiate and direct their own learning. After all, this is certainly not the way most people were taught. They fear that if their subordinates are given greater freedom to explore reality on their own,

they will learn wrong things or will not learn the right things in the proper sequence. We must put less emphasis on learning "the right facts," and more on learning how to learn. Even if we do temporarily mislearn a few things, in the long run the practice in experimentation and imagination will be greatly to our benefit.

- *Become deeply knowledgeable about your subject.* Only when people make themselves fully familiar with a particular situation can they detach themselves enough to get an original view of it.
- *Defer judgment.* It is important to make wild guesses, to juggle improbable relationships, to take intellectual risks, to take a chance on appearing ridiculous. Refrain from making judgments too early.
- *Be flexible.* Shift your point of view; to dream up new ideas for things, imagine as many possible solutions to a particular problem as possible.
- *Be self-evaluative.* When a person comes up with a creative idea, he or she is always a minority of one. History is replete with examples of ideas that were rejected for years before people began to realize their worth. Therefore, the creative person must be one who knows his or her own mind and is relatively independent of the judgment of others. To become a good judge of their own thinking, people must practice making many judgments.
- *Ask yourself lots of open-ended questions.* One extensive study showed that 90 percent of the time the average teacher asks questions to which there can be only one right answer, which the teacher already knows. Questions that pique curiosity and allow many possible right answers were asked only 10 percent of the time. Realize that you were probably taught that way, and take steps to rectify the tendency.
- *Learn to cope with frustration and failure.* Thomas Edison tried more than 2,000 combinations of metal before he found just the right kind for the electric element in his first light bulb.

Another factor in learning ability that has been studied is motivation to learn (Botwinick, 1977). It has been suggested that persons in middle and late adulthood are less motivated to learn than younger people. For example, it often appears that they are anxious when placed in a laboratory situation for testing their learning ability. To the extent that this is true, their ability to learn is underestimated.

It has also been found in laboratory experiences that older adults are more likely than younger adults to make the "omission error." That is, when they suspect they may be wrong, they are more likely to refrain from responding at all, and therefore are scored as having not learned the task. But when asked what they think the answer is, they are often right.

An Applied VIEW

The Lifelong Learning Resource System

As work environments undergo more and faster changes, there is a growing emphasis on learning how to learn, rather than on mastering a specific skill that may become obsolete. Secondary education or even a college education may no longer suffice for an entire career. Workers require "regular booster shots of education and training" (Abeshouse, 1987, p. 23).

Knowles (1989) made a marked distinction between teaching aimed at children and youths (pedagogy) and the teaching of adults (androgogy). Adults differ from younger persons in the following ways:

- *The need to know.* Adults need to know why they need to learn something before undertaking it.
- *The learners' self-concept.* Adults have a self-concept of being responsible for their own decisions, for their own lives.
- *The role of the learners' experience.* Adults come into an educational activity with both a greater volume and a different quality of experience than youths.
- *Readiness to learn.* Adults become ready to learn those things they need to know and be able to do in order to cope effectively with their real-life situations.
- *Orientation to learning.* In contrast to children's and youths' subject-centered orientation to learning (at least in school), adults are life-centered (or task-centered or problem-centered) in their orientation to learning.
- *Motivation.* Although adults are responsive to some external motivators (better jobs, promotions, higher salaries, and the like), the most potent motivators are internal pressures (the desire for increased job satisfaction, self-esteem, quality of life, and the like).

Also, the meaningfulness of the task affects motivation. It is clear that the motivation for middle-aged and elderly adults is different from that of younger adults, and many experiments have not taken this into consideration in studying learning ability.

Decline in cognitive ability due to aging can often be offset through motivation and new learning experiences. This is shown by the growing number of adults who return to formal education in middle adulthood.

Why are more and more adults going back to school? In the past, children could be educated to deal with a society and workplace that would remain essentially unchanged for their entire lives. Today the rate of change and innovation is too rapid. Fifty-year-old men and women who were born before the computer was being invented, and certainly didn't learn about computers in school as children, are now routinely asked to use them at work. It is now commonplace for people to return to school in order to advance or even maintain their present career. Also, sometimes an adult returns to school in order to learn a new skill or hobby that will be enjoyable during retirement.

Women in particular are going back to school in large numbers. Middle-aged women of today were not encouraged to pursue higher education when they were young. Some women are trying to catch up to be competitive with their male counterparts. Other women may return to school, not to study accounting or computer science, but to study literature or history, just to broaden their knowledge and for their own personal enjoyment. Many need occupational training to support themselves and their families after a divorce.

The education system is having to adapt to this change. Most adults cannot afford to quit their current jobs to go back to school. More schools are now offering evening and part-time programs. Many schools offer courses that can be taken at home, in some cases taking advantage of technology such as TV or computers.

Not all new learning by middle-aged adults takes place in a formal school setting. Employees in many different types of work settings are asked to keep abreast of new innovations. Other social experiences, such as practicing a religion, going to a library, watching television, and serving as a volunteer, involve new learning. Learning is now more than ever a lifelong task.

The beautiful thing about learning is that nobody can take it away from you.

Anon

Guided Review

10. Despite extensive research on intelligence during adulthood, investigators do not agree on the state of intellectual ability. For instance, Terman's longitudinal study showed an increase in IQ scores with age among his gifted population. Horn's studies, however, show decline in _____ intelligence, with an increase in _____ intelligence.

11. According to Horn, fluid intelligence depends on the proper functioning of the nervous system. Crystallized intelligence indicates the cumulative effects of _____ and _____ on task performance.

12. Memory is closely related to intelligence. Prospective memory (the ability to retrieve an intention to act that has been stored in long-term memory) may _____ in middle adulthood.

13. Highly creative people like to do their own planning, are the most _____ when unusual circumstances arise, and can tolerate uncertainty and _____ better than others.

14. Today more adults are going back to school because the rate of change and _____ in our society is so rapid.

Patterns of Work

As the "baby boom" generation enters middle age, many changes are beginning to occur in the workplace. Fewer and fewer new young workers will be available to enter the workforce. Employers will find themselves with a larger number of older workers. This shrinking labor pool is leading many employers to pay more attention than ever to the welfare of their employees. Some of the new issues of the late 1990s were child care, elderly care, home-based work, nontraditional work schedules, and the spiraling cost of health-care benefits.

O'Connor and Wolfe (1991) have identified several factors that enable adults to experience personal growth during the mid-life transition that results in positive emotional outlook and enthusiasm for career. Examples of these factors are understanding and changing organization of one's career, ego development, and commitment to learning. Other studies have found that some changes in adults' life structure are best accounted for by a process of shifting one's internal models (Wolfe & others, 1990). An example of this notion is moving from the existing structure of an adult's self and world to a commitment to new choices that help form a new structure.

Employers are also attempting more creative approaches to development and training. In the past, employers have tended to spend the majority of their training and development resources on younger employees. Perhaps this is just a matter of employers being unaware of the problems and concerns of their older employees. Or perhaps money and time invested in younger employees were considered better spent than that on older employees.

But in recent years, a trend has emerged among employers to recognize some of the concerns of middle-aged employees. Among them are the following:

- Awareness of advancing age and awareness of death

- Awareness of body changes related to aging

- Knowing how many career goals have been or will be attained

- Search for new life goals

Answers

10. fluid, crystallized 11. culture, learning 12. decrease 13. resourceful, ambiguity 14. innovation

- Marked change in family relationships

- Change in work relationships

- Sense of skills and abilities becoming outdated

- Feeling of decreased job mobility and increased concern for job security

Businesses have responded to these issues with continuing education, seminars, workshops, degree programs, and other forms of retraining. Employers are beginning to have an increasing appreciation for the contribution of older workers. There is growing recognition that each individual has different career choices, patterns, and promotional opportunities (Sterns & Miklos, 1995). As the labor pool shrinks, the welfare of the older, established workforce becomes more valuable. Another concern is the midcareer crisis.

Special Problems of the Working Woman

It is probably not news to you that the problems facing women in the workplace are different from those of men. But what actual difference does being a woman make? A review of this literature reveals the following four major problem areas.

Sexual Harassment on the Job

Sexual harassment can take many forms (Gelfand & others, 1995), such as verbal sexual suggestions or jokes; leering; "accidentally" brushing against your body; a "friendly" pat, squeeze, or pinch, or arm around you; catching you alone for a quick kiss; explicit propositions backed by the threat of losing your job; and forced sexual relations.

Although harassment of professional women has received considerable media attention in recent years (e.g., Justice Thomas' nomination hearings), blue-collar women have even more difficulty with this problem. Many women who work in the trades report that their marriages are strained by their jobs; not only do their husbands not like their nontraditional occupation, but they are unwilling to support them against the sex discrimination and harassment they suffer (Dinnerstein, 1992; Grossman & Chester, 1990).

Most blue-collar women have been verbally harassed (88 percent), and many have been pinched, fondled, and otherwise physically assaulted (28 percent). They have little support from their supervisors; in fact, 20 percent of the perpetrators are the supervisors. These women also suffer discrimination: Their competence is questioned, the job requirements are stiffer, they are denied advancement, and necessary job information is withheld. They have little support for their complaints (Schroedel, 1990).

Fiske and Glick (1995) theorized that male sexual harassment in the workplace results from a combination of factors: ambivalent motives on the part of men and male gender stereotyping of women and jobs. Ambivalence refers to both hostile and mild motives, and the complex interaction of these motives with gender stereotyping promotes different types of sexual harassment. Some women do not consider their personal experiences with sexual harassment as a form of sex discrimination (Murrell & others, 1995). However, both sexual harassment and sexual discrimination result in negative work attitudes for women.

Equal Pay and Promotion Criteria

The Equal Pay Act was passed in 1963 and states that men and women in substantially similar jobs in the same company should get the same pay. Under this act, the complainant may remain anonymous while the complaint is being investigated.

In spite of these legal protections, women make less money on the average than men and are less often promoted to management-level jobs. Why? Male prejudice is one reason, no doubt, but there are probably others. Among the several explanations that have been offered (but for which little current research evidence exists) are: Women may be absent more from work due to illness of children and are much more likely to take parenthood leave; many women seem to have greater anxiety about using computers than males; and women take less math in school.

Career and/or Family

The increase in working mothers has created a need for childcare in this country. Uttal (1999) reports that many mothers, regardless of ethnic background, prefer leaving their infants and young children with relatives rather than in day care. Despite this expressed preference, significantly more African-American and Mexican-American mothers use relative child care than Anglo-American mothers. Uttal suggests this trend is due to a variety of factors such as individual family needs, economic needs, and extended family relationships. The research reported on the dual-career family in chapter 14 applies here as well.

Travel Safety

Working women are exposed to a considerable number of hazards to which the average housewife and mother is not subjected. Crimes against women are no longer limited to the inner city but now occur in suburban and even rural areas with a high frequency.

These four problems are gradually being recognized in the workplace, and there is hope that they will be alleviated.

The Midcareer Crisis

Midcareer crisis A stage that some persons go through in middle age during which they come to question their career and personal goals and dreams.

Considerable attention is now being given to the crisis many people undergo in the middle of their careers. For some it is a problem of increasing anxiety, which is troublesome but no serious problem. For others a **midcareer crisis** is a reality, and it is truly threatening.

A number of changes in the middle years are not caused by work: the awareness of advancing age, the death of parents and other relatives, striking changes in family relationships, and a decrease in physical ability. Other changes are entirely work related.

Coming to Terms with Attainable Career Goals

By the time a person reaches the age of 40 in a professional or managerial career, it is pretty clear whether she or he will make it to the top of the field. If individuals haven't reached their goals by this time, most adjust their level of aspirations and, in some cases, start over in a new career. Many, however, are unable to recognize that they have unrealistic aspirations and thus suffer from considerable stress.

Even people whose career patterns are stable, such as Catholic priests, often have a midcareer letdown. Nor is this crisis restricted to white-collar workers. Many blue-collar workers, realizing that they have gone about as far as they are going to go on their jobs, suffer from depression.

This is also the time when family expenses, such as college education for teenage children, become great. If family income does not rise, this obviously creates a conflict, especially if the husband is the sole provider for the family. If the wife goes back to work, other types of stress often occur. Forthofer and associates (1996) found that marital problems are associated with work loss, specifically financial loss. Based on the average earnings of participants in this study, work loss related to marital problems came to approximately $6.8 billion per year. The authors suggest that family interventions be targeted at the prevention of marital problems to provide both psychosocial and economic benefits to society.

The Change in Work Relationships

Relationships with fellow employees obviously change when one has come to the top of one's career. Some middle-aged adults take a mentoring attitude toward younger employees, but others feel resentful toward the young because they still have a chance to progress. When people reach their forties and fifties, they often try to establish new relationships with fellow workers, and this contributes to the sense of conflict.

A Growing Sense of Outdatedness

In many cases, an individual has to work so hard just to stay in a job that it is impossible to keep up-to-date. Sometimes a younger person, fresh from an extensive education, will join the firm and will know more about modern techniques than the middle-aged person does. These circumstances usually cause feelings of anxiety and resentment in the older employee because he or she is afraid of being considered incompetent. A good example is society's heavy reliance on computers to help people manage many aspects of their business and personal lives. Today, very young children are taught how to use a computer in school and at home. Older adults did not have this training and thus many feel challenged by the complexities of computers. Czaja and Sharit (1998) found that without computer training experience, older people often felt uncomfortable and ineffective with computers. However, after only a three-day training period most reported that they felt much more comfortable using a computer.

Inability to Change Jobs

Age discrimination in employment starts as early as age 35 in some industries and becomes pronounced by age 45. A federal law against age discrimination in employment was passed in 1968 to ease the burden on the older worker, but to date the law has been poorly enforced on both the federal and state levels. Many employers get around the law simply by telling older applicants that they are "overqualified" for the available position.

The Generativity Crisis

Erikson suggested that people in the middle years ought to be in the generativity stage. This is a time when they should be producing something of lasting value, making a gift to future generations. In fact, this is definitely a concern for middle-aged workers. The realization that the time left to make such a contribution is limited can come with shocking force. Braverman and Paris (1993) found that at midlife, using work as a defense against dealing with emotional conflicts tends to break down, and problems of childhood can re-emerge as mid-life crises.

The generativity crisis is similar to the identity crisis of late adolescence in many ways. Both often produce psychosomatic symptoms such as indigestion and extreme tiredness. Middle-aged persons often get chest pains at this time. These symptoms are rarely caused by organic diseases in people younger than 50 and usually are due to a depressed state associated with career problems.

The resolution of this crisis, and of other types of crises that occur during early and middle adulthood, depends on how the person's personality has developed during this period. In the following section, we continue our examination of this topic, which began in chapter 14.

Some Suggestions for Dealing with the Midcareer Crisis

Levinson and others found that a fair number of workers experience a stressful mid-life transition. One major way of dealing with it is for the middle-aged worker to help younger employees make significant contributions. Furthermore, companies are taking a greater responsibility for fostering continuing education of their employees. More equitable patterns of responsibilities in the home are also developing among dual-career middle-aged couples, although there are many exceptions (Coltrane & Ishii-Kuntz, 1992; Dancer & Gilbert, 1993).

We should continue the type of job transfer programs for middle-aged people that we now have for newer employees. Although sometimes the changes can be threatening, the move to a new type of job and the requisite new learning experiences can bring back a zest for work.

Perhaps the federal government should consider starting midcareer clinics. Such clinics could help workers reexamine their goals, consider job changes, and provide information and guidance. Another solution might be the establishment of "portable pension plans" that would move with workers from one company to another so they would not lose all they have built up when they change jobs.

Can you imagine any other remedies?

Guided Review

15. A number of concerns face middle-aged employees. These concerns include knowing how many career goals have been or will be reached, changes in family relationships, change in work relationships, feelings of decreased job _____ and concern for job _____.

16. Some middle-aged workers may experience a _____ crisis upon the realization that there may be limited time remaining for them to make contributions for future generations.

17. Some of the problems facing women in the workplace are _____ _____, equal pay, and travel safety.

18. Some women in the workplace experience _____, resulting in a questioning of competence, tougher job requirements, and blocks to career advancement.

CONCLUSION & SUMMARY

What is true of personality and social development appears to be true, though probably to a lesser extent, of physical and mental development: What you expect is what you get. If you expect

- your weight to go up,
- your muscles to grow flabby and weak,
- your senses to dull,
- your climacteric to be disruptive,
- your intelligence to drop,
- your creativity to plummet, and
- your sexual interest and ability to decline, they probably will.

This is called the self-fulfilling prophecy. People who take a positive outlook, who enthusiastically try to maintain their bodies and minds, have a much better chance at success. They are also better able to deal with the stresses that life naturally imposes on us all. This is not to say that we can completely overcome the effects of aging. It means that through our attitudes, we can learn to deal with them more effectively.

This phenomenon is also seen in the world of work. There are, of course, major changes that occur to most workers as they age, but the disruption of these alterations will usually be more severe if the person is sure they are going to be. Many workplaces are establishing programs to help their employees deal with these stresses. Of particular concern are the special problems that afflict female but not male workers.

What kinds of physical changes affect people in middle adulthood?

- Health concerns in middle adulthood include increasing weight and lower metabolism.
- In the middle period of adulthood there is a common but often unnecessary decline in muscular ability, due in part to a decrease in exercise.
- Sensory abilities—vision, hearing, smell, and taste—begin to show slight declines in middle adulthood.
- The climacterium, the loss of reproductive ability, occurs at

menopause for women but at much older ages for most men.

What are the main factors affecting a person's intellectual development in middle adulthood?

- Horn suggests that although fluid intelligence deteriorates with age, crystallized intelligence does not.
- * Sternberg suggests three types of intelligence: analytical, creative, and practical.
- Baltes has proposed a dual-process model of intelligence, which suggests a decline in the mechanics of intelligence (classification skills, logical reasoning), yet an increase in the pragmatics of intelligence (social wisdom).
- Creativity, important in a rapidly changing world, manifests itself at different peak periods throughout adulthood.
- Learning in middle adulthood can be enhanced through motivation, new learning experiences, and changes in education systems.

Answers

15. mobility, security 16. mid-life 17. sexual harassment 18. discrimination

What are the patterns of work that we most often see in this life stage?

- In recent years, a trend has emerged among employers to recognize some of the concerns of middle-aged employees.

- Four major problem areas are related to working women: sexual harassment on the job, equal pay and promotion criteria, career and/or family, and travel safety.
- Considerable attention is now being given to the crisis many people

undergo in the middle of their careers.
- One major way of dealing with the mid-life crisis is for the middle-aged worker to help younger employees make significant contributions.

KEY TERMS

Basal metabolism rate (BMR)
Climacteric
Climacterium
Crystallized intelligence

Dual-process model
Fluid intelligence
Hormone replacement therapy (HRT)
Male change of life

Menopause
Midcareer crisis
Olfactory sense
Self-fulfilling prophecy

WHAT DO YOU THINK?

1. When you look at the physical shape your parents and grandparents are in, and their attitudes toward the subject, do you see evidence of the self-fulfilling prophecy?
2. If you are a female and have not yet gone through menopause, what

do you anticipate your feelings will be about it?
3. If you are a male, can you imagine what women facing menopause must be feeling?
4. What are some ways that our society might foster the creative abilities of its adult citizens?

5. What are some ways that our society might foster the learning of its adult citizens?
6. What remedies can you think of for the midcareer crisis?

CHAPTER REVIEW TEST

1. Basal metabolism rate refers to
   a. the minimum amount of energy an individual tends to use after exercising.
   b. the minimum amount of energy an individual tends to use when in a resting state.
   c. the maximum amount of energy an individual tends to use after exercising.
   d. the maximum amount of energy an individual tends to use when in a resting state.

2. For persons over age 50, even one or two drinks each day can be dangerous, because they can cause
   a. permanent liver damage.
   b. irreversible kidney damage.
   c. clogged arteries.
   d. enlargement of the left ventricle of the heart.

3. During middle adulthood, how does one's vision change?
   a. The lens becomes more elastic.

   b. The cornea decreases in curvature and thickness.
   c. The iris responds less well to light.
   d. The ability to focus on nearby objects increases.

4. Due to physical changes in middle adulthood, our vision can be affected in what ways?
   a. Eyes do not adapt to sudden intense light or darkness as effectively.
   b. Detection of certain colors can be more difficult.
   c. There is a heightened risk of eye diseases.
   d. All of the answers are correct.

5. During middle adulthood, how does hearing ability change?
   a. Higher frequencies need to be louder to be heard.
   b. Lower frequencies need to be louder to be heard.
   c. The ability to hear human speech remains constant.

   d. The ability to listen to speech in a crowded environment declines, while the ability to listen to someone alone without background noise increases.

6. Hormone replacement therapy has offered relief for women who experience serious problems with
   a. mid-life crises.
   b. menopause.
   c. weight loss.
   d. fertility.

7. What type of intelligence deteriorates with age, to some extent?
   a. Learned
   b. Natural
   c. Crystallized
   d. Fluid

8. What is an example of crystallized intelligence?
   a. Arithmetical reasoning
   b. Letter grouping
   c. Recalling paired associates
   d. Dominoes

9. People who like to do their own planning, make their own decisions, are flexible, and are able to stand their ground in the face of criticism demonstrate traits of a
   a. highly creative person.
   b. career-oriented person.
   c. person with strong cognitive abilities.
   d. person who has successfully individuated him/herself from significant others.

10. An aid to creativity is
    a. self-initiated learning.
    b. deferring judgment and being flexible.
    c. self-evaluation.
    d. All of the answers are correct.

11. While being tested on paired associate learning tasks the group most at a disadvantage if the amount of time available for response is not sufficient is the
    a. group in early adulthood.
    b. group in middle adulthood.
    c. group in late adulthood.
    d. All groups would be at a disadvantage.

12. Groups of middle-aged and elderly subjects are tested on their ability to remember associations between two lists of words. How are they most likely to respond when they suspect they may be wrong?
    a. Take an educated guess.
    b. Refrain from responding.
    c. Confer with other group members.
    d. State that they do not know the answer.

13. Research indicates that adults need to know why they need to learn something before undertaking it, that they have a self-concept of being responsible for their own decisions, and that they are life-centered in their orientation to learning. These findings highlight the difference between children and adults in
    a. cognitive abilities.
    b. level of individuation.
    c. self-fulfillment.
    d. the learning process.

14. A factor in learning ability during middle adulthood is motivation to learn. It is important for researchers to keep in mind that _____ affects an adult's level of motivation.
    a. level of education
    b. meaningfulness of the task
    c. interest
    d. external distractions

15. Consequences of discrimination against women in the workplace include
    a. stiffer job requirements.
    b. inability to advance in their career.
    c. questioning of a woman's competence.
    d. All of the answers are correct.

16. When an accountant 20 years younger than Dan joined his marketing firm, Dan felt resentful and anxious because he feared he would be considered incompetent. Dan has a growing sense of
    a. job distress.
    b. outdatedness.
    c. the "gold watch" syndrome.
    d. job reluctance.

Answers

1.b 2.d 3.c 4.d 5.a 6.b 7.d 8.a 9.a 10.d 11.c 12.b 13.d 14.b 15.d 16.b

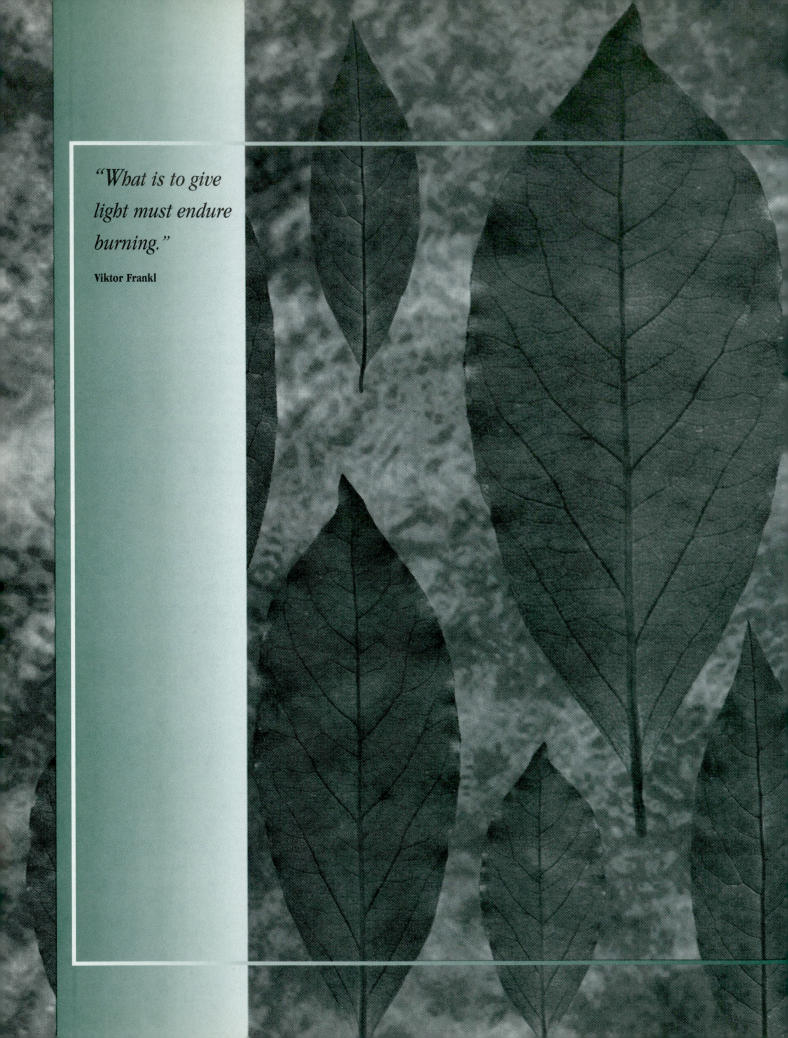

"What is to give light must endure burning."

Viktor Frankl

CHAPTER 16

Psychosocial Development in Middle Adulthood

Chapter Outline

Recently, a middle-aged woman friend shared some reflections with me: I remember walking to school one day in the second grade, chatting with my girlfriend's mother as she escorted us. I told her that I had noticed how much more quickly the day seemed to pass than it used to. Seven seemed a very advanced age to me then, so I was sure this phenomenon was related to being finally grown-up. Later that year we moved into a new house in a new community. Moving day was very exciting. The real grown-ups were very busy, so the most entertaining thing I had to do was to sit around and think about my life. Moving seemed to have wrapped up the first part of my life into a discrete little package. And it came to me that there I was, almost 8 years old, and I didn't have a feeling for all that time. I promised myself, as I sat in our old, soft maroon chair, holding some of my accumulated possessions dislocated by their recent journey, that five years later to the day I would sit again in the same spot, in the same position, holding the same objects. Then, I figured, with all the awareness born of old age, I would really know what five years would feel like. And five years later I did just that.

I am still trying to comprehend or capture a sense of time passing. Now only the units have changed. Every once in a while I hold very still and try to catch 20 years. Twenty years feel like those five did long ago. Twenty from now, if I'm lucky, I'll be staring my death in the face. It's all so odd. Somewhere inside I was all grown-up when I was 7. That "me" hasn't really aged or changed much, and it's still watching as the world wrinkles on the outside. Days are minutes, months are weeks, and years are months. I'll probably be menopausal in the morning!

Quoted by Lila Kalinich ✺

Chapter Objectives

After reading this chapter, you should be able to answer the following questions.

◆ How do adults in general deal with stress?

◆ What are the typical patterns of marriage in the family during middle adulthood?

◆ What are the main factors that affect sex and love among middle-aged people?

◆ What happens to personality during the adult years: does it typically change or remain continuous?

Dealing with the Stresses of Adulthood

We have included this section in the middle adult part of our book because the stresses of adulthood are different in one important way: More and more, adults are expected to deal with stress entirely on their own. True, adults can and should expect help from others, but an increasing number of crises call for independent decisions and actions. For example, many more families today exist in a state of ongoing, unending crisis. These families often have only one parent, who is unable to work and therefore is below the poverty level, and who has one or more handicapped or highly disruptive children.

As should be clear by now, stress has many sources, regardless of your age. Mainly, stress is due to change. It is the nature of human development to produce

General adaptation syndrome
A set of reactions that occur in animals in response to all toxic substances. Involves three stages: alarm, resistance, and exhaustion.

Alarm reaction Selye's term for a "call to arms" of the body's defensive forces.

Stage of resistance Selye's term for the body's reaction that is generally a reversal of the alarm reaction.

Stage of exhaustion Selye's term for the body's physiological responses that revert to their condition during the stage of alarm.

inexorable change in every aspect of our existence. This situation is difficult enough when we are young, but at least then we have the support of parents, teachers, and other adults, as well as a more resilient body. More stress does seem to occur as we get older. As we move from early to late adulthood, we must rely more and more on knowledge and insight to avoid having a stressful life.

The General Adaptation Syndrome

In 1936 Hans Selye (the father of stress research) was studying a little-known ovarian hormone, which led to the discovery of the **general adaptation syndrome** (Selye, 1956, 1975). In one of the experiments, hormones from cattle ovaries were injected into rats to see what changes would occur. Selye was surprised to find that the rats had a broad range of reactions:

- The cortex became enlarged and hyperactive.

- A number of glands shrank.

- Deep bleeding ulcers occurred in both the stomach and upper intestines.

Further experiments showed that these reactions occurred in response to all toxic substances, regardless of their source. Later experiments also showed them occurring, although to a lesser degree, in response to a wide range of noxious stimuli, such as infections, hemorrhage, and nervous irritation.

Selye called the entire syndrome an **alarm reaction.** He referred to it as a generalized "call to arms" of the body's defensive forces. Seeking to gain a fuller understanding of the syndrome, he wondered how the reaction would be affected if stress were present for a longer period of time. He found that a rather amazing thing happens. If the organism survives the initial alarm, it enters a **stage of resistance.** In this second stage, an almost complete reversal of the alarm reaction occurs. Swelling and shrinkages are reversed; the adrenal cortex, which lost its secretions during the alarm stage, becomes unusually rich in these secretions; and a number of other shock-resisting forces are marshalled. During this stage, the organism appears to gain strength and to have adapted successfully to the stressor.

If the stressor continues, however, a gradual depletion of the organism's adaptational energy occurs (Selye, 1982). Eventually this leads to a **stage of exhaustion.** Now the physiological responses revert to their condition during the stage of alarm. The ability to handle the stress decreases, the level of resistance is lost, and the organism dies. Figure 16.1 portrays these three stages. Table 16.1 lists the physical and psychological manifestations of the three stages.

As you grow older, your ability to remain in the resistance stage decreases. Activity over the years gradually wears out your "machine," and the chances of sustaining life are reduced. As we will discuss in chapter 17, no one dies of old age. Rather, they succumb to some stressor because their ability to resist it has become weakened through aging.

Figure 16.1

The general adaptation syndrome.

Selye compared his general adaptation stages with the three major stages of life. Childhood, he said, is characteristic of the alarm stage. Children respond excessively to any kind of stimulus and have not yet learned the basic ways to resist shock. In early adulthood, a great deal of learning has occurred, and the organism knows better how to handle the difficulties of life. In middle and old age, however, adaptability is gradually lost, and eventually the adaptation syndrome is exhausted, leading ultimately to death.

Selye suggested that all resistance to stress inevitably causes irreversible chemical scars that build up in the system. These scars are signs of aging. Thus, he said, the old adage that you shouldn't "burn the candle at both ends" is supported by the body's biology and chemistry. Selye's work with the general adaptation syndrome has also helped us to discover the relationship between disease and stress.

Risk and Resilience

Resilience The ability to recover from highly stressful situations.

Risk factors Stressors that individuals experience.

Protective factors Characteristics of resilient individuals that protect them from stress.

Individuals who deal well with stress and who have few psychological, behavioral, or learning problems as a result of it are said to have **resilience** (see chapter 10). In recent years, researchers have become interested in studying the characteristics of resilient individuals. The stressors that individuals experience are called **risk factors.** Risk factors include poverty, chronic illness, parental mental illness and drug abuse, exposure to violence through war or some of the tragedies in the inner cities, and the family experiences of divorce and teenage motherhood. Researchers have been interested in identifying **protective factors** (characteristics of resilient individuals that protect them from stress). Three kinds of protective factors have been found so far: family environments, support networks, and personality characteristics (Hauser & Bowlds, 1990). Recent research indicates that women tend to suffer

TABLE 16.1 SELYE'S STRESS ADAPTATION SYNDROME

Stage	Function	Physical Manifestations	Psychological Manifestations
Stage I: Alarm reaction	Mobilization of the body defensive forces.	Marked loss of body weight. Increase in hormone levels. Enlargement of the adrenal cortex and lymph glands.	Person is alerted to stress. Level of anxiety increases. Task-oriented and defense-oriented behavior. Symptoms of maladjustment, such as anxiety and inefficient behavior may appear.
Stage II: Stage of resistance	Optimal adaptation to stress.	Weight returns to normal. Lymph glands return to normal size. Reduction in size of adrenal cortex. Constant hormonal levels.	Intensified use of coping mechanisms. Person tends to use habitual defenses rather than problem-solving behavior. Psychosomatic symptoms may appear.
Stage III: Stage of exhaustion	Body resources are depleted and organism loses ability to resist stress.	Weight loss. Enlargement and depletion of adrenal glands. Enlargement of lymph glands and dysfunction of lymphatic system. Increase in hormone levels and subsequent hormonal depletion. If excessive stress continues, person may die.	Personality disorganization and a tendency toward exaggerated and inappropriate use of defense mechanisms. Increased disorganization of thoughts and perceptions. Person may lose contact with reality, and delusions and hallucinations may appear. Further exposure to stress may result in complete psychological disintegration involving violence or stupor.

Source: Adapted from *Adult Health Nursing* by Carol Ren Kneisl and SueAnn Wooster Ames. Addison-Wesley, Menlo Park, Calif., 1986.

Cultural Stress: Membership in a Minority Group

Dave Mack, an urban worker in Chicago, observes that a variety of differences exist among Asian people living in America, and these differences can cause intense stress. Referring to someone as an "Asian" may be misleading. The Chinese are proud of their vast history and the cultures it has spawned. Koreans also possess a rich, though separate, history. Filipinos, Burmese, and Vietnamese, though possibly educated in Chinese schools, nevertheless associate with some Asians while dissociating with others. For instance, among Southeast Asian people, a great deal of animosity exists between Cambodians and the Hmong.

These attitudes of cultural pride provoke endless problems, especially in our large cities. Mack tells of a group of Vietnamese waiting for a bus in the rain after a basketball game. They got on the bus when it arrived, just as some

Chinese people appeared at the bus stop. Since another bus was not immediately available to transport everyone, the Vietnamese bus driver ordered his riders off of the bus and into the rain so that the Chinese people could get onto the bus first.

Assimilation into urban American culture, itself a smorgasbord of ethnicities all within a few square miles, often proves immensely stressful for all involved. The tension also involves how far one should go in regard to becoming "American." Is there such a thing as an "ethnic American"? Should people who immigrate into America be expected to set aside cultural conflicts for the sake of their new home? Given the stress that is bound to result from such an acclimation, is it worth the cost? Is it harder if you are middle aged or older than it would be for younger people?

more from domestic violence than men. Umberson and associates (1998) found that women who suffered from domestic violence reported feeling much less personal control over their lives. Men, however, did not report any diminished sense of self-control. Of course, a weakness of all self-report studies is the possibility that one group is unwilling to reveal their true feelings because of societal pressures. In addition, Ratner (1998) found that women also suffered from health problems if they developed psychopathology or drug addiction as a result of domestic abuse.

Prevention

Psychologists have been enthusiastic about identifying risk and protective factors in the hope that this knowledge will contribute to the prevention of psychological difficulties. Successful prevention programs reduce the occurrence of maladjustment and clinical dysfunction by reducing risk factors (when possible) and enhancing protective factors and effective coping strategies. Primary prevention programs try to eliminate problems before they begin. Secondary prevention programs intervene during the early stages of a problem to reduce its severity or the length of time it will last.

Prevention programs vary in whether they are directed toward all children and adolescents in a particular school or city, or whether only students identified to be at particular risk are invited. Among adolescents, prevention programs are most often delivered in the schools or in a community agency. School-based programs have been effective in building social skills and reducing at-risk behaviors. Effective programs have been developed for reducing the onset, use, and abuse of cigarettes, marijuana, and alcohol, reducing teen pregnancy, curbing dropout rates, improving academic performance, and reducing delinquent behavior (Kazdin, 1993). According to research by the Carnegie Council on Adolescent Development (1995), families, schools, and community organizations must work together to reduce risks, enhance protective factors, and promote healthy adolescent development.

Unfortunately, prevention programs are still limited and are not able to prevent the occurrence of mental disturbance. Psychotherapy, psychiatric hospitalization, and medications are needed to improve dysfunction for those individuals already suffering from mental disturbance.

A relevant source on dealing with stress is the book by Benson, H. and Proctor, W. *Beyond the relaxation response*. New York: Berkeley (1985). It outlines a stress reduction program that has helped millions of people live healthier lives.

Another good book on this subject is *Flow* by Csikszentmihalyi, M. New York: Harper & Row (1990). "This book summarizes, for a general audience, decades of research on the positive aspects of human experience."

The period in a marriage after which there is no longer a need to care for children is often a time for pursuing dreams that were previously impractical.

Guided Review

1. Hans Selye outlined three stages of a general adaptation syndrome. These include: alarm reaction, a stage of _____, and a stage of exhaustion.
2. Each of Selye's stages can be understood in terms of its _____, physical manifestations, and _____ manifestations.
3. The stressors that people feel are called risk factors, whereas the characteristics that increase resilience are called _____ factors.
4. _____ prevention programs try to eliminate problems before they begin.

Marriage and Family Relations

In this section, we consider four important aspects of middle-aged life today: relationships in marriage, relationships with aging parents, relationships with brothers and sisters, and divorce. Although not all would agree, we define this part of life as going from 35 to 64 years of age.

Marriage at Middle Age

Mid-life transition Levinson's term for the phase that usually lasts for five years and generally extends from age 40 to 45.

Middle age is often a time when husbands and wives reappraise their marriage. The **mid-life transition** (a period during which people seriously reevaluate their lives up to that time) often causes a person to simultaneously examine current relationships and consider changes for the future. Often, whatever tension that exists in a marriage is suppressed while the children still live at home. As they leave to go off to college or to start families of their own, these tensions are openly expressed.

Emotional divorce Sometimes a couple learns to "withstand" each other, rather than live with each other. The only activities and interests that they shared were ones that revolved around the children.

Sometimes couples learn to "withstand" each other rather than live with each other. The only activities and interests they share are ones that revolved around the children. When the children leave, they are forced to recognize how far apart they have drifted. In effect, they engage in **emotional divorce.** Often the experience of divorce can be thought of as a cluster of small divorces (Steefel, 1992).

Empty nest syndrome Refers to the feelings parents may have as a result of their last child leaving home.

But most couples whose marriages have lasted this long have built the type of relationship that can withstand reappraisal, and they continue for the rest of their lives. U.S. Census data (1996) suggest that the highest rates for separation and divorce occur about five years after the beginning of the marriage. The period after the children leave home is like a second honeymoon for many. After the initial period of negative emotions that follow this disruption of the family, often called the **empty nest syndrome,** married couples can evaluate the job they have done with their children. They can pat themselves on the back for a job well done and then relax now that a major life goal has been accomplished. They then realize that they have more freedom and privacy and fewer worries. They usually have more money to spend on themselves. And this period after the children leave home is now much longer than it used to be. Husbands and wives now can look forward to spending 20 or 30 years together as a couple rather than as a large family.

The Happy Marriage

What does research have to say about the components of a happy, or at least a lasting, marriage? Gottman and Krokoff (1989) conducted a longitudinal study looking at the types of interactions between husband and wife and the effect on marital satisfaction. Earlier research suggested that there was always more negative interaction in unhappy marriages than in happy marriages. An exception to this appears to be

Answers

1. resistance 2. function, psychological 3. protective 4. Primary

An Applied View

Marriage Therapy in Middle Adulthood

Iwanir and Ayal (1991) suggest that the mid-life phase in the marital relationship is a complicated transition period, one that challenges the flexibility and coping skills of every couple. If a couple finds their marriage to be in trouble (the authors call this "Separation/Divorce Initiation" or S/DI), they recommend a three-step process to help. The steps include: (1) assessment of the relationship's stamina and the function of the S/DI; (2) treating symptoms and reactions to the traumatic event in an "emergency intervention" mode; and (3) steps and techniques to help the couple overcome the traumatic effects of the S/DI and to rebuild their relationship on a more appropriate basis (p. 609).

Three wonderful descriptions of middle-aged marriage are: (1) Breslin's *Table money*. New York: Ticknor & Fields. An empathetic tale of matrimony, alcoholism, and the struggle to attain maturity, focusing on a poor middle-aged Irish American couple; (2) Guest's *Ordinary people*. New York: Ballantine. The evocative story of the relationships among a middle-aged couple, their teenage son, and his psychiatrist; (3) Hansberry's *A raisin in the sun*. New York: Modern Library, 1995. This moving drama portrays the inner lives of an African-American family.

the marriages of Chinese people. Shek (1995 a & b) found that although Chinese men feel happier in their marriages the longer they last, the opposite was true for the women in this large study of 1,500 subjects.

Gottman and Krokoff decided to look at the effect of different types of negative interactions rather than one global category. They found that certain types of conflict may in fact be positive factors in a happy, lasting marriage. They also found that certain types of conflict, particularly defensiveness, stubbornness, and withdrawal on the part of the husband, indicated that a marriage was in trouble. Gottman and Krokoff assigned to the wife the role of manager of marital disagreements and suggested that she get her husband to "confront areas of disagreement and to openly vent disagreement and anger" (p. 50). Most husbands tend to try to avoid relational confrontations (Moyers & Bly, 1990). Therefore, overcoming this reluctance can have extremely beneficial long-term effects on the marriage.

Another factor related to marital satisfaction is parenting satisfaction. Rogers and White (1998) found that high marital quality in couples was associated with significantly higher rates of parenting satisfaction. In other words, if a couple has a strong marriage, they are more likely to be content in their parenting roles.

Many married couples look forward to their "golden years" of marriage, those years purported to be the happiest. Unfortunately, Glen (1998) found no empirical evidence that the average couple experiences greater happiness in their later years.

The Unmarried Individual

About 1 in 20 people in middle age have never been married (U.S. Census, 1996). In general, a person who has never married by middle age will not get married. Such people tend either to have very low or very high education levels. At the low extreme, of those who have less than five years of school, one person in seven has never married. The factors that kept these people from completing school, such as mental illness or other handicaps, are probably the same ones that make them less likely to get married. At the other extreme, 13 percent of middle-aged women with 17 or more years of education have never been married.

A number of possible explanations could account for this. These women may choose higher education and a career over marriage. They may believe marriage will hold them back. A cultural factor may be at work, because some men feel threatened by women with more education than they have. Perhaps women who delay marriage to pursue an education end up having a smaller pool of available men to choose from, because men die, on the average, at an earlier age. Finally, the number of persons who live together without marrying is rapidly increasing (see figure 16.2).

Relationships with Aging Parents

Middle age is also a time when most people develop improved relationships with their parents. Middle-aged children, most of them parents themselves, gain a new perspective on parenthood and so reevaluate the actions taken by their own parents.

Figure 16.2

The number of unmarried couples in the United States is climbing rapidly.

Relationships and roles among the generations are always changing.

Also, grandchildren can strengthen bonds that may have weakened when their parents left home when they were young adults.

In many cases, however, the relationship begins to reverse itself. As elderly parents grow older, they sometimes become as dependent on their middle-aged children as those children once were on them. Most people fail to anticipate the costs and emotional strains that the aging of their parents can precipitate. This can lead ultimately to new sources of tension and rancor in the relationship. Often, early family experiences may have a positive or negative affect on the later relationship between adult children and their aging parents (Whitbeck & others, 1994). For example, young children who have close relationships with their parents, and whose parents provided consistent care, will have more positive later relationships.

The most frequently cited problem of middle-adult women is not menopause or aging, but caring for their aging parents and parents-in-law (James, 1990). This is not so surprising when we realize that it is virtually always the daughter(s) in the family who is responsible for the care of the elderly parents (Kendig & others, 1992). Green (1991) found that the daughter who is the primary caretaker relies on siblings, especially her sisters if she has them, for emotional support. These sisters typically feel guilty about not doing enough. On the average, brothers provide less help and feel less guilty about it. Recent findings have maintained the idea that social support is of foremost importance to daughters who are the primary caregivers for aging parents

In industrial societies, close relationships among siblings tend to be optional, based on the siblings' desires to be friendly toward one another or not. In nonindustrial societies, sibling relationships are based on the constraints that cultural norms impose. Such norms demand that siblings should behave in certain ways toward each other. These differences, in large part, are due to differences in economic structure.

Nonindustrial societies tend to be agrarian, village-centered, and relatively poor. Because resources are limited in such societies, sibling cooperation is necessary to accomplish tasks, to maintain family functioning, and to attain economic goals. In these societies, a greater number of siblings exists and they are expected to fulfill certain responsibilities. Siblings share caretaking and act as educational and socializing agents for each other's children. Parents usually have this role in industrial societies. In these societies, sibling relationships are secondary to spouse-spouse and parent-child relationships.

In nonindustrial societies, sister-brother and brother-brother relationships are closest, whereas sister-sister relationships are closest in industrial societies. Control mechanisms exist in nonindustrial societies to deal with tension and conflicts, such as an emphasis on the authority of older children over younger siblings.

(Pohl & others, 1994). By social support the authors mean emotional, financial, or other support offered by friends and family. Daughters may feel more positive about caregiving when they have secure income, health, marital status, and educational level. It seems that the demands on women to fulfill the role of family nurturer are deeply rooted and powerful. Of course, as more women enter the workplace, and as more of them become assertive about equitable family responsibilities, this pattern may well change, with males assuming more of the burden.

Caserta & others (1996) examined caring for elderly parents or in-laws and have proposed a multidimensional view of this burden. The authors determined several aspects of the caregiving task, such as the emotional strain, the time constraints involved (e.g., amount of time elderly relatives depend on one's care), and physical health of the caregiver. The well-being of the caregiver, therefore, is important to the person receiving the care. Because the burden of caregiving is not easily measured, each of the various dimensions should be considered as having a possible effect on the relationship. We will deal here with two other features of family life in middle adulthood: relationships with siblings and the problems of divorce.

Relationships with Siblings

Developmental psychology has, for some time now, recognized the importance of sibling relationships for a child's cognitive and social growth. But do these special relationships stop contributing to a person's development after adolescence? Does the relationship slowly decline in importance as one ages? Are the characteristics of the relationship the same in middle adulthood as they were in childhood? Psychological research has recently begun to focus on some of these questions.

Sibling relationships have the potential to be the most enduring that a person can have. You don't usually meet your spouse until young adulthood or at least adolescence. Your parents usually pass away before you do. You usually pass away before your children do. But most siblings are born within a few years of each other, and such a relationship can last 60, 80, or even 100 years!

One would hope that a growing maturity would lessen rivalry. Certainly adult siblings are faced with more serious and important tasks than are childhood siblings. For example, most middle-aged siblings must make mutual decisions concerning the care of their elderly parents and eventually deal with the aftermath of their death.

Another consideration is the effect of changing family patterns on sibling relationships. Couples now are having fewer or even no children. Children will therefore be less available to parents for companionship and psychological support. On the other hand, parents and their siblings will be living longer, more active lives. The obvious conclusion is that sibling relationships will become more and more important in the future.

Friendships

Middle age is a time when friendships become fewer and more precious. Actually, the findings of Carstensen (1992) suggest that individuals begin narrowing their range of social partners long before middle age. The most dramatic decline occurs between the ages of 18 and 30. In early adulthood, interaction frequency with acquaintances and close friends begins to decline while at the same time it increases with spouses and siblings. It would seem that at about age 30, individuals choose a select few relationships from which to derive support, self-definition, and a sense of stability. Emotional closeness, however, increases throughout adulthood in relationships with relatives and close friends. These relationships with a select few, then, become increasingly close and satisfying during the middle adult years. Further, the idea that face-to-face contact is necessary for closeness cannot be supported. In fact, many parents report feeling close to their adult children after they have moved out of the house.

The Middle-Aged Divorced Person

Mid-life divorce has become an important focus of researchers. For example, several (Knoester & Booth, 2000; Smock & others, 1999) have found the relationship between divorce and economic status for women to be more complicated than had been thought. Whether or not a woman's financial status changes as a result of divorce depends on a number of factors.

The divorce rates are higher for second or subsequent marriages, for African-Americans, and for those who are less educated and who have lower earning ability. Mid-life is a time when a divorce is less likely to occur—most divorces take place during the first five years of marriage and the number tapers off rapidly after that (see figure 16.3). Nevertheless, the proportion of divorced persons in mid-life is relatively high, because many who divorced earlier have never remarried. Men and women over 40 experience significantly more turmoil and unhappiness than younger people at the same stage of divorce (Chiriboga, 1989). The reasons are clear: length of time of marriage, complex economic and property linkages, a web of social relationships, and a generally higher standard of living.

In respect to the last point, it should be noted that women, especially at mid-life, are often hard hit economically by divorce. The National Longitudinal Survey found they experience significant declines in income, increased rates of poverty, and dramatic lifestyle changes upon separation, divorce, or widowhood; generally they do not recover unless they remarry (Hoffman & Duncan, 1988). Furthermore, because most women who divorce at mid-life are already working, they have little room to maneuver for more income after divorce. This is especially true for African-American women, because the only notable increase in workforce participation after divorce is for white women (Morgan, 1991).

More and more children are living in homes without fathers. More than half of single-parent mothers are not receiving full child support and half of those are not receiving any. Whereas 68 percent of white women were awarded child support, only 35 percent of African-American women and 41 percent of Latina women received such awards (Crohan & others, 1989). Until recently, child support was awarded mainly because of the mother's limited income. Now, most states use a specific formula that relates child support to both parents' incomes. This requires both parents to provide adequate financial support regardless of which parent has custody of the child (Cancian & Meyer, 1996).

Figure 16.3

This chart of divorces in the United States shows that most divorces occur within the first five years of marriage, with the peak at three years. Interestingly, the same pattern is found in most other societies, ranging from contemporary Sweden to the hunting and gathering groups of southwest Africa.

U.S. Bureau of the Census.

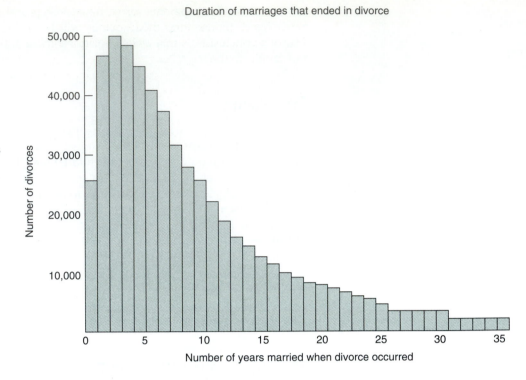

Duration of marriages that ended in divorce

A discomforting finding of White (1992) is that children of divorce, even after they have left home and their parents enter middle age, receive significantly less support (child care, advice, transportation, loans, and so forth) than do children whose parents have remained married. Remarriage does not seem to increase or decrease this support deficit.

In general, new divorce laws were considered to have a liberating effect on women. Until the liberalization of divorce laws and attitudes, women usually had no choice but to endure a difficult and sometimes even abusive marriage. Cultural norms allowed men much more moral latitude, the so-called double standard. Women basically just had to put up with it.

Before liberalization, it was necessary to establish "reasonable grounds" for divorce, such as adultery or physical abuse. Women who were granted divorces were almost always awarded larger alimony settlements than they receive today, to make up for the loss of income. This was necessary because women lagged far behind men in their earning potential, and often women stayed at home to raise the children and run the household while the husband advanced a career. A woman could not survive a divorce if it left her and her family destitute.

In 1970 the divorce laws were liberalized in California, a change soon followed across the country. This was the introduction of a **no-fault divorce.** A major facet of the new laws was supposed to be their gender neutrality. Men and women are treated equally under the divorce law, and this includes the division of property and alimony. But perhaps these laws were premature. Men and women did not in 1970, and still do not today, live in an economically equitable system. Men still possess a competitive advantage in earning potential, and the culture still holds women responsible for raising the children and running the household. When a divorce judge divides up the property equally, grants little or no alimony, and provides inadequate child support, it is the woman and children who suffer.

This is particularly true of the middle-aged homemaker. The courts seldom give much recognition to the years spent running the household while the husband invested time in advancing a career. Such a woman cannot reasonably be expected to compete with others who have been gaining experience in the marketplace while she stayed at home.

No-fault divorce The law that lets people get divorced without proving some atrocious act by one of the spouses. In legal language, this is known as an irretrievable breakdown of a marriage.

Another effect is that no-fault divorce laws mandate an even division of property. This often means that the family house must be sold. Before these laws, the house was almost always given to the woman and her children. Besides being an economic burden, the loss of the house has psychological consequences for the development of the children. The dislocation often requires that the children leave their school, neighborhood, and friends. And this usually comes just after the divorce, a period of tremendous stress for any child.

Some indications show that reform is on the way. In California the rules for division of property and spousal support are being revised. More things are now being considered family assets, to be divided equally, such as the major wage earner's salary, pension, medical insurance, and future earning power. In addition, some states have now become aggressive at pursuing husbands who are delinquent on child support payments. Their names are being published and a part of their wages is being withheld and given to the ex-wife. Massachusetts is even considering paying spouses the money lost through delinquent payments and reimbursing the state through taxes and wage garnishments of the other spouse.

Divorce will probably never be the "civilized" process that the early proponents of no-fault divorce laws hoped it would become. At best, we can expect the suffering of spouses to become more equal, and the suffering of the children to be reduced.

Marriage and family life are closely related to two other factors that play an important role in middle age: sex and love.

Guided Review

5. During middle age, marriage is sometimes affected by emotional _____ (which means drifting apart while still married).
6. After the initial period of negative emotions that follow after the children leave home, called the "_____ _____ syndrome," couples can evaluate the job they have done in raising their family.
7. Certain types of conflict in a marriage can be positive and are particularly beneficial if the _____ is willing to confront areas of disagreement.
8. It is unlikely that a middle-aged person who has never married will marry. Such people tend to have either very high or very low levels of _____.
9. One of the most challenging problems facing middle-adult women is that their parents or parents-in-law are now _____ on them.
10. New divorce laws were considered to have a _____ effect on women. These laws, however, have had the result of impoverishing many women.

Sex and Love in Middle Adulthood

At mid-life, minor physiological changes occur in both male and female sexual systems. For the male, there may be lower levels of testosterone, fewer viable sperm, a decrease in sex steroids affecting muscle tone and the cardiovascular system, slight changes in the testes and prostate gland, and a change in the viscosity and volume of ejaculate (Hunter & Sundel, 1989). There is usually a need to spend more time and to give more direct stimulation to the penis to attain erection. None of these changes is sufficient to alter significantly the man's interest and pleasure in a sexual and sensual life.

Answers

5. divorce 6. empty nest 7. husband 8. education 9. dependent 10. liberating

Many couples find that when they reach middle age, their relationship becomes more romantic.

An award-winning novel that examines, among other aspects of middle age, several views of sexuality, is Tom Wolfe's *The bonfire of the vanities.* New York: Farrar, Straus & Giroux. With his customary verve, Wolfe looks inside the heads of five men and two women, all New Yorkers in early middle age, and shows us how they think.

For the female, the reduction in estrogen occurring during and after menopause may cause changes, such as less vaginal lubrication and possible vaginal irritation at penetration, that can eventually affect the ease and comfort of sexual intercourse. Sexual arousal may be somewhat slower after the fifth decade, but orgasmic response is not impaired. As with the males, females may need more time and appropriate stimulation for vaginal lubrication and orgasmic responsivity. Some studies have found a reduction of female interest and desire, whereas others have found a decrease in frequency of intercourse (Cutler & others, 1987).

Sexuality at middle age also has a relationship to depression: before menopause, women have higher levels of depression than men (Bebbington & others, 1998). These researchers found that after menopause, however, this is no longer so. "There was a clear reversal of the sex difference in prevalence of depression in those over age 55" (p. 9).

A report on frequency of sexual activity among the adults of all ages, the Janus Report, gives a picture that weakens the stereotype that as we grow older, we become more inactive sexually. As table 16.2 illustrates, there is a small increase in sexual activity in the middle years, as compared with early adulthood. For men, middle age is a time when opportunity, if not desire, is at a peak. For women, age makes little difference across the adult lifespan. These findings are supported by Deacon and associates (1995), who found that the physical and pathological changes associated with advancing age do not necessarily reduce the opportunity to enjoy sex.

Generally speaking, attitudes toward love remain constant into middle age, however, Butler and associates (1995) learned that older adults differ in their conceptions of love from younger adults in several important ways: "Specifically, greater age was related to lower agreement with items thought to reflect passive, dependent love (Mania) and all-giving, selfless love (Agape), and these tendencies were more pronounced in females than in males. Furthermore, the age-related decrease in agreement with Mania items was more pronounced among those who were currently in love" (p. 292).

Another way of looking at conceptions of love may be seen in Robert Sternberg's expansion of his triangular theory of love (see chapter 14). He suggests (2000) that through young adulthood, everyone develops a personal "love story." He has identified a number of these love stories, for example:

TABLE 16.2 FREQUENCY OF SEXUAL INTERCOURSE BY AGE

| | Ages (Years) | | | | | | | | | |
| | 18 to 26 | | 27 to 38 | | 39 to 50 | | 51 to 64 | | 65+ | |
	M	F	M	F	M	F	M	F	M	F
N =	254	268	353	380	282	295	227	230	212	221
a. Daily	15%	13%	16%	8%	15%	10%	12%	4%	14%	1%
b. A few times weekly	38	33	44	41	39	29	51	28	39	40
c. Weekly	19	22	23	27	29	29	18	33	16	33
d. Monthly	15	15	8	12	9	11	11	8	20	4
e. Rarely	13	17	9	12	8	21	8	27	11	22
Active = lines a + b	53%	46%	60%	49%	54%	39%	63%	32%	53%	41%
At Least Weekly = lines a through c	72%	68%	83%	76%	83%	68%	81%	65%	69%	74%

- The travel story ("I believe that beginning a relationship is like starting a journey that promises to be both exciting and challenging.")

- The gardening story ("I believe any relationship that is left unattended will not survive.")

- The horror story ("I find it exciting when I feel my partner to be somewhat frightened of me.")

- The business story ("I believe close relationships are like good partnerships.")

- The pornography story ("It is very important to be able to satisfy all my partner's sexual desires and whims.") (2000, p. 54)

Sternberg argues that even when couples have similar values and interests, they may still have love problems because they are operating from significantly different love stories.

The experts pretty well agree on the nature of physical alterations that occur through the middle years of adulthood. Much less agreement exists, however, on the course of personality development in these years.

An Applied View

Are You a Good Lover?

I want to step out of my role as an author for a moment to write as a psychotherapist (John Dacey). Since 1973, I have had a small practice—no more than two or three clients a week—mostly consisting of marriage counseling. In the course of trying to help individuals to improve or save their marriages, one question almost inevitably occurs to the client: "Am I a good lover?" At first, most men will say that they think they are. As they become more trusting and self-analytical in the counseling setting, the majority realize they have serious doubts about the question. Women are much more likely to be aware of a lack of confidence in this area right from the beginning. I have met very few people, within my practice or in my social life, who are without doubts about themselves as a lover.

The problem is, it's a bad question. In fact, there's no such thing as a good lover.

I believe we can get a lot of help in understanding this issue from the contextualist approach (see chapter 1). As you will recall, this model recommends that we consider several criteria when examining human relationships:

- *Bidirectional causation*. Most human behavior is the result of *interactions* with others. That is, I do what I do because you did what you did because I did what I did, and so on. There is seldom one clear initial cause of why we behave as we do. I have found that in helping my clients, the question should not be "Am I a good lover?" but rather "Are we good lovers to each other?"
- *Historical imbeddedness*. All actions are meaningful only in the context of the historical time in which they occur. There are times during a relationship

when the partners take good care of each other, sexually and otherwise. There are other times, when one or both are sick, tired, or distracted, and then, for a time at least, they are not good lovers to each other. Remember the biopsychosocial model: over time, all three factors (biological, psychological, social) will play a role in how good a partner we are able to be.

- *Goodness of fit*. No matter how much a person might want to be a good lover, the relationship is limited by the extent to which it fits the needs of the two partners. All lovers differ in their preferences, tastes, interests, and values. Some difference in these areas is likely to add spice to the interaction. But if the differences are too great, then the level of intimacy is necessarily limited, and the individuals will be unable to be good lovers to each other no matter how much they might try. They are likely to continuously invalidate each other's personality, which inevitably causes great pain.
- *Probability*. Human interactions are complex, and ever-changing. As a result, no one is a good lover all of the time. All we can hope for is that the components that make up our partnership allow us to be good lovers to each other *most of the time*. It seems to me that the greatest joy in life is to participate in a loving relationship that has a high probability of success. Only then are we likely to have much chance of being a "good lover."

Guided Review

11. Cutler et al. claimed that low _____ levels are associated with decreased sexual interest for women.
12. The Janus Report indicates that the stereotype that people become less _____ sexually as they age is not supported by the Januses' research.
13. Robert Sternberg has argued that the success of the adult intimate relationships depends on the level of compatibility of the partners' _____.

Personality Development: Continuous or Changing?

In earlier chapters, we have examined the controversy over whether personality is stable or changing. This debate is concerned with middle adulthood, too.

Continuity versus Change

The man who views the world at 50 the same as he did at 20, has wasted 30 years of his life.

Muhammad Ali

Most of us have heard someone say, "Oh, he's been like that ever since he was a baby!" Such a comment doesn't sound like a philosophical statement, but think about what it implies. It implies that individuals can remain basically the same throughout their lifespan. This is the fundamental question that the issue of change versus continuity of development addresses. Do human beings really change very much over the course of their lives, or do we all stay pretty much the same? It is the focus of great debate by child-development and lifespan psychologists alike because of its implications.

If we assume that people remain the same regardless of what happens to them as their life continues, then the period of early childhood takes on great meaning. Several of the developmental theorists we have discussed (e.g., Freud and Piaget—see chapter 2) have focused much of their attention on the early years of childhood in the belief that what happens to a person during childhood determines much of what will happen to him or her in the future.

Conversely, others (e.g., Erikson and other adult development theorists—see chapter 2) believe that because people are constantly changing and developing, all life experiences must be considered important. In that case, early childhood becomes a somewhat less significant period in the whole of development, and adolescence and adulthood come more into focus. It also implies that getting children "off on the right foot" is not enough to ensure positive development. These are just some of the implications of the debate about personality continuity versus change.

In the study of adulthood, the issue of continuity versus change gets even more complex. In general, two distinct theoretical positions influence the study of adult personality. Some theorists feel that adults remain basically the same—that the adult personality is stable. This is continuity in adult development. Other theorists view the adult as constantly in a process of change and evolution. That is what the position of change refers to.

The study of continuity versus change in adulthood is complicated by the many ways that the issue is studied. Some researchers look at pieces of the personality (personality traits) as measured by detailed questionnaires. They argue that the answers to such questionnaires assess adult personality. These researchers are known as **trait theorists.**

Trait theorists Researchers who look at pieces of the personality (personality traits), as measured by detailed questionnaires.

Others note that such questionnaires measure only parts of the personality. They argue that adult personality is much more complicated than any list of personality traits. What is interesting to them is how those traits fit with the whole of the person. Beyond that, they are also interested in how an adult's personality interacts with

Answers

Stage theorists   Researchers who believe that research based on personality traits is too narrow in focus and that we must also look at the stages of change each person goes through.

the world around him or her. They believe that research based on personality traits is too narrow in focus and that we must also look at the stages of change each person goes through. These researchers are known as **stage theorists.** The old saying, "you can't see the forest for the trees," sums up their position—the parts prevent you from seeing the whole.

The differences in how to go about measuring adult personality complicate the study of continuity and change in adulthood. Researchers use extremely different methods of measuring adult personality and then relate their findings to support either the position of continuity or change. In general, trait theorists have found that the adult personality remains the same: Their work supports continuity (Costa & McCrae, 1995). These researchers summed up their findings in the title of an article: "Still Stable after All These Years." They recently proposed that personality traits are organized hierarchically, with narrow traits combining to define broad factors (Costa & McCrae, 1995 a & b). For example, it is common that a person who is kind, unselfish, and empathizes with others is a very compassionate person. Researchers looking at the whole of the adult personality through extensive interviews found support for the notion of change in adulthood (Levinson, 1990a, 1990b).

The study of continuity versus change in adult psychology has important implications, just as it does in childhood psychology. The findings of personality studies add to our knowledge of what "normal" adult development means. Yet as we have seen, the studies vary in their definitions of what adult personality is and how it should be measured. Not surprisingly, studies also differ in what they tell us about normal adult development. Theorists have different answers to the question: "If nothing very unusual happens (like a catastrophe), how will the adult personality develop?"

Trait theorists like McCrae and Costa might say, "If nothing unusual happens, then the adult personality will stay relatively the same. Normal adult personality development is really the maintenance of personality." Levinson, Vaillant, and Erikson, looking at the whole of the adult, would respond differently (see also chapter 14). They might say, "The adult personality naturally and normally develops through change. Normal adult personality development is a continual process of growth and change."

Who is right? We suggest you read our summary of the studies that each camp provides, and try to make up your own mind. We begin with Daniel Levinson's theory, as it applies to middle age.

Seasons of a Man's Life: Levinson

This section continues a discussion of Levinson's theory that was begun in chapter 14. Figure 16.4 reproduces that part of his theory that applies to middle adulthood.

Settling Down

The settling down phase usually extends from age 33 to 40. At this time, most men have pretty well decided what occupation they choose to pursue. During this period, most men attempt to achieve two tasks: (1) establish a niche in society, and (2) advance up the ladder of the occupational group. During this phase, the male attempts to overcome his dependency on his mentor and slowly is able to "become his own man." This is a step in the direction of greater individuation, in that the man thinks less and less as others want him to, and more and more as his own views dictate. He is now ready to go into the third phase of his adulthood, the mid-life transition.

The Mid-Life Transition

The mid-life transition, which usually lasts for five years, generally extends from age 40 to 45. It involves three major developmental tasks:

• The review, reappraisal, and termination of the early adult period.

• Decisions on how the period of middle adulthood should be conducted.

Figure 16.4

Levinson's theory—middle age.

From *The Seasons of a Man's Life* by Daniel Levinson, copyright © 1978 by Daniel J. Levinson. Used by permission of Alfred A. Knopf, a division of Random House, Inc.

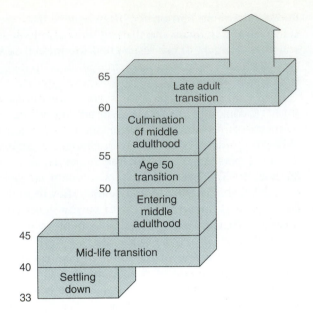

You might enjoy reading the third in Updike's definitive series about the ordinary American male adult: *Rabbit is rich*. New York: Knopf. In this volume, Rabbit reaches middle age.

- Dealing with the polarities that are the source of deep division in the man's life at this stage. These polarities, which represent the continual struggle toward greater individuation, are (1) young/old, (2) destruction/creation, (3) masculinity/femininity, and (4) attachment/separation.

Young/Old Young/old is the major polarity to be dealt with during the mid-life transition. Levinson referred to Freud's disciple, Carl Jung (1966), who suggested that the experience of thousands of generations of human beings has gradually produced deep-seated ideas that each of us must learn to deal with. The major one is that although we begin to grow old even at birth, we are also interested in maintaining our youth, if only to avoid the ultimate consequence of our mortality: death.

In tribal symbolism, the word young represents fertility, growth, energy, potential, birth, and spring. Old, on the other hand, encompasses termination, death, completion, ending, fruition, and winter. Until the age of 40, the man has been able to maintain his youthful self-image. Through producing and raising children, and in some cases through a creative product such as a book, invention, or painting, he has been able to see himself as part of a new and youthful recycling of life. Subconsciously, at least, he has been able to maintain the myth of immortality.

At about the time of his 40th birthday, he is confronted with evidence of his own declining powers. He is no longer able to run, play tennis, or shoot basketballs as effectively as he could in his twenties. He sometimes forgets things, and his eyesight may not be as good. Even more damaging to his hope for immortality is the illness of his friends. Heart attacks, strokes, and other serious illnesses are more frequent among people of his age. In many cases, his parents suffer serious illnesses, or even die. These events lead to one inevitable realization: He is going to die, and perhaps in the not-too-distant future. Even the 32 years left him (on the average) do not seem like much, because over half of life is now already past.

A sense of wanting to leave a legacy now emerges. Most individuals want to feel that their life has made some difference, and they want to leave something behind them that can be remembered. Therefore, it is typical at this time that the individual becomes more creative and often works harder than he has in the past to make a contribution considered worthwhile by those who follow him.

Destruction/Creation The male going through a mid-life transition realizes not only the potential of the world to destroy but also his own capacity to be destructive. He recognizes the evil within himself and his own power to hurt, damage, and injure himself and others. He knows, if he is honest with himself, that he has not only hurt others inadvertently but sometimes with clear purpose. He sees himself as both victim and villain in the "continuing tale of man's inhumanity to man" (Levinson, 1978, p. 224).

The more honest he is with himself, the more he realizes how tremendous is his capacity to destroy. This honesty has a bonus, however: In recognizing his power to be destructive, he begins to realize how truly powerful he can be in creating new and useful forms of life. As with the young/old polarity, he now attempts to strike a new balance between his destructive and creative sides.

Masculinity/Femininity Levinson again borrowed from Jung, using his concept that all persons have a masculine and feminine side and that they emphasize one over the other because of the demands of society. This emphasis often costs us greatly. A rich adulthood can be achieved only by compensating for that part of us that was denied during our childhood. In most males, the feminine side has typically been undernourished and now must come to the fore if they are to be all they are capable of being.

According to Levinson, in early adulthood, femininity has a number of undesirable connotations for the male. To the young man, masculinity connotes bodily prowess and toughness, achievement and ambition, power, and intellectuality. Also to the young man, the feminine role represents physical ineptness, incompetence and lack of ambition, personal weakness, and emotionality. Now is the time when the polarity between these self-concepts must be seen and reconciled.

The male who is to achieve greater individuation now recognizes that these dichotomies are false and that he does indeed have a feminine side that must also be nourished. The mature male is able to allow himself to indulge in what he before has disparaged as feminine aspects of his personality. Such a male feels secure enough in his masculinity to enjoy his ability to feel, to nurture, to be dependent. Levinson suggests such men are now freer to assume more independent relationships with their mothers, to develop more intimate love relationships with peer women, and to become mentors to younger men and women alike.

Attachment/Separation By the attachment/separation process, Levinson meant that each of us needs to be attached to our fellow members of society but also to be separate from them. As the human being develops, a fascinating vacillation occurs between each of these needs. In childhood a clear-cut attachment to mother and later to family exists. Children need support because of their incompetence in dealing with the complexity of the world around them. Nevertheless, children do begin the separation process by forming attachments to their peers.

During adolescence, this need switches toward an emphasis on separateness from family, as the individual proceeds through the identity moratorium. During this time, most adolescents need to separate themselves not only from their parents but also from the entire society around them in order to try out new ways of being. This need vacillates back toward attachment during early adulthood. The ultimate goal, of course, is interdependence (see chapter 6).

Throughout their twenties and thirties, most men are involved in entering the world of work and in family and have a strong attachment to others who can help them be successful in these goals. Now, in the mid-life transition, a new separateness, perhaps a second adolescence, takes place. The man, especially the successful man, begins to look inside and to gain greater awareness of his sensual and aesthetic feelings. He becomes more in touch with himself by being temporarily less in touch with the others around him.

Because the men interviewed so extensively by Levinson and his colleagues were between the ages of 35 and 45, their study of adult development ends at the mid-life transition. Levinson recognized, however, that a great deal is still to be learned about development after this stage. He ends his book by encouraging those who are attempting to develop theory and research on the periods following this stage of life.

Seasons of a Woman's Life: Levinson

More recently, Levinson (1990b) turned his attention to female progress toward maturity. For his research, he selected three groups of women between the ages of 35 and 45. One-third are homemakers whose lives have followed the traditional family-centered pattern, one-third are teachers at the college level, and one-third are businesswomen. He saw these women as representing a continuum from the domestic orientation to the public orientation, with the college teachers being somewhere in between. Each of the 45 women has been interviewed eight to ten times by the research staff (half of whom are female) for a total of 15 to 20 hours.

Of greatest importance is the finding that females go through a sequence of stages very similar to the stages experienced by the males who were studied. Each gender may be seen as going through an alternating series of structure-building and structure-changing stages. Levinson found, for example, that men in their late thirties want to "become their own man." He also found that at just this time, women desire to "become their own woman"; that is, they want greater affirmation both from the people in their world and from themselves.

Although male and female growth toward maturity may be in similar stages, Levinson and his associates also believed that major differences exist between the genders within these similar stages. Sociohistorical differences are important. For women, the central themes are gender splitting, the traditional marriage enterprise, and the emerging gender revolution.

Gender Splitting

Gender splitting Levinson's term; all societies support the idea that there should be a clear difference between what is considered appropriate for males and for females; gender splitting appears to be universal.

All societies support the idea that a clear difference should exist between what is considered appropriate for males and for females: **Gender splitting** appears to be universal. Women's lives have traditionally been devoted to the domestic sphere; men's to the public sphere. Human societies have seen a need for females to stay at home to protect the small number of offspring (compared with other species) while the male goes about being the "provisioner" (getting the resources the family needs outside of the home).

The Traditional Marriage Enterprise

Traditional marriage enterprise Levinson's term. The main goal of this type of marriage is to form and maintain a family.

In the final analysis, everyone gets married because they believe they can have a better life by doing so. Some exceptions may occur, but they are probably rare. At any rate, the main goal of the **traditional marriage enterprise** is to form and maintain a family. Gender splitting is seen as contributing to this goal.

Being supportive of the husband's "public" role—that is, getting resources for the family—is seen by the woman as a significant part of her role. When she goes to work, this goal is not largely different. Levinson reported that it is still a source

For women, an important transition appears to occur at about 30 years of age. The transition involves a period of self-evaluation that usually leads to greater satisfaction with life.

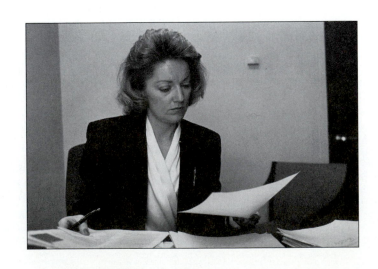

of conflict when a female does get to be the boss. Women pay a heavy price for the security this role affords. Many find it dangerous to develop a strong sense of self.

The Gender Revolution

Gender revolution Levinson's term; the meanings of gender are changing and becoming more similar.

But the meanings of gender are changing and becoming more similar. This is because young and middle-aged adults have so much more work to do. The increase in life expectancy has created a large group, the elderly, who consume more than they produce. This, together with the decrease in birthrate, has brought many more women out of the home and into the workplace. Two other factors have also been at work in creating the **gender revolution:** the divorce rate and the increase in the educational levels of women. This has resulted in a "split dream" for women—to devote themselves to the nurturing of their children *and* to have a fulfilling career. For many women, the attempt to do both brings on role overload. At every transitional point—starting a career, becoming 30, the mid-life "correction"—this conflict arises. "Are the children old enough for me to go back to work?" "Do I stay at home so my husband can fulfill his dream?" It's a big concern for many women.

In his study of women, Levinson found support for the existence of the same stages and a similar mid-life crisis as for men (Levinson, 1986). A major study of women's development (Reinke & others, 1985) used a methodology similar to Levinson's and found important transitions in the lives of women, but not exclusively clustered around the mid-life period (ages 40 to 45). Instead, women described important transitions in their lives at ages 30, 40, and 60.

We are, in Levinson's opinion, at a cultural crossroads. The old division of female homemakers and male providers is breaking down, but no clear new direction has yet appeared. Researchers will be watching this dramatic change closely.

Levinson operated from the viewpoint of psychology. The next theory is that of a psychiatrist, most of whom are trained in the Freudian tradition. As we shall see, that makes for a rather different view of adult personality development.

Generativity versus Stagnation: Erikson

Let us turn now to a theory that is considered a classic. In this final section, we will put forth Erikson's explanation of personality development in middle adulthood: generativity versus stagnation.

A Sociocultural View

Does Having a "Mid-Life Crisis" Depend on Your Ethnic Background?

Over the years, a number of researchers have noticed that people of color are less likely to report having had a "mid-life crisis" than are whites. A number of hypotheses have been proposed as to why this might be so (can you guess what they might be?). In their extensive review of the literature, however, DeVries and Gallagher (1994) refuted this conclusion. They believed that encountering a mid-life crisis depends mainly on one's socioeconomic status, and the higher that is, the more likely is the individual to feel that she or he has been through such an experience. Because persons of color are more likely to be in the lower socioeconomic level, they are less likely to report the experience:

> Mid-life crises are an affliction of the relatively affluent: rosy illusions are easier to maintain when a person is already somewhat shielded from reality.

Just as childhood is often constricted among the poor, who early in life face adult realities and burdens, so middle age may be eclipsed by a premature old age brought on by poverty and poor health. Among working-class people, for whom strength and stamina may mean earning power, middle age may begin at thirty-five rather than the forty-five often cited by respondents drawn from the sedentary middle class (1994, p. 74).

In DeVries and Gallagher's view, then, just as "the moratorium of youth" we considered in chapter 11 is mainly experienced by middle- and upper-class adolescents, the so-called mid-life crisis is primarily a problem for those who have the time and money to afford it. Can you think of any other life crises that may pertain only to one socioeconomic group? How about one ethnic group?

Generativity   Erikson's term for the ability to be useful to ourselves and to society.

Generativity means the ability to be useful to ourselves and to society. As in the industry stage, the goal here is to be productive and creative. However, productivity in the industry stage is a means of obtaining recognition and material reward. In the generativity stage, which takes place during middle adulthood, one's productivity is aimed at being helpful to others. The act of being productive is itself rewarding, regardless of recognition or reward. Erikson added that generativity is

> that middle period of the life cycle when existence permits you and demands you to consider death as peripheral and to balance its certainty with the only happiness that is lasting: to increase, by whatever is yours to give, the good will and the higher order in your sector of the world. (1978, p. 124)

Although Erikson certainly approved of the procreation of children as an important part of generativity for many people, he did not believe that everyone needs to become a parent in order to be generative. For example, some people, who from misfortune or because of special and genuine gifts in other directions, cannot apply this drive to offspring of their own and instead apply it to other forms of altruistic concern and creativity (Erikson, 1968).

At this stage of adulthood some people become bored, self-indulgent, and unable to contribute to society's welfare; they fall prey to **stagnation.** Such adults act as though they were their own only child. People who have given birth to children may fail to be generative in their parenthood and come to resent the neediness of their offspring.

Stagnation   According to Erikson, the seventh stage of life (middle-aged adulthood) tends to be marked either by generativity or by stagnation—boredom, self-indulgence, and the inability to contribute to society.

In terms of promoting generativity, Wacks (1994) has suggested that each individual has an "inner elder-child," which combines both shame and fear of aging with a childlike appreciation of life and wisdom. Although he refers to an "elder-child," Wacks found that this phenomenon occurs in the middle years of adulthood. By nurturing this inner elder-child, the individual can gain maturity by learning from life experiences, including those that are painful or fearsome. This can help in integrating the young self with the older self at mid-life, that in turn tends to foster more generative attitudes.

Although generativity may provide great satisfaction to those who reach it, theorists have suggested that the picture is not as clear as it might appear (McAdams & others, 1993). In a cross-sectional study that looked at generativity across age groups, McAdams and associates examined four different features of generativity: generative concern, commitments, action, and narration. They found some evidence for Erikson's hypothesis that generativity is relatively low in young adulthood, peaks at mid-life, and declines in the older years. These researchers reported that several studies have suggested differences between men and women. Most men appear to become fixed in the industry stage, doing work merely to obtain the social symbols of success. Most women, these studies suggested, become fixed in the identity stage, confused and conflicted about their proper role in life, which prevents them from achieving intimacy and reaching the stage of generativity. Is Erikson's more optimistic view correct or not? Only more sophisticated investigation of the question will resolve it.

Becoming generative is not easy. It depends on the successful resolution of the six preceding Eriksonian crises we have described in this book. People who are able to achieve generativity have a chance to reach the highest level of personhood in Erikson's hierarchy: integrity. We will examine that stage in chapter 18.

As you can see, all of the theories described thus far hold that as we age we go through many important changes. Let us turn now to the other side of the coin: the position that the adult personality is made up of traits that remain continuously stable, in most cases, throughout adulthood.

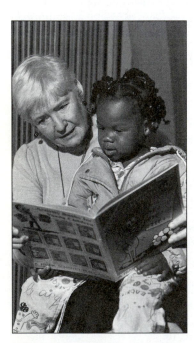

Generativity, Erikson's term for the major goal of the middle years of adulthood, includes coming to understand those who are different from you and desiring to make a lasting contribution to their welfare.

Continuous Traits Theory

In their extensive study of men at mid-life, McCrae and Costa (1984; see also Costa & McCrae, 1995a & b) found no evidence of personality change over the adult years, nor any evidence for the existence of mid-life crisis. The research measured the stability of several different personality traits over a period of six years (a longitudinal study) and also looked at those same personality traits in a cross-age population (a cross-sectional analysis).

At the first testing, McCrae and Costa administered several personality inventories to men ranging in age from 17 to 97. When they combined the data they gathered from the inventories, they defined three major personality traits that they feel govern the adult personality: neuroticism, extroversion, and openness to experience. Each of those three traits is supported by six subtraits or "facets" (see figure 16.5). The three major traits together are termed the **NEO model of personality.** The researchers found relative stability of those traits throughout male adulthood.

Neuroticism is described as an index of instability or a predisposition for some kind of breakdown under stress. Behaviors associated with this trait include the following:

- A tendency to have more physical and psychiatric problems (without medical problems).

- Greater tendencies to smoke and drink.

- More general unhappiness and dissatisfaction with life.

Extroversion, the tendency to be outgoing and social, is the second global trait found by McCrae and Costa. Extroversion seems to spill over into almost all aspects of the personality, because it implies an overriding interest in people and social connections.

Openness to experience, the third general trait, is exactly that: an openness to new ideas, fantasies, actions, feelings, and values. Overall, a lack of rigidity in regard to the unfamiliar characterizes openness to experience.

The researchers noted that although habits, life events, opinions, and relationships may change over the lifespan, the basic personality of an individual does not (McCrae & Costa, 1984). They thought that people who experience a mid-life crisis probably have the personality makeup that biases them toward that behavior. The Costa and McCrae research, however, lacks consideration of the reciprocal nature of influence of a person with his or her environment. Even so, the rigor of McCrae and Costa's work warrants careful consideration from those interested in personality development across the lifespan.

NEO model of personality
McCrae and Costa's theory that there are three major personality traits, which they feel govern the adult personality.

Figure 16.5

Schematic representation of the three-dimensional, 18-facet NEO (neuroticism, extroversion, openness) model of McCrae and Costa.

From R. McCrae and P. Costa, Jr., *Emerging Lives, Enduring Disposition: Personality in Adulthood.* Copyright © 1984 Little, Brown and Company, Boston, MA. Reprinted by permission of the authors.

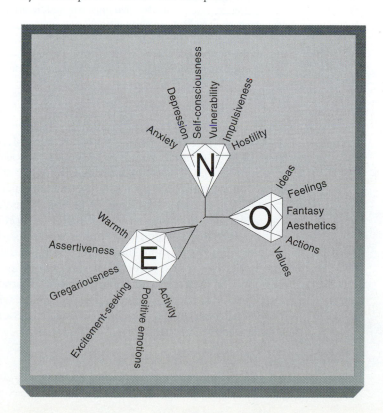

An Informed View

Traits versus Stages

As you can see, a clear conflict exists between the trait researchers and the positions of the three stage theorists. It appears that they cannot both be correct, although the truth may lie somewhere in between. We have devoted much more space to the stage theories. In part this is because they have received so much attention in the popular press, as well as by scholars. It is also because we are biased toward them. (It is certainly obvious throughout this book that we have a great deal of admiration for the ideas of Erikson.)

Whatever the case may be, the important thing is that, through discussion, further reading, and observation, you try to come to your own opinion. What do you think?

If you would like to have a more informed opinion on this issue, you might want to read one of the articles on the subject referenced in this chapter (e.g., Levinson, McCrae & Costa).

You might also wish to learn more about it by going to our web site at http://www.mhhe.com/dacey5.

Guided Review

14. Two theoretical positions influence the study of personality. Trait theorists believe that adults remain basically the same and _____ theorists believe that the adult is constantly changing and evolving.
15. In his discussion on mid-life transition, Daniel Levinson identifies four polarities that are a source of division in the life of a middle-adult man. These polarities are young/old, destruction/creation, masculinity/femininity, and _____.
16. From his studies on women, Levinson stated that the stages of women's development are similar to the stages for men, but he found three women's themes: _____ _____, the traditional marriage enterprise, and the emerging gender revolution.
17. McCrae and Costa refer to "an index of instability or a predisposition for some kind of breakdown under stress" as _____.
18. Erikson saw generativity (the ability to be useful to ourselves and society) versus _____ as the challenge for middle adulthood.
19. According to McCrae and Costa, _____, extroversion, and openness to experience are the three traits they found to be stable in middle-aged adult males.
20. In the study of college-educated women's personality by Stewart and Ostrove, it was learned that their confidence in their personal efficacy (increased, decreased) with age.

Finally, in an article summarizing the best of previous research, Stewart and Ostrove (1998) surveyed what we know about college-educated women's personality in middle age. They conclude that there are some important changes in personality that typically occur among these women from early adulthood, most significantly ". . . an increased sense of personal identity and confidence in personal efficacy, paralleled with somewhat increased preoccupation with aging itself" (p. 1191). They recommend that further study also look at changes in personality in poor women. As to men, they state, "Perhaps the early adoption of a confident and authoritative stance, associated with cultural expectations of men, means that middle age for men involves more acknowledgement of doubt and vulnerability. Perhaps, too, the social changes of recent years will mean that young men who make major investments in domestic life will experience middle age differently than their fathers did" (p. 1192).

Answers

14. stage 15. attachment/separation 16. gender splitting 17. neuroticism 18. stagnation 19. neuroticism 20. increased

CONCLUSION & SUMMARY

Dealing with change is as serious a challenge in mid-life as at any other time. Learning new ways to get along with one's spouse, parents, siblings, and children is necessary at this time of life. Considerable debate occurs over whether personality changes much during this period. Some think it goes through a series of predictable changes; others view it as continuous with earlier life. Workers often experience a "mid-life crisis" at this time, and women workers have an additional set of burdens to handle. Yet with any luck, we make it safely through middle age and move on to late adulthood.

How do adults generally deal with stress?

- Many life events, including major events and daily hassles, contribute to stress in our lives.
- Selye's concept of the general adaptation syndrome includes the stages of alarm reaction, resistance, and exhaustion.
- It is not unusual for disease to result from stress.
- People who are exposed to many risk factors but develop few behavioral or psychological problems are called resilient.

What are the typical patterns of marriage in the family during middle adulthood?

- Middle age offers a time for marriage reappraisal, which proves positive for most couples.

- Middle age is also a time when most people develop improved relationships with their parents, though in some cases the relationship begins to reverse itself when those parents become dependent on their middle-aged children.
- Sibling relationships have the potential to be the most enduring that a person can have, with the relationship between sisters being strongest. It is usually one of these sisters who cares for the elderly parents.
- Reducing the number of one's friends begins in early adulthood. A deepening of the friendships that remain begins in middle age and goes on throughout the rest of life.
- Liberalization of divorce laws has improved the position of women following divorce; however, Weitzman argues that serious inequity still exists.

What are the main factors that affect sex and love among middle-aged people?

- Frequency of sexual intercourse as well as marital satisfaction appear to increase over the middle years.
- Some minor changes in sexual physiology occur for both sexes, but usually these need not hamper sexual satisfaction.
- Being a good lover is not a personality trait, but rather the result of interaction with another person.

What happens to personality during the adult years: does it typically change or remain continuous?

- Research by trait theorists such as Kagan, and McCrae and Costa generally supports the notion that human beings remain fairly stable throughout life.
- By contrast, theorists such as Erikson, Levinson, and Vaillant argue that human beings are best described as constantly changing and developing throughout life.
- Levinson suggested that most men go through a mid-life transition in which they must deal with the polarities between young and old, masculinity and femininity, destruction and creation, and attachment and separation.
- Levinson also suggested that females go through a similar experience to that of males, with some notably different influences.
- Erikson's theory placed middle adulthood within the stage labeled "generativity versus stagnation." Generativity means the ability to be useful to ourselves and to society without concern for material reward.
- McCrae and Costa defined three major personality traits that they feel govern the adult personality: neuroticism, extroversion, and openness to experience.
- In the study of college-educated women's personality by Stewart and Ostrove, it was learned that sense of personal identity and their confidence in their personal efficacy increased with age.

KEY TERMS

Alarm reaction
Emotional divorce
Empty nest syndrome
Gender revolution
Gender splitting
General adaptation syndrome
Generativity

Mid-life transition
NEO model of personality
No-fault divorce
Protective factors
Resilience
Risk factors

Stage of exhaustion
Stage of resistance
Stage theorists
Stagnation
Traditional marriage enterprise
Trait theorists

WHAT DO YOU THINK?

1. In what ways does Selye's concept for the general adaptation syndrome play a part in your life? In the lives of your friends?
2. What is the best way for middle-aged people to take care of their ailing, elderly parents?
3. What changes would you make in our divorce laws?
4. Why is the mid-life transition so stressful for some men and not for others?
5. What are the main differences between male and female personality development during the middle adult years?
6. Who's right, the stage theorists or the trait theorists?

CHAPTER REVIEW TEST

1. If a person is alerted to stress, the level of anxiety increases, and task-oriented and defense-oriented behavior takes place, the person is experiencing the psychological manifestations of
   a. alarm reaction.
   b an anxiety attack.
   c defense mechanisms.
   d denial.

2. According to Selye, your ability to remain in the resistance stage decreases when you are
   a experiencing optimum drive.
   b experiencing an alarm reaction.
   c an adolescent.
   d growing older.

3. Under continual stress, the gradual depletion of an organism's adaptational energy eventually leads to
   a stage of resistance.
   b stage of exhaustion.
   c collapse of the nervous system.
   d increased energy.

4. Francis and Joan have drifted apart over the years but remain married to each other because of their children. Their relationship illustrates the
   a. functional marriage.
   b. practical marriage.
   c. functional divorce.
   d. emotional divorce.

5. According to Gottman and Krokoff's longitudinal research on marital interactions, those who tend most to avoid relational confrontations are
   a. divorcing couples.
   b. couples married for more than 25 years.
   c. husbands.
   d. wives.

6. What is the most frequently cited problem of middle-aged adult women?

   a. Aging
   b. Menopause
   c. Caring for their children
   d. Caring for their aging parents

7. Research suggests that a typical characteristic of a sibling relationship in middle adulthood is
   a. growing distance.
   b. increased animosity.
   c. mutual caring for elderly parents.
   d. rivalry over the inheritance.

8. Because the no-fault divorce laws do not account for an inequitable economic system, who suffers most financially by divorce?
   a. The middle-aged homemaker
   b. The career oriented woman
   c. The middle-aged father
   d. The adult children

9. The notion that adult personality changes over time is supported by
   a. stage theorists.
   b. transition theorists.
   c. trait theorists.
   d. lifespan theorists.

10. Trait theory is to _____ as stage theory is to

    _____.
    a. lifespan development; stair step transition
    b. continuity in adult development; change in adult development
    c. change in adult development; continuity in adult development
    d. stair step transition; lifespan development

11. The _____ that occur during Levinson's mid-life transition represent the continual struggle toward greater individuation.
    a. attachments
    b. separations
    c. level of intimacy
    d. polarities

12. The idea that a clear difference exists between what is appropriate for males and for females is referred to as
    a. gender splitting.
    b. the gender revolution.
    c. role strain.
    d. the traditional marriage.

13. McCrae and Costa argued that although habits, life events, opinions, and relationships may change over the lifespan, the basic _____ of an individual does not.
    a. value
    b. orientation
    c. personality
    d. coping mechanisms

14. According to Erikson, during the generativity stage one's productivity is aimed at
    a. career advancement.
    b. material rewards.
    c. being helpful to others.
    d. recognition.

15. McCrae and Costa defined three major personality types as neuroticism, extroversion, and
    a. introversion.
    b. openness to experience.
    c. outdatedness.
    d. None of the above.

16. In the study of college-educated women's personality by Stewart and Ostrove, it was learned that their sense of personal identity and their confidence in their personal efficacy
    a. decreased with age.
    b. increased with age.
    c. was unaffected by aging.
    d. is almost double that of men of the same age.

Answers

1.a 2.d 3.b 4.d 5.c 6.d 7.c 8.a 9.a 10.b 11.d 12.a 13.c 14.c 15.b 16.b

PART **IX**

Late Adulthood

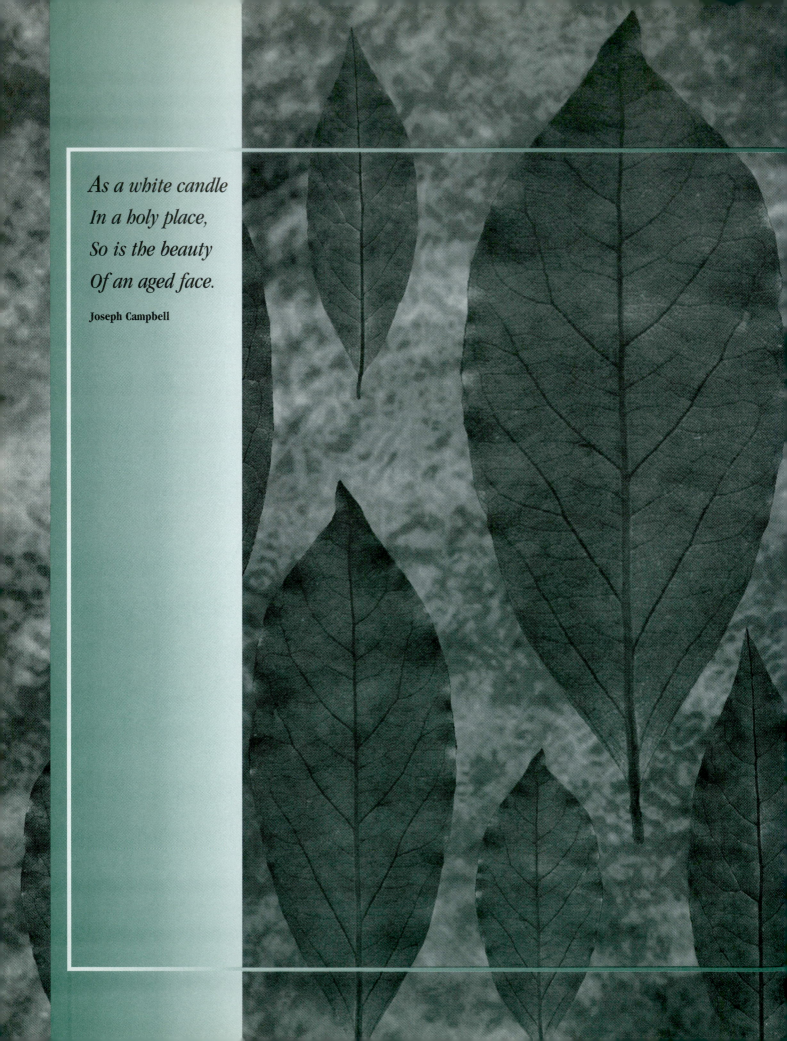

As a white candle
In a holy place,
So is the beauty
Of an aged face.

Joseph Campbell

CHAPTER 17

Even when he was very old and ill, Winston Churchill's fabled sense of humor never left him. In addition, it was only in his later years that he found time to sharpen his artistic skills, which brought him world renown in that realm. He was an excellent example of how fruitful the last third of life can be.

A nd just as young people are all different, and middle-aged people are all different, so too are old people. We don't all have to be exactly alike.... There are all kinds of old people coping with a common condition, just as kids in puberty when their voices start cracking.

Every one of them is different. We old folks get arthritis, rheumatism, our teeth fall out, our feet hurt, our hair gets thin, we creak and groan. These are the physical changes, but all of us are different. And I personally feel that you follow pretty much the pattern of your younger years. I think that some people are born young and some people are born old and tired and gray and dull.... You're either a nasty little boy turned old man or a mean little old witch turned old or an outgoing, free-loving person turned old. As for myself, I feel very excited about life and about people and color and books, and there is an excitement to everything that I guess some people never feel.... I have a lot of friends who are thirty-year-old clods. They were born that way and they'll die that way.... But me, I'm happy, I'm alive, and I want to live with as much enjoyment and dignity and decency as I can, and do it gracefully and my way if possible, as long as possible.

M.F.K. Fisher

A special session of the British House of Lords was being held to honor Winston Churchill on his ninetieth birthday. As he descended the stairs of the amphitheater, one member turned to another and said, "They say he's really getting senile." Churchill stopped, and leaning toward them, said in a stage whisper loud enough for many to hear, "They also say he's deaf!" ❂

Although positive, these vignettes remind us of the stereotypes of old age as being a rather negative stage of life. Multiple-choice and true-false tests given to college students have shown that this and other stereotypes continue to exist (Harris & others, 1996). How much truth is there to them? Must growing old mean decline? Must the teeth and hair fall out, the eyes grow dim, the skin wrinkle and sag? Must intelligence, memory, and creativity falter? Must old age be awful?

Or is there actually only a relatively slight decline in capacity, a decline greatly exaggerated by our values and presumptions? Many elderly people seem to be having the time of their lives! Could it be that the negative aspects of aging are largely the result of a self-fulfilling prophecy (people expect to deteriorate, so they stop trying to be fit, and then they do deteriorate)? Could most of us in our later years be as capable as those famous few who seem to have overcome age and remained vigorous into their nineties and beyond? In chapter 17, we will investigate these questions.

The questions that introduced this chapter concern most of the 23 million men and women over 65 who constitute 12 percent of our population today. In 1900 the over-65 population was 3 million, only 3 percent of the total. By the year 2040 it will have reached 20 percent (see figure 17.1). Such questions should also concern those of us who hope to join their ranks some day. In the next section we look at the answers to these questions, as revealed by considerable new research.

Chapter Objectives

After reading this chapter you should be able to answer the following questions.

◆ Must we age and die?
◆ What are the key aspects of physical development among the elderly?
◆ How is cognitive development affected by old age?

Must We Age and Die?

It is never too late to be what you might have been.

George Eliot

"Nothing is inevitable except death and taxes," the old saying goes. But is death inevitable? True, no one so far has attained immortality; the oldest known person in the United States, as certified by the Social Security Administration, is 114 years old. And, of course, the vast majority of the people who have ever lived are dead.

But not all organisms die. Some trees alive today are known to be more than 2,500 years old; they have aged but show no sign of dying. Bacteria apparently are able to live indefinitely, as long as they have the requirements for their existence. The fact is, we are not sure why we age, and until we are, we cannot be certain that aging and death are absolutely inevitable. Nor can we overlook those who appear to age well, which is often referred to as "successful" or "robust" aging (Garfein & Herzog, 1995). Robustly aging individuals report greater social contact and better health and vision than those who age less successfully.

Figure 17.1

Age distribution of U.S. population, selected years.

Source: Social Security Administration.

A Sociocultural View   *Percentage of Elderly in Japan Soon to Be Much Higher Than Here*

As can be seen in figure 17.2, the percentage of the Japanese population over the age of 65 was about the same as the United States in 1990 (about 12 percent). By the year 2020, however, when the percentage of U.S. elderly will have risen by 3 percent, Japan's will have increased by 13 percent. That means that 25 percent of all Japanese will be elderly.

Two factors account for most of the increase in Japan (Kakuchi, 1997). The country is known for its excellent health care and nutrition. The Japanese also have a greatly decreased birthrate. For example, the percentage of those 14 or younger has dropped from 35 in 1955 to about 15 percent today. Can you imagine what the impact of this huge change will be on Japanese social conditions?

Figure 17.2

A comparison of the percentage of elderly persons in the United States and Japan from 1990 to 2020. More than a fourth of the Japanese population is projected to be older than 65 by 2020.

Japan Information Network

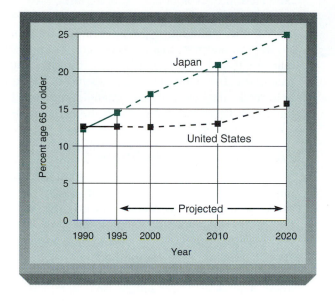

Physiological Theories of Aging

It is apparent that organisms inherit a tendency to live for a certain length of time. An animal's durability depends on the species it belongs to. The average human lifespan of approximately 70 years is the longest of any mammal. Elephants, horses, hippopotamuses, and asses are known to live as long as 50 years, but most mammals die much sooner.

Some doctors are fond of stating that "no one ever died of old age." This is true. People die of some physiological failure that is more likely to occur the older one gets. One likely explanation of aging is that the various life-support systems gradually weaken. Illness and death come about as a cumulative result of these various weaknesses. Seven different physiological factors have been suggested as accounting for this process.

Wear and Tear Theory

Wear and tear theory   The theory that aging is due to the cumulative effects of hard work and lifelong stress.

The **wear and tear theory** seems the most obvious explanation for aging, but there is actually little evidence for it. To date, no research has clearly linked early deterioration of organs with either hard work or increased stress alone.

A complex interaction, however, may be involved. It is known that lower rates of metabolism are linked to longer life and that certain conditions, such as absence

This olive tree found in Greece is more than 2,500 years old. Do you think it's possible that it might live forever?

of rich foods, cause a lower metabolism. Therefore, the lack of the "good life" may prolong life. On the other hand, it is also known that poor people who seldom get to eat rich foods tend to die at an earlier age than middle-class or wealthy people. Therefore, the evidence on this theory is at best conflicting.

Aging by Program

According to the **aging by program** theory, we age because it is programmed into us. It is hard to understand what evolutionary processes govern longevity (if any). For example, the vast majority of animals die at or before the end of their reproductive period, but human females live 20 to 30 years beyond the end of their reproductive cycles. This may be related to the capacities of the human brain. Mead (1972) argued that this extra period beyond the reproductive years has had the evolutionary value of helping to keep the children and grandchildren alive. For example, in times when food is scarce, older people may remember where it was obtained during the last period of scarcity. On the other hand, it may be that we humans have outwitted the evolutionary process and, due to our medical achievements and improvements in lifestyle, are able to live on past our reproductive usefulness.

Another enduring hypothesis, originally proposed by Birren (1960), is known as the "counterpart" theory. According to this concept, factors in human existence that are useful in the earlier years become counterproductive in later years. An example is the nonreplaceability of most cells in the nervous system. The fact that brain cells are not constantly changing enhances memory and learning abilities in the earlier years, but it also allows the nervous system to weaken because dead cells are not replaced.

Homeostatic Imbalance

It may be a failure in the systems that regulate the proper interaction of the organs, rather than wear of the organs themselves, that causes aging and ultimately death. These homeostatic (feedback) systems are responsible, for example, for the regulation of the sugar and adrenaline levels in the blood. Apparently there is not a great deal of difference in the systems of the young and the old when they are in a quiet state. It is when stress is put on the systems (death of a spouse, loss of a job, a frightening experience) that we see the effects of the elderly **homeostatic imbalance.** The older body simply isn't as effective, qualitatively or quantitatively, in reacting to these stresses. Figure 17.3 shows graphically the relationship between problems with the homeostatic systems and the competence of the organism to react effectively to dangers in the environment.

Cross-Linkage Theory

The proteins that make up a large part of cells are composed of peptides. When cross-links are formed between peptides (a natural process of the body), the proteins are altered, often for the worse. For example, **collagen** is the major connective tissue in the body; it provides, for instance, the elasticity in our skin and blood vessels. When its proteins are altered, skin and vessels are adversely affected. This is known as the **cross-linkage theory.**

Accumulation of Metabolic Waste

Although the connection has not been clearly established as yet, it may be that waste products resulting from metabolism build up in various parts of the body and contribute to the decrease in competence of those parts. Examples of this effect of the **accumulation of metabolic waste** are cataracts on the eye, cholesterol in the arteries, and brittleness of bones.

Autoimmunity

With increasing age, there is increasing **autoimmunity,** the process by which the immune system in the body rejects the body's own tissue. Examples of this are rheumatoid arthritis, diabetes, vascular diseases, and hypertension. It may be that, with age, the body's tissues become more and more self-rejecting.

Aging by program The theory that all animals seem to die when their "program" dictates.

Homeostatic imbalance The theory that aging is due to a failure in the systems that regulate the proper interaction of the organs.

Collagen The major connective tissue in the body; it provides the elasticity in our skin and blood vessels.

Cross-linkage theory Proteins that make up a large part of cells are composed of peptides. When cross-links are formed between peptides, the proteins are altered, often for the worse.

Accumulation of metabolic waste Waste products resulting from metabolism build up in various parts of the body.

Autoimmunity The process by which the immune system in the body rejects the body's own tissue.

Figure 17.3

Homeostasis and health. Progressive stages of homeostasis from adjustment (health) to failure (death).

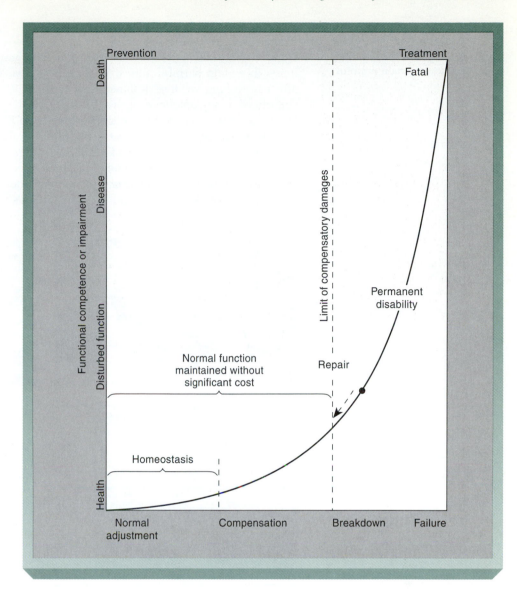

Antigens The substances in the blood that fight to kill foreign bodies.

This may be the result of the production of new **antigens,** blood that produces antibodies, which in turn fight to kill foreign bodies. These new antigens may come about for one of two reasons:

• Mutations cause the formation of altered RNA or DNA.

• Some cells may be "hidden" in the body during the early part of life. When these cells appear later, the body does not recognize them as its own, and forms new antigens to kill them. This in turn may cause organ malfunction.

Patients with a confirmed diagnosis of such ailments are usually instructed to begin drug therapy and change their lifestyles according to prescribed instructions (Clyman & Pompei, 1996 a & b). If patients continue to suffer from disabling pain, surgery is an alternative solution. However, elderly people who are bedridden, wheelchair-bound, or have heart disease are not often candidates for surgery. Fortunately, doctors are considering alternate treatments that may be effective.

Accumulation of Errors

Accumulation of errors As cells die, they must synthesize new proteins to make new cells. As this is done, occasionally an error occurs. Over time, these errors mount up and may finally grow serious enough to cause organ failure.

As cells die, they must synthesize new proteins to make new cells. As this is done, occasionally an error occurs. Over time these errors mount up. This **accumulation of errors** may finally grow serious enough to cause organ failure.

Genetic Theories of Aging

Gene theory   The theory that aging is due to certain harmful genes.

Gene theory also suggests that aging is programmed but says that the program exists in certain harmful genes. Whatever the reason, little doubt exists that genes affect how long we live. Kallman and Jarvik's (1959) research into identical twins still offers strong evidence of this. They found that monozygotic twins (those born from the same egg) have more similar lengths of life than do dizygotic twins (those born from two eggs). This effect is illustrated in figures 17.4 and 17.5.

There is a distinct group of adults that does not fit neatly into any theory of aging. They are called the centenarians; those people 100 or older who do not succumb to common causes of death for persons their age. What factors contribute to the survival of these men and women? Smith's (1997) research suggested that,

Figure 17.4

One-egg twins at the ages of 12, 17, 67, and 91 years (note the long separation of these twins between the ages of 18 and 66).

Figure 17.5

One-egg twins at the ages of 5, 20, 55, and 86 years.

although these men and women are not necessarily more robust than their contemporaries (whom they've outlived), they are relatively resistant to illnesses such as cancer and circulatory diseases.

Effects of the Natural Environment on Aging

Our genes and the physiology of our organs greatly affect the length of our lives. This may be seen in the extreme accuracy with which insurance companies are able to predict the average number of deaths at a particular age. A mathematical formula to predict the number of deaths within a population was produced as early as 1825 by Gomertz. The formula is still quite accurate except for the early years of life.

Today many fewer deaths occur in early childhood, because vaccines have eliminated much of the danger of diseases at this age. This shows that the natural environment is also an important factor in the mortality rate. Many of today's elderly would have died in childhood had they been born in the early part of the nineteenth century.

Considering mortality rates for specific cultures rather than world population shows the effects of the environment more specifically. Starvation in Africa and earthquakes in Guatemala obviously had a tragic effect on the mortality rates of those two countries. Some evidence indicates that the nuclear testing in the Pacific in the 1950s is affecting the aging process of some of the residents there. Little or no evidence exists, however, to suggest that the radiation we are all exposed to every day is having any impact on aging. It remains to be seen if events such as the nuclear accident at Three Mile Island will have adverse effects.

Other Modifiers of Aging

In addition to genetic, physiological, and natural environmental factors that indirectly affect the individual's rate of aging, other factors can modify a person's level of ability more directly. Many of these modifiers interact with one another in complex ways. Some of the major modifiers are training, practice, motivation, nutrition, organic malfunction, illness, injury, stress level, educational level, occupation, personality type, and socioeconomic status.

For example, although it appears that social networks (the number and extent of friendships a person has) do not directly affect the survival of elderly people, they are related to their quality of life. Within nursing homes, those who tend to be aggressive and verbally agitated have poor social networks and generally lack intimacy with their fellow patients. Figure 17.6 summarizes the relationships between the hypothesized factors that affect aging of physical and mental systems. These include two genetic, five physiological, and five environmental factors, as well as twelve other modifiers of human abilities. You could find no clearer example of the biopsychosocial model at work!

It is a well-established fact that gender affects aging: women live approximately six years longer than men (Legato, 1998). This is surprising given that women

A Sociocultural View

The Role of Relatives in the Health of Persons of Color

A number of studies have indicated that although African-American and Latino elderly are more susceptible than whites to health problems, if their relatives are involved in their lifestyle choices, this difference is greatly lessened. For example, persons of color are more susceptible to diabetes and hypertension, in part because they often have inadequate diets (too much sugar and fat, not enough fresh vegetables, etc.). Relatives can make sure that appropriate foods are purchased and properly prepared. They can also provide informal health care and intervene with health services to ensure that help is provided to the elderly when needed.

Figure 17.6

Influences on adult mental and physical systems.

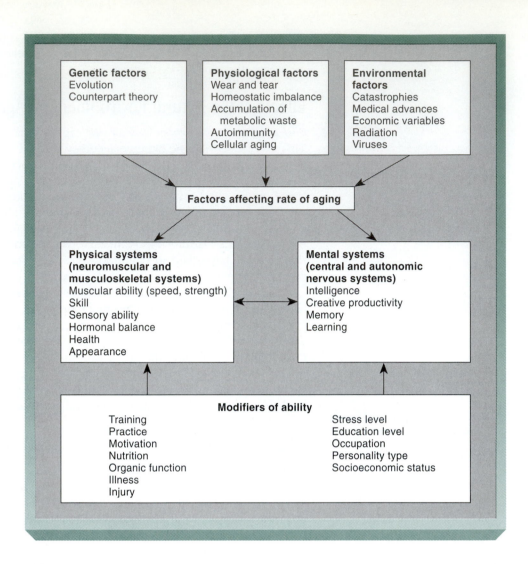

suffer from more gender-specific diseases and ailments than men do. For example, women have higher incidences of autoimmune disease such as lupus; as well as more reported cases of multiple sclerosis, migraine headaches, osteoporosis, and colon cancer.

Before reading the next section, you might try your hand at the true-false test on the topic of aging in the box—An Applied View: The Facts on Aging Quiz.

Guided Review

1. Theorists have proposed three generic explanations for aging and death: physiological aspects, _____ aspects, and environmental aspects.
2. Within the physiological aspects, one of the explanations is called the _____ and _____ theory, meaning that hard work and stress gradually destroy body parts.
3. The other physiological aspects are: aging by program, homeostatic imbalance, _____ theory, accumulation of metabolic waste, autoimmunity, and accumulation of errors.
4. The impact of the environment on aging and death helps us understand that our genes and the _____ of our organs affects the length of our lives.
5. Those people 100 years old or older are called _____.

Answers

1. genetic 2. wear, tear 3. cross-linkage 4. physiology 5. centenarians

The Facts on Aging Quiz

Mark the items T for true or F for false.

1. A person's height tends to decline in old age.

2. More older persons (over 65) have chronic illnesses that limit their activity more than younger persons.

3. Older persons have more acute (short-term) illnesses than persons under 65.

4. Older persons have more injuries in the home than persons under 65.

5. Older workers have less absenteeism than younger workers.

6. The life expectancy of African-Americans at age 65 is about the same as whites.

7. The life expectancy of men at age 65 is about the same as women's.

8. Medicare pays over half of the medical expenses for the aged.

9. Social Security benefits automatically increase with inflation.

10. Supplemental Security Income guarantees a minimum income for needy aged.

11. The aged do not get their proportionate share (about 11%) of the nation's income.

12. The aged have higher rates of criminal victimization than persons under 65.

13. The aged are more fearful of crime than are persons under 65.

14. The aged are the most law abiding of all adult groups, according to official statistics.

15. There are two widows for each widower among the aged.

16. More of the aged vote than any other age group.

17. There are proportionately more older persons in public office than in the total population.

18. The proportion of African-Americans among the aged is growing.

19. Participation in voluntary organizations (churches and clubs) tends to decline among the healthy aged.

20. The majority of the aged live alone.

21. About 3 percent less of the aged have incomes below the official poverty level than the rest of the population.

22. The rate of poverty among aged African-Americans is about three times as high as among aged whites.

23. Older persons who reduce their activity tend to be happier than those who remain active.

24. When the last child leaves home, the majority of parents have serious problems adjusting to their "empty nest."

25. The proportion of widowed is decreasing among the aged.

The key to the correct answers is simple: Alternating pairs of items are true or false (i.e., 1 and 2 are true, 3 and 4 are false, 5 and 6 are true, etc.; and 25 is true).

Physical Development

In this section, we consider development from the standpoints of reaction time, sensory abilities, other body systems, health, and appearance.

Reaction Time

It is obvious that physical skills decline as people grow older. This appears to be especially true of manual dexterity. Although older people are able to perform short, coordinated manual tasks, a long series of tasks such as playing a stringed instrument becomes increasingly difficult for them. Famed Spanish guitarist Andrés Segovia and pianist Vladimir Horowitz are notable exceptions.

Is this because the human nervous system is deteriorating through aging? To answer this question, psychologists have completed numerous studies of "reaction time," the time between the onset of a stimulus and the actual muscle activity that indicates a reaction to it. Studying reaction time is a scientific way of separating the effects of the central nervous system from the ability of the rest of the body to perform manual tasks.

We can conclude that variables other than sheer neural or motor activities account for most change in physical skills over time. One example of an alternative

Seniors usually find that their coordination declines with the years, and so they often quit playing sports. Now there is a strong movement to reverse this trend.

Ageism The prejudice that the elderly are inferior to those who are younger.

factor is ageism. It has been shown that young people process and respond to the speech of older people in stereotypical ways such as "baby talk" or pandering (Giles & others, 1992). This type of prejudice is known as **ageism.**

Because they are often treated in a condescending way, elderly persons sometimes behave in a less competent manner than they are capable of. Ageism is a prejudice that can seriously affect the elderly, lowering the quality of their lives. Furthermore, it robs our society of the diverse contributions that might otherwise be made by elderly persons, if their feelings of self-esteem and competence were not undermined by this prejudice.

What are some things you could do to fight this unfair attitude? For example, how might you help change the stereotype that senility is normal in the elderly?

Other factors that influence the reaction time of the elderly are motivation, depression, anxiety, response strategies, and response style. Older adults can improve their ability in any of these areas if they desire.

Sensory Abilities

Sensory functioning may be among the important determinants of individual differences in cognitive performance. Lindenberger and Baltes (1994) see old age as often being a time of "sensory deprivation"—reduced opportunities for stimulating exchanges with the environment. Lack of sensory stimulation is one of many factors that emerges during later phases of life, and helps regulate the process of aging. Such late-life factors of development are powerful influences, and may account for developmental changes in old age. We look at some of those changes in the following paragraphs.

Vision

We are always the same age inside.

Gertrude Stein

A number of problems may affect the eye as the adult ages. The lenses may become less transparent, thicker, and less elastic. This tends to result in farsightedness. The illumination required to perceive a stimulus also increases with age. Retina changes almost never occur before the age of 60; however, some have argued that conditions that affect the retina may occur without causing noticeable changes in the eye.

Increasing age often brings a heightened risk for such problems (Learning to see, 2000). The main concerns are:

- Floaters, also known as floating spots, are actually particles suspended in the jelled substance that fills the eyeball. They are annoying, but generally do not impair vision. However, a severe "floating" problem accompanied by flashes of light could indicate a more serious condition called retinal detachment.

- Dry eye, stemming from diminished tear production, can usually be eased with drops. There are also several procedures that stop tear drainage and conserve moisture.

- Senile macular degeneration is the thinning of the layers of the retina and rupturing of tiny blood vessels in this part of the eye. Sufferers experience faded, distorted, or blurred central vision. Advances in laser surgery have shown promise in treating diseases of the retina such as this.

- Cataracts are the leading cause of blindness in people over 65. They occur when the eye lens clouds, impairing vision. If cataracts become large enough, they can be removed, usually by laser surgery.

- Glaucoma results from increased pressure caused by fluid within the eye. If left untreated, the disease can damage the optic nerve and lead to blindness. Eye drops, pills, and several surgical procedures can ward off fluid build-up and/or drain the eye. Glaucoma usually has no symptoms and can only be detected through an eye exam.

A number of factors can cause the body to become shorter and stiffer with age.

Psychosocial adjustment to decline in vision, however, does not go unnoticed in late adulthood (Davis & others, 1995). Psychosocial factors such as depression, satisfaction with life, social support, self-esteem, stress, and motivation are all related to age-related decline in visual capabilities.

At any rate, with recent improvements in ophthalmology and optical surgery, the declining ability of the human eye need not greatly affect vision in older age (with the single exception of poor night vision, which hampers driving).

Does society have the responsibility to provide transportation for people when it takes away their licenses? If not, does government have any responsibility to help such people? What's your view? To widen your understanding, you might interview several young adults who will bear the brunt of the cost for elderly transportation, and some older adults who will be isolated without it.

Hearing

Decline in hearing ability may be a more serious problem than decline in vision. However, we seem to be much less willing to wear hearing aids than we are to wear glasses, perhaps because we rely on vision more.

There is evidence to support that older adults have more difficulty understanding spoken language when background noise is present (Tun, 1998). Spoken sentences were presented to older and younger adults in quiet; and with different levels of background noise. Both groups performed similarly in quiet; however, the older adults could not tolerate as much background noise as the younger adults. These findings suggest that older adults have more difficulty inhibiting distracting noises which therefore impacts their ability to process speech.

Speech

A common perception about older adults is that they tend to talk about more off-topic and irrelevant details than younger adults. James and associates (1998) investigated this perception and found that when talking about autobiographical information, the older adults spoke more off-topic than the younger adults. This was not true, however, for describing pictures. James and associates concluded that older people valued communicating about their life experiences and, therefore, produced more speech. The relative unimportance of the pictures resulted in the older adults producing more precise speech.

Smell

Some atrophy of olfactory fibers in the nose occurs with age. When artificial amplifiers are added, however, the ability of the older people to recognize foods by smell is greatly improved.

An Informed VIEW   *When Should the Elderly Lose Their License?*

By 2020, up to one out of every five Americans will be 65 or older, and the vast majority will possess a driver's license. This is of concern because statistics show that accidents caused by drivers over the age of 75 equal or surpass those of teenagers, who have been considered the most dangerous group of drivers. A number of states are moving to monitor older drivers more aggressively. However, in those cases where a license is denied or revoked, the drivers may find themselves stranded without crucial transportation (Harvard Health Letter, 1999).

If you would like to have a more informed opinion on this issue, you might want to read one of the articles on the subject referenced in this chapter (e.g., Harvard Health Letter).

You might also wish to learn more about it by going to our web site at http://www.mhhe.com/dacey5.

Taste

Studying the effects of aging on the sense of taste is difficult because taste itself is so dependent on smell. About 95 percent of taste derives from olfactory nerves. It is clear, however, that there is decline in tasting ability among the elderly (Cowart & others, 1994). Whereas young adults have an average of 250 taste buds, elderly adults have an average of no more than 100.

Other Body Systems

Included in the category of body systems are the skeletal system, skin, teeth, hair, and locomotion (ability to move about).

Skeletal System

Although the skeleton is fully formed by age 24, changes in stature can occur for many reasons. Because the entire skeletal system becomes tighter and stiffer, the aged frequently have a small loss of height. Diseases of the bone system such as arthritis are probably the result of changes in the collagen in the bones with age.

Diseases such as osteoporosis can be very crippling. In this regard there is good news. Studies at Tufts University indicate strong evidence that if people over 50 (men as well as women) increase their daily intake of calcium to 1,200 milligrams and their vitamin D intake to about 500 international units, they can substantially decrease their risk of osteoporosis (Howe, 1997).

Skin

Collagen is also a major factor in changes in the skin because continuous stretching of collagen causes it to lengthen and the skin begins to lose its elasticity with age. The skin becomes coarser and darker, and wrinkles begin to appear. Darkness forms under the eyes, more because of a growing paleness of the skin in the rest of the face than because of any change in the under-eye pigmentation. Years of exposure to the sun also contribute to these effects.

Another important cause of the change in skin texture has to do with the typical weight loss among the elderly. They have a tendency to lose fat cells, which decreases the pressure against the skin itself. This tends to cause sagging, folds, and wrinkles in the skin.

Teeth

The loss of teeth is certainly one physical aspect that may occur in older adults. Even when corrective measures are taken, the surgery involved and the adjustment to dentures have a major impact on the person's self-image. In most cases, the loss of teeth is more the result of gum disease than decay of the teeth themselves. Education, the use of fluorides, the use of new brushing techniques, and daily flossing likely will make this aspect of aging far less of a problem in the future.

Hair

Probably the most significant signature of old age is change of the hair. Thinness, baldness, grayness, stiffness, and a growing amount of facial hair in women are all indications of growing old. Hormonal changes are undoubtedly the main culprit here. Improvements in hair coloring techniques and hair implants may make it possible to avoid having "old-looking" hair (for those to whom this is important).

Locomotion

It is generally assumed that the decrease in locomotion by older adults is due to aging. A recent study, however, suggests that although older people do indeed walk more slowly, the pattern of coordination between their limbs remains essentially the same as for younger adults. In fact, a study by Sharpe and associates (1997) indicates positive results for older adults who participate in bi-weekly levels of physical activity. Compared to non-active adults, these men and women reported overall improvements in their physical functioning.

Areas of improvement included walking speed, mental outlook, muscle strengthening, pain reduction, and increased flexibility.

Health

Illness is not a major cause of death until one reaches the thirties, and only then among African-American females. This is probably because they generally receive fewer preventive health services, and because medical treatment is frequently delayed until the later stages of disease. Not until adults reach the age of 40 does ill health, as opposed to accidents, homicide, and suicide, become the major cause of death. Arteriosclerotic heart disease is the major killer after the age of 40 in all age, sex, and race groups.

Another major cause is "cerebrovascular accidents" such as strokes. Due to a new treatment, victims who receive a clot-busting drug treatment known as tissue plasminogen activator (TPA) in time have a much better chance of surviving and recovering from the effects of a stroke. Symptoms that indicate need for a quick administration of the therapy (call 911) include paralysis of part of the body, drooping of facial muscles, and/or impairment of speech or motor abilities.

Alcoholism

For adults aged 60 or older, both continuation of problem drinking and late-onset problem drinking are known to occur. Unfortunately, alcohol abuse is often difficult to recognize in elderly adults, who may exhibit conditions related to aging in general. For those taking medications, alcohol may cause them to suffer from negative reactions or may interfere in the aging process.

Prostate Cancer

Until recently, one of the leading causes of death among men, prostate cancer, was seen as unrelated to lifestyle (Harvard Men's Health Watch, 1997). New research has discovered links between a number of behaviors and the disease. These dangerous behaviors are:

- Eating excessive dietary fat (red meat is the leading culprit).

- Drinking too much alcohol (those who had more than 22 drinks a week had a 40 percent greater risk than light drinkers, and for those who had 57 or more, the risk was 90 percent higher).

- Smoking (even light smoking is risky).

- Too little exercise (those who burned 4,000 calories per week cut their risk in half).

Alzheimer's Disease

Alzheimer's disease is one of the two most common forms of dementia that affect the elderly, and is probably the single greatest source of affliction and debilitation. For example, more than half of those over 85 (the fastest growing age cohort) suffer from the disease (Shute, 1997). On the other hand, a study of men in their 90s and over 100 found that few of them have the affliction (Lauman, 1999). Apparently those who have Altzheimer's in their 80s tend to die from it, and those who live longer are more likely to be blessed with healthy brains.

The German neurologist Alois Alzheimer discovered the disease in 1906, but it did not gain attention until the 1970s. Researchers have announced that they have found a gene that is implicated in the cause. This does not, however, mean they have found a cure for it. Alzheimer's is difficult to diagnose and even more difficult to treat.

Relatively few of its symptoms respond to any type of treatment, and then only in the earliest stages. Alzheimer's disease usually follows a 6- to 20-year course (Eastman, 1997). Symptoms include the deterioration of one's ability to learn, handle complex tasks, remember how to travel around familiar places, follow conversations, remember ordinary words, control behavior, or perform basic tasks of daily life (Costa, 1997).

Alzheimer's differs from what is called multi-infarct dementia in several ways. Those who exhibit signs of multi-infarct dementia are likely to remain stable for long periods of time or show signs of improvement, then suddenly develop new symptoms. The symptoms associated with Alzheimer's begin slowly and become steadily worse.

The normal brain consists of billions of nerve cells (neurons), which convey messages to one another chemically by way of branchlike structures called dendrites and axons. Neuron groups generate specific chemical transmitters that travel between cells at the synapses. Although Alzheimer's victims look normal externally, their brains are undergoing severe changes. Brain autopsies unmask severe damage, abnormalities, and even death of neurons. Once neurons die, they can never be replaced. Current research on Alzheimer's, however, is developing medications that might actually preserve the health of nerve cells before they die. Researchers hope one day to be able to identify very early, presymptomatic cases of the disease and treat the individual with these medications in order to prevent the appearance of symptoms of the disease (Eastman, 1997).

Several theories have been put forth to explain the causes of Alzheimer's. Some theorists believe that a virus causes the disease, whereas others think that environmental factors are involved. A popular theory is that an overabundance of metal accumulation in the neurons, mainly aluminum, causes it. Some dispute this theory because although we all ingest aluminum, our bodies reject it by refusing to digest it. There is also some indication that Alzheimer's burns holes in the cells, thus impairing their function. Administering large doses of vitamin E may help prevent the disease and may slow its progress. All of these possibilities are currently being studied scientifically.

It now appears that Alzheimer's may be transmitted genetically, because we know that a sibling of an Alzheimer's patient has a 50 percent chance of contracting the disorder. Almost all persons with Down syndrome, a genetic disorder, will develop Alzheimer's disease if they live long enough. It may be that a defective gene makes a person likely to get it if environmental conditions are present.

It is also known that Alzheimer's does not discriminate on the basis of ethnicity (Exploring the Environment, 1996). Women are somewhat more likely to contract the disease, but to date it is not known why, and some research has shown that being female is not a risk factor.

The president of the Alzheimer's Association reports that the cost of caring for an Alzheimer's patient in the home is $18,000 to $20,000 per year, whereas nursing home care may reach anywhere from $40,000 to $70,000 per year (Alzheimer's Association, 1999). The financial burden is usually placed on the patient's family, because neither Medicare nor most private health care insurance covers the cost of the long-term care these patients need. As a result, seven out of ten Alzheimer's patients live at home and nearly 75 percent of homecare is provided by family and friends (Alzheimer's Association, 1999). Another alternative to chronic care is the adult-care facility. These programs provide help with daily tasks such as feeding, washing, toileting, and exercising.

Until recently the outlook has been bleak for patients and families suffering with Alzheimer's. Breakthroughs appear to be on the horizon on three fronts (Eastman, 2000):

- New ways to combat key enzymes that contribute to Alzheimer's.

- New understanding of how to immunize people against a protein that becomes abnormal.

- The emergence of human gene therapy capable of vitalizing damaged brain cells.

Two books that offer many suggestions on how to care for Alzheimer's patients at home are: (1) Carly Hellen's *Alzheimer's disease: Activity-focused care,* Butterworth-Heinemann, Woburn, MA. (2) The Alzheimer's Association's *Activity programming for persons with dementia,* Chicago, IL.

Not all the news is good, however. A recent study (NIA News, 2000) found that low-dose regimen of the steroid prednisone, an anti-inflammatory drug, is not effective in the treatment of Alzheimer's disease. The study, one of the first from a number of clinical trials trying to determine the usefulness of anti-inflammatory agents to prevent or treat Alzheimer's, suggests that not all classes of such drugs may slow the rate at which people develop the disease or suffer cognitive decline.

If you desire further information on what is known about the disease, write to the Alzheimer's Association, 70 East Lake Street, Suite 600, Chicago, Illinois, 60601. You can also go to the National Institute on Aging, Alzheimer's Disease Education And Referral (ADEAR) Center web site at www.alzheimers.org.

The Gastric System

For years doctors have assumed that digestive problems of the elderly have been the result of a decline in the secretion of gastric acids. Reasoning that the elderly seem to get ulcers as readily as younger people, Hurwitz and associates (1997) tested a group of 250 elderly and found only a small percent to be low secreters. This is good news for older adults because it means they do not have to worry about absorption rates of the medications they need to take, among other concerns.

The Relationship between Physical and Mental Health

In their study of the general health of 1,139 elderly persons living in an urban community, Gerson and associates (1987) made a number of interesting findings:

- A strong relationship exists between physical and mental health.

- Married men have better health than unmarried men (married women are not healthier than unmarried women). This may be because their wives take care of them, or because they feel responsible to their families to maintain their health.

- Social resources are strongly associated with mental health for women, but less so for men. Probably women are more likely than men to use their social resources to help them maintain their mental health. Many men hate to admit to their friends that they are having a mental disturbance, because it is not considered "manly."

- Economic resources are clearly related to mental health. As previously pointed out, this is especially true for African-American women.

An Applied VIEW

New Research Shatters a Long-Standing Belief about Neurons

According to the National Institute on Aging (NIA, 1999), scientists have always thought that neurons were formed only during the fetal period and for a short time after birth. Once a person had his or her full complement of neurons, that was that—the adult human body could not create new ones.

This past year that belief changed dramatically. Researchers discovered that the human brain does indeed retain the ability to generate neurons throughout life (Eriksson, 1998). In this study, cancer patients received injections of a compound called BrdU, which was used for diagnostic purposes. The BrdU was incorporated into the cells' DNA as they divided. Upon examining brain tissue from the patients after death, the investigators found . . . that these adult brains contained dividing neuronal stem cells. By demonstrating that new neurons can be generated in the adult brain, it may now be possible to stimulate intrinsic brain repair mechanisms to replace neurons and glial cells lost through age, trauma, and disease. Alzheimer's and Parkinson's diseases, strokes, and spinal cord injuries are all characterized by neuronal dysfunction and death. Finding ways to stimulate the formation of new brain and spinal cord neurons may one day lead to novel therapeutic approaches for these and other conditions.

Source: NIA (1999). *Progress report and Alzheimer's disease.* Washington, D.C.: United States Department of Health and Human Services, NIH Publication No. 99-4664.

An Applied View

Gateball and the Japanese Elderly

Gateball, developed in post–World War II Japan, is a team sport combining elements of golf and croquet. It employs strategies that exercise both mind and body. Although the object is to score the most points, a great deal of emphasis is placed on the individual's contributions to the team as opposed to individual achievement.

In addition to these benefits, gateball also provides a social outlet, building relationships around a common interest. Gateball has become immensely popular among "silver agers," as older people are called by the Japanese. In a modern, crowded, industrial country like Japan, with early retirement and the highest life expectancy in the world, gateball provides a way for seniors to continue their lifelong pattern of group participation in something worthwhile.

Observations of gateball players in action found people who share information, laughter, and a relaxed sense of belonging. When a player who hadn't been there for some time reappeared, he or she was warmly welcomed back. Exchange of food occurs routinely on the break, and people often encourage others to take some home with them.

In America, this kind of community spirit among seniors is evidenced in some sports (such as golf and bowling), but the stereotype of the elderly person in the rocking chair remains pervasive. Sports provide a means by which older people can remain healthy as well as connected to other people. It is another important lesson we might glean from Japanese culture.

Recent findings further refute the stereotype that elderly people are less health conscious (Anderson, 1996). In fact, elderly patients tend to worry about well-being more than younger patients, but what they worry about is not necessarily of concern. For example, elderly people may worry about getting enough fiber in their diet and disregard the very real danger of falling.

Health and Retirement

Muller and Boaz (1988) stated: "Many studies of the retirement decision have found that poor health increases the probability of retirement. Yet doubts have been expressed whether self-reported deterioration of health is a genuine cause of retirement, rather than a socially acceptable excuse" (p. 52). These researchers studied the actual health status of retirees and found support for the idea that the majority of those who say they are retiring for health reasons are telling the truth. Research conducted by Smith and Moen (1998) indicates that the decision to retire is influenced by the retiree's spouse. Although most retirees view their spouse's influence as a major factor, spouses frequently assume their influence has little effect.

Health unquestionably affects the physical abilities of adults across the age range. Yet it is also clear that social circumstances are the main factor in health in the older years. Thus, the healthiness of adults appears to be more a result of the cultural conditions in which they find themselves than of their age.

Appearance

All of the physical factors treated earlier have an effect on the person's self-concept, but none has a stronger impact than physical appearance. Appearance is of great importance in the United States. A youthful appearance matters a great deal and to women more than to men. Females are affected by the "double standard" of aging— a somewhat overweight, greying man is "distinguished-looking," whereas a woman with the same traits is "growing old." Thus women are more likely to use diet, exercise, clothing, and cosmetics to maintain their youthful appearance. Nevertheless, significant changes in physical appearance occur with age that cannot be avoided.

As you can see from the data presented in this chapter, a certain amount of physical decline happens in later life, but it does not occur until most people are quite advanced in age. And with the new medical technologies and marked trend toward adopting more healthy living styles, you can expect to see a much more capable elderly population. Will this happy news also be true for cognitive development?

Guided Review

6. Physical abilities such as reaction time are not only affected by the aging process but also by motivations, depression, anxiety, _____ _____, response style, and ageism.

7. All five senses decline with age but hearing ability may be a more serious problem than _____, because people are less likely to wear a hearing aid than they are _____.

8. Because of continuous stretching of _____, the skin begins to lengthen and lose its elasticity with age.

9. One developing breakthrough in treatments for Alzheimer's disease, a serious mental loss in some elderly persons, is in the discovery of new ways to combat key (germs, enzymes).

10. Research indicates that Alzheimer's disease may be transmitted (genetically, socially), because we know that a (grandparent, sibling) of an Alzheimer's patient has a 50 percent chance of contracting the disorder.

11. When it comes to appearance in aging, there is a _____ _____ for men and for women.

Cognitive Development

In chapter 15, we described the changes in intelligence that develop across the adult lifespan, focusing on middle age. In this chapter we take a closer look at old age. The major question is whether a significant decline in cognitive competence tends to occur as we become elderly. A review of the research on this question reveals a serious conflict. Salthouse (1990) stated it well:

> Results from psychometric tests and experimental tasks designed to assess cognitive ability frequently reveal rather substantial age-related declines in the range from 20 to 70 years of age.... On the other hand, adults in their 60s and 70s are seldom perceived to be less cognitively competent than adults in their 20s and 30s, and in fact, many of the most responsible and demanding leadership positions in society are routinely held by late middle-aged or older adults. (p. 310)

Cognitive Ability in the Elderly: Tests versus Observations

So wherein lies the truth—in the results of tests, or in our observations of actual performance? As we said, the answer is not simple. What factors could account for this discrepancy? Currently there are four hypotheses, each of which play a part (Salthouse, 1990):

- *Differences in type of cognition.* Intelligence tests tend to measure specific bands of cognitive ability, whereas assessments of real-life activities probably also include noncognitive capacities, such as personality traits. Thus some aspects of IQ may decline without causing lowered performance on the job, for example.

- *Differences in the representativeness of the individuals or observations.* Many examples exist of elderly persons who can perform admirably even into their nineties, but do these individuals really represent the average elderly person? Probably not. It is also probable that only the most competent individuals are able to survive in such demanding situations. Those who are less competent will have dropped out of the competition at an earlier age. Therefore, when

Answers

6. response strategies 7. vision, glasses 8. collagen 9. enzymes 10. genetically, sibling 11. double standard

An Applied VIEW

A Comparison of Physical Abilities

One of the best ways of comprehending adult development is to do a miniseries of experiments of your own. In this activity, you can compare the physical development of friends and relatives with just a few simple pieces of equipment. Pick at least three people in at least two age groups. The results might surprise you. You may find that you need to alter the instructions of the following experiments to make it more convenient for you to do the study. This is perfectly all right, as long as you make sure that each test is the same for every person who takes it. The greater the variety of the adults you enlist in the study, in factors such as age, sex, and religion, the more interesting your results will be.

Muscular strength. Several of the following tests require a heavy table. Simply have each subject grasp a leg of the table with one hand and raise the leg off the ground 3 inches. Subjects who can hold it up 3 inches for 30 seconds have succeeded in step 1. Now have them try to hold it up another 3 inches, and if they succeed they get credit for step 2 (each step must be done for 30 seconds). In step 3 they must hold it at a height of 1 foot, in step 4 they must hold it at a height of 1½ feet, and in step 5 at a height of 2 feet. Record one point for each step successfully completed.

Vision. The subject should be seated at the table with chin resting on forearms and forearms resting on the table. Set a magazine at a distance of 2 feet and ask the subject to read two lines. Next 3 feet, then 4 feet, then 5 feet, and finally at 6 feet. One point is given for each step.

Hearing. The subject is seated with his or her back to the table. You will need some instrument that makes the same level of noise for the same period of time. For example, a portable radio might be turned on a brief moment and turned back off, each time at the same volume. A clicker might be used. Whatever you use, make the standard noise at 2 feet behind the subject and have him or her raise a hand when the sound is heard. Then make the sound at 4 feet, 6 feet, 10 feet, and 20 feet. You may need to vary these distances, depending on the volume of the instrument you are using.

Be sure to vary the intervals between the noises that you make, so that you can be sure the subject is really hearing the noise when you make it. Give points for each appropriate response.

Smell, Taste, and Touch. For these three tests, you will need five cups of equal size. The cups should hold milk, cola, soft ice cream, yogurt, and applesauce. Each food should be chilled to approximately the same temperature. Blindfold subjects and ask them to tell you what the five substances are.

Reaction Time. For this test you will need three squares, three circles, three triangles; one of each is 1 inch high, 2 inches high, and 3 inches high. Make them of cardboard, plastic, or wood. Arrange the nine figures in random order in front of the subject. Tell the subject that when you call out the name of one of the figures (e.g., a large square), he or she is to put a finger on it as quickly as possible. Call out the name of one of the figures, and time the response. Repeat this test five times, calling out a different figure each time, and compute the total time required for the five trials.

Reaction Time. Again arrange the nine pieces randomly in front of the subject. You will call out either the shape ("circle") or a size ("middle-size"). The subject puts the three circles or the three middle-size pieces in a pile as quickly as possible. Repeat this experiment five times, using a different designator each time, and compute the total time the task requires.

Health. Ask subjects to carefully count the number of times they have been in the hospital. Give them one point if they have been hospitalized 10 times or more, two points for 5 through 9 times, three points for 3 times, four points for no more than 1 time, five points if they have never been hospitalized for any reason (pregnancy should not be counted).

Health. Ask subjects to carefully remember how many times they have visited a doctor within the past year. Give one point for 4 or more times, two points for 3 times, three points for 2 times, four points for 1 time, five points for no visits at all.

Compare the scores for each test for persons within the age groups you have chosen. Do you see any patterns? Are the results of aging evident? What other conclusions can you draw?

---

we examine the abilities of successful older persons, we may be studying only the "cream of the crop." Finally, it seems likely that observed competence represents only one type of cognitive ability (balancing the company's books, reading music), whereas intelligence testing involves several (verbal, math, reasoning, and other abilities).

- *Different standards of evaluation.* Most cognitive tests tend to push individuals to their limits of ability. Assessments of real-life tasks, those with which people are quite familiar (such as reading the newspaper), may require a lower standard of testing.

- *Different amounts of experience.* Doing well on an intelligence test requires one to employ traits that are not used every day, such as assembling blocks so that they resemble certain patterns. The skills assessed in real-life situations are more likely to be those the individual has practiced for years. For example, driving ability may remain high if the person continues to drive regularly as she ages. Young adults may type well because they have greater dexterity, but older typists may do just as well because they are better able to anticipate the text they are typing.

Each of these hypotheses seeks to explain the discrepancy between tested ability and actual performance as being the result of faulty research techniques. Many other writers have suggested that perhaps the elderly really are inferior in cognitive competence to younger persons but that they find ways to compensate for their lost cognitive abilities. Thus older persons are able to maintain performance levels even as ability is waning. Unfortunately, no one has suggested how such compensation might be achieved, so this hypothesis is doubtful.

Another aspect of cognitive decline has proven of great interest to psychologists. It is referred to as terminal drop.

Terminal Drop

Terminal drop The period of from a few weeks up to two years before a person's death, during which his or her intelligence is presumed to decline rapidly.

Birren was the first to discuss **terminal drop** (1964). He defined it as the period preceding the person's death, from a few weeks up to two years prior. This research looks at the relationship, not between intelligence and age (which is the number of years from birth till the time of testing), but between intelligence and survivorship (which is the number of years from the time of testing until death). The hypothesis is that the person's perception, consciously or unconsciously, of impending death may cause the decline in intelligence. This perception causes the person to begin withdrawing from the world. Consequently, performance on an intelligence test drops markedly.

According to Birren,

> The individual himself may or may not be aware in himself of diffuse changes in mood, in mental functioning, or in the way his body responds. Terminal [drop] may be paced by a disease initially remote from the nervous system, such as a cancer of the stomach. Thereafter, over a series of months, a rapid sequence of changes might be observed in overt behavior or in measured psychological characteristics of the individual. It is as though at this point the physiology of the individual had started on a new phase, that the organism is unable to stop (p. 280).

Some researchers have questioned whether terminal drop pervades all cognitive abilities or is restricted to specific ones. In a study designed to answer this question, White and Cunningham (1988) found terminal drop to apply to a shorter period than five years and to be more restricted than was previously thought. They reached the following conclusions:

> Only vocabulary scores for those who died at age 70 or less and within two years of testing were affected by terminal drop. . . . Thus the terminal drop phenomenon may be limited to abilities that typically are relatively unaffected by age, such as vocabulary or other verbal abilities. Furthermore, the effects may be restricted to a time period much closer to death than had been originally proposed (p. 141).

Small and Backman (1997) studied the effects of terminal drop among the very old (ages 75 to 95). They found that ". . . episodic memory and verbal skill may be particularly sensitive in predicting such effects" (p. 309).

Researchers have come to several different conclusions concerning the effect of age on intelligence level.

One final warning: Although virtually all studies described here use IQ tests to measure intelligence, the two are not identical. IQ involves school-related abilities, whereas intelligence is made up of these and many other abilities (e.g., spatial ability and "street smarts"). It is not possible at present to discern how much this discrepancy affects the research. Another mental trait that is hard to study, but is even more vital to understand and cultivate, is creativity.

Creativity

In chapter 15, we concluded that quantity of creative production probably drops in old age but that quality of production may not. This is based on studies of actual productivity. But what about potential for production? Might it be that the elderly are capable of great creativity but that, as with IQ, factors like motivation and opportunity prevent them from fulfilling this ability? That is the question addressed by the next set of studies we'll discuss.

Cross-Sectional Studies of Creative Productivity

The first large-scale study to look at the creative productivity of typical people at various ages who are still alive was completed by Alpaugh and associates (Alpaugh & Birren, 1977). They administered two batteries of creativity tests to 111 schoolteachers aged 20 to 83. Their findings supported the idea that creativity does decline with age. One major criticism of their research is that the tests they used are probably not equally valid for all age groups. The younger subjects are more likely to have had practice with these types of materials than the older ones. For example, the study of creativity is relatively new, so the tests used to measure it have been designed recently. Thus those who attended school more recently are more likely to have encountered such tests than those who graduated many years ago. Such familiarity would provide an advantage to the younger subjects in the study.

Jaquish and Ripple (1980) attempted to evaluate the effects of aging while avoiding the problem of using age-related materials. These researchers gathered

An Applied View — *Ways to Keep Memory Functioning*

Memory loss is one of the signs of aging that causes people the most concern. A 50-year-old may worry about forgetfulness, whereas a 70-year-old may fear that this forgetfulness is actually a sign of Alzheimer's disease. In a society that is full of information, such as written words, television, and computer technology, it is not surprising that people feel a sense of overload, and a sense of fear when they can't remember where they parked their car. What may be surprising, however, are the recent findings that memory doesn't really diminish over the years.

Although brain changes do occur with age, these changes do not necessarily mean that memory loss will be the result. Rather, it simply takes older people longer to learn, and requires more effort to store memory for quick recall later. It is the stresses and distractions in the environment that keep people from retrieving details more easily. In the right environment, one that includes physical and mind-stimulating activities and reduced stress, the memory of healthy people in their seventies and eighties can expand.

Photographs can aid memory, but also can induce false

memory in older adults (ages 60 to 75). Angell and associates (1997) found that viewing photographs can prompt better recall in both older and younger adults (ages 16 to 22). However, older adults were more likely to "remember" an event in which they had not participated but only had viewed in a photograph.

Studies have shown that people who feel good about themselves and who feel a sense of control in their lives are better prepared to maintain their mental abilities. Self-help classes for memory improvement are one way in which older people can take an active role in strengthening their memory capacities. Although some people believe that drugs or herbs can improve memory, there is no convincing proof that substances work. Taking the initiative to exercise their minds, older people may still occasionally forget where they put their slippers, but they won't soon forget the essentials.

Research indicates that the time right after retirement can be a period of creative growth, as the individual turns from the demands of a work schedule to the opportunities offered by an artistic endeavor.

data on six age groups across the lifespan: 10 to 12 years (61 people); 13 to 17 years (71 people); 18 to 25 years (70 people); 26 to 39 years (58 people); 40 to 60 years (51 people); and 61 to 84 years (39 people). The study had a total of 350 subjects.

The definition of creativity in this study was restricted to the concepts of fluency, flexibility, and originality; these are collectively known as divergent thinking abilities (see Parkhurst, 1999, for a discussion of definitions of creativity). These three traits

Reseach indicates that the elderly years can be a period of creative growth, as the individual turns from the demands of family and work to the opportunities offered by an artistic endeavor.

were measured through the use of an auditory exercise, which was recorded on cassette. Known as the Sounds and Images Test, it elicits responses to the "weird" sounds presented on the tape. Responses are then scored according to the three traits of divergent thinking. The researchers believe that this test is so unusual that no age group is likely to have had more experience with it than any other.

A number of interesting findings have resulted from this study, as you can see in table 17.1. On all three measures of divergent thinking, the scores generally increased slightly across the first five age groups. Scores for the 40- to 60-year-old group increased significantly, whereas scores for the 61- to 84-year-old group decreased significantly below the scores of any of the younger age groups. Furthermore, when decline in divergent thinking did occur, it was more pronounced in quantity than in quality. That is, greater age differences occurred in fluency (a measure of quantity) than in originality (a measure of quality). Finally, it is not known to what extent the oldest subjects were affected by hearing loss, particularly of high and low tones. This could be an alternative explanation of the findings for this oldest group.

Probably the most important finding of the study had to do with the relationship between divergent thinking and self-esteem, which was measured by the Coopersmith Self-Esteem Inventory. Table 17.1 indicates that self-esteem follows a pattern quite similar to the other three traits.

Of special interest is the relationship between self-esteem and divergent thinking for the oldest group: The correlations were moderately high in every case. This indicates that self-esteem may have a positive effect on creative abilities over the years, or that creativity may enhance self-esteem, or both. Jaquish and Ripple (1980) concluded that

> There is much more plasticity in adult development than has been traditionally assumed. Such an interpretation should find a hospitable audience among those people concerned with educational intervention. If the creative abilities of older adults were to be realized in productivity, it would be difficult to overestimate the importance of the formation of new attitudes of society, teachers in continuing adult education programs, and in the older adults themselves (p. 152).

The Stages of Life during Which Creativity May Best Be Cultivated

In this final section we present Dacey's theory (1989b) that there are certain critical periods in life during which creative ability can be cultivated most effectively. Its relevance to the study of late adulthood will be obvious. Table 17.2 presents a list of these periods for males and females.

TABLE 17.1 MEANS FOR DIVERGENT THINKING AND SELF-ESTEEM SCORES

Age Group	Fluency Mean	Flexibility Mean	Originality Mean	Self-Esteem Mean
18–25	31	19	19	34
26–39	30	18	19	37
40–60	36	21	20	38
61–84	22	15	15	32

From G. Jaquish and R. E. Ripple, "Cognitive Creative Abilities Across the Adult Life Span" in *Human Development*. Copyright © 1980. S. Karger AG, Basel, Switzerland. Reprinted by permission of the publisher.

TABLE 17.2 PEAK PERIODS OF LIFE DURING WHICH CREATIVITY MAY MOST READILY BE CULTIVATED

For Males	For Females
1. 0–5 years old	0–5 years old
2. 11–14 years old	10–13 years old
3. 18–20 years old	18–20 years old
4. 29–31 years old	29–31 years old
5. 40–45 years old	40 (37?)–45 years old
6. 60–65 years old	60–65 years old

Reprinted with the permission of Lexington Books, an imprint of The Free Press, a Division of Simon & Schuster, Inc., from *Fundamentals of Creative Thinking* by John S. Dacey. Copyright © 1989 by Lexington Books.

The basic premise of this theory is that a person's inherent creativity can blossom best during a period of crisis and change. The six periods chosen in table 17.2 are ages at which most people experience stress due to life changes.

The table presents a new theory, and thus it must be considered speculative. Nevertheless some direct evidence supports it (Esquivel, 1995; Hennessey, 1995). Some excellent research from the fields of personality and cognitive development also indicates that these periods are more volatile than any others.

Included in the theory is the concept that major gains in creative performance are less likely with each succeeding period. That is, what happens to the person in the early years is far more influential than what happens in the later years. The older people become, the less likely they are to have a sudden burst of highly creative production.

The Sixth Peak Period

Evidence for the first five peak periods has been presented earlier in this book. The first period is mentioned in chapter 7 (although not called creativity per se), the second and third in chapter 12, the fourth in chapter 14, and the fifth in chapter 16. The rationale for the sixth period, from 60 to 65, is reviewed here.

For most men and for a growing number of women, this is the period in which retirement occurs. Even if a woman has not been in the labor force, she has many adjustments to make because of her husband's retirement. Thus most adults are faced with a major adjustment of self-concept at this time in their lives.

Although some do not adjust well and begin withdrawing from society, others take advantage of the change to pursue creative goals that had previously been impossible for them. Obviously a majority of the "young old" (the new term for those who are aged 60 to 70) do not suddenly become creative, but a substantial number do. Of the several thousand highly productive people he studied, Lehman (1953, 1962) found more than 100, or almost 5 percent, whose major productivity began in the years after 60.

This is not to say that maintaining or increasing creative performance in one's later years is easy. There are inherent problems that are not readily overcome. Psychologist B. F. Skinner (1983), who had a 60-year-long career of highly creative achievement, stated that productivity is difficult for the elderly because they tend to lose interest in work, find it hard to start working, and work more slowly:

> It is easy to attribute this change to them, but we should not overlook a change in their world. For motivation, read reinforcement. In old age, behavior is not so strongly reinforced. Biological aging weakens reinforcing consequences. Behavior is more and more likely to be followed by aches and pains and quick fatigue. Things tend to become "not worth doing" in the sense that the aversive consequences exact too high a price. Positive reinforcers become less common and less powerful. Poor vision closes off the world of art, faulty hearing the enjoyment of highly fidelitous music. Foods do not taste as good, and erogenous tissues grow less sensitive. Social reinforcers are attenuated. Interests and tastes are shared with a smaller number of people (p. 28).

It is increasingly clear that creativity may blossom at any age. This theory of "the peak periods of creative growth" is not meant to disparage that fact. Solid evidence indicates, however, that the best opportunities lie in the six periods identified by the theory. Are there also periods in the development of gender roles in later life that have special importance? of sexuality? of family relations? of work and retirement? We'll examine these questions in the next chapter.

Wisdom

One final point: What is the relationship between intelligence and creativity, and how do they relate to the highest level of human cognition, **wisdom?** In table 17.3, Robert Sternberg's (1990) comparison of the three is presented. He makes a fascinating comparison of wisdom, intelligence and creativity, for each of the relevant aspects of life: knowledge; mental processes; intellectual styles; personality; motivation; and environmental context (see chapter 2).

As you can see in table 17.3, the phrase "going beyond" typifies the concept of creativity. Robert Kegan, in his groundbreaking book *In Over Our Heads* (1994), suggests that as the average lifespan continues to increase, we will be "going beyond" more and more, simply because more people live to old age:

> A hundred years ago the average American lived to the middle forties. Today the average American lives more than twenty years longer, an entire generation longer for each individual life. What might the individual generate given an additional generation to live? My candidate: a qualitatively new order of consciousness. I suggest we are gradually seeing more adults working on a qualitatively different order of consciousness than did adults one hundred years ago because we live twenty or more years longer than we used to (p. 352).

Baltes and Staudinger (2000) offer a somewhat different view of the concept of wisdom; they find it to be ". . . an expert knowledge system concerning the fundamental pragmatics of life. These include knowledge and judgment about the meaning and conduct of life and the orchestration of human development toward excellence while attending conjointly to personal and collective well-being" (p. 122). The phrase "tend jointly to personal and collective well-being" really means the same thing as the concept of "going beyond" employed above by Sternberg and Kegan. Baltes and Staudinger suggested that wisdom is the result of five factors:

Wisdom   The superior insight and judgment that can only come from experience.

Two books that delve into cognitive functioning in old age are: (1) Sarton's *As we are now.* New York: Norton. A novel in the form of the diary of a retired schoolteacher. (2) Skinner and Vaughan's *Enjoy old age: A program of self-management.* New York: Norton. In this book, the grandfather of behaviorism explains how to use behavior modification to better handle the problems of aging.

TABLE 17.3 SUMMARY, SIMPLIFIED COMPARISON AMONG WISDOM, INTELLIGENCE, AND CREATIVITY

	Construct		
Aspect	**Wisdom**	**Intelligence**	**Creativity**
Knowledge	Understanding of its presuppositions and meanings as well as its limitations	Recall, analysis, and use	Going beyond what is available
Processes	Understanding of what is automatic and why	Automatization of procedures	Applied to novel tasks
Primary intellectual style	Judicial	Executive	Legislative
Personality	Understanding of ambiguity and obstacles	Eliminating ambiguity and overcoming obstacles within conventional framework	Tolerance of ambiguity and redefinition of obstacles
Motivation known	To understand what is known and what it means	To know and to use what is known	To go beyond what is
Environmental context	Appreciation in environment of depth of understanding	Appreciation in environment of extent and breadth of understanding	Appreciation in environment of going beyond what is currently understood

From *Wisdom* by R. J. Sternberg. Copyright © 1990, Cambridge University Press, New York. Reprinted with the permission of Cambridge University Press.

- Intelligence, including both fluid and crystallized types.
- Personality traits, such as openness to experience, generativity (see Erikson's theory in chapter 16), and a continuing willingness to meet life's challenges (Bandura, 1997).
- The personality-intelligence interface, which includes creativity and social intelligence.
- Life experience.
- Age (by and large, the older the person, the greater the wisdom).

Guided Review

12. Discrepancies between the results of tests and our observations of cognitive abilities may be due to differences in type of cognition, differences in the representation of the individuals or observations, different standards of _____, and different amounts of experience.
13. Training can increase abilities in older adults. However, about two years before death, a _____ _____ in mental functioning often occurs.
14. It is suggested that a decline in intelligence in the later years may be caused by the person's _____ of impending death.
15. Jaquish and Ripple found in their studies on creativity that there is a correlation between _____ and creativity.
16. Dacey sees creativity as blossoming during periods of _____ and _____.
17. Wisdom is different from both creativity and intelligence, in that it has a focus on _____.
18. Baltes and Staudinger suggest that wisdom is the result of intelligence, personality, the intelligence-personality interaction, life experience, and _____.

Answers

12. evaluation (or testing)   13. terminal drop   14. perception   15. self-esteem   16. crisis, change   17. understanding   18. age

CONCLUSION & SUMMARY

At the beginning of this chapter we asked, "Must growing old mean decline?" The answer is that some decline is inevitable, but the picture is much less gloomy than we have been led to believe. The loss of mental and physical abilities is, on the average, relatively slight; some individuals experience only moderate physical loss and no cognitive loss at all. For many older adults, compensatory skills and abilities may replace lost capacities. The same is true for personal and social development.

Here once again we run into the bugaboo of all human development: the self-fulfilling prophecy. Because American society has been changing rapidly for many decades, older adults are frequently viewed as incompetent—their experience appears to have little relevance in "modern times." Yet carefully controlled laboratory measurements of their abilities make clear that their losses may be relatively slight.

Perhaps as we learn to understand the aging process, and as the process is better understood by the public in general, the majority of adults will not assume that their abilities must undergo severe decline. In such a situation, the quality of life of the elderly surely will improve greatly, and because we could reasonably expect an increase in the productive contributions of seniors, all of society would benefit!

Must we age and die?

- A variety of physiological theories regarding aging and death exist. These include aging by program, homeostatic imbalance, and cross-linkage theories.
- Gene theory also suggests that aging is programmed but says that the program exists in certain harmful genes.
- The natural environment is also an important factor in mortality (e.g., now fewer elderly mortalities are due to the spread of influenza).
- Major modifiers of ability such as training, nutrition, illness, stress level, and personality type also affect one's rate of aging.

What are the key aspects of physical development among elderly?

- Although reaction time appears to decline with age, Elias and others have pointed to several reasons for this decline.
- We may conclude that variables other than sheer neural or motor activities account for most change in physical skills over time. These include ageism, motivation, depression, anxiety, response strategies, and response style.
- Changes in sensory abilities, the skeletal system, skin, teeth, hair, and locomotion are noticeable in late adulthood.
- Even though hormone production slows down during late adulthood, a detriment in one area is often compensated for by some other gland.
- Probably the single greatest scourge of the elderly, and in many ways the most debilitating, is Alzheimer's disease.
- A strong relationship exists between physical and mental health.

How is cognitive development affected by old age?

- A number of factors have been suggested as explaining the difference between tested and observed changes in elderly cognition. These include differences in type of cognition, the representativeness of the individuals or observations, standards of evaluation, and amounts of experience.
- The person's perception, consciously or unconsciously, of impending death may cause a decline in intelligence in the later years. This is called terminal drop.
- Creativity is evidenced in late adulthood and in some cases may be strongest during this time. Although quantity of creative production probably drops in old age, the quality of creative production and potential ability probably do not.
- Wisdom refers to going beyond what is known to an understanding of the implication of things. It is the result of intelligence, personality, the intelligence-personality interaction, life experience, and age.

KEY TERMS

Accumulation of errors
Accumulation of metabolic waste
Ageism
Aging by program
Antigens

Autoimmunity
Collagen
Cross-linkage theory
Gene theory

Homeostatic imbalance
Terminal drop
Wear and tear theory
Wisdom

WHAT DO YOU THINK?

1. Which of the explanations of why we age and die do you find most persuasive?
2. Which factors do you believe most strongly affect aging: physiological, genetic, environmental, or some others?
3. Regarding the decline of physical systems, which has the greatest impact on the person's life: reaction time, sensory abilities, other body systems, hormonal balance, health, or appearance? Why?

4. Johnny Kelly of Boston ran the Boston Marathon every year until he was well into his eighties. Why do some people seem to age so much better than others?

5. Regarding the decline of cognitive systems, which has the greatest impact on the person's life: intelligence, creativity, memory, or learning? Why?

6. Programs in which young people meet regularly with elderly adults seem to have rewards for all involved. By what other means might we better tap the knowledge and creativity of the elderly?

7. Which is more important to society, intelligence, creativity, or wisdom?

CHAPTER REVIEW TEST

1. The counterpart theory holds that
   a. the aging process is programmed.
   b. factors that are useful in the earlier years become counterproductive in later years.
   c. early deterioration is due to hard work and a stressful lifestyle.
   d. the aging process is due to alterations in cell proteins.

2. One explanation of aging is that the various life-support systems gradually weaken and that death comes about as a cumulative result of these various weaknesses. This refers to which aspect of aging?
   a. Genetic
   b. Environmental
   c. Physiological
   d. Human abilities

3. According to the cross-linkage theory, what happens to collagen, the major connective tissue in the body that provides elasticity in our skin, as we grow older?
   a. It becomes a waste product as a result of a metabolism build-up in the body.
   b. It causes early aging.
   c. It contributes to our body's tissues becoming more self-rejecting.
   d. Our skin wrinkles because the proteins of collagen are altered.

4. A failure in the body's systems to regulate the proper interaction of organs is known as
   a. cross-linkage theory.
   b. autoimmunity.
   c. homeostatic imbalance.
   d. counterpart theory.

5. Studies of monozygotic twins showing that they have more similar lengths of life than do dizygotic twins are evidence of which aspect of aging?
   a. Human ability
   b. Environmental
   c. Physiological
   d. Genetic

6. In examining the effects of the environment on aging, one factor that has contributed to lower mortality rates in Western culture is
   a. better diet.
   b. changes in the evolutionary process.
   c. the increased use of vaccines in early childhood.
   d. None of the above.

7. Stress level, educational level, motivation, and personality type are examples of
   a. genetic factors.
   b. physiological factors.
   c. environmental factors.
   d. modifiers of ability.

8. Ageism can be defined as
   a. the study of late adulthood.
   b. the study of human development as one ages.
   c. a type of prejudice toward older adults.
   d. physical changes from middle to older adulthood.

9. Breakthroughs that appear to be on the horizon for combating Alzheimer's include:
   a. new ways to combat key enzymes that contribute to cell damage.
   b. new understanding of how to immunize people against a protein that becomes abnormal.

c. the emergence of human gene therapy.
   d. All of the above.

10. Alzheimer's disease is
    a. one of the two most common forms of dementia that affect the elderly, and is probably the single greatest source of affliction and debilitation.
    b. caused largely by bacteria.
    c. suffered most by people whose IQ is the top third of the population.
    d. strongly regressive.

11. Research indicating that there is a strong positive relationship between the length of survivorship and high level of intellectual ability is known as the
    a. terminal drop theory.
    b. cross-linkage theory.
    c. homeostasis theory.
    d. the aging by program theory.

12. According to terminal drop theory, a person's perception of _____ causes the person to begin withdrawing from the world and, consequently, performance on an IQ test drops markedly.
    a. personal health
    b. impending death
    c. intellectual abilities
    d. interpersonal abilities

13. Jaquish and Ripple (1980) found a positive relationship between self-esteem and _____ for the oldest group of subjects.
    a. divergent thinking
    b. originality
    c. flexibility
    d. fluency

14. According to the theory of Baltes and Staudinger, wisdom is the result of
    a. life experience.
    b. age.
    c. personality and intelligence.
    d. All of the above.

15. Dacey (1989b) proposed that there are certain _____ in life during which creative ability can be cultivated most effectively.
    a. work-related experiences
    b. critical periods
    c. ages
    d. educational experiences

16. According to Dacey's research, a peak period during life in which female creativity may most readily be cultivated is
    a. 10 to 13 years old.
    b. 18 to 20 years old.
    c. 29 to 31 years old.
    d. All of the above.

Answers

1. b 2. c 3. d 4. c 5. d 6. c 7. d 8. c 9. d 10. a 11. a 12. b 13. a 14. d 15. b 16. d

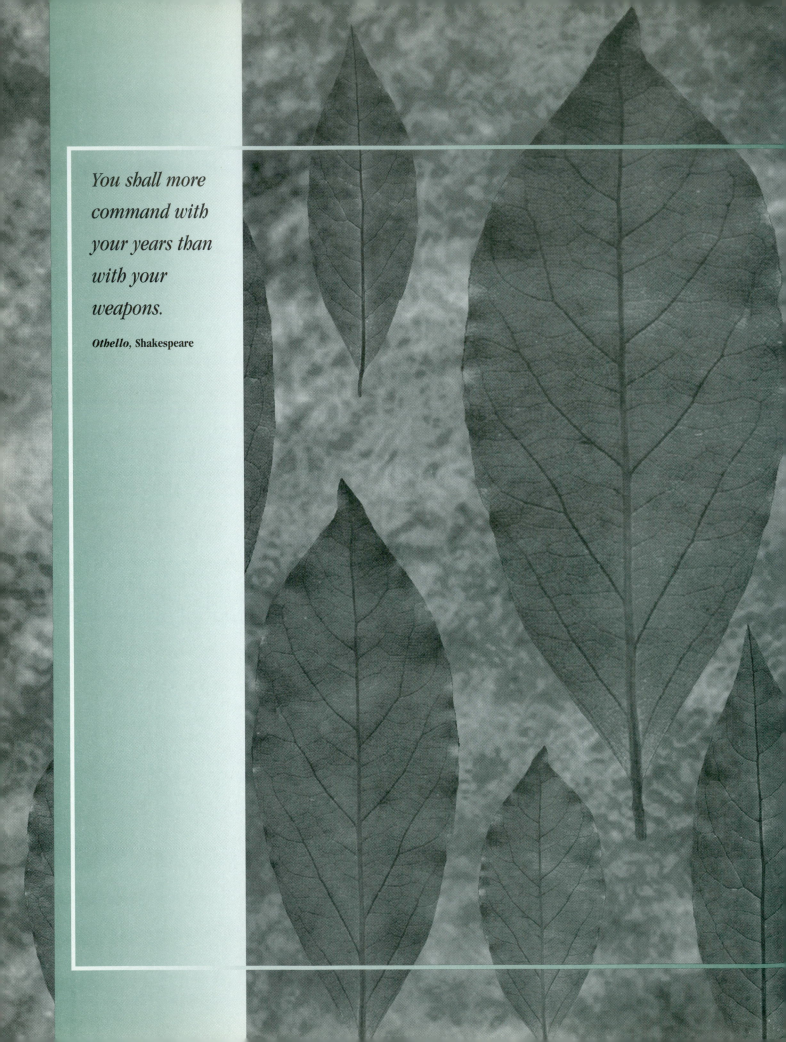

You shall more command with your years than with your weapons.

Othello, Shakespeare

CHAPTER 18

Psychosocial Development in Late Adulthood

Getting married in 1948 I married into a world that had a very definite definition of marriage. I married into a man-oriented society, where the man was the provider, the center, the whatnot, and the woman circled around the man. But I married Ruby Dee; Ruby had some other ideas about marriage. [Laughs.] There were one or two other extra things on her agenda that I didn't know about, but when they came up I saw no reason to challenge her. For example, after our first baby was born and we moved down to Mount Vernon, New York, I remember Ruby standing washing dishes one day and saying to me, quite confidently, "You know, I'm not going to do this the rest of my life." I said, "No? What are you going to do?" She said, "Well, I'm going to be an actor. I'm still going to act." I said, "Yes." She said, "I'm going to go to acting school." And I said, "Well, okay." And at that time we didn't have much money, so we decided that Ruby would go to acting school and I would stay home and sometimes wash the dishes and take care of the baby. And when Ruby came home she would teach me what she learned at the acting class.

Now, when I stepped into the marriage I didn't think of that, but that happened. And over the years I think the central thing that I've learned is how to more easily open my life and let Ruby in. I think women are much more generous in letting people into their lives than men—although I might be wrong. I think that men come with a sense that they are the complete embodiment of what God intended should represent value, virtue, power, and all that sort of thing, and that women, to some degree, are there to service and serve them—that's how women fulfill themselves. Gradually my wife and the circumstances of the time led me to a different understanding, and I'm glad for that, because it made me a broader and a deeper and a much richer person. It has enriched my spirit, my spirituality. It means also—and this is the best part of it all—that I learned a lesson a long time ago, and the lesson is, "The way to make a man rich is to decrease his wants." I learn more and more every day what not to want and how not to want it. To me that is the regimen of the spirit.

Actor and biographer Ossie Davis, age 78

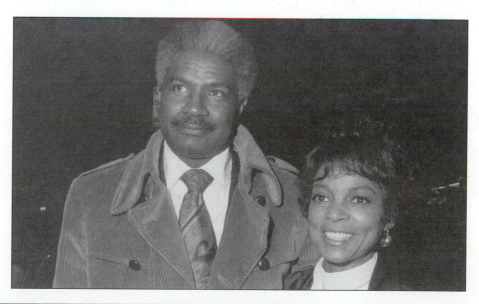

Actor and biographer Ossie Davis, age 78, and wife, Ruby Dee.

Research on the aging process got an encouraging boost from the American Psychological Association recently. This parent organization for psychologists formed the Continuing Committee on Aging (Abeles, 1997). The purpose of the committee is to foster ". . . research on normal and pathological aging; foster the development of a science of gender, ethnicity and aging; support psychological practice in nursing homes. . . " (p. 2), as well as other elderly concerns such as memory (Murray, 1997a), depression (DeAngelis, 1997), social priorities (Murray, 1997b), and the stress of caregiving to ill spouses (Murray, 1997c). In 1997, the keynote address to the APA annual convention was given by Nobel Laureate Elie Wiesel, who emphasized the need for gratitude to the elderly for their role in helping us remember the lessons of the past, such as has been the case with the Holocaust (Sleek, 1997). He defended the right of the elderly and other often-victimized populations. These efforts by the APA to focus on elderly issues should help us deal with the problems caused by the mushrooming of the numbers of those in this age group, particularly in the area of social development.

Chapter Objectives

After reading this chapter, you should be able to answer the following questions.

◆ How do social relationships develop during late adulthood?
◆ What are major factors affecting the older worker?
◆ Is personality development any different among older adults?

Social Development

This section is devoted to five aspects of social development: gender roles, sexuality, families, the older worker, and retirement.

Gender Roles

You might think that when people reach old age, their gender roles will have become pretty well fixed. In fact, researchers generally agree with the statement by Sales (1978) that this is not so:

> When people enter their sixties, they enter a new and final stage in the life cycle. At this point they confront the loss of many highly valued roles, the need to establish a new life structure for the remaining years, and the undeniable fact of life's termination. Widowhood and retirement are the central role transitions likely to occur at this time, but the death of friends and relatives also diminishes one's social network. Although people are aware of the inevitability of these role losses as they enter old age, their often abrupt reality may result in severe role discontinuity (p. 185).

To sum up, the major concern for gender roles among the elderly is **role discontinuity.** See the accompanying box for several questions you should keep in mind as you read the theories and research summaries that follow.

A number of gerontologists have noted that people in late adulthood experience a **crossover** in gender roles. Older men become more like women, and older women become more like men. They do not actually cross over—they just become more like each other. For example, this is what Neugarten (1968) found in her groundbreaking studies of aging men and women. She stated that "women, as they age, seem to become more tolerant of their own aggressive, egocentric impulses; whereas men, as they age, [become more tolerant] of their own nurturative and affiliative impulses" (p. 71).

The differences between men and women, so many of which seem to be based on sexuality, are no longer as important. With the barriers breaking down, older

The "crossover effect" concerns the tendency of men to do more things that are considered feminine, such as washing the dishes, and for women to do more things that are considered masculine, such as taking charge of repairs to the home.

Role discontinuity   Abrupt and disruptive change caused by conflicts among one's various roles in life.

Crossover   Older men become more like women, and older women become more like men.

An Informed VIEW

Is Role Discontinuity Inherent in Growing Old?

Role discontinuity occurs when people experience an abrupt change in their style of life and their role in it. Is this a natural part of growing old? Should we expect our world to shrink and our power to erode? Or is this just a stereotype of old age? Is role discontinuity a problem only for the poor, who have less control over their lives than the wealthy? Does high intelligence make a difference? How about gender? What's your view?

If you would like to have a more informed opinion on this issue, you might want to read one of the articles on the subject referenced in this chapter (e.g., Haan, AARP).

You might also wish to learn more about it by going to our web site at http://www.mhhe.com/dacey5.

---

men and women seem to have more in common with each other, and thus may be more of a solace to each other as they deal with the disruptive changes of growing old. This is not to say that men and women reverse gender roles. Rather, they move toward androgyny (see chapter 14), accepting whatever role, male or female, is appropriate in the situation.

On the basis of data obtained by University of California at Berkeley, Norma Haan (1989) concluded that the gender-role changes that result from aging generally lead toward greater candor with others and comfort with one's self. For the most part, she said, "people change, but slowly, while maintaining some continuity" (p. 25).

Friendships among the elderly also show gender-role differences (AARP, 1997). Although older men and women are alike in that they rarely terminate friendships, they differ in several ways:

- Men tend to trust their best friend more.

- On the other hand, men have less personal conversations with their male friends than do women with their female friends.

- Women place relationships at the top of their list, whereas for men, topical subjects such as sports, politics, and career are most important.

Sexuality

The question of whether to allow residents of nursing homes to engage in sex has been a growing problem as elders' attitudes toward sex change.

Prior to the 1980s, most reports on sex among the elderly agreed that sexual practices drop off sharply in old age. For example, Pearlman (1972) reported that only 20 percent of elderly males have sex two times or more per month. Serious doubts exist, however, about the reliability of these reports. Society disapproves of the idea of sex among the elderly, so it may be that many do not report what actually goes on.

Although perceptions about sexuality among the elderly may be somewhat distorted by such reports, a recent study conducted by Hillman and Stricker (1996) revealed another factor that influences attitudes toward elderly sexuality. People with close contact to their grandparents tend to have a more permissive attitude toward elderly sexuality than those who are less involved with their grandparents. Further, the older the subjects in this study, the greater their overall knowledge about elderly sexuality, which in turn was linked to acceptance of this sexuality. Close contact with elderly relatives and others may disprove commonly held assumptions about sex and aging.

The Janus Report

An investigation that collected data on frequency of sexual activity among the elderly, the Janus Report (Janus & Janus, 1993) gives a picture that weakens the stereotype of the sexually inactive elder even more. According to this research, in the last decade of this century, there is little difference in the practices of young adults and elderly adults! In fact, this study found rather minor differences among any of its four age groups. Either the adults in the Janus study were more honest in reporting what they actually do, or some great changes in sexual attitudes among older Americans have occurred in recent years.

Sex and the "Old-Old"

In a fascinating study restricted to people 80 to 102 years old by Bretschneider and McCoy (1988), we get a look at the sexual activities of those elderly who used to be thought totally inactive. Table 18.1 gives us some surprises. In previous years (the "past section" in table 18.1), the men claim to have engaged in intercourse more than the women, but no difference occurred in enjoyment. In their present lives, 63 percent of the men and 30 percent of the women say they have intercourse at least sometimes, and 76 percent of the men and 39 percent of the women say they enjoy it at least mildly. Another interesting finding of this study is that the men reported having their first intercourse at an average age of 22 and women at age 25. What a difference from today's figures (see chapter 13)!

Widowhood and Sexuality

A number of factors account for gender differences in attitudes and interest in sex. For example, women outlive men by approximately seven years. Most married women will become widows because they marry men nearly four years older than themselves. In contrast, most men in society will not become widowers unless they reach age 85. Due to this imbalance of elderly males and females, it is more difficult for women to find sexual partners in their aging years.

Whether or not a woman is sexually active depends mainly on her marital status. Men have generally had more opportunity for extramarital sexual relations than

TABLE 18.1 REPORTED FREQUENCY AND ENJOYMENT OF SEXUAL INTERCOURSE BY 80- TO 102-YEAR-OLD MEN AND WOMEN IN THE PAST (YOUNGER YEARS) AND IN THE PRESENT

	Entire Sample		Frequency							
			Never		Sometimes		Often		Very Often	
	N	%	n	%	n	%	n	%	n	%
Past										
Men	92	92	3	3	3	3	60	65	26	28
Women	90	88	2	2	10	11	70	78	8	9
Present										
Men	80	80	30	38	27	34	21	26	2	3
Women	80	78	56	70	16	20	8	10	0	0

	Entire Sample		Enjoyment							
			None		Mild		Moderate		Great	
	N	%	n	%	n	%	n	%	n	%
Past										
Men	91	91	3	3	5	6	23	25	60	66
Women	92	90	5	5	9	10	34	37	44	48
Present										
Men	79	79	19	24	11	14	21	27	28	35
Women	82	80	50	61	10	12	13	16	9	11

From *Archives of Sexual Behavior* by J. G. Bretschneider and N. L. McCoy, 17(2): 117, 1988. Reprinted with permission from Kluwer Academic/Plenum Publishers.

women, due to the *differential opportunity structure*. This means that due to social disapproval and more rigid rules enforced by parents, peers, and the legal system, women have not had the same access to sex as men have had.

Impotency

Impotency The inability to engage in the sexual act.

One of the biggest fears in males of increasing age is **impotency.** Physical changes, nonsupportive partners and peers, and internal fears may be enough to inhibit or terminate sexual activity in males. It may become a self-fulfilling prophecy (if you think something is going to happen, there is a greater likelihood that it will).

Sleep laboratory experiments have shown that many men in their sixties to eighties who have labeled themselves as impotent regularly experience erections in their sleep. In many cases a man is capable of having intercourse, but a physical condition such as diabetes impedes it. New types of prosthetic devices can remedy a variety of psychological and physical problems. Although recent findings have hastened the pursuit of wonder drugs, prosthetic devices may be the best solution (Benson, 1996). The newest drug, Viagra, may change this.

Prostatectomy The removal of all or part of the male prostate gland.

One pervading myth is that surgery of the prostate gland inevitably leads to impotency. Many elderly men experience pain and swelling of this small gland, and a **prostatectomy** (removal of all or a part of this gland) is sometimes necessary. Most impotency that results from the removal of this gland is psychological rather than physical.

Most sexual problems that women experience are due to hormonal changes. The vaginal walls begin to thin, and intercourse may become painful, with itching and burning sensations. Estrogen pills and hormone creams relieve many of these symptoms. Further, if women believe that sexual activity ceases with menopause and aging, it probably will. Although women have fewer concerns about sex, they are often worried about losing their attractiveness, which can also have a negative effect on their sex lives.

Generative love Most characteristic of parenthood, a time during which sacrifices are gladly made for the sake of the children.

Existential love The capacity to cherish the present moment, perhaps first learned when we confront the certainty of our own personal death.

At any rate, it is quite likely that there is a real decline in sexual activity among the elderly. Men are often concerned about their ability to consummate intercourse. They also worry about their loss of masculinity, in terms of looks and strength. The literature on sex among the elderly, however, shows a new attitude emerging. Datan and colleagues (1987) described well the difference between **generative love** and **existential love:**

> We believe that existential love, the capacity to cherish the present moment, is one of the greatest gifts of maturity. Perhaps we first learn this love when we first confront the certainty of our own personal death, most often in middle adulthood. Generative love is most characteristic of parenthood, a time during which sacrifices are gladly made for the sake of the children. However, it is existential love, we feel, that creates the unique patience and tenderness so often seen in grandparents, who know how brief the period of childhood is, since they have seen their own children leave childhood behind them.
>
> We have not yet awakened to the potential for existential love between old women and old men, just as we are not yet prepared to recognize the pleasures of sexuality as natural to the life span, particularly to the postparental period.
>
> Those old people who have had the misfortune of spending their last days in nursing homes may learn that love can be lethal. We have been told of an old woman and an old man who fell in love. The old man's children thought this late flowering was "cute"; however, the old woman's children thought it was disgraceful, and over her protests, they removed her from the nursing home. One month later she registered her final protest: she died (p. 287).

Out of all the hundreds and hundreds of studies of monkeys, one finding applies to every type: From the largest gorilla to the tiniest spider monkey, they all spend about four hours a day in "grooming." Grooming refers to their different ways of touching—stroking, removing bugs, hugging, sex. It is obviously genetic. It seems likely that we humans have something in common with them. We all need to be touched, too. The elderly get less touching than the rest of us, perhaps because they are not seen as being attractive. But they need physical contact just as much as everyone else.

The Elderly and Their Families

The familial relationship undergoes changes in membership, organization, and role during the aging process. Due to improved health care, individuals can expect to live longer, which means that married couples will have more years together after their children leave home. Though exceptions (those who are divorced, childless, or who never married) occur, most middle-aged couples go through similar stages in the life cycle. Following are the four basic phases:

1. The child-rearing stage

2. The stage of childlessness before retirement

3. The retirement stage

4. Widowhood and widowerhood

The duration of each stage in the life cycle, and the ages of the family members for each stage, vary from family to family. Childbearing patterns have a lot to do with life in the late stages of life. Couples who complete their families in their early years will have a different lifestyle when their last child leaves home than couples with "change of life" babies, who may have a dependent child at home when they are ready to retire. This can pose serious economic problems for those retirees on fixed incomes, trying to meet the staggering costs of education. In addition, with children in the home, saving for retirement is difficult.

Retirement may bring about changes for both spouses, but wives who have not properly prepared themselves emotionally and financially for retirement may find it particularly stressful. Retirement generally signifies a decrease in income and a lowering of the standard of living, but it may take a while before some of these problems are noticed. Household duties may change, with the husband generally helping more.

Although many changes affect the elderly family, in some marriages it may be true that the more things change the more they stay the same. Studies have shown that among elderly married couples, certain factors contribute to the well-being of the relationship that, in turn, promote a stable, satisfying marriage. It has been found, however, that those situations in which one spouse suffers a long-term illness do tend to have more problems (Wickrama & others, 1997). As couples change over time, it will be interesting to see whether the interactional processes in the long-term marriage also change, or if they remain stable despite individual development.

Conflict is an inevitable part of any relationship that lasts over time. The relationship between elderly parents and their adult children is no exception. Clarke and associates (1999) conducted a study of aging parents and their middle-aged children. They were specifically interested in the emergence of common conflict themes. They found six types of conflict:

• communication and style of interaction

• lifestyle choices and habits

• parenting practices and values

• religion, ideology, and politics

• work habits

• standards of household maintenance

Interesting generational differences were found. For example, older parents more often reported conflicts over habits and lifestyle choices than their adult children did. The children more often reported communication conflicts and interaction style conflicts.

Finally, gender differences were found between older married husbands and wives as to the importance of support from family and friends (Lynch, 1998). Support from children was perceived by women as most positive, whereas spousal support was perceived as most important to men.

Widowhood

With women outliving men by large margins, the wife is most often the survivor. Only half of women over 65 are living with a partner. Many widows have to take on additional duties, including managing household finances and janitorial tasks, and some will have to seek employment. Widowhood affects social relationships with family and friends. Often a widow is the "fifth wheel" in social settings, and former relationships may dissipate. Fortunately, new social activities and friends emerge and replace the old ones.

Howie (1992–1993) suggested that we consider widowhood to be a normal part of aging for women. Thus the ideal focus is shifted from bereavement to concern with the social implications of the extended years of widows' lives. Women should regard widowhood with the understanding that it is yet another passage in the process of aging and dying.

Remarriage is an alternative to the loneliness that most widows and widowers feel after losing their spouse. However, remarriage rates for senior citizens are low, and it is not an option for most. The reasons for not remarrying include the following:

- Many of the elderly view it as improper.

- Children may oppose remarriage.

- Social Security laws penalize widows who remarry.

- There are three single women for every single man over age 65.

In her study of older widows' attitude toward remarriage, Talbot (1998) learned that two-thirds of the sample said they were still interested and attracted to men. However 55 percent were strongly opposed to remarriage. Only 15 percent of the sample felt favorably toward remarriage.

Seniors who choose to remarry, however, enjoy much success if the ingredients of love, companionship, financial security, and offspring consent are present. Accepting the remarriage of a parent can be difficult, even for adult children of older parents. Ganong and associates (1998) studied the responses of adult children to vignettes portraying the later life remarriage of an older parent. The vignettes described situations in which either the parent or the stepparent needed help. Overall, Ganong and associates found that the adult children felt an obligation to help either their parent or their stepparent, but the obligation felt toward stepparents was not as great.

Care of Elderly Parents

Developmental psychologists have become much more interested in caregiving to elders in recent years. Variables studied have included stress caused by living alone or in nursing homes (Naleppa, 1996; Ponder & Pomeroy, 1996; Tirrito, 1996; Stephens & Townsend, 1997), abuse (Hwalek & others, 1996; Neale & others, 1996), and coping strategies (Davis & others, 2000; DeVries & others, 1997; Kramer & others, 1999; Mok & Mui, 1996).

Elderly people identify their adult children, when they have them, as the primary helpers in their lives. When these people have both an adult son and an adult

For those who want to work with older adults, put *Promoting successful aging* at the top of your reading list. Roth and Atherton have written a readable book that is half about theory and research and half about the specific strategies for dealing with the needs of the elderly.

A Sociocultural View

Caregiving for Elderly in Swarthmore, Pennsylvania, and Botswana, Africa

Draper and Keith (1992) were perplexed by the question, "Why is care for the elderly such a problem for Americans?" Draper had recently returned from studying the lifestyle of the !Kung people of Botswana and decided to do a comparison study with Keith of elder care in Swarthmore, a Philadelphia suburb.

Older residents of Swarthmore are extremely worried about their care, especially with regard to loss of health, which generates feelings of fear. The researchers learned that for many of the elders, need for care is a primary reason for moving into Swarthmore. They do so to be near a child or relative who could supervise their eventual move into a retirement home should professional care prove necessary. The problem is that whether they moved into Swarth-

more (to be near relatives), or moved out of Swarthmore (to enter a retirement community), the costs to the older person usually involve loss of ties to their communities.

In contrast, elders of the !Kung villages "age in place." They do not retire, relocate, or enter age-graded elder care institutions. Indeed, they have no other place to go. The !Kung were asked, "For an old person, what makes a good life?" One-third responded, "If you have a child to take care of you, you have a good life." Care is almost always provided by one's children and community.

For the people of Swarthmore, technologically superb care is available, but its benefits must be weighed against the loss of community ties and personal autonomy. For the !Kung, social needs and physical care are compatible.

---

daughter, elderly people most often name the son as the primary helper (Kramer & others, 1999). This is surprising, because as we pointed out in chapter 16, care of elderly parents is almost always undertaken by daughters, if the elderly persons have any. The role that men play in caregiving, however, should not be overlooked. While they are not likely to be the primary caretakers of elderly parents, sons do contribute to their care in significant ways (Marks, 1996).

In the past, elder care was most often done by unmarried daughters, if there were any. They were expected to do this because it was assumed that the work would be easier for them, because they had no responsibilities for husband or children. In fact, married women report that their married status makes caregiving for their elderly parents easier, because of the support they receive.

It is not only the biological daughters of elderly parents who provide caretaking support. Davis and associates (1999) found no differences between care provided by daughters and by daughters-in-law. They suggest that it is the quality of the interactions with the older person that is most significant and not the relation to the person.

Caring for the elderly has been associated with many risk factors for the caregivers involved. Depression and stress are two of the most common risk factors cited in the literature. The degree of stress and depression experienced has been associated with specific caregiver characteristics. For example, Meshefedjian and associates (1998) found that the closer the relationship of the caregiver to the elderly person, the higher the caregiver scored on a test of depression. In addition, the less education caregivers have, the more likely they are to be depressed. Lawrence and associates (1998) also found that having a close relationship with the elderly person resulted in increased perceptions of overload by the caregiver. Not only is the closeness of the relationship (i.e., parent/child) a factor in caregiver mental health, but the quality of these associations between them is also important. Poor interactions between caregivers and those in their care even result in verbally and physically aggressive behaviors in adults (Cohen-Mansfield & Werner, 1998). Researchers have also found that the number of difficulties encountered in one's role as a caregiver is related to stress and burden. For example, Riedel and associates (1998) found that caregivers who reported many types of difficulty in their role experienced higher levels of burden than caregivers who reported only one type of difficulty.

An Applied View   Assisted Living for Older Adults

For many people, the move to a new home is often an exciting and highly anticipated event. People dream of continued happiness in their new dwelling and look forward to creating new and happy memories there. For older adults, however, the move to a senior complex or assisted living facility can be a very different experience. This experience can be either positive or negative, depending on the person's attitude and ability to adjust to the new living environment. Those older adults who are successful in their adjustment accept that they are aging and view assistance as a natural part of old age. When older adults make positive adaptive responses to their new setting, they welcome such conveniences as meal preparation and housekeeping. To an elder who has not made a positive adjustment, these conveniences may be viewed as humiliating dependence on others.

There are many factors that can affect a person's successful adjustment to an assisted living facility. These factors are important when considering relocation. Michelson (1998) lists five factors that elderly persons should consider during relocation. The first is the person's home and what it means to him/her. Michelson suggests that adequate time and preparation is given to "grieve the closing of a home." The second is loss, which is considered inevitable in old

age. A person relocating to an assisted living facility must be prepared to face the losses incurred due to aging on a daily basis. For example, bedridden residents or those in wheelchairs serve as daily reminders of the aging process and may "trigger additional feelings of personal loss" in an individual. The third factor is the individual's response or adaptation to aging. When a person demonstrates positive adaptation to the aging process, he/she experiences successful aging. The fourth factor pertains to the changes within the individual and whether these changes warrant additional assistance. For example, are there cognitive changes, health changes or changes in the individual's support system, which may require assistance from the assisted living facility staff? Finally, the fifth factor to consider is how the elderly person feels about moving. A more positive adjustment to the assisted living facility will occur if the individual "perceives that his or her choice will offer more gains than losses."

The decision to move from one's home to an assisted living community is often a difficult one. Experts suggest that making it highly personalized and considering all of the various needs of the elderly person can make a smoother transition.

As indicated, there are clear risks of stress and depression for the caregiver when placed in this role. Many researchers have studied the caregiver role to find ways in which to ease the burden of such a responsibility. Recent research by Chang and associates (1998) points to spiritual and religious beliefs as beneficial for coping with caregiving responsibilities. Caregivers who employed such beliefs reported better relationships with those in their care, as well as less feelings of religion/spirituality in coping with caregiving for disabled elders. Shared responsibility in caregiving has also been found to be beneficial for caregivers. Lower stress levels and lower levels of depression were reported by those family caregivers who used adult day care to assist with caregiving responsibilities (Zarit & others, 1998).

What about the situation in which the elders have no children, or at least none who are willing or able to care for them? Research indicates that elderly individuals who have no kin tend to substitute a close friend whom they persuade to take the place of the absent relative. Most family and close friends still feel that they ought to take care of the elderly in their own homes if possible. Racial and ethnic variations play a role in who should be responsible for caring for the older generation, however, Lee and associates (1998) found that African-American elderly were more likely to expect to be cared for by their children than elderly white parents. Burr and Mutchler (1999) found that elderly Latinos were also more likely to agree that the younger generation should care for them.

It is not always the younger generation that provides caretaking for elderly persons. Often this role is taken by the spouse of the elderly person. Kramer and associates (1999) studied older husbands who cared for their ailing wives. They found that these men did less well than men married to healthy wives in the following areas: marital interactions, social integration, household responsibilities and well-being. These findings confirm that it is more stressful to be in a relationship with an ailing person than with a healthy person. Caring for an elderly person with dementia has been found to be the most stressful situation of all. Ory and associates (1999) found that caregivers of dementia patients spend significantly more time each week in their role than other types of caregivers. Dementia caregivers experience more caregiver strain and report higher levels of physical and mental health problems.

Another option for elderly care is a nursing home facility. If a family does choose long-term care for an elderly parent, how do they choose the right nursing home for that parent? Several studies have examined both positive and negative characteristics of nursing homes. Castle and Fogel (1998) compared nursing homes that employ restraint to those that are restraint free. Overall, the restraint-free facilities were smaller with a lower occupancy rate, had a "richer mix of nursing staff," and were likely to employ more full-time equivalent registered nurses. Cohen-Mansfield and Werner (1998) found that, not surprisingly, nursing homes which had enhanced environments such as an outdoor nature environment produced more positive evaluations by both residents and their families.

The Changing Role of the Grandparent

In today's world, with increased life expectancy, grandparenthood has become a unique experience within the family system (Pruchno, 1999; Drew & Smith, 1999; King & Elder, 1998). Grandparenthood is positively linked to the mental health and morale of elderly persons. For example, in a classic study, Neugarten and Weinstein (1964) examined styles of grandparenting and created categories for five general styles: "formal," "the fun seeker," "the surrogate parent," "the reservoir of family wisdom," and "the distant figure." An interesting finding was that the fun seeker and the distant figure emerged as the most popular styles of grandparenting. Both exclude an emphasis on authority. Many grandparents preferred a grandparent-grandchild relationship in which their role was simply to enjoy being with their grandchildren rather than feeling responsible as co-parents with their adult children.

Today, however, many grandparents play a more integral part in the lives of their grandchildren. A survey completed by the American Association of Retired Persons (AARP, 2000) concluded that the state of American grandparenting is strong. More than 8 out of 10 grandparents in the study had seen a grandchild in the previous month. Eleven percent of those studied are regular caregivers.

Recent research by Pruchno (1999) reveals that a growing number of grandparents are raising their grandchildren alone. The parents of these children, the middle generation, are usually absent. This absence is due to many reasons such as parental death, substance abuse, or incarceration. Pruchno found that African-American and white grandmothers differed in two important ways. First, it is more common for the African-American grandmothers to have peers who are also raising grandchildren alone. Second, a household containing multiple generations living together is not an uncommon condition for black grandmothers. These two findings may explain why black grandmothers experienced fewer emotional burdens from their caregiving role than white grandparents did.

Grandparents are also playing a bigger role as day-care providers for their grandchildren. Most grandparents hope to have a positive effect on their grandchildren. King and Elder (1998) identified several factors that predicted how effective a grandparent believed he/she was in the life of his/her grandchild. Some factors that were predicted to be effective are participation in church, living close by, having a small number of grandchildren, and having known one's own grandparents.

Erikson (1963) explained, in his stage of generativity, the significance of grandchildren to grandparents. Erikson believed that generativity referred to providing a better life for future generations and that not having reached the stage of generativity would cause stagnation and self-absorption in the individual (see chapter 16). The personal development of grandparents is furthered by their close rapport with younger generations and vice versa. When this vital relationship is disrupted, as it usually is in the case of divorce, the suffering of grandparents can be agonizing (Gray & Geron, 1995).

An Applied VIEW

Do You Know Your Grandparents?

Are your grandparents still alive? Even though you have probably known them for many years, you may not know them very well. Try answering the questions below for one set of your grandparents, and if possible, check your answers with them to get your GKQ (Grandparent Knowledge Quotient).

1. What's your grandmother's favorite activity?
2. In total, how many rings do your grandparents wear?
3. What color are your grandfather's eyes?
4. Where does your grandfather eat lunch?
5. What is your grandmother's favorite TV show?

6. In what year did your grandparents meet?
7. For whom did your grandmother vote for president in 1996?
8. Does your grandfather know how to prepare asparagus?
9. Who is your grandfather's favorite relative?
10. Name some of either of your grandparents' favorite movie stars.

You might try making up a test like this about yourself and asking your grandparents, parents, siblings, and friends to respond to it. It should be interesting to see which of them knows you best.

The Older Worker

Only a small percentage of all older adults are in the labor force—about 11 percent. Many of these retirements were due to forced retirement. Today, only airline pilots and public safety workers such as fire fighters and police can be forced to retire because of their age; however, not many people want to continue working past 65. For example, a large steel corporation that has never had mandatory retirement finds that less than 1 percent of their 40,000 workers stay on past 65. The average age of retirement at this company is below 62. Of those who do wish to stay on, most seem able to do a good job of meeting their requirements (Clay, 1996).

Performance

As this society ages through greater longevity, the aging of the baby boom generation, and decreased birth rates, some of the stereotypes about aging are coming under closer scrutiny. An excellent series of longitudinal studies performed by Erdman and associates (1985), which yielded a sample of more than 7,000 subjects, has provided an in-depth look at this and other aspects of the relationships between old age and work. The stereotype that age equals declining performance is getting more research attention because the number of workers in the last two decades of their careers will grow 41 percent while the number of workers 16 to 35 years old will decline slightly (Johnston, 1987).

The stereotype is bolstered by research on aging that demonstrates a decline in abilities such as dexterity, speed of response, agility, hearing, and vision. If all these abilities decline, then one may conclude that job performance must decline with age. McEvoy and Cascio (1989) conducted an extensive meta-analysis (a study that compiles the results of many other studies) of 96 studies and found no relationship between age and job performance. It made no difference whether the performance measure was ratings or productivity measures, nor whether the type of job was professional or nonprofessional.

What explanation is there for these results? How does the older worker deal with the mild decline of physical abilities that affects most elderly persons? Experience is one answer. There is said to be no substitute for it, and it is certainly valued by employers. Other reasons cited are that older workers have lower absenteeism, turnover, illness, and accident rates (Kacmar & Ferris, 1989; Martocchio, 1989). They also tend to have higher job satisfaction and more positive work values than younger workers. These qualifications seem to offset any decreases in physical ability that increasing age causes.

Retirement

"I just don't want to retire," said Charlie, a 65-year-old shipping clerk. "But you've worked hard, and you should get the fruits of your labor," said his boss. "Fruits of my labor, my backside! I know lots of guys, as soon as they retire, they get sick or something and then they die. I know if I retire I'm gonna die. I'm gonna die!" Despite his protestations, Charlie was retired. Three months later he was dead.

For many people, retirement is a welcome relief from a frustrating and boring job. For others, it is just as difficult as being unemployed. Retirement requires changing the habits of an adult lifetime. This probably explains why more than 11 percent of those 65 and over are employed.

Nevertheless, the great majority of the elderly do not choose to work. Research conducted by Smith and Moen (1998) indicates that the decision to retire is influenced by the retiree's spouse. Although most retirees view their spouse's influence as a major factor, the spouses frequently assume their influence has little effect. The decision is a complicated one, but many people now feel they have enough financial security so that they need not work. Health may be the biggest factor. Retirement seems to be harder on males than females. Many feel that they have nothing to do, although their wives still have a job. The home still must be taken care of, the meals cooked, the clothes cleaned. Most older wives have already adjusted to a reduction in their roles because their children have left home. For men, the change usually comes all at once.

Retirement and Leisure

How you view retirement depends on the work and leisure experiences you have had up to the point of retirement. The leisure activities pursued throughout life play a crucial role in your social adjustment later on. The relationships among work, retirement, and leisure can be seen in figure 18.1.

The type of work you do directly affects how you spend leisure time, in two ways. The scheduling of work affects when leisure time is available. A person who works second or third shift might be unable to take part in activities that are often thought of as evening activities, such as dining and dancing. Second, the content of work may influence how much time will be left over for leisure activities. Persons with physically draining positions may be too tired to do anything but nap after work. On the other hand, a person with a desk job may choose physically challenging activities during leisure hours.

When leisure is no more than an extension of work experiences and attitudes, it performs what leisure theorists call a spillover function. For example, some people try to relax by performing some of their easier tasks at home—the "stuffed briefcase" syndrome. Conversely, when leisure time is engaged in to make up for disappointment and stress at work, it is described as a compensatory function. An example would be excessive partying at the end of the workday or week.

Figure 18.1

The interrelatedness of work, leisure, and retirement. Solid lines denote the direct influence of (1) work on leisure, and (2) work and leisure upon retirement. Broken lines suggest a possible feedback influence whereby preferences for uses of leisure time may affect choice of jobs, and the availability of more time in retirement may affect content of leisure activities.

From Robert Havighurst, "Perceived Life Space" in *Contributions to Human Development* 3:93–112 (1963). S. Karger AG, Basel, Switzerland. Reprinted by permission of the publisher.

Making Retirement More Enjoyable

An excellent source of information on the elderly is the American Association of Retired Persons (AARP). With about 30 million members, this powerful group publishes materials that may interest you. Write to them at National Headquarters, 601 E Street NW, Washington, DC 20049.

The belief is growing that retired persons are an important resource to the community. Numerous efforts have been made in recent years to tap this powerful resource. A number of national programs now make an effort to involve retired persons in volunteer and paid work of service to society.

Recent surveys seem to indicate that the "golden years" are not so golden for many retired persons. But with improving health conditions (see chapter 17), improved understanding of the nature of life after 65, and a considerable increase in government involvement, the lives of retirees have a far better chance of being fruitful.

Contrary to the stereotype, getting old need not, and usually does not, mean being lonely. In fact, the elderly, most of whom have a good deal of free time, often use it to develop their social lives. We now move to a discussion about their personal development.

Guided Review

1. Many changes occur in late adulthood, including role _____ (an abrupt and disruptive change in role) and "crossover" of sex roles.
2. In late adulthood, the gender role of older men becomes (more; less) like that of women, and women's role becomes (more; less) like that of men.
3. The child-launching phase, the childless preretirement period, the retirement phase, and _____ are stages most middle-aged and aged couples can anticipate.
4. Most family and close friends feel that the best place to take care of the elderly is (in a hospital; in a nursing home; in their own homes).
5. Five general styles of grandparenting have been identified by Neugarten and Weinstein (1964): formal, fun seeking, _____ _____, reservoir of family wisdom, and distant figure.
6. Although some decline in dexterity, speed, and agility occurs in older workers, _____ may be one of the reasons that job performance does not generally decline among these workers.
7. Leisure theorists write about two functions for leisure: a spillover function and a _____ function.
8. Retirement is (more; less) difficult for females than for males.

Personal Development

Two points of view have received most interest in the field of personality development in the elderly: those of the Committee on Human Development and those of Erik Erikson. Although dated, these two bodies of research are still respected by personality experts and so must be included in this chapter.

The Committee on Human Development

What are the effects of aging on personal development? The Committee on Human Development, consisting of gerontologist Bernice Neugarten and her associates at the University of Chicago, has been responsible for some of the most highly respected research on this topic (e.g., Havighurst & others, 1968; Neugarten, 1968).

Adults between the ages of 54 and 94 who were residents of Kansas City were asked to participate in a study of change across the adult lifespan. The sample is somewhat biased in that it represents only white persons who were living on their own (i.e., not institutionalized) at the time of the study. They were somewhat better educated and of a higher socioeconomic group than is typical for this age group. Nevertheless, the sample is reasonably well balanced, and because of the thoroughness with which these persons were studied, this research has become a classic in the field of adult psychology. Neugarten summarized the findings:

Answers

1. discontinuity 2. more, more 3. widowhood 4. in their own homes 5. surrogate parent 6. experience 7. compensatory 8. less

- In the middle years (especially the fifties), a change occurs in the perception of time and death and the relationship of the self to them. Introspection, contemplation, reflection, and self-evaluation become important aspects of life. People at this age become more interested in their "inner selves."

- Perception of how well one can control the environment undergoes a marked change:

> Forty-year-olds, for example, seem to see the environment as one that rewards boldness and risk-taking, and to see themselves as possessing energy congruent with the opportunities perceived in the outer world. Sixty-year-olds, however, perceive the world as complex and dangerous, no longer to be reformed in line with one's wishes, and the individual as conforming and accommodating to outer-world demands (1968, p. 140).

- *Emotional energy* declines with age. Tests showed that intensity of emotion invested in tasks undergoes a definite decline in the later years.

- *Gender-role reversals* also occur with age (discussed earlier in this chapter).

- *Age-status* becomes more rigid with development. Age-status refers to society's expectations about what is normal at various ages. These expectations change not only with advancing years, but according to the particular society and to the historical context. For example, in 1940 a woman who was not married by age 22 was not considered unusual, but if she had not married by the time she was 27, people began to worry. In the late 1980s, the expected age of marriage is much less rigid. This holds only for the United States; in Samoa, for example, concern arises if a person is not married by age 15.

What is the optimum pattern of aging in terms of our relationships with other people? The Committee on Human Development has also investigated this question. For many years, there have been two different positions on this question, known as the activity theory and the disengagement theory.

According to the **activity theory,** human beings flourish through interaction with other people and through keeping physically active. They are unhappy when, as they reach the older years, their contacts with others shrink as a result of death, illness, and societal limitations. Those who are able to keep up the social activity of their middle years are considered the most successful.

Activity theory   Human beings who are able to keep up the social activity of their middle years are considered the most successful.

Erikson believes that the character of the old Swedish doctor in Ingmar Bergman's famous film, *Wild Strawberries,* excellently reflects the eight stages he proposes.

Disengagement theory The most mature adults are likely to gradually disengage themselves from their fellow human beings in preparation for death.

Disengagement theory contradicts this idea. According to this position, the belief that activity is better than passivity is a bias of the Western world. This was not always so; the Greeks, for example, valued their warriors and athletes but reserved the highest distinction for such contemplative philosophers as Sophocles, Plato, and Aristotle. Many people in the countries of the Eastern Hemisphere also hold this view. According to disengagement theory, the most mature adults are likely to gradually disengage themselves from their fellow human beings in preparation for death. They become less interested in their interactions with others and more absorbed in internal concerns. They accept the decreasing attention of a society that views them as losing power.

Does this mean that the tendency toward disengagement is more normal than the tendency toward activity? It is now believed that what has appeared to be disengagement is instead a temporary transition from the highly active role of the middle-aged adult to the more sedate, spiritually oriented role of the elderly person. Most humans truly enjoy social contact, so disengagement from one's fellows may be the result of traumatic experience or a physiologically caused mental disturbance such as clinical depression. On the other hand, activity theory, with its emphasis on social involvement, is now considered too general (Marshall, 1994). For example, many people may reduce social contacts, but keep active with solitary hobbies. Activity per se has not been found to correlate with a personal sense of satisfaction with life. Carstensen (1995, 1996) offered a resolution of the debate with her **socio-emotional selectivity theory.** She suggested that humans use social contact to obtain physical survival, information they need, the maintenance of a sense of self

Socio-emotional selectivity theory According to this theory, humans use social contact for four reasons: to obtain physical survival, to get information they need, to maintain a sense of self, and to acquire pleasure and comfort.

Clearly the group on the left is enjoying itself more than the woman on the right, but does that mean that the disengagement theory is wrong?

An Applied VIEW

How Their Attitudes Can Affect the Way People Think

What's in an attitude? A great deal, according to those who knew Sister Mary, a nun who lived to be 101 years of age (Snowdon, 1997). Even more remarkable than her longevity is her resilience. Although she had brain lesions common to Alzheimer's disease, she had high scores on cognitive tests shortly before her death. Much of Sister Mary's success was attributed to her active lifestyle and optimistic attitude. She worked full time as a teacher until she was 77. After that, she worked part-time for several years, until retiring at age 84. Sister Mary loved to read and used a magnifying glass to pore over books, maps, and newspapers. Not only did she keep her mind active, but she kept her spirit active as well. In her final years, she gave lessons to others about how to age with grace, dignity, joy, and beauty. Her story offers strong evidence for the activity theory.

An Applied View

Getting Perspective on Your Thinking

If you hope to be the kind of person who ends his or her life with a sense of integrity, the time to begin is right now. You don't get to be a happy elderly person unless you plan and work for it. You can do this in many ways, but we have some suggestions to pass along to you.

Whenever you are about to make an important decision, follow these four steps:

1. Come to some tentative conclusion about what you should do.

2. Close your eyes and picture yourself as a 75-year-old woman or man.

3. Imagine yourself explaining your decision to that old person, and try to picture her or him telling you what she or he thinks about what you have decided.

4. If you don't like what you hear, rethink the decision and go through this process again.

Use this technique to get a better perspective on your thinking; you will be surprised by how much wisdom you already have.

---

and pleasure and comfort. These goals exist throughout life, but the importance of each shifts with age. For the elderly, the need for physical survival so important in infancy and the need for information from others in younger adulthood become less important. The need for emotional support grows. They tend to get this support from relatives and close friends (their "social convoys," as they have been called) more and more, and less and less from casual acquaintances such as coworkers. In fact, this is true of anyone who is threatened, such as terminally ill young people. Joseph Cardinal Bernardin, when dying of cancer, expressed it this way (*Time,* 2000):

> I now realized that when I asked my doctor for the test results, I had to let go of everything. . . . One of the things I have noticed about illness is that it draws you inside yourself. When we are ill, we tend to focus on our own pain and suffering. We may feel sorry for ourselves or become depressed (p. 21).

Further, the challenges faced in later life can be quite different. For example, Kling and associates (1997) have investigated elderly coping with loss of home, community relocation, and caring for a mentally ill adult child. Other research that has evaluated altered coping skills of the late adult population (and ways to improve these skills) have been completed by Heckhausen (1997) and Tabourne (1995). Thus the elderly appear to be disengaging, but in fact they are simply becoming more selective about with whom they wish to spend their social time. Carstensen's socio-emotional selectivity theory appears to explain the changes that occur better than either disengagement or activity theory.

Erikson

Erikson believed that resolution of each of the first seven crises in his theory should lead us to achieve a sense of personal **integrity.** Older adults who have a sense of integrity feel their lives have been well spent. The decisions and actions they have taken seem to them to fit together—their lives are integrated. They are saddened by the sense that time is running out and that they will not get many more chances to make an impact, but they feel reasonably well satisfied with their achievements. They usually have a sense of having helped to achieve a more dignified life for humankind.

The acceptance of human progress, including one's own, is essential for this final sense of integrity. This is the path to wisdom, which Erikson defined as "the detached and yet active concern with life itself in the face of death itself" (1978, p. 26).

In three words I can sum up everything I've learned about life. It goes on.

Anonymous

Integrity The resolution of each of the first seven crises in Erikson's theory should lead us to achieve a sense of personal integrity. Older adults who have a sense of integrity feel their lives have been well spent.

When people look back over their lives and feel that they have made many wrong decisions, or more commonly, that they have frequently not made any decisions at all, they tend to see life as lacking integrity. They feel **despair,** which is the second half of this last stage of crisis. They are angry that there can never be another chance to make their lives make sense. They often hide their fear of death by appearing contemptuous of humanity in general, and those of other religions and races in particular. As Erikson put it, "Such despair is often hidden behind a show of disgust" (1968, p. 140).

Erikson (1978) provided a panoramic view of his life-cycle theory in an analysis of Swedish film director Ingmar Bergman's famous film *Wild Strawberries*. In this picture, an elderly Swedish doctor goes from his hometown to a large city, where he is to be honored for 50 years of service to the medical profession. On the way, he stops by his childhood home and, resting in an old strawberry patch, begins an imaginary journey through his entire life, starting with his earliest memories. In the ruminations of this old man, Erikson saw clear and specific reflections of the eight stages he proposed.

Erikson demonstrated through Bergman's words that, like his other seven stages, this last stage involves a life crisis. Poignantly, the old doctor struggles to make sense out of the events of his life. He is ultimately successful in achieving a sense of integrity. The film is well worth seeing, and Erikson's analysis makes it an even more meaningful experience.

Despair When people look back over their lives and feel that they have made many wrong decisions, or more commonly, that they have not made any decisions at all.

To better understand what if feels like for an individual to reach late adulthood, you may want to read the following books: (1) Malcolm Cowley's *The view from 80* (New York: Penguin) is a personal account the author wrote when he was 82 years old. Critic Donald Hall describes this book as "Eloquent on the felt disparity between an unchanged self and the costume of altered flesh"; (2) *Coming of age,* written by Simone de Beauvoir, is a magnificent psychological study that provides an intense look at what it means, rather than how it feels, to become old.

Guided Review

8. Researchers with the Committee on Human Development found that adults between the ages of 54 and 94 changed their perception of how well they could control the environment and that there was a marked decline in the _____ _____ they invested in tasks as they aged.
9. _____ theory and _____ theory offer explanations of ways in which people cope with aging.
10. According to the disengagement theory, most adults will disengage themselves from their fellow human beings in preparation for _____.
11. According to Carstensen's socio-emotional selectivity theory, humans use social contact for four reasons: to obtain physical survival, to get information they need, to maintain a _____ _____ _____, and to acquire pleasure and comfort.
12. Erikson suggests that as we look back over our lives, if we see our lives as having been _____, we have achieved the goal of his final stage of life.

CONCLUSION & SUMMARY

Many changes happen during later adulthood. A "crossover" effect in gender roles occurs, sexual activity changes, and the nature of family relationships undergoes several alterations.

As we leave the industrial age and enter the age of information processing, the nation's older workers experience an incredibly different environment from that of their predecessors of 50 years ago. Even retirement is a much-changed

adventure. As in each of the preceding chapters, life appears as never-ending change but change with discernible patterns. Perhaps more stress takes place in old age than before, but more effective techniques are also available for dealing with it.

How do social relationships develop during late adulthood?

• A number of gerontologists have noted that people in late adulthood experience a "crossover" in gender roles: Older men become more like women, and older women become more like men.
• White summarizes that in late adulthood males are generally more sexually active than females but that declining activity in the female is usually attributable to

declining interest or illness in the male partner.

- Elderly people identify their adult children, when they have them, as the primary helpers in their lives. When these people have both an adult son and an adult daughter, elderly people most often name the son as the primary helper, although the daughter usually does most of the caregiving.

What are major factors affecting the older worker?

- Research suggests four basic phases through which most middle-aged and aged couples pass: child-launching,

childless preretirement, retirement, and widowhood.

- Although older people show less interest in working than younger people, discrimination and stereotypes about older workers underestimate their desire to help.
- Men usually find retirement more difficult than do women.

Is personality development any different among older adults?

- Neugarten's work on the effects of aging on personal development reveals that elderly people become more interested in their "inner

selves," perceptions of the environment change, psychic energy declines, gender-role reversals occur, and age-status becomes more rigid.

- The Committee on Human Development investigated patterns of aging, including activity theory and disengagement theory. Today, the more accepted explanation of elderly social behavior is Carstensen's socio-emotional selectivity theory.
- For Erikson resolution of each of the first seven stages in his eight-stage theory should lead people to achieve a sense of integrity in the last stage. If not, they experience despair.

KEY TERMS

Activity theory
Crossover
Despair
Disengagement theory

Existential love
Generative love
Impotency
Integrity

Prostatectomy
Role discontinuity
Socio-emotional selectivity theory

WHAT DO YOU THINK?

1. Traditionally in Western society, elderly men marrying young women has been more accepted than elderly women marrying young men. Why do you believe these attitudinal differences arose?
2. What is your position on sex in old-age institutions? Should there be any restrictions at all?

3. Which aspect of your family life do you most fear facing a change with as you get old?
4. What are some ways that the experience of older workers facing mandatory retirement could best be used in our society?
5. Some have said that whereas Erikson's first seven stages describe

crises in which action should be taken, the last stage, integrity versus despair, is merely reactive. All he has the elderly doing is sitting in a rocking chair and looking back over their lives. Do you believe that this criticism is valid?

CHAPTER REVIEW TEST

1. In late adulthood, crossover in sex roles means that
   a. older men and women identify with each other more.
   b. older men become more like women and older women become more like men.
   c. older men take on roles most often associated with women.
   d. older women take on roles most often associated with men.

2. Whether or not an older woman is sexually active depends mainly on her
   a. level of interest.
   b. marital status.

c. perception of her children's attitudes.
d. number of interpersonal relationships.

3. Examples of experiences that may inhibit or terminate sexual activity in adult men include
   a. physical changes.
   b. nonsupportive partners and peers.
   c. internal fears.
   d. All of the answers are correct.

4. What is the first phase of the life cycle most middle-aged couples go through?
   a. Widowhood

b. The retirement phase
c. The child-launching phase
d. The childless preretirement period

5. John and Sarah are the parents of three children and provide an example of generative love. They
   a. gladly make many sacrifices for the sake of the children.
   b. cherish the time they have with their children at present.
   c. expose their children to the culture and traditions of their ancestry.
   d. are committed to spending all their time with the children.

6. The reason most often given by widowers for not remarrying is
   a. many widows view remarriage as improper.
   b. children may oppose remarriage.
   c. there are three single women for every single man over age 65.
   d. All of the above.

7. Ganong and associates found that the obligation adult children feel toward helping their parent or their stepparent
   a. is much greater toward the parent.
   b. is about equal.
   c. is somewhat greater toward the parent.
   d. is usually greater toward the stepparent.

8. Older workers make valued employees for all of the following reasons, except lower
   a. absenteeism.
   b. turnover.
   c. accident rates.
   d. job skills.

9. Research conducted by Smith and Moen (1998) indicates that the decision to retire is primarily influenced by the retiree's
   a. spouse.
   b. job expectancies.

   c. sense of well-being.
   d. level of education.

10. Retirement may be most stressful for men because:
    a. they wish they could stay working.
    b. they feel they now have nothing to do.
    c. they worry over Social Security benefits.
    d. None of the above.

11. According to leisure theorists, a spillover function refers to
    a. when leisure is no more than an extension of work experiences and attitudes.
    b. when leisure time is engaged in to make up for disappointment and stress at work.
    c. when leisure time is spent worrying about stressful events at work.
    d. when leisure time takes away from time to be spent at work.

12. The idea that there are societal expectations about what is normal at various stages refers to
    a. gender roles.
    b. socialization.
    c. age-status.
    d. role continuity.

13. According to Carstensen socio-emotional selectivity theory,

    humans use _____
    _____ to obtain physical survival, information they need, the maintenance of a sense of self, and pleasure and comfort.
    a. psychological engagement
    b. social contact
    c. emotional reflection
    d. social love

14. When adults distance themselves from other human beings in preparation for death and become less interested in their interactions with others, it is referred to as
    a. disengagement theory.
    b. separation theory.
    c. distantiation.
    d. personal engagement theory.

15. For Erik Erikson, we are led to a sense of personal integrity by
    a. personal well-being.
    b. a sense of self-control.
    c. achievement.
    d. a sense that life has been well spent.

16. According to Erikson, people who are contemptuous of humanity
    a. have psychologically disengaged.
    b. have been socially rejected.
    c. are preparing for an attack.
    d. are looking back over their lives and hiding their fear of death.

Answers

1. b 2. b 3. d 4. c 5. a 6. d 7. c 8. d 9. a 10. b 11. a 12. c 13. b 14. a 15. d 16. d

I have touched my dead mother in dreams—her plump shoulder against my own. She tells me how to live, assures me the blue couch was a good choice."

Lisa Glatt

CHAPTER 19

Dying and Spirituality

As I said, you got to check out some time; you can't stay here forever. . . . Well, you just hope you go with a little dignity, that you don't have to suffer from Alzheimer's or die slowly in a rest home alone somewhere. I thought it was very interesting when I was in Bora Bora for six months. I was down there making a movie. . . . I did not live with the company, but found a house by myself up a road. There was a family next door—Polynesian natives—and the old lady of the house was there and she was dying. She suddenly said, "I'm going to die," and went to bed for three days and died. I remember at her funeral that everybody was dressed in white; it was like a wedding almost. And I was talking to them about it and they said, "Oh, yes, the fathers and the mothers are the most respected. They just go and die when they're ready." I said, "Geez, does that really go on like this all the time?" They said, "That's the way this society works." There are no old age homes, no old people wandering around, you know, suffering to death. Isn't it a strange thing, I thought to myself. What a respect for age that we don't have. . . . Like I say, life is like a hotel. We all check in and we all check out. Seems to me that the Polynesian approach to checking out is a great deal better than ours.

Actor Jason Robards, age 72 ✿

Chapter Objectives

After reading this chapter, you should be able to answer the following questions.

◆ What is the role of death in life?

◆ What is the purpose of "grief work"?

◆ What are the factors that cause and determine the nature of suicide?

◆ What is the meaning of "successful dying"?

◆ How do psychologists define the nature of spirituality?

The Role of Death in Life

Americans, who have long been accused of abhorring the subject of death, are now giving it considerable attention.

In this section, we review research and theory from the social and physical sciences to examine three major concerns: What is death? How do we deal with the death of others? How do we deal with our own death?

What Is Death?

The matter of my friend rests heavy upon me.
　　How can I be salved?
　　How can I be stilled?
　　My friend, who I loved, has turned to clay.
　　Must I, too, lie me down
　　Not to rise again for ever and ever?

Gilgamesh, c. 2000 B.C.E.

Since the first historian, Homer, began recording the lives of the Greeks, the meaning of death has been a central issue.

In the movies, death is almost invariably portrayed in the same sequence: Dying people make a final statement, close their eyes, fall back on the pillow or into the arms of a loved one, and are pronounced dead. In fact, death rarely occurs that way. In most cases, the person dies gradually. Death is a state, but dying is a process.

Ascertaining when people are truly and finally dead has been a medical problem for centuries. For example, in the early 1900s, Franz Hartmann claimed to have collected approximately 700 cases of premature burial or "close calls." In 1896 the "Society for the Prevention of Premature Burial" was founded. Fear of premature burial was so strong that in 1897 in Berlin, a patent was granted for a life signal device that sent up a warning flag and turned on a light if movement was detected inside the coffin.

We no longer have any serious problem in determining whether a person is dead. But determining exactly when death occurred has come to be of even greater importance because of organ donations. All the body's systems do not cease simultaneously, so disagreements exist over which system is most significant in judging whether a person is dead.

The more absolute death seems, the more authentic life becomes.

John Fowles

The Leading Causes of Death in the United States

In figure 19.1 we see listed the nine major causes of death for persons of all ages. The rates are given for males and females, and some of the differences in rates between the two are interesting. (Cerebrovascular diseases pertain to the heart and blood vessels, pulmonary diseases have to do with the lungs.)

Four Types of Death

Today, four types of death are recognized: clinical death, brain death, biological or cellular death, and social death.

Clinical Death

In one sense, the individual is dead when his or her respiration and heartbeat have stopped. This is the aspect of dying referred to in the movies when the doctor turns and sadly announces, "I'm sorry, but he's gone." Actually, **clinical death** is the least useful to the medical profession and to society at large because it is unreliable.

Due to the advent of **cardiopulmonary resuscitation (CPR),** many individuals whose lungs and heart had ceased to function have been saved. In other cases, spontaneous restarting of the heart and lungs has occurred after failure.

Clinical death The individual is dead when his or her respiration and heartbeat have stopped.

Cardiopulmonary resuscitation (CPR) A technique for reviving an individual's lungs and/or heart that have ceased to function.

Figure 19.1

Death rates by cause and sex, United States.

Statistics from *Statistical Abstract of the United States,* 1995 (p. 95) by U.S. Bureau of the Census, 1995, Washington, DC: U.S. Government Printing Office.

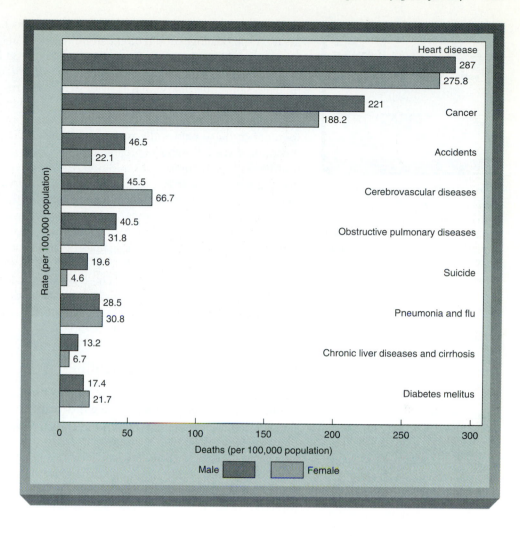

Brain Death

Brain death   Death of the brain occurs when it fails to receive a sufficient supply of oxygen for a short period of time (usually eight to ten minutes).

Death of the brain occurs when it fails to receive a sufficient supply of oxygen for a short period of time (usually 8 to 10 minutes). The cessation of brain function occurs in three stages: First the cortex stops, then the midbrain fails, and finally the brain stem ceases to function. When the cortex and midbrain stop operating, **brain death** has occurred, and the person enters an irreversible coma. The body can remain alive in this condition for a long time, because the autonomic processes such as breathing and heart beat are governed by the brain stem. Consciousness and alertness, however, will never be regained (Kammerman, 1988).

Biological Death

Biological death   Death occurs when it is no longer possible to discern an electrical charge in the tissues of the heart and lungs.

The cells and the organs of the body can remain in a functioning condition long after the failure of the heart and lungs. **Biological death** occurs when it is no longer possible to discern an electrical charge in the tissues of the heart and lungs.

Social Death

Social death   The point at which a patient is treated essentially as a corpse, although perhaps still "clinically" or "biologically" alive.

Sudnow (1967) was the first to suggest the concept of **social death,** which, "within the hospital setting, is marked at that point at which a patient is treated essentially as a corpse although perhaps still 'clinically' or 'biologically' alive" (p. 74). He cites cases in which body preparation (e.g., closing the eyes, binding the feet) were started while the patient was still alive, to make things easier for the staff. Also, in some cases, family members have signed autopsy permissions while the patient was still alive.

It is possible to ensure that all or part of your body will be donated for use after your death, usually by a designation on your driver's license. Have you done this? If not, what are your reasons for refraining?

Legal death Condition defined as "unreceptivity and unresponsivity, no movements or breathing, no reflexes, and a flat electroencephalogram (EEG) reading that remains flat for 24 hours."

Electroencephalogram (EEG) A graphic record of the electrical activity of the brain.

So when is a person really dead? If a person has suffered brain death, but the heart is still beating, should the heart be removed and used for a transplant operation?

One complex case (Goldsmith, 1988) involved the Loma Linda University Medical Center, famous for its work in the area of organ transplants. They attempted to initiate a program that would provide scarce organs for transplants. In this program, healthy hearts and other organs would be taken from babies born with anencephaly, a condition in which part or all of the brain is missing at birth. Ninety-five percent of these babies die within one week. When the anencephalic infants were born, they were flown to Loma Linda and given traditional "comfort care" (warmth, nutrition, and hydration). In addition, they were put on artificial breathing support for a maximum of seven days. The hospital maintained that they were put on respirators until a technical definition of brain death could be ascertained. But critics contended that this was done because the organs needed the time to mature for a successful transplant to occur. A storm of controversy ended the program before any donations could be made. Critics accused the hospital of "organ farming." The hospital argued that it was not only trying to increase the number of organ donors for infants but also giving the families of anencephalic babies an opportunity to "turn their tragedy into something good." With the advent of more advanced technology, the distinction between life and death becomes blurred, and the ethical considerations grow increasingly complex.

The Legal Definition of Death

In 1968 the Harvard Ad Hoc Committee to Examine the Criteria of Brain Death suggested the following criteria for **legal death:** "Unreceptivity and unresponsivity, no movements or breathing, no reflexes, and a flat **electroencephalogram (EEG)** reading that remains flat for 24 hours."

Such criteria preclude the donation of organs in most cases, because the organs would probably suffer irreparable damage in the 24 hours needed to check the EEG. Others have suggested that the time at which the cerebral cortex has been irreparably damaged should be accepted as the time when organs can be removed from the body (Jefko, 1980).

Organ donation is not the only difficulty involved. An increasing number of cases illustrate the ethical problem created by maintaining the life of comatose individuals with the support of technical equipment. A number of medical personnel, philosophers, and theorists have suggested that maintaining life under these conditions is wrong. What do you think?

Although scientists may disagree on the exact nature of death itself, we have been learning a great deal about how people deal, and how they should deal, with the death of their loved ones. We turn to that subject now.

Dealing Successfully with the Death of Others

Until this century, people were used to seeing death. It was considered a normal part of life. Half of all children died before their tenth birthday, one-third within their first year. Only in recent decades have the rates of death from all causes declined so much. Even the number of deaths from the scourge of AIDS is decreasing (CDC, 1996).

In modern Western societies, death comes mostly to the old. For example, 55 percent of all males are age 65 or over when they die, and almost a third are past 75. The mortality rate has declined in our country from 17 per 1,000 population in 1900 to slightly less than 9 per 1,000 today (U.S. Census, 1996). For the first time in history, a family may expect to live 20 years (on the average) without one of its members dying.

An important exception should be noted: the huge number of children who are losing their mothers to AIDS (CDC, 1996). As of 2000, 125,000 children and 21,000 adolescents will have suffered this fate. Four out of five of them are from African-American or Latino families.

The causes of overall lower mortality are clear: virtual elimination of infant and child mortality, and increasing control over the diseases of youth and middle age. For this reason, the subject of death became more and more taboo in the first half of this century. Probably as a result, social scientists spent little time studying our reactions to it or trying to find better ways to help us deal with it. Fortunately, in recent decades, this has changed.

Grief Work

No one ever told me that grief felt so like fear. I am not afraid, but the sensation is like being afraid. The same fluttering in the stomach, the same restlessness, the yawning. I keep on swallowing.

C. S. Lewis

Grief has a great deal in common with fear, and most grieving people really are afraid, at least unconsciously. They are frightened by the strength of their feelings and they often fear that they are losing their sanity. They feel that they cannot go on, that their loss is so great that their own lives are in danger.

Grief not only follows death; when there is advance warning, it frequently precedes it. Fulton (1977) found that anticipatory grief has four phases: depression, a heightened concern for the ill person, rehearsal of death, and finally an attempt to adjust to the consequences that are likely to occur after the death.

The topic of anticipatory grief has received increasing attention lately. Major debates have occurred about its exact nature. For example, Hill and associates (1988) found that those widows who had anticipated their husband's death reported a higher level of mental health than those who had not. Most researchers agree that a forewarning of the impending death of a loved one can have therapeutic consequences:

- Avoiding the shock and fear that often accompanies sudden death.

- Being able to make plans for the future that won't be regarded as betrayals.

- Expressing thoughts and feelings to the dying loved ones, thereby avoiding a sense of lost opportunity.

- A time to prepare for the changes ahead.

Pathological Grieving

The process of grieving, painful as it is, is experienced and resolved by most individuals. In some cases, however, morbid grief reactions occur that prevent the successful conclusion of this life crisis. Three types of these grief reactions are: delayed reaction, distorted reaction, and pathological mourning.

Anticipatory grief, which precedes the sick person's death, is usually very difficult. It often provides a number of benefits to the grieving, however.

Delayed Reaction

In some cases, the intense reaction of the first stage is postponed for days, months, and in some cases years. In these cases, it is common for some seemingly unrelated incident to bring to the surface an intense grieving, which the individual does not even recognize as grief. Take, for example, the case of a 42-year-old man who underwent therapy to deal with an unaccountable depression. It was soon discovered that when he was 22, his 42-year-old mother committed suicide. Apparently, the occurrence of his own 42nd birthday brought to the surface all the feelings that he had managed to repress since that time.

Distorted Reactions

In most cases, distorted reactions are normal symptoms carried to an extreme degree. They include adopting the behavior traits of the deceased, such as aspects of the deceased's fatal illness and other types of psychosomatic ailments, particularly colitis, arthritis, and asthma.

An example we know of is a young man whose mother died of lymphomic cancer. At her death, she had large boils on her neck. Some weeks after she died, her son discovered lumps on his neck that quickly developed into boils. On examination, they were found to be benign. In fact, it was determined that they were entirely psychosomatic. That is, the doctors decided that the only explanation of their existence was the great stress in the young man's mind over the loss of his mother.

An Applied View — *A Personal Experience of One of the Authors with Delayed Reaction*

I am stepping out of my role as an author to relate an experience of mine that is relevant to this discussion of the function of grief. In April 1957 I joined the U.S. Navy and sailed to the Mediterranean for a six-month tour of duty on an oil supply ship. In early November I returned home to a joyful reunion with my family. After this wonderful weekend at home, I returned to my ship. Two days later I received a telegram informing me of a tragedy: My mother, two younger brothers, and two younger sisters had been killed in a fire that had destroyed our house. My father and three younger brothers and a sister had escaped with serious burns.

On the long train ride home from the naval port, I recall thinking that, as the oldest, I should be especially helpful to my father in the terrible time ahead. I was also aware of a curious absence of dismay in myself.

In our medium-sized upstate New York town, the catastrophe was unprecedented, and expressions of grief and condolences were myriad. People kept saying to me, "Don't try to be so brave. It's good for you to let yourself cry." And I tried to, but tears just wouldn't come.

At the funeral, the caskets were closed, and I can remember thinking that maybe, just maybe, this was all just a horrible dream. I distinctly remember one fantasy about my brother Mike. He was born on my first birthday and in the several years before the fire, I had become especially close to him. I imagined that he had actually hit his head trying to escape and had wandered off to Chicago with a case of amnesia and that no one was willing to admit that

they didn't know where he was. I knew this wasn't true, but yet I secretly clung to the possibility. After a very difficult period of time, our family gradually began a new life. Many people generously helped us, and eventually the memories faded.

Several times in the years that followed, I went to doctors because of a stomachache, a painful stiff neck, or some other malady that couldn't be diagnosed physically. One doctor suggested that I might be suffering from an unresolved subconscious problem, but I doubted it.

Then one night in 1972, 15 years after the fire, I was watching *The Waltons' Christmas,* a television show in which the father of a close family is lost and feared dead. Although dissimilar from my own experience, this tragedy triggered an incredible response in me. Suddenly and finally it occurred to me: "My God, half my family is really gone forever!" I began sobbing and could not stop for more than three hours. When I finally stopped, I felt weak and empty, relieved of an awful burden. In the days that followed I believe I went through a clear-cut "delayed grief" reaction.

Therefore, the answer to the question, at least in my experience, is clear: Grief work really is essential, and we avoid it only at the cost of even greater pain. My father died some years ago, and my grief was immediate and intense. I cannot help but feel that my emotional response that time was considerably more appropriate and healthy.

John Dacey

To learn more about dealing with death, you may want to read one of the following books: (1) A Pulitzer Prize-winning novel related to this topic is Agee's, *A death in the family.* This novel focuses on the effect of a man's death on his young son; (2) Becker's, *The denial of death* provides a brilliant analysis of the human failure to acknowledge death, and explores the theories of Freud, Rank, Jung, Fromm, and others. Becker was awarded the Pulitzer Prize for this work; (3) One of Freud's most famous works, *Totem and taboo,* explains how psychoanalysis looks at death and dying.

The ultimate distorted reaction is depression so deep that it causes the death of a surviving loved one. This is especially likely to happen to widowers (Martikainen & Valkonen, 1996).

Pathological Mourning

In pathological mourning the process is not skipped but is prolonged and intensified to an abnormal degree (disabling distress is experienced for more than a few years) (Wortman & Davis, 1997). Frequently, the person suffering from pathological mourning tries to preserve every object of the deceased in perpetual memory.

An example of this illness is the man who worked hard with his wife to renovate an old cottage they had bought in order to live by a lake not far from their home. A few days before they were going to move in, she died of a heart attack. Many months later, friends noticed that he would disappear for several days at a time. One friend followed him to the cottage and found that he had created a shrine to her memory in it. Her clothes and other possessions were laid out in all the rooms, and her picture was on all the walls. Only after extensive therapy was he able to go through a more normal grief, give up the shrine, and move on with his life.

The Role of Grief

Most psychologists who have examined the role of grief have concluded that it is an essential aspect of a healthy encounter with the crisis of death. They believe that open confrontation with the loss of a loved one is essential to accepting the reality of a world in which the deceased is no longer present. Attempts to repress or avoid thoughts about the loss are only going to push them into the subconscious, where they will continue to cause problems until they are dragged out and accepted fully.

And yet, dealing with grief is also costly. For example, the mortality rate among grieving persons is seven times higher than a matched sample of nongrieving persons. On the other hand, the Japanese are most reticent about public grief and yet seem to suffer no ill effects from this reticence. The Balinese frequently laugh at the time of death, because, they say, they are trying to avoid crying; yet they seem to be psychologically healthy. Some cultures employ "keeners" who wail loudly so that the bereaved will not have to do so themselves.

An Applied View — Dealing with Grief and Associated Anger

Many people suffering from grief and the anger that often accompanies it believe that their only option is to "wait it out" and "just get through it." As one client we know put it, "I can't believe I'm so weak that I can't get past this!" In fact, grief sufferers have a number of options; most of these activities can provide relief from their pain, often by turning it to some good:

- Join a volunteer program. For example, those who have lost a loved one in a drunk driving incident can join Mothers Against Drunk Driving.
- Volunteer to do work for a friend or neighbor who needs the help.
- Find physical outlets for painful feelings—anything from an exercise club to beating the carpets with a broom.
- Talk about feelings with a trusted friend or relative.
- Seek psychotherapeutic help. There are specialists who are trained to help with grief and anger.
- Join a support group. In addition to groups that deal generally with grief or anger, there are specialty groups such as groups for those who have lost a child or are related to a suicide victim.
- Work for a hotline such as those operated by the Good Samaritans.
- Learn to meditate.
- Join a yoga class.

Research by Wortman and Silver (1997) on the grief response found that a number of widely held beliefs are not supported by the evidence. They concluded that:

- A significant proportion of those who report little or no distress or depression after the death of a loved one also did not experience physical maladies as a result.

- Delayed grief does exist but it is extremely rare.

- Many physicians refrain from prescribing antidepressants and anti-anxiety drugs, believing that loss must equal suffering.

- Arriving at some philosophical reason for the loss of a loved one only rarely results in a lessening of distress. People who struggle to learn "Why me?" tend to have more distress than those who do not look for answers.

- The idea that grieving normally ends after one year is false; there is wide variation in the length of time people need to recover from loss.

- People often feel that they should cover up their grief if it goes on over a year, because others are made uncomfortable by it. This attitude of "grin and bear it" often prevents sufferers from getting the psychological help that can ease their burden.

The Role of the Funeral

One of the hardest aspects of dealing with the death of a loved one is deciding how the funeral (if there is to be one) is to be conducted. Funerals have always been an important part of American life, whether the elaborate burial rituals practiced by Native Americans, or the simple funerals of our colonial forebears.

Once the intimate responsibility of each family, care for the dead in the United States has been transferred to a paid service industry. The need for this new service was brought about by changes in society during the first part of this century. The more mobile, urbanized workforce had less family support and less time to devote to the task of caring for the dead. In a relatively short time, funeral homes and funeral directors became the accepted form of care for one's dead relatives.

This commercialization of care for the dead has had mixed results. During the 1950s and 1960s, funeral homes came under stinging criticism for their expense and their lack of sensitivity to the needs of the surviving family members. The bereaved often felt that the funeral directors were more interested in dramatic and expensive presentations of the body than in what might be best for the family members.

In your opinion, what are the appropriate arrangements for a funeral? Are you in favor of formal religious services? Why or why not?

Dealing Successfully with One's Own Death

Having nearly died, I've found death like that sweet feeling that people have that let themselves slide into sleep. I believe that this is the same feeling that people find themselves in whom we see fainting in the agony of death, and I maintain that we pity them without cause. If you know not how to die, never trouble yourself. Nature will in a moment fully and sufficiently instruct you; she will exactly do that business for you; take you no care for it.

Michel de Montaigne

Why is the acceptance of death so painful to so many of us? Why does it come up in every developmental stage, only to be partially resolved and partially denied?

Many people find dying a much harder experience than Montaigne would have us believe it is. Many dying patients feel seriously depressed before their deaths, and a large number have suicidal feelings. Among the reasons for these depressions are the following:

- Medication-induced mood alterations

- Awareness of how little time is left

A Sociocultural VIEW

The Funeral in Other Times and Countries

Looking at the funeral practices of former cultures shows us not only how they buried their dead but also something about their values.

Ancient Egypt

Upon the death of the head of the house in ancient Egypt, women would rush frantically through the streets, beating their breasts from time to time and clutching their hair. The body of the deceased was removed as soon as possible to the embalming chambers, where a priest, a surgeon, and a team of assistants proceeded with the embalming operation. (The Egyptians believed in the life beyond; embalming was intended to protect the body for this journey.) While the body was being embalmed, arrangements for the final entombment began. When the mummified corpse was ready for the funeral procession and installation in its final resting place, it was placed on a sledge drawn by oxen or men and accompanied by wailing servants, professional mourners simulating anguished grief, and relatives. It was believed that when the body was placed in an elaborate tomb (family wealth and prestige exerted an obvious influence on tomb size), its spirits would depart and later return through a series of ritualistic actions.

Ancient Greece

Reverence for the dead permeated burial customs during all phases of ancient Greek civilization. Within a day after death the body was washed, anointed, dressed in white, and laid out in state for one to seven days, depending on the social prestige of the deceased. Family and friends could view the corpse during this time. For the funeral procession, the body was placed on a bier carried by friends and relatives and followed by female mourners, fraternity members, and hired dirge singers. Inside the tomb were artistic ornaments, jewels, vases, and articles of play and war. Like the Egyptians, the ancient Greeks prepared their tombs and arranged for subsequent care while they were still alive. About 1000 B.C.E. the Greeks began to cremate their dead. Although earth burial was never entirely superseded, the belief in the power of the flame to free the soul acted as a strong impetus to the practice of cremation. A choice of burial or cremation was available during all the late Greek periods.

The Roman Empire

Generally speaking, the Romans envisioned some type of afterlife and, like the Greeks, practiced both cremation and earth burial. When a wealthy person died, the body was dressed in a white toga and placed on a funeral couch, feet to the door, to lie in state for several days. For reasons of sanitation, burial within the walls of Rome was prohibited; consequently, great roads outside the city were lined with elaborate tombs erected for the well-to-do. For the poor, there was no such magnificence; for slaves and aliens, there was a common burial pit outside the city walls.

Anglo-Saxon England

In Anglo-Saxon England (approximately the time when invading Low German tribes conquered the country in the fifth century), the body of the deceased was placed on a bier or in a hearse. On the corpse was laid the book of the Gospels as a symbol of faith and the cross as a symbol of hope. For the journey to the grave, a pall of silk or linen was placed over the corpse. The funeral procession included priests bearing lighted candles and chanting psalms, friends who had been summoned, relatives, and strangers who deemed it their duty as a corporal work of mercy to join the party. Mass was then sung for the dead, the body was solemnly laid in the grave (generally without a coffin), the mortuary fee was paid from the estate of the deceased, and liberal alms were given to the poor.

Colonial New England

Burials and funeral practices were models of simplicity and quiet dignity in eighteenth century New England. Upon death, neighbors (or possibly a nurse if the family was well-to-do) would wash and lay out the body. The local carpenter or cabinetmaker would build the coffin, selecting a quality of wood to fit the social position of the deceased. In special cases, metal decorations imported from England were used on the coffin. In church, funeral services consisted of prayers and sermons said over the pall-covered bier. Funeral sermons often were printed (with skull and crossbones prominently displayed) and circulated among the public. The funeral service at the grave was simple, primarily a brief prayer followed by the ritual commitment of the body to the earth. The filling of the grave, with neighbors frequently supplying the necessary labor because there were no professional gravediggers, marked the formal end of the early-colonial funeral ceremony.

Let's hope it won't happen, but what would you do if you were called upon to organize a funeral tomorrow? Would you know whom to notify? How would you arrange for the preparation and disposition of the body? What kind of ceremony, religious or otherwise, would you ask for? What would you do about a funeral home, a cemetery plot, and the will and death benefits of the deceased?

Perhaps you could discuss this with some of your friends or classmates, to see how they would feel. Notice how you feel about opinions that differ from yours.

Source: Turner & Helms (1989, pp. 492–93).

- Feelings of isolation from relatives and friends who are withdrawing

- Feelings of grief for the losses that are close at hand

- Feelings of disillusion and resentment over injustice

Depression is sometimes described as cognitive withdrawal because many patients have a decreasing ability and motivation to process stimuli as death nears (see terminal drop, chapter 17).

Must dying, then, always be such an unhappy experience? European psychiatrist Elisabeth Kübler-Ross is the most famous student of the process of death. Her three books on the subject have all been best sellers: *On Death and Dying* (1969), *Death—The Final Stage of Growth* (1975), and *To Live Until We Say Good-bye* (1978). Kübler-Ross discovered that, far from wanting to avoid the topic of death, many dying patients have a strong urge to discuss it. She interviewed hundreds of terminally ill persons. On the basis of these interviews, she developed a five-stage theory, describing the emotions that underlie the process of dying. The stages in her theory are flexible, in that people can move through them quickly, slowly, or not at all. Some fluctuation occurs between the stages, but by and large people tend to move through them in sequential order. They are portrayed in figure 19.2.

Kübler-Ross's stage theory was the first to counter the common assumption that it is abnormal to have strong emotions during the dying process. However, no empirical confirmation that this particular sequence of stages is universal exists. Her theory overlooks the effects of personality, ethnic, or religious factors. For example, people in some cultures such as some Native American and Asian ethnic groups view death as just another stage of existence, and do not encourage dread of it. So, should we accept Kübler-Ross' model or not? The biological, psychological, and social aspects of the process of dying are obviously very complex. We will need to know much more—knowledge gained through careful research—before we can answer this question. We can say that her theory, like all good theories, has at least provided us with five constructs (the five stages) to help guide that research.

Another theory, also based on observation and also describing five stages, is that of Saunders (1989). Her suggested stages are shock, awareness of loss, withdrawal, healing, and renewal. The similarities with Kübler-Ross' stages are noteworthy. Wortman and Silver (1989) agree with the themes presented by Kübler-Ross and Saunders but urge that they do not occur in set stages in all individuals. Rather, these studies find that the themes are intermingled, ending with some people on a positive note and others react finally with anger and/or depression. As to the latter, some have urged that it is the right reaction. We are reminded of Dylan Thomas' famous lines of poetry (*Collected Poems,* 1971), addressed to his father:

**Do not go gentle into that dark night—
Rage, rage against the dying of the light!**

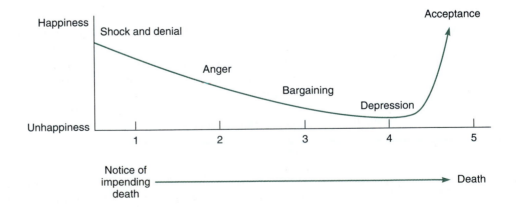

Figure 19.2

Kübler-Ross' stages of dying.

From E. Kübler-Ross, *On Death and Dying,* Macmillan, New York, 1969.

No matter how well prepared we are, death is always sad and stressful. Most of the time, though, we know that we can do nothing about it, and so we must accept the inevitable. How different it is when the death was not inevitable but was chosen by the person because life had become no longer worth living.

Guided Review

1. Currently four different definitions of death exist: clinical death (stoppage of respiration and heart), brain death (cessation of cortex and midbrain activity), _____ death (not possible to discern electrical changes in tissues of heart and lungs), and _____ death (person treated essentially as dead).

2. The criteria for legal death is unreceptivity, no movements or breathing, no reflexes, and a flat _____ reading that remains flat for 24 hours.

3. The causes in Western society for lower mortality rates are the reduction of infant and child mortality and increasing control over the _____ of youth and middle age.

4. In addition to normal grief, there are three types of morbid grief reactions: _____ grief, distorted reactions, and _____ mourning.

5. Anticipatory grief is characterized by four phases: _____, a heightened concern for the ill person, _____ of death, and an attempt to adjust to the consequences that will occur after death.

6. Most psychologists believe that grief is essential as a part of a _____ encounter with death, but the forms that healthy grief might take have not yet been studied well empirically.

7. People may feel depressed before their own death because they are experiencing feelings of loss for friends and family, as well as feeling a sense of _____ over injustice.

8. Elisabeth Kübler-Ross argues that dying has five stages. These stages are shock and denial, anger, _____, depression, and acceptance.

To better understand how we, as individuals, handle our own death, read: (1) Kübler-Ross' *On death and dying,* a classic in this field; (2) Tolstoy's *The death of Ivan Illich,* a novel about a man who learns that he has terminal cancer, and his lonely journey into understanding the meaning of life and the ability to accept his own death.

Suicide: The Rejection of Life

As you will see, we are beginning to learn more about how and why suicides happen. This information will surely help us in our efforts to prevent such unfortunate deaths.

The Overall Picture

Suicide and attempted suicide among adolescents are growing national problems (Holinger & others, 1987) and an increasingly common response to stress and depression among young persons (Dempsey, 1994). Suicide now ranks as the second leading cause of death among persons age 15 to 19, and many experts believe that if no suicides were "covered up," it would be the leading cause. The rates were higher for whites than for non-whites (USDHHS, 1996). Younger adults today have generally higher rates of suicide than their grandparents did at that age (Conwell, 1995; Centers for Disease Prevention and Control, 1996). Teenagers have become not only more suicidal but apparently more reckless and self-destructive in general. As the suicide rate has risen steadily over the past 20 years, so too has the rate for motor vehicle accidents (the leading cause of death), accidents of other types, and homicides (U.S. Bureau of the Census, 1992).

Answers

1. biological, social 2. electroencephalogram (EEG) 3. diseases 4. delayed, pathological 5. depression, rehearsal 6. healthy 7. resentment 8. bargaining

Although suicide rates for teenagers have risen 72 percent since 1988, the rate for most other age groups has decreased. It would be safe to say that although the United States as a whole has become slightly less suicidal, teenagers and young people in general (age 30 and under) have become dramatically more suicidal. The increase has risen most steadily and most consistently among teenagers. It should be noted, however, that teen suicidal deaths rank high because teens have a relatively low rate of death from other causes (Swedo & others, 1991).

Two other groups are much more prone to suicide, however: the so-called middle-old and old-old groups. Although the suicide rate for 15- to 24-year-olds is high—12.5 per 100,000—the rate for those 75 and older is almost double that, with males accounting for almost all the difference (U.S. National Center for Health Statistics, 1996). In fact, the older single white male is by far the person most likely to die from suicide (USDHHS, 1996). Accordingly, since older people make up the fastest growing portion of the population, the number of suicides among the elderly will continue to rise (Conwell & others, 1990). Glass and Reed (1993) stated that although teenage suicides receive significantly more media attention, elderly people are at higher risk for suicide than any other age group.

For the elderly, poor health is often a cause of suicide because it causes depression. Poor health is used as a way of covering up suicide. Furthermore, Leibson and associates (1999) warn that older people with serious depression often do not provide accurate health information when questioned in research studies. It was found that illnesses reported by doctors records were more accurate in describing a depressed state than the person's self-report. Loneliness is a second major factor. Effects of factors and forces on the behavior of people are important to understanding the causes leading to suicide (Mishara, 1996). It should be noted that for unstable individuals, even minor changes in their life patterns can push them either toward committing suicide or inhibit their tendency to do so.

There is the story of an elderly retiree from the police force who had made an excellent adjustment to leaving the force. When he discovered that he had a large brain tumor, however, he became very depressed at the thought of leaving his wife, children, and nine grandchildren, to all of whom he was deeply attached. One day, after asking his wife to go to the store for his favorite candy, he shot himself. His wife discovered him and threw away his pistol. She told the paramedics she saw a man fleeing from her house. The "case" remained unsolved, and she was able to bury her husband in a Catholic cemetery.

The Influence of Gender on Suicide

At all ages, major gender differences exist. The rate for males is much higher due to the type of suicidal behavior engaged in, the methods used, the lethality of the attempt, and the degree of psychiatric disturbance present. Males and females are two very different suicidal types. Universally, males are about four times more likely

Males are three to four times more likely to die of suicide attempts than are females.

to die of suicide than females (Statistical Abstract of the U.S., 1995). Attempt rates show even more dramatic gender differences, but in the opposite direction. Failed attempts at suicide among females are much higher than for males (Woodruff-Pak, 1988). A major reason for the high survival rate among females is the method used. Whereas males often resort to such violent and effective means as firearms and hanging, females tend to choose less violent and less deadly means, such as pills. Male suicide attempters are considered significantly more disturbed than female attempters (Blum & others, 1992). Males are usually more committed to dying and therefore succeed far more often.

In light of the increase of suicides among the elderly, the prevention of suicide is gaining more attention (Cattell & Jolley, 1995). Health care professionals can play an important role in suicide prevention. Examining the practical role of the community in the lives of the elderly is a good beginning in these prevention efforts.

It should be noted, however, that although some elderly people may contemplate suicide, many have successfully resisted the urge to commit it. Older adults have certain coping abilities and reasons for living that enable them to face many demands of advanced age (Range & Stringer, 1996). One possible reason that more men than women die by their own hands is that older women are able to list more reasons for living than are men. In fact, Range and Stringer reported that older women often have greater ability to cope than they even realize. The authors suggest that suicide prevention strategies target men and encourage the development of deterrents to suicide.

Guided Review

9. Suicide and attempted suicide is an increasingly common response to _____ and depression among young people.
10. The suicide rate for men and women over 70 years of age is almost _____ as high as for men and women between the ages of 15 and 24 years.
11. Younger adults today have generally (lower, higher) rates of suicide than their grandparents did at that age.
12. For the elderly, _____ _____, depression, and _____ are some of the major factors of suicide.

An Applied View

The Danger Signs of Suicide

- Sudden changes in mood or behavior.
- Pulling away from family and friends.
- Marked increase or decrease in sleeping.
- Becoming "accident prone."
- Talking about death or suicide, or heightened interest in reading about them.
- Heightened interest in music or art that deals with death.
- Giving away favorite possessions.
- Impetuous desire to get affairs in order.
- Abrupt drop in school or work performance.
- Impulsive drug and alcohol abuse.
- Changes in personal hygiene.

- Lack of interest in food.
- Unusual anger, anxiety, or apathy.
- Hypochondria.
- Inability to concentrate.
- Experience of serious personal loss.
- Previous history of suicide attempts.

No single one of these signs is in itself a clear indication of suicidal ideation. Several of them, however, are cause for concern. Anyone talking about committing suicide should be taken seriously and a mental health professional should be consulted, even when you feel sure the person is "only talking about it to get attention or sympathy."

Answers

9. stress 10. twice 11. higher 12. poor health; loneliness

An Applied View — My Attempts at Suicide (by Anonymous)

My first psychiatrist told my parents that my psychological tests indicated that I was potentially suicidal. I was 14 then. At 22, I had made five suicide attempts and had been in six mental institutions, which add up to 29 months as a mental patient and five years of intensive therapy. My diagnosis was borderline schizophrenia, chronic depression, and sadomasochism. Why? How had I become so obsessed with suicide?

When I flash back on my adolescent days, I remember feeling ugly, socially awkward, stuck away in an all-girls' boarding school reading Camus and Hesse, unpopular, and stupid! In fact, I was not quite as dreadful as all that, but in my mind I was. I felt different. I once wrote, "I'm at the bottom of an upside-down garbage can and it's so ugly." The world was horrible, but I was the worst part of it.

Suicide was my escape. Unsuccessful suicide attempts put me in the care of others who delicately forced me to confront my feelings of sadness and anger. I had to learn to share with others and sometimes that was what I secretly wanted. Two of my attempts, however, were calculated, purposeful acts. Despite what shrinks may say, I wanted to be dead, not taken care of.

What did death mean to me? One of my earliest memories is sitting on moss-covered ground in a grove of pines, reading *The Prayer for the Dead* with my basset hound curled up beside me. Suicide meant escape from hell on earth. No other purgatory could be worse than this one. Even if I were reincarnated, I would end up being some "lowly animal" with the kind of mind that could not plague me with frightening, lonely, depressing thoughts. I clung to my friends and family, but it only increased my anger and self-contempt. I treated those people as my keepers who temporarily saved me from being left alone with my tormenting mind.

The final blow hit in Boston. I gradually withdrew from the few friends I had as well as my family. Death had grown so close that I no longer felt that I had much time. It was impossible to commit myself to anyone or anything. I was reserved, yet few people could sense how obsessed I was with death. Signs of affection terrified me because I knew I could not let anyone count on me. I needed death if life became too unbearable.

It finally did. I had become so passive that I no longer made contact with people. They had to call me. So much time had elapsed since I had felt close to someone that it seemed my "disappearance" would not really upset anyone. In addition to this, I was convinced that I was too stupid to handle academics or even a menial job (even though I had two jobs at the time). On a day when I knew no one would try and reach me, I took three times the lethal dosage of Seconal.

I was found 24 hours later and came out of a coma after 48 more. My arm was paralyzed. This time, I was placed in a long-term hospital. Another try at life began.

With the help of an excellent therapist and the patient love of those whom I had thus far rejected, I have started once more. It has been two years since I took the pills. I think I know why people bother to live now.

"Successful" Dying

Death and dying, by whatever means, are not one of our favorite topics, but they do have an important place in our study of life. In the next section of this chapter, we will discuss two of the ways we humans have to deal with death in a mature and satisfying way.

Death with Dignity

So, my judges, face death with good hope, and know for certain that no evil can happen to a good man, either in life or after death.

Socrates

Euthanasia Means a "good death." There are two types: passive euthanasia, in which the patient's legal instructions are carried out by the medical team, and active euthanasia, in which the patient's life is ended in ways that are now illegal.

No doubt most people would rather not suffer serious physical pain when they die, and many would prefer to avoid the emotional pain that often attends death. Until recently, however, only a few had any choice. Today, great debates have formed around two alternatives, both of them a form of **euthanasia.** There are two types of euthanasia (which means a "good death" in Greek). Passive euthanasia refers to refraining from continuing efforts to sustain a faltering life, such as turning off life-

Physician-assisted suicide
Doctors give patients death-inducing drugs.

support systems. These methods are either covered by a living will or are determined by the patient's legal representative. Active euthanasia means actively ending a life, either through directly killing the patient or by **physician-assisted suicide** (PAS). In PAS, it is against the law everywhere for the physician to actually give the patient a death-inducing drug. In Holland doctors do administer such drugs, but without legal protection (they aren't prosecuted). In Oregon, there is a law allowing doctors to prescribe such drugs, but the patients must take it themselves.

On 30 September 1976, Governor Edmund Brown, Jr., of California signed the "Natural Death Act," the first death with dignity law in the nation. The statute states the right of an adult to sign a written directive instructing her or his physician to withhold or withdraw life-sustaining procedures in the event of a terminal condition. The law contains specific definitions for "terminal condition," "life-sustaining procedure," and "qualified patient." The directive must be drawn up in the form set forth by the statute. It must be signed and dated by an adult of sound mind and witnessed by two persons not related by blood or entitled to the estate of the declarant.

Since then all but 10 states have established such procedures. In June 1990 the Supreme Court ruled that because the desires of a Missouri woman who has been lying in a coma since 1983 had not been made explicit through a living will, she could not be allowed to die despite her parents' wishes. However, the Court has ruled that when procedures established within each state are followed, the "right to die" would be constitutional.

Almost 80 percent of Americans die in hospitals, and 70 percent of those deaths involve some aspect of medical technology such as breathing, feeding, and waste elimination equipment. Hence it is essential that those who do not want to be maintained on life-support systems if they become terminal put their wishes in writing according to their state's laws. Open communication with one's doctor is also essential (Lynn & others, 1996).

Physician-Assisted Suicide

Whatever you want to do, do it now. There are only so many tomorrows.

Anne Morrow Lindbergh

Today there is also a serious debate taking place over the appropriateness of physician-assisted suicide (Foreman, 1996). In this case, someone on the medical team typically injects an overdose of morphine, which quickly brings on unconsciousness and death. Those who support it claim a number of advantages for it: time of death is up to the patient; it can be used by those for whom the hospice or hospital is inappropriate; and death is painless if the patient is given a high enough dose of morphine. Shapiro (2000) describes the experience of a Dutch doctor, Dr. Herbert Cohen:

> "He performed euthanasia between 50 and 100 times until he gave up his family practice a few years ago. Sometimes, he brought flowers. Sometimes his patient gave him a bottle of wine and they toasted death together. Often, a minister present read the 23rd Psalm. Yet each time, Cohen says about helping the patient die, 'it is a mountain you have to climb'" (p. 148).

Others suggest that its limitations are: it is an extreme way to end suffering; some family members may be made to feel guilty; it may interfere with healing in relationships; it is opposed by most major religions; and it could be abused in order to save money. In a letter to the Supreme Court from his deathbed (Woodward & McCormick, 1996, p. 62), Cardinal Bernardin wrote, "As one who is dying, I have especially come to appreciate the gift of life. Creating a new right to assisted suicide will endanger society and send a false signal that a less than 'perfect' life is not worth living."

At this time, the American public seems to favor physician-assisted suicide. Polls have found that two-thirds of the American public wants legislation permitting some form of the practice (Taylor, 1995). The American Medical Association's Council of Ethical and Judicial Affairs (Goodman, 1998) has proposed new guidelines for the optimal use of directives. The guidelines urge the use of detailed worksheets in tailoring end-of-life care to the specific preferences of the patient. They proposed a process that physicians should be required to follow when educating their patients about death and dying. It remains to be seen whether or not these directives will be enacted.

The Hospice: "A Better Way of Dying"

The "death ward" in most hospitals is not a nice place to be. The atmosphere is one of hushed whispers and fake smiles. No children below the age of 12 are allowed. Medications to control the pain are usually given on a schedule rather than as needed. Machines are used to continue life at all costs, though the patient may

The modern hospice is organized to afford a more "natural death" to the dying. Although this woman knows she does not have long to live she is able to maintain a positive attitude with the help of the hospice staff.

desire death. Viewing a typical American death ward made British historian Toynbee conclude that "Death is un-American."

In reaction to this, some have reached back to the Middle Ages, when religious orders set up havens in which dying pilgrims could come to spend their last days. The modern **hospice** was established to provide for a more "natural" death for those who are terminally ill. The first U.S. hospice opened in New Haven, Connecticut, in 1971. Since then the National Hospice Organization has been formed to help promulgate this movement.

The hospice is not a new type of facility; it is a new philosophy of patient care in the United States (although not new in Europe). Hospices do pioneering work in such neglected areas as the easing of pain and psychological counseling of patients and their families. Even before patients begin to suffer pain, which in diseases such as cancer can be excruciating, they are given a mixture of morphine, cocaine, alcohol, and syrup so they come to realize that pain can be controlled. Known as "Brompton's Mixture," this concoction is used only when the patient's need is severe; it is very effective in alleviating both pain and the fear accompanying it. A major goal of the hospice is to keep the person's mind as clear as possible at all times.

The hospice program movement has now grown to the point that it supports its own journal. Articles in the *Hospice Journal* often provide supplementary information about special issues concerning the terminally ill. For example, an article on hospice care for patients with AIDS (Schofferman, 1987) delved into additional issues of concern: irrational fear of contagion, homophobia (fear of homosexuals) by friends and relatives, and special difficulties in caring for substance abusers.

One of the major questions now being considered is whether the hospice should continue as a separate facility run solely for that purpose or become a standard part of all major hospitals. Currently, hospice programs in the United States are primarily home-based care, with the sponsorship of such programs evenly divided between hospitals and community agencies. Many insurance programs now cover hospice care. Although many assume hospices deal only with the elderly, as can be seen in figure 19.3, nearly one-third of the patients are younger than 65.

Whatever the case, for most of us, dying is frightening and, ultimately, very hard to understand. To come to terms with it, we almost always rely on our spiritual rather than our cognitive powers.

Hospice   Services aimed at relieving suffering of terminally ill patients.

Figure 19.3

Growth of hospices in the United States.

Guided Review

13. A law was passed in California in 1976 that allows death with dignity, which means that adults have the right to legally state their rejection of _____ procedures when they are in a terminal condition.
14. The hospice was established to provide a more _____ death for people who are terminally ill.
15. The hospice movement contributes to the death with dignity movement by providing relief from distressing symptoms and providing a _____ _____ for the terminal patient.
16. One of the major goals of the hospice is to keep the patient's _____ as clear as possible.

Spirituality

There is but one true philosophical problem, and this is suicide:
Judging whether life is or is not worth living amounts to answering
the fundamental question of philosophy.

Albert Camus

Spirituality is concerned not only with whether life is worth living but why it is worth living. It may involve the attempt to better understand the reasons for living through striving to know the intentions of a Supreme Being. An example is reading inspired books such as the Bible, the Koran, and Native American writings. Another is trying to discern the purposes and goals of some universal life force by, for example, examining historical trends in biological changes of species. In any case, spirituality includes all of our efforts to gain insight into the underlying, overriding forces of life. For many, it is the only justification for morality.

How important a role does spirituality play in the lives of typical American adults? One way this question has been investigated is through looking at religious participation and at religious attitudes. These factors are sometimes misleading, but together they offer one part of the answer to the question.

Religious Participation

Americans have always been highly religious. This statement is supported by numerous Gallup polls (Gallup, 1998). A majority of the elderly consider religious practice to be of major importance in their lives. According to surveys, 96 percent of those over 65 believe in God, and 82 percent report that religion plays a significant role in their lives.

Religious values become stronger with age. For example, the percentage of people who express strong religious beliefs increases from 35 percent among young adults to 47 percent in middle age to 66 percent among the elderly. Attending services once or more each month grows among these three age groups from 50 percent to 67 percent to nearly 75 percent (Russell, 1989). Furthermore, the influence of religion appears to be highly related to a sense of well-being in elderly persons.

In their study of 836 elderly persons, Koenig and associates (1988) attempted to clear this up. They looked at nonorganizational practices (prayer, Bible reading, etc.) and subjective religious feelings, as well as organized religious practices. They found moderately strong correlations between morale and all three religious measures. The relationships were especially strong for women and for those over 75.

An Applied View — If You Had Your Life to Live Over Again, What Would You Do Differently?

This question was recently asked of 122 retired persons by DeGenova (1992). She discovered that her sample chose the pursuit of education more than any other area. This emphasis on education among retirees may be because they feel their lack of education led to missed or limited opportunities. Although these people indicated they would have spent more time doing a variety of things, they said that they would have spent less time worrying about work.

This poem describes the feelings of one 81-year-old lady, Nadine Stair, on the topic:

If I had my life to live over,
I'd like to make more mistakes next time.
I'd relax, I would limber up. I would be sillier
than I have been this trip. I would take fewer
things seriously. I would take more chances.
I would climb more mountains and swim more
rivers. I would eat more ice cream and less

beans. I would perhaps have more actual troubles,
but I'd have fewer imaginary ones.
You see, I'm one of those people who live sensibly
and sanely hour after hour, day after day. Oh, I've
had my moments, and if I had it to do over again,
I'd have more of them. In fact, I'd try to have
nothing else. Just moments, one after another,
instead of living so many years ahead of each day.
I've been one of those persons who never goes
anywhere without a thermometer, a hot water
bottle, a raincoat, and a parachute. If I had to do
it again, I would travel lighter than I have.
If I had my life to live over, I would start
barefoot earlier in the spring and stay that way
later in the fall.
I would go to more dances.
I would ride more merry-go-rounds.
I would pick more daisies!

Spirituality does appear to develop with age. A number of theories have been offered as to how and why this is so. Among them, four views have come to receive highest regard: those of Viennese psychoanalysts Viktor Frankl and Carl Jung, sociobiologist E. O. Wilson, and theologian James Fowler.

Frankl's Theory of Spirituality

Frankl (1967) described human life as developing in three interdependent stages according to the predominant dimension of each stage.

1. The *somatic* (physical) *dimension.* According to the somatic dimension, all persons are motivated by the struggle to keep themselves alive and to help the species survive. This intention is motivated entirely by instincts. It exists at birth and continues throughout life.

2. The *psychological dimension.* Personality begins to form at birth and develops as a result of instincts, drives, capacities, and interactions with the environment. The psychological dimension and the somatic dimension are highly developed by the time the individual reaches early adulthood.

Religious life is of great importance to many of the elderly.

Dr. Victor Frankl, survivor of six years in a Nazi concentration camp, has made many contributions to the field of psychology and spirituality.

3. The *noetic dimension*. The noetic dimension has roots in childhood but primarily develops in late adolescence. It is spiritual not only in the religious sense but also in the totality of the search for the meaningfulness of life. This aspect distinguishes humans from all other species. The freedom to make choices is the basis of responsibility. Reason exists in the noetic realm. Conscience, which greatly affects the meaningfulness that we discover in life, resides in the noetic.

Frankl believed that development in the physical and personality dimensions results from the total sum of the influences bearing upon an individual. The noetic, on the other hand, is greater than the sum of its parts. This means that we as adults are responsible for inventing (or reinventing) ourselves! Whatever weaknesses our parents may have given us, we can and should try to overcome them. They need not govern our lives.

Jung's Theory of Spirituality

Jung (1971), a student of Freud's, agreed to a large extent with his mentor's description of development in the first half of the human life. But he felt that Freud's ideas were inadequate to describe development during adulthood. Jung saw spiritual development as occurring in two stages.

The First Half of Life

In each of the Jungian functions of thinking, feeling, sensing, and intuiting, the personality develops toward individuation (see chapter 14). Most people are well individuated by the middle of life, at approximately age 35; that is, we are most different from each other at this age.

The Second Half of Life

The goal of human development in the second half of life is just the opposite. Here a movement toward wholeness or unity of personality is the goal. Somewhere around mid-life, the individual should begin to assess the various systems of his or

Dr. Carl Jung, a student of Freud's, introduced many concepts into psychology, including the anima and animus (his concepts of the female and male soul).

her personality and come to acknowledge the disorganized state of these systems. There should be a turning inward or self-inspection that marks the beginning of true adult spirituality. The goals of this introspection are:

- discovering a meaning and purpose in life;

- gaining a perspective on others, determining values and activities in which one is willing to invest energy and creativity; and

- preparing for the final stage of life—death.

Spirituality in the second half of life develops as a complement to the first half of life. By nourishing one's undeveloped side of life, one comes to a recognition of the spiritual and supernatural aspects of existence. For men, this means developing the **anima** and for females the **animus.**

In contrast to the self-determination of spirituality seen in Frankl's and Jung's psychological points of view, sociobiology sees spirituality as determined almost entirely by instinct, that is, as a function of the genes.

Wilson's Theory of Spirituality

The predisposition to religious belief is the most complex and powerful force in the human mind and in all probability an ineradicable part of human nature.

Edward Wilson

Harvard sociobiologist Edward O. Wilson, the leading spokesperson for the sociobiological point of view (see chapter 13), argued that religion and spirituality are inseparable. Together they grant essential benefits to believers. He argued that all societies, from hunter-gatherer bands to socialist republics, have religious practices with roots that go back at least as far as the Neanderthal period.

For example, he argued that even modern Russian society, which is still largely anticlergy and pro-socialism, is as much a religious society as any other. Wilson (1978) cited one of Lenin's closest disciples, Grefori Pyatakov, who describes what it is to be "a real Communist"—one who

> will readily cast out from his mind fears in which he has believed for years. A true Bolshevik has submerged his personality in the collectivity, the "Party," to such an extent that he can make the necessary effort to break away from his opinions and convictions and can honestly agree with the "Party"—that is the test of a true Bolshevik (p. 184).

Wilson said that in this statement we see the essence of religious spirituality. Humans, he argued, have a need to develop simple rules for handling complex problems. We also have a strong need for an unconscious sense of order in our daily lives. We strongly resist attempts to disrupt this order, which religion almost always protects.

Religion is one of the few uniquely human behaviors. Rituals and beliefs that make up religious life are not seen among any other animals. Some scientists, notably Lorenz and Tinbergen, argued that animal displays, dances, and rituals are similar to human religious ceremonies. Wilson believed this comparison was wrong; animal displays are for the purpose of communicating (sexual desire, etc.), but religious ceremonies intend far more than mere communication.

Their goal is to "reaffirm and rejuvenate the moral values of the community" (Wilson, 1978, p. 179). Furthermore, religious learning is almost entirely unconscious. Most religious tenets are taught and deeply internalized early in life. Early teaching is a necessity if children are to learn to subvert their natural self-interests to the interest of society.

Anima   The female side of the personality. Males tend to repress it until later in life.

Animus   The male side of the personality. Females tend to repress it until later in life.

Once we truly know that life is difficult—once we truly understand and accept it—then life is no longer difficult. Because once it is accepted, the fact that life is difficult no longer matters.
M. S. Peck

The sociobiological explanation of spirituality, then, is that through religious practice, the survival of practitioners is enhanced. Those who practice religion are more likely to stay alive (or at least they were in the past) than those who do not practice religion.

Wilson believed that even a person's willingness to be controlled may be genetic. Although all societies need some rebels, they also require that the vast majority of people be controllable, typically through religious and political beliefs. Therefore, Wilson believed that over the long run genes that favor willingness to be controlled have been favored by natural selection.

The potential for self-sacrifice can be strengthened in this manner because the willingness of individuals to relinquish rewards or even surrender their own lives will favor group survival. The Jonestown mass suicide, for example, appears to have occurred because of the group's hope to remain united in afterlife. This concept of self-sacrifice is also the basis for Weinrich's (1987) assertion that homosexuality is an altruistic behavior (see chapter 13).

Religions usually favor survival of their believers. This is not always true, though, and is true to differing degrees. It has been estimated that there have been more than 100,000 different religious faiths since humankind began. Obviously most have failed.

Some religions are even contrary to the survival needs of their believers. The Shaker religion, which disallows sexual intercourse to any of its participants, is an example. Shakerism lasted in this country for no more than two centuries. It flourished in the nineteenth century, but only a very few believers exist today. With no new recruits, it seems doomed to extinction. This, Wilson argued, is always the case for those religions that do not somehow enhance the vitality and hardiness of the groups that support them. The constant pursuit of a better chance for survival is why new ones are started.

Religions, according to the sociobiological point of view, develop through three steps:

Objectification Wilson's term for the person's perception of reality.

Commitment People devote their lives to objectified ideas. They are willing under any circumstances to help those who have done the same.

Mythification Stories are developed that tell why members of a religion have a special place in the world. These stories are rational and enhance the person's understanding of the physical as well as the spiritual world.

1. **Objectification.** First, a perception of reality is described. Objectification occurs, which includes images and definitions that are easy to understand. Examples are good versus evil, heaven versus hell, and the control of the forces of nature by a god or gods.

2. **Commitment.** People devote their lives to these objectified ideas. Out of this commitment, they are willing under any circumstances to help those who have done the same.

3. **Mythification.** In mythification, stories are developed that tell why the members of the religion have a special place in the world. These stories are rational and enhance the person's understanding of the physical as well as spiritual world. The stories include explanations of how and why the world, as well as the religion, came to be. In earlier, less sophisticated religions, the faith is said to have been founded at the same time as the beginning of the race. These rarely include all-powerful or all-knowing gods. In less than one-third of the known religions is there a highly placed god, and in even fewer is there a notion of a moral god who has created the world. In the later religions, God is always seen as male, and almost always as the shepherd of a flock.

Not surprisingly, Wilson saw science as taking the place of theology today, because science has explained natural forces more effectively than theology. In fact, he asserted that science has explained theology itself. Although he saw theology as being phased out, he argued that the demise of religion is not at all likely. As long as religions make people more likely to survive and propagate themselves, Wilson suggested, they will enjoy worldwide popularity.

Wilson's theory attempted to explain spiritual development within societies. Theologian James Fowler has offered a description of the development of faith throughout the life cycle of individuals without regard to the culture in which faith forms.

Fowler's Theory of Spirituality

James Fowler (1993, 2000) offered a theoretical framework built on the ideas of Piaget, Erikson, and Kohlberg. He believed strongly that cognitive and emotional needs are inseparable in the development of spirituality. Spirituality cannot develop faster than intellectual ability and also depends on the development of personality. Thus Fowler's theory of faith development integrates the role of the unconscious, of needs, of personal strivings, and of cognitive growth. As he described it (1993):

> Faith develops with the establishment of new centers of value, new images of power, and new master stories that coalesce in stages and advance toward a point where there is maximal individuation of the self and corresponding minimization of the personal ego as the point from which evaluations are made (p. 27).

Fowler saw faith developing in six steps. He said that the stages in faith development can be delayed indefinitely, but the person must have reached at least a certain minimal age at each stage in order to move on to a succeeding stage. His six stages are as follows:

Intuitive-projective faith
The first developmental step of Fowler's theory of faith. In this stage, the individual focuses on surface qualities, as portrayed by adult models.

1. **Intuitive-projective faith.** For intuitive-projective faith, the minimal age is 4 years. In this stage, the individual focuses on surface qualities, as portrayed by adult models. This stage depends to a great extent on fantasy. Conceptions of God or a supreme being reflect a belief in magic.

Mythical-literal faith Fantasy ceases to be a primary source of knowledge at this stage, and verification of facts becomes necessary.

2. **Mythical-literal faith.** For mythical-literal faith, minimal age is 5 to 6 years. Fantasy ceases to be a primary source of knowledge at this stage, and verification of facts becomes necessary. Verification of truth comes not from actual experience but from such authorities as teachers, parents, books, and tradition. Faith in this stage is mainly concrete, and depends heavily on stories told by highly credible storytellers. For example, the traditional story of Adam and Eve is taken quite literally.

Poetic-conventional faith
Faith is still conventional and depends on a consensus of opinion of other, more authoritative persons.

3. **Poetic-conventional faith.** For poetic-conventional faith, minimal age is 12 to 13 years. The child is entering Piaget's codification stage. Faith is still conventional and depends on a consensus of opinion of other, more authoritative persons. Now the person moves away from family influence and into new relationships. Faith begins to provide a coherent and meaningful synthesis of these relationships.

    Individuals become aware of symbolism and realize that there is more than one way of knowing truth. Learned facts are still taken as the main source of information, but individuals in Stage 3 begin to trust their own judgment and the quality of selected authorities. Nevertheless, they do not yet place full confidence in their own judgment.

Individuating-reflective faith
Individuals in stage four begin to assume responsibility for their own beliefs, attitudes, commitments, and lifestyle.

4. **Individuating-reflective faith.** For individuating-reflective faith, minimal age is 18 to 19 years. Youths in stage 3 are unable to synthesize new areas of experience because depending on others in the community does not always solve problems. Individuals in Stage 4 begin to assume responsibility for their own beliefs, attitudes, commitments, and lifestyle. The faith learned in earlier stages is now disregarded, and greater attention is paid to one's own experience. Those individuals who still need authority figures have a tendency to join and become completely devoted to clubs and cults.

Paradoxical-consolidation faith In this stage, such elements of faith as symbols, rituals, and beliefs start to become understood and consolidated.

5. **Paradoxical-consolidation faith.** For paradoxical-consolidation faith, minimal age is 30. In this stage such elements of faith as symbols, rituals, and beliefs start to become understood and consolidated. The person begins to realize that other approaches to dealing with such complex questions as the supernatural and supreme being can be as valid as her

or his own. The individual at this stage considers all people to belong to the same universal community and has a true regard for the kinship of all people.

Universalizing faith The final developmental step of Fowler's theory of faith. Here the individual lives in the real world but is not of it. Such persons do not merely recognize the mutuality of existence; they act on the basis of it.

6. **Universalizing faith.** For universalizing faith, minimal age is 40 years. As with Kohlberg's final stage, very few people ever reach this level. Here the individual lives in the real world but is not of it. Such persons do not merely recognize the mutuality of existence; they act on the basis of it. People at this stage appear to be truly genuine and lack the need to "save face" that exists at the lower stages.

Stage 6, as described by Fowler, compares closely with a hypothetical Stage 7 of morality proposed by Kohlberg (see chapter 9). Although he never found anyone at a Stage 7 level of morality, Kohlberg believed that theoretically there should be a stage for those few persons who rise above the purely cognitive and achieve a place where they transcend logic. These individuals, who are rare indeed, come to understand why one should be just and ethical in a world that is unjust. A burning love of universal humankind presses them always to act in truly moral ways.

The development of spirituality and morality appears to be parallel all along the sequence, especially in the Kohlberg and Fowler models. At the early levels, the orientation is basically selfish; ethical thinking and behavior are virtually nonexistent. The child is "good" only to please more powerful persons.

Religion is for those who are afraid to go to Hell. Spirituality is for those who have already been there.

An elderly recovering alcoholic

At the second two levels, concern for the opinion of the community in general takes over. "What will people think!" is uppermost in religion as well as in moral decisions. Only if and when the highest levels are reached do true spirituality and morality emerge. And for a few individuals at the highest level, the distinction between the moral and the spiritual no longer exists.

Why do people vary so much in level of spirituality? Can the biopsychosocial model help us answer this question? Do you believe that Fowler's ideas would apply to Eastern cultures? What's your opinion?

Guided Review

17. _____ is concerned with whether life is worth living and why it is worth living.
18. For many Americans religion is connected to spirituality. The influence of religion appears to be highly related to a sense of _____ in elderly persons.
19. Victor Frankl looks at spirituality, and especially the third or _____ dimension, as directed toward transcending training and aspiring to higher levels of thought and behavior.
20. Carl Jung sees life in two halves, with the _____ second half of life directed toward finding meaning and _____, and preparing for death.
21. Wilson argues that the evolutionary or survival value of spirituality develops in three stages. These stages are objectification, commitment, and _____.
22. Fowler, like Piaget, Erikson, and Kohlberg, includes stages of development and a _____ age for each stage in his theory of faith development.
23. Fowler sees faith developing in six stages: intuitive-projective, _____ poetic-conventional, individuating-reflective, paradoxical-consolidation, and _____.

Answers

17. Spirituality 18. well-being 19. noetic 20. spiritual, purpose 21. mythification 22. minimal 23. mythical-literal, universalizing

CONCLUSION & SUMMARY

"The distinction between the moral and the spiritual no longer exists." What a wonderful goal to choose as a means of living the good life. It is probably also the best way to ensure a successful death. We sincerely hope that having read this book will contribute in some small way to your achievement of those two preeminent goals!

What is the role of death in life?

- Today, four types of death are recognized: clinical death, brain death, biological or cellular death, and social death.
- In modern Western societies, death comes mostly to the old.

What is the purpose of "grief work"?

- Grief both follows and can precede the death of a loved one.
- In some cases, morbid grief reactions occur that prevent the successful conclusion of the life crisis. These are known as delayed reactions, distorted reactions, and pathological reactions.
- Most psychologists who have examined the role of grief have concluded that it is a healthy aspect of the crisis of death.
- Funerals have always been an important part of American life. Research has indicated that the rituals surrounding funerals have therapeutic benefits that facilitate the grieving process.
- Kübler-Ross has offered five stages of dying: shock and denial, anger, bargaining, depression, and acceptance.

What are the factors that cause and determine the nature of suicide?

- Suicide rates for those over 75 is double that of adolescents with the older white male most likely to take his life.
- Males and females are very different regarding suicide with men being more likely to die than women.

What is the meaning of "successful dying"?

- The hospice movement and "death with dignity" legislation have provided people with more control over their own death, making it a bit easier to accept.

How do psychologists define the nature of spirituality?

- In recent decades, participation in religious activities has been changing in a number of ways.
- The elderly practice their religions to a greater degree than other adults.
- Theories of spirituality have been presented by Frankl, Jung, Wilson, and Fowler.
- Fowler has incorporated the work of Erikson, Piaget, and Kohlberg in his theory of the development of faith, which proceeds through six stages.

KEY TERMS

Anima
Animus
Biological death
Brain death
Cardiopulmonary resuscitation (CPR)
Clinical death
Commitment

Electroencephalogram (EEG)
Euthanasia
Hospice
Individuating-reflective faith
Intuitive-projective faith
Legal death
Mythical-literal faith

Mythification
Objectification
Paradoxical-consolidation faith
Physician-assisted suicide
Poetic-conventional faith
Social death
Universalizing faith

WHAT DO YOU THINK?

1. It has been suggested that people in Western society typically are more fearful of death than are members of Eastern cultures. If so, what factors contribute to our more frightened attitude?
2. Most of us think of grief as something that happens to us. Do you think it makes sense to describe it as "work"?
3. How do you feel about the idea of "successful death"?
4. Are there some old people—those who have lost their spouse and all their friends or those who are undeniably terminal—who should be allowed to take their own lives? Should these people be helped to have a "ceremony of death"?
5. In this chapter we have suggested two ways of making death more dignified. Can you think of any others?
6. Are you satisfied with your own level of religious participation? What do you think you should do differently?
7. How would you define your own spirituality?
8. Fowler states that there is a certain minimal age for each of his stages of spiritual development. What kinds of experience do you think would move a person from one stage to the next?

CHAPTER REVIEW TEST

1. If brain death occurs, a person still remains alive in this condition because
   a. autoplasia stimulates the autonomic processes.
   b. neuroplasia stimulates the autonomic processes.
   c. the autonomic processes are governed by the brain stem.
   d. the autonomic processes are governed by the cortex.

2. Legal death occurs when
   a. respiration and heartbeat have stopped.
   b. the brain fails to receive sufficient amount of oxygen.
   c. there is an unreceptivity and unresponsivity, no movements or breathing, no reflexes, and a flat electroencephalogram reading that remains flat for 24 hours.
   d. it is no longer possible to discern an electrical charge in the tissues of the heart and lung.

3. The phases of anticipatory grief are
   a. depression, a heightened concern for the ill person, rehearsal of death, and an attempt to adjust to the consequences that are likely to occur after the death.
   b. depression and rehearsal of death.
   c. a heightened concern for the ill person, rehearsal of death, and an attempt to adjust to the consequences that are likely to occur after the death.
   d. depression, a heightened concern for the ill person, and rehearsal of death.

4. Knowledge of the impending death of a loved one can have which therapeutic consequences?
   a. Avoidance of shock
   b. Ability to plan for the future
   c. Time to prepare for impending changes
   d. All of the answers are correct.

5. According to Kübler-Ross' theory, dying need not be a(n) _____ experience.
   a. religious
   b. unexpected
   c. unhappy
   d. expensive

6. A young man, whose father died from lung cancer, is displaying grief known as distorted reaction. He has
   a. experienced grieving stages that are prolonged and intensified to an abnormal degree.
   b. developed some of the same symptoms his father had, which his doctor determined were entirely psychosomatic.
   c. created a shrine in memory of his father.
   d. experienced anticipatory grief.

7. Why do many dying patients feel depressed before their deaths?
   a. Medication-induced mood alterations
   b. Feelings of isolation from relatives and friends who are withdrawing
   c. Awareness of how little time is left
   d. All of the answers are correct.

8. Of all adult groups, older single white males are the most likely to die of
   a. cancer.
   b. heart disease.
   c. accident.
   d. suicide.

9. The law that grants an adult the right to instruct his or her physician to withhold or withdraw life-sustaining procedures in the event of a terminal condition is known as a
   a. "right to life" law.
   b. "living will" law.
   c. "death with dignity" law.
   d. None of the answers are correct.

10. Home-based care for the dying is known as the
    a. Visiting Nurses program.
    b. hospice program.
    c. behavioral medicine program.
    d. home-health program.

11. Whether life is worth living and why it is worth living is the major premise of
    a. spirituality.
    b. religion.
    c. separation anxiety.
    d. None of the answers are correct.

12. In what stage in Frankl's theory of spirituality are persons motivated by the struggle to keep themselves alive and to help the species survive?
    a. Somatic dimension
    b. Psychological dimension
    c. Noetic dimension
    d. None of the answers are correct.

13. In Fowler's theory of spirituality, stages in _____ can be delayed indefinitely, but the person must have reached a certain minimal age at each stage to move on to a succeeding stage.
    a. psychological growth
    b. spiritual belief
    c. faith development
    d. commitment

14. According to Fowler, what is the minimal age at which a person can gain universalizing faith?
    a. 12 to 13 years old
    b. 18 to 19 years old
    c. 30 years old
    d. 40 years old

15. According to Jung, by the age of 35, most people are well
    a. established.
    b. prepared for life's work.
    c. individuated.
    d. on their way to developing a wholeness of personality.

16. The sociobiological point of view states that we develop religion through what steps?
    a. Objectification, commitment, mythification
    b. Commitment and mythification
    c. Objectification and mythification
    d. Objection and commitment

Answers

1. c 2. c 3. a 4. d 5. b 6. b 7. d 8. d 9. c 10. b 11. a 12. a 13. c 14. d 15. c 16. a

Glossary

A

Absorbent mind Montessori's term for a child's ability to absorb experiences from the environment (0 to 6 years) (Ch. 7).

Accommodation Piaget's term to describe the manner by which cognitive structures change (Ch. 2).

Accumulation of metabolic waste Waste products resulting from metabolism build-up in various parts of the body, contributing greatly to the decreasing competence of those parts (Ch. 17).

Accumulation-of-errors theory As cells die, they must synthesize new proteins to make new cells. As this is done, occasionally an error occurs. Over time, these errors mount up and may finally grow serious enough to cause organ failure (Ch. 17).

Activity theory Human beings flourish through interaction with other people. They are unhappy when, as they reach the older years, their contacts with others shrink as a result of death, illness, and societal limitations. Those who are able to keep up the social activity of their middle years are considered the most successful (Ch. 18).

Adaptation One of the two functional invariants in Piaget's theory (Ch. 2).

Adolescent egocentrism The reversion to the self-centered thinking patterns of childhood that sometimes occurs in the teen years (Ch. 11).

Adoption To take a child of other parents voluntarily as one's own (Ch. 3).

Adult Attachment Interview (AAI) Evaluates adults' responses to questions about attachment (Ch. 6).

Afterbirth Stage three of the birth process during which the placenta and other membranes are discharged (Ch. 4).

Ageism The prejudice that the elderly are inferior to those who are younger (Ch. 17).

Age-status Refers to society's expectations about what is normal at various ages (Ch. 18).

Aggression Hostile or destructive behavior directed at another (Ch. 10).

Aging by program The theory that all animals seem to die when their "program" dictates (Ch. 17).

AID Artificial insemination by donor (Ch. 3).

AIDS (Acquired Immune Deficiency Syndrome) A condition caused by a virus that invades the body's immune system, making it vulnerable to infections and life-threatening illnesses (Chs. 4 and 12).

Alarm reaction Selye's term for a "call to arms" of the body's defensive forces (Ch. 16).

Alleles Different forms of a gene (Ch. 3).

Amniocentesis A process that entails inserting a needle through the mother's abdomen, piercing the amniotic sac and withdrawing a sample of the amniotic fluid (Ch. 4).

Anal stage Freud's belief that the anus is the main source of pleasure during the age 1½ to 3 years (Ch. 2).

Androgogy The science of teaching adults (Ch. 15).

Androgyny Functional level of gender-role identifications that incorporate male and female qualities (Ch. 14).

Anima The female side of the personality. Males tend to repress it until later in life (Ch. 19).

Animism Children consider objects as alive and conscious that adults consider inert (Ch. 7).

Animus The male side of the personality. Females tend to repress it until later in life (Ch. 19).

Anorexia nervosa A syndrome of self-starvation that mainly affects adolescent and young adult females (Ch. 11).

Anoxia (lack of oxygen) A condition that possibly can cause brain damage or death if it occurs during the birth process (Ch. 4).

Anticipatory images Piaget's term for images (including movements and transformation) that enable the child to anticipate change (Ch. 7).

Antigens The substances in the blood that fight to kill foreign bodies (Ch. 17).

Apgar A scale to evaluate a newborn's basic life signs administered one minute after birth and repeated at three-, five- and ten-minute intervals; it uses five life signs—heart rate, respiratory effort, muscle tone, reflex irritability, and skin color (Ch. 5).

Apnea Brief periods when breathing is suspended (Ch. 5).

Artificial insemination by donor (AID) (Ch. 3).

Artificialism Children attribute human life to inanimate objects (Ch. 7).

Assimilation Piaget's term to describe the manner in which we incorporate data into our cognitive structures (Ch. 2).

Attachment Behavior intended to keep a child (or adult) in close proximity to a significant other (Ch. 6).

Au pair Young women, often English, who provide child care services (Ch. 8).

Authoritarian parents Baumrind's term for parents who are demanding and want instant obedience as the most desirable child trait (Ch. 8).

Authoritative parenting style The most common parenting style, in which parents are sometimes authoritarian and sometimes permissive, depending to some extent on the parents' mood. Parents believe that both parents and children have rights but that parental authority must predominate (Ch. 12).

Autoimmunity The process by which the immune system in the body rejects the body's own tissue (Ch. 17).

Autonomy Infants realize that they have a share in controlling their interactions with others (Ch. 6).

Autosexuality The love of oneself; the stage at which the child becomes aware of himself or herself as a source of sexual pleasure, and consciously experiments with masturbation (Ch. 12).

B

Babbling Infant produces sounds approximating speech between 5 and 6 months (Ch. 5).

Basal metabolism rate (BMR) The minimum amount of energy an individual tends to use when in a resting state (Ch. 15).

Battered Child Syndrome Classic physical abuse (Ch. 10).

Bilingualism Students are taught partly in English and partly in their own language (Ch. 7).

Biological death Death occurs when it is no longer possible to discern an electrical charge in the tissues of the heart and lungs (Ch. 19).

Biopsychosocial interactions A term for the idea that development proceeds by the interaction of biological, psychological, and social forces (Chs. 1 and 14).

Biopsychosocial theory of homosexuality The theory that homosexuality is caused by some factor in a person's DNA that affects temperament, which in turn interacts with psychological and social factors to determine sexual orientation (Ch. 12).

Blastocyst When the fertilized egg reaches the uterus (about 7 days), it's known as a blastocyst (Ch. 4).

Brain death Death of the brain occurs when it fails to receive a sufficient supply of oxygen for a short period of time (usually eight to ten minutes) (Ch. 19).

Breech birth A birth in which the baby is born feet first, buttocks first, or in a crosswise position (transverse presentation) (Ch. 4).

Bulimia nervosa This disorder is characterized by "episodic binge-eating accompanied by an awareness that the eating pattern is abnormal, fear of not being able to stop eating voluntarily, and depressed mood and self-deprecating thoughts following the eating binges" (Ch. 11).

Bullies Those who have aggressive reaction patterns and have considerable physical strength (Ch. 10).

C

Capacitation Removal of layer surrounding sperm (Ch. 3).

Cardiopulmonary resuscitation (CPR) A technique for reviving an individual's lungs and/or heart that have ceased to function (Ch. 19).

Cellular differentiation Embryonic cells are destined for specific functions (Ch. 4).

Centration A feature of preoperational thought—the centering of attention on one aspect of an object and the neglecting of any other features (Ch. 7).

Cesarean section A surgery performed to deliver the baby through the abdomen if for some reason the child cannot come through the birth canal (Ch. 4).

Child abuse Commonly includes physical abuse, sexual abuse, emotional abuse, physical neglect, emotional neglect, and educational neglect (Ch. 10).

Children at risk Children who give early signs of physical or psychological difficulties; unless helped by appropriate intervention, may continue to experience problems, perhaps with increasing intensity, throughout the lifespan (Ch. 4).

Chlamydia Bacterial infection that may cause infertility; now the most common STI, with about 5 to 7 million new cases each year. There often are no symptoms; it is diagnosed only when complications develop (Chs. 3 and 12).

Cholesterol A substance in the blood that adheres to the walls of the blood vessels, restricting the flow of blood and causing strokes and heart attacks (Ch. 13).

Chorionic villi sampling (CVS) A procedure in which a catheter (small tube) is inserted through the vagina to the villi and a small section is suctioned into the tube (Ch. 4).

Chromosome failure Biological changes such as enlarged breasts in males and abnormal body hair in females (Ch. 14).

Classification The process by which concrete operational children can group objects with some similarities within a larger category (Chs. 7 and 9).

Climacteric Refers to a relatively abrupt change in the body, brought about by changes in hormonal balances (Ch. 15).

Climacterium Refers to the loss of reproductive ability (Ch. 15).

Clinical death The individual is dead when his or her respiration and heartbeat have stopped (Ch. 19).

Closed adoption Natural parents know nothing about the adopting parents (Ch. 3).

Cognitive structures Piaget's term to describe the basic tools of cognitive development (Ch. 2).

Collagen The major connective tissue in the body; it provides the elasticity in our skin and blood vessels (Ch. 17).

Commitment The third phase in Perry's theory, in which the individual realizes that certainty is impossible but that commitment to a certain position is necessary, even without certainty; For Fowler, the third step in the birth of a religion, in which people devote their lives to objectified ideas. They are willing under any circumstances to help those who have done the same (Chs. 13 and 19).

Competence Children's sense of self-esteem related to athletic competence, likability by peers, physical appearance, and behavioral conduct (Ch. 10).

Concrete operational period Piaget's third stage of cognitive development during which children begin to employ logical thought processes with concrete material (Ch. 9).

Conservation Children conserve the essence of something even though surface features change (Chs. 7 and 9).

Constructed knowledge Belenky's fifth phase of women's thinking; characterized by an integration of the subjective and procedural ways of knowing (types 3 and 4) (Ch. 13).

Continuity The lasting quality of experiences; development proceeds steadily and sequentially (Ch. 1).

Controlled scribbling Drawing in which children carefully watch what they are doing, whereas before they looked away (Ch. 7).

Convergent thinking Thinking used to find one correct answer (Ch. 11).

Cooing Early language sounds that resemble vowels (Ch. 5).

Coordination of secondary schemes Infants combine secondary schemes to obtain a goal (Ch. 5).

Coregulation A sharing of decision making between parent and child (Ch. 8).

Crawling Locomotion in which the infant's abdomen touches the floor and the weight of the head and shoulders rests on the elbows (Ch. 5).

Creeping Movement is on hands and knees and the trunk does not touch the ground; creeping appears from 9 months in most youngsters (Ch. 5).

Critical thinking Those mental processes that help us to solve problems and make decisions (Ch. 9).

Cross-linkage theory A theory of aging stating that the proteins that make up a large part of cells are composed of peptides. When cross-links are formed between peptides (a natural process of the body), the proteins are altered, often for the worse (Ch. 17).

Crossover Older men become more like women, and older women become more like men (Ch. 18).

Cross-sectional studies This method compares groups of individuals of various ages at the same time in order to investigate the effects of aging (Ch. 1).

Crowds Groups known for certain values, attitudes, or activities (Ch. 12).

Cryopreservation Freezing embryos for future use (Ch. 3).

Crystallized intelligence Involves perceiving relationships, educing correlates, reasoning, abstracting, concept of attainment, and problem solving, as measured primarily in unspeeded tasks involving various kinds of content (semantic, figural, symbolic) (Ch. 15).

Cultural constructivism When children use the particular environment around them, they construct their own world view (Ch. 2).

Culture Those values, beliefs, and behaviors characteristic of a large group of people, for example, those of Hispanic origin (Ch. 2).

Cumulative continuity When a person's interactional style is reinforced by the environment, thus sustaining it across the lifespan (Ch. 16).

Cystic fibrosis Chromosomal disorder producing a malfunction of the exocrine glands (Ch. 3).

Cytogenetics The study of chromosomes (Ch. 3).

Cytomegalovirus (CMV) A virus that can cause damage ranging from mental retardation, blindness, deafness, and even death. One of the major difficulties in combatting this disease is that it remains unrecognized in pregnant women (Ch. 4).

D

Day care Locations providing services and care for children (Ch. 8).

Decentering The process by which concrete operational children can concentrate on more than one aspect of a situation (Ch. 9).

Decoding The technique by which we recognize words (Ch. 9).

Deferred imitation Imitative behavior that continues after the disappearance of the model to be imitated (Ch. 7).

DES (diethylstilbestrol) In the late 1940s and 1950s, DES (a synthetic hormone) was administered to pregnant women supposedly to prevent miscarriage. It was later found that the daughters of the women who had received this treatment were more susceptible to vaginal and cervical cancer (Ch. 4).

Descriptive studies Information is gathered on subjects without manipulating them in any way (Ch. 1).

Despair The counterpart to integrity in the last stage of Erikson's theory. When people look back over their lives and feel that they have made many wrong decisions, or more commonly, that they have not made any decisions at all (Ch. 18).

Developing readers Children who are beginning to understand the relationship between sound and symbol and pay close attention to the print in their efforts at decoding (Ch. 9).

Developmental contextualism Focuses not only on the interactions between heredity and environment but

the changes resulting from the interactions (Ch. 2).

Developmental risk Children who may be susceptible to problems because of some physical or psychological difficulty ("at-risk" children) (Ch. 4).

Developmentally delayed A term that describes children who experience a developmental lag because of either physical or psychological causes; these children usually "catch up" (Ch. 7).

Diethylstilbestrol Drug administered to pregnant women to help them hold embryo or fetus; later found to increase the risk of genital cancer in the daughters of these women (Ch. 4).

Differential opportunity structure Due to social disapproval and more rigid rules enforced by parents, peers, and the legal system, women have not had the same access to sex that men have had (Ch. 18).

Difficult children Term to describe restless, irritable children; associated with Chess and Thomas (Ch. 6).

Dilation Stage one of the birth process during which the cervix dilates to about 4 inches in diameter (Ch. 4).

Discontinuity Behaviors that are apparently unrelated to earlier aspects of development (Ch. 1).

Disengagement theory According to this position, the most mature adults are likely to gradually disengage themselves from their fellow human beings in preparation for death. They become less interested in their interactions with others, and more concerned with internal concerns (Ch. 18).

Distantiation The readiness of all of us to distance ourselves from others when we feel threatened by their behavior (Ch. 14).

Divergent thinking Thinking used when a problem to be solved has many possible answers. What are some ways that a school curriculum can enhance creative thinking at the junior and senior high school levels? (Ch. 11).

DNA Deoxyribonucleic acid; the chemical structure of the gene that accounts for our inherited characteristics (Ch. 3).

Dominant The tendency of a gene to be expressed in a trait (Ch. 3).

Down syndrome Genetic abnormality caused by a deviation on the twenty-first pair of chromosomes (Ch. 3).

Drawing Piaget's use of the term to indicate a growing symbolic ability (Ch. 7).

Dual-career family A family in which both the mother and the father are working, usually full time (Ch. 13).

Dualism Perry's initial phase of ethical development, in which "things are either absolutely right or absolutely wrong" (Ch. 13).

Dual-process model A model of intelligence that says there may be a decline in the mechanics of intelligence, such as classification skills and logical reasoning, but that the pragmatics are likely to increase (Ch. 15).

DUPE Problem-solving model (Determine a problem exists, Understand its nature, Plan for its solution, and Evaluate the solution) (Ch. 9).

E

Easy children Term used to describe calm, relaxed children; associated with Chess and Thomas (Ch. 6).

Ectoderm The outer layer of the embryo that will give rise to nervous system, among other developmental features (Ch. 4).

Ectopic pregnancy A pregnancy in which the fertilized egg attempts to develop in one of the fallopian tubes; this is sometimes referred to as a tubal pregnancy (Ch. 4).

Egg donor Woman either donates or sells eggs (Ch. 3).

Ego One of the three structures of the psyche according to Freud; mediates between the id and the superego (Ch. 2).

Egocentric speech Piaget's term to describe children's speech when they do not care to whom they speak (Ch. 5).

Egocentrism Child focuses on self in early phases of cognitive development; term associated with Piaget (Chs. 5 and 7).

Electroencephalogram (EEG) A graphic record of the electrical activity of the brain (Ch. 19).

Embryo transfer A form of assisted reproduction (Ch. 3).

Embryonic period Third through the eighth week following fertilization (Ch. 4).

Emergent readers Children who can identify letters and recognize some common words; they know what books "do" and they attempt to read by using semantic and syntactic cues (Ch. 9).

Emotional divorce Sometimes a couple learns to "withstand" each other, rather than live with each other. The only activities and interests that they shared were ones that revolved around the children. When the children leave, they are forced to recognize how far apart they have drifted; in effect, they are emotionally divorced (Ch. 16).

Emotional energy   The emotional feelings invested in various life tasks (Ch. 18).

Emotional maltreatment   A form of chld abuse (Ch. 10).

Empty nest syndrome   Refers to the feelings parents may have as a result of their last child leaving home (Ch. 16).

Encoding   Translating speech sounds into meaningful language (Ch. 9).

Endoderm   The inner layer of the embryo that will give rise to the lungs, liver, and pancreas, among other developmental features (Ch. 4).

Endometriosis   A condition in which tissue normally found in the uterus grows in other areas, such as the fallopian tubes (Ch. 3).

Entrainment   Term used to describe the rhythm that is established between a parent's and an infant's behavior (Ch. 6).

Equilibration   Piaget's term to describe the balance between assimilation and accommodation (Ch. 2).

Escape   Perry's term for refusing responsibility for making any commitments. Because everyone's opinion is "equally right," the person believes that no commitments need be made, and so escapes from the dilemma (Ch. 13).

ESL   English as a Second Language (Ch. 7).

Estrogen replacement therapy (ERT)   A process in which estrogen is given in low levels to a woman experiencing severe problems with menopause (Ch. 15).

Ethology   The study of behavior in natural settings (Ch. 6).

Euthanasia   Means a "good death." There are two types: passive euthanasia, in which the patient's legal instructions are carried out by the medical team, and active euthanasia, in which the patient's life is ended in ways that are now illegal (Ch. 19).

Existential love   The capacity to cherish the present moment, perhaps first learned when we confront the certainty of our own personal death (Ch. 18).

Explicit memory   Those events that we consciously remember (Ch. 5).

Expressive language   Language that children use to express their own ideas and needs (Ch. 7).

Expulsion   Stage two of the birth process during which the baby passes through the birth canal (Ch. 4).

External fertilization   Fertilization occurs outside of the woman's body (Ch. 3).

Extinction   Refers to the process by which conditioned responses are lost (Ch. 2).

F

Failure-to-thrive (FTT)   A condition in which the weight and height of infants consistently remain far below normal (the bottom 3 percent of height and weight measures) (Ch. 5).

Fallopian tubes   Passageway for the egg once it is discharged from the ovary's surface (Ch. 3).

False beliefs   Failure to understand the reasoning of others (Ch. 9).

Fastmapping   Techniques to help children detect word meanings (Ch. 7).

Fetal alcohol syndrome (FAS)   Refers to babies when their mothers drink alcohol during pregnancy; they manifest four clusters of symptoms: psychological functioning, growth factors, physical features, and structural effects (Ch. 4).

Fetal period   The period extending from the beginning of the third month to birth (Ch. 4).

Fetoscopy   A procedure in which a tiny instrument called a fetoscope is inserted into the amniotic cavity, making it possible to see the fetus (Ch. 4).

Fluid intelligence   Involves perceiving relationships, educing correlates, maintaining span of immediate awareness in reasoning, abstracting, concept formation, and problem solving, as measured in unspeeded as well as speeded tasks involving figural, symbolic, or semantic content (Ch. 15).

Forceps delivery   A procedure in which the physician, for safety, will withdraw the baby with forceps during the first phase of birth (Ch. 4).

Fragile X syndrome   A sex-linked inheritance disorder in which the bottom half of the X chromosome looks as if it is ready to fall off; causes mental retardation in 80 percent of the cases (Ch. 3).

Friend   A nonfamilial relationship that offers feelings of warmth and support (Ch. 10).

Functional invariants   In Piaget's theory, functional invariants refer to the psychological mechanisms of adaptation and organization (Ch. 2).

G

Gamete intrafallopian transfer (GIFT)   Sperm and egg are placed in fallopian tube (Ch. 3).

Gender identity   The conviction that one belongs to the sex of birth (Ch. 8).

Gender revolution   Levinson's term; the meanings of gender are changing and becoming more similar (Ch. 16).

Gender role   Culturally acceptable sexual behavior (Ch. 8).

Gender-role reversals   Older men see themselves and other males as becoming submissive and less authoritative with advancing years. Conversely, older women see themselves and other women as becoming more dominant and self-assured as they grow older (Ch. 18).

Gender-role stereotypes   Stereotypes that associate males and females with rigid categories of behavior and/or appearance (Ch. 14).

Gender splitting   Levinson's term; all societies support the idea that there should be a clear difference between what is considered appropriate for males and for females; gender splitting appears to be universal (Ch. 16).

Gender stereotypes   Beliefs about the characteristics associated with male or female (Ch. 8).

Gene theory   The theory that aging is due to certain harmful genes (Chs. 8 and 17).

General adaptation syndrome   Refers to a set of reactions that occur in animals in response to all toxic substances, regardless of their source. Involves three stages: alarm, resistance, and exhaustion (Ch. 16).

Generative love   Most characteristic of parenthood, a time during which sacrifices are gladly made for the sake of the children (Ch. 18).

Generativity   Erikson's term for the ability to be useful to ourselves and to society (Chs. 2 and 16).

Genital herpes   An incurable sexually transmitted infection, with about 500,000 new cases every year (Ch. 12).

Genital stage   Freud's belief in a resurgence of a strong sex drive from 12 years and beyond (Ch. 2).

Genotype   An individual's genetic composition (Ch. 3).

German measles (rubella)   A typically mild childhood disease caused by a virus; pregnant women who contract this disease may give birth to a baby with a defect: congenital heart disorder, cataracts, deafness, mental retardation. The risk is especially high if the disease appears early in the pregnancy (Ch. 4).

Germinal period   The first two weeks following fertilization (Ch. 4).

Glaucoma   Results from a buildup of pressure inside the eye due to excessive fluid. The resulting damage can destroy one's vision (Ch. 15).

Gonorrhea   Well-known venereal infection accounting for between 1.5 and 2 million cases per year (Ch. 12).

Goodness of fit   Compatibility between parental and child behavior; how well parents and their children get along (Ch. 6).

Group marriage   A marriage that includes two or more of both husbands and wives, who all exercise common privileges and responsibilities (Ch. 14).

H

Habituation   A process in which stimuli that are presented frequently cause a decrease in an infant's attention (Ch. 5).

Handedness   Children's preference for using one hand over the other (Ch. 7).

Head Start   Early intervention program intended to provide educational and developmental services to disadvantaged children (Ch. 7).

Hemophilia   A genetic condition causing incorrect blood clotting; called the "bleeder's disease" (Ch. 3).

Hepatitis B   A viral infection transmitted through sex or shared needles (Ch. 12).

Herpes simplex   An infection that usually occurs during birth; a child can develop the symptoms during the first week following the birth. The eyes and nervous system are most susceptible to this disease (Ch. 4).

Heterosexuality   Love of members of the opposite sex (Ch. 12).

Heterozygous   Different alleles for a trait (Ch. 3).

Holophrase   Children's first words that usually carry multiple meanings (Ch. 5).

Holophrastic speech   The use of one word to communicate many meanings and ideas (Ch. 5).

Homelessness   Those who live in shelters, or on the street, or parks (Ch. 8).

Homeostatic imbalance   The theory that aging is due to a failure in the systems that regulate the proper interaction of the organs (Ch. 17).

Homosexual marriage   Though not accepted legally, the weddings of homosexuals are now accepted by some religions (Ch. 14).

Homosexuality   Love of members of one's own sex (Ch. 12).

Homozygous   Identical alleles for a trait (Ch. 3).

Hormonal balance   One of the triggering mechanisms of puberty that may be used to indicate the onset of adolescence (Ch. 11).

Hospice   A facility and/or program dedicated to assisting those who have accepted the fact that they are dying and desire a "death with dignity." Provides pain control and counseling but does not attempt to cure anyone (Ch. 19).

Human Genome Project   The attempt to identify and map the 50,000 to 100,000 genes that constitute the human genetic endowment (Ch. 3).

Human immunodeficiency virus (HIV)   The virus that leads to AIDS (Ch. 12).

I

Id   One of the three structures of the psyche according to Freud; the source of our instinctive desires (Ch. 2).

Identity crisis   Erikson's term for those situations, usually in adolescence, that cause us to make major decisions about our identity (Chs. 2 and 11).

Imaginary audience   Adolescents' perception that the world is constantly scrutinizing their behavior and physical appearance (Ch. 11).

Imitative behavior   The tendency of infants to mimic the behavior of others (Ch. 5).

Implantation   Fertilized egg attaches and secures itself to uterine wall (Chs. 3 and 4).

Impotency   The inability to engage in the sexual act (Ch. 18).

Impulsivity   A child's lack of ability to delay gratification (Ch. 10).

In vitro fertilization   Fertilization that occurs "in the dish"; an external fertilization technique (Ch. 3).

Independent readers   Children who can read ably and without assistance using all of the cueing systems (Ch. 9).

Individuating-reflective faith   The fourth developmental step of Fowler's theory of faith. Individuals in stage four begin to assume responsibility for their own beliefs, attitudes, commitments, and lifestyle (Ch. 19).

Individuation   Refers to our becoming more individual; we develop a separate and special personality, derived less and less from our parents and teachers and more from our own behavior (Chs. 8 and 14).

Infantile amnesia   Our inability to recall events from early in life (Ch. 5).

Infertility   An inability to achieve pregnancy after two years (Ch. 3).

Inner speech   Serves to guide and plan behavior (Ch. 5).

Insecure parents   Those parents who believe everything they do inevitably influences their child's destiny; they feel overwhelmed by the difficulties of parenting (Ch. 8).

Instrumental conditioning   Skinner's form of conditioning in which a reinforcement follows the desired response; also known as operant conditioning (Ch. 2).

Integrity   The resolution of each of the first seven crises in Erikson's theory should lead us to achieve a sense of personal integrity. Older adults who have a sense of integrity feel their lives have been well spent. The decisions and actions they have taken seem to them to fit together (Ch. 18).

Interaction   Behaviors involving two or more people (Ch. 6).

Interactional continuity   Exists when a person's style evokes reciprocal responses from others in ongoing social interaction, thereby sustaining the behavior pattern across the lifespan when a similar interactive event occurs (Ch. 16).

Intergenerational continuity   Term used to describe the connection between childhood experiences and adult behavior (Ch. 6).

Internal fertilization   A natural process in which fertilization occurs within the woman (Ch. 3).

Intimacy   Erikson's stage that represents the ability to relate one's deepest hopes and fears to another person and to accept another's need for intimacy in turn (Ch. 14).

Intimidated parents   Those parents who lack the ability to be firm with their child (Ch. 8).

Intrauterine device   Usually a plastic loop inserted into the uterus as a contraceptive device (Ch. 3).

Intuitive-projective faith   The first developmental step of Fowler's theory of faith. In this stage, the individual focuses on surface qualities, as portrayed by adult models (Ch. 19).

Irreversibility   The inability to reverse thinking, that is, to solve a problem and then proceed in reverse, tracing the steps back to the original question or premise (Ch. 7).

Isolation   The readiness all of us have to isolate ourselves from others when we feel threatened by their behavior (Ch. 14).

IUGR   Intrauterine growth retardation, a condition that can occur when the mother's nutrient supply during pregnancy is too low (Ch. 4).

K

Klinefelter syndrome   Males with the XXY chromosomal pattern (Ch. 3).

Knowledge-acquisition components   Sternberg's term for those components that help us to learn how to solve problems in the first place (Ch. 9).

L

Language explosion Rapid acquisition of words beginning at 18 months (Ch. 5).

Latency Freud's belief that the sex drive becomes dormant at 5 to 12 years (Ch. 2).

Lateralization Refers to a preferred side of the brain for a particular activity (Ch. 7).

Learning A process that results in the modification of behavior (Ch. 10).

Learning theory of homosexuality The belief that homosexuality is the result of learned experiences from significant others (Ch. 12).

Legal death Condition defined as "unreceptivity and unresponsivity, no movements or breathing, no reflexes, and a flat electroencephalogram (EEG) reading that remains flat for 24 hours" (Ch. 19).

Life course Levinson's term. Life refers to all aspects of living—everything that has significance in a life; course refers to the flow or unfolding of an individual's life (Ch. 14).

Life cycle Levinson's term The life cycle is a general pattern of adult development, whereas the life course is the unique embodiment of the life cycle by an individual (Ch. 14).

Life structure Levinson's term. The underlying pattern or design of a person's life at a given time (Ch. 14).

Longitudinal studies The experimenter makes several observations of the same individuals at two or more times in their lives. Examples are: determining the long-term effects of learning on behavior; the stability of habits and intelligence; and the factors involved in memory (Ch. 1).

M

Male change of life Change in hormonal balance and sexual potency (Ch. 15).

Manipulative experiments The experimenter attempts to keep all variables (all the factors that can affect a particular outcome) constant except one, which is carefully manipulated (Ch. 1).

Maturation The process of physical and mental development due to physiology (Ch. 11).

Maximum growth spurt The period of adolescence when physical growth is at its fastest (Ch. 11).

Meiosis Cell division in which the number of chromosomes is halved (Ch. 3).

Menarche Onset of menstruation (Ch. 11).

Menopause The cessation of menstruation (Ch. 15).

Mentoring The act of assisting another, usually younger, person with his or her work or life tasks (Ch. 14).

Mesoderm The middle layer of the embryo that gives rise to muscles, skeleton, excretory system (Ch. 4).

Mesosystem The relationship among microsystems (Ch. 1).

Metacognition The theory of mind that refers to children's ability to construct their own ideas of how their minds work (Ch. 7).

Metacognitive experiences Responses to cognitive stimuli (Ch. 7).

Metacognitive knowledge A child's knowledge and beliefs, gained from experience about cognitive matters (Ch. 7).

Metacomponents Sternberg's term for those components that help us to plan, monitor, and evaluate our problem-solving strategies (Ch. 9).

Metalinguistic awareness A capacity to think about and talk about language (Ch. 9).

Microsystem The home or school (Ch. 1).

Midcareer crisis A stage that some persons go through in middle age during which they come to question their career goals, discover that their dreams for advancement may be unrealistic, and their relations with fellow employees are changing (Ch. 15).

Mid-life transition Levinson's term for the phase that usually lasts for five years and generally extends from age 40 to 45 (Ch. 16).

Miscarriage The term that describes when a pregnancy ends spontaneously before the twentieth week (Ch. 4).

Mitosis Cell division in which the number of chromosomes remains the same (Ch. 3).

Modeling Bandura's term for observational learning (Ch. 2).

Monogamy The standard marriage form in the United States and most other nations, in which there is one husband and one wife (Ch. 14).

Moral dilemma A modified clinical technique used by Kohlberg in which a conflict is posed for which subjects justify the morality of their choices (Ch. 9).

Motor skills Skills (both gross and fine) resulting from physical development enabling children to perform smooth and coordinated physical acts (Ch. 7).

Multiple intelligence Gardner's theory that attributes seven types of intelligence to humans (Ch. 9).

Mutations Abrupt hereditary changes (Ch. 3).

Mythical-literal faith The second developmental step of Fowler's theory of faith. Fantasy ceases to be a primary source of knowledge at this stage, and verification of facts becomes necessary (Ch. 19).

Mythification Stories are developed that tell why members of a religion have a special place in the world. These stories are rational and enhance the person's understanding of the physical as well as the spiritual world (Ch. 19).

N

Nanny Frequently former nurses who provide child-care services, often English (Ch. 8).

Naturalistic experiments In these experiments, the researcher acts solely as an observer and does as little as possible to disturb the environment. "Nature" performs the experiment, and the researcher acts as a recorder of the results (Ch. 1).

Negative reinforcement Refers to those stimuli whose withdrawal strengthens behavior (Ch. 2).

Neglect A form of child abuse (Ch. 10).

NEO model of personality McCrae and Costa's theory that there are three major personality traits, which they feel govern the adult personality (Ch. 16).

Neonate The term for an infant in the first days and weeks after birth (Ch. 5).

Neurological assessment Identifies any neurological problem, suggests means of monitoring the problem, and offers a prognosis about the problem (Ch. 5).

New York Longitudinal Study Long-term study by Chess and Thomas of the personality characteristics of children (Ch. 6).

Noetic dimension Frankl's third stage of human development has roots in childhood but primarily develops in late adolescence. It is spiritual, not only in the religious sense but in the totality of the search for the meaningfulness of life (Ch. 19).

No-fault divorce The law that lets people get divorced without proving some atrocious act by one of the spouses. In legal language, this is known as an irretrievable breakdown of a marriage (Ch. 16).

Normal range of development The stages of pubertal change occur at times that are within the normal range of occurrence (Ch. 11).

Novice phase Period of ages 17–33 that includes early adult transition, according to Levinson (Ch. 14).

Numeration The process by which concrete operational children grasp the meaning of number, the oneness of one (Ch. 9).

Nurturing parenting style The style of parenting in which parents use indirect methods such as discussion and modeling rather than punishment to influence their child's behavior. Rules are kept to a minimum (Ch. 12).

O

Object permanence Refers to children gradually realizing that there are permanent objects around them, even when these objects are out of sight (Ch. 5).

Objectification Fowler's term for the first step in the birth of a religion in which a perception of reality is described (Ch. 19).

Observational learning A term associated with Bandura, meaning that we learn from watching others (Ch. 10).

Olfactory sense The sense of smell, which uses the olfactory nerves in the nose and tongue (Ch. 15).

One-time, one-group studies Studies carried out only once on one group of subjects (Ch. 1).

Open adoption Natural parent has considerable input into the adoption process (Ch. 3).

Operant conditioning Skinner's form of conditioning in which a reinforcement follows the desired response; also known as instrumental conditioning (Ch. 2).

Oral stage Freud's belief that the mouth is the main source of pleasure from age 0 to 1½ years (Ch. 2).

Organ reserve Refers to that part of the total capacity of our body's organs that we do not normally need to use (Ch. 13).

Organization One of the two functional invariants in Piaget's theory (Ch. 2).

Organogenesis The formation of organs during the embryonic period (Ch. 4).

Overextensions Children's tendency to apply a word too widely (Ch. 7).

Overregulation Children's inappropriate use of language rules they have learned (Ch. 7).

Ovulation Egg bursts from the surface of the ovary (Ch. 3).

P

Paradoxical-consolidation faith The fifth developmental step of Fowler's theory of faith. In this stage, such elements of faith as symbols, rituals, and beliefs start to become understood and consolidated (Ch. 19).

Pedagogy The science of teaching children (Ch. 15).

Peer Refers to youngsters who are similar in age to other children, usually within 12 months of one another (Ch. 10).

Peer victimization A form of abuse in which a child is frequently the target of peer aggression (Ch. 10).

Pelvic inflammatory disease (PID) Infection that often results from chlamydia or gonorrhea, and frequently causes prolonged problems, including infertility (Chs. 3 and 12).

Performance components Sternberg's term for those components that help us to execute the instructions of the metacomponents (Ch. 9).

Permissive parenting style Parents have little or no control over their children and refrain from disciplinary measures (Chs. 8 and 12).

Personal fable Adolescents' tendency to think of themselves in heroic or mythical terms (Ch. 11).

Phallic stage Freud's belief that the sex organs become the main source of pleasure from age 3 to 5 years (Ch. 2).

Phenotype The observable expression of gene action (Ch. 3).

Phenylketonuria (PKU) Chromosomal disorder resulting in a failure of the body to break down the amino acid phenylalanine (Ch. 3).

Phonological cues Using sounds to form words (Ch. 9).

Phonology Describes how to put sounds together to form words (Ch. 7).

Physical abuse A form of child abuse (Ch. 10).

Placenta The placenta supplies the embryo with all its needs, carries off all its wastes, and protects it from danger (Ch. 4).

Play An activity that children engage in because they enjoy it for its own sake (Ch. 8).

Poetic-conventional faith The third developmental step of Fowler's theory of faith. Faith is still conventional and depends on a consensus of opinion of other, more authoritative persons (Ch. 19).

Polyandry A marriage in which there is one wife but two or more husbands (Ch. 14).

Polygamy A marriage in which there is one husband but two or more wives (Ch. 14).

Polygenic inheritance Many genes contribute to the formation of a particular trait (Ch. 3).

Positive reinforcement Refers to those stimuli whose presentation as a consequence of a response strengthens or increases the rate of the response (Ch. 2).

Postnatal depression The low or "down" feeling many women experience a few days after giving birth (Ch. 4).

Pragmatic cues Practical signals used to discover meaning (Ch. 9).

Pragmatics Describes how we learn to take part in a conversation (Ch. 7).

Precociousness The ability to do what others are able to do, but at a younger age (Ch. 11).

Prematurity A condition that occurs less than 37 weeks after conception and is defined by low birth weight and immaturity (Ch. 4).

Prenatal learning Possibility that the fetus learns while in the womb (Ch. 4).

Preoperational Piaget's second stage of cognitive development, extending from about 2 to 7 years (Ch. 7).

Prepared childbirth Combination of relaxation techniques and information about the birth process; sometimes called the Lamaze method after its founder (Ch. 4).

Prepared environment Use of age-appropriate materials to further cognitive development (Ch. 7).

Primary circular reactions Infants repeat some act involving their bodies; term associated with Piaget's theory (Ch. 5).

Procedural knowledge Belenky's fourth phase of women's thinking; characterized by a distrust of both knowledge from authority and the female thinker's own inner authority or "gut" (Ch. 13).

Prodigiousness The ability to do qualitatively better than the rest of us are able to do; such a person is referred to as a prodigy (Ch. 11).

Project Head Start Programs intended to provide educational and developmental services to preschool children from low-income families (Ch. 7).

Prosocial behavior Refers to such behaviors as friendliness, self-control, and being helpful (Ch. 10).

Prostatectomy The removal of all or part of the male prostate gland (Ch. 18).

Protective factors Characteristics of resilient individuals that protect them from stress (Ch. 16).

Psychoanalytic theory Freud's theory of the development of personality (Ch. 2).

Psychoanalytic theory of homosexuality Freud's theory suggests that if the child's first sexual feelings about the parent of the opposite sex are strongly punished, the child may identify with the same-sex parent and develop a permanent homosexual orientation (Ch. 12).

Psychological dimension The second stage of Frankl's theory of human development, in which personality begins to form at birth and develops as a result of instincts, drives, capacities, and interactions with the environment (Ch. 19).

Puberty A relatively abrupt and qualitatively different set of physical changes that normally occur at the beginning of the teen years (Ch. 11).

Punishment Usually refers to a decrease in the frequency of a response when certain unpleasant consequences immediately follow it (Ch. 2).

R

Random scribbling Drawing in which children use dots and lines with simple arm movements (Ch. 7).

Realism Refers to when children learn to distinguish and accept the real world (Ch. 7).

Received knowledge Belenky's second phase of women's thinking; characterized by being awed by the authorities but far less affiliated with them (Ch. 13).

Receptive language Language that children use to show an understanding of words without necessarily producing them (Ch. 7).

Recessive A gene whose trait is not expressed unless paired with another recessive gene, for example, both parents contribute genes for blue eyes (Ch. 3).

Reciprocal interactions Similar to transactional model; recognizes the child's active role in its development; I do something to the child, the child changes; as a result of the changes in the child, I change (Chs. 1 and 5).

Reflective listening A method of talking to others; you rephrase the person's comments to show you understand (Ch. 12).

Reflex When a stimulus repeatedly elicits the same response (Ch. 5).

Reinforcement Usually refers to an increase in the frequency of a response when certain pleasant consequences immediately follow it (Ch. 2).

Relativism The second phase in Perry's theory. An attitude or philosophy that says anything can be right or wrong depending on the situation; all views are equally right (Ch. 13).

Representation Child's growing ability to engage in abstract thinking (Ch. 7).

Reproductive images Mental images that are faithful to the original object or event being represented; Piaget's term for

images that are restricted to those sights previously perceived (Ch. 7).

Repudiation Striving toward a state of identity means committing to one life style and repudiating (giving up) all the other possibilities, at least for the present (Ch. 11).

Resiliency The ability to recover from either physiological or psychological trauma and return to a normal developmental path (Ch. 1).

Resilient children Children who sustain some type of physiological or psychological trauma yet remain on a normal developmental path (Ch. 10).

Respiratory distress syndrome (RDS) A problem common with premature babies that is caused by the lack of a substance called surfactant, which keeps the air sacs in the lungs open (Ch. 5).

Retreat According to Perry's theory of ethical development, when someone retreats to an earlier ethical position (Ch. 13).

Rh factor An incompatibility between the blood types of mother and child; if the mother is Rh-negative and the child is Rh-positive, miscarriage or even infant death can result (Ch. 4).

Risk factors Stressors that individuals experience (Ch. 16).

Role discontinuity Abrupt and disruptive change caused by conflicts among one's various roles in life (Ch. 18).

S

Scaffolding Helping children move from initial difficulties with a topic to a point where, with help, they gradually learn to perform the task independently (Chs. 2 and 5).

Scheme Piaget's term to describe the patterns of behavior that infants use to interact with their environment (Ch. 2).

Secondary circular reactions Infants direct their activities toward objects and events outside themselves (Ch. 5).

Secular trend The phenomenon (in recent centuries) of adolescents entering puberty sooner and growing taller and heavier (Ch. 11).

Self-concept Children know who they are and what makes them different from everyone else (Chs. 8 and 10).

Self-control Restraint exercised over impulses, emotions, and desires (Ch. 10).

Self-esteem Children possess feelings of confidence and satisfaction with one's self (Chs. 8 and 10).

Self-fulfilling prophecy Making an idea come true simply by believing it will (Ch. 15).

Semantic cues Readers relate words to what they signify (Ch. 9).

Semantics Describes how to interpret the meaning of words (Ch. 7).

Senile macular degeneration This disease of the retina is a leading cause of blindness, beginning as blurred vision and a dark spot in the center of the field of vision (Ch. 17).

Sensitive periods Certain times in the lifespan when a particular experience has a greater and more lasting impact than at another time (Chs. 1 and 7).

Sensitive responsiveness Refers to the ability to recognize the meaning of a child's behavior (Ch. 6).

Sensorimotor period Piaget's term for the first of his cognitive stages of development (0 to 2 years) (Ch. 5).

Sequential (longitudinal/cross-sectional) studies A cross-sectional study done at several times with the same groups of individuals (Ch. 1).

Seriation The process by which concrete operational children can arrange objects by increasing or decreasing size (Ch. 9).

Sex cleavage Youngsters of the same sex tend to play and do things together (Ch. 8).

Sexual abuse Any sexual activity between a child and adult, whether by force or consent (Ch. 10).

Sexually transmitted diseases (STD) Class of diseases that may cause infertility (Ch. 3).

Sexually transmitted infections A class of infections that are transmitted through sexual behavior (Ch. 12).

Siblings Brothers and sisters (Ch. 8).

Sickle-cell anemia A chromosomal disorder resulting in abnormal hemoglobin (Ch. 3).

Silence Belenky's first phase of women's thinking, characterized by concepts of right and wrong (Ch. 13).

Sleeping disorder A child who does not sleep readily and wakes repeatedly (Ch. 5).

Slow-to-warm-up children Term used to describe children with low intensity of reactions; may be rather negative when encountering anything new (Ch. 6).

Social (cognitive) learning theory Bandura's theory that refers to the process whereby the information we glean from observing others influences our behavior (Ch. 2).

Social death The point at which a patient is treated essentially as a corpse, although perhaps still "clinically" or "biologically" alive (Ch. 19).

Social perspective-taking The idea that children's views on how to relate to others emerge from their personal theories about the traits of others (Ch. 10).

Socialization Refers to the need to establish and maintain relations with others and to regulate behavior according to society's demands (Ch. 8).

Socialized speech Piaget's term for the time when children begin to exchange ideas with each other (Ch. 5).

Socio-emotional selectivity theory According to this theory, humans use social contact for four reasons: to obtain physical survival, to get information they need, to maintain a sense of self, and to acquire pleasure and comfort. For the elderly the last two are most important (Ch. 18).

Solidarity Erikson's term for the personality style of persons who are able to commit themselves in concrete affiliations and partnerships with others and have developed the "ethical strength to abide by such commitments, even though they may call for significant sacrifices and compromises" (Ch. 14).

Somatic dimension The first stage of Frankl's theory of human development, in which all persons are motivated by the struggle to keep themselves alive and to help the species survive (Ch. 19).

Sperm The germ cell that carries the male's 23 chromosomes (Ch. 3).

Sperm donor Male either donates or sells sperm (Ch. 3).

Spina bifida A genetic disorder resulting in the failure of the neural tube to close (Ch. 3).

Stability A belief that children's early experiences affect them for life (Ch. 1).

Stage of exhaustion Selye's term for the body's physiological responses that revert to their condition during the stage of alarm (Ch. 16).

Stage of resistance Selye's term for the body's reaction that is generally a reversal of the alarm reaction (Ch. 16).

Stage theorists Researchers who believe that research based on personality traits is too narrow in focus and that we must also look at the stages of change each person goes through (Ch. 16).

Stagnation According to Erikson, the seventh stage of life (middle-aged adulthood) tends to be marked either by generativity or by stagnation—boredom, self-indulgence, and the inability to contribute to society (Ch. 16).

State of identity If individuals were in a state of identity (an ideal circumstance), the various aspects of their self-image would be in agreement with each other; they would be identical (Ch. 11).

STD (sexually transmitted diseases) A major cause of infertility (Ch. 3).

Stillbirth The term used to describe, after the twentieth week, the spontaneous end of a pregnancy if the baby is born dead (Ch. 4).

Stress Anything that upsets our equilibrium—both psychological and physiological (Ch. 10).

Structure building Levinson's term. During structure-building periods, individuals face the task of building a stable structure around choices they have made (Ch. 14).

Structure changing Levinson's term. A process of reappraising the existing life structure and exploring the possibilities for new life structures characterizes the structure-changing period (Ch. 14).

Subculture A subgroup within a culture, in this case a social culture (Ch. 12).

Subjective knowledge Belenky's third phase of women's thinking; characterized by some crisis of male authority that sparked a distrust of outside sources of knowledge, and some experience that confirmed a trust in women thinkers themselves (Ch. 13).

Sudden infant death syndrome (SIDS) Death of an apparently healthy infant, usually between 2 and 4 months of age; thought to be a brain-related respiratory problem (Ch. 5).

Superego One of the three structures of the psyche according to Freud; acts as a conscience (Ch. 2).

Surrogacy motherhood One woman carries another woman's embryo (Ch. 3).

Symbolic play The game of pretending; one of five preoperational behavior patterns (Ch. 7).

Symmetry An infant's capacity for attention; style of responding influences interactions (Ch. 6).

Synchrony The ability of parents to adjust their behavior to that of an infant (Ch. 6).

Syntactic cues Using language rules to combine words into sentences (Ch. 9).

Syntax Describes how we learn to put words together to form sentences (Ch. 7).

Syphilis A sexually transmitted infection that presents a great danger in that in its early stage there are no symptoms. If untreated, it can be fatal (Chs. 4 and 12).

T

Telegraphic speech Initial multiple-word utterances, usually two or three words (Ch. 5).

Temperament A child's basic personality that is now thought to be discernible soon after birth; how a child interacts with the environment (Chs. 6 and 10).

Temporizing An aspect of Perry's theory of ethical development, in which some people remain in one position for a year or more, exploring its implications but hesitating to make any further progress (Ch. 13).

Teratogens Any agents that can cause abnormalities, including drugs, chemicals, infections, pollutants, and the mother's physical state (Ch. 4).

Terminal drop The period of from a few weeks up to two years before a person's death, during which his or her intelligence is presumed to decline rapidly (Ch. 17).

Tertiary circular reaction Repetition with variation; the infant is exploring the world's possibilities (Ch. 5).

Thalidomide A popular drug prescribed during the early 1960s that was later found to cause a variety of birth defects when taken by women early in their pregnancy (Ch. 4).

Theory of mind Children's realization that others' thoughts affect their behavior (Ch. 7).

Toxoplasmosis Caused by a protozoan, it may cause damage to the nervous system; transmitted by animals, especially cats (Ch. 4).

Traditional marriage enterprise Levinson's term. The main goal of this type of marriage is to form and maintain a family (Ch. 16).

Trait theorists Researchers who look at pieces of the personality (personality traits), as measured by detailed questionnaires (Ch. 16).

Transformation Children learn to think about what they shouldn't do in different terms (Ch. 10).

Transition Levinson's concept that each new era begins as an old era is approaching its end. That "in-between" time is a transition (Ch. 14).

Transition-linked turning points The precursors and outcomes of a variety of transitions. A constellation of events that define the transition period or the timing and sequence of events that occur within a transitional period. For example, puberty and school events are frequently studied as key transitions signaling the entry into adolescence (Ch. 11).

Treatment The variable that the experimenter manipulates (Ch. 1).

Triarchic model of intelligence A three-tier explanation of intelligence proposed by Robert Sternberg (Ch. 9).

Trophoblast The outer surface of the fertilized egg (Ch. 4).

Turner syndrome Females with the XO chromosomal pattern (Ch. 3).

U

Ultrasound The use of sound waves to produce an image that enables a physician to detect structural abnormalities (Ch. 4).

Umbilical cord Contains blood vessels that go to and from the mother through the arteries and veins supplying the placenta (Ch. 4).

Uniform growth Montessori's term to describe the developmental period in which children show considerable stability (Ch. 7).

Universalizing faith The final developmental step of Fowler's theory of faith. Here the individual lives in the real world but is not of it. Such persons do not merely recognize the mutuality of existence; they act on the basis of it (Ch. 19).

V

Validation Fromm's term for the reciprocal sharing of deep secrets and feelings that allows people to feel loved and accepted (Ch. 14).

Vocables Consistent sound patterns to refer to objects and events (Ch. 5).

W

Wear and tear theory The theory that aging is due to the cumulative effects of hard work and lifelong stress (Ch. 17).

Whole Language A method in which students learn to read by obtaining the meaning of words, with phonics being introduced when needed from context (Ch. 7).

Z

Zone of proximal development The distance between a child's actual developmental level and a higher level of potential development with adult guidance (what children can do independently and what they can do with help) (Ch. 2).

Zygote The fertilized egg (Ch. 3).

Zygote intrafallopian transfer (ZIFT) The fertilized egg (the zygote) is transferred to the fallopian tube (Ch. 3).

References

A. A. R. P. (September–October, 1997). Friendship facts. *Modern Maturity,* 41.

A.A.R.P. (February 2000). Grandparents and kids: getting along fine. Washington DC: *AARP Bulletin,* 21.

Abeles, N. (1997). A victory for the aging community. *APA Monitor, 28* (10), 2.

Abeshouse, R. P. (1987). *Lifelong learning, Part I: Education for a competitive economy.* Washington, DC: Roosevelt Center for American Policy Studies.

Abravanel, E. & DeYoung, N. (1991). Does object modeling elicit imitative like gestures from young infants? *Journal of Experimental Child Psychology, 52,* 22–40.

Adams, G., Montemayor, R., & Gullotta, T. (1996). Psychosocial development during adolescence: The legacy of John Hill. In G. Adams, R. Montemayor, & T. Gullotta (Eds.), *Psychosocial development during adolescence.* Thousand Oaks, CA: Sage.

Adams, H. E., Wright, L. W., & Lohr, B. A. (1996). Is homophobia associated with homosexual arousal? *Journal of Abnormal Psychology, 105* (3), 440–445.

Adolph, K. (1997). Learning in the development of infant locomotion. *Monographs of the Society for Research in Child Development, 262* (3).

Agbayewa, M., Oluwafemi, M. Stephen, A., & Wiggins, S. (1998). Socioeconomic factors affecting suicide in elderly populations in British Columbia. *The Canadian Journal of Psychiatry, 43* (8), 829–835.

Ahrons, C. (1994). The effects of the postdivorce relationship on paternal involvement: A longitudinal view. *American Journal of Orthopsychiatry, 63,* 441–450.

Aiken, L. (1998). *Human development in adulthood.* NY: Plenum.

Ainsworth, M. (1973). The development of infant-mother attachment. In B. Caldwell and H. Riccuti (Eds.). *Review of child development research.* Chicago: U. of Chicago Press.

Ainsworth, M. (1979). Infant-mother attachment. *American Psychologist, 34,* 932–937.

Ainsworth, M. & Bowlby, J. (1991). An ethological approach to personality. *American Psychologist, 46,* 333–341.

Akhtar, N., Carpenter, M., & Tomasello, M. (1996). The role of discourse novelty in early word learning. *Child Development, 67,* 635–645.

Alexander, G. & Korenbrot, C. (1995). The role of prenatal care in preventing low birth weight. *The Future of Children, 5* (1), 103–120.

Allen, B. P. (1995). Gender stereotypes are not accurate: A replication of Martin (1987) using diagnostic vs. self-report and behavioral criteria. *Sex Roles, 32* (9/10), 583–600.

Al-Mabuk, C. P. A. & Enright, R. D. (1995). Forgiveness education with parentally love-deprived late adolescents. *Journal of Moral Education, 24,* 427–444.

Al-Mateen, C. S., Brookman, R., Best, A. M., & Singh, N. N. (1996). Inquiring about sexual abuse. *Journal of the American Academy of Child & Adolescent Psychiatry, 35* (4), 407–408.

Alpaugh, P. K. & Birren, J. E. (1977). Variables affecting creative contributions across the adult life span. *Human Development, 20* (4), 240–248.

Alpaugh, P., Renner, V., & Birren, J. (1976). Age and creativity. *Educational Gerontology, 1,* 17–40.

Alsaker, F. (1995). Is puberty a critical period for socialization? *Journal of Adolescence, 18,* 427–444.

Alsaker, F. (1996). Annotation: The impact of puberty. *Journal of Child Psychology and Psychiatry and Allied Disciplines, 37* (3), 249–258.

Altman, L. (1994). High H.I.V. levels raise risks to newborns. *New York Times,* August 17.

Alva, S. A. & Jones, M. (1994). Psychosocial adjustment and self-reported patterns of alcohol use among Hispanic adolescents. *Journal of Early Adolescence, 14,* 432–448.

Alves, J. (1993). Transgressions and transformations: Initiation rites among urban Portuguese boys. *American Anthropologist, 95* (4), 894–928.

Alzheimer's Association Annual Report. (1996). *A world without Alzheimer's.* Washington, DC: Alzheimer's Association.

Alzheimer's Association. (1999). *President's report.* Silver Springs, MD: Alzheimer's Disease Education.

Amabile, T. M., Hennessey, B. A., & Grossman, B. S. (1986). Social influence on creativity: The effects of contracted-for reward. *Journal of Personality & Social Psychology, 50* (1), 14–23.

American Academy of Pediatrics. (1998). Guidance for effective discipline. *Pediatrics, 101* (4), 723–728.

American Academy of Pediatrics. (2000). Changing concepts of Sudden Infant Death Syndrome: Implications for infant sleeping environment and sleep position. *Pediatrics, 105* (3), 650–656.

American Academy of Pediatrics. (2000). Diagnosis and evaluation of the child with attention-deficit/hyperactivity disorder. *Pediatrics, 105* (5), 1158–1170.

American Academy of Pediatrics. (2000). Fetal alcohol syndrome and alcohol-related neurodevelopmental disorders. *Pediatrics, 106* (2), 358–361.

American Association of Retired Persons. (1990a, January). FDA warns against dietary supplement. *A.A.R.P., 31* (1), 7.

American Association of Retired Persons. (1990b, January). Study links alcohol to heart damage. *A.A.R.P., 31* (1), 7.

American Heart Association. (1998). *Diet and the heart.* Washington, DC: AHA.

American Psychiatric Association. (1994). *Diagnostic and statistical manual mental disorders* (4th ed.), Washington, DC: author.

Anderson, E. G. (1996). Worrying about health: A uniquely American pastime? *Geriatrics, 51* (9), 56–60.

Anderson, J., Crawford, C., Nadeau, J., & Lindberg, T. (1992). Was the Duchess of Windsor right? A cross cultural review of the socioecology of ideals of female body shape. *Ethology and Sociobiology, 13* (3), 197–227.

Anderson, L. (June 5, 1998). Prodding teenagers into action: Programs try to boost level of fitness, exercise. Boston: *Boston Globe,* p. 1.

Anderson, L. & Krathwohl, D. (To be published, 2001). *A taxonomy for learning, teaching, & assessing: A revision of Bloom's taxonomy of educational objectives.* Reading, MA: Addison-Wesley-Longman.

Angell, K. E., Gross, W., Johnson, M. S., Koutstaal, W., & Schacter, D. L. (1997). False recollection induced by photographs: A comparison of older and younger adults. *Psychology and Aging, 12* (2) 203–215.

Angier, N. (1993). Map of all chromosomes to guide genetic hunters. *The New York Times,* December 16.

Annie E. Casey Foundation. (1995). State profiles of child well-being. *Kids Count Data Book.* Boston, MA.

Apgar, V. (1953). A proposal for a new method of evaluation of the newborn infant. *Anesthesia and Analgesia, 32,* 260–267.

Arcus, D., Gardner, S., & Anderson, C. (1992). Infant reactivity, maternal style, and the development of inhibited and uninhibited behavioral profiles. *Temperament and environment.* Symposium at the biennial meeting of the International Society for Infant Studies.

Arnett, J. (1996). What it means to be an adult. *Journal of Adult Development, 3* (1), 38–47.

Ary, D., James, L., & Biglan, A. (1999). Parent-daughter discussions to discourage tobacco use: Feasibility and content. *Adolescence, 34* (134),

Aslin, R., Jusczyk, P., & Pisoni, D. (1998). Speech and auditory processing during infancy: Constraints on and precursors to language. In W. Damon (Series Ed.) & D. Kuhn & R. Siegler (Volume Eds.), *Handbook of child psychology: Volume 2. Cognition, perception, and language.* New York: John Wiley.

Astington, J. (1993). *The child's discovery of mind.* Cambridge, MA: Harvard University Press.

Atkinson, D. (1999). The three R's of children of alcoholics: Rules, roles, roads. *Journal of Health Education., 30* (4), 254–255.

Avery, M. E. & Litwack, G. (1983). *Born early.* New York: Little, Brown.

Azar, B. (1996). Some forms of memory improve as people age. *APA Monitor, 27* (11), 27.

Azar, B. (1996). Project explores landscape of midlife. *APA Monitor, 27* (11), 26.

Azar, B. (1997a). More research needed on the leading causes of death. *APA Monitor, 28* (10), 31.

Azar, B. (1997b). Be careful how you define intelligence. *APA Monitor, 28* (10), 37.

Azar, B. (1999). E. O. Wilson to speak at APA's convention. *APA Monitor, 30* (4), 17.

Azar, B. (1999 October). Mom's stress may affect early child development. *APA Monitor,* p. 20.

Bailey, J. (1991). A genetic study of male sexual orientation. *Archives of General Psychiatry, 48,* 1089–1096.

Bailey, J. M., Pillard, R. C., Neale, M. C., & Agyei, Y. (1993). Heritable factors influence sexual orientation in women. *Archives of General Psychiatry, 50,* 217–223.

Bailey, J. M. & Pillard, R. C. (1991). A genetic study of male sexual orientation. *Archives of General Psychiatry, 48,* 1089–1096.

Baillargeon, R. (1987). Object permanence in 3½ and 4½ month old infants. *Developmental Psychology, 23,* 655–664.

Baker, K. (1999). How can we best serve LEP students? A reply to Nicholas Meier and Stephen Krashen. *Phi Delta Kappan, 80* (9), 707–710.

Balcazar, H. & Mattson, S. (2000). Nutrition. In S. Mattson and J. Smith (Eds.), *Core curriculum for maternal-newborn nursing.* Philadelphia: W. B. Saunders.

Balch, G. I. (1998). Exploring perceptions of smoking cessation among high school smokers: Input and feedback from focus groups. *Preventive Medicine: An International Devoted to Practice and Theory, 27* (5), A55–A63.

Baltes, P., Lindenberger, U., & Staudinger, U. (1998). Lifespan theory in developmental psychology. In R. M. Lerner (Ed.), *Handbook of child psychology: Volume 1. Theoretical models of human development.* New York: John Wiley.

Baltes, P. B. & Blates, M. M. (Eds.). (1990). *Successful aging: Perspectives from the behavioral sciences.* Cambridge: Cambridge University Press.

Baltes, P. B. & Shaire, K. (1993). The aging mind: Potential and limits. *The Gerontologist, 33* (5), 580–594.

Baltes, P. B. & Staudinger, U. M. (2000). Wisdom: A metaheuristic (pragmatic) to orchestrate mind and virtue toward excellence. *American Psychologist, 55* (1), 122–136.

Baltes, P. B., Sowarka, D., & Kliegl, R. (1989). Cognitive training research on fluid intelligence in old age: What can older adults achieve by themselves? *Psychology and Aging, 4* (2), 217–221.

Baltimore, D. (1994). What is the Genome project? In N. Cooper (Ed.), *The human genome project.* Mill Valley, CA: University Science Books.

Bandura, A. (1986). *Social foundations of thought and action.* Englewood Cliffs, NJ: Prentice-Hall.

Bandura, A. (1997). *Self-efficacy: The exercise of control.* New York: Freeman.

Bandura, A. & Walters, R. (1963). *Social learning and personality development.* New York: Holt, Rinehart & Winston.

Bandura, A., Ross, D., & Ross, S. (1963). Imitation of film-mediated aggressive models. *Journal of Abnormal and Social Psychology, 66,* 3–11.

Banks, J. (1993). Multicultural education: Development, dimensions, and challenges. *Phi Delta Kappan,* September, 22–28.

Banks, J. & Banks, C. A. (Eds.). (1993). *Multicultural education: Issues and perspectives.* Boston: Allyn and Bacon.

Bankston, C. L. & Caldas, S. J. (1998). Family structure, schoolmates, and racial inequalities in school achievement. *Journal of Marriage and the Family, 60,* 715–723.

Barchers, S. (1994). *Teaching language arts.* New York: West.

Barnes, G. M., Farrell, M. P., & Banerjee, S. (1994). Family influences on alcohol abuse and other problem behaviors among black and white adolescents in a general population sample. *Journal of Research on Adolescence, 4,* 183–201.

Barnes, J. (1998). Mental health promotion: A developmental perspective. *Psychology, Health & Medicine. Special Issue: Health promotion and mental health, 3* (1), 55–69.

Barry, D. (1993). Screen violence and America's children. *Spectrum, 66* (3), 37–42.

Bartlett, S. (1997). No place to play: Implications for the interactions of parents and children. *Journal of Children and Poverty, 3* (1).

Barton, L., Hodgman, J., & Pavlova, Z. (1999). Causes of death in the extremely low birth weight infant. *Pediatrics, 103* (2), 446–451.

Bartsch, K. & Wellman, H. (1995). *Children talk about the mind.* New York: Oxford University Press.

Baumrind, D. (1967). Child-care practices anteceding three patterns of preschool behavior. *Genetic Psychology Monographs, 75,* 43–88.

Baumrind, D. (1971). Current patterns of parental authority. *Developmental Psychology Monographs, 4,* 1–103.

Baumrind, D. (1986). *Familial antecedents of social competence in middle childhood.* Unpublished manuscript.

Baumrind, D. (1991). The influence of parenting style on adolescent competence and substance use. Special Issue: The work of John P. Hill: I. Theoretical, instructional, and policy contributions. *Journal of Early Adolescence, 11* (1), 56–95.

Baumrind, D. (1991). To nurture nature. *Behavioral and Brain Sciences,* XIV, 386.

Baumrind, D. (1993). The average expectable environment is not good enough: A response to Scarr. *Child Development, 64* (5), 1299–1317.

Baumrind, D. (1995). Commentary on sexual orientation: Research and social policy implications. Special Issue: Sexual orientation and human development. *Developmental Psychology, 31* (1), 130–136.

Beall, A. E. & Sternberg, R. J. (1995). The social construction of love. *Journal of Social and Personal Relationships, 12* (3), 417–438.

Bebbington, P. & others. (1998). The influence of age and sex on the prevalence of depression conditions. *Psychological Medicine, 28* (1), 9–19.

Becoming A Nation of Readers: The report of the commission on reading. (1984). Washington, DC: National Academy of Education, National Institute of Education, and Center for the Study of Reading.

Begley, S. (August 21, 1999). Why the young kill. *Newsweek.*

Belenky, M., Clinchy, B., Goldberger, N., & Tarule, J. (1986). *Women's ways of knowing.* New York: Basic Books.

Belsky, J. (1996). Parent, infant, and social-contextual antecedents of father-son attachment security. *Developmental Psychology, 32* (5), 905–913.

Bem, S. (1975). Androgyny vs. the light little lives of fluffy women and chesty men. *Psychology Today, 9* (4), 58–59, 61–62.

Bem, S. (1995). Dismantling gender polarization and compulsory heterosexuality: Should we turn the volume down or up? *Journal of Sex Research, 32* (4), 329–334.

Bem, S. (1996). Exotic becomes erotic. *Psychological Review, 103* (2), 320–335.

Bem, S. (1999). *An unconventional family.* New Haven, CT: Yale University Press.

Bengston, V. L. & Robertson, J. L. (Eds.). (1985). *Grandparenthood.* Beverly Hills, CA: Sage.

Benson, G. S. (1996). Editorial: Male sexual dysfunction—pitfalls, pills and prostheses. *The Journal of Urology, 156,* 1636.

Bergman, S. (1991). Men's psychological development. *Work in Progress:* No. 48. Wellesley, MA: The Stone Center, Wellesley College, 1–13.

Berk, L. (1997). *Infant, children, adolescents.* Needham Heights, MA: Allyn & Bacon.

Berko, Gleason, J. (1997). *The development of language.* Boston: Allyn and Bacon.

Berzonsky, M. & Kuk, L. (2000). Identity status, identity processing style and transition to university. *Journal of Adolescent Research, 15* (1), 81–98.

Bingham, C. R. & Crockett, L. J. (1996). Longitudinal adjustment patterns of boys and girls experiencing early, middle, and late sexual intercourse. *Developmental Psychology, 32* (4), 647–658.

Birren, J. (1960). Behavioral theories of aging. In N. Shock (Ed.), *Aging.* Washington, DC: American Association for the Advancement of Science.

Birren, J. (1964). *The psychology of aging.* Englewood Cliffs, NJ: Prentice-Hall.

Bishop, J. & Waldholz, M. (1990). *Genome.* New York: Simon & Schuster.

Bito, H., Tsien, R. W., & Deisseroth, K. (1996). Signaling from synapse to nucleus: Postsynaptic CREB phosphorylation during multiple forms of hippocampal synaptic plasticity. *Neuron,* Jan. 16 (1), 89–101.

Bjorklund, D. (1997). In search for a metatheory for cognitive development (or, Piaget is dead and I don't feel so good myself). *Child Development, 68* (1), 144–148.

Bjorklund, D. (2000). *Children's thinking: Developmental function and individual differences.* Belmont, CA: Wadsworth.

Blackman, J. (1997). *Medical aspects of developmental disabilities in children birth to three.* Gaithersburg, MD: Aspen Publications.

Blass, E. & Ciaramitaro, V. (1994). A new look at some old mechanisms in human newborns. *Monographs of the Society for Research in Child Development, 59* (1), Serial No. 239.

Bloom, B. (1956). Taxonomy of educational objectives. *Handbook I: Cognitive domain.* New York: McKay.

Bloom, L. (1998). Language acquisition in its developmental context. In D. Kuhn & R. Siegler (Eds.), *Handbook of child psychology.* Volume 5. New York: John Wiley.

Bloom, L. (2000). Language acquisition in its developmental context. In W. Damon (Series Ed.) & D. Kuhn & R. Siegler (Volume Eds.), *Handbook of child psychology: Volume 2, Cognition, perception, and language.* New York: John Wiley.

Blum, R. W., Harmon, B., Harris, L., Bergeisen, L., & Resnick, M. (1992). American-Indian-Alaska native youth health. *Journal of the American Medical Association, 267,* 1637–1644.

Blumenkrantz, D. (1992a). *Fulfilling the promise of children's services.* San Francisco: Jossey-Bass.

Blumenkrantz, D. (1992b). *Rite of passage experience.* Glastonbury, CT: R.O.P.E.

Blumenkrantz, D. (1996). *The rite way: Guiding youth to adulthood and the problem of communitas.* Michigan: University of Michigan Press.

Blumenkrantz, D. & Gavazzi, S. (1993). Guiding transitional events for children and adolescents through a modern day rite of passage. *Journal of Primary Prevention, 13* (3), 199–212.

Blustein, D. (2000). *The interface of work and relationships.* Manuscript under review.

Blustein, D. & Flum, H. (1999). A self-determination perspective of exploration and interest in career development. In M. Savackas & A. Spokane, Eds., *Vocational interests.* Palo Alto, CA: Davies-Black Publishing.

Bly, Robert. (1990). *Iron John.* Reading, MA: Addison-Wesley.

Bock, R. (1993). *Understanding Klinefelter syndrome.* Washington, DC: U.S. Department of Health and Human Services.

Bodmer, W. & McKie, R. (1995). *The book of man.* New York: Scribner.

Boehm, K., Schondel, C., Marlowe, A., & Manke-Mitchell, L. (1999). Teens' concerns: A national evaluation. *Adolescence, 34* (135).

Bogenschneider, K., Wu, M., Raffaelli, M., & Tsay, J. (1998). "Other teens drink, but not my kid": Does parental awareness of adolescent alcohol use protect adolescents from risky consequences? *Journal of Marriage and the Family, 60,* 356–373.

Boivin, M. & Hymel, S. (1997). Peer experiences and social self-perceptions: A sequential model. *Developmental Psychology, 33* (1), 135–145.

Booth, D. (1994). *Classroom voices: Language-based learning in the elementary school.* New York: Harcourt Brace.

Borgman, R. (1986). "Don't come home again:" Parental banishment of delinquent youths. *Child Welfare, 65* (3), 295–304.

Bornstein, J. M. (1986). Retraining the older worker: Michigan's experience with senior employment services. Special issue: Career counseling of older adults. *Journal of Career Development, 13* (2), 14–22.

Bornstein, M. (1992). Perception across the life cycle. In M. Bornstein & M. Lamb (Eds.), *Developmental psychology: An advanced textbook* (3rd ed.). Hillsdale, NJ: Erlbaum.

Bornstein, M. (1995). Parenting infants. In M. Bornstein (Ed.), *Handbook of parenting* (Vol. 3). Hillsdale, NJ: Lawrence Erlbaum.

Bornstein, M. & Arterberry, M. (1999). Perceptual development. In M. Bornstein & M. Lamb (Eds.), *Developmental psychology: An advanced textbook.* Mahwah, NJ: Lawrence Erlbaum.

Borum, R. (1996). Improving the clinical practice of violence risk assessment. *American Psychologist, 51,* 945–956.

Botwinick, J. (1977). Intellectual abilities. In J. E. Birren & K. W. Schaie (Eds.), *Handbook of the psychology of aging.* New York: Van Nostrand Reinhold.

Botwinick, J. (1984). *Aging and behavior* (3rd ed.) New York: Springer.

Bouchard, T. (1994). Genes, environment, and personality. *Science, 264,* 1700–1791.

Bowlby, J. (1969). *Attachment.* New York: Basic Books.

Bowlby, J. (1982). Attachment and loss: retrospect and prospect. *American Journal of Orthopsychiatry, 52,* 664–678.

Bowlby, J. (1988). *A secure base.* New York: Basic Books.

Boyer, E. (1990). Giving dignity to the teaching profession. In D. Dill & Associates (Eds.), *What teachers need to know.* San Francisco: Jossey-Bass.

Brabeck, M. (1983). Moral judgment: Theory and research on differences between males and females. *Developmental Review, 3,* 274–291.

Bradway, K., Thompson, C., & Graven, S. (1958). Preschool IQs after 25 years. *Journal of Educational Psychology, 49,* 278–281.

Brady, B. A. & Gray, D. D. (1988). Employment services for older job seekers. *The Gerontologist, 27,* 565–568.

Bransford, J. & Stein, B. (1993). *The IDEAL problem solver.* New York: Freeman.

Braverman, S. & Paris, J. (1993). The male mid-life crisis in the grown-up resilient child. *Psychotherapy, 30,* 651–656.

Brazelton, T. B. & Cramer, B. (1990). *The earliest relationship.* Reading, MA: Addison-Wesley.

Brazelton, T. B. & Nugent, K. (1995). *Neonatal Behavioral Assessment Scale.* London: MacKeith Press.

Brazelton, T. B., Christophersen, E., Frauman, A., Gorski, P., Poole, J., Stadtler, A., & Wright, C. (1999). Instruction, timeliness, and medical influences affecting toilet training. *Pediatrics, 103* (6), 1353–1358.

Bredekamp, S. & Copple, C. (Eds.). (1997). *Developmentally appropriate practice in early childhood programs.* Washington, DC: National Association for the Education of Young People.

Brelis, M. (July 3, 1998). Lewd hazing on cutter detailed. Boston: *Boston Globe,* B1, 4.

Brenner, A. (1984). *Helping children cope with stress.* San Diego, CA: Lexington Books.

Bretschneider, J. G. & McCoy, N. L. (1988). Sexual interest and behavior in healthy 80 to 102 year olds. *Archives of Sexual Behavior, 17* (2), 109–129. New York: Plenum Press.

Brisk, M. (1998). *Bilingual education.* Mahwah, NJ: Erlbaum.

Broberg, A., Wessels, H., Lamb, M., & Hwang, C. (1997). Effects of daycare on the development of cognitive abilities in 8-year-old: A longitudinal study. *Developmental Psychology, 33* (1), 62–69.

Brody, G., Stoneman, Z., & McCoy, J. (1992). Associations of maternal and paternal direct and differential behavior with sibling relationships: Contemporaneous and longitudinal analyses. *Child Development, 63,* 82–92.

Brody, G. H., Stoneman, Z., & Flor, D. (1996). Parental religiosity, family processes, and youth competence in rural, two-parent African American families. *Developmental Psychology, 32* (4), 696–706.

Brody, J. (2000). What could be good about morning sickness? *Plenty.* New York Times, June 6, D7.

Brodzinsky, D., Lang, R., & Smith, D. (1995). Parenting adopted children. In M. Bornstein (Ed.), *Handbook of parenting* (Vol. 3). Hillsdale, NJ: Erlbaum.

Bronfenbrenner, U. (1978). *The ecology of human development.* Cambridge, MA: Harvard University Press.

Bronfenbrenner, U. (1989). Ecological systems theory. *Annals of Child Development, 6,* 187–249.

Bronfenbrenner, U. & Morris, P. (1998). The ecology of developmental processes. In R. M. Lerner (Ed.), *Handbook of child psychology: Volume 1. Theoretical models of human development.* New York: John Wiley.

Bronson, M. (1995). *The right stuff for children birth to 8.* Washington, DC: National Association for the Education of Young People.

Bronson, M. (2000). *Self-regulation in early childhood.* New York: Guilford.

Bronson, M., Pierson, D., & Tivnan, T. (1984). The effects of early education on children's competence in elementary school. *Evaluation Review, 8* (5), 615–627.

Brooks, J. & Lewis, M. (1976). Midget, adult and child: infants responses to strangers. *Child Development, 47,* 323–332.

Brooks-Gunn, J. (1987). Pubertal processes. In V. B. Van Hasselt & M. Hersen (Eds.), *Handbook of adolescent psychology.* New York: Pergamon.

Brooks-Gunn, J., Peterson, A., & Eichorn, D. (1985). The study of maturational timing effects in adolescence. *Journal of Youth and Adolescence, 14* (3), 149–161.

Brown, B., Dolcini, M., & Leventhal, A. (1997). Transformations in peer relationships at adolescence: Implications for health-related behavior. In J. Schulenberg & J. L. Maggs (Eds.), *Health risks and developmental transitions during adolescence* (pp. 161–189). New York, NY: Cambridge University Press.

Brown, B. B. (1990). Peer groups and peer cultures. In S. Feldman & G. Elliot (Eds.), *At the threshold: The developing adolescent.* Cambridge, MA: Harvard University Press.

Brown, B. R., Baranowski, M. D., Kulig, J. W., & Stephenson, J. N. (1996). Searching for the Magic Johnson effect: AIDS, adolescents, and celebrity disclosure. *Adolescence, 31* (122), 253–264.

Brown, J. K. (1982). Cross-cultural perspectives on middle-aged women. *Current Anthropology, 23* (2), 143–156.

Brown, R. (1973). *A first language: The early stages*. Cambridge, MA: Harvard University Press.

Brown, S. L. & Booth, A. (1996). Cohabitation versus marriage: A comparison of relationship quality. *Journal of Marriage and Family, 58* (8), 668–678.

Bruner, J. (1966). *Toward a theory of instruction*. Cambridge, MA: Harvard University Press.

Brunstein, J. C., Dangelmayer, G., & Schultheiss, O. C. (1996). Personal goals and social support in close relationships: Effects on relationship mood and marital satisfaction. *Journal of Personality and Social Psychology, 71* (5), 1006–1019.

Buchanan, D. (1992). Outward Bound goes to the inner city. *Educational Leadership, 50* (4), 38–39.

Bulkin, W. & Lukashok, H. (1988). Rx for dying. *New England Journal of Medicine, 318*, 376–378.

Burchinal, M., Roberts, J., Riggins, R., Zeisel, S., Neebe, E., & Bryant, D. (2000). Relating quality of center-based child care to early cognitive and language development longitudinally. *Child Development, 71* (2), 339–357.

Bureau of the Census. (1996). *Statistical Abstract of the United States*. Washington, DC: Author.

Burke, J. & Hagedorn, J. M. (1995). Are gangs created by a need for family? In R. Del Campo & D. S. Del Campo (Eds.), *Taking sides: Clashing views on controversial issues in childhood and society* (pp. 360–376). Guilford, CT: The Dushkin Publishing Group, Inc.

Burkhardt, S. & Rotatori, A. (1995). *Treatment and prevention of childhood sexual abuse*. Washington, DC: Taylto & Francis.

Burr, J. A. & Mutchler, J. E. (1999). Race and ethnic variation in norms of filial responsibility among older persons. *Journal of Marriage & the Family, 61* (3), 674–687.

Bursik, K. (1995). Gender-related personality traits and ego development: Differential patterns for men and women. *Sex Roles, 32* (9/10), 601–615.

Burton, L. M. (1992). Black grandparents rearing children of drug-addicted parents: Stressors, outcomes, and social service needs. *The Gerontologist, 32* (6), 744–751.

Butler, R., Walker, W., Skowronski, J., & Shannon, L. (1995). Age responses to the love structures scale. *International Journal of Aging and Human Development, 40* (4), 281–296.

Byne, W. (1994, May). The biological evidence challenged. *Scientific American*, 50–55.

Cabrera, N., Tamis-LeMonda, C., Bradley, R., Hofferth, S., & Lamb, M. (2000). Fatherhood in the twenty-first century. *Child Development, 71* (1), 127–136.

Cahill, M. & Salomone, P. R. (1987). Career counseling for work life extension: Integrating the older worker into the labor force. *Career Development Quarterly, 35* (3), 188–196.

Cairns, R. (1998). The making of developmental psychology. In R. M. Lerner (Ed.), *Handbook of child psychology: Volume 1. Theoretical models of human development*. New York: John Wiley.

Calhoun. K. & Wilson, A. (2000). In L. Szuchman & F. Muscarella, Eds. (2000). *Psychological perspectives on human sexuality*. NY: Wiley.

Call, V., Sprecher, S., & Schwartz, P. (1995). The incidence and frequency of marital sex in a national sample. *Journal of Marriage and the Family, 57* (3), 639–652.

Callow, R. (1994). Classroom provision for the able & the exceptionally able. *Journal on Support-for-Learning, 9* (4), 151–154.

Cameron-Jones, M. & O'Hara, P. (1995). Mentors' perceptions of their roles with students in initial teacher training. *Cambridge Journal of Education, 25* (2), 189–199.

Campbell, B. & Gaddy, J. (1987). Rates of aging and dietary restrictions: Sensory and motor function in the Fischer 344 rat. *Journal of Gerontology, 42* (2), 154–159.

Campbell, F. & Ramey, C. (1994). Effects of early intervention on intellectual and academic achievement: A follow-up study of children from low-income families. *Child Development, 65*, 684–698.

Cancian, M. & Meyer, D. R. (1996). Changing policy, changing practice: Mothers' incomes and child support orders. *Journal of Marriage and the Family, 58* (8), 618–627.

Cannister, M. W. (1999). Mentoring and the spiritual well-being of late adolescents. *Adolescence, 34* (136), 769–779.

Capacchione, L. (1989). *The creative journal for children*. Boston: Shambhala.

Carnegie Corporation of New York. (1995). *Great Transitions: Preparing Adolescents for a New Century*. Carnegie Council on Adolescent Development.

Carnevali, D. L. & Patrick, M. (Eds.). (1986). *Nursing management for the elderly* (2nd ed.). Philadelphia: J. B. Lippincott.

Carney, J. (1993). "Is it really so terrible here?" Karl Menninger's pursuit of Erik Erikson. Special Issue: Erik H. Erikson. *Psychohistory-Review, 22* (1), 119–153.

Carstensen, L. (1992). Social and emotional patterns: Support for socioemotional selectivity theory. *Psychology and Aging, 7* (3), 331–338.

Carstensen, L. L. (1995). Evidence for a life-span theory of socioemotional selectivity. *Current Directions in Psychological Science, 4* (5), 151–156.

Carstensen, L. L., Gottman, J. M., & Levensen, R. W. (1995). Emotional behavior in long-term marriage. *Psychology and Aging, 10* (1), 140–149.

Casas, J. & Pytluk, S. (1995). Hispanic identity development: Implications for research and practice. In J. Ponterotto, J. Casas, L. Suzuki, & C. Alexander (Ed.), *Handbook of multicultural counseling*. Thousand Oaks, CA: Sage.

Case, R. (1998). The development of conceptual structures. In W. Damon (Series Ed.) and D. Kuhn & R. Siegler (Volume Eds.), Volume 4, *Handbook of child psychology*. New York: John Wiley.

Caserta. M. S., Lund, D. A., & Wright, S. D. (1996). Exploring the caregiver burden inventory (CBI): Further evidence for a multidimensional view of burden. *International Journal of Aging and Human Development, 43* (43), 21–34.

Casey, M. B., Nuttall, R., & Pezaris, E. (1997). Mediators of gender differences in mathematics college entrance test scores. *Developmental Psychology, 33* (4), 669–680.

Casper, L. & Bryson, K. (1999). Growth in single father's outpace this growth and single mothers. *United States Department of Commerce News*. Washington: Department of Commerce.

Caspi, A. (1998). Personality development across the life-course. In W. Damon (Series Ed.) & N. Eisenberg (Vol. Ed.), *Handbook of child psychology: Volume 3. Social, Emotional, and Personality Development*. New York: John Wiley.

Caspi, A., Belsky, J., & Silva, P. (1992). Childhood experience and the onset of menarche: A test of a sociobiological model. *Child Development, 63* (1), 47–58.

Caspi, A., Bem, D. J., & Elder, G. H. Jr. (1989). Continuities and consequences of interactional styles across the life course. *Journal of Personality, 57* (2), 375–406.

Cassidy, J., Kirsch, S., Scolton, K., & Parke, R. (1996). Attachment and representations of peer relationships. *Developmental Psychology, 32* (5), 892–904.

Castle, N. G. & Fogel, B. (1998). Characteristics of nursing homes that are restraint free. *The Gerontologist, 38* (2) 181–188.

Cattell, H. & Jolley, D. J. (1995). One hundred cases of suicide in elderly people. British *Journal of Psychiatry, 166*, 451–457.

Cauffman, E. & Steinberg, L. (1996). Interactive effects of menarcheal status and dating on dieting and disordered eating among adolescent girls. *Developmental Psychology, 32* (4), 631–635.

Ceci, S. (1996). *On intelligence*. Cambridge, MA: Harvard University Press.

Centers for Disease Control (CDC). (1995). *Reproductive Health*. Atlanta: Centers for Disease Control and Prevention.

Centers for Disease Control (CDC). (2000). *Sexually transmitted diseases sourcebook*. Atlanta: CDC.

Centers for Disease Control (CDC). (2000). Tobacco use among middle and high school students–United States, 1999. (January 28). *Morbidity and Mortality Weekly Report* (Washington, DC), 49–53.

Centers for Disease Prevention and Control (1996). *Teenage suicide*. Atlanta: CDC.

Chall, J. (1983). *Stages of reading development*. New York: McGraw-Hill.

Chall, J., Jacobs, V., & Baldwin, L. (1990). *The reading crisis: Why poor children fall behind*. Cambridge, MA: Harvard University Press.

Chamberlain, P. & Patterson, G. (1995). Discipline and child compliance in parenting. In M. Bornstein (Ed.), *Handbook of parenting*. Hillsdale, NJ: Erlbaum.

Chandler, M., Sokol, B., & Wainryb, C. (2000). Beliefs about truth and beliefs about rightness. *Child Development, 71* (1), 91–97.

Chang, B. H., Noonan, A. E., & Tennstedt, S. L. (1998). The role of religion/spirituality in coping with caregiving for disabled elders. *The Gerontologist, 38* (4), 463–470.

Checkley, K. (1997). The first seven . . . and the eighth. *Educational Leadership, 5* (1), 8–13.

Chen, X., Rubin, K., & Li, D. (1997). Relation between academic achievement and social adjustment: Evidence from Chinese children. *Developmental Psychology, 33* (3), 518–525.

Chen, Z. & Siegler, R. (2000). Across the great divide: Bridging the gap between understanding of toddlers' and older children's thinking. *Monographs of the Society for Research in Child Development,* Serial No. 261, 65 (2).

Cherlin, A., Furstenberg, F., Chase-Lansdale, P., Kiernan, K., Robins, P., Morrison, D., & Teitler, J. (1991). Longitudinal studies of effects of divorce in Great Britain and the United States. *Science, 252,* 1386–1389.

Cherry, S. (1992). *Understanding pregnancy and childbirth.* New York: Collier.

Chess, S. & Thomas, A. (1987). Know your child. New York: Basic Books. *Child Development, 71* (4), 1018–1032.

Children's Defense Fund (1989). *A day in the lives of some teens.* Washington, DC: Children's Defense Fund.

Children's Defense Fund. (1995). *The state of America's children yearbook.* Washington, DC: Children's Defense Fund.

Children's Defense Fund. (1996). *The state of America's children yearbook.* Washington, DC: Children's Defense Fund.

Children's Defense Fund. (2000). *AIDS and children.* Washington, DC: Children's Defense Fund.

Chiriboga, D. A. (1989). Mental health at the midpoint. In S. Hunter & M. Sundel (Eds.), *Midlife myths.* Newbury Park, CA: Sage.

Christ, G. (2000). *Healing children's grief: Surviving a parent's death from cancer.* New York: Oxford.

Cicchetti, D. & Toth, S. (1998). Perspectives on research and practice in developmental psychopathology. In W. Damon (Series Ed.) & I. Sigel & K. Renninger (Volume Eds.), *Handbook of child psychology: Volume 4. Child psychology in practice.* New York: John Wiley.

Cigarette smoking among adults. (June 15, 1992). *Journal of the American Medical Association, 267* (3), 3133.

Cillessen, A. & Bukowski, W. (Eds.). (2000). Recent advances in the measurement of acceptance and rejection in the peer system. *New Directions for Child and Adolescent Development, 88* (Summer).

Clarke, E., Preston, M., Raksin, J., & Bengtson, V. (1999). Types of conflicts and tensions between older parents and adult children. *The Gerontologist, 39* (3), 261–270.

Clarke-Stewart, K., Allhusen, V., & Clements, D. (1995). Nonparental caregiving. In M. Bornstein (Ed.), *Handbook of parenting.* Hillsdale, NJ: Erlbaum.

Clay, R. (1996, December). Some elders thrive on working into late life. *APA Monitor, 35,* 12.

Clay, R. (1997). Laughter may be no laughing matter. *APA Monitor, 28* (9), 18.

Clifford, B., Gunter, B., & McAleer, J. (1995). *Television and children.* Hillsdale, NJ: Erlbaum.

Clifford, P., Tan, S., & Gorsuch, R. (1991). Efficacy of a self-directed behavioral health change program: Weight, body, composition, cardiovascular fitness, blood pressure, health risk and psychological mediating variables. *Journal of Behavioral Medicine, 14* (3), 303–323.

Clifton, R., Perris, E., & Bullinger. (1991). Infants' perception of auditory space. *Developmental Psychology, 27,* 187–197.

Clyman, B. B. & Pompei, P. (1996a). Osteoarthritis: New roles for drug therapy and surgery. *Geriatrics, 51* (9), 32–36.

Clyman, B. B. & Pompei, P. (1996b). Osteoarthritis: What to look for, and when to treat it. *Geriatrics, 51* (8), 36–41.

Cochran, S. V. & Rabinowitz, F. E. (1996). Men, loss, and psychotherapy. *Psychotherapy, 33* (4), 593–600.

Coffey, P., Leitenberg, H., Henning, K., & Turner, T. (1996). Mediators of the long-term impact of child sexual abuse: Perceived stigma, betrayal, powerlessness, and self-blame. *Child Abuse and Neglect, 20* (5), 447–455.

Coffey, P., Leitenberg, H., Henning, K., & Turner, T. (1996). The relation between methods of coping during adulthood with a history of childhood sexual abuse and current psychological adjustment. *Journal of Consulting and Clinical Psychology, 64* (5), 1090–1093.

Cohen, J. (Feb. 7, 1997). The genomics gamble. *Science, 275,* 767–772.

Cohen-Mansfield, J. & Marx, M. S. (1992). The social network of the agitated nursing home resident. *Research on Aging, 14* (1), 110–123.

Cohen-Mansfield, J. & Werner, P. (1998). Predictors of aggressive behaviors: A longitudinal study in senior day care centers. *Journal of Gerontology, 53B* (5), P300–P310.

Cohn, R. (1979). Age and the satisfactions from work. *Journal of Gerontology, 34,* 264–272.

Coie, J. & Dodge, K. (1998). Aggression and antisocial behavior. In W. Damon (Series Ed.) & N. Eisenberg (Volume Ed.), *Handbook of child psychology: Volume 3. Child psychology in practice.* New York: John Wiley.

Col, N. F., Eckman, M. H., Kara, R. H., Pauker, S. G., Goldberg, R. J., Ross, E. M., Orr, R. K., & Wong, J. B. (1997, April 9). Patient-specific decisions about hormone replacement therapy in postmenopausal women. *Journal of the American Medical Association, 277,* (14), 1140–1147.

Cole, E. & Rothblum, E. (1990). Commentary on "Sexuality and the midlife woman." *Psychology of Women Quarterly, 14* (4), 509–512.

Cole, M. (1996). *Cultural psychology.* Cambridge, MA: Harvard University Press.

Cole, M. (1999). *Culture in development.* In M. Bornstein & M. Lamb (Eds.), *Developmental psychology: An advanced textbook.* Mahwah, NJ: Erlbaum.

Cole, M. & Cole, S. (1996). *The development of children.* New York: Freeman.

Cole, R. (1998).The genome and the human genome project. In T. Peters, *Genetics: Issues of social justice.* Cleveland, Ohio: Pilgrim Press.

Cole, T. (1991). The specter of old age: History, politics, and culture in an aging America. In B. Hess & E. Markson (Eds.), *Growing old in America* (pp. 23–38). New Brunswick, NJ: Transaction.

Coles, R. (1970). *Erik Erikson: The growth of his work.* Boston: Little, Brown.

Coles, R. (1997). *The moral intelligence of children.* Boston: Random House.

Collins, M. F. & Weatherburn, D. (1995). Unemployment and the dynamics of offender populations. *Journal of Quantitative Criminology, 11* (3), 231–245.

Collins, N. L., Dunkel-Schetter, C., Lobel, M., & Scrimshaw, S. C. M. (1993). Social support in pregnancy: Psychosocial correlates of birth outcomes and postpartum depression. *Journal of Personality and Social Psychology, 65* (6), 1243–1258.

Collins, P. (1993). The interpersonal vicissitudes of mentorship: An exploratory study in the field of supervisor-student relationship. *Clinical Supervisor, 11* (1), 121–135.

Collins, W., Harris, M., & Susman, A. (1995). Parenting during middle childhood. In Marc Bornsteinn (Ed.), *Handbook of parenting, Volume 1: Applied and practical parenting.* Mahwah, NJ: Lawrence Erlbaum.

Coltrane, S. & Ishii-Kuntz, M. (1992). Men's housework: A life course perspective. *Journal of Marriage and the Family, 54,* 43–57.

Compas, B., Hinden, B. R., & Grehardt, C. (1995). Adolescent development: Pathways and processes of risk and resilience. *Annual Review of Psychology, 46,* 265–293.

Comstock, G. (1993). The medium and society: The role of television in American society. In G. Berry & Asamen, J. (Eds.), *Children and television.* Newbury Park, CA: Sage.

Comstock, G. & Paik, H. (1991). *Television and the American child.* New York: Academic.

Comstock, G. & Paik, H. (1994). The effects of television violence on antisocial behavior: A meta-analysis. *Communication Research, 21,* 269–277.

Comstock, G. & Scharrar, E. (1999). *Television.* San Diego: Academic Press.

Conwell, Y. (1995). Suicide among elderly persons. *Psychiatric Services, 46* (6), 563–572.

Conwell, Y., Rotenberg, M., & Caine, E. D. (1990). Completed suicide at age 50 and over. *Journal of the American Geriatrics Society, 38,* 640–644.

Cook-Deegan, R. (1995). The gene wars: *Science. politics, and the human genome.* New York: Norton.

Cooksey, E. C. & Fondell, M. M. (1996). Spending time with his kids: Effects of family structure on fathers' and children's lives. *Journal of Marriage and the Family, 58* (8), 693–707.

Cooksey, E. C., Rindfuss, R. R., & Guilkey, D. K. (1996). The initiation of adolescent sexual and contraceptive behavior during changing times. *Journal of Health and Social Behavior, 37* (1), 59–74.

Cooney, T. & Mortimer, J. (1999). Family structure differences the timing of leaving home: Exploring mediating factors. *Journal of Research on Adolescence, 9* (4), 367–393.

Cooper, N. (Ed.). (1994). *The human genome project.* Mill Valley, CA: University Science Books.

Cooper, T., Berseth, C., Adams, J., & Weisman, L. (1998). Actuarial survival in the premature infant less than 30 weeks' gestation. *Pediatrics, 101* (6), 975–978.

Coronary disease attributable to sedentary lifestyle. (September 19, 1990). *Journal of the American Medical Association, 328* (8), 574–578.

Costa, F. M., Jessor, R., Donovan, J. E., & Fortenberry, J. D. (1995). Early initiation of sexual intercourse: The influence of psychosocial unconventionality. *Journal of Research on Adolescence, 5* (1), 71–91.

Costa, P. T. & McCrae, R. R. (1995). Domains and facets: Hierarchical personality assessment using the revised NEO

Personality Inventory. *Journal of Personality Assessment, 64* (1), 21–50.

Cote, J. E. & Levine, C. (1988). The relationship between ego identity status and Erikson's notions of institutionalized moratoria, value orientation stage, and ego dominance. *Journal of Youth and Adolescence, 17* (1), 81–100.

Cowan, N., Nugent, L., Elliott, E., Ponomarev, I., & Saults, J. (1999). The role of attention in the development of short-term memory: Age differences in the verbal span of apprehension. *Child Development, 70* (5), 1082–1097.

Cowart, B. J., Yokomukai, Y., & Beauchamp, G. K. (1994). Bitter taste in aging: Compound-specific decline in sensitivity. *Physiology and Behavior, 56* (4), 1237–1241.

Cox, H. (1988). *Later life.* Englewood Cliffs, NJ: Prentice-Hall.

Cox, M., Owen, M., Henderson, V. K., & Margand, N. (1992. Prediction of infant-father and infant-mother attachment. *Developmental Psychology, 28,* 474–483.

Cox, M., Paley, B., Burchinal, M., & Payne, C. (1999). Marital perceptions and interactions across the transition to parenthood. *Journal of Marriage and the Family, 61,* 611–625.

Craig, J. & Rollman, G. (1999). Somesthesis. In J. Spence, J. Darley, and D. Foss (Eds.), *Annual Review of Psychology, 50,* 305–331.

Craig, T. K. J. (1996). Adversity and depression. *International Review of Psychiatry, 8* (4), 341–353.

Craig-Bray, L., Adams, G. R., & Dobson, W. R. (1988). Identity formation and social relations during late adolescence. *Journal of Youth and Adolescence, 17* (2), 173–188.

Creeden, J. E. (1990). Environmental and behavioral factors affecting fraternity drinking. *Journal of College Student Development, 31,* 465–467.

Crick, N. (1996). The role of overt aggression, relational aggression, and prosocial behavior in the prediction of children's future social adjustment. *Child Development, 67,* 2317–2327.

Crick, N., Casas, J., & Ku, H. (1999). Relational and physical forms of peer victimization in preschool. *Developmental Psychology, 35* (2), 376–385.

Crick, N., Casas, J., & Mosher, M. (1997). Relational and overt aggression in preschool. *Developmental Psychology, 33* (4), 579–588.

Criqui, M. H. (1990). Comment on Shaper's "Alcohol and mortality." *British Journal of Addiction, 85* (7), 854–857.

Crohan, S. E., Antonucci, T. C., Adelman, P. K., & Coleman, L. M. (1989). Job characteristics and well-being at mid-life: Ethnic and gender comparisons. *Psychology of Women Quarterly, 13,* 223–235.

Crouter, A. C., Perry-Jenkins, M., Huston, T. L., & McHale, S. M. (1987). Processes underlying father involvement in dual-earner and single-earner families. *Developmental Psychology, 23,* 431–440.

Crowley, J. E. (1986). Longitudinal effects of retirement on men's well-being & health. *Journal of Business and Psychology, 1* (2), 95–113.

Cruickshank, D., Bainer, D., & Metcalf, K. (1995). *The act of teaching.* New York: McGraw-Hill.

Csikszentmihalyi, M. & Rathunde, K. (1998). In R. M. Lerner (Ed.), *Handbook of child psychology: Volume 1. Theoretical models of human development.* New York: John Wiley.

Culp, M., Clyman, M., & Culp, R. (1995). Adolescent depressed mood, reports of suicide attempts, and asking for help. *Adolescence, 30,* 827–837.

Curtis, H. & Barnes, N. S. (1994). *Invitation to biology.* New York: Worth.

Curtis, J. M. & Curtis, M. J. (1993). Factors related to susceptibility and recruitment by cults. *Psychological Reports, 73,* 451–460.

Cutler, G. B. & Chrousos, G. P. (1999). *Variability in Hormone Concentrations and Self-Reported*

Cutler, W., Schleidt, W., & Friedmann, E. (1987). Lunar influences on the reproductive cycle in women. *Human Biology, 59,* 959–972.

Czaja, S. & Sharit, J. (1998). Age differences in attitudes toward computers. *Journal of Gerontology, 53B* (5), 329–340.

D'Augelli, A. & Patterson, C. (1995). Lesbian, gay, and bisexual identities over the lifespan. *Psychological Perspectives.* New York: Oxford University Press.

Dacey, J. (1993). Reducing dropout rate in inner city middle school students through instruction in self-control. *Journal of Research in Middle Level Education,* Fall, 109–116.

Dacey, J. (1998). A history of the concept of creativity. In H. Gardner & R. Sternberg, (Eds.), *Encyclopedia of creativity.* San Francisco: Academic Press.

Dacey, J. & Fiore, L. (2000). *Your anxious child.* San Francisco: Jossey-Bass.

Dacey, J. & Kenny, M. (1997). *Adolescent development* (2nd ed.). Boston: McGraw-Hill.

Dacey, J. & Lennon, K. (1998). *Understanding creativity: The interplay of biological, psychological and social forces.* San Francisco: Jossey-Bass.

Dacey, J., Amara, D., & Seavey, G. (Winter 1993). Reducing dropout rate in inner city middle school children through instruction in self control. *Research on Middle Level Education, 17* (1), 111–119.

Dacey, J., deSalvatore, L., & Robinson, J. (Winter 1997). The results of teaching middle school students two relaxation techniques as part of a conflict prevention program. *Research in Middle Level Education, 20* (2), 91–102.

Dacey, J. S. (1986). *Adolescents today* (3rd ed.). Glenview, IL: Scott, Foresman.

Dacey, J. S. (1989a). *Fundamentals of creative thinking.* Lexington, MA: D.C. Heath/Lexington Books.

Dacey, J. S. (1989b). Peak periods of creative growth across the life span. *The Journal of Creative Behavior, 24* (4), 224–247.

Dacey, J. S. (1989c). Discriminating characteristics of the families of highly creative adolescents. *The Journal of Creative Behavior, 24* (4), 263–271.

Dacey, J. S. & Packer, A. (1992). *The nurturing parent: How to raise a creative, loving, responsible child.* New York: Fireside/Simon & Schuster.

Damasio, A. (1999). *The feeling of what happens.* New York: Harcourt Brace & Company.

Damon, W. (1995). *Greater expectations.* New York: The Free Press.

Dancer, L. & Gilbert, L. (1993). Spouses' family work participation and its relation to wives' occupational level. *Sex Roles, 28* (3/4), 127–145.

Darkenwald, G. & Novak, R. (1997). Classroom age competition and academic achievement in college. *Adult Education Quarterly, 47* (3/4), 108.

Darling-Hammond, L. (1994). Performance-based assessment and educational equity. *Harvard Educational Review, 64* (1), 5–30.

Darrach, B. (1992). The war on aging. *Life, 15* (10), 32–45.

Datan, N. (1995). Corpses, lepers, and menstruating women: Tradition, transition, and the sociology of knowledge. *Feminism & Psychology, 5* (4), 449–459.

Datan, N., Rodeheaver, D., & Hughes, F. (1987). Adult development and aging. *Annual Review of Psychology, 38,* 153–180.

Davidson, J. M. (1989). Sexual emotions, hormones, and behavior. *Advances, 6* (2), 56–58.

Davis, C., Lovie-Kitchin, J., & Thompson, B. (1995). Psychosocial adjustment to age-related macular degeneration. *Journal of Visual Impairment and Blindness, 89* (1), 16–27.

Davis, C., Woodside, D., Olmsted, M., & Kaptein, S. (1999). Psychopathology in the eating disorders: The influence of physical activity. *Journal of Applied Biobehavioral Research, 4* (2), 139–156.

Davis, K. J., Sloane, P. D., Mitchell, C. M., Pressier, J., Grant, L., Hawes, M. C., Lindeman, D., Montgomery, R., Long, K., Phillips, C., & Koch, G. (2000). Specialized dementia programs in residential care settings. *Gerontologist, 40* (1), 32–42.

De Casper, A., Lecanuet, J., Busnel, M., & Granier-Deferre, C. (1994). Fetal reactions to recurrent maternal speech. *Infant Behavior and Development, 17* (2), 159–164.

Deacon, S., Minichiello, V., & Plummer, D. (1995). Sexuality and older people: Revisiting the assumptions. *Educational Gerontology, 21* (5), 497–513.

DeAngelis, T. (1997). Elderly may be less depressed than the young. *APA Monitor, 28* (10), 25.

DeGenova, M. K. (1992). If you had your life to live over again, What would you do differently? *International Journal of Aging and Human Development, 34* (2), 135–143.

Dekovic, M. & Janssens, J. (1992). Parents' child-rearing style and child's sociometric status. *Developmental Psychology, 28,* 925–932.

Del Vecchio, M., Zhou, H., Tully, T., & Yin, J. C. (1995). CREB as a memory modulator: Induced expression of a dCREB2 activator insoform enhances long-term memory in drosophila. *Cell, 81* (1), 107–215.

Dellman-Jenkins, M., Lambert, D., Fruit, D., & Dinero, T. (1986). Old and young together. *Childhood Education,* 206–212.

Dempsey, C. L. (1994). Health and social issues of gay, lesbian, and bisexual adolescents. *Families in Society, 75* (3), 160–167.

DeVries, B., Davis, C. G., Wortman, C. B., & Lehman, D. R. (1997). Long-term psychological and somatic consequences of later life parental bereavement. *Omega: Journal of Death & Dying, 35* (1), 97–117.

DeVries, H. M., Hamilton, D. W., Lovett, S., & Gallagher-Thompson, D. (1997). Patterns of coping preferences for male and female caregivers of frail older adults. *Psychology & Aging, 12,* 263–267.

di Mauro, D. (1995). *Sexuality research in the United States: An assessment of social and behavioral sciences.* New York: The Social Science Research Council.

Diamant, L. & McAnulty, R. D. (1995). *The psychology of sexual orientation behavior & identity.* Westport, CT: Greenwood Press.

Diamond, A. (2000). Close interrelation of motor development and cognitive development and of the cerebellum and prefrontal cortex. *Child Development, 71* (1), 44–56.

Diehl, M., Willis, S. L., & Schaie, K. W. (1995). Everyday problem solving in older adults. *Psychology and Aging, 10* (3), 478–491.

Dinnerstein, M. (1992). *Women between two worlds: Reflections on work and family.* Philadelphia: Temple University Press.

DiPetro, J., Hodgson, D., & Costigan, K. (1996). Fetal antecedents of infant temperament. *Child Development, 67,* 2568–2583.

Dishion, T. J., Andrews, D. W., & Crosby, L. (1995). Antisocial boys and their friends in early adolescence: Relationship characteristics, quality, and interactional process. *Child Development, 66,* 139–151.

Dixon, R. & Lerner, R. (1999). History and systems in developmental psychology. In M. Bornstein & M. Lamb (Eds.), *Developmental psychology: An advanced textbook.* Mahweh, NJ: Lawrence Erlbaum.

Donner, M. (1997, Feb.). A genetic basis for the sudden infant death sex ratio. *Medical Hypotheses, 2,* 137–142.

Dori, G. A. & Overholser, J. C. (1999). Depression, hopelessness, and self-esteem: Accounting for suicidality in adolescent psychiatric inpatients. *Suicide & Life-Threatening Behavior, 29* (4), 309–318.

Dorn, L. D., Nottelmann, E. D., Susman, E. J., & Inoff-Germain, G. (1999), Variability in hormone concentrations. *Journal of Youth and Adolescence, 12* (4), 343–350.

Douglas, A., Johnstone, H., & Russell, J. (2000). Sex-steroid induction of endogenous opoid inhibition on oxytocin secretory responses to stress. *Journal of Neuroendocrinology, 12* (4), 343–350.

Dragoi, V. & Staddon, J. (1999). The dynamics of operant conditioning. *Psychological Review, 106* (1), 20–61.

Dranoff, S. M. (1974). Masturbation and the male adolescent. *Adolescence, 9* (34), 16–176.

Draper, P. & Keith, J. (1992). Cultural contexts of care: Family caregiving for elderly in America and Africa. *Journal of Aging Studies, 6* (2), 113–134.

Drew, L. & Smith, P. (1999). The impact of parental separation/divorce on grandparent-grandchild relationships. *International Journal of Aging and Human Development, 49* (1), 61–78.

Dumont, M. & Provost, M. A. (1999). Resilience in adolescents: Protective role of social support, coping strategies, self-esteem, and social activities on experience of stress and depression. *Journal of Youth and Adolescence, 28* (3), 343–363.

Duncan, G. & Brooks-Gunn, J. (2000). Family poverty, welfare reform, & child development. *Child Development, 71* (1), 188–196.

Duncan, G., Brooks-Gunn, J., & Klebanov, P. (1994). *Child Development, 65,* 296–318.

Dunn, J. (1994). Experience and understanding of emotions, relationships, and membership in a particular culture. In Paul Ekman & Richard Davidson (Eds.), *The nature of emotion.* Oxford University Press, 1994.

Dunn, J., Brown, J., & Maguire, M. (1995). The development of children's moral sensibility: Individual differences and emotion understanding. *Developmental Psychology, 31,* 649–659.

Dunn, J., Slomkowski, C., & Beardsall, L. (1994). Sibling relationships from the preschool period through middle childhood and early adolescence. *Developmental Psychology, 30* (3), 315–324.

Durham, M. G. (1998). Dilemmas of desire: Representations of adolescent sexuality in two teen magazines. *Youth and Society, 29* (3), 369–389.

Duvall, E. (1971). *Family development.* Philadelphia: Lippincott.

Eakes, G. (1995). Chronic sorrow: The lived experience of parents of chronically mentally ill individuals. *Archives of Psychiatric Nursing, 9* (2), 77–84.

Eastman, P. (1997). Slowing down Alzheimer's. *American Association of Retired Persons Bulletin, 38,* 1–6.

Eastman, P. (January 2000). Scientists piecing Alzheimer's puzzle. *AARP Bulletin, 41* (1), 18–19.

Eccles, J. & Roeser, R. (1999). School and community influences on human development. In M. Bornstein & M. Lamb (Eds.), *Developmental psychology: An advanced textbook.* Mahwah, NJ: Erlbaum.

Edwards, C. (1995). Parenting toddlers. In M. Bornstein (Ed.), *Handbook of parenting.* Hillsdale, NJ: Erlbaum.

Edwards. R. & Usher, R. (1997). University adult education in the postmodern moment. *Adult Education Quarterly, 47,* (3/4), 153.

Eilenberg, J., Fullilove, M., Goldman, R. G., & Mellman, L. (1996). Quality and use of trauma histories obtained from psychiatric outpatients through mandated inquiry. *Psychiatric Services, 47* (2), 165–169.

Eisdorfer, C. & Wilkie, F. (1973). Intellectual changes and advancing age. In L. Jarvik (Ed.), *Intellectual functioning in adults.* New York: Springer.

Eisenberg, N. (1992). *The caring child.* Cambridge, MA: Harvard University Press.

Eisenberg, N. & Fabes, R. (1998). Prosocial development. In W. Damon (Series Ed.) & N. Eisenberg (Volume Ed.), *Handbook of child psychology: Volume 3, Social, emotional, and personality development.* New York: John Wiley.

Eisenberg, N., Fabes, R., Murphy, M., Karbon, K., & Smith, M. (1999). The relation of children's dispositional empathy-related responding to their emotionality, regulation, and social functioning. *Developmental Psychology, 32* (2), 195–209.

Eisenberg, N., Martin, C., & Fabes, R. (1996). Gender development and gender effects. In D. Berliner & R. Calfee (Eds.), *Handbook of educational psychology.* New York: Macmillan.

Ekman, P. & Davidson, R. (Eds.). (1994). *The nature of emotions.* New York: Oxford University Press.

Elder, G. (1998). Theories of human development: Contemporary perspectives. In R. M. Lerner (Ed.), *Handbook of child psychology: Volume 1. Theoretical models of human development.* New York: John Wiley.

Elias, M., Elias, P., & Elias, J. (1977). *Basic processes in adult developmental psychology.* St. Louis: Mosby.

Eliason, M. J. (1995). Accounts of sexual identity formation in heterosexual students. *Sex Roles, 32* (11/12), 821–834.

Elkind, D. (1978). *The child's reality: Three developmental themes.* Hillsdale, NJ: Erlbaum.

Elkind, D. & Bowen, R. (1979). Imaginary audience behavior in children and adolescents. *Developmental Psychology, 15,* 38–44.

Elliott, S., Kratochwill, T., Littlefield, J., & Travers, J. (1996). *Educational psychology: Effective teaching, effective learning.* Dubuque, IA: Brown/Benchmark.

Elliott, S., Kratochwill, T., Littlefield, J., & Travers, J. (2000). *Educational psychology: Effective teaching, effective learning.* Dubuque, IA: Brown/Benchmark.

Ely, R. (1997). Language and literacy in the school years. In J. Gleason (Ed.), *The development of language.* Needham, MA: Allyn and Bacon.

Emde, R., Plomin, R., Robinson, J., Corley, R., DeFries, J., Fulker, D., Reznick, J., Campos, J., Kagan, J., & Zahn-Waxler, C. (1992). Temperament, emotions, and cognition at fourteen months: The MacArthur, Longitudinal Twin Study. *Child Development, 63* (6), 1437–1455.

Eng, T. R. & Butler, W. T. (Eds.). (1997). *The hidden epidemic: Confronting sexually transmitted diseases.* Washington, DC: National Academy Press.

Engstrom, P. F. (1986). Cancer control objectives for the year 2000. In L. E. Mortenseon, P. F. Engstrom, & P. N. Anderson (Eds.), *Advances in cancer control.* New York: Alan R. Liss.

Enright, R. D., Levy, V. M., Harris, D., & Lapsley, D. K. (1987). Do economic conditions influence how theorists view adolescents? *Journal of Youth and Adolescence, 16* (6), 541–560.

Erikson, E. (1958). *Young man Luther: A study in psychoanalysis and history.* New York: Norton.

Erikson, E. (1959). Growth and crises of the healthy personality. *Psychological Issues, 1.*

Erikson, E. (1963). *Childhood and society* (2nd ed.). New York: Norton.

Erikson, E. (1968). *Identity: Youth and crisis.* New York: Norton.

Erikson, E. (1969). *Gandhi's truth: On the origins of militant nonviolence.* New York: Norton.

Erikson, E. (1975). *Life, history, and the historical movement.* New York: Norton.

Erikson, E. (1978). *Adulthood.* New York: Norton.

Eriksson, P. S., Perfilieva, E., Bjork-Eriksson, T., Alborn, A. M., Nordborg, C., Peterson, D. A., & Gage, F. H. (1998). Neurogenesis in the adult human hippocampus. *Nature-medicine, 4* (11), 1313–1317.

Escarce, M. (1995). A cross-cultural study of Nepalese neonatal behavior. In K. Nugent,

B. Lester, & T. B. Brazelton, (Eds.), *The cultural context of infancy*. Norwood, NJ: Ablex.

Eskilson, A. & Wiley, M. (1999). Solving for the X: Aspirations and expectations of college students. *Journal of Youth and Adolescence, 28,* (1), 51–57.

Esquivel, G. B. (1995). Teacher behaviors that foster creativity. Special Issue: Toward an educational psychology of creativity: I. *Educational Psychology Review, 7* (2), 185–202.

Etounga-Manguelle, D. (2000). Does Africa need a cultural adjustment program? In L. Harrison & S. Huntington (Eds.), *Culture matters*. New York: Basic Books.

Evaluation of covert video surveillance in the diagnosis of Munchausen Syndrome by Proxy: Lessons from 41 cases. *Pediatrics, 105* (6), 1305–1312.

Everaerd, W., Laan, E., & Spiering, M. (2000). Male sexuality. In L. Szuchman & F. Muscarella, Eds. (2000). *Psychological perspectives on human sexuality*. NY: Wiley.

Ewert, A. & Heywood, J. (1991). Group development in the natural environment: Expectations, outcomes, and techniques. *Environment and Behavior, 23* (5), 592–615.

Exploring the environment. (Spring, 1996). *Alzheimer's Association National Newsletter, 16* (1), 4a.

Fagerstrom, R. (1994). Correlation between depression and vision in aged patients before and after cataract operations. *Psychological Reports, 75,* 115–125.

Fagot, B. (1995). Parenting boys and girls. In M. Bornstein (Ed.), *Handbook of parenting*. Hillsdale, NJ: Erlbaum.

Fagot, B., Leinbach, M., & O'Boyle, C. (1992). Gender labeling, gender stereotyping, and parenting behaviors. *Developmental Psychology, 28,* 225–230.

Fantz, R. (1961). The origin of form perception. *Scientific American, 204,* 66–72.

Farrell, M. & Strang, J. (1991). Substance use and misuse in childhood and adolescence. *Journal of Child Psychology and Psychiatry and Allied Disciplines, 32* (1), 109–128.

Federal Bureau of Investigation (FBI). (2000). *Uniform crime reports for the U. S.* Washington: FBI.

Feinbloom, R. (1993). *Pregnancy, birth, and the early months* (2nd. ed.). Reading, MA: Addison-Wesley.

Feldman, B. (1995). The search for identity in late adolescence. In M. Sidoli & G. Bovensiepen (Eds.), *Incest fantasies and self-destructive acts: Jungian and post-Jungian psychotherapy in adolescence*. New Brunswick, NJ: Transaction Publishers.

Feldman, D. (1979). The mysterious case of extreme giftedness. In A. H. Passow (Ed.), *The gifted and the talented: Their education and development*. Chicago: Univ. of Chicago Press (NSSE).

Feldman, D. H. (1994). *Beyond universals in cognitive development* (2nd ed.). Norwood, NJ: Ablex Publishing Corporation.

Feldman, S. S., Fisher, L., Ranson, D. C., & Dimiceli, S. (1995). Is "what is good for the goose good for the gander?" Sex differences in relations between adolescent coping and adult adaptation. *Journal of Research on Adolescence, 5,* 333–359.

Feldman, S. S., Rosenthal, D. R., Brown, N. L., & Canning, R. D. (1995). Predicting sexual experience in adolescent boys from peer rejection and acceptance during childhood. *Journal of Research on Adolescence, 5,* 387–411.

Ferber, R. (1985). *Solve your child's sleep problems*. Simon & Schuster.

Ferguson, T., Stegge, H., Miller, E., & Olsen, M. (1999). Guilt, shame, and symptoms in children. *Developmental Psychology, 35* (2), 347–357.

Fergusson, D. M. & Lynskey, M. T. (1996). Adolescent resiliency to family adversity. *Journal of Child Psychology and Psychiatry and Allied Disciplines, 37* (3) 281–292.

Ferris, P. (1997). *Dr. Freud: A life*. Washington, DC: Counterpoint.

Field, T. (1990). Infancy. Cambridge, MA: Harvard University Press.

Fingerman, K. (1995). Aging mothers' and their adult daughters' perceptions of conflict behaviors. *Psychology & Aging, 10,* 639–649.

Finkel, S., Costa, E., Silva, J., Cohen, G., Miller, S., & Sartorius, N. (1996). Behavioral and psychological signs and symptoms of dementia: A consensus statement on current knowledge and implications for research and treatment. *International Journal of Geriatric Psychiatry, 12* (11), 1050–1061.

Finkelhor, D. (1996, August). *Keynote Address*. Presented at the International Congress on Child Abuse and Neglect. Dublin, Ireland.

Fischbach, G. (1992). Mind and brain. *Scientific American, 267* (3), 48–60.

Fischer, A. & Shaw, C. (1999). African Americans' mental health and perceptions of racist discrimination: The moderating effects of racial socialization experiences and self-esteem. *Journal of Counseling Psychology, 46* (3), 395–407.

Fiske, S. T. & Glick, P. (1995). Ambivalence and stereotypes cause sexual harassment: A theory with implications for organizational change. *Journal of Social Issues, 51* (1), 97–115.

Flannery, D. J., Vazsonyi, A. T., & Rowe, D. C. (1996). Caucasian and Hispanic early adolescent substance use: Parenting, personality, and school adjustment. *Journal of Early Adolescence, 16,* 71–89.

Flavell, J. (1963). *The developmental psychology of Jean Piaget*. New York: Van Nostrand.

Flavell, J. (1998). Social cognition. In W. Damon (Series Ed.) & D. Kuhn & R. Siegler (Volume Eds.), *Handbook of child psychology: Volume 2. Cognition, perception, and language*. New York: John Wiley.

Flavell, J. (1999). Cognitive development: Children's knowledge about the mind. In J. Spence, J. Darley, & D. Foss (Eds.), *Annual Review of Psychology*. Palo Alto, CA: Annual Reviews.

Flavell, J. Beach, D., & Chinsky, J. (1966). Spontaneous verbal rehearsal in a memory task as a function of age. *Child Development, 37,* 282–299.

Floyd, F., Stein, T., Harter, K., Allison, A., & Nye, C. (1999). Gay, lesbian, and bisexual youths: Separation-Individuation, parental attitudes, identity consolidation, and well-being. *Journal of Youth and Adolescence, 28* (6), 719–725.

Fodor, I. & Franks, V. (1990). Women in midlife and beyond: The new prime of life? *Psychology of Women Quarterly, 14,* 445–449.

Ford, K. & Norris, A. E. (1995). Factors related to condom use with casual partners among urban African-American and Hispanic males. *AIDS Education and Prevention, 7* (6), 494–503.

Fordham, S. & Ogbu, J. U. (1986). Black students' school success: Coping with the burden of "acting white." *Urban Review, 18,* 176–206.

Foreman, J. (1996, June 16). Doctors and patients at the end of life. *The Boston Globe,* 23.

Foreman, J. (1999, August 2). Miracle before birth. *The Boston Globe,* pp. C1, 4.

Forthofer, M. S., Markman, H. J., Cox, M., Stanley, S., & Kessler, R. C. (1996). Associations between marital distress and work loss in a national sample. *Journal of Marriage and the Family, 58* (8), 597–605.

Fouad, N. & Brown, M. (2000). The role of race and social class in development. In S. Brown & R. Lent, Eds., *Handbook of counseling psychology*. New York: Wiley.

Fowler, J. (1993). Response to Helmut Reich: Overview or apologetic? *International Journal for the Psychology of Religion, 3* (3), 173–179.

Fowler, J. W. (2000). *Becoming adult, becoming Christian*. San Francisco: Jossey-Bass.

Fox, J. (1997). *Primary health care of children*. St. Louis: Mosby.

Fraiberg, S. (1980). *Clinical studies in infant mental health: The first year of life*. New York: Basic.

Fraiberg, S., Adelson, E., & Shapiro, V. (1987). Ghosts in the nursery: A psychoanalytic approach to the problems of impaired mother-infant relationships. In L. Fraiberg (Ed.), *Selected writings of Selma* (pp. 100–136). Columbus: Ohio State University Press.

Frankl, V. (1967). *Psychotherapy and existentialism*. New York: Simon & Schuster.

Frankland, P. W., Blendy, J. A., Coblentz, J., Marowitz, Z., Scheutz, G., Silva, A. J., & Kogan, J. H. (1997). Spaced training induces normal long-term memory in CREB mutant mice. *Current Biology, 17* (1), 1–11.

Freitag, M., Belsky, J., Grossman, K., Grossman, K., & Scheueerer, H. (1996). Continuity in parent-child relationships from infancy to middle childhood and relationships with friendship competence. *Child Development, 67,* 1437–1454.

Freud, A. (1968). Adolescence. In A. E. Winder & D. L. Angus (Eds.), *Adolescence: Contemporary studies*. New York: American Book.

Freud, A. & Dann, S. (1951). An experiment in group upbringing. *Psychoanalytic Study of the Child, 6,* 127–168.

Freud, S. (1955). Totem and taboo. In J. Strachey (Ed. and Trans.), *The standard edition of the complete psychological works of Sigmund Freud* (Vol. 13). London: Hogarth Press (Original work published 1914).

Freud, S. (1966). *The complete introductory lectures on psychoanalysis*. Translated and edited by James Strachey. New York: Norton.

Fricker, H., Hindermann, R., & Bruppacher, R. (1995). The Aarau study on pregnancy and the newborn: An epidemiologic investigation of the course of pregnancy in

996 Swiss women, and its influence on newborn behavior using the Brazelton scale. In K. Nugent, B. Lester, and T. B. Brazelton (Eds.), *The cultural context of infancy*. Norwood, NJ: Ablex.

Friedan, B. (1963). *The feminine mystique*. New York: W. W. Norton.

Friedman, S. (1996). Reproductive conflicts in incest victims: An unnoticed consequence of childhood sexual abuse. *Psychoanalytic Quarterly, 65* (2), 383–388.

Frisch, R. E. (1988). Fatness and fertility. *Scientific American, 258* (3), 88–95.

Fromm, E. (1955). *The sane society*. New York: Holt, Rinehart & Winston.

Fromm, E. (1968). *The art of loving*. New York: Harper & Row.

Fulton, R. (1977). *General aspects*. In N. Linzer (Ed.), Understanding bereavement and grief. New York: Yeshiva University Press.

Funk, J. B. (1993). Reevaluating the impact of video games. *Clinical Pediatrics, 32* (2) 86–90.

Furnham, A. & Weir, C. (1996). Lay theories of child development. *Journal of Genetic Psychology, 157* (2), 211–226.

Furstenberg, F. F. (1990). The new extended family. In K. Pasley & M. Ihinger-Tallman (Eds.), *Remarriage and stepparenting*. New York: Guilford.

Gabriel, T. (1997, January 5). Pack dating: For a good time, call a crowd [New York Times Magazine]. *The New York Times*, pp. 22–23, 38.

Gagnon, J. H. & Simon, W. (1969). They're going to learn on the street anyway. *Psychology Today, 3* (2), 46 ff.

Gagnon, J. H. & Simon, W. (1987). The sexual scripting of oral genital contacts. *Archives of Sexual Behavior, 16* (1), 1–25.

Galen, B. & Underwood, M. (1996). A developmental investigation of social aggression among children. *Developmental Psychology, 33* (4), 589–600.

Gallup, G. (1988). *The Gallup poll*. New York: Random House.

Galton, F. (1870). *Hereditary genius*. New York: Appleton.

Galton, F. (1879). Psychometric experiments. *Brain, 2*, 148–162.

Ganong, L., Coleman, M., McDaniel, A. K., & Killian, T. (1998). Attitudes regarding obligations to assist an older parent or stepparent following later-life remarriage. *Journal of Marriage and the Family 60*, 595–610.

Ganzel, A. (1999). Adolescent decision making: The influence of mood, age, and gender on the consideration of information. *Journal of Adolescent Research, 14* (3), 289–295.

Garbarino, J. (1999). *Lost boys: Why our sons turn violent and how we can save them*. New York: The Free Press.

Garbarino, J. & Benn, J. (1992). The ecology of childbearing and childrearing. In J. Garbarino (1992). *Children and families in the social environment*. New York: Aldine.

Garcia Coll, C. (1990). Developmental outcome of minority infants: A process-oriented look into our beginnings. *Child Development, 61*, No. 2, 270–289.

Garcia Coll, C., Lamberty, G., Jenkins, R., McAdoo, H., Crnic, K., Wasik, B., & Garcia, H. (1996). An integrative model for the study of developmental competencies in minority children. *Child Development, 67*, 1891–1914.

Garcia, M., Shaw, D., Winslow, E., & Yaggi, K. (2000). Destructive sibling conflict and the development of conduct problems in young boys. *Developmental Psychology, 36* (1), 44–53.

Gardner, H. (1982). *Art, mind and brain*. New York: Basic.

Gardner, H. (1983). *Frames of mind: the theory of multiple intelligences*. New York, NY: Basic Books

Gardner, H. (1991). *The unschooled mind*. New York: Basic.

Gardner, H. (1993). *Creating minds*. New York: Basic.

Gardner, H. (1993). *Frames of mind: The theory of multiple intelligences*. New York: Basic Books.

Gardner, H. (1995). *Leading minds: An anatomy of leadership*. New York: Basic Books.

Gardner, H. (1997). *Extraordinary minds*. New York: Basic.

Gardner, H. & Winner, E. (1982). Children's conceptions (and misconceptions) of the arts. In H. Gardner, *Art, mind, and brain*. New York: Basic Books.

Garfein, A. J. & Herzog, A. R. (1995). Robust aging among the young-old, old-old, and oldest-old. *Journal of Gerontology: Social Sciences, 50B* (2), S77–S87.

Garland, A. F. & Zigler, E. (1993, February). Adolescent suicide prevention: Current research and social policy implications. *American Psychologist*, 169–182.

Garner, R. (1992). Learning from school texts. *Educational Psychologist, 27* (1), 53–64.

Garnier, H. & Stein, J. (1998). Values and the family: Risk and protective factors for adolescent problem behaviors. *Youth and Society, 30* (1), 89–120.

Garratt, D., Roche, J., & Tucker, S. (1997). *Changing experiences of youth*. London: Sage.

Garrod, A., Smulyan, L., Power, S., & Kilkenny, R. (1995). *Adolescent portraits*. Needham Heights, MA: Allyn & Bacon.

Garvey, C. (1990). *Play*. Cambridge, MA: Harvard University Press.

Garvey, M. J. & Schaffer, C. B. (1994). Are some symptoms of depression age dependent? *Journal of Affective Disorders, 32*, 247–251.

Gary, F., Moorhead, J., & Warren, J. (1996). Characteristics of troubled youths in a shelter. *Archives of Psychiatric Nursing, 10* (1), 41–48.

Gavazzi, S. & Blumenkrantz, D. (1993). Facilitating clinical work with adolescents and their families through the rite of passage experience program. *Journal of Family Psychotherapy, 4* (2), 47–67.

Ge, X., Best, K. M., Conger, R. D., & Simons, R. L. (1996). Parenting behaviors and the occurrence and co-occurrence of adolescent depressive symptoms and conduct problems. *Developmental Psychology, 32* (4), 717–731.

Ge, X., Conger, R. D., Cadoret, R. J., Neiderhiser, J. N., Yates, W., Troughton, E., & Stewart, M. A. (1996). The developmental interface between nature and nurture: A mutual influence model of child antisocial behavior and parent behaviors. *Developmental Psychology, 32* (4), 574–589.

Geary, D. & Bjorklund, D. (2000). Evolutionary developmental psychology. *Child Development, 71* (1), 57–65.

Geary, D., Bow-Thomas, C., Lin, F., & Siegler, R. (1996). Development of arithmetical competencies in Chinese and American children: Age, language, and schooling. *Child Development, 67*, 2022–2044.

Geis, J. A. & Klein, H. A. (1989). The relationship of life satisfaction to life change among the elderly. *The Journal of Genetic Psychology, 151* (2), 269–271.

Gelb, M. (1996). *Thinking for a change*. London: Aurum Press.

Gelfand, M. J., Fitzgerald, L. F., & Drasgow, F. (1995). The structure of sexual harassment: A confirmatory analysis across cultures and settings. *Journal of Vocational Behavior, 47*, 164–177.

Gelman, R. & Baillargeon, R. (1983). A review of some Piagetian concepts. In P. Mussen (Ed.), *Handbook of child psychology*. Volume 3. New York: Wiley.

Gerhardt, C. A., Compas, B. E., Connor, J. K., & Achenbach, T. M. Association of a mixed anxiety-depression syndrome and symptoms of major depressive disorder during adolescence. *Journal of Youth & Adolescence, 28* (3), 305–323.

Gerson, L. W., Jarjoura, D., & McCord, G. (1987). Factors related to impaired mental health in urban elderly. *Research on Aging, 9* (3), 356–371.

Gfellner, B. B. (1994). A matched group comparison of drug use and problem behavior among Canadian Indian and white adolescents. Special Issue: Canadian research on early adolescence. *Journal of Early Adolescence, 14*, 24–48.

Gfroerer, J., Wright, D., & Kopstein, A. (1997). Prevalence of youth substance abuse: The impact of methodological differences between two national surveys. *Drug & Alcohol Dependence, 47* (1), 19–30.

Gibson, E. & Walk, R. (1960). The visual cliff. *Scientific American, 202*, 64–71.

Giles, H., Coupland, N., Coupland, J., Williams, A., & Nussbaum, J. (1992). *Intergenerational talk and communication with older people*.

Gilligan, C. (1982). *In a different voice*. Cambridge, MA: Harvard University Press.

Gilligan, C., Lyons, N., & Hanmer, T. (1990). *Making connections: The relational worlds of adolescent girls at Emma Willard School*. Cambridge, MA: Harvard University Press.

Gilovich, K. D. & Miller, L. (1994). Combining adult and adolescent female incest survivors in a weekend retreat. *Journal of Child Sexual Abuse, 3* (2), 15–30.

Gitlin, T. (1987). *Years of hope, days of rage*. New York: Bantam Books, Inc.

Glass, J. C., Jr. & Reed, S. E. (1993). To live or die: A look at elderly suicide. *Educational Gerontology, 19*, 767–778.

Gleick, J. (1992). *Genius: The life and science of Richard Feynman*. New York: Pantheon.

Glen, N. (1998). The course of marital success and failure in five American 10-year marriage cohorts. *Journal of Marriage and the Family, 60* (August), 569–576

Gold, P. E., Jones, M. G., Korol, D. L., Manning, C. A., & Wilkniss, S. M. (1997). Age-related differences in an ecologically based study of rote learning. *Psychology and Aging, 12* (2) 372–375.

Goldman-Rakic, P. (1999). Working memory and the mind. The Editors of Scientific American, *The Scientific American Book of The Brain*. New York: The Lyons Press.

Goldsmith, M. F. (1988). Anencephalic organ donor program suspended; Loma Linda report expected to detail findings. *Journal of the American Medical Association, 260,* 1671–1672.

Goleman, D. (1985). *Vital lies, simple truths: The psychology of self-deception.* New York: Simon & Schuster.

Goleman, D. (1995). *Emotional intelligence.* New York: Bantam.

Golinkoff, R. & Hirsh-Pasek, K. (2000). *How babies talk.* New York: Dutton.

Goode, E. (2000). Most ills are a matter of more than one gene. *The New York Times,* June 27, pp. D1, D6.

Goodman, K. (1998). End-of-life algorithms. *Psychology, Public Policy, and Law, 4* (3), 719–727.

Gopnik, A., Meltzoff, A., & Kuhl, P. (2000). *The scientist in the crib.* New York: Morrow.

Gorski, P. (1999). Toilet raining guidelines: Parents—The role of parents in toilet training. *Pediatrics, 103* (6), 1362–1363.

Gosse, G. H. & Barnes, M. J. (1994). Human grief resulting from the death of a pet. *Anthrozoos, 7* (2), 103–112.

Gottlieb, G. (1997). *Synthesizing nature-nurture.* Mahwah, NJ: Erlbaum.

Gottlieb, G., Wahlsten, D., & Lickliter, R. (1998). The significance of biology for human development: A developmental psychobiological systems view. In R. M. Lerner (Ed.), *Handbook of child psychology: Volume 1. Theoretical models of human development.* New York: John Wiley.

Gottman, J. M. & Krokoff, L. J. (1989). Marital interaction and satisfaction: A longitudinal view. *Journal of Consulting and Clinical Psychology, 57,* 47–52.

Graber, J. A. & Brooks-Gunn, J. (1996). Transitions and turning points: Navigating the passage from childhood through adolescence. *Developmental Psychology, 32* (4), 768–776.

Graber, J. A., Petersen, A. C., & Brooks-Gunn, J. (1996). Pubertal processes: Methods, measures, and models. In J. A. Graber, J. Brooks-Gunn, et al. (Eds.), *Transitions through adolescence: Interpersonal domains and context* (pp. 23–53). Mahwah, NJ: Lawrence Erlbaum Associates, Inc.

Graham, B. (1994). Mentoring and professional development in careers services in higher education. *British Journal of Guidance and Counselling, 22* (2), 261–271.

Graham, S. (1994). Motivation in African-Americans. *Review of Educational Research, 64* (1), 55–117.

Graham, S. & Hudley, C. (1994). Attributions of aggressive and nonaggressive African American male early adolescents: A study of construct accessibility. *Developmental Psychology, 30,* 365–373.

Grant, L. What sexual revolution? (1999). In R. Nye, Ed. *Sexuality.* London: Oxford.

Gray, C. A. & Geron, S. M. (1995). The other sorrow of divorce: The effects on grandparents when their adult children divorce. *Journal of Gerontological Social Work, 23* (3/4), 139–159.

Green, A. H. (1995). Comparing child victims and adult survivors: Clues to the pathogenesis of child sexual abuse. *Journal of the American Academy of Psychoanalysis, 23* (4), 655–670.

Green, C. P. (1991). Clinical considerations: Midlife daughters and their aging parents. *Journal of Gerontological Nursing, 17* (11), 6–12.

Greenberger, E. & Chen, C. (1996). Perceived family relationships and depressed mood in early and late adolescence: A comparison of European and Asian Americans. *Developmental Psychology, 32* (4), 707–716.

Greene, K., Rubin, D. L., Hale, J. L., & Walters, L. H. (1996). The utility of understanding adolescent egocentrism in designing health promotion messages. *Health Communication, 8* (2), 131–152.

Greenfield, J. (1999). Cultural change and human development. In E. Turiel (Ed.), *Development and cultural change: Reciprocal processes.* San Francisco, CA: Jossey-Bass.

Greenfield, P. & Suzuki, L. (1998). Culture and human development: Implications for parenting, education, pediatrics, and mental health. In W. Damon (Series Ed.) & I. Sigel & K. Renninger (Volume Eds.), *Handbook of child psychology: Volume 4. Child psychology in practice.* New York: John Wiley.

Greenhouse, L. (2000). Justices deny gandparents visiting rights. *New York Times,* June 6, 1,15.

Greenspan, S. (1995). *The challenging child.* Reading, MA: Addison-Wesley.

Greenspan, S. & Benderly, B. (1997). *The growth of the mind.* Reading, MA: Addison-Wesley.

Grisso, T. & Tomkins, A. (1996). Communicating violence risk assessment. *American Psychologist, 51* (9), 928–930.

Grossman, H. Y. & Chester, N. L. (1990). *The experience and meaning of work in women's lives.* Hillsdale, NJ: Erlbaum.

Grusec, J., Goodnow, J., & Cohen, L. (1996). Household work and the development of concern for others. *Developmental Psychology, 32* (6), 999–1007.

Grusec, J., Goodnow, J., & Kucynski, L. (2000). New directions in analyses of parenting contributions to children's acquisition of values. *Child Development, 71* (1), 205–211.

Guberman, S. (1996). The development of everyday mathematics in Brazilian children with limited formal education. *Child Development, 67,* 1609–1623.

Guelzow, M. G., Bird, G. W., & Koball, E. H. (1991). An exploratory path analysis of the stress process for dual career men and women. *Journal of Marriage and the Family, 53* (2), 151–164.

Guilford, J. P. (1975). Creativity: A quarter century of progress. In I. A. Taylor & J. W. Getzels (Eds.), *Perspectives in creativity.* Chicago: Aldine.

Gutman, D. (1973, December). Men, women and the parental imperative. *Commentary,* 59–64.

Guttmacher, A. & Kaiser, I. (1986). *Pregnancy, birth and family planning.* New York: Signet.

Guyer, B., Hoyert, D., Martin, J., Ventura, S., MacDorman, M., & Strobino, D. (1998). Annual summary of vital statistics—1998. *Pediatrics, 104* (6), 1229–1246.

Gyulay, J. (1989). What suicide leaves behind. *Special Issue: The death of a child. Counseling and Values, 35* (2), 104–113.

Haan, N. (1976). ". . . change and sameness . . ." reconsidered. *International Journal of Aging and Human Development, 7,* 59–65.

Haan, N. (1981). Common dimensions of personality development. In D. M. Eichorn (Ed.), *Present and past in middle life.* New York: Academic Press.

Haan, N. (1989). Personality at midlife. In S. Hunter & M. Sundel (Eds.), *Midlife myths.* Newbury Park, CA: Sage.

Hack, M., Klein, N., & Taylor, H. (1995, Spring Issue) Long-term developmental outcomes of low birth weight infants. *Future of Children, 5* (1),176–196.

Haignere, C. S., Culhane, J. F., Balsley, C. M., & Legos, P. (1996). Teachers' receptiveness and comfort teaching sexuality education and using non-traditional teaching strategies. *Journal of School Health, 66* (4), 140–144.

Haith, M. & Benson, J. (1998). Infant cognition. In W. Damon (Series Ed.) & D. Kuhn & R. Siegler (Volume Eds.), *Handbook of child psychology: Volume 2. Cognition, perception, and language.* New York: John Wiley.

Hajcak, F. & Garwood, P. (1989). Quick-fix sex: Pseudosexuality in adolescents. *Adolescence, 23* (92), 75–76.

Hakuta, K. (1986). *Mirror of language: The debate of bilingualism.* New York: Basic Books.

Hakuta, K. & McLaughlin, B. (1996). Bilingualism and second language learning: Seven tensions that define the research. In D. Berliner & R. Calfee (Eds.), *Handbook of educational psychology.* New York: Macmillan.

Halford, G. S. (1989). Reflection on 25 years of Piagetian cognitive psychology, 1963–1988. *Human Development, 32,* 325–357.

Haliburn, J. (2000). Reasons for adolescent suicide attempts. *Journal of the American Academy of Child & Adolescent Psychiatry, 39* (1), 13–14.

Hall, D., Eubanks, L., Swarnalatha, M., Kenney, R., & Johnson, S. (2000).

Hall, G. S. (1904). *Adolescence.* (2 vols.) New York: Appleton-Century-Crofts.

Hallman, R. (1967). Techniques for creative teaching. *Journal of Creative Behavior, 1* (3), 325–330.

Hamby, S. & Sugarman, D. (1999). Acts of psychological aggression against a partner and their relation to physical assault and gender. *Journal of Marriage and the Family, 61* (2), 959–970.

Hamer, D. (1993). A linkage between diva markers on x chromosome & male sexual orientation. *Science, 261,* 321–327.

Hamilton, C. (2000). Continuity and discontinuity of attachment from infancy through adolescence. *Child Development, May/June, 71* (3), 690–694.

Hamilton, S. F. & Darling, N. (1996). Mentors in adolescents' lives. In K. Hurrelmann, S. F. Hamilton, et al. (Eds.), *Social problems and social contexts in adolescence: Perspectives across boundaries* (pp. 199–215). New York, NY: Aldine De Gruyter.

Hammond, W. A. & Romney, D. M. (1995). Cognitive factors contributing to adolescent depression. *Journal of Youth Adolescence, 24,* 667–682.

Hammond, W. R. & Yung, B. (1993). Psychology's role in the public health response to assaultive violence among young African-American men. Special Issue: Adolescence. *American Psychologist, 48* (2), 142–154.

Harding, J. (1998). *Sex acts: practices of femininity and masculinity.* London: Sage.

Harris, A. C. (1994). Ethnicity as a determinant of sex role identity: A replication study of item selection for the Bem Sex Role Inventory. *Sex Roles, 31* (3/4), 241–273.

Harris, D. K., Changas, P. S., & Palmore, E. B. (1996). Palmore's first facts on aging quiz in a multiple-choice format. *Educational Gerontology, 22,* 575–589.

Harris, J. & Fiedler, C. (1988). Preadolescent attitudes toward the elderly. *Adolescence, 23,* 335–340.

Harris, J. & Liebert, R. (1992). *Infant & child.* Englewood Cliffs, NJ: Prentice-Hall.

Harrison, H. (1983). *The premature baby book.* New York: St. Martins.

Harrison, L. (2000). Why culture matters. In L. Harrison & S. Huntington (Eds.), *Culture matters.* New York: Basic Books.

Harry, J. (1986). Sampling gay men. *Journal of Sex Research, 22,* 21–34.

Hart, C. (1998). 50% of fragile X patients lack telltale signs. *AAP News, 14* (6), 1, 16.

Hart, C. (2000). Genome project likely to bring new responsibilities to pediatricians. *AAP News, 16* (2), 1, 10.

Hart, D., Hofmann, V., Edelstein, W., & Keller, M. (1997). The relation of childhood personality types to adolescent behavior and development: A longitudinal study of Icelandic children. *Developmental Psychology, 33* (2), 195–205.

Hart, J. (2000). Statistics say abuse hits close to home. *Boston Globe,* May 30, B1, B8.

Harter, S. (1993). Visions of self: Beyond the Me in the mirror. In J. Jacobs (Ed.), *Developmental perspectives on motivation.* Lincoln, Nebraska: University of Nebraska Press.

Harter S. (1998). The development of self-representations. In W. Damon (Series Ed.) & N. Eisenberg (Volume Ed.), *Handbook of child psychology: Volume 3. Child psychology in practice.* New York: John Wiley.

Harter, S. (1998). The development of self-representations. In W. Damon (Series Ed.) & N. Eisenberg (Volume Ed.), *Handbook of child psychology: Volume 3, Social, emotional, and personality development.* New York: John Wiley.

Hartup, W. (1996). The company they keep: Friendships and their developmental significance. *Child Development, 67,* 1–13.

Harvard Health Letter. (1991). Elderly drivers. Cambridge, MA: Harvard University Press.

Harvard Health Letter (1999). Driving licenses and the elderly. Cambridge, MA: Harvard University.

Harvard Men's Health Watch. (1997, October). Prudence and the prostate. *Harvard Men's Health Watch, 2* (3), 5–7.

Harvey, E. (1999). Short-term and long-term effects of early parental employment on children of the National Longitudinal Survey of Youth. *Developmental Psychology, 35* (2), 445–459.

Hastings, P., Zahn-Waxler, C., Robinson, J., Usher, B., & Bridges, D. (2000). The development of concern for others in children with behavior problems. *Developmental Psychology, 36* (5), 531–546.

Hauser, S. T. & Bowlds, M. K. (1990). In S. Feldman & G. Elliot (Eds.), *At the threshold: The developing adolescent.* Cambridge, MA: Harvard University Press.

Hauser-Cram, P., Pierson, D., Klein Walker, D., Tivnan, T. (1991). *Early education in the public schools.* San Francisco: Jossey-Bass.

Havighurst, R., Neugarten, B., & Tobin, S. (1968). Disengagement and patterns of aging. In B. Neugarten (Ed.), *Middle age and aging.* Chicago: University of Chicago Press.

Hawkins, R. D., Kandel, E. R., & Siegelbaum, S. A. (1993). Learning to modulate transmitter release: Themes and variations in synaptic plasticity. *Annual Review of Neuroscience, 16,* 625–665.

Hawkins, R. D. & Kandel, E. R. (1996). Long-term potentiation is reduced in mice that are doubly mutant in endothelial and neuronal nitric oxide synthase. *Cell, 87,* 6.

Hayne, H. & Rovee-Collier, C. (1995). The organization of reactivated memory in infancy. *Child Development, 66,* 893–906.

Hayward, M. D. (1986). The influence of occupational characteristics on men's early retirement. *Social Forces, 64* (4), 1032–1045.

Heckert, D. A., Nowak, T. C., & Snyder, K. A. (1998). The impact of husbands' and wives' relative earnings on marital disruption. *Journal of Marriage and the Family, 60* (4), 690–703.

Heckhausen, J. (1997). Developmental regulation across adulthood: Primary & secondary control of age-related challenges. *Developmental Psychology, 33* (1), 176–187.

Heimann, B. & Pittenger-Khushwant, K. (1996). The impact of formal mentorship on socialization and commitment of newcomers. *Journal of Managerial Issues, 8* (1), 108–117.

Heller, S., Larrieu, J., D'Imperio, R., & Boris, N. (1999). Research on resilience to child maltreatment: Empirical considerations. *Child Abuse & Neglect, 23* (4), 321–338.

Henig, R. *The monk in the garden.* Boston: Houghton Mifflin.

Hennessey, B. A. (1995). Social, environmental, and developmental issues and creativity. Special Issue: Toward an educational psychology of creativity: I. *Educational Psychology Review, 7* (2), 163–183.

Henning, K., Leitenberg, H., Coffey, P., & Turner, T. (1996). Long-term psychological and social impact of witnessing physical conflict between parents. *Journal of Interpersonal Violence, 11* (1), 35–51.

Henrich, C., Brown, J., & Aber, J. (2000). Evaluating the effectiveness of school-based violence prevention: Developmental approaches. *Social Policy Report, SRCD 13* (3).

Henry, B., Caspi, A., Moffit, T. E., & Silva, P. A. (1996). Temperamental and familial predictors of violent and nonviolent criminal convictions: Age 3 to age 18. *Developmental Psychology, 32* (4), 614–623.

Henry, D. (1999). Resilience in maltreated children: Implications for special needs adoption. *Child Welfare, 78* (5), 519–540.

Herbert, J. & Hayne, H. (2000). Memory retrieval by 18–30 month-olds: Age-related changes in representational flexibility. *Developmental Psychology, 36* (4), 473–484.

Herman-Giddens, M., Slora, E., Wasserman, R., Bourdony, C., Koch, G., & Hasemeier, C. (1997). Secondary sexual characteristics and menses in young girls in office practice: A study from the pediatric research office settings network. *Pediatrics, 99* (4), 505–518.

Hersch, P. (1991a, April). Teen epidemic. *American Health,* 42–45.

Hersch, P. (1991b, May). Sexually transmitted diseases are ravaging our children. *American Health,* 42–52.

Hertz, R. (1989). Dual-career corporate couples: Shaping marriages through work. In B. Risman & P. Schwartz, (Eds.), *Gender in intimate relationships.* Belmont, CA: Wadsworth.

Hertz, R. (1991). Dual career couples and the American dream: Self-sufficiency and achievement. *Journal of Comparative Family Studies, 22* (2), 247–262.

Hertzog, C. (1989). Influences of cognitive slowing on age differences in intelligence. *Developmental Psychology, 25,* 636–651.

Hertzog, C., Kidder, D. P., Mayhorn, C. B., Morrell, R. W., & Park, D. C. (1997). Effect of age on event-based and time-based prospective memory. *Psychology and Aging, 12* (2) 314–327.

Hetherington, E. & Parke, R. (1999). *Child psychology.* New York: McGraw-Hill.

Hetherington, E. M., Stanley-Hagan, M., & Anderson, E. (1989). Marital transitions: A child's perspective. *American Psychologist, 44,* 303–312.

Hetherington, M. & Stanley-Hagan, M. (1995). Parenting in divorced and remarried families. In M. H. Bornstein (Ed.), *Children and parenting* (Vol. 4). Hillsdale, NJ: Erlbaum.

HHS News (1997). *Early identification of Alzheimer's disease.* Washington: U.S. Department of Health and Human Services.

HHS News. (1997). *Teen sex down, new study shows.* Washington, DC: U.S. Department of Health and Human Services.

Hiebert, E. & Raphael, T. (1996). Psychological perspectives on literacy and extensions to educational practice. In D. Berliner & R. Calfee (Eds.), *Handbook of educational psychology.* New York: Macmillan.

Hill, C. D., Thompson, L. W., & Gallagher, D. (1988). The role of anticipatory bereavement in older women's adjustment to widowhood. *The Gerontologist, 28* (6), 7–12.

Hill, J. P. (1987). Central changes during adolescence. (Society for Research on Adolescence) Research on Adolescents and their families. In W. Damon (Ed.), *New directions in child psychology.* San Francisco: Jossey-Bass.

Hill, J. P. & Holmbeck, G. N. (1986). Disagreements about rules in families with seventh-grade girls and boys. *Journal of Youth and Adolescence, 16* (3), 221–246.

Hillman, J. L. & Stricker, G. (1996). Predictors of college students' knowledge of and attitudes toward elderly sexuality: The relevance of grandparental contact. *Educational Gerontology, 22,* 539–555.

Hinde, R. (1991). Relationships, attachment, and culture: A tribute to John Bowlby. The effects of relationships on relationships. *Infant Mental Health Journal, 12* (3), 154–163.

Hinde, R. (1992). Developmental psychology in the context of other behavioral sciences. *Developmental Psychology, 28* (6), 1018–1029.

Hinde, R. (1993). A comparative study of relationship structure. *British Journal of Social Psychology, 32* (3), 191–207.

Hines, A. M. (1997). Divorce-related transitions, adolescent development, and the role of the parent-child relationship: A review of the literature. *Journal of Marriage and the Family, 59* (2), 375–388.

Hochhauser, M. & Rothenberger, J. (1992). *AIDS education*. Dubuque, Iowa: Wm. C. Brown.

Hodgman, J. (1998). Apnea of prematurity and risk for SIDS. *Pediatrics, 102* (4), 969–970.

Hoffman, K. & Stage, E. (1993). Science for all: Getting it right for the 21st century. *Educational Leadership, 50* (5), 27–31.

Hoffman, M. (2000). *Empathy and moral development*. New York: Cambridge University Press.

Hoffman, S. & Duncan, G. (1988). What are the economic consequences of divorce? *Demography, 25*, 641–645.

Hoffmann, J. P. & Johnson, R. A. (1998). A national portrait of family structure and adolescent drug use. *Journal of Marriage and the Family, 60* (4), 633–645.

Holden, C. (1987). Alcoholism and the medical cost crunch. *Science, 235*, 1132–1133.

Holinger, P. C., Offer, D., & Ostrov, E. (1987). Suicide and homicide in the United States: An epidemiologic study of violent death, population changes, and the potential for prediction. *American Journal of Psychiatry, 144* (2), 215–219.

Holland, J. L. (1973). *Making vocational choices: A theory of careers*. Englewood Cliffs, NJ: Prentice-Hall.

Holmbeck, G., Paikoff, R., & Brooks-Gunn (1995). Parenting adolescents. In M. Bornstein (Ed.), *Handbook of parenting: Volume 1, Children and parenting*. Mahwah, NJ: Lawrence Erlbaum.

Honan, W. H. (1997, March 16). Drug arrests rise 18% on major college campuses, survey finds. *The New York Times*, p. 25.

Horgan, J. (1993, June). Eugenics revisited. *Scientific American, 268* (6), 122–131.

Horn, J. L. (1975). *Psychometric studies of aging and intelligence*. New York: Raven Press.

Horn, J. L. (1978). Human ability systems. In P. B. Baltes (Ed.), *Life-span development and behavior* (Vol. 1). New York: Academic Press.

Horn, J. L., Donaldson, G., & Engstrom, R. (1981). Apprehension, memory, and fluid intelligence decline in adulthood. *Research on Aging, 3* (3), 33–84.

Horowitz, F. (2000). Child development and PITS: Simple questions, complex answers, and developmental theory. *Child Development, 71* (1), 1–10.

Horwitz, A., White, H., & Howell-White, S. (1996). Becoming married and mental health. *Journal of Marriage and the Family, 58* (4), 895–907.

Horwitz, A. V. & White, H. R. (1998). The relationship of cohabitation and mental health: A study of a young adult cohort. *Journal of Marriage and the Family, 60* (4), 505–514.

Household and Family Characteristics. (1999). *Married adults still in the majority*.

Washington: Office of the U.S. Census Bureau.

Howard, P. (2000). *The owner's manual for the brain*. Austin, Texas: Bard Press.

Howard-Glenn, H. (2000). Newborn biological/behavioral characteristics and psychosocial adaptations. In S. Mattson & J. Smith (Eds.), *Core curriculum for maternal-newborn nursing*. Philadelphia: W. B. Saunders.

Howe, P. (1997, October). Study of elders favors calcium, vitamin D. Boston, MA: *The Boston Globe*, A12.

Howie, L. (1992–93). Old women and widowhood: A dying status passage. *Omega, 26* (3), 223–233.

Hu, S. (1995). Xq28 linkage between sexual orientation in males but not females. *Nature Genetics, 11* (2), 248–256.

Huerta, R., Mena, A., Malacara, J. M., & De Leon, J. D. (1995). Symptoms at perimenopausal period: Its association with attitudes toward sexuality, life-style, family function, and FSH levels. *Psychoneuroendocrinology, 20* (2), 135–148.

Hulicka, I. (1967). Short-term learning and memory. *Journal of the American Geriatrics Society, 15*, 285–294.

Hulit, L. & Howard, M. (1997). *Born to talk*. Needham Heights, MA: Allyn & Bacon.

Hunt, T. & Lindley, C. J. (1989). *Testing older adults*. Washington, DC: Center for Psychological Services.

Hunter, S. & Sundel, M. (1989). Midlife myths. Newbury Park, CA: Sage.

Huston, A. & Wright, J. (1998). Mass media and children's development. In W. Damon (Series Ed.) & I. Sigel & K. Renninger (Volume Eds.), *Handbook of child psychology: Volume 4. Child psychology in practice*. New York: John Wiley.

Huttenlocher, J., Haight, W., Bryk, A., Seltzer, M., & Lyons, T. (1991). Early vocabulary growth: Relation to language input and gender. *Developmental Psychology, 27*, 236–248.

Huttenlocher, P. (1994). Synaptogenesis in the human cerebral cortex. In G. Dawson & K. Fischer (Eds.), *Human behavior and the developing brain*. New York: Guilford.

Hwalek, M., Neale, A., Goodrich, C., & Quinn, K. (1996). The association of elder abuse and substance abuse in the Illinois elder abuse system. *The Gerontologist, 36* (5), 694–700.

Hyde, J. S. & DeLamater, J. (1997). *Understanding human sexuality* (6th ed.). New York: McGraw-Hill.

Igoa, C. (1995). *The inner world of the immigrant child*. Mahwah, NJ: Erlbaum.

Isakson, K. & Jarvis, P. (1999). The adjustment of adolescents during the transition into high school: A short-term longitudinal study. *Journal of Youth and Adolescence, 28* (1), 1–16.

Isley, S., O'Neil, R., Clatfelter, D., & Parke, R. (1999). Parent and child expressed affect and children's social competence: Modeling direct and indirect pathways. *Developmental Psychology, 35* (2), 547–560.

Iwanir, S. & Ayal, H. (1991). Midlife divorce initiation. *Contemporary Family Therapy, 13* (6), 609–623.

Izard, C. (1982). *Measuring emotions in infants*

and young children. New York: Cambridge University Press.

Izard, C. (1994). Intersystems connections. In Paul Ekman & Richard Davidson (Eds.), *The nature of emotion*. Oxford University Press.

Izard, C., Fantauzzo, C., Castle, J., Haynes, O., Rayias, M., & Putnam, P. (1995). The onogeny and significance of infants' facial expressions in the first 9 months of life. *Developmental Psychology 31* (6), 997–013.

Jackson, H. & Nuttall, R. (1997). *Childhood abuse: Effects on clinicians' personal and professional lives*. Thousand Oaks, CA: Sage.

Jackson, J. (1996). *Genetics and you*. Totowa, NJ: Humana Press.

Jackson, J. S. & Gibson, R. C. (1985). Work and retirement among the black elderly. In Z. S. Blou (Ed.), *Current perspectives on aging and the life cycle: Vol. 1: Work, retirement, and social policy*. Greenwich, CN: JAI Press.

Jacobvitz, D. B. & Bush, N. F. (1996). Reconstructions of family relationships: Parent-child alliances, personal distress, and self-esteem. *Developmental Psychology, 32* (4), 732–743.

James, L. E., Burke, D. M., Austin, A., & Hulme, E. (1998). Production and perception of "verbosity" in younger and older adults. *Psychology and Aging, 13* (3), 355–367.

James, M. (1990). Adolescent values clarification: A positive influence on perceived locus of control. *Journal of Alcohol and Drug Education, 35* (2), 75–80.

James, S. H. & Nims, D. R. (1996). A catalog of psychiatric medications used in the treatment of child and adolescent mental disorders. *School Counselor, 43* (4), 299–307.

Janus, S. & Janus, C. (1993). *The Janus report on sexual behavior*. New York: Wiley.

Jaquish, G. & Ripple, R. E. (1980). Cognitive creative abilities across the adult life span. *Human Development, 34* (2), 143–152.

Jasper, M. (2000). Antepartum fetal assessment. In S. Mattson & J. Smith (Eds.), *Core curriculum for maternal-newborn nursing*. Philadelphia: W. B. Saunders.

Jeffreys, S. (1998). Behavior. In R. Nye (Ed.), *Sexuality*. London: Oxford.

Jefko, W. (1980). Redefining death. In E. Schneiderman (Ed.), *Death: Current perspectives*. Palo Alto, CA: Mayfield.

Jennings, J. & Kamarck, T. (1997). Aging or disease? *Psychology and Aging, 2* (2), 239.

Jennings, J. R., Kamarck, T., Manuck, S., & Everson, S. A. (1997). Aging or disease? Cardiovascular reactivity in Finnish men over the middle years. *Psychology and Aging, 12* (2), 225–238.

Jessor, R., Van Den Boss, J., Vanderryn, J., Costa, F. M., et al. (1995). Protective factors in adolescent problem behavior: Moderator effects and developmental change. *Developmental Psychology, 31* (4), 923–933.

Jeynes, W. H. (1999). Effects of remarriage following divorce on the academic achievement of children. *Journal of Youth & Adolescence, 28* (3), 385–393.

Jezel, D. R., Molidor, C. E., & Wright, T. L. (1996). Physical, sexual, and psychological abuse in high school dating relationships:

Prevalence rates and self-esteem issues. *Child and Adolescent Social Work Journal, 13* (1), 69–87.

Johnson, B., Shulman, S., & Collins, W. A. (1991). Systemic patterns of parenting as reported by adolescents: Developmental differences and implications for psychosocial outcomes. *Journal of Adolescent Research, 6* (2), 235–252.

Johnson, M. (1998). The neural basis of cognitive development. In W. Damon (Series Ed.) & D. Kuhn & R. Siegler (Volume Eds.), *Handbook of child psychology: Volume 4. Child psychology in practice.* New York: John Wiley.

Johnson, M. (1999). *Developmental cognitive neuroscience.* London: Blackwell.

Johnson, M. (2000). Functional brain development in infants: Elements of an interactive specialization framework. *Child Development, 71* (1), 75–81.

Johnson, T. P., Aschkenasy, J. R., Herbers, M. R., & Gillenwater, S.A. (1996). Self-reported risk factors for AIDS among homeless youth. *AIDS Education and Prevention, 8* (4), 308–322.

Johnston, L., O'Malley, P. M., & Bachman, J. G. (1996). National survey results on drug use from the monitoring the future study, 1975–1994. *Vol. II: College students and young adults.* Washington, DC: National Institute on Drug Abuse.

Johnston, W. B. (1987). *Workforce 2000: Work and workers for the 21st century.* Indianapolis, IN: Hudson Institute.

Jones, S. (1993). *The language of genes.* New York: Anchor Books.

Jones, S. (1996). Imitation or exploration: Young infants' matching of adults' oral gestures. *Child Development, 67,* 1952–1969.

Julian, T., Mc Kenry, P., & McKelvey, M. (1992). Components of men's well-being at mid-life. *Issues in Mental Health Nursing, 13* (4), 285–299.

Jung, C. G. (1996). *The spirit in man, art and literature.* NY: Ballinger Foundation.

Jung, C. G. (1933). *Modern man in search of a soul.* New York: Harcourt, Brace & World.

Jung, C. G. (1971). *The portable Jung.* (Joseph Campbell, Ed.). New York: Viking Press.

Kacmar, K. M. & Ferris, G. R. (1989). Theoretical and methodological considerations in the age-job satisfaction relationship. *Journal of Applied Psychology, 74* (2), 201–207.

Kaestner, K. H., Schmid, W., Gass, P., Schutz, G., & Blendy, J. A. (1996). Targeting of the CREB gene leads to up-regulation of a novel CREB mRNA isoform. *EMBO Journal, 15* (5), 1098–1106.

Kagan, J. (1994). *Galen's prophecy: Temperament in human nature.* New York: Basic Books.

Kagan, J. (1997). Temperament and the reactions to unfamiliarity. *Child Development, 68* (1), 139–143.

Kagan, J. (1998). Biology and the child. In W. Damon (Series Ed.) & N. Eisenberg (Vol. Ed.), *Handbook of child psychology: Volume 3. Social, emotional, and personality development.* New York: John Wiley.

Kagan, J. (1998). *Three seductive ideas.* Cambridge, MA: Harvard University Press.

Kail, R. (1990). *The development of memory in children.* New York: Freeman.

Kakuchi, S. (1997, September 27). Graying of Japan. *The Boston Globe,* A3.

Kallman, F. & Jarvik, L. (1959). Individual differences in constitution and genetic background. In J. Birren (Ed.), *Handbook of aging and the individual.* Chicago: Univ. of Chicago Press.

Kamino, K., Tateishi, K., Satoh, T., Nishiwaki, Y., Yoshiiwa, A., Miki, T., Ogihara, T., & Sato, N. (1997). Elevated amyloid beta protein (1–40) level induces CREB phosphorylation at serine-133 via p44/42 MAP kinanse (Erk1/2)-research, *Biochemical and Biophysical Research Communications, 232* (3), 637–645.

Kammerman, J. B. (1988). *Death in the midst of life.* Englewood Cliffs, NJ: Prentice-Hall.

Kaplowitz, P. & Oberfield, S. (1999). Reexamination of the age limit for defining when puberty is precocious in girls in the United States: implications for evaluation and treatment. *Pediatrics, 104* (4), 936–941.

Karp, S. A., Holmstrom, R. W., Silber, D. E., & Stock, L. J. (1995). Personalities of women reporting incestuous abuse during childhood. *Perceptual and Motor Skills, 81* (3), 955–965.

Kart, C. S., Metress, E. K., & Metress, S. P. (1988). *Aging, health and society.* Boston: Jones & Bartlett Publishers, Inc.

Kassebaum, N. (1994). Head Start: Only the best for America's children. *American Psychologist, 49* (2), 123–126.

Kastenbaum, R. & Kastenbaum, B. (1989). *The encyclopedia of death.* Phoenix: Oryx Press.

Kaufman, A. & Wang, J. (1992). Gender, race, and education differences on the K-BIT at ages 4 to 90 years. *Journal of Psychoeducational Assessment, 10* (3), 219–229.

Kaufman, A. S., Reynolds, C. R., & McLean, J. E. (1989). Age and WAIS-R intelligence in a national sample of adults in the 20- to 74-year age range: A gross-sectional analysis with education level controlled. *Intelligence, 13* (3), 235–253.

Kaufman, J. C., McLean, J. E., Kaufman, A. S., & Kaufman, N. L. (1994). White, black, and Hispanic differences on fluid and crystallized abilities by age across the 11- to 94-year range. *Psychological Reports, 75* (3), 1279–1288.

Kazdin, A. (1993). Adolescent mental health. *American Psychologist, 48* (2), 127–141.

Kazdin, A. E. (Ed.). (1997). *Encyclopedia of psychology.* Washington, DC: American Psychological Association.

Kegan, R. (1994). *In over our heads.* Cambridge, MA: Harvard University Press.

Kellogg, B. (2000). Fetal development. In S. Mattson and J. Smith (Eds.), *Core curriculum for maternal-newborn nursing.* Philadelphia: W. B. Saunders.

Kellogg, R. (1979). *Children's drawings/children's minds.* New York: Avon.

Kelly, J. & Hansen, D. (1990). Social interactions and adjustment. In V. VanHasselt & M. Herson (Eds.), *Handbook of adolescent psychology.* New York: Pergamon, 131–146.

Kendall-Tackett, K., Williams, L., & Finkelhor, D. (1993). Impact of sexual abuse on children: A review and synthesis of recent empirical studies. *Psychological Bulletin, 113* (1), 164–180.

Kendig, H., Hashimoto, A., & Coppard, L. (Eds.). (1992). *Family support for the elderly: The international experience.* Oxford: Oxford University Press.

Kerns, K., Klepac, L., & Cole, A. (1996). Peer relationships and preadolescents' perceptions of security in the child-mother relationship. *Developmental Psychology, 32* (3), 457–466.

Kerns, K., Tomich, P., Aspelmeier, J., & Contreras, J. (2000). Attachment-based assessments of parent-child relationships in middle childhood. *Developmental Psychology, 36* (5), 614–626.

Kid and Media@The New Millenium. Menlo Park, CA: Kaiser Family Foundation.

Kidder, L. H., Lafleur, R. A., & Wells, C. V. (1995). Recalling harassment, reconstructing experience. *Journal of Social Issues, 51* (1), 53–67.

Kiebler, M., Lee, C. J., Lev-Ram, V., Tsien, R. Y., Kandel, E. R., Hawkins, R. D., & Arancio, O. (1996). Nitric oxide acts directly in the presynaptic neuron to produce long-term potentiation in cultured hippocampal neurons. *Cell, 87* (6), 1025–1035.

Kielsmeier, J. C. (1996). Walkabout: More than summer school. *Education and Urban Society, 28* (2), 167–175.

Kim, K., Smith, P., & Palermitti, A. (1997). Conflict in childhood and reproductive development. *Evolution and Human Behavior, 18* (2), 109–142.

Kim, U. (1990). Indigenous psychology: Science and applications. In R. Brislin (Ed.), *Applied cross-cultural psychology.* Newbury Park, CA: Sage.

Kimmel, D. (1974). *Adulthood and aging.* New York: Wiley.

Kimmel, D. C. & Weiner, I. B. (1985). *Adolescence: A developmental transition.* Hillsdale, NJ: Erlbaum.

Kindlon, D. & Thompson, M. (1999). *Raising Cain: Protecting the emotional life of boys.* New York: Ballantine Books.

King, I. (1914). *The high school age.* Indianapolis: Bobbs-Merrill.

King, K. (2000). Common teen suicide myths undermine prevention programs. *American Academy of Pediatrics News* (February). Elk Grove Village, IL: American Association of Pediatricians.

King, V. (1994). Nonresident father involvement and child well-being. *Journal of Family Issues, 15* (1), 78–96.

King, V. & Elder, G. H. (1998). Perceived self-efficacy and grandparenting. *Journal of Gerontology, 53* (5), 249–257.

Kinsey, A., Pomeroy, W., Martin, C., & Gebhard, P. (1948). *Sexual behavior in the human male.* Philadelphia: Saunders.

Kinsey, A., Pomeroy, W., Martin, C., & Gebhard, P. (1953). *Sexual behavior in the human female.* Philadelphia: Saunders.

Kinsman, S., Romer, D., Furstenberg, F, & Schwarz, D. (1998). Early sexual initiation. *Pediatrics, 102* (5), 1185–1192.

Kitzmann, K. (2000). Effects of marital conflict on subsequent triadic family interactions and parenting. *Developmental Psychology, 36* (1), 3–13.

Kivett, V. R. (1991). Centrality of the grandfather role among older rural black and white men. *Journal of Gerontology, 46* (5), 250–258.

Klassen, A. D., Williams, C. J., & Levitt, E. E. (1989). *Sex and morality in the U.S.: An empirical enquiry under the auspices of the Kinsey Institute*. Middletown, CT: Wesleyan University Press.

Klatsky, A. (1999). Moderate drinking and reduced risk of heart disease. *Alcohol Research & Health, 23* (1), 15–23.

Klein, N. (1978, October). Is there a right way to die? *Psychology Today, 12,* 122.

Klein, R. (1991). Age-related eye disease, visual impairment, and driving in the elderly. *Human Factors, 33* (5), 521–525.

Kliegl, R., Smith, J., & Baltes, P. (1989). Testing-the-limits and the study of adult age differences in cognitive plasticity of a mnemonic skill. *Developmental Psychology, 25* (2), 247–256.

Kliegl, R., Smith, J., & Baltes, P. (1990). On the locus and process of magnification of age differences during mnemonic training. *Developmental Psychology, 26* (6), 894–904.

Kling, K., Seltzer, M., & Ryff, C. (1997). Distinctive late-life challenges. *Psychology & Aging, 12* (2), 288–295.

Klonof-Cohen, H. (May, 1997). Sleep position and sudden infant death in the United States. *Epidemiology, 3,* (2), 327–329.

Kneisl, C. R. & Ames, S. W. (1986). *Adult health nursing: A biopsychosocial approach*. New York: Addison-Wesley.

Knoester, C. & Booth, A. (2000). Barriers to divorce: When are they effective? *Journal of Family Issues, 21* (1), 78–99.

Knopf, M. (1993). Having shaved a kiwi fruit. *Psychological Research, 53* (3), 203–224.

Knopf, M. & Neidhardt, E. (1989). Aging and memory for action events. *Developmental Psychology, 25* (5), 780–786.

Knowles, M. (1989). *The adult learner: A neglected species*. Houston: Gulf.

Knox, D., Zusman, M., & Nieves, W. (1998). College students' homogamous preferences for a date and mate. *College Student Journal, 32* (4), 482–484.

Knox, R. A. (1997, February 10). Growing older. Boston, MA: *The Boston Globe,* C1.

Koberg, C., Boss, R., Chappell, D., & Ringer, R. (1994). Correlates & consequences of protege mentoring in a large hospital. *Group & Organization Management, 19* (2), 219–239.

Koch, H. (1960). The relation of certain formal attributes of siblings to attitudes held toward each other and toward their parents. *Monographs of the Society for Research in Child Development, 25* (4). Chicago: University of Chicago Press.

Kochanska, G. Mutually responsive orientation between mothers and their young children: Implications for early socialization. *Child Development, 68* (1), 94–11.

Koenig, A., Cicchetti, D., & Rogosch, F. (2000). Child compliance/noncompliance and maternal contributors to internalization in maltreating and nonmaltreating dyads.

Koenig, H. G., Kvale, J. N., & Ferrell, C. (1988). Religion and well-being in later life. *The Gerontologist, 28* (1), 18–20.

Kogan, N. (1983). Stylistic variation in childhood and adolescence: Creativity, metaphor, cognitive styles. In P. H. Mussen (Ed.), *Handbook of child psychology* (Vol. 3). New York: Wiley.

Kohlberg, L. (1966). A cognitive-developmental

analysis of children's sex-role concepts and attitudes. In E. Maccoby (Ed.), *The development of sex differences*. Palo Alto, CA: Stanford University Press.

Kohlberg, L. (1975). The cognitive-developmental approach to moral education. *Phi Delta Kappan, 56,* 670–677.

Kohlberg, L. (1981). *The philosophy of moral development*. New York: Harper & Row.

Kohlberg, L. (1996). A cognitive-developmental analysis of children's sex-concepts and attitudes. In E. Maccoby (Ed.), *The Development of Sex Differences*. Palo Alto, CA: Stanford University Press.

Kolata, G. (1990). *The baby doctors*. New York: Dell.

Kolata, G. (1998). *Clone*. New York: Wm. Morrow.

Kopp, C. (1993). *Baby steps*. New York: Freeman.

Korf, B. (1996). *Human Genetics: A problem-based approach*. Cambridge, MA: Blackwell.

Kosan, L. (February 2000). Young girls and their parents cope with an earlier onset of puberty. *The Boston Parents' Paper*. Boston, MA.

Koss, M., Gidycz, C., & Wisniewski, N. (1987). The scope of rape: Incidence and prevalence of sexual aggression and victimization in a national sample of higher education students. *Journal of Consulting and Clinical Psychology, 55,* 162–170.

Kowal, K. & Kramer, I. (1997). Children's understanding of parental differential treatment. *Child Development, 68* (1), 113–126.

Kozol, J. (1991). *Savage inequalities*. New York: Crown.

Kramer, B. J. & Lambert, J. D. (1999). Caregiving as a life course transition among older husbands: A prospective study. *Gerontologist, 39* (6), 658–667.

Krause, N. & Wray, L. (1991). Psychosocial correlates of health and illness among minority elders. *Generations, 15,* 25–30.

Kruger, A. (1994). The midlife transition: Crisis or chimera? *Psychological Reports, 75,* 1299–1305.

Kübler-Ross, E. (1969). *On death and dying*. New York: Macmillan.

Kübler-Ross, E. (1975). *Death: The final stage of growth*. Englewood Cliffs, NJ: Prentice-Hall.

Kübler-Ross, E. & Warshaw, W. (1978). *To live until we say goodbye*. Englewood Cliffs, NJ: Prentice-Hall.

Kuhn, D. (2000). Does memory development belong on an endangered topic list? *Child Development, 71* (1), 21–25.

Kurdek, L. (1998). Relationship outcomes and their predictors: Longitudinal evidence from heterosexual married, gay cohabiting, and lesbian cohabiting couples. *Journal of Marriage and the Family, 60* (4), 553–568.

Labouvie-Vief, G. & Lawrence, R. (1985). Object knowledge, personal knowledge, and processes of equilibration in adult cognition. *Human Development, 28,* 25–39.

Lachman, M. E. (1992). Improving memory and control beliefs through cognitive restructuring and self-generated strategies. *Journal of Gerontology, 47* (5), 293–299.

Ladd, G. & LeSieur, K. (1995). Parents and children's peer relationships. In Marc Bornsteinn (Ed.), *Handbook of parenting, Volume 4: Applied and practical parenting*. Mahwah, NJ: Lawrence Erlbaum.

Lamb, M. (1998). Nonparental child care: Context, quality, correlates, and consequences. In W. Damon (Series Ed.) & I. Sigel & K. A. Renninger (Volume Eds.), *Handbook of child psychology: Volume 4: Child psychology in practice*. New York: John Wiley.

Lamb, M., Hwang, C., Ketterlinus, R., & Fracasso, M. (1999). Parent-child relationships. In M. Bornstein & M. Lamb (Eds.), *Developmental psychology: An advanced textbook*. Mahwah, NJ: Erlbaum.

Lamb, M. E. (1987). *The father's role: Cross-cultural perspectives*. Hillsdale, NJ: Erlbaum.

Langer, E. (1993). A mindful education. *Educational Psychologist, 28* (1), 43–50.

Langlois, J., Ritter, J., Casey, R., & Sawin, D. (1995). Infant attractiveness predicts maternal behaviors and attitudes. *Developmental Psychology, 31,* 464–472.

Lansdown, R. & Walker, M. (1991). *Your child's development from birth through adolescence*. New York: Knopf.

Larivee, S., Normandeau, S., & Parent S. (2000). The French connection: Some contributions of French-language research in the post-Piagetian era. *Child Development, 71* (4), 823–839.

Larson, R. W., Richards, M. H., Moneta, G., Holmbeck, G., & Duckett, E. (1996). Changes in adolescents' daily interactions with their families from ages 10 to 18: Disengagement and transformation. *Developmental Psychology, 32* (4), 744–754.

Lattal, K. (1992). B. F. Skinner and psychology. *American Psychologist, 47* (11), 1269–1272.

Lauer, R. H., Lauer, J. C., & Kerr, S. T. (1990). The long-term marriage: Perceptions of stability and satisfaction. *International Journal of Aging and Human Development, 31* (3), 189–195.

Lauman, E. O., Gagnon, J. H., Michael, R. T., & Michaels, S. (1994). *The social organization of sexuality: Sexual practices in the United States*. Chicago, IL: The University of Chicago Press.

Lawrence, R. H., Tennstedt, S. L., & Assmann, S. F. (1998). Quality of the caregiver-care recipient relationship: Does it offset negative consequences of caregiving for family caregivers? *Psychology & Aging, 13* (1), 150–158.

Leaper, C., Anderson, K., & Sanders, P. (1998). Moderators of gender effects on parents' talk to their children: A meta-analysis. *Developmental Psychology, 34* (1), 3–27.

"Learning to see the inevitable signs of aging." (2000). *Better Vision Institute*. <http://www.visionsite.org/press/ageeyes/htm.>

Lease, K. P. & Robbins, S. B. (1994). Relationships between goal attributes and the academic achievement of Southeast Asian adolescent refugees. *Journal of Counseling Psychology, 41* (1), 45–52.

LeBlanc, A. N. (1994, August 14). While Manny's locked up [The New York Times Magazine]. *The New York Times,* pp. 26–33, 46, 49, 53.

Leboyer, F. (1975). *Birth without violence*. New York: Knopf.

Lee, G. R., Peek, C. W., & Coward, R. T. (1998). Race differences in filial responsibility expectations among older parents. *Journal of Marriage and the Family, 60* (3), 404–412.

Leeming, F., Dwyer, W., & Oliver, D. (1996).

Issues in adolescent sexuality. Needham Heights, MA: Allyn & Bacon.

Legato, M. (1998). *Gender-specific aspects of human biology for the practising physician*. Armonk, NJ: Futura.

Lehman, H. C. (1953). *Age and achievement*. Princeton, NJ: Princeton University Press.

Lehman, H. C. (1962). The creative production rates of present versus past generations of scientists. *Journal of Gerontology, 17,* 409–417.

Lehman, H. C. (1964). The relationship between chronological age and high level research output in physics and chemistry. *Journal of Gerontology, 19,* 157–164.

Leiblum, S. R. (1990). Sexuality and the midlife woman. *Psychology of Women Quarterly, 14* (4), 495–508.

Leibson, C., Garrard, J., Mitz, N., Waller, L., Indritz, M., Jackson, J., Rolnich, S., & Luepke, L. (1999). The role of depression in the association between self-rated physical health and clinically defined illness. *The Gerontologist, 39* (3), 291–298.

Leitenberg, H., Detzer, M., & Srebnik, D. (1993). Gender differences in masturbation and the relation of masturbation experience in preadolescence and/or early adolescence to sexual behavior and sexual adjustment in young adulthood. *Archives of Sexual Behavior, 22* (2), 87–98.

Leland, J. (1998). The Secret Life of Teens, Newsweek, June 16, p. 121.

Lemerise, E. & Arsenio, W. (2000). An integrated model of emotion processes and cognition in social information processing. *Child Development, 71* (1), 107–118.

Leonard, M. (1997, March 23). Fleeting memories. *The Boston Globe*, pp. E1–E2.

Lerner, R. (January, 1991). Changing organism—context relations as the basic process of development: A developmental contextual perspective. *Developmental Psychology, 27* (1), 27–32.

Lerner, R., Fisher, C., & Weinberg, R. (2000). Toward a science for and of the people: Promoting civil society through the application of developmental science. *Child Development, 71* (1), 11–20.

Lerner, R. M. (1995). *America's youth in crisis: Challenges and options for programs and policies*. Thousand Oaks, CA: Sage.

Lerner, R. M. (1996). Relative plasticity, integration, temporality, and diversity in human development: A developmental contextual perspective about theory, process, and method. *Developmental Psychology, 32,* 781–786.

Lerner, R. M. (Ed.). (1998). Theoretical models of human development. *Handbook of Child Psychology* (5th ed.), Vol. 1.

Lerner, R. M. & Korn, M. E. (1997). Developmental psychology: Theories. In A. E. Kayolin (Ed.), *Encyclopedia of Psychology*. Washington, DC: A.P.A.

Lerner, R. M. & Simi, N. L. (1997). A holistic, integrated model of risk and protection in adolescence: A developmental contextual perspective about research, programs, and policies. *Paper presented at a conference on "Developmental science and the holisitic approach: A symposium followed up at the Royal Swedish Academy of Sciences,"* Wiks Castle, Sweden, May 24–27.

Lesesne, T., Chance, R., & Buckman, L. (1995).

Pasages: Young adults coming of age. *Journal of Reading, 38* (5), 406–410.

LeVay, S. (1993). *The sexual brain*. Cambridge, MA: The MIT Press.

LeVay, S. & Hamer, D. (1994). Evidence of a biological influence in male homosexuality. *Scientific American, 270* (5), 43–49.

Levensen, R. W., Carstensen, L. L., & Gottman, J. M. (1993). Long-term marriage: Age, gender, and satisfaction. *Psychology and Aging, 8* (2), 301–313.

Levinson, D. (1978). *The seasons of a man's life*. New York: Knopf.

Levinson, D. (1986). A conception of adult development. *American Psychologist, 41* (1), 3–13.

Levinson, D. (1990a). A theory of life structure development in adulthood. In C. N. Alexander & E. J. Langer (Eds.), *Higher states of human development* (pp. 35–54). New York: Oxford University Press.

Levinson, D. (1990b). *Seasons of a woman's life*. Presented at the 98th annual convention of the American Psychological Association, Boston.

Lewis, C. (1963). *A grief observed*. New York: Seabury Press.

Lewis, K. G. & Moon, S. (1997). Always single and single again women: A qualitative study. *Journal of Marital and Family Therapy, 23* (2), 115–134.

Lewis, M. (1997). *Altering fate: Why the past does not predict the future*. New York: Guilford.

Lewis, M. (2000). The promise of dynamic systems approaches for an integrated account of human development. *Child Development, 71* (1), 36–43.

Lewis, M. & Brooks-Gunn, J. (1979). *Social cognition and the acquisition of self*. New York: Plenum.

Lewis, M., Feiring, C., & Rosenthal, S. (2000). Attachment over time. *Child Development, May/June 71* (3), 707–720.

Lewkowicz, D. (1996). Infants' response to the audible and visual properties of the face: 1. Role of lexical-syntactic content, temporal synchrony, gender, and manner of speech. *Developmental Psychology, 32* (2), 347–366.

Li, W., Tully, T., & Kalderon, D. (1996). Effects of a conditional drosophila PKA mutant on olfactory learning and memory. *Learning and Memory, 2* (6), 320–333.

Lickona, T. (1996). Eleven principles of effective character education. *Journal of Moral Education, 25,* 93–100.

Liebert, R., Sprafkin, J. N., & Lieberet, R. (1992). *The early window*. New York: Pergamon.

Liebert, R. M., Sprafkin, J. N., & Davidson, E. (1988). *The early window*. New York: Pergamon.

Liem, J., James, J., O'Toole, J., & Boudewyn, A. (1997). Assessing resilience in adults with histories of childhood sexual abuse. *American Journal of Orthopsychiatry, 67* (4), 594–605.

Lillie-Blanton, M., Bowie, J., & Ro, M. (1996). African American women: Social factors and the use of preventive health services. In M. M. Falik, K. S. Collins, et al. (Eds.), *Women's health: The Commonwealth Fund survey* (pp. 99–122). Baltimore, MD: Johns Hopkins University Press.

Lindenberger, U. & Baltes, P. B. (1994). Sensory

functioning and intelligence in old age: A strong connection. *Psychology and Aging, 9* (3), 339–355.

Lips, H. (2001). *Sex and gender*. Mountain View, CA: Mayfield.

Little, T. & Lopez, D. (1997). Regularities in the development of children's causality beliefs about school performance across six sociocultural contexts. *Developmental Psychology, 33* (1), 165–175.

Lockman, J. & Thelen, E. (1993). Introduction. *Child Development, 64* (4), 953–960.

Luthar, S., Cicchetti, D., & Becker, B. (2000). The construct of resilience: A critical evaluation and guidelines for future work. *Child Development*, May/June, *71* (3), 543–562.

Lutz, C. & Przytulski, K. (1997). *Nutrition and diet therapy*. Philadelphia: F. A. Davis Co.

Lutz, D. & Sternberg, R. (1999). Cognitive development. In M. Bornstein & M. Lamb, (Eds.), *Developmental psychology: An advanced textbook*. Mahwah, NJ: Erlbaum.

Lynch, S. (1998). Who supports whom? How age and gender affect the perceived quality of support from family and friends. *The Gerontologist, 38* (2), 231–238.

Lynskey, M. & Fergusson, D. (1997). Factors protecting against the development of adjustment difficulties in young adults exposed to childhood sexual abuse. *Child Abuse & Neglect, 21* (12), 1177–1190.

Lytton, H., Singh, J., & Gallagher, L. (1995). Parenting twins. In M. Bornstein (Ed.), *Handbook of parenting* (Vol. 1). Hillsdale, NJ: Erlbaum.

Maccoby, E. (1988). Social emotional development and response to stressors. In Norman Garmezy & Michael Rutter (Eds.), *Stress, coping and development in children*. Baltimore: Johns Hopkins.

Maccoby, E. (1998). *The two sexes: Growing up apart, growing up together*. Cambridge, MA: Belknap Press.

Maccoby, E. & Jacklin, C. (1974). *The psychology of sex differences*. Stanford University Press.

Mack, J. E. & Hickler, H. (1982). *Vivienne: The life and suicide of an adolescent girl*. New York: New American Library.

MacRae, H. (1992). Fictive kin as a component of the social networks of older people. *Research on Aging, 14* (2), 226–247.

Madaus, G. (1994). A technological and historical consideration of equity issues associated with proposals to change the nation's testing policy. *Harvard Educational Review, 64* (1), 76–95.

Magid, K. & McKelvey, C. (1987). *High risk: Children without a conscience*. New York: Bantam.

Main, M. (1996, April). Introduction to the special section on attachment and psychopathology: Overview of the field of attachment. *Journal of Consulting and Clinical Psychology, 64* (2), 237–242.

Main, M. & Goldwyn, R. (In press). Interview-based adult attachment classifications: Related to infant-mother and infant-father attachment. *Developmental Psychology*.

Malina, R. M., & others. (1998). Television viewing, physical activity and health-related fitness. *Journal of Adolescent Health, 23* (5), 318–325.

Malloy, M. & Freeman, D. (2000). *Birth weight and gestational age.* Mahwah, NJ: Erlbaum.

Malonebeach, E., Zarit, S., & Farbman, D. (1995). Variability in daily events & mood of family caregivers to cognitively impaired elders. *International Journal of Aging & Human Development, 41,* 151–167.

Malowald, M. (1992). To be or not to be a woman: Anorexia nervosa, normative gender roles, and feminism. *Journal of Medicine and Philosophy, 17* (2), 233–251.

Manchester, W. (1983). *The last lion: Winston Spencer Churchill.* Boston: Little, Brown.

Manning, M. & Baruth, L. (1996). *Multicultural education of children and adolescents.* Needham Heights: Allyn and Bacon.

Manuck, S. B., Kamarck, T. W., Kasprowicz, A. S., & Waldstein, S. R. (1993). Stability and patterning of behaviorally evoked cardiovascular reactivity. In J. J. Blascovich, E. S. Katkin, et al. (Eds.), *Cardiovascular reactivity to psychological stress & disease* (pp. 111–134). Washington, DC: American Psychological Association.

Marcia, J. E. (1980). Identity in adolescence. In J. Adelson (Ed.), *Handbook of adolescent psychology.* New York: Wiley.

Marcia, J. E. (1983). Some directions for the investigation of ego development in early adolescence. *Journal of Early Adolescence, 3* (3), 215–223.

Marks, N. F. (1996). Caregiving across the lifespan: National prevalence and predictors. *Family Relations: Journal of Applied Family & Child Studies, 45* (1), 27–36.

Marrs, R., Bloch, L., & Silverman, K. (1997). *Dr. Richard Marrs fertility book.* New York: Delacorte.

Marsh, H. W. & Richards, G. E. (1988). The outward bound bridging course for low-achieving high school males: Effect on academic achievement and multidimensional self-concepts. *Australian Journal of Psychology, 40* (3), 281–298.

Marshall, E. (Nov. 29, 1996). The human genome hunt scales up. *Science, 274,* 1456.

Marshall, J. R. (1994). The diagnosis and treatment of social phobia and alcohol abuse. *Bulletin of the Menninger Clinic, 58* (2A), A58–A66.

Marshall, L. (1981). Auditory processing in aging listeners. *Journal of Speech and Hearing Disorders, 46,* 226–240.

Marshall, V. & Levy, J. (1990). Aging and dying. In R. Binstock & L. George (Eds.), *Handbook of aging and the social sciences.* San Diego, CA: Academic Press.

Marsiglio, W. (1992). Stepfathers with minor children living at home. *Journal of Family Issues, 13* (2), 195–214.

Martikainen, P. & Valkonen, T. (1996). Mortality after the death of a spouse: Rates and causes of death in a large Finnish cohort. *American Journal of Public Health, 86* (8), 1087–1093.

Martin, D. H., Mroczkowski, T. F., Dalu, Z. A., McCarty, J., Jones, R. B., & Hopkins, S. J. Azithromycin for Chlamydial Infections Study Group (1992). A controlled trial of a single dose of Azithromycin for the treatment of chlamydial urethritis and cervicitis. *New England Journal of Medicine, 327* (13), 921–925.

Martocchio, J. J. (1989). Age-related differences in employee absenteeism: A meta-analysis. *Psychology and Aging, 4,* 409–414.

Maslow, A. (1987). *Motivation and personality.* (Revised by R. Frager, J. Fadiman, C. McReynolds, & R. Cox.) New York: Harper & Row.

Masoro, E. J. (1984). Nutrition as a modulator of the aging process. *Physiologist, 27* (2), 98–101.

Massachusetts Department of Public Health. (1991). *Adolescents at risk 1991: Sexually transmitted diseases.* Boston, MA: Author.

Masters, W. & Johnson, V. (1966). *Human sexual response.* Boston: Little, Brown.

Masters, W. & Johnson, V. (1970). *Human sexual inadequacy.* Boston: Little, Brown.

Masters, W. H., Johnson, V. E., & Kolodny, R. C. (1986). *Masters and Johnson on sex and human loving.* Boston: Little, Brown.

Masters, W. H., Johnson, V. E., & Kolodny, R. C. (1995). *Human sexuality* (5th ed.). New York: HarperCollins College Publishers.

Matthews, K., Wing, R., Kuller, L., Meilahn, E., Kelsey, S., Costello, E., & Caggiula, A. (1990). Influences of natural menopause on psychological characteristics and symptoms of middle-aged healthy women. *Journal of Consulting and Clinical Psychology, 58* (3), 345–351.

Mattson, S. (2000). Ethnocultural considerations in the childbearing period. In S. Mattson and J. Smith (Eds.), *Core curriculum for maternal-newborn nursing.* Philadelphia: W. B. Saunders.

Matusow, A. J. (1984). *The unraveling of America.* New York: Harper & Row.

Mazess, R. B. (1982). On aging bone loss. *Clinical Orthopaedics and Related Research, 165,* 239–252.

McAdams, D. P., de St. Aubin, E., & Logan, R. L. (1993). Generativity among young, midlife, and older adults. *Psychology and Aging, 8* (2), 221–230.

McCandless, B. & Bardarah, J. (1991). The church confronting adult depression: A challenge. Special issue: Depression and religion. *Counseling and Values, 35* (2), 104–113.

McCary, J. (1978). *McCary's human sexuality.* New York: Van Nostrand Reinhold.

McClintock, M. & Herdt, G. (1996). Rethinking puberty: The development of sexual attraction. *Current Directions in Psychological Science, 5,* 178–183.

McCrae, R. & Costa, P. T., Jr. (1984). *Emerging lives, enduring dispositions: Personality in adulthood.* Boston: Little, Brown.

McEvoy, G. M. & Cascio, W. F. (1989). Cumulative evidence of the relationship between employee age and job performance. *Journal of Applied Psychology, 74,* 11–17.

McGaugh, J. L. & Guzowski, J. F. (1997). Antisense oligodeoxynucleotide-mediated disruption of hippocampal cAMP response element binding protein levels impairs consolidation of memory for water maze training. *Proceedings of the National Academy of Sciences, 94* (6), 2693–2698.

McGaugh, J. L., Coleman-Mesches, K., & West, M. A. (1997). Opposite effects on two different measures of retention following unilateral inactivation of the amygdala. *Behavioral Brain Research, 86* (1), 17–23.

McGhee, P. (1979). *Humor: Its origin and development.* San Francisco: Freeman.

McGhee, P. (1988). The role of humor in

enhancing children's development and adjustment. *Journal of Children in Contemporary Society, 20,* 249–274.

McGhee, P. & Panoutsopoulou, T. (1995). The role of cognitive factors in children's metaphor and humor comprehension. *International Journal of Humor Research, 3* (2), 119–146.

McGue, M., Sharma, A., & Benson, P. (1996). The effect of common rearing on adolescent adjustment: Evidence from a U.S. adoption cohort. *Developmental Psychology, 32* (4), 604–613.

McKusick, V. (1992). *Mendelian inheritance in man: Catalogs of autosomal dominant, autosomal recessive, and X-linked phenotypes* (10th ed.). Baltimore: Johns Hopkins University Press.

McLaughlin, S. (1998). *Introduction to language development.* San Diego: Singular Publishing.

McNeill, J. (1995). *Freedom, glorious freedom.* Boston: Beacon.

Mead, M. (1972, April). *Long living in cross-sectional perspective.* Paper presented to the Gerontological Society, San Juan, Puerto Rico.

Mech, E., Pryde, J., & Rycraft, J. R. (1995). Mentors for adolescents in foster care. *Child & Adolescent Social Work Journal, 12* (4), 317–328.

Meltz, B. (November 18, 1999). Guns, gimmicks, and gizmos abound, but so do some happier choices. *The Boston Globe,* F1, F4.

Menyuk, P., Liebergott, J., & Schultz, M. (1995). *Early language development in full-term and premature infants.* Mahwah, NJ: Erlbaum.

Meshefedjian, G., McCusker, J., Bellavance, F., & Baumgarten, M. (1998). Factors associated with symptoms of depression among informal caregivers of demented elders in the community. *The Gerontologist, 38* (2), 247–253.

Meshot, C. & Leitner, L. (1992–93). Adolescent mourning and parental death. *Death Studies, 17* (4), 319–332.

Meston, C. M., Trapnell, P. D., & Gorzalka, B. B. (1996). Ethnic and gender differences in sexuality: Variations in sexual behavior between Asian and non-Asian university students. *Archives of Sexual Behavior, 25* (1), 33–72.

Michael, R., Gagman, J., Laumann, E., & Kolata, G. (1994). *Sex in America.* Boston: Little, Brown.

Michels, P. J., Johnson, N. P., Mallin, R., Thornhill, J. T., et al. (1999). Coping strategies of alcoholic women. *Substance Abuse, 20* (4), 237–248.

Michelson, S. (1998). "Do I belong here?" Making a home in later life. *Journal of Geriatric Psychiatry, 31,* 73–78.

Mintz, B. I. & Betz, N. E. (1988). Prevalence and correlates of eating disordered behaviors among undergraduate women. *Journal of Counseling Psychology, 35* (3), 463–471.

Mischel, H. & Mischel, W. (1983). The development of children's knowledge of self-control strategies. *Child Development, 54* (4), 603–619.

Mishara, B. L. (1996). A dynamic developmental model of suicide. *Human Development, 39* (1), 181–194.

Mitchell, C. M., O'Neil, T. D., Beals, J., Dick, R. W., Keane, E., & Manson, S. M. (1996). Dimensionality of alcohol use among American Indian adolescents: Latent structure, construct validity, and implications for developmental research. *Journal of Research on Adolescence, 6* (1), 151–180.

Mok, B. & Mui, A. (1996). Empowerment in residential care for the elders: The case of an aged home in Hong Kong. *Journal of Gerontological Social Work, 27* (1/2).

Molina, B. S. G. & Chassin, L. (1996). The parent-adolescent relationship at puberty: Hispanic ethnicity and parent alcoholism as moderators. *Developmental Psychology, 32* (4), 675–686.

Montero, I., Ruiz, I., & Hernandez, I. (1993). Social functioning as a significant factor in women's help-seeking behavior during the climacteric period. *Social Psychiatry and Psychiatric Epidemiology, 28* (2), 178–183.

Montessori, M. (1967). *The absorbent mind.* New York: Dell.

Montgomery, R., Haemmerlie, F., & Zoellner, S. (1996). The "imaginary audience," self-handicapping and drinking patterns among college students. *Psychological Reports, 79* (3), 783–785.

Moon, R., Patel, K., & Shaefer, S. (2000). Sudden infant death specific SIDS mortality: United States, 1991 versus 1995. *Pediatrics, 105* (66), 1227–1235.

Moore, B. N. & Parker, R. (1986). *Critical thinking.* Mountain View, CA: Mayfield Publishing Co.

Moore, E. W., McCann, H., & McCann, J. (1985). *Creative and critical thinking.* Boston, MA: Houghton Mifflin.

Moore, G. (1983). *Developing and evaluating educational research.* Boston: Little, Brown.

Moore, K. & Persaud, T. (1998). *Before we are born: Essentials of embryology and birth defects.* Philadelphia: Saunders.

Moore, M. (1997). *Nutritional care.* St Louis: Mosby.

Moore, R. (1995). Psychological factors and the etiology of binge eating. *Addictive Behaviors, 20* (6), 713–723.

Moran, B. (2000). Maternal infections. In S. Mattson and J. Smith (Eds.), *Core curriculum for maternal-newborn nursing.* Philadelphia: W. B. Saunders.

Morgan, L. A. (1991). *After marriage ends: Economic consequences for midlife women.* London: Sage.

Morris, J. (1974, July). *Conundrum.* Ms., 57–64.

Moshman, D. (1998). Cognitive development beyond childhood. In W. Damon (Ed.) *Handbook of child psychology.* NY: Wiley.

Moskowitz, B. (1979). The acquisition of language. *Scientific American, 239,* 92–108.

Mullaly, L. (2000). Psychology of pregnancy. In S. Mattson and J. Smith (Eds.), *Core curriculum for maternal-newborn nursing.* Philadelphia: W. B. Saunders.

Muller, C. F. & Boaz, R. F. (1988). Health as a reason or a rationalization for being retired? *Research on Aging, 10* (1), 37–55.

Mullis, R., Hill, L., Wayne, E., & Readdick, C. (1999). Attachment and social support among adolescents. *Journal of Genetic Psychology, 160* (4), 500–502.

Murphy, S. A. (1996). Parent bereavement stress and preventive intervention following the violent deaths of adolescent or young adult children. *Death Studies, 20* (5), 441–452.

Murray, B. (1997a). Our 20s appear to be the age we can't forget. *APA Monitor, 28* (10), 24.

Murray, B. (1997b). Elderly people alter their social priorities as they age. *APA Monitor, 28* (10), 25.

Murray, B. (1997c). Psychologists help ease caregivers' stress. *APA Monitor, 28* (10), 26.

Murray, B. (1999). Boys to men: Emotional miseducation. *APA Monitor, 30* (7), 1, 38.

Murrell, A. J., Olson, J. E., & Frieze, I. H. (1995). Sexual harassment and gender discrimination: A longitudinal study of women managers. *Journal of Social Issues, 51* (1), 139–149.

Muscari, M. (1998). Prevention: Are we really reaching today's teens? *American Journal of Maternal/Child Nursing, 4* (2), 87–91.

Muuss, R. E. (1996). *Theories of adolescence* (7th ed). New York: McGraw-Hill.

Nakonezny, P. A., Shull, R. D., & Rodgers, J. L. (1995). The effect of no-fault divorce law on the divorce rate across the 50 states and its relation to income, education, and religiosity. *Journal of Marriage and the Family, 57* (2), 477–488.

Naleppa, M. (1996). Families and the institutionalized elderly. *Journal of Gerontological Social Work, 27* (1/2).

Narvaez, D., Getz, I., Rest, J., & Thoma, S. (1999). Individual moral judgment and cultural ideologies. *Developmental Psychology, 35* (2), 478–488.

National Cancer Institute. (2000). Press release: *Questions and answers about hormone replacement therapy.* Bethesda, MD: National Institutes of Health.

National Center for Education Statistics. (1992). *American education at a glance.* Washington, DC: Office of Educational Research and Improvement.

National Center for Health Statistics. (1995). *Healthy people 2000.* Hyattsville, MD: Public Health Service.

National Council of Teachers of Mathematics. (1989). *Curriculum and evaluation standards for school mathematics.* Reston, VA.

National Institute for Health Statistics. (1994). *Obesity in the American population.* Washington, DC: U.S. Government Printing Office.

National Institute on Aging News. (2000). *Alzheimer's disease research update.* National Institute on Aging, ADEAR Center Email Address: ADEAR@alzheimers.org.

National Institute on Aging. (1993). Forgetfulness in old age: It's not what you think. *Age page.* U.S. Department of Health and Human Services.

National Institute on Aging. (1999). *Progress report and Alzheimer's disease.* Washington, DC: United States Department of Health and Human Services, NIH Publication No. 99-4664.

National Television Violence Study. (1996). Studio City, CA: Mediascape.

Neale, A., Hwalek, M., Goodrich, C., & Quinn, K. (1996). The Illinois elder abuse system: Program description & administrative findings. *The Gerontologist, 36* (3), 502–511.

Nelson, W., Hughes, H., Katz, B., & Searight, R. (1999). Anorexic eating attitudes and behaviors of male and female college students. *Adolescence, 34* (135), 621–633.

Neugarten, B. & Moore, J. (1968). The changing age-status system. In B. Neugarten (Ed.), *Middle age and aging.* Chicago: Univ. of Chicago Press.

Neugarten, B. (Ed.). (1968). Middle age and aging. Chicago: University of Chicago Press.

Neugarten, B. L. & Weinstein, K. K. (1964). The changing American grandparent. *Journal of Marriage and the Family, 26* (1), 199–206.

Neumann, I., Wigger, A., Torner, L., & Landgraf, R. (2000). Brain oxytocin inhibits basal and to stress-induced activity of the hypothalamo-pituitary-adrenal axis in male and female rats. *Journal of Neuroendocrinology, 12* (3), 235–243.

Newcomb, M., Bukowski, W., & Pattee, L. (1993). Children's peer relations: A meta-analytic review of popular, rejected, neglected, controversial, and average sociometric status. *Psychological Bulletin, 113* (1), 99–128.

Newman, D., Caspi, A., Moffitt, T., & Silva, P. (1997). Antecedents of adult interpersonal functioning: Effects of individual differences in age 3 temperament. *Developmental Psychology, 33* (2), 206–217.

NIA News (2000). Scientists zero in on enzyme at work in Alzheimer's disease. Washington: National Institute on Aging, web site www.alzheimers.org/nia.

NICHD Early Child Care Research. (1998). Early child care and self-control, compliance, and problem behavior at twenty-four and thirty-six months. *Child Development, 69,* 1145–1170.

NICHD Early Child Care Research. (1999). Child care and mother-child interaction in the first 3 years of life. *Developmental Psychology, 35* (6), 1399–1413.

NICHD Early Child Care Research. (2000). The relation of child care to cognitive and language development. *Child Development, 71* (4), 960–980.

Nightingale, E. O. & Goodman, M. (1990). *Before birth.* Cambridge, MA: Harvard U. Press.

NIH (2000). The estrogen-progesterone regimen. Washington: The National Institutes of Health.

Niijhuis, J. (Ed.). (1992). *Fetal behavior: Developmental and perinatal aspects.* New York: Oxford University Press.

Nilsson, L., Furuhjelm, M., Ingleman-Sundberg, A., & Wirsen, C. (1993). *A child is born.* New York: Delacorte.

Nilsson, L. G. (1995). Dissociated effects of elaboration on memory of enacted and non-enacted events. *Psychological Research, 36* (2), 225–233.

Noam, G. (1998). Clinical-developmental psychology: Toward developmentally differentiated interventions. In W. Damon (Series Ed.) & I. Sigel & K. Renninger (Volume Eds.), *Handbook of child psychology: Volume 4. Child psychology in practice.* New York: John Wiley.

Nolinske, T. (1995). Multiple mentoring relationships facilitate learning during fieldwork. *American Journal of Occupational Therapy, 49* (1), 39–43.

Nolinske, T. L. (1995). The value of the mentor-protégé relationship as perceived by the mentor, the protégé and the protégé's boss. *Dissertation Abstracts International: Section B: The Sciences & Engineering, 55* (8-B), 3623.

Nugent, K., Lester, B., & Brazelton, B. (1995).

The cultural context of infancy. Norwood, NJ: Ablex.

Nurmi, J. (1992). Age differences in adult life goals, concerns, and their temporal extension: A life course approach to future-oriented motivation. *International Journal of Behavioral Development, 15* (4), 487–508.

Nuttall, R. & Nuttall, E. (1980). *Family coping and disasters.* Boulder, CO: National Hazards Research Applications.

Nuttall, R. & Nuttal, E. (1980). *The impact of disaster on coping behaviors of families.* Unpublished manuscript. Boston College.

O'Connor, D. & Wolfe, D. M. (1991). From crisis to growth at midlife: Changes in personal paradigm. *Journal of Organizational Behavior, 12,* 323–340.

O'Conor, A. (1995). Breaking the silence. In G. Unks (Ed.), *The gay teen.* New York: Routledge.

Olds, S., London, M., & Ladewig, P. (1996). *Maternal-newborn nursing.* Reading, MA: Addison-Wesley.

Olweus, D. (1982). Development of stable aggression reaction patterns in males. In R. Blanchard & C. Blanchard (Eds.), *Advances in the study of aggression.* Vol. 1 New York: Academic.

Olweus, D. (1993). *Bullying at school: What we know and what we can do.* Cambridge, England: Oxford.

Olweus, D. (1995). Bullying or peer abuse at school: Facts and interventions. *Current directions in psychological science, 4* (6), 196–200.

Ono, H. (1998). Husbands' and wives' resources and marital dissolution. *Journal of Marriage and the Family, 60* (4), 674–689.

Ornstein, R. & Sobel, D. (1987). *The healing brain.* New York: Simon & Schuster.

Ory, M., Hoffman, R. R., Yee, J. L., Tennstedt, S., & Schulz, R. (1999). Prevalence and impact of caregiving: A detailed comparison between dementia and nondementia caregivers. *Gerontologist, 39* (2), 177–185.

Osofsky, J. (1995). The effects of exposure to violence on young children. *American Psychologist, 50* (9), 782–788.

Ossip-Klein, D. J., Doyne, E. J., Bowman, E. D., Osborn, K. M., McDougall-Wilson, I. B., & Neimeyer, R. A. (1989). Effects of running or weight lifting on self-concept in clinically depressed women. *Journal of Consulting and Clinical Psychology, 57* (1), 158–161.

Ottesen, C. C. (1993). *L. A. Stories.* Yarmouth, ME: Intercultural Press.

Ovando, C. & Collier, V. (1998). *Bilingual and ESL classroom: Teaching in multicultural contexts.* New York: McGraw Hill.

Overton, W. (1998). Developmental psychology: Philosophy, concepts, and methodology. In R. M. Lerner (Ed.), *Handbook of child psychology: Volume 1. Theoretical models of human development.* New York: John Wiley.

Owens, R. (1996). *Language development.* Boston: Allyn and Bacon.

Owens, W. (1953). Aging and mental abilities. *Genetic Psychology Monographs, 48* (1), 3–54.

Oyserman, D. & Markus, H. (1990). Possible selves in balance: Implications for

delinquency. *Journal of Social Issues, 46* (2), 141–157.

Packer, A. (Winter, 2000). *Teens and tobacco.* FCD Update. Needham, MA: FCD Educational Services.

Palmer, C. T. & Tiller, C. F. (1995). Sexual access to females as a motivation for joining gangs: An evolutionary approach. *The Journal of Sex Research, 32* (2), 213–217.

Palmore, E. (1985). How to live longer and like it. *Journal of Applied Gerontology 4,* (2) 1–8.

Palmore, E. B., Nowlin, J. B., & Wang, H. S. (1985). Predictors of function among the old-old: A 10-year follow-up. *Journal of Gerontology, 40* (2), 244–250.

Paris, S. & Cunningham, A. (1996). Children becoming students. In D. Berliner & R. Calfee (Eds.), *Handbook of educational psychology.* New York: Macmillan.

Park, S., Belsky, J., Putnam, S., & Crnic, K. (1997). Infant emotionality, parenting, and 3-year inhibition: Exploring stability and lawful discontinuity in a male sample. *Developmental Psychology, 33* (2), 218–227.

Parke, R. (1996). *Fatherhood.* Cambridge, MA: Harvard University Press.

Parke, R. & Brott, A. (1999). *Throwaway dads.* Boston: Houghton Mifflin.

Parke, R. & Buriel, R. (1998). Socialization in the family: Ethnic and ecological perspectives. In W. Damon (Series Ed.) & N. Eisenberg (Volume Ed.), *Handbook of child psychology: Volume 3. Child psychology in practice.* New York: John Wiley.

Parkhurst, H. B. (1999). Confusion, lack of consensus, and the definition of creativity as a construct. *Journal of Creative Behavior, 33* (1), 1–21.

Patterson, C. (1995). Special section: Sexual orientation & human development. *Developmental Psychology, 31* (1), 3–140.

Patton, W. & McMahon, M. (1999). *Career development and systems theory.* Pacific Grove, CA: Brooks/Cole.

Paul, R. W. (1987). Dialogical thinking. In J. B. Baron & R. J. Sternberg (Eds.), *Teaching thinking skills.* New York: W. H. Freeman.

Pearlman, C. (1972, November). Frequency of intercourse in males at different ages. *Medical Aspects of Human Sexuality, 16* (1), 92–113.

Perkins, D., Jay, E., & Tishman. (1993). Introduction: New conceptions of thinking. *Educational Psychologist, 28,* (1), 67–85.

Perkins, D. F., Luster, T., Villarruel, F., & Small, S. (1998). An ecological, risk-factor examination of adolescents' sexual activity in three ethnic groups. *Journal of Marriage and the Family, 60* (4), 660–673.

Perls, T. T., Silver, M. H., & Lauerman, J. F. (1999). *Living to 100: Lessons in living to your maximum potential at any age.* New York, NY: Basic Books.

Perozynski, L. & Kramer, L. (1999). Parental beliefs about managing sibling conflict. *Developmental Psychology, 35* (2), 489–499.

Perry, W. (1968a). *Forms of intellectual and ethical development in the college years.* New York: Holt, Rinehart & Winston.

Perry, W. (1968b, April). *Patterns of development in thought and values of students in a liberal arts college: A*

validation of a scheme. Washington, DC: U.S. Department of Health, Education, and Welfare, Office of Education, Bureau of Research. Final report.

Perry, W. (1981). Cognitive and ethical growth. In A. Chickering (Ed.), *The modern American college.* San Francisco: Jossey-Bass.

Peters, J. (1997). *When mothers work.* Reading, MA: Addison-Wesley.

Petersen, A., Leffert, N., & Graham, B. (1995). Adolescent development and the emergence of sexuality. *Suicide and Life Threatening Behavior, 25* (1), 4–17.

Petersen, A. C., Compas, B. E., Brooks–Gunn, J., Stemmler, M., Ey, S., & Grant, K. E. (1993, February). Depression in adolescence. *American Psychologist* (2), 155–168.

Petersen, A. C., Crockett, I., Richards, M., & Boxer, A. (1988). A self-report measure of pubertal status. *Journal of Youth and Adolescence, 17* (1), 117–134.

Peterson, C. (1999). Grandfathers' and grandmothers' satisfaction with the grandparenting role: Seeking new answers to old questions. *The International Journal of Aging and Human Development, 48* (3), 191–216.

Petherbridge, J. (1996). Debriefing work experience: A reflection on reflection? *British Journal of Guidance & Counseling, 24* (2), 243–257.

Pfaff, W. (1997). *The future of the U.S. as a great power.* Pittsburgh: Carnegie Council on Ethics and International Affairs.

Phares, V. (1992). Where's poppa? The relative lack of attention to the role of fathers in child and adolescent psychopathology. *American Psychologist, 47,* 656–664.

Phinney, J. S. & Alipuria, L. L. (1990). Ethnic identity in college students from four ethnic groups. *Journal of Adolescence, 13,* 171–183.

Phinney, J. S. (1996). When we talk about American ethnic groups, what do we mean? *American Psychologist, 51* (9), 918–927.

Piaget, J. (1926). *The language and thought of the child.* New York: Harcourt, Brace, and World.

Piaget, J. (1932). *The moral judgment of the child.* New York: Macmillan.

Piaget, J. (1951). *Play, dreams, and imitation in childhood.* New York: Norton.

Piaget, J. (1952). *The origins of intelligence in children.* New York: International Universities Press.

Piaget, J. (1966). *Psychology of intelligence.* Totowa, NJ: Littlefield, Adams, & Co.

Piaget, J. (1967). *Six psychological studies.* New York: Random House.

Piaget, J. (1973). *The child and reality.* New York: Viking.

Piaget, J. & Inhelder, B. (1969). *The psychology of the child.* New York: Basic.

Picard, C. L. (1999). The level of competition as a factor for the development of eating disorders in female collegiate athletes. *Journal of Youth and Adolescence, 28* (5), 583–594.

Pike, A., McGuire, S., Hetherington, E. M., Reiss, D., & Plomin, R. (1996). Family environment and adolescent depressive symptoms and antisocial behavior: A multivariate genetic analysis. *Developmental Psychology, 32* (4), 590–603.

Pilote, R. A. (1998). Adolescent bulimia nervosa-Part 1: Adolescent problem behaviors. *Youth and Society, 30* (1), 89–120.

Pinker, S. (1994). *The language instinct.* New York: Morrow.

Pinker, S. (1997). *How the mind works.* New York: W. W. Norton.

Pipher, M. (1994). *Reviving Ophelia.* New York: Ballantine.

Pipp-Siegel, S. & Foltz, C. (1997). Toddlers' acquisition of self/other knowledge: Ecological and interpersonal aspects of self and other. *Child Development, 68* (1), 69–79.

Pi-Sunyer, F. X. (1994). The fattening of America. *The Journal of the American Medical Association, 272* (3), 238.

Pizer, H. (Ed.). (1983). *Over fifty-five, healthy and alive.* New York: Van Nostrand Reinhold.

Plomin, R., DeFries, J., McClearn, G., & Rutter, M. (1997). *Behavioral genetics: A primer* (3d. ed.). New York: Freeman.

Plomin, R., Emde, R., Braungart, J., Campos, J., Corley, R., Fulker, D., Kagan, J., Reznick, J., Robinson, J., Zahn-Waxler, C., & DeFries, J. (1993). Genetic change and continuity from fourteen to twenty months: The MacArthur Longitudinal Twin Study. *Child Development, 64* (5), 1354–1376.

Plomin, R., Reiss, D., Hetherington, E. M., & Howe, G. (1994). Nature and nurture: Genetic contributions to measures of the family environment. *Developmental Psychology, 30* (1), 32–43.

Plomin, R., Reiss, D., Hetherington, E. M., & Howe, G. (1995). Nature and nurture: Genetic contributions to measures of the family environment. *Developmental Psychology, 30* (1), 32–43.

Plotkin, H. (1997). *Evolution in mind: An introduction to evolutionary psychology.* Cambridge, MA: Harvard University Press.

Pohl, J. M., Given, C. W., Collins, C. E., & Given, B. A. (1994). Social vulnerability and reactions to caregiving in daughters and daughters-in-law caring for disabled aging parents. *Health Care for Women International, 15* (3), 385–395.

Polak, A. & Harris, P. (1999). Deception by young children following noncompliance. *Developmental Psychology, 35* (2), 561–568.

Pollack, W. (1998). *Real boys: Rescuing our sons from the myths of boyhood.* New York: Henry Holt.

Pollak, S., Cicchetti, D., Hornung, K., & Reed, A. (2000). Recognizing emotion in faces: Developmental effects of child abuse and neglect. *Developmental Psychology, 35* (5), 679–688.

Pollock, R. (1995). A test of conceptual models depicting the developmental course of informal mentor protege relationships in the work place. *Journal of Vocational Behavior* (46), 146–162.

Ponder, R. & Pomeroy, E. (1996). The grief of caregivers. *Journal of Gerontological Social Work, 27* (1/2). The Haworth Press, Inc.

Popenoe, D. (1996). *Life without father.* New York: Martin Kessler Books.

Powell, C. (1996). *My American journey.* New York: Random House.

Pritham, U. & Sammaons, L. (1993). Korean's women's attitudes toward pregnancy and prenatal care. *Health Care, Women Int, 14,* 145.

Prosser, J. & McArdle, P. (1996). The changing mental health of children and adolescents: Evidence for a deterioration? *Psychological Medicine, 26* (4), 715–725.

Pruchno, R. (1999). Raising grandchildren: The experiences of black and white grandmothers. *The Gerontologist, 39* (2), 209–221.

Purugganan, O., Stein, R., Silver, E., & Benenson, B. (2000). Exposure to violence among urban school-aged children: Is it only on television? *Pediatrics, 106* (4), 949–953.

Putman, M. (2000). Risks associated with gestational age and birth weight. In S. Mattson & J. Smith (Eds.), *Core curriculum for maternal-newborn nursing.* Philadelphia: W. B. Saunders.

Range, L. M. & Stringer, T. A. (1996). Reasons for living and coping abilities among older adults. *International Journal of Aging and Human Development, 43* (1), 1–5.

Ratner, P. A. (1998). Modeling acts of aggression and dominance as wife abuse and exploring their adverse health effects. *Journal of Marriage and the Family, 60,* 453–465.

Raymo, C. (1996). Searching for a metaphor for the miraculous. *The Boston Globe,* January 15, C1.

Reed-Victor, E. & Stronge, J. (1997). Building resiliency: Constructive directions for homeless education. *Journal of Children and Poverty, 3* (1), 67–91.

Regoli, R. & J. Hewitt. (1991). *Delinquency in society.* New York: McGraw Hill.

Reimer, M. (1996). "Sinking into the ground": The development and consequences of shame in adolescence. *Developmental Review, 16* (4), 321–357.

Reinke, B., Ellicott, A., Harris, R., & Hancock, E. (1985). Timing of psychosocial change in women's lives. *Human Development, 28* (2), 259–280.

Reisberg, L. (Jan. 28, 2000). Student stress is rising, especially among women. *The Chronicle of Higher Education,* A52+.

Remafedi, G. (1988). Homosexual youth. *Journal of the American Medical Association, 258* (2), 222–225.

Rensberger, B. (1996). *Life itself: Exploring the realm of the living cell.* NY: Oxford University Press.

Restak, R. (1991). *The brain has a mind of its own.* New York: Crown.

Reyes, B. (1997, October 13). More marrying outside of racial group, data show. Boston: *The Boston Globe* (Associated Press), p. A1.

Rhodes, S. (1983). Age-related differences in work attitudes and behavior: A review and conceptual analysis. *Psychological Bulletin, 93* (3), 328–367.

Rich, M. (1999). Pediatricians should educate parents, youth about media's effects. *AAAP News, 13* (5), 28–29.

Ridley, M. (2000). *Genome.* New York: Harper Collins.

Riedel, S. E., Fredman, L., & Langenberg, P. (1998). Associations among caregiving difficulties, burden, and rewards in caregivers to older post-rehabilitation patients. *Journal of Gerontology, 53B* (3), 165–174.

Rierdan, J., Koff, E., & Stubbs, M. (1988). *A longitudinal analysis of body image as a predictor of the onset and persistence of adolescent girls' depression.* Working Paper

No. 188, Wellesley College Center for Research on Women.

Robak, R. W. & Weitzman, S. P. (1994–95). Grieving the loss of romantic relationships in young adults: An empirical study of disenfranchised grief. *Omega Journal of Death and Dying, 30* (4), 269–281.

Roberts, L. J. & Leonard, K. E. (1998). An empirical typology of drinking partnerships and their relationship to marital functioning and drinking consequences. *Journal of Marriage and the Family, 60* (4), 515–526.

Robins, L. & Rutter, M. (1990). *Straight and devious pathways from childhood to adulthood.* Cambridge, England: Cambridge University Press.

Roche, J. & Ramsbey, T. W. (1993). Premarital sexuality: A five-year follow-up study of attitudes and behavior by dating stage. *Adolescence, 28* (109), 67–80.

Roche, J. & Tucker, S. (1997). *Youth in society.* London: Sage.

Rodgers, J., Harris, D. F., & Vickers, K. B. (1992). Seasonality of first coitus in the United States. *Social Biology, 39* (1/2), 1–14.

Rodkin, R. & Farmer, T. (2000). Heterogeneity of popular boys: Antisocial and prosocial configurations. *Developmental psychology, 36* (1), 14–24.

Rogers, S. J. & White, L. (1998). Satisfaction with parenting: The role of marital happiness, family structure, and parents' gender. *Journal of Marriage and the Family, 60,* 293–308.

Rogoff, B. (1990). *Apprenticeship in thinking: Cognitive development in social context.* New York: Oxford University Press.

Rogosh, F., Cicchetti, D., Shields, A., & Toth, S. (1995). Parenting dysfunction in child maltreatment. In M. Bornstein (Ed.), *Handbook of parenting.* Mahwah, NJ: Erlbaum.

Ronge, L. (1998). Early fetal alcohol diagnosis helps patients over lifetime. *AAP News,* October, 14–16.

Rose, L. (Sept., 1995). The 27th Annual Phi Delta Kappa/Gallup Poll of the Public's Attitudes Towards the Public Schools. *Phi Delta Kappan, 77* (1), 41–59.

Rose, S. (1990). *Neurobiology of learning and memory.* NJ: World Scientific.

Rose, S., Feldman, J., Wallace, I., & McCarton, C. (1991). Information processing at 1 year: Relation to birth status and developmental outcome during the first 5 years. *Developmental Psychology, 27,* 723–737.

Rosen, E. I. (1987). *Bitter choices: Blue-collar women in and out of work.* Chicago: Univ. of Chicago Press.

Rosenthal, S. (1996, July). Identifying risk-taking in teen girls. *Ob. Gyn. News,* p. 12.

Rosin, H. M. (1990). The effects of dual career participation on men: Some determinants of variation in career and personal satisfaction. *Human Relations, 43* (2), 169–182.

Ross, H. (1996). Negotiating principles of entitlement in sibling property disputes. *Developmental Psychology, 32* (1), 90–101.

Ross, H. M. (1994). "Meanings adult daughters attach to a parent's death": Comment. *Western Journal of Nursing Research, 16* (4), 361–362.

Ross, R., Paganini-Hill, A., & Wan, P. (2000). Effective hormone replacement therapy on cancer risk. *Journal of the National Cancer Institute, 92,* 328–335.

Rossi, A. S. (Ed.). (1994). *Sexuality across the life course*. Chicago: The University Chicago Press.

Rothbart, M. (1994). Emotional development: Changes in reactivity and self-regulation. In Paul Ekman & Richard Davidson (Eds.), *The nature of emotion*. Oxford University Press, 1994.

Rothbart, M., & Bates, J. (1998). Temperament. In W. Damon (Series Ed.) & N. Eisenberg (Vol. Ed.), *Handbook of child psychology: Volume 3. Social , Emotional, and Personality Development*. New York: John Wiley.

Rothbaum, F., Weisz, J., Pott, M., Miyake, M., & Morelli, G. (2000). Attachment and culture: Security in the United States and Japan. *American Psychologist, 55* (10), 1093–1104.

Rotheram-Borus, M. J. (1993). Biculturalism among adolescents. In M. E. Bernal, G. P. Knight, et al. (Eds.), *Ethnic identity: Formation and transmission among Hispanics and other minorities* (pp. 81–102). Albany, NY: State University of New York Press.

Rowland, D. L., Greenleaf, W. J., Dorfman, L. J., & Davidson, J. M. (1993). Aging and sexual function in men. *Archives of Sexual Behavior, 22* (6), 545–557.

Rubin, K., Bukowski, W., & Parker, J. (1998). Peer interactions, relationships, and groups. In W. Damon (Series Ed.) & N. Eisenberg (Volume Eds), *Handbook of child psychology: Volume 4. Child psychology in practice*. New York: John Wiley.

Rubin, K., Coplan, R., Nelson, L., Cheah, C., & Lagace-Sequin, D. (1999). Peer relationships in childhood. In M. Bornstein & M. Lamb (Eds.), *Developmental psychology: An advanced textbook*. Mahwah, NJ: Erlbaum.

Rubin, R. (1995). *Maternal identity and maternal experience*. New York: Springer.

Rubin, S. S. & Schechter, N. (1997). Exploring the social construction of bereavement: Perceptions of adjustment and recovery in bereaved men. *American Journal of Orthopsychiatry, 67* (2), 279–289.

Ruble, D. & Martin, C. (1998). Gender development. In W. Damon (Series Ed.) & N. Eisenberg (Volume Ed.), *Handbook of child psychology: Volume 3. Child psychology in practice*. New York: John Wiley.

Ruffman, T. & Keenan, T. (1996). The belief-based emotion of surprise: The case for a lag in understanding relative to false belief. *Developmental Psychology, 32* (1), 40–49.

Rushton, J. & Ankney, C. D. (1997). Brain size and cognitive ability. *Psychonomic Bulletin and Review, 3* (1), 21–36.

Russell, C. H. (1989). *Good news about aging*. New York: Wiley.

Rutter, M. (1983). School effects on pupil progress: Research findings and policy implications. *Child Development, 54,* (1), 1–29.

Rutter, M. (1988). Stress, coping, and development: some issues and some questions. In Norman Garmezy and Michael Rutter (Eds.), *Stress, coping and development in children*. Baltimore: Johns Hopkins.

Rutter, M. (1995). Maternal deprivation. In Marc Bornsteinn (Ed.), *Handbook of Parenting. Volume 4: Applied and Practical Parenting*. Mahwah, NJ: Lawrence Erlbaum.

Rutter, M. (1997). Nature-nurture integration: The example of antisocial behavior. *American Psychologist, Vol. 52* (4), 390–398.

Rutter, M. & Rutter, M. (1993). *Developing minds: Challenge and continuity across the lifespan*. New York: Basic Books.

Rutter, M. & Rutter, M. (1993). *Developing minds: Challenge and continuity across the lifespan*. New York: Basic Books.

Ryan, G. & Lane, S. (1997). *Juvenile sexual offending*. San Fransisco: Jossey-Bass.

Ryan, R. M. (1995). Psychological needs and the facilitation of integrative processes. *Journal of Personality, 63* (3), 397–427.

Rycek, R., Stuhr, S., McDermott, J., Benker, J., & Schwartz, M. (1998). Adolescent egocentrism and cognitive functioning during late adolescence. *Adolescence, 33* (132), 745–749.

Rymer, R. (1993). *Genie: A scientific tragedy*. New York: Harper.

Saal, H. (1998). Alternative therapies for Down syndrome: Fact or false hope. *AAP News, 14* (5), 16.

Saarni, C., Mumme, D., & Campos, J. (1998). Emotional development: Action, communication, and understanding. In W. Damon (Series Ed.) & N. Eisenberg (Vol. Ed.), *Handbook of child psychology: Volume 3. Social, Emotional, and Personality Development*. New York: John Wiley.

Sadker, M. & Sadker, D. (1994). *Failing at fairness: How America's schools cheat girls*. New York: Scribners.

Sadler, T. W. (1995). *Langman's medical embryology*. (7th ed.). Baltimore: Williams and Wilkins.

Sales, E. (1978). Women's adult development. In I. Fieze (Ed.), *Women and sex roles*. New York: W. W. Norton.

Salthouse, T. (1990). Cognitive competence and expertise in aging. In *Handbook of the psychology of aging*. New York: Academic Press.

Saltus, R. (2000, July 4). The man who fixes brains. *The Boston Globe,* pp. 1, 2.

Saluter, A. F. (1991). *Marital status and living arrangements: March 1991*. Current Population Reports, P-20 (No. 461). Washington, DC: Bureau of the Census.

Sameroff, A. & Haith, M. (1996). *The five to seven year shift*. Chicago: Univerity of Chicago Press.

Samuelson, L. & Smith, L. (2000). Grounding development in cognitive processes. *Child Development, 71* (1), 98–106.

Sanday, P. R. (1990). *Fraternity gang rape: Sex, brotherhood, and privilege on campus*. New York: New York University Press.

Sanders, G. F. & Mullis, R. L. (1988). Family influences on sexual attitudes and knowledge as reported by college students. *Adolescence, 23* (92), 837–846.

Sansavini, A., Bertoncici, J., & Giovanelli, G. (1997). Newborns discriminate the rhythm of multisyllabic words. *Developmental Psychology, 33* (1), 3–11.

Santelli, J., Brener, N., Lowry, R., Bhatt, A., & Zabin, L. (1998). Multiple sexual partners among U.S. adolescents and young adults. *Family Planning Perspectives, 30* (6), 271–275.

Sanyika, D. (1996). Gang rites and rituals of initiation. In L. C. Mahdi, N. G. Christopher, & M. Meade (Eds.), *Gang behavior*. Chicago: Open Court.

Saul, J. (1997). Adult education and religion. *Adult Education Quarterly, 47* (3/4), 169.

Saunders, J. B. (1989). The efficacy of treatment for drinking problems. Special issue: Psychiatry and the addictions. *International Review of Psychiatry, 1* (1), 121–137.

Savage, M. P. & Holcomb, D. R. (1999). Adolescent female athletes' sexual risk-taking behaviors. *Journal of Youth and Adolescence, 28,* 595–602.

Savin-Williams, R. C. (1995). An exploratory study of pubertal maturation timing and self-esteem among gay and bisexual male youths. Special Issue: Sexual orientation and human development. *Developmental Psychology, 31* (1), 56–64.

Savin-Williams, R. C. & Berndt, T. J. (1990). Friendship and peer relations. In S. Feldman & G. Elliot (Eds.), *At the threshold: The developing adolescent*. Cambridge, MA: Harvard University Press.

Schacter, D. (1996). *Searching for memory*. New York: Basic Books.

Schaie, K. W. (1994). The course of adult intellectual development. *American Psychologist, 49* (4), 304–313.

Schaie, K. W. & Hertzog, C. (1983). Fourteen-year cohort-sequential analyses of adult intellectual development. *Developmental Psychology, 19* (4), 531–543.

Schairer, C. & others. (2000). Menopausal estrogen and estrogen-progestin replacement therapy and breast-cancer risk. *Journal of the American Medical Assoication, 283* (4), 485–491.

Scharlach, A. E. & Fuller-Thomson, E. (1994). Coping strategies following the death of an elderly parent. *Journal of Gerontological Social Work, 21* (3/4), 85–100.

Scheidlinger, S. (1994). A commentary on adolescent group violence. *Child Psychiatry and Human Development, 25* (1), 3–11.

Schirrmacher, R. (1998). *Art and creative development for young children*. Albany, NY: Delmar Publishers.

Schneider, W. & Bjorklund, D. (1998). Memory. In D. Kuhn & R. Siegler (Eds.), *Handbook of child psychology*. Volume 5. New York: John Wiley.

Schneider, W., & Pressley, M. (1997). *Memory development between two and twenty*. Mahwah, NJ: Lawrence Erlbaum.

Schoem, D. (1991). *Inside separate worlds: Life stories of young Blacks, Jews, and Latinos*. Ann Arbor: University of Michigan Press.

Schofferman, J. (1987). Hospice care of the patient with AIDS. *The Hospice Journal, 3,* 51–84.

Schroedel, J. R. (1990). Blue-collar women: Paying the price at home on the job. In H. Y. Grossman & N. L. Chester (Eds.), *The experience and meaning of work in women's lives*. Hillsdale, NJ: Erlbaum.

Schulenberg, J., Wadsworth, K. N., O'Malley, P. M., Bachman, J. G., & Johnston, L. D. (1996). Adolescent risk factors for binge drinking during the transition to young adulthood: Variable- and pattern-centered approaches to change. *Developmental Psychology, 32,* (4), 659–673.

Schulz, R. & Ewen, R. B. (1988). *Adult development and aging: Myths and emerging realities*. New York: Macmillan.

Schwartz, D., Dodge, K., & Coie, J. (1993). The emergence of chronic peer victimization in boys' play groups. *Child Development, 64* (6), 1755–1772.

Scott, D. (Ed.). (1988). *Anorexia and bulimia.* New York: New York University Press.

Sears, W. & Sears, M. (1994). *The birth book.* Boston: Little, Brown.

Sebald, H. (1977). *Adolescence: A social psychological analysis* (2nd ed.). Englewood Cliffs, NJ: Prentice-Hall.

Sege, I. (1999, March 6). A $50,000 dilemma on campus. *The Boston Globe,* pp. A1, A 9.

Sege, I. (May 6, 1998). Life on the straight edge. Boston: *Boston Globe,* E1.

Seidman, S. (2000). *An educator's guide to adoption.* Silver Springs, MD: Celebrate Adoption.

Seifer, R., Schiller, M., & Sameroff, A. (1996). Attachment, maternal sensitivity, and infant temperament during the first year of life. *Developmental Psychology, 32* (1), 12–25.

Selman, R. (1980). *The growth of interpersonal understanding.* New York: Academic.

Selman, R. L. & Schultz, L. H. (1990). *Making a friend in youth: Developmental theory and pair therapy.* Chicago: University of Chicago Press.

Seltz, J. (2000). Teen brains *are* different. Boston: *Boston Globe,* May 28, E 1,5.

Selye, H. (1956). *The stress of life.* New York: McGraw-Hill.

Selye, H. (1975, October). Implications of stress concept. *New York State Journal of Medicine,* 2139–2145.

Selye, H. (1982). History and present status of the stress concept. In L. Goldberger & S. Breznitz (Eds.), *Handbook of stress: Theoretical and clinical aspects.* New York: The Free Press.

Seppa, N. (1996, August). Rwanda starts its long healing process. *APA Monitor,* p. 14.

Seppa, N. (1997, March). What defines a man today? *APA Monitor,* pp. 1, 12.

Serakan, U. (1989). Understanding the dynamics of self-concept of members in dual-career families. *Human Relations, 42* (2), 97–116.

Serbin, L., Powlishta, K., & Gulko, J. (1993). The development of sex typing in middle childhood. *Monographs of the Society for Research in Child Development, 58* (2).

Shackleford, T. & Buss, D. (1997). Marital satisfaction in evolutionary psychological perspectives. In R. Sternberg & M. Hojjat, Eds., *Satisfaction in close relationships.* NY: Guilford.

Shade, B. (1987). Ecological correlates of the educative style of Afro-American children. *Journal of Negro Education, 56,* 88–99.

Shahtahmasebi, S., Davies, R., & Wenger, G. C. (1992). A longitudinal analysis of factors related to survival in old age. *The Gerontologist, 32* (3), 404–413.

Shanker, A. (1995). *Where we stand.* New York Times.

Shapiro, B. (1997). Researchers questions the way society grieves. *APA Monitor, 28* (10), 36.

Shapiro, J. (2000). Euthanasia's home. *Annual Editions: Aging.* Sluice Dock, CT: Dushkin/McGraw-Hill.

Sharpe, P. S., Jackson, K. L., White, C., Vaca, V., Hickey, T., Gu, J., & Otterness, C. (1997). Effects of a one-year physical activity intervention for older adults at congregate nutrition sites. *The Gerontologist, 37* (2), 208–215.

Shatz, C. (1996). Emergence of order in visual system development. *Journal of Physiology, 90* (3–4), 141–150.

Shatz, C. (1999). The developing brain. In The Editors of Scientific American, *The Scientific American Book of the Brain.* New York: The Lyons Press.

Sheehy, G. (1992). *The silent passage: Menopause.* New York: Random House.

Shek, D. T. L. (1995a). Gender differences in marital quality and well-being in Chinese married adults. *Sex Roles, 32* (11/12), 699–715.

Shek, D. T. L. (1995b). Marital quality and psychological well-being of married adults in a Chinese context. *The Journal of Genetic Psychology, 156* (1), 45–56.

Sheley, J. F., Zhang, J., Brody, C. J., & Wright, J. D. (1995). Gang organization, gang criminal activity, and individual gang members' criminal behavior. *Social Science Quarterly, 76* (1), 53–68.

Shields, P. & Rovee-Collier, C. (1992). Long-term memory for context-specific category information at six months. *Child Development, 63,* 245–259.

Shifrin, D. (1998). Three-year study documents nature of television violence. *AAP News, 14* (8), 23.

Shin, Y. (1999). The effects of a walking exercise program on physical function and emotional state of elderly Korean women. *Public Health Nursing, 16* (2), 146–154.

Shore, B. (1996). *Culture in mind: Cognition, culture, and the problem of meaning.* New York: Oxford University Press.

Shore, R. (1997). *Rethinking the brain: New insights into early development.* New York: Families and Work Institute.

Shute, N. (1997). Why do we age? *U.S. News and World Report, 123* (7), 55–57.

Shweder, R. (1991). *Thinking through cultures.* Cambridge, MA: Harvard University Press.

Siegel, J. & Shaughnessy, M. (1995). There is a first time for everything: Understanding adolescence. *Adolescence, 30* (117), 217–221.

Siegler, I. (1975). The terminal drop hypothesis: Fact or artifact? *Experimental Aging Research, 1,* 169.

Siegler, R. (1996). *Emerging minds: The process of change in children's thinking.* New York: Oxford University Press.

Siegler, R. (1998). *Children's thinking.* (3d ed.). Upper Saddle River: Prentice Hall.

Siegler, R. (2000). The rebirth of children's learning. *Child Development, 71* (1), 26–35.

Sigelman, C. K., Estrada, A. L., Derenowski, E. B., & Woods, T. E. (1996). Intuitive theories of human immunodeficiency virus transmission: Their development and implications. *Journal of Pediatric Psychology, 21* (4), 555–572.

Silver, J. (1998). Housing for older adults: Supporting the transition to a new home. *Journal of Geriatric Psychiatry, 31,* 3–5.

Silverstein, L. B. (1991). Transforming the debate about child care and maternal employment. *American Psychologist, 46* (10), 1025–1032.

Simms, M., Dubowitz, H., & Szilagyi, M. (2000). Health care needs of children in the foster care system. *Pediatrics, 106* (4), 909–918.

Simons, R. L., Gordon, L. C., Conger, R. D., & Lorenx, F. O. (1999). Explaining the higher incidence of problems among children of divorce compared with those in two-parent families. *Journal of Marriage and the Family, 61* (1), 1020–1033.

Simonton, D. K. (1975). Age and literary creativity. *Journal of Cross-cultural Creativity, 6* (2), 259–277.

Simonton, D. K. (1976). Biographical determinants of achieved eminence. *Journal of Personality and Social Psychology, 33* (2), 218–276.

Simonton, D. K. (1977a). Creativity, age and stress. *Journal of Personality and Social Psychology, 35,* 791–804.

Simonton, D. K. (1977b). Eminence, creativity and geographical marginality. *Journal of Personality and Social Psychology, 35,* 805–816.

Simonton, D. K. (1993). Blind variation, chance configurations, and creative genius. *Psychological Inquiries, 4* (2), 225–228.

Sims, J. M. (1996). The use of voice for assessment and intervention in couples therapy. *Women and Therapy, 19* (3), 61–77.

Skinner, B. F. (1938). *The behavior of organisms.* New York: Macmillan.

Skinner, B. F. (1953). *Science and human nature.* New York: Macmillan.

Skinner, B. F. (1968). *The technology of teaching.* New York: Appleton-Century-Crofts.

Skinner, B. F. (1971). *Beyond freedom and dignity.* New York: Knopf.

Skinner, B. F. (1974). *About behaviorism.* New York: Knopf.

Skinner, B. F. (1983). *A matter of consequences.* New York: Knopf.

Skinner, B. F. (1984). The shame of American Education. *American Psychologist* (September), 947–954.

Skinner, B. F. (1986). Some thoughts about the future. *Journal of the Experimental Analysis of Behavior* (March), 229–235.

Slaby, R. (1990, Spring). Gender concept development legacy. *New Directions for Psychology, 47,* 21–29.

Sleek, S. (1997). Weisel emphasizes need to thank elderly. *APA Monitor, 28* (10), 23.

Slomkowski, C. & Dunn, J. (1996). Young children's understanding of other people's beliefs and feelings and their connected communication with friends. *Developmental Psychology, 32* (3), 442–447.

Small, B. & Backman, L. (1997). Cognitive correlates of mortality. *Psychology and Aging, 12* (2), 309–314.

Small, S. A. & Luster, T. (1994). An ecological, risk-factor approach to adolescent sexual activity. *Journal of Marriage and the Family, 56,* 181–192.

Smith, B. & Blass, E. (1996). Tast-mediated calming in premature, preterm, and full-term infants. *Developmental Psychology, 32* (6), 1084–1089.

Smith, B. K. (1989). *Grandparenting in today's world.* Austin, TX: Hogg Foundation for Mental Health.

Smith, D. (1997). Centenarians: Human longevity outliers. *The Gerontologist, 37* (2), 200–207.

Smith, D. B. & Moen, P. (1998). Spousal influence on retirement: His, her and their perceptions. *Journal of Marriage and the Family, 60,* 734–744.

Smith, D. W. E., Seibert, C. S., Jackson, F. W., & Snell, J. (1992). Pet ownership by elderly people: Two new issues. *International Journal of Aging and Human Development, 34* (3), 175–184.

Smith, J. & Baltes, P. (1999). Lifespan perspectives on development. In M. Bornstein & M. Lamb (Eds.), *Developmental psychology: An advanced textbook* (pp. 47–73). Mahwah, NJ: Erlbaum.

Smith, K. (2000). Normal childbirth. In S. Mattson & J. Smith (Eds.), *Core curriculum for maternal-newborn nursing*. Philadelphia: W. B. Saunders.

Smith, R. (1990). *A theoretical framework for explaining the abuse of hyperactive children*. Unpublished doctoral dissertation, Boston College, Chestnut Hill, MA.

Smith, R. (1997). *Cosby: The life of a comedy legend*. Amherst, NY: Prometheus Books.

Smock, P., Manning, G., & Gupta, S. (1999). The effect of marriage in divorce on women's economic well-being. *American Sociological Review, 64* (6), 794–812.

Smotherman, W. & Robinson, S. (1996). The development of behavior before birth. *Developmental Psychology, 33* (3), 425–434.

Snowdon, D. (1997). Aging and Alzheimer's disease: Lessons from the nun study. *The Gerontologist, 37* (2), 150–156.

Snyder, H., Sickmund, M., & Poe-Yamagata, E. (1996). *Update on violence*. Washington, DC: Office of Justice.

South, S. J. (1993). Racial and ethnic differences in the desire to marry. *Journal of Marriage and the Family, 55* (3), 357–370.

Spence, A. (1989). *Biology of human aging*. Englewood Cliffs, NJ: Prentice-Hall.

Sprecher, S. (1999). "I love you more today than yesterday." *Journal of Personality and Social Psychology, 76* (1), 46–53.

Springer, S. & Deutsch, G. (1998). *Left brain, right brain*. New York: Freeman.

Sroufe, L. A., Cooper, R., & DeHart, G. (1992). *Child development*. New York: Knopf.

St. Peters, M., Fitch, M., Huston, A., Wright, J., & Eakins, D. (1991). Television and families: What do young children watch with their parents? *Child Development, 62*, 1409–1423.

Stambrook, M. & Parker, K. (1987). The development of the concept of death in childhood. *Merrill-Palmer Quarterly, 33* (2), 133–157.

Statistical Abstract of the United States. (1995). *Gender and suicide*. Washington: U.S. Government Printing Office.

Steefel, N. M. (1992). A divorce transition model. *Psychological Reports, 70* (2), 155–160.

Steers, W. N., Elliot, E., Nemiro, J., & Ditman, D. (1996). Health beliefs as predictors of HIV-preventive behavior and ethnic differences in prediction. *Journal of Social Psychology, 136* (1), 99–110.

Stein, C. H., Wemmerus, V. A., Ward, M., Gaines, M. E., Freeberg, A. L., & Jewell, T. C. (1998). "Because they're my parents": An intergenerational study of felt obligation and parental caregiving. *Journal of Marriage and the Family, 60* (4), 611–622.

Steinberg, L. (1990). Autonomy, conflict, and harmony in the family relationship. In S. Feldman & G. Elliot (Eds.), *At the threshold: The developing adolescent*. Cambridge, MA: Harvard University.

Stephens, M. & Townsend, A. (1997). Stress of parent care. *Psychology & Aging, 12* (2), 376–386.

Stepp, L. (2000). *Our last best shot*. New York: Riverhead.

Stern, D. (1990). *Diary of a baby*. New York: Harper Collins.

Stern, D., Rahn, M. L., & Chung, Y. P. (1998). Design of work-based learning for students in the United States. *Youth & Society, 29* (4), 471–502.

Stern, M. & Karker, K. (1992). Modifying the premature stereotype in mothers of premature and ill full term infants. *Journal of Clinical Child Psychology, 21* (1), 76–82.

Sternberg, R. (1986). *Intelligence applied*. New York: Harcourt Brace Jovanovich.

Sternberg, R. (1988). *The triarchic mind: A new theory of human intelligence*. New York: Viking.

Sternberg, R. (1990). *Metaphors of mind: Conceptions of the nature of intelligence*. New York: Cambridge University Press.

Sternberg, R. (1996). *Successful intelligence*. New York: Simon & Schuster.

Sternberg, R. (2000). What's your love story? *Psychology Today, 32* (4), 52–59.

Sternberg, R. & Davidson, J. (1995). *The nature of insight*. Cambridge, MA: M. I. T. Press.

Sternberg, R. & Lubart, T. (1995). *Defying the crowd: Cultivating creativity in a culture of conformity*. New York: Free Press.

Sternberg, R. J. (2000). Cross-disciplinary verification of theories: The case of the triarchic theory. *History of Psychology, 3* (2), 177–179.

Sternberg, R. J. (Ed.). (2000). *Handbook of intelligence*. New York, NY: Cambridge University Press.

Sternberg, R. J. (1986). The triangular theory of love. *Psychological Review, 93* (1), 129–135.

Sternberg, R. J. (1990). *Wisdom*. New York: Cambridge University Press.

Sterns, H. L. & Miklos, S. M. (1995). The aging worker in a changing environment: Organizational and individual issues. *Journal of Vocational Behavior, 47* (2), 248–268.

Stevens, J. C. & Cain, W. S. (1987). Old-age deficits in the sense of smell as gauged by thresholds, magnitude matching, and odor identification. *Psychology and Aging, 2*, 36–42.

Stevens-Simon, C. & Kaplan, D. (1998). Teen childbearing trends. *Pediatrics, 102* (5), 1205–1207.

Steward, E. (1995). *Beginning writers in the zone of proximal development*. Hillsdale, NJ: Lawrence Erlbaum.

Stewart, A. & Ostrove, J. (November, 1998). Women's personality in middle-age. *American Psychologist, 53* (11), 1185–1195.

Stimmel, B. (1991). *The facts about drug use*. New York: Consumer Report Books.

Stipek, D. & Ryan, R. (1997). Economically disadvantaged preschoolers: Ready to learn but further to go. *Developmental Psychology, 33* (4), 711–723.

Stolberg, S. (2000). Despite ferment, gene therapy progresses. *The New York Times*, June 6, D1, D4.

Stoller, E. P., Forster, L. E., & Duniho, T. S. (1992). Systems of parent care within sibling networks. *Research on Aging, 14* (1), 28–49.

Stoppard, M. (1993). *Conception, pregnancy and birth*. New York: DK Publishing.

Stossel, S. (May, 1997). The man who counts the killings. *Atlantic Monthly, 279* (5), 86–104.

Strasburger, V. & Donnerstein, E. (1999). Children, adolescents, and the media. *Pediatrics, 103* (1), 129–149.

Strawbridge, W. & Wallhagen, M. (1992). Is all in the family always best? *Journal of Aging Studies, 6* (1), 81–92.

Strough, J., Berg, C., & Sansone, C. (1996). Goals for solving everyday problems across the lifespan: Age and gender differences in the salience of interpersonal concerns. *Developmental Psychology, 32* (6), 1106–1115.

Subcommittee on Health and the Environment. (1987). *Incidence and control of chlamydia*. Washington, DC: U.S. Government Printing Office.

Substance Abuse and Mental Health Services Administration. (1999). *Cigar smoking*. Washington, DC: Substance Abuse and Mental Health Services Administration.

Sudnow, D. (1967). *Passing on*. Englewood Cliffs, NJ: Prentice-Hall.

Sue, S. & Sue, D. W. (1991). *Counseling the culturally different: Theory and practice*. New York: Wiley.

Sugarman, L. (1986). *Lifespan development: Concepts, theories and interventions*. New York: Methuen.

Sullivan, M. (1997). *The Boston College Chronicle*, Chestnut Hill, MA, pp. 1, 5.

Sullivan, T. & Schneider, M. (1987). Development and identity issues in adolescent homosexuality. *Child and Adolescent Social Work Journal, 4* (1), 13–24.

Super, D. E. (1983). Assessment in career guidance: Toward truly developmental counseling. *Personnel and Guidance Journal, 61* (4), 555–562.

Super, D. E. (1990). A life-span, life-space approach to career development. In D. Brown, L. Brooks, & others (Eds.), *Career choice and development*. San Francisco: Jossey-Bass.

Swarr, A. E. & Richards, M. H. (1996). Longitudinal effects of adolescent girls' pubertal development, perceptions of pubertal timing, and parental relations on eating problems. *Developmental Psychology, 32* (4), 636–646.

Swedo, S., Rettew, D., Kuppenheimer, M., Lum, D., Dolan, S., & Goldberger, E. (1991). Can adolescent suicide-attempters be distinguished from at-risk adolescents? *Pediatrics, 88* (5), 620–629.

Szkrybalo, J. & Ruble, D. (1999). "God made me a girl": Sex-category constancy judgments and explanations revisited. *Developmental Psychology, 35* (2), 392–402.

Szuchman, L. & Muscarella, F., Eds. (2000). *Psychological perspectives on human sexuality*. NY: Wiley.

Tabourne, C. (1995). The effects of a life review program on disorientation, social interactions and self-esteem of nursing home residents. *International Journal of Aging & Human Development, 41* (2), 251–266.

Tada, W. & Stiles, J. (1996). Developmental changes in children's analysis of spatial patterns. *Developmental Psychology, 32* (5), 951–970.

Tada, W. & Stiles, J. (1997). Developmental changes in children's analysis of spatial patterns. *Developmental Psychology, 32* (5), 951–970.

Tager-Flusberg, H. (1997). Putting words together: Morphology and syntax in the preschool years. In J. Gleason (Ed.), *The development of language*. Boston: Allyn and Bacon.

Talbot, M. (1998). Older widows' attitudes towards men and remarriage. *Journal of Aging Studies, 12* (4), 429–449.

Tamborlane, W. (1997). *Children's nutrition*. New Haven: Yale University Press.

Tamborlane, W. (Ed.). (1997). *The Yale guide to children's nutrition*. New Haven: Yale University Press.

Tanner, J. M. (1989). *Fetus into man*. Cambridge, MA: Harvard University Press.

Tapley, D. & Todd, W. D. (Eds.). (1988). *Complete guide to pregnancy*. New York: Crown.

Tardif, T. & Wellman, H. (2000). Acquisition of mental state language in Mandarin- and Cantonese-speaking children. *Developmental Psychology, 36* (1), 25–43.

Tate, D., Reppucci, N., & Mulvey, E. (1995). Violent juvenile delinquents. *American Psychologist, 50* (9), 777–781.

Taub, H. (1975). Effects of coding cues upon short-term memory. *Developmental Psychology, 11* (2), 254.

Taylor, M. (1996). The development of children's beliefs about social and biological aspects of gender. *Child Development, 67,* 1555–1571.

Taylor, N. (1995). Gay and lesbian youth. In T. DeCrescenzo. (Ed.), *Helping gay and lesbian youth*. New York: Haworth.

Taylor, R. D. (1996). Adolescents' perceptions of kinship support and family management practices: Association with adolescent adjustment in African American families. *Developmental Psychology, 32* (4), 687–695.

Taylor, R. D., Casten, R., Flickinger, S. M., Roberts, D., & Fulmore, C. D. (1994). Explaining the school performance of African-American adolescents. *Journal of Research on Adolescence, 4* (1), 21–44.

Temple, C. (1993). *The brain*. New York: Penguin.

Terman, L. M. (1925). *Genetic studies of genius*. Stanford, CA: Stanford University Press.

Thelen, E. (1995). Motor development: A new synthesis. *American Psychologist, 50* (2), 79–95.

Thoma, S. & Rest, J. (1999). The relationship between moral decision making and patterns of consolidation and transition in moral judgment development. *Developmental Psychology, 35* (2), 323–334.

Thomas, R. (1992). *Comparing theories of child development*. Belmont, CA: Wadsworth.

Thompson, P. (1998). Adolescents from families of divorce: Vulnerability to physiological and psychological disturbances. *Journal of Psychosocial Nursing, 36,* 34–41.

Thompson, R. (1998). Early sociopersonality development. In W. Damon (Series Ed.) & N. Eisenberg (Vol. Ed.), *Handbook of child psychology: Volume 3. Social, Emotional, and Personality Development*. New York: John Wiley.

Thompson, R. (1999). The individual child: Temperament, emotion, self, and personality. In M. Bornstein & M. Lamb (Eds.), *Developmental psychology: An advanced textbook*. Mahwah, NJ: Erlbaum.

Thompson, R. (2000). The legacy of early attachment. *Child Development, 71* (1), 145–152.

Thorndike, R., Hagan, E., & Satler, J. (1985). *The Stanford-Binet Intelligence Scale* (4th ed.). Chicago: Riverside.

Thornton, S. (1995). *Children solving problems*. Cambridge, MA: Harvard University Press.

Tingus, K. D., Heger, A. H., Foy, D. W., & Leskin, G. A. (1996). Factors associated with entry into therapy in children evaluated for sexual abuse. *Child Abuse and Neglect, 20* (1), 63–68.

Tirrito, T. (1996). Mental health problems and behavioral disruptions in nursing homes. *Journal of Gerontological Social Work, 27* (1/2), 73.

Todd, J., Friedman, A., & Karinki, P. (1990). Women growing stronger with age: The effect of status in the U.S. and Kenya. *Psychology of Women Quarterly, 14* (4), 567–577.

Tolbert, H. A. (1996). Psychoses in children and adolescents: A review. *Journal of Clinical Psychiatry, 57* (3), 4–8.

Tomada, G. & Schneider, B. (1997). Relational aggression, gender, and peer acceptance: Invariance across culture, stability over time, and concordance among informants. *Developmental Psychology, 33* (4), 601–609.

Townsend, A. & Franks, M. (1995). Binding ties: Closeness and conflict in adult children's caregiving relationships. *Psychology & Aging, 10* (3), 343–350.

Travers, J., Elliott, S., & Kratochwill, T. (1993). *Educational psychology: Effective teaching, effective learning*. Dubuque, IA: Brown/Benchmark.

Tronick, E. (1989). Emotions and emotional communication in infants. *Child Development, 44,* 112–119.

Troumbley, P., Burman, K., Rinke, W., & Lenz, E. (1990). A comparison of the health risk, health status, self motivation, psychological symptomatic distress, and physical fitness of overweight and normal weight soldiers. *Military Medicine, 155* (9), 424–429.

Tully, T. & Yin, J. C. (1996). CREB and the formation of long-term memory. *Current Opinion on Neurobiology, 6* (2), 264–268.

Tun, P. (1998). Fast noisy speech: Age difference in processing rapid speech with background noise. *Psychology and Aging, 13* (3), 424–434.

Turiel, E. (1998). The development of morality. In W. Damon (Series Ed.) & D. Kuhn & R. Siegler (Volume Eds.), *Handbook of child psychology: Volume 2. Cognition, perception, and language*. New York: John Wiley.

Turner, J. S. & Helms, D. B. (1989). *Contemporary adulthood*. New York: Holt, Rinehart & Winston.

Tversky, A. & Kahneman, D. (1981). The framing of decisions and the psychology of choice. *Science, 211,* 453–458.

Twomey, L., Taylor, J., & Furiss, B. (1983). Age changes in the bone density and structure of the lumbar vertebral column. *Journal of Anatomy, 136* (1), 15–25.

U.S. Bureau of the Census. (1992). *Vital statistics*. Washington, DC: U.S. Government Printing Office.

U.S. Bureau of the Census. (1995). *Statistical Abstract of the United States*. Washington, DC: Government Printing Office.

U.S. Bureau of the Census. (1996). *Statistical Abstract of the United States*. Washington, DC: Government Printing Office.

U.S. Department of Commerce. (1999). *Vital statistics*. Washington, DC: U.S. Government Printing Office.

U.S. Department of Health and Human Services. (1982). *Television and behavior: Ten years of scientific progress and implications for the eighties*. Washington, DC: U.S. Government Printing Office.

U.S. National Center for Health Statistics. (1986). *Advance data from vital and health statistics, No. 125*. DHHS Pub. No. (PHS) 86–1250. Hyattsville, MD: Public Health Service.

U.S. National Center for Health Statistics. (1992). *Aging in the eighties*. Washington, DC: U.S. Government Printing Office.

U.S. Public Health Service. (1995). *Monthly statistics report, 43.*

Uhlenberg, P., Cooney, T., & Boyd, R. (1990). Divorce for women after midlife. *Journals of Gerontology, 45* (1), 3–11.

Umberson, D., Anderson, K., Glick, J., & Shapiro, A. (1998). Domestic violence, personal control, and gender. *Journal of Marriage and the Family, 60* (3), 442–452.

Unger, R. & Crawford, M. (1996). *Woman and gender: A feminist psychology*. New York: McGraw-Hill.

Uttal, L. (1999). Using kin for child care: Embedment in the socioeconomic networks of extended families. *Journal of Marriage and the Family, 61* (4), 845–857.

Uvnas, M. (1998). Oxytocin may mediate the benefits of positive social interaction and emotions. *Psychoneurocrinnology, 23* (8), 819–835.

Uzgiris, U. & Raeff, C. (1995). Play in parent-child interactions. In M. Bornstein (Ed.), *Handbook of parenting*. Hillsdale, NJ: Erlbaum.

Vaillant, G. (1977). *Adaptation to life*. Boston: Little, Brown.

Valsiner, J. (1998). The development of the concept of development: Historical and epistemiological perspectives. In R. M. Lerner (Ed.), *Handbook of child psychology: Volume 1. Theoretical models of human development*. New York: John Wiley.

van Hoof, A. (2000). The identity status approach: In need of fundamental revision and qualitative change. *Developmental Review, 19* (4), 622–647.

VanderZanden, J. (1989). *Human development* (4th ed.). New York: Knopf.

Vanfear, C. & Zietlow, P. (1991). Toward a contingency approach to marital interaction: An empirical integration of three approaches. *Communication Monographs, 27* (1), 26–35.

Vartanian, L. (1997). Separation-individuation, social support, and adolescent egocentrism: An exploratory study. *Journal of Early Adolescence, 17* (3), 245–270.

Vaughan, V. & Litt, I. (1990). *Child and adolescent development: Clinical implications*. Philadelphia, PA: W. B. Saunders.

Verbrugge, L. M. (1989). The twain meet: Empirical explanations of sex differences in health and mortality. *Journal of Health and Social Behavior, 30* (3), 282–304.

Vigil, J. D. (1996). Street baptism: Chicano gang initiation. *Human Organization, 55,* 149–153.

Von Eye, A. & Schuster, C. (2000). The odds of resilience. *Child Development,* May/June, *71* (3), 563–566.

Voydanoff, P. & Donnelly, B. (1998). Parents' risk and protective factors as predictors of parental well-being and behavior. *Journal of Marriage and the Family, 60,* 344–355.

Vygotsky, L. S. (1962). *Thought and language.* Cambridge, MA: MIT Press.

Vygotsky, L. S. (1978). *Mind in society.* Cambridge, MA: Harvard University Press.

Wachowiak, F. & Clements, R. (1997). *Emphasis Art.* Reading, MA: Addison Wesley.

Wacks, V., Jr. (1994). Realizing our inner elder-child. *Journal of Humanistic Psychology, 34* (4), 78–100.

Wade, N. (2000). Now, the hard part: Putting the genome to work. *The New York Times,* June 27, pp. D1, D4.

Wakschlag, L. & Hans, S. (1999). Relation of maternal responsiveness during infancy to the development of behavior problems in high-risk youths. *Developmental Psychology, 35* (2), 569–579.

Wakschlag, L., Chase-Lansdale, P. & Brooks-Gunn, J. (1996). Not just "Ghosts in the Nursery": Contemporaneous intergenerational relationships and parenting in young African-American families. *Child Development, 67,* 2131–2147.

Waldholz. M. (1992, December 11). Scientists near the end of race to discover a breast-cancer gene. *The Wall Street Journal.*

Walker, L. (2000). Psychology and domestic violence around the world. *American Psychologist, 54* (1), 21–29.

Walker, L., Hennig, K., & Krettenauer, T., (2000). Parent and peer contexts for children's moral reasoning development. *Child Development, 71* (4), 1033–1048.

Wallace, J. B. (1992). Reconsidering the life review: The social construction of talk about the past. *The Gerontologist, 32* (1), 120–125.

Wallerstein, J. (1988). *Children of divorce.* Corte Modera, CA: Center for the Family in Transition.

Wallerstein, J. S. & Corbin, S. B. (1999). The child and the vicissitudes of divorce. In R. M. Galatszer-Levy, L. Kraus, et al., (Eds.), *The scientific basis of child custody decisions* (pp. 73–95). New York, NY: John Wiley & Sons, Inc.

Walsh, M. (1992). *Moving to nowhere.* New York: Auburn House.

Walther, R. R. & Harber, L. C. (1984). Expected skin complaints of the geriatric patient. *Geriatrics, 39* (1), 67.

Warabi, T., Kase, M., & Kato, T. (1984). Effect of aging on the accuracy of visually guided saccadic eye movement. *Annals of Neurology, 16,* 449–454.

Warhol, J. (Ed.). (1998). *New perspectives in early emotional development.* Skillman, NJ: Johnson & Johnson Pediatric Institute.

Warren, S. B. (1992). Lower threshold for referral for pyschiatric treatment for adopted adolescents. *Journal of the American Academy of Child and Adolescent Psychiatry, 31* (4), 518–524.

Washington, A. E., Arno, P. S., & Brooks, M. A. (1986). The economic cost of pelvic inflammatory disease. *Journal of the American Medical Association, 225* (13), 1021–1033.

Waterman, A. (1999). Identity, the identity statuses, and identity status development: A contemporary statement. *Developmental Review, 19* (4), 591–621.

Waters, E. & Cummings, E. M. (2000). A secure base from which to explore close relationships. *Child Development, 71* (1), 164–172.

Waters, E., Hamilton, C., & Weinfield, N. (2000). The stability of attachment security from infancy to adolescence and early adulthood: General introduction. *Child Development,* May/June, *71* (3), 678–683.

Waters, E., Merrick, S., Treboux, D., Crowell, J., & Albersheim, L. (2000). Attachment security in infancy and early adulthood: A twenty-year longitudinal study. *Child Development,* May/June, *71* (3), 684–689.

Watson, J. (1924). *Behaviorism.* New York: Norton.

Watson, M. (1995). The relation between anxiety and pretend play. In A. Slade & D. Wolf, (Eds.), *Children at play.* New York: Oxford University Press.

Weber, M. (1904). *The protestant ethic and the spirit of capitalism.* New York: Charles Scribner's Sons.

Wechsler, D. (1955). *Manual for the Wechsler adult intelligence test.* New York: Psychological Corp.

Wechsler, D. (1958). *The measurement and appraisal of adult intelligence.* Baltimore: Williams & Wilkins.

Wechsler, D. (1981). *Wechsler adult intelligence scale* (revised). New York: Psychological Corporation.

Wechsler, D. (1989). *Wechsler preschool and primary scale of intelligence* (revised). San Antonio, TX: Psychological Corporation.

Wechsler, D. (1991). *Wechsler intelligence scale for children* (3rd ed.). San Antonio, TX: Psychological Corporation.

Wechsler, H. (1996). Alcohol and the American college campus: A report from the Harvard School of Public Health. *Change, 7/8,* 20–25, 60–62.

Wechsler, H., Molnar, B., Davenport, A., & Baer, J. (1999). College alcohol use: A full or empty glass? *Journal of American College Health, 47,* 247–252.

Wechsler, H., Rigotti, N. A., Gledhill-Hoyt, J., & Lee, H. (1998). Increased levels of cigarette usage among college students: A cause for national concern. *Journal of the American Medical Association, 280* (19), 1673–1678.

Weeks, D. (1989). Death education for aspiring physicians, teachers, and the funeral directors. *Death Studies, 13* (1), 17–24.

Weigel, D., Devereux, P., Geoffrey, L., & Ballard-Reisch, D. (1998). A longitudinal study of adolescents' perceptions of support and stress: Stability and change. *Journal of Adolescent Research, 13* (2), 158–177.

Weiner, B. (1990). History of motivational research in education. *Journal of Educational Psychology, 82,* 616–622.

Weiner, I. B. (1992). *Psychological disturbance in adolescence* (2d ed.) New York: Wiley.

Weinfield, N., Sroufe, A., & Egeland, B. (2000). Attachment from infancy to early adulthood in a high-risk sample: Continuity, discontinuity, and their correlates. *Child Development,* May/June, *71* (3), 695–702.

Weinraub, M. & Gringlas, M. (1995). Single parenthood. In M. Bornstein (Ed.), *Handbook of parenting. Volume 3.* Mahwah, NJ: Lawrence Erlbaum.

Weinrich, J. D. (1987). A new sociobiological theory of homosexuality applicable to societies with universal marriage. *Ethology and Sociobiology, 8* (1), 37–47.

Weisner, T. (2000). Culture, childhood, and progress in sub-Saharan Africa. In L. Harrison & S. Huntington (Eds.), *Culture matters.* New York: Basic Books.

Weiss, L., Farrar, E., & Petrie, H. (1989). *Dropouts from school: Issues, dilemmas, and solutions.* Albany, NY: State University of New York Press.

Weissberg, R. & Greenberg, M. (1998). School and community competence-enhancement and prevention programs. In W. Damon (Series Ed.) & I. Sigel & K. Renninger (Volume Eds.), *Handbook of psychology: Volume 4. Child psychology in practice.* New York: John Wiley.

Weissbourd, R. (1996). *The vulnerable child.* Reading, MA: Addison Wesley.

Weitzman, B., Knickman, J., & Shinn, M. (1990). Pathways to homelessness among New York City families. *Journal of Social Issues, 46* (4), 125–140.

Welte, J. W. & Mirand, A. L. (1995). Drinking, problem drinking and life stressors in the elderly general population. *Journal of Studies on Alcohol, 56* (1), 67–73.

Werker, J. & Tees, R. (1999). Influences on infant speech processing: Toward a new synthesis. In J. Spence, J. Darley, & D. Foss (Eds.), *Annual Review of Psychology.* Palo Alto: Annual Reviews.

Werner, E. & Smith, R. (1992). *Overcoming the odds: High risk children from birth to adulthood.* Ithaca: Cornell University Press.

Wertheimer, M. (1962). Psychomotor coordination of auditory-visual space at birth. *Science 134,* 213–216.

Wertsch, J. & Tulviste, P. (1992). L. S. Vygotsky and contemporary developmental psychology. *Developmental Psychology, 28* (4), 548–557.

Whalen, C. K., Henker, B., Hollingshead, J., & Burgess, S. (1996). Parent-adolescent dialogues about AIDS. *Journal of Family Psychology, 10* (3), 343–357.

Whisett, D. & Land, H. (1992). Role strain, coping and marital satisfaction of stepparents. Families in Society: *The Journal of Contemporary Human Services, 14,* 79–91.

Whitaker, R. & Dietz, W. (1997). Predicting obesity in young adulthood from childhood and parental obesity. *New England Journal of Medicine, 337* (13), 869–873.

Whitbeck, L., Hoyt, D. R., & Huck, S. M. (1994). Early family relationships, intergenerational solidarity, and support provided to parents by their adult children. *Journal of Gerontology: Social Sciences, 49* (2), S85–S94.

Whitbeck, L. B. & Hoyt, D. R. (1991). Campus prestige and dating behaviors. *College Student Journal, 25* (4), 457–469.

Whitbeck, L. B., Simons, R. L., & Kao, M. (1994). The effects of divorced mothers' dating behaviors and sexual attitudes on the sexual attitudes and behaviors of their adolescent children. *Journal of Marriage and the Family, 56* (5), 615–621.

Whitbourne, S. K. (1996). *The aging individual: Physical and psychological perspectives*. New York, NY: Springer Publishing Company, Inc.

White, D. (1997, October 15). The change that comes over men. Boston: *The Boston Globe*, p. D1.

White, L. (1992). The effect of parental divorce and remarriage on parental support for adult children. *Journal of Family Issues, 13* (2), 234–250.

White, M. (1994). *Stranger at the gate*. New York: Simon & Schuster.

White, N. & Cunningham, W. R. (1988). Is terminal drop pervasive or specific? *Journals of Gerontology, 43* (6), 141–144.

White, T. (1975). *Breach of faith*. NY: Atheneum.

Whitehead, A. & Mathews, A. (1986). Factors related to successful outcome in the treatment of sexually unresponsive women. *Psychological Medicine, 16* (2), 373–378.

Whitehurst, G. & Lonigan, C. (1998). Child development and emergent literacy. *Child Development, 69*, 848–872.

Whiting, W. L. IV & Smith, A. D. (1997). Differential age-related processing limitations in recall and recognition tasks. *Psychology and Aging, 12* (2) 216–224.

Who's Who Special Report. (1997). *What parents of top teens don't know about their kids*. Lake Forest, IL: Educational Communications.

Wickrama, K. A. S., Lorenz, F. O., Conger, R. D., & Elder, G. H. (1997). Marital quality and physical illness: A latent growth curve analysis. *Journal of Marriage and the Family, 59* (1), 143–155.

Wiederman, M. W., Pryor, T., & Morgan, C. D. (1996). The sexual experience of women diagnosed with anorexia nervosa or bulimia nervosa. *International Journal of Eating Disorders, 19* (2), 109–118.

Wiegman, O. & van Schie, E. (1998). Video game playing and its relations with aggressive and prosocial behaviour. *British Journal of Social Psychology, 37* (3), 367–378.

Wierson, M., Long, P., & Forehand, R. (1993). Toward a new understanding of early menarche. *Adolescence 28* (112), 913–924.

Wilgoren, J. (1999). Quality daycare, early, is tied to achievement as an adult. *The New York Times*, A16.

Wilkie, J. R., Ferree, M. M., & Ratcliff, K. S. (1998). Gender and fairness: Marital satisfaction in two-earner couples. *Journal of Marriage and the Family, 60*, 577–594.

Will, J., Self, P., & Data, N. (1976). Maternal behavior and perceived sex of infant. *American Journal of Orthopsychiatry, 46*, 135–139.

William, G. & Wagner, W. (1996). Optimal development in adolescence: What is it and how can it be encouraged? *The Counseling Psychologist, 24* (3), 360–399.

Williams, K. & Bird, M. (1992). The aging mover: A preliminary report on constraints to action. *International Journal of Aging and Human Development, 34* (4), 271–297.

Willimon, W. & Naylor, T. (1995). *The abandoned generation*. Grand Rapids, MI: Eerdmans.

Willis, S. & Nesselroade, C. (1990). Long-term effects of fluid ability training in old-old age. *Developmental Psychology, 26* (6), 905–910.

Willis, S. & Schaie, K. W. (1986). Training the elderly on the ability factors of spatial orientation and inductive reasoning. *Psychology and Aging, 1* (3), 239–247.

Wilson, B. F. & Clarke, S. C. (1992). Remarriages: A demographic profile. *Journal of Family Issues, 13* (2), 123–141.

Wilson, E. O. (1978). *Sociobiology*. Cambridge, MA: Harvard University Press.

Wilson, J. (1993). *The moral sense*. New York: Free Press.

Wilson, S. M. & Medora, N. P. (1990). Gender comparisons of college students' attitudes toward sexual behavior. *Adolescence, 25* (99), 615–627.

Wingerson, L. *Mapping our genes*. (1990). New York: Plume.

Witter, F. (1993). Epidemiology of prematurity. In F. R. Witter & L. G. Keith (Eds.), *Textbook of prematurity: Antecedents, treatment, & outcome*. Boston: Little, Brown.

Woititz, J. (1990). *Adult children of alcoholics*. Lexington, MA: Health Communications, Inc.

Wolfe, D., O'Connor, D., & Crary, M. (1990). Transformations of life structure and personal paradigm during the midlife transition. *Human Relations, 43* (10), 957–973.

Wolff, P. (in press). Why is psychoanalysis still interesting?

Wolfinger, N. (1998). The effects of parental divorce on adult tobacco and alcohol consumption. *Journal of Health and Social Behavior, 39*, 254–269.

Wolford, B., McGee, T., Raque, T., & Coffey, O. D. (1996). Collaboration works for at-risk and delinquent youths. *Corrections Today* (August), 109–112.

Wolfson, M. (1989). *A review of the literature on feminist psychology*. Unpublished manuscript, Boston College, Chestnut Hill, MA.

Wolpert, L. (1991). *The triumph of the embryo*. New York: Oxford University Press.

Woodruff-Pak, D. (1988). *Psychology and aging*. Englewood Cliffs, NJ: Prentice-Hall.

Woodward, A. & Markman, E. (1998). Early word learning. In D. Kuhn & R. Siegler (Eds.), *Handbook of child psychology. Volume 2*. New York: John Wiley.

Woodward, K. & McCormick, J. (Nov 25, 1996). The art of dying well. (how Cardinal Joseph Bernardin set model for dying with grace)(Cover Story). *Newsweek, 128*, 22, 60.

Wortman, C. & Silver, R. (1989). The myths of coping with loss. *Journal of Consulting and Clinical Psychology, 57*, 349–357.

Wright, J., Huston, A., Reitz, A., & Piemyat, S. (1994). Young children's perceptions of television reality: Determinants and developmental differences. *Developmental Psychology, 30* (2), 229–239.

Wright, V. (February 2000). Knowledge, counseling can help prevent job injuries among teens. *American Association of Pediatrics News*. Elk Grove Village, IL: AAP.

Wright, V. (November, 1999). Sleeping in adult beds risky for kids under 2. *AAP News, 15* (11), 32.

Wright, W. (1998). *Born that way: Genes, behavior, personality*. New York: Knopf.

Wyckoff, A. (1999). Consider religious, ethnic customs when diagnosing child abuse. *AAAP News, 13* (5),18–19.

Wyers, N. (1987). Homosexuality in the family: Lesbian and gay spouses. *Social Work, 32*, 143–148.

Yan, W. & Gaier, E. L. (1994). Causal attributions for college success and failure. *Journal of Cross-Cultural Psychology, 25* (1), 146–158.

Young, M. H., Miller, B. C., Norton, M. C., & Hill, E. J. (1995). The effect of parental supportive behaviors on life satisfaction of adolescent offspring. *The Journal of Marriage and the Family, 57* (3), 813–822.

Young, R. A., Paseluikho, M. A., & Valach, L. (1997). The role of emotion in the construction of career in parent-adolescent conversations. *Journal of Counseling and Development, 76* (1), 36–44.

Yule, G. (1996). *The study of language*. Cambridge: Cambridge University Press.

Yuochi, S., Mischel, W., & Peake, P. (1990). Predicting adolescent cognitive and self-regulatory competencies from preschool delay of gratification. *Developmental Psychology, 26* (6), 978–986.

Yurgelun, T. (November/December, 1998). Brain abnormalities in chronic schizophrenia. *Psychology Today*, 56–59.

Zarit, S., Stephens, M., Townsend, A., & Greene, R. (1998). Stress reduction for family caregivers: Effects of adult day care use. *Journal of Gerontology, 53B* (5), 267–277.

Zerbe, K. J. (1992). The Phoenix rises from eros, not ashes: Creative collaboration in the lives of five impressionist and postimpressionist women artists. *Journal of the American Academy of Psychoanalysis, 20* (2), 295–315.

Zigler, E. & Finn-Stevenson, M. (1999). Applied developmental psychology. In M. Bornstein & M. Lamb, (Eds.), *Developmental psychology: An advanced textbook*. Mahwah, NJ: Erlbaum.

Zigler, E. & Hall, N. (2000). *Child development and social policy*. New York: McGraw-Hill.

Zigler, E. & Muenchow, S. (1992). *Head Start*. New York: Crown.

Zigler, E. & Styfco, S. (1994). Head Start: Criticisms in a constructive context. *American Psychologist, 49* (2), 127–132.

Zippay, A. (1995). Exploring employment skills and social networks among teen mothers. *Child & Adolescent Social Work Journal, 12* (1), 51–69.

Zwillich, T. (1996a). Pregnant teens who work don't drop out. *Ob/Gyn. News* (July), p. 17.

Zwillich, T. (1996b). Simple screen for alcohol use in pregnant teens. *Ob/Gyn. News* (July), p. 17.

Credits

LINE ART/TABLES

CHAPTER 1
Fig. 1.2: From John F. Travers, *The Growing Child,* Scott, Foresman and Company, Glenview, IL, 1982. Reprinted by permission of the author.
Table 1.2: From John F. Travers, *The Growing Child,* Scott Foresman and Company, Glenview, IL, 1982. Reprinted by permission of the author.

CHAPTER 2
Table 2.1: From John F. Travers, *The Growing Child,* Scott, Foresman and Company, Glenview, IL, 1982. Reprinted by permission of the author.
Table 2.2: From *Childhood and Society* by Erik H. Erikson. Copyright 1950, © 1963 by W. W. Norton & Company, Inc., renewed © 1978, 1991 by Erik H. Erikson. Used by permission of W. W. Norton & Company, Inc.; From *Childhood and Society* by Erik Erikson published by Hogarth Press. Used by permission of The Random House Group Limited.
Fig. 2.2: From R. Lerner, *Developmental Psychology,* Vol. 27, 1991, p. 27–32, Figure 1, p. 30. Copyright 1991 by the American Psychological Association. Reprinted with permission.

CHAPTER 3
Table 3.1: From John F. Travers, *The Growing Child,* Scott, Foresman and Company, Glenview, IL, 1982. Reprinted by permission of the author.
Fig. 3.1: From John F. Travers, *The Growing Child,* Scott, Foresman and Company, Glenview, IL, 1982. Reprinted by permission of the author.
Fig. 3.2: From John F. Travers, *The Growing Child,* Scott, Foresman and Company, Glenview, IL, 1982. Reprinted by permission of the author.
Fig. 3.3: From John F. Travers, *The Growing Child,* Scott, Foresman and Company, Glenview, IL, 1982. Reprinted by permission of the author.
Fig. 3.6: From John F. Travers, *The Growing Child,* Scott, Foresman and Company, Glenview, IL, 1982. Reprinted by permission of the author.
Table 3.4: From John F. Travers, *The Growing Child,* Scott, Foresman and Company, Glenview, IL, 1982. Reprinted by permission of the author.

CHAPTER 4
Fig. 4.5: Modified from K. L. Moore and T.V.N. Persaud, *The Developing Human: Clinically Oriented Embryology,* 5th ed. Copyright © 1993 W. B. Saunders Company, Philadelphia, PA. Reprinted by permission.

CHAPTER 5
Fig. 5.2: From *The Conscious Brain* by Steven Rose, copyright © 1973 by Steven Rose. Used by permission of Alfred A. Knopf, a division of Random House, Inc.
Table 5.3: Adapted from Shore, R. (1997). *Rethinking the brain: New insights into early development.* New York: Families and Work Institute.
Table 5.4: From John F. Travers, *The Growing Child,* Scott, Foresman and Company, Glenview, IL, 1982. Reprinted by permission of the author.
Table 5. 5: From John F. Travers, *The Growing Child,* Scott, Foresman and Company, Glenview, IL, 1982. Reprinted by permission of the author.
Table 5.6: From John F. Travers, *The Growing Child,* Scott, Foresman and Company, Glenview, IL, 1982. Reprinted by permission of the author.

CHAPTER 6
Table 6.3: Source: From John Bowlby, "Attachment and Loss: Retrospect and Prospect" in *American Journal of Orthopsychiatry,* 52:664–678. Reprinted with permission from the *American Journal of Orthopsychiatry.* Copyright © 1982 by the American Orthopsychiatry Association, Inc.

CHAPTER 7
Fig. 7.1: From John F. Travers, *The Growing Child,* Scott, Foresman and Company, Glenview, IL, 1982. Reprinted by permission of the author.
Fig. 7.4: From John F. Travers, *The Growing Child,* Scott, Foresman and Company, Glenview, IL, 1982. Reprinted by permission of the author.
Fig. 7.5: From John W. Santrock and Steve R. Yussen, *Child Development: An Introduction,* 4th ed. Copyright © 1989 Wm. C. Brown Communications, Inc., Dubuque, Iowa. All rights reserved. Reprinted by permission.
Table 7.2: From John F. Travers, *The Growing Child,* Scott, Foresman and Company, Glenview, IL, 1982. Reprinted by permission of the author.

CHAPTER 8
Table 8.3: From Laura E. Berk, *Child Development,* 4th Edition. Copyright © 1997 by Allyn & Bacon. Reprinted/adapted by permission.
Table 8.4: From Bronson, M. B. 1995. *The Right Stuff for Children Birth to 8: Selecting Play Materials to Support Development,* Washington, DC: NAEYC. Reprinted with permission from the National Association for the Education of Young Children.

CHAPTER 9
Table 9.1: From John F. Travers, *The Growing Child,* Scott, Foresman and Company, Glenview, IL, 1982. Reprinted by permission of the author.
Fig. 9.2: From John F. Travers, *The Growing Child,* Scott, Foresman and Company, Glenview, IL, 1982. Reprinted by permission of the author.
Table 9.3: From Elliott, Kratochwill, Littlefield, and Travers, *Educational Psychology: Effective Teaching, Effective Learning,* Copyright 2000, McGraw-Hill. Used by permission of The McGraw-Hill Companies.
Table 9.4: From Elliott, Kratochwill, Littlefield, and Travers, *Educational Psychology: Effective Teaching, Effective Learning,* Copyright 2000, McGraw-Hill. Used by permission of The McGraw-Hill Companies.
Table 9.5: Based on L. Kohlberg, "A Cognitive-Developmental Analysis of Children's Sex-Role Concepts and Attitudes" in *The Development of Sex Differences,* edited by E. Maccoby, Stanford University Press, Stanford, CA, 1966.
Table 9.6: Based on data from Owens, 1996.

CHAPTER 12
Cartoon: © The New Yorker Collection 1991. Edward Koren from cartoonbank.com. All rights reserved.
Fig.TA12.1: © The New Yorker Collection 1991 Edward Koren from cartoonbank.com. All Rights Reserved.
Table 12.2: 1995 National Survey of Family Growth and 1995 National Survey of Adolescent Males.
Table 12.3: Leeming and Associates (1996), *Issues in Adolescent Sexuality.* Needham Heights, MA: Allyn & Bacon.

CHAPTER 12.4
Table 12.4: Center for Disease Control, Surveillance Report, Vol. 12, No. 1, 2000.
Table 12.5: Reproduced with the permission of The Alan Guttmacher Institute from: The Alan Guttmacher Institute, *Teenage Pregnancy: Overall Trends and State-by-State Information,* New York: The Alan Guttmacher Institute, 1999.
Table 12.6: Substance Abuse & Mental Health Services Administration, 1999 National Household Survey on Drug Abuse, 1999.

CHAPTER 13
Table 13.1: Bureau of the Census, 1996.
Table 13.2: From John Dacey, *Adult Development.* Scott, Foresman and Company, Glenview, IL, 1982. Reprinted by permission of the author.

CHAPTER 14
Table 14.1: From "Marital Status and Living Arrangements: March 1998" in Current Population Reports, P-20 (No. 514), U.S. Bureau of the Census, Washington, DC, 1999.
Fig. 14.2: From *The Seasons of a Man's Life* by Daniel Lcvinson, copyright © 1978 by Daniel J. Levinson. Used by permission of Alfred A. Knopf, a division of Random House, Inc.; Reprinted by permission of Sterling Lord Literistic, Inc. Copyright 1975 by Daniel Levinson
Table 14.4: From R. J. Sternberg, "The Triangular Theory of Love" in *Psychological Review,* 93:119–135. Copyright 1986 by the American Psychological Association. Adapted with permission.

CHAPTER 15
Fig. 15.2: From J. L. Horn, "Remodeling Old Models of Intelligence" in *Handbook of Intelligence: Theories, Measurements, and Applications,* edited by B. B. Wolman, Wiley & Sons, New York, 1985.
Fig. 15.4: Data from H. C. Lehman, *Age and Achievement,* Princeton University Press, Princeton, NJ, 1953.
Fig. 15.5: Data from W. Dennis, "Creative Productivity Between 20 and 80 Years," in *Journal of Gerontology* 21:1–8, 1966.
Box 15.5: NIA (1999). Progress report and Alzheimer's disease. Washington, DC: United States Department of Health and Human Services, NIH Publication No. 99-4664.

CHAPTER 16
Table 16.1: Adapted from *Adult Health Nursing* by Carol Ren Kneisl and SueAnn Wooster Ames. Addison-Wesley, Menlo Park, Calif., 1986.
Fig. 16.3: U.S. Bureau of the Census.
Table 16.2: From *The Janus Report on Sexual Behavior* by S. Janus and C. Janus. Copyright © 1993 Wiley & Sons, New York. Reprinted by permission of John Wiley & Sons, Inc.
Fig. 16.4: From *The Seasons of a Man's Life* by Daniel Levinson, copyright © 1978 by Daniel J. Levinson. Used by permission of Alfred A. Knopf, a division of Random House, Inc.; Reprinted by permission of Sterling Lord Literistic, Inc. Copyright 1975 by Daniel Levinson
Fig. 16.5: From R. McCrae and P. Costa, Jr., *Emerging Lives, Enduring Disposition: Personality in Adulthood.* Copyright © 1984 Little, Brown and Company, Boston, MA. Reprinted by permission of the authors.

CHAPTER 17

Fig. 17.1: Social Security Administration.
Fig. 17.2: Japan Information Network.
Fig. 17.3: From Paola S. Timiras, *Developmental Physiology and Aging*, MacMillan Publishing Company, 1972. Used with permission of Paola S. Timiras.
Table 17.2: From G. Jaquish and R. E. Ripple, "Cognitive Creative Abilities Across the Adult Life Span" in *Human Development*. Copyright © 1980. S. Karger AG, Basel, Switzerland. Reprinted by permission of the publisher.
Table 17.3: Reprinted with the permission of Lexington Books, an imprint of The Free Press, a Division of Simon & Schuster, Inc., from *Fundamentals of Creative Thinking* by John S. Dacey. Copyright © 1989 by Lexington Books.
Table 17.4: From *Wisdom* by R. J. Sternberg. Copyright © 1990, Cambridge University Press, New York. Reprinted with the permission of Cambridge University Press.

CHAPTER 18

Table 18.1: From *Archives of Sexual Behavior* by J. G. Bretschneider and N. L. McCoy, 17(2): 117, 1988. Reprinted with permission from Kluwer Academic/Plenum Publishers.
Fig. 18.1: From Robert Havighurst, "Perceived Life Space" in *Contributions to Human Development* 3:93–112 (1963). S. Karger AG, Basel, Switzerland. Reprinted by permission of the publisher.

CHAPTER 19

Fig. 19.1: Statistics from *Statistical Abstract of the United States,* 1995 (p. 95) by U.S. Bureau of the Census, 1995, Washington, DC: U.S. Government Printing Office.
Fig. 19.2: From E. Kubler-Ross, *On Death and Dying*, Macmillan, New York, 1969.

PHOTOS

PART OPENERS

Page xii: Photo by Kristen Dacey-Iwai. **1:** © Lori Adamski Peek/Stone Images; **2:** © John Fortunato/Stone Images; **3:** © Laura Dwight/Photo Edit; **4:** © H. Armstrong Roberts; **5:** © Lori Adamski Peek/Stone Images; **6:** © PhotoDisc website; **7 and 8:** © Michael Newman/Photo Edit, Inc.; **9:** © David Young-Wolff/Photo Edit

CHAPTER 1

Page 3: © Neil Michel/Axiom; **6 (top left):** © Bettmann/CORBIS; **p. 6 (top right):** © AP/Wide World Photos; **p. 6 (bottom left):** © Everett Collection; **p. 6 (bottom right):** © CORBIS; **p. 12:** © Andy Sacks/Stone Images; **p. 8:** © Michael Newman/ Photo Edit, Inc.

CHAPTER 2

Page 26: © A. Barrington Brown/Science Source/Photo Researchers, Inc.; **p. 27 (top):** © Bettmann/CORBIS; **p. 27 (bottom):** © Vol. 9/CORBIS; **p. 30:** © Bettmann/CORBIS; **p. 31:** © Vol. 66/PhotoDisc; **p. 32:** Courtesy of Andrew Schwebel; **p. 35:** Courtesy of James Wertsch; **p. 38:** © Christopher Johnson/Stock Boston

CHAPTER 3

Page 49: © Robert Brenner/Photo Edit, Inc.; **p. 51a:** © Walter Dawn/Photo Researchers, Inc.; **p. 51b:** © SIU/SPL/Photo Researchers, Inc.; **p. 56:** © AP/Wide World Photos; **p. 58:** © Mark Richards/Photo Edit; **p. 63:** © Walter Hodges/Stone Images; **p. 64:** © A. Sieveking/Petit Format/Photo Researchers, Inc.; **p. 65:** © The Granger Collection; **p. 67:** © Charles Thatcher/Stone Images

CHAPTER 4

Page 73: © Nancy McKenna/Photo Researchers, Inc.; **p. 74 (top):** © Don W. Fawcett/Photo Researchers, Inc.; **p. 74 (bottom):** © Omikron/Photo Researchers, Inc.; **p. 77 (top):** © Omikron/Photo Researchers, Inc.; **p. 77 (bottom):** © Petit Format/Photo Researchers, Inc.; **p. 78:** © Petit Format/Photo Researchers, Inc.; **p. 81:** © Michael Okoniewski/The Image Works; **p. 83:** © John Griffin/The Image Works; **p. 85:** Courtesy of A. P. Streissguth, S. K. Clarren, and K. L. Jones, "Natural History of the Fetal Alcohol Syndrome: A Ten-Year Follow-Up of Eleven Patients" in *Lancet; 2,* 85–92, July 1985; **p. 86:** © Saturn Stills/Science Photo Library/Photo Researchers, Inc.; **p. 92:** © Doug Martin/Photo Researchers, Inc.; **p. 94:** © Vol. 52/CORBIS

CHAPTER 5

Page 101: © Myrleen Ferguson/Photo Edit, Inc.; **p. 108 (all):** Courtesy of Dr. Tiffany Field and *Science.* From Field, et al., Model and Infant Expressions from "Discrimination and Imitation of Facial Express by Neonates" in *Science,* fig. 2, Vol. 218, pp. 179–81, October 8, 1982. Reprinted by permission of the American Association for the Advancement of Science.; **p. 110:** © Michael Newman/Photo Edit, Inc.; **p. 111:** © John Travers; **p. 112:** © Robert Brenner/Photo Edit, Inc.; **p. 115:** © Myrleen Ferguson/Photo Edit, Inc.; **p. 116:** © Enrico Ferorelli; **p. 119:** © Vol. 63/PhotoDisc; **p. 120:** © Barbara Rios/Photo Researchers, Inc.; **p. 125:** © Myrleen Ferguson/Photo Edit, Inc.

CHAPTER 6

Page 131: © PhotoDisc website; **p. 132:** © Suzanne Szasz/Photo Researchers, Inc.; **p. 134 and 135:** © PhotoDisc website; **p. 137:** © Sandra Johnson/Index Stock; **p. 141:** © Stone Images; **p. 148:** © Julie O'Neil/Index Stock

CHAPTER 7

Page 155: © Dennis O'Clair/Stone Images; **p. 156 and 157:** © John Travers; **p. 160:** © PhotoDisc website; **p. 161:** © Vol. 124/CORBIS; **p. 162:** © Sharon L. Fox/Index Stock; **p. 164:** © Palmer & Brilliant/Index Stock; **p. 170:** © Robert Knowles/ Black Star; **p. 172:** © Skjold Photographs; **p. 179:** © Elizabeth Crews

CHAPTER 8

Page 183: © Pedro Call/Stock Market; **p. 185:** © Alan Abramowitz/Stone Images; **p. 188:** © Elizabeth Crews; **p. 189:** © Lori Adamski Peek/Stone Images; **p. 190:** © Jonathan Nourok/Photo Edit, Inc.; **p. 192 (left):** © Nancy Lutz/Index Stock; **p. 192 (right):** © Carol Palmer/Index Stock; **p. 196:** © Ulrike Welsch/Photo Researchers, Inc.; **p. 199:** © Erika Stone/Photo Researchers, Inc.; **p. 202:** © Elizabeth Crews/The Image Works

CHAPTER 9

Page 213: © Skjold Photographers; **p. 217:** © Elizabeth Crews; **p. 219:** © Mimi Forsyth/Monkmeyer; **p. 221:** © Vol. 41/PhotoDisc; **p. 226:** © Mary Kate Denny/Stone Images; **p. 228:** © Myrleen Fertuson/Photo Edit, Inc.; **p. 239:** © John Travers

CHAPTER 10

Page 245: © Vol. 70/PhotoDisc; **p. 253 (top):** © Richard Hutchings/Photo Researchers, Inc.; **p. 253 (bottom):** © Vol. 45/PhotoDisc; **p. 256:** © Elizabeth Crews; **p. 257:** © Elizabeth Crews/The Image Works; **p. 261:** © PhotoDisc website; **p. 265:** © Bob Kalman/The Image Works

CHAPTER 11

Page 275: © PhotoDisc website; **p. 277:** © CORBIS website; **p. 281:** © AKG/Photo Researchers, Inc.; **p. 284:** © Giraudon/Art Resource, NY; **p. 290:** © David Young-Wolff/Photo Edit, Inc.; **p. 291:** © Kansas City Star/Liaison Agency; **p. 295:** © Susan Toog-Wagner/Photo Researchers, Inc.; **p. 297:** © Jonathan Nourok/Photo Edit, Inc.; **p. 299 (top):** © Tony Freeman/Photo Edit, Inc.; **p. 299 (bottom):** © The Granger Collection

CHAPTER 12

Page 310: © Myrleen Ferguson Cate/Photo Edit, Inc.; **p. 313:** © PhotoDisc website; **p. 317:** © Bettmann/CORBIS; **p. 322:** © Matthew Mendelsohn/CORBIS; **p. 326:** © Richard Hutchings/Photo Edit, Inc.; **p. 329:** © Steve Starr/Stock Boston

CHAPTER 13

Page 335: © Jason Laure; **p. 339:** © Spencer Grant/Index Stock; **p. 350:** © Vol. 105/CORBIS

CHAPTER 14

Page 355: © Bobbi Carrey/Index Stock; **p. 359:** © Alden Pellett/The Image Works; **p. 364:** © Vol. 78/PhotoDisc; **p. 365:** © Charles Gatewood/The Image Works; **p. 366:** © Bob Daemmrich/The Image Works; **p. 367 (left):** © AP/Wide World Photos; **p. 367 (right):** © Jaye R. Phillips/Index Stock; **p. 370:** © Michael Newman/Photo Edit, Inc.; **p. 374:** © Toni Michaels

CHAPTER 15

Page 383: © Toni Michaels; **p. 391:** © CORBIS; **p. 392:** © Dion Ogust/The Image Works; **p. 394:** © Bob Stitzer/Photo Edit, Inc.

CHAPTER 16

Page 409: © Ulrike Welsch; **p. 411:** © Elizabeth Crews/The Image Works; **p. 416:** © Toni Michaels; **p. 422:** © Toni Michaels/The Image Works; **p. 424:** © Nita Winter/The Image Works

CHAPTER 17

Page 431: © Syndicated Feature/The Image Works; **p. 434:** © B. Grunzweig/Photo Researchers, Inc.; **17.4 and 17.5:** From Birren, *The Handbook of Aging and the Individual.* Copyright © The University of Chicago Press; **p. 439:** © Toni Michaels; **p. 441:** © Barbara Rios/Photo Researchers, Inc.; **p. 449:** © Toni Michaels; **p. 451:** © Elizabeth Crews

CHAPTER 18

Page 459: © CORBIS; **p. 460:** © Tony Freeman/Photo Edit; **p. 461:** © Frank Siteman/Index Stock; **p. 472:** © The Museum of Modern Art Film Stills Archive; **p. 473 (left):** © Frank Siteman/Index Stock; **p. 473 (right):** © Toni Michaels

CHAPTER 19

Page 480: © The Granger Collection; **p. 482:** © Toni Michaels; **p. 483:** © Mark Richards/Photo Edit; **p. 486:** © Michael Okoniewsk/The Image Works; **p. 490:** © Hank Morgan/Photo Researchers, Inc.; **p. 494:** © Al C. Ampanie/The Image Works; **p. 497:** © Paul Conklin/Photo Edit, Inc.; **p. 498 (top):** © Keystone/The Image Works; **p. 498 (bottom):** © Keystone/The Image Works

Name Index

Wertsch, J., 35
Whitaker, 215
Whitbeck, L., 411
Whitbourne, S. K., 383
White, C., 442
White, D., 385
White, H. R., 357
White, L., 410, 414
White, N., 449
Whitehurst, G., 240
Whiting, W. L., 391
Who's Who Special Report, 309
Wickelgren, 390
Wickrama, K. A. S., 464
Wiederman, M. W., 316
Wigger, A., 371
Wiles, M., 371
Wilke, F., 394
Wilke, J. R., 350
Wilkniss, S. M., 391
Will, J., 200
Williams, A., 440
Williams, L., 267
Wilogran, J., 195
Wilson, A., 371
Wilson, E. O., 499
Wilson, J., 250

Wing, R., 385
Winslow, E., 189
Wirsen, C., 77
WISC-111, 220
Woititz, J., 382
Wolfe, D., 397
Wolfe, D. M., 397
Wolfe, T., 416
Wolfinger, N., 310
Wolford, B., 329
Wolfson, M., 370
Wolpert, L., 51, 54
Wong, J. B., 385
Woods, T. E., 323
Woodside, D., 466
Woodward, A., 126
Woodward, K., 494
Wortman, C., 485, 488
WPPSI-R, 220
Wright, D., 327
Wright, J., 261, 262
Wright, J. D., 328
Wright, L. W., 282, 283
Wright, S. D., 412
Wright, T. L., 319
Wright, V., 114, 293
Wu, M., 327

Wyckoff, A., 266
Wyers, N., 359

Y

Yaggi, K., 189
Yeats, W. B., 385
Yee, J. L. 468
Yin, J. C., 390
Yokomukai, Y., 442
Yoshiiwa, A., 389
Young, R. A., 310
Yule, G., 124
Yurgelun-Todd, D., 296
Yussen, S., 166

Z

Zabin, L., 318
Zahn-Waxler, C., 143, 263
Zarit, S., 467
Zeisel, S., 195
Zhang, J., 328
Zhou, H., 390
Zigler, E., 170, 185, 195
Zoellner, S., 296

Subject Index

Page numbers followed by *b, f,* and *t* indicate boxes, figures, and tables, respectively.